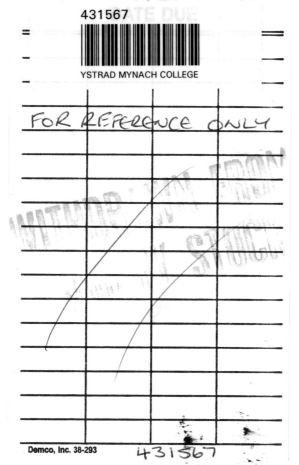

THE LAW SOCIETY'S CONVEYANCING HANDBOOK
14TH EDITION

THE LAW SOCIETY'S CONVEYANCING HANDBOOK
14th Edition

General Editor

Frances Silverman

LLM Solicitor

Consultant Editors

Annette Goss
Peter Reekie
Anne Rodell
Michael Taylor
Bernadette Whitters

Editorial Board

Helen Davies, *Solicitor, Peters Langsford Davies*
Kenneth Edwards, *Solicitor*
Philip Freedman LLB, *Solicitor, Mishcon de Reya*
Emma Slessenger, *Solicitor, Allen & Overy LLP*

*nominated by the Law Society's
Conveyancing and Land Law Committee*

The Law Society

First published January 1992
2nd edition 1993
3rd edition 1994
4th edition 1995
5th edition 1996
6th edition 1997
7th edition 1999
8th edition 2001
9th edition 2002
10th edition 2003
11th edition 2004
12th edition 2005
13th edition 2006
14th edition 2007

R 346.410438 ISBN-13: 978-185328-603-2
431567. ISSN 1350-1852

Copyright in the Standard Conditions of Sale and the Standard Commercial Property Conditions of Sale (Appendices V.9 and V.10) is jointly held by the Law Society and the Solicitors Law Stationery Society Ltd.

Materials in Appendix IX are Crown copyright. Crown copyright material is reproduced here with the permission of the Controller of HMSO and the Queen's Printer for Scotland.

The Law Society is also grateful to the Council of Mortgage Lenders for its kind permission to reproduce the material in Appendix VI.

The forms and guidance in Appendix VII appear with the kind permission of HM Revenue and Customs.

Published in 2007 by the Law Society
113 Chancery Lane, London WC2A 1PL

Typeset by Columns Design Ltd, Reading
Printed by TJ International Ltd, Padstow, Cornwall

Contents

B. PRE-EXCHANGE

C. EXCHANGE

D. TITLE

. PRE-COMPLETION

V. FORMS AND PRECEDENTS

VI. COUNCIL OF MORTGAGE LENDERS GUIDANCE

VII. STAMP DUTY LAND TAX AND VAT

Preface to the 1992 edition

Conveyancing is a much maligned art – an easy option in the eyes of many practitioners. If this is true, why is it that the Legal Practice Directorate and Professional Ethics Department of the Law Society have a constant stream of telephone calls and letters from practitioners anxious to know how to solve conveyancing problems? The idea of this book originated from the Law Society's Land Law and Conveyancing Committee who felt that the time had come to publish a work which attempted to deal with and resolve the many problems encountered on a daily basis by practitioners. The aim of this book, therefore, is to present in readable form a ready reference handbook of the practice of conveyancing. The book does not pretend to be a comprehensive guide to the law – for this the reader is, at various points throughout the text, referred to specialist works dealing with particular areas, but it does seek to deal fully with the practice of conveyancing and to provide guidance on resolving problems which may be encountered by practitioners. The text is, therefore, divided into sections which deal with the conveyancing transaction in chronological sequence. Chapters have been included on matters which, although peripheral to the main issue, nevertheless impinge on it, e.g. advertising, property selling, costs, undertakings and remedies. Although the book does contain some specialist sections, e.g. the purchase of licensed premises, milk quotas in agricultural land, it is intended as a handbook for the general practitioner and does not, therefore, cover in detail specialist areas pertaining to commercial transactions. It does, however, seek to gather together some information which is not found either in other conventional conveyancing texts or in some cases at all, this aspect particularly concentrating on the resolution of practical problems and provision of checklists and guidelines. Precedents are not included within the text since the practitioner has ample scope for finding precedents in many other published works. Some commonly encountered practical areas are no longer dealt with by trainee solicitors during their Finals course, and in such areas, e.g. residential security of tenure, the book aims to provide the solicitor with a brief résumé of the law with reference to a specialist work on the subject should that be required.

It is hoped that this book will form the practitioner's first point of reference and to that end extensive appendices include the text of many of the matters to which a practitioner has cause to refer during the course of each working day, e.g. HM Land Registry Practice Notes, addresses of authorities for the purpose of making searches, stamp duty tables, the Formulae for exchange of contracts.

It is of course vital that any book which purports to be an essential working tool in the hands of a busy practitioner should be up to date with both law and practice. The decision has, therefore, been taken by the Law Society that this book will be completely revised and updated regularly in order to ensure that the practitioner has available to him in one volume the very latest information relating to conveyancing.

No offence is intended to female members of the profession by references in the text to the solicitor as 'he', for which please read 'he or she' as appropriate. To include the words 'he or she' on every occasion where such reference appears would have the effect of extending the text by a considerable amount which in turn would have adverse repercussions on the publication price of the book.

I would like to acknowledge with thanks the permission of HM Land Registry and the Inland Revenue for publication of their various leaflets and guidance notes which appear in the appendices to the book.

I would also like to thank Linklaters and Paines for their help with sections on milk quotas and VAT, Withers for their assistance in preparing the text on agricultural land, Chris Jowett of the Halifax Building Society for his help in relation to mortgages, Martin Wood of HM Land Registry for his assistance with points on registered land, and Tony Donell who read through each section of the manuscript before publication.

I should also record my appreciation to the staff of the Law Society, in particular Joanna Davies-Evitt and Carl Upsall who have been responsible for the co-ordination of the text, preparation of appendices and index and eventual publication of the text itself.

Finally my thanks go to Trevor Aldridge, Margaret Anstey, Murray Ross, Philip Freedman, and Kenneth Edwards who comprised the Editorial Board for this book. They had the unenviable task of sitting through monthly meetings to discuss and correct my indecipherable manuscript. Without their constant help, support and encouragement this book might not have seen the light of day.

The law is stated as at 1 December 1991.

Frances Silverman
Rowfold Grange
West Sussex

Preface to the 14th edition

After more than a year of frantic preparation and anticipation, home information packs have now become part of the daily conveyancing routine and although the major part of the text for this new edition had to be prepared before the packs became compulsory, the book has been updated to reflect the latest version of this new requirement. The other major change which merits mention is the replacement of the Solicitors' Practice Rules 1990 by the Solicitors' Code of Conduct 2007 and all references to the former have been removed and replaced by the new version – a marathon task in itself. The section on stamp duty land tax has had another makeover and hopefully now presents a clear and useful guide to this tricky subject.

My thanks go to the consulting editors who have updated the various sections of the book – Annette Goss, Peter Reekie, Anne Rodell, Michael Taylor, and Bernadette Whitters; and also to the Editorial Board – Helen Davies, Kenneth Edwards, Philip Freedman and Emma Slessenger for their continuing support and help with this edition.

At the Law Society and the Solicitors Regulation Authority, my thanks go to Diane Latter, Angela Doran, Derek Mitchell, and Bronwen Still.

For their help with the updating of this edition, I would also like to thank Trevor Hellawell (environmental issues), Peter Camp (financial services, mortgage fraud, money laundering), Birketts Solicitors (agricultural land and agricultural tenancies), Chris Baker (commonhold), David Jordan (VAT), Alan Riley (stamp duty land tax), and Jane Hanney (licensing).

For their help with permissions and updating this edition, I would like to thank the following organisations: British Sugar, Council of Mortgage Lenders, the Land Registry, National Radiological Protection Board, and Rural Payments Agency.

Any errors which remain in the book are my responsibility alone.

The law is stated as at 1 July 2007.

Frances Silverman
Rowfold
West Sussex

About the authors

Chris Baker is a partner with Davies Arnold Cooper. He has experience in a wide variety of commercial, retail and residential property transactions, particularly development projects. Prior to coming to the UK Chris practised law in Australia for a number of years. Chris has particular expertise with commonhold. He is the author of *A Practical Guide to Commonhold* (Legalease) and is the Home Builders Federation representative on the commonhold consultative working group.

Peter Camp is a solicitor and is visiting Professor (Chair of Ethics) at the College of Law. He is also Principal of Educational & Professional Services, which provides training and consultancy services to the solicitors' and accountants' professions. Peter is a former member of the Law Society's Financial Services Taskforce. Amongst his numerous publications are: *Solicitors and Financial Services: A Compliance Handbook* (Law Society, 2002); *Cordery on Solicitors* (where he contributes sections on financial services and solicitors' accounts) and *Solicitors and Money Laundering: A Compliance Handbook* (Law Society, 2nd edn, 2007); *Solicitors and the Accounts Rules: A Compliance Handbook* (Law Society, 2006); and *Companion to the Solicitors' Code of Conduct 2007* (Law Society, 2007).

Helen Davies is a solicitor and partner at Peters Langsford Davies and Law Society Council Member for Gwent and the South West. Helen specialises in residential and small scale commercial property, business transfers and some agricultural property. She is also chair of the Regulatory Affairs Board, governor of Plymouth University, chair of County Environmental Trust and a member of the Law Society's HIPs Task Force.

Kenneth Edwards was admitted as a solicitor in 1961 and from 1965 practised at Cardens in Brighton specialising in building society law. Kenneth also acted as external Head Office Solicitor to the former Alliance Building Society. He continued in that capacity until the 1980s and played a significant part in the merger with Leicester Building Society. As a member of the Law Society's Conveyancing and Land Law Committee, Kenneth was involved in the bringing together of the Law Society's Standard Conditions of Sale and National Conditions of Sale and the documentation for the Law Society's TransAction scheme (he wrote part of the text for the Buyer's Guide). As member of a joint Law Commission Committee, he authored a paper 'Deposits; no time for a change'. He is a past President of Sussex Law Society.

Philip Freedman is a solicitor and senior property partner at Mishcon de Reya. He is a member of various committees at the Law Society, including the Conveyancing and Land Law Committee, the Standard Conditions of Sale Working Party, the Joint Advisory Committee of the Land Registry and the Law Society, the Local Searches Joint Working Party of the Law Society and the Local Government Association. Philip is also chair of the Commercial Leases Working Group, a member of the RICS Working Party on the PACT Scheme and a member of the British Property Federation

Working Party on Short Leases. His publications include *Service Charges: Law and Practice* (Jordans, 2002).

Annette Goss is a solicitor and worked in private practice as a conveyancer and property lawyer before joining the Government Legal Service. She has worked as a solicitor for the Crown Estate and is currently the land registrar at the Land Registry, Nottingham (East) Office. Annette has been involved in designing and developing a professional training course with Michael Taylor on land registration law and practice for Land Registry staff, and has also prepared and delivered lectures and seminars to Land Registry staff, legal practitioners, academics and other members of the legal profession.

Jane Hanney is a solicitor and director of Magna Law Ltd, a niche firm of solicitors specialising in food law, licensing, health and safety, and environmental law with particular emphasis on the food and drink/agriculture sector. Jane is a member of the Law Society Food Law Group, an associate member of the Chartered Institute of Environmental Health and co-author of Licensing for Conveyancers (Law Society, 2005). She also lectures regularly in her areas of expertise.

James Harbottle trained with Allen & Overy in the City and qualified in their property department in 1994. He worked for Burges Salmon from 1996 before joining Birketts in September 2000. His strongest areas of practice are in agricultural, equestrian and commercial property. James is a member of the Agricultural Law Association and a professional member of the CLA.

Trevor Hellawell is a solicitor and legal training consultant with 15 years' experience training in environment law. He works with the College of Law, lawyers and other professionals, Landmark Information Group, the Ministry of Defence and several other clients, particularly in the engineering sector. Trevor was formerly a member of the Law Society's Planning and Environmental Law Committee and is the author of the *Environmental Law Handbook* (6th edn, Law Society, 2005) and *Blackstone's Guide to Contaminated Land* (OUP/Blackstone, 2000).

Dave Jordan is a retired VAT consultant with many years' experience, including 14 years with HM Revenue and Customs.

Professor Peter Reekie is a property training consultant with Penningtons and visiting professor at the College of Law. Peter was admitted as a solicitor in 1976 and spent some years in private practice dealing with residential and commercial property work. He is director of Peter Reekie Associates Co. Ltd, which provides legal training and related services to lawyers and other professionals, and was formerly managing director of Legal Network Television. He writes for publication and lectures extensively at property law conferences, seminars and related events, and is consultant materials editor for the College of Law's Structured Commercial Property Programme.

Alan Riley is a solicitor and property law consultant, formerly with Halliwells LLP and the College of Law (Chester) as a senior lecturer. He now provides legal training, professional support and property law information services to law firms throughout the country. He is co-writer and publisher of *Commercial Property Information Update* and has co-written *Leasehold Liability – A Guide to the 1995 Act* (Jordans) and *Commercial Property and Business Leases* (Jordans).

Anne Rodell is an associate director of design at the College of Law, currently teaching property law and practice at the College's Guildford and Moorgate centres. She qualified as a solicitor in 1989 and from 1989 to 1998 was an assistant solicitor in the real estate department of Linklaters, specialising in commercial property matters. In August 2003 Anne joined the College of Law as a tutor specialising in property law and practice and is currently designing three commercial property courses for the LPC.

Frances Silverman is a solicitor and formerly a Reader at the College of Law. She has been author of the Law Society's *Conveyancing Handbook* since first publication in 1992. Frances is also author of several other books on conveyancing, sits as a part-time Chairman of Employment Tribunals and of the Leasehold Valuation Tribunal, and is a founder member of the Institute of Expert Witnesses.

Emma Slessenger is a solicitor and real estate professional support lawyer at Allen & Overy LLP. She has been a member of the Law Society's Conveyancing and Land Law Committee since 1998 and a member of the editorial board of the *Conveyancing Handbook* since 2002. She is a founder member of the London Property Support Lawyers Group and was closely involved with its development of the Commercial Property Standard Enquiries. She was co-editor of the *Landlord and Tenant Factbook* (Sweet & Maxwell) from 1996 to 2004 and co-author of *Leasehold Liability: the Landlord and Tenant* (Covenants) Act 1995 (Jordans). Emma is a member of the editorial board of the *Landlord and Tenant Review* (Sweet & Maxwell) and in 2004 was appointed as the precedents editor of the *Conveyancer and Property Lawyer* (Sweet & Maxwell). She writes and lectures widely on real estate issues.

Michael Taylor is a solicitor and the senior assistant Land Registrar at the Land Registry, Birkenhead (Rosebrae) office. Michael spent some years as a conveyancing and property lawyer in private practice before joining the Land Registry. Michael has been involved in designing and developing a professional training course with Annette Goss on land registration law and Practice for Land Registry staff, and has also prepared and delivered lectures and seminars to Land Registry staff, legal practitioners, academics and other members of the legal profession.

Bernadette Whitters is an Associate Professor at the College of Law, currently lecturing on property law and conveyancing at the College's Guildford centre. She qualified as a solicitor in 1980 and from 1980 to 1985 was the Assistant Company Solicitor at the Provident Financial Group, specialising in commercial and residential property matters. In November 1985, Bernadette joined the College of Law as a lecturer specialising in property law and conveyancing. From August 1995 to April 2003 she was responsible for devising, scripting and presenting the residential and commercial property programmes produced by Legal Network Television (LNTV), a wholly owned subsidiary of the College of Law. Bernadette has also devised and presented a number of continuing professional development courses and has written and contributed to a number of College publications.

Table of cases

Table of statutes

Table of statutory instruments

Table of European legislation

AA. New developments

AA.1   Home information packs

AA.1.1. The first phase of the introduction of the home information pack (HIP) began on 1 August 2007, when the requirement for the 'responsible person' to have a pack at the first point of marketing for a dwelling with four bedrooms or more was introduced (see A26 and A27). Since those chapters were written, the second phase has begun, and the requirement was extended on 10 September 2007 to dwellings with three or more bedrooms. See **www.homeinformation-packs.gov.uk** for further details.

AA.1.2. The Law Society has announced the release of further HIP products in September 2007 to provide a range of flexible delivery solutions for solicitors in addition to its online HIP product developed with MDA. The new products developed by the Law Society and the OyezStraker Group allow solicitors to order HIP components by phone, fax and email (the bureau service) and supplies kits including a binder and guidelines on the compilation of a HIP using the Law Society's TransAction forms (the starter kit).

AA.1.3. The Royal Institution of Chartered Surveyors (RICS) has agreed to a 'stay' of the judicial review they brought to challenge specific points relating to the Department for Communities and Local Government's implementation of the requirement to include an energy performance certificate (EPC) in a HIP. At the time of going to press, if an EPC is required in a HIP it must not be more than 12 months old. A consultation on the age of an EPC in a HIP is anticipated at the end of 2007.

AA.1.4. Further phases to bring in the requirement to have a HIP and a date by when a HIP is required at the first point of marketing for all types of dwellings are anticipated during the lifetime of this 14th edition of the Handbook.

AA.1.5. Lenders have indicated in the press that their view on acceptance of personal searches has not changed following the introduction of HIPs. There is no formal statement by the Council of Mortage Lenders (CML), but it appears from the stories reported in the press that enquiries of local authority carried out by personal search will be accepted if it is checked by a solicitor and backed by their professional indemnity insurance. Lenders' specific requirements regarding personal searches are given in Part 2 of the CML Lenders' Handbook.

AA.2. Energy performance certificates

AA.2.1. The requirements to assess and record the energy performance of buildings is being phased in according to the timetable given in A27. The requirement to have an EPC for dwellings is being phased in with HIPs.

AA.3. Law Society's Protocol and TransAction forms

AA.3.1. In July 2007 the Law Society released a new series of TransAction forms that may be used to create a HIP and to facilitate the conveyancing process. This edition of the Handbook was updated before the forms became available, and still refers to the previous editions of the TransAction forms – Seller's Property Information Form, Seller's Leasehold Information Form, etc.

AA.3.2. The explanatory notes for solicitors explaining the purpose of the new TransAction forms is reproduced in Appendix V.13.

AA3.3. The National Conveyancing Protocol is under review by the Law Society, and so the 14th edition of the Handbook continues to refer to the existing 5th edition of the Protocol.

AA.4. Solicitors' Code of Conduct 2007

AA.4.1. This edition has been updated to reflect the rules of the Solicitors' Code of Conduct 2007 which replaced the Solicitors' Practice Rules 1990. Selected Rules which are relevant to conveyancing are reproduced in Appendix I.1.

AA.4.2. The Solicitors Regulation Authority (SRA) are currently analysing the responses to a consultation on the provisions of Rule 3, particularly 3.07–3.15. The reason is to look at the restrictions on solicitors to act on behalf of the buyer and the seller. The consultation closed on 26 July 2007. See **www.sra.org.uk** for details.

AA.4.3. The SRA made minor amendments to Rule 18 on 10 August 2007 to allow for solicitors' obligations under the HIPs regime. The amended Rule is included in the Appendix to this book.

AA.4.4. The Law Society announced that some of the guidance which accompanied the Solicitors' Practice Rules 1990 in *The Guide to the Professional Conduct of Solicitors 1999* ('the Guide') will continue to be useful to solicitors after 1 July 2007, although it has ceased to be 'guidance from the regulator'. The annexes to Chapter 25 of the Guide remain available on the Law Society's website in the 'good practice' section. Some of this material continues to reproduced in the appendices to this Handbook.

AA.5. Law Society's business leases

AA.5.1. The Law Society is reviewing its business leases to make them consistent with the aims of the Code for Leasing Business Premises in England and Wales 2007. It is anticipated that revised leases will be available early in 2008.

AA.6. Consumers, Estate Agents and Redress Act 2007

AA.6.1. The Act requires estate agents to belong to an independent ombudsman scheme (currently voluntary). It also requires estate agents to keep records of their dealings with clients for six years. In addition the Act gives powers to the Office of Fair Trading to inspect files and consider an agents fitness to practice.

AA.6.2. The Act gained Royal Assent on 19 July 2007, but the provisions relevant to estate agents are not expected to come into force until April 2008.

AA.7. Adverse possession – Pye v. United Kingdom

AA.7.1. The Grand Chamber of the European Court of Human Rights gave its ruling on *J.A. Pye (Oxford) Ltd and J.A. Pye (Oxford) Land Ltd* v. *United Kingdom* (application no. 44302/02) on 30 August 2007. The Chamber ruled that there had been no breach by the UK Government of Article 1 of the European Convention of Human Rights. Pye Ltd had sought compensation from the government for the loss of its land, valued at £10 million, by adverse possession to a farmer (Mr and Mrs Graham) who had continued to occupy the land after their grazing licence had expired.

AA.7.2. HM Land Registry issued 'Additional practice affecting Practice Guide 5: Adverse possession of unregistered land and transitional provisions for registered land in the Land Registration Act 2002' on 14 September 2007. It is the Land Registry's view that the decision of the Grand Chamber in *Pye* does not affect the decision in *Beaulane Properties* v. *Palmer* [2006] EWHC 1071 (Ch) and therefore the requirement to show inconsistent use continues.

AA.8. Land registration

AA.8.1. The Land Registry's Practice Guides are regularly revised and updated to take account of changes in law and changes to Land Registry practice. Up to date versions are available on the Land Registry website (**www.landregistry.gov.uk/publications**).

AA.8.2. Mental Capacity Act 2005 introduces lasting powers of attorney which replace enduring powers of attorney as from 1 October 2007. No new enduring powers of attorney can be created on or after that date although existing enduring powers will remain in force. See D2.9.36 for further information as to lasting powers and Land Registry Practice Guide 9 for the Registry's requirements where a transfer or other deed is executed under a lasting power of attorney.

AA.8.3. A Land Registry consultation exercise is expected on proposals to amend the

Land Registration Rules 2003. A further Land Registry consultation exercise is planned to deal with the introduction of two additional triggers for compulsory first registration.

AA.9. Electronic conveyancing

AA.9.1. The Land Registry's consultation exercise on its proposals for Land Registration (Network Access) Rules 2007 and Land Registration (Electronic Communications) Order 2007 has now been completed and a report of the consultation is awaited. A report of the trial of a limited version of the chain matrix service in Bristol, Portsmouth and Fareham is also expected.

AA.9.2. Further consultation exercises will deal with the remaining secondary legislation required to operate an e-conveyancing system and the fees payable in respect of new e-conveyancing services. Full details of the proposals will be set out in the respective consultation papers. Details will also be available on the website (**www.econsultations.e-conveyancing.gov.uk**).

AA.9.3. The first phase of the more extensive e-conveyancing pilot is scheduled to commence in 2008. The Land Registry proposes to introduce electronic DS1s and to extend its e-lodgement facilities. The second phase of the pilot will include an enhanced version of the chain matrix service.

AA.9.4. Up to date information about developments in e-conveyancing and the services available are on the e-conveyancing website (**www.landregistry. gov.uk/e-conveyancing**).

A. PRELIMINARY MATTERS

A1. Taking instructions

1.1. Objectives

1.1.1. The purpose of taking instructions is to obtain sufficient information from the client to enable the solicitor to conduct the whole transaction: it will be necessary to consult the client further during the course of the transaction, but taking full instructions at an early stage will obviate the need to contact the client frequently to confirm minor details. Checking minor details with the client is not cost effective nor does it inspire the client with confidence in the solicitor's ability to do the work.

1.1.2. A further objective is to obtain an overall view of the transaction in order to give the client full and proper advice appropriate to the circumstances: unless full instructions are taken the solicitor is in danger of overlooking matters which are relevant to the transaction, e.g. insuring the property, or the inheritance tax implications of co-ownership.

Taxation consequences

1.1.3. Regard must always be paid to the taxation consequences of the proposed transaction whether or not these are mentioned to the solicitor by the client. Failure to do so may result in an action for breach of contract or negligence by the client against the solicitor.[1]

1. See *Hurlingham Estates Ltd* v. *Wilde*, *The Times*, 3 January 1997.

1.2. Where have the instructions come from?

1.2.1. Instructions to act may be accepted provided there is no breach of Rules 1 and 2 Solicitors' Code of Conduct 2007 (Rule 1 – core duties; Rule 2 – client relations). Thus instructions must be declined *inter alia* in the following circumstances:

(a) where to act would involve the solicitor in a breach of the law, e.g. a fraudulent conveyance;

(b) where the solicitor would be involved in a breach of the rules of conduct, e.g. dealing with more than one prospective buyer without disclosing this to all prospective buyers;

(c) where a conflict of interest exists or is likely to exist;

(d) where the solicitor lacks the expertise to carry out the client's instructions competently;

(e) where the solicitor does not have sufficient time to devote to the client's affairs;

(f) where the instructions are tainted by duress or undue influence, e.g. an elderly client is 'persuaded' by her relatives to sell the family home;

(g) where the solicitor, one of his partners, employees or close relatives holds some office or appointment the holding of which might lead the client or the general public to infer that the solicitor had some influence over the outcome of the matter, e.g. a solicitor who is a member of the local planning committee should not accept instructions to act in a planning appeal against the authority of which he is a member;

(h) where another solicitor has already been instructed in the matter and that other solicitor's retainer has not been terminated;

(i) where the client's freedom of choice to instruct the solicitor of his choosing has been impaired in some way, e.g. the client has received a discount from a builder on the condition that a certain solicitor is instructed.

1.2.2. Subject to the exceptions outlined above the solicitor cannot decline to act on the basis of the colour, race, national or ethnic origins of the client[1] nor on the basis of the client's sex or sexual orientation, marital status,[2] disability,[3] religion, belief or age.[4]

1.2.3. Instructions which have been obtained through a referral from an estate agent, mortgage broker or other third party may be accepted provided there is compliance with Rule 9 Solicitors' Code of Conduct 2007 (referrals of business). The solicitor may pay referral fees to introducers provided that the arrangement complies with Rule 9.02 Solicitors' Code of Conduct 2007 (financial arrangements with introducers).

1.2.4. If instructions are received indirectly through a third party, confirmation of the instructions must be obtained directly from the client in order to clarify the client's exact requirements and to ensure that the instructions are not tainted by duress or undue influence.

1.2.5. The solicitor should be alert to the possibilities of mortgage fraud and should adhere to the guidelines issued by the Law Society in its leaflet 'Green Card Warning on Property Fraud II' (see Appendix III.3).

1. Race Relations Act 1976, Rule 6 Solicitors' Code of Conduct 2007 (equality and diversity).
2. Sex Discrimination Act 1975 and Rule 6 Solicitors' Code of Conduct 2007 (equality and diversity).
3. Disability Discrimination Act 1995, Rule 6 Solicitors' Code of Conduct 2007 (equality and diversity).
4. Rule 6 Solicitors' Code of Conduct 2007 (equality and diversity).

1.3. Taking instructions in person

1.3.1. The client's name and address and the identity of the other party to the transaction should be requested before the first interview, or at the start of the first interview, in order to check for possible conflicts of interest. At the interview the client should be provided with written information regarding the cost of the transaction and details of whom to contact if the client has a complaint. The client should be asked to sign a copy of the document thereby acknowledging receipt.

1.3.2. Wherever possible instructions should be obtained from the client in a personal interview. This will enable the solicitor to clarify areas of doubt concerning the transaction, enable the client to ask questions about matters which worry him, and establish a confident working relationship between the solicitor and his client.

1.3.3. Where the solicitor is instructed by one person to act on behalf of that person and another, e.g. as co-sellers, the non-instructing client's authority to act and consent to the transaction should be confirmed directly with the person concerned.

1.3.4. If the interviewer is not the person who will conduct the transaction on the client's behalf, the client should be introduced to or at least told the name and status within the firm of the person who will be effecting the client's business and of the person whom he may contact should the need arise and whom the client should contact in the event of a problem or complaint arising about the solicitor's services.[1]

1.3.5. Under the terms of the Protocol, the solicitor who is acting for the seller is required to obtain his client's answers to the Seller's Property Information Form, to obtain from his client any relevant documents relating to, e.g. guarantees, building regulation consent, etc., and to ask his client to complete the Fixtures Fittings and Contents Form. He must also obtain details of all financial charges over the property (including second and subsequent mortgages, improvement grants and discounts repayable to the local authority), and ascertain the identity of all persons aged over 17 who are resident in the property in order to establish whether or not such persons have an interest in the property.

1.3.6. Where the client has been referred to the solicitor under an agreement authorised by Rule 9.02 Solicitors' Code of Conduct 2007, the client must be given, in writing, all the relevant information concerning the referral, including the existence of the financial arrangement with the introducer and the amount of any payment to the introducer. Where the introducer is paying the solicitor to provide services to the introducer's customers, the client must also be informed of the amount the introducer is paying for the solicitor's services and the amount the client is required to pay the introducer. The written notice must also contain a statement that the advice given to the client will be independent and confirm that the information disclosed by the client will not be disclosed to the introducer unless the client consents.[1]

1. *Ibid.*

1.4. **Instructions taken by telephone, etc.**

1.4.1. Where instructions are received by telephone the solicitor must still carry out the conflict of interest enquiries referred to in A1.3.1.

1.4.2. If instructions are received by telephone, e-mail or by any other non-face-to-face method, consideration must be given to Consumer Protection (Distance Selling) Regulations 2000 (SI 2000/2334) (as amended by Consumer Protection (Distance Selling) (Amendment) Regulations 2005 (SI 2005/689)).

1.4.3. The regulations apply where a 'supplier' (the solicitor) is providing services to a 'consumer' (an individual instructing the solicitor on personal business). Corporate clients instructing a solicitor on company business are not consumers within this definition.

1.4.4. A 'distance contract' is one which is concluded under 'an organised sales or services provision scheme', e.g. in response to an advertisement or where there is no physical communication up to and at the moment when the contract is concluded. Instructions received by letter or e-mail may fall within this definition of a distance contract.

1.4.5. Contracts relating to financial services are exempted from the regulations but contracts to provide conveyancing services are not currently exempt.

1.4.6. Where the regulations apply certain information must be supplied to the client in writing (regs.7 and 8). Most of the information required would be contained in a client care letter (e.g. name of solicitor, price, description of service to be provided) but in order to comply with the regulations it is suggested that, in cases where the regulations do or might apply, a clause is included in the client care letter to state that the contract between the solicitor and client will not be concluded until the client signs and returns a copy of the client care letter to the solicitor.

1.4.7.   Further, the client care letter must provide the client with information as to how the client's right to cancel may be affected if the client agrees to performance of the services beginning less than seven working days after the contract was concluded (reg. 8 as amended by SI 2005/689). Where the solicitor provides this information before the solicitor provides the services and the client agrees to the performance starting before the end of the cooling-off period, the client has no right to cancel under the regulations. Where, however, the information is provided 'in good time' during the performance of the services, the client will have a cooling-off period of seven working days starting on the day the contract is concluded and ending seven working days later or when the performance is completed, whichever is the sooner (regs. 12 and 13 as amended).

1.4.8.   It is also essential for the client care letter to obtain the client's agreement to exclude reg. 19 which states that if the services provided under the contract are not performed within a maximum of 30 days from the date of the contract, the contract is treated as if it had not been made.

1.4.9.   Where the client has been referred to the solicitor under an agreement covered by Rule 9 Solicitors' Code of Conduct 2007, the client must be told the details of the agreement and the level of payment made by the solicitor.

1.5.   Identity of the client

1.5.1.   A solicitor who purports to act on behalf of a client impliedly warrants to third parties with whom he has dealings (e.g. the other party's solicitor) that he has the client's authority to act. If he does not have the client's authority he may be liable to the third party for breach of warranty of authority.[1] For this reason a solicitor may want to check the identity of a client with whom he is not familiar.

1.5.2.   Checking the client's identity may serve as a precaution against mortgage fraud (see A24) and money laundering (see A23) and establishes that the client is the person who he says he is, thus ensuring that the solicitor has the client's authority to act in the transaction.

1.5.3.   The Law Society released guidance on money laundering in January 2004 and further anti-money laundering guidance for solicitors undertaking property work in December 2005. The guidance takes into account the changes introduced by Money Laundering Regulations 2003 (SI 2003/3075), which came into effect on 1 March 2004. The regulations extend to conveyancing and they require solicitors to obtain satisfactory evidence of their client's identity (see A23).

1.5.4.   Proceeds of Crime Act 2002 came into effect in February 2003. It includes an extended offence of money laundering and as a result solicitors should:

- enquire of the client how their transactions are to be funded; and

- consider whether they will accept cash payments for property and if so, to what limit.

Lender's requirements

1.5.5. When acting for a lender under the terms of the Lenders' Handbook (see Appendix VI.2), the identity of the client must be verified in accordance with the requirements of paragraph 3.3. of the Handbook.

1. See *Penn* v. *Bristol & West Building Society* [1997] 3 All ER 470.

1.6. Using checklists

1.6.1. Although checklists cannot be expected to cover every eventuality in every transaction they are useful in standard transactions to ensure that all necessary information is acquired during the course of the interview.

1.6.2. Checklists focus the interviewer's mind on the relevant information, which minimises preparation time and ultimately saves time in the interview itself, but do need to be used sympathetically so that the client does not feel he is being processed in an impersonal way.

1.6.3. Where checklists are used it is helpful to have them printed on a distinct colour of paper so that they are easily located in the file either by the solicitor himself or by another member of his staff who has to work on the file.

1.6.4. A reminder of the matters which will be raised at a first interview with a client is set out in A1.7–1.9 below. Standard checklists for sellers and buyers may be compiled from these guidelines to suit the individual requirements of particular firms.

1.7. Acting for the seller

1.7.1.

	Item	Reason for question	Further reference
(a)	Date instructions taken.	Record keeping.	
(b)	Full names, addresses of seller(s) and buyer(s) and home and business telephone numbers.	Needed in contract and for contact with client.	
(c)	Name and address of person at estate agents	For contact.	

	Item	Reason for question	Further reference
(d)	Find out where title deeds are and obtain client's authority to obtain them if in the hands of a third party.	To deduce title.	Deducing title, D1.
(e)	Ask clients for title number (if known).	To obtain official copy entries of the title.	Investigation of title, D2.
(f)	Name of other parties' solicitors or representatives.	For contact.	Dealing with non-solicitors, A5.
(g)	Do we act for the other party also?	Conflict of interest, breach of Rule 3.	Acting for both parties, A10.
(h)	Full address of property to be sold.	Needed in contract.	
(i)	Situation of property – position of footpaths/ railways/rivers, etc.	Need for plan or special searches.	Pre-contract searches and enquiries, B10.
(j)	Tenure: freehold/leasehold.	Needed in contract.	
(k)	Price.	Needed in contract, Stamp Duty Land Tax (SDLT) considerations.	
(l)	Has any preliminary deposit been paid? If so, how much? Receipt obtained?	Take account in calculating deposit on exchange.	Preliminary deposits, A12.
(m)	Which fixtures are to be removed?	Needed in contract.	Fixtures and fittings, B22.
(n)	Which fittings are to remain? Additional price for fittings?	Needed in contract and may affect SDLT. Need to supply Fixtures, Fittings and Contents Form to client.	Fixtures and fittings, B22.

Item	Reason for question	Further reference
(o) Anticipated completion date.	To advise client on likely duration of transaction and to assess urgency of matter. To discuss redemption of present mortgage, i.e. interest charges up to end of month.	
(p) Present/proposed use of property.	Planning aspects/restrictive covenants.	
(q) Does the transaction attract VAT?	May be needed in contract and client may need advice.	VAT, A16.
(r) Who is resident in the property?	Occupiers' rights, overriding interests.	Seller's investigation of title, B3.
(s) Is the transaction dependent on the purchase?	Synchronisation.	Exchange, section C.
(t) Any other terms agreed between parties?	Needed in contract.	
(u) Any correspondence between the parties?	Existence of a contract, or other terms agreed.	Form of contract, B11.
(v) Vacant possession/ details of tenancies.	Needed in contract.	
(w) Advice as to costs.	Required by Rule 2.	Estimate of costs, A8.
(x) Interest on deposit.	Deposit interest considerations.	Deposit, B17.
(y) Do a financial calculation, including costs.	To ensure the client can afford the transaction.	
(z) Time taken in interview.	Time costing/ recording.	
(aa) Did we act on purchase?	Look at old file prior to interview to gain relevant information.	

Item	Reason for question	Further reference
(bb) Are there any outstanding mortgages? How much and to whom?	Calculation of financial statement and will normally need to be redeemed on completion.	
(cc) Ask for seller's mortgage account number or reference.	Needed in order to obtain deeds from lender and to obtain a preliminary redemption statement.	
(dd) Advise seller not to cancel mortgage repayments or insurance until completion.	So that redemption figure obtained on completion is not higher than presently anticipated.	
(ee) How much deposit required?	Advise client on dangers of reduced deposit, use of deposit in related purchase.	Deposit, B17.
(ff) What is to happen to the proceeds of sale?	Accounting to the client, investment advice.	Financial services, A4. Post-completion, section G.
(gg) Does the sale attract CGT?	Advise the client.	Capital gains tax, A15.
(hh) Obtain answers to Seller's Property Information Form and completion of Fixtures, Fittings and Contents Form.	To supply the buyer with this information.	Pre-contract searches and enquiries, B10.
(ii) Discuss advantage of making a local search and enquiries and any other relevant searches.		Pre-contract searches and enquiries, B10.
(jj) Check identity of client.	A precaution against mortgage fraud and money laundering.	A1.4. Money laundering, A23. Mortgage fraud, A24.

1.8. Acting for the buyer

1.8.1.

Item	Reason for question	Further reference
(a) Date instructions taken.	Record keeping.	
(b) Full names and addresses of seller(s) and buyer(s) and home and business telephone numbers.	Needed in contract and for contact with client.	
(c) Name and address of person at estate agents.	For contact.	
(d) Name of other parties' solicitors or representatives.	For contact.	Dealing with non-solicitors, A5.
(e) Do we act for the other party also?	Conflict of interest, breach of Rule 3.	Acting for both parties, A10.
(f) Full address of property to be bought.	Needed in contract.	
(g) Situation of property – position of footpaths/railways/ rivers, etc.	Need for plan or special searches.	Pre-contract searches and enquiries, B10.
(h) Tenure: freehold/leasehold.	Needed in contract.	
(i) Price.	Needed in contract, SDLT considerations.	
(j) Has any preliminary deposit been paid? If so, how much? Receipt obtained?	Take account in calculating deposit on exchange.	Preliminary deposits, A12.
(k) Which fixtures are to be removed?	Needed in contract.	Fixtures and fittings, B22.
(l) Which fittings are to remain? Additional price for fittings? Apportionment of purchase price?	Needed in contract and may affect SDLT.	Fixtures and fittings, B22.

Item	Reason for question	Further reference
(m) Anticipated completion date.	To advise client on likely duration of transaction and to assess urgency of matter. Effect of date on first payment under mortgage.	
(n) Present/proposed use of property.	Planning aspects/ restrictive covenants.	
(o) Does the transaction attract VAT?	May be needed in contract and client may need advice.	VAT, A16.
(p) Who is resident in the property?	Occupiers' rights, overriding interests.	Seller's investigation of title, B3.
(q) Is the transaction dependent on the sale of another property?	Synchronisation.	Exchange, section C.
(r) Any other terms agreed between the parties?	Needed in contract.	
(s) Any correspondence between the parties?	Existence of a contract, or other terms agreed.	Form of contract, B11.
(t) Vacant possession/ details of tenancies.	Needed in contract.	
(u) Advice as to costs.	Required by Rule 2.	Estimate of costs, A8.
(v) Interest on deposit.	Deposit interest considerations.	Deposit, B17.
(w) Do a financial calculation, including costs.	To ensure the client can afford the transaction.	
(x) Time taken in interview.	Time costing/ recording.	
(y) How will the deposit be funded?	Is bridging finance needed? Need to give notice if funds invested? Client's authority if undertaking to be given.	Deposit, B17.

	Item	Reason for question	Further reference
(z)	How is the balance of the price to be funded? Has the client obtained a mortgage certificate or offer? Does client have outstanding mortgage on any other property?	Advice on sources of finance and/or tax relief on interest. Lenders may insist that all outstanding mortgages are repaid as a condition of the new loan.	Financial services, A4.
(aa)	Survey arrangements.	Advise the client.	Surveys, A13.
(bb)	Insurance: Property? Life? Contents? Other? e.g. employee liability.	Advise the client.	Insurance, C3.
(cc)	How is property to be held by co-owners?	Advise the client.	Joint purchasers, A9.
(dd)	Custody of deeds.	Instructions needed if property not mortgaged.	Post-completion, section G.
(ee)	Client's present property?	Need to give notice to determine tenancy? Penalty on mortgage redemption.	
(ff)	Check client's identity	A precaution against mortgage fraud and money laundering and required by the Lenders' Handbook.	A1.5. Money laundering, A23. Mortgage fraud, A24.
(gg)	Stamp Duty Land Tax	Advise client of responsibility to complete Land Tax Return.	Post-completion, section G.

1.9.   Instructions in special cases

1.9.1.   Additional information will be required where the transaction concerns a newly constructed property, is leasehold, or is a dealing with part only of the seller's property. Further checklists to deal with these situations are contained in sections I (new properties), J (sales of part), and K (leaseholds).

1.9.2.   If it appears that the property (or part of it) comprises a flying freehold, the client should be warned of the possible difficulties in obtaining finance for the property as many lenders are reluctant to accept a flying freehold as security for a loan.[1]

1.9.3.   If the client is to act as a guarantor to another client's debts (e.g. on a mortgage or as surety to a lender), it may be necessary to consider separate representation for the guarantor in order to avoid any conflict of interests (see A10).

1.   See paragraph 5.5 of the Lenders' Handbook (Appendix VI.2).

1.10.   After the interview

1.10.1.   Instructions should be confirmed to the client in writing.[1] The letter should include:

(a)   information relating to the name and status of the person who will be carrying out the work for the client and the name of the person who has overall responsibility for the matter;

(b)   details of whom the client should contact in the event of a complaint about the solicitor's services;

(c)   an explanation of how the client will be kept informed of progress;

(d)   information as to costs and disbursements including liability for third party costs;

(e)   a repetition of the advice regarding any agreement under Rule 9 Solicitors' Code of Conduct 2007 (referrals of business) (where relevant);

(f)   information regarding the payment of stamp duty land tax, see A1.10.4;

(g)   advice regarding the evidence of identification needed under money laundering legislation and information about the acceptable means of payment;

(h)   a résumé of the information received and advice given at the interview in order to ensure that no misunderstanding exists between solicitor and client;

(i)   confirmation of any action agreed to be taken by the solicitor;

(j)   a reminder to the client of anything which he promised to do, e.g. obtain service charge receipts;

(k)   a request for a payment on account in relation to disbursements; and

(l)   a copy of the Law Society's client leaflets (where appropriate): 'Your Guide to Buying a Home' and 'The Clients Charter'; or your firm's own leaflets.

1.10.2. Provided that the checklist used contains a note of the time expended on the interview, and that a full written record of the interview exists in the form of a follow-up letter to the client, a detailed attendance note may be dispensed with.

1.10.3. If not already done, contact should be established with the representatives of the other parties involved in the transaction, e.g. other solicitor, estate agent, lender. If the identity of the other party's solicitor is not known, his or her status should be checked with the Law Society. If a licensed conveyancer, their status can be checked with the Council for Licensed Conveyancers. This is also a requirement of paragraph 3.2 of the Lenders' Handbook.

1.10.4. The client care letter sent to the buyer following the interview should also make the following points regarding the completion of the land tax return form:

- that it is the client's duty to submit the form within the time limit of 30 days, although the solicitor may send the form on behalf of the client;

- that there are penalties for a failure to submit the form on time (£100 for up to three months delay, thereafter £200 together with tax related penalty if there is a failure to file for twelve months);

- if the firm does complete the form on behalf of the client, the form will be completed based on information provided by the client and that the client is responsible for the accuracy of the information and for any penalty which may be incurred if the form is returned for correction;

- that failure to submit the form on time may result in delays in registering the purchase of the property;

- the client is liable for the payment of any tax due and where there are co-buyers the liability is joint and several;

- that if the solicitor is named on the form as 'tax agent' the solicitor will not accept any responsibility for the form, he will merely be the person with whom HM Revenue and Customs will communicate and to whom the land transaction return certificate will be sent;

- that HM Revenue and Customs may enquire into the transaction and the client may be liable to pay additional tax after any enquiry;

- that should an enquiry take place, any costs incurred by the solicitor will be additional to those paid for the conveyancing transaction;

- that the client should keep any documents relating to the transaction for a minimum period of six years;

- that any documents in the solicitor's possession will be available for a minimum period of six years and what will happen to them after that period has expired.

1.10.5. For the seller:

    (a) obtain title deeds;

(b)   send for official copy entries of the title (registered land);

    (c)   ask estate agent for copy of the particulars;

    (d)   requisition local search and enquiries and other searches (if so instructed by the client);

    (e)   investigate title before drafting contract;

    (f)   prepare abstract or epitome of title (unregistered interest in land);

    (g)   make Land Charges Department search against seller;

    (h)   check seller's replies to the Seller's Property Information Form.

1.10.6.   For the buyer:

    (a)   make search applications appropriate to the property and its location (if not to be supplied by seller);

    (b)   deal with buyer's mortgage and survey arrangements if required;

    (c)   check the identity of the buyer(s);

    (d)   check the identity of the seller's representative if not known;

    (e)   obtain estate agent's particulars;

    (f)   consider draft contract when received from seller.

1.   See guidance to Rule 2.02 Solicitors' Code of Conduct 2007; this information must be given in a clear and readily accessible form. In Protocol cases the specimen letters contained in the Protocol documentation may be adapted for use in this situation. See also the Law Society's guidance, 'Your clients – your business', issued January 2006.

1.11.   Lost title deeds

1.11.1.   If it appears that the client's title deeds to unregistered land have been lost or destroyed, it may be possible to obtain voluntary registration of the title at the Land Registry.

1.11.2.   An application for first registration made by a person who is unable to produce a full documentary title must be supported by satisfactory evidence of the applicant's entitlement to apply, together with, where appropriate, evidence to account for the absence of documentary evidence of title.[1]

1.   Land Registration Rules 2003, r.27; and see Land Registry Practice Guide 2.

1.12.   Adverse possession

1.12.1.   If it appears that the land or any part of it may have been acquired by adverse possession it may be possible to obtain voluntary registration of the title at the Land Registry. Land Registration Act 2002 has not changed the substantive law as to what constitutes adverse possession, for example the requirements of factual possession and the intention to possess. Where appropriate, reference should be made to the relevant specialist texts. Reference may also be made to G3.4.4 and G3.10 and Land Registry Practice Guides 4 and 5.

A2. Property selling

2.1. General principles

2.1.1. Property selling may be carried out by a solicitor:

- as part of his practice, either through the solicitor's own office or through a separate Solicitors Estate Agency Ltd (SEAL);

- through an individual practice formed for property selling;

- through a joint property selling practice (formed with other firms of solicitors and distinct for all purposes including indemnity rules, accounts rules, practice rules and conflict provisions through a recognised body).

2.1.2. In selling property the solicitor is still acting as a solicitor and therefore remains bound by Solicitors' Code of Conduct 2007, Solicitors' Accounts Rules 1998, and all other rules, regulations and principles of conduct which affect solicitors in practice.

2.1.3. A solicitor may carry out such valuation as may be necessary to give advice to the client on the price at which the property should be sold, and to prepare the sale particulars. The solicitor may provide structural surveys and formal valuations through the firm but must ensure that the relevant staff have the appropriate level of competence; see Rule 18 Solicitors' Code of Conduct 2007.

2.1.4. Property selling may be carried on either as part of the solicitor's business or as a separate business but in the latter case Rule 21 Solicitors' Code of Conduct 2007 (separate businesses) must be observed (see A2.13 and Appendix I.1).

2.1.5. Fees earned by the solicitor through property selling which is carried on through the solicitor's practice or a SEAL must be included in his gross fees return.

2.1.6. Paragraphs A2.2–2.12 apply where property selling is carried on as part of the solicitor's business.

2.2.   Advertising

2.2.1.   Subject to compliance with Rule 7 Solicitors' Code of Conduct 2007 (publicity), a solicitor may advertise that he undertakes property-selling work and/or may advertise a specific property which he has been instructed to sell.

2.2.2.   An entry or advertisement of a solicitor who undertakes a property-selling service may appear in a directory or 'Yellow Pages' under the heading of 'estate agents' or 'solicitors'.

2.2.3.   Unsolicited visits and telephone calls may be made to a current or former client, another lawyer, an existing or potential professional or business connection, or a commercial organisation or public body. Unsolicited visits and telephone calls to the general public are expressly prohibited by Rule 7.03 Solicitors' Code of Conduct 2007.

2.2.4.   Solicitors may place 'for sale' boards outside properties which they have been instructed to sell provided that the boards comply with current statutory requirements and with Rule 7 Solicitors' Code of Conduct 2007.

2.3.   Employment and remuneration of unqualified staff

2.3.1.   Unqualified, i.e. non-solicitor, staff may be employed to deal with property selling but they cannot enter into partnership with the solicitor.

2.3.2.   Fee sharing with a genuine employee is permitted by Rule 8 Solicitors' Code of Conduct 2007 as is fee sharing with an estate agent who is acting as a sub-agent on the sale of a property. But this must not be used to disguise a 'partnership' by a solicitor with a non-qualified person.

2.4.   Premises used for property selling

2.4.1.   A department or branch office which is used mainly for property selling may be described as an 'estate agency' or 'property centre' or by any other suitable description, provided that the description is not misleading.

2.4.2.   Rule 5 Solicitors' Code of Conduct 2007 (business management in England and Wales) relating to the supervision and management of a firm applies equally to property selling.

2.4.3.   A 'property display centre' is a separate office or premises where a solicitor alone or in association with other firms of solicitors, displays or disseminates information relating to the selling of property, but where no other business of a solicitor's firm, particularly negotiating, is conducted. See paragraph 5 guidance to Rule 18 Solicitors' Code of Conduct 2007 (property selling).

2.4.4. The firms operating a joint property display centre may establish a joint service company to carry out the necessary administrative functions concerned with the running of the centre, but the service company cannot carry on any legal practice nor have any dealings with the actual selling of property.

2.4.5. A joint property display centre cannot be used to carry on any part of the solicitors' professional practice. Any stationery used for writing to the property buying and selling public must be the stationery of the individual property selling firm, and not the notepaper of the joint property display centre. However, the centre's name and logo may appear on the notepaper. The words 'regulated by the Solicitors Regulation Authority' must also appear.

2.5.　SEALs

2.5.1. A SEAL is a joint solicitors' property-selling practice. It must be a corporate body recognised under Administration of Justice Act 1985, s.9, by the Law Society (a 'recognised body'). It must be owned by at least four firms of solicitors with no principals in common and none of which has a controlling majority of the shares. It must not itself undertake conveyancing work and must be physically separate from its participating practices.

2.5.2. A SEAL may provide a full range of estate agency services, i.e. act as agent for the seller and provide mortgage services for the buyer.

2.5.3. If the SEAL is acting for the seller on the sale of a property, and

    (a)　the SEAL is providing mortgage related services to the buyer; or

    (b)　a participating firm is doing the conveyancing for the buyer;

the buyer and seller must give their written informed consent, and different individuals must deal with the work for seller and buyer; see Rule 3.11–3.14 Solicitors' Code of Conduct 2007 and paragraphs 80–81 guidance to Rule 3.

2.6.　**Written agreement as to remuneration**

2.6.1. When accepting instructions to act in the sale of a property, a solicitor must give the client a written statement containing the following information:

    (a)　the amount of the solicitor's remuneration, or its method of calculation;

    (b)　the circumstances in which the remuneration becomes payable;

    (c)　the amount of any disbursements which are to be separately charged, or the basis on which they will be calculated, and the circumstances in which they may be incurred;

    (d)　whether VAT is payable and whether it is included in the estimate or fixed fee;

    (e)   whether or not the solicitor is to be a sole agent;

    (f)   the identity of the property to be sold;

    (g)   the interest to be sold;

    (h)   the price to be sought;

    (i)   an explanation of the phrases 'sole selling rights', 'ready willing and able purchaser' (or similar phrases), if used in the agreement.

2.7. Amount of remuneration

2.7.1. The amount of commission charged by the solicitor for selling a property is a matter for agreement between the solicitor and his client.

2.7.2. Unless the client signs an agreement in relation to charges under Solicitors Act 1974, s.57, the amount of the commission may be subject to the remuneration certificate procedure. The client may in any event be entitled to taxation of the bill by the court.

2.7.3. A composite fee for both property selling and conveyancing may be quoted or advertised, but must be clearly expressed.

2.8. Application of Estate Agents Act 1979

2.8.1. Estate Agents Act 1979 does not apply to solicitors who are engaged in property selling, but Property Misdescriptions Act 1991 does. This latter Act makes it an offence for a person selling property to attach a misleading description to the property which is being sold. The liability is similar to that incurred under Trades Descriptions Act 1968. Solicitors' Code of Conduct 2007 imposes on solicitors similar duties and obligations to those to which estate agents are subject under regulations made under the 1979 Act.

2.9. Insurance

2.9.1. Property-selling activities must be covered by the terms of the solicitors' insurance policy.

2.10. Declining instructions to act

2.10.1. Instructions must be declined where there would be a breach of Rule 1 or 2 Solicitors' Code of Conduct 2007.

2.10.2. Where the solicitor is asked to sell a property of a type which he is unused to handling he should either decline the instructions or place the property with a subagent who is experienced in that type of property.

2.10.3. There may be occasions when a conflict of interest arises between the solicitor and his client when the solicitor is engaged in selling the property as well as undertaking the legal work. As in any situation where a conflict arises or is likely to arise, the solicitor must decline to act or should cease to act further in the transaction. Attention is also drawn to the Law Society's guidance relating to mortgage fraud (see A24 and Appendix III.3).

2.11. Introductions and referrals

2.11.1. Provided there is compliance with Rule 9 Solicitors' Code of Conduct 2007 (referrals of business) a solicitor may have an arrangement with an estate agent in relation to the sale of property (see A7).

2.12. Commissions from third parties

2.12.1. Any commission received by a solicitor as a result of the client having entered into, e.g. an endowment mortgage, is subject to Rule 2.06 Solicitors' Code of Conduct 2007 (client relations).

2.13. Property selling as a separate business

2.13.1. Rule 21 Solicitors' Code of Conduct 2007 permits a solicitor to control, actively participate in or operate (in each case alone, or by or with others) a separate business, including a property-selling business, provided that there is compliance with the provisions of Rule 21 which are summarised below.

2.13.2. The property-selling (estate agency) business must be carried out from premises which are clearly differentiated from that of any premises of the solicitor in England and Wales. If the estate agency business shares premises or reception staff with any English or Welsh practice of the solicitor, the customers of the estate agency business must be informed that, as customers of the estate agency business, they do not enjoy the statutory protection afforded to clients of a solicitor and that the estate agency is not regulated by the Solicitors Regulation Authority.

2.13.3. The property-selling business must not be held out or described in such a way as to suggest that the property-selling business is carrying on a practice regulated by the Solicitors Regulation Authority.

2.13.4. All parperwork, documents, records and files relating to customers of the estate agency business must be kept separately from those relating to the solicitor's practice. Money held for the estate agency business and its customers must not be held in the solicitor's client account.

2.13.5.   If the only services provided to the seller are property-selling services through a SEAL, the solicitor may act for the buyer in the purchase of the property provided that the conditions listed in Rule 3.13 Solicitors' Code of Conduct 2007 are complied with. In particular, the buyer and the seller must give their written and informed consent to the arrangement and different individuals must deal with the work on behalf of the seller and buyer. Alternatively, the solicitor may do conveyancing work for the seller where the separate business has provided mortgage services to the buyer provided Rule 3.13 is complied with.

2.14.   Acting for a buyer

2.14.1.   Neither the solicitor nor the firm may act in the conveyancing for a buyer of any property sold through the estate agency unless the conditions set out in Rule 21.05(f) Solicitors' Code of Conduct 2007 have been complied with:

(a) the firm must share the ownership of the estate agency with at least one other business in which neither the individual solicitor nor the firm has any financial interest;

(b) no person in the firm has dealt with the sale of the seller's property for the separate business; and

(c) the buyer has given written consent to the firm acting after the firm's financial interest in the sale going through has been explained to the buyer.

A3. Advertising

## 3.1.	Solicitors' Code of Conduct 2007

3.1.1.	A solicitor may publicise his practice provided that the publicity complies with Rule 7 Solicitors' Code of Conduct 2007 (publicity). The main points of Rule 7 are summarised in A3.3–A3.8.

## 3.2.	Compliance with Consumer Credit (Advertisements) Regulations 2004

3.2.1.	The contents of advertisements relating to the provision of credit and related services must comply with Consumer Credit (Advertisements) Regulations 2004 (SI 2004/1484) which are summarised below. These regulations apply in circumstances where, e.g. the solicitor is advertising his services and indicates that he can obtain mortgage finance for a client. These regulations do not apply to advertisements for mortgages which are a first charge on the borrower's home but they will apply to advertisements for second mortgages. If the firm publishes a credit advertisement it must ensure that the advertisement complies with the regulations.

3.2.2.	*Summary of the Regulations:*

1.	Every credit advertisement must be written in plain and intelligible language; be easily legible (or, in the case of any information given orally, clearly audible), and specify the name of the advertiser.

2.	Unless one of the exceptions in Regulation 4(1)(b) applies, e.g. the advertisement is published on the radio, the advertisement must specify a postal address at which the advertiser may be contacted.

3.	Where security will be required the advertisement must specify the nature of the security and, where the security required is a mortgage over the debtor's home, the advertisement must contain the following warning: *Your home may be repossessed if you do not keep up repayments on a mortgage or any other debt secured on it.* Where the loan is being used to pay debts due to other creditors, the advertisement must also contain the following warning: *Think carefully before securing other debts against your home*.

4.   Where the advertisement relates to loans under equity release schemes secured on the debtor's home, the advertisement must state: *Check that this mortgage will meet your needs if you want to move or sell your home or you want your family to inherit it. If you are in any doubt, seek independent advice*.

5.   The warnings must be given no less prominence than the other issues required in the advertisement.

6.   The APR must be specifically mentioned and given greater prominence than the mention of any other charge.

7.   The advertisement must also include the issues listed in Schedule 2 of the Regulations:

     (a)   The amount of credit which may be provided under a consumer credit agreement or an indication of the maximum amount and the minimum amount of credit which may be provided;

     (b)   a statement of any requirement to place on deposit any sum of money in any account with any person;

     (c)   in the case of an advertisement relating to credit to be provided under a debtor-creditor-supplier agreement, where the advertisement specifies goods, services, land or other things having a particular cash price, the acquisition of which from an identified dealer may be financed by the credit, the cash price of such goods, services, land or other things;

     (d)   a statement as to whether an advance payment is required and if so the amount or minimum amount of the payment expressed as a sum of money or a percentage;

     (e)   in the case of an advertisement relating to running-account credit, a statement of the frequency of the repayments of credit under the advertised transaction and of the amount of each repayment stating whether it is a fixed or minimum amount, or a statement indicating the manner in which the amount will be determined;

     (f)   in the case of other credit advertisements, a statement of the frequency, number and amounts of repayments of credit;

     (g)   a statement indicating the description and amount of any other payments and charges which may be payable under the transaction advertised;

     (h)   in the case of an advertisement relating to fixed-sum credit which is repayable at specified intervals or in specified amounts, the total amount payable by the debtor, being the total of any advance payments, the amount of credit repayable by the debtor, and the amount of the total charge for credit.

3.3. Matters prohibited by Solicitors' Code of Conduct 2007

3.3.1. Rule 7.01 provides that publicity must not be misleading or inaccurate.

3.3.2 Rule 7.03 generally prohibits unsolicited visits or telephone calls to the general public.

3.3.3. Unsolicited visits and telephone calls may be made to a current or former client, another lawyer, an existing or potential professional or business connection, or a commercial organisation or public body (subject to any legal requirements such as those under Data Protection Act 1998).

3.4. Application of Solicitors' Code of Conduct 2007

3.4.1. Rule 7 (publicity) applies to all forms of publicity including the name or description of the firm, stationery, advertisements, brochures, websites, directory entries, media appearances, press releases promoting a practice and direct approaches to potential clients and other persons, and whether conducted in person, in writing or in electronic form.

3.5. Property selling

3.5.1. Publicity in relation to any other business or activity carried on by the firm (e.g. property selling) must comply with Rule 7 Solicitors' Code of Conduct 2007.

3.5.2. The solicitor would be able to describe himself as a 'solicitor', 'estate agent' or 'solicitor and estate agent' in an advertisement which relates to his property-selling activities, and may be listed under the heading of 'solicitors' or 'estate agents' in a directory.

3.6. Advertising the solicitor's charges

3.6.1. Any publicity relating to the solicitor's charges or basis of charging must be clearly expressed.

3.6.2. All publicity relating to charges must make it clear whether disbursements and VAT are included.

3.7. Advertising placed by third parties

3.7.1. Where advertisements are placed by third parties which advertise the services of solicitors to whom work may be referred, the solicitor remains responsible for the advertisement. Such advertisements should therefore be checked carefully by the solicitor before publication. If the solicitor becomes aware of a breach, the solicitor must take steps to have the publicity changed or withdrawn. Solicitors must not authorise any other person to conduct publicity for the solicitors' practice in a way which would be contrary to Rule 7.

3.8. Professional stationery

3.8.1. Requirements for professional stationery are set out in Rule 7.07 Solicitors' Code of Conduct 2007. All firms are required to put 'regulated by the Solicitors Regulation Authority' on their letterhead and fax headings.

A4. Financial services

4.1. Activities within Financial Services and Markets Act 2000

4.1.1. Financial Services and Markets Act 2000 (FSMA) has made major changes to the regulation of the financial services industry. Of necessity, these changes will affect solicitors and since the consequences of providing investment services (referred to in the 2000 Act as 'regulated activities') without authorisation can amount to a criminal offence, solicitors must ensure that any activity caught by the Act is undertaken in an appropriate manner. The Act came into force on 1 December 2001.

The following activities may involve a solicitor in regulated activities:

(a) advising a client about obtaining a regulated mortgage, an insurance contract (e.g. endowment, mortgage protection, defective title, household contents or building policies) an ISA or a pension mortgage;

(b) where a property sale is linked to the sale of a business in the form of a sale of company shares;

(c) where shares in a management company are transferred on completion;

(d) where the sale of a property for a client leads to the client looking for advice on how to invest the proceeds of sale.

4.1.2. It is a criminal offence to carry on 'regulated activities' as defined in Financial Services and Markets Act (Regulated Activities) Order 2001, without authorisation. Since 1 December 2001, authorisation must be obtained from the Financial Services Authority. Large numbers of firms of solicitors will fall outside the requirements to be authorised provided they undertake regulated activities strictly in accordance with the statutory exclusions or exemptions.

4.2. Regulated activities

4.2.1. 'Regulated activities' are defined in Financial Services and Markets Act (Regulated Activities) Order 2001 (RAO).

4.2.2.   A regulated activity is potentially undertaken when a solicitor is involved in any one of the activities referred to in articles 5–61 RAO and relating to any one of the specified investments listed in articles 74–89. The most common activities will be advice on the merits of buying or selling a specified investment or arranging on behalf of a client the sale or purchase of a specified investment. Shares, endowment policies and other insurance contracts, regulated mortgages and ISAs constitute common specified investments.

4.2.3.   Advising the client on or arranging the following products does not constitute a regulated activity:

    (a)   a bank or building society account;

    (b)   unregulated mortgages.

4.2.4.   Generic investment advice is not within the definition of regulated activities in the RAO. Generic advice is advice about general categories of investment, as opposed to specific investments. Recommendations to the client that 'it would be wise to invest capital in equity shares/unit trusts' or 'you should take out a life insurance policy' are both examples of generic advice. A recommendation to the client that he should 'invest £5,000 in x unit trusts' or to 'take out a regulated life insurance policy for a 15-year term with y insurance company who do a very good policy' is, however, specific investment advice falling within the definition of a 'regulated activity'.

4.2.5.   'Arranging deals in investments' is a regulated activity within the Act. A solicitor who is involved in arrangements which lead to a client taking out a regulated life insurance policy is potentially carrying on a regulated activity even if he had given no advice about the policy.

4.2.6.   Solicitors who arrange deals in investments can avoid the need for authorisation by showing that certain exclusions contained in the RAO apply. The most important are as follows:

    (a)   Arrangements made with or through an authorised person (i.e. one authorised by the Financial Services Authority under the FSMA) where:

        (i)   the transaction is entered into on advice given to the client by an authorised person; or

        (ii)   it is clear in all the circumstances that the client, in his capacity as an investor, is not seeking and has not sought advice from the person as to the merits of the client entering the transaction (or if the client has sought advice the solicitor has declined to give it but has recommended the client to seek advice from an authorised person).

    It is important to note, however, that the above exclusion does not apply to an insurance contract nor does it apply if the solicitor receives from any person other than the client any pecuniary reward or advantage, for which he does not account to the client, arising out of his entering into the transaction. The Solicitors Regulation Authority (SRA) has taken the view that retaining commission with the informed consent of the client in accordance with Rule 2.06 Solicitors' Code of Conduct 2007 does represent 'accounting to the client' and the benefit of the exclusion will still apply in these circumstances.

(b) Introductions: where a person introduces a client to an authorised or exempt person and the introduction is made with a view to the provision of independent advice. Note that like the exclusion in (a) above this exclusion does not apply to insurance contracts.

4.2.7. Solicitors should note that the exclusion arising from the use of an authorised person only applies to arranging; it does not apply to investment advice. Further, none of the exclusions apply to the advice or arrangements where the investment product is an insurance contract (see A4.1.1 for examples of such contracts). Where the activity involves advice or the exclusion for arranging is not available for any reason, an alternative means of avoiding the need for authorisation is to use Part XX FSMA which contains provisions relating to 'exempt regulated activities' carried on by members of a profession which is supervised and regulated by a designated professional body (DPB). The SRA is a DPB.

4.2.8. Section 327 FSMA provides that the prohibition against carrying on regulated activities contained in the Act does not apply to the carrying on of a regulated activity by a member of a profession if certain conditions apply:

(a) the person must be a member of a profession or controlled or managed by one or more such members;

(b) the person must not receive from anyone other than his client any pecuniary reward or other advantage, for which he does not account to his client, arising out of his carrying on of any of the activities;

(c) the manner of the provision of any service in the course of carrying on the activities must be incidental to the provision by him of professional services;

(d) only regulated activities permitted by the DPB's rules may be carried out.

4.2.9. The SRA has issued rules (Solicitors' Financial Services (Scope) Rules 2001), covering the requirements of (d) above. These rules limit the scope of solicitors benefiting from Part XX. The prohibited activities include:

(a) market making;

(b) buying, selling, subscribing or underwriting as principal where the firm holds itself out as engaging in the business of buying investments with a view to selling them;

(c) acting as a trustee or operator of a regulated CIS;

(d) acting as a stakeholder pension scheme manager;

(e) entering into a regulated mortgage contract as lender or administering a regulated mortgage contract unless this is in the firm's capacity as a trustee or PR and the borrower is a beneficiary;

(f) entering into regulated home reversion or home purchase plans as plan providers (see A4.4).

4.2.10. There are further restrictions on using Part XX where the investment is a packaged product. These are defined as long term insurance contracts (including endowment policies), units or shares in regulated Collective Investment Schemes (e.g. unit trusts or shares in Open Ended Investment Companies) or an investment trust savings scheme, whether or not held within an ISA or PEP or a stakeholder pension scheme. Where such investments are acquired, firms cannot use the 'incidental' exception in Part XX but, where possible, should use an authorised person. Firms may, however, pass on and endorse the advice of an authorised person within Part XX.

4.3. Mortgages

4.3.1. Under article 61(1) RAO, entering into a regulated mortgage contract as lender is a regulated activity. Further, under article 61(2), administering a regulated mortgage contract where the contract was entered into by way of business is also a regulated activity. A regulated mortgage is one where:

(a) the lender provides credit to an individual or trustees;

(b) the obligation to repay is secured by a first legal mortgage on land in the UK;

(c) at least 40% of that land is used or intended to be used as or in connection with a dwelling by the borrower, a beneficiary of the trust or related person.

Note, purely commercial mortgages or mortgages on overseas property will be unregulated.

4.3.2. Financial Services and Markets Act 2000 (Regulated Activities) (Amendment) (No. 1) Order 2003 amended the RAO with regard to regulated mortgages. It extended the definition of regulated activities to 'arranging regulated mortgage contracts' and 'advising on regulated mortgage contracts' in addition to entering into as lender and administering a regulated mortgage. The changes relating to regulated mortgages came into force on 31 October 2004.

4.3.3. Solicitors' Financial Services (Scope) Rules 2001 have been amended to prevent solicitors from using Part XX FSMA in relation to the activity of advising on regulated mortgage. Consequently, it will not be possible for the 'incidental' route to avoid authorisation to be used for advice. It will, however, be possible for solicitors to endorse the advice of an authorised person where such endorsement is incidental to other work.

4.3.4. Arranging regulated mortgages will be excluded where the arrangement is with or through an authorised person (the same conditions as noted above will apply) or where the arrangement consists of an introduction to an authorised person with a view to the provision of independent advice.

4.3.5. A further exclusion has been added where an introduction is made to an authorised lender or broker. To benefit from this exclusion, before the introduction the following must be disclosed to the client:

(a) details of any fee or commission to be received or commission to be received for introducing the client; and

(b) an indication of any other reward or advantage to be received arising out of the introduction

This additional exclusion does not require the introduction to be made with a view to the provision of independent advice.

4.3.6. Enforcing mortgages falls within the definition of 'administering' a mortgage. If the mortgage is regulated this will potentially be a regulated activity. However, there is an exclusion where the administration is pursuant to an agreement with an authorised person. Enforcing mortgage terms on behalf of an authorised commercial lender should, therefore, be excluded.

4.3.7. A solicitor who is involved in obtaining mortgage finance for a client will be acting as a mortgage broker under Consumer Credit Act 1974. For this activity, the solicitor needs to hold a licence under the 1974 Act. The Law Society holds a group licence from the Director General of Fair Trading which covers all solicitors acting within the ordinary course of practice. Normally, therefore, a solicitor does not need to hold an individual licence.

4.4. Regulated home reversion plans and regulated home purchase plans

4.4.1. A 'regulated home reversion plan' is a form of equity release arrangement under which a person buys all or part of a qualifying interest in land (other than timeshare accommodation) in the UK from an individual who is entitled under the arrangement to occupy at least 40% of the land in question as or in connection with a dwelling. The arrangement specifies one or more qualifying termination events, on the occurrence of which that entitlement will end.

4.4.2. A 'regulated home purchase plan is an arrangement under which a purchaser buys a qualifying interest or an undivided share of a qualifying interest in land (other than timeshare accommodation) in the UK and the interest is held on trust for the purchaser and other individual(s) as beneficial tenants in common. The arrangement provides for the obligation of the individual(s) to buy the interest bought by the purchaser over the course of or at the end of a specified period. The individual(s) or a related person will be entitled under the arrangement to occupy at least 40% of the land in question as or in connection with a dwelling during that period.

4.4.3. Regulated home purchase plans are forms of Islamic financing arrangements designed to enable the purchase of a home in a way that is acceptable under Islamic law.

4.4.4. Financial Services and Markets Act 2000 (Regulated Activities) (Amendment) (No.2) Order 2006 (SI 2006/2383) amended the RAO with regard to home reversion and home purchase plans. With effect from 1 April 2007 these are specified investments and activities such as arranging and advising on such plans are now regulated. Entering into and administering such plans will also be regulated activities.

4.4.5. Solicitors' Financial Services (Scope) Rules 2001 have been amended to prevent solicitors using Part XX FSMA 2000 in relation to recommending particular plans but solicitors can endorse the advice of an authorised person where such endorsement incidental to other work.

4.4.6. Similar exclusions to those available for regulated mortgages apply (see A4.3.4 and A4.3.5).

4.5. Insurance contracts

4.5.1. As a result of the Insurance Mediation Directive, regulation has been extended to all activities relating to the selling and administration of insurance contracts. Advice on and arrangements made for the acquisition or disposal of all insurance contracts are now caught as regulated activities. Further, assisting in the administration and performance of such contracts (including claims handling) will also be caught as a regulated activity. These provisions came into force on 14 January 2005.

4.5.2. Conveyancers will be affected by this change where, as part of their conveyancing, they give advice on or make arrangements for a client to acquire a life policy as part of mortgage arrangements (endowment or term policies) or where they arrange indemnity policies such as defective title insurance, contaminated land insurance, lender/title insurance, household contents insurance or building insurance. Further, solicitors who assist clients in claims handling will also potentially be involved in regulated activities (although acting in relation to claims handling for an insurance company will generally be excluded).

4.5.3. It is unlikely that any of the general exclusions will apply (the authorised person and the introductions exclusions expressly cannot apply to insurance contracts). Consequently unauthorised solicitors who wish to be involved in insurance mediation (advice on, arrangements for or administration of insurance contracts) will need to do so as 'exempt regulated activities'. If the insurance involves 'long term insurance contracts excluding pure protection policies' (e.g. endowment policies or pension policies) there are restrictions on the use of the exempt regime (see A4.2.10). No advice (beyond passing on or endorsing the advice of an authorised person) should be given where such a product is to be acquired. Arrangements should be limited to 'execution only' arrangements (i.e. where it is clear on reasonable grounds that the client is not relying on the firm as to the merits or suitability of that transaction).

4.5.4. For other insurance products (e.g. term assurance policies or indemnity policies) advice, arrangements or administration can be undertaken by a firm if these activities are incidental to the conveyancing transaction. Solicitors' Financial Services (Scope) Rules 2001 have been amended to require solicitors who wish to undertake insurance mediation services to:

    (a)   appoint a compliance officer, and

    (b)   be registered in the register maintained by the Financial Services Authority.

4.6.   Trustees and personal representatives

The solicitor who is a trustee or personal representative

4.6.1. If a solicitor, in his capacity as a trustee, buys or sells investments for the trust or estate he may be excluded under the RAO, provided he is acting as a principal. Where a solicitor who is a trustee or personal representative advises his fellow trustees or personal representatives or makes arrangements for the acquisition or disposal of investments for his co-trustees or personal representatives or a beneficiary, the RAO provides further exclusions (article 66). These exclusions only apply if the trustee is not remunerated for the arranging or advice in addition to any remuneration received for acting as trustee or personal representative. Article 66 expressly provides that a person is not to be regarded as receiving additional remuneration merely because his remuneration is calculated by reference to time. Article 66 does not apply to insurance mediation activities where such activities are undertaken for reward. This means that solicitors are unlikely to be able to use article 66 for activities relating to insurance contracts.

Trustees or personal representatives will 'manage' the investments belonging to the trust or estate. The RAO makes it clear, however, that only 'discretionary management' will be caught as a regulated activity. Non-discretionary management will not be a 'regulated activity'. Non-discretionary management will occur when either the firm acts for outside trustees or where a solicitor or employee of the firm is a joint trustee or personal representative with someone from outside the firm. Discretionary management is only likely where a solicitor is a sole trustee or personal representative or where the solicitor is jointly acting as such with someone from within the firm. Article 66 excludes 'discretionary management' where such is undertaken by a person acting as a trustee or personal representative. In addition to the condition relating to 'no additional remuneration' noted above for advising and arranging, solicitors must not hold themselves out as providing a management service if they wish to benefit from this exclusion.

If the article 66 exclusion does not apply, it is open to solicitors who are trustees or personal representatives to show that their activities fall within the general exemption contained in Part XX FSMA as noted above.

The solicitor who is acting for trustees or personal representatives

4.6.2. It should be noted that the exclusion contained in article 66 only applies where a solicitor is a trustee or a personal representative – it does not apply if the solicitor merely acts for trustees or personal representatives. In these circumstances, arrangements can be excluded by using the authorised person exclusion noted in A4.2.6 or arrangements and advice may fall within the incidental exemption contained in Part XX FSMA.

4.7. Commissions

4.7.1. Life assurance companies and the providers of some other types of investment product pay commissions to intermediaries on the sale of their products. A solicitor who introduces a client to an authorised person will usually receive a commission for the introduction.

4.7.2. Any commission received by the solicitor is subject to Rule 2.06 Solicitors' Code of Conduct 2007 (see Appendix I.1 and N1.8). As noted above, a number of the exclusions from the need for authorisation require solicitors to account for any commission. If a solicitor retains commission without the client's consent (even if the commission is not more than the £20 *de minimis* allowed for in Conduct Rule 2.06) these exclusions in the RAO and the Act will not apply. Solicitors risk committing a criminal offence if they undertake regulated activities without being authorised and without the benefit of an appropriate exclusion.

4.8. Compliance

4.8.1. The SRA has issued Solicitors' Financial Services (Conduct of Business) Rules 2001 applicable to solicitors seeking exemption under Part XX. These rules have been amended to reflect the compliance obligations where a solicitor undertakes insurance mediation.

4.8.2. The Rules include obligations relating to:

- *Status disclosure.* Requiring firms to indicate in writing that they are not authorised by the FSA but are regulated by the SRA. Where insurance mediation is undertaken a compulsory statement indicating that the firm's name is included on the FSA register is required.

- *Execution of transactions.* Requiring firms to keep records of instructions received and instructions given.

- *Record of commissions.* Requiring firms to keep records of commissions received and records of how such commission has been accounted for.

- *Execution only transactions – packaged products.* Requiring firms to give written confirmation of execution only transactions involving packaged products.

- *Insurance mediation activities.* Requiring firms to inform clients whether or not any recommendation is given on the basis of a fair market analysis of the type of product and requiring firms to give clients a demands and needs statement setting out the client's demands and needs and an explanation of why a particular insurance contract was recommended.

Where a buyer insists upon a seller obtaining an insurance product, e.g. defective title insurance, the solicitor acting for the seller will have to comply with these requirements if the solicitor is involved in insurance mediation. This will be so even if the policy is to be taken out in the buyer's name. However, if the buyer's solicitor advised upon and arranges the insurance at the cost of the seller, the buyer's solicitor will be involved in insurance mediation and as such will have to comply with the Conduct of Business Rules.

4.8.3. Breach of the Scope Rules can amount to a criminal offence where firms undertake unauthorised regulated activities. Further, the FSA can order the firm to cease undertaking any regulated activities. Breach of the Conduct of Business Rules, whilst not amounting to a criminal offence, can lead to disciplinary action by the SRA or Legal Complaints Service.

A5. Dealing with non-solicitors

5.1. Licensed conveyancers

5.1.1. When dealing with a licensed conveyancer who is not known personally to the solicitor, a check on the identity of the conveyancer should be made with the Council for Licensed Conveyancers (see Appendix VIII.2 for address).

5.1.2. The solicitor should ensure that he deals either directly with the licensed conveyancer or with a person working under the immediate supervision of such a person.

5.1.3. Licensed conveyancers are bound by rules relating to conduct, discipline, insurance and accounts which are similar to those which bind solicitors. It is therefore normally possible to deal with a licensed conveyancer as if the conveyancer was a fellow solicitor subject to the best interests of the solicitor's client.

5.2. Law Society Formulae and undertakings

5.2.1. The Protocol, the Law Society Formulae for Exchange of Contracts and the Code for Completion by Post (see Appendix II) may be used in dealings with licensed conveyancers. Licensed conveyancers have no equivalent sanction to the court's control over the conduct of solicitors, but the Law Society recommends that they are nevertheless treated by solicitors as being on an equal footing with themselves. It is therefore normally possible to rely on undertakings given by such persons.

5.3. Employment of licensed conveyancers by solicitors

5.3.1. A solicitor may employ a licensed conveyancer as a conveyancing clerk or in some other capacity. Work done by the licensed conveyancer must be done as an integral part of the solicitor's practice and is subject to all the practice rules. The licensed conveyancer may be named in the solicitor's publicity (including stationery) provided that his status is made clear. A solicitor may not enter into partnership with a licensed conveyancer nor share his fees with him (except under the exception to Rule 8 Solicitors' Code of Conduct 2007 (fee sharing) which permits fees to be shared with a genuine employee).

5.3.2.   As with any transaction, the overriding concern is for the best interests of the client. In any situation where there is doubt over the conduct of the matter, guidance should be sought from the Professional Ethics Guidance Team.

5.4.   Unqualified conveyancers

5.4.1.   Under Solicitors Act 1974, s.22 (as amended), it is an offence for an unqualified person to draw up or prepare *inter alia* a contract for sale, transfer, conveyance, lease or mortgage relating to land unless that person can prove that the act was not done in expectation of fee, gain or reward.

'Qualified persons'

5.4.2.   The only persons who are 'qualified' under section 22 are solicitors, barristers, notaries public, licensed conveyancers, authorised practitioners, and some public officers. An unqualified person acting in breach of the section commits a criminal offence and his 'client' may be guilty of aiding and abetting the offence.

5.4.3.   A solicitor acting for the other party to the transaction could also be guilty of procuring the commission of an offence by inviting the unqualified person to submit a contract or conveyance.

5.4.4.   Courts and Legal Services Act 1990 contains provisions enabling 'authorised practitioners' (as defined in the Act) to conduct conveyancing services on behalf of their customers. Rules regulating the conduct of authorised practitioners have not yet been made.

5.5.   Dealing with unqualified persons

5.5.1.   The Law Society has published guidance for solicitors who are asked to deal with unqualified conveyancers which are summarised below. See further Appendix IV.5.

5.5.2.   A solicitor should refuse to have any dealings with an unqualified person unless he has clear evidence that no offence under section 22 will be committed.

5.5.3.   At the outset of a transaction which apparently involves an unqualified person the solicitor should write to the unqualified person drawing attention to the Law Society's guidelines and asking for satisfactory evidence that no offence will be committed. The solicitor's client should also be informed of the situation.

5.5.4.   Drafts of suitable letters are set out in the guidelines.

5.5.5.   A letter from a qualified person confirming that he will prepare the relevant documents will be satisfactory evidence that no offence will be committed and the solicitor may proceed with the transaction.

5.5.6.   The Protocol can be used with unqualified persons, but no sanctions would lie against them in the event of a breach.

5.5.7.   There are provisions in Land Registration Rules 2003 whereby a conveyancer can satisfy evidential requirements by giving a relevant certificate. The term 'conveyancer' includes a solicitor, licensed conveyancer, a fellow of the Institute of Legal Executives, or duly certificated notary public.[1]

1.   Land Registration Rules 2003, r.217 as amended.

5.6.   Undertakings

5.6.1.   Undertakings should not be accepted from unqualified persons since there is no method of enforcing them. Thus where, e.g. a seller who is represented by an unqualified person has a mortgage subsisting at completion, the buyer's solicitor must require the seller to produce a signed Form DS1 at completion and must not accept an undertaking for its discharge. This may mean that the seller has to obtain bridging finance to repay the loan before completion or that the seller's lender will have to attend at completion. A solicitor who accepts an undertaking from an unqualified person may be in breach of his duty of care to his own client and thus liable to make good to the client any loss sustained as a result of a dishonoured undertaking.

5.7.   Completions and agency work

5.7.1.   There is no duty on a solicitor to undertake agency work by way of completions by post or to attend to other formalities on behalf of third parties who are not clients and who are represented by an unqualified person. A solicitor who does undertake such work should only do so after having agreed in writing with the unqualified person the precise extent of the solicitor's duties and agreed fee for such services. Where a considerable amount of work is undertaken on behalf of the unqualified person's client there is a danger of the solicitor being in breach of Rule 3 Solicitors' Code of Conduct 2007 since he may effectively be acting for both parties in the transaction.

5.8.   The contract

5.8.1.   It will be necessary for special provisions to be inserted in the draft contract to take account of the fact that the other party is not represented by a qualified person.

Clauses to deal with the following matters should be inserted in the contract:

(a) personal attendance by an unrepresented seller at completion to take up the deeds and purchase price because Law of Property Act 1925, s.69, only applies when a document containing a receipt for the purchase price is handed over by a qualified person or by the seller himself;

(b) payment of the deposit either to an estate agent who is a member of a recognised professional body, or to the buyer's solicitor in the capacity of stakeholder. An alternative to these arrangements would be to insert a condition in the contract providing for the deposit to be placed in a bank or building society deposit account in the joint names of seller and buyer.

5.9. Pre-contract enquiries

5.9.1. The answers to pre-contract enquiries and any other enquiries (including requisitions on title) given by an unrepresented seller should be signed by the seller in person. Although an unqualified person may have the seller's express authority to answer such enquiries on his behalf, an action in misrepresentation (should such become necessary) will more easily be sustained if the answers have been signed by the seller personally.

5.10. Powers of attorney

5.10.1. Any power of attorney which purports to give the unqualified person power to deal with a matter on behalf of his or her 'client' should be carefully checked to ensure its validity and effectiveness for its purported purpose (see B23).

5.11. Acting for the lender

5.11.1. A solicitor acting for a lender where the borrower is represented by an unqualified person is under no obligation to undertake work which the buyer's solicitor should normally assume (e.g. drafting the purchase deed) and should not render the unqualified person additional assistance. However, in such a situation the solicitor must bear in mind that the interests of his lender client in obtaining a good title to the property are paramount. The advance cheque should be drawn in favour of a solicitor, licensed conveyancer or person properly authorised to receive the money by the borrower. On redemption of a mortgage similar principles apply.

5.12. Authorised practitioners

5.12.1. Authorised practitioners are entitled to carry out conveyancing services on behalf of their clients pursuant to Courts and Legal Services Act 1990 and the regulations made under that Act (none of which have been made as yet). Conveyancing services must be carried out under the supervision of a qualified solicitor. Authorised practitioners are subject to similar rules relating to the handling of clients' money as those which affect solicitors and are also bound to honour undertakings given by them or their staff. They may, therefore, be regarded in the same light as licensed conveyancers. In cases of doubt or difficulty assistance should be sought from the Professional Ethics Guidance Team.

A6. In-house solicitors

6.1. Acting for the lay employer
6.2. Acting for fellow employees

6.3. Acting for third parties

6.1.   Acting for the lay employer

6.1.1.   A solicitor who is employed by a non-solicitor employer must comply with Solicitors' Code of Conduct 2007 (see in particular Rules 12 and 13) and all the other rules of professional conduct.

6.1.2.   Under Rule 20 (requirements of practice) a practising certificate will be needed where the in-house solicitor:

  (a)   is held out or employed as a solicitor or lawyer (e.g. where the solicitor's name and qualifications appear on the employer's notepaper); or

  (b)   carries out reserved work prohibited to unqualified persons by Solicitors Act 1974 (e.g. drawing a contract for the sale of land for fee or reward); or

  (c)   fulfils the role of a 'person qualified to supervise' under Rule 5.02 Solicitors' Code of Conduct 2007; or

  (d)   authorises the withdrawal of money from a client account.

6.1.3.   If an employed solicitor uses his employer's stationery it must be clear that the stationery is being used by a solicitor on legal professional business and that the solicitor is responsible for the contents of the letter.

6.1.4.   Rule 13 Solicitors' Code of Conduct 2007 (in-house practice) places restrictions on the type of work which an employed solicitor may undertake. In general he is prohibited from doing work for anyone other than his employer.

6.2.   Acting for fellow employees

6.2.1.   An employed solicitor may carry out conveyancing on behalf of a fellow employee provided that the work is permitted by his contract of employment and is done free of charge to the fellow employee. The conveyancing must also relate to or arise out of the work of the employee client, i.e. it must be a job-related move. Before accepting the instructions to act the employed solicitor must ensure that the fellow employee does not wish to instruct another solicitor or licensed conveyancer (see Rule 13.02 Solicitors' Code of Conduct 2007).

6.3. **Acting for third parties**

6.3.1. If his contract of employment permits him to do so an employed solicitor may undertake work on behalf of private clients in his own time. In this respect he will be treated as a principal in private practice and must comply with Solicitors' Code of Conduct 2007, Accounts Rules and Indemnity Rules. If he practises from home, compliance with Rule 20 Solicitors' Code of Conduct 2007 (requirements of practice) will be required and he may need to register his home address with the Law Society as a practising address. Because of the danger of conflict of interests private work must not be undertaken for clients and customers of the employer.

6.3.2. Where acting in a conveyancing transaction for a fellow employee (see A6.2.1) an employed solicitor may also act for a joint owner/buyer and for a lender. A lender may require an indemnity from the employer or insurance cover similar to that required under Solicitors' Indemnity Rules 2006.

A7. Introductions and referrals

7.1.   Rule 9 Solicitors' Code of Conduct 2007

7.1.1.   A solicitor may have an arrangement with a third party for the introduction of clients to the solicitor by the third party, or the referral of clients to the third party by the solicitor. Such arrangements are permitted by Rule 9 Solicitors' Code of Conduct 2007 (referrals of business) provided that there is no breach of any of the rules of conduct.

7.1.2.   Rule 9 applies to any arrangement made by a solicitor with, e.g. an estate agent, bank, building society or mortgage broker for the introduction of clients to the solicitor from such third parties or the referral of clients to the third parties by the solicitor but not to introductions and referrals between firms of solicitors.

7.2.   Maintaining the independence of the solicitor

7.2.1.   It is of paramount importance that the solicitor should remain independent of any third party to or from whom referrals are made so that the client may be given impartial and objective advice by the solicitor.

7.2.2.   It should also be noted that Rule 19 Solicitors' Code of Conduct 2007 (financial services) prevents a solicitor from acting as an appointed representative in respect of introductions and referrals made in the field of investment business, other than by having a separate business which is the appointed representative of an independent financial adviser.

7.2.3.   No arrangement with an introducer should affect the solicitor's duty to communicate directly with the client to obtain or confirm instructions, in the process of providing advice and at all appropriate stages of the transaction.

7.2.4.   Where the solicitor is being paid for his or her services by the introducer rather than by the client there is a danger of conflict of interests arising, and the solicitor must decline to act if such a conflict arises or is likely to arise.

7.3.   Reliance by the solicitor on limited sources of business

7.3.1.   If a solicitor allows himself to become reliant on a limited source or sources of business from introducers there is a danger that the advice given by him to his introduced clients will be influenced by the solicitor's need to maintain his source of business, to the extent that the advice will not be impartial and may not be in the best interests of that particular client.

7.3.2. Solicitors are advised to review their sources of business at regular intervals (see guidance to Rule 9 Solicitors' Code of Conduct 2007), to ensure that the solicitor does not become too reliant on one introducer as a source of work.

7.3.3. Factors to be taken into account in reviewing the arrangements include:

(a) whether the solicitor has complied with Rule 9;

(b) whether the solicitor has given referred clients independent advice, which has not been affected by the interests of the introducer; and

(c) the amount and proportion of the firm's income arising as a result of each referral arrangement.

7.4. Referral agreements

7.4.1. All referral arrangements must be in writing and available for inspection by the Solicitors Regulation Authority.

7.4.2. Under the agreement, the introducer must undertake to comply with Rule 9 Solicitors' Code of Conduct 2007.

7.4.3. Where an introducer wishes to publicise the services of solicitors to whom the introducer will refer work, the publicity must comply with Rule 7 Solicitors' Code of Conduct 2007 (publicity). The solicitor remains responsible for any publicity. Such publicity should therefore be checked carefully by the solicitor before publication.

7.4.4. The agreement with the introducer must not include any provision which would compromise, infringe or impair any of the solicitor's duties set out in Solicitors' Code of Conduct 2007 or allow the introducer to influence or constrain the solicitor's professional judgement in relation to the advice given to the client.

7.4.5. The agreement must provide that before making a referral the introducer must give the client all relevant information concerning the referral, in particular:

(a) the fact that the introducer has a financial arrangement with the solicitor; and

(b) the amount of any payment to the introducer which is calculated by reference to that referral; or

(c) where the introducer is paying the solicitor to provide services to the introducer's customers:

(i) the amount the introducer is paying the solicitor to provide those services; and

(ii)   the amount the client is required to pay the introducer.

7.4.6.   If the solicitor has reason to believe that the introducer is breaching any of the terms of the agreement the solicitor must take all reasonable steps to ensure that the breach is remedied. If the introducer continues to breach the agreement the solicitor must terminate it.

7.4.7.   Potential introducers should be made aware of the terms on which the solicitor will accept instructions from an introducer and the fees that will be charged to an introduced client.

7.5.   Confirming the client's instructions

7.5.1.   Any instructions received from or through an introducer must be confirmed directly with the client by sending or giving the client written terms of business. If the client was referred to the solicitor under an agreement covered by Rule 9 Solicitors' Code of Conduct 2007, the client must be informed of the agreement between the introducer and the solicitor and must be given the information specified in Rule 9.02(g) Solicitors' Code of Conduct 2007.

7.5.2.   Before accepting instructions to act for a client referred under an agreement under Rule 9 Solicitors' Code of Conduct 2007, the solicitor must give the client, in writing, all relevant information concerning the referral, in particular:

(a)   the fact that the solicitor has a financial arrangement with the introducer; and

(b)   the amount of any payment to the introducer which is calculated by reference to that referral; or

(c)   where the introducer is paying the solicitor to provide services to the introducer's customers:

(i)   the amount the introducer is paying the solicitor to provide those services; and

(ii)   the amount the client is required to pay the introducer;

(d)   a statement that any advice given by the solicitor will be independent and that the client is free to raise questions on all aspects of the transaction; and

(e)   confirmation that any information disclosed to the solicitor will not be disclosed to the introducer unless the client consents; but that where the solicitor is also acting for the introducer in the same matter and a conflict of interests arises, the solicitor might be obliged to cease acting.

7.5.3.   This disclosure is required as soon as the referral is made and the solicitor will normally be expected to write to the client with the information before the first interview. If, due to lack of time, the disclosure is made at the first interview, it should be made at the start of the first interview and confirmed in writing.

7.6. Fees and commissions

7.6.1. Rule 9 Solicitors' Code of Conduct 2007 also applies to agreements which constitute 'financial arrangements'. A financial arrangement includes any payment to an introducer in respect of a referral, and any agreement under which the solicitor is paid by the introducer to provide services to the introducer's customers. 'Payment' includes any consideration but does not include normal hospitality, proper disbursements, or normal business expenses.

7.6.2. Any commission received by the solicitor who has referred a client to a third party is subject to Rule 2.06 Solicitors' Code of Conduct 2007 (client relations) under which rule the solicitor must account to the client for any commission which exceeds £20 unless the client, having been informed of the amount of the commission, consents to the solicitor keeping the commission.

7.6.3. Clients must be charged the correct amount for local searches. Any discount or rebate offered to a solicitor on a disbursement amounts to a reduction in the cost of that disbursement and must be passed to the client. This is irrespective of the amount of the rebate or 'commission'. If the full amount is charged to the client, the solicitor will have misled the client by overstating the cost of the disbursement and effectively will have overcharged (see *Law Society* v. *Adcock and Mocroft* [2006] EWHC 3212 (Admin)).

7.7. Referrals by the solicitor to a third party

7.7.1. A solicitor who recommends a client to a third party must do so in good faith, judging what is in the client's best interests. Any agreement entered into whereby the solicitor recommends clients to a third party must not restrict the solicitor's freedom to recommend clients to other third parties if this would be in the best interests of the client.

A8. Estimate of costs

8.1. Duty to give estimate

8.1.1. A solicitor must, at the outset and as the matter progresses, give a client the best information possible about the likely costs of the transaction including the cost of compliance with SDLT requirements. See Rule 2 Solicitors' Code of Conduct 2007 (client relations).

8.1.2. If it is not possible to give an estimate, a general forecast of the approximate costs should be given.

8.1.3. A solicitor must explain at the outset any payments the client is likely to have to make, e.g. search fees and Land Registry fees. Where possible the solicitor must give details of the probable costs.

8.1.4. Any information about costs must be clear and confirmed in writing. See Rule 2.05 Solicitors' Code of Conduct 2007.

8.2. Residential conveyancing

8.2.1. In residential conveyancing it is normally possible to give the client an estimate of the costs of the transaction.

8.3. Commercial transactions

8.3.1. A precise estimate of costs may not be possible in the context of commercial transactions; nevertheless the client should still be given a general forecast of likely costs and the method of calculation of those costs at the outset of the transaction, and informed if that figure is likely to vary substantially.

8.4. Bills payable by a third party

8.4.1. Where the client is or will become liable to pay a bill presented by a third party, e.g. to a landlord's solicitor for consent to assignment, the solicitor should obtain an estimate of the third party's bill at the outset of the transaction and should inform the client of the amount of the estimate. If the estimate appears to be an unreasonably high figure, negotiations to attempt to reduce it should be undertaken before a substantial amount of work in the transaction has taken place. Money should be obtained from the client on account of the third party's costs before an undertaking to pay is given.

8.4.2.   If the client is entitled to be indemnified by a third party, e.g. by a tenant seeking a licence to assign, an estimate of the costs should be given to the third party's solicitor. Such an estimate should be as firm as possible in the circumstances, but may be qualified by a statement to the effect that the estimate has been given on the basis that the matter proceeds without unforeseen complications.

8.5.   Giving an estimate

8.5.1.   Any information about costs must be clear and confirmed in writing (Rule 2.05 Solicitors' Code of Conduct 2007). In order to avoid misunderstandings it is preferable only to give an estimate in writing or, if oral, confirm the estimate in writing immediately.

8.5.2.   In residential conveyancing it is frequently not possible to avoid giving an estimate over the telephone. In such circumstances it should be made clear to the prospective client that the estimate is given on the basis of information supplied by the client and may be subject to variation if unknown factors later emerge which complicate the transaction.

8.5.3.   The estimate should be as comprehensive as possible and should be clear as to whether VAT and/or disbursements are included in the given figure.

8.5.4.   The client should be warned that if unforeseen complications arise, the estimate may be revised.

8.5.5.   Minor expenses, e.g. postage and telephone, which are part of the solicitor's overheads, are to be included in the estimate and must not be added as a disbursement.

8.5.6.   The estimate should state whether or not it covers the cost of completing the SDLT form.

8.5.7.   Charges specified in the estimate for local and other searches must be as accurate as possible. The client must not be charged more than the cost of obtaining the search from the local search agency. Any attempt to recover a higher payment from the client or for the solicitor to take a commission from the agency will be a breach of Solicitors' Code of Conduct 2007 (see A7.6.3).

8.6. Change in circumstances

8.6.1. If events occur which cause the original estimate to become inaccurate the solicitor must immediately inform the client in writing of the change in circumstances and should revise his estimate accordingly.

8.6.2. Failure to advise the client of a change in the likely level of fees may render the solicitor liable to prosecution for giving misleading information relating to charges under Consumer Protection Act 1987, s.20.

8.7. Quotations for costs

8.7.1. The solicitor should make it clear to the client that an estimate for costs is not a fixed price ('a quotation') for the work unless it is the solicitor's intention to charge a fixed price which will not be altered in any circumstances.

8.7.2. Where a quotation is given the solicitor is not at liberty to charge the client more than the fixed fee even if the transaction turns out to be more difficult or complex than had been anticipated. Petty expenses such as postage and telephone must not be added as disbursements to the fixed fee.

8.7.3. It is recommended that if a fixed fee is quoted the client is informed of that fee in writing and told that the quotation will be valid for a stated period, e.g. three months. If the solicitor has not been instructed by the client within this period he will then be entitled to issue a revised quotation.

8.7.4. Money received for or on account of an agreed fee must not be paid into a client account.[1] It must be paid into an office account.

8.7.5. A quotation for costs which has been accepted by the client may be subject to Solicitors Act 1974, s.57, which provides that it must:

    (a) be in writing;

    (b) embody all the terms of the agreement;

    (c) be signed by the client or his agent;

    (d) be reasonable in amount and in lieu of ordinary profit costs.

8.7.6. Remuneration certificates are not available to a client where a section 57 agreement has been made, but he may seek taxation of the bill in the normal way. The agreement is enforceable by the solicitor under the ordinary principles of contract law.

1. See Rule 19(5) Solicitors' Accounts Rules 1998.

8.8. VAT on solicitors' charges

8.8.1. Where a firm is registered, VAT will be chargeable to the client on the solicitor's bill and on some disbursements paid by the solicitor on the client's behalf, depending upon the 'place of supply' for the VAT purposes.

8.8.2.   Where the services are 'closely related to land' such as conveyancing, the 'place of supply' is the place where the land/building is situated (regardless of where the customer is). This could mean that VAT registration in another member state of the EU is required.

8.8.3.   Where any other legal services are provided, the 'place of supply' is where the customer is domiciled. For UK customers and individuals in other EU member states, UK VAT at standard rate is therefore chargeable. For businesses registered in another member state, no VAT is charged provided the customer's VAT registration number is quoted on the firm's invoice, and for customers outside the EU, no UK VAT is chargeable.

8.8.4.   When giving an estimate or quotation of costs to the client the solicitor should make it clear whether or not that estimate or quotation includes VAT. If no mention of VAT is made the client is entitled to assume that the quoted figure is inclusive of VAT.[1]

8.8.5.   Where an individual or firm is registered for VAT, the firm's VAT registration number must appear on the bills issued by the firm or, if a separate tax invoice is issued, on the tax invoice.

8.8.6.   Where the client's bill is reduced by the amount of commission which the solicitor has earned, e.g. on an endowment policy taken out by the client, VAT may be charged on the net amount of the bill, providing that the commission set off is correctly shown on the face of the invoice. Customs' VAT Notes No. 1 1988/89, item 6, published in April 1988 states the following:

> 'Many traders when charging fees to their clients reduce the amount by taking into account commission they receive from third parties. For example, a financial adviser provides guidance on insurance to a client; the insurance company pays the adviser a commission and the adviser passes on the benefit to the client by charging a lower fee.
>
> In the past, traders have accounted for output tax on the full value of their supply before any deductions for commission. HM Revenue and Customs have reviewed this ruling, and from now on you need only account for output tax on the fee shown on the invoice.'

8.8.7.   In March 1990 Customs issued an agreed statement setting out two methods which may be used in respect of the format of invoices for set-offs of commission:

Method 1

Fee	110.00
Rebate equivalent to commission received	10.00
Fee	100.00
VAT @ 17.5%	17.50
Total	117.50

(Note: commission must be described as a rebate when using this method.)

Method 2

Fee net of £10 commission	100.00
VAT @ 17.5%	17.50
Total	117.50

8.8.8. HM Revenue and Customs are currently reviewing the treatment of commissions and whether the value of the supply is the gross amount chargeable before set-off of commissions, with VAT being calculated on that value, and any commission being set off against the gross fee.

8.8.9. The Law Society issued the following in the *Gazette* ([1992] *Gazette*, 9 September):

> '**VAT and commission**
>
> The question of the effect on the application of VAT to a bill for professional services rendered to a client on the receipt of commission from a third party has recently been the subject of correspondence between the VAT subcommittee of the revenue law committee and HM Revenue and Customs.
>
> Until agreement can be reached and revised guidance is published, Customs have advised that members could continue to rely upon the practice outlined in item 6 of VAT Notes No. 1 1988/89, namely to charge VAT after netting off any commission using one of the methods set out in A8.8.7 above.'

8.8.10. Rule 2 Solicitors' Code of Conduct 2007 (client relations) obliges solicitors to account to their client for any commission they receive, subject to a *de minimis* threshold of £20.

1. Value Added Tax Act 1994, s.89.

A9. Joint purchasers

9.1. Advising the client

9.1.1. When acting for joint purchasers, it is essential to clarify their intentions as to the method by which they are to hold the property. The solicitor should explain the different methods of co-ownership to the clients in language appropriate to their level of understanding and should advise as to the most suitable type of co-ownership to meet the particular situation. A separate trust deed should be completed to express the clients' wishes. Also a note of the clients' wishes should be made on the file so that appropriate steps may be taken to implement the clients' instructions in the purchase deed (see E1).

9.1.2. Instructions should be obtained from both (or all) co-purchasers.[1]

9.1.3. Where the intending co-purchasers are not married to each other nor in a civil partnership[2] it may be necessary to advise each party independently about their rights in the property to be purchased. Solicitors should be alert to the possibility of a conflict of interests arising between the two clients in this situation (see A9.8).

1. See *Penn v. Bristol & West Building Society* [1997] 3 All ER 470.
2. Civil Partnership Act 2004.

9.2. Co-ownership or sole ownership?

9.2.1. In the vast majority of cases a husband and wife or civil partners should be advised to hold a property as co-owners and this is usually a requirement of any major lending institution. This requirement by lenders for co-ownership by spouses, civil partners and co-habitees is irrespective of the contribution which each party will make to the mortgage repayments. A contra-indication to co-ownership by a married couple, etc may exist where one or both of the parties is individually wealthy and where consideration must be given to the equalisation of estates for inheritance tax purposes. Sole legal ownership may be considered prudent if one of the parties is in a 'high-risk' category of unincorporated business where the potential consequences of bankruptcy may need to be considered.

9.2.2. A non-owning spouse/civil partner will have rights under Family Law Act 1996 (see A9.2.3) and/or a beneficial interest through contribution to the purchase price of the property (see A9.2.4). But neither of these methods of protection is as secure as co-ownership of the legal estate.

9.2.3. Where one spouse or civil partner owns the matrimonial home in his or her sole name the non-owning party has a statutory right of occupation under section 30 Family Law Act 1996. The non-owning party cannot be evicted without the leave of the court and, if not in occupation, the court can enforce the non-owning party's right by ordering that they be allowed into occupation of the property (section 33 of the Act). To ensure that the Family Law Act right of occupation can be enforced against a person buying or taking a mortgage from the owning party, the right should be protected by registration of either a Class F land charge under Land Charges Act 1972 or a homes rights notice at the Land Registry. If the right has been protected by registration the court's powers under section 33 1996 Act may be exercised against the new owner of the property. Under section 33(5) the court has the power to order that the right of occupation should extend beyond the termination of the marriage as a result of the death or divorce of the owning spouse, or the termination of the civil partnership.

Co-owners

9.2.4. Where two or more persons buy property together, each contributing to the purchase price and/or mortgage repayments, and the title to the property is held in the name of only one of the buyers, the non-owning party may have a beneficial interest in the property under a resulting or constructive trust.[1] The non-owning party has a right to occupy the property under section 12 Trusts of Land and Appointment of Trustees Act 1996 which can be enforced against the owner by court order under section 14 of that Act. In addition the court has power to make an occupation order under Family Law Act 1996, s. 33 in cases where the applicant does not have home rights but does have a beneficial interest in the property. Where the title to the property is registered, a sale or mortgage will be registered free from the beneficial interest unless registration is prevented by a restriction in the proprietorship register.[2] If, however, the owner of the beneficial interest is in occupation of the property at the time of the purchase or mortgage, the beneficial interest may override the disposition of the registered title under the provisions of Schedule 3 paragraph 2 Land Registration Act 2002. If the title to the property is unregistered the buyer or mortgagee will be bound by the beneficial interest if they had notice of it at the time of the disposition.[3] However, whether the title is registered or unregistered the beneficial interest can be overreached if the sale or mortgage is entered into by all the trustees being at least two in number or a trust corporation.[4] In most cases where a buyer or mortgagee becomes aware of a beneficial interest he will insist that the seller appoints a second trustee to enter into the disposition with him. When the interest is overreached, the person with the beneficial interest will no longer be able to enforce it against the property.

9.2.5. Unmarried purchasers, whether co-habitees, brother and sister or merely friends who are joining together to purchase a property, should normally be advised to hold the property as co-owners since the existence of a beneficial or overriding interest may be costly and difficult to establish in the event of a dispute between the parties. Many lenders will insist that the legal estate is held jointly in these circumstances.

Civil partners

9.2.6. Civil Partnership Act 2004 which provides for registration of a civil partnership for same-sex couples came into force on 5 December 2005. If a couple choose to register their partnership their property rights both during the partnership and in the event of the partnership being dissolved will be governed by the Act.

9.2.7. With regard to the initial purchase of the property the couple should consider whether or not both partners will appear on the legal title in the same way as any other co-owners and, where appropriate, a trust deed should be drawn up. Once the partnership has been registered, the provisions of Chapter 3 of the Act relating to property and financial relations will come into effect. Under section 65 a civil partner making a substantial contribution in money or money's worth to property, which is either co-owned with the other civil partner or owned entirely by the other civil partner, will acquire a share or an enlarged share in that property. When dealing with a purchase from a sole owner who is in a civil partnership there is a possibility that the other partner has acquired a beneficial interest in the property by direct or indirect contributions.

9.2.8. The provisions of section 30 Family Law Act 1996 apply to civil partners (Civil Partnership Act 2004, s. 82). See A9.2.3.

9.2.9. When a civil partnership is brought to an end the provisions of Chapter 3 and Schedule 5 provide for the adjustment of property rights similar to the rights available on divorce. The ex-partners' ownership of any property will be determined in accordance with the provisions of the Act and not in accordance with any agreement or trust deed entered into before the partnership was registered.

9.2.10. Consideration should always be given to the question of taking out a joint life policy to protect the mortgage over the lives of both spouses/co-habitees even where the property is held in one name alone or where the mortgage repayments are made by one party alone. The joint lives policy will protect the repayments of the mortgage even in the event of death of the non-owning or non-earning spouse/co-habitee.

1. The claimant must be able to prove that he or she made a contribution to the property and the size of that contribution; see *National Westminster Bank plc* v. *Malhan* [2004] EWHC 847 where the court decided that the claimant had failed to prove that she had savings of £31,000 in 1986 which, she alleged, she had used to pay the balance of the purchase price of the house.
2. Land Registration Act 2002, s.26. See also Land Registration Rules 2003, r.94(1) which requires the registered proprietor to apply for a restriction in Form A where the estate is subject to a trust of land.
3. 'Notice' includes actual notice, constructive notice and imputed notice. See *Hunt* v. *Luck* [1902] 1 Ch 428; *Kingsnorth Finance Co. Ltd* v. *Tizzard* [1986] 1 WLR 783.
4. Law of Property Act 1925, s.2(2). See also *City of London Building Society* v. *Flegg* [1988] AC 54.

9.3. The choices

9.3.1. In law co-ownership of land can usually only exist through the medium of a trust of land. The legal estate will thus be held by joint tenants on trust for themselves (and possibly other persons) in equity. The legal joint tenancy is not severable and there must be a minimum of two trustees (and maximum of four) in order to deal with the legal estate.[1]

9.3.2. In equity there is a choice between holding as joint tenants or as tenants in common.

9.3.3. The capacity of the buyers, whether as joint tenants or tenants in common, must be expressly stated in the purchase deed or in a separate trust deed. Panel 11 of Form TR1 (transfer of whole registered title(s)) contains a declaration of trust to be completed where there is more than one transferee.[2] A transfer containing such a declaration of trust must be executed by the buyers. An express declaration of trust may also be made in the additional provisions panel of the Land Registry form (e.g. panel 12 of TR1). In this event, the form must be signed or executed by the buyers.[3] Details of the trust will not appear on the register.[4]

1. Law of Property Act 1925, s.1(6) and s.34.
2. See *Huntingford* v. *Hobbs* [1992] EGCS 38 and *Stack* v. *Dowden* [2007] UKHL 17 as to the effect of declarations in earlier forms of transfer that the survivor of the transferees was entitled to give a valid receipt for capital money.
3. Law of Property Act 1925, s.53(1).
4. Land Registration Act 2002, s.78.

9.4. Joint tenants

9.4.1. Where co-owners hold the beneficial interest as joint tenants, none of the co-owners will be entitled to a distinct or separate proportion of that interest: each one owns all of it. The main distinguishing feature of the joint tenancy is the right of survivorship which leads to the interest accruing to the ultimate sole surviving joint tenant. Because no distinct part of the interest belongs to any individual tenant, no part of it will belong to the estate of a deceased joint tenant and, where the co-owners were married to each other or in a civil partnership, will not attract inheritance tax. An interest in a joint tenancy cannot be left by will, the deceased's share passing automatically to the surviving joint tenant(s). A beneficial joint tenancy can be severed which has the effect of converting it into a tenancy in common if there were only two joint tenants.[1]

1. An express declaration of joint tenancy will result in the joint owners being given equal shares in the event of a severance: *Goodman* v. *Gallant* [1986] Fam 106. However, if there was no express declaration, the severance of the joint tenancy may result in the property being divided according to the contributions made by the joint owners. Where there is no express declaration a transfer into joint names will infer both a legal and beneficial joint tenancy. Cases where the court will hold that the parties intended that their beneficial interests would differ from their legal interests would be very unusual: see *Stack* v. *Dowden* [2007] UKHL 17.

9.5. Tenants in common

9.5.1. Where a tenancy in common exists, each co-owner holds a quantified proportion of the beneficial interest which is capable of being disposed of *inter vivos* or by will or passes on the intestacy of the deceased tenant in common. The proportionate share in the property which belonged to a deceased tenant in common is subject to inheritance tax rules.

9.5.2. Unless the contrary is stated or evidence to the contrary is proved, a court will assume that tenants in common hold the beneficial interest in proportion to the parties' original contributions to the property.[1] In order to avoid subsequent disputes and litigation it is desirable that the proportionate shares of each tenant in common are expressly agreed and recorded in a deed of trust (or certified copy transfer) which is signed by the co-owners. In unregistered land an express declaration as to the proportionate shares may be included in the purchase deed. If the parties cannot agree on the amount of their respective shares separate advice for one or all of them is necessary. Unless the proportions in which the beneficial interest is held are clearly stated, it may be difficult to determine the ownership of the proceeds of sale when the property is ultimately sold. This will present problems for the solicitor if, e.g. the property is sold and the proceeds are to be divided as a result of a matrimonial or civil partnership breakdown. See the Law Society's guidance on conflicts of interest post *Etridge* in Appendix IV.8.

9.5.3. One drawback to an express statement of the beneficial interest is that it cannot be changed except by deed. If, for example, a deed of trust stated that a husband owned 70% of the equitable interest and his wife 30%, but the wife subsequently paid off the whole mortgage on the house using money which she had inherited on the death of one of her parents, the wife might feel that she had become entitled to a larger proportion of the beneficial interest through her contribution to the mortgage but, unless a new deed of trust is drawn up, redefining the proportionate shares of the parties, on sale of the property, the wife would still be entitled only to her original 30%. An alternative solution is that the whole or part of one joint owner's beneficial interest can be transferred to the new owner in writing, signed by the person transferring.[2]

9.5.4. A tenancy in common can be devised by will or will pass on intestacy. Where property is held by this method the parties should be advised as to the desirability of making a will.

9.5.5. Where a tenancy in common is created the deed should make specific provision relating to the appointment of a new trustee in the event of the death of one co-owner. In the absence of such a provision the provisions of Trusts of Land and Appointment of Trustees Act 1996, s.19 may operate to give beneficiaries who are of full age and competence the right to nominate a new trustee.

1. *Springette* v. *Defoe* [1992] NPC 34; *Savill* v. *Goodall* [1992] NPC 153.
2. Law of Property Act 1925, s.53.

9.6. Suitability of each method

Joint tenancy

9.6.1. The automatic right of survivorship may make this method of co-ownership both suitable and attractive to prospective co-owners who are married to each other or in a civil partnership. However, a joint tenancy may not be appropriate for a married couple or civil partners where one or both of the buyers is individually wealthy, where equalisation of estates for inheritance tax purposes is a consideration or where one or both of the parties has children from a previous relationship who might expect to inherit on their parent's death. Survivorship rights may well not be intended by co-owners who are not married to each other or not in a civil partnership, and would not normally be considered suitable when dealing with property held in a business partnership.

Tenancy in common

9.6.2. Prospective co-owners who are not married to each other or not in a civil partnership will usually be advised to hold by this method. This is also the most appropriate method by which partnership property can be dealt with. Consideration should be given to this method where the contributions made by each of the co-owners to the purchase price are in unequal proportions and where the parties are married to each other but one (or both) of them has children from a previous relationship whom the parent might reasonably expect to inherit on the death of their natural parent.

9.7. Gifts

9.7.1. Where the purchase price of the property is supplied by one party alone, but the property is purchased in the joint names of the person who paid the purchase price and another, equity generally deems the property to be held on a resulting trust on behalf of the buyer, unless there is an indication to the contrary (such as an express declaration of trust in the transfer), or the circumstances are within the limited cases where a presumption of advancement applies.

9.8. Co-habitees

9.8.1. All co-habitees whether they are spouses, civil partners, co-habitees or joint purchasers may need to be advised independently about their respective rights in the property to be purchased. Solicitors should be alert to the possibility of a conflict of interests arising in this situation.

9.8.2. It is advisable for co-habitees who are to be co-owners to enter into a separate deed of trust which sets out their respective interests in the property. The rights and obligations conferred by this document can only be altered by the execution of a further deed of trust but this disadvantage is outweighed by the advantage of having certainty as to the parties' rights and interests.

9.8.3.   In *Oxley* v. *Hiscock* [2004] EWCA Civ 546, the Court of Appeal provided guidance on the steps to be taken when acting for co-habitees:

- the solicitor should always enquire about the source of the funds for the purchase and the future liability for the repayment of the mortgage;

- if there is evidence that the purchase is actually a joint acquisition or that others may be acquiring rights under a potential constructive trust, the client(s) should be advised either to purchase the property as legal co-owners and/or to record their arrangement in a trust deed;

- when drafting the transfer and/or trust deed decisions have to be made as to whether the equitable interest is to be held as joint tenants or tenants in common.

9.8.4.   If the property is to be purchased in the sole name of one co-habitee, the other should be advised (where appropriate) to protect his or her interest by lodging an application for registration of an appropriate restriction at the Land Registry.[1]

1.   Land Registration Rules 2003, r.92 and Sched.4 (e.g. Form A and Form II restrictions).

A10. Acting for both parties

10.1. Conflict of interests

10.1.1. As a general principle of professional conduct a solicitor or firm of solicitors should not accept instructions to act for two or more clients in the same transaction where there is a conflict or a significant risk of a conflict between the interests of those clients.[1]

10.1.2. Neither should a solicitor or his firm continue to act for two or more clients if a conflict of interests arises between those clients.[2]

1. See Rule 3 Solicitors' Code of Conduct 2007 (conflict of interests).
2. *Ibid.*

10.2. Rule 3 Solicitors' Code of Conduct 2007 (conflict of interests)

10.2.1. Subject to certain exceptions, acting for both parties in a conveyancing transaction at arm's length is generally prohibited by Rule 3.07 Solicitors' Code of Conduct 2007. The rule should be considered carefully before a decision is taken to act for more than one party.

10.2.2. In most circumstances, therefore, a solicitor who is asked to act for both parties to a transaction will decline to act for both either because of the potential conflict of interest between the parties or because of the application of Rule 3.07 Solicitors' Code of Conduct 2007.

10.2.3. A solicitor must not act for both parties in a conveyancing transaction where the prohibitions in Rule 10.06(3) and (4) Solicitors' Code of Conduct 2007 apply, that is where a contract race is being run.

10.2.4. Provided there is no conflict of interest the same solicitor may act for both seller and buyer where the transaction is not at arm's length (e.g. a transaction between parties who are related by blood, adoption or marriage or living together: see paragraph 73 guidance to Rule 3 Solicitors Code of Conduct 2007).

10.3.   **Exceptions to Rule 3**

10.3.1.   A solicitor must not act for seller and buyer:

(a)   without the written consent of both parties;

(b)   if a conflict of interest exists or arises; or

(c)   if the seller is selling or leasing as a builder or developer.

If a builder or developer acquires a property in part exchange, and sells it on without development, he or she is not selling as a builder or developer for the purpose of Rule 3.

10.3.2.   Subject to A10.3.1, a solicitor may act for both seller and buyer, but only if:

(a)   both parties are established clients (the test here is an objective one, i.e. whether a reasonable solicitor would regard the person as an established client. A person who is related by blood, adoption or marriage or who is living with an established client counts as an established client. A seller or buyer who instructs the solicitor for the first time is not an established client. A person who is selling or buying jointly with an established client counts as an established client); *or*

(b)   the consideration is £10,000 or less and the transaction is not the grant of a lease (the value of any property taken in part exchange must be taken into account in calculating the consideration); *or*

(c)   seller and buyer are represented by two separate offices in different localities and

    (i)   different solicitors who normally work at each office, conduct or supervise the transaction for seller and buyer; and

    (ii)   no office of the practice (or an associated practice) referred either client to the office conducting his or her transaction; *or*

(d)   the only way in which the solicitor is acting for the buyer is in providing mortgage related services; *or*

(e)   the only way in which the solicitor is acting for the seller is in providing property selling services through a SEAL.

10.3.3.   When a solicitor's practice (including a SEAL) acts in the property selling for the seller and either acts for the buyer on the purchase or provides mortgage related services to the buyer, the following additional conditions must be met:

(a)   different individuals must conduct the work for the seller and the work for the buyer; and if the individual conducting the work needs supervision, they must be supervised by different solicitors; *and*

(b)   the solicitor must inform the seller in writing, before accepting instructions to deal with the property selling, of any services which might be offered to a buyer, whether through the same practice or any practice associated with it; *and*

(c)   the solicitor must explain to the buyer, before the buyer gives consent to the arrangement:

    (i)   the implications of a conflict of interests arising; *and*

    (ii)   the solicitor's financial interest in the sale going through; *and*

    (iii)   if the solicitor proposes to provide mortgage related services to the buyer through a SEAL which is also acting for the seller, that the solicitor cannot advise the buyer on the merits of the purchase.

10.4.   Mortgages

Standard mortgages

10.4.1.   A mortgage is a standard mortgage where:

    (a)   it is provided in the normal course of the lender's activities;

    (b)   a significant part of the lender's activities consists of lending; and

    (c)   the mortgage is on standard terms.

10.4.2.   A solicitor may act for both lender and borrower in a standard mortgage provided there is no conflict of interests, the mortgage instructions do not go beyond Rule 3.19 Solicitors' Code of Conduct 2007 (which sets out details of the type of instructions which can be accepted) and, where the property is to be used solely as the borrower's private residence, the approved certificate of title set out in the annexe to Rule 3 is used.

10.4.3.   The provisions in Rule 3 also apply to non-residential mortgages but the certificate of title can be in any form recognised by the Board of the Solicitors Regulation Authority or which complies with Rule 3.19.

Individual mortgage

10.4.4.   An individual mortgage is any mortgage other than a standard mortgage (see A10.4.1 above). The lender and borrower must be separately represented and the grant of an individual mortgage at arm's length; see Rule 3.16(b) Solicitors' Code of Conduct 2007.

Acting for seller, buyer and lender

10.4.5.   A solicitor, or solicitors practising in associated practices, must not act for seller, buyer and lender in the same transaction unless no conflict of interest exists or arises, and, in the case of a standard mortgage, the solicitor has given written notification of the circumstance to the lender.

10.5. **Contract races**

10.5.1. If the transaction involves a contract race the same firm may not act for two or more prospective buyers, nor may the firm act for both seller and one of the prospective buyers. See Rule 10.06 Solicitors' Code of Conduct 2007 (relations with third parties).

10.6. **Merger of firms**

10.6.1. As a result of a merger or amalgamation a firm may find that it is acting for both seller and buyer in the same transaction. Unless the circumstances of the transaction fall within one of the exceptions to Rule 3, see Rule 3.09 and Rule 3.10 Solicitors' Code of Conduct 2007, the firm should cease to act for one or both of the parties from the date of the merger. If none of the exceptions apply, the firm may continue to act for one party only if the duty of confidentiality to the other is not at risk (see Rule 3.15 Solicitors' Code of Conduct 2007).

Rule 4.04

10.6.2. The merged firm may continue to act for both established clients if both clients have been informed of the situation and have consented to the merged firm continuing to act. For informed consent the client must be aware that the firm might hold material information in relation to their matter which the firm cannot disclose. In addition it must also be reasonable in all the circumstances of the case for the firm to continue acting.

10.6.3 Where the firm has been acting for two or more clients in compliance with Rule 3 (conflict of interest) and can no longer fulfil the requirements of Rule 3, the firm may continue to act for one client with the consent of the other, provided that the firm complies with Rule 4.04.

10.6.4. New instructions received for clients of the merged firm will be subject to the provisions of Rule 3 Solicitors' Code of Conduct 2007.

10.7. **Solicitor who moves to another firm**

Client's pending business is taken over by the new firm

10.7.1. In these circumstances the solicitor may find that his new firm is already acting for the other party to the transaction and a situation analogous to that which occurs on a merger of firms pertains. The provisions of Rule 4.04 must be complied with.

10.7.2. On moving to the new firm the solicitor may find he is now acting for the buyer in a transaction where he had previously been acting for the seller in the same transaction (or vice versa): although in this situation there is no question of the same solicitor or same firm acting for both parties, the solicitor, while working for his previous firm, will have acquired information which is confidential to his (now) former client and which may affect or prejudice the way in which he handles the transaction for the client of the new firm. In order to preserve his duty of confidentiality to his former client the solicitor should not act for the client of the new firm in this transaction, but there is no objection to the matter being handled by another fee-earner in the solicitor's new firm provided that adequate safeguards are put in place in accordance with Rule 4.04 to ensure that the confidential information is safeguarded.

10.8. Property selling

10.8.1. See A10.3.3 where the solicitor conducts property selling as part of the firm's own solicitor's business.

10.8.2. Where the solicitor conducts property selling through a separate jointly owned business and the solicitor does not do the seller's conveyancing or does the seller's conveyancing under one of the exceptions in Rule 3.11 Solicitors' Code of Conduct 2007, he may do the buyer's conveyancing. Alternatively the solicitor may do a seller's conveyancing where the estate agency business provides mortgage services to the buyer. The buyer and the seller must give their written informed consent and different individuals must deal with the work for seller and buyer; see Rule 3.13.

10.8.3. If any of the circumstances in Rule 3.09 apply (established clients; consideration of £10,000 or less; representation by two separate offices) the firm may sell the property, provide mortgage related services, and act for the seller and buyer in the conveyancing provided that Rules 3.10 and 3.13 are complied with. This does not apply where there is more than one prospective buyer: see Rules 10.06(3)–(4) Solicitors' Code of Conduct 2007.

10.9. Joint borrowers

10.9.1. Where joint borrowers are obtaining a mortgage for the purchase of property, there is no objection to the same solicitor advising both of them, provided that their interests coincide. Where, however, one party is acting as surety for the other's debts, e.g. a wife who is guaranteeing her husband's mortgage of the matrimonial home to secure the husband's business debts, the parties' interests will almost certainly be in conflict with each other. In these circumstances, separate and independent advice must be given to each party. It may be possible for the same solicitor to advise both clients in these circumstances, but each client should be seen separately and the advice given to each party must be consistent with that party's interests.[1] When instructions are being carried out under the terms of the Lenders' Handbook, paragraph 8 of the Handbook will normally prohibit the same solicitor from advising any borrower who does not benefit personally from the loan or any guarantor or any non-owning occupier. Such persons must have independent advice (also see A10.4).

1. See *Barclays Bank plc* v. *O'Brien* [1993] 4 All ER 417; *Midland Bank plc* v. *Serter* [1994] EGCS 45; *Clark Boyce* v. *Mouat* [1993] 3 WLR 1021, PC; *Banco Exterior Internacional* v. *Mann* [1995] 1 All ER 936, CA. Also see *Bank Melli Iran* v. *Samadi Rad* [1995] 2 FLR 367, where the court said that a wife who had been advised separately by a different solicitor in the firm which was also advising her husband had not received 'independent' advice.

A11. Mortgages: acting for lender and borrower

11.1. General principles

11.1.1. The buyer's lender will frequently instruct the buyer's solicitor also to act for him in connection with the grant of the mortgage. The same situation commonly occurs in relation to the discharge of an existing mortgage when acting for a seller client.

11.1.2. As soon as the solicitor accepts instructions to act for the lender he is acting for both parties in one transaction (i.e. for both lender and borrower) and owes a duty to both clients.[1] Their respective interests are not necessarily identical and need to be separately considered.

11.1.3. Subject to A10.4, acting for both parties is permissible provided that no conflict of interest arises between the two clients.

11.1.4. The lender's instructions to act and (in the case of a purchase) terms of offer must be carefully scrutinised to ensure that there is no conflict or potential conflict between the interests of the lender and the buyer/seller.

11.1.5. In many cases the lender's instructions will require the solicitor to observe the terms of the Lenders' Handbook (which is certified for compliance with Rule 3 Solicitors' Code of Conduct 2007 (conflict of interests)).

11.1.6. A solicitor may not act for a lender where the terms of the lender's instructions exceed the limitations imposed by Rules 3.19 and 3.20 Solicitors' Code of Conduct 2007.

1. *Mortgage Express v. Bowerman & Partners* [1995] 2 All ER 769, CA.

11.2. Conflict of interests

11.2.1. If a conflict should occur the solicitor must decline to act (or to continue to act) for both parties unless he can, with the consent of one party, continue to act for the other.

11.3.   Examples of conflict

11.3.1.   Conflict may arise if, for example:

    (a)   the terms of the mortgage offer are inequitable;

    (b)   instructions reveal that the buyer would be in breach of one of the terms of the offer;

    (c)   the buyer/seller is unable to comply with the lender's terms;

    (d)   the buyer is offering inadequate security.

11.3.2.   A conflict will also arise if the buyer's solicitor becomes aware that the buyer is misrepresenting the purchase price to the lender, e.g. where the buyer and seller have agreed that the actual purchase price of the property will be lower than that shown in the contract and purchase deed, or where the buyer receives an inducement such as a free holiday to persuade him to buy the property. Solicitors have a duty of confidentiality to their clients, but this does not affect their duty to act in the best interests of each client. Subject to the instructions received from the particular lender concerned, any information regarding variations to the purchase price should be forwarded to the lender with the consent of the buyer. If the buyer will not consent to the information being disclosed to the lender the solicitor must cease to act for the lender and must consider carefully whether he is able to continue to act for the buyer. Any attempt to defraud the lender may lead to criminal prosecutions of both the buyer and the buyer's solicitor. The solicitor would also be guilty of unprofessional conduct. If a solicitor is aware that his client is attempting to perpetrate fraud in any form he should immediately cease to act for that client. Attention is drawn to the Law Society's Property Fraud Warning Card II (Appendix III.3).

11.4.   Confidentiality

11.4.1.   If a conflict does arise between the borrower and his lender where the same solicitor is acting for both parties it should be borne in mind that all information received by the solicitor from his client is confidential and cannot be disclosed to the lender without the client's consent. Knowledge acquired in the course of acting for the client is not imputed to the lender.[1] Where, for example, the solicitor is told by his borrower client that the client intends to breach the terms of the mortgage offer by letting the premises to a tenant, the solicitor, when informing the lender that he can no longer act for him, must tell the lender that the reason for the termination of the retainer is because a conflict of interests has arisen, but is not at liberty to disclose the nature of the conflict without the borrower client's consent.

1. *Halifax Mortgage Services Ltd.* v. *Stepsky, The Times,* 27 June 1995.

11.5.   Individual mortgages

11.5.1.   The solicitor must not act for both lender and borrower in an individual mortgage at arm's length; see Rule 3.17 Solicitors' Code of Conduct 2007.

11.5.2.   An individual mortgage is defined by Rule 3.17 Solicitors' Code of Conduct 2007 as any mortgage other than a standard mortgage. A standard mortgage is one on standard terms provided in the normal course of the lender's activities.

11.5.3.   Subject to the general principles of conflict of interests it would be possible to act in an individual mortgage which is not at arm's length (e.g. a loan between father and son), but it is advisable to ensure that the borrower receives independent advice about the terms of the loan.

11.6.   Lender's costs

11.6.1.   See N1.

11.7.   Sureties

11.7.1.   Where the lender requires a surety to enter into the transaction, the surety should be advised to take independent advice before signing the security document. This is of particular importance where the intended surety is the wife of the borrower since the courts take the view that a security should not be enforced against a married woman unless the lender can show that he has taken reasonable steps to show that she understood the transaction.[1] Under the terms of the Lenders' Handbook (paragraph 8) a solicitor cannot act for both the borrower and a surety without the lender's consent and the surety must have independent advice.

11.7.2.   If the proceeds of a life policy fall into the deceased's estate (e.g. because the policy was not formally assigned to the lender) the surety has no claim against the deceased's estate.

1. See *Barclays Bank plc* v. *O'Brien* [1993] 3 WLR 786, HL; *CIBC Mortgages* v. *Pitt* [1993] 3 WLR 802, HL.

11.8.   Mortgage fraud

11.8.1.   Mortgage fraud can occur in either a residential or commercial transaction and can assume many different guises. Solicitors must be alert to the possibility of fraud and should be careful not to participate, even unknowingly, in a transaction where such a fraud is being perpetrated (see A24 and Appendix III.3).

11.9. Ownership of documents and confidentiality

11.9.1. The following guidance relates to the position where the same firm of solicitors acted for the buyer/borrower and for the lender on a contemporaneous purchase and mortgage and the lender asks to see documents on the 'conveyancing file'.

11.9.2. Where all the documentation is kept on one file, the solicitor will have to sort through the file to determine ownership of the various papers.

11.9.3. The documents which the lender will be entitled to see fall into two categories. The first category is documents prepared or received by the solicitor on behalf of the lender. The second category is documents prepared or received by the solicitor on behalf of the borrower which, it is considered, the lender is nonetheless entitled to see. The rationale is that these documents relate to that part of the solicitor's work where the lender and borrower can be said to have a common interest, i.e. the deduction of title, the acquisition of a good title to the property and ancillary legal issues, such as the use of the property. Examples of the most common items in these two categories are set out below.

11.9.4. Documents held by the solicitor on behalf of the lender are:

(a) the lender's instructions to the solicitor;

(b) copy mortgage deed;

(c) copy report on title;

(d) any correspondence between the solicitor and the lender or between the solicitor and a third party written or received on the lender's behalf.

11.9.5. Documents held by the solicitor on behalf of the borrower which the lender is entitled to see include:

(a) contract for sale;

(b) property information form/enquiries before contract;

(c) abstract or epitome of title/official copy entries of the title;

(d) requisitions on title;

(e) draft purchase deed;

(f) draft licence to assign (where appropriate);

(g) Land Registry application forms.

11.10. The CML Lenders' Handbook for England and Wales

Introduction

11.10.1. The Lenders' Handbook forms the contract between the solicitor (or licensed conveyancer) and lender where the solicitor (or licensed conveyancer) is representing a lender who has agreed to be a party to the Lenders' Handbook. A number of major lenders have agreed to be parties to the Lenders' Handbook and other mortgage lenders may instruct solicitors to act on the terms of the Lenders' Handbook. The instructions apply whether or not the solicitor is acting for both borrower and lender or for the lender only.

11.10.2. Modifications of the instructions specific to the transaction in hand will be notified to the solicitor in the lender's written instructions to the solicitor and/or in Part 2 of the Lenders' Handbook.

11.10.3. It is the solicitor's responsibility to ensure that the property has a good and marketable title which can safely be accepted by the lender as security and that the property is validly charged to the lender to secure the advance made to the borrower.

11.10.4. Communications between the solicitor and the lender must be in writing (or confirmed in writing) and must quote the mortgage account or roll number, the borrower's name and initials, the address of the property and the solicitor's reference.

11.10.5. Documents contained in the 'joint file' (as defined in the Lenders' Handbook) must be retained by the solicitor for at least six years from the date of the mortgage. The borrower is not permitted to have documents from the file without the lender's consent. Equally, the lender is not permitted to have documents from the file without the borrower's consent. Each would be entitled to certified copies, but the lender only to those documents relevant to its retainer because of the right of the borrower to confidentiality (see A11.9.4 and A11.9.5).

11.10.6. The solicitor must use the lender's standard documentation the wording of which must not be varied without the lender's consent.

A12. Preliminary deposits

12.1.	General law	12.3.	New properties
12.2.	Payment to estate agents	12.4.	Action by solicitor

12.1. General law

12.1.1. There is no requirement in law for either party to pay a preliminary deposit since neither party is committed to the sale and purchase until contracts have been exchanged.

12.2. Payment to estate agents

12.2.1. An estate agent will sometimes ask a prospective buyer to pay a preliminary deposit as an indication of the buyer's good intentions to proceed with negotiations. The buyer should be advised to resist pressure from the agent to make such a payment since no advantage to the buyer derives from it.

12.2.2. If a preliminary deposit is to be paid the buyer should ensure that the agent has the seller's authority to take the deposit. Without such authority the buyer has no recourse against the seller if the agent misappropriates the money.[1]

12.2.3. A signed receipt must be obtained in respect of any preliminary deposit which is paid, a copy of which should be placed on the solicitor's file for reference. The terms of the receipt should be scrutinised before signature to ensure that the deposit will be refundable if the transaction does not proceed.

12.2.4. Any preliminary deposit paid is normally fully refundable to the buyer if the transaction does not proceed.

12.2.5. Preliminary deposits are usually paid to the estate agent who will hold the money in the capacity of agent for the seller. Interest on a preliminary deposit which exceeds £500 may be payable under Estate Agents Act 1979.

12.2.6. Where a preliminary deposit is taken by a solicitor who is acting as an estate agent, consideration should be given to holding that deposit in the capacity of agent for the buyer in accordance with the Solicitors' Property Group Code of Practice.[2]

1. See *Sorrell* v. *Finch* [1977] AC 728.
2. See **www.solicitorspropertygroup.co.uk**.

12.3. New properties

12.3.1. A seller who is a builder or developer will invariably require a prospective buyer to pay a preliminary deposit. In this situation the payment of the deposit may operate as an option to purchase a numbered plot at a stated price, the seller promising that he will not sell that plot elsewhere nor raise the price provided that contracts are exchanged within a stated period. Here the buyer may have little choice but to pay the deposit, but a receipt should always be obtained and a copy of it placed on the buyer's solicitor's file for reference. The terms of the receipt should be scrutinised to ascertain whether the deposit is refundable to the buyer if he later changes his mind and withdraws from the transaction. Since this type of preliminary deposit often buys an option on a numbered plot it is not unusual to find that the deposit is not returnable to the buyer in any circumstances, although it will be credited as part of the purchase price if the matter proceeds.

12.4. Action by solicitor

12.4.1. The solicitor should always enquire whether a preliminary deposit has been paid, and if so how much and to whom. A copy of the receipt should be obtained and a note of the amount of the deposit made on the file so that this may be taken into account when calculating the balance of deposit needed on exchange.

12.4.2. The solicitor should also enquire whether the prospective buyer has signed any authority or other documents held by the estate agent which may be relevant to the contract.

A13. Surveys

13.1. When should a survey be commissioned?

13.1.1. Ideally the buyer should always have a survey carried out before exchange of contracts, but many buyers, particularly first-time buyers for whom the expense of a survey is a major consideration, do not commission an independent survey, preferring to rely instead on the valuation undertaken by their lender. Most lenders disclose their written valuation reports to their customers.

13.1.2. The home information pack will contain a home condition report covering the state and condition of the property (see A26). Some lenders may not be willing to rely on this report and may continue to require a separate valuation before making a mortgage offer.

13.1.3. In the case of commercial premises a buyer will have much more detailed concerns relating to the structure, use, and floor loading capabilities of the property. Compliance with statutory requirements must also be checked. The comments contained in the following paragraphs do not reflect the detail required in a commercial transaction.

13.2. Reasons for a survey

13.2.1. The *caveat emptor* rule places on the buyer the onus of discovering any physical faults in the property agreed to be sold. For this reason alone, a survey is always advisable in order to discover physical defects which are not readily apparent on inspection of the property by the lay client, except perhaps where a property in the course of construction is being purchased with the benefit of structural defects insurance.

13.2.2. In addition to the above the surveyor's report should:

    (a) confirm whether or not the value of the property equates with the price agreed to be paid for it;

    (b) point out any major structural defects which exist;

    (c) give the buyer early warning of potential structural problems or major repair work which will be required in the foreseeable future so that these may be taken into account in deciding whether the buyer is able and/or prepared to undertake the responsibility for such future expenditure;

(d) bring to the attention of the buyer's solicitor the existence of factors which may be indicative of third party rights or overriding interests over the property and which need to be the subject of further enquiries by the solicitor;

(e) point out minor matters which may need remedial work in the near future;

(f) confirm whether or not the boundaries on the ground correspond with those shown in the title deeds.

13.3.   Advice to the client

13.3.1. If the client has not already instructed a surveyor, the reasons for having a survey done and the limitations of the home condition report (if one has been provided) should be explained to the client. A note should be made on the file that the client was so advised and of the client's decision following the receipt of the advice. The advice given should include information relating to the different types of survey available and their relative cost.

13.3.2. The client should be advised to commission a survey as soon as a firm offer has been accepted by the seller. The results of the survey must be obtained before exchange of contracts since once exchange has taken place the client will no longer have the right to withdraw from the transaction on the grounds of a physical defect in the property. The results of the survey may reveal matters which will require further investigation by the buyer's solicitor, or even give grounds for the negotiation of a reduction in the purchase price, both of which must, where appropriate, be conducted before a binding contract is entered into.

13.3.3. Although there is no reported decision on the point, it is possible that a court might hold that a solicitor who had not advised a client to have a survey done was in breach of his duty of care towards his client or in breach of Supply of Goods and Services Act 1982, s.13 which implies an obligation to perform a contract for services with reasonable skill and care.

13.3.4. If the solicitor does go through the surveyor's report prepared for the client, he is expected to exercise his own judgment and expertise in relation to the interpretation of the report and should emphasise to the client the limitations on the advice which can be given by the solicitor about the report (i.e. that he is looking at the report as a lawyer and not as a surveyor).

13.4.   Types of survey

13.4.1. In broad terms the client has three options open to him:

(a) to rely on the valuation made by his lender;

(b)   to commission a 'Home Buyer's Valuation and Survey Report';

(c)   to instruct an independent surveyor to do a full structural survey.

Valuation

13.4.2. This will be undertaken by the buyer's lender in order to establish whether the property being purchased will be adequate security for the amount of the loan. The buyer pays the cost of this valuation and is usually permitted to see the valuer's report, but the report will not necessarily reveal sufficient information about the state of the property to allow the buyer to make a reasoned judgment as to whether or not to proceed with his purchase. Where the amount required by the buyer on mortgage represents a high percentage of the purchase price of the property, the interests of the buyer and his lender in the valuation broadly coincide, in that if the value of the property does not provide adequate security for the loan, then neither does it represent a wise investment for the client. In these circumstances therefore it may be considered that a lender's valuation report alone will provide sufficient protection of the client's interests. A valuation alone may also be considered adequate in circumstances where the client is purchasing a property in the course of construction which is to be covered by a structural defects insurance scheme.

Home Buyer's Valuation and Survey Report

13.4.3. This option represents a compromise between the mortgage valuation and the full survey and is thus an attractive option for a client who, for reasons of expense or otherwise, is reluctant to commission a full survey. In many cases the buyer's lender will agree (for an additional fee) to instruct the lender's valuer to undertake the survey concurrently with the mortgage valuation with consequent savings in time and expense for the client. This type of survey may provide adequate information for the client who is purchasing an ordinary suburban property built within the last 100 years, but the client should not be misled into thinking that the survey result is an absolute guarantee of the state and condition of the property. Although of much more value to the client than a mere valuation, this type of survey is still relatively superficial in scope.

Full survey

13.4.4. The potential expense of a full survey deters many clients from choosing this option. The client might be reminded that £500 abortive expense on a survey is preferable to discovering that £30,000 worth of structural repairs needs to be done to the property he has just purchased without the benefit of a survey. This option is undoubtedly the most expensive of the three on offer, the exact expense and value to the client depending on what the surveyor has been instructed to investigate. A full survey will only reveal the true state and condition of the entire property if the surveyor is correctly instructed to investigate all aspects of the property.

Guidelines

13.4.5. The need for a full structural survey may be indicated by the presence of one or more of the following factors:

(a) the property is of a high value;

(b) the amount of the buyer's intended mortgage represents a low proportion of the purchase price, e.g. less than 70%;

(c) the property is more than 100 years old;

(d) the buyer intends to alter or extend the property after completion;

(e) the property is not of conventional brick and mortar construction;

(f) the proximity of the property to features which may cause subsidence or other structural problems, e.g. mines, filled-in gravel pits, rivers, vibration damage from aircraft or railways;

(g) the property is not detached.

Surveys in special cases

13.4.6. A surveyor, even when instructed to carry out a full structural survey, will not normally investigate drainage or electrical systems. A property which does not have the benefit of mains drainage will require a separate drainage survey from an expert in that field, since the cost of repair or replacement of a private drainage system can be prohibitive. Liability for escaping effluent can also involve civil and criminal penalties. If the electric wiring system in the property has not been inspected during the past five years a report on the adequacy and safety of the electrical installations may also be desirable. Where environmental issues are relevant, e.g. on purchases of development land, a separate environmental survey may also be desirable to ensure that the land does not harbour any hazardous substances which may incur liability on the landowner under Environmental Protection Act 1990 or Environment Act 1995. The local authority for the area can supply information relating to the presence of radon in the area. The National Radiological Protection Board publishes definitive maps, provides information on radon, and offers a written report on the radon potential for a property (see B25.6.6).

Flats and other attached properties

13.4.7. Where the property to be purchased is a flat or is a property which is structurally attached to neighbouring property, a full survey is desirable. The structural soundness of the property being bought is in these circumstances dependent on the soundness of the neighbouring property also, and the surveyor must therefore be instructed to inspect the adjoining property (if possible) as well as the property actually being purchased.

Water supply pipes

13.4.8.   The owner or occupier of land may be responsible for the maintenance of a water supply pipe which crosses privately owned land before joining the publicly maintained mains supply pipe. A full structural survey may not deal with the water supply system (particularly where the pipes supplying the property being surveyed pass through or under adjoining property). The client may be advised to obtain a separate survey of the water supply pipes from his water supply company. A fee may be payable for this service.

13.5.   Surveyor's liability

13.5.1.   The surveyor owes a duty of care to his client to carry out his survey with reasonable skill and care. This common law duty is reinforced by Supply of Goods and Services Act 1982, s.13 which implies into a contract for services a term that the work will be carried out with reasonable skill and care.

13.5.2.   Where a client suffers loss as a result of a negligent survey an action can be sustained against his surveyor, subject to the validity of any exemption clause which may have formed part of the surveyor's terms of work. The normal rules relating to remoteness of damage apply; thus the client will not sustain a successful action unless the area of the client's complaint lies within the scope of what the surveyor was instructed to do, and hence the importance of giving full and explicit instructions when the survey is commissioned.

13.5.3.   An exclusion clause which seeks to limit or to exclude the surveyor's liability in contract or tort will be subject to the reasonableness test in Unfair Contract Terms Act 1977, s.11. Where a lay client has suffered loss the burden of showing that the clause satisfies the reasonableness test will be a difficult one for the surveyor to discharge,[1] but the clause may give some protection where the client who commissioned the survey was experienced in the property field.[2]

13.5.4.   Where the client suffers loss after having relied on a lender's valuer's report an action in tort may lie against the surveyor. No action in contract can be sustained because, the survey having been commissioned by the lender, there is no contractual relationship between the buyer and the surveyor. The success of such an action may again depend on the validity of any exclusion clause contained in the valuation; however, it was held by the House of Lords in *Smith v. Eric S Bush (a firm)*; *Harris* v. *Wyre Forest District Council*[3] that a valuer instructed by a lender to carry out a mortgage valuation of a modest house, in the knowledge that the buyer would rely on the valuation without obtaining an independent survey, owed a duty of care to the buyer to exercise reasonable care and skill in carrying out the valuation. Similarly in *Beresforde* v. *Chesterfield Borough Council*,[4] where the lender presented the valuer's report to the buyer on its own headed notepaper, the Court of Appeal allowed the buyer to proceed with a claim based on loss arising out of an allegedly negligent valuation directly against the lender. However, the court's decision in this case was interlocutory and as no trial took place it cannot be assumed that a lender will always be liable in such circumstances. The decisions in these cases may assist lay purchasers of ordinary modestly priced houses or small businesses,[5] but may not assist in other circumstances where it would be reasonable to assume that the buyer would commission his own independent survey.

13.5.5. A complaint about a negligent valuation/survey made in-house by a lender may be investigated by the Building Societies' Ombudsman provided the complainant is an existing borrower from that lender.[6]

1. See *Yianni* v. *Edwin Evans & Sons* [1982] 1 QB 438.
2. See *Stevenson* v. *Nationwide Building Society* (1984) 272 EG 663.
3. [1990] 1 AC 831, HL.
4. [1989] 39 EG 176.
5. See *Qureshi* v. *Liassides* (unreported 22 April 1995). See commentary in *Estates Gazette*, 11 November 1994, p.123.
6. *Halifax Building Society* v. *Edell* [1992] Ch 436.

13.6. Lenders' Handbook[1]

13.6.1. Paragraph 4 of the Lenders' Handbook requires the solicitor to check that certain assumptions made by the valuer in his report are correct.

13.6.2. The solicitor is recommended by the Lenders' Handbook to advise the buyer client that the valuation may contain omissions or inaccurate information.

1. Part 1 of the Lender's Handbook is reproduced as Appendix VI.2.

A14. Stamp Duty Land Tax

14.1. Introduction

14.1.1. Stamp Duty Land Tax (SDLT) replaced Stamp Duty in relation to transactions completing on or after 1 December 2003.[1]

14.1.2. SDLT is a tax on transactions (not on documents) and applies, with minor exceptions, to all transactions affecting land within the UK.

14.1.3. The tax applies irrespective of where the transaction was completed (i.e. offshore completions are no longer exempted) and whether or not the transaction was evidenced by a document.

14.1.4. The purchaser (as defined in Finance Act 2003, s.43(4)) is responsible for the payment and the submission of the self-assessment land transaction return form to HM Revenue and Customs. Unless it is submitted online, the purchaser (or his attorney) must personally sign the form.

14.1.5. Where there are joint purchasers the liability for payment is joint and several.

14.1.6. The 'purchaser' will normally be the buyer in a land transaction or the tenant under a lease but note that a landlord who pays a premium on surrender of a lease will also fall within the definition of a purchaser.

14.1.7. The SDLT form and payment must be submitted within 30 days of the date when the charge to tax arises.

14.1.8. Penalties and interest are payable for late payment and criminal penalties including imprisonment and fines exist for tax evasion and fraud. The investigation powers of HM Revenue and Customs last for a period of up to 20 years.

14.1.9. The document evidencing the land transaction is not required to be submitted with the land transaction return.

14.1.10. Unlike its predecessor, stamp duty, SDLT is not always a single one-off payment. For example, in the case of a lease, a further charge to tax can arise on the exercise of a rent review. It is therefore essential that a copy of the SDLT return and associated papers are safely retained.

14.1.11. Where ownership of land is transferred by means of a transfer of shares in a limited company, the maximum tax payable by the purchaser is 0.5% stamp duty on the shares transferred.

14.1.12. If the transfer of the ownership of a company is made within the triggers for withdrawal of acquisition, group or company reconstruction relief, the selling company must make an amendment return within 30 days of the transfer and pay any tax previously relieved (Finance Act 2003, Sched.7).

1.   See A14.31 for transitional provisions and examples of transactions which may still be subject to stamp duty.

14.2. Time of payment

14.2.1. Payment of SDLT is due within the same timescale that a land transaction return is made; namely within 30 days of the 'effective date' of the relevant land transaction (Finance Act 2003, s.86).

14.2.2. Although the effective date will normally be the date of completion, the charge to tax arises when the purchaser has 'substantial benefit of the contract'. In the following circumstances this will give rise to a charge to tax before actual completion:

    (a)   payment of (normally) at least 90% of the purchase price;

    (b)   the purchaser or a connected person having the right to occupy the land, including under a licence;

    (c)   the purchaser or a connected person having the right to receive rents;

    (d)   payment by the purchaser or a connected person of rent.

14.3. Chargeable transactions

14.3.1. For SDLT purposes a land transaction is a transaction which consists of the acquisition of a chargeable interest in land in the UK. An acquisition of a chargeable interest includes its creation, the surrender or release of a chargeable interest, and the variation of a chargeable interest.

14.3.2. Chargeable interests in land are defined in section 48 Finance Act 2003 and comprise:

(a) an estate, interest, right or power in or over land in the UK; or

(b) the benefit of an obligation, restriction or condition affecting the value of any such estate, interest, right or power;

other than an exempt interest.

14.3.3. Section 48(2)–(5) Finance Act 2003 provides details of exempt interests, which include any security interest (such as a mortgage or charge), a licence to use or occupy land, and a tenancy at will. The acquisition of an exempt interest is not a land transaction and therefore does not involve SDLT.

14.3.4. For a land transaction to be chargeable to SDLT, there must be chargeable consideration. This is consideration in money or money's worth given for the subject matter of the transaction directly or indirectly by the purchaser (Finance Act 2003, s.50 and Sched.4).

14.3.5. Certain land transactions, although involving the acquisition of a chargeable interest, are specifically exempt from payment of SDLT (see A14.5 and Finance Act 2003, Sched.3).

14.3.6. Transactions where no money passes may still be chargeable, where non-monetary consideration is given. This may include the provision of services, goods or works, or the assumption of debt. Where the consideration consists of services, goods or works, the market value of such items will be attributed as the consideration on which SDLT will be levied.

14.3.7. The transfer of land where no money consideration passes, but where the land is subject to a mortgage or other financial charge, continues to be treated as a transfer for consideration. The consideration is taken to be the amount of debt assumed and is charged to SDLT accordingly. Where jointly owned land is subject to a mortgage and there is a transfer of equity, the amount of debt assumed is taken to be a proportion of the outstanding mortgage corresponding to the proportion of the equity share acquired.

14.3.8. The value of chattels is not liable to SDLT.

14.4. Linked transactions

14.4.1. Where transactions are linked (whether or not there is a gap in time between them) the chargeable consideration is aggregated and charged to SDLT at the rate applicable to the total combined price paid.

14.4.2. Where an earlier linked transaction has been notified to HM Revenue and Customs, credit is given for the amount of tax already paid and only the top-up tax is payable on each subsequent linked transaction.

14.4.3. It is therefore always necessary to keep records of SDLT returns to provide evidence of tax paid.

14.5. Exempt transactions

14.5.1. The principal exemptions from SDLT are:

    (a)   transfers on divorce or dissolution of a civil partnership;

    (b)   gifts;

    (c)   other transfers for no chargeable consideration;

The last category would include a transfer to a beneficiary out of a trust where, but for the trust, the beneficiary would otherwise be absolutely entitled to the land (Finance Act 2003, Sched.16), and a partition of jointly owned land where there is no consideration paid between the participants (Finance Act 2003, Sched.4).

14.5.2. Transactions where the consideration does not exceed the zero-rate band (see A14.11) are not exempt from SDLT and may still be required to be notified to HM Revenue and Customs on a land transaction return form.

14.5.3. A land transaction that is exempt is not chargeable to SDLT and does not need to be notified to HM Revenue and Customs on a land transaction return form. However, where an exempt land transaction (or document evidencing the land transaction) is required to be registered at the Land Registry, a self-certificate in form SDLT 60 must be completed. This form is not submitted to HM Revenue and Customs but must be submitted to the Land Registry to enable registration to proceed (Finance Act 2003, s.79(3)(b)). Where registration at the Land Registry is not required, there is no statutory requirement on a purchaser to complete a self-certificate. However, best practice is to require the purchaser to complete a self-certificate in all cases and to retain it with the purchaser's SDLT records.

14.5.4. Note that if a transaction is 'relieved' rather than exempted (see A14.6) an SDLT return must be made together with a claim for relief.

14.6. Relieved transactions

14.6.1. In the following cases the transaction may be relieved from SDLT but it is still necessary to make an SDLT return and to claim relief expressly:

(a) alternative property finance mortgages effected by resale or sale and leaseback (Finance Act 2003, ss.72 and 73);

(b) group, reconstruction and acquisition reliefs which apply to companies either at least 75% subsidiaries of one another, or both of another company. Qualifications apply in various circumstances and in all cases clawback of relief applies for three years from the transaction or longer where an agreement to transfer out of the group is made within three years, but the company leaves the group more than three years later (Finance Act 2003, Sched.7);

(c) residential properties in Disadvantaged Areas (DA) (i.e. those areas defined as 'Enterprise Areas' by the Chancellor in his 2002 Pre-Budget Report). The 2003 Budget announced and from 10 April 2003 brought into effect the full reliefs sanctioned by the EU for Disadvantaged Areas. The same provisions are re-enacted under Finance Act 2003, s.57 and Sched.6. Since 17 March 2005 this relief applies only to residential property (see A14.12.5);

(d) registered charities acquiring land for charitable purposes may claim full relief from SDLT. However, the relief is subject to clawback if the land ceases to be used for charitable purposes (Finance Act 2003, s.68);

(e) compulsory purchase and for performance by public bodies of planning matters (Finance Act 2003, ss.60 and 61);

(f) sale and leaseback (or lease and leaseback): the leaseback element is relieved where full SDLT has been paid on the sale and the property leased back forms all or part of the land that was the subject of the sale (Finance Act 2003, s.57A).

Residential property relief

14.6.2. A series of reliefs relating to residential property is granted by Schedule 6A Finance Act 2003. Subject to qualifications, these allow various classes of property trader to take property into stock or in part exchange without payment of SDLT. In all cases, the property taken in part exchange must be second-hand and must have been the main or only residence of the seller at some time in the two years prior to the date of purchase. In the case of a sale by personal representatives the qualifying period is the two years prior to the date of death. The amenity land surrounding the second-hand house should not normally exceed 0.5 hectares. If the curtilage is greater than 0.5 hectares, the value of the property will have to be apportioned between the value of the property comprising 0.5 hectares and the excess. Full relief will be granted on the qualifying area and SDLT charged at the normal rate on the excess. In each case the buyer must be a company genuinely trading in the relevant sector. A house building company or an associated company taking a property in part exchange will have to insert its Construction Industry Scheme number on the land transaction return when claiming Schedule 6A relief.

14.6.3. House builder's relief on second-hand houses bought in part exchange is only available where there is a related sale of one of the builder's new houses which is intended to be the only or main residence of the buyer. A new house is a building (or part of a building) which has been constructed or adapted for use as a single dwelling. Once the property is acquired, a house building company is free to deal with the property as it sees fit, but on re-sale, the buyer will be liable to SDLT at the normal rate. A buyer of a new house from a house builder in part exchange for his own second-hand property will not receive any relief from SDLT on the purchase.

14.6.4. Under Finance Act 2003, Sched.6A, paras.2–4, property traders, chain breaker companies and traders buying from personal representatives may all claim relief from SDLT on their purchases. Under Finance Act 2003, Sched.6A, paras.5 and 6, employers and relocation companies may buy an employee's existing house to facilitate relocation for a new job with either the same or a new employer or at a new location to which the employee cannot reasonably travel from the existing house. The purchases under Finance Act 2003, Sched.6A, paras.5 and 6 must be made by companies in the relevant business and do not permit directors or others to occupy the properties. Before reselling the properties, the relieved buyers may only carry out such work to make them clean and safe and may not normally spend more than £10,000 on those works. In default, the relief is lost. Where 3% of the value of the property exceeds £10,000, this amount may be spent on the permitted works, up to a maximum of £20,000.

14.6.5. Certain acquisitions by registered social landlords (Finance Act 2003, s.71) and certain leases granted by registered social landlords (Finance Act 2003, s.128) are exempt.

14.6.6. Certain right-to-buy transactions (Finance Act 2003, Sched.9) are exempt for qualifying purchases by sitting tenants.

14.6.7. Collective enfranchisement by leaseholders (Finance Act 2003, s.74) where the transferee is an RTE company may result in a zero charge to SDLT. Section 74 enables the right-to-buy tenants to divide the purchase price by the number of flats in respect of which the right is being exercised. This lower figure determines the rate of SDLT (which may be 1% or zero) that is then applied to the gross price.

Non-residential property relief

14.6.8. Finance Act 2003 provides the following reliefs for non-residential property:

    (a)   where both parties are public bodies (section 66);

    (b)   by bodies for national purposes, including historic buildings, museums etc. (section 69);

    (c)   transactions resulting from alterations to parliamentary constituency boundary changes (section 67);

(d) transactions as a result of the demutualisation of insurance companies and building societies (sections 63 and 64);

(e) the initial transfer of assets to a limited liability partnership (section 65);

(f) public/infrastructure projects where a public body transfers to a private body;

(g) public projects exempted from stamp duty.

14.6.9. The provisions of Finance Act 2003 should be checked to ensure that the transaction meets the requirements for relief.

14.7. Option agreements

14.7.1. Agreements granting options and rights of pre-emption are chargeable transactions in their own right.

14.7.2. SDLT is payable on any fee for the grant of an option or right of pre-emption. A further liability arises on the exercise of the option or right and the two transactions are normally linked (see A14.4).

14.7.3. On submission of each land transaction return, the buyer must determine the consideration for the land transaction concerned and calculate the SDLT due, deducting the tax already paid and paying any balance of tax, penalties and interest due to accompany the return forms.

14.8. Sub-sales

14.8.1. Care needs to be taken not to incur SDLT on the first limb of a sub-sale (Finance Act 2003, ss.45 and 45A). For example, B enters into a contract for the purchase of land from A (the 'main contact'). B then enters into a second contract (the 'sub-sale contract') to sell the same land to C, so that either A transfers direct to C, or there are simultaneous transfers from A to B and from B to C. Provided the two contracts complete at the same time (or are 'substantially performed' at the same time), B will incur no liability for SDLT. In such cases, completion of the main contract, or its substantial performance, will be disregarded for the purposes of SDLT (see Finance Act 2003, s.45(3)). C will incur a liability for SDLT on the aggregate of the amount B is obliged to pay to A under the main contract, and the amount C is obliged to pay to B for the benefit of the sub-sale contract.

14.8.2. However, if the main contract is substantially performed prior to its completion (e.g. where B enters into occupation of the property before transfer to C), or the completion of the sub-sale contract is delayed beyond completion of the main contract, the main contract will give rise to a land transaction, and B must submit a land transaction return and pay any SDLT due. Both purchasers will become liable to submit a land transaction return and to pay any SDLT due on the consideration payable under the relevant contract.

14.8.3. Group companies cannot claim relief on sub-sales by one to another (Finance Act 2003, s.45A(9)).

14.8.4. Care needs to be taken with sub-sales not to infringe SDLT avoidance regulations contained in section 75A Finance Act 2003.[1] In a case where the sub-sale contract is made at a price that is lower than the consideration payable under the main contract, the sub-purchaser will nevertheless be charged to SDLT at the higher main contract price.

1. Stamp Duty Land Tax (Variation of the Finance Act 2003) Regulations 2006 (SI 2006/3237).

14.9.   **Exchanges of land**

14.9.1. Both parties to an exchange of freehold and leasehold interests in land are liable to SDLT at the appropriate rate on the market value of the interest in land each acquires (Finance Act 2003, s.47).

14.9.2. The tax will be payable on the full market value of the interest regardless of the amounts specified in the documentation if they do not represent the market values.

14.9.3. Reliefs are available for house builders acquiring second-hand houses in part exchange for new ones of their own construction (see A14.6).

14.10.   **Contract and conveyance**

14.10.1. Despite particular provisions for option agreements and sub-sales, the general rule is that SDLT will not be payable on contracts for the sale of land where the transaction is perfected by conveyance (Finance Act 2003, ss.44 and 45).

14.11.   **Rates of SDLT**

14.11.1. SDLT is calculated in accordance with the rate tables contained in Finance Act 2003, s.55 for capital payments. Schedule 6 gives the rates applicable to property in a Disadvantaged Area (DA) and Schedule 5 gives the charge on lease rents. Solicitors can perform a post code and ward search on the HM Revenue and Customs website to determine whether land falls within a DA (see B10 for more information on this search).

Rate for residential freehold property

14.11.2. SDLT is calculated as a percentage of the whole of the consideration paid:

Not more than £125,000	0% (outside a DA)
Not more than £150,000	0% (within a DA)
More than £125,000 but not more than £250,000	1%
More than £250,000 but not more than £500,000	3%
More than £500,000	4%

14.11.3. Where the property is partly within a DA, the zero-rate band threshold applicable to the part within the DA is £150,000.

Rate for non-residential or mixed freehold property

14.11.4. SDLT is calculated as a percentage of the whole consideration paid:

Not more than £150,000	0%
More than £150,000 but not more than £250,000	1%
More than £250,000 but not more than £500,000	3%
More than £500,000	4%

14.12. **Calculating SDLT**

14.12.1. Several methods of calculation of tax are available to solicitors:

(a) longhand from the rate tables;

(b) on-screen software tools either free-standing or embedded in SDLT forms software;

(c) online calculation tools available on the Stamp Office website at **www.hmrc.gov.uk/so**.

14.12.2. Solicitors should take care to ensure that the calculation and result are accurate and correct and that the buyer checks the return and figures before signing the land transaction return form.

14.12.3. Calculation of SDLT depends not only on the price, value or consideration for the land but also on which current tax rates apply, the type of property, and whether or not the land lies in a DA.

14.12.4. It is important to distinguish between residential and non-residential property because different rates of SDLT apply (Finance Act 2003, s.116):

(a) a residential property is property which is used or has been adapted for use as a single dwelling, even if the single dwelling is part of a larger building;

(b)   amenity land forming part of the garden or grounds of the building, a garage (detached or integral), parking space and (domestic) garden shed are all included within the definition of residential property;

(c)   a single transaction involving six or more dwellings is not residential;

(d)   institutional property used as residential accommodation for school pupils, students, the armed forces or as a principal residence for more than 90% of the occupants is residential property;

(e)   institutional property used as accommodation for higher education halls of residence, children's homes, care and/or treatment and psychiatric homes, hospitals, prisons and hotels is not residential;

(f)   where land is used for residential purposes no account shall be taken of any other use;

(g)   where land is not used, but is suitable for a particular residential or nonresidential use, it will be treated as within that class.

14.12.5. For contracts for the acquisition of non-residential land made or varied on or after 17 March 2005, DA relief is abolished (see A14.6.1(c)).

14.12.6. Mixed use land is land which combines both residential and non-residential property. Where that land is situated outside a DA, non-residential tax rates apply (Finance Act 2003, Sched.6). When mixed use land is within or partly within a DA a just and reasonable apportionment has to be made as between the use and as to the location.

14.12.7. When land is outside a DA and is either wholly non-residential or mixed use, the whole property is treated as non-residential and the £150,000 zero-rate threshold applies.

14.12.8. Where non-residential land is partly within a DA, the value of the property which is not exempt must be taken as a just and reasonable apportionment of the whole. The SDLT rate bands then apply to that value.

14.12.9. Where land within a DA is residential then the £150,000 zero-rate band applies to it.

14.12.10. Where ownership of land is transferred by means of a transfer of shares in a limited company, the maximum tax payable by the purchaser is 0.5% stamp duty on the shares transferred.

14.12.11. If the transfer of the ownership of a company is made within the triggers for withdrawal of acquisition, group or company reconstruction relief, the selling company must make an amendment to its original return within 30 days of the transfer and pay any tax previously relieved (Finance Act 2003, Sched.7).

14.13. **Fixtures and fittings**

14.13.1. All those buildings, plants and fixtures which common sense and the doctrine of annexation dictate are part of the land, remain so under SDLT. Those fittings which are easily and obviously portable are not annexed to the land.

14.13.2 HM Revenue and Customs has clarified the types of fixtures that it will regard as annexed and not susceptible to an apportionment of the price for chattels, and gives a list of similar items usually regarded as fittings (see SDLT Manual at Appendix VII.3).

14.13.3. The guidance provided in SDLT Bulletin 6 is neither conclusive nor finite. While the examples given relate principally to residential property, the same principles apply to non-residential property.

14.13.4. A buyer should consider whether the apportionment between price and chattels can be justified to HM Revenue and Customs on enquiry and whether any tax saved justifies possible enquiries, tax-related penalties, and interest.

14.14. **Leases**

14.14.1. The duty payable on a premium and on the lease rent are calculated separately (Finance Act 2003, Sched.5).

14.14.2. The duty payable on a premium paid for the grant or transfer of a lease is calculated in the same way as on a capital payment for a freehold, but the operation of the zero-rate band on the grant of a lease depends on the level of rent under the lease. If the lease rent is more than £600 a year, all the premium is charged to SDLT at 1% or above, the zero-rate band being inapplicable.

14.14.3. Although the premium may be taxed at 1% or more of the price paid, the rent under the lease will not necessarily give rise to further charge to SDLT. Lease rents continue to be separately taxed and SDLT charged either alone or as well as the SDLT levied on the premium paid.

14.14.4. Payment of a reverse premium is not chargeable consideration and is ignored for calculation of tax.

14.14.5. The total SDLT payable on grant of a lease is the sum of tax payable on premium and on rent.

SDLT on rents

14.14.6. The relevant zero-rate band (for either residential or non-residential property) may be used twice in determining the actual SDLT payable for any one lease. This will occur when the zero-rate band is applied first to calculating the tax on the premium, where the rent is less than £600 a year; and second to establish whether the Net Present Value (NPV) of the lease rents exceeds the relevant threshold. If the NPV does exceed the threshold, SDLT is charged on the rent.

14.14.7. SDLT on the excess of NPV of the rent over the relevant zero-rate band thresholds (£125,000 for residential property and £150,000 for non-residential property) is all charged at 1%.

14.14.8. As SDLT is rounded down, the excess of NPV needs to exceed £100 before the first £1 of tax is payable on lease rent. The calculation of 1% of less than £100 produces less than £1 and is therefore rounded down to nil.

Net Present Value of the lease rents

14.14.9. The Net Present Value (NPV) of a lease is the product of multiplying the rent in pounds sterling by the term in years and discounting the result by the current Treasury Discount Rate. The current Treasury Discount Rate is 3.5%. NPV is an accepted mathematical formula for calculating on principles of compound discount.

14.14.10. There are several ways of working out the NPV for rents under a lease:

    (a)   longhand, using pen, paper and HM Revenue and Customs Individual Year Factor and Cumulative Factor tables or calculator;

    (b)   using the NPV function on Microsoft Excel spreadsheet software;

    (c)   using the lease tax calculator tool on the HM Revenue and Customs website at **www.hmrc.gov.uk/so**.

14.14.11. The NPV of a lease will only be accurate if the correct number of years and rent levels are entered into the formula:

    (a)   no account is taken of either break options or rights to extend the term (Finance Act 2003, Sched.17A, para.2);

    (b)   if the term is known and is a fixed number of years, enter the number of whole years during which rent is paid;

    (c)   if the term is indefinite (e.g. a periodic tenancy), the term is deemed to be one year (Finance Act 2003, Sched.17A, para.4).

14.14.12. Calculation of the NPV of a lease involves ascertainment of the annual rent throughout the term. Rents may be unascertained, ascertainable, or certain for any period (Finance Act 2003, Sched.17A, para.7). The way in which rents are treated for the purpose of the NPV calculation varies accordingly. If the annual rent is a fixed amount, calculating the NPV should be relatively straightforward. If all or part of the rent is uncertain at the outset, complications arise.

14.13.13. Only the first five years' rental payments are relevant to the NPV calculation, since the rent for year six and beyond is taken to be equal in all cases to the highest rent payable in any consecutive 12-month period in the first five years.

14.14.14. Complications arise when the rent payable within the first five years is either uncertain, or unascertained at the outset. Where rent varies in accordance with a provision in the lease (whether by way of a fixed increase, or by the operation of a rent review), or is contingent, uncertain or unascertained (whether fixed, subject to review, or turnover), the following rules:

    (a)   rent for the first five years. As regards calculating the rent payable for the first five years of the term, there must be added to any fixed amount of rent made payable by the lease a reasonable estimate (as under Finance Act 2003, s.51) of any rent that is contingent, uncertain or unascertained (e.g. because the rent is wholly or partly a turnover rent, or there is an open market rent review within the first five years);

    (b)   rent for years six, seven, eight etc. As regards calculating the rent payable after the end of the fifth year of the term, the rent is to be taken in every case (even where there are later fixed increases) as being equal to the highest amount payable during any consecutive period of 12 months during the first five years of the term.

No account is to be taken for these purposes of any provision for rent to be adjusted in accordance with the retail price index.

14.14.15. HM Revenue and Customs regard the term of a lease to be its contractual term or, if shorter, the time running from the date of the grant. However, rent review dates which, as a result of this interpretation, fall within the final three months of the fifth year running from the date of the grant can be ignored (see Finance Act 2003, Sched.17A, para.7A). The commonplace backdating of the term commencement date to the quarter day immediately preceding the grant of the lease will not therefore normally result in the rent for the fifth year being partly unascertained.

14.14.16. The amount of rent used in the calculation must be increased by VAT on the rent if the landlord has made a valid election to waive the VAT exemption prior to the effective date of the transaction, otherwise the rent is entered net into the NPV calculation. Where service charge under a lease is stated separately from the rent, only the rent is entered in the NPV calculation. Where a single figure is specified in the lease for rent, service charge and any other sums, the whole amount is included as rent for determining the NPV of the lease.

14.14.17. Using the appropriate numbers, NPV can be calculated using one of the methods suggested above to establish whether or not any lease duty is payable. Where longhand or manual calculation of NPV is preferred, the tables provided by HM Revenue and Customs for Individual Year and Cumulative Year Factors should be used:

    (a)   the Individual Year Factor table is used for calculating NPV during the first five years of the term where rent is unascertained at the time of the return. Rent changes for each year should be calculated separately by multiplying the rent for the year by the Individual Year Factor for that year. The results for each year are then added together to give the NPV for the period;

(b) the Cumulative Factor table is used for both fixed rent during the first five years of the term and where NPV is being calculated for the period from year six to the end of the term at a certain rent. Multiply the fixed rent by the Cumulative Factor for the appropriate number of years to give the NPV required.

14.14.18. The tables and detailed instructions for their use are given in SDLT Bulletin 6.

14.15. Further returns of SDLT on leases

14.15.1. Where the rent for any period within the first five years of the term is not certain at the outset, the NPV of the lease will initially have been calculated (and any SDLT paid) on the basis of an estimate of that rent. In such cases, a further return may need to be made within 30 days of the earlier of the date when the rent becomes certain or the fifth anniversary of the commencement of the term (Finance Act 2003, Sched.17A, para.8). A new determination of the NPV under the lease will be made in exactly the same way as for the original return, inserting the ascertained rent into the calculation. If the outcome is that the original NPV calculation was correct (because the ascertained rent matches the original estimate) nothing further is required to be done. If the outcome of the new determination is that SDLT becomes payable where none was before (e.g. because the NPV now exceeds the zero-rate threshold), or that additional SDLT becomes payable (because the actual NPV exceeds the original estimate), a further return must be filed. If the outcome results in SDLT having been overpaid on the original return (because the original estimate was excessive) a claim for a repayment can be made.

14.15.2. After the fifth anniversary of the commencement of the term, it should not normally be necessary to make further returns in respect of the original grant of a lease. However, an exception is made for abnormal rent increases occurring after the end of the fifth year of the term (Finance Act 2003, Sched.17A, para.14). Abnormal increases of rent may be due to a scheduled rent review, or may be systemic (because of, e.g. a turnover rent or royalty rent), or may simply arise because the lease is varied by agreement. In broad terms, an abnormal increase is one which sees the rent increase by more than 20% each year (so that, over a five-year period, the rent doubles).[1] Schedule 17A, para.15 sets out a formula to determine whether a rent increase is abnormal. The effect of there being an abnormal increase is that a new lease is deemed to have been granted in consideration of the rent increase. It is treated as being linked with the original term.

14.15.3. Further returns may be required after the end of the term. Special provisions under paragraphs 3 and 4 Schedule 17A Finance Act 2003 deal with leases that are granted for a fixed term and then until determination, and those granted for fixed terms that are extended by operation of law.

14.15.4. Where a lease continues after its contractual expiry date (e.g. because the tenant enjoys statutory security of tenure), it is treated as if it were a lease for the original term of years plus one year (hence a six-year lease will become a seven-year lease). If it continues beyond the first extra year, it is treated as if it were a lease for the original term of years plus two years (hence a six-year lease will become a seven-, then an eight-year lease). At the start of each additional year, a new determination of the NPV of the lease (with its added year(s)) needs to be made. If the outcome of the new determination is that the NPV of the lease now exceeds the zero-rate threshold (£150,000 in commercial property cases), SDLT becomes payable within 30 days of the start of the year. If the NPV of the lease had originally exceeded the threshold on grant (so that tax had been paid), additional tax becomes payable by virtue of the additional year(s). Where tax, or additional tax, becomes payable as a result of these rules, a tax return must be made within 30 days of the date on which the lease is treated as being for a longer term. Where a lease has been assigned, it is the assignee's responsibility to pay the additional tax, and to comply with the requirement to file returns arising out of the holding over. These rules only apply to leases that were originally subject to SDLT.

14.15.5. A lease for an indefinite term (such as a periodic tenancy) is treated at first as a lease for a term of one year. However, if the tenancy remains in place beyond the first year, it is treated in the same way as if the lease was for a fixed term that had been extended by operation of law.

14.15.6. Certain transfers and assignments of leases will trigger either a clawback or the end of relief enjoyed since grant (Finance Act 2003, Sched.17A, para.11). In those circumstances, either the transferor or transferee or both may need to make returns (Finance Act 2003, Sched.17A, para.12):

(a) the transferor will need to make an amendment return if the transfer triggers withdrawal of a relief claimed (such as a group relief or charities relief);

(b) the transferee will need to make a full return (as on grant of a lease) when on the transfer the property ceases to be entitled to the relief claimed since grant of the lease (such as charitable use or social landlord relief);

(c) a transferee's return will require a full land transaction return as at grant of lease and calculation of SDLT on both premium paid on transfer and on the lease rents. However, the NPV calculation is only for the period from the effective date of the transfer to the end of the term.

Tax is not chargeable retrospectively for the period when the tenant was eligible for the relevant relief.

1. Note that long rent-free periods and stepped rents may also mean that smaller increases are treated as 'abnormal'.

14.16. Surrenders

14.16.1. The surrender of a term of years is treated as an assignment of a lease and will therefore only be a notifiable transaction if a consideration is paid (by the landlord) exceeding the relevant zero-rate band or the consideration does not exceed the zero-rate band, but the lease was originally granted for seven or more years. The landlord will then need to make a land transaction return within 30 days of the effective date of the surrender (Finance Act 2003, Sched.17A, para.16).

14.16.2. Payment of a reverse premium by the tenant does not count as chargeable consideration (Finance Act 2003, Sched.4). A surrender made for no consideration is self-certifiable.

14.16.3. In the case of a surrender and re-grant (whether express or implied), a full land transaction return is required in relation to the re-grant as for any new grant. However, in calculating SDLT payable, a form of allowance (overlap relief) is given for the SDLT already paid in respect of the unexpired term surrendered (Finance Act 2003, Sched.17A, para.9). Overlap relief works so that, when calculating the NPV of the newly granted lease, the tenant is able to reduce the amount of rent to be brought into the calculation by deducting rents that would otherwise have been payable during the overlapping period of the surrendered and new terms. Such rents have already effectively been taxed as part of the surrendered lease and so should not be taxed again. Overlap relief only applies where the surrendered lease, was itself subject to SDLT.

14.17. Leases as linked transactions

14.17.1. Leases may be linked transactions in the same way as any other land transactions and will then be subject to the aggregation of premiums paid and of rents used in calculating NPV. Only the aggregation of premium will be subject to an increase in the relevant rate of tax, since rents are taxed at a flat rate of 1%.

14.17.2. New grants of lease between the same or connected parties may be treated as linked transactions, if they form part of a single scheme, arrangement or series of transactions. Where successive leases of the same or substantially the same premises are treated as linked transactions, the successive terms take effect as a single lease (Finance Act 2003, Sched.17A, para.5).

14.18. Agreement for lease

14.18.1. An agreement for lease is a notifiable transaction if the agreement is substantially performed (e.g. the tenant takes up occupation). The date of substantial performance is the effective date of the transaction. A notional lease is treated as having been granted on the effective date on the terms of, and at the rent payable under, the actual lease. A land transaction return relating to the notional lease must be made, and tax paid, in the standard way (Finance Act 2003, Sched.17A, para.12A).

14.18.2. When completion of the lease takes place, the actual lease may need to be notified, a further return may be required, and any additional tax may be payable. The actual lease operates as a notional surrender of the notional lease. The tenant can use overlap relief (see A14.16.3) to reduce the NPV of the actual lease as if an actual surrender and re-grant had occurred. In some cases, the operation of overlap relief may reduce the NPV of the actual lease to nil, in which case the actual lease is self-certifiable.

14.19. Partnership property

14.19.1. An acquisition of land by a partnership is chargeable to SDLT in the usual way. However, measures were introduced by Finance Act 2004 to apply SDLT to certain partnership transactions which had initially been excluded from the scope of the tax. As from 23 July 2004, SDLT became chargeable in the following additional circumstances:

(a) where an interest in land is transferred into a partnership, either by an existing partner or by some other person in exchange for an interest in that partnership;

(b) where partnership property includes an interest in land and arrangements are in place so that either an existing partner transfers (for money or money's worth) all or part of his partnership interest to a person who is or becomes a partner, or a person becomes a partner and an existing partner reduces his partnership share (or ceases to be a partner) and withdraws money or money's worth from the partnership; and

(c) where a partnership transfers an interest in land to a partner or former partner.

In those circumstances, a share of the relevant partnership property is taken to have been acquired.

14.19.2. Provision is made in each case for calculating the value of the relevant share of partnership property acquired (Finance Act 2003, Sched.15, Part 3). That value is based on the proportion of market value transferred making allowance for a share already held. Formulae for calculation of tax liability according to circumstance are specified.

14.19.3. As from 19 July 2006, the provisions of A14.19.1(b) only apply to transfers of partnership shares in property investment partnerships (i.e. partnerships whose sole or main activity is in investing or dealing in interests in land). This means that transfers of partnership shares in ordinary professional partnerships are no longer chargeable to SDLT.

14.19.4. For most transfers of partnership property, general exemptions and reliefs apply, but may be subject to special rules on calculation of value.

14.20. Land transaction returns

14.20.1. Every relevant notifiable transaction must be reported to HM Revenue and Customs and the details provided in standard form.

14.20.2. Reporting transactions may be conducted in paper form, by delivering a land transaction return to HM Revenue and Customs, or electronically through the online SDLT filing service.

14.20.3. Returns comprise five separate forms for buyers to use[1] (but not necessarily for the same transaction) and an HM Revenue and Customs certificate. Forms SDLT1–4 comprise the self-assessment return.[2] The forms are accompanied by explanatory notes, which can be viewed and downloaded from **www.hmrc.gov.uk/so** or using the CD 'Stamp Duty Land Tax' available from the HM Revenue and Customs order line.

14.20.4. Original paper forms SDLT1–4, SDLT6 and SDLT60, payslips and explanatory leaflets may be obtained from the HM Revenue and Customs order line:

HMRC Contact Centre
PO Box 37
St Austell
PL35 5YN
Tel. 0845 302 1472
Fax. 01726 201015

14.20.5. Electronic versions of SDLT1–4, SDLT6 and SDLT60 are also available. Alternatively, proprietary software is available for firms to generate their own forms. These must however be printed in identical format to the official forms.

14.20.6. Except where the online service is used, the form must be signed by the buyer personally (not by his solicitor) or by the buyer's attorney. The latter must be duly appointed in writing for the specific purpose of signing SDLT declarations.

14.20.7. No documents are sent with the form.

14.20.8. The form submitted, if on paper, must be an original (not a photocopy) with a unique identifier number.

14.20.9. If the land transaction return is one of those statistically or otherwise sampled (normally within nine months of the submission of the return), it is important that the taxpayer and any agents concerned in the transaction are able to provide any requested information and documents called for by the Board of HM Revenue and Customs. For this reason alone it is important to retain workings and calculation results on file with all other documents relevant to any tax calculation for the mandatory period of six years.

1. HM Revenue and Customs have also provided non-statutory schedules for transactions involving multiple properties or subject to multiple leases which are available from their website or the Manchester Complex Transactions Unit.
2. Stamp Duty Land Tax (Administration) Regulations 2003 (SI 2003/2837).

14.21. **Subsequent returns**

14.21.1. Where circumstances or facts come to light after the original land transaction return has been made, as many subsequent land transaction returns as necessary must be submitted. For example, a further return must be submitted for each subsequent linked transaction or for the draw down of each parcel of land. Each subsequent return must be signed by the buyer declaring its truth and complete-ness (Finance Act 2003, s.81A).

14.21.2. On each occasion, tax must be recalculated and consideration for all elements of the series of transactions aggregated: total tax recalculated, credit given for tax already paid and the balance tendered.

14.22. **Price unascertainable**

14.22.1. Where the price to be paid under a chargeable transaction is uncertain or contingent and all or some part of the price will not be paid until more than six months after the effective date, the buyer may apply to HM Revenue and Customs to defer payment (Finance Act 2003, s.90). While application to defer is pending, the buyer should make a return, but need not pay SDLT on the deferred amount. On notification of the decision by HM Revenue and Customs, payment should be made in accordance with the decision unless an appeal is lodged against the decision. Otherwise the terms of the decision should be complied with in all respects for original and amendment or further returns

14.23. **The forms**

14.23.1. Form SDLT1 is required for every notifiable transaction. For most residential and simple non-residential land transactions comprising freehold only or not reporting a new lease, only form SDLT1 will need to be completed. On form SDLT1, financial statistics for the transaction are given and the self-assessed tax is declared.

14.23.2. Form SDLT2 is required where there are more than two sellers or two buyers. A separate form SDLT2 is required for each additional party. Form SDLT2 must be signed by the buyer named in it. Additional sellers do not need to sign, although their details must be supplied to HM Revenue and Customs.

14.23.3. Form SDLT3 may be required to provide full information about the land transferred and a separate form SDLT3 will be required for each additional parcel of land after the first. The first parcel is reported on SDLT1, but may be continued in form SDLT3 if space is insufficient.

14.23.4. SDLT4 is the form on which further details of complex and commercial transactions are reported, including sales of companies where part of the price is apportioned to land. The form is also used for reporting details of new leases granted and for additional data for corporate buyers.

14.23.5. A SDLT payslip and payment of tax must accompany any land transaction return. If payment is made by cheque, the cheque must state the SDLT1/payslip unique identifier number.

14.23.6. SDLT6 is the explanatory notes booklet which accompanies the forms to assist in their completion.

14.23.7. SDLT60 is the form of self-certificate which is made where a transaction is not notifiable. This form must be signed by the buyer and is not sent to HM Revenue and Customs. The form is accompanied by explanatory notes.

14.24. Submission of the forms

14.24.1. The completed land transaction return, comprising SDLT1 and as such of forms SDLT 2–4 as are necessary, is sent to the HM Revenue and Customs Data Capture Centre (see Appendix VIII.2 for address). Returns should be submitted only to the address specified on form SDLT1 and in accordance with those instructions.

14.24.2. For the data capture facility to work, SDLT forms, payslips and cheques should not be folded or stapled. Only original form SDLT1 and payslips may be submitted, although forms SDLT2–4 may be copied. Data should be aligned within the boxes in the forms to ensure forms can be scanned and to avoid automatic rejection of the return.

14.24.3. When HM Revenue and Customs is satisfied that a land transaction return has been made and the details are not manifestly inaccurate or the tax incorrect, the taxpayer or his agent will be issued with an HM Revenue and Customs certificate in form SDLT 5. This certificate acknowledges receipt of the return, but is not conclusive evidence either that the return is correct or that liability to SDLT has been satisfied. Certificates are issued without prejudice to the HM Revenue and Customs enquiry and enforcement powers available to the Board.

14.24.4. Where the online filing service is used, HM Revenue and Customs issue an electronic SDLT 5 certificate. Online filing of a tax return generates a receipt which is sent online within a few minutes. This can be printed for submission to HM Land Registry with the application for registration. HM Revenue and Customs will also provided a paper SDLT 5 certificate, but this should be sent to the taxpayer, or kept on file, and is not to be sent to HM Land Registry.

14.24.5. The buyer may stipulate that the HM Revenue and Customs certificate is returned to him, or to the property address, or to a specified agent.

14.24.6. The SDLT60 form of self-certificate must be signed by the buyer making a declaration of truth and completeness. This form does not need to be submitted to HM Revenue and Customs.

14.24.7. It is important that both taxpayer and agent retain copies of land transaction return certificates and SDLT60 forms for future reference and in case of requests for production.

14.25. Amendment returns

14.25.1. When a taxpayer or any other person concerned in the preparation or submission of a land transaction return becomes aware of a factual inaccuracy in a return (e.g. that the return is incorrect, incomplete, or that the tax has been overpaid or underpaid or assessed), the taxpayer must make an amendment return within 30 days. Compliance, penalty and enforcement provisions apply to amendment returns as for original land transaction returns (Finance Act 2003, s.80).

14.26. Keeping records

14.26.1. From the outset of the transaction, it is advisable to ensure that full records of transactions are maintained. There is a duty to keep and preserve records to enable a complete and correct land transaction return, self-certificate or claim[1] to be made and delivered.[2] The documents which should be retained include:

    (a)   all materials relating to valuation and/or price;

    (b)   all documents and information relating to apportionments for chattels;

    (c)   accounts records for funds received and disbursed;

    (d)   documents demonstrating allowable costs;

    (e)   calculations for assessment of SDLT.

14.26.2. All documents relevant to a SDLT transaction and necessary for determination of value and assessment of the tax may be required by HM Revenue and Customs for enquiry purposes.[3] The required records must be retained for six years after either any enquiry has been completed or HM Revenue and Customs no longer has the power to enquire into the return or self-certificate

14.26.3. Once completed, the land transaction return forms should be copied and the copies retained. On-screen and online forms lend themselves to electronic archiving.

14.26.4. All documents relevant to a SDLT transaction and return must be retained for six years. This duty applies to all persons concerned with the relevant land transaction. Even in a straightforward purchase of a residential property, there may be issues of valuation and apportionment of chattels which necessitate the retention of specific information. A paper record of all monetary movements within the transaction or a confirmed electronic accounts record should be included in the retained documentation.

14.26.5. In practice, retention of the whole file, including accounts records and copies of the land transaction return forms, payslip and certificate or SDLT60, may be an easier alternative.

14.26.6. The duty to retain documents, in either paper or electronic form extends to all persons concerned in a transaction. The duty extends to specifically proscribing destruction of documents.

14.26.7. The penalty for failure to keep records is £3,000 unless HM Revenue and Customs is satisfied that the information contained in the destroyed documents can be proved by other documentary evidence (section 93).

1. Finance Act 2003, Sched.11A, Part 3.
2. Finance Act 2003, Sched.10, para.9 and Sched.11, Part 2.
3. Finance Act 2003, Sched.10 and Sched.11, Part 2.

14.27. Refunds

14.27.1. Claims for refunds not made in a return can be made by letter and the claimant must maintain all supporting evidential and transactional records to substantiate the claim (Finance Act 2003, Sched.11A, para.2).

14.28. Acting as the buyer's agent and acting for the lender

14.28.1. The taxpayer must consent to the appointment of an agent and for HM Revenue and Customs to conduct correspondence about the land transaction return with the agent. This consent is given on form SDLT1.

14.28.2. The question of agency has several implications for solicitors:

    (a)   does the solicitor necessarily know enough about the buyer's affairs to be able to conduct correspondence with HM Revenue and Customs for SDLT purposes?

    (b)   can the solicitor be sure that he acts for the client in all relevant transactions?

    (c)   has any necessary disclosure been full and frank?

If the answer to any question is not an unequivocal affirmative, it may be sensible for the solicitor to decline to act as the client's agent.

14.28.3. Where there are multiple buyers, deciding whether or not it is appropriate to act as an agent may be even more difficult.

14.28.4. Where the solicitor acts only for the lender and not for the buyer, a decision must be made concerning the administration of submitting the land transaction return, receiving the certificate and submission of any Land Registry applications. The options open to the lender and the lender's solicitor are:

    (a)   lender's solicitor acts as buyer's agent;

    (b)   lender permits buyer's solicitor to act as its agent for making the land transaction return, obtaining the certificate, with or without also making the Land Registry application;

    (c)   lender's solicitor acts as buyer's agent only for limited purpose of submitting the completed land transaction return and obtaining the certificate.

14.28.5. Whichever of the alternatives is adopted by the lender, the lender's solicitor will need to ensure that the buyer and/or his solicitor fully understand(s) what is required of each party and gives any necessary undertakings. In particular, the lender's solicitor will need to ensure that he undertakes no obligation or liability in connection with any tax affairs of the buyer and that this is clear to both the buyer and his solicitor and to HM Revenue and Customs.

14.29. Land Registry applications

14.29.1. No document effecting or evidencing a land transaction may (unless exempt from certification) be registered at the Land Registry, recorded or reflected in an entry in the register without a certificate as to compliance with SDLT (Finance Act 2003, s.79). See Land Registry Practice Guide 49 for details of the Registry's cancellation policy.

14.29.2. In those cases where the land transaction can be self-certified to the Land Registry, the completed form SDLT60 must accompany the application for registration. The original will be returned if a certified copy accompanies the application for registration. Self-certificates are not conclusive of the fact that the transaction was not notifiable or that no tax was due. HM Revenue and Customs has full enquiry and enforcement powers in relation to form SDLT 60.

14.29.3. The fact that a transaction is not registrable at the Land Registry does not preclude a subsequent HM Revenue and Customs enquiry into the transaction. In such a case, it is advisable for the buyer to complete a SDLT60 form on completion and to retain the form for six years.

14.30. Enforcement and penalties

14.30.1. HM Revenue and Customs may enquire into any land transaction return or self-certificate (Finance Act 2003, Sched.11). To instigate an enquiry it must give notice of the enquiry to the buyer within nine months after the latest of either the actual date of filing the return or making the self-certificate and within nine months after the last amendment was made.

14.30.2. The enquiry may extend to whether tax is chargeable or whether the transaction was chargeable or notifiable and to the amount of tax chargeable (Finance Act 2003, Sched.10, para.12 and Sched.11, para.7).

14.30.3. On at least 30 days' notice, HM Revenue and Customs can require the buyer to produce documents for the purpose of the enquiry, but the documents must be within the taxpayer's possession or power and may normally be copies unless HM Revenue and Customs, by notice, requires originals. HM Revenue and Customs may specify the information and form as it reasonably requires. However, the buyer is not obliged to provide information or documents relating to any pending appeal by him or referral to the Special Commissioners to which he is a party.

14.30.4. The penalty for failure to produce documents on notice is £50 and either £30 a day determined by an officer of the Board or £150 a day if determined by the Court (Finance Act 2003, Sched.11, para.16).

14.30.5. During an enquiry the taxpayer may amend his land transaction return. The amendments will take effect unless HM Revenue and Customs in its notice of closure of enquiry states that the amendments have been taken into account. If so, the notice of closure specifying liability of the buyer applies.

14.30.6. Authorised HM Revenue and Customs officers have the power to call in writing for documents and information which are reasonably required to establish tax liability or the amount of tax due from a taxpayer (Finance Act 2003, Sched.13). Documents and information may be required from:

    (a)   the taxpayer, including companies which have ceased to exist and deceased taxpayers (within six years after the death);

    (b)   a third party (but not more than six years after the taxpayer's death);

    (c)   a tax accountant in relation to clients' tax affairs (if the tax accountant has been convicted of a tax offence or had a SDLT penalty imposed);

    (d)   an auditor or tax adviser when acting as tax accountant (disclosing advice to or identity of client/taxpayer and not disclosed to HM Revenue and Customs elsewhere).

14.30.7. HM Revenue and Customs must adhere to the limitations of its power to call for information so that:

    (a)   notices to barristers, advocates and solicitors must be made by HM Revenue and Customs Board (not an authorised officer) where information is required from them as a third party or tax accountant;

    (b)   the person must be given a reasonable opportunity to make documents and information available before HM Revenue and Customs applies to Commissioners for consent to issue notice;

(c)   where notice is served on any other person, a copy must be given to the taxpayer.

14.30.8. Documents and information outside the scope of an HM Revenue and Customs notice (Finance Act 2003, Sched.13, Part 4) include:

(a)   personal and journalistic material;

(b)   documents relating to a pending tax appeal;

(c)   documents more than six years old at the date of the notice;

(d)   documents subject to legal privilege;

(e)   auditors' and tax advisers' own papers in connection with acting under a statutory appointment.

14.30.9. To obtain information relating to the tax liability and amount of tax due, the Board of HM Revenue and Customs may:

(a)   give any person written notice (in prescribed form) requiring delivery of documents and information;

(b)   obtain a court order for delivery of documents where reasonably believing a serious fraud has been committed; or

(c)   on oath obtain a warrant (expiring after 14 days) to enter and search premises, with force if necessary.

Offences and penalties

14.30.10. Contravening the provisions of the Finance Act is a criminal offence.

14.30.11. The most serious of the offences created under Finance Act 2003 is fraudulent evasion of tax for which the sanctions are:

(a)   on summary conviction – imprisonment for a maximum of six months or a fine up to the statutory maximum or both; and

(b)   on conviction on indictment – imprisonment for a maximum of seven years or an unlimited fine or both (Finance Act 2003, s.95).

14.30.12. There is a lesser offence of assisting preparation or delivery of incorrect information, return, or other document knowing that it is incorrect and likely to be used for tax purposes. This does not need to result in non-payment or under-payment of SDLT and the penalty is a maximum fine of £3,000 (Finance Act 2003, s.96).

14.30.13. The offences relating to documents are:

(a) falsification, concealment or destruction of documents or information; and

(b) causing or permitting falsification, concealment or destruction.

14.30.14. The sanctions for offences relating to documents are:

(a) on summary conviction – a fine of up to the statutory maximum;

(b) on conviction on indictment – imprisonment for a maximum of two years or an unlimited fine or both.

14.30.15. Defences for document related offences are:

(a) acting more than two years after notice or order was made and HM Revenue and Customs has not notified of unsatisfactory compliance; and

(b) acting more than six months after HM Revenue and Customs requested information and the HM Revenue and Customs Board has refused consent to serve notice.

Tax payments, tax underpayments and penalties

14.30.16. There is a regime of penalties for various failures by the taxpayer unless with reasonable excuse, in which case HM Revenue and Customs may allow extra time to effect the necessary act (Finance Act 2003, s.97). The defaults within the scope of the penalties include: late delivery of returns, non-payment or under-payment of tax, or failure to amend. Penalties are without prejudice to any criminal proceedings and civil penalties and criminal sanctions are cumulative (Finance Act 2003, s.99).

14.30.17. The penalties for late submission of land transaction returns (Finance Act 2003, Sched.10) are as follows:

(a) up to three months late: £100;

(b) more than three months late: £200;

(b) more than 12 months late: flat-rate penalty and tax-related penalty up to amount of tax due (so the total may be double tax and flat-rate penalty).

14.30.18. The penalty for submitting incorrect return applies where the land transaction return is incorrect or is not corrected. If the original return is fraudulently or negligently made or correction is not made in a reasonable time, the buyer is liable to a tax-related penalty not exceeding the amount of the underpayment.

14.30.19. Interest is payable both by the taxpayer on late payments and underpayments, but also by HM Revenue and Customs on repayments of SDLT. The tax must be paid at the time of making a land transaction return, whether the original return, an amendment return, a return on withdrawal of relief or a further return in respect of lease rents (Finance Act 2003, s.86). Penalties to which the buyer is liable must also be paid when submitting the return. Payment is treated as having been made on the day it was received by HM Revenue and Customs where a cheque is tendered and is paid on first presentation to the paying bank (Finance Act 2003, s.92).

14.30.20. Interest is payable at the applicable rate on unpaid tax and penalties for the period from 30 days after the latest date for submission of the relevant return until the date of payment (Finance Act 2003, ss.87 and 88). HM Revenue and Customs pays interest at the applicable rate on repayment of tax and penalties for the period from the date the funds were lodged with it to the date of repayment (Finance Act 2003, s.89).

14.31. Stamp duty

14.31.1. There are only two occasions when land transaction documents must still be produced to HM Revenue and Customs:

    (a) documents witnessing a transaction subject to stamp duty and completing after 1 December 2003 under Stamp Act 1891 as amended; and

    (b) documents which should have been stamped under the Stamp Act regime and are required to be produced in evidence and/or where the court does not exercise its discretion to admit.

14.31.2. Finance Act 2003 does not repeal the former stamp duty legislation nor is it superseded for all transactions. Those transactions which were historically stamp duty transactions at the making of the contract do not become transactions subject to SDLT merely through the passing of time.

14.31.3. Transactions which were not completed before 1 December 2003 and which are the culmination of contracts entered into under the stamp duty regime remain so, unless some action is taken to alter or novate the contract. This action only affects SDLT liability if taken on or after the first relevant date for contracts on sale, or on or after 17 April 2003 for grants of options or rights of pre-emption.

14.31.4. Documents evidencing those transactions still subject to stamp duty remain subject to submission to HM Revenue and Customs for adjudication, production or impress. Submission of documents for stamping should be accompanied by forms L(A)451 delivering particulars of the transaction, Stamps 61 and payment. Where the transaction comprises land and other assets, the declaration of apportionment of price between the land and other assets continues to be made on form Stamps 22 (see Appendix VII.2).

14.32. Certificates of value

14.32.1. Transitional documents still requiring production to the HM Revenue and Customs (see A14.31) and those below the zero-rate band threshold still require the relevant certificate of value.

14.32.2. Transactions still subject to stamp duty (see A14.31) will also be subject to the rate bands relevant for the date of the contract when calculating stamp duty payable.

14.32.3. Where the transaction is subject to SDLT, a certificate of value will not be required. The land transaction return will contain all the information required to ascertain the value and appropriate rate of tax, even if this is 0%. A certificate will still be issued by HM Revenue and Customs in the usual way.

A15. Capital Gains Tax

15.1. **Liability to CGT**
15.2. **The principal private dwelling house exemption**
15.3. **Chargeable gains**

15.4. **Business premises**
15.5. **Charities**
15.6. **Time of disposal**

15.1. Liability to CGT

15.1.1. A liability to CGT may arise on the disposal of an interest in land. A seller's solicitor should be aware of the possibility of potential liability and advise his client accordingly. Similarly, a buyer who is purchasing property other than for use as his principal private dwelling should be made aware of potential tax liability which may be incurred in his subsequent disposal of the property.

15.1.2. The definition of 'chargeable assets' within Taxation of Chargeable Gains Tax Act 1992 includes an interest in the proceeds of sale of land held by co-owners. Thus a disposition by a beneficial joint owner of his equitable interest in land could give rise to a charge to CGT.[1]

15.1.3. Some transactions which are incidental to the sale of land also give rise to a charge to CGT, e.g. where a separate payment is made for the release or modification of an easement or covenant.

15.1.4. For the purposes of the Act, a sale and leaseback transaction is technically treated as two separate disposals, but in practice HM Revenue and Customs may regard them as one, namely the part disposal of land by the seller of the freehold.

15.1.5. Subject to certain reliefs, gifts fall within the meaning of 'disposal'.

1. *Kidson* v. *Macdonald* [1974] Ch 339.

15.2. The principal private dwelling house exemption

15.2.1. The disposal of an individual's principal private dwelling house including garden or grounds is exempt from CGT. Up to 0.5 hectare (including the site of the house) is within the exemption.[1]

15.2.2. To qualify for the exemption the seller must have lived in the dwelling house as his only or main residence throughout his period of ownership. A degree of permanence and expectation of continuity is required for the exemption to be claimable. A short period of residence (e.g. of a few months) may not qualify for relief.[2]

15.2.3.   Certain periods of absence are disregarded when deciding the question of residence:[3]

    (a)   the last 36 months of ownership;

    (b)   by extra-statutory concession, the first 12 months of ownership (in order to facilitate the sale of another property). If there are good reasons for this period exceeding one year, which are outside the individual's control, it will be extended up to a maximum of two years;

    (c)   any period(s) not exceeding three years in total throughout the period of ownership. Absence within this exception may be for any reason, e.g. an extended holiday and can be made up of several separate periods of absence provided that the total under this exception does not exceed three years;

    (d)   any period(s) during which the individual was working outside the UK. This exception applies to employees only, not to self-employed persons;

    (e)   any period(s) not exceeding four years in total during which the individual was prevented from living in his dwelling house because he was required by his conditions of employment to live elsewhere. This exception would be applicable, e.g. to a headmaster who was required to live in accommodation provided by the school, or to an employee who was temporarily seconded to a branch office beyond commuting distance from his home.

15.2.4.   The periods of absence outlined above are cumulative, and if exceeded a proportion of the exemption relative to the length of the absence in proportion to the length of ownership of the property will be lost and the non-exempt part chargeable to CGT.

15.2.5.   Where a dwelling house has grounds of more than 0.5 hectare, the excess is prima facie taxable, but HM Revenue and Customs have a discretion to allow land in excess of 0.5 hectare to be included within the principal private dwelling house exemption if the extra land can be shown to be necessary for the reasonable enjoyment of the house.

15.2.6.   The sale of land alone, where the ownership of the house is retained, enjoys the benefit of the exemption so long as the land sold does not exceed 0.5 hectare. It should be noted that if the house is sold and land retained, a subsequent sale of the land will usually attract CGT.

Duality of user

15.2.7.   Where part of a principal private dwelling house is used for business purposes, e.g. a doctor who has a consulting room in his home, a proportion of the exemption may be lost, relative to the area of the 'business premises' in relation to the total area of the dwelling house. If, however, a 'duality of user' can be shown, the full exemption may be available. Thus a person who works from home, but who does not have a separate room for his business which the other members of the family are prohibited from entering, may still take full advantage of the principal private dwelling house exemption.

15.2.8.   Only one exemption is available to married couples. Where a married couple own more than one house an election must be made as to which property is to take the benefit of the exemption. An election in respect of one property is not irrevocable and can be switched, e.g. if it appears that one property is increasing in value at a faster rate than the other.

15.2.9.   The principal private dwelling house exemption is available where the disposal is made by trustees provided that the person in occupation of the property was a person who was entitled to be in occupation under the terms of the settlement, e.g. a tenant for life.[4]

15.2.10. Tenants in common may be liable for CGT on their respective shares in the equitable interest in the property.

15.2.11. An individual who buys his dwelling house in the name of a company will not be able to claim the principal private dwelling house exemption.

1. Taxation of Chargeable Gains Act 1992, s.222.
2. *Goodwin* v. *Curtis*, *The Times*, 14 August 1996.
3. Taxation of Chargeable Gains Act 1992, s.223.
4. Taxation of Chargeable Gains Act 1992, s.28(1) and (2).

15.3. **Chargeable gains**

15.3.1.   Any gain is chargeable at the highest rate at which the individual pays income tax, subject to the availability of proper relief. Corporations pay CGT at the corporation tax rate applicable to them, subject to roll-over relief. Separate taxation is applied to married couples; each spouse therefore has his or her own annual allowance for CGT purposes.

Guidelines

15.3.2.   When taking instructions from an individual in relation to the sale of a dwelling house, the answers to the following four questions will indicate to the solicitor whether there is likely to be a CGT liability on the property. If the client's answers to all the questions set out below match the suggested answers, there is unlikely to be a CGT liability arising out of the transaction. If any of the client's answers differ from those suggested, further enquiries should be raised with the client.

  1.   Question: Did you move into the house immediately after you bought it?
       Answer: Yes.

2. Question: Have you lived anywhere else since moving into this house?
   Answer: No.
3. Question: Does the house and the garden cover more than 0.5 hectare?
   Answer: No.

(The answer to this question may already be apparent from the estate agent's particulars of the property.)

4. Question: Do you own another house?
   Answer: No.

15.4. Business premises

15.4.1. Subject to certain reliefs, business premises are subject to CGT. The matter should be referred to the client's accountant for him to check the correct apportionment of the purchase price as between the property and any goodwill paid for the business.

15.5. Charities

15.5.1. Generally charities are exempt from CGT.

15.6. Time of disposal

15.6.1. The time of disposal of the property affects the year of assessment for the calculation of gains and losses for CGT purposes. A disposal of an interest in land is made at the time of the contract and not at the later time of completion.[1] However, no charge to tax arises unless the contract is completed, since until completion there will have been no disposal within the tax. Where a contract is conditional, the disposal is made at the time when the contract becomes unconditional, or in the case of an option, when it is exercised.[2] See Taxation of Chargeable Gains Act 1992, s.144 for more about options and in particular the treatment of a payment for the grant of an option.

1. Taxation of Chargeable Gains Act 1992, s.28(1).
2. Taxation of Chargeable Gains Act 1992, s.28(2).

A16. Value Added Tax

16.1. VAT on property transactions

The charge to tax

16.1.1. VAT at standard rate has been chargeable on certain commercial property transactions since 1 April 1989. Non-compliance with the legislation (where relevant) will involve the client in heavy penalties and interest payments, as well as unforeseen VAT liability. An exempt transaction can have implications for recovery of input tax incurred up to 10 years prior to the transaction. It is therefore essential that the relevance of VAT to a transaction is considered at an early stage and the client advised accordingly.

16.1.2. Generally VAT will not be chargeable on transactions involving residential property but may be relevant to both freehold and leasehold commercial property and to land. This chapter does not deal with problems associated with the self-supply of services.

16.2. Residential property

16.2.1. The sale of an existing building (i.e. not new) which is a dwelling or is used for a qualifying residential purpose or qualifying charitable purpose is generally exempt from VAT. However, zero-rating may apply if it:

- has been empty for 10 years or more and has just been renovated; or

- has just been converted from a non-residential building; or

- is a protected building and has undergone a substantial reconstruction; or

- it is a first grant of a major interest (freehold or lease if over 21 years) in a new dwelling, or a building for use for 'qualifying residential purposes' or 'qualifying charitable purposes'.

The detailed conditions for zero-rating must be met. The benefit of zero-rating is that VAT on costs may be recovered, whereas with an exempt transaction, it may not.

16.2.2. The Standard Conditions of Sale provide that all sums payable under the contract are exclusive of VAT, and in the case of residential property no further provisions as to VAT are normally necessary.

16.2.3. 'Qualifying residential purposes' include premises which are used as a hospice; accommodation for the armed forces; a children's home; a care home; and the accommodation element of a residential school, a monastery or nunnery and any other residential premises which is the sole or main residence of at least 90% of its residents. Specifically excluded from this category are hospitals, prisons and hotels or similar accommodation. 'Qualifying charitable purposes' include use as a village hall or similar or use by a charity otherwise than in the course or furtherance of a business.

Supply of construction work

16.2.4. The construction or development of new dwellings, qualifying residential or qualifying charitable property is zero-rated. A garage built at the same time as the dwelling for use with it will usually also benefit from zero-rating. Services supplied to a registered housing association for the conversion of a non-residential building are also zero-rated. Work of converting a non-residential property into residential property and of converting, for example, a house into flats, and renovation of a dwelling which has been empty for three years or more, is chargeable at the 5% rate.

16.2.5. Time share, holiday, and other accommodation with restrictions on its occupation does not fall within the zero-rated category, where standard rating often applies.

16.2.6. A residential developer, building new houses and flats for sale, will be able to recover his input tax (e.g. on agents', solicitors', architects' and other professional fees) since the sale of a major interest in his property to a private buyer will be zero-rated. The buyer pays no VAT on his purchase. The same position applies to sales of substantially reconstructed listed buildings and the first sale of buildings converted into residential from non-residential property. It should be noted that certain purchases, including white goods, fitted furniture except in kitchens, and carpets are specifically blocked for input tax recovery purposes in the hands of a developer, and builders must charge VAT at standard rate, even if the project is otherwise zero-rated.

16.2.7. Subsequent sales by private individuals or commercial organisations will be exempt from VAT.

16.2.8. Owners of residential accommodation who did not construct the building in question, and who subsequently sell the building in the course of a business, will be making an exempt supply with no right to opt to tax.

Change of use

16.2.9. If the use of a building designed as a dwelling is subsequently changed to a non-residential use, this has no immediate VAT consequences. If, however, the use of a building intended for a qualifying residential purpose as defined above (i.e. a communal residential building) or qualifying charitable (non-business) use is changed to a non-residential or non-charitable use within 10 years of its construction, a charge to VAT at the standard rate arises in order to claw back the VAT on building/purchase costs which would have been charged if there had not initially been a qualifying residential or charitable use. The value of the charge to VAT is dependent on how many years the building has been used for qualifying purposes, e.g. if five out of 10 years are left then the charge would be 50% of the original VAT cost.

16.3. **Mixed developments**

16.3.1. Where only part of a building qualifies for zero-rating, e.g. a shop with a residential flat above, the non-zero-rated element of the building construction (in the example given, the shop) will be standard rated and a supply of the property will either be exempt or standard rated, subject to the election to waive exemption, or if the building is under three years old and the transaction is the freehold sale. The proceeds received from the development must be apportioned between the two differently rated parts of the building on a fair and equitable basis. There is no set method for determining apportionment of common areas of the building, e.g. foundations and roof, although any fair and reasonable method will usually be accepted. As a precaution the client should be advised to seek clearance from HM Revenue and Customs before development is commenced.

16.4. **Land**

16.4.1. The sale of a freehold interest in land (without buildings or civil engineering works on it), grant of a lease, or of a licence is generally exempt from VAT, subject to the right in most cases (except outright sales of freeholds in new buildings or civil engineering works under three years old which are standard rated in any case) to exercise the option to tax. The grant of certain short term rights over land, such as car parking, mooring of boats, storage of aircraft, sporting rights over land, or the right to fell and remove standing timber and certain other supplies listed in Item 1, Group 1, Schedule 9 VATA 1994 attract VAT at the standard rate.

16.5. **Commercial property**

16.5.1. The freehold sale of a new building (within three years of the date of completion) is standard rated (see A16.6). Other dealings with commercial property are exempt subject to the election to waive exemption (commonly known as the option to tax). If the option to tax has been exercised and notified to HM Revenue and Customs within 30 days the standard rate will apply, or if the property is a new freehold to which the compulsory standard rate charge applies on a mandatory basis. The sale of a let property by a VAT-registered seller to a VAT-registered buyer who elects to waive the VAT exemption for the property and notifies it to HM Revenue and Customs prior to the tax point for the transaction, may be treated as the sale of a business as a going concern so that VAT will not be chargeable. In addition, since 18 March 2004, the buyer must notify the seller that his option to tax is not subject to the statutory block under paragraph 2(3AA), Schedule 10 VATA 1994. Clearance for transfer of a going concern transaction is not generally provided by HM Revenue and Customs for straightforward transactions and reference should be made to HM Revenue and Customs VAT Notice 700/9. It is advisable for the seller to ensure the buyer provides evidence of having opted to tax by the relevant date, and the buyer will also require to see that the seller has opted to tax.

16.5.2. The Standard Commercial Property Conditions, Second Edition, provide as a standard provision that the sale of the property is exempt from VAT and that the seller will not exercise the option to tax. However, optional provisions are also included enabling the contract to provide for the sale to be standard-rated for VAT or to be treated as a transfer of a going concern (see A16.15).

16.6. Freehold sales of new commercial buildings

16.6.1. Every freehold sale of a new commercial property (including civil engineering works) before it is completed and within the first three years after its completion attracts VAT at standard rate unless a sale as a transfer of a property letting business as a going concern can be arranged – see A16.15.

16.6.2. 'Completion' of the building is either the date of the architect's certificate of practical completion or the date when the building was first fully occupied, whichever first occurs.

16.6.3. The buyer of such a building must therefore raise additional enquiries of the seller to ascertain whether the transaction (and any subsequent disposal of the building by the buyer) will attract VAT and the parties must agree on the contractual provisions which are to be inserted relating to the payment of VAT.

Guidelines

16.6.4. (a) Matters to be considered on taking instructions:

　　　(i)　will the sale be a standard rated supply so that VAT will be chargeable (whether as a 'new' commercial building or as a result of the election to waive exemption having been exercised)?

　　　(ii)　if not, what evidence (if any) is needed to satisfy HM Revenue and Customs that the sale will be an exempt or zero-rated supply or a transfer of a going concern?

(iii) if the sale is exempt from VAT, is the building subject to the Capital Goods Scheme (was the building purchased, constructed, renovated or fitted out by the seller, or predecessor, within the last 10 years at a cost in excess of £250,000, and did the seller incur VAT at that time)?

(b) Additional enquiries:

(If the contract requires the buyer to pay VAT he will want to be certain that VAT is chargeable and will also wish to have evidence to establish whether or not there is a mandatory charge to VAT on a subsequent sale. If the contract does not require the buyer to pay VAT he may be inclined not to raise the issue with the seller, but he should still ensure that the supply is in fact an exempt supply and that he has sufficient evidence to establish that a future sale by him will be exempt.)

(i) why does the seller consider that the sale is a standard-rated supply?

(ii) please provide a copy of the architect's certificate of practical completion;

(iii) when was the building first fully occupied?

(iv) what evidence is available to verify the date when the building was first fully occupied?

(v) please confirm that if VAT is paid on completion the seller will at that time deliver a VAT invoice to the buyer;

(vi) has the seller previously elected to waive his exemption from VAT or does he intend to do so before completion?

(vii) if the answer to question (vi) is 'yes', please confirm that the exercise of the option to tax has been or will be notified to HM Revenue and Customs within 30 days of its being made. The buyer's solicitor should request a copy of the option to tax document and of the letter of notification to ascertain the extent of the land to which the option will apply and to check that it is valid. It should also be noted that it is HM Revenue and Customs' policy to acknowledge receipt of an option to tax and this can therefore be acceptable evidence;

(viii) if the purchase is by way of a transfer of a going concern, is the building subject to the capital goods scheme? If so, please provide details of the initial deduction or subsequent adjustments, if any. See also A16.8.20.

(Note that if the seller agrees not to charge VAT, the contract should either specify that the price stated is inclusive of any VAT or should expressly provide that the seller has not elected to waive the VAT exemption in respect of the property and agrees not to do so.)

(c) The deposit:

If the seller's solicitor receives the deposit in the capacity of 'agent for the seller', a VAT tax point arises on exchange of contracts in relation to the amount of the deposit. If the deposit is held as 'stakeholder' the tax point for both the deposit and the balance of the purchase price will not arise until completion. This can be particularly important when dealing with the transfer of a going concern rules (see A16.15), or purchase of a property at auction.

16.6.5. A special condition on the printed version of the Standard Conditions of Sale Form provides that the sale is exclusive of VAT (see Appendix V.9).

16.7. Commercial leases

16.7.1. Commercial leases are normally treated as giving rise to exempt supplies by the landlord to the tenant, and no VAT will be payable on the premium or rent unless the landlord has exercised his option to waive the VAT exemption in respect of the building on or before completion or before rent is paid (or invoiced if earlier). If the landlord exercises that option, he must account to HM Revenue and Customs for VAT on the rent from all tenants of the building whether or not he obtains that VAT from the tenant. The landlord will normally want the tenant to pay the VAT, but whether the tenant will be liable to do so depends upon the date and wording of the lease. If the landlord makes the election after the grant of the lease, he can compel the tenant to pay VAT in addition to the rent unless there is anything in the lease to the contrary (and for this purpose a contrary provision must expressly refer to VAT; a general reference to the tenant not being liable to pay for tax on rent will not preclude the landlord from holding the tenant liable to pay the VAT).[1] Conversely, where a lease is granted after the landlord has elected to waive the VAT exemption for the building, the rent specified in the lease will be inclusive of VAT unless the lease states otherwise.[2] If the landlord exercises his option to tax during the term of a lease which expressly exonerates the tenant from paying VAT, or exercises his option and then grants a lease which is silent as to VAT, the landlord will have to account to HM Revenue and Customs for VAT as if the rent payable by the tenant was inclusive of VAT, i.e. with VAT at 17.5%, seven forty-sevenths of the rent will be regarded as VAT.

16.7.2. Any lease which might be subject to VAT should contain a covenant by the tenant to pay to the landlord any VAT chargeable on the rent or on any payment made under the lease in addition to the rent. The clause should also provide that in any situation where the tenant is required by the lease to reimburse the landlord for expenditure incurred by the landlord, e.g. for insurance premiums or service charge, the tenant should also reimburse any VAT paid by the landlord in respect of those payments unless VAT on those payments is recoverable by the landlord. Generally the VAT treatment of the service charge follows the rent, i.e. if the rent is standard rated, so is the service charge.

16.7.3.   Where in a lease a landlord has covenanted not to elect for VAT during the currency of the lease, that covenant, being personal in nature, may not be binding on a subsequent purchaser of the reversion unless a direct covenant has been entered into by that purchaser. It is therefore safer for the tenant to negotiate a lease which includes a covenant given by the landlord that he will undertake to obtain a non-opting covenant from any buyer.

Exempt tenants

16.7.4.   If the tenant of a lease makes exempt supplies he will be seriously disadvantaged by having to pay VAT on his rent (since he will not be able to recover some or all of that VAT). An exempt tenant in a market dominated by taxable tenants should consider taking a valuer's advice about the consequences of the VAT implications in his lease.

Guidelines

16.7.5.   (a)   'Options to tax' checklist for landlords:

Consider:

(i)   how much irrecoverable VAT has the landlord incurred/does the landlord incur?

(ii)   the VAT status of tenants/potential tenants/purchasers;

(iii) the short- and long-term consequences of exercising an option which is only revocable in limited circumstances (generally within three months, provided that no input tax has been recovered or output tax charged, or after 20 years in both cases with the written permission of HM Revenue and Customs);

(iv)   the consequences of agreeing a premium rent with an exempt tenant;

(v)   the costs of any additional administration which would be incurred in collecting VAT and issuing VAT invoices;

(b)   Reminders for tenants:

(i)   check whether or not VAT is included in the rent;

(ii)   remember that if the lease is silent section 89 VATA 1994 could apply;

(iii) if the tenant makes taxable supplies only, the main adverse consequence of paying VAT on his rent may be a cash flow disadvantage, set against which there may also be cash benefits for the tenant, e.g. the recovery of VAT on his service charge payments;

(iv)   if the tenant makes exempt or mainly exempt supplies he may be seriously disadvantaged by having to pay VAT on his rent since he will not be able to recover some or all of that VAT.

Purchases subject to leases

16.7.6.   The leases to which the property is subject should be checked to discover whether the buyer will be able to charge VAT should he wish to exercise his option to tax. The following matters should also be considered:

(a)   does the lease expressly provide that VAT is payable in addition to rent and other payments made or consideration given by the tenant or if not will section 89 apply?

(b)   will the landlord be able to recover from the tenant VAT on supplies received from a third party? or

(c)   is the landlord under an obligation to attempt to recover VAT from HM Revenue and Customs before he can look to the tenant for indemnity?

(d)   are all other sums referred to in the lease expressed to include any VAT which will be chargeable?

(e)   are the rent review provisions adequate if the landlord decides to elect to tax?

1.   Value Added Tax Act 1994, s.89.
2.   Value Added Tax Act 1994, s.10.

16.8.   **The option to tax**

16.8.1.   Where a transaction involving a commercial building or land is exempt from VAT the seller or landlord normally has the right to elect to waive the VAT exemption for the building, with a result that VAT will be chargeable both on the rents received from lettings and on the proceeds of any sale (see A16.5).

16.8.2.   The option to tax relates to the landlord's interest in an entire building. Thus an election made by a landlord who owns a whole office block affects all his tenants. Buildings which are linked by covered walkways or internal access are treated as one building as are complexes consisting of a number of units grouped around a fully enclosed concourse. If a tenant wishes to sub-let premises the VAT treatment does not depend upon the landlord's election to waive exemption. The tenant must himself elect to waive exemption if he wishes to charge VAT to the sub-tenant and retain the right to recover input tax charged to him by the landlord.

16.8.3.   An option to tax cannot be exercised retrospectively. When ownership of the building changes hands, the new owner must make his own election to tax. A transfer by one company to a subsidiary or holding company will be a change of ownership giving rise to a fresh election to tax so long as the transferee company is not in the same VAT group as the transferor. Normally such a transfer would have to be at the market price, that price being subject to VAT, so that the VAT on the purchase would be irrecoverable by the transferee if it did not itself make the election unless the transferee was occupying the building for the purposes of its taxable business.

16.8.4. A common problem encountered is where the owner of the property has charged VAT on rent but there is no formal option to tax in place. Where the option to tax was exercised prior to 1 March 1995 and the total rental income was under £20,000 pa, then there was no requirement to notify the election to HM Revenue and Customs. In cases where the election took place subsequent to that date and VAT has been charged, HM Revenue and Customs will generally accept that the election was exercised but there was a failure to notify it, and a belated notification will usually be accepted. Alternatively it could be argued that as no notification was made, the election is invalid and the supply should be exempt from VAT.

16.8.5. Written notice of an election must be given to the Commissioners not later than 30 days from the date of the election or such later date as may be agreed with them. This can be done by a letter to HM Revenue and Customs or on Form VAT1614 (available from the HM Revenue and Customs website – see Appendix VIII.2). The letter (or Form VAT1614) must include a clear description of the property involved including the building name and postcode. Plans or maps should be supplied where available, particularly if these are necessary to identify the land and buildings. The letter (or Form VAT1614) should be signed by an appropriately authorised person, for example, a director, a partner (or trustee), an authorised administrator or by a sole proprietor.[1] In cases where any other person notifies the election, it must be accompanied by a letter of authority signed by the 'taxable person'. There is a specialist Option to Tax Unit, at Portcullis House, 21 India Street, Glasgow, G2 4DZ.

16.8.6. An election which is under three months or over 20 years old can be revoked upon application to HM Revenue and Customs and obtaining their agreement in writing. If the election is under three months old, no output VAT must have arisen, no input VAT must have been reclaimed and no 'transfer of a going concern' treatment applied to the land in question. The first revocations of elections exercised in 1989 will be possible in 2009, and HM Revenue and Customs have issued a consultation paper on the subject which is available on their website, together with responses.

16.8.7. A buyer who has had to pay VAT on his purchase may wish to charge VAT on a letting or a subsequent disposition of the property by him in order to recover the VAT which he incurred on his purchase. VAT incurred before the date of election is irrecoverable (except with the consent of HM Revenue and Customs) unless no exempt supplies have been made in the meantime; thus the buyer's election to tax must normally be made before or at least within 30 days of completion, particularly where the building is bought subject to existing tenancies.[2] Similar considerations apply to developers who have incurred substantial input tax as a result of construction work on the building.

16.8.8. Exempt or partially exempt tenants, e.g. those whose business is in the financial sector, banks, building societies, etc., will be reluctant to pay VAT on their rent because they cannot usually recover the tax in full.

16.8.9. Persons who wish to make an election may need to seek permission from HM Revenue and Customs *before* they elect when the land or buildings concerned have *already* been the subject of an exempt supply by them, usually an exempt letting. If HM Revenue and Customs are satisfied that there would be a 'fair and reasonable' attribution of input tax between the exempt supplies already made and the taxable supplies to be made following the election, the person will be authorised to waive exemption on the land or buildings from a current date. Alternatively, prior consent is not needed provided the conditions for automatic consent published by HM Revenue and Customs are met (see VAT Notice 742A, para.5.1). Under the capital goods scheme, recovery of some of the VAT incurred on the land or buildings may then follow by means of annual adjustments and, usually, a 10-year period beginning with the time the VAT was incurred.

16.8.10. The option to tax applies only to commercial buildings. It does not therefore apply to dwellings: relevant residential buildings; relevant charitable buildings (other than use as an office); pitches for residential caravans; facilities for mooring a residential houseboat; sales of land to a DIY housebuilder; or sales of land to a housing association where the housing association has provided a certificate that it intends to use the land for residential development.

16.8.11. In addition, the option to tax is disapplied in the case of a commercial building sold to a buyer who intends to convert it into dwellings, unless the buyer will make zero-rated supplies in respect of either the freehold sale or lease in excess of 21 years in the converted property, and agrees in writing to VAT remaining chargeable (in which case the buyer can recover the VAT). It must be the immediate buyer who carries out the conversion.

Statutory block to the option to tax

16.8.12. A statutory provision intended to counter tax avoidance in this area (e.g. lease and leaseback between associated traders) can catch 'innocent' transactions. The provisions are complex and the following is only a summary. If it appears that a transaction may be caught by the provisions, reference to the detail of the legislation is essential and specialist advice may be necessary. The disapplication of the option to tax could have serious effects on the viability of a development as it may result in the recovery of input tax incurred on the project being forfeited.

16.8.13. Paragraphs 2(3AA) and 3A of Schedule 10 VATA 1994 were inserted by Finance Act 1997 and apply to supplies made on or after 19 March 1997. These paragraphs provide that where the grant of an interest in property is between connected parties, and the recipient is unable to recover at least 80% of their input tax under the partial exemption rules, then the option to tax is disapplied and the grant is exempt. Paragraph 2(3AA) provides that where an option to tax has been made a supply will not be treated as a taxable supply in situations where:

    (a)   the grant giving rise to the supply was made by a person ('the grantor') who was a developer of the land; and

    (b)   at the time of the grant, it was the intention or expectation of either:

        (i)   the grantor; or

        (ii)   a person responsible for financing the grantor's development of the land for exempt use,

    that the land would become exempt land.

16.8.14. A grant of land made by any person in relation to any land is a grant made by a 'developer' if:

    (a)   the land or building or part of a building on that land is an asset which can be treated as a capital item in respect of which the input tax incurred is subject to adjustment under the capital goods scheme (see A16.8.20);

    (b)   that person or the person financing the development, intended or expected that either of them or a person connected with either of them, would be occupying the land for an ineligible purpose during the capital goods scheme adjustment period applicable to it.

16.8.15. A person does not occupy for eligible purposes unless he is a taxable person. A taxable person must also occupy the land for the purpose of making supplies which are in the course or furtherance of his business and the supplies are taxable supplies (whether zero-, lower- or standard-rated) such that any input tax of his which was wholly attributable to those supplies would be input tax for which he would be entitled to a credit. HM Revenue and Customs' rule of thumb is that at least 80% of the person's supplies must be taxable.

16.8.16. Occupation of land by a body to which section 33 VATA 1994 applies (local authorities and various other statutory bodies) is occupation of the land for eligible purposes to the extent that the body occupies the land other than for the purposes of a business. Occupation of land by a government department (within the meaning of VATA 1994, s.41) is also occupation of the land for eligible purposes.

16.8.17. 'Funding the development of the property' includes all the following:

    (a)   directly or indirectly providing funds for meeting the whole or any part of the cost of the grantor's development of the land or building;

    (b)   directly or indirectly procuring the provision of such funds by another;

    (c)   directly or indirectly providing funds for discharging, in whole or in part, any liability that has been or may be incurred by any person for or in connection with the raising of funds to meet the cost of the grantor's development of the land or building;

    (d)   directly or indirectly procuring that any such liability is or will be discharged, in whole or in part, by another.[3]

16.8.18. References to the provision of funds for a purpose referred to in paragraph 3A(4) include:

    (a)   the making of a loan of funds that are or are to be used for that purpose;

    (b)   the provision of any guarantee or other security in relation to such a loan;

    (c)   the provision of any of the consideration for the issue of any shares or other securities issued wholly or partly for raising those funds; or

    (d)   any other transfer of assets or value as a consequence of which any of those funds are made available for that purpose.[4]

Transitional provisions

16.8.19. The rules above apply to supplies made on or after 19 March 1997 unless the supply arises from a 'relevant pre-commencement grant'.

A 'relevant pre-commencement grant' is a grant which was either made before 26 November 1996; or made after 26 November 1996 but before 30 November 1999 in pursuance of an agreement in writing entered into before 26 November 1996 on terms fixed in that agreement.[5]

Capital goods scheme

16.8.20. The following types of land are covered by the capital goods scheme:

    (a)   land or a building or part of a building, or a civil engineering work or part of a civil engineering work, where the value of the interest supplied to the owner, by a taxable supply is £250,000 or more (excluding any part of that value consisting of rent);

    (b)   a building or part of a building where the owner's interest in, right over or licence to occupy it is treated as self-supplied to him. The value of the supply must be £250,000 or more;

    (c)   a building where the aggregate value of the land on which the building is constructed and the goods and services in connection with the construction supplied to the owner by way of taxable (standard-rated) supply is £250,000 or more;

    (d)   a building which the owner alters, or an extension or an annexe which he constructs, where additional floor area is 10% or more of the original floor area before the work was carried out. The value of all taxable (standard-rated or lower-rated) supplies of goods and services, made or to be made to the owner on or after 3 July 1997 for, or in connection with, the alteration, etc., must be £250,000 or more;

(e)   a refurbishment of property costing more than £250,000 where the goods or services involved are supplied to the landlord on or after 3 July 1997. Refurbishment includes fitting out but is otherwise undefined. This gives rise to a practical difficulty in distinguishing between refurbishment and repair.

16.8.21.   Where a buyer inherits the balance of the seller's capital goods scheme adjustment period, as is the case where a building is acquired under the transfer of a going concern rules, the method of scheme adjustments for that balance of the adjustment period must be agreed in advance with HM Revenue and Customs. Enquiries should therefore be raised with the seller as to whether there is an existing capital goods scheme adjustment period. If so, the seller must be asked to supply details of the cost of the property, of the VAT initially recovered by the seller, any subsequent adjustments to that recovery and the timing of the intervals in the adjustment period.

1.   See Business Brief 17/99, dated 5 August 1999.
2.   But, see the decision in *Higher Education Statistics Agency Ltd* v. *Customs and Excise Commissioners* [2000] STC 332 where it was held that the relevant date when an election had to be made by is the date of payment of the deposit. In the case of HESA the election to tax was made after the deposit was paid at auction but prior to completion. HESA were found liable to pay VAT on the purchase price.
3.   VATA 1994, Sched. 10, para.3A(4).
4.   VATA 1994, Sched. 10, para.3A(5).
5.   See s.37(5) Finance Act 1997.

16.9.   Surrenders

16.9.1.   Surrenders in the course of a business are exempt from VAT. They may be taxable if the tenant has exercised his option to tax in respect of his leasehold interest.[1]

16.9.2.   If the tenant has exercised his option to tax in respect of his leasehold interest, and if the landlord is paying the tenant for the surrender, the tenant is making a standard rated supply of an interest in the land. Where the consideration for the surrender is other than in money VAT is payable on the value of the interest surrendered. Thus if the landlord in return for the surrender grants a long lease to the tenant, VAT is payable on the value of the surrendered lease, but a precise value may be difficult to assess. If a proposal involves a surrender by operation of law, liability to VAT should be agreed in writing before the surrender is made.

16.9.3.   Variations to a lease will be treated as being part of the supply of the lease. Variations will therefore be exempt unless the landlord has opted to tax, in which case the lease and the variations will be subject to VAT at the standard rate. A variation of a lease is regarded as the surrender of the lease and the grant of another in its place. HM Revenue and Customs have published a revised

Statement of Practice which will apply in circumstances where a deemed surrender and re-grant occur by operation of law (see Appendix VII.5).

1. *Lubbock Fine & Co.* v. *Commissioners of Customs and Excise* (Case C-63/92) [1994] STC 101.

16.10. Charities

16.10.1. The construction or first grant of a major interest in a building which is constructed or converted from non-residential use for use for a 'relevant charitable purpose' is zero-rated. Where the charity is using the premises for the purpose of a business carried on by it (e.g. a shop run by the charity where goods are sold to the public or a school where fees are charged for attendance), the rules for commercial property apply as this is not a use for a relevant charitable purpose.

16.10.2. A landlord is prevented from exercising the election to waive exemption where the building is to be occupied for a charity solely for a relevant charitable purpose, other than as an office.

16.10.3. Legislation also provides for zero-rating of the construction of a charitable use 'annexe', providing that the annexe is capable of functioning independently from the existing building and the main access to the annexe is not through the existing building or vice versa. The main difficulty in this area is whether the building constitutes an 'annexe' or is rather an 'extension' or 'enlargement', in which case standard-rating applies. There has been considerable case law on this issue and it is recommended that professional advice be sought before the charity issues the necessary certificate for zero-rating to the builder. In the case of both purchase and construction of qualifying buildings, for zero-rating to apply the supply must be to the charity which will use the building for qualifying purposes and must be supported by a certificate.

16.11. Conversions and renovations

16.11.1. The cost of reconstruction, alteration or enlargement of an existing building generally attracts VAT at the standard rate. However, the sale by a developer of a major interest in a building which has been converted to a dwelling or for residential use from a non-residential building is zero-rated. A 'major' interest is a freehold sale or the grant of a lease for over 21 years. However, there are problems in applying the zero rate where the non-residential premises contained residential accommodation prior to the conversion, such as in the case of a converted public house. In such cases the zero rate only applies to the extent that an additional dwelling is formed not containing any part of the pre-existing residential accommodation.

16.11.2. The reduced rate of VAT (5%) is chargeable on works for the conversion of a property into a different number of dwellings; conversions of dwellings into residential communal homes; and the renovation of dwellings that have been empty for at least three years with effect from 11 May 2001. This covers the qualifying conversion/renovation services, and building materials supplied with those services. In addition, from 1 August 2001 the sale of the freehold, or the premium or first payment of rent on a lease in excess of 21 years, in a renovated dwelling which has been empty for 10 years or more prior to the sale is zero-rated.

16.12. Listed buildings

16.12.1. Alterations to listed and other protected buildings (scheduled monuments) which required and have received listed building consent are zero-rated, whereas repairs and maintenance to such buildings is standard-rated. The grant of a major interest in a substantially reconstructed protected building is zero-rated. If a building is simply in a conservation area it does not qualify for the zero rating.

16.13. Agricultural land

16.13.1. The option to tax applies to agricultural land in a broadly similar way to other kinds of land whereas before 1995 an option to tax agricultural land affected adjacent land. Marshland and moorland which is used for grants of sporting rights comes within the definition of agricultural land in this context. Agricultural dwelling houses are exempt and no option to tax can be exercised in respect of them, but an apportionment of their value will have to be made where they are part of a sale of agricultural land. See also B8.

16.14. Sporting rights

16.14.1. Where sporting rights are sold as part of the sale of freehold land, the whole supply is treated as exempt subject to the option to tax, unless the value of the sporting rights is more than 10% of the total value in which case an attribution must be made and standard rate VAT accounted for on the sporting rights. In the case of supplies of sporting rights where the freehold of the land over which they are to be exercised is not sold to the same person, VAT at standard rate applies.

16.15. Property sold as a going concern

16.15.1. Where property is sold as a transfer of a going concern (TOGC), the transaction will only be outside the scope of VAT if the buyer satisfies all the criteria for relief. If he does not do so, the seller will be liable for VAT.

16.15.2. To qualify for relief there simply needs to be a transaction involving the sale of assets which puts the buyer in a position to carry on the business previously conducted by the seller. The relief may therefore be lost if the buyer contracts a sub-sale or re-sells the property within a short period.

16.15.3. It should be noted that there are special provisions relating to the sale of a 'new' or elected property, in that the buyer must also opt to tax in order for the transaction to be treated as the transfer of a going concern.

16.15.4. In addition, with effect from 18 March 2004, in order for the property to qualify as part of the transfer of a going concern, the buyer must also provide a notice to the seller, confirming that the buyer's option to tax is not subject to the statutory block (see A16.8.10). If the option to tax is not exercised or this notice is not provided, then the property must be treated as standard-rated, outside the 'transfer of a going concern' provisions, although a transitional period, effective to 30 June 2004, allowed transfer of a going concern treatment if the notice was not provided but the conditions were otherwise met – i.e. the option to tax was not blocked.

16.16. Summary checklist of application of VAT to property transactions

Type of dealing	Rate of tax
A. Freehold sales	
Buildings designed as dwellings built or converted and sold by developer.	Zero.[1]
Communal residential buildings sold by developer.	Zero.[1]
Non-business charitable buildings sold by developer.	Zero.[1]
Domestic and other non- commercial buildings sold by others.	Exempt.
New commercial buildings.	Standard.[2]
Other commercial buildings.	Exempt subject to option.
B. Leases[3]	
New buildings or converted from non-residential buildings where dwellings, communal residential buildings or non-business charitable buildings if for more than 21 years where built by and granted by developer.	Zero on premium or first payment of rent, exempt thereafter.[1]
Similar to above but lease for 21 years or less.	Exempt.

Type of dealing	Rate of tax
Domestic and non-commercial buildings granted by other than developer.	Exempt.
New commercial buildings.	Exempt subject to option.
Other commercial buildings.	Exempt subject to option.
Assignments.	Exempt subject to option.
Surrenders.	Exempt subject to option.
Reverse surrenders.	Exempt subject to option.

C. Listed buildings

Approved alterations to dwellings, communal residential and non-business charitable buildings.	Zero.
Other work on similar buildings.	Standard.
Freehold sales by developer of substantially reconstructed similar buildings.	Zero.[1]
Leases for more than 21 years from developer of substantially reconstructed similar buildings.	Zero on premium or first payment of rent, exempt thereafter.[1]
Any works to commercial listed buildings.	Standard.
Sales and leases of substantially reconstructed commercial listed buildings.	Exempt subject to option.

D. Building land

Sales and leases.	Exempt subject to option.[4]

E. Refurbished buildings

Sales and leases of residential buildings.	Exempt.[5]
Sales and leases of non-residential buildings.	Exempt subject to option.

F. Conversions

Freehold sale by developer of conversion from non-residential building into dwelling or communal residential building.	Zero.[1]
As above but grant of lease for over 21 years.	Zero on premium or first rent, exempt thereafter.[1]

Type of dealing	Rate of tax
Construction services supplied to registered housing association on conversion of non-residential building into a dwelling or communal residential building.	Zero.
Conversion of a property into a different number of dwellings (e.g. house into flats or vice versa) or of a dwelling into residential communal homes.	5%

G. Building services

Construction of new buildings designed as dwellings (including sub-contractors' services).	Zero.
Construction of communal residential and non-business charitable buildings provided an appropriate certificate is obtained from the customer, and the customer is the person using the building for qualifying purposes.	Zero.
Construction of new commercial buildings.	Standard.
Repairs and alterations.	Standard.
Demolition.	Standard unless part of a single zero-rated construction for new build dwellings, etc.
Professional services.	Standard.
Renovations of dwellings which have been empty for at least three years.	5%

H. Civil engineering work

New work.	Standard.
Repairs, maintenance and alteration of existing buildings.	Standard.

I. Options

Option to undertake a transaction which itself is chargeable to VAT.	Standard on option fee.

1. Zero on first grant, subsequent supplies exempt.
2. All freehold sales are taxable at standard rate while building remains 'new'.
3. In relation to leases, 'grant' includes assignment.
4. Except for sales to housing associations where a certificate for residential development is supplied or sales to DIY housebuilders, where the option to tax is not available.
5. Unless the property has been empty for 10 or more years when freehold sale, or lease over 21 years is zero-rated.

A17. Tax relief on mortgages

17.1. **Introduction**   17.3. **Companies**
17.2. **Business premises**

17.1. Introduction

17.1.1. Tax relief on the interest element of mortgage repayments relating to the purchase of an individual's private dwelling house ceased to be available as from 6 April 2000.

17.2. Business premises

17.2.1. Where a loan is taken out in respect of the purchase or improvement of business premises interest on that loan may qualify as an allowable expense of the business for tax purposes and thus some element of tax relief will be obtained against an individual's income tax liability or a company's corporation tax liability.

17.3. Companies

17.3.1. A company which takes out a loan for the purchase or improvement of business premises may obtain corporation tax relief on the interest element of the loan provided it is an allowable business expense.

A18. Transfers on breakdown of marriage or civil partnership

18.1. Introduction

18.1.1. Special considerations apply to the transfer of property between husband and wife on the breakdown of a marriage. This chapter does not deal with giving advice on the terms of the settlement between husband and wife, only on its implementation (see the guidance on Undue Influence in Appendix IV.8). Similar considerations are relevant on the breakdown of a civil partnership.

Conflict of interests

18.1.2. Even in cases where the settlement is amicable and is not made pursuant to a court order in matrimonial proceedings, the parties must be independently advised because of the inevitable risk of conflict of interests which arises in this situation.

18.2. Acting for the transferor

Mortgages

18.2.1. The solicitor acting for the transferor should ascertain the extent of existing mortgages over the property to be transferred. It must be decided whether the property is to be transferred free of the mortgage to the other spouse, and if so, whether the transferring spouse will redeem the mortgage or will continue to make repayments. If the property is to be transferred free of the mortgage, steps must be taken to discharge those charges before completion of the transfer. This may involve advising the transferor about refinancing and taking a new loan secured over another property in order to discharge his indebtedness over the property to be transferred. The lender's consent to the transfer will be required if either the mortgage deed requires it or if the borrower-spouse is to be released from his or her covenant under the mortgage. The borrower's continuing liability under the mortgage may affect his or her ability to obtain another loan on a different property. Arrangements must be made for the continuation of payments under the mortgage. Any life policy taken out in connection with an existing mortgage should be checked to ascertain the name(s) of the person(s) insured under the policy. If the property is to be transferred free of the mortgage to which the policy related, a re-assignment of the policy should be effected on discharge of the mortgage. If the benefit of the policy is to be transferred, the consent of the lender should be obtained and the insurance company notified of the change. The transfer of the benefit of the policy may attract CGT liability (see A15).

Outstanding discount on purchased local authority housing

18.2.2. A disposal of property which had been bought from a local authority under the provisions of Housing Act 1985, Pt. V made in pursuance of an order under Matrimonial Causes Act 1973, s.24 does not trigger the repayment of discount provisions under Housing Act 1985.[1] Thus no discount is repayable where the property is transferred under a court order for the transfer or a property adjustment order made under section 24. Where the court order is for the sale of the property under Matrimonial Causes Act 1973, s.24A a proportion of the discount may be repayable if the property is sold within three years after its purchase from the local authority.

1. Housing Act 1985, s.160(1)(*c*).

18.3.　Acting for the transferee

18.3.1. The transferee's solicitor should undertake the normal pre-contract searches and enquiries to ensure that no adverse entries exist which might adversely affect the property or its value (see B10).

18.3.2. Any charge which had been registered to protect the spouse's rights of occupation under Family Law Act 1996 ceases to be effective on issue of a divorce decree absolute unless an order under section 33(5) of the Act has been made and registered.

18.3.3. In appropriate cases advice should be given in relation to raising finance to purchase the share in the property to be transferred.

18.3.4. If the property is to be transferred subject to an existing mortgage, the lender's consent to the transfer must be obtained if the borrower is to be released from the covenant and/or if the mortgage so requires and arrangements made for the continuance of payments under the mortgage. If the benefit of a life policy is to be transferred, the lender's consent may be necessary and notice of the transfer must be given to the insurance company after completion.

18.3.5. Where the transferred property is mortgaged, consideration should be given to the protection of the mortgage by either an endowment policy or a mortgage protection policy. A lender may also insist that a policy to insure against the transferor's subsequent insolvency is acquired.

18.3.6. Transfers made in connection with divorce settlements do not attract Stamp Duty Land Tax (see A14.5.1).

18.3.7. A transfer of land between spouses for which 'value' is not given, that is, full consideration or something like it, in some form may be set aside by the court, under Insolvency Act 1986, ss.339–342 at the request of the trustee in bankruptcy if the transferring spouse becomes bankrupt within five years of the transfer. The solvency of the transferring spouse at the time of the transfer may be a material factor in the decision whether the transfer can or should be set aside, so the transferee spouse may want to get a declaration of solvency from the transferor at the time when the transfer is made. The transferee might also want to consider the possibility of insuring against the risk of the transferor's becoming bankrupt within five years. Should the transferee want to mortgage or sell the property within five years, this should not cause difficulties because of the amendments made to the 1986 Act by Insolvency (No.2) Act 1994 (see Appendix IV.3).

18.4. Public funding

18.4.1. The cost of conveyancing work necessary to give effect to the terms of a court order will usually be covered by the client's public funding certificate. This applies equally to consent orders and the work which is undertaken to implement such orders.[1]

1. See *S* v. *S* (*Legal Aid Taxation*) [1991] Fam Law 271; *Copeland* v. *Houlton* [1955] 3 All ER 178.

18.5. Mentally incapacitated party

18.5.1. Where a property adjustment order or an order for sale has been made and one of the adult parties lacks mental capacity, the provisions of the Practice Note, 'Ancillary Relief Orders: Conveyancing for Mentally Incapacitated Adults', issued by the Official Solicitor on 3 January 2006, must be followed (see Appendix IX.4).

18.5.2. Before the property can be sold, either the authority of the Court of Protection must be obtained or, where the incapacitated party is a trustee of a jointly owned property, an order appointing a substitute trustee must be made. Where the party is a sole owner of the property and a receiver has been appointed, the receiver will apply for authority to sell the property. (See Court of Protection Practice Note 4.) Where no receiver has been appointed the Court of Protection will authorise someone to act on the owner's behalf.

18.5.3. If the incapacitated party is a co-owner, section 22(2) LPA 1925 prevents the disposition of the legal estate in land so long as one trustee is a patient. The sale can only take place if there is another person authorised to act under an Enduring Power of Attorney, or if another trustee is appointed by either the family court or by the county court where the estate fund does not exceed the county court limit. A copy of the order appointing the new trustee must be produced to the Land Registry with the application to register the transfer (see generally B7).

18.6. Lenders' Handbook

18.6.1. The provisions of paragraph 16.3 of the Lenders' Handbook must be observed in appropriate cases (see Appendix VI.2).

A19. The National Conveyancing Protocol

19.1. Aim of the Protocol

19.1.1. The Protocol for domestic conveyancing was first introduced in March 1990 in an attempt to standardise and streamline the procedures involved in domestic transactions. The fifth edition took effect on 30 November 2004.

19.1.2. The Protocol does not take account of home information packs or the new TransAction forms. It is currently under review by the Law Society.

19.2. Domestic transactions

19.2.1. Solicitors are recommended to use the Protocol in all domestic transactions and should agree with the other party's solicitor at the outset of each transaction whether or not the Protocol will be used in that transaction.

Developers

19.2.2. Not all of the Protocol procedures will be appropriate for use when a developer is selling individual houses on an estate but, as far as possible, developers who have chosen to use the Protocol should adhere to the Protocol procedures, having notified the buyer's solicitors of any changes which have been made.

Local authority transactions

19.2.3. The Law Society's Local Government Group recommends that a local authority which is selling property should consider whether or not the transaction is one where it is appropriate to use the Protocol in whole or in part. In cases where the authority dispenses with a formal contract of sale use of the Protocol may not be appropriate.

19.3. Departure from the Protocol

19.3.1. If the Protocol is not being used in a residential transaction, or is to be substantially varied, the solicitor who intends to depart from the Protocol must inform the solicitor acting for the other party of this fact at the earliest opportunity. For the avoidance of doubt, variations to the Protocol should be recorded in writing between the parties. A departure from the Protocol when it has been agreed that it should be used in the transaction, or a failure to notify the other party of a departure from the Protocol, may be professional misconduct. If the parties have agreed that the Protocol will be used, a solicitor must give notice to the solicitor acting for the other party if, during the course of the transaction, it becomes necessary to depart from Protocol procedures.

19.4. Standard Conditions of Sale

19.4.1.   The Standard Conditions of Sale will be used to form the basis of the contract of sale in transactions which are regulated by the Protocol. The drafting of the Standard Conditions reflects the requirements of the Protocol, and thus an amendment to the Standard Conditions may itself be a departure from the Protocol which will need to be notified to the other party.

19.5. Disclosure of related transactions

19.5.1.   When a solicitor is instructed to buy or sell a residential property on behalf of his client he will explain the use of the Protocol to the client and will discuss with him the advantages and disadvantages of disclosing information to the other party about the progress of any related sale or purchase transaction. Disclosure of such information may be helpful to the other party but might not be helpful to the solicitor's own client if, e.g. the client was experiencing difficulties in selling his own property. Disclosure of information about related transactions can only be made with the client's consent, and the client's refusal to give such consent is not deemed to be a departure from the Protocol and written notice does not have to be served on the other party.

19.6. Non-solicitors

Licensed conveyancers

19.6.1.   Where it is in the interests of a client that the Protocol procedures are followed, a licensed conveyancer acting for the other party should be invited to adopt them. Licensed conveyancers are to be regarded in the same light as solicitors; it is therefore possible to rely on a licensed conveyancer's agreement to use the Protocol in a transaction.

Unqualified persons

19.6.2.   There is no reason why an unqualified person should not agree to comply with the Protocol procedures and use the related standard forms in the course of a transaction but no sanction would lie against such a person who departed from the Protocol. Not all of the standard forms are available to unqualified persons. Since undertakings cannot be accepted from unqualified persons it follows that an exchange of contracts using the Law Society formulae and completion using the Code for Completion by Post (both required under the Protocol) cannot be used when dealing with an unqualified person (see A5).

19.7. Text of the Protocol

19.7.1. The full text of the Protocol is set out in Appendix II.1, and the procedures referred to in the Protocol are dealt with in context in other sections of this book.

19.8. Use of forms

19.8.1. Where the Protocol is used the Standard Conditions of Sale should be used to form the basis of the agreement between the parties. While the Standard Agreement for Sale (front and back pages of the printed form) may be reproduced on a solicitor's word processor, the text of the Conditions themselves, for copyright reasons, may not (see A21).

19.8.2. Pre-contract enquiries under the Protocol are conducted using the Seller's Property Information Form, which may be reproduced on a solicitor's word processor as may the Fixtures, Fittings and Contents Form and the Completion Information and Requisitions on Title Form.

19.8.3. New TransAction forms (TA1–TA15) have been published by the Law Society to support solicitors acting for sellers and buyers after the commencement of duties under Housing Act 2004, ss.155–159 on 1 August 2007. For further details, see A26 and Appendix V.13. The general licence granted to solicitors to reproduce the Protocol forms (Seller's Property Information Form, Seller's Leasehold Information Form, etc.) is extended to these new forms.

19.8.4. Any form which is reproduced under the general licence outlined above, which applies to solicitors only, must be presented in a format as close as possible to the original form with no textual alterations and must state in a prominent position 'This form is part of the Law Society's TransAction Scheme'. The forms may not be photocopied except for the purpose of taking a file copy.

A20. Interest on clients' money

20.1. Solicitors' Accounts Rules 1998

20.1.1. A solicitor who holds money on behalf of a client may be required to pay the client interest or a sum in lieu of interest on the money he is holding. The circumstances when the client is entitled to interest and the amount of that interest are governed by Solicitors' Accounts Rules 1998 a summary of which is set out below. The text of Part C of the Rules appears in Appendix I.2.

20.1.2. The Rules can be varied by agreement in writing between the solicitor and his client, but contracting out is never appropriate if it is against the client's interests (Rule 27 Solicitors' Accounts Rules 1998).

20.1.3. If a solicitor pays a lender's cheque into his client account in anticipation of completing the mortgage and completion is postponed, the mortgage instructions may make the solicitor liable to pay interest at the mortgage rate if the money is not returned to the lender within the time stipulated in the lender's instructions.

20.2. Deposits in conveyancing transactions

20.2.1. The Rules apply to all money held by a solicitor on behalf of a client, including a deposit held by a solicitor whether as agent for the seller or as stakeholder.

20.2.2. Where the Rules apply, interest must be paid to the client irrespective of whether the money was held in a deposit or current account.

20.3. Stakeholder deposits

20.3.1. A deposit which is held in the capacity of stakeholder does not belong to either client until completion, but an entitlement to interest on that deposit arises under Rule 26 Solicitors' Accounts Rules 1998.

20.3.2. In the absence of express agreement to the contrary the interest will follow the stake.

20.3.3. Standard Condition 2.2.6 provides for the seller to receive the interest earned on a stakeholder deposit, provided the contract is completed but not if it is rescinded (see Appendix V.9).

20.4.   Designated accounts

20.4.1. Where client money is held in a separate designated client account, the solicitor must account to the client for the interest actually earned on that account. A separate designated client account is a deposit or share account for money relating to a single client.

20.5.   General client account

20.5.1. If the money is held in a general client account the duty to pay interest depends on the amount of money held and the period for which it is held, but there is no requirement to pay interest if the amount calculated is £20 or less.

Table of minimum balances

20.5.2. No interest need be paid if the money held does not exceed the amounts set out in the table below for times not exceeding the periods shown.

Time in weeks	Amount
8	£1,000
4	£2,000
2	£10,000
1	£20,000

20.6.   Sums exceeding £20,000

20.6.1. If a sum exceeding £20,000 is held for one week or less, a solicitor is not required to pay interest unless it is fair and reasonable to do so in all the circumstances. Although this part of the rule allows some discretion to be exercised by the solicitor in deciding whether or not to pay interest, such discretion should be exercised in the client's favour. Thus, if a sum of £1,000,000 were held on behalf of a client for two days, the considerable amount of interest which would accrue during that short time should be paid to the client.

20.7.   Intermittent amounts

20.7.1. There will be occasions when the solicitor either holds money intermittently for the client, or when the amount being held varies from time to time. In these circumstances the solicitor must account to the client for interest where it would be fair and reasonable to do so, having regard to the amounts of money held and to the length of time for which it is held. The discretion permitted by this rule should be exercised in favour of the client.

20.8. Rate of interest

20.8.1. The rate of interest (for money not held in a separate designated client account or held on a general client account) is the same rate as would have been payable if the money had been kept in a separate designated client account. Where money is held in a separate designated client account (which should be a deposit account with a major clearing bank or a deposit or share account with a building society) the amount of interest payable is the sum actually earned on that money while on deposit. However, for money held in a general client account, Rule 25(2) Solicitors' Accounts Rules 1998 requires payment (if higher) of the rate of interest payable on money placed on deposit on similar terms by a member of the business community.

20.8.2. Accrued interest on a contractual deposit held under the terms of the Standard Conditions of Sale is defined by Standard Condition 1.1.1.(a) (see Appendix V.9). The difference between a fair sum in lieu of interest and any higher rate payable in respect of a much larger general account may be retained by the solicitor.

20.9. Trustees

20.9.1. Money held by a solicitor which belongs to a trust (not being a controlled trust) of which the solicitor is a trustee, where the solicitor is acting for the trust, is client money and the interest provisions described above apply. If interests arises under a controlled trust (see Rule 2(2)(h) Solicitors Accounts Rules 1998), all of the interest must be paid to the beneficiaries (see Rule 15, note (vi) and Rule 24, note (x) Solicitors' Accounts Rules 1998).

20.10. Client's right to certificate

20.10.1. A client who feels that he ought to have been paid interest on money held on his behalf by his solicitor may apply to the Legal Complaints Service for a certificate as to whether or not interest ought to have been paid and, if so, the amount of that interest.

20.11. Tax on interest

20.11.1. In some circumstances deduction of tax at source may be applicable to interest which is paid on clients' money. The Law Society guidance on this matter is set out in full in Appendix IV.6.

A21. Reproduction of standard forms

21.1. **Standard Conditions of Sale and Standard Commercial Property Conditions**
21.2. **Protocol forms**

21.3. **Enquiries of Local Authority forms**
21.4. **Land Registry forms**

21.1. Standard Conditions of Sale and Standard Commercial Property Conditions

21.1.1. Solicitors may reproduce on their own word processors the agreement for sale which incorporates the Standard Conditions of Sale or Standard Commercial Property Conditions by reference but are not permitted to reproduce (whether on a word processor or by other means of reproduction) the text of the General Conditions of Sale without express permission from the copyright holder. Copyright is jointly held by the Law Society and the Solicitors' Law Stationery Society (OYEZ). Enquiries relating to copyright should, in the first instance, be addressed to Law Society Publishing (for address see Appendix VIII.2). The Conditions are reproduced in Appendix V.9 and V.10.

21.2. Protocol forms

21.2.1. It is in the interests of both the solicitor and his client that uniformity of presentation should be maintained where forms form part of the TransAction scheme.

21.2.2. The forms are Law Society copyright but may be reproduced by a solicitor on a word processor in a version which resembles the printed form as closely as possible. No additions, deletions, adaptations or alterations of the text of the printed version must be made. Additionally each word-processed copy must bear in a prominent position the following phrase 'This form is part of the Law Society's TransAction Scheme' in order to indicate to a person who reads the form that the document is a genuine reproduction of a Protocol form.

21.3. Enquiries of Local Authority forms

21.3.1. A general licence has been granted to solicitors to reproduce CON 29R Enquiries of Local Authority (2007) and CON 29O Optional Enquiries of Local Authority (2007) on word processors provided that the quality of the form produced is of a standard acceptable to local authorities.

21.3.2. As a general guideline, reproduction on paper which weighs no less than 80gsm, at a resolution of no less than 300 dpi, in 12 point Roman typeface should satisfy these requirements. The local authority has the right to reject a form which does not meet an acceptable standard of reproduction.

21.3.3. The forms may be reproduced on separate sheets of A4 paper. Permission has been granted for practitioners to reproduce and submit to the local authority only the front page of the printed CON 29R and CON 29O. The local authority may insist that the format of the printed form is followed as closely as is possible and in particular that the boxes which appear on the front page of the printed form are reproduced in the word-processed version.

21.4. Land Registry forms

21.4.1. Land Registry forms may be downloaded free of charge from the Land Registry website **www.landregistry.gov.uk** and may be freely reproduced for use within the firm. They may also be obtained from a law stationer or commercial software organisation.

21.4.2. All Land Registry forms are Crown copyright and all rights are reserved. The forms may not be sold to a third party in hard copy or machine readable format.

21.4.3. Schedule 1 forms may be reproduced in accordance with rule 210 of the Land Registration Rules 2003 and must be printed on durable A4 size paper. Electronically reproduced forms need to comply with the requirements of rule 211.

21.4.4. Documents for which no form is prescribed must be in such form as the registrar may direct or allow.[1]

21.4.5. Any queries about adaptation of forms and the Registry's checking and approval service should be made to the Forms Unit, Land Registry, 32 Lincoln's Inn Fields, London, WC2A 3PH. Telephone no. 0207 166 4405.

21.4.6. Detailed guidance on reproduction of Land Registry forms can be found in Land Registry Practice Guide 46.

1. Land Registration Rules 2003, r.212.

A22. Electronic conveyancing

22.1. Introduction

22.1.1. Land Registration Act 2002 (the Act) provides the statutory framework for the development and regulation of a system of electronic conveyancing (e-conveyancing). Further subordinate legislation will provide the detail as to how the system will work.

22.1.2. The fundamental objective underpinning the Act is set out in paragraph 1.5 of the Law Commission Report 'Land Registration for the Twenty-First Century' (Law Com. No. 271):

> '... the register should be a complete and accurate reflection of the state of the title of the land at any given time, so that it is possible to investigate title to land online, with the absolute minimum of additional enquiries and inspections.'

22.1.3. Further information, details of the strategy for the implementation of electronic conveyancing in England and Wales and the timeline for the e-conveyancing programme are available on the e-conveyancing website at **www.landregistry.gov.uk/e-conveyancing**.

22.1.4. E-conveyancing is being developed incrementally. As part of that development, the Land Registry plans to continue to improve and extend its existing electronic services.

22.2. Electronic services

22.2.1. Land Registry Direct is an internet based service that provides the facility to view registers of title and to obtain register information from the Land Registry database via instant online access. It enables account holders to view registers and title plans from their own computers, make searches online, view online documents referred to on the register and print official copies. The security controls of Land Registry Direct restrict its use to authorised customers on the terms of its conditions of use. Details of this service are available at **www.landregistrydirect.gov.uk**.

22.2.2. Land Registration Rules 2003, rr.14 and 132, give the registrar authority to permit electronic delivery of applications without the need for paper application forms. This system of electronic lodgement of non-dispositionary applications is being introduced in a number of phases. Applications such as the noting of the death of a joint proprietor, a change of name on marriage, a change of property description and applications for the entry of a restriction or unilateral notice may be lodged electronically using Land Registry Direct. In certain circumstances the Land Registry will also provide completion documentation electronically via Land Registry Direct.

22.2.3.   The simplest applications to deal with electronically are those that do not contain deeds. As enhancements continue to be made to the system it will also provide for the electronic lodgement of applications containing electronically signed deeds and documents. The Land Registry has indicated that charges will be among the first electronic documents to be introduced.

22.2.4.   The Land Registry is working with a number of lenders on a system of electronic discharges (EDs). This system involves a lender's computer sending an electronic message to the Land Registry's computer instructing the removal of the relevant charge entries. The lenders involved in using this system aim to generate an ED within five working days from receipt of the redemption monies. On receipt of the message, if electronic validation is successful, the Land Registry computer will automatically remove the relevant entries from the register of the title. For further information see G1.11.

22.2.5.   Electronic requisitions may now be raised by the Land Registry. If an e-mail address is provided on a Land Registry application form, requisitions will generally be sent to that e-mail address.

22.2.6.   The Land Registry provides an electronic payment facility. Payment by variable direct debit can be used for any application lodged by post, telephone or via e-services.

22.2.7.   For more information on available electronic services see Land Registry Practice Guides 23 (electronic lodgement of applications), 31 (discharges of charges), 45 (receiving and replying to notices by e-mail) and 59 (receiving and replying to requisitions by e-mail).

22.3.   E-conveyancing: the statutory framework

22.3.1.   The Act provides the statutory framework for a system of e-conveyancing in which the transfer and creation of interests in registered land will be made by electronic means.

22.3.2.   The provisions set out in the Act, Part 8 and Sched.5, provide for:

(a)   electronic dispositions being deemed to comply with statutory and common law requirements as to deeds and documents;

(b)   the creation of and access to a secure electronic communications network;

(c) power to require the use of electronic conveyancing; and

(d) the provision of a system of electronic settlement in relation to transactions involving registration.

22.3.3. The Act also provides that an electronic document when lodged will record the time and date when it takes effect and bear the electronic signature of each person who needs to authenticate it. Each signature will need to be certified. Registration and certification authorities will be required for the issue of such digital signatures.

22.3.4. These e-conveyancing provisions will not become operative until further subordinate legislation is passed. The Act obliges the Lord Chancellor to consult 'as appropriate' on most of the secondary legislation that will be required.

22.3.5. The first part of the consultation exercise on the secondary legislation required to operate an e-conveyancing system contained proposals for the Land Registration (Network Access) Rules 2007 and the Land Registration (Electronic Communications) Order 2007. The second part of the consultation provides more detail on e-conveyancing processes and services. A further consultation is expected to deal with proposals for the new fee structure in respect of such new e-conveyancing services. Further information is available on the e-conveyancing consultations website at **www.econsultations. e-conveyancing.gov.uk**.

22.4. E-conveyancing: implementation

22.4.1. The Land Registry is planning a staged approach to the implementation of a fully interactive e-conveyancing system in which documents created by practitioners and 'executed' electronically will result in automatic changes to the register. There will be further consultation with practitioners and other interested parties as the programme develops. New services will generally be introduced as pilots and/or trials to test the systems and procedures before extending and rolling out such services.

Chain matrix prototype

22.4.2. The Land Registry introduced its limited version of the chain matrix in March 2007. This chain matrix provides information that enables users to see the progress of other transactions in their chain online. The prototype of the chain matrix service has enabled the Land Registry to test the system and assess its impact before enhancing and developing the service further.

E-conveyancing pilot

22.4.3. A more extensive e-conveyancing pilot is planned for 2008. This will require the introduction of appropriate secondary legislation, the development of the secure electronic communications network, the use of effective electronic signatures and a revised fee structure.

22.4.4.   An enhanced chain matrix will enable users to signal their readiness to exchange contracts and complete electronically. Users will also be able to navigate to other parts of the service via the chain matrix and send electronic documents between the parties.

22.4.5.   Further development of the chain matrix system will enable a validation service to be introduced. This will check the data in the contract, transfer and charge documents lodged electronically against Land Registry records. It will enable any discrepancies, for example in the names of the registered proprietors or the address of the property, to be dealt with at an early stage and errors corrected online.

22.4.6.   A notional register view showing how the register would look if the transaction completed on the basis of the draft documentation lodged will also be available to the conveyancers acting for the parties.

22.4.7.   A secure electronic communications network will enable users to communicate with the Land Registry and each other. It is expected that different levels of access to the system may be given to different users and a network access agreement will define the nature of the transactions that a particular user may undertake through the network.

22.4.8.   It is expected that a number of channel access services will be available to enable users to access the central e-conveyancing service. Providers of such services may include organisations such as the Land Registry and commercial providers, for example the National Land Information Service channel providers.

A full e-conveyancing system

22.4.9.   A fully interactive e-conveyancing system will require the provision of a system of electronic settlement. An electronic funds transfer (EFT) service will enable funds to be transferred automatically at exchange and completion and allow for the automatic processing of Stamp Duty Land Tax in respect of electronic documents. The Land Registry has announced its intention to procure an EFT system to underpin its e-conveyancing service.

22.4.10.   Completion with simultaneous registration will enable the current registration gap, that is the current period between the completion of a transaction and its subsequent registration at the Land Registry, to be eliminated. The system will also need to provide for the automatic registration of company charges at companies house.

22.4.11.   Whilst the ultimate aim of e-conveyancing is to achieve completion with registration, the Land Registry has indicated that, initially, the system will not provide for automatic registration on completion. A conveyancer will need to apply electronically for registration.

22.4.12. Once a fully interactive e-conveyancing service is in place it is anticipated that the paper-based and electronic systems of conveyancing will co-exist for a period. Before introducing rules to make e-conveyancing compulsory the Act provides that a draft of such rules must be laid before and approved by resolution of each House of Parliament after appropriate consultation.

A23. Money laundering

23.1. What is money laundering?

23.1.1. Money laundering is the process through which criminals attempt to conceal the true origin or ownership of the proceeds of their criminal activities so as to retain control over them and ultimately make it appear as though the proceeds come from a legitimate source. Solicitors should be alert to the possibility of their clients using them to launder money, which may expose the solicitors themselves to criminal offences. Failure to report a client where there is a suspicion that a money laundering offence may be, or has been, committed can result in the solicitor being prosecuted, as can assisting a money launderer.

23.1.2. Solicitors are advised to study *Money Laundering: Guidance for Solicitors* (Pilot – January 2004) (as amended by subsequent guidance on the case of *Bowman* v. *Fels* [2005] EWCA 226 Civ), which is available at **www.sra.org.uk**. See also *Solicitors and Money Laundering: A Compliance Handbook* by Peter Camp, published by Law Society Publishing (second edition, April 2007).

23.2. The offences

The current offences relating to money laundering are contained in Proceeds of Crime Act 2002. References to section numbers in the following paragraphs are references to Proceeds of Crime Act 2002. The offences carry a penalty of between five and 14 years' imprisonment. The offences divide into three categories.

Offences where the firm is involved in a client matter or transaction

23.2.1. It is an offence:

(a) to acquire, use or possess the proceeds of criminal conduct (section 329);

(b) to conceal, disguise, convert, transfer or remove from the UK the proceeds of criminal conduct (section 327);

(c) to be involved in an arrangement which facilitates the acquisition, retention, use or control of another person's criminal property, where there is knowledge or suspicion that this is the case (section 328).

23.2.2. Criminal property is defined as the benefit (or representation of the benefit) of a person's criminal conduct, i.e. any conduct which constitutes a crime in the UK, or if undertaken abroad, would have constituted a crime if committed in the UK. A new defence came into effect on 15 May 2006 and applies where there are reasonable grounds for believing the conduct occurred abroad and it was not unlawful conduct in that overseas jurisdiction (and was not of a description prescribed by Order). It is necessary for the alleged offender to know or suspect that it does constitute or represent such a benefit (section 340).

23.2.3. A defence is available where disclosure of knowledge or suspicion is made to the Serious Organised Crime Agency (SOCA) or to a Nominated Officer, i.e. a firm's Money Laundering Reporting Officer (MLRO) (section 338).

Offences following a disclosure report made to the SOCA or to the firm's Nominated Officer (section 333)

23.2.4. It is an offence to disclose to any person (including your own client) that a report has been made to the SOCA or to the firm's MLRO in circumstances where this is likely to prejudice an investigation (tipping off). There is a defence available to professional legal advisers who may make a disclosure to a client in connection with the giving of legal advice. The defence is lost if the disclosure is made 'with the intention of furthering a criminal purpose', i.e. the legal adviser's intention, not the client's intention.

23.2.5. Further, once a report has been made to the SOCA or to the MLRO it may be an offence to continue to act for the client without the consent of the SOCA or the MLRO. The MLRO can only give consent if he has disclosed details to the SOCA and the SOCA has, in turn, either given consent for the firm to continue to act or the SOCA has not, before the end of seven working days of the MLRO's disclosure, refused consent to continue to act.

Offences involving a failure to disclose knowledge or suspicion of money laundering (section 330)

23.2.6. It is an offence for a person who knows or suspects or who has reasonable grounds for knowing or suspecting that another is engaged in money laundering not to disclose that information where the information came to him in the course of business in the regulated sector. On 1 March 2004 the definition of the regulated sector was extended to include 'the provision by way of business of legal services which involves participation in a financial or real property transaction'. Conveyancing transactions will be within the 'regulated sector' for these purposes. The section provides that a person does not commit an offence if he is a professional legal adviser and the information came to him in privileged circumstances.

23.3.   Money laundering and conveyancers

23.3.1.   Solicitors involved in property transactions are at particular risk – many of the typical day-to-day transactions in the property department could, potentially, bring a solicitor within the ambit of the legislation. The Law Society has issued specific guidance for conveyancing practitioners (December 2005) – this guidance is available online.

23.3.2.   The following are specific areas of concern.

(a) **Use of client account**

Money launderers will find it difficult to pass money through banks and financial institutions without providing a good reason. Passing money through a solicitor's client account with repayment on a 'clean' client account cheque is a useful laundering transaction. Solicitors should take particular care where property transactions are aborted after the payment of substantial sums into client account (i.e. payments made for a deposit or purchase price) or where costs are paid twice (particularly if the second payment is from a third party indicating that they had agreed to pay the client's costs).

(b) **Purchase of property with suspect funds**

Once money has been cleaned as a result of passing sums through a number of transactions, the money launderer will wish to invest the laundered funds in such a way that no one will suspect the asset to be the indirect benefit from crime. Property purchase is an ideal investment – particularly commercial property which will bring in a rental income as well as potentially giving rise to a capital gain. Solicitors acting on the conveyancing will be facilitating the acquisition, use, retention and control of ciminal property in these cases and can be guilty of an offence if they do so with knowledge or suspicion. Solicitors who defend clients charged with criminal offences should be particularly alert to the danger of money laundering if their firms also undertake property work.

(c) **Tax evasion and welfare benefit fraud**

The notional proceeds of tax evasion or welfare benefit fraud (i.e. the amount of money equal to the savings in tax or benefit received) are criminal property. Information regarding tax evasion and/or welfare benefit fraud may come to light during a conveyancing retainer. Where there is knowledge or suspicion that assets (including bank balances) have been acquired after the date of any such evasion or fraud, solicitors should be cautious and consider possible money laundering implications. Real property itself may be criminal property if it has been purchased using funds which are criminal property or purchased using a mortgage which is subject to monthly payments from a bank account containing the notional proceeds of a crime. Any subsequent sale of the property would amount to money laundering. Abuse of the Stamp Duty

Land Tax procedure may also give rise to money laundering implications, e.g. through misleading apportionment of the purchase price.

(d) **Mortgage fraud**

The proceeds of a mortgage fraud will inevitably be criminal property. A solicitor who assists a client in mortgage fraud will be facilitating the acquisition of criminal property within section 328. It is not necessary for the solicitor to know that the client is committing a mortgage fraud. The solicitor can be guilty under section 328 if he suspects that the circumstances will lead to fraud. Further, even if a solicitor is not involved in the mortgage application, completing a purchase using the proceeds of a mortgage fraud will facilitate the retention, use or control of criminal property. A solicitor who therefore proceeds to completion suspecting that the client has been engaged in mortgage fraud is at risk of prosecution under section 328.

23.4. The conduct issues

23.4.1. Note (xi) to Rule 15 Solicitors' Accounts Rules 1998 warns solicitors that they should not provide banking facilities for third parties (including clients of the firm) as this might lead to assisting money launderers.

Disclosure and legal professional privilege

23.4.2. Legal professional privilege may prevent solicitors from reporting their suspicions. The Court of Appeal in *Bowman* v. *Fels* (2005) EWCA Civ 226 confirmed that common law legal professional privilege is not overriden by the authorised disclosure defence. Consequently, before making a disclosure to the authorities, a solicitor must consider whether any knowledge or suspicion arises as a result of legal professional privilege. If it does, no disclosure can be made without a client waiver, and before that waiver can be obtained, the solicitor would have to consider the tipping-off offences. However, privilege does not extend to information communicated in order to further a criminal purpose.

23.5. Money Laundering Regulations 2003

23.5.1. The Regulations (SI 2003/3075) were passed as a result of the Second European Money Laundering Directive (Council Directive 2001/97/EC of 4 December 2001) and came into force on 1 March 2004.

Scope of the 2003 Regulations

23.5.2. The Regulations apply if a person is carrying on 'relevant business' which includes:

    (a)   regulated activities within the meaning of Financial Services and Markets Act 2000;

    (b)   any of the following activities when carried on by way of business:

        (i)   operating a bureau de change;

        (ii)   transmitting money (or any representation of monetary value) by any means; or

        (iii) cashing cheques which are made payable to customers;

    (c)   estate agency work;

    (d)   any activities of a person who acts as an insolvency practitioner; or

    (e)   the provision by way of business of advice about the tax affairs of another person;

    (f)   the provision by way of business of legal services by a body corporate or unincorporate or, in the case of a sole practitioner, by an individual and which involves participation in a financial or real property transaction (whether by assisting in the planning or execution of transactions or otherwise by acting for, or on behalf of, a client in any such transaction);

    (g)   the provision by way of business of services in relation to the formation of a company or the formation, operation or management of a company or trust.

Systems and training to prevent money laundering (Regulation 3)

23.5.3.   When conducting relevant business, no business relationship is to be formed or one-off transaction carried out unless the solicitor maintains:

    (a)   identification procedures;

    (b)   record-keeping procedures;

    (c)   internal reporting procedures;

    (d)   such other procedures of internal control and communication as may be appropriate for the purposes of forestalling and preventing money laundering;

    (e)   procedures for employees who handle relevant business to be trained in details of the law and the recognition and handling of suspect transactions.

23.5.4.   The maximum penalty for failing to comply with these provisions is two years in prison.

23.5.5.   A business relationship means any arrangement the purpose of which is to facilitate the carrying out of transactions on a frequent, habitual or regular basis where the total amount of any payment to be made is not known or capable of being ascertained at the outset.

23.5.6. Any transaction which is not carried out in the course of an established business relationship is regarded as a 'one-off transaction'.

Identifying the client (Regulations 4 and 5)

23.5.7. These regulations apply in all cases where the solicitor is forming a business relationship with his client. They also apply to one-off transactions where the value of the transaction is €15,000 or more, or where the solicitor knows or suspects that the transaction involves money laundering.

23.5.8. The solicitor must, as soon as is reasonably practicable after first contact, ask the client for production of satisfactory evidence of identity or take steps which will result in evidence being produced. If satisfactory evidence of identity is not produced, the transaction must not proceed any further (Regulation 4(3)(c)). Chapter 3 of *Money Laundering: Guidance for Solicitors* (Pilot – January 2004) contains detailed guidance on how identity can be established. The Law Society has also produced *Money Laundering: A Guide for Clients* (February 2004) which explains the requirements of the regulations to clients.

Record-keeping procedures (Regulation 6)

23.5.9. Records must be kept for five years after completion of the transaction of the evidence obtained of identity and of all transactions carried out by the client.

Internal reporting (Regulation 7)

23.5.10. Internal reporting procedures are necessary where persons are employed who are handling relevant business or where the solicitor practises in partnership. In such cases, there must be a person within the firm to whom all information about known or suspected money launderers is to be given, 'the Nominated Officer'. The Nominated Officer will probably be a partner. Anyone in the firm must disclose to the Nominated Officer any information or matter which comes into his possession in the course of relevant business, as a result of which he knows or suspects or has reasonable grounds for knowing or suspecting that a person is engaged in money laundering. Where such disclosure is made, the Nominated Officer must determine whether it does give rise to such knowledge or suspicion and, if so must report to the SOCA.

Reporting to the SOCA

23.5.11. All reports are dealt with nationally by the SOCA. Section 339 Proceeds of Crime Act 2002 allows the Secretary of State by order to prescribe the form and manner of disclosure reports. At the time of writing no such order has been made. It is therefore recommended that reports are made on the standard form which can be found at **www.soca.gov.uk**.

23.6.   **Summary**

23.6.1.   The law and regulations on money laundering are complex and far-reaching.

23.6.2.   In the context of conveyancing, the solicitor must ensure that he properly identifies his client at the outset of the transaction, and has in place procedures for recording that information and a 'reporting officer' within the firm.

23.6.3.   The source of any large cash payments from a client must be verified. It may be prudent to include a sentence in the client care letter to the effect that the solicitor will not accept cash payments from the client in excess of a stated amount (e.g. £500).

23.6.4.   The solicitor should also be wary of the client who withdraws from a transaction without good reason after payment of the deposit and requires his deposit to be returned to him. This is one example of how money may be laundered through a solicitor's client account.

23.6.5.   Any suspicious circumstance involving the handling of client's money must be reported to the firm's reporting officer.

A24. Mortgage fraud

24.1. Guidance from the Law Society

24.1.1. Solicitors need to be alert to the possibility of a mortgage fraud. The Law Society has issued the following guidance to solicitors:

- Property Fraud Warning Card II ('Green Card'), Appendix III.3.

- Mortgage Fraud – variation in purchase price.

The following paragraphs outline the most common types of fraud and the solicitor's duty in relation to a suspected fraud.

24.2. Solicitor's duty

24.2.1. The Law Society's guidance on mortgage fraud states that if a solicitor is aware that his or her client is attempting to perpetrate fraud in any form, he or she must immediately cease acting for that client.

24.2.2. Rule 2.01 Solicitors' Code of Conduct 2007 states that:

'... you must refuse to act or cease acting for a client in the following circumstances:

(a)   when to act would involve you in a breach of the law or a breach of the rules of professional conduct;'

24.2.3. Failure to comply with the Rule carries with it the risk of criminal prosecution (for having aided and abetted a fraud) and/or civil action (breach of contract or negligence by, e.g. a lender who suffers loss) and of being disciplined for breach of the Code of Conduct.

24.2.4. A solicitor may be guilty of conspiracy to defraud by undertaking the conveyancing work for a client who is himself engaged in a fraudulent transaction. The solicitor's active knowledge of or participation in the fraud is not necessary; if the work involved in the conveyancing falls below the standard expected of a normal solicitor, this may indicate that the solicitor had no genuine belief in the transaction in which he was acting and imply that the solicitor was involved in the conspiracy. A solicitor who is found guilty of fraud is likely to be struck off the Roll.

24.3.   **Types of fraud**

Status

Income

24.3.1.   The borrower overstates his income in the mortgage application, usually with the sole aim of securing a higher mortgage. A solicitor who knows that his client is unemployed or that there are substantial arrears owing on the client's current mortgage should be alert to the possibility of mortgage fraud but is not under a duty to inform the lender of this fact unless the lender's instructions expressly require him to do so.[1]

Identity

24.3.2.   The borrower conceals his true identity, perhaps to disguise the fact that he has another subsisting mortgage. Fraud can also occur where a husband forges his wife's signature (or vice versa). An indication of this type of fraud is where the solicitor is asked to contact the husband at his business address rather than his home address. Another example in this category is the sale at an inflated price to an individual by a company controlled by him. This device is used to raise additional finance for the company. This type of fraud is sometimes carried out on a large scale and often involves other fraud, e.g. tax, improvement grants. Instructions to purchase or transfer the property into the name of nominees may indicate a fraud of this type. In all cases where the client is not personally known to the solicitor, it may be prudent to check the identity of the client. Where there are co-buyers (e.g. husband and wife), instructions must be confirmed from both of them.[2]

Property

Price reduction

24.3.3.   The price to be shown in the purchase deed is less than that agreed to be paid by the buyer, or situations where the client instructs that a reduced price has been agreed to take account of an allowance for 'repairs to the property'. In some cases, the amounts shown in the contract and purchase deed will be identical but fraud occurs because the full amount of the purchase price is never in fact paid, e.g. the buyer says he has paid money directly to the seller, or that part of the price has been set off by the buyer against money owed to him by the seller.

Fraudulent valuations

24.3.4.   Where it appears that the valuation of the property is higher than might be expected for a property of that type or is considerably higher than the figure in a recent (say within the last 12 months) disposal of the property. A solicitor is not an expert in valuations and cannot be expected to advise on the accuracy of a valuation obtained by the client; nevertheless, a valuation which is patently out of line with the apparent value of the property may give rise to suspicion.

Roll-over fraud

24.3.5. This occurs where the borrower sells a property to an associate at an inflated price. As a result, the associate is able to obtain a higher mortgage. No repayments are made under the mortgage. Before the lender is able to repossess the property, it is sold to another associate for a higher figure, and so on.

Use of sub-sales

24.3.6. A client instructs a solicitor in the purchase of a property for, say, £100,000. The solicitor is told that the property, currently owned by Y, is to be bought in the name of B who is selling to C at a price of £160,000. B and C are either the same person (using assumed identities) or associated persons. Y may also be a party to the fraud, although in some cases he may be an innocent seller. C obtains a mortgage of £150,000 based on the higher value and secures an immediate profit of £50,000. The balance between the original sale price and the higher sub-sale price is never paid, or is said to be paid direct by B to C, or is allegedly set off by B against money owed to him by C. A simultaneous exchange of contracts followed by a quick completion is often a feature of these transactions. The lender is then left with a property worth only £100,000 as security for the loan.[3] A variation on this theme is where A grants a lease to B at a ground rent; B then assigns the lease to C at a premium. The purpose of this type of transaction is to give C a legal interest on which he can then obtain a mortgage.

Money paid direct

24.3.7. A deposit or balance of the purchase price which is paid (or said to be paid) direct to the seller from the buyer may indicate a mortgage fraud.

1. *Penn* v. *Bristol & West Building Society* [1997] 3 All ER 470.
2. *Bristol & West Building Society* v. *Kramer*, *The Independent*, 26 January 1995.
3. *Ibid.*

24.4. **The conduct issues**

24.4.1. A solicitor must act in the best interests of the client. Where he is acting for both the buyer and his lender, he owes a duty to both. There is a duty to report to the lender any alteration in the purchase price and any other information specifically identified in the lender's instructions.[1]

24.4.2. The solicitor's duty of confidentiality means that the buyer/borrower must consent to disclosure being made to the lender. This situation may give rise to a conflict of interests between the lender client and the buyer client. The solicitor cannot then continue to act for both clients and cannot continue to act for one client without the consent of the other. The safest course of action to adopt is to cease to act for both clients in these circumstances. Where the solicitor is obliged to cease to act for the lender, he should return the papers to the lender, stating that they are returned on the grounds of conflict of interests. However, in the Law Society's *Money Laundering: Guidance for Conveyancers*, it is stated that the principles of client confidentiality would usually mean that the lay client would need to waive their confidentiality before the mortgage company could be informed. If there was no valid retainer because of the crime/fraud exception, the solicitor can tell the mortgage company without the client's permission. If knowledge or suspicion is formed during the course of the retainer with the mortgage company the solicitor will have a duty to advise the Lender because the information is relevant to the Lender's decision to make the loan.

24.4.3. Mortgage funds obtained using fraudulent means will be the proceeds of crime. Solicitors must appreciate that knowledge or suspicion of a client's mortgage fraud may require action to be taken under Proceeds of Crime Act 2002 (see A23 above).

1. *Alliance & Leicester Building Society* v. *Edgestop Ltd* [1994] 2 EGLR 229; *Bristol & West Building Society* v. *May, May and Merriman* [1997] 3 All ER 206.

A25. Rentcharges

25.1. Definition

25.1.1. A rentcharge is generally defined as being a periodic sum issuing out of land which arises other than out of a landlord/tenant relationship.

25.1.2. Since 22 August 1977 rentcharges have not, with limited exceptions, been able to be created (see Rentcharges Act 1977, s.2 and A25.5).

25.1.3. If a rentcharge is created in fee simple or for a fixed term of years it is a legal interest which is binding on a subsequent buyer of the land charged irrespective of notice where the title to the land is unregistered.

25.1.4. A rentcharge for life (e.g. created under a settlement) is equitable only.

25.2. Title

25.2.1. On a sale of unregistered land subject to a rentcharge, in the absence of a provision to the contrary in the contract, the document creating the rentcharge must be abstracted in addition to a 15-year-old good root of title and subsequent documentation.

25.2.2. On first registration of land which is subject to a rentcharge, the rentcharge is noted in the charges register of the title to the land (see Land Registration Rules 2003, r.35(1)).

25.3. Transfer

25.3.1. The benefit of an existing rentcharge must be transferred by deed.[1] The benefit of a covenant for payment of the rentcharge must be expressly assigned. In the absence of express assignment, the obligation to pay remains, but would be unenforceable by action for its recovery other than by distress or re-entry.[2]

---

1. Where the rentcharge is registered, Form TR1 should be used and the necessary express assignment of the benefit of the covenant for payment should be inserted in the Additional Provisions Panel of Form TR1.
2. *Grant* v. *Edmondson* [1931] 1 Ch 1.

25.4. **Extinction**

25.4.1. The three main ways in which a rentcharge can come to an end are:

(a) by release by the owner of the rentcharge to the owner of the land charged;

(b) by merger when the owner of the rentcharge and the owner of the land charged become the same person;

(c) by redemption under Rentcharges Act 1977.

25.4.2. Except for rentcharges which are exempted under Rentcharges Act 1977, the 1977 Act provides that every rentcharge will be extinguished at the expiry of the period of 60 years from 22 August 1977 or on the date when it first becomes payable, whichever is later.

25.4.3. On compulsory redemption of a rentcharge and on proof that an applicant has paid the rentcharge price either to the person entitled to payment or into court, the Secretary of State will issue a redemption certificate. Where a rentcharge is redeemed by agreement or surrender, a deed of release should be drawn up and signed by the parties. Where the land subject to the rentcharge is registered, an application to cancel notice of the rentcharge should be made to the Land Registry.

25.5. **Creation of new rentcharges**

25.5.1. Rentcharges Act 1977 prevents the creation of new rentcharges after 22 August 1977, except in the following circumstances:[1]

(a) those which give effect to trusts in the case of family charge under Schedule 1, Trusts of Land and Appointment of Trustees Act 1996;

(b) creation of an estate rentcharge;

(c) a rentcharge created under any Act in connection with works on land;

(d) a rentcharge created under an order of the court.

1. Rentcharges Act 1977, s.2(3).

25.6. **Estate rentcharges**

25.6.1. An estate rentcharge[1] is a rentcharge created for the purposes either:

(a) of making covenants to be performed by the owner of the land affected enforceable by the rent owner against the owner for the time being of the land; or

(b) of meeting the costs of performance by the rent owner of covenants for the provision of services, the carrying out of maintenance or repairs, or effecting insurance or the making of a payment for the benefit of the land affected by the charge.

25.6.2. Rentcharges created under (a) above represent one method of providing for the effective enforcement of positive covenants. Rentcharges under (b) above are a useful method of reserving service charges out of freehold sales, e.g. where a management company covenants to maintain amenity areas or to provide services, although some lenders are reluctant to lend money on the security of a property which is subject to such a charge.

25.6.3. The rentcharge must represent a payment for the performance by the rent owner of a covenant (e.g. for insurance, etc., under (b) above) which is reasonable in relation to that covenant. If this provision is not complied with, the rentcharge will not be a valid estate rentcharge unless the amount reserved is only nominal.

25.6.4. It appears, however, that the wording of the rentcharge does not have to be expressed to require a reasonable sum, it is sufficient that the actual sum should be reasonable. Where the amount is no more than 100% of the expenditure incurred on behalf of owners of properties on an industrial estate this has been held to be reasonable.[2]

1. Rentcharges Act 1977, s.2(4).
2. *Orchard Trading Estate Management Ltd* v. *Johnson Security Ltd* [2002] 2 EGLR 1.

25.7. Apportionment

25.7.1. By Rentcharges Act 1977, s.4, the owner of land affected by a rentcharge which also affects other land not owned by him may in certain circumstances apply to the Secretary of State for a certificate apportioning the rent between the two parcels of land. A similar procedure exists for the apportionment of a rentcharge on a sale of part of land.

25.7.2. By Standard Condition 4.5 and Standard Commercial Property Condition 6.5 the buyer is not entitled to object to an informal apportionment of a rentcharge as being a defect in title.

25.7.3. The Land Registry's requirements are set out in its Practice Guide 56.

25.8. Registration of rentcharges

25.8.1. If a rentcharge capable of subsisting as a legal interest is granted out of a registered title, then, in accordance with the fundamental principles of registration of title, the disposition must be completed by registration to be legally effective.[1] The compulsory first registration provisions do not apply to rentcharges. They may, however, be registered voluntarily.[2]

25.8.2. If it appears to the registrar that a right to determine a registered rentcharge is exercisable he may enter notice of the fact in the register.[3] An application for such an entry must be supported by evidence to satisfy the registrar that the applicant has the right to determine the rentcharge and that the right is exercisable.[4]

1. Land Registration Act 2002, s.27(1) and (2)(b).
2. Land Registration Act 2002, s.3.
3. Land Registration Act 2002, s.64.
4. Land Registration Rules 2003, r.125.

A26. Home information packs

26.1. Housing Act 2004 duties

26.1.1. Housing Act 2004 (HA 2004) received Royal Assent on 18 November 2004. Part 5 of HA 2004 (ss.148–178) provides for duties in relation to home information packs. These duties are being brought into effect for certain properties in phases (see A26.2) and the detailed content of home information packs is prescribed by regulations (see A26.3).

26.1.2. The person responsible for complying with the Act (a 'responsible person' (HA 2004, s.151)) is the person who markets the property. That is, either the seller or the person 'acting as estate agent' on behalf of the seller.

26.1.3. The definition of 'acting as estate agent' will cover the activities of solicitors involved in property selling. The person must be acting in the course of a business and must be acting 'in pursuance of marketing instructions from the seller'. 'Marketing instructions' include instructions to sell the property by auction or tender (HA 2004, s.150). A property is put on the market when 'the fact that it is or may become available for sale is, with the intention of marketing the property, first made public in England and Wales by or on behalf of the seller' (HA 2004, s149(2)).

26.1.4. The basic duties placed on the responsible person are:

    (a)   to have in his possession or under his control, a home information pack for the property which complies with the regulations (HA 2004, s.155); and

    (b)   to provide a copy of the home information pack or of specified documents within the pack when requested to do so by potential buyers (s.156(1)). The copy must be provided within a period of 14 days beginning with the day on which the request is made (s.156(9)). The copy may only be provided in electronic format if the potential buyer agrees to receive it in that format (s.156(11)).

26.1.5. These duties do not apply to the seller if there is another person responsible for marketing the property whom the seller believes has the home information pack in his possession (HA 2004, s.155(2) and s.156(6)). If the seller is asked to provide a copy of the pack in this situation he must take reasonable steps to inform the potential buyer that the request should be made to the other person (HA 2004, s.156(7)).

26.1.6. The obligation to provide a copy of the pack does not apply where the responsible person believes that the person making the request:

(a) is unlikely to have sufficient means to buy the property;

(b) is not genuinely interested in buying a property of a general description which applies to the property; or

(c) is not a person to whom the seller is likely to be prepared to sell the property (HA 2004, s.156(4)).

The exceptions in s.156(4) do not authorise the doing of anything which constitutes an unlawful act of discrimination.

26.1.7. It is lawful to charge a fee to cover the reasonable costs of making and sending a paper copy of the pack to the potential buyer (HA 2004, s.156(8)). Where a fee is charged, the pack must be provided to the potential buyer within a period of 14 days beginning with the day on which the fee is paid or the terms agreed by the buyer (HA 2004, s.157(5)(a)).

26.1.8. The seller may impose conditions on potential buyers, or instruct his estate agent to do so, regarding the use or disclosure of any information contained in the home information pack (HA 2004, s.157(3)). Any conditions must be notified to the potential buyer before the end of a period of 14 days beginning with the day of the request (HA 2004, s.157(4)(a)(ii)). Where conditions have been imposed, the pack must be provided within a period of 14 days beginning with the day on which the potential buyer agreed to those conditions (HA 2004, s.157(5)(a)).

26.1.9. In addition to the above, where a responsible person provides a potential buyer with a copy of any document within the home information pack, or allows a potential buyer to inspect any document within the pack, he must ensure that the document is authentic and complies with the requirements of the regulations (HA 2004, s.159 (4) and (5)).

26.1.10. Electronic copies of the home information packs must not be used unless the potential buyer agrees to receive the pack in electronic format (HA 2004, s.156(11)).

26.1.11. None of the foregoing duties apply to residential property which is not available (and is marketed as not available) with vacant possession (HA 2004, s.160). The one exception to this rule is where two or more dwellings in a subdivided building are being sold as a single property with none of them being available for sale as a separate lot. If one of the dwellings is being sold with vacant possession then the duty to provide a home information pack arises in respect of the whole property (HA 2004, s.171(2); see also A26).

26.2   Implementation and transitional arrangements

26.2.1.   Regulations[1] made under HA 2004 provide for the detailed content of home information packs, their assembly, and enforcement. The central document in a home information pack, the energy performance certificate (EPC), is also subject to separate but related regulations[2] (see also A27).

26.2.2.   Home Information Pack (No.2) Regulations 2007 came into effect on 2 July 2007 and allow that the duties under HA 2004, ss.155–159 will come into effect in phases. The first phase began on 1 August 2007 and brings in the duties in HA 2004, s.155-159 for properties marketed as having 'four or more bedrooms'.[3]

26.2.3.   Further commencement orders are anticipated to bring in the HA 2004 duties for residential property with three or more bedrooms, and finally for all residential property marketed with vacant possession (with the exception of those properties listed in Part 6 of the Regulations (see A26.6). When these orders are made is dependent on the Department for Communities and Local Government's figures for the number of accredited domestic energy assessors. A similar phased introduction is applied to the energy performance regulations.

26.2.4.   Regulation 33 allows for the phased introduction by commencement orders. The commencement date will differ depending on the number of bedrooms the property is marketed as having. Regulation 33 states the duties to have and provide a home information pack do not arise in relation to a property where:

'(a)   the property is put on the market by or on behalf of the seller before the commencement date;

(b)   action taken at any time during the period starting with 1 June 2006 and ending before the commencement date by or on behalf of the seller, made public the fact that the property was on the market;

(c)   such action was taken with the intention of selling the property before the commencement date; and

(d)   such action was sustained to a reasonable extent after it was put on the market, during the period starting with 1 June 2006 and ending before the commencement date.'

26.2.5.   A further transitional arrangement is outlined in regulation 34. This allows that, until 1 January 2008, the duties in HA 2004, s.155–159 will only apply once the EPC and recommendation report, or the predicted energy assessment (PEA), is in the possession of the responsible person. To rely on this exception all the conditions in regulation 34(2) and (3) must be met:

(a)   the property is put on the market before 1 January 2008;

(b)   requests complying with regulation 18 for all required documents, not just the EPC or PEA, are delivered in accordance with regulation 19 before the property is marketed;

(c)   the responsible person continues to make all reasonable efforts to obtain required documents:

(i)   before a property is marketed; and

(ii)   within 28 days of marketing the property; and

(iii) after the first 28 days until the duties to provide a home information pack under the HA 2004 ending when a property is taken off the market or sold.

26.2.6.   If a seller has not provided a home information pack containing an EPC to the buyer in accordance with regulation 34, a further duty will arise[4] for the seller to provide an EPC free of charge to the buyer or tenant before the contract is entered into.

1. Home Information Pack (No.2) Regulations 2007 (SI 2007/1667).
2. Energy Performance of Buildings (Certificates and Inspections) (England and Wales) Regulations 2007 (SI 2007/991) as amended by Energy Performance of Buildings (Certificates and Inspections) (England and Wales) (Amendment) Regulations 2007 (SI 2007/1669).
3. Housing Act 2004 (Commencement No.8) (England and Wales) Order 2007 (SI 2007/1668). See A26.6 for the exceptions.
4. Energy Performance of Buildings (Certificates and Inspections) (England and Wales) (Amendment) Regulations 2007, regulation 4.

26.3.   **Content of a pack**

Regulations

26.3.1.   Home Information Pack (No.2) Regulations 2007 (SI 2007/1667) came into effect on 2 July 2007. The regulations cover:

(a)   the content of the home information pack;

(b)   assembly and accuracy of the home information pack;

(c)   exceptions to the duty to provide a home information pack;

(d)   enforcement of the regulations.

26.3.2.   The content of the home information pack is strictly controlled. The seller is only allowed to include the documents and information which are 'required' or 'authorised' by the regulations. 'Required' documents must be included and 'authorised' documents may be included. If the seller chooses to provide additional information outside the 'required' and 'authorised' categories, it must be made clear that the extra documents and information do not form part of the home information pack. The home information pack must be kept 'separate and clearly distinguished' from any other document (reg.4(3)).

26.3.3.   Unless the regulations allow for an official copy of a document to be included in the home information pack, all documents must be original versions or true copies of them (regs.5 and 6). Where documents contain a map, plan or drawing in which colours are used, the copy plan will be considered to be a true copy if the colours are reproduced with sufficient accuracy to enable them to be identified (reg.5(2)).

26.3.4. Only one original home information pack need be prepared with buyers being provided with copies of it (reg.6). All copies of the pack, or of the pack documents, must be true copies, or where the document is an official copy, either a true copy or another official copy.

26.3.5. The pack documents must be in English where the property is in England. Where the property is in Wales, the pack may be in English, Welsh or a combination of these languages.

26.3.6. Where the sale involves the creation of a new interest, for example the creation of a commonhold or lease of a newly created flat, the sale statement must be completed as if the interest was already in existence, that is, as if the lease had already been created (reg.10). The title of the superior estate from which the interest is being created must be deduced to comply with regulation 8(e), (f) and 9(j).

Required documents and information

26.3.7. Regulation 8(a)–(l) and lists the documents and information which are 'required' in the home information pack. The Schedules to the regulations prescribe the information that must be included in these required documents (see Appendix IX.5). The home information pack index must be the first document in the pack, followed by the EPC and/or for property not physically complete, a PEA. The remaining required items can appear in a pack in any order:

(a) home information pack index (Schedule 1);

(b) EPC and recommendation;

(c) for property which is not physically complete – a PEA (Schedule 2);

(d) a sale statement (Schedule 3);

(e) for property with registered title – an official copy of the title register and an official copy of the title plan;

(f) for property with unregistered title – a certificate of an official search of the index map and 'such other documents on which the seller can reasonably be expected to rely in order to deduce title';

(g) the replies to: enquiries of local authority (Schedule 7); drainage and water enquiries (Schedule 8); and to a search of the local land charges register;

(h) where property is being sold in the circumstances set out in HA 2004, s.171(2), any leases or licences to which the property is subject or will be subject following completion of the sale (e.g. the sale of the freehold of two linked properties, house and granny-flat, one with vacant possession and other tenanted);

(i) for leasehold property (Schedule 5):

    (i)   the lease;

    (ii)   the name and address of the current landlord and any managing agents or other managers;

    (iii) any management regulations;

    (iv) details of any amendments proposed in relation to the lease or management regulations;

    (v)   a summary of current or proposed works and agreements affecting the property and financial contribution to the cost;

    (vi) a summary or statements of service charges supplied in the last 36 months;

    (vii) most recent requests for payment (relating to the 12 months preceding the first point of marketing) for service charges, ground rent and insurance;

(j)   for new leasehold interests:

    (i)   the lease or terms of the lease proposed;

    (ii)   estimates of service charges, ground rent and insurance expected for the 12 months following completion;

(k)   for commonhold property (Schedule 4):

    (i)   an official copy of the title register and official copy of the title plan relating to the common parts;

    (ii)   official copy of the commonhold community statement;

    (iii) any additional rules or regulations made for managing the commonhold which are not included in the commonhold community statement;

    (iv) any amendments proposed to the commonhold community statement and any amendments to any other rules or regulations for managing the commonhold;

    (v)   most recent requests for payment of the commonhold assessment, reserve fund, and insurance received in the last 12 months;

    (vi) name and address of current or proposed managing agents and/or other managers;

    (vii) summary of current or proposed works affecting the property and/or common parts;

(l)   for new commonhold interests:

    (i)   the commonhold community statement or terms of the commonhold community statement proposed;

(ii)   estimates of commonhold assessment, reserve fund, and insurance payments expected for the 12 months following completion.

Authorised documents and information

26.3.8. In addition to the 'required' documents and information, a home information pack may also include any of the 'authorised' documents and information listed in regulation 9(a)–(p) and Schedule 10 (see Appendix IX.5):

    (a)   a home condition report which complies with Schedule 9 (this can only be provided by a member of a home inspectors certification scheme which has been approved by the Secretary of State under Part 8 of the regulations;

    (b)   any documentary evidence of any safety, building, repair or maintenance work carried out since the date of the home condition report;

    (c)   any policy, warranty or guarantee for defects in the design, building or conversion of the building;

    (d)   any information about standards to which the property has been built;

    (e)   an accurate translation in any language of any pack document;

    (f)   an additional version of any document, in any other format such as Braille or large print;

    (g)   a summary or explanation of any pack document;

    (h)   information identifying the property, e.g. a description, photograph or maps;

    (i)   information about a pack document, e.g. source of supply, complaints procedures;

    (j)   if the property is or includes a registered estate, official copies of any documents referred to in the individual register;

    (k)   additional information relating to a commonhold specified in Schedule 4, para.3;

    (l)   additional information relating to leaseholds as specified in Schedule 5;

    (m)   search reports (other than those required by reg.8) relating to matters such as common land, rights of access, ground stability (for example coal mining, tin mining, salt extraction), environmental hazards and flooding, telecommunication services, utility services, transport services and roads, liability to repair buildings outside of the property (for example chancel repairs);

    (n)   searches relating to another dwelling house in the vicinity of the property which contain information of interest to a potential buyer;

    (o)   any document referred to in a search report included in the pack under reg.8(j), (k) and (l) or under reg.9(m) and (n);

(p) information which relates to the list given in Schedule 10 and which would be of interest to potential buyers (see Appendix IX.5)

Using the Law Society's TransAction forms with home information packs

26.3.9. The Law Society has created a new suite of forms based on the previous TransAction forms (such as the Seller's Property Information Form and Seller's Leasehold Information Form) to facilitate the preparation of home information packs and the conveyancing transaction following acceptance of an offer. These forms may be viewed on the Law Society's website at **www.lawsociety.org.uk**. Explanatory notes for solicitors regarding the use of these forms are reproduced in Appendix V.13.

26.3.10. Form TA1 Home Information Pack Index and Form TA2 Sale Statement meet the requirements of Schedule 1 and Schedule 2 of regulations. Other forms, such as Form TA3 Required Leasehold Information and Form TA4 Required Commonhold Information, provide a convenient way to present in a home information pack names and addresses and summaries of information, which may not otherwise be contained in a formal document supplied by the seller or managing agent. Completing Form TA5 Proof of Requests for Missing Documents and Information is a way to demonstrate in a pack that the responsible person has met the requirements of the regulations in relation to items missing from a home information pack (see A26.4).

26.3.11. Form TA6 Property Information is purposefully brief to allow for its use as a possible 'authorised' document in a home information pack. It is similar in some respects to the 'Home Use Form' published in draft by the Department for Communities and Local Government.

26.3.12. Forms TA6–TA11 may be used as 'authorised' forms in a home information pack, although it is less likely that the detailed Form TA11 will be used in pack. The content of these forms is 'authorised' by Schedule 10 of the regulations.

26.3.13. Form TA6 is only for use in a pack but forms TA7–TA11 may also be used in non-home information pack transactions. Form TA11 replaces the Seller's Property Information Form, and Forms TA12 and TA13 are designed for use later in a transaction.

26.3.14. Form TA10 Fittings and Contents is a new edition of the previous Fixtures, Fittings and Contents Form (fourth edition). It is similar in some respects to the 'Home Contents' form published in draft by the Department for Communities and Local Government.

26.3.15. Forms TA14 Leasehold Information Request and TA15 Commonhold Information Request are designed to help gather information for inclusion in a home information pack. These forms may be sent to those in possession of this information (the seller and managing agents for example), but they will not be included in a home information pack.

26.3.16. The new TransAction forms do not include the warnings and advice which appeared on the first page of the some of the previous editions of the Trans Action forms, such as the Seller's Property Information Form. The Law Society is preparing some notes that may be given by solicitors to seller at the same time as the seller is asked to complete the forms. These notes will be available from the Law Society's website.

26.4. Documents missing from a pack

Unobtainable documents

26.4.1. Under regulation 20 the following documents may be omitted from the home information pack if, after making all reasonable efforts and enquiries, the responsible person believes that the document no longer exists or that it cannot be obtained from or created by any person:

(a) any predicted energy assessments (see reg.8(c));

(b) any documents relied on to deduce unregistered title (see reg.8(f)(ii));

(c) any required commonhold information (see reg.8(g));

(d) any required leasehold information (see reg.8(h));

(e) any leases or licences for dwelling houses to which HA, 2004, s.171(2) applies (see reg.8(i)).

Energy information

26.4.2. Regulation 16 allows the property to be marketed without the energy perform-ance certificate or predicted energy assessment if:

(a) the first point of marketing occurs on or after 1 January 2008;

(b) regulation 20 does not apply;

(c) the request for the document was delivered at least 14 days before the first point of marketing;

(b) the responsible person continues to use all 'reasonable' efforts to obtain the certificate within 28 days of the point of first marketing;

(c) it is included in the home information pack as soon as reasonably practicable; and

(d) proof of the request is included in the home information pack (a proof of request must comply with regulation 18(2)).

26.4.3. As part of the transitional arrangements, until 1 January 2008 the duty to provide a home information pack and EPC only applies once the EPC is available, provided that it was commissioned before the property was marketed. In this case the seller must provide the energy performance certificate before the contract is entered into (see A26.2).

Unavailable documents

26.4.4.   In certain circumstances the responsible person is allowed to market a property for a period of up to 28 days with a home information pack from which certain of the regulation 8 documents are omitted. For this exception to apply the conditions of in regulation 17 must be met. The conditions are:

(a)   the request for the document was delivered before the first point of marketing;

(b)   the responsible person believes (on reasonable grounds) that the document will be obtained within 28 days from the first point of marketing and uses all reasonable efforts to obtain the document before then;

(c)   it is reasonable to expect the document to be obtained before the expiry of the 28-day period if reasonable efforts are used;

(d)   the responsible person continues to use all reasonable efforts to obtain the document if it cannot be obtained within the 28-day period;

(e)   the home information pack index contains a statement of

(i)   the steps taken to obtain the document;

(ii)   the date by which the responsible person expects to obtain the documents;

(iii)   the reason for any delay which has occurred or is likely to occur in relation to the provision of the document;

(iv)   if delayed again, the further date by when the responsible person expects to obtain the document (Schedule 1, para.(f));

(f)   a proof of the request (complying with regulation 18(2)) is included in the pack.

26.5.   Assembly and accuracy of packs

26.5.1.   The home information pack must be available before the 'first point of marketing', that is the date on which the duty arises under HA 2004, s.155(1).

26.5.2.   If the property is taken off the market and then put back on the market within a year of the 'first point of marketing', no further 'first point of marketing' arises (reg.3(3)) so the original home information pack can be used.

26.5.3.   If the property is taken off the market and is put back on the market after the end of a period of one year from the 'first point of marketing', then another 'first point of marketing' will arise and the home information pack must be up to date to that point (reg.3(4)). When property is taken off the market because a buyer has been found and is put back on the market within 28 days of the offer being withdrawn, no further 'first point of marketing' will arise and the existing home information pack can still be used.

26.5.4. Regulations 13 and 15 contain provisions governing the order and age of the documents included in the home information pack at the first point of marketing. Under regulation 13 the pack must be arranged so that the first documents in the pack are, in order:

    1.   the Home Information Pack Index; and

    2.   the EPC and recommendation and /or the PEA.

The remaining documents may appear in any order.

26.5.5. The EPC and recommendation report and the PEA must be no more than 12 months old at the first point of marketing. The documents listed in regulation 8(e), (f)(i), (g), (h), (j), (k) and (l) must not be more than three months old at the first point of marketing (reg.15) (see Appendix IX.5). All other documents can be more than three months old but must be the most recent version. If any document has been amended since its issue that amendment must also be included in the pack (reg.15(3)).

26.5.6. Where the responsible person either amends a required document or obtains a further version of it, he must include the amended version in the pack and remove the earlier version. The point at which the document is amended becomes the 'first point of marketing' for that document (reg.21).

26.5.7. If the property is not physically complete before the first point of marketing but becomes so before the sale is completed, the home information pack must be updated to include an energy performance certificate and recommendation report (reg.22).

26.5.8. Authorised documents may (rather than must) be updated (reg.23).

26.5.9. If the responsible person is not the seller, the responsible person must provide the seller with a copy of any of the home information pack documents so that the seller can check its accuracy (reg.24).

26.6.   Exceptions from HA 2004 duties

26.6.1. Regulations 25–34 list a number of situations in which a home information pack does not have to be provided.

Non-residential premises

26.6.2. The sale of non-residential premises is excluded from the duties in HA 2004, ss.155–159. For the purposes of this exclusion, non-residential premises are:

  (a) property where the most recent use is or was primarily non-residential;

  (b) a dwelling-house which, from the manner in which it is marketed, will clearly be converted for primarily non-residential use by the time the sale has been completed.

26.6.3. If a question arises as to whether the property for sale is classed as 'non-residential premises' for the purposes of the duties contained in HA 2004, ss.155–159, regulation 25(c) states that premises will be non-residential premises if:

  '(a) the total area of land is 5 hectares or more; and

  (b) the most recent use of the land is or was primarily for one or more of the following purposes:

  (i) horticulture or cultivation;

  (ii) the breeding and keeping of animals or livestock; or

  (iii) as grazing land or woodlands.'

Holiday accommodation

26.6.4. The duties under ss.155–159 do not apply to the sale of holiday accommodation (reg.27).

Mixed sales

26.6.5. Where residential property is being sold with business property and, at the first point of marketing, the seller does not intend to accept an offer to sell the residential property in isolation from the business property, HA 2004, ss.155–159 will not apply (reg.28).

Dual use of a dwelling-house

26.6.6. Where the most recent use of the property was both residential and business use and the property is being marketed on the basis that it is suitable for both uses, a home information pack need not be provided (reg.29).

Portfolios of properties

26.6.7. There is no duty to provide a home information pack where a number of residential properties are being sold in a portfolio and the seller does not intend to accept an offer to buy one of the properties in isolation from the others (reg.30).

Unsafe properties and demolition

26.6.8. Where residential properties are being sold in an unsafe condition in that they pose a serious risk to the health and safety of occupants and visitors, or where properties are being sold as suitable for demolition and redevelopment, there is no duty to provide a home information pack (regs.31 and 32).

26.7.   Enforcement

26.7.1.   The duty to provide the home information pack will be enforced by the local weights and measures authority (HA 2004, s.166). It has the power to require the production of a home information pack (HA 2004, s.167) and, in the event of a breach of the duties in sections 155 and 156, it has power to issue a penalty charge notice (HA 2004, s.168). The penalty charge is £200 (reg.35).

26.7.2.   A potential buyer who commissions his own version of any of the prescribed documents, because he has not been provided with an authentic copy within the prescribed period, may recover any reasonable fee paid by him from the responsible person (HA 2004, s.170).

26.8.   Further information

26.8.1.   Procedural guidance on the home information pack and energy performance regulations is published by the Department for Communities and Local Government. The guidance and information regarding the implementation of home information packs in England and Wales can be found at **www.homeinformationpacks.gov.uk**.

26.8.2.   Information and guidance on issues relating to home information packs for solicitors can be found on the Law Society's website at **www.hips.lawsociety. org.uk**. The Law Society has also created its own home information pack product to be used in conjunction with its revised TransAction forms.

A27. Energy performance of buildings

27.1. The energy performance of buildings directive

27.1.1. The European Union directive on the energy performance of buildings ('the directive')[1] came into force on 4 January 2003. Its objective is 'to promote the improvement of the energy performance of buildings within the Community, taking into account outdoor climatic and local conditions, as well as indoor climate requirements and cost-effectiveness'.

27.1.2. The directive lays down requirements regarding a general framework for calculation of the energy performance of buildings, the application of minimum requirements for energy performance, energy certification of buildings and the regular inspection of air-conditioning systems and boilers.

27.1.3. The obligations to be met under the directive are to 'ensure that when buildings are constructed, sold or rented out, an energy performance certificate is made available to the owner or the prospective buyer or tenant, as the case may be'.

1. Directive 2002/91/EC of the European Parliament and of the Council of 16 December 2002 on the energy performance of buildings.

27.2. The Regulations

27.2.1. Energy Performance of Buildings (Certificates and Inspections) (England and Wales) Regulations 2007 (as amended)[1] ('the regulations') implement Articles 7, 9 and 10 of the directive. The duties required by the regulations are subject to a phased implementation (see A27.3). This implementation is complicated by the inclusion of energy performance certificates (EPCs) in home information packs and the duties of the 'responsible person' to make the pack available at the 'first point of marketing'.

27.2.2. The regulations create new duties for sellers and landlords prior to any agreement for sale or rent, and new duties on the construction of buildings and on the completion of certain modifications to existing buildings. The regulations will, in time, affect the majority of buildings in England and Wales.

27.2.3. For the purposes of the regulations a building means: 'a roofed construction having walls, for which energy is used to condition the indoor climate, and a reference to a building includes a reference to a part of building which has been designed or altered to be used separately.'

27.2.4. The regulations include provision for the:

- creation and supply of EPCs and recommendation reports;
- inclusion of an 'asset rating' or attachment of a copy of an EPC to the written particulars given to prospective buyers where a home information pack is required under Housing Act (HA) 2004, ss.155–159;
- production and display of display energy certificates (DECs);
- accreditation of energy assessors;
- creation of a register or registers to store certificates and reports;
- inspections of air-conditioning systems; and
- enforcement of duties.

27.2.5. Articles 3–6 of the directive have already been implemented in England and Wales by separate regulations[2] and the Building Regulations have been amended to allow for the establishment of standard methods to assess energy performance (see also B24.8).

1. Energy Performance of Buildings (Certificates and Inspections) (England and Wales) Regulations 2007 (SI 2007/991) as amended by Energy Performance of Buildings (Certificates and Inspections) (England and Wales) (Amendment) Regulations 2007 (SI 2007/1669).
2. Building and Approved Inspectors (Amendment) Regulations 2006 (SI 2006/652).

27.3 Implementation and transitional provisions

27.3.1. The regulations are subject to a phased implementation and the timetable at A27.3.4 provides further detail as to these phases.

27.3.2. The first phase of the implementation has been aligned with the phased introduction of home information packs (see A.26). An EPC must be included in a home information pack and the 'responsible person' under HA 2004 is under a duty to make the pack available at the 'first point of marketing'.

27.3.3. EPCs will, in time, be required where property is sold without being marketed, for example, on sales of local authority housing and sales between family members. The certificates will apply to both commercial and residential property.

27.3.4. Schedule 1 (as amended)[1] of the regulations provides for the phased introduction of duties to provide an EPC, dependant on the use and size of the building and whether it is newly constructed. An outline of the intended phased implementation from 1 January 2008 is detailed below:

- 1 January 2008
    - on construction of all new dwellings
- 6 April 2008
    - on the sale of buildings other than dwellings with a floor area of 500m^2 or more
    - on the rent of buildings other than dwellings with a floor area of 500m^2 or more
    - on construction of all new non-dwellings
- 1 October 2008
    - on the sale or rent of all buildings

1. Schedule 1 is amended by the Energy Performance of Buildings (Certificates and Inspections) (England and Wales) (Amendment) Regulations 2007 (SI 2007/1669).

27.4. Energy performance certificate and recommendation report

27.4.1. The EPC must be issued by an energy assessor accredited to produce EPCs for the particular category of buildings concerned (see A27.7). In most cases it will be prepared following a physical inspection of the building. The energy assessor's inspection will involve the compilation of various details of a building, including size, type, age, construction materials, insulation, roof type, heating systems, and amount and type of glazing.

27.4.2. The information gathered during the inspection and the criteria applied to it will differ depending on whether the building is or will be a dwelling and whether it is newly constructed.[1] The certificate is generated from this data using a standard software package and must contain the information specified in reg.11. An example of an EPC for a marketed sale of a dwelling is reproduced in Appendix IX.6.

27.4.3. An EPC for an existing dwelling will contain the asset rating, reference information (including the unique reference number as stored on the central register), date, estimated energy use, details of the energy assessor, details on how to complain, and general advice on energy efficiency. It must also be accompanied by a recommendation report.

Asset rating

27.4.4. The asset rating is a main element of the EPC. It is a numerical indicator of the amount of energy estimated to meet the needs of a standard use of a building. In some circumstances it may be supplied separately to the EPC (see A27.8.4). It comprises two graphs illustrating the energy efficiency rating (how energy efficient the home is) and the environmental impact rating (in terms of carbon dioxide emissions) of the building.

27.4.5. The asset rating of a building is calculated according to a government approved methodology. The rating is expressed by a number between 1 and 100 (with 100 being the most efficient) and, graphically, by coloured bands labelled A–G (with A being the most efficient) similar to the ratings given to household white goods.

27.4.6. The asset rating is calculated by comparing various details of a building to a model of how energy efficient a building of that type and size ought to be. It does not record the actual energy consumption of a building.

Recommendation report

27.4.7. A recommendation report is prepared by the energy assessor who carries out the energy assessment and such a report must accompany the EPC. The report must make recommendations for the improvement of the energy performance of the building. For each improvement the cost of making it and the typical saving gained by making it are given. The asset rating graphs in the EPC show the 'potential' ratings which could be achieved for the building if all the recommendations are acted upon.

Registration and validity

27.4.8. The EPC and recommendation report, and the data collected to generate it, must be entered by the energy assessor on a central register prior to supplying it to the person who commissioned the EPC. It must remain stored in the register for a period of at least 20 years (reg.31).

27.4.9. An EPC for an existing dwelling remains valid for a period of 10 years, except when the duty to supply a home information pack under HA 2004, ss.155–159 applies. In this case the EPC must be no more than 12 months old at the first point of marketing (see A26.5.5). The age of the EPC in these circumstances is under review by the government.

27.4.10. The central register for EPCs commissioned where a home information pack is required under HA 2004 and home condition reports (HCRs) is maintained by the Landmark Information Group (**www.hcrregister.com**). The EPC for a building can be viewed and printed using this website by entering the unique reference number that appears on the EPC.

27.4.11. A form of EPC to be used in the marketing of dwellings is available from the Department for Communities and Local Government website at **www.communities.gov.uk**. The form of EPC for non-dwellings, newly constructed buildings and buildings to which major modifications have been made may differ from the form of EPC for existing dwellings.

1. Regulation 17A Building Regulations 2000 (SI 2000/2531) as inserted by reg.15 Building and Approved Inspectors (Amendment) Regulations 2006 (SI 2006/652) give the authority to approve assessment methodologies to the Secretary of State. Details of these methodologies are given in a circular issued by the Department for Communities and Local Government at **www.communities. gov.uk**.

27.5. Predicted energy assessment (PEA)

27.5.1. The PEA is a 'required' document in a home information pack for residential dwellings that are not physically complete at the first point of marketing (see A26.3.7). The content of a PEA is prescribed in Home Information Pack (No.2) Regulations 2007 (SI 2007/1667), Sched.2. The main element of the PEA is an 'asset rating' which is expressed on the PEA in the same way as it is in an EPC (see A27.4.4).

27.5.2. Unlike an EPC, the PEA is not compiled by means of a physical inspection of the building. It is generated based on the plans and specifications of a building to be constructed.

27.5.3. The PEA does not need to be created by an energy assessor and it does not need to be entered and stored on a central register.

27.6. Display energy certificate (DEC) and advisory report

27.6.1. The DEC is required for large buildings occupied by public authorities or other institutions providing public services to a large number of people. Regulation 16 provides for occupiers of such buildings to have a valid advisory report and to display a valid DEC in a prominent place.

27.6.2. The DEC and advisory report are created by an energy assessor accredited to produce EPCs for the particular category of building concerned (see A27.7). The DEC illustrates the energy performance of a building based on actual energy used and contains an operational rating (reg.15). The advisory report makes recommendations for the improvement of the energy efficiency of such a building.

27.7. Energy assessors

27.7.1. An EPC must be created by an energy assessor who is a member of an accreditation scheme approved by the Secretary of State. The energy assessor must be accredited to produce EPCs for the particular category of building concerned (reg.25).

27.7.2. There are a number of accreditation schemes for domestic energy assessors that have been approved by the Secretary of State. These include schemes run by the following companies and organisations (see Appendix VIII.2):

- Building Research Establishment

- Elmhurst

- NES

- Northgate

- Royal Institution of Chartered Surveyors (RICS)

- EPC Ltd

- Quidos

- Home Inspector Certification Ltd

27.7.3. Such accreditation schemes must contain adequate provision for indemnity arrangements and for facilitating the resolution of complaints (reg.25).

27.7.4. Further accreditation schemes for buildings that are not dwellings and newly constructed buildings are to be approved by the Secretary of State (see **www.communities.gov.uk/epbd** for the most up-to-date list of accreditation schemes).

27.8. Duties of the seller

27.8.1. The seller of a building must make available to any potential buyer a copy of a valid EPC and recommendation report free of charge at the earliest opportunity and before entering into a contract for sale (reg.5(2)). The earliest opportunity will be the sooner of the following events:

- when following a request, written information about the building is made available to the potential buyer; or

- when following a request, the building is viewed by a potential buyer.

27.8.2. The seller's duty to make an EPC and recommendation report available to any prospective buyers does not apply (reg.5(3)) if the seller reasonably believes that the prospective buyer:

- is unlikely to have sufficient means to buy the building; or

- is not genuinely interested in buying a building of a general description which applies to the building; or

- is not a person to whom the seller is prepared to sell the building.

27.8.3. An EPC provided by the seller is valid if it is no more than 10 years old and no other EPC has been created since it was made, unless the EPC is provided in circumstances where the duty to supply a home information pack under HA 2004, ss.155–159 applies. In this case an EPC is only valid if it is not more than 12 months old and no other EPC has been created since it was made.

27.8.4. When a building is marketed for sale and the duties in HA 2004, ss.155–159 apply to the property, the person giving any written particulars to potential buyers must attach either an EPC or an asset rating (reg.6).[1]

27.8.5. The seller has a duty under reg.5(5) to ensure that the person who ultimately becomes the buyer of the building has a valid copy of the EPC and recommendation report free of charge.

1. See reg.6 as to the specific requirements and definition of written particulars.

27.9.   Duties of the landlord

27.9.1. The prospective landlord of a building must supply to any potential tenant a valid EPC and recommendation report free of charge at the earliest opportunity and before entering into a contract for tenancy is made. The earliest opportunity will be the sooner of the following events:

- when following a request, written information about the building is made available to the potential tenant; or

- when following a request, the building is viewed by a potential tenant.

27.9.2. The landlord's duty to make an EPC and recommendation report available to any prospective tenant does not apply (reg.5(3)) if the landlord reasonably believes that the prospective tenant:

- is unlikely to have sufficient means to rent the building; or

- is not genuinely interested in renting a building of a general description which applies to the building; or

- is not a person to whom the landlord is prepared to rent the building.

27.9.3. The landlord has a duty under reg.5(5) to ensure that the person who ultimately becomes the tenant of the building has a valid copy of the EPC and recommendation report free of charge.

27.10.   Duties on construction

27.10.1. Regulation 8 and Sched.2 relate to EPCs on construction and provide that where a building is erected, or a building is modified to change the number of parts for separate use, the person carrying out the work shall on completion:

- supply an EPC to the owner of the building; and

- give to the local authority notice to that effect.

27.10.2. The duty to provide an EPC does not apply to buildings whose construction is not yet complete.

27.11. Exemptions

27.11.1. Regulation 4 provides that the following buildings do not require an EPC:

- buildings which are used primarily or solely as places of worship;

- temporary buildings with a planned time of use of two years or less;

- industrial sites, workshops and non-residential agricultural buildings with low energy demand;

- stand-alone buildings with a total useful floor area of less than 50m² which are not dwellings.

27.11.2. Under reg.7 the duty to provide an EPC and recommendation report may not apply where buildings are to be demolished.

27.12. Enforcement

27.12.1. The local Weights and Measures Authority is responsible for the enforcement of the duties under the regulations (reg.38). An authorised officer of an enforcement authority has power to require the production of documents for inspection (reg.39) and, in the event of a breach of duty, has the power to issue a penalty charge notice (reg.40). The amount of the penalty charge is determined according to the category of building and the breach concerned (reg.43). An appeal against such a penalty charge notice lies to the county court (reg.45).

27.12.2. Regulation 42 provides a defence where an EPC is unobtainable. A seller, landlord or builder (or person responsible for the construction of a new building) will not be liable to a penalty charge notice for not having or supplying an EPC if he can demonstrate that he made a proper request for an EPC at least 14 days before the relevant time at which he was required to have the same available and that despite all reasonable attempts he did not have the same in his possession or control at that time.

27.12.3. There is also provision to avoid a double penalty where a £200 penalty charge is levied for failure to provide a compliant home information pack (reg.41).

27.13. Further information

27.13.1. The website of the Department of Communities and Local Government contains further information and guidance on the implementation of the regulations (see **www.communities.gov.uk/epbd**).

B. PRE-EXCHANGE

B1. Pre-contract negotiations

1.1. Effect of 'subject to contract'

1.1.1. The phrase 'subject to contract' may no longer be of great importance in view of the fact that Law of Property (Miscellaneous Provisions) Act 1989, s.2, requires the contract for the sale of land to be in writing and signed by both parties. It is unlikely that a contract would inadvertently be entered into by correspondence between the parties (see B1.6.3).

1.1.2. The inclusion of the phrase 'subject to contract' will normally act as a suspensory condition which will prevent the formation of a binding contract until such time as the effect of the condition is removed, e.g. on exchange.

1.1.3. Once introduced, the phrase will continue to govern subsequent correspondence until its effect is expressly or impliedly removed. It is thus not essential that every item of pre-contract correspondence carries the suspensory condition.

1.2. A contract already exists

1.2.1. The phrase 'subject to contract' can only give protection to the parties where no contract exists. If a contract has already come into existence the phrase cannot invalidate or eradicate that contract.

1.3. Removal of suspensory condition

1.3.1. The condition will normally remain in effect until removed with the consent of both parties on exchange. It cannot be removed unilaterally.[1]

1.3.2. However, care should be taken to ensure that the wording of correspondence or telephone conversations does not imply the current existence of a contract which will negate the effect of the 'subject to contract' formula.[2]

1.3.3. The phrase should thus be used with care and not regarded as a magic formula which will protect the parties in all circumstances.

1. *Sherbrooke* v. *Dipple* (1980) 255 EG 1203.
2. See *Griffiths* v. *Young* [1970] Ch 675; *Michael Richards Properties Ltd* v. *Corporation of Wardens of St. Saviour's Parish Southwark* [1975] 3 All ER 416.

1.4.   Protracted negotiations

1.4.1. In *Cohen* v. *Nessdale*,[1] it was held that the phrase 'subject to contract' continued to govern negotiations despite an interval of some eight months; however, it is unwise to rely on this decision as the continued protection of the phrase cannot be guaranteed in all circumstances.

1.4.2. Where negotiations for the property have become interrupted or protracted a solicitor should not rely on the continued effect of the phrase 'subject to contract'. When negotiations recommence after an interval the 'subject to contract' formula should be repeated in all subsequent correspondence to ensure its continued protection pending the resolution of the negotiations.

1. [1982] 2 All ER 97.

1.5.   Contract denied

1.5.1. Difficulties have in the past arisen over the use of the phrase 'subject to contract'[1] and some solicitors prefer to use the words 'contract denied' in preference to 'subject to contract'. However, there is no reported decision on the effect of the phrase 'contract denied' and the phrase should therefore, for safety's sake, be regarded as being similar in operation and effect to the words 'subject to contract'.

1. See *Law* v. *Jones* [1974] Ch 112; *cf. Tiverton Estates* v. *Wearwell Ltd* [1975] Ch 146.

1.6.   Need for written contract

1.6.1. In most cases the requirement for a written contract for the sale of land will be satisfied by the formal exchange of contracts by the parties, following negotiations conducted by their respective solicitors (see B11).

1.6.2. To ensure that no contract inadvertently comes into existence before the parties are ready to exchange it is customary to qualify all pre-contract correspondence with the words 'subject to contract' or 'contract denied'.

1.6.3. In exceptional cases an exchange of correspondence may satisfy the requirements of section 2 Law of Property (Miscellaneous Provisions) Act 1989, but only where:

(a)   the letters set out or incorporate all the terms of the agreement; and

(b)   there is an intention that the exchange of letters will result in a binding contract.[1]

Correspondence which is headed 'subject to contract' cannot fulfil the above conditions.[2]

1.   *Commission for the New Towns* v. *Cooper (Great Britain) Ltd* [1995] 26 EG 129, CA.
2.   *Ibid.*

1.7.   Collateral contracts

1.7.1.   Section 2 Law of Property (Miscellaneous Provisions) Act 1989 requires that all agreed terms be incorporated into the written contract. As a result, a contract will be invalid if it omits any of the terms agreed between the parties.

1.7.2.   One way around this rule was for the party attempting to enforce the contract to argue that the omitted terms form a collateral contract, and do not have to be included in the main contract. The courts are increasingly reluctant to accept such argument so care should be taken to include all the terms in the main contract.

1.7.3.   In *Grossman* v. *Hooper*,[1] Chadwick LJ used the example of the sale of a house and carpets and curtains. If the parties have agreed that the sale of the house will be without the carpets and curtains and later they enter into a separate agreement for the sale of the carpets and curtains, this later agreement could be regarded as independent of the property contract. However, if the agreement for the sale of the house includes the carpets and curtains, the terms relating to the chattels must be included or incorporated into the property contract. If the terms are omitted, the property contract will not satisfy section 2 Law of Property (Miscellaneous Provisions) Act 1989.

1.7.4.   It may be possible to avoid this problem by including a clause in the property contract to the effect that all matters agreed in correspondence between the parties' solicitors should be deemed to be included in that contract.[2]

1.   *Grossman* v. *Hooper* [2001] 2 EGLR 82.
2.   *Jones* v. *Forest Fencing* [2001] NPC 165.

1.8.   Lock-out agreements

1.8.1.   A lock-out agreement where the seller agrees not to negotiate with any third party for a specified period of time is capable of being a valid collateral contract and does not need to satisfy the requirements of Law of Property (Miscellaneous Provisions) Act 1989, s.2.[1] A lock-in agreement, i.e. to negotiate with these parties only, is never valid.[2]

1.8.2. Breach of a lock-out agreement does not give rise to a claim for substantial damages nor for long-term injunctive relief.[3]

1. *Pitt* v. *PHH Asset Management Ltd* [1993] EGCS 127; *Walford* v. *Miles* [1992] 2 AC 128, HL.
2. *Courtney & Fairburn Ltd* v. *Tolaini Bros Ltd* [1975] 1 WLR 297.
3. *Moroney* v. *Isofam Investments SA* [1997] EGCS 178; *Tye* v. *House* [1997] 41 EG 160, CA.

B2. Contract races

2.1. Solicitors' Code of Conduct 2007

2.1.1. Where a seller's solicitor is asked by his client to deal simultaneously with more than one prospective buyer he is required to comply with Rule 10.06 Solicitors' Code of Conduct 2007 (relations with third parties).

2.1.2. Compliance with the Rule is mandatory and breach thereof can lead to disciplinary action being taken against the solicitor.

2.1.3. The Rule applies irrespective of whether the prospective buyers are supplied with their contracts simultaneously or whether contracts are issued to different prospective buyers one after the other. The supply of documentation such as a plan of the land or Land Registry title number in order to facilitate the transfer of the premises to a buyer is covered by the Rule. As the Rule prohibits 'dealing' with more than one prospective buyer, it is not necessary for each prospective buyer to be supplied with a 'contract', nor need each contract be in identical terms. The Rule applies to both domestic and commercial transactions. The Rule also applies where the seller's solicitor knows that the second (and subsequent) buyer(s) are being dealt with directly by the seller without the solicitor's involvement.

2.1.4. Where, having supplied a prospective buyer with a draft contract or other documentation, the seller later receives a further offer for the property which later offer he would prefer to accept, the seller may accept the second offer but his solicitor should give notice of withdrawal to the first prospective buyer's solicitor prior to dealing with the second prospective buyer and submitting draft papers to him. If notice of withdrawal is given, Rule 10.06 does not apply. Similarly, if the first prospective buyer's solicitor returns the papers to the seller's solicitor before papers are submitted to the second prospective buyer, only one buyer would be in possession of draft papers at any given time, thus a contract race does not exist and Rule 10.06 does not apply. The Rule does not apply to the distribution of auction papers to potential bidders or their solicitors, but does apply where a prospective buyer by private treaty is part of a draft contract and the seller then decides to put the property into auction.

2.1.5. Where information is provided for an estate agent or for a home information pack provider only as part of the home information pack, the solicitor will not have 'dealt' with the prospective buyers and Rule 10.06 will not apply. However, providing additional information, either directly or indirectly through an estate agent or home information pack provider, will normally amount to a 'dealing'.

2.2.   **Solicitor acting for seller**

2.2.1.   Where a solicitor is acting for the seller he must explain to his client that the solicitor is required to comply with the Conduct Rule referred to above, and if the seller refuses to allow the solicitor to make the notification the solicitor must decline to act; see Rule 10.06(1) and (2) Solicitors' Code of Conduct 2007.

2.3.   **Disclosure of race to buyers**

2.3.1.   If the seller instructs the solicitor to deal with more than one prospective purchaser, other than in a sale by auction or tender, the solicitor must at once disclose the seller's decision direct to the solicitor acting for each prospective buyer or (where no solicitor is acting) to the prospective buyer(s) in person. Such disclosure should be made immediately by the most suitable means but if made face to face, or by telephone, the solicitor should consider confirming the instruction in writing. Prior to making the disclosure the client's authority must be obtained. If the client refuses to give his authority the solicitor must refuse to act.

2.3.2.   The solicitor's obligation under Rule 10.06 will also arise where, to the solicitor's knowledge, the seller deals directly with another prospective buyer (or their conveyancer) or the seller instructs another solicitor to deal with another prospective buyer.

2.3.3.   Since buyers are themselves wary of entering into contract races, the seller should also be warned of the danger of losing the prospective buyers altogether if a race is commenced. It is normally preferable to avoid a contract race if at all possible.

2.4.   **Acting for seller and buyer**

2.4.1.   Even where a solicitor would normally be entitled to act for both the seller and buyer, e.g. because the situation falls within one of the exceptions set out in Rule 3.10 Solicitors' Code of Conduct 2007, the contract race gives rise to a significant risk of conflict of interests between the two clients and the solicitor must not continue to act for both; see Rule 10.06(3) Solicitors' Code of Conduct 2007.

2.5.   Acting for more than one buyer

2.5.1.   Where forms of contract are submitted to more than one prospective buyer, a solicitor must not accept instructions to act for more than one such buyer; Rule 10.06(4) Solicitors' Code of Conduct 2007.

2.6.   Licensed conveyancers

2.6.1.   Licensed conveyancers may be regarded in the same light as solicitors; thus, for the purpose of the Rule, disclosure of a contract race to a licensed conveyancer can be treated as disclosure of the race to the client of the conveyancer. Disclosure of the existence of the race must, however, be made directly to the buyer if that buyer is represented by an unqualified person. Authorised practitioners may be regarded in the same light as licensed conveyancers.

B3. Seller's investigation of title

3.1. Seller's investigation of title

3.1.1. Having obtained official copy entries of the title (registered land) or the seller's title deeds or a copy of them (unregistered land), the seller's solicitor should investigate title before drafting the contract for sale. The manner and method of such investigation is dealt with in D2. Existing land/charge certificates no longer have any legal status and thus their loss/absence is not a matter of concern.

3.2. Reasons for investigation

3.2.1. The investigation of the title by the seller's solicitor at this stage of the transaction is a precautionary measure to ensure that:

(a) the seller is the owner of or is otherwise entitled to sell the whole of the estate in accordance with the instructions given to his solicitor;

(b) any incumbrances on the title can be revealed in the draft contract in order to satisfy the seller's duty of disclosure;

(c) any defects in the title may be spotted and appropriate steps taken to rectify them before exchange of contracts;

(d) any consents which may be necessary from third parties may be obtained;

(e) any requisitions on title by the buyer can be anticipated, and if necessary an appropriate special condition may be included in the draft contract.

3.2.2. Not all covenants noted on the register at first registration will be binding. The Registrar is not required to check the validity of a covenant on first registration. Rule 35 Land Registration Rules 2003 requires him 'to enter a notice in the register of the burden of any interest which appears from his examination of title to affect the registered estate'. If the applicant for first registration wishes to have a particular covenant omitted from the register he must produce evidence that the covenant is void due to its lack of registration under Land Charges Act 1972.[1] Unless such an application is made the Registrar will enter a notice of the covenant on the register.

1. See G3.4.6–3.4.8 for further details of Land Registry requirements.

3.3. **Registered titles**

3.3.1. Obtain up-to-date official copy entries of the title and check to ensure that no entries have been made which will affect the seller's right to sell the property as instructed, e.g. there may be a restriction or a caution against dealings on the register. (Although cautions against dealings were abolished with prospective effect by Land Registration Act 2002, existing cautions were unaffected.)

3.3.2. On first registration of the title positive covenants may have been omitted from the register; in such a case the seller will need to take an indemnity covenant from the buyer and provide the buyer with a copy of the transfer which imposed the covenants in order to prove the need for indemnity. This latter will involve the inspection of pre-registration title deeds.

3.4. **Unregistered titles**

3.4.1. Check when the compulsory registration order came into force in the area and that no dealings which would have induced registration have occurred since that date. The date of compulsory registration for each district is set out in Land Registry Practice Guide 51.

3.4.2. In most cases the land will require registration after completion of this transaction. Although this will primarily be the responsibility of the buyer, this factor should be borne in mind by the seller's solicitor in his pre-contract investigation of title so that any areas of difficulty which might be the subject of a requisition by the Land Registry may be clarified.

3.4.3. If it transpires that the land should have been registered on a previous disposition, an immediate application for late registration must be made by the seller's solicitor, a full disclosure of the situation being made to both the seller and the buyer's solicitor. Title will then need to be dealt with as if the seller's title was awaiting registration at the Land Registry (see B4).

3.4.4. An index map search should be made to ensure that no part of the land has already been registered without the owner's knowledge and that no caution against first registration affects the land (see B10).

3.4.5. A Land Charges Department search should be made against the name of the seller to ensure that no incumbrances exist other than those revealed by the title deeds (see B10).

Freeholds

3.4.6. (a) Decide which document is to be used as the root of title, and check the validity of the chain of title forwards from that time.

(b) Does the root document refer to any earlier documents which the buyer may be entitled to call for?

(c) Are there any pre-root covenants which need to be disclosed to the buyer?

(d) Are all documents within the chain correctly stamped and executed?

(e) Watch for change of names, e.g. on marriage or change of a company name. Obtain evidence of the changes if necessary.

(f) If in doubt as to the effectiveness of restrictive covenants, options or third party rights revealed by the title, a Land Charges Department search should be made to clarify the position.

(g) Obtain copies of any necessary death certificates or grants of representation.

Existing leaseholds

3.4.7. Law of Property Act 1925, s.44 limits the right of an intended lessee or assignee of an existing lease to require production of the reversionary title or titles. This limitation, however, does not apply to:

(a) registered land or a term of years to be derived out of registered land; or

(b) a contract for the grant of a lease to which the compulsory registration provisions apply.[1]

Where the lease falls outside the compulsory registration provisions and there is little or no premium payable for its assignment the buyer may be content not to insist on deduction of the reversionary title.

3.4.8. Problems may, however, arise if the title to the freehold was not called for on the original grant of the lease. The following points should be checked:

(a) Is a marked copy of the freehold title available or can it be obtained? If not, check that the contract excludes the buyer's right to deduction of the freehold.

(b) Check the chain of title from the lease (or sub-lease) including evidence of surrenders and copies of any necessary consents, e.g. to assignments or alterations.

(c) Is consent to this assignment required? If so, obtain the names of referees from the buyer's solicitor and forward them to the landlord's solicitor. Obtain a firm estimate from the landlord's solicitor before giving an undertaking for costs.

(d) Is the freehold or superior leasehold title registered? Whether or not this is so can be ascertained by making an index map search. Where the freehold or superior title is registered official copy entries of the title can be obtained by the buyer. This may overcome the limitation posed by the seller being unable to deliver the freehold or superior leasehold title.

1. Law of Property Act 1925, s.44; as amended by Land Registration Act 2002, Sched.11, para.2.

3.5. **Title in name of sole owner**

3.5.1. Instructions will have revealed whether anyone other than the seller is living at the property. If there is, consideration should be given to the question of whether the occupants have any rights in the property which may impede the seller's intention of selling with vacant possession.

Is the seller married or in a civil partnership?

3.5.2. The seller's spouse or civil partner may have statutory rights of occupation under Family Law Act 1996 and/or a beneficial interest in the property through a contribution to the purchase price. Enquiries should also be made to ascertain whether the non-owning spouse or civil partner has the benefit of an occupation order under Family Law Act 1996.

Homes rights

3.5.3. Current registration of such rights can be verified by inspecting official copy entries of the title (registered land) or by making a Land Charges Department search against the seller (unregistered land). Even if such rights are not presently protected by registration the spouse or civil partner may still effect a registration at any time until actual completion.

Rights are already registered

3.5.4. It will be a condition of the contract that such registration is removed before completion.[1] Negotiations must be entered into with the spouse's or civil partner's solicitors for the removal of the charge and a satisfactory solution obtained before exchange of contracts.

Rights in existence but not registered

3.5.5. It is unsafe to assume that the spouse or civil partner will not exercise the right to register a charge under Family Law Act 1996 and instructions should be obtained directly from the spouse or civil partner (through a separate solicitor if there is any possibility of conflict of interests) to confirm their acquiescence in the proposed sale. A formal release of rights and agreement not to enforce any such rights against the seller should be prepared for signature before exchange by the non-owning spouse or civil partner.

3.5.6. A registration under Family Law Act 1996 can be removed on production of:

(a) an application made by the person with the benefit of the rights;

(b) a divorce decree absolute or dissolution order for a civil partnership;

(c) a court order to that effect;

(d) the death certificate of the spouse;

unless an order under s.33(5) of the Act has been made and registered.

Beneficial interests

3.5.7.   If it is thought that the spouse or civil partner may also be entitled to a beneficial interest in the property it should be assumed that the property is held by the seller on constructive trust for himself and his spouse or civil partner. The spouse's or civil partner's independent confirmation of agreement to the sale must be obtained and the spouse or civil partner joined as a party to the contract. A solicitor would be well advised to explain to the spouse or civil partner that his/her written consent to the sale is required, that giving such consent may affect his/her legal rights and that the spouse or civil partner should obtain independent advice before signing the release. The dangers of negligence and undue influence should also be noted where the owning spouse or civil partner 'persuades' the non-owning spouse or civil partner to consent to the transaction (see Appendix IV.8).

3.5.8.   Suggested form of wording for release of rights:

  (a)   'In consideration of the buyer entering this agreement I (*name of spouse or civil partner*) agree:

     (i)   to the sale of the property on the terms of this agreement; and

     (ii)   that I will not register rights in relation to the property, whether under Family Law Act 1996 or otherwise, and that I will procure before completion the removal of any registration made by me; and

     (iii) that I will vacate the property by the completion date.'[2]

  or

  (b)   'In consideration of your today entering into a contract with (*name of owning spouse or civil partner*) for the purchase of the property known as (*insert address of property to be sold*), I agree:

     (i)   to release any beneficial interest which I may have in the property (such interest, if any, being transferred to the proceeds of sale of the property), such release to be effective from the date of completion of the sale of this property;

     (ii)   to procure the cancellation of any registration which may have been effected by me or on my behalf on or before completion, including any registration in respect of rights of occupation which I may have under Family Law Act 1996; and

     (iii) to vacate the property by the completion date.'[3]

Sharers and co-habitees

3.5.9.   Sharers and co-habitees may be able to establish a beneficial interest in the property through contribution to the purchase price. Investigation must be made of the exact status of each occupier. If necessary a release of rights should be obtained, or they may be joined as parties to the contract. The solicitor should advise the sharer/co-habitee in similar terms to those suggested in B3.5.7. Enquiries should also be made to ascertain whether the non-owning occupier has the benefit of an occupation order under Family Law Act 1996, s.33.

Overriding interests

3.5.10. Persons in actual occupation of registered land may have overriding interests.[4] A formal release of such rights should be obtained. The occupiers may also be joined as contracting parties.

3.5.11. If the existence of a beneficial interest is suspected, the buyer's solicitor may request the appointment of a second trustee to overreach the interest (see B3.6.2).

Tenants

3.5.12. If vacant possession is to be given of the property on completion effective steps must be taken to terminate the tenancies.

3.5.13. If vacant possession is not to be given on completion full details of the tenancies must be obtained since disclosure of the tenancies must be made in the draft contract. Accurate information will be required by the buyer in relation to the amount of rent payable by the tenants, the dates of rent reviews, and the effect of any security of tenure legislation on the tenancies.

1. Family Law Act 1996, Sched.4, para.3(1).
2. This clause should be included in the contract of sale.
3. This clause may either be incorporated in the contract or drawn up as a separate document and attached to the contract. In either case the clause should be signed by the non-owning spouse.
4. Land Registration Act 2002, Sched.1, para.2, Sched.3, para.2 and Sched.12, para.8.

3.6. **Death of a joint proprietor**

Registered land

Registration of restriction

3.6.1. A restriction in either Form A or the earlier Form 62 registered in the proprietorship register indicates that the equitable interest was held on a tenancy in common and two trustees will be needed to transfer the legal estate. A buyer will normally insist that the seller obtains the appointment of a new trustee or the removal of the restriction before taking a transfer from him. If he does not do this then, on lodging his application for registration of the transfer, the buyer would need to produce to the Land Registry such evidence as will satisfy the Registrar that the registered estate is no longer subject to a trust of land.[1] Such evidence might comprise a statutory declaration by the sole survivor that in stated circumstances the declarant has become entitled legally and beneficially to the registered land, that he has not incumbered his undivided share, and that he has not received notice of any incumbrance upon the undivided share of the deceased proprietor. A certificate by the seller's conveyancer will be accepted in place of a declaration if the conveyancer is able to speak from his knowledge of all the relevant facts.

Appointment of second trustee

3.6.2. The seller's solicitor may be appointed as the new trustee provided that there is no conflict of interest between the instructing client and the other person(s) now entitled to the remainder of the property. The appointment of the second trustee should be dealt with as a matter of urgency so that there are two trustees named in the contract. If there is difficulty over the appointment of a second trustee the contract may include a clause providing that a second trustee will be appointed prior to execution of the purchase deed, the existing trustee contracting alone at this stage of the transaction. This latter situation should be avoided if possible because it is less satisfactory to the buyer who in contracting with one trustee alone has no guarantee that the matter will proceed smoothly to completion.

No restriction registered

3.6.3. Where no restriction is registered the equitable interest may be presumed to have been held under a joint tenancy and the sole surviving joint tenant may sell on production of the death certificate of the deceased.[2]

Unregistered land

3.6.4. Check the document under which the joint owners acquired the property to ascertain whether it was held on a joint tenancy or tenancy in common.

Tenancy in common

3.6.5. The existence of two trustees of the legal estate gives the buyer the assurance that any subsisting beneficial interests will be overreached on completion, thus removing any doubt which may exist as to whether the deceased had disposed of his interest in the property during his lifetime (see above).

Joint tenancy

3.6.6. Check the deed by which the joint tenants bought the property to ensure that no memorandum of severance is endorsed on it and make a bankruptcy search in the Land Charges Department to establish that no bankruptcy proceedings were or are pending against either joint tenant (see B10). Provided that these conditions are satisfied, the sole survivor may sell with a certificate that he is a sole beneficial owner on production of the death certificate of the deceased joint tenant. Again, provided that these conditions are satisfied, the personal representatives of a last surviving joint tenant can convey the land on production of the grant so long as the conveyance contains a statement that the survivor was solely and beneficially entitled to the property. If the joint tenancy has been severed or if bankruptcy proceedings are pending the tenancy must be treated as a tenancy in common and dealt with by the appointment of a second trustee (see above).

1. Land Registration Rules 2003, r.99.
2. Land Registration Rules 2003, r.164.

3.7. Breach of restrictive covenant/other defect in title

Restrictive covenants

3.7.1. If the breach cannot be remedied, e.g. by obtaining belated consent of the person entitled to the benefit of the covenant, consider obtaining restrictive covenant indemnity insurance in an appropriate sum.

Other defects in title

3.7.2. Defects which can be remedied, e.g. the appointment of a new trustee or missing stamp duties should be rectified as soon as possible and in any event before exchange of contracts. Defects which are irremediable will have to be revealed in the draft contract and insurance cover obtained as appropriate (see B6).

3.8. Planning

3.8.1. Although not strictly a matter of title, the seller's solicitor should check at this stage that any necessary planning or building regulation consents have been obtained and complied with. If not with the deeds copies of such consents should be requisitioned from the local authority for the buyer's use.

3.9. Donatio mortis causa

3.9.1. It is possible, although extremely rare, for the seller to have acquired the land through a *donatio mortis causa*.[1] In such a case there will be no documentary evidence of the devolution of title from the deceased to the present seller. Proof of the validity of the seller's title will have to be shown to the buyer; it may be possible to do this by means of a statutory declaration made by the seller.

1. See *Sen* v. *Headley* [1991] 2 All ER 636.

3.10. Action after investigation of title

Registered land

3.10.1. Official copy entries of the title and any other supporting documentation, e.g. evidence of tenancies or overriding interests should be prepared for delivery to the buyer with the draft contract.

Unregistered land

3.10.2. An epitome of title should be prepared for delivery to the buyer with the draft contract.

B4. Seller's title awaiting registration

4.1. The nature of the problem

4.1.1. A seller, after completion of a recent purchase of registered land, may seek to sell the land to a third party before registration of his own transfer has been completed at the Land Registry. As such, he will not at that stage be the registered proprietor of the land.

4.1.2. A similar problem exists where, having bought unregistered land which is subject to compulsory registration, the seller wishes to sell that land before his application for first registration has been completed. In this latter situation he should not sell on his unregistered title to the buyer, leaving the buyer to apply for registration on completion of his purchase, since the seller's title will become void if no application for registration is made by the seller within two months of the completion of his own purchase.[1] A safer course of action is for the seller to submit his application to the registrar for first registration and then to sell on with registration of title pending.

1. Land Registration Act 2002, s.7; and see *Pinekerry* v. *Needs (Contractors)* (1992) 64 P&CR 245.

4.2. Seller's right to deal with land

4.2.1. The seller is entitled to exercise owner's powers in relation to a registered estate if he is the registered proprietor or entitled to be registered as the proprietor.[1]

1. Land Registration Act 2002, s.24.

4.3. Delay

4.3.1. In practice, if the buyer were to insist that completion of his purchase be delayed until the seller became the registered proprietor of the land through completion of the pending application for registration, the transaction might be delayed which would result in adverse practical and financial consequences for both parties. The buyer will normally agree to complete provided that the seller's own title to the land is registered at some time before the buyer's application for registration is completed.

4.3.2. The buyer's lender must be informed of the position and his requirements observed.

4.4. Contractual condition for deduction of title

4.4.1. The seller must prove to the buyer's satisfaction that the seller is a person who is entitled to be registered as proprietor of the land concerned. This is normally achieved by producing to the buyer official copy entries of the title (which will show the seller's predecessor as registered proprietor), together with a copy of the transfer and a copy of the Land Tax Certificate from the registered proprietor to the seller, appropriate evidence as to those matters upon which the register is not conclusive, a clear Land Registry search against the title, and evidence that the seller lodged a correct application for registration preferably within the priority period afforded by his own search.

4.4.2. Where the land is presently unregistered, the buyer will insist on deduction of the unregistered title together with evidence that the seller has lodged a properly completed application form for first registration of the title. Deduction of title by this method requires the insertion of a special condition to this effect in the contract.

4.4.3. The contract should require the seller to expedite the application and assist the buyer in answering any requisitions which might be raised by the Land Registry in relation to the pending registration.

4.4.4. If the contract requires the buyer to purchase the seller's existing equitable interest in the property (the seller does not have the legal estate until registration is complete), the seller must be required to give an undertaking to transfer the legal estate to the buyer on completion of the seller's registration of title.

4.4.5. Any clause in the contract which relates to obligations that remain in existence after completion will not merge on completion under Standard Condition 7.4.

4.5. Provision for payment of interest by buyer

4.5.1. In order to discourage the buyer from delaying completion by insisting on the seller actually becoming registered as proprietor it is not uncommon to find a contractual provision to the effect that if the buyer does insist on the seller completing his own registration before completion of the sale to the buyer, the buyer will pay interest on the balance of the purchase price at the contract rate for the period between the agreed contractual completion date and actual completion. The Court of Appeal has upheld such a provision.[1]

1. *P & O Overseas Holdings Ltd* v. *Rhys Braintree Ltd* [2002] EWCA Civ 296.

4.6. Protection of the buyer

4.6.1. The buyer may insist that the seller includes a provision in the contract whereby he agrees to expedite his application for registration and that he will assist the buyer by answering any requisitions relating to the pending application which are raised by the Land Registry. Such a condition should be expressed so that it remains extant after completion of the buyer's contract and does not merge with the transfer on completion. Some risks are inherent in this situation and the buyer should protect his contract by registration.

4.7. Protection of the lender

4.7.1. The mortgage, until registration, takes effect only as a charge on the equitable interest and will not comply with the provisions of Building Societies Act 1986. The borrower would, however, be estopped from denying the validity of the charge.[1]

1. *First National Bank plc* v. *Thompson* [1995] NPC 130.

B5. Seller's duty of disclosure

5.1.   Reasons for disclosure

5.1.1.   It is an implied term of a contract for the sale of land that the seller is selling free from incumbrances. If this is not to be so the seller must reveal the incumbrances to which the property is subject. Failure to disclose incumbrances may give the buyer the right to rescind the contract and to claim damages.

5.2.   What must the seller disclose?

5.2.1.   As an exception to the *caveat emptor* principle the seller is under a duty to disclose to the buyer latent incumbrances and defects in his title. This duty exists irrespective of whether the buyer raises enquiries about such matters.

Meaning of latent

5.2.2.   Legally a defect is latent if it is not apparent, but the distinction between latent and patent defects is, in practice, unclear: see, e.g. *Yandle & Sons* v. *Sutton*[1] where a right of way which was apparent on inspection of the property was nevertheless held to be a latent defect. A seller should err on the side of caution and make a full disclosure of defects and incumbrances.

Law of Property Act 1969, s.24

5.2.3.   Although a defect is not latent if the buyer has constructive notice of it under Law of Property Act 1925, s.198, the effect of Law of Property Act 1969, s.24 is to place a duty on the seller to reveal matters which are registered at the Land Charges Department. A buyer who enters into a contract knowing of an irremovable incumbrance impliedly agrees to take subject to that incumbrance (i.e. cannot rescind because of it), but the effect of section 24 is that mere registration under Land Charges Act 1972 is not knowledge for this purpose.

Occupiers

5.2.4.   A buyer of an unregistered title who inspects the property will be deemed to have notice of the rights of occupiers.[2] Where the title is registered, the rights of occupiers may be overriding interests. It is uncertain whether the rights of occupiers fall within the duty of disclosure. Following *Williams & Glyn's Bank Ltd* v. *Boland*[3] the accepted view is that a full disclosure of occupiers' rights should be made.

Local land charges

5.2.5. Unless the contract provides to the contrary, the duty of disclosure includes matters which would be revealed by a local land charges search. Where the contract does not contain an effective clause excluding such matters from the duty of disclosure the seller should make a local land charges search before drafting the contract.[4]

Matters outside the seller's knowledge

5.2.6. It was held in *Re Brewer & Hankin's Contract*[5] that the seller's duty of disclosure may extend even to matters of which he was unaware. However, standard contractual conditions will normally exclude the seller's liability for non-disclosure in these circumstances (see Standard Condition 3, Appendix V.9). Knowledge acquired by the seller's solicitor in the course of acting for his client is imputed to the seller.[6]

Overriding interests

5.2.7. The seller is under a duty to disclose latent overriding interests. In practice a disclosure of all overriding interests known to the seller should be made (see G3.11.6–G3.11.8).

1. [1922] 2 Ch 199.
2. *Hunt* v. *Luck* [1902] 1 Ch 428.
3. [1981] AC 487.
4. *Rignall Developments Ltd* v. *Halil* [1988] Ch 190.
5. (1889) 80 LT 127.
6. *Strover* v. *Harrington* [1988] Ch 390.

5.3.   Matters falling outside the duty of disclosure

Matters known to the buyer

5.3.1. There is no duty to disclose matters which are already known to the buyer, but the seller must ensure that the buyer has actual knowledge of such matters and cannot assume that a matter is within the buyer's knowledge. Even where an incumbrance is contained within one of the title deeds supplied to the buyer with the draft contract or appears on the register in registered land, the buyer's knowledge of the incumbrance cannot be assumed and the seller should take steps, whether by inclusion of a contractual condition or otherwise, specifically to draw the defect to the buyer's attention.

Matters apparent on inspection

5.3.2.   Matters which can readily be discovered on an inspection of the property do not fall within the duty of disclosure.[1]

Physical defects

5.3.3.   Physical defects, whether latent or patent, do not generally fall within the duty of disclosure, but the buyer may seek a remedy in misdescription if the contractual description of the land is rendered inaccurate through this omission.[2] Rescission may also be available to a buyer who, through the non-disclosure of a physical defect, is unable to use the land for the specific purpose for which it was sold.[3] The deliberate concealment of a known physical defect may give rise to an action in the tort of deceit.[4]

Planning matters

5.3.4.   Planning matters are not matters of 'title' and are therefore not strictly within the duty of disclosure. It is, however, considered good practice to make disclosure of such matters.

1. But see *Yandle & Sons* v. *Sutton* [1922] 2 Ch 199.
2. *Re Puckett & Smith's Contract* [1902] 2 Ch 258.
3. It is rare for the contract to state the purpose of the buyer's use specifically.
4. *Gordon* v. *Selico Co. Ltd* (1986) 278 EG 53.

5.4.   Non-disclosure by buyer

5.4.1.   As a general rule a prospective buyer who is not already in a fiduciary relationship with his seller owes no duty of disclosure to his seller. Exceptionally such a duty may exist, e.g. *English* v. *Dedham Vale Properties,*[1] where the buyer was held liable to account to the seller for profit ultimately received from an undisclosed planning application made by the buyer.

1. [1978] 1 WLR 93.

5.5.   Consequences of non-disclosure

5.5.1.   The buyer's remedies for non-disclosure will be rescission of the contract if the non-disclosure is judged to be substantial. If the non-disclosure is not substantial the buyer can be forced to complete and will obtain his remedy through an abatement in the purchase price. A substantial non-disclosure is one where its effect is substantially to deprive the buyer of his bargain. A remedy may also lie in misrepresentation since non-disclosure effectively amounts to a misrepresentation by silence.[1]

1. *Pankhania* v. *Hackney London Borough Council* [2002] All ER (D) 22.

5.6. Contractual exclusion clauses

5.6.1. Clauses which purport to exclude liability for non-disclosure and misrepresentation are common, e.g. Standard Condition 7.1 (Appendix V.9), and as far as the latter is concerned are subject to the reasonableness test in Unfair Contract Terms Act 1977.[1] Their effectiveness in protecting the seller cannot therefore be guaranteed. Some restriction of the seller's duty of disclosure may be felt desirable but a total exclusion of liability would probably not be upheld by the courts save in exceptional circumstances. See also the impact of Unfair Terms in Consumer Contracts Regulations 1999, in B11.10.

1. *Pankhania* v. *Hackney London Borough Council* [2002] All ER (D) 22.

5.7. Conclusion

5.7.1. Despite the various recognised exceptions to the duty of disclosure outlined above, a prudent seller will make a full disclosure of all defects and incumbrances to the buyer, protecting himself where necessary by the inclusion of appropriate contractual clauses to prevent the buyer from exercising a right to rescind in respect of the disclosed matters. Some restriction of the seller's duty of disclosure may be incorporated by way of an exclusion clause in the contract, but care must be exercised to ensure that the clause is reasonable in the light of the circumstances of the particular transaction.

B6. Defective title and restrictive covenant insurance

6.1. Discovery of defects

6.1.1. The seller's solicitor should make a full investigation of the seller's title prior to drafting the contract for sale. Any potential defects in that title must be disclosed to the buyer in the contract and accepted by him, otherwise the seller may be called upon to remove the incumbrance.

6.1.2. Where it appears that a defect in title exists which is not remediable, the seller's solicitor may consider obtaining defective title insurance to cover liability arising out of the defect. Many, but not all, defects can be insured against in this way.

6.1.3. Before obtaining the policy the seller's instructions should be obtained, authorising the solicitor to proceed with this course of action. The seller should be fully advised of the problem and of the likely cost of a policy.

6.1.4. Some lenders insist on the borrower obtaining an indemnity policy against the seller's insolvency, for example where it is apparent that a voluntary transaction has been effected within the past five years. A typical policy will cost a minimum of £175.

6.2. Financial Services and Markets Act 2000

6.2.1. Since 14 January 2005, solicitors who advise clients about obtaining defective title insurance may be involved in activity regulated by Financial Services and Markets Act 2000. It is a criminal offence to carry on 'regulated activities' without authorisation from the Financial Services Authority.

6.2.2. Solicitors may advise upon and arrange indemnity policies where the activity is incidental to the conveyancing transaction but the solicitor must comply with Solicitors' Financial Services (Scope) Rules 2001, i.e. the firm must appoint a compliance officer and be registered with the Financial Services Authority. All firms of solicitors have been registered by the Law Society in the Financial Services Authority's register (see A4.4.1).

6.3.   Obtaining a policy

6.3.1.   Countrywide Legal Indemnities offers a policy which has been negotiated by the Law Society. Some other major insurance companies will issue policies to cover defects in title. To ensure that a proper premium, commensurate with the risk involved, is paid, quotations should be obtained from more than one company.

6.3.2.   The defect in title is the seller's responsibility because he will be contractually bound to prove a good title to his buyer. The seller should therefore normally expect to meet the costs of obtaining the policy. If the policy is obtained at the request of the buyer it may be possible to negotiate to share the expense with him. In any event the contract should deal with the liability for the expense of obtaining such a policy.

6.3.3.   The policy will be a single premium policy the benefit of which will attach to the land. The policy should be mentioned in the contract (if the policy is available at that time) and handed over to the buyer on completion to be kept in a safe place with the documents of title.

6.4.   Information needed by insurance company

6.4.1.   Before issue of the policy the insurance company will need to assess the risk involved. As a general rule, defects which have occurred in the recent past, e.g. during the last 15 years will be more expensive and difficult to insure against than those which occurred many years ago. The seller's solicitor should be prepared to provide the insurance company with the following information or documents:

    (a)   the precise nature of the defect;

    (b)   where relevant, a copy of the document in which the defect appears;

    (c)   the date when the defect arose, or date when the problem giving rise to the defect occurred;

    (d)   what steps (if any) have been taken to remedy the defect;

    (e)   whether any third party has taken steps to assert rights against the land because of the defect;

    (f)   an approximate estimate of the amount of cover needed.

6.5.   Restrictive covenants

6.5.1.   The breach of a restrictive covenant affecting the title is a common reason for needing defective title insurance. In some cases the need for the policy will arise, not because a covenant has been broken, but because some contemplated action with or on the land will cause a breach. For example, it is common to find a restrictive covenant which prevents use of the property except as a single private dwelling house and the client wishes now to convert the property into flats, which action would cause a breach of covenant. In such a case it may be possible to obtain an insurance policy which will cover liability for the future breach of covenant. Where the seller is contracting to sell with planning permission for development, he should obtain and bear the cost of the policy; in other cases this matter will be the buyer's responsibility.

6.5.2.   Apart from the matters listed in B6.4, the insurance company will also need the following information or documents:

(a)   a copy of the document imposing the covenant or, if this is not available, a copy of the exact wording of the covenant;

(b)   the exact nature of the breach which has occurred or details of the action which is contemplated which will cause the breach;

(c)   the date when the covenant was imposed;

(d)   whether or not the covenant is registered on the charges register of the title (or as a Class D(ii) charge in unregistered land where the covenant was imposed after 1925);

(e)   the nature of other properties in the immediate neighbourhood. This is to enable the insurance company to assess the risk of enforcement of the covenant more precisely. Taking the example given above of a potential breach being caused by a conversion of a dwelling into flats, if many of the neighbouring properties have already been converted into flats, the likelihood of this particular covenant being enforced if breached is more remote than if the surrounding properties remain in single owner-ship. A plan which shows the property in the context of the surrounding locality is often useful;

(f)   a copy of any planning permission which permits the development to be undertaken by the client and copies of any objections which were lodged in respect of the application;

(g)   what steps have been taken (if any) to trace the person(s) with the benefit of the covenant and the results of those enquiries. The identity of the person who has the benefit of the covenant should be revealed if known, but steps should not be taken to approach that person without the prior consent of the insurance company since such an approach may have an adverse effect on the outcome of the situation and the conse-quent insurance risk;

(h)   details of any complaints which have been received from persons with the benefit of the covenants.

6.5.3.   Before arranging insurance, check that the covenant is binding on the title, either by registration under Land Charges Act 1972 or by the registration of a notice against the title at the Land Registry. Covenants noted on the register at first registration will not necessarily be binding. Under Rule 35 Land Registration Rules 2003, the Registrar is not required to check the validity of a covenant at first registration and covenants will be entered in the register unless the applicant for first registration makes an application to have the covenant omitted from the register. (see G3.4.6–G3.4.8 as to the Land Registry's requirements in this respect).

6.6.   Accepting the policy when acting for the buyer

6.6.1.   Where a buyer is asked to accept a policy taken out by the seller or his predecessor which purports to cover liability for a defect or breach consideration should be given to the following matters:

(a)   check that full disclosure of all relevant facts was made to the insurer prior to the issue of the policy;

(b)   ensure that the policy enures to the benefit of successors and is not restricted to a named person;

(c)   check that the policy covers the defect or breach in question;

(d)   check that the amount of cover offered by the policy appears to be adequate;

(e)   if the policy is already in existence enquire whether any claims have been made under the policy and the result of those claims;

(f)   ensure that the original policy will be handed over on completion. Where the policy has been taken out by a developer to cover the building of several properties, an examined or certified copy of the policy should be handed over on completion;

(g)   where a policy already exists, consideration should be given to taking an express assignment of the benefit of the policy from the seller and, after completion, giving notice of the assignment to the insurance company;

(h)   obtaining any proposed lender's approval to the policy terms and amount of cover.

6.7.   Positive covenants

6.7.1.   Similar considerations apply where indemnity has been given in relation to a positive covenant.

6.8.   Lenders' Handbook

6.8.1.   The Lenders' Handbook outlines a number of situations in which indemnity insurance will be required by the lender. The terms on which the lender will accept a policy are contained in paragraph 9 of the Handbook (see Appendix VI.2).

B7. Capacity

7.1.   Introduction

7.1.1.   In general a seller cannot convey a legal estate unless that estate is vested in him, although in very limited cases he may, under a power, convey a legal estate vested in some other person, e.g. a lender exercising a power of sale.

7.1.2.   Although the nature of the seller's capacity no longer affects the extent of the covenants which are implied in the buyer's favour in the purchase deed, certain points relating to the seller's capacity to deal with the interest in land which he is purporting to dispose of still need to be addressed. These points are outlined in the paragraphs below. Implied covenants are discussed in M9.[1]

7.1.3.   A registered proprietor has unfettered powers of disposition.[2] A buyer of registered land is concerned only to ensure that any restrictions on the register are complied with. The statutory provisions have effect only for the purpose of preventing the title of a buyer being questioned (and do not affect the lawfulness of a disposition).[3] The seller will in any event be bound to comply with any fiduciary duties he has, but a buyer is not concerned with them unless they are reflected in a restriction on the register. For example, if trustees were to sell land in breach of trust, in the absence of a restriction on the register, the transfer could not be impeached but the trustees would be liable to the beneficiaries of the trust for the breach. Where the title to the property is registered with title absolute, and there is no restriction placed on the proprietorship register, the seller is deemed to have the capacity to transfer the land (subject to the provisions relating to alteration of the register) and further enquiry into the seller's capacity is in such cases unnecessary.

1.   See Law of Property (Miscellaneous Provisions) Act 1994 and M9.
2.   Land Registration Act 2002, s.26(1).
3.   Land Registration Act 2002, s.26(2).

7.2. Provision for capacity in the contract

7.2.1. For contracts entered into on or after 1 July 1995, it is no longer necessary to state the seller's capacity in the contract.[1]

1. See Law of Property (Miscellaneous Provisions) Act 1994 and M9.

7.3. Beneficial owner

7.3.1. A beneficial owner is a single estate owner who owns the whole of the legal and equitable interest in the property for his own benefit. Either an individual or a corporation may satisfy this requirement. No other person must have any beneficial interest in the interest in land if the capacity of beneficial owner is to apply. Co-owners cannot satisfy this requirement since they hold the property on a trust of land.[1]

7.3.2. If it appears that someone other than the seller named in the contract is in occupation of the property, the buyer must make full enquiries about the status of such occupier in order to establish what interest he has in the property and to establish whether or not the seller is in fact a beneficial owner.

7.3.3. An occupier may claim a beneficial interest in the property through, e.g. contributing to the purchase price. In such a case, it will be necessary for a second trustee to be appointed to act with the seller in order to overreach the beneficial interest of the occupier.[2] Alternatively (or additionally) it may be thought desirable for the occupier to sign a release of his or her rights. Such a release may be included as a contractual term, in which case the occupier will need to sign the contract before exchange. The validity of such disclaimers seems to have met with the court's approval.[3]

7.3.4. In registered land the rights of persons in actual occupation may be overriding interests.[4] If so, a buyer will take subject to these rights (including those which are capable of registration but which are not in fact registered). However, where the sale is by trustees, the rights arising under the trust will be overreached provided the capital money arising is paid to at least two trustees or a trust corporation.

7.3.5. In unregistered land a buyer is deemed to buy with notice of occupiers' rights, other than those capable of registration but which are not registered as land charges;[5] thus the buyer needs to inspect the property and to make full enquiries about the rights of any occupiers.

7.3.6. A surviving co-owner may be a beneficial owner (see B7.4).

1. See *Re Robertson's Application* [1969] 1 All ER 257.
2. See *City of London Building Society* v. *Flegg* [1988] AC 54; *Lloyds Bank* v. *Rossett* [1991] 1 AC 107.
3. *Appleton* v. *Aspin* [1988] 1 WLR 410.
4. Land Registration Act 2002, Sched.1, para.2 and Sched.3, para.2.
5. *Hunt* v. *Luck* [1902] 1 Ch 428.

7.4. **Trustees of land**

7.4.1. Where land is held on a trust of land any conveyance or transfer of the land must be made by the trustees, being at least two individuals or a trust corporation, in order to overreach the equitable interests of the beneficiaries.

7.4.2. Co-owners hold land on a trust of land.[1]

7.4.3. Where a trust of land exists, whether expressly created or arising under statute (e.g. on intestacy), the trustees are under a duty to consult with, and, so far as is consistent with the general interests of the trust, give effect to the wishes of the adult competent beneficiaries who are entitled to a beneficial interest in possession of the land, when exercising their powers under the trust (e.g. to sell the land).[2] A trust which is created by an *inter vivos* disposition (but not by will) can expressly exclude the duty to consult.[3] A buyer is not concerned to check compliance with the obligation to consult.[4] In registered land the buyer is only concerned to see that the terms of any restriction on the register are complied with.

7.4.4. Where the trust was expressly created, a power to postpone the sale is implied and cannot be excluded by contrary provision in the trust instrument.[5]

7.4.5. Where the trust arises under statute (e.g. on intestacy), the trustees have a power (but not a duty) to sell the land.[6]

7.4.6. Difficulties may arise if there are only two acting trustees who disagree over the decision to sell, since one trustee alone cannot transfer the legal estate. It may therefore be necessary in these circumstances to apply to the court under Trusts of Land and Appointment of Trustees Act 1996, s.14 to resolve the dispute. On an application under this section the court may make any order it thinks fit (including an order for sale), and thus may, but is not obliged to, order the sale of the property.

7.4.7. In making such an order the court must have regard to the factors listed in section 15 Trusts of Land and Appointment of Trustees Act 1996 including the purpose of the trust and the interests of any secured creditor or beneficiary.

7.4.8. If a disposition creating a trust of land requires the trustees to obtain the consents of a person or persons before exercising their power of sale, the buyer is only concerned to see that a maximum of two consents have been obtained (even if the trust deed requires a greater number) and is never concerned with the consents of persons suffering mental incapacity. Where a person whose consent is required is not of full age, the buyer is not concerned to see that such consent has been obtained, but the trustees must obtain the consent of a parent or guardian of the under age beneficiary.[7] In registered land the buyer is only concerned to see that the terms of any restriction on the register are complied with.

7.4.9. Trustees' powers to sell, mortgage, and grant leases are the same as those of an absolute owner but they must exercise those powers having regard to the rights of the beneficiaries.[8]

7.4.10. Trusts of Land and Appointment of Trustees Act 1996 has converted existing trusts for sale into 'trusts of land'. From 1 January 1997, co-owners hold land on a trust of land (formerly trust for sale).

7.4.11. Where the purpose of the trust is to sell the land it is still possible to create an express trust for sale. The requirement for the trustees to sell must however be expressly stated since it is no longer implied under the general law.

1. Law of Property Act 1925, ss.34 and 36.
2. Trusts of Land and Appointment of Trustees Act 1996, s.11.
3. *Ibid.* s.11(2).
4. *Ibid.* s.16(1).
5. *Ibid.* s.4(1).
6. *Ibid.* Sched.2.
7. *Ibid.* s.10.
8. *Ibid.* s.6.

7.5. Personal representatives

7.5.1. Personal representatives have all the powers of trustees of land but are only entitled to exercise those powers during the administration.[1] They are not, however, subject to sections 10, 11 and 14 Trusts of Land and Appointment of Trustees Act 1996 (duties to obtain consents, consultation with beneficiaries and the court's power of sale).[2]

7.5.2. Their powers are joint as to land, whether freehold or leasehold; therefore all proving personal representatives must be made parties to the contract and purchase deed (conveyance, lease, etc.).[3] A single proving personal representative may, however, act on his own.

7.5.3. The buyer should always see a copy of the grant to ascertain the names of all of the proving personal representatives.

7.5.4. In registered land a buyer is only concerned to see that the terms of any restriction on the register are complied with.

1. Administration of Estates Act 1925, s.39.
2. Trusts of Land and Appointment of Trustees Act 1996, s.18.
3. Law of Property (Miscellaneous Provisions) Act 1994, s.16.

7.6. Settled land

7.6.1. The following sub-paragraphs should be read in the light of Trusts of Land and Appointment of Trustees Act 1996 which abolishes the creation of new strict settlements (with very limited exceptions) on or after 1 January 1997. The Act is not retrospective in effect and existing strict settlements are unaffected by the legislation. Land which is held under Universities and Colleges Estates Act 1925 will continue to be settled land and is unaffected by the 1996 Act.

7.6.2. The tenant for life is the person in whom the legal estate in settled land is vested via the vesting instrument. Where there is no tenant for life, or he is a minor, the legal estate is vested in statutory owners who are usually the trustees of the settlement. The tenant for life (or, if none, the statutory owners) will therefore be the seller of settled land, but the trustees of the settlement must be joined as parties to the purchase deed in order to give a valid receipt for capital moneys arising and thus to overreach the interests of the beneficiaries.

7.6.3. The trust deed itself is generally 'behind the curtain' and thus of no concern to a buyer. The buyer is bound and entitled to assume that the person in whom the legal estate is vested by the vesting instrument is the person rightfully entitled to the legal estate and that the persons named as trustees are the properly constituted Settled Land Act trustees.

7.6.4. A sale or other disposition of settled land can only be made for the purposes of the settlement and must be made for the best consideration in money reasonably obtainable.[1] Unless expressly extended by the terms of the settlement certain restrictions on dispositions are imposed by Settled Land Act 1925. The main restrictions relate to mortgages and leases, e.g. the Act permits leases for building or forestry to be granted for a term not exceeding 999 years, for mining, not exceeding 100 years, and for agricultural or occupational purposes, not exceeding 50 years. Powers to grant options to purchase or to take a lease and to grant easements are limited by Settled Land Act 1925, s.51. A disposition which is not authorised either by the Act or by the terms of the settlement is void, even if the buyer was unaware of the settlement.[2]

7.6.5. Where settled land is registered, the tenant for life (or statutory owners) will be registered as proprietor and appropriate restrictions are entered on the proprietorship register.[3] A buyer is only concerned to see that the terms of the restrictions are complied with.

1. Settled Land Act 1925, s.39(1).
2. *Weston* v. *Henshaw* [1950] Ch 510; *cf. Re Morgan's Lease; Jones* v. *Norsesowicz* [1972] Ch 1.
3. Land Registration Rules 2003, r.186 and Sched.7.

7.7. Mortgagees

7.7.1. In order to sell the property the lender must have an express or implied power of sale and that power must have arisen and become exercisable. A power of sale is implied in every mortgage made by deed unless expressly excluded.[1] A legal mortgage must be made by deed.[2] It therefore follows that a lender who has taken a legal mortgage will always have a power of sale unless (exceptionally) that power has been expressly excluded. An equitable mortgage need not be made by deed;[3] it will therefore be necessary to check carefully the existence of the lender's power to sell. In some cases an equitable mortgage may give the lender an irrevocable power of attorney which would give the lender power to convey the legal estate vested in the borrower in exercise of the power of sale.

7.7.2. Under Land Registration Act 2002, s.52, subject to any entry in the register to the contrary, the proprietor of a registered charge is to be taken to have the powers of disposition conferred by law on the owner of a legal mortgage. Conversely, the owner of a charge which is not substantively registered has no power of sale.

7.7.3. As far as a buyer is concerned, he need only check the existence of the power of sale and that it has arisen. The power of sale arises on the legal date for redemption of the mortgage which is usually specified to be a date early on in the mortgage term (e.g. one month after creation of the mortgage).

7.7.4. A lender who is exercising his power of sale must ensure that:

(a) his power of sale exists;

(b) the power has arisen; and

(c) the power has become exercisable.

7.7.5. The lender's power becomes exercisable if one of the three following conditions is met:[4]

(a) notice requiring payment of the principal money has been served on the borrower and default has been made in payment of the principal money for three months; or

(b) some interest under the mortgage is in arrears and unpaid for two months after becoming due; or

(c) there has been breach of some other provision contained in the mortgage deed or Law of Property Act 1925.

7.7.6. A lender who sells in a situation where his power has arisen but not become exercisable will nonetheless pass good title to the buyer but may be liable in damages to the borrower.

Borrowers

7.7.7. Subject to any contractual restriction in the mortgage (e.g. restricting further the limited statutory power to grant leases of the property) which may be reflected by a restriction on the register of the title, a borrower may be treated as a beneficial owner.

1. Law of Property Act 1925, s.101.
2. Law of Property Act 1925, s.85.
3. But must be in writing and signed by both parties to satisfy Law of Property (Miscellaneous Provisions) Act 1989, s.2.
4. Law of Property Act 1925, s.103.

7.8.   **Charities**

7.8.1.   If there is no restriction on the proprietorship register, a buyer may safely deal with the charity as if it were an absolute owner. If there is a restriction on the register, the following subparagraphs should be considered. Reference should also be made to Land Registry Practice Guide 14.

7.8.2.   Unless a charity is an exempt charity, no disposition (the term disposition applies to the transfer or conveyance of land and not to the contract for sale)[1] can be made by the charity without an order of the court or Charity Commissioners unless all the following conditions are satisfied:[2]

(a)   the trustees must obtain a written report about the proposed disposition from a qualified surveyor (FRICS, ARICS, SVA or ASVA);

(b)   the property is advertised for the period and in the manner advised by the surveyor;

(c)   the trustees decide that in the light of the surveyor's report they are satisfied that the terms of the disposition are the best that can be obtained;

(d)   prescribed words are inserted in both the contract and purchase deed.

7.8.3.   The prescribed words must be in one of the following forms:

(a)   the land transferred (or as the case may be) is held by [(proprietors) in trust for] (charity), an exempt charity; or

(b)   the land transferred (or as the case may be) is held by [(proprietors) in trust for] (charity), a non-exempt charity, but this transfer (or as the case may be) is one falling within paragraphs (a), (b) or (c) of section 36(9) Charities Act 1993; or

(c)   the land transferred (or as the case may be) is held by [(proprietors) in trust for] (charity), a non-exempt charity, and this transfer (or as the case may be) is not one falling within paragraphs (a), (b) or (c) of section 36(9) Charities Act 1993, so the restrictions on disposition imposed by section 36 of that Act apply to the land.[3]

Note that when there is no trust (i.e. the land is the corporate property of the registered proprietor charity) the words 'XXXX in trust for' are omitted.

7.8.4.   Where the prescribed words are included in the disposition, the buyer and persons who subsequently acquire the property for money or money's worth are entitled to rely on the conclusiveness of the facts stated and rely on a certificate in the purchase deed that the trustees have power under the trusts of the charity to effect the disposition and that they have complied with the provisions of Charities Act 1993, s.36 so far as applicable to it. The buyer may also rely on such a certificate where the land is registered with a restriction in Form 12 or Form E.[4]

Dealing with land owned by a charity

7.8.5. When dealing with land owned by a charity the following points should be checked:

(a) is the transaction authorised by the statute or deed which governs the charity?

(b) is the charity exempt? If so, the transaction can proceed without delay.

If not an exempt charity:

(c) can the trustees give the certificate referred to in B7.8.4?

(d) if not, has an order of the court or the Charity Commissioners been obtained?

7.8.6. Where an order is needed it must either be obtained before exchange of contracts or the contract must be made conditional on the order being obtained.[5]

7.8.7. The purchase deed containing the certificate must be signed by the charity trustees, or by two or more of them acting under an authority given by the trustees.[6] In the case of a corporate charity this usually means the directors. It is not sufficient for the deed to be sealed by the company in the presence of a director and the secretary.

7.8.8. Land held on charitable, ecclesiastical and public trusts ceased to be settled land and became subject to a 'trust of land' on 1 January 1997 (with the exception of land to which Universities and College Estates Act 1925 applies).[7]

1. *Osborn and Co. Ltd* v. *Dior; Marito Holdings SA* v. *Borhane* CA [2003] All ER (D) 185 (Jan).
2. Charities Act 1993, ss.37–40.
3. Land Registration Rules 2003, r.180.
4. Land Registration Rules 2003, Sched.4.
5. See B13.
6. See Charities Act 1993, s.82.
7. Trusts of Land and Appointment of Trustees Act 1996.

7.9. Companies

7.9.1. A company which is regulated by the Companies Acts may deal with land so long as the transaction is within the scope of the objects clause of its memorandum of association. In favour of a person dealing with a company the validity of an act done by a company shall not be called into question on the ground of lack of capacity by reason of anything in the company's memorandum. The good faith of the buyer is irrelevant and it is no longer necessary to make a company search to ensure that the power to conduct the transaction exists.[1] A company may hold property jointly with another company or individual.[2] Where a company applies to become the proprietor of registered land, details of the company's powers must be supplied to the registrar[3] and, if those powers are limited, an appropriate restriction will be entered on the register. A buyer is only concerned to see that the terms of any restriction are complied with.

7.9.2.   The powers of a company incorporated by Royal Charter are not restricted by the terms of its Charter; it may therefore be regarded as having the same powers as an individual.

7.9.3.   The powers of a company which is incorporated by some other statute are governed by the enabling statute which should in each case be checked and the requisite procedures followed. A transaction outside the terms of the statute will be void.

7.9.4.   The powers of a foreign company should be expressly checked and the requisite procedures followed. Checks may include confirmation from a lawyer entitled to practise in the jurisdiction in which the foreign company was incorporated that the company exists in law and has power to buy, sell and hold land, etc. (see E4).

Transactions between a company and one of its directors

7.9.5.   Companies Act 1985, s.320, applies to arrangements under which a director acquires an asset from the company. The word 'arrangement' covers freehold and leasehold transactions and options made between the director and the company. Transactions under which the company purchases assets from one of its directors are also covered by section 320(1)(*b*). Under these provisions, a transaction to which the section applies must be sanctioned by the company in general meeting. The company's approval should be obtained before exchange of contracts, but a retrospective approval, obtained before completion, will validate the transaction. The resolution should identify the property, the buyer and the price and may approve the transaction on such other terms as the board of directors may agree. A private company may pass a written resolution (without holding a formal meeting) provided that the vote is unanimous. Where a formal meeting is held, a bare majority will suffice to pass the resolution. Minor transactions, defined as those which are below £2,000 in value or those with a value of between £2,000 and £100,000 where the value represents less than 10% of the company's assets, do not need approval. The term 'director' includes persons connected with the director so that a transfer by a company to a director's wife or to another company with which the director is associated will invoke the provisions of the section. The consequences of failure to comply with section 320 are contained in section 322: broadly, the transaction is voidable at the instance of the company. The company is entitled to be compensated for any loss it has suffered as a result of the unapproved transaction and to account for any gain.

Transactions before company formed

7.9.6.   A person who purports to act on behalf of a company or as agent for it at a time when the company has not been formed will be personally liable on the contract, Companies Act 1985, s.36C(1). This provision can result in the solicitor acting on a sale or purchase for a company in the process of incorporation becoming personally liable for the contract and being entitled to enforce the contract.[4]

1. Companies Act 1989, s.108.
2. Bodies Corporate (Joint Tenancy) Act 1899, s.1.
3. See Land Registration Rules 2003, rr.181 and 183.
4. *Braymist Ltd* v. *Wise Finance Co. Ltd* [2002] 2 All ER 333, CA.

7.10. Minors

7.10.1. A person aged under 18 years cannot hold a legal estate in land but may hold an equitable interest. If, however, there is no restriction on the register of the title, the buyer is entitled to assume that the seller has full capacity. A conveyance to a minor alone takes effect as an agreement to create a trust of land and in the meantime to hold the land on trust for him. A contract for sale to a minor is binding on him unless repudiated by him during minority or within a reasonable time after attaining majority.[1]

1. See Minors' Contracts Act 1987.

7.11. Persons suffering from mental disability

7.11.1. A contract for the sale or purchase of land, entered into by a person who is suffering from mental incapacity sufficient to deprive him of understanding of the nature of the transaction, is voidable at the option of the incapacitated party, provided he can prove that at the time of the transaction the other contracting party was aware of the disability.[1]

7.11.2. Once a receiver is appointed under Mental Health Act 1983, s.99, the patient loses all contractual capacity and any purported *inter vivos* disposition by him is void. The receiver has power, subject to the court's approval, to deal with the patient's property.[2]

7.11.3. On the appointment of a receiver a restriction is not normally entered on a registered title unless the receiver or other authorised person requests its entry. Where the receiver is registered as proprietor a restriction is automatically entered.[3] The restriction would usually prevent registration of any disposition unless made pursuant to an order of the court under Mental Health Act 1983. On a dealing with registered land, the registrar will require a copy of the order which provides the receiver's authority to act.

7.11.4. Practice Note 'Ancillary Relief Orders: Conveyancing for Mentally Incapacitated Adults', should be consulted when transferring land pursuant to a property adjustment order or sale order made on a divorce, nullity or judicial separation in matrimonial proceedings (see A18.5).

1. *Broughton* v. *Snook* [1938] Ch 505.
2. See Mental Health Act 1983, ss.95 and 96.
3. Land Registration Act 2002, s.42(1)(a).

7.12.   Universities and colleges

7.12.1.   Universities and Colleges Estates Act 1925 confers powers to sell and exchange land and to purchase land as an investment on the universities of Oxford, Cambridge and Durham (and their respective colleges) and on Winchester and Eton Colleges and restrictions are entered in registered land reflecting the limitations on their powers under the statutes governing them. Other universities and colleges may be educational charities and are subject to the rules on charities outlined above.

7.13.   Local authorities

7.13.1.   A local authority may acquire land, inside or outside its own area, for the purpose of any of its functions under any Public General Act or for the benefit, improvement or development of its area. Power to acquire land for the provision of accommodation is given by Housing Act 1985, s.17. Powers of compulsory purchase of land are conferred by many statutes and are outside the scope of this book.

7.13.2.   Ministerial consent is required for certain disposals of land by a local authority. In such a case, consent must be obtained before contracts are exchanged, or alternately the contract made conditional on such consent being forthcoming. A conveyance made without the requisite consent may be void. In certain cases a buyer is entitled to assume that the transaction is within the powers of the local authority and does not have to investigate whether or not ministerial approval has been given. Under Housing Act 1988, s.44 (which does not apply to right to buy sales and leases), any disposal of residential property by a local authority for which the consent of the Secretary of State for the Environment is required is void if made without consent unless:

(a)   the disposal is in favour of an individual or two or more individuals; and

(b)   the disposal comprises only a single house or flat.

7.13.3.   The protection afforded by Local Government Act 1972, s.128 does not apply in respect of residential premises unless both these conditions are satisfied. Where the land is registered, a buyer is only concerned to see that the terms of any restriction are complied with.

7.14.   Parish and community councils

7.14.1.   Land may be acquired by such a council (whether inside or outside its own area) for the purposes of any of its functions under Local Government Act 1972 or any other Public General Act.

7.14.2. Ministerial consent is required for disposals of land, but buyers from parish and community councils are protected against breach of the consent provisions.[1]

1. Local Government Act 1972, s.128.

7.15. Building societies, friendly societies, trade unions

7.15.1. A building society may acquire and hold land for the purpose of its business or for commercial purposes under Building Societies Act 1986, ss.16 and 17. It will also have power to sell land as a lender where it has lent money on mortgage and the lender's power of sale has become exercisable (see B7.7).

7.15.2. Registered friendly societies and industrial and provident societies have power to buy, sell and hold land, subject to the rules of each individual society.

7.15.3. Property belonging to a trade union is usually vested in trustees on trust for the union. Powers of acquisition and disposition are subject to the rules of the union, the general law relating to trustees, and some special provisions contained in Trade Union and Labour Relations Act 1974, s.2.

7.16. Fiduciary relationships

7.16.1. Where a fiduciary relationship exists between the parties to the transaction, there is a presumption of constructive fraud which is rebuttable on proof (by the dominant party to the relationship) that the transaction was at a fair price (an independent valuation is highly desirable), that all the circumstances of the transaction were known to the subordinate party, and that each party received, or was given a proper opportunity to take, independent legal advice. The transaction is prima facie voidable at the instance of the subordinate party.

7.16.2. A fiduciary relationship is deemed to exist in dealings between the following persons:

   (a) solicitor and client;

   (b) trustee and beneficiary;

   (c) parent and child (where the influence of the parent over the child may be held to have endured beyond the child's majority);

   (d) doctor and patient;

   (e) religious advisor and disciple;

   (f) teacher and pupil;

   (g) fiancés (but not between husband and wife).

7.16.3. A fiduciary relationship may exist in circumstances other than those listed above, but is not presumed to exist, and the dominance of one party over the other would have to be proved before the court would apply the doctrine of constructive fraud.[1]

7.16.4. If a solicitor is asked to act in dealings between any of the parties listed in B7.16.2, or in any other situation where he feels that the relationship between the contracting parties may be classed as fiduciary, he should ensure that:

(a) an independent valuation of the property is obtained;

(b) all the facts pertaining to the transaction are known by and understood by both parties;

(c) the parties are separately represented (see A10).

1. See, e.g. *Lloyds Bank* v. *Bundy* [1975] QB 326 (fiduciary relationship proved to have existed between bank manager and customer).

7.17. One-man companies

7.17.1. It is permitted for a company to have only one shareholder. That shareholder may also be a director of the company. If he is the only director a second person must be appointed to act as company secretary.

7.18. Administration procedures

7.18.1. If a company is in administration, any sale of property will be carried out by either an administrative receiver or by an administrator, depending upon the date of the charge under which the appointment is made. If the charge was entered into before 15 September 2003 (when the relevant provisions of Enterprise Act 2002 came into force and amended Insolvency Act 1986) the creditor may appoint an administrative receiver. If the charge was made after the provisions came into force, an administrator will be appointed. Administrative receiverships still exist for charges created before 15 September 2003 but will become less important as time passes.

7.18.2. Both administrators and administrative receivers must be qualified insolvency practitioners.

7.18.3. When buying a property from an administrator or an administrative receiver, the validity of the appointment should be checked, including:

(a) the validity of the floating charge under which the appointment was made and that the charge is a qualifying floating charge under paragraph 14 Schedule B1 Insolvency Act 1986 amended by Schedule 16 Enterprise Act 2002;

(b) that the charge covered the whole or substantially the whole of the company's property;

(c) that the charge is not likely to be invalidated, e.g. for want of registration, or fraudulent preference;

(d) that the appointment does not exceed any powers in the charge;

(e) that the administrator or the administrative receiver has power to conduct the transaction in question;

(f) in a case where two receivers have been appointed, whether they are able to act jointly and severally or jointly only.

7.18.4. A certified copy of the appointment should be obtained by the buyer since this is one of the documents that will have to be produced to the Land Registry on registration of the transfer: see Land Registry Practice Guides 35 and 36.

7.18.5. As a matter of practice the administrator or the administrative receiver may decline to give any warranties or covenants and may seek to exclude his personal liability. A buyer may, where appropriate, prefer to take a transfer from the lender in exercise of his power of sale where the buyer will benefit from the limited covenants given by lenders and will also have the guarantee of over-reaching subsequent incumbrances.

7.18.6. An administrator has the same powers as an administrative receiver under Insolvency Act 1986 and he acts as an agent of the company and an officer of the court. His main function is to rescue the company as a going concern, but he does have the power to realise assets in order to make a distribution to creditors. An administrator's appointment will terminate automatically after 12 months unless it is extended by the court or by consent.[1]

1. Insolvency Act 1986, Sched.B1, paras.76–86 as amended by Enterprise Act 2002, Sched.16.

7.19.   Attorneys

7.19.1. A power of attorney can be general (giving the attorney power to do anything that the donor can lawfully do) or specific (giving the attorney power to sell a specific property).

7.19.2. Where the seller is a beneficial owner he can delegate his power to sell land to an attorney by using a general power of attorney.[1]

7.19.3. Where the land is held by co-owners the land is held on a trust of land. A trustee with a beneficial interest in the land can appoint an attorney using a general power or a general trustee power and can appoint his sole co-trustee to be his attorney. The attorney must make a statement that the donor is beneficially entitled either at the time of the disposition or within three months following the disposition.[2]

7.19.4. A trustee who is not beneficially entitled under the trust should use a general trustee power. He can appoint his sole co-trustee to be his attorney; however, the power will be limited to a maximum period of 12 months.[3]

7.19.5.   If a sole co-trustee has been appointed to be an attorney using a general power or a general trustee power of attorney, he cannot give a good receipt for the purchase price and overreaching will not operate. In such a case the donor should appoint a third party to act as attorney.

7.19.6.   The buyer must insist on seeing the original or a certified copy of the power of attorney and he must carry out a bankruptcy search against the donor. Provided that the buyer is not aware of any event that would revoke the power, the buyer will get a good title.

7.19.7.   At completion the buyer must collect a certified copy of the power of attorney.

7.19.8.   Where the property is registered see B23.7 and Land Registry Practice Guide 9 for the Land Registry's requirements on registration of a purchase from an attorney.

7.19.9.   When the person who bought from the attorney comes to sell an unregistered property, his buyer will want to ensure that the power had not been revoked prior to the sale by the attorney. He can conclusively presume that it was not revoked if the sale by the attorney took place within 12 months of the power being granted. If the sale took place more than 12 months after the date of the power then the current buyer must obtain a statutory declaration from his seller stating that the seller was not aware of any revocation of the power at the time of his purchase. This statutory declaration must be produced either before the sale to the buyer or within three months of that sale having taken place.

7.19.10.   For example, on 1 January 1990, A, an unregistered owner, appointed B to be his attorney. On 1 July 1990, A, through his attorney, sold his property to C. In 2006, C is selling the property to D. D can presume that the power had not been revoked before the sale to C because the sale took place within 12 months of the power having been granted. However, if the sale to C had taken place on 1 July 1991, D would require a statutory declaration from C stating that he, C, had no knowledge of any revocation of the power at the time of his purchase from the attorney. The statutory declaration must be prepared at the time of the sale to D or within three months of that sale having taken place.

1.   Powers of Attorney Act 1971, s.10.
2.   Trustee Delegation Act 1999, s.1.
3.   Trustee Delegation Act 1999, s.5.

B8. Agricultural land

8.1.   Introduction

8.1.1.   The procedure when buying agricultural land will be similar to that employed when buying any piece of freehold or leasehold land (as appropriate). The following paragraphs merely draw attention to some matters to which particular attention needs to be paid because of the nature of agricultural land. For more detailed information reference should be made to a specialist text on the subject.

8.2.   Plans

8.2.1.   The boundaries of agricultural land need to be checked carefully so that both parties understand clearly and precisely the extent of the land to be sold or let. The seller and buyer and/or their respective surveyors should inspect the land and agree the boundaries which should be marked on a plan to be attached to the contract and, in due course, the form of lease or transfer. It is essential that the plan should be of sufficiently large scale (e.g. 1:2500) and dimensions to identify the land and its salient features clearly. In order to satisfy Land Registry requirements a large scale Ordnance Survey map must be used for this purpose. The route of any services and other easements which cross the land should be identified.

8.2.2.   Where possible 'T' marks should be marked on the plan to indicate the future responsibility for maintenance of boundaries with specific reference in the wording of the lease or transfer to those responsibilities. Where no definite indications as to boundaries exist, reference may be made to the common law presumptions, e.g. where there is a hedge and ditch boundary, the boundary lies on the far side of the ditch from the hedge. At common law the *ad medium filum* rule applies to roads and rivers.

8.2.3.   Rights of way and access to the property should be checked including individual field access points.

8.3. Pre-contract searches

8.3.1. The situation of the land may indicate that some of the less usual pre-contract searches should be undertaken, e.g. rivers, railways (see B10). A commons registration search should always be undertaken. It will also be necessary for the buyer's solicitor to require the local authority to answer some of the questions on Part II of Enquiries of Local Authority Search Form. Particular attention should be paid to questions relating to public rights of way. The buyer should be made aware of the possibility of future modification orders arising in relation to public rights of way.

8.3.2. If only part of land which enjoys rights of common is being sold, an apportionment of those rights between the two parcels of land may be considered.

8.3.3. Specific enquiries should be raised with the seller about sites of special scientific interest or other environmental designations where the local search replies indicate that such a site is included in the land to be bought.

8.3.4. A search may be made with the owning authority where it is necessary to establish the routes of pipelines and cables passing under, through or over the property.

8.3.5. A chancel repair liability search may be necessary (see B10).

8.3.6. Any index map search made against the property should be supplemented by a search of the index of relating franchises and manors held by the Land Registry.

8.3.7. Geological workings may necessitate searches, e.g. for coal, oil, sand and gravel.

8.3.8. An agricultural credits search should be carried out where the transaction includes the purchase of argricultural machinery and equipment. See B8.12.

Enquiries of the seller

8.3.9. In addition to the normal pre-contract enquiries, a form of agricultural tenancy enquiries may be required where the land to be bought includes tenanted property and some of the following additional enquiries may be relevant to the purchase:

    (a) planning enquiries concerning agricultural buildings and whether or not they fall within the Agricultural General Development Order;

    (b) enquiries concerning listed buildings and scheduling under Ancient Monuments and Archaeological Areas Act 1979;

    (c) information should be sought on all grant or subsidy schemes relating to the property ascertaining whether the conditions applicable to them have been properly observed and ensuring no money will become repayable;

B

(d)   enquiries concerning single farm payment entitlement and other quotas which may benefit the property and whether they are transferable to the buyer;

(e)   enquiries concerning boundaries and their maintenance;

(f)   enquiries relating to services benefiting the property (especially water supplies);

(g)   enquiries relating to sites of special scientific interest or other environmental designations whether or not these come to light in answers to a local search;

(h)   enquiries relating to abstraction and discharge licences granted by the Environment Agency under Water Resources Act 1991, Environmental Protection Act 1990 or Environment Act 1995;

(i)   enquiries as to the history of the occurrence of notifiable diseases on the property;

(j)   specific enquiries relating to sporting rights;

(k)   enquiries relating to the existence of standing timber felling licences and grant conditions.

8.3.10.   Particular attention should be paid to matters arising in (c) and (d) above in view of the introduction on 1 January 2005 of the single farm payment scheme under the European Commission's review of the agricultural subsidy system. Most transactions in agricultural land will involve either the transfer or lease of single farm payment entitlement units. In normal circumstances a buyer should expect to acquire an entitlement unit for each eligible hectare comprised in the land to be purchased or let.

8.3.11.   The buyer should ensure the seller provides an up-to-date copy of the seller's Rural Payments Agency register of entitlement units. Once this has been reviewed by the buyer's surveyor, contract provisions should be agreed to deal with the price for the entitlement units and the mechanics of transfer. The buyer should review and agree the terms of the required RLE1 Form which must be submitted to the Rural Payments Agency not less than six weeks prior to the agreed transfer date. It is essential that the notification timetable is agreed with a view to meeting:

(a)   the scheme year application date (normally on or about 15 May); and

(b)   the requirement under the scheme for the claimant to occupy the relevant holding for a 10-month period.

A failure to consider the timing of notification may give rise to a significant loss of support income in the relevant claim year.

8.4. Planning

8.4.1. The authorised use of the land under Town and Country Planning Act 1990 should be ascertained. This information may be revealed in answers to enquiries of the local authority where planning permissions have been granted or a certificate confirming lawful use has been obtained from the planning authorities. In the absence of these the seller should be asked to disclose detailed information on the use of the property. Any restrictions on the use of the property should be discussed by the buyer's solicitor with his client to ensure that they do not conflict with the client's requirements. It is unusual for a seller to give a warranty in the contract relating to the authorised use of the property.

8.4.2. In most cases a change of use to agricultural use needs no consent. In some cases the erection of agricultural buildings does not require consent.

8.4.3. Particular care should be taken to establish whether any dwelling on the property is subject to any occupancy restriction, requiring occupation by someone employed or last employed in agriculture.

8.5. Taxation consequences

8.5.1. If the transaction involves the sale of a business as a going concern, value added tax should not be paid where both the seller and the buyer are registered for VAT. The VAT rules for a going concern transaction are more rigorous where land is included. If the buyer is not registered but the seller is, the seller must charge VAT on the assets which are subject to VAT at the standard rate, unless the buyer registers for VAT and also elects to waive exemption prior to the tax point for the transaction being reached, in which case no VAT is charged. The buyer must also satisfy the seller that their option to tax is not blocked. See A16.15.4. This may include the agricultural land if the option to tax has effect in relation to it.[1] In other cases value added tax may be payable on the transaction, in which case an appropriate clause to this effect needs to be included in the contract.

8.5.2. This type of transaction will often raise taxation issues in relation to capital gains tax and/or corporation tax as well as inheritance tax. Both the seller and the buyer should ensure they take appropriate advice before the structure of the transaction is finalised.

1. Value Added Tax Act 1994, s.40 and VAT (Special Provisions) Order 1995 (SI 1995/1268).

8.6. Grants and subsidies

8.6.1. The buyer should enquire of the seller whether any grants or subsidies have been received or are payable in respect of the land. If any part of these grants or subsidies is repayable on sale of the land, the seller should be required to fulfil this obligation before completion.

8.6.2. If the buyer is intending to purchase any entitlements from the seller under the single farm payment scheme, the buyer should ask the seller to disclose all information held by the seller relevant to the scheme. The buyer should pay particular attention to any restrictions applying to entitlements held by the seller which were allocated to the seller from the UK national reserve. Entitlements do not attach to land and, as a result, will not automatically transfer to the buyer on completion of the purchase of the property. See B8.3.10.

8.6.3. The buyer should take advice from a surveyor on the environmental issues arising under cross compliance, the entry level scheme and the higher level scheme in so far as these relate to the property being purchased.

8.7. Growing crops, livestock, machinery

8.7.1. The seller must agree with the buyer which items of livestock and/or plant and machinery are to be included in the sale. A valuation of these items is often required and the contract should contain an appropriate clause to cover the valuation issues. A schedule of items to be included in the sale should be annexed to the contract.

8.7.2. Similarly agreement must be reached between the parties relating to growing crops, i.e. whether the seller is to be entitled to return to the property after completion in order to harvest his crops, or whether ownership of and responsibility for the growing crops will pass to the buyer on completion. Where the buyer is to take over responsibility for livestock and/or growing crops he may require the seller to give a warranty in the contract that the seller will use his best (or reasonable) endeavours to maintain standards of good husbandry and/or cross compliance over the land until completion. The buyer may consider it prudent to employ a veterinary surgeon to inspect livestock and to certify their state of health. The seller may be required to produce current vaccination certificates for livestock (where appropriate) and livestock passports. It should be noted that a contract to fell and remove standing timber is a contract for the sale of an interest in land which is, by Law of Property (Miscellaneous Provisions) Act 1989, s.2, required to be in writing.

8.8. Water

8.8.1. If the land currently has a water abstraction licence under Water Resources Act 1991, enquiries should be raised to confirm that the benefit of the licence is assignable; a condition providing for the licence to be assigned to the buyer must then be included in the contract. The buyer must then notify the water authority of the change of ownership of the licence within 15 months of completion. Failure to do so results in the licence becoming void and there is no guarantee that a new licence will be granted. Forms supplied by the Environment Agency (in duplicate and accompanied by a plan of the land) may be used to notify the Environment Agency of the assignment. Assignment of a licence is only possible where the buyer takes over the whole of the land to which the licence applies. If the licence relates to only part of the land sold, no assignment is possible and the buyer will need to apply for an apportionment of the existing licence with the seller's co-operation. The contract should contain an appropriate clause to deal with any proposed apportionment.

8.8.2. Where the water supply to the property is metered, the water authority must, in addition to being notified of the change of ownership, be asked to read the meter on the day of completion, in order that apportioned accounts can be sent to seller and buyer.

8.8.3. Some or all of the following enquiries may need to be raised in connection with the water supply to the property:

(a) does the property have a mains water supply?

(b) if there is a mains water supply, does the mains pipe (which is maintained by the water company) run through the property or immediately adjacent to the property in a public highway?

(c) if there is no direct access to the mains water pipe, how is the property connected to the mains, who owns and is liable for the private spur, and does the property have the benefit of private easements for the continued use of the pipe, its maintenance, repair and replacement and the taking of water through it?

(d) where is the mains water meter?

(e) if the property has a private water supply its source should be identified and enquiries raised as to whether the source supplies this property exclusively;

(f) are special water uses required, e.g. for spray irrigation?

(g) if the property is supplied by a private water source from an adjoining property enquiries should be raised to ascertain the contractual rights and obligations of the parties.

8.9.   Tenancies

8.9.1. In order to fulfil his duty of disclosure the seller must give the buyer full details of any tenancies or licences which affect the property. Such details having been supplied, the buyer is, by Standard Condition 3.3.2(a) and Standard Commercial Property Condition 4.1.2 (current editions), deemed to enter the contract knowing and accepting the tenancy terms. By Standard Condition 3.3.2(e), it is the buyer's responsibility to check the effects of any security of tenure legislation affecting such tenancies. Some tenant farmers may have significant protection under Agricultural Holdings Act 1986 or some protection under

Agricultural Tenancies Act 1995 (see K8), and farm workers living in tied accommodation may be protected by Rent (Agriculture) Act 1976 or Housing Act 1988 (see K6).

8.9.2. If the property is sold subject to existing tenancies the buyer should covenant with the seller to observe and perform those conditions which remain to be observed and performed by the landlord and to indemnify the seller against them.

8.10. Wayleave agreements

8.10.1. Any wayleave agreements which affect the property (e.g. for pylons, pipelines, etc.) may be expressly assigned to the buyer with the consent of the appropriate authority. Wayleave payments need only be apportioned if they are of substance. Generally a plan of the property sold can be sent to the utility company after completion and they will apportion the wayleave and issue refunds and demands as appropriate.

8.10.2. The utility companies generally offer a pre-contract search where a buyer wishes to establish exactly what wayleaves exist over the property.

8.11. Quotas

8.11.1. Milk quota must be expressly transferred to the buyer. This topic is further considered in B9. The sale of milk quotas is a standard-rated supply of services for VAT purposes if it is done in the course of a business and the seller is VAT registered. If the quota is sold together with the land, HM Revenue and Customs have indicated that they will treat it as a simple supply of the land.

8.11.2. Sugar beet contracts with British Sugar plc are not quotas. They are standard form contracts agreed through the NFU under the industry's Inter Professional Agreement (IPA). They are personal to the grower and except in limited circumstances provided in the IPA or where special dispensation has been given by British Sugar plc, they cannot be assigned (in whole or in part) or charged or dealt with in any way. All changes are subject to the agreement of British Sugar without which the contract may be terminated. All queries or proposed changes should be referred to British Sugar plc, Weston Centre, 10 Grosvenor Street, London, W1K 4QY.

8.12. Agricultural credits search

8.12.1. A fixed or floating charge made by a farmer in favour of a bank over agricultural stock or assets is void against anyone other than the farmer himself unless the charge is registered with the Land Registry within seven days of its execution.[1]

8.12.2. A person who is buying farming stock or assets or a mortgagee who is lending money on the security of such items should make an agricultural credits search at the Land Registry in order to check the existence and validity of subsisting charges. The search should be made by the buyer before contracts are exchanged in order to find out whether any charges affect the property; in such a case the seller must be required to provide evidence of their discharge at completion. A further search is advised, to be made just before completion, to ensure that no further charges have been registered since the date of the earlier search.

8.12.3. The search is made by submitting Form AC6 in duplicate to Agricultural Credits, Plumer House, Tailyour Road, Crownhill, Plymouth PL6 5HY (DX 8249 Plymouth 3). No personal or telephone search facilities currently exist. Current search fees are listed in Appendix IX.1.

8.12.4. A certificate of search is conclusive but affords no priority period in favour of the searcher. A copy of the memorandum of an agricultural charge can be obtained on application on Form AC5.

8.12.5. An agricultural credits search can only be made against a private individual. Where the seller is a company, the buyer should make a search at Companies House to establish whether any floating charges exist over the company's farming stock or assets.

8.12.6. For more information see Land Registry Practice Guide 63.

1. Agricultural Credits Act 1928, s.9.

8.13. Company search

8.13.1. If buying or leasing land from a limited company or granting a mortgage to a limited company, a company search will normally be desirable. This search should be made before exchange of contracts and updated before completion, particularly where farming stock or assets form part of the sale (see E2.10).

8.14. Post-exchange matters

Mortgages

8.14.1. Appropriate releases should be obtained from the seller or the relevant chargee in relation to any mortgages which affect the property being sold.

8.14.2. Where a floating charge is discovered against a company seller, a certificate of non-crystallisation should be obtained from the relevant lender at completion.

Duplicate purchase deed

8.14.3.   When a part only of agricultural land is sold or where the buyer is giving indemnities to the seller, it is advisable to have the purchase deed drawn up in duplicate, the duplicate being kept by the seller as evidence of, e.g. restrictive covenants imposed on the buyer. This is essential if the seller's title is not yet registered at the Land Registry.

Completion statement

8.14.4.   In addition to the normal requirements for a completion statement (see E4) the following may need to be considered on a dealing with agricultural land:

(a)   VAT on vatable supplies, e.g. farming stock and assets, sporting or fishing rights, entitlement units and quota;

(b)   apportionment of agricultural rents, cottage rents, wayleave payments, sporting or fishing rents;

(c)   payment for fittings being purchased;

(d)   payment for any seeds, cultivations or labour at valuation (plus VAT if applicable);

(e)   allowance for any agreed retentions for holdover;

(f)   where VAT is payable, a separate VAT invoice should be supplied with the completion statement on receipt of the VAT from the buyer;

(g)   payment for entitlements.

8.15.   **Post-completion matters**

8.15.1.   On the sale of the whole or part of a freehold which is subject to an agricultural tenancy, written notice of the change of ownership should be served on the tenant including details of any rent apportionment.

8.15.2.   Transfer forms for the transfer of milk quota must be registered with the Rural Payments Agency after completion (see B9).

8.15.3.   Transfer forms for the transfer of entitlements must be registered with the Rural Payments Agency.

8.15.4.   If the benefit of a grant is taken over with the granting authority's consent, registration of the new owner must be made in accordance with the granting authority's requirements.

8.15.5.   Notice of transfer of a water abstraction licence must be given to the Environmental Agency within 15 months of the transfer.

8.16.   Environmental aspects

8.16.1.   Any discharge which may pollute controlled waters will require a licence/ consent from the Environment Agency under Water Resources Act 1991. Discharge from slurry tanks or yard washing may be sufficiently contaminated to require such a consent.[1]

8.16.2.   Enquiries should be made as to whether the agricultural processes carried out on the property fall within the scope of the regulations made under Environmental Protection Act 1990 as amended or other statutes governing the environment.

8.16.3.   Enquiries should be raised as to whether the property has been the subject of a past land use which has left residual contamination likely to interfere with the buyer's proposed use of the property or which may cause pollution.

8.16.4.   Consideration should be given to the Waste Management (England and Wales) Regulations 2006 (SI 2006/937) which regulate the licensing of the disposal of agricultural waste on the property.

1.   See Control of Pollution (Silage, Slurry and Agricultural Fuel Oil) Regulations (SI 1991/324).

8.17.   Sporting and other rights

8.17.1.   Occasionally sporting rights are reserved by the seller. These may include game under Ground Game Acts, deer (not included in Ground Game Acts) and fishing rights for the seller and his licensees. The rights will include rights of access both to exercise the sporting rights and to retrieve fallen game, any damage caused being made good by the seller. The terms of the contract should be checked to see which, if any, of such rights are being reserved by the seller.

8.17.2.   If it is likely that minerals are contained under the land being sold, consideration should be given to their reservation to the seller, including, where appropriate, rights to work and take away the minerals. A bare reservation of minerals does not allow either seller or buyer to work them. Alternatively, a restrictive covenant may be imposed on the buyer preventing him from working any minerals in the land. If this is done a buyer who wished in the future to work the minerals would have to seek a release of the covenant from the seller (or his successor in title), but no further transfer of the mineral rights would be needed.

8.17.3.   Unless there is a specific reservation in the purchase deed, most incorporeal hereditaments (including a lordship of the manor) will pass with the land. Lordships and manorial rights are sometimes reserved to the seller when land is sold since they are saleable commodities in themselves.

8.17.4.   The reservation of sporting rights, minerals and incorporeal hereditaments all impact on the value of the interest being transferred or leased. The buyer should ensure that appropriate valuation advice is taken where the seller requires reservations of this kind.

8.17.5. Certain sporting rights are now separately registrable under sections 3 and 27 Land Registration Act 2002: see Land Registry Practice Guide 16. An application for registration of such rights should be made in the usual way.

B9. Milk quotas

9.1.   General principles

9.1.1.   Milk quotas were introduced in the UK on 2 April 1984 to regulate the quantity of milk and milk products being produced in the EU. Farms producing milk and other milk products were given an allocation (a quota) the amount of which was normally based on their production levels in 1983. A levy may be payable if a producer exceeds his quota. Quota attaches to the land and will thus pass to a buyer or tenant of the land. Further information and *A Guide to Milk Quotas* can be found at **www.rpa.gov.uk**.

9.2.   Buying land with quota attached

Pre-contract enquiries

9.2.1.   Additional pre-contract enquiries will be necessary to establish:

   (a)   the exact amount of quota attaching to the land;

   (b)   the composition of the quota (i.e. does it include direct sales, or wholesale quota?);

   (c)   that the seller is the freehold owner of the whole holding to which the quota attaches;

   (d)   that the quota does not attach to any land outside the land agreed to be sold;

   (e)   that if the seller is not the freehold owner of the entire holding, all other persons with an interest in the holding, such as landlords or lenders, who will be affected by the disposal of the quota have signified their agreement to the disposal on Form MQ/1; or

   (f)   if an apportionment of the quota has been made within the previous six months and notified to the Rural Payments Agency by means of Form MQ/8.

9.2.2.   If a third party, other than persons referred to in (e) above, has an interest in the land (e.g. lender or trustee) that person's consent to the transfer of the quota should be required on Form MQ/1.

9.2.3. The seller should be required to supply the buyer with his most recent computer print-out from the Rural Payments Agency[1] which will show the allocation of quota and the registration of the quota in the seller's name. The seller will also need to produce his latest statement from his purchaser(s) of milk, showing deliveries to date, to assess the used/unused element of the quota to be sold.

9.2.4. To assist the buyer in dealing with future transfers of quota or claims for compensation from tenants, the seller's records relating to livestock cropping in 1983 and details of the use of the land and buildings, tenant's improvements and rent paid in 1983 should be produced to the buyer and handed over to him on completion.

9.2.5. A seller who sells milk direct to the public must have a licence, a copy of which should be supplied to the buyer and arrangements made for the transfer of the licence to the buyer on completion. Farmhouse cheesemakers are classified as direct sellers if they use their own milk for cheese production within a single business entity. If a farmhouse cheesemaker buys milk directly from a producer or processes his own milk in a separate business entity, the cheesemaker must be approved by the Rural Payments Agency to act as a purchaser. The producer will need to ensure that the quota is registered with the farmhouse cheesemaker to cover deliveries.

The contract

9.2.6. The contract must contain a clause dealing with the transfer of the quota to the buyer (see B1 and B11). Wording similar to that set out below will be appropriate for this purpose:

> 'The seller is the proprietor of wholesale/direct sales quota for [volume] of quota per annum. On completion the seller shall hand over to the buyer an application form for the transfer of the said quota duly signed and completed so far as the seller is able together with a signed statement as required by the Rural Payments Agency and thereafter shall use his best endeavours to obtain the transfer of the said quota to the buyer by providing any further evidence as the Agency shall require.'

The purchase deed

9.2.7. The purchase deed must contain a clause assigning the benefit and burden of the specified amount of quota to the buyer.

Completion

9.2.8. On completion (in addition to normal completion requirements) the buyer must ensure that such of the following documents as are relevant to the transaction are handed over:

    (a) completed Form MQ/1 (consent to transfer of quota);

    (b) any documentation relevant to an apportionment of quota;

    (c)   the quota notification from the Rural Payments Agency;

    (d)   the seller's records for 1983;

    (e)   a direct seller's licence.

Post-completion

9.2.9.   The buyer must give notice of change of occupation to the Rural Payments Agency on a quota transfer form (Form MQ/1). If the change happens at the end of the quota year, MQ/1 forms must be received by 31 March of the quota year to which the transfer relates.

9.2.10.   The buyer should also be advised to keep accurate records of his milk production, use of land, tenant's improvements, etc., for use in future transfers or disputes relating to a tenant's right to compensation.

9.3.   **Sales of part of land**

9.3.1.   Where a buyer buys part of the seller's land he will become entitled to a proportionate amount of the quota attaching to the holding. If the parties (including interested parties) cannot agree on the apportionment of the quota taking account of areas used for milk production then the matter must be referred to arbitration:

    (a)   where apportionment is to be carried out by arbitration the transferor and transferee may, by arrangement, appoint an arbitrator, and the transferee must give notice of such appointment to the Rural Payments Agency within 14 days of the appointment; or

    (b)   the transferor or transferee may apply to the President of the Royal Institution of Chartered Surveyors (RICS) for the appointment of an arbitrator. The party which makes the application must, within 14 days of making the application, notify the Rural Payments Agency of the application. The arbitrator will base his award on the areas used for milk production during the last five-year period in which production took place. A fee will be charged by the RICS; or

    (c)   where neither of the above have taken place, the Rural Payments Agency may make application to the President of RICS for the appointment of an arbitrator.

9.3.2.   The provisions in B9.2 will also be relevant to a sale of part of a holding. In particular the contract must contain a clause to deal with the transfer of the quota. Provisions similar to those set out below will be appropriate:

    '(a)   in addition to the property the seller shall transfer on completion … litres of wholesale/direct sales quota;

    (b)   on completion the seller shall hand over to the buyer's solicitors an application form for the transfer of the said quota duly signed and completed (so far as the seller is able) together with a signed statement the contents of which are in accordance with the provisions of the relevant regulations.[1] The documentation shall be submitted to the Rural Payments Agency forthwith;

(c)   if the seller fails to hand over the requisite forms the buyer may rescind the contract and the seller shall repay the deposit money to the buyer;

(d)   the seller shall supply the buyer and the Rural Payments Agency (or as appropriate) with all necessary evidence required to substantiate the amount of quota transferred with the property and shall use the seller's best endeavours to obtain a transfer of that share of the quota.'

1.   Dairy Produce Quotas Regulations 2005 (SI 2005/465) as amended by Dairy Produce Quotas (Amendment) Regulations 2006 (SI 2006/120); Dairy Produce Quotas (Wales) Regulations 2005 (SI 2005/537); Dairy Produce Quotas (General Provisions) (Amendment) Regulations 2005 (SI 2005/466).

9.4.   Selling land with the benefit of quota

9.4.1.   The seller should be prepared to supply the buyer with the information specified in B9.2.1 and, on completion, such of the documents listed in B9.2.8 as are relevant. The contract and purchase deed must contain a clause dealing with the transfer of the quota (see B9.2.6).

9.5.   Tenancies

9.5.1.   Clauses to deal with the following matters should be considered for inclusion in any tenancy agreement which relates to land which has the benefit of quota:

(a)   prohibition of alienation of the quota by the tenant;

(b)   maintenance of milk production on the land to prevent loss of quota;

(c)   the benefit of the quota on termination of the tenancy;

(d)   tenant's rights to compensation for loss of quota at the end of the tenancy.

9.5.2.   The quota will revert to the landlord on termination of the tenancy but the tenant may be entitled to compensation for the loss of the quota. Where the quota reverts to the landlord Form MQ/1 needs to be completed and sent to the Rural Payments Agency. The landlord can only retain the quota until transfer to another active producer unless he is himself an active producer.

9.5.3.   Agricultural tenancies are explained in more detail in K8.

9.6.   Compensation payable to tenants for loss of quota

9.6.1.   Agriculture Act 1986 provides for payment by the landlord to certain agricultural tenants on termination of a tenancy which is subject to the provisions of

Agricultural Holdings Act 1986. Agricultural Tenancies Act 1995 applies to farm business tenancies entered into on or after 1 September 1995. The 1995 Act entitles a tenant to compensation at the end of a tenancy for physical improvements made to a holding and for intangible advantages which increase the value of the holding, provided they are left behind by a departing tenant and the landlord's written consent to the improvements has been obtained. Intangible advantages include milk quota obtained during the course of a tenancy. For tenancies covered by the 1995 Act the milk quota provisions in section 13 and Schedule 1 Agriculture Act 1986 do not apply.

Eligible tenants

9.6.2.   To be eligible for compensation under Agriculture Act 1986 a tenant must:

     (a)   have the quota registered in his own name (not in the name of a company or partnership through which the tenant carries on business); and

     (b)   have been in occupation of the land as tenant on 2 April 1984; or

     (c)   have succeeded to a tenancy since 2 April 1984 under the succession provisions of Agricultural Holdings Act 1986, so long as the party from whom the tenant succeeded was himself in possession on 2 April 1984.

9.6.3.   Assignors of tenancies assigned after 2 April 1984 are not eligible, but the assignee is, subject to satisfying the qualifications outlined above.

9.6.4.   The statutory entitlement to compensation relates to only one transfer of occupation. There is no entitlement on subsequent transfers. It is therefore open to a landlord to determine the terms under which new tenants can enjoy the quota attached to the holding, i.e. whether they will be charged for quota at the beginning of the tenancy and whether or not they will be entitled to any payment at the end of the tenancy. If the land being vacated comprises only part of the tenant's holding there is an apportionment of the quota for compensation purposes.

Calculation of payment

9.6.5.   Payment is calculated by taking:

     (a)   the value of the allocated quota in excess of the standard quota for the land (or if allocated quota is less than the standard quota a proportionate reduction is made); and

     (b)   the value of the tenant's fraction of the standard quota; and

     (c)   the value of the transferred quota (this will be the entire value where the tenant has borne the whole cost of the transfer and proportionately where the tenant has only borne part of the cost).

Valuation of quota

9.6.6.   Value is defined as the value at the termination of the tenancy taking into account available evidence of the value of the quota including the value of the land with and without quota.

9.6.7.   Standard quota is calculated by multiplying the relevant number of hectares by the prescribed quota per hectare.

9.6.8.   Prescribed quota is defined by Milk Quota (Calculation of Standard Quota) (Amendment) Order 1992 (SI 1992/1225) as 7,140 litres per hectare. There is a lower figure for land in less favoured areas (areas eligible for hill livestock compensatory allowance) and different figures apply for different breeds.

9.6.9.   The relevant number of hectares is the average number of hectares used during the relevant period (the period to which allocated quota was determined, normally 1983) for feeding of dairy cows kept on the land.

Method of assessing quantum

9.6.10.   The quantum of compensation (called the 'tenant's fraction') is ascertained by comparing the annual rental value of the tenant's dairy improvements and fixed equipment with the rent paid for the land during the relevant period.

9.6.11.   The formula used is

$$\frac{r}{r+R}$$

where r = the annual rental value at the end of the relevant period of the tenant's dairy improvement and fixed equipment and R = the rent of the land.

9.6.12.   Liability for compensation does not arise until the termination of the tenancy but either landlord or tenant may at any time prior to termination seek determination of the standard quota or the tenant's fraction by agreement or arbitration.

9.6.13.   The procedure for claiming compensation is similar to that for claiming tenant right under Agricultural Holdings Act 1986.

9.7.   Quota transfers without land

9.7.1.   The notification of a transfer without land is effected on form MQ1 to be received by 31 March in the quota year to which the transfer relates.[1]

9.7.2.   The transferee must meet the definition of a producer at the operative date of the transfer.

Applying for approval

9.7.3.   An application for approval is made using form MQ/1 (*Application for approval to transfer quota without land*). The form should be received by 31 March in the quota year to which the transfer relates.

Used and unused quota

9.7.4. The transferor and transferee must agree how much quota is used or unused. When calculating how much of the original wholesale quota is used it is necessary to take into account deliveries which have already been made with the butterfat adjustment.

9.7.5. If used quota is transferred with unused quota, the Rural Payments Agency will:

(a)   permanently transfer the unused quota to the new owner (the transferee);

(b)   recalculate their ongoing and permanent butterfat bases to take account of the newly-acquired unused quota for the current quota year;

(c)   leave the used quota with the transferor for the remainder of the quota year in question. The used quota will be moved to the transferor as unused quota following the end of the quota year.

Geographical restrictions on transfers

9.7.6. Quota cannot be transferred to or from any of these groups of Scottish islands:

(a)   the islands of Orkney, except for the island of Stronsay; or

(b)   the islands of Jura, Gigha, Arran, Bute, Great Cumbrae and Little Cumbrae, the Kintyre peninsula south of Tarbert and the areas of land within the Argyll and Bute District comprising those parts of the parishes of Dunoon and Kilmun and Inverchaolain.

9.7.7. These groups of islands form separate units of production and are known as 'ring-fenced areas'. A temporary transfer of quota is permitted where it increases quantities available to dairy enterprises within the ring-fenced areas. Quota may be transferred temporarily or permanently within each ring-fenced area, and may be leased into a ring-fenced area, provided the normal requirements are met. Quota may not be transferred, either permanently or temporarily, outside a ring-fenced area.

Changes in butterfat base after a permanent transfer

9.7.8. 'Permanent' butterfat base is the figure attached to permanent quota, after being adjusted for transfers, permanent conversions and special allocations. If the butterfat base of any wholesale quota transferred in is higher or lower than the transferor's ongoing or permanent butterfat base, the new ongoing or permanent butterfat base will be recalculated as the weighted average of the butterfat base of the quota transferred in and the transferee's existing quota and butterfat base. A quota holder who has leased in quota and then leases/permanently transfers quota out, will have their ongoing butterfat base reweighted after each quota movement.

Confirmation of transfer

9.7.9. The Rural Payments Agency will write to the transferor to confirm:

(a) that the transfer has been entered on the quota register;

(b) the changes to the transferor's quota and permanent and ongoing butterfat bases (where applicable);

(c) the details of the producers and purchaser(s) involved.

9.7.10. They will also notify the purchaser of the change in the amount of quota registered with them and the changes to the producer's permanent and ongoing butterfat bases. The Rural Payments Agency will also write to the transferee (and transferee's purchaser, where appropriate) to confirm the results of the transfer in.

Temporary reallocation of quota

9.7.11. Farmers affected by herd movement restrictions can apply for a temporary reallocation of quota using Form MQ/16. For details see Form MQ/16A Explanatory Notes.

1. See Council Regulation (EC) 1788/2003, Art.18.

B10. Pre-contract searches and enquiries

10.1. Reason for making searches and enquiries

10.1.1. Subject to the seller's duty of disclosure,[1] it is up to the buyer to make sure of his bargain. Thus the buyer needs to find out as much about the property as possible before he commits himself to a binding contract to purchase the property. At common law the seller is generally under no obligation to disclose physical defects in the property to the buyer; therefore if the seller does not reveal information about the physical aspects of the property the buyer must obtain such information from other sources, much of which can be obtained through making proper pre-contract searches and enquiries.[2] The buyer should also be advised to arrange for a survey to be carried out to discover physical defects in the property. A solicitor's failure to make appropriate searches may give rise to liability in negligence to the buyer if as a result the buyer suffers loss.[3] However, the seller must not fraudulently conceal known defects or reply dishonestly to questions on pre-contract enquiries or information forms.

10.1.2. The introduction of the home information pack does not change the basic principle that sales of land are on a *caveat emptor* basis (see A26).

1. Discussed in B5. The common law duty of disclosure is often modified by contractual condition, e.g. Standard Condition 3.
2. See Standard Commercial Property Conditions of Sale (Second Edition) 3.1.2(d) on 'searches and enquiries which a prudent buyer would have made before entering into the contract'. Reproduced in Appendix V.10.
3. *Cooper v. Stephenson* (1852) Cox M & H 627.

10.2. Who should make the searches and enquiries?

10.2.1. The onus of making searches rests with the buyer, but in some cases the seller may make all appropriate pre-contract searches and pass the results of these searches to the buyer as part of the pre-contract package. When the home information pack is introduced, the seller will provide some searches and enquiries in the pack, however the sale will still be on a *caveat emptor* basis. It will frequently assist the progress of the transaction if the seller chooses to instigate pre-contract searches on behalf of the buyer and thus gives the buyer a complete package of documentation at an early stage in the transaction, but he is not obliged to do so. The liability provisions on Forms CON 29R and CON 29O (see Appendix V.7) acknowledge a duty of care in negligence by the council to a buyer who relies on replies obtained from another party.

10.2.2. In any case where the seller does not make all the appropriate pre-contract searches, the buyer should do so. Since the risk of buying the property subject to undiscovered defects broadly rests with the buyer, it is up to the buyer to ensure that all necessary pre-contract searches have been made, whether by the buyer himself, or by the seller on the buyer's behalf.

10.3. When should searches and enquiries be made?

10.3.1. Where the searches and enquiries are being undertaken by the seller's solicitor, they should be put in hand in sufficient time to ensure that their results will be available to send to the buyer with the draft contract. Where it is anticipated that delay in receiving the search result will be experienced this may mean that it is necessary to submit a search application as soon as instructions for the sale of the property are received notwithstanding that a buyer has not at that time been found for the property. In other cases the search application need not be submitted until a buyer for the property has been found since, the more recent the date of the search result, the more benefit it will be to the buyer. If the buyer's solicitor is to make searches, he should put his searches in hand as soon as firm instructions to proceed are received from his client. The buyer's solicitor, on receipt of the home information pack (if appropriate) and/or the pre-contract package from the seller's solicitor, should check which searches (if any) have been made by the seller, and immediately submit additional search forms if he considers that any additional searches need to be made to meet the requirements of the particular transaction. Search applications should always be submitted without delay since some authorities take a long time to reply to them. It is unwise for a buyer to exchange contracts before having analysed the results of his pre-contract searches; thus delay in submitting search applications may result in delay to the transaction itself. (See also A26.)

10.4. Which searches and enquiries should be made?

10.4.1. Details of the searches and enquiries listed below are contained in B10.5.

Home information pack

10.4.2. For details of the searches which are required to be included in the home information pack and for those which may be included, see A26.

All transactions

10.4.3.   The following searches are regarded as 'usual' and should be undertaken in every transaction:

- search of the local land charges register;
- enquiries of the local authority and, if appropriate, optional enquiries;
- standard drainage and water enquiries of the water service company;
- pre-contract enquiries of the seller.

Registered land

10.4.4.   In addition to the searches and enquiries listed in B10.4.3, official copy entries of the title must be obtained.

Unregistered title

10.4.5.   In addition to the searches and enquiries listed in B10.4.3, a Land Charges Department search against the name of the seller and prior estate owners whose names appear on the abstract or epitome of title should be undertaken.

Other common searches and enquiries

10.4.6.   Other common searches and enquiries in addition to those listed in B10.4.3 are:

- coal mining search;
- index map search if dealing with unregistered title or an unregistered interest in registered land;
- environmental data search;
- Disadvantaged Areas search (checking relief from stamp duty land tax);
- any of the less usual searches which may be applicable in the circumstances (see B10.6).

10.5.   Summary of usual searches and enquiries

10.5.1.   Local land charges search

- **When to make:** in every transaction.
- **Form:** LLC1 in duplicate (LLC1 is a prescribed form provided for by Local Land Charges Rules 1977, Schedule 1, form C).
- **Search methods:**
  - National Land Information Service Channel (NLIS, see B10.17);

- post/DX to local authority;
- personal search.

- **Plan:** needed if land cannot be clearly identified from postal address.

- **Fee:** yes. See Local Land Charges (Amendment) Rules 2003 (SI 2003/2502). Personal search: £11.00 (plus £1.00 for each additional plot of land up to a maximum for additional plots of £16.00). Official search: £4.00 for searches requested by electronic means, £6.00 for other requests, plus £1.00 for each additional plot of land included in the search up to a maximum of £16.00.

- **Summary of information to be obtained from search:** the most important are: some planning decisions, compulsory purchase orders, financial charges affecting the property, tree preservation orders.

- **Protection given by search:** none. Search result only shows state of register at time when search is made but warning of impending land charges can sometimes be obtained by making an Enquiries of Local Authority search on Form CON 29R (see B10.5.2). A third party can take benefit of search made by someone else (e.g. a seller can make a search to pass the result to buyer or his lender). Local Land Charges Act 1975, s.10 provides compensation in limited circumstances where there is an error on the search certificate, or where a matter is binding on the land but is not revealed by the search, because it was not registered at the time of the search. An entry is binding on the land whether or not it is revealed by the search.

- **Personal search facility:** there is a statutory right to make a personal search, but local authorities do not guarantee the accuracy of the result. It should only be undertaken where time does not permit an official search to be made. Some lenders will not accept personal searches and, if a personal search is undertaken, clients should be warned that it is not guaranteed by the local authority.

- **Special points:** can be made personally or by agent, but the result is not guaranteed. Insurance may be available if exchange has to take place before result of search received.

10.5.2. *Standard and optional enquiries of local authority*

- **When to make:** standard enquiries in every transaction, optional enquiries where appropriate.

- **Form:** the enquiry form CON 29 is split into two forms and both should be submitted in duplicate (see Appendix V.7):
  - CON 29R Enquiries of Local Authority (2007).
  - CON 29O Optional Enquiries of Local Authority (2007).

- **Search methods:**

    – National Land Information Service Channel (NLIS, see B10.17);

    – post/DX to local authority;

    – personal search.

    In view of local government boundary changes, care should be exercised to ensure that the search forms are sent to the correct local authority.

- **Plan:** always include a plan with search requests. Some local authorities have specific requirements in relation to the submission of forms and plans (e.g. Cornwall County and District Councils). Non-compliance with these procedures may result in delay in receiving the answers to enquiries.

- **Fee:** yes. Contact the relevant authority for details. Fees will differ between authorities and between standard and optional enquiries. VAT is payable on a personal search but not on one made by post. See also the special points below.

- **Summary of information to be obtained:** relates only to the property being searched against. Matters which affect neighbouring properties are not disclosed in the search replies.

    – *from standard enquiries:* planning and building regulations; roads; land for public purposes; land for road works; drainage agreements and consents; road schemes; railway schemes; traffic schemes; outstanding notices; infringements of building regulations; notices, orders, directions and proceedings under planning acts; conservation areas; compulsory purchase; contaminated land; radon gas. See Appendix V.7 for the full enquiries.

    – *from optional enquiries:* road proposals by private bodies; public paths and byways; advertisements; completion notices; parks and countryside; pipelines; houses in multiple occupation; noise abatement; urban development areas; enterprise zones; inner urban improvement areas; simplified planning zones; land maintenance notices; mineral consultation areas; hazardous substance consents; environmental and pollution notices; food safety notices; hedgerow notices; common land and town and village greens.

- **Protection given by search:** the buyer is bound by matters even if not discovered by search. The authorities 'do not accept legal responsibility for an incorrect reply, except for negligence. Any liability for negligence will extend to the person who raised the enquiries and the person on whose behalf they were raised. It will also extend to any other person who has knowledge (personally or through an agent) of the replies before the time when he purchases, takes a tenancy of, or lends money on the security of the property or (if earlier) the time when he becomes contractually bound to do so' (extract from the notes to Forms CON 29R and CON 29O, see Appendix V.7).

- **Personal search facility:** some authorities permit personal searches, but do not guarantee the accuracy of the result; it should only be undertaken where time does not permit an official search to be made. Even where facilities are granted for personal searches, these may not cover all the matters normally covered by Forms CON 29R and CON 29O and may not be acceptable to the buyer's lender.

   There are limitations on personal searches and some lenders will not accept them. The accuracy of a personal search depends on the ability and diligence of the searcher. It is not guaranteed by the local authority. If a personal search is undertaken, clients should be told of this and advised of the limitations on personal searches and their possible implications.

- **Special points:** can be made personally or by agent, but the result is not guaranteed. Insurance is available if exchange has to take place before result of search received, but check lender's requirements. Where a local authority refuses to answer a question relating to whether or not a property abuts a public highway consideration should be given to undertaking a commons registration search (see B10.5.7) and to making an inspection of the property.

   The fee requested from the client in respect of the local land charges search and the enquiries of the local authority must accurately reflect the fee charged by the local authority or the local search agents used by the solicitor. It is not acceptable to charge the client an enhanced fee. It is also not acceptable to charge the client an enhanced fee which is paid to the local search agent in exchange for a commission payment from the local search agent to the solicitor.

- **Notes:** both the local search and enquiries of the local authority contain questions relating to planning matters. In most cases the local authority to whom the search application is submitted will also be the planning authority for the area who will therefore answer the planning enquiries on the standard forms. In a few cases, e.g. new town development corporations, the planning authority is separate from the local authority and planning enquiries have to be separately addressed to the planning authority. If in doubt, telephone the local authority prior to submitting the search application in order to check the position.

10.5.3. *Standard drainage and water enquiries*

- **When to make:** standard enquiries in every transaction, optional enquiries where appropriate.

- **Form:** CON 29DW (2007) Standard Drainage and Water Enquiries (see Appendix V.6).

- **Search methods:**

  - National Land Information Service Channel (NLIS, see B10.17);

  - post/DX to relevant company(ies) (see Appendix VIII.2 for addresses);

  - fax – 24 hour expedited search is available from all companies.

  Care should be exercised to ensure that the search forms are sent to the correct company. In some cases enquiries will need to be made of more than one company. The website **www.drainageandwater.co.uk** has a postcode search facility that will return the correct company for a property.

- **Plan:** insisted on by some water service companies, always needed if land cannot be clearly identified from postal address.

- **Fee:** yes. Contact the appropriate regional water service company for details or visit **www.drainageandwater.co.uk**. All regional water service companies answer standard drainage and water enquiries (and for a higher fee, answer an expedited standard search made by fax). Also, at the time of going to press, both Severn Trent and Thames Water offer a 'commercial search' at a higher fee. Solicitors should be aware that the Law Society has only been involved in approving the form and content of the standard drainage and water search. Some areas, such as those served by Dee Valley plc water supply, may be subject to further administrative charges – always check with the appropriate water service company before sending fees.

- **Summary of information to be obtained from search:** location of public sewers within boundaries of the property or its vicinity; whether foul water and surface drainage from property drain to a public sewer; whether any sewers or proposed sewers are adopted; location of public water mains and whether the property is connected; the basis of charging for sewerage and water supply to the property (see Appendix V.6 for full enquiries).

- **Protection given by search:** The standard drainage and water enquiries were aimed primarily at residential property but were not intended to exclude commercial properties, however when first launched the liability was limited to £5,000. Following representations from the profession and discussion between the Law Society and the regional water service companies, an interim measure was agreed in September 2002 – an increase in professional indemnity cover maintained by most water companies to £2 million for commercial property transactions. Some companies do not offer the increased level of cover. Solicitors are advised to check the level of liability cover with individual water service companies before making a search.

- **Personal search facility:** none.

- **Special points:** protection extends to the person, company or body who is the recipient of the report with an actual or potential interest in the property. The property may be located where two different water companies separately provide water and sewerage services. Check carefully for this before submitting the search form to avoid unnecessary delays.

10.5.4. Pre-contract enquiries of seller

- **When to make:** in every transaction.

- **Form:**

  – Seller's Property Information Form (fourth edition) for domestic freehold properties and leasehold properties;

  – Seller's Leasehold Information Form (third edition) for domestic leasehold properties;

  – new TransAction forms have been made by the Law Society (see A26 and Appendix V.13;

  – Commercial Property Standard Enquiries (second edition) (CPSE) (available from the Practical Law Company's website, **www.practicallaw.com**);

  – Other forms from legal stationers are also available.

  In domestic leasehold cases, both the Seller's Property Information Form and the Seller's Leasehold Information Form must be submitted; the information on these two forms does not overlap and answers to both sets of enquiries will be needed by the buyer.

- **Search methods:** send to seller's solicitor.

- **Plan:** no.

- **Fee:** no.

- **Summary of information to be obtained from:**

  – *Seller's Property Information Form:* ownership of boundaries; disputes about the property; occupiers' interests; planning requirements; guarantees affecting the property; approximate completion date; fixtures and fittings; details of notices received by the seller which affect the property.

  – *Seller's Leasehold Information Form:* management company information; landlord's details; maintenance charges; notices; consents; complaints; building insurance; decoration; alterations; occupation; enfranchisement; fire certificates; differences from letting arrangements of other units in the building; problems with maintenance charges; whether the property is part of a conversion; planning permission or established use certificates.

- *Commercial Property Standard Enquiries (general – for all transactions):* boundaries and extent; party walls; rights benefiting the property; adverse rights affecting the property; title policies; access to neighbouring land; access to and from the property; physical condition; contents; utilities and services; fire certificates and means of escape; planning and building regulations; statutory agreements and infrastructure; statutory and other requirements; environmental; occupiers and employees; insurance; rates and other outgoings; capital allowances; value added tax; transfer of a business as a going concern; other VAT treatment; standard-rated supplies; exempt supplies; zero-rated supplies; transactions outside the scope of VAT; notices; disputes.

- **Protection given by search:** none. Seller may be liable in misrepresentation for inaccurate replies.

- **Personal search facility:** none.

- **Special points:** solicitors are required to check the client's replies to Part 1 of the Seller's Property Information Form and the Seller's Leasehold Information Form and to complete and sign Part 2 of the forms. The Law Society has stated that checking the answers given in Part 1 of the form is part of the solicitor's duty as a prudent conveyancer. Failure to do this may amount to inadequate professional service and may be professional negligence (*McMeekin* v. *Long* [2003] 29 EG 120). As a result, Part 2 of the forms must be completed in every case. Completion of Part 2 requires the solicitor to check the information provided by the client in Part 1 and to check the other information in the solicitor's possession, e.g. past and current files, deeds, etc. Where questions have been answered in the terms 'not so far as the seller is aware', this will imply that the seller and his solicitor have made investigations and have no actual knowledge of any defect (*William Sindall plc* v. *Cambridgeshire County Council* [1994] 3 All ER 932). To be adequate, these investigations must cover the seller's personal knowledge as well as the contents of such files, deeds, etc., as are in the firm's personal possession and any other reasonable investigations.

In addition, solicitors acting for the buyer should not accept a Seller's Property Information Form or a Seller's Leasehold Information Form which has not been properly completed. Acceptance may amount to a failure to carry out all the usual enquiries and the solicitor will be in breach of his duty to the buyer client and to any lender client for whom he is also acting.

Enquiries additional to those on the prescribed forms should only be raised where relevant and necessary to the particular transaction. Do not raise additional enquiries about matters that can be resolved by a survey or personal inspection of the property. Seller's replies should be factual and accurate and not based on statements of opinion. The seller's solicitor must take his client's instructions before answering the enquiries.

The seller may supply replies as part of pre-contract package or home information pack, in which case it is unnecessary for buyer to send form to seller. In other cases buyer should send forms to seller as soon as possible at the start of the transaction, and seller should reply as quickly as possible.

In commercial property cases where CPSEs are used it is standard practice for the solicitor to submit the request form to the seller's solicitors (usually via email) while the CPSEs referred to in the request are available to all parties on the Practical Law Company's website (**www.practicallaw.com**).

10.5.5. *Official copy entries of the title*

- **When to make:** in every registered land transaction.

- **Form:**

  – OC1 Application for Official Copies of Register/Title Plan and/or certificate in Form C1.

  – OC2 Application for Official Copies of Documents Only.

- **Search methods:**

  – National Land Information Service Channel (NLIS, see B10.17);

  – Land Registry Direct (**www.landregistrydirect.gov.uk**);

  – post/DX/fax to the Land Registry (see Appendix VIII.1 for addresses);

  – telephone – application can be made by a credit account holder 8.30am–6.00pm Monday to Friday and 8.30am–1.00pm Saturdays and on the national number 0870 908 8063 or 0870 908 8069 for the telephone centre for Wales (specialising in Welsh place names and offering a Welsh speaking service). This number deals with all telephone applications irrespective of where the land is situated.

- **Plan:** no.

- **Fee:** yes, see Land Registration Fee Order 2006 (see Appendix IX.3).

- **Summary of information to be obtained from search:** up-to-date copy of entries affecting seller's title.

- **Special points:** the application is usually made by the seller who supplies the results to the buyer. For more information see Land Registry Practice Guide 11.

10.5.6. *Land Charges Department search*

- **When to make:** in all cases when dealing with unregistered land. Strictly not relevant to land registered with an absolute title but sensible for seller's solicitor to make search against his own client's name to ensure no bankruptcy proceedings pending.

- **Form:**

  - Form K15 Application for an Official Search: not applicable to registered land.

  - Form K16 Application for an Official Search (bankruptcy only).

- **Search methods:**

  - National Land Information Service Channel (NLIS, see B10.17);

  - Land Registry Direct (**www.landregistrydirect.gov.uk**);

  - post/DX to Land Charges Department, Plymouth (see Appendix VIII.2 for address);

  - personal search at Plymouth address only (see Appendix VIII.2 for address).

- **Plan:** none.

- **Fee:** £1 per name for written applications, £2 per name for telephone, fax and computer searches.

- **Summary of information to be obtained from search:** this is the quickest method of checking that no bankruptcy proceedings are registered against a client (although it must be borne in mind that bankruptcy entries are normally cancelled automatically after five years). In addition, in unregistered land, information relating to incumbrances over the land, e.g. post-1925 restrictive covenants, second and subsequent mortgages, estate contracts, and home rights.

- **Protection given by search:** full search: 15 working days from date of official search certificate provided completion takes place within this period. Where an entry is revealed which appears to be irrelevant to the transaction in hand, the seller's solicitor may be asked to certify that the entry does not apply to the transaction (by endorsing the search certificate to this effect). Such endorsement does not alter the legal significance of the search result, but an unqualified endorsement by the seller's solicitor would commit him to personal liability if loss were subsequently suffered by the buyer resulting from that particular entry.

- **Personal search facility:** at Land Charges Department, Plymouth only, but no protection given by personal search.

- **Special points:** the effect of Law of Property Act 1969, s.24 (by displacing the 'registration is notice' rule contained in Law of Property Act 1925, s.198) is to place the burden of disclosure of incumbrances on the seller and thus renders this search strictly unnecessary at the pre-contract stage of the transaction. Since the search needs to be made against all estate owners of the land whose names are revealed in the evidence of title, it is only possible for a buyer to make proper searches if title is deduced to him before exchange. These points notwithstanding it is advisable for the buyer to make a search at least against the seller's name at this stage in order to ensure that no bankruptcy or other financial charges are pending against the seller and that no Class F charge protecting the seller's spouse's or civil partner's home rights have been registered at that time. Additionally, if the documentation supplied by the seller reveals the existence of restrictive covenants which if valid would impede the buyer's proposed use of the land, a check may be made against the name of the person on whom the burden of the covenants was imposed to check whether the covenants were registered as Class D(ii) land charges (if not the covenants are not enforceable against a subsequent purchaser if entered into after 1925). To take advantage of the protection period afforded by the search it will usually need to be repeated shortly before completion. In registered land, bankruptcy entries or a notice protecting a spouse's or civil partner's home rights will be entered on the register and so revealed by official copy entries of the title so long as those copies are up to date.

- For more information see Land Registry Practice Guide 63.

10.5.7. *Commons registration search*

This information is now obtained by making optional enquiry 22 'Common land, town and village greens' on Form CON 29O Optional Enquiries of Local Authority (2007) (see B10.5.2).

10.5.8. *Coal mining search*

- **When to make:** in any case where the property is situated in an 'Affected Area' in which coal mining takes place or has done so in the past. To determine whether a coal mining search is required, conveyancers should consult *Coal Mining and Brine Subsidence Claim Searches: Directory and Guidance* (Law Society, 2006). Solicitors may also check online using a post code search service operated freely by the Coal Authority at **www.coalminingreports.co.uk**.

- **Form:** CON 29M (2006) coal and brine search form.

- **Search methods**:

    - National Land Information Service Channel (NLIS, see B10.17);

    - the Coal Authority's Mining Report Online Service (**www. coalminingreports.co.uk**);

    - fax (an expedited 48-hour service is available to credit account customers or where the full fee is paid in advance);

– post/DX to the Coal Authority (see Appendix VIII.2 for address).

- **Plan:** yes.

- **Fee:** Current fees for residential property are £24.00 for postal or telephone applications and £20.00 for online applications. Fees for nonresidential searches up to a maximum of 25 hectares in extent, are £50.00 inclusive of VAT irrespective of the method of application. Fees information is available from the Coal Authority by telephone, 0845 762 6848 and at **www.coalminingreports.co.uk**, or from your NLIS channel.

- **Summary of information to be obtained from search:** whether the property is in an area where coal mining has taken or is likely to take place; the existence of underground coal workings and mine entries which may cause problems with subsidence; whether compensation for subsidence has been paid in the past or repairs carried out or any claim is current.

- **Protection given by search:** Any liability of the Coal Authority for negligence in giving mining reports shall be for the benefit of not only enquirers but also a person (being a purchaser for the purpose of section 10(3) Local Land Charges Act 1975) who or whose agent had knowledge before the relevant time (as defined in that section) of the contents of the mining report. Such extension of liability to another (who did not purchase the mining report from the Authority) is limited to a purchaser, lessee or mortgagee of the property and not others (e.g. other recipients of reports on title, etc.). Full Terms and Conditions and guidance on liability can be found on the Coal Authority's website (**www.coalminingreports.co.uk**). All residential reports include insurance cover for the property owner of up to £20,000 in respect of loss of value as a result of there being a material change in the mining information in a subsequent residential report. It is intended to cover loss suffered as a result of changes in the coal mining database at any time during the insured person's ownership of the property. Where the search is obtained by the seller, the buyer will receive the benefit of the insurance cover. Similar cover applies to 'residential-search-not-required' certificates.

- **Personal search facility**: none.

- **Special points:** disused mines exist in many areas where coal mining has not been carried on within living memory. The dangers of subsidence exist in any area where mining has at some time taken place. Provisions for compensation for subsidence are complex: in some cases, once a sum has been paid in compensation, no further claim can be sustained despite further subsidence damage to the land.

  From 30 September 2003 the Coal Authority has offered an interpretive report service for residential property. Under the service the applicant will be provided with detailed analysis and advice about mine shafts revealed in the initial report, including a risk assessment as to whether, in the opinion of the Coal Authority, the main building of the property is inside the possible zone of ground movement from any reported mine entry. This service will be offered at an additional cost if the initial report discloses a mine shaft.

10.5.9. Index map search

- **When to make:** in all cases when buying an interest in unregistered land. It is also useful when buying an area of land comprised in more than one registered title.

- **Form:** SIM Application for an Official Search of the Index Map.

- **Search methods:**

  – National Land Information Service Channel (NLIS, see B10.17);

  – Land Registry Direct (**www.landregistrydirect.gov.uk**);

  – post/DX/fax/telephone to the Land Registry (see Appendix VIII.1 for addresses).

- **Plan:** a suitable plan may be needed, see Land Registry Practice Guide 10.

- **Fee:** see Land Registration Fee Order 2006 (see Appendix IX.3).

- **Summary of information to be obtained from search:** whether the land is already registered or is subject to a pending application or caution against first registration or existence of a registered rentcharge or affecting franchise.

- **Protection given by search:** none, although if search result is inaccurate, a right to indemnity may arise (see M7).

- **Personal search facility:** not available.

- **Special points:** if it is discovered that the land is already registered or that a compulsory registration order came into force before the date of the most recent conveyance on sale on the title the seller must be asked to rectify the situation before this transaction proceeds. For more information, see Land Registry Practice Guide 10.

10.5.10. Environmental Data Search

- **When to make:** there is no professional obligation to undertake an environmental data search in the course of property transactions. Solicitors must, however, consider whether contamination is an issue in every transaction and advise clients of the potential liabilities associated with environmental issues, without overstating them. In all commercial transactions, and in residential cases where contamination is considered a potential issue, solicitors may consider making specific pre-contract enquiries of the seller, and other enquiries of statutory and regulatory bodies and if there is a possibility that the site is contaminated, or the buyer or lender requests one, an environmental data search may be made, see B25 and the *Environmental Law Handbook, 5th edition* (Law Society, 2002).

- **Form:** there is no standard form.

- **Search methods:**

    - National Land Information Service (NLIS, see B10.17);

    - online with search providers (see Appendix VIII.2);

    - post to search providers (see Appendix VIII.2);

    - fax to search providers (see Appendix VIII.2);

    - Environment Agency search (**www.environment-agency.gov.uk**).

- **Plan:** it is essential to confirm the location of the land by reference to a plan (paper or online) or by grid reference.

- **Fee:** From £25 to £200 (differs for residential or commercial).

- **Summary of information to be obtained from search:** (depending on provider) all information held by regulatory bodies, a detailed land use survey highlighting current and historic uses, floodplain data, risk assessment.

- **Protection given by search:** none.

- **Personal search facility:** none.

- **Special points:** the purpose of this search is to establish that there is no cause for concern regarding environmental issues or, if there is a concern, to inform further enquiries and advice to the client. For further guidance see B25, Appendix III.1 and the *Environmental Law Handbook* (Law Society, 2002).

10.5.11. *Disadvantaged Areas Search (Relief from SDLT)*

- **When to make:** when acting for the buyer or seller of residential property, a search should be made to determine whether a property is located within a designated disadvantaged area. This will be necessary in every:

    - purchase of residential property where the purchase price does not exceed £150,000;

    - lease of residential property with an average annual rent of more than £600.

    From 17 March 2005 Disadvantaged Areas Relief is not available for non-residential land transactions.

The purchase of six or more separate dwellings as a single transaction is classed as a non-residential transaction and SDLT is payable at the appropriate rate.

Section 116 Finance Act 2003 defines residential, commercial, and mixed-use property. In mixed-use property (part residential and part non-residential) the value has to be apportioned and the £150,000 limit applied to the residential part.

The scope of the exemption is such that it applies to property which on 7 May 1998 was situated in specified qualifying wards included in the current indices of deprivation for England and Wales (Indices of Deprivation 2000).

The exemption will apply to a property falling outside a qualifying ward if on 27 November 2001 it had the same postcode as land which on 7 May 1998 was within a qualifying ward.

Where a property is partly inside a qualifying ward, the purchase price must be apportioned and the part outside will be subject to SDLT.

This complicated definition can give rise to a number of problems, not least that searches currently available to establish whether property falls within a qualifying ward for the purposes of disadvantaged areas SDLT exemption are not always conclusive.

- **Form:** not applicable.

- **Search method for properties with a postcode:**

  - check the postcode lies in a disadvantaged area by using the postcode search on the HM Revenue and Customs website (**www.hmrc.gov.uk/so/pcode_search.htm**);

  - check which ward the property was located in on 7 May 1998 by visiting **www.neighbourhood.statistics.gov.uk** and searching against the property's postcode;

  - check the ward is listed on the HM Revenue and Customs website (**www.hmrc.gov.uk/so/disadvantaged.htm**).

If the results of these three checks are positive, then the property is exempt.

If the postcode search is positive but the ward search shows part or all of the property is outside the relevant ward, the property will still be exempt if the property on 27 November 2001 had the same postcode as land which on 7 May 1998 fell within a qualifying ward.

Warning: The HM Revenue and Customs postcode search is not complete, and is therefore inconclusive. If the postcode search shows that the property is outside a designated area or no postcode is found it may be prudent to follow the steps for properties without postcodes below.

- **Search method for properties without a postcode:**

  – check with the local authority to find out which ward the property was located in on 7 May 1998. Maps showing wards as at 1998 can be viewed as pdf files on **www. neighbourhood.statistics. gov.uk**;

  – check whether the ward is listed on the HM Revenue and Customs website (**www.hmrc.gov.uk/so/disadvantaged.htm**);

  – obtain a copy of the 7 May 1998 boundary ward map from the Ordnance Survey Boundaries Service (Tel. 023 8030 5092) and check that the property is within the boundaries shown. The Neighbourhood Statistics website also holds pdf files of the 1998 ward boundary maps.

  If the results of these checks above show the property within the ward, it is exempt. Any part outside the ward is subject to SDLT.

- **Alternative search method**

  The procedures to ascertain whether a property qualifies for the relief can be time-consuming and not always conclusive. An alternative may be to submit a good plan of the property together with the relevant transaction document to either HM Revenue and Customs Stamp Taxes Enquiry Line or in writing to the offices in Worthing or Manchester (complex transactions) and seek written advice. However, you are only able to obtain a binding opinion of the SDLT due if you inform the HM Revenue and Customs of everything they need to know about the transaction. If advice is sought, HM Revenue and Customs will assist, but any opinion they give will be an informal opinion and will not bind them. Telephone enquiries made on the Stamp Taxes Helpline on 0845 603 0135 may also be of general assistance.

- **Plan:** a copy of the 7 May 1998 ward map clearly showing the property within a ward boundary.

- **Fee:** none.

- **Summary of information to be obtained from search:** an indication of whether the property falls within one of the designated areas that qualify for relief.

- **Protection given by search:** none.

- **Personal search facility:** not applicable. Telephone queries may be directed to the Stamp Taxes Helpline on tel. 0845 603 0135.

- **Special points:** a contract providing for the transfer of six or more properties is classed as non-residential. Schedule 6 Finance Act 2003 determines how property situated partly within and partly outside a designated disadvantaged area is to be treated for the purposes of the relief (queries may be referred to HM Revenue and Customs Stamp

Taxes Office). The European Commission granted approval for the Disadvantaged Areas Relief on 21 January 2003, and its approval is valid until 31 December 2006.

- **Claiming the relief:** For transactions affected by SDLT, relief will be claimed by completing form SDLT1. Box 9 of the form deals with reliefs. No supporting documents or evidence need accompany the return. After the HM Revenue and Customs certificate has been issued, some claims will be checked. At this point the client or solicitor may be asked to provide evidence to substantiate the claim, which may include:

    – the full postcode for the property being transferred;

    – a full photocopy of the transfer document;

    – a copy of the contract or sale agreement;

    – evidence that consideration for the transaction did not exceed £150,000;

    – if the document is a lease, a payment in respect of the rent element;

    – if possible, a copy of the ward map with the location of the property clearly marked.

10.6.   Less usual searches and enquiries

10.6.1.   The buyer's solicitor must in all cases be alert to the need to make additional searches since his client will normally be bound by any matters which those searches would have revealed if made. If a less usual search is not made, in circumstances where it would have been relevant, and as a result of this omission the client suffers loss, the buyer's solicitor will be liable in negligence.[1] In some cases the seller's solicitor may make the appropriate searches and supply the results to the buyer's solicitor, but it remains the buyer's solicitor's duty to ensure that all the correct searches have been undertaken and that their results are satisfactory. A summary of some of the less usual pre-contract searches appears below.

10.6.2.   *Waterways*

- **When to make:** where a river, stream or canal passes through or adjoins the property.

- **Form:** letter.

- **Search methods:**

    – National Land Information Service Channel (NLIS, see B10.17);

    – for rivers, streams or brooks post to the Environment Agency (see Appendix VIII.2 for address);

– for canals post to the British Waterways Board (see Appendix VIII.2 for address).

• **Plan:** yes.

• **Fee:** yes.

• **Summary of information to be obtained from searches:** ownership of river banks and canals; liability for repairs of and maintenance of river banks and canals; fishing rights; licences to abstract water; drainage rights; liability for flooding from rivers; rights of way affecting towpaths along sides of canals.

• **Protection given by searches:** none.

• **Personal search facility:** none.

• **Special points:** The local authority may be responsible for smaller waterways within its own area. Although a search may be requested electronically through an NLIS channel, the response will arrive by post/DX.

10.6.3. Underground railways

• **When to make:** land adjoins railway, railway passes through land, property built close to underground railway network.

• **Form:** letter.

• **Search methods:**

– National Land Information Service Channel (NLIS, see B10.17);

– post to appropriate underground authority (see Appendix VIII.2 for addresses).

• **Plan:** yes.

• **Fee:** yes.

• **Summary of information to be obtained from search:** ownership of track, routes of underground tunnels.

• **Protection given by search:** none.

• **Personal search facility:** not available.

• **Special points:** although a search may be requested electronically through an NLIS channel the response will arrive by post/DX.

10.6.4. Overground railways

There is no statutory basis for response to property enquiries by the railway industry in Great Britain. The main infrastructure controller is Network Rail (formerly Railtrack plc) and a variety of train operators use the track, occupy stations and other railway land. None of these bodies has a system to respond to search letters. Network Rail does not respond to enquiries. Network Rail has answered a series of frequently asked questions at **www.networkrail.co.uk/Property/FAQ.htm**. Information can also be obtained from the reply to enquiry 3.5 'Nearby Railway Schemes', on Form CON 29R Enquiries of Local Authority (2007). This will give details of railways within 200m of the proposed property.

10.6.5. *Tin mining*

- **When to make:** mainly applicable to land to be purchased in West Devon or Cornwall.

- **Form:** letter.

- **Search methods:**

    – National Land Information Service Channel (NLIS, see B10.17);

    – post to Cornwall Consultants (see Appendix VIII.2 for address).

- **Plan:** yes.

- **Fee:** yes.

- **Summary of information to be obtained from search:** presence of disused underground workings which could cause subsidence damage.

- **Protection given by search:** none.

- **Personal search facility:** not available.

- **Special points:** although a search may be requested through an NLIS channel, the response will arrive by post/DX.

10.6.6. *Clay mining*

- **When to make:** mainly applicable to land to be purchased in Dorset, West Devon or Cornwall.

- **Form:** letter.

- **Search methods:**

    – National Land Information Service Channel (NLIS, see B10.17);

    – post to Kaolin and Ball Clay Association (see Appendix VIII.2 for address).

- **Plan:** yes.

- **Fee:** yes.

- **Summary of information to be obtained from search:** presence of workings which could cause subsidence damage.

- **Protection given by search:** none.

- **Personal search facility:** not available.

- **Special points:** although a search may be requested through an NLIS channel, the response will arrive by post/DX.

10.6.7. *Brine*

- **When to make:** land to be purchased in Cheshire, Greater Manchester or Droitwich (Hereford & Worcester). See also *Coal Mining and Brine Subsidence Claim Searches: Directory and Guidance* (Law Society 2006) available from **www.coalminingreports.co.uk**.

- **Form:** on the combined CON 29M (2006) coal and brine search form.

- **Search methods:**

  – National Land Information Service Channel (NLIS, see B10.17);

  – post or DX to the Coal Authority (see Appendix VIII.2 for address);

  – telephone to the Coal Authority's customer service team on 0845 762 6848.

- **Plan:** yes.

- **Fee:** yes.

- **Summary of information to be obtained from search:** presence of disused brine extraction workings which could cause subsidence damage; an indication of whether there have been any claims for damage made by the owner or a previous owner against the Brine Board for past or suspected past damage; whether the Board has made a 'once-and-for-all' payment commuting the property from any further claim for compensation: such a commutation will usually result in the value of the property being reduced and making it difficult to mortgage. If the search result reveals that a claim for compensation has been lodged but not yet adjudicated the buyer must after completion give notice of the change of ownership to the Board.

- **Protection given by search:** none.

- **Personal search facility:** not available.

- **Special points:** although a search may be requested through an NLIS channel, the response will arrive by post/DX.

10.6.8. *Limestone*

- **When to make:** land to be purchased in Dudley, Sandwell, Walsall or Wolverhampton.

- **Form:** letter.

- **Search methods:**

B

- National Land Information Service Channel (NLIS, see B10.17);

- post to local, district or metropolitan council.

- **Plan:** yes.

- **Fee:** yes.

- **Summary of information to be obtained from search:** presence of disused underground workings which could cause subsidence damage.

- **Protection given by search:** none.

- **Personal search facility:** not available.

- **Special points:** although a search may be requested through an NLIS channel, the response will arrive by post/DX.

10.6.9. Rent registers

- **When to make:** land to be purchased is subject to a Rent Act 1977 tenancy.

- **Form:** CON 29E Request for a search of the register kept pursuant to section 79 Rent Act 1977 (in duplicate).

- **Search methods:** post to the relevant Rent Assessment Panel (see Appendix VIII.2).

- **Plan:** no.

- **Fee:** £1.

- **Summary of information to be obtained from search:** the form of enquiry is as follows: 'Are there any, and if so what, subsisting entries in the Register in respect of the above property or any part of it kept pursuant to Section 79 of the Rent Act 1977, as amended by Paragraph 43 of Schedule 25 to the Housing Act 1980?'. Such entries will be disclosed by the search.

- **Protection given by search:** the replies are furnished in the belief that they are correct but on the distinct understanding that neither the President nor any member of his staff is legally responsible therefore, except in negligence.

- **Personal search facility:** not available.

- **Special points:** if a rent is registered, it is an offence for the landlord to charge more than the registered rent for the property. Rent charged in excess of the registered amount is recoverable by the tenant. Registration of a revised rent can normally only be made after two years have elapsed since the last registration. There are now five Rent Assessment Panels covering England, and one covering Wales. For details of their coverage, visit the website of the Residential Property Tribunal Service (**www.rpts.gov.uk**). Form CON 29E was agreed between the Law

Society of England and Wales and the Department of the Environment, it has not been updated since 1996.

10.6.10. *Chancel repair liability*

The cost of repairing the chancel of a parish church is generally met by either the parochial church council, the representative body of the church in Wales, other ecclesiastical bodies, or educational establishments. In some rare instances, however, landowners are liable for the costs of such repair.[2]

10.6.11. Where the liability is not recorded in the title deeds, consideration should be given as to whether it is appropriate to make enquiries.

10.6.12. Enquiries may be made using commercial products that determine if a property is located in a parish where there remains a potential to enforce chancel repair liability, but these products are not property specific.

10.6.13. Property specific enquiries may be made by conducting a personal search or 'FOI paid for search' of the Record of Ascertainments held by the National Archives. For details, see National Archives Legal Records Information Leaflet 33 and 'Information from the Archive L1', both available from **www.nationalarchives.gov.uk**. It is understood that these records are incomplete.

10.6.14. Insurance may be considered as an option following the results of a search, or as an alternative to searching. Insurers may require confirmation that no enquiries of the local church have been made regarding chancel repair liability. (See A4, B6 and C3.)

10.6.15. Schedules 1 and 3 to Land Registration Act 2002 provide that a right in respect of the repair of a church chancel is an interest which overrides first registration and a disposition of a registered title. This liability will retain its overriding status until 13 October 2013. After this date a purchaser will generally only be bound by the liability if it has been protected by an entry on the register or, in the case of unregistered land, a caution against first registration has been registered or the liability is referred to in the title deeds (see Land Registry Practice Guide 66 as to overriding interests losing automatic protection in 2013).

10.6.16. *Search of the index of relating franchises and manors*

- This search will not be required in most conveyancing transactions but may be appropriate when dealing with agricultural land (see B8.3.6). The application should be made in form SIF.

- For more details see Land Registry Practice Guide 13.

---

1. See *G & K Ladenbau (UK) Ltd* v. *Crawley & De Reya* [1978] 1 All ER 682.
2. See *Aston Cantlow and Wilmcote with Billesley Parochial Church Council* v. *Wallbank* [2004] 1 AC 546.

10.7. **Results of searches**

10.7.1. On receiving the results of searches the buyer's solicitor must check the answers given to ensure that the information supplied complies with his client's instructions. Any reply which is unclear must be pursued with the appropriate authority (or seller in the case of pre-contract enquiries) until a satisfactory explanation is received. Failure to pursue an unsatisfactory reply which results in loss being suffered by the client may result in the buyer's solicitor being liable to his own client in negligence.[1] Any reply which is for any reason not satisfactory must be referred to the client for further instructions. Contracts should not be exchanged until satisfactory results of all searches have been received. A summary of the information received from the searches should be communicated to the buyer by his solicitor.

10.7.2. When reporting back to the client it is essential that the client is made aware of the type of issues that cannot be identified from the local search and enquiries.

1.   *Computastaff* v. *Ingledew Brown Bennison Garrett & Co.* (1983) 133 NLJ 598.

10.8. **Checklist**

10.8.1. *Making searches*

   (a)   Decide which searches need to be made and which method is most appropriate.

   (b)   Is a plan required, is it accurate, and is it on a sufficiently large scale to identify the property and the surrounding area clearly?

   (c)   What questions (in addition to those on the printed form) need to be asked?

   (d)   Correct application form and fee?

   (e)   Correct address for submission of the search?

   (f)   Diarise the file and chase up delayed responses.

10.8.2. *Search replies*

   (a)   Analyse the answer to each question – does it accord with what you would expect to find and with what the client wants?

      –   If it does: place a tick in the margin against that question.

      –   If it does not: place a cross in the margin by the question, pursue the question with the relevant authority until a satisfactory reply is received, then replace the cross with a tick, take the client's further instructions if the ultimate reply is not satisfactory.

   (b)   Where an answer contains information which should be communicated to the client or on which the client's further instructions are needed, place a 'C' in the margin beside that question and contact the client.

(c) Do not exchange contracts until all search replies have been received and all answers are marked with a tick.

(d) Consider whether the results of any searches require an insurance policy to be taken out to cover potential liabilities. Remember that the negotiation of an insurance policy may constitute 'arranging' within Financial Services Act 1986.

10.9. Liability on searches

Local land charges

10.9.1. Where a person suffers loss as a result of an error in an official certificate of search, compensation may be payable under Local Land Charges Act 1975, s.10.

Pre-contract enquiries of the seller

10.9.2. An incorrect reply to pre-contract enquiries may lead to liability in misrepresentation. A reply expressed in terms such as 'the seller is not aware (etc.)' may import a warranty that the seller has made reasonable enquiries relating to the matter in question.[1] Any exclusion clause purporting to avoid or minimise liability for misrepresentation will be subject to the reasonableness test in Unfair Contract Terms Act 1977, s.11 and cannot therefore be guaranteed to afford protection to the seller.[2] Even a carefully worded reply to an enquiry, insisting upon *caveat emptor*, may not excuse the seller from a misrepresentation.[3] Where the erroneous reply stems from the seller's solicitor's negligence he will be liable to his own client,[4] he may also owe a duty of care to the buyer under *Hedley Byrne* v. *Heller* principles.[5] Knowledge acquired by the solicitor while acting on his client's behalf is imputed to the client (regardless of whether the client had actual knowledge of the matter in question); thus a seller may be liable in misrepresentation to the buyer for a statement made by his solicitor without his knowledge. In such a case indemnity against the seller's liability could be sought from the seller's solicitors.[6] Where the answers to the enquiries are to be completed by the seller personally (and not by his solicitor), e.g. the Seller's Property Information Form in Protocol cases, the seller's solicitor should advise his client to complete the form with care, since an inaccurate or misleading reply could lead to liability in misrepresentation.[7] The seller should also be advised of the need to notify the buyer if circumstances change, thus rendering inaccurate the original reply given to a question on the search form. The seller's solicitor must complete and sign Part 2 of the Seller's Property Information Form in Protocol cases and may be liable for losses suffered by the seller as a result of errors in the Seller's Property Information Form, Part 1, which the solicitor has not checked and corrected. See B10.5.4.

1. *William Sindall plc* v. *Cambridgeshire County Council* [1996] 3 All ER 932.
2. See Standard Condition 7.1. Some forms of pre-contract enquiries also contain an exclusion clause. See also *Walker* v. *Boyle* [1982] 1 All ER 634.
3. *Morris* v. *Jones* [2002] EWCA Civ 1790.
4. *Cemp Properties* v. *Dentsply* [1989] 35 EG 99.
5. *Hedley Byrne & Co. Ltd* v. *Heller & Partners Ltd* [1964] AC 465 and *Wilson* v. *Bloomfield* (1979) 123 SJ 860.
6. See *Strover* v. *Harrington* [1988] Ch 390.
7. See *McMeekin* v. *Long* [2003] All ER (D) 124. It was held that the Longs should have answered yes to a question on the Seller's Property Information Form asking whether there were any neighbourhood disputes. See also *Sykes and another* v. *Taylor-Rose and another* [2004] All ER (D) 468. The sellers were not under a duty to disclose to the buyers their knowledge that a murder had occurred at the property.

10.10. Relying on searches made by a third party

10.10.1. In relation to enquiries of local authorities on Forms CON 29R and CON 29O and those other enquiries whose terms and conditions include similar provisions as to liabilities, the results of searches are not personal to the searcher; thus their benefit may be transferred to a third party. Where the seller makes pre-contract searches and passes their results to the buyer, the buyer and his lender may in such cases take the benefit of the results. The buyer must check that the seller has undertaken all the searches and enquiries which the buyer deems necessary for the transaction in hand and, if not, he must effect the additional searches himself. If the buyer is not satisfied with the results of the searches made by the seller because, e.g. he considers that they are out of date, or that insufficient questions have been raised, he should repeat the search himself.

10.10.2. There are limitations on personal searches and some lenders will not accept them. The accuracy of a personal search depends on the ability and diligence of the searcher. It is not guaranteed by the local authority. If a personal search is undertaken, clients should be told of this and advised of the limitations on personal searches and their possible implications.

10.11. Inspection of the property

10.11.1. Inspection of the property should be undertaken by the client in all cases. There is no obligation on the solicitor, either in law or conduct, to carry out an inspection in every transaction, but he should do so if his client so requests or if matters reported by the client's inspection give rise to suspicion on the part of the buyer's solicitor. The client should be advised to look for (and to report their existence to his solicitor) any of the following matters:

    (a)   a discrepancy or uncertainty over the identity or boundaries of the property;

    (b)   evidence of easements which adversely affect the property;

    (c)   the existence and status of non-owning occupiers;

    (d)   discrepancy between the fixtures and fittings which the client understood to belong to the property and those actually existing.

10.11.2. It is useful for the client to take a plan of the property with him in order to check its accuracy. An appointment to inspect should be arranged with the seller. The client's surveyor may be able to obtain the necessary information whilst carrying out a survey, but must be instructed to do so.

10.11.3. A solicitor who carries out an inspection on behalf of his client may be liable in negligence if he fails to discover a matter which he ought reasonably to have discovered,[1] for example, the existence of a right of way crossing the property, but the solicitor should stress to the client that the inspection has been carried out by the solicitor in his role as solicitor, and that he does not profess to have the same knowledge about, for example, structural defects in the property as possessed by a surveyor.

1.   *Barclay-White v. Guillaume & Sons* [1996] EGCS 123.

10.12. Tithes

10.12.1. Tithes were abolished in 1936. The 60-year annuities which replaced them were themselves extinguished by Finance Act 1977. There is therefore no need to consider any search for tithes.

10.13. Company search

10.13.1. Where either the seller or buyer is a corporate body a company search prior to exchange should be undertaken in order to check that the company actually does exist. Company searches are discussed in E2.

10.14. Assignment of guarantees

10.14.1. Where the answers to pre-contract enquiries reveal that the property has the benefit of a structural defects policy (for example, NHBC, Zurich, Premier Guarantee) or other guarantee (such as, for woodworm or damp treatment) the benefit of which will pass to the buyer on completion, consideration should be given to whether a formal assignment of the benefit of the policy or guarantee will be needed.

10.15. Properties without mains drainage

10.15.1. Some rural properties may not have the benefit of mains drainage. The client's surveyor should be asked to ascertain the type of drainage provided at the property and if necessary a drainage survey may need to be undertaken to ensure that the system is functional and adequate to meet the needs of the property and its occupants. In some cases it will be necessary to obtain the consent of the Environment Agency for the operation of the drainage system (because the system may discharge effluent into the land or into an adjacent watercourse). The seller should be asked to supply a copy of any such consents in his possession. It may be necessary to transfer such consents to the buyer on completion.

Cesspools

10.15.2. A cesspool is a covered watertight tank used for receiving and storing sewage. It has no outlet but must be regularly emptied either by the local authority or by a private contractor. The tank must be, and remain, impervious to the ingress of groundwater or surface water and to leakage. No consent from the Environment Agency is required for a cesspool.

Septic tanks

10.15.3. A septic tank is a sewage system (usually consisting of two or three chambers) in which the sewage is retained for sufficient time to allow it to partially break down (anaerobic decomposition) before the contents are discharged. Discharge may be by soakage into the ground. The effluent cannot be discharged into a watercourse without further treatment. Environment Agency consent may be required for discharge into the ground.

Package sewage treatment plants

10.15.4. Package sewage treatment plants are similar to septic tanks but treat the sewage to a higher standard than the latter before discharging the effluent. Environment Agency consent is required for the discharge.

Environment Agency consent

10.15.5. Under Water Resources Act 1991, Environment Agency consent is required for any discharge of sewage effluent into a watercourse, lake or pond, and may also be required for any discharge into or onto land. Separate consent is required under Land Drainage Act 1991 if the discharge is made into a main river. An administration charge is made by the Environment Agency for an application for consent together with an annual fee to cover monitoring and other costs.

10.16. Lenders' Handbook

10.16.1. When acting under the terms of the Lenders' Handbook paragraph 5.2 gives details of the pre-contract searches which must be made (see paragraph 5.2.4 for specific details on mining searches). Note that except where the search result carries a priority period the search must not be more than six months old at the date of completion. The lender's specific requirements should also be checked since some lenders will not accept personal searches or search insurance.

10.17. **National Land Information Service (NLIS)**

Introduction

10.17.1. The National Land Information Service (NLIS) brings together and delivers land and property related information held by many different organisations. It delivers integrated land and property information search facilities that support the conveyancing process and can assist the same through faster and more accurate property identification available through the National Land and Property Gazetteer (NLPG).

10.17.2. Conveyancing searches are requested and delivered, where possible, electronically. Conveyancers can retrieve land and property information from the Land Registry and conduct local authority searches, as well as searching for other information – such as coal mining activity, utility services, environmental or geological data – relating to the property.

How the process works

10.17.3. The NLIS hub acts as the gateway to the information held by NLIS data providers such as local authorities, the Land Registry and the Coal Authority. It also provides workflow management, which tracks all requests for information from the channels and responses from data providers.

10.17.4. There are three channels licensed by government to provide NLIS services to solicitors and licensed conveyancers:

- Jordans Ltd – **www.jordans.co.uk**;

- Searchflow – **www.searchflow.co.uk**; and

- TM Property Service Ltd – **www.TMsearch.co.uk**.

These channels act as e-retailers, interacting directly with practitioners via the Internet.

The search request process

10.17.5. The solicitor submits a search request via a secure Internet connection to a channel which, in turn, passes it to the hub. The hub interrogates each of the appropriate data providers concurrently, and reports back to the channel, which formats and presents the consolidated search results for delivery to the practitioner. The whole process is streamlined, and in some cases only takes a matter of minutes to complete.

Information

10.17.6. Further information may be found on the websites of the National Land Information Service (**www.nlis.org.uk**) and the National Land and Property Gazetteer (**www.nlpg.org.uk**). Contact details for the channels can be found in Appendix VIII.2.

B11. Form of contract

11.1. Statutory provisions

11.1.1. Law of Property (Miscellaneous Provisions) Act 1989 repealed Law of Property Act 1925, s.40. The 1989 Act requires all contracts for the sale or other disposition of land or an interest in land to be made in writing and signed by the parties. The writing must incorporate all the terms which have been expressly agreed by the parties and the document must then be signed by or on behalf of all the parties. Where contracts are to be exchanged each part of the contract must contain all the agreed terms and be signed by the appropriate party. It is possible for the signed document to refer to another document which itself contains the agreed terms. If the document does not contain all the agreed terms an order for rectification may be sought.[1]

11.1.2. The requirement for a written contract does not apply to contracts:

(a) to grant a lease for a term not exceeding three years taking effect in possession without a fine;

(b) made at public auction.

Joining two documents together to satisfy the section

11.1.3. Where the signed document does not itself contain all the agreed terms it is possible to join two (or more) documents together in order to constitute a complete contract and thus satisfy the statutory requirements. There is little case law on this point under the 1989 Act,[2] but the rules which applied to the joining of documents under Law of Property Act 1925, s.40 (predecessor to section 2) will not necessarily be applied to actions brought under section 2 of the 1989 Act.[3] It is possible, e.g. to draft a contract which incorporates the Standard Conditions of Sale or Standard Commercial Property Conditions[4] by reference without setting out the full text of those conditions. In such a case the Standard Conditions or Standard Commercial Conditions (as appropriate) will be deemed to be incorporated as part of the contract although contained in a different document from that which was signed by the parties. Since the court's interpretation of this aspect of section 2 is as yet unknown, it is not possible to speculate in what circumstances the court will allow documents to be joined together to form a contract. It should be borne in mind that failure to satisfy the requirements of section 2 results in there being no contract at all between the parties, and the court has no equitable jurisdiction to allow the enforcement of a contract which does not meet the statutory requirements.[5] Care should therefore be taken to ensure that the contract does satisfy section 2 and to this end it is recommended that the full text of the general conditions of sale which are being used (e.g. the Standard Conditions of Sale) is set out in the contract itself.[6] See also B1.7 and B1.8.

Resulting, implied and constructive trusts

11.1.4. Section 2(5) Law of Property (Miscellaneous Provisions) Act 1989 states that nothing in section 2 shall affect the 'creation or operation of resulting, implied or constructive trusts'. A constructive trust will arise if there is evidence that the parties had concluded an agreement. In such a case the courts will be able to give effect to the agreement by enforcing the constructive trust. However, if there are any preconditions to the agreement, e.g. the landlord's consent is required to an assignment, then the trust will not come into being until the condition has been satisfied.[7]

Proprietary estoppel

11.1.5. Section 2 Law of Property (Miscellaneous Provisions) Act 1989 will also not apply where claims are based on proprietary estoppel. Proprietary estoppel is often argued as an alternative where it may not be possible to show the common intention needed to establish constructive trusts. An estoppel may arise where a property owner makes a representation to another party which is relied on by that other party and which leads that other party to act to their detriment.[8] The representation usually relates to the current or future ownership of land or of interests in land. If the party to whom the representation has been made acts to their detriment in reliance on that representation, the representation cannot be revoked and the courts will enforce it despite the lack of a written agreement. In *Crabb* v. *Arun District Council* [1976] 1 Ch 179, Lord Denning explained that proprietary estoppel '… will prevent a person insisting on his strict legal rights … when it would be inequitable for him to do so having regard to the dealings which have taken place between the parties'. In various cases the courts have accepted a wide range of 'acts to the detriment' including: the expenditure of money on a property in which the claimant had been led to believe she had an interest,[9] looking after the property owner and working in his house and garden,[10] continuing in the property owner's employment[11] and selling land without reserving a right of way over it.[12]

1. *Wright* v. *Robert Leonard Developments Ltd* [1994] EGCS 69.
2. *Raymond Ruddick* v. *Paul Ormston* (2005) (unreported) LTL 24/11/2005. The High Court refused to join two documents written on separate pages of a diary, one signed by the seller and the other by the buyer. The pages were written as separate, self-contained documents. Even if they could have been joined, the court went on to decide that they would not have complied with 1989 Act, s.2(1) because the completion date, which had been agreed by the parties, was not specified in the written agreement.
3. See *Firstpost Homes Ltd* v. *Johnson* [1995] 1 WLR 1567.
4. See Appendices VI.12 and VI.14.

5. See however *Pagemanor* v. *Ryan* [1998] NPC 37 where a buyer under contract which did not fulfil s.2 obtained an alternative remedy in quasi-contract. See also *Nweze and another* v. *Nwoko* [2004] EWCA Civ 379, in which the Court of Appeal decided that an oral compromise of a dispute, a term of which was that one party would sell a property at the best price available, was not a contract for the sale of land and was not caught by Law of Property (Miscellaneous Provisions) Act 1989, s.2.
6. See *B. Ltd* v. *T. Ltd* [1991] NPC 47 where it was held that incorporation of the National Conditions of Sale by reference did satisfy s.2 of the Act. See also *Commission for New Towns* v. *Cooper, The Independent,* 15 March 1995, CA where it was held that an exchange of letters did not satisfy s.2.
7. *Representative Body for the Church in Wales* v. *Newton* [2005] EWHC 681; 16 EGCS 145, QBD.
8. See *Taylor Fashions Ltd* v. *Liverpool Victoria Trustees Co. Ltd* [1982] 1 QB 133. See also *Cobbe* v. *Yeomans Row Management Ltd* [2006] EWCA Civ 1139.
9. See *Pascoe* v. *Turner* [1979] 1 WLR 431.
10. See *Re Basham* [1986] 1 WLR 1498.
11. See *Greasley* v. *Cooke* [1980] 1 WLR 1306 and *Gillett* v. *Holt* [2001] Ch 210.
12. See *Crabb* v. *Arun DC* [1976] 1 Ch 179.

11.2.   Satisfying the statutory requirements

11.2.1.   The statutory requirements are normally satisfied by the preparation by the seller's solicitor of a formal contract. The contract is usually prepared in two identical parts based on the Standard Conditions of Sale or Standard Commercial Property Conditions as amended to fit the particular circumstances of the transaction. A summary of both sets of Standard Conditions is contained in B12 and the conditions are set out on Appendix V.9 and V.10. The contract comes into being when exchange of contracts takes place. For signature and exchange of contracts see section C.

Collateral contracts

11.2.2.   To be enforceable, options, equitable mortgages[1] and side letters issued in connection with sale of land transactions also need to satisfy the requirements of section 2. This will mean that these documents need to be in writing and signed by both parties. An agreement not to negotiate with any other buyer (a 'lock-out' agreement) can be enforceable as a separate collateral contract provided good consideration is given. This type of agreement does not fall within the scope of section 2.[2] A 'lock-in' agreement (i.e. to negotiate with these buyers only) is not an enforceable contract.[3] Also see B1.7 and B1.8.

Variation of contract

11.2.3.   A variation of a contract to which section 2 applies must itself comply with the section.[4]

1. *United Bank of Kuwait plc* v. *Sahib* [1996] NPC 12.
2. *Pitt* v. *PHH Asset Management Ltd* [1993] EGCS 127.
3. *Courtney & Fairburn* v. *Tolaini Bros* [1975] 1 WLR 297.
4. *McCausland* v. *Duncan Lawrie* [1996] NPC 94. An exception to this is a variation of the payments to be made under a mortgage which are not required to satisfy the section: *Target Holdings* v. *Priestly* [1999] *Gazette,* 6 May.

11.3. **Contents of the contract**

11.3.1. In addition to the formal parts, i.e. date, parties, signature, the contract comprises two main elements:

(a) the particulars, which describe the physical extent of the property to be sold and its tenure; and

(b) the conditions which set out the terms on which the seller is prepared to sell the property.

11.4. **The particulars**

11.4.1. These must contain a clear description of the physical extent of the property to be sold and whether the estate to be sold is freehold or leasehold. The title number of a parcel of registered land is its sole distinguishing feature and thus must be referred to in the particulars. The class of title under which the land is registered (e.g. absolute) must also be included in order to give the buyer an accurate description of the estate which is being sold. Where the boundaries are well defined and the property has a regular postal address, the postal address may suffice to describe the land itself. In other cases a more detailed description may be necessary, referring where appropriate to the measurements of the property and/or a plan (see B21). Any inaccuracy in the particulars may give rise to an action in misdescription or misrepresentation (see section M).

11.5. **Conditions of sale**

Open contract rules

11.5.1. Where a contract makes no reference to a particular matter the contract is said to be 'open' on this point and is thus governed by the open contract rules which are laid down either by common law or by statute. Some of the open contract rules are satisfactory in operation, e.g. the rules for deduction of title on the sale of unregistered freeholds, and are invariably used without alteration. Others, e.g. the time for completion, which under the open contract rules is set at 'a reasonable time after the contract', are less satisfactory and are frequently altered by special condition in the contract itself. The Standard Conditions of Sale normally vary the open contract rules, but may themselves require amendment to suit the particular circumstances of the transaction.

Standard Conditions of Sale

11.5.2. Assuming that the Standard Conditions of Sale have been used to form the basis of the contract, special conditions will still be needed to deal with any variations which are required, and any features peculiar to the particular transaction. Even in the most straightforward transaction special conditions will invariably be required to deal with the matters listed below.

Checklist of usual special conditions

11.5.3.

Condition to deal with	Reason for inclusion	Standard Condition	Reference
Title	Buyer is entitled to know what title is being offered.	SC 4.1 SCPC 6.1	Section D
Deposit	No provision at common law, variation of general conditions may be required.	SC 2.2 SCPC 2.2	B17
Interest on deposit	Interest is payable under Solicitors' Accounts Rules.	SC 2.2.6	A20
Completion date	Open contract rule and general conditions not satisfactory.	SC 6.1 SCPC 8.1	Section F
Title guarantee	Defines scope of implied covenants for title.	SC 4.6.2 SCPC 6.6.2	M9
Incumbrances	Seller's duty of disclosure.	SC 3 SCPC 3	B5
Fixtures and fittings	To create an obligation and to avoid disputes between the parties.	SC 10 SCPC 12	B22

Condition to deal with	Reason for inclusion	Standard Condition	Reference
Vacant possession	Implied by common law unless stated to the contrary. Normally included for certainty and must deal with requirement for completion to take place at the property if so required.	SC Special condition 4 SCPC Special condition 2	B3

11.6. Full/limited title guarantee

11.6.1. The seller can sell with either full or limited title guarantee irrespective of the capacity in which he could have sold the property under the pre 1 July 1995 law (Law of Property (Miscellaneous Provisions) Act 1994). The guarantees apply to the sale of both freehold and leasehold property and on the grant of a lease. They can also be used on the transfer of personal property including intellectual property and rights in shares. The extent of the warranties given under the full and limited title guarantees is discussed in M9.[1]

11.6.2. On the front of the Standard Contract form the seller should specify whether he sells with full or limited title guarantee. Should the seller fail to specify the nature of the title guarantee, Standard Condition 4.6.2, and Standard Commercial Property Condition 6.6.2, provide that the seller will sell with full title guarantee. In addition, Special Condition 2 of the standard conditions of sale provides that the seller will sell with either full or limited title guarantee as specified on the front page of the contract.

11.6.3. The warranties given under the full and limited guarantees can be amended in the agreement. If the seller is concerned about incumbrances he should disclose them in the contract and ensure that the buyer agrees to take the property subject to them. See also Standard Condition 4.6.2. Under s.6 of the 1994 Act (as amended by Land Registration Act 2002) the sale of a registered title will also be subject to any matters entered on the register of title at the time of the disposition. As a result any such matters will not be covered by the title guarantee.

11.6.4. If the seller is a beneficial owner he will usually provide full title guarantee. If the seller is a trustee, personal representative or mortgagee, he will usually provide a limited title guarantee.

11.6.5. Where the disposition is of an interest the title to which is registered the seller will not be liable under any of the covenants for title for anything which at the time of the disposition was entered in the register in relation to that interest.[2]

1. Land Registration Rules 2003, rr. 67 to 69, incorporate the provisions as to implied covenants into registered conveyancing.
2. Law of Property (Miscellaneous Provisions) Act 1994, s.6 as inserted by Land Registration Act 2002, Sched.11, para.31.

11.7. Drafting the contract

11.7.1. Although drafting the contract is the prerogative of the seller, the relative bargaining strength of the parties rarely permits the seller to draft a contract which is entirely to his own satisfaction. Contract drafting is therefore an exercise in the art of compromise. The seller must seek to preserve his own interests without misleading the buyer, but will frequently have to include or concede some terms which favour the buyer in order to achieve a prompt conclusion to the transaction. A solicitor, whether acting for seller or buyer, who obstinately insists on the total protection of his own client's interests in the contract terms will at best prolong the transaction unnecessarily or at worst find that negotiations break down entirely and in neither case can he be said to be providing a proper service to his client. Where the Protocol is used amendments of the standard terms should be kept to a minimum.

11.8. Style of drafting

11.8.1. The contract must clearly state what the seller is offering to sell and on what terms including price. Use of anachronistic language should be avoided but clarity must not be sacrificed for brevity. Conditions should only be included where they are relevant and necessary and not through force of habit. Bearing in mind that it is the solicitor's duty to draft a contract which will avoid disputes or litigation between the parties, it becomes a matter of judgment as to the extent of the inclusion of clauses which cater for unforeseen eventualities.

Guidelines

(a) Does the contract describe clearly what is to be sold?

(b) Is a plan necessary?

(c) Does the contract accord with the client's instructions as to the conditions on which the property is to be sold?

(d) Are the conditions concise and unambiguous?

11.9. Looking at the contract from the buyer's point of view

11.9.1. No two draftsmen will ever produce identically worded contracts for the sale of the same property. Drafting is a personal skill and the draftsman's choice of words must be respected by the buyer's solicitor. Amendments should not be made to suit the individual whim of the buyer's solicitor but should be confined to those which are necessary and relevant to the particular transaction. The primary questions in looking at the contract from the buyer's point of view are:

(a)   does the clause accord with the client's instructions? and

(b)   does the clause do what it is intended to do?

11.9.2.   If the answers to these questions are in the affirmative – leave the wording alone. If not, alter the clause until it does meet the above criteria.

11.9.3.   Amendments should be clearly inserted on both copies of the draft contract in a distinctive colour.

11.10.   Unfair Terms in Consumer Contracts Regulations 1999

11.10.1.   Unfair Terms in Consumer Contracts Regulations 1999 (SI 1999/2083) affect all contracts (oral or written) made between a seller or supplier and a consumer (this latter expression applies to individuals only). Unlike Unfair Contract Terms Act 1977, the 1999 Regulations do apply to land contracts,[1] including mortgages and tenancy agreements. Agreements for financial services made between an individual and his broker are also potentially within the Regulations. The EU Directive (93/13/EEC), from which the English Regulations derive, intended land contracts to be included within its scope.

Situations in which the Regulations apply

11.10.2.   The Regulations do not apply to a contract for sale made between two private individuals but catch contracts made between a corporate or business seller and a private individual. Thus contracts for new houses or plots on a building estate where the seller is a developer and the buyer a private individual are potentially affected since in these circumstances the contract is usually in standard form and there is little or no freedom for the buyer to negotiate terms. Similarly mortgages, where the lender is in business and the borrower is not, are caught, as also are sales by mortgagees.

11.10.3.   Tenancy agreements and contracts for financial services are potentially within the scope of the Regulations.

Effect of the Regulations

11.10.4.   If a term is held to be unfair, that term is to be treated as void, but the rest of the contract remains binding on the parties, so long as it is capable of continuing without the offending term.

11.10.5. A term will be regarded as unfair if, contrary to the requirement of good faith, it causes a significant imbalance in the parties' rights and obligations arising under the contract to the detriment of the consumer. Various factors, similar to those contained in Unfair Contract Terms Act 1977, are contained in the Regulations to act as guidelines as to whether 'good faith' exists, e.g. the strength of the bargaining position of the parties, the circumstances surrounding the contract, and whether the consumer has received any special inducement, such as a discount, to agree to the term.

11.10.6. The burden of proof will lie on the consumer to show that a term included in the contract which was not individually negotiated between the parties is unfair.

11.10.7. The Regulations also require all contracts to be drafted in plain intelligible language. See also A21 for information on the reproduction of the contract.

1.   *Khatun* v. *Newham London Borough Council* [2003] EWHC 2326.

B12. Standard Conditions of Sale and Standard Commercial Property Conditions

12.1. Standard Conditions of Sale

12.1.1. Most contracts for the sale of residential property will be made either on the Standard Conditions of Sale Form or by reference to the Standard Conditions.

12.1.2. The text of the Standard Conditions of Sale (fourth edition) are set out in Appendix V.9. Individual conditions are referred to in context in the text of this book.

12.1.3. The Standard Conditions of Sale (fourth edition) came into force on 13 October 2003.

12.2. Standard Commercial Property Conditions

12.2.1. The Standard Commercial Property Conditions (second edition) are based on the Standard Conditions of Sale (fourth edition) but apply to commercial transactions. The full text of the conditions is set out in Appendix V.10. Many of the conditions in the Standard Commercial Property Conditions are identical in wording to their Standard Conditions counterparts, but there are some notable exceptions. The method of calculating compensation for late completion under Standard Commercial Property Condition 9.3 is not based on the concept of relative fault. The Standard Commercial Property Conditions are intended for use in more complex commercial transactions and the Standard Conditions may be appropriate for simple commercial transactions.

12.3. Incorporating Standard Conditions of Sale

12.3.1. To satisfy Law of Property (Miscellaneous Provisions) Act 1989, s.2 a contract for the sale or other disposition of land must be in writing, incorporating all the terms which have been agreed between the parties. These terms will normally include the Standard Conditions of Sale or the Standard Commercial Property Conditions. Where a solicitor prepares a contract on a word processor or by other duplicated means incorporation of either set of the Standard Conditions by reference may satisfy the requirements of section 2 (but see B11.1.3). Failure to satisfy section 2 means that no contract exists between the parties.[1]

12.3.2. The Standard Commercial Property Conditions are drafted in two parts. Only Part I will automatically be incorporated into the contract. An express condition is needed if it is desired also to incorporate Part II.

1. See *B Ltd* v. *T Ltd* [1991] NPC 47.

12.4. Using Standard Conditions of Sale

12.4.1. Not all of the Standard Conditions will be appropriate for use in every transaction. Solicitors should, in every transaction, give careful thought to the application of the conditions and expressly amend those which are inappropriate to the particular circumstances of the current transaction. As in all cases, amendments should be restricted to those which are essential to meet the circumstances of an individual case.

12.5. Protocol

12.5.1. The Standard Conditions of Sale (fourth edition) are one of the standard documents forming part of the Law Society's National Conveyancing Protocol (see A19). The proposed use by the seller's solicitor of a different form of conditions would be a departure from the Protocol which would need to be disclosed to the buyer's solicitor at the commencement of the transaction. The drafting of the Standard Conditions mirrors the requirements of the Protocol; thus an amendment to the Standard Conditions may itself be a departure from the Protocol requiring notification to the other party. Since the aim of the Protocol is to simplify and speed up the conveyancing process it is recommended that in transactions where the Protocol is being used, solicitors alter the Standard Conditions as little as possible, subject to their paramount duty of acting in the best interests of their client.

B13. Conditional contracts

13.1. When are conditional contracts appropriate?

13.1.1. Conditional contracts carry with them some risks and uncertainties which make them inappropriate for everyday use, but they may be considered for use in the following circumstances:

(a) where the buyer has not had the opportunity before exchange of contracts to make searches and enquiries or to conduct a survey or where his mortgage arrangements have not been finalised;

(b) where the contract is dependent on planning permission being obtained for the property;

(c) where the sale requires the consent of the Charity Commissioners under Charities Act 1993 (see B7.8);

(d) where the sale is dependent on permission being obtained from a third party, e.g. ministerial consent, landlord's consent;

(e) where the parties wish to be bound to a contract but there is some other unresolved matter which prevents commitment to an unconditional contract for the time being, e.g. the seller has to get in part of the legal estate.

13.2. Desirability of conditional contracts

13.2.1. Conditional contracts are generally not desirable since they leave an element of doubt as to the very existence and validity of the contractual obligations between the parties. Most of the situations in which conditional contracts are proposed for use benefit the buyer more than the seller (e.g. 'subject to planning permission'), and the seller should resist the suggestion of entering a conditional contract if at all possible. A conditional contract may, however, be inevitable where the seller needs the consent of the Charity Commissioners to the sale under Charities Act 1993 since an unconditional contract which is entered into without such consent is not lawful.

13.2.2. Conditional contracts should never be used where one or both of the parties has an unconditional sale or purchase contract which is dependent on the conditional contract. In this situation, if the conditional contract were to be rescinded for non-fulfilment of the condition, this would give rise to great difficulties in the fulfilment of the linked unconditional contract and may result in a breach of that contract.

13.2.3. Before agreeing to enter a conditional contract the seller should consider whether there are any viable alternative solutions. Where it has been suggested that the sale is 'subject to planning permission', it may be preferable to delay exchange until the results of the planning application have been received by the buyer, rather than enter into a hastily drafted conditional contract. An alternative solution may be to grant the buyer for a nominal consideration an option to purchase the property to be exercised within a stated period.

13.3.   Conditions precedent and subsequent

Conditions precedent

13.3.1. A condition precedent has the effect of suspending the operation of the contract until the terms of the condition have been met. If the condition has not been fulfilled by the appropriate time limit, the party with the benefit of the condition may withdraw and the contractual obligations of the parties never come into existence.

Conditions subsequent

13.3.2. Where the contract is subject to a condition subsequent, the contractual obligations of the parties arise on the creation of the contract and continue to exist until terminated by the party with the benefit of the condition on its non-fulfilment.

13.3.3. If the wording of the condition reads 'subject to x', this indicates a condition precedent.

13.3.4. If the wording of the condition reads 'until x', this indicates a condition subsequent.

13.4.   Requirements for a valid conditional contract

Certainty

13.4.1. The terms of the condition must be clear and certain. In *Lee-Parker* v. *Izzet (No.2)*,[1] an agreement to sell a freehold house 'subject to the buyer obtaining a satisfactory mortgage' was held to be void because the word 'satisfactory' was too nebulous and there was thus no certainty regarding the circumstances in which the buyer would validly be able to withdraw from the contract. It should be noted, however, that not all 'subject to mortgage' clauses will suffer the same fate. A similarly worded clause in *Janmohamed* v. *Hassam*[2] was held to be valid.

Time for performance

13.4.2. It was held in *Aberfoyle Plantations Ltd* v. *Cheng*[3] that the time for performance of the condition is of the essence and cannot be extended either by agreement between the parties or by the court. The same case also laid down the rules relating to the time for performance of the condition which are summarised as follows:

(a) where the contract contains a completion date, the condition must be fulfilled by that date, irrespective of whether time was of the essence of the contractual completion date;

(b) if a time is stated for the fulfilment of the condition, that time limit must be complied with or the contract will fail;

(c) if no time limit is specified the condition must be fulfilled within a reasonable time. This provision is patently unsatisfactory since it leaves room for argument about what is a reasonable time.

1. [1972] 2 All ER 800.
2. (1976) 241 EG 609.
3. [1960] AC 115.

13.5. Withdrawal from the contract

13.5.1. Only the party with the benefit of the condition may withdraw from the contract, and only for reasons connected with the condition. No other reason will justify withdrawal, although there is no obligation on the resiling party to prove that he is being reasonable in exercising his rights to withdraw. It is a question of construction of the condition itself as to whether a party may withdraw before performance of the condition.[1]

1. *Tesco Stores Ltd* v. *William Gibson & Co. Ltd* (1970) 214 EG 835.

13.6. Waiver of the condition

13.6.1. Where the condition benefits one party only, it may be waived unilaterally. In other cases the waiver amounts to a variation of the contract and requires the consent of both parties. If to remove the condition takes away the whole purpose of the contract, the whole contract will fail for uncertainty.

13.7. Drafting

13.7.1. The drafting of a condition requires extreme care to ensure that the requirements outlined in B13.4 have been satisfied. No such provision is included in the Standard Conditions of Sale although a contract to assign a lease may be conditional on the landlord's consent being obtained under Standard Condition 8.3.

13.7.2.   *Guidelines*

(a)   Consider the precise event(s) on which the contract is to be made conditional.

(b)   By what time must the condition be fulfilled? (Bear in mind that the specified time limit cannot be extended.)

(c)   Consider the precise terms on which the party with the benefit of the condition may rescind.

(d)   Ensure that there are no loopholes which would enable one party to escape from the contract other than for the non-fulfilment of the event(s) contemplated in (a) above.

(e)   Use an established precedent, tailoring it to fit your exact requirements.

(f)   Take your time: a condition which is hastily drafted may contain unforeseen errors.

(g)   Having drafted your 'perfect' condition, leave it on the desk overnight and review the wording objectively in the cold light of day. Does the condition achieve its objectives? Is it clear and certain? Do any unforeseen or unwanted consequences flow from the wording?

Precise terms for rescission

13.7.3.   'Subject to searches'

(a)   Which searches?

(b)   Which adverse entries will give rise to the right to rescind?

(c)   By when must the search result(s) be received?

(d)   Can buyer rescind if he changes his mind and never makes search applications?

13.7.4.   'Subject to mortgage'

(a)   Specify name of lender(s) to whom application made.

(b)   Specify amount of required advance.

(c)   Specify acceptable interest rates.

(d)   Should the buyer be entitled to rescind if the mortgage offer is subject to conditions or a retention – what conditions attached to the offer would be acceptable/unacceptable?

(e)   Time limit by which application must be determined?

(f) Can buyer rescind if he changes his mind and never puts in an application for a mortgage?

13.7.5. 'Subject to survey'

(a) Named surveyor?

(b) What type of survey?

(c) Which defects revealed by survey report will entitle buyer to withdraw?

(d) Should a financial limit be placed on the entitlement to rescind? E.g. buyer can rescind if survey reveals defects which exceed £x in total. If so who assesses the value?

(e) Time limit for obtaining result of survey.

(f) Can buyer rescind if he changes his mind and never instructs the surveyor?

13.7.6. 'Subject to planning permission'

(a) Form of application to be agreed between the parties.

(b) What conditions attached to the consent would entitle the buyer to rescind?

(c) Can buyer rescind if he changes his mind and never puts in a planning application?

(d) Time limit for result of application.

(e) Which party is to make the application and pay the fee?

(f) The non-applying party should agree in writing not to oppose the application and to support it.

(g) Is the application to be for outline or detailed permission?

(h) Which party is to pay the architect's and other professional fees in connection with the application?

B14. Sub-sales

14.1. Definitions

14.1.1. In this section of the text only, the following expressions have the meanings set out below:

    (a) 'the buyer' means the person who has contracted to buy land and who is selling the land under a sub-sale contract before completion of his own purchase;

    (b) 'the seller' means the person from whom the buyer (as defined above) is purchasing the land and in whom the legal title to the property will be vested pending completion;

    (c) 'the third party' means the person who is buying the land from the buyer (as defined above) under the sub-sale contract.

14.2. Buyer's position pending completion

14.2.1. A buyer who has exchanged contracts for the purchase of property is the owner of the beneficial interest in the land, but does not obtain the legal estate until registration of the transfer to him (or completion in the case of unregistered land).

14.3. Contractual restriction on sub-sales

14.3.1. Where a buyer intends to sell the property to a third party by way of sub-sale he must ensure that his existing contract to purchase the land contains no restriction which would prevent the sub-sale. Standard Condition 1.5 and Standard Commercial Property Condition 1.5 both state that the buyer is not entitled to transfer the benefit of the contract. As a result the seller cannot be forced to transfer the title to anyone other than the buyer named in the contract. This provision will not prevent sub-sales of freeholds nor sub-assignments of leases. However, the buyer will have to complete the second transaction separately and subsequent to his own purchase. The provision does however provide protection on the grant of a lease as the seller (landlord) cannot be forced to grant the lease to anyone other than the buyer (tenant) in the contract. A seller should resist a buyer's request to remove Condition 1.5 from the contract, because its presence ensures that the seller will take the benefit of the covenants given by the first tenant on grant of a lease.

14.3.2. If a restriction against sub-sales is included in the buyer's contract, he will be able to contract to resell the land to a third party, but will have to complete this second transaction separately and subsequent to his own purchase.

14.3.3. Provided there is no such restriction, the buyer may enter a contract for sale with a third party, prior to completion of his own purchase. In such a case, the buyer may, if he wishes, draft the transfer document to reflect the sub-sale (i.e. the seller transfers direct to the sub-purchaser with the original buyer joining in as a party to transfer his beneficial interest in the estate being transferred). Provided the buyer's transfer is technically correct, the seller cannot refuse to sign even if he had previously been unaware of the sub-sale.

14.3.4. Where there is a restriction on sub-sales in the contract it may be possible for the buyer to assign the benefit of his contract with the seller to the third party and then to complete the purchase as nominee for the third party. Because the buyer will have the right to occupation on completion of his purchase, he will be liable for the relevant Stamp Duty Land Tax (SDLT) and the subsequent transfer to the third party will also be brought into charge to tax. If the assignee fails to complete, the buyer (assignor) may find himself in a position where he is unable to force the seller to transfer the property to the buyer because the assignment is binding on all parties, including the seller (see *Scammell* v. *Dicker* [2005] EWCA Civ 405).

14.4. Special conditions in the sub-sale contract

14.4.1. Special conditions may need to be inserted in the sub-sale contract to deal with the following matters.

The contract

14.4.2. When drafting the sub-sale contract, care must be taken to take account of any relevant provisions in the principal contract, e.g. as to length of a notice to complete; the buyer needs to be in a position to give the third party a notice to complete expiring not later than the date of expiry of any notice to complete which the buyer receives from the seller.

Title

14.4.3. The third party should be required by contractual condition to accept the buyer's entitlement to be registered by the production of official copy entries of the seller's registered title, and the contract between seller and buyer. In unregistered land the buyer, having investigated title with his own seller, can usually satisfy Law of Property Act 1925, s.44 by supplying a good root of title and subsequent documentation, but will need to produce his own purchase contract to the third party as evidence that he can compel the seller to convey the legal estate.

The purchase deed

14.4.4. The purchase deed will usually consist of a transfer or conveyance from the seller direct to the third party. The buyer will need to be made a party to the document in order to transfer his equitable interest in the property to the third party.

Apportionment of the price

14.4.5. Where the amount payable by the third party exceeds the consideration due from the buyer to the seller, the purchase deed will need to contain an apportionment of the price as between buyer and seller, with a receipt for their respective portions being given by each.

14.5. Completion

14.5.1. Depending on the arrangements which have been made between the parties, special provisions may need to be considered in relation to actual completion of the transaction, e.g.

    (a)   where completion is to take place;

    (b)   transmission of the money;

    (c)   custody of deeds;

    (d)   undertakings for the discharge of the seller's mortgage(s) over the property.

14.6. Stamp Duty Land Tax

14.6.1. Under the stamp duty regime, an intermediate buyer of land who entered into a sub-sale contract was often able to arrange that completion was effected by the owner/seller conveying land direct to the sub-purchaser and thus saving or reducing his liability to tax. Similar arrangements can be made under Stamp Duty Land Tax (SDLT), but care needs to be taken (see A14.8).

14.6.2. Sections 45 and 45A Finance Act 2003 provide for both the main contract and sub-sale contract to be fully chargeable to tax unless the two contracts complete or are substantially performed at the same time. Finance Act 2003, by introducing the concepts of the effective date of a transaction and substantial performance meant that resting on contracts as a device for postponing the charge to duty has disappeared.

14.6.3. Where an intermediate buyer of land substantially performs the main contract (for example, where he enters into occupation of the land, or commences to develop it), the contract becomes a land transaction and is subject to SDLT. Its effective date is the date of substantial performance. Completion may not take place until the owner conveys the (now possibly developed) land to the sub-purchaser. At such time, a further land transaction occurs. The transfer to the sub-purchaser is a land transaction. Its effective date is the date of transfer. Both purchasers will become liable to submit a land transaction return and to pay any SDLT due on the consideration payable under the relevant contract.

14.6.4. Group relief is not allowable for sub-sales between group companies.

14.7. Registration of third party

14.7.1. Whether the transaction proceeds by way of a direct transfer from the seller to the third party or by two separate purchase deeds, the third party will still be able to effect registration of his own title at the Land Registry without needing to insist that the buyer obtains a registered title in his own name first. Where two purchase deeds have been executed, the third party will need to produce the transfer from the seller to the buyer to the Registry as proof of the devolution of title (see B4).

14.8. Protection of sub-sale contract

14.8.1. The third party is in a more vulnerable position than a normal buyer since completion of his contract is dependent on the buyer's completion of his own contract with the seller. It may therefore be advisable for the third party to protect his contract by registration. Registration of a contract for sale as a class C(iv) land charge can only be effected against the owner for the time being of an unregistered legal estate, i.e. the seller (see C5.3). When the title is registered protection is by the entry of notice in the register of the title.

14.9. Notice to complete

14.9.1. The buyer cannot serve a notice to complete on the third party unless and until he has completed his own contract with the seller. Until this happens the buyer is not 'ready able and willing' to complete within the terms of Standard Condition 1.1.3[1] or Standard Commercial Property Condition 1.1.3. This problem can be overcome by the insertion of a special condition in the contract which allows the buyer to serve a notice notwithstanding that he has not yet completed his own contract. Once a notice to complete is served, time will be of the essence of the contract; the buyer should therefore not serve such a notice unless he is confident that he can complete his own purchase (from the seller) within the time limit which he has imposed on the third party.

1. See generally *Cole* v. *Rose* [1978] 3 All ER 1121.

14.10. Capital Gains Tax

14.10.1. Where a Capital Gains Tax liability is incurred by either the seller or buyer as a result of the sale(s) HM Revenue and Customs treats a sub-sale transaction as being two separate sales (even if completed by one deed), the sale from seller to buyer being regarded as having taken place before the transaction between the buyer and the third party (see A15).

14.11. VAT

14.11.1. The VAT implications of a sub-sale will also need to be considered and provision made in the contract for the responsibility for payment of VAT where applicable (see A16).

B15. Supply of evidence of title before exchange

15.1. **Supply of evidence of title before exchange**

15.2. **Registered land**
15.3. **Unregistered land**

15.1. Supply of evidence of title before exchange

15.1.1. Having investigated title prior to drafting the contract it will be possible in most cases for the seller to supply the buyer with evidence of title concurrently with the draft contract. Where the Protocol is being used, the seller is obliged to supply his evidence of title to the buyer at this stage of the transaction (Protocol, para. 4.4, see Appendix II.1).

15.1.2. The supply of such evidence of title before exchange is recommended as it will enable the buyer to obtain a comprehensive view of the property which he is buying and will obviate delays after exchange since problems which arise on the title will be brought to light and dealt with at an early stage in the transaction.

15.1.3. Where this is done, it is common for the seller to include a contractual condition which precludes the buyer's right to raise requisitions on the evidence of title. Such a condition does not bind the buyer's lender. Such a condition will exclude the normal contractual condition allowing requisitions to be raised within a certain time after exchange of contracts (see Standard Condition 4.2.1 and Standard Commercial Property Condition 6.2). Where such a condition is included in the contract the buyer must obtain satisfactory answers to his queries on the evidence of title before exchange of contracts. He will not be able to rescind the contract after exchange if he discovers a defect arising out of the evidence of title which was supplied to him prior to exchange. The buyer should ensure that any condition excluding his right to raise requisitions should be limited to requisitions upon the evidence of title actually supplied by the seller prior to exchange of contracts. It should not prohibit requisitions being raised on undisclosed matters which are only revealed by pre-completion searches at the Land Registry or the Land Charges Department.

15.2. Registered land

15.2.1. Up-to-date official copy entries of the title together with supporting documents, e.g. evidence of overriding interests, tenancies, title plan, etc., should be supplied by the seller at his own expense. The copies supplied to the buyer must be *original* official copies. Photocopies of official copies do not satisfy this requirement.

15.3. **Unregistered land**

15.3.1. An epitome of title together with clear photocopies of the documents referred to in it should be supplied to the buyer.

B16. Undertakings for bridging finance

16.1. General points on undertakings

16.1.1. An undertaking is a promise by a solicitor (or a member of the solicitor's staff) to do, or to refrain from doing, something. The promise is enforceable against the solicitor personally, even where the promise was given by a member of staff and not by the solicitor himself. An undertaking given in the firm's name binds all the partners. Undertakings are binding because they are given and no other considerations impinge on their enforceability; thus the normal period of limitation of actions imposed by the Limitation Acts does not apply and an undertaking may be enforced against the giver irrespective of the fact that the normal limitation period has expired.[1]

16.1.2. Failure to honour an undertaking is professional misconduct.[2]

16.1.3. Because of the personal liability which attaches to undertakings it is important that both the giver and recipient of the promise understand precisely what the terms of the promise are. To avoid any misunderstanding it is recommended that undertakings are always given in writing. Any ambiguity in the terms of the promise is construed against the giver of the undertaking. The guidelines contained in the Law Society's Undertakings Warning Card should be observed (see Appendix III.4).

16.1.4. An undertaking is enforceable because it has been given and thus needs no consideration for its validity, although in practice consideration will often be present.

16.1.5. A promise to give an undertaking is enforceable as an undertaking.

16.1.6. A solicitor is responsible for honouring any undertaking given by his staff. In order to ensure that no undertaking is given which is outside the control of the solicitor to perform it is recommended that undertakings should only be given by partners in the firm, or by other staff with the prior consent of a partner.

16.1.7. Where an undertaking is given by a member of staff without having obtained or exceeding the requisite authority from a partner, the firm will still be bound to honour that undertaking unless the recipient was aware of the lack of authority on the part of the giver.

16.1.8. Any exclusion of the personal liability of the giver of the undertaking must be clear and explicit. Such undertakings should be regarded with great caution since the primary value of the undertaking, i.e. its enforceability may have been seriously eroded by the exclusion clause. A solicitor may give an undertaking on behalf of a client provided that the wording of the undertaking makes it clear that the primary responsibility for performance of the promise lies with the client and not with the solicitor.

16.1.9. The solicitor must ensure that whatever is promised by the undertaking is capable of performance and is totally within his own control to perform. An undertaking will be enforceable even if the circumstances which prevailed at the time when the undertaking was given subsequently change. Any change in circumstances which potentially affects the fulfilment of an undertaking must be notified to the recipient and, if necessary, the terms renegotiated to ensure that whatever promise has been given is capable of performance.[3]

16.1.10. An undertaking to do something which is not within the direct control of the giver should, if it is appropriate to give such an undertaking at all, only be given in qualified form, e.g. an undertaking to procure the client's signature to a document is not totally within the solicitor's own control since he cannot force the client to sign; thus the undertaking should be worded on the basis that the solicitor will use his best (or reasonable) endeavours to procure the required signature.

16.1.11. Undertakings given by licensed conveyancers or authorised practitioners are enforceable as if they were given by solicitors.

16.1.12. Undertakings given by unqualified persons who are not acting through a solicitor's practice are only enforceable under the ordinary law of contract and should never be accepted.

Guidelines

(a) Obtain the client's irrevocable written authority before giving an undertaking.

(b) Ensure the wording of the undertaking is clear, unambiguous, and totally capable of performance.

(c) Only give written undertakings, signed or authorised by a partner.

(d) Mark the client's file conspicuously to ensure that the undertaking is not overlooked.

(e) When the undertaking has been fulfilled obtain a written release from the recipient.

1. *Bray v. Stuart West & Co.* [1989] EGCS 60.

2. Rule 10.05 Solicitors' Code of Conduct 2007.
3. *Udall* v. *Capri Lighting Ltd* [1997] 3 All ER 262.

16.2. Bridging finance for the deposit

16.2.1. Where bridging finance is being extended for the deposit on the client's purchase the bank or other lender will normally require the solicitor to give an undertaking to repay the loan, usually out of the proceeds of sale of the client's existing property.

16.2.2. Such an undertaking should only be given where:

(a) the solicitor is sure that sufficient funds will be available on completion to repay the loan with interest;

(b) the solicitor knows the client well enough to feel confident of making a binding commitment on that client's behalf;

(c) the client has given his irrevocable authority for the undertaking to be given. If in doubt, obtain the authority in writing.

16.3. When should the undertaking be given?

16.3.1. Until contracts have been exchanged on the client's related sale transaction there is no guarantee that any funds will be available to repay the loan. Ideally, therefore, such an undertaking should not be given until contracts have been exchanged on the sale. In practice it may be necessary to give the undertaking shortly before exchange in order to ensure the availability of funds for a simultaneous exchange on both sale and purchase contracts. The undertaking should not be given until negotiations for the sale contract are close to the point of exchange, with no outstanding unresolved problems.

16.4. Terms of the undertaking

16.4.1. The Law Society has agreed a form of wording for use by solicitors when giving undertakings to banks for bridging finance. The full form of this undertaking is set out in Appendix V.2.

16.4.2. Even where an undertaking is presented to the solicitor in the standard form or a familiar and frequently used form of wording, the entire wording should be read carefully in the light of the particular transaction to ensure that the wording is appropriate for those circumstances. If the wording is not wholly appropriate to the circumstances in hand, the undertaking should be amended to reflect the particular requirements of the transaction.

16.4.3. Confine the terms of the undertaking to repayment:

(a) of a stated figure, plus interest on that sum if so instructed;

(b) from a defined source, e.g. the proceeds of sale of a named property;

(c) of the net proceeds of sale, having defined what is understood by the word 'net', i.e. after deduction of specified loans, estate agents' commission, solicitor's fees, disbursements on the sale and purchase, and any other known and defined liabilities which will reduce the amount available to repay the loan;

(d) when the proceeds of sale are actually received by the solicitor. This protects the solicitor against having to honour the undertaking in circumstances where the sale of the property is completed but for some reason the funds are never received by him, e.g. the client intercepts the money and absconds with it.

16.5.   Change of circumstances

16.5.1. If, having given an undertaking, the circumstances of the client's sale and purchase transactions change, e.g. the consideration for the sale is reduced to take account of a structural defect, the terms of the undertaking must be considered carefully to ensure that they are still capable of performance. The recipient of the undertaking must be informed of the changed circumstances irrespective of whether they affect the obligations covered by the undertaking. Where the undertaking has become impossible of performance because of the changed circumstances the solicitor must renegotiate the undertaking to obtain either a release of his obligations or a form of wording which is capable of performance in the light of the current situation.

16.6.   Checklist

16.6.1.   (a) Do I know the client well enough to feel confident about giving the undertaking?

(b) Have I got the client's irrevocable written authority to give the undertaking?

(c) Has the client disclosed all subsisting mortgages and liabilities which will or might affect the amount of money which will be available to discharge the loan?

(d) Is there sufficient equity to repay the loan with interest?

(e) Are the terms of the undertaking totally acceptable?

(f) Are negotiations for the client's sale sufficiently firm and advanced to make it safe to give the undertaking?

(g) Has the undertaking been authorised by a partner?

(h)   Has the cover of the client's sale file been clearly marked to show that an undertaking has been given, to whom, and for what amount?

16.7.   Loan guarantees

16.7.1.   A solicitor who gives an undertaking which is effectively a guarantee of a loan being taken out by the client will be bound by that undertaking even if it is not given 'in the normal course of practice'. Such an undertaking may, however, be outside the scope of the solicitors' indemnity insurance.

B17. Deposit

17.1. Is a deposit necessary?

17.1.1. In law a deposit is unnecessary and neither common law nor statute provides for such to be payable. The payment of a deposit is a purely customary arrangement which is expressly incorporated into the contract for the benefit of the seller.

Purpose of deposit

17.1.2. The payment of a deposit acts as part payment of the purchase price, demonstrates the buyer's good intentions of completing the contract, and gives the seller leverage to ensure the fulfilment of the contract since he is usually able to forfeit the deposit if the buyer defaults, thereby recouping part or all of the loss occasioned by the buyer's default.

17.2. How much deposit?

17.2.1. No deposit at all is payable unless the contract expressly makes provision for one.

17.2.2. The Standard Conditions of Sale provide for a deposit of 10% of the purchase price and chattels price. This figure will apply unless specifically amended. The Standard Commercial Property Conditions provide for a 10% deposit of the purchase price and this will apply unless specifically amended.

17.2.3. In recent years deposits of less than 10% have become more widespread in residential transactions due in part to the increase in 95% or 100% mortgage offers to buyers, and to the fact that high property prices, with consequently high deposits, place an unfair financial burden on the buyer whilst over-compensating a seller who forfeits that deposit on the buyer's default.

17.2.4. It is clearly to the seller's advantage to demand a 10% deposit; if, however, he is asked by the buyer to accept a reduced amount the following factors should be considered:

(a) the risk of the sale going off, with the consequent need to forfeit the deposit to compensate for loss;

(b) the buyer's mortgage arrangements – are they firm and settled? Is the offer of advance for the whole of the purchase price (taking into account the amount of the reduced deposit)?

(c) the likely amount of loss which the seller would suffer if the buyer were to default, e.g. cost of bridging finance or interest needed to complete a related purchase, length of time and costs of resale of the property.

17.2.5. The seller's solicitor must explain the consequences of taking a reduced deposit to his client and obtain his client's express authority before agreeing the reduction with the buyer's solicitor or representative. *Morris* v. *Duke Cohan*[1] suggests that it may be professional negligence for a solicitor to accept a reduced deposit without the client's express authority.

17.2.6. If a reduced deposit is taken on exchange, the contract should provide for the balance of the 10% to become immediately payable on service of a notice to complete.[2]

17.2.7. Only in exceptional circumstances should the transaction proceed without any deposit being taken. Examples might include family transactions or sales to sitting tenants.

17.2.8. Deposits in excess of 10% are very rare, and cannot be justified in normal circumstances. The risk is that a defaulting buyer may be able to obtain repayment of the whole of an excessive deposit (not just the amount in excess of 10%).[3]

17.2.9. The amount of the deposit actually payable on exchange will take into account any preliminary deposit already paid, but, unless the contract provides otherwise,[4] is calculated exclusive of the value of chattels which are to be paid for in addition to the purchase price of the land.

1. (1975) 119 SJ 826.
2. See Standard Condition 6.8.3.
3. See *Dojap Investments Ltd* v. *Workers Trust and Merchant Bank Ltd* [1993] AC 573 where the forfeiture of a 24% deposit was held to be a penalty.
4. See Standard Condition 2.2.1.

17.3. How is the deposit to be funded?

17.3.1. The answer to this question should be obtained when initial instructions are taken from the client. It is safest to assume at this stage that the seller will require a full 10% deposit, and if the buyer wishes to pay a reduced deposit the matter will have to be raised during negotiations with the seller's solicitor.

From an investment account

(a) How much notice does the buyer need to give to withdraw his funds without losing a significant amount of interest?

(b) Ensure sufficient money is transferred to a short-term investment account in time for it to be immediately available on exchange.

Bridging finance

17.3.2. Bridging finance from a bank or other lender will often be needed in a situation where the purchase is dependent on a related sale:

(a) It should be apparent at an early stage in the transaction that bridging finance will be required and arrangements should be made as soon as possible so that the money is immediately available when required on exchange.

(b) An undertaking to repay the bridging loan out of the proceeds of sale of the client's existing property will often be required from the solicitor. Should an undertaking be given and, if so, are its terms acceptable?

(c) Has the client been properly advised about the costs and risks of bridging finance, e.g. high interest rate payable over an uncertain period if the sale goes off, arrangement fees?

(d) Tax relief on the amount of the bridging finance is available where the loan is taken on a separate loan account, but not where the loan is taken by way of overdraft on a current account. If the client has a high cash flow passing through his current account it may be more cost effective to forgo the tax relief and take advantage of the lower interest rates payable on the current account.

Deposit guarantee

17.3.3. Check buyer's eligibility – the conditions of the scheme may provide, e.g. that the scheme is not available for first-time buyers, or that the deposit must not exceed either 10% of the purchase price or £15,000, or that the completion date in the contract must not be more than six weeks from the date of exchange.

17.3.4. The seller's agreement to use of the scheme must be obtained as soon as possible and arrangements put in hand to obtain the guarantee so that it is available to be handed to the seller on exchange of contracts.

17.3.5. Before agreeing to accept deposit by way of guarantee the seller should consider:

(a) the fact that he may not be able to use the deposit towards the deposit on his own purchase (depending on the scheme used) although this factor will be of no consequence if a deposit guarantee is to be used in that transaction also;

(b) the consequences (including costs and delay) of attempting to enforce payment through the scheme if the reasons for the buyer's ultimate default are either disputed or not covered by the scheme.

Lenders' deposit-free schemes

17.3.6. The terms of these schemes vary from lender to lender. The terms of the particular scheme should be considered carefully by both parties before a decision to use them is taken. In particular the seller should have regard to the possible consequences (including costs and delay) if the reasons for the buyer's ultimate default are either disputed or not covered by the scheme.

17.4. Clearing funds

17.4.1. Under Standard Condition 2.2.4 the deposit is payable by direct credit or by a cheque drawn on the solicitor's or licensed conveyancer's client account. The buyer's solicitor must therefore ensure that he receives the amount of the deposit from his own client in sufficient time to allow the client's cheque to be cleared through the solicitor's clients' account before drawing the cheque in favour of the seller for the deposit or authorising the direct credit.

17.4.2. Under Standard Commercial Property Condition 2.2.2 the deposit is payable by direct credit only. The Conditions require that the direct credit arrive not later than the date of the contract in cleared funds at the bank nominated by the seller's solicitors (see Conditions 1.1.1(g), 2.2.1 and 2.2.2). This may be impossible to fulfil if exchange takes place in the late afternoon. Agreeing between solicitors to send the money the next working day may avoid the buyer's solicitor being in breach of the undertaking implied in Formula B but will not operate to amend the contract because of Law of Property (Miscellaneous Provisions) Act 1989 s.2 – so (a) his client will technically be in breach of contract and (b) is the seller entitled to the overnight interest which his solicitor has forgone?

17.5. Capacity in which deposit is held

17.5.1. The deposit is held in one of the three capacities listed below:

(a) agent for the seller;

(b) agent for the buyer;

(c) stakeholder.

17.5.2. In the absence of contrary agreement solicitors and estate agents hold in the capacity of agent for the seller, but an auctioneer holds as stakeholder.[1] This general rule may be varied by express contractual condition.

17.5.3. The capacity of agent for the buyer is rarely used since in most situations the seller will be reluctant to agree to the deposit being held in this way. It may, however, be necessary to use this capacity where the seller is represented by an unqualified person.

17.5.4. If the deposit is held as agent for the seller, the agent may hand the money over to the seller before completion. In this situation the seller can use the money towards the deposit on his own purchase, but where this occurs the buyer may have difficulty in recovering the money if the seller defaults on completion. The buyer should be advised of the risks involved in agreeing to the deposit being held in the capacity of agent.

17.5.5. A stakeholder is the principal for both parties and where this capacity is used the money may be handed to either party without the consent of the other provided the stakeholder is confident that circumstances exist which justify his decision to make payment. Normally, however, the stakeholder should not part with the money until completion or other resolution of the matter.

17.5.6. Most deposits are paid to the seller's solicitor in the capacity either of agent for the seller or stakeholder.

17.5.7. The Standard Conditions of Sale (Condition 2.2.6) and Standard Commercial Property Conditions (Condition 2.2.2) generally provide for the deposit to be held as stakeholder and this is the capacity recommended by the Law Society.[2] The capacity of agent for the seller will, however, apply if the seller is to use all or part of the deposit towards the deposit on his related residential transaction in England and Wales (Standard Condition of Sale 2.2.5), and may be necessary in some circumstances where an exchange under the Law Society's Formula C is contemplated; see B17.9.6.

17.5.8. Where the seller is represented by an unqualified person the buyer's solicitor should ensure that he or a reputable estate agent holds the deposit (in either case in the capacity of stakeholder) or that it is placed in a deposit account in a bank or building society in the joint names of seller and buyer.

Fiduciary vendors

17.5.9. Where the sellers are selling as trustees the money arising from the sale will be trust money and should never be outside the control of the trustees.[3] This requirement will be satisfied if the deposit is paid to some person in the capacity of agent for the seller.

17.5.10. Where the deposit or any part of it is proposed to be held as agents of the seller, it is recommended that the buyer client should be advised of the risks involved in agreeing to this.

1. *Edgell* v. *Day* (1865) LR 1 CP 80; *Ryan* v. *Pilkington* [1959] 1 All ER 689.
2. [1975] *Gazette*, 184.
3. [1957] *Gazette*, 327.

17.6. Solicitor holding the deposit

17.6.1. The money is client money and must be placed in a client account in accordance with Solicitors' Accounts Rules 1998.

17.7. Interest on the deposit

17.7.1. Whether the money is held in the capacity of agent for the seller or stakeholder interest may be payable under Part C Solicitors' Accounts Rules 1998 (see Appendix I.2).

17.7.2. Where the money is held as stakeholder interest is payable on the stake money under the provisions of Solicitors' Accounts Rules 1998. It is up to the parties to decide which of them should be entitled to the interest on the stake money and an appropriate clause must be included in the contract to deal with the payment of interest in these circumstances. The Law Society's recommended form of wording for such a clause is as follows: 'The stakeholder shall pay to the seller/buyer a sum equal to the interest the deposit would have earned if placed on deposit (less costs of acting as stakeholder).' In the absence of an agreement the interest follows the stake under Rule 26 Solicitors Accounts Rules 1998.

17.7.3. Standard Condition 2.2.6 provides that where the deposit, or part of it, is held in the capacity of stakeholder, interest on the deposit will be payable to the seller on completion. If the buyer negotiates an agreement that he is to be credited with interest on the deposit, a special condition must be inserted in the contract to that effect. Standard Commercial Property Condition 2.2.2 contains provisions similar to Standard Condition 2.2.6.

17.8. Deposits paid to estate agents

17.8.1. At common law an estate agent holds the deposit as agent for the seller, but this capacity may be changed to stakeholder by express contractual provision.

17.8.2. In whichever capacity the deposit is held the risk of its loss through the default of the agent generally falls on the buyer.[1]

17.8.3. This risk has been minimised by Estate Agents Act 1979, s.16 which requires agents to carry insurance to cover clients' money. 'Clients' money' is defined by section 12 of the 1979 Act to include any contract or pre-contract deposit.

17.8.4.   The money must be placed in a clients' account (section 14 Estate Agents Act 1979), and is held on trust by the agent for the person who is or who will become entitled to the money. Since the money is trust money it will not vest in a trustee in bankruptcy should the agent be made bankrupt.[2]

17.8.5.   An estate agent who holds in the capacity of agent for the seller is under a duty to account to the client for interest on any deposit exceeding £500.[3] It is not clear whether an estate agent who holds in the capacity of stakeholder is subject to the provisions relating to the payment of interest.

1.   *Sorrell* v. *Finch* [1977] AC 728.
2.   Estate Agents Act 1979, s.13(1).
3.   Estate Agents (Accounts) Regulations 1981 (SI 1981/1520), reg.7.

17.9.   Contractual terms relating to the deposit

17.9.1.   Standard contractual conditions will normally provide for the seller's solicitor to hold a 10% deposit as stakeholder, the deposit to be paid by direct credit or solicitor's cheque (see Standard Condition 2.2.1 and 2.2.4 and Standard Commercial Property Condition 2.2.2).

17.9.2.   The standard clauses represent the safest method both of payment and of holding the deposit. Variations of these provisions by express contractual term is possible but should only be done where the substituted term is necessary to meet the circumstances of the individual transaction and sufficiently safeguards the interests of both parties.

17.9.3.   Variation of the standard provisions may be required where the seller is represented by an unqualified person, or where a less than 10% deposit is being taken. In the latter case provision should be included in the contract for the balance of the 10% to become immediately payable in the event of a notice to complete being served so that the seller is able to forfeit the full 10% sum should it become necessary to do so. (See Standard Condition 7.5.2.)

17.9.4.   Any preliminary deposit which was paid to an estate agent before exchange should be handed over to the solicitor who is holding the deposit once exchange has taken place. If this does not occur the seller will technically be in breach of contract because the contract requires the solicitor to hold 'the deposit', and this may in turn cause problems for a buyer who seeks the recovery of his deposit on the seller's default. In practice estate agents are reluctant to part with the preliminary deposit, seeking to retain it in part payment of their commission. The solicitor who is to hold the deposit should check the terms on which any preliminary deposit is held by the estate agent to ascertain if it can be taken into account in the completion statement.

Checklist for contract terms

(a)   How much deposit is required in total?

(b) Has a preliminary deposit been paid – if so, how much and to whom?

(c) Who is to hold the deposit and in which capacity?

(d) Method of payment?

(e) If in cash, provide for payment by banker's draft or equivalent.

(f) If less than 10%, provide for balance to be immediately payable on service of a completion notice.

17.9.5. The Protocol and the Standard Conditions of Sale recognise the existing practice in many areas for the deposit received on the sale of the property to be used to pay the deposit on the purchase of another property.

17.9.6. The presence of Standard Condition 2.2.6 may mean that a special condition will be necessary if the Law Society's Formula C is used on exchange of contracts and the person at the end of the chain will not agree to the deposit being held as stakeholder. In this event, it would be necessary for all parties in the chain to be notified and a special condition would be required only in the last contract in the chain. It is suggested that this should be:

> 'The deposit shall be paid to the seller's solicitor as agent for the seller and Standard Condition 2.2.6 is varied accordingly.'

17.10.

Methods of payment of deposit

17.10.1. The seller may insist on the payment of the deposit in cash unless he has agreed to accept some other method of payment.[1] Standard Condition 2.2.4 requires payment to be made by direct credit or solicitor's cheque only, except where the contract is made at auction. Standard Commercial Property Condition 2.2.2 requires payment only by direct credit except at sales by auction where other methods of payment are acceptable.

17.10.2. Solicitors should be wary of accepting a deposit in cash because of the dangers of money laundering (see A23).

17.10.3. If a cheque taken in payment of the deposit bounces, this constitutes a fundamental breach of contract which gives the seller the option either of keeping the contract alive for the benefit of both parties, or of treating the contract as discharged by the breach, and in either event of suing for damages.[2] A separate cause of action arises out of the cheque itself. The contract should be drafted to indicate precisely what the rights of the parties are in the event of the dishonour of the deposit cheque.

17.10.4. The option of treating the contract as discharged is of little consolation to a seller who, on the strength of his sale contract, has exchanged contracts for the purchase of another property. Provision should therefore be made in the contract to ensure that the deposit is only payable by a method which will be honoured on presentation, e.g. banker's draft or solicitor's clients' account cheque.

1.   *Johnston* v. *Boyes* (1898) 14 TLR 475.
2.   *Millichamp* v. *Jones* [1983] 1 All ER 267, and see Standard Condition 2.2.2.

17.11.   Using the deposit to fund another transaction

17.11.1.   A seller who is a builder or developer, or one who is involved in the purchase of another property, may wish to use part or all of the deposit received from his sale before completion of that transaction takes place.

17.11.2.   The deposit may only be used by the seller in this way if it is held in the capacity of agent for the seller.

17.11.3.   Although totally satisfactory for the seller, this situation is less than satisfactory for the buyer who may find that he has difficulty in recovering his money if the sale is not completed through the default of the seller or if the seller goes bankrupt or absconds with the money. The buyer should be advised of these risks.

17.11.4.   Before agreeing to allow the seller to have use of the deposit pending completion the buyer should try to ensure that the contract contains some protection for him against the seller's default. In an exceptional case it would be possible for the buyer to secure the deposit by taking an equitable charge over the seller's existing and new properties. Such a charge would need to be protected by registration of a notice (registered land) or Class C(iii) land charge (unregistered land) to bind a purchaser and could only be enforced by a court order for the sale of the property.

17.11.5.   Standard Condition 2.2.5 allows the seller to use all or part of the deposit to fund his own deposit on a related residential transaction in England and Wales but for no other purpose. No equivalent provision is contained in the Standard Commercial Property Conditions.

17.12.   Buyer's lien

17.12.1.   From the moment when he pays the deposit to the seller in the capacity of agent (but not stakeholder) the buyer has a lien over the property for the amount of the deposit. The lien is only enforceable by a court order for sale of the property and must be protected by a notice (registered land) or Class C(iii) land charge (unregistered land) in order to bind a purchaser. If the buyer is in occupation his lien may be an overriding interest in registered land.[1]

17.12.2. If the buyer defaults on completion he has no right to the return of his deposit. This is subject to the court's discretion to order the return of a deposit under Law of Property Act 1925, s.49(2).

17.12.3. If the contract is terminated for any other reason the buyer has a lien which may be enforced either by the buyer himself or by a person claiming under him.[2]

17.12.4. When the reason for non-completion of the sale is a defect in the seller's title the lien extends to the deposit, interest, and the costs of investigating title, and where the sale is by auction under the direction of the court, costs incurred by the buyer in connection with the auction are also included.[3]

17.12.5. A buyer who pays a deposit to a stakeholder is not entitled to recover through his lien the costs of an unsuccessful action for specific performance brought against him by the seller.[4]

1. Land Registration Act 2002, Sched.1, para.2 and Sched.3, para.2.
2. *Levy* v. *Stogdon* [1898] 1 Ch 478.
3. *Holliwell* v. *Seacombe* [1906] 1 Ch 426.
4. *Combe* v. *Lord Swaythling* [1947] Ch 625.

17.13. Deposits paid direct to the seller

17.13.1. A buyer's solicitor should be wary of a situation in which the buyer has apparently paid a deposit directly to the seller. This may indicate the existence of a mortgage fraud (see A24).

17.13.2. The Protocol envisages the deposit being passed by the buyer's solicitor to the seller's solicitor. Solicitors are reminded of the Law Society's guidance on mortgage fraud (see Appendices IV.3 and V.5). In many cases of such fraud, the deposit is allegedly paid direct between the parties.

17.13.3. A solicitor should not confirm to another solicitor that deposit payments have been made or received unless the moneys have been paid into that solicitor's client account or that solicitor has actual evidence that the payment has been made or received by a third party.

17.13.4. Solicitors are reminded of Rule 4 Solicitors' Code of Conduct 2007 (confidentiality and disclosure). Any solicitor with a query about a suspected mortgage fraud should contact the Professional Ethics Guidance Team for advice.

B18. Liquor licensing and food safety

18.1. The new licensing regime: Licensing Act 2003

18.1.1. Significant changes were introduced to the licensing laws in England and Wales by Licensing Act 2003, which came into effect on 24 November 2005. This Act created a single integrated scheme for licensing premises which sell alcohol, provide regulated entertainment or provide late night refreshment. This was achieved by amalgamating the six previous licensing regimes – for alcohol, public entertainment, cinemas, theatres, late night refreshment houses and night cafes. Under the new regime, the system of separate licences for different activities was replaced by a single licence – the premises licence – which authorises the use of any premises, part of premises or place for any or all of the 'licensable activities'.

18.1.2. The licensable activities covered by the Act are:

    (a) the sale by retail of alcohol;

    (b) the supply of alcohol by clubs;

    (c) the provision of regulated entertainment (including cinemas and theatres);

    (d) the provision of late night refreshment.

Thus, the premises licence replaced the old justices' on and off licences, late night refreshment licences and all entertainment licences – public entertainment, theatre and cinema licences.

18.1.3. At the same time, a new system of personal licences was also introduced which is portable, allowing the licence holder to move from one licensed premises to another without any procedural requirements other than the requirement to notify a change of address.

18.1.4. Club premises certificates replaced club registration certificates and temporary event notices are now used instead of occasional permissions and occasional licences.

18.2. Licensing objectives

18.2.1. The legislation focuses on the promotion of four fundamental statutory licensing objectives. These are:

(a) the prevention of crime and disorder;

(b) public safety;

(c) the prevention of public nuisance; and

(d) the protection of children from harm.

These objectives establish the criteria to be used by the licensing authorities in determining or reviewing licence applications.

18.3. Licensing authority

18.3.1. The responsibility for alcohol licensing transferred under the new law from the magistrates' courts to the local authorities, which were already responsible for the licensing of public entertainment and late night refreshment. Thus, the new legislation provides for local decision making so that determinations reflect local circumstances and take into account local discretion.

18.3.2. Under Licensing Act 2003, each licensing authority is required to determine and publish a statement of its licensing policy every three years, which must be kept under review and revised when necessary.

18.3.3. The purpose of the licensing policy statement is to set out the criteria which are used in determining licence applications and provide transparency to all those involved in a licence application. This will thus specify the attitude of the authority on licensing issues and will provide guidance to potential applicants or existing licence holders. As each authority's statement reflects local circumstances there are differences between the different statements. Different local authorities will therefore take different views on similar issues, and those advising in transactions involving licensed premises should accordingly acquaint themselves with the licensing policy of the area in which those premises are located.

18.3.4. It should be noted that some licensing authorities have adopted cumulative impact policies as part of their licensing policy statement. Such policies create a rebuttable presumption against the grant of new licences or material variations to a licence within a particular area, because the area is already saturated with certain types of premises. However, in determining applications for premises situated in such areas, the licensing authority must still consider the merits of each individual application and, where grant of a licence or variation would be unlikely to add significantly to the cumulative impact of licensed premises on the promotion of the licensing objectives, the licence should be granted.

18.4. Licensing register

18.4.1. Each authority is required to maintain a licensing register detailing applications made to and authorisations issued by the licensing authority.

18.4.2. The licensing register will contain a record of:

    (a)   each premises licence issued;

    (b)   each club premises certificate issued;

    (c)   personal licences issued for those resident (at the time of application) in the licensing authority area;

    (d)   all temporary event notices received.

18.4.3. The register will also include a record of:

    (a)   applications to vary;

    (b)   applications to transfer;

    (c)   applications to review;

    (d)   changes of name and address of licence holders;

    (e)   surrender of licences.

18.4.4. Every formal application will be recorded in the register. The register will be the starting point for the solicitors acting in any transaction involving licensed premises.

18.4.5. This register is available to the public and the licensing authority must provide facilities for inspection during office hours. Inspection is free and copies of entries are to be provided at a reasonable charge. Many licensing authorities maintain an online licensing register which is searchable.

18.5. Premises licence

18.5.1. A premises licence is required to cover all the licensable activities that take place at an establishment. Once granted the premises licence remains valid indefinitely until such time as it is revoked or surrendered. Practitioners should be aware however that it will lapse in circumstances of the licence holder's death, insolvency or insanity. The licence is not subject to renewal but an annual payment to the licensing authority is required.

18.5.2. A premises licence is required for a wide range of premises, including:

    (a)   pubs and bars;

    (b)   restaurants;

    (c)   nightclubs;

    (d)   supermarkets, off licences, and shops making retail alcohol sales;

    (e)   hotels;

    (f)   late night refreshment premises;

    (g)   non-qualifying clubs (see B18.9);

    (h)   cinemas;

    (i)   theatres.

18.5.3. Applications for a premises licence can be made by anyone over the age of 18 (including companies, partnerships, etc.), who is carrying on, or proposes to carry on, a business that involves licensable activities on the premises. The application form for a premises licence incorporates an 'operating schedule' which sets out the nature and times of the licensable activities being provided together with the steps being taken to meet the licensing objectives outlined above. It is vitally important that the applicant considers these steps very carefully as they will be translated into conditions on the licence.

18.5.4. Where the premises licence specifies the provision of alcohol, the application also needs to specify the 'designated premises supervisor'. This person will have to hold a personal licence (see B18.8) and will be the point of contact for the premises for the licensing authorities, or the police or fire services if problems occur at the premises. A designated premises supervisor may supervise more than one premises provided they can ensure that the licensing objectives are met and the licensing law and licence conditions are complied with.

18.5.5. A premises licence application also needs to be accompanied by a set of current floor plans for the premises on a scale of 1:100, unless it has been previously agreed with the relevant licensing authority in writing that an alternative scale is acceptable.

18.5.6. All applications must be advertised in the local press and on the premises and notified to the responsible authorities. Objections (which are referred to as 'relevant representations') to premises licence applications may be made by responsible authorities and interested parties.

Responsible authorities

18.5.7. Responsible authorities are defined as the following in relation to the area in which the premises are situated:

(a)   the chief officer of police;

(b)   the fire authority;

(c)   the health and safety authority;

(d)   the local planning authority;

(e)   the environmental health authority;

(f)   the body recognised as being responsible for protection of children from harm;

(g)   any licensing authority other than the relevant licensing authority.

Interested parties

18.5.8.   Interested parties are defined as any of the following:

(a)   a person living in the vicinity of the premises;

(b)   a body representing persons who live in that vicinity;

(c)   a person involved in a business in the vicinity of the premises;

(d)   a body representing persons involved in such businesses.

Objections

18.5.9.   Any objections raised must relate to one or more of the four licensing objectives.

18.5.10.   If relevant representations are received, the licensing authority must hold a hearing, unless all parties agree that a hearing is not necessary, in order to consider the representations and determine the application.

18.5.11.   If no relevant representations have been received, then provided the application has been lawfully made and properly advertised and notified, the licensing authority must grant the licence subject only to those conditions which are consistent with the operating schedule.

18.6.   Regulated entertainment

18.6.1.   Regulated entertainment is defined as the provision of entertainment or entertainment facilities subject to conditions and exemptions as set out in the Act.

Entertainment

18.6.2.   The descriptions of entertainment given in the Act are:

(a)   the performance of a play (including a rehearsal if the public are admitted);

(b)   an exhibition of a film;

(c)   an indoor sporting event;

(d)   boxing or wrestling entertainment (indoor and outdoor);

(e)   a performance of live music;

(f)   any playing of recorded music;

(g)   a performance of dance;

(h)   entertainment similar to live music, recorded music or dance;

where the entertainment described takes place in the presence of an audience and is provided in order to entertain the audience.

Entertainment facilities

18.6.3.   Entertainment facilities are described as facilities for enabling people to take part in entertainment consisting of:

(a)   making music (vocal or instrumental or both);

(b)   dancing;

(c)   entertainment similar to making music or dancing;

where the facilities are provided for the purpose of being entertained.

18.6.4.   Whereas under Licensing Act 1964 there was a requirement for the entertainment to be 'public', under the 2003 Act it is not just public entertainment which is licensable but also private entertainment if it is provided for 'consideration and with a view to profit'.

18.7.   **Late night refreshment**

18.7.1.   Under Licensing Act 2003 all establishments (apart from exempt categories) that provide hot food and hot drinks to the public for consumption either on or off the premises between the hours of 11 pm and 5 am must be licensed. This means that, not only premises which were licensed as 'late night refreshment houses' under the old licensing regime, but also hot food takeaways which were not previously subject to any licensing requirements require a premises licence.

18.7.2.   The following types of late night refreshment are exempt from the requirement for a premises licence:

(a)   hot drinks distributed by a machine that is operated solely by the customer;

(b)   hot food or hot drink supplied free of charge, where there is also no charge for admission to any premises, or a charge for some other item to obtain the hot food or hot drink;

(c) hot food or hot drink supplied by a registered charity or by a person authorised by a registered charity (registered under Charities Act 1993, or not required by this Act to be registered);

(d) hot food or hot drink supplied on a moving vehicle (for example: trains, coaches, limousines);

(e) hot food or hot drink supplied to members and guests of recognised clubs that hold a club premises certificate;

(f) hot food or hot drink supplied to hotel and bed and breakfast guests;

(g) refreshments in staff canteens, where the staff are required to work between 11 pm and 5 am.

18.8.   Personal licence

18.8.1. One of the major changes of Licensing Act 2003 was the introduction of personal licences, which are issued to individuals and which authorise the holder to sell or supply alcohol or to authorise the sale or supply of alcohol for consumption on or off premises for which a premises licence is in force. No sale of alcohol can be made except by a personal licence holder or under their authorisation.

18.8.2. A personal licence relates only to the sale/supply of alcohol under a premises licence. It does not permit the holder to sell/supply alcohol from anywhere, only from establishments operating under a premises licence or at temporary events.

18.8.3. A personal licence is not required for other licensable activities such as the provision of regulated entertainment or late night refreshment or for the sale/supply of alcohol under a club premises certificate.

18.8.4. An applicant for a personal licence must fulfil the following qualifying criteria in order to obtain a personal licence:

(a) be aged 18 or over;

(b) possess a recognised qualification;

(c) have not had a personal licence revoked in the previous five years;

(d) either the police have not raised any objections to the grant; or

(e) if the police have raised objections, the licensing authority has decided not to act on the objection; and

(f) the appropriate fee has been paid.

18.8.5. As part of the application process, in order to satisfy the police that they do not have a criminal record, the applicant must submit a criminal conviction certificate or a criminal record certificate or the results of a subject access search of the police national computer.

B

18.8.6. The licence is valid for ten years initially, unless it is surrendered by the holder, revoked by the licensing authority, or forfeited or suspended by the court. At the end of the ten-year period, the holder may apply for renewal of the licence which may be renewed at ten-yearly intervals thereafter.

18.8.7. There is no need to apply for a new licence when a personal licensee moves as these licences are portable and may be used anywhere in England and Wales.

18.9. Club premises certificates

18.9.1. Licensing Act 2003 preserves aspects of earlier licensing legislation as it applied to 'registered members clubs', where technically there are no retail sales of alcohol to club members.

18.9.2. Under the new legislation, clubs which satisfy certain qualifying conditions are classed as 'qualifying clubs' and require a club premises certificate. An application for this certificate is very similar to an application for a premises licence and requires the inclusion of an operating schedule and also needs to be advertised and notified to responsible authorities. However, there is no requirement for a designated premises supervisor to be specified on this type of licence, and also no requirement for those supplying alcohol under the club premises certificate to hold a personal licence.

18.10. Transfer of premises licence

18.10.1. When a business involving licensable activities is sold to a new owner it will be necessary to transfer the premises licence. The 2003 Act provides that any person or company that is eligible to apply for a premises licence may apply to have a premises licence transferred to them. Such a transfer will only change the identity of the licence holder and will not alter the licence in any other way.

18.10.2. An application to transfer must be notified to the chief officer of police. In exceptional circumstances, where the police believe that the transfer may undermine the crime prevention objective, they may object to the application, but this is expected to be rare. Objections to a transfer cannot be made by other responsible authorities or interested parties. In the absence of police objections, the transfer must be granted.

18.10.3. Under Licensing Act 1964, when buying licensed premises the standard practice was to apply for a protection order or interim authority which would have effect on the completion date or shortly beforehand. This enabled the buyer to carry on business at the premises as soon as the purchase was finalised. An application for transfer would then be made at a later stage.

18.10.4. Under the new legislation there is no provision that specifically replaces either a protection order or an interim authority. However, in order to enable continuity and ensure there is no interruption to business at the premises during determination of the transfer, it is possible to request that the application for transfer be given immediate effect, i.e. from the date it is received by the licensing authority, until formally determined or withdrawn.

18.10.5. An application for immediate effect will normally require the consent of the current licence holder. However, this may be waived if the applicant can demonstrate that he has taken all reasonable steps to obtain the consent and can show that he is in a position to use the premises immediately for the licensable activities authorised by the licence.

18.10.6. To avoid any problems with respect to obtaining the consent of the holder of the premises licence to an immediate transfer, it may be sensible for the contract for sale to include the agreement of the licence holder to the buyer making an application for transfer with immediate effect (Licensing Act 2003, s.43) on or before the completion date.

18.11. Variation of premises licence

18.11.1. The holder of a premises licence may apply to vary the licence by, for example, altering conditions attaching to the licence, or changing the hours of operation, or changing the authorised licensable activities permitted. An application to vary the actual premises may also be made, provided it is a minor change. However, it is not possible to vary substantially the premises to which the licence relates. Any substantial change would require an application for a new licence.

18.11.2. The procedure for an application to vary is essentially the same as for the original grant and must also be advertised and notice of the application given to each responsible authority. Responsible authorities and interested parties may object to the variation on grounds relating to the licensing objectives. In the absence of any objection the variation will be granted.

18.12. Provisional statements

18.12.1. Under the 1964 Act, there were only two grounds on which the licensing justices could refuse a final grant for a licence which had been obtained provisionally. Those grounds were the failure to complete the works in accordance with the approved plans, or where the licensee was deemed not to be a fit and proper person. Investors who had obtained a provisional grant therefore had reassurance that the licence would be granted when the premises had been completed. Provisional statements under the new legislation do not provide the same degree of assurance.

18.12.2. The application for a provisional statement must be accompanied by plans, details of the work to be carried out and details of the proposed licensable activities. The procedure for advertisement and hearing of these applications is similar to that which applies to a new premises licence. Accordingly, there will be a hearing if there are objections and the licensing authority can then issue a provisional statement expressing its view. It would indicate, for example, that it would be necessary to attach conditions to the licence or to exclude some of the proposed licensable activities if, in its view, the licensing objectives required those amendments.

18.12.3. The holder of such a statement knows that when he applies for a full premises licence he is likely to obtain a grant in accordance with the statement. There is still however an opportunity for further objection when that application is made. The licensing authority can only entertain such an objection, however, if it is satisfied that it could not have been raised at the provisional stage.

18.12.4. As an alternative to applying for a provisional statement, there is nothing to prevent an application being made for a full premises licence before new premises are constructed or existing premises are extended or changed, provided the relevant information is available. If the licence were granted it would not have immediate effect, but the date when it would become effective would be included in the licence.

18.13. Interim authorities

18.13.1. A premises licence lapses on the death, mental incapacity or insolvency of the licence holder. As there may be a delay before a new premises licence holder can be appointed, there are provisions under Licensing Act 2003 to permit the continuation of the authorisations under a premises licence until a formal transfer can occur. This arrangement is called an 'interim authority' and allows the licensable activities to continue until transfer.

18.13.2. In these circumstances an 'interim authority notice' should be submitted to the relevant licensing authority within seven days of the lapse of the premises licence. The effect of giving an interim authority notice is to reinstate the premises licence from the time the licensing authority receives the notice and for the person giving the notice to become the licence holder. The maximum period for which an interim authority notice may have effect is two months. An application for transfer to a new licence holder must, therefore, be made within this time period.

18.13.3. Where a premises licence has lapsed due to death, incapacity or insolvency of the holder or has been surrendered, it is also possible under Licensing Act 2003, s.50, for anyone who is eligible to apply for a premises licence, to apply for a transfer of the licence with immediate effect. Such an application must be made within seven days of the lapse of the licence and can only be made where there is no interim authority notice in force. The effect of this application is to reinstate the licence from the time the application was received by the licensing authority.

18.14. Review of licences

18.14.1. A new provision introduced by Licensing Act 2003 was the 'review' process. Under this provision an interested party or a responsible authority may, at any time following the grant of a premises licence or club premises certificate, apply to the licensing authority for a review of the licence, if they consider that there is an issue relating to one of the licensing objectives occurring at that particular premises. However, licensing authorities are not permitted to initiate their own reviews of premises licences or club premises certificates.

18.14.2. The licensing authority is required to advertise any application to review it receives for a period of 28 days during which time the licence holder, interested parties and responsible authorities may make representations. A hearing must then be held within 20 working days of the end of this period.

18.14.3. Following a review hearing, the licensing authority has a range of powers. It may decide that no action is necessary for the promotion of the licensing objectives, or it may decide that only informal action, such as informal warnings or recommendations for improvements within a specified time, is the most appropriate way forward.

18.14.4. However, where the licensing authority considers that formal steps are required, it may take any of the following actions:

(a) modify (add, alter or omit) the conditions of the licence;

(b) exclude a licensable activity from the licence;

(c) remove the designated premises supervisor;

(d) suspend the licence for a period not exceeding three months;

(e) revoke the licence.

18.14.5. Modifications of conditions and exclusion of licensable activities may be imposed either permanently or for a temporary period of up to three months.

18.15. Closure orders

18.15.1. The government in advocating this new regime argued that the flexibility and additional scope of the extended licensing hours would be counterbalanced by rigorous new powers of enforcement.

18.15.2. The police had had powers to close premises licensed for the sale of alcohol if there was likely to be disorder or disturbance. Initially this could be for a period of up to 24 hours after which the police could then apply to the magistrates for a review of the closure order.

18.15.3. Under Licensing Act 2003 this power of closure was extended to all licensed premises. Under this legislation the police can apply to the magistrates for an order closing premises in a specified area where disorder is anticipated. Alternatively, as before, the police can close specified premises. The period is again up to 24 hours with the possibility for extended periods of 24 hours until such time as the order is reviewed by the magistrates' court. Where these powers are used the licensing authority must review the premises licence following the procedure set out in B18.14.

18.16. Pre-contract enquiries

18.16.1. In view of the provisions summarised above, the following enquiries should be made of the seller by those proposing to acquire licensed premises:

(a)   to supply a copy of the premises licence;

(b)   to supply a plan of the premises as incorporated in the licence;

(c)   to supply a copy of any application which has been submitted for a variation of the premises licence;

(d)   to establish that no alterations have been made to the premises since the licence has been granted;

(e)   to supply a copy of any provisional statement which has been issued in connection with the property;

(f)   to obtain confirmation that the designated premises supervisor (as specified in the licence) remains on the premises;

(g)   to provide details of all personal licensees currently working on the premises;

(h)   to confirm that no closure orders or applications for closure orders have been made in relation to the premises;

(i)   to ascertain the outcome of any reviews by the licensing authority in relation to the premises licence, or whether any review is pending;

(j)   to confirm any current capacity limit on the premises;

(k)   to specify the number of temporary event notices held at the premises (including their duration) in the current year and to provide copies of any notifications which have been given on future temporary events;

(l)   to provide a copy of the receipt for the current annual fee;

(m)   to confirm the rateable value of the premises;

(n)   to obtain confirmation that the licence holders have complied with the terms of their licence and any mandatory conditions which apply to the premises; and

(o)   to require copies of any correspondence between either responsible authorities or interested parties that might indicate the possibility of an application to review the licence.

18.17. Register of interest

18.17.1. Provision is made for freeholders, licence holders, occupiers and others with prescribed interests in premises situated in a licensing authority's area to register their interest with the licensing authority. On payment of a fee they are then entitled to be notified of any changes made in the licensing register in the following 12 months.

18.18. Food premises licensing/approval

Introduction: history and the new legislation

18.18.1. New EU food hygiene legislation came into force in the UK on 1 January 2006. This affects all food businesses including manufacturers, processors, distributors, retailers, caterers and primary producers.

18.18.2. Prior to the introduction of this new legislation, most food premises were legally required to be registered with their local authority under the Food Premises (Registration) Regulations 1991 (as amended), made under the Food Safety Act 1990. Certain other types of food premises, generally manufacturers and wholesalers of products of animal origin, such as dairies, meat products manufacturers or wholesale fish markets that were subject to product-specific regulations, were required to be approved by the local authority and generally their products had to display a health mark or be accompanied by a health certificate. In addition, operating meat plants were required to be licensed. The new food hygiene legislation replaces and amends this prior legislation and, accordingly, the previous registration/licensing requirements no longer apply.

18.18.3. The new food hygiene legislation is less prescriptive and introduces risk-based procedures based on the application of Hazard Analysis and Critical Control Points (HACCP) principles and requires food premises to be either registered or approved. As it is contained in EU Regulations, it is directly applicable in the UK and there is no requirement for it to be implemented by national legislation.

18.18.4. New UK legislation (Food Hygiene Regulations (England) 2006 (SI 2006/14)) is, however, necessary in order to identify the offences under the new legislation, provide for the enforcement of the EU Regulations, and revoke the existing food hygiene legislation. The 2006 Regulations came into force on 11 January 2006.

18.18.5. A 'food business' is defined as any undertaking whether for profit or not and whether public or private, carrying out any stage of production, processing and distribution of food. This includes businesses involved in primary production in many cases for the first time.

18.18.6. A 'food business operator' is the natural or legal person(s) responsible for ensuring that the requirements of food law are met within the food business under their control.

18.18.7. The Hygiene Regulations do not apply to all food activities and consequently the following are exempt from registration/approval:

(a) primary production for domestic use;

(b) the domestic preparation, handling or storage of food for private domestic consumption;

(c) the direct supply, by the producer, of small quantities of primary products to the final consumer or to local retail establishments directly supplying the final consumer;

(d) collection centres and tanneries which fall within the definition of food business only because they handle raw material for the production of gelatine or collagen.

18.18.8. The rules that apply to a food business will depend on the type of food handled or sold. The requirements are therefore different depending on which of the following categories applies to the business:

(a) restaurants, caterers and businesses selling food to the final consumer;

(b) businesses (other than restaurants, caterers and businesses selling food to the final consumer) manufacturing food not of animal origin;

(c) businesses (other than restaurants, caterers and businesses selling food to the final consumer) making or handling foods of animal origin.

Restaurants, caterers, businesses selling food to the final consumer and other food businesses processing or handling foods of non-animal origin.

18.18.9. Restaurants, caterers and other businesses selling food to the final consumer must register their food businesses with their local authority. (Where food is sold to the final consumer there is no distinction made between food of animal origin and that which is not of animal origin.)

18.18.10. Other food businesses processing or handling foods of non-animal origin also require registration. The registration requirements are the same as for restaurants, caterers, etc., selling to the final consumer but they are classified separately because other requirements under the EU food hygiene legislation are slightly different.

18.18.11. If the food business establishment is located in more than one local authority area, it must be registered with each authority separately. Moveable establishments such as burger vans and ice cream vans should be registered by the food business operator with the local authority in whose area the vehicle is normally kept. Vehicles and stalls used to transport, prepare or sell food, should register with the local authority where the stocks of food are normally kept.

18.18.12. Registrations are to be made on a standard form and must provide full details of all the activities undertaken. These forms are available from the relevant local authority and are usually available online.

18.18.13. For new businesses, registration forms need to be submitted at least 28 days before food operations commence. Once establishments are registered, the food business operator must ensure that the local authority has up-to-date information on the establishments by notifying it of any subsequent changes such as change of food business operator or change to the food operations undertaken. Such notifications should be made in writing as soon as possible and in any event no later than 28 days after the change occurred.

18.18.14. If a food business is already registered under the current legislation and no changes have been made since registration or the last inspection visit, then no further action is required in order to comply with the new legislation. If there have been any changes, then it is necessary to notify the relevant local authority. Notification of a change to the operator of a food business establishment should be made by the new business operator.

18.18.15. As well as the registration requirements, food business operators must also comply with general hygiene requirements set out in EU Regulation 852/2004 and establish, implement and maintain food safety management procedures based on HACCP principles.

Other businesses processing or handling foods of animal origin

18.18.16. Foods of animal origin include fresh meat (including game meat), minced meat, meat products, meat preparations, shellfish, fish and fishery products, milk and dairy products, eggs and egg products, rendered animal products and miscellaneous products including frogs' legs and snails.

18.18.17. From 1 January 2006 food businesses that handle food of animal origin (with some exceptions for wild game meat) must be approved by the competent authority (either the Food Standards Agency or local food authorities). If a food business requires approval it does not require registration as well. Approval replaces both previous approvals and licences.

18.18.18. Food businesses falling into this category include catering and retail butchers supplying to the catering trade and/or other establishments (unless the supply is on a marginal, localised and restricted basis), slaughterhouses, cutting plants, game handling establishments, meat processing facilities, and retail and wholesale cold stores. Premises which make food containing both products of plant origin and processed products of animal origin do not require approval but do need to be registered.

18.18.19. Under the new Hygiene Regulations a food business handling food of animal origin will need to be re-assessed for approval even if it is already approved or licensed. However, the current approval/licence will continue until the re-assessment is carried out and the food business operator need not take any action until contacted by the competent authority.

18.18.20. New businesses are required to apply for approval to the relevant enforcement authority.

B

18.18.21. Food businesses which were previously licensed by the local authority to supply game for the domestic market or to produce minced meat and meat preparations for the domestic market, and cold stores where there was no previous licence requirement will need to be approved under the new Regulations.

18.18.22. As well as approval of establishments, food business operators must also comply with general hygiene requirements set out in the Regulations and establish, implement and maintain food safety management procedures based on HACCP principles. In addition products of animal origin have to bear an identification mark.

18.18.23. The above requirements apply to these food businesses irrespective of the throughput of the premises.

Butchers' shops

18.18.24. Prior to 1 January 2006, butchers' shops selling both unwrapped raw meat and ready to eat foods were required to be licensed annually. The regulations requiring this were repealed from 1 January 2006 and thus a butchers' shop licence is no longer required. However, butchers' shops are subject to the new EU hygiene regulations and will therefore be required to register with the local authority in the same way as other food businesses selling food to the final consumer.

Register

18.18.25. The local authority is required to keep a list of food business establishments registered with it. This list is available for inspection by the general public at all reasonable times. The list contains the following information:

    (a)   name of food business operator;

    (b)   name of food business;

    (c)   address of food business establishment;

    (d)   particulars and nature of the food business.

B19. Mortgage offers

19.1. **Acceptance of offer**
19.2. **Conditions attached to offer**
19.3 **Islamic mortgages**
19.4. **Duty of confidentiality**

19.5. **Consumer Credit Act 1974**
19.6. **Discharge of existing mortgage**

19.1. Acceptance of offer

19.1.1. Where the client is purchasing a property with the aid of mortgage finance, the solicitor must ensure that the client has received and (where necessary) accepted a satisfactory offer of a mortgage before advising the client to exchange contracts.

19.1.2. From 31 October 2004 mortgages are regulated by the Financial Services Authority (FSA) under Financial Services and Markets Act 2000. Advice given to the client about the terms of a mortgage offer and/or arranging a regulated mortgage may be regulated activity within the terms of the Act (see A4). Unless a regulated mortgage is arranged by a person who is authorised under the Act or with a (properly authorised) financial institution, it will be unenforceable without the leave of the court (see A4.3).

19.1.3. Giving generic advice regarding different types of mortgage and their suitability for the client is not within the definition of a regulated activity. However, providing specific advice about different providers and mortgage products is a regulated activity (see A4.2.4). Provided the solicitor follows the Scope Rules and Conduct of Business Rules issued by the Law Society, the advice given will fall within the 'exempt regulated activities' provision of Part XX Financial Services and Markets Act 2000 (see A4.2.7).

19.1.4. Financial Services and Markets Act 2000 (Regulated Activities) (Amendment) (No.2) Order 2006 (SI 2006/2383) came into effect on 6 April 2007. The regulations extend the FSA remit to 'home reversion plans' (where the home owner sells all or part of the home in exchange for a lump sum or income and continues to live in the house rent-free) and to *Ijara* and *Diminishing Musharaka* products (a rental-purchase arrangement compatible with Sharia law – see B19.3).

19.2. Conditions attached to offer

19.2.1. Before acceptance of the offer or committing his client to the purchase, the solicitor should ensure that the client understands the conditions attached to the mortgage offer and the terms of the mortgage and will be able to comply with them. Conditions may be general, e.g. a condition that the property must not be let without the lender's consent, or special, having application to this offer only, e.g. a condition that the buyer obtains an endowment policy as security for the mortgage. The mortgage offer, even if formally accepted, may be subject to a condition allowing the lender to withdraw the offer even after exchange. The solicitor should check the offer to see whether this is the case and whether or not the lender requires a formal acceptance of the offer.

19.2.2. If the conditions attached to the mortgage offer are not wholly acceptable to the client, e.g. the offer requires the client to take out a new endowment policy when the client would be better advised to extend and re-assign an existing policy, an attempt should be made to renegotiate the terms with the lender. Such a term may be invalid under Part IV Courts and Legal Services Act 1990. In extreme cases an alternative source of finance may need to be investigated.

19.2.3. If the mortgage is being entered into under an equity release scheme, the client may require advice as to the scheme's suitability for the client's particular needs from a specialist financial adviser. These schemes are designed to provide the borrower with a regular income or lump sum secured against property. The loan will be repaid when the property is sold on the borrower's death. They are not generally suitable for a borrower who intends to move house again during his lifetime.

19.2.4. In this situation, where the buyer's solicitor has also been instructed to act for the lender, a conflict exists between the interests of the buyer client and the lender client. Unless such conflict can be resolved to the satisfaction of both clients, the solicitor cannot continue to act for either, unless with the consent of one client he is permitted to continue to act for the other. The solicitor's duty of confidentiality towards his client may prevent him from continuing to act for either client in this situation.

19.2.5. If it comes to the notice of the solicitor that the client will be in breach of the terms of the mortgage offer, e.g. where the purchase price for the property has been misrepresented to the lender, the lender must be informed of the problem (see A11). The duty to inform the lender exists throughout the transaction, not just at the time when the offer is being considered. Failure to inform the lender of circumstances in which it appears that the buyer client is attempting to perpetrate a fraud on the lender may lead to the criminal prosecution of the solicitor and to disciplinary proceedings being taken against him. It may also invalidate the solicitor's indemnity insurance if the solicitor has acted dishonestly.[1] This gives rise to a conflict of interests between the buyer client and the lender client since the lender may, in the light of the information received, choose to adjust the terms of the mortgage offer to the detriment of the buyer client. Attention is drawn to the Law Society's guidelines on mortgage fraud which are reproduced in Appendix V.5 and Law Society's Property Fraud Warning Card in Appendix III.3.

1. See *Shultari* v. *Solicitors Indemnity Fund Ltd* [2004] All ER (D) 327.

19.3 Islamic mortgages

19.3.1. There are two basic Sharia compliant schemes for providing finance to assist in the purchase of property. The *Murabaha* involves a bank purchasing the property on behalf of the buyer and then reselling it to the buyer at a higher price. The buyer pays for the property by instalments. The repayment term is usually short (around 15 years). *Murabaha* arrangements satisfy the requirements of a regulated mortgage and are therefore regulated by the FSA.

19.3.2. For buyers who require greater flexibility the *Ijara* and Diminishing *Musharaka* schemes permit a bank to buy the property and then to lease it to the buyer. The bank agrees to transfer the property to the buyer at the end of the term of the lease. Both of these schemes came under the FSA regulation on 6 April 2007 when Financial Services and Markets Act 2000 (Regulated Activities) (Amendment) (No.2) Order (SI 2006/2383) came into effect.

19.3.3. Rule 3 Solicitors' Code of Conduct 2007 (conflict of interest) provides that a solicitor may act for both the borrower and the lender in a conveyancing transaction where the transaction is a standard mortgage and no conflict of interest arises (see Rule 3.17). If the mortgage is an individual mortgage, in that material terms of the mortgage have been negotiated separately between the lender and the borrower, the parties must be separately represented (see Rule 3.16(2)(b)). With *Ijara* and Diminishing *Musharaka* schemes some of the terms of the mortgage may be negotiated between the parties which will bring the mortgage within the definition of an individual mortgage. In addition, as both of these schemes operate on the basis that the lender sells the property to the buyer over a period of time, a solicitor acting for both parties may be in breach of Rule 3.07.

19.3.4. It is a fundamental principle of common law, which Rule 3 Solicitors' Code of Conduct 2007 reflects, that a solicitor cannot act for both parties where there is a conflict of interests. For so long as, and to the extent that, any property finance product (including Sharia compliant products) gives rise to a conflict of interests, Rule 3 will apply to prevent a solicitor from acting for both parties.

19.3.5. Buyers using Islamic mortgages do not incur multiple payments of SDLT. Individual buyers were exempted from double taxation in 2005 by virtue of Finance Act 2003, s.71A (as amended). Purchases by companies and partnerships were given the same exemption under Finance Act 2006, s.168 which came into effect on 20 July 2006.

19.3.6. The Right to Buy scheme introduced by the Housing Act 1980 is incompatible with the use of Islamic mortgages as it requires ownership of the property to pass directly from the seller to the buyer. The ODPM issued a consultation paper, *Non-standard mortgages for purchasing social dwellings* in March 2005 proposing amendments to the legislation.

19.4. Duty of confidentiality

19.4.1. In any of the above circumstances where a conflict of interests exists between the buyer client and the lender client the solicitor, acting in his capacity of adviser to the buyer, may only disclose the nature of the conflict to the lender with the consent of the buyer client. Disclosure of information without the buyer client's consent will be a breach of the solicitor's duty of confidentiality (see also A24).

19.5. Consumer Credit Act 1974

19.5.1. Consumer Credit Act 1974, s.58 may be applicable if the mortgage is:

(a)   for a sum less than £25,000;

(b)   to be granted to an individual or partnership by a non-exempt lender; and

(c)   is not a loan for the purchase of land.

19.5.2. Consumer Credit Act 1974 does not generally apply to loans exceeding £25,000 and, by regulations made under the Act,[1] loans granted by most major banks, building societies and insurance companies are exempted from the provisions of the Act.[2]

19.5.3. The requirements of section 58 will thus not normally be relevant in circumstances where the buyer client is purchasing land with the assistance of a first mortgage from an institutional lender. Where, however, the client already owns the land in question and is refinancing or taking out a second or subsequent mortgage the provisions of section 58 should be borne in mind, particularly where the solicitor is acting also for the lender.

19.5.4. Section 58 provides that the borrower must be given a 'cooling-off' period (normally of 14 days) after the mortgage documentation has been sent to him by the lender. The purpose of this period is to allow the borrower to reflect on and to take independent advice on the terms of the loan without being subjected to pressure from the lender or anyone acting on behalf of the lender. During the 'cooling off' period neither the lender nor anyone acting on his behalf (which includes the solicitor acting for the lender) may make contact with the borrower, whether by letter, telephone or any other means of communication. During this time the solicitor may speak or write to his borrower client if the client approaches him, but client contact should not be initiated by the solicitor whilst the consideration period is running. Failure to comply with this provision will render the mortgage unenforceable except with leave of the court, which will not automatically be granted. Thus a solicitor who is acting for a lender in circumstances where section 58 applies must establish precisely when the consideration period begins to run and must not prejudice the enforceability of the loan by voluntarily contacting his client during this period.

1. Consumer Credit (Exempt Agreements) Order 1989 (SI 1989/869). This financial limit has been repealed by Consumer Credit Act 2006, s.2(1)(b) from a date to be appointed. This is expected to come into force on 6 April 2008.
2. Consumer Credit Act 1974, s.16A gives the Secretary of State power to provide by order for the exemption of consumer credit agreements where the debtor has a high net worth. Consumer credit agreements entered into wholly or predominantly for a debtor's business purposes where the credit provided exceeds £25,000 will also be exempted from regulation under Consumer Credit Act 1974, s.16B from a date to be appointed. This is expected to come into force on 6 April 2008.

19.6. Discharge of existing mortgage

19.6.1.   It is usually a term of a mortgage offer for a first mortgage over property that any existing mortgage which the client has should be discharged on or before completion of the new loan. The solicitor must ensure the buyer client is aware of and can comply with this condition.[1]

19.6.2.   Some lenders charge interest on an existing loan until the end of the calendar month notwithstanding that the mortgage is repaid earlier. Since this extra amount of interest can add up to a considerable sum, the solicitor should enquire of the lender whether such interest will be charged on the discharge of the existing mortgage and advise his client accordingly.

1. See para 5.8 of the Lenders' Handbook (see Appendix VI.2).

B20. Auctions

20.1. Acting for the seller

20.1.1. Where property is to be sold by auction the contract generally consists of particulars, describing the land to be sold, conditions stating the terms of the sale, and a memorandum of the sale which will be signed by or on behalf of the buyer at the auction itself.

20.1.2. The special conditions of the contract are normally prepared by the seller's solicitor in conjunction with the auctioneer who will prepare the particulars of sale. The contract will frequently incorporate the Standard Conditions of Sale although many auctioneers have their own general conditions of sale and some have adopted the Common Auction Conditions (RICS, second edition, 2005).

20.1.3. The seller of residential property by auction is obliged to produce a home information pack for prospective buyers (see A26).

20.2. Preparing the contract

20.2.1. In addition to the usual contractual clauses particular attention should be paid to the matters listed below. Most of these matters are normally dealt with either in the auctioneers' general conditions, the Common Auction Conditions, the Standard Conditions of Sale or by the Standard Commercial Property Conditions but it is advisable to check their relevance to the particular property concerned and to ensure that any necessary amendments or additions to the Standard Conditions are included in the special conditions of the contract. Some, but not all, of the matters listed below are included in the Common Auction Conditions, Standard Condition 2.3 and in Standard Commercial Property Condition 2.3.

Reserve price

20.2.2. By Sale of Land by Auction Act 1867, s.5 the contract must state whether or not the property is subject to a reserve price. Unless a reserve is placed on the property the auctioneer will be bound to sell to the highest bidder.

Right to bid

20.2.3. Where the property is subject to a reserve price the seller may, under Sale of Land by Auction Act 1867, reserve the right to bid at the auction. This right when reserved by special condition in the contract may be exercised by the seller or his agent.

The auctioneer's control over the bidding

20.2.4. In order to avoid uncertainty the contract should make it clear whether the auctioneer has the right to refuse a bid; or to fix the amount of bids; and should contain provisions whereby the auctioneer may settle any dispute which arises over the bidding.

Payment of deposit

20.2.5. The contract should provide for the amount of the deposit to be paid, the time when it is to be paid, and the methods of payment which are acceptable. It is usual at an auction to provide for a full 10% deposit to be paid. At common law the deposit must be tendered in cash.[1] Standard Condition 2.2.1 and Standard Commercial Property Condition 2.2 provide for a 10% deposit to be payable but do not limit the methods of payment (Standard Condition 2.2.4 does not apply to auction contracts); therefore unless this condition is amended the seller would have to accept payment by the buyer's own cheque with the attendant risks of that cheque not being honoured on presentation. Under the Common Auction Conditions the deposit must be paid to the auctioneer by cheque or banker's draft drawn on an approved bank. It will be held as stakeholder unless a special condition provides otherwise (Common Auction Condition 2.2).

Seller's right to withdraw from auction

20.2.6. In the absence of a special condition it is uncertain whether the seller is entitled to withdraw the property from auction once bidding has commenced unless the sale is subject to a reserve price. Under the Common Auction Conditions, the auctioneer may, without explanation, refuse to accept a bid.

Retraction of bids by buyer

20.2.7. It is common to include a condition precluding the retraction of a bid once made. Such a condition is probably unenforceable at common law under the general principles of offer and acceptance. A bid made at auction is an offer, and the offeror (buyer) is free to withdraw his offer at any time until acceptance by the auctioneer. Acceptance takes place with the fall of the hammer. It should be noted that auction contracts are excluded from the provisions of Law of Property (Miscellaneous Provisions) Act 1989, s.2 (requiring a contract for the sale of land to be in writing); an auction contract will therefore be binding and enforceable even if oral and no memorandum is signed.

Division of property into lots

20.2.8.   If required, an express right to divide the property into separate lots should be included in the contract.

Buyer's right to rescind

20.2.9.   Where the buyer has not been given the opportunity to make searches or to inspect copies of searches made by the seller prior to the auction, it may be felt appropriate to include a provision which allows the buyer to rescind within a certain time if the results of his searches are not satisfactory. The inclusion of such a condition will introduce an element of uncertainty into the contract, which is not primarily in the interests of the seller. Any such condition must be carefully drafted to ensure that it will not render the contract void for uncertainty and will not allow the buyer to escape from the contract except in precisely worded given circumstances. Under Common Auction Condition 4.2, where no documents were made available before the auction, evidence of title must be provided within five business days of the contract. The buyer then has seven business days to raise requisitions. If the title is not satisfactory the buyer can withdraw from the contract. Condition 8 deals with the consequences of rescission.

Tenancies

20.2.10.   The seller's duty of disclosure requires that accurate details of all tenancies to which the property is subject must be revealed in the contract.

Inspection of title deeds and searches

20.2.11.   It is common to include a clause in the auction particulars which entitles any prospective buyer to inspect the title deeds and any searches which have been made by the seller. The clause should provide for a time and place for the inspection.

1.   *Johnston* v. *Boyes* (1898) 14 TLR 475.

20.3.   **Other preparatory steps by the seller**

20.3.1.   In addition to the preparation of the contract the seller's solicitor should, before the auction, undertake the preparatory steps in B20.3.2–20.3.4 (see also A26).

Searches

20.3.2.   A buyer will frequently not have sufficient time before the auction in which to make the usual searches and enquiries. In order to avoid having to include a clause in the contract entitling the buyer to rescind if the results of searches are not satisfactory, it is preferable for the seller to undertake such searches himself and to make them available for inspection by prospective buyers both before the auction and at the sale itself. A local authority search and enquiries may be requisitioned by the seller's solicitor, as well as any other searches which are relevant to the particular transaction. The seller's solicitor should also prepare and make available answers to standard enquiries before contract.

Title

20.3.3.   As with the preparation of any draft contract, the seller's solicitor should investigate his client's title prior to drafting the contract so that any imperfections may either be disclosed in the contract or put right before the auction takes place. Particular care is needed to ensure that full details of any existing tenancies are obtained.

Inspection of deeds

20.3.4.   It is helpful to the buyer if the seller can allow a prospective buyer an opportunity to inspect the title deeds and search results at the seller's solicitor's office or other named place at a convenient time prior to the auction. The deeds and search results should also be available for inspection at the auction itself.

20.4.   Attending the auction

20.4.1.   The seller's solicitor should attend the auction in order to make the title deeds and search results available for inspection to prospective buyers and to answer any queries which may arise.

20.5.   Memorandum of sale

20.5.1.   The memorandum of sale is usually annexed to the printed auction particulars and conditions. It is common to include a condition that the buyer will sign the memorandum immediately after the sale. The auctioneer has implied authority to sign on behalf of both seller and buyer. An auctioneer's clerk has no such implied authority but may be expressly authorised to sign for one or both of the parties. As far as the buyer is concerned, the auctioneer's authority is limited to 'the time of the sale' which expression has no legal definition but must be taken to mean either at the sale itself or within a short time afterwards. In *Chaney* v. *Maclow*[1] the auctioneer's signature, effected at the auctioneer's own offices some two hours after the sale, was held to bind the buyer; *cf. Bell* v. *Balls*[2] where a signature made one week after the sale was not effective to bind the buyer. If the buyer refuses to sign and the auctioneer will not sign as the buyer's agent the seller cannot force the buyer to sign, because an oral agreement to put a contract into writing and to sign it cannot be enforced by specific performance, but it seems that damages may be recovered for breach of such a condition.[3] It should be noted that auction contracts are excluded from the provisions of Law of

Property (Miscellaneous Provisions) Act 1989, s.2 (requiring a contract for the sale of land to be in writing); an auction contract will therefore be binding and enforceable even if oral and no memorandum is signed.

20.5.2. Under the Common Auction Conditions, the buyer must sign the sale memorandum and pay the deposit immediately. If he fails to do so, the auctioneer may either sign the memorandum on the buyer's behalf or offer the property for sale again.

1. [1929] 1 Ch 461.
2. [1897] 1 Ch 663.
3. See *Wood* v. *Midgely* (1854) 5 De GM & G 41.

20.6.   **Acting for the buyer**

Searches

20.6.1. In frequent circumstances the buyer may not instruct his solicitor in sufficient time to permit the usual searches and enquiries to be undertaken. In these circumstances and when a home information pack is not available (see A26) the buyer's solicitor should at least attempt to make enquiries of local authority in the usual way. If there is insufficient time to do this, the buyer's solicitor should make enquiries of local authority in person or through an agent, unless the results of these enquiries are otherwise available from the seller's solicitor or the auctioneer.

20.7.   **Survey**

20.7.1. Where time permits the buyer should be advised to have the property surveyed prior to the auction.

20.8.   **Contract and title**

20.8.1. A copy of the auction particulars, containing the contract terms, should be obtained and scrutinised prior to the auction. Where searches have not been made by the buyer it should be ascertained whether the contract contains a provision allowing the buyer to rescind if the results of searches undertaken after the auction are adverse. If no such provision is included, the buyer should be advised of the consequences of entering a contract without having made searches and enquiries.

20.8.2. The seller's solicitor will often allow the buyer the opportunity to inspect the title deeds (and sometimes also searches which he has undertaken) before the auction. The buyer's solicitor should inspect the deeds and make such further enquiries as are relevant to the property at the earliest possible opportunity. The buyer may take the benefit of searches requisitioned by the seller, but reliance on such searches is inadvisable if the search results are more than two months old. If inspection of the deeds is not possible prior to the auction the buyer's solicitor should attend the auction and make such inspection before the bidding commences.

20.8.3. The terms of an auction contract are often less favourable to the buyer than would be the case in a sale by private treaty. Auction contract terms are generally non-negotiable as far as the buyer is concerned and therefore the terms of the contract need to be carefully scrutinised before the auction and the buyer advised about the consequences of any adverse terms. Occasionally, the special conditions of the contract will be altered by an oral statement made at the time of the auction itself and the buyer should be advised to listen carefully and note the effect of any such amendments. Examples of terms which might be onerous to the buyer include the following:

(a) terms precluding the buyer's right to raise enquiries or requisitions after the auction;

(b) restrictions on sub-sales by the buyer;

(c) obligations on the buyer to pay the arrears of rent or service charge on a leasehold property;

(d) terms requiring the buyer to reimburse the seller for search fees and/or the cost of supplying an engrossment of the transfer deed;

(e) on the sale of a freehold reversion of a block of flats, terms excluding any warranty by the seller that the provisions of Landlord and Tenant Act 1987 have been complied with. See K9.

20.8.4. Any information supplied by the seller to the potential buyers prior to the auction must be accurate. Despite the terms of the contract, inaccuracies in any documents provided by the seller may lead to an action in misrepresentation.[1]

1. *Pankhania* v. *Hackney London Borough Council* [2002] All ER (D) 22.

20.9. Finance

20.9.1. The buyer should be warned of the possibility of abortive expenditure if his bid is not successful. As the contract to purchase will come into existence at the time of the auction itself it is essential that the buyer's financial arrangements have been finalised prior to the auction. Arrangements must be made for the deposit to be available at the auction, in cash (banker's draft) if this is required by the auction particulars.

20.10. **Insurance**

20.10.1. The buyer should also make arrangements for the property to be placed on insurance cover from the moment of the fall of the auctioneer's hammer since, depending on the terms of the contract, risk in the property may pass to him at this time.

20.11. **Rights of first refusal**

20.11.1. If the property to be sold at auction is affected by Landlord and Tenant Act 1987 which gives the tenants of some leasehold flats the right to purchase the landlord's reversionary interest (see K9) the landlord must comply with section 5B Landlord and Tenant Act 1987 (as amended by Housing Act 1996). This section requires the landlord to serve notice on at least 90% of the qualifying tenants between four and six months before the auction. Failure to comply with the Act is a criminal offence.

20.12. **VAT**

20.12.1. The auctioneer usually holds deposits for the seller as agent. This means that when the hammer goes down, a tax point is created for the transaction. Therefore, if the property is subject to the election to waive exemption, and it is intended to make the purchase under the TOGC rules (so that no VAT is payable) the purchaser must exercise their election to waive exemption and notify it to HM Revenue and Customs prior to the day of auction, otherwise TOGC procedures cannot be invoked. If the purchase does not take place, the purchaser can then revoke the election to waive exemption (see A16).

B21. Plans

21.1. **When is a plan necessary?**
21.2. **Preparing the plan**
21.3. **Showing features on the plan**

21.4. **Referring to the contract plan**

21.1. When is a plan necessary?

21.1.1. Before drafting the contract the seller's solicitor should consider whether it is necessary to identify or describe the property by reference to a plan. On receipt of the draft contract from the seller's solicitor, the buyer's solicitor should also consider whether a plan is required. The buyer is entitled to demand a plan on the purchase deed (at the seller's expense) only if the description of the property through the contract and evidence of title is inadequate without one; therefore this matter must be addressed at the pre-contract stage. In other circumstances the buyer might be able to insist on the inclusion of a plan provided that he offered to prepare and pay for it. The buyer's solicitor may need a plan of the property in order to make pre-contract searches and enquiries (see B10).

21.1.2. A plan must be used on a sale of part of land (which includes the grant of leases of flats) and may be desirable in other cases, e.g. where the boundaries of the property are not self-evident, but should not be used indiscriminately (see Land Registry Practice Guide 40). The sale of the whole of a registered title can usually be described adequately by reference to its title number and, where applicable, its postal address.

21.1.3. Land Registration Rules 2003, r.213, provides that a document lodged at the Land Registry dealing with part of the land in a registered title must have attached to it a plan identifying clearly the land dealt with. However, if the land dealt with is identified clearly on the title plan it may instead be described by reference to that title plan. On building estates, the seller should normally submit his estate layout plan to the Land Registry for approval before the sale of the individual plots is commenced. Any changes in the approved estate layout plan should be notified by the seller to the Land Registry. See Land Registry Practice Guide 41.

21.1.4. Whatever type of plan is used it must be of sufficient size and scale to enable the boundaries and other features of the property to be readily identified.[1] A plan on a scale of 1:1250 will suffice for most cases, but a larger scale will usually be required for sales of flats or the division of buildings into separate units.

21.1.5. Boundaries shown on the majority of plans prepared by the Land Registry are general boundaries only and do not therefore show the exact line of the boundaries.[2] The registered proprietor may apply to the Land Registry for the exact line of the boundary, or any part of the boundary, to be determined. The application must be made in Form DB.[3] For further guidance as to the evidence to be lodged in support of the application see Land Registry Practice Guide 40.

21.1.6.   A plan will be required where the sale is by reference to a fence line or where the boundaries of the property are otherwise unclear. In such a case the parties should be asked to agree the boundaries (if necessary by a site inspection and with the co-operation of the owner of neighbouring property) and the fence line or boundary should be staked out on the site.

21.1.7.   For the possible requirement for a new plan on the first registration of a lease following an assignment where the lease has more than seven years to run, see K11.8.7.

1.   See *Scarfe* v. *Adams* [1981] 1 All ER 843; *Gillen* v. *Baxter and another* [2003] PLSCS 235; and *Horn and another* v. *Philips and another* (CA, 18 December 2003).
2.   Land Registration Act 2002, s.60. See also *Chadwick and others* v. *Abbotswood Properties Ltd and others* [2004] EWHC 1058, and Land Registry Practice Guide 40.
3.   Land Registration Rules 2003, r.118 and Land Registration Act 2002, s.60.

21.2.   Preparing the plan

21.2.1.   Plans used in deeds may emanate from a variety of sources. Generally, any plan that has been professionally prepared and is drawn accurately to a scale referred to below should be satisfactory for use in a deed. Hand drawn sketches should not be used.

21.2.2.   There are some occasions where a professionally drawn plan may be unsuitable, e.g. if it was drawn for an architectural or engineering purpose (large scale) or it was drawn for a location plan or road map (small scale). The most commonly acceptable base plans for use in any deed lodged for registration are copies of Ordnance Survey maps (see B21.2.7) or copy estate layout plans approved by the Land Registry (see B21.1.3).

21.2.3.   Where a plan is required for any new deed or for any application lodged at the Land Registry it should be prepared having regard to the following guidelines:

- it should be drawn to and show its actual scale;
- show its orientation (for example, a north point);
- use preferred scales of 1/1250–1/500 for urban properties;
- use preferred scales of 1/2500 for rural properties (fields and farms etc);
- not based on a scale of imperial measurement (for example 16 feet to 1 inch);
- not reduced in scale (see B21.2.4);
- not marked or referred to as being for identification only;

- not show statements of disclaimer used under Property Misdescriptions Act 1991;

- show sufficient detail to be identified on the Ordnance Survey map;

- show its general location by showing roads, road junctions or other landmarks;

- show the land of the property including any garage or garden ground;

- show buildings in their correct (or intended) position;

- show access drives or pathways if they form part of property boundaries;

- show the land and property clearly (for example by edging, colouring or hatching);

- have edgings of a thickness that do not obscure any other detail;

- show separate parts by suitable plan markings (house, parking space, dustbin space);

- identify different floor levels (where appropriate);

- show intricate boundaries with a larger scale or inset plan;

- show measurements in metric units only, to two decimal places;

- show undefined boundaries accurately and where necessary, by reference to measurements;

- show measurements that correspond, so far as possible, to scaled measurements.

Note: The Land Registry does not consider it necessary to specify in any deed or on any plan the area of the property described.

21.2.4. Where it is clear that the plan contained in a deed or copy deed is a reduced copy of the original, the reduced plan is acceptable provided:

- the original scale has been deleted; or

- the plan has been endorsed with a statement to the effect that it is a reduced copy (or in the case of a copy deed, a reduced copy of the plan to the original deed); or

- the actual scale is stated in place of the original scale.

21.2.5. The Land Registry will reject any dealing of part or lease application in respect of registered land which contain plans that have been reduced from their original scale that still bear the original scale endorsement.

21.2.6. Any plan attached to a certified copy of an original deed must not be a reduced copy of the original. It must be identical to the original in all respects.

21.2.7. Current Ordnance Survey mapping is only available from authorised Ordnance Survey Stockists (see **www.ordnancesurvey.co.uk** for details).

21.2.8. The Land Registry is not authorised to supply Ordnance Survey maps.

21.2.9. Where the value or complexity of the transaction justifies the expense, an architect or surveyor may be instructed to prepare a plan. The client's authority should be obtained prior to incurring such expenditure.

21.2.10. If there is any doubt as to the size or extent of the property an inspection should be carried out and measurements taken.

21.2.11. Guidance on the preparation of plans can be found in Land Registry Practice Guide 40.

21.3. Showing features on the plan

21.3.1. The plan must be clearly drawn so that it is capable of being read in isolation from the accompanying contract or purchase deed. The wording of the contract or purchase deed will, however, need to make reference to the plan and its various features and this point should be borne in mind when the plan is drawn, e.g. a right of way may be more easily described in words in the contract if its beginning and end points are marked 'A' and 'B' on the plan in addition to the demarcation of the route.

Points to note

21.3.2.   (a)   Markings should be clear and precise.

(b)   Land to be sold should be outlined or coloured in red.

(c)   Retained land (if any) should be outlined or coloured in blue.

(d)   Other land referred to should be coloured or hatched in distinct colours other than red or blue. If possible it is best to avoid the use of green on a plan where red has already been used since the most common form of colour blindness relates to the inability to distinguish between these two colours. See Land Registry Practice Guide 40 as to its preferred practice for colouring plans.

(e)   The ownership of boundaries should be indicated by 'T' marks with the 'T' on the side of the boundary line within the land which bears responsibility for the maintenance of the boundary. In the absence of a specific request the Land Registry will only show 'T' marks on the title plan if referred to in a covenant or other provision in the transfer.

(f)   Rights of way and routes of services should be tinted or marked with broken or dotted lines of a distinct colour, with each end of the route being additionally identified with separate capital letters.

(g)   Where the plan is to scale the scale should be shown.

(h) If the plan is not to scale, metric measurements should be shown along each boundary. An imperial measurement can be used in addition to the metric measurement provided that the metric measurement is placed first and the imperial measurement is in characters no larger than the metric figures.

(i) A compass point indicating the direction of north should be shown.

(j) A key should be included to explain the meaning of the various colours and lines used on the plan.

21.4. Referring to the contract plan

21.4.1. The contract (and subsequent purchase deed) may refer to the plan as being 'for identification purposes only', or will describe the land as being 'more particularly delineated on the plan'. These two phrases are mutually exclusive and a combination of the two serves no useful purpose.[1]

'Identification purposes only'

21.4.2. Where there is a discrepancy between the land shown on the plan and the contract description and the plan has been described as being for identification purposes only, the verbal description of the land will normally prevail over the plan. The court may, however, refer to such a plan to define the boundaries of the property where the verbal description is unclear.[2]

'More particularly delineated'

21.4.3. In the event of a discrepancy between the verbal description of the land and the plan, the plan will prevail over the words where the phrase 'more particularly delineated' has been used. This phrase should not be used unless the plan is to scale.

21.4.4. A plan which is included in the purchase deed but which is not referred to by use of one of the above phrases may be looked at in order to identify the land only if the description of the property as afforded by the purchase deed and other available evidence (e.g. title deeds) is unclear.[3]

Registered land

21.4.5. A transfer or lease of part of the land in a registered title must have attached to it a plan identifying clearly the land transferred or leased (unless such land is clearly defined on the seller's title plan).[4] A plan described as 'for identification purposes only' does not meet this requirement.

1. *Neilson* v. *Poole* (1969) 20 P&CR 909.
2. See *Wiggington & Milner Ltd* v. *Winster Engineering Ltd* [1978] 3 All ER 436.
3. *Leachman* v. *L & K Richardson Ltd* [1969] 3 All ER 20.
4. Land Registration Rules 2003, r.213.

B22. Fixtures and fittings

22.1. Distinction between fixtures and fittings

Fixtures

22.1.1. Fixtures are generally items which are attached to and form part of the land and which will therefore be included as part of the property on sale of the land unless the seller expressly reserves the right to remove them.

Fittings

22.1.2. Fittings or chattels do not form part of the land and so are not included as part of the property on sale of the land unless the seller expressly agrees to leave them behind.

Practical distinction

22.1.3. The legal distinction between fixtures and fittings as outlined in the above subparagraphs is quite clear. The practical distinction between the two categories is sometimes less obvious. Movable objects which are not attached to the land, e.g. carpets, curtains and free-standing furniture clearly fall within the definition of fittings, but items which are attached to the land such as gas boilers and satellite dishes are not always classified as fixtures. Case law in this area is unclear and there have been reported cases where items such as greenhouses, garden ornaments, plumbed-in kitchen appliances and even freezers have been held to be fixtures, and other cases where the same items have been held to be fittings.[1]

1. See *TSB Bank* v. *Botham* [1996] EGCS 149, and *Elitestone* v. *Morris* [1997] 2 All ER 513.

22.2. Need for certainty in contract

22.2.1. In view of the uncertainty of the status of some items in law it is essential that in appropriate circumstances the contract deals expressly with:

(a) fixtures which the seller intends to remove on or before completion (including, where appropriate, the tenant's right to remove tenant's trade fixtures);

(b) compensation for the buyer if the seller causes damage in the course of the removal of fixtures;

(c) fittings which are to remain at the property;

(d) any additional price which the buyer is to pay for the fittings;

(e) the apportionment of the purchase price to exclude from the total the price paid for the fittings;

(f) deferment of passing of title to fittings until completion because in the absence of such a condition Sale of Goods Act 1979, s.18 will provide that title to the fittings passes to the buyer on exchange;

(g) a warranty that fittings are free of incumbrances (e.g. subsisting hire-purchase agreements). Although Sale of Goods Act 1979, s.12 will imply such a warranty its express inclusion in the contract prevents the matter from being overlooked by the seller (see Standard Condition 10).

22.2.2. Disputes over the unexpected removal of fixtures and fittings are common and frequently cost more to resolve than the value of the disputed items. The buyer may require the seller to supply written confirmation that fixtures and fittings which were seen by the buyer on inspection of the property will not be removed from the property and are included in the sale, or in appropriate cases the contract may contain a warranty given by the seller that he has not removed any fixtures from the property since a stated date.

22.2.3. The estate agent's particulars should be scrutinised to see which items are listed as being included or excluded from the sale, and checked with the client to ensure their accuracy.

22.2.4. When taking instructions it will be necessary to ascertain from the client which items are to be removed, which items he expects to remain at the property, and whether any price in addition to the price of the land is required for the fittings.

22.2.5. The Standard Conditions of Sale contract form provides for a list of items being sold to the buyer to be attached to the contract.

22.3. Apportionment of purchase price

No SDLT on chattels

22.3.1. The sale of chattels, including chattels which although attached to the land have not become fixtures, does not attract SDLT unless included in the conveyance. The value of chattels which have been included in the purchase price of the land may therefore be subtracted from the total purchase price and ignored in deciding whether reduced rates of SDLT for transactions not exceeding £500,000 can be claimed in the transfer, thereby effecting a reduction in the value of the land and a possible consequent reduction in the rates and/or amount of SDLT payable by the buyer.

22.3.2. This apportionment of the purchase price between the land and the chattels is of most value to the buyer when the value of the land and chattels together is marginally above one of the current SDLT thresholds.

Consequences of over-valuation

22.3.3. Only the fair value of the chattels may be deducted from the purchase price for this purpose (see the guidance from HM Revenue and Customs SDLT Manual in Appendix VII.3). Any over-valuation of the price of the chattels is a fraud on HM Revenue and Customs which may render both the solicitor and his client liable to criminal sanctions. Such conduct would also be conduct unbefitting the solicitor which could result in disciplinary proceedings being brought against him. A further consequence of the over-valuation is that the contract for the sale of the land would be unenforceable by court action since it could be construed by the courts as being a contract to defraud HM Revenue and Customs, such contracts being unenforceable on the grounds of public policy.[1]

22.3.4. If the draft contract does not make provision for the apportionment of the purchase price in a situation where such apportionment would be appropriate, the buyer should, as a matter of courtesy, seek the seller's consent before making the necessary adjustment to the contract.

1. See *Saunders* v. *Edwards* [1987] 2 All ER 651.

22.4. Protocol

22.4.1. Paragraph 2.9 of the Protocol requires the seller's solicitor to obtain information relating to fixtures and fittings from the seller, using the standard Fixtures, Fittings and Contents Form (replaced by Form TA10 Fittings and Contents). The completed form should then be sent to the buyer's solicitors with the draft contract (Protocol, para. 4.4). See Appendix II.1 for the full text of the Protocol.

22.5. Guidelines

22.5.1. In order to avoid future disputes between the parties the solicitor is advised to check with the client which items are included/excluded from the sale and whether any additional price is payable for the included items. Items which would normally be considered to be fixtures (e.g. fitted wardrobes) should not be charged for in addition to the contract price nor removed from the property unless there is an express reservation of the right to do so in the contract. Items which are normally removable as fittings, e.g. carpets, will not be included in the contract unless the parties agree to their inclusion, possibly at a price additional to the sum payable for the land. Where there are items which may be regarded either as fixtures or fittings depending on the circumstances, e.g. a greenhouse, the solicitor will need to make further enquiries of his client and should consider express mention of these items in the contract for the avoidance of doubt. In residential transactions use of the Form TA10 Fittings and Contents is strongly recommended. This form, the contents of which will be agreed by the parties, will be annexed to and form part of the contract.

22.6. Passing of title to chattels

22.6.1. Under Standard Condition 10 both the risk and title in chattels does not pass to the buyer until completion.

22.6.2. Under Standard Commercial Property Condition 12 title in chattels remains with the seller until completion but risk passes on exchange. It may be difficult for a buyer to obtain insurance over chattels which he does not own.

B23. Powers of attorney

23.1. When is a power needed?

23.1.1. The solicitor should consider the preparation of a power of attorney for his client if the client:

(a) is elderly and/or physically infirm; or

(b) is likely to be unavailable at the time when it will be necessary to obtain his signature to documents.

23.2. What type of power?

General power under Powers of Attorney Act 1971

23.2.1. This type of power will give the attorney authority to deal with all of the donor's assets including the sale or purchase of property.

Special power under Powers of Attorney Act 1971

23.2.2. A special power will give the attorney authority to deal only with the matters specified in the power and thus may be limited to, e.g. the sale of a named property. Except where it is intended to allow the attorney to assume complete control of the donor's affairs this type of power would be more appropriate than a general power in the context of the sale or purchase of land.

Enduring power under Enduring Powers of Attorney Act 1985

23.2.3. This type of power must be executed in the form prescribed by the Enduring Powers of Attorney (Prescribed Forms) Regulations (SI 1990/1376). It is not revoked on the subsequent mental incapacity of the donor. This power cannot be used by a trustee to confer power on his sole co-trustee where, e.g. property is jointly owned by husband and wife and one party wishes to appoint the other as his or her attorney during a period of absence abroad. See Trustee Delegation Act 1999. No new enduring powers of attorney can be created after 30 September 2007: see Mental Capacity Act 2005.

23.2.4. A power which is executed under a prescribed form which is not current at the time of execution is probably not valid and a new power using the form prescribed by the current regulations must be executed. Acts done by the attorney under an invalid power can be ratified by execution of a deed of ratification by the donor, provided the donor is still mentally capable.

Security powers

23.2.5. A security power under Powers of Attorney Act 1971, s.4 may be taken by a lender who has taken an equitable mortgage in order to give him a power to sell the property if the borrower defaults on the mortgage. This type of power is irrevocable and may be incorporated in the mortgage document or given by separate deed.

Trusts and powers of attorney

23.2.6. Prior to 1 March 2000, if a trustee (including a co-owner) wished to appoint an attorney to act in connection with a sale or purchase of a property, he could not use a general power of attorney. The donor had to use a specific power of attorney under Trustee Act 1925, s.25. This was limited in duration to 12 months. In addition the power could not be used by a trustee to delegate to his sole co-trustee, in such a case he would have to use an enduring power of attorney under Enduring Powers of Attorney Act 1985.

23.2.7. From 1 March 2000 a trustee who is beneficially entitled under the trust (e.g. a co-owner) can now use a general power (Trustee Delegation Act 1999, s.1). He can also appoint his sole co-trustee to be his attorney. If the trustee is not beneficially entitled under the trust, section 5 of the 1999 Act states that he can use a general power but that it must be limited to a period of 12 months, and the trustee can appoint his sole co-trustee to be his attorney. In either case, if a sole co-trustee has been appointed, the attorney cannot give a valid receipt for capital money and overreaching will not operate. Where there are only two trustees a third party should be appointed to act as attorney. Since the 1999 Act, an enduring power of attorney can no longer be used by a trustee to appoint a sole co-trustee to act as attorney (s.4).

Lasting powers of attorney

23.2.8. These are discussed in D2.9.36.

23.3.   Who should be the attorney?

23.3.1. The client should be advised of the consequences of giving a power of attorney, i.e. that the attorney will (depending on the terms of the power) have a wide authority and discretion to deal with the client's affairs. Only a person whom the client trusts absolutely should be considered for appointment as attorney. The solicitor may be appointed as attorney provided that no conflict of interests exists between himself and his client(s). The solicitor should advise the client of his charges in relation to so acting. The limitations on the appointment of an attorney in the case of trust property have been noted above.

23.4. When should the appointment be made?

23.4.1. The power of attorney should be drawn up and executed as soon as the decision to appoint an attorney has been made. This is necessary because it is courteous to inform the other party to the transaction at the earliest opportunity that the documents will be signed under a power of attorney.

23.5. The client who already has a power

23.5.1. Where a client comes to the solicitor with an existing power of attorney, the solicitor should examine the power to ascertain its type and validity for the transaction proposed.

23.6. Informing the other party of the appointment

23.6.1. It is courteous to inform the other party to the transaction at the earliest opportunity that the documents will be signed under a power of attorney. A copy of the power should be supplied to the other party as soon as possible so that its validity and suitability for the transaction in progress may be confirmed.

23.6.2. Except in the case of a security power or an enduring power which has been registered with the Court of Protection, if the power will be more than 12 months old at the date when it is purportedly exercised, the person who buys from the attorney will need to make a statutory declaration immediately after completion stating that he believed the power to be valid and had no knowledge of its revocation at the time of its exercise. See Powers of Attorney Act 1971, s.5.

23.7. Statutory declarations and Land Registry requirements

23.7.1. Except in the case of a security power or an enduring power which has been registered with the Court of Protection, if the power was more than 12 months old at the date it was purportedly exercised, Powers of Attorney Act 1971 provides that when the person who buys from the attorney comes to sell the property he must provide a statutory declaration to his buyer stating that he (the purchaser from the attorney) had no knowledge of any revocation of the power at the time he bought the property (see Powers of Attorney Act 1971, s.5). This provision envisages that the title would remain unregistered after the purchase from the attorney. As the title will be subject to first registration the Land Registry requirements must be complied with.

23.7.2. When acting for the buyer it is important to bear in mind the Land Registry practice regarding powers of attorney. If the power is more than 12 months old at the date of the sale by the attorney, or if it is an enduring power which was registered at the Court of Protection more than 12 months before the transaction, the Land Registry may require evidence of the non-revocation of the power (Land Registration Rules 2003, r.62). If the Land Registry does call for evidence it will require the buyer from the attorney to provide either:

- a statutory declaration stating that the buyer from the attorney was not aware of any revocation of the power at the date of the transaction; or

- a certificate in Form 2 signed by the buyer's conveyancer.

23.7.3. It is the buyer from the attorney who must provide the declaration or certificate, not the attorney nor the seller's solicitor. It is the knowledge of the person dealing with the attorney which is relevant under Powers of Attorney Act 1971.

23.7.4. In all cases the Land Registry will require evidence of the power of attorney which should either be:

- Form 1 completed by the buyer's conveyancer; or

- the original power of attorney; or

- a certified copy of the power of attorney.

23.7.5. For more details see Land Registry Practice Guide 9.

B24. Planning

24.1. Relevance of planning to the transaction

24.1.1. Heavy penalties may ensue from breach of planning legislation; it is therefore important to check at the start of a transaction that any necessary planning requirements have been or will be complied with. It may also be necessary to check whether any restrictive covenants on the property conflict with the present structure(s) and/or use, and if so whether consent to the buildings and/or their current use/or a release or indemnity insurance has been obtained.

24.1.2. The development of land will normally require the grant of planning permission. Development is defined by Town and Country Planning Act 1990 (as amended) as 'the carrying out of building, engineering, mining or other operations in, on, over or under land, or the making of any material change in the use of any buildings or other land'. This definition encompasses the erection of new buildings, the demolition of and alterations and additions to existing buildings, fish farming and in certain circumstances changing the use of a building.

24.1.3. A house which has been in multiple occupation will need planning permission for use as a single dwelling unless it has been occupied by not more than six residents living together as a single household (including a household where care is provided for residents). See Class C3 Town and Country Planning (Use Classes) Order 1987.

24.2. Acting for the seller

24.2.1. Although planning matters do not necessarily fall within the seller's duty of disclosure, the buyer's solicitor will raise various enquiries about planning matters and will be reluctant to proceed with the transaction unless he can be reassured that the buildings and use of the property satisfy current planning regulations. In Protocol cases, a number of matters pertaining to planning will be revealed by the seller on the Seller's Property Information Form which is supplied to the buyer. The following matters should therefore be checked either from the documents in the solicitor's possession, from information obtained from the client, or from the local planning authority (usually the district council):

(a) the date when the property was first built;

(b) whether any additions, alterations or extensions have been made to the property or within its grounds since the property was first built and, if so, the date of each addition, etc.;

(c) if the property has been built or any alteration to it has been made within the past four years, either that planning consent was obtained (either expressly or by virtue of General Permitted Development Order) or was not required. Any conditions attached to the planning consent should, if possible, be checked to ensure that they have been complied with. Proceedings to enforce planning restrictions in respect of development which consists of 'building works' must normally be taken within four years of the breach;

(d) if the property is leasehold, in addition to (c) above, whether any additions, alterations, etc., have been made since the date of the grant of the lease and, if so, whether any restriction on development contained in the lease has been complied with;

(e) what the property is used for, whether any material change of use to the property has occurred during the past 10 years and, if so, whether the appropriate consent has been obtained. There is a 10-year time limit on the enforcement of breach of planning control through change of use. If no enforcement proceedings are taken within the 10-year period the previously unlawful use becomes an authorised use. The change of use from one use class to another requires consent, as does the change from use as a single dwelling house to use of the premises for multiple occupation or sub-division into separate units;

(f) where alterations or additions to the property have been made within the past 12 months, whether building regulation consent has been obtained and complied with (see B24.7);

(g) whether the property is a listed building or in a conservation area. Special provisions apply to such buildings and areas and the restrictions on development are more stringent than those applied in other cases. Where a building is listed, separate listed building consent may be required.

24.2.2. Any irregularity in the planning situation should ideally be corrected by the seller before contracts are exchanged. Realistically this may not always be possible and the seller may have to reveal the irregularity to the buyer who, depending on the nature of the problem, may be prepared to proceed with the transaction subject to a reduction in the price or an indemnity against liability given by the seller in the contract.

24.2.3. Paragraph 2.8 of the Protocol requires the seller's solicitor to obtain copies of all relevant planning decisions and to submit these to the buyer's solicitor as part of the pre-contract documentation (see Appendix II.1 for the full text of the Protocol).

24.3. Acting for the buyer

24.3.1. The matters itemised in B24.2.1 should be raised as pre-contract enquiries with the seller. Any irregularity revealed by the seller's answers should either be corrected at the seller's expense or, depending on the nature of the breach, an indemnity taken from the seller in the contract. Liability for breach of planning legislation enures with the land; thus any breach which exists on completion will become the responsibility of the buyer.

24.3.2. Instructions should be taken from the buyer in relation to the following matters:

(a) does the buyer's intended use of the property correspond with its present authorised use? If not, will planning permission be required for the buyer's intended use and is it realistic to expect that consent from the local planning authority would be forthcoming?

(b) is it apparent on inspection of the property that new buildings or alterations have been made within the last four years? If so, check with the seller whether planning consent for the new buildings was needed/ obtained/ complied with;

(c) does the buyer intend to alter the property in any way after completion? If so, will the proposed alterations require planning consent or consent from the person with the benefit of an existing restrictive covenant against development and is it realistic to expect that such consent(s) will be forthcoming?

24.3.3. The answers to the local search and enquiries should be checked carefully to ensure that no breach of planning law is revealed in those answers. Any matters of doubt should be clarified with the local authority and the seller before the matter proceeds to exchange of contracts.

24.3.4. Where the client's instructions reveal that his proposals for the property will require planning permission to be obtained, it should first be ascertained whether or not the client would wish to proceed with his purchase in the event of an application for permission being refused by the local authority. If the client would not wish to pursue his purchase in such circumstances, he should be advised either to delay exchange until planning permission for his proposed development is obtained, or to ask the seller to make the contract conditional on obtaining such consent (see B13). Even where the client is prepared to take the risk of planning permission ultimately being refused, he should be advised about the procedure for making such application (including the costs) and the consequences of developing the land without permission. The register of planning applications maintained by the local authority under Town and Country Planning Act 1990 may be inspected to obtain an insight into the authority's policy for the area, and thus the likelihood of obtaining permission for the proposed development. Generally an authority will not permit development which conflicts with its development plan documents for the area, e.g. industrial development would not be permitted in an area designated for residential use or vice versa.

24.3.5. Even where the client's proposals will not require planning permission, consideration should still be given to the necessity for building regulation consent (for building works of any description) and compliance with or insurance against any restrictive covenants on the property which would prevent the client's intended development.

24.3.6. If the seller has made additions or alterations to the property, the local authority has the right to reconsider the council tax banding of the property when it changes hands.

24.4. Matters which do not require specific planning permission

24.4.1. Certain matters which would otherwise fall within the definition of development (and thus require planning permission) are specifically excluded from that definition by the Act itself or by General Permitted Development Order. A summary of the main cases where permission is not required either by the statute or by regulation is listed below. In any case of doubt, the Act and the various regulations made under it should be checked, and/or advice sought from the planning department of the local authority:

   (a) maintenance works to buildings, e.g. painting the exterior;

   (b) internal works which do not materially affect the appearance of the exterior, e.g. sub-dividing a room by the erection of a non-load-bearing partition wall;

   (c) the use of buildings or land within the curtilage of a dwelling house for any purpose incidental to the use of the dwelling house, e.g. using an existing outhouse as a playroom. The 'curtilage' of a dwelling house is the land immediately surrounding the house and except where the grounds are large will normally encompass the whole of the garden area;

   (d) change of use within the same use class as specified by Town and Country Planning (Use Classes) Order 1987 (as amended), e.g. changing from use as a newsagent's shop to an ironmonger's shop. Changing a single dwelling house into two or more units is a material change of use which requires planning permission, as is a change from one use class to another, e.g. changing from use as a shop to use as an office;

B

(e)   development which falls within Town and Country Planning (General Permitted Development) Order 1995, e.g. erection of fences (subject to a height restriction), some demolition works, development within the curtilage of a dwelling house. This latter provision will permit the building of a small extension to an existing dwelling house without the need for express planning permission but is subject to strict conditions on the extent and siting of the extension; once the size limit for extensions under General Permitted Development Order has been used, all further extensions to the house require express permission. The conditions attached to General Permitted Development Order must be strictly observed, and if they cannot be complied with express permission for the development is needed. The local authority has power to restrict General Permitted Development Order in whole or in part in relation to its area. Before the client proceeds to effect works which ostensibly fall within the Order it should be confirmed that the relevant part of the Order is in force in the area concerned.

24.4.2.   Enquiries of the local authority, which will be undertaken in every transaction, contain several questions relating to planning matters. The answers to these questions should be analysed carefully by the buyer's solicitor.

24.4.3.   Special rules apply to listed buildings and the provisions outlined above may not apply.

24.5.   Enforcement of planning breaches

24.5.1.   The time limits for the enforcement of planning breaches are:

- in the case of building operations, four years from the date that the operations were substantially completed;

- in the case of a change of use to a single dwelling house, four years from the date the change of use commenced;

- in the case of any other breach, e.g. unauthorised change of use or failure to comply with a condition attached to planning permission, 10 years from the date of the breach.

24.5.2.   On the expiry of the time limit, if no enforcement action has been taken, the operation or use becomes lawful. The commencement of enforcement actions, i.e. the issue of an enforcement notice, prior to the expiry of the time limit, stops time running and will prevent the breach from becoming lawful.

24.6   Planning rules which apply in special cases

24.6.1.   If the land is covered by a Special Development Order, or is within an enterprise zone or a simplified planning zone, special rules apply which alter the general law.

24.6.2. In some cases the rules relating to the need for planning permission are relaxed within these special zones, in others parts of General Permitted Development Order may be restricted. The replies to enquiries of the local authority will reveal whether or not the property is affected by any of these special zonings. If so, the provisions of the relevant Order should be checked before advice is given to the client on the need for planning permission.

24.7 Building Regulations

24.7.1. Building Regulations compliance is necessary whenever building works are to be undertaken. The need for this is separate from planning consent and is required even where the development falls within the General Permitted Development Order and does not require express planning permission.

24.7.2. The regulations cover various aspects of the structure including its structural stability, fire resistance and means of escape, weather resistance, sound resistance, ventilation, drainage, heating and energy performance, stairways, ramps and guards and facilities for disabled people and the safety of glazing.

24.7.3. Since 1 April 2002 the regulations have applied to the installation of replacement windows and doors. All replacement windows, roof lights, and glazed doors will have to be covered by either a certificate issued by the Local Authority Building Control or by FENSA. The Glass and Glazing Federation has established a self-assessment scheme, FENSA, and FENSA members must carry out the work to the appropriate standard and can then issue a certificate with the local authority within 10 days of the work being completed. These provisions apply to contracts entered into on or after 1 April 2002. The provisions will apply to orders placed before 1 April 2002 if the work was not completed before 1 July 2002. The solicitor needs to check that the appropriate consents are available (appropriate questions are included in the third edition of the seller's property information form).

24.7.4. From 31 December 2004 certain building works which involve electrical installations and amendments to existing installations require Building Regulations consent and must be carried out by an electrician whose qualifications are listed within the approved qualifications list in amended Building Regulations 2000 (SI 2000/2531) (as amended by Building (Amendment) (No. 3) Regulations 2004).

24.7.5. Certain buildings do not need Building Regulations consent, for example, certain detached buildings not used for sleeping and some extensions, provided they are under certain size restrictions. In addition the construction of a greenhouse, porch, conservatory (with transparent or translucent roof), covered yard or car port are exempt from Building Regulation control where the floor area of the addition does not exceed 30 square metres. The installation of heat producing appliances when carried out by an approved installer does not require consent.

24.7.6. A person who intends to undertake building works must make an application for consent before starting work. There are two forms of application, the Full Plans Application and the Building Notice method. For a Full Plans application detailed plans are required and full details of the construction must be submitted. The Building Notice differs from the Full Plans Application in that all that is necessary is the completion and submission of a simple form describing the proposed work. With the Building Notice application the Building Control Surveyor will inspect the work on site and will expect any problems to be rectified immediately.

24.7.7. A key element of building control is the inspections conducted by the Building Control Officer. Statutory inspections have to be carried out at specified stages in the construction and the Building Control Officer may also inspect at other stages in the construction.

24.7.8. The Local Authority issues a Certificate of Compliance when the building work is finished and the final inspection has taken place. This confirms that the work is in accordance with the regulations. In some cases an independent building inspector will carry out the inspections and issue the Certificate of Compliance to the local authority. It is essential that a copy of this certificate is provided to the buyer on the sale of the property.

24.7.9. Proceedings for breach of Building Regulations must generally be taken within 12 months of the infringement. However in some circumstances the local authority may be able to enforce the regulations outside the 12-month time limit.[1] A buyer should therefore seek confirmation of compliance with the regulations in respect of works completed since the property was built and if this is not available the buyer should consider insurance against the risk of enforcement.[2] Although enforcement action under section 36(1) or (2) Building Act 1984 cannot be taken outside of the 12-month time limit, the Building Control Department may still be able to obtain an injunction under section 36(6).[3] The buyer could ask the seller to obtain a Regularisation Certificate from the Building Control Department at the Local Authority. The Building Control Officer will inspect the property and provide a list of work required to bring the building up to the correct standard. Depending upon the level of work required the buyer might choose to ask the seller to carry out the work prior to completion, negotiate a reduction in the purchase price to cover the cost of carrying out the work after completion or withdraw from the transaction. The buyer's lender may also need to be informed.

1. Building Act 1984, s.36(1) and Public Health Act 1936, s.65.
2. See Building Act 1984, s.36(6).
3. *Cottingham* v. *Attey Bower & Jones* [2000] PNLR 557.

24.8 Energy performance certificates

24.8.1. Energy Performance of Buildings (Certificates and Inspections) (England and Wales) Regulations 2007 (SI 2007/991)[1] ('the regulations') amend the

Building Regulations and place sellers, landlords and builders under an obligation to provide an energy performance certificate (EPC) to prospective buyers and tenants[2] (see A27 for further details as to their requirements and their phased implementation).

24.8.2.   The EPC contains an assessment of the energy efficiency of a building and provides recommendations for the improvement of the energy performance of the building.[3] The EPC will give the building an asset rating ranging from A–G, with A being the most efficient.

24.8.3.   EPCs should be shown on request to any prospective purchaser or tenant and should be provided to the ultimate purchaser or tenant before they enter into the contract.[4]

24.8.4.   The EPC must be provided by an energy assessor who is a member of an accreditation scheme approved by the Secretary of State[5] for that particular category of building.

24.8.5.   Where Housing Act 2004 places a seller under a duty to provide a home information pack, each pack must contain an EPC (see A26). In addition, the marketing particulars must either include the asset rating of the building or the EPC must be attached.[6]

24.8.6.   Further information and guidance and the form of the certificate to be used in the marketing of dwellings is available from the Department for Communities and Local Government website at **www.communities.gov.uk**.

24.8.7.   EPCs will, in time, be required where dwellings are sold without being marketed, for example sales of local authority housing and sales between family members. EPCs will also be required for commercial and residential properties (see A27.3).

24.8.8.   EPCs have a life of 10 years but where the certificate is included in a home information pack it must be no more than 12 months old at the first point of marketing[7] (see A26). This 12-month limit is to be the subject of consultation and may change.

24.8.9.   As the use of the home information pack is being phased in, the provision of EPCs for homes is also being phased in. Dwellings containing four or more bedrooms marketed on or after 1 August 2007 require an EPC. It is expected that the requirement for a home information pack will be extended to all residential properties with vacant possession by 1 January 2008. All other new homes will require an EPC from 1 January 2008. Similarly the obligation to include the asset rating or attach the EPC to the marketing particulars is also being phased in. As part of the transitional arrangements, until 1 January 2008, the duty to provide a home information pack and EPC only applies once the EPC is available, provided that it was commissioned before the property was marketed. However, the seller must provide the buyer with the EPC before the contract is entered into.

1. As amended by Energy Performance of Buildings (Certificates and Inspection) (England and Wales) (Amendment) Regulations 2007 (SI 2007/1669).
2. Reg.5.
3. Reg.10.
4. Reg.5.
5. Reg.25.
6. Reg.6.
7. Reg.11.

24.9. Environmental issues

24.9.1. Where a planning application is made for 'environmentally sensitive development' as defined in Town and Country Planning (Environmental Impact Assessment) (England and Wales) Regulations 1999 (SI 1999/293) (as amended), the local planning authority may require the applicant to submit an environmental statement with his application. Some local authorities ask for an environmental assessment to be submitted in connection with all applications for major development irrespective of the above Regulations.

B25. Environmental issues

25.1. Introduction

25.1.1. The legislation which focussed most practitioners' minds on environmental matters – the contaminated land regime – was brought into effect in England on 1 April 2000 and in Wales on 1 July 2001. It applies to all land, whether residential, commercial, industrial or agricultural. It can affect owners, occupiers, developers and lenders. The legislation, which is contained in Part IIA Environmental Protection Act 1990 (EPA 1990) and in regulations and statutory guidance issued under it, is retrospective. See Contaminated Land (England) Regulations 2006 (SI 2006/1380); Contaminated Land (Wales) Regulations 2001 (SI 2001/2197); and DEFRA Circular 01/2006.

25.1.2. Solicitors should be aware of the provisions of Part IIA EPA 1990 and the contents of the Law Society's Contaminated Land Warning Card (see Appendix III.1). This chapter includes an outline of the potential liabilties and gives further information on the steps recommended in the Warning Card.

25.2. Environmental risks

Legal liabilities

25.2.1. A buyer may inherit a number of legal liabilities on purchasing a property. The liability for the remediation of contaminated land is the most acute, but not the only, risk faced by buyers.

25.2.2. The full implications of environmental law in property transactions are explained in the *Environmental Law Handbook* by Trevor Hellawell (Law Society). Liabilities may emerge under a number of statutes and in a number of ways. Most of the liabilities mentioned below are more relevant to commercial transactions, but some may also be significant in residential cases.

25.2.3. Issues may emerge under the following legislation and common law principles:

- the nature conservation regime contained in Wildlife and Countryside Act 1981, Parts I and II as amended by Countryside and Rights of Way Act 2000;

- Pollution Prevention and Control Act 1999 and Pollution Prevention and Control (England and Wales) Regulations 2000;

- the waste regulatory regime under Environmental Protection Act 1990, Part II;

- the contaminated land regime under Environmental Protection Act 1990, Part IIA;

- the statutory nuisance regime under Environmental Protection Act 1990, Part III;

- the water pollution legislation in Water Resources Act 1991;

- the sewer discharge legislation in Water Industry Act 1991;

- the common law of nuisance.

The particular issue of contaminated land

25.2.4. Land may become contaminated as a result of past or present industrial use: leakages of liquids from storage tanks, washings from site plant and equipment, spillages from delivery wagons, or wastes and liquids being deposited (deliberately or inadvertently) on site from a potentially contaminative industrial process or other historic land use.

25.2.5. Contamination is not only a result of industrial waste, it may result from such things as leakages of oil from storage tanks for domestic heating systems, or waste oils from car engines, or other polluting matter disposed of on the land from DIY activities.

25.2.6. Details of which sites are determined as contaminated are available from the local authority (or Environment Agency if a special site). However, a negative reply to the local authority enquiries does not guarantee that the site is uncontaminated. Such an answer may merely mean that the site has not been inspected or that such pollution as does exist is not so serious as to meet the Part IIA definitions.

25.2.7. An offence is committed if those required to do so fail to remediate contaminated land when so instructed (Environmental Protection Act 1990, Part IIA). The liability to remediate land may arise as a result of substances already in the land at completion, which are giving rise to a risk of significant harm to persons or things nearby.

25.2.8. If the original polluter of the land cannot be found, the current owner or occupier may be served with a remediation notice requiring the land to be cleaned up. An offence is committed if he fails to comply, and the authorities can do the necessary works themselves and recover the costs from the person served with the notice.

25.2.9. A further problem is that a buyer can himself be determined as the 'original polluter'. This is because the original polluter is defined as 'any of the persons who [caused or] knowingly permitted the [contaminating substances] to be in, on or under the land'. Allowing something to remain on land if you could remove it amounts to permitting it to be on the land.

25.2.10. Actual knowledge of the contamination, turning a blind eye to an obvious risk of the presence of contamination, or failing to make enquiries for fear of discovering the truth would all amount to having the required knowledge.

25.2.11. Accordingly, if a buyer knew, or ought to have known, or realised, or could have found out, that there was contamination on the site, he may be liable as an original polluter.

25.2.12. There may also be leakages of substances onto the ground after completion in respect of which the buyer client may be deemed to be the 'original polluter' of the land.

25.2.13. Detailed provisions in Part IIA exclude a seller from any further liability for contamination if a reduction in the purchase price was negotiated to take account of particular contamination and remediation, or if a site is sold with full information about its contaminated history. These exclusions are likely to be relevant in most commercial transactions, the effect being that liability for contamination tends to run with the land.

25.2.14. Where there is no original polluter, the liability will fall on the owner or occupier for the time being.

Non-legal risks and liabilities

25.2.15. In addition to the legal risks mentioned above, environmental issues which may concern a buyer might include:

- flooding;
- radon gas;
- other health effects;
- invasive weeds and other pests;
- potential resale value.

25.3. Contaminated land warning card

25.3.1. Following the implementation of Part IIA EPA 1990 the Law Society issued a Warning Card on Contaminated Land (Appendix III.1). The advice contained in the Warning Card is intended to conform to best practice and not to constitute a professional requirement for solicitors.

25.3.2. The Warning Card requires solicitors, in every conveyancing transaction, to exercise their professional judgement in each case as to whether environmental liability is likely to be an issue.

25.3.3. The Warning Card also contains a series of steps that can be taken by solicitors to conform with best practice in conveyancing. Steps 1 and 2 should be routinely followed by solicitors acting in all types of conveyancing cases.

25.3.4. Steps 3 and 4 are recommended in all commercial conveyancing cases, and in those residential cases where solicitors consider that contamination is likely to be a risk. Steps 5 and 6 are recommended in commercial cases where steps 3 and 4 have revealed a risk of contamination. Steps 7 and 8 are for consideration where there are unresolved problems in any conveyancing case.

25.4. Step 1 – advising the client

25.4.1. In every conveyancing case, solicitors should advise the client of:

- the possibility of acquiring an interest in contaminated land;

- the potential liabilities associated with contaminated land;

- the range of other legal and non-legal risks outlined above;

- the steps that can be taken to assess the risks.

25.4.2. Solicitors may consider a standard paragraph added to the client care letter, a leaflet which can be sent at the start of the matter, or a meeting to discuss the issues.

25.4.3. If the client does not wish the solicitor to underake any environmental enquiries, solicitors should confirm the initial advice (and the fact that no investigations have been requested or made) to the client and any lender. Whatever the wishes of the borrower, some lenders may require such investigation.

25.5. Step 2 – specific enquiries of the seller

25.5.1. The extent and type of enquiries will depend on whether the land and property to be transferred is for domestic residential or commercial use.

25.5.2. The following are examples of some of the enquiries that may be made of the seller in domestic residential transactions:

- whether the seller is aware of any potentially contaminative use of the site or previous accidents, incidents or spillages;

- whether the site has been used for landfill or waste disposal purposes;

- details of previous owners or occupiers and activities carried out by them;

- whether there have been any disputes, or circumstances which may give rise to any disputes with neighbours or regulatory bodies regarding the state of the land;

- what (if any) planning consents have been issued in respect of the site, what conditions they contained regarding contamination and its remediation, and details of any works carried out to comply with the conditions.

25.5.3. It may be possible to check any such information whenever acting for a buyer of new property from a developer who will offer facilities for inspection of the documentation. There is an incentive in Part IIA Environmental Protection Act 1990 for the developer to give full and clear information to a buyer to enable him reasonably to assess the risk of contamination on the site at purchase.

25.5.4. The Commercial Property Standard Enquiries (second edition) include enquiries to make of the seller with regard to environmental issues. In general, the enquiries to make of a seller in commercial transactions include:

- the need for, and compliance with, all consents, licences, authorisations and permits in relation to any activities or processes conducted on the site, etc.;

- any contact or disputes with the regulatory bodies;

- details of any pollution incidents or accidents affecting the site and copies of any reports, correspondence, court orders, notices (including in particular remediation, charging or works notices) or recommendations relating to such accidents or incidents and details of any remedial work carried out including certificates of satisfactory completion;

- details of any environmental impairment liability insurance or any application therefor (whether or not the proposal was accepted by the insurers);

- disclosure of any consultants' or other report on the environmental risk assessment of the property or the seller's business;

- whether the seller is aware of any potentially contaminative current or previous use of the site or neighbouring sites;

- whether the site or any adjoining sites have been used for landfill or waste disposal;

- details of previous owners or occupiers and activities carried on by them;

- what (if any) planning consents have been issued in respect of the site, what conditions they contained regarding contamination and its reme-diation, and details of any works carried out to comply with the conditions.

25.5.5. There are two possible responses to these enquiries:

(a) *Replies are forthcoming.* The replies may need specialist interpretation by a surveyor or environmental consultant. Further, more detailed investigation may be needed if there are specific areas of concern;

(b) *The seller resists.* If the seller issues the blanket reply 'not so far as the seller is aware, please rely on own investigations and surveys', the buyer client must consider whether to undertake his own alternative investiga-tions. The seller must also be aware that in giving such a response he may be impliedly warranting that he has himself already undertaken enquiries.

25.6. Step 3 – enquiries of statutory and regulatory bodies

25.6.1. The Warning Card states that Step 3 should be taken in 'all commercial cases, and if contamination is likely to be a risk in residential cases (e.g. redevelop-ment of brown field land)'.

25.6.2. Solicitors should make full searches of any public registers regarding the site and adjacent land. The main bodies to contact (see Appendix VIII.2 for details) are:

- Natural England (and Scottish and Welsh equivalents) (nature conser-vation designations);

- Environment Agency (licences, registers and prosecutions);

- local authority (registers and information on contaminated land and any relevant planning consents and hazardous substance information);

- Health and Safety Executive (incidents and accidents);

- sewerage undertakers (consents and registers);

- British Coal (mining activities and abandoned mine leakage issues).

25.6.3. Enquiries of these bodies should be made regarding any:

- information held by them about the site, any investigations or inspec-tions made of it or adjacent land, details of any accidents, incidents or complaints and an indication of whether there is any intention to serve any notices in respect of the land;

- accidents, incidents and complaints by regulators or others relating to adjacent land.

25.6.4. Forms CON 29R and CON 29O Enquiries of Local Authority (see Appendix V.7) request information regarding notifications or entries on registers maintained under various statutes and regulations, including Part IIA Environmental Protection Act 1990. However, such notification procedures and register entries need only appear if land is actually identified and determined as contaminated. If land is not formally so identified or determined, no information will be held on the registers nor need be revealed in answer to the enquiries.

25.6.5. Information regarding the actual state of the land (albeit not yet 'contaminated') may be in the possession of the authority and may be of interest to a buyer. In such cases, consideration should be given to widening the scope of the enquiry and the wording of the questions to require disclosure of any 'information relating to the environment' at the relevant target site. Such information must be provided in compliance with Environmental Information Regulations 2004 (SI 2004/3391).

Radon

25.6.6. Radon is a naturally occurring radioactive gas which is present in the ground and is found at low levels in all buildings. The recommended limit for radon in UK homes is called the Action Level. A Radon Affected Area is declared when the estimated percentage of dwellings at or above the Action Level is 1% or more. The answer to question 3.13 of Form CON 29R Enquiries of Local Authority (2007) will reveal whether a property is in a Radon Affected Area. If this is the case, the seller should be asked for the results of any radon measurements made in the property.

25.6.7. The Health Protection Agency (formerly the National Radiological Protection Board (NRPB)) offers an information service to provide information on the radon potential of a dwelling (see Appendix VIII.2 for contact details).

25.7. Step 4 – independent site history investigation

25.7.1. The Warning Card states that Step 4 should be taken in 'all commercial cases, and if contamination is likely to be a risk in residential cases (e.g. redevelopment of brown field land)'. This step may include:

- obtaining a site investigation report from a commercial search company;

- desktop studies of the site involving consideration of old maps, plans, photographs and local physical and anecdotal evidence, to evaluate potential risks;

- consideration of contaminated land profiles available on the Environment Agency website, which outline the usual types of contamination associated with certain types of land use (e.g. landfill, railway yards, gasworks, munitions factories, etc.).

25.7.2. Residential and commercial search products are offered by a number of providers (see below) or through an NLIS channel:

- Environment Agency (**www.environment-agency.gov.uk**);

- Groundsure Ltd (**www.groundsure.co.uk**);

- Landmark Information Group (**www.landmark-information.co.uk**);

- Sitescope (**www.sitescope.co.uk**) (part of Landmark Information Group).

25.7.3. Search providers offer an initial risk assessment of the information provided in a report. Different providers offer different forms of risk assessment. An assessment might include a professional opinion on whether the property will be determined as contaminated land within the meaning of Part IIA Environmental Protection Act 1990 and whether there is likely to be any effect on the value of the property.

25.7.4. Solicitors should note that any such risk assessment is based purely on the publicly available information. No assessment of the actual site is undertaken. Also, there are matters contained in the report, which may affect a client's decision that are not taken into account in the risk assessment at all. Moreover, no mapping or information service is able to determine, for instance, whether there had been a spillage of domestic heating oil in the back garden. Enquiries of the seller or the local authority may still be necessary here and practitioners should not assume that a risk assessment that gives the property a clear report means there is no problem. If problems are evident on the search, the providers will usually indicate what further steps should be taken before deciding to buy and these can help the solicitor and client decide how next to proceed.

25.7.5. In most cases, the search will reveal no entries of any concern. Keeping the search with the file or deeds in electronic form will assist if future reference needs to be made in relation to the information disclosed. There would be no need to inform the lender where the search result is clear.

25.7.6. In some cases, the search will reveal entries that may be of some concern to the buyer. The solicitor should discuss these issues with the client to decide how to proceed, if necessary following consideration of any risk assessment, to ascertain the degree of risk posed by a revealed entry.

25.7.7. The mere fact that information reveals an entry, or a potentially contaminative historical use, does not necessarily mean that there is a problem with the land, merely that there may be, and this possibility may require further investigation.

25.7.8. The decision whether to proceed, undertake further investigations or withdraw must be the client's, and it will frequently depend on factors unrelated to the environmental information revealed by the search. Factors such as the cost of the further investigations, the difficulty and delay involved in undertaking them, the accuracy and helpfulness of the further information revealed, the general timescale of the transaction and the client's attitude to risk will all influence the decision.

25.7.9. Often, the next step after obtaining a report is simply to acquire further information (especially as it may be easily obtainable from an obvious source), rather than to consider an actual site inspection at significant additional cost.

25.7.10. Next steps could be to contact the relevant agency or local authority. The local authority will have assessed their area for the purposes of Part IIA and may have records of the steps taken by a developer to make the land safe which in most cases would avoid the need for a site investigation. Enquiries could also be directed towards the developer.

25.7.11. Until the actual extent of a potential problem is investigated and revealed by an intrusive ground investigation, no solicitor can advise fully on its implications, and reports are only designed to provide the information to enable solicitors to identify the next questions. A ground investigation is highly unlikely ever to be undertaken in a routine domestic transaction, and thus the client will ultimately be required to take a view on the basis of information alone. In these circumstances a solicitor cannot provide the client with conclusive answers. If the client wishes to proceed the solicitor should advise the client to seek assistance from a specialist.

25.7.12. If the property which is the subject of the report is to be charged as security for a loan, the solicitor should contact the lender to report the findings and indicate (if it be the case) that further investigations are ongoing. Solicitors should ask the lender whether they require any further steps to be taken. The report should only be sent to the lender with a recommendation that it is referred to the lender's valuer for consideration in extreme cases. The report should be kept with any documentary records along with other important searches.

25.8. Step 5 – full site investigation

25.8.1. The Warning Card recommends this step in 'commercial cases where there is a likelihood that the site is contaminated'. It would be very rare to undertake this step in residential cases, in which case the solicitor should consider Step 7.

25.8.2. The scope for detailed surveys of potentially contaminated sites will depend on agreeing the cost with the client and weighing the cost against the potential risks.

25.8.3. The cost of an investigation might be shared between the buyer and the seller as it may be in the seller's interests that the buyer knows the state of the site at completion.

25.8.4. Where there is a substantial risk of contamination, the investigation costs may well be acceptable to an intending buyer or lessee. For sites with a lower degree of prima facie risk, the client may prefer to limit the investigation to a 'desk survey'. If the desk survey reveals problems that need further investigation, then a thorough site survey involving test boreholes and sampling may be advisable.

25.8.5. The solicitor should be consulted regarding the terms of engagement of the environmental consultant to ensure that the client gets a report which is useful and reliable as a basis for risk assessment. It is important that the client is made aware of the risks of having no survey, or one that does not cover contamination issues.

25.9. Step 6 – contractual protections

25.9.1. Step 6 is to consider contractual protections against the seller. These may include:

- requiring the seller to make a specifically quantified and earmarked payment or price reduction, to take account of the potential liability;

- requiring the seller to provide full information about the contamination to the buyer in the contract;

- agreeing a formula whereby remediation costs are shared between potential polluters;

- seeking appropriate warranties as to the state of the site at completion;

- seeking an indemnity against future liabilities or reductions in value due to the state of the land at completion;

- requiring remediation by the seller before completion;

- obtaining assignment of any environmental insurance policies which may cover the site (or obtaining fresh cover).

Specific payments or price reductions

25.9.2. The buyer may seek a reduction in the price (as opposed to a retention) to cover the cost of remediation or clean-up, or any perceived blighting effect on value. Alternatively, the buyer may want the seller to make a payment towards the cost of remediation.

Requiring the provision of full information

25.9.3. The provision of full information on a voluntary basis is a way in which a seller can establish precisely that full information has been given to a buyer in relation to the presence of contaminants on the site, their nature and concentration.

25.9.4. The provision of this information would have the effect of removing the seller from the category of person eligible to receive a remediation notice in respect of contaminated land, thus leaving the buyer to foot the seller's share of the cost in addition to any they would already have to bear. There is thus a clear incentive for a seller to give the information and a corresponding incentive for the buyer to know exactly the state of the site and take decisions about whether to proceed and if so, at what price.

Agreements on liabilities

25.9.5. The parties may wish to agree between themselves how they wish to apportion any liability for contamination.

25.9.6. Any such agreement will be honoured by the authority, and all its decisions regarding contaminated land liability will be taken with the intention of effecting the agreement.

25.9.7. Such agreements may need to specify in percentage terms what proportion of any remediation work required or agreed is to be borne by the respective parties.

25.9.8. It is suggested that any indemnities regarding contaminated land which are intended to amount to an 'agreement on liabilities' for the purposes of Part IIA Environmental Protection Act 1990 be kept separate in the documentation from other environmental provisions. In addition, modification may be required of any inconsistent provisions contained in Standard Condition 3.

25.9.9. When considering the extent of any indemnities to be given, not only is it essential to decide who must take the risk of all existing contamination, but also the effect of any future contamination, the effects of any future development of the land, which may release earlier contamination and the risks of changes in environmental legislation. Standards of clean-up need to be agreed, as do the respective contributions. A sliding scale over three to five years may be appropriate as may threshold and cap arrangements for levels of expenditure.

Retention by buyer

25.9.10. Alternatively, the buyer may prefer to complete on the basis of a retention from the price sufficient to cover any likely costs of remediation or clean-up. This will enable the buyer to carry out the remediation works rather than rely upon the seller and this has advantages in terms of quality control and project management.

Indemnities

25.9.11. The seller might be required to indemnify the buyer against the costs of remediation or clean-up or against any damages, loss or injury resulting from any past contamination or pollution of the soil or any water courses or aquifers.

25.9.12. Caps on the level of indemnity are common, and they are only as good as the credit of the person giving them.

B

25.9.13. Phased indemnities are becoming more common – an arrangement whereby the seller remains liable for the first year, but the buyer gradually assumes part of the risk as the years go by until after, say, 10 years, the buyer is wholly liable.

25.10. Step 7 – withdrawal from the purchase

25.10.1. This step should be considered in residential or commercial cases when any of steps 1 to 6 above result in 'unresolved problems'.

25.10.2. At any stage in the above process, a buyer must be prepared to walk away from the transaction if:

- the risks are too great;
- the information is too hard to find; or
- the seller is too resistant to negotiation.

25.11. Step 8 – advising insurance

25.11.1. This step should be considered in residential or commercial cases when steps 1 to 6 above result in 'unresolved problems' and when the client does not wish to withdraw.

25.11.2. In commercial cases, new insurance cover may be available to the buyer against the risks of liability resulting from contamination or pollution. This will usually only be granted following an environmental risk assessment by specialist consultants appointed or approved by the insurance companies. It may be a requirement that any contamination found be cleaned up and an annual environmental audit of pollution control procedures carried out.

25.11.3. Several companies in the insurance market offer cheaper products designed to cover the risk that residential property may be designated as contaminated within the meaning of Part IIA. However, these are limited in scope.

25.11.4. Other insurers offering cover for homeowners are the National House-Building Council (NHBC) by means of Buildmark Cover, which is offered for new and converted homes that are registered with it and Zurich Building Guarantees in respect of new, converted and rental homes. It should be noted that this cover is limited in its ambit and application.

Earlier insurance cover: assignment of the policy?

25.11.5. In commercial cases, the availability of insurance cover in respect of past polluting events should also be considered and investigated with the seller in pre-contract enquiries.

25.11.6. Although the current practice of insurers is to limit or exclude liability for such events, older public liability and third party liability policies were wide enough to cover them and there may still be residual cover under old policies.

25.11.7. If this is possible or likely, specialist brokers might be called in to carry out an investigation into past insurance policies. If cover is available to the seller under these older policies, the indemnity clause in the contract should be coupled with an assignment of the benefit of this policy.

25.12. Advice to sellers

25.12.1. From the seller's point of view, achieving a clean break from the liabilities attaching in particular to a commercial site may not always be possible. In particular, liability may continue for:

- breaches of the consents committed while the seller was the site-owner and operator (commercial sites only);

- breaches of waste legislation while in possession (commercial sites only);

- contaminated land (on the person who originally caused or knowingly permitted substances to be on the site pre-sale) (commercial and residential sites);

- statutory nuisances caused or continued (commercial and residential sites);

- water pollution offences caused or knowingly permitted (commercial and residential sites);

- sewage discharge offences (commercial sites only);

- civil liability (as co-defendant for damage caused or continued during the period of ownership (commercial and residential sites).

25.12.2. In respect of most of these liabilities (all save for contaminated land) there is no easy way to shift liability on to a buyer other than by asking for indemnities, which the buyer is unlikely to give. A more important strategy is to ensure (perhaps by incoming and outgoing audits) what the state of play is when the site is sold on, so as to be able successfully to determine who did in fact cause a pollution incident, should there ever be a dispute.

25.12.3. As far as contaminated land is concerned, sellers should take close note of those clauses in the legislation that would exclude a seller from liability if:

- contract documents specifically reflect the payment (often in the form of a price reduction) of a specific sum for remediation;

- the land is sold in circumstances where full information is provided to the buyer about the contamination on the site;

- the seller and buyer agree on a contractual formula for dealing with any liabilities which emerge;

and ensure that the paperwork is drafted in such a way as to maximise the chance of exclusion.

B26. Boundaries and easements

26.1. Checking boundaries

26.1.1. The burden of discovering the identity and ownership of boundaries usually lies with the buyer since Condition 4.4.1 Standard Conditions of Sale and Standard Commercial Property Condition 6.3.1 will (unless excluded from the contract) relieve the seller of the obligation to define precisely their route or to prove title to their ownership.

26.1.2. The buyer's solicitor should therefore check the boundaries as shown on the title deeds, accompanying plans, and (where supplied) the estate agent's particulars. Where from investigation of the above documents the boundaries are unclear or a discrepancy exists, further enquiries should be undertaken to clarify the position.

26.1.3. The client should be asked to check the boundaries by a site inspection or the client's surveyor should specifically be asked to undertake this task in the course of his own inspection of the property. The solicitor is not generally under an obligation to inspect the property but may need to do so where a discrepancy or query over the boundaries exists which is not resolved by inspection of the deeds and plans or by other enquiries made by the solicitor. An inspection may be required in the case of the purchase of a newly constructed property to ensure that the site plans accord with the property as it stands on the ground. Where the solicitor does accept the obligation of inspecting the property he will be liable in negligence if he does not carry out that duty with proper care.[1]

26.1.4. The following enquiries and investigations may also assist to determine the extent and ownership of boundaries:

(a) specific pre-contract enquiries of the seller;

(b) application of the common law presumptions (see B26.2.2–B26.2.7);

(c) a site inspection of the property;

(d) an inspection of pre-root or pre-registration title deeds (if available);

(e) an Index Map search at the Land Registry (see B10);

(f) inspection of Ordnance Survey maps.

Ordnance Survey maps

26.1.5. It is the practice of Ordnance Survey maps to show the centre line of boundary features as the boundary. These maps may therefore give a general indication of the placing of a boundary subject to tolerances of scale but will not show the precise delineation of the boundary.

'T' marks

26.1.6. Plans attached to conveyances and transfers may indicate the ownership of boundaries by the use of 'T' marks. The stem of the 'T' should rest on the relevant boundary, the 'T' being on the side of the boundary which is responsible for its maintenance.[2]

26.1.7. The Lenders' Handbook, para. 6.2 requires the solicitor to ensure that the boundaries of the property are clearly defined by reference to a suitable plan or description.

26.1.8. Boundary agreements entered into for the purpose of clarifying the boundary, rather than for the conveyance of land, need not comply with section 2 Law of Property (Miscellaneous Provisions) Act 1989.[3]

26.1.9. In boundary disputes where the definition of the parcels in a conveyance or transfer is not clear, the court will take into account the physical features on the ground when determining where the boundary lies.[4]

1. See *Barclay-White* v. *Guillaume & Sons* [1996] EGCS 123.
2. See *Seeckts* v. *Derwent* [2004] EWHC 1913, Ch.
3. *Joyce* v. *Rigolli* [2004] EWCA Civ 79. See also *Neilson* v. *Poole* (1969) 20 P&CR 909.
4. *Chadwick and others* v. *Abbotswood Properties Ltd and others* [2004] EWHC 1058.

26.2. **Evidence of boundaries**

Registered land

26.2.1. Provided that provisions relating to the ownership of boundaries were clearly set out in the documentation accompanying the application for registration, these will be recorded on the register of the title. The extent of the boundaries shown on the title plan will usually not show the exact position since boundaries shown on plans drawn by the Land Registry are general boundaries only unless shown on the register as determined.[1]

Common law rebuttable presumptions as to boundaries

The ad medium filum rule

26.2.2. A person who owns land abutting on a private or public highway is presumed to own the soil or sub-soil respectively of the highway up to the middle line. The surface of a public highway is vested in the highway authority. Registered titles do not show ownership of the sub-soil to the centre of an adopted road even where expressly included in the transfer.

The hedge and ditch rule

26.2.3. Where two properties are separated by a hedge and a man-made ditch, the boundary line is presumed to lie on the far side of the ditch from the hedge.[2]

Foreshore

26.2.4. In the absence of contrary evidence, the boundary of land adjoining the sea lies at the top of the foreshore. The foreshore is that part of the shore lying between the ordinary high and low water marks. Land below the medium line of the foreshore belongs to the Crown.

Non-tidal rivers and streams

26.2.5. The *ad medium filum* rule applies so that the owners of properties on either bank of the stream or river own the bed up to the middle of the stream or river. The owner of the river is also presumed to own the right to fish in the river but this presumption may be rebutted and it is common to find that fishing rights have been separately sold to third parties.

Tidal rivers and sea inlets

26.2.6. The bed and foreshore of a tidal river is prima facie vested in the Crown subject to the public's rights of navigation and fishing. The Crown's rights extend to that point in the river where the tide ebbs and flows, beyond which point the *ad medium filum* rule applies.

Trees

26.2.7. A tree belongs to the owner on whose land it was planted even if its trunk, roots or branches extend on to a neighbouring property. Where it cannot be established who planted the tree (e.g. because the trunk straddles the boundary of the land) ownership may be inferred from the circumstances. Regular maintenance (e.g. lopping or topping) by one person may be indicative of ownership by that person.

Accretion and diluvion

26.2.8. Where land is bounded by water the land owner's boundary extends to that land as added to by accretion or lost by diluvion (erosion). This doctrine applies only where the changes in the boundary are gradual and imperceptible in the ordinary course of nature. It does not apply where a substantial and recognisable change in the boundary has suddenly taken place.[3] The doctrine applies to registered land unless an agreement as to its operation has been noted in the register.[4]

1. Land Registration Act 2002, s.60 and see Land Registration Rules 2003, r.118 and Land Registry Practice Guide 40 as to applications for a boundary to be determined. See also *Clements and others* v. *Goodacre* [2004] All ER (D) 120. In cases of difficulty specialist texts should be consulted. See also D2.5.2.
2. See *Alan Wibberley Building Ltd* v. *Insley, The Times*, 30 April 1999.
3. *Southern Centre for Theosophy Inc.* v. *State of South Australia* [1982] 1 All ER 283.
4. Land Registration Act 2002, s.61.

26.3. Party walls

Party Wall Act 1996

26.3.1. Party Wall Act 1996 in substance re-enacts London Building Acts (Amendment) Act 1939 which previously only applied to London. The provisions of the 1996 Act apply throughout England and Wales.

New party structures

26.3.2. Section 1 requires a building owner to give at least one month's notice if he wishes to build a party structure where none exists. If the adjoining owner consents within 14 days, the wall is to be built half on the land of each owner or in such position as they agree. The expense of building is agreed between them or in an appropriate proportion considering the use and the cost of labour and materials. If consent is not forthcoming, the building owner may only build on his land. He may, subject to certain conditions, place footings below the land of the adjoining owner. He must compensate the adjoining owner and any occupier for any damage caused. Any dispute which arises is to be determined in accordance with the dispute resolution procedure in section 10.

Existing party structures

26.3.3. Section 2 gives a building owner wide powers to deal with party structures. Rebuilding may be to a height of not less than two metres where the wall is not used by the adjoining owner. A building owner may not cause unnecessary inconvenience and must compensate the adjoining owner and occupier for any loss or damage caused. If he opens any part of the adjoining land or building, he must maintain hoarding or shoring for its security. He must usually make good all damage caused to adjoining premises, internal furnishings and decorations, and may be required to pay expenses in lieu. He must also pay a fair allowance for disturbance and inconvenience.

Procedure

26.3.4. Section 3 requires a building owner to serve the adjoining owner with a party structure notice stating the building owner's name and address, details of the proposed work and the date on which it is to start at least two months before any proposed work is to start. Section 20 defines 'owner' to include anyone with a tenancy for more than a year and any purchaser under an agreement for purchase or lease. The notice ceases to have effect if work is not started within 12 months and if it does not proceed with due diligence. If an adjoining owner does not consent to the notice within 14 days, a dispute arises and section 10 applies. An adjoining owner may serve a counter notice within one month requiring the owner to build chimney breasts, recesses or other such works. The works must be specified and plans, sections and particulars must accompany the counter notice. The counter notice may require the existing height of the wall to be maintained if a building owner proposes to reduce it to not less than two metres. A building owner must comply with a counter notice unless this would injure him, cause unnecessary inconvenience or delay. If he does not consent to the counter notice within 14 days, section 10 applies. The procedure differs where a building owner wants to construct special foundations. If the adjoining owner does not consent, they may not be put in.

Dispute resolution procedure

26.3.5. Where a dispute arises, it is to be settled by surveyors (section 10). Both parties must agree on the appointment of a surveyor or appoint their own surveyor and the two surveyors must select a third surveyor. Either of the other two may then call on him to settle the matter. All appointments must be in writing and cannot be rescinded. Provision is made to deal with the situation where a surveyor dies, becomes incapable of acting, or refuses or neglects to act effectively. An award cannot authorise interference with an easement of light or rights in the party wall but may deal with the right, time and manner of carrying out work and any other matter arising from the dispute. The surveyor's award is conclusive, subject to the right of either party to appeal to the county court within 14 days of the date of the award. The court may rescind or modify the award.[1]

Payment for the work

26.3.6. The building owner generally pays for all work. Where work is due to lack of repair, required by the adjoining owner or the latter makes use of the work, he must pay or contribute to the cost of the work. The building owner must serve him with an account within two months of completion. If the adjoining owner objects within one month, the matter is to be settled under section 10. Security for costs may be required before any work starts.

Miscellaneous

26.3.7. A building owner who proposes to excavate and construct a building or structure within three to six metres of any building or structure of the adjoining owner may, and must if required by the adjoining owner, strengthen or safeguard at his own expense the foundations of the adjoining owner if certain conditions are met. Finally, the Act gives rights to enter and remain on land for carrying out works and an occupier who refuses to permit this may be guilty of an offence.

1. See *Young and another* v. *Bemstone Ltd* [2004] All ER (D) 108 for an example of a dispute under s.10(b) which was referred to the county court.

26.4. **Hedgerows**

26.4.1. Hedgerow Regulations 1997,[1] reg. 3 prevents or inhibits the removal of hedge-rows growing in or adjacent to common land, a nature reserve, a SSSI, or land used for agriculture, forestry, or the keeping of horses, ponies or donkeys. Optional enquiry 21 on Form CON 29 (Part II) asks: 'if there are entries in the record under reg. 10, how can they be obtained, and where can the record be inspected?'

26.4.2. The Regulations apply where a hedgerow has a continuous length of at least 20 metres (or if less than 20 metres must meet by intersection or junction another hedgerow). They do not apply to hedgerows within or marking the boundary of a domestic curtilage.

26.4.3. The local planning authority has power to prevent the removal of an 'important hedgerow' which is defined by regulation 4 as one which has existed for 30 years or more and which satisfies at least one of the criteria set out in Part II of Schedule 1 to the Regulations. These criteria relate to archaeological/historical matters and to wildlife/landscape considerations.

26.4.4. An owner (which includes a tenant) who wishes to remove a hedgerow which is covered by the Regulations must serve a 'hedgerow removal notice' on the local planning authority. The form of notice is specified in Schedule 4 and must include a plan. The local planning authority may then either serve a notice saying that the hedgerow can be removed or serve a 'hedgerow retention notice'. If no notice has been served at the expiry of 42 days, the hedgerow can be removed.

26.4.5. Exceptions, where hedgerow removal is permitted, include:

    (a)   making a new access to replace an existing access;

    (b)   making a temporary access in an emergency;

    (c)   national defence;

    (d)   development for which planning permission has been granted;

    (e)   flood defence or land drainage;

    (f)   work preventing plant or tree pests;

    (g)   felling, etc., to prevent obstruction with electric lines;

    (h)   proper management.

26.4.6. An appeal against a retention notice lies to the Secretary of State for Environ-ment within 28 days. It is an offence to remove a hedgerow without the necessary permission.

26.4.7. As an alternative to prosecution the local planning authority can serve a notice requiring a new hedge to be planted. The local planning authority can apply for an injunction in the county court or High Court to restrain an actual or apprehended offence.

High hedges

26.4.8. Anti-social Behaviour Act 2003 gives the owner or occupier of a domestic property the right to complain to the local authority on the grounds that a high hedge (as defined in the Act) is adversely affecting the reasonable enjoyment of his property. A fee is payable.

26.4.9. If the local authority decides that the complaint is justified, it can issue a remedial notice requiring, for instance, that the hedge owner cut back the hedge. This notice cannot require the hedge to be reduced to a height of less than two metres. Failure to comply with a remedial notice can lead to a fine of up to £1,000 and the court can order the hedge owner to carry out the works with additional fines if the order is not complied with.

26.4.10. For more information, see the relevant sections of website of the Department for Communities and Local Government: **www.communities.gov.uk**.

1. SI 1997/1160.

26.5. **Checking easements**

Acting for the buyer

26.5.1. During the pre-contract stage, the buyer's solicitor must check the title and all the other documents in his file to ensure that the buyer will have the benefit of all the easements necessary for the enjoyment of the property and that there are no easements existing over the property that might impede the buyer's use and enjoyment of it. The Standard Conditions of Sale and the Standard Commercial Property Conditions provide that the buyer will take the property subject to incumbrances discoverable by inspection of the property (Standard Condition 3.1.2(b) and Standard Commercial Property Condition 3.1.2(b)).

Acting for the seller

26.5.2. From the seller's point of view, he must make sure that the contract discloses all the incumbrances that will bind the buyer after the purchase. To comply with this duty the seller's solicitor must also investigate the existence of easements over the property being sold.

Discovering easements

26.5.3. To discover easements the solicitor needs to:

- inspect the official copy of the register or the title deeds;

- if the title is unregistered, carry out a search at the Land Charges Department to check whether any D(iii) (equitable easement) land charges are registered;

- if acting for the seller, make enquiries of the seller client as to the rights his neighbours and others enjoy over the property being sold and the rights he enjoys over adjoining property;

- if acting for the buyer, instruct the buyer to make a personal inspection of the property to look for evidence of any easements, e.g. rights of way, rights to light, drainage, right to park, both enjoyed by the property and exercised over it.

26.6. Creation of easements

26.6.1. Easements can be created by express grant (either by deed or in writing), by implication on the sale of part of a property, or by prescription. The enforceability of easements depends upon their mode of creation and whether they have complied with the appropriate requirements regarding registration.

Express easements

26.6.2. To be legal, an express easement must be for an interest equivalent to an estate in fee simple absolute in possession or a term of years absolute.[1] It must also be created by deed.[2] If the easement is not granted for the equivalent of a legal estate (e.g. a determinable easement) or it is in writing, it can only take effect in equity. If in writing, the written agreement must comply with Law of Property (Miscellaneous Provisions) Act 1989, s.2.

Unregistered land

26.6.3. An express legal easement is binding on the land. Its existence should be discoverable from the deeds and it may also be obvious on an inspection of the property. If the easement is created in writing it can only be equitable and, to be enforceable against subsequent owners of the property, it requires registration as a D(iii) land charge. A search at the Land Charges Department should reveal its existence. If the D(iii) land charge has not been registered, it will be void against a purchaser of the legal estate for money or money's worth.[3]

Registered land

26.6.4. The creation of an express easement by deed over a registered title is a registrable disposition and must be completed by registration to take effect at law.[4] Prior to the implementation of Land Registration Act 2002 the creation of an easement by deed also needed to be completed by registration. So all express easements created by deed, which were created after the title was registered should appear on the title of the servient property. Equitable easements must be protected by an entry in the register. Under Land Registration Act 1925 protection was either a notice or caution. Under Land Registration Act 2002 an equitable easement should be protected by notice. For more information see Land Registry Practice Guide 62 which deals with the registration of easements under Land Registration Act 2002.

Implied easements

26.6.5. Implied easements come into existence on the sale of part of a property.[5] See J1.3.1 as to the creation of implied easements under the rule in *Wheeldon* v. *Burrows* and Law of Property Act 1925, s.62. Implied easements over unregistered land are legal easements and as such are binding on subsequent owners of the property. Where the land is registered, implied easements do not need to be completed by registration to take effect at law.[6]

Prescriptive easements

26.6.6. Easements created by prescription are legal easements which come into existence as the result of a long period of use. Easements created by prescription over unregistered land are legal easements and therefore are binding on the owner of the land. Where the land is registered, prescriptive easements take effect as legal interests. This is so whether created before or after the implementation of Land Registration Act 2002. Unlike expressly granted easements, prescriptive easements do not need to be registered to take effect at law.

1. Law of Property Act 1925, s.1(2)(a).
2. Law of Property Act 1925, s.52(1).
3. Land Charges Act 1972, s.4.
4. Land Registration Act 2002, s.27(1). The application to register the benefit and/or burden of the easements should be made in Form AP1 (Land Registration Rules 2003, Rule 90).
5. *Wheeldon* v. *Burrows* (1879) 12 Ch 31.
6. Land Registration Act 2002, s.27(7).

26.7. Easements as overriding interests in registered land

First registration

26.7.1. All legal easements existing at the date of first registration are overriding interests to which the land is subject.[1] Under Land Registration Act 1925, equitable easements that were openly exercised and enjoyed could take effect as overriding interests.[2] Under Land Registration Act 2002, only legal easements can be overriding interests. Expressly granted easements, whether legal or equitable, will be entered on the register on first registration in view of the Registrar's obligation to enter the burden of any interest appearing from his examination of the title to affect the registered estate.[3]

Dispositions of registered land

26.7.2. Any easement which was an overriding interest immediately before the coming into force of Land Registration Act 2002 retains its overriding status indefinitely. This will include both legal easements and equitable easements that were openly exercised and enjoyed.[4]

26.7.3. Easements expressly granted on or after 13 October 2003 must be completed by registration to operate at law. If not registered they take effect only in equity. Such equitable easements are not overriding interests and must be protected by way of notice if they are to bind a subsequent owner of the land. Implied easements and prescriptive easements do not require to be completed by registration to be legal easements and will take effect as overriding interests.

26.7.4. The only easements capable of overriding dispositions are:

(a) easements that were overriding interests when the Act came into force on 13 October 2003; and

(b) those arising by implication or prescription.

26.7.5. For dispositions of registered land registered on or after 13 October 2006, a buyer of registered land for valuable consideration will not be bound by an implied or prescriptive easement arising after the Act came into force that is an overriding interest unless:

(a) the buyer knows of it; or

(b) it is obvious from a reasonable inspection of the land; or

(c) it has been exercised within one year of the date of purchase.[5]

26.7.6. Most implied and prescriptive easements will be used on a regular basis and will not be at risk of losing their status. However, if a person has the benefit of an easement that does not meet the requirements above, he should apply for his interest to be protected by the entry of a notice against the servient land.[6]

26.7.7. Where the servient land is unregistered, consideration should be given to making an application for entry of a caution against first registration (see G3.4.9–G3.4.12).

1. Land Registration Act 2002, ss.11(4)(b) and 12(4)(c), and Sched.1, para.3.
2. See *Celsteel Ltd* v. *Alton House Holdings Ltd* [1985] 2 All ER 562 and *Thatcher* v. *Douglas* [1996] 146 NLJ 282.
3. Land Registration Rules 2003, r.35 and Land Registration Rules 1925, r.40.
4. Land Registration Act 2002, Sched.12.
5. Land Registration Act 2002, Sched.3, para.3(1) and Sched.12, para.10.
6. For further guidance see Land Registry Practice Guide 19 on notices, restrictions and the protection of third party rights and Practice Guide 52 as to easements acquired by prescription (both available at **www.landregistry.gov.uk**).

26.8. Access to neighbouring land

26.8.1. Access to Neighbouring Land Act 1992 allows the court to grant the applicant a temporary right of access to another person's land for the purpose of carrying out basic preservation work, i.e. work necessary to protect, repair or maintain (but not to improve) the applicant's property. The fact that the repairs would be substantially more expensive to carry out without access to the neighbour's land is not itself a ground for making the order. For an order to be made, the proposed works must be either impossible or substantially more difficult to carry out without an access order. The applicant need not be the owner of the land in question.

26.8.2.   The county court must refuse an access order where it is satisfied that the respondent or any other person would suffer interference with or disturbance of his use or enjoyment of the land to such a degree that it would be unreasonable to make the order.

26.8.3.   An order, if made, will be binding on successors in title of the respondent, provided it is registered. Although the applicant need not own the land, if he does the Act does not seem to provide for the benefit of the order to enure for the benefit of successors in title to the applicant's land. Where the land is unregistered an application under the Act is registrable as a pending action, an order as a writ and order. Where the land is registered, an application under the Act can be protected by either an agreed or unilateral notice. An order under the Act can only be protected by an agreed notice.[1]

26.8.4.   The Act contains provisions for compensation for loss of privacy, inconvenience, pecuniary loss, damage or injury. Except where the dominant land concerned is residential, payment of a fee for the access may be ordered by the court.

26.8.5.   Pre-completion searches at the Land Registry (or the Land Charges Department in the case of unregistered land) will identify cases where access orders have been registered under the Act.

26.8.6.   It is not possible to contract out of the provisions of the Act.

1.   Land Registration Rules 2003, r.80.

26.9.   Vehicular access over land

26.9.1.   The driving of a vehicle over common or other land is prohibited by section 193(4) Law of Property Act 1925 and section 34 Road Traffic Act 1988 makes it a criminal offence to drive a motor vehicle over land which is not a road but which is a restricted byway, or land over which a bridleway or public footpath runs. These offences are committed if the vehicle is driven on the land without lawful authority. It was therefore assumed that it was not possible to obtain an easement by prescription to drive over such land as easements by prescription could only be acquired in respect of activities which were capable of being carried out lawfully. However, the House of Lords in *Bakewell Management Ltd* v. *Brandwood*[1] decided that in a situation in which the owner of the land *could* have granted such an easement (i.e. had the legal right to grant it) then it is possible for an easement to drive vehicles over the land to be acquired by prescription provided that there has been a long and uninterrupted use of the right.

26.9.2.   Where the benefiting or burdened land is registered, an application to note the benefit and/or burden of the easement should be made to the Land Registry in the usual way.[2] Land Registry Practice Guide 52 deals with easements claimed by prescription and statutory rights of way for vehicles.

1.   *Bakewell Management Ltd* v. *Brandwood* [2004] UKHL 14.
2.   Where the benefiting land is registered the application should be made in Form AP1. Where the benefiting land is not registered the application against the registered servient land should be made in either Form AN1 or UN1.

C. EXCHANGE

C1. Preparing to exchange

<table>
<tr><td>1.1.</td><td>**Introduction**</td><td>1.3.</td><td>**Reporting to the buyer**</td></tr>
<tr><td>1.2.</td><td>**Checklist**</td><td></td><td></td></tr>
</table>

1.1. Introduction

1.1.1. On exchange a binding contract will come into existence, after which time neither party will normally be able to withdraw from the contract without incurring liability for breach. It is therefore essential to check that all outstanding queries have been resolved and that both parties' financial arrangements are in order before the client is advised to commit himself to the contract.

1.2. Checklist

1.2.1. Although the checklist below largely reflects matters which are of concern to a buyer, many of the items will also be of concern to a seller. The seller should pay particular attention to those items marked with an asterisk.

Searches

(a) Have all necessary searches and enquiries been made?

(b) Have all the replies to searches and enquiries been received?

(c) Have all search and enquiry replies been checked carefully to ensure that the replies to individual questions are satisfactory and accord with the client's instructions?

(d) Has Part 2 of the Sellers' Property Information Form or Part 2 of the Sellers' Leasehold Information Form been signed by the seller's solicitor?

*(e) Have all outstanding queries been resolved satisfactorily?

Survey

(a) Has a survey of the property been undertaken?

(b) Is the result of that survey satisfactory?

Mortgage arrangements

(a) Has a satisfactory mortgage offer been made and (where necessary) accepted by the client?

(b)   Are arrangements in hand to comply with any conditions attached to the advance, e.g. in relation to an endowment policy?

(c)   Taking into account the deposit, the mortgage advance (less any retention) and the costs of the transaction (including SDLT, Land Registry fees and other disbursements), has the client sufficient funds to proceed with the purchase?

* (d)   Have arrangements been made to discharge the seller's existing mortgage(s)?

* (e)   If the transaction is a sale of part, has the seller's lender (if any) agreed to release the property to be sold from the mortgage?

Deposit

* (a)   How much (if any) preliminary deposit has been paid?

* (b)   How much money is needed to fund the deposit required on exchange?

(c)   Has a suitable undertaking been given in relation to bridging finance?

* (d)   To whom is the deposit to be paid?

NB: Where Formula C is to be used for exchange, the deposit may have to be paid to someone other than the immediate seller.

(e)   Have the deposit funds been obtained from the client and cleared through clients' account?

NB: Standard Condition 2.4 requires that payment is to be made only by a cheque drawn on a solicitor's or licensed conveyancer's client account or by direct credit. Standard Commercial Property Condition 2.2 requires payment be made by direct credit.

The contract

* (a)   Have all outstanding queries been satisfactorily resolved?

* (b)   Have all agreed amendments been incorporated clearly in both parts of the contract?

* (c)   Has the approved draft been returned to the seller?

* (d)   Is a clean top copy of the contract available for signature by the client?

* (e)   Have the terms of the contract been explained to the client?

* (f)   Has the list of fixtures and fittings been agreed between the parties?

Insurance

(a)   Have steps been taken to insure the property immediately on exchange?

* (b)   If the buyer is to rely on the seller's insurance policy, has the buyer's interest been noted on that policy?

(c)   Have steps been taken to obtain any life policy required under the terms of the buyer's mortgage offer?

Completion date

*   Has a completion date been agreed?

Method of exchange

*   Which method of exchange is most suitable to be used in this transaction?

Synchronisation

*   Where the client requires a simultaneous exchange on both sale and purchase contracts, are both transactions and all related transactions in the chain also ready to proceed?

Signature of contract

*   Has the client signed the contract?

Occupiers

*   Has the concurrence of all non-owning occupiers been obtained?

1.3.   Reporting to the buyer

1.3.1.   When the buyer's solicitor has completed his investigations into the property (including having finalised any amendments to the draft documentation) he should prepare and send or give to his client a report on the proposed purchase which should explain to the client (in language appropriate to the client's level of understanding) the nature of the solicitor's investigations into the property and its legal title, the results of these investigations, the terms of the contract and the mortgage offer, and a summary of conclusions or advice to the client.

1.3.2.   An example of such a report is set out in Appendix V.12. The precise content of the report will vary from transaction to transaction and in the case of commercial property a more detailed report may be desirable. A report on leasehold property should explain the terms of the lease to the client (see K3).

C2. Signature of contract

2.1. Requirement for signature

2.1.1. Both parties must sign the contract (or each must sign one of two identical copies) in order to satisfy Law of Property (Miscellaneous Provisions) Act 1989, s.2. Such signature need not be witnessed.

2.2. Signature by the client

2.2.1. Ideally the client should be asked to sign the contract in the presence of his solicitor, the solicitor first having ensured that the client understands and agrees to the terms of the contract.

2.2.2. In cases where it is not practicable for the client to sign in the solicitor's presence, the contract may be sent to the client for signature with an accompanying letter which clearly explains where and how the client is required to sign the document. If not already done, the letter should explain the terms of the contract in language appropriate to the client's level of understanding, and also request a cheque for the deposit indicating by which date the solicitor needs to be in receipt of cleared funds. The client should be asked to return the signed contract to the solicitor as soon as possible. (There is an example report on proposed purchase at Appendix V.12.)

2.3. Signature by solicitor on behalf of client

2.3.1. A solicitor needs his client's express authority to sign the contract on behalf of the client.[1]

2.3.2. Unless the solicitor holds a valid power of attorney, it is recommended that such an authority be obtained from the client in writing, the client previously having been informed of the legal consequences of giving such authority (i.e. signature implies authority to proceed to exchange, and exchange creates a binding contract). Failure to obtain authority may render the solicitor liable in damages for breach of warranty of authority.[2]

1. *Suleman v. Shahsavari* [1989] 2 All ER 460.
2. *Ibid.*

2.4.   **Special cases**

Co-owners

2.4.1. One co-owner may sign the contract on behalf of all the co-owners, but the solicitor should ensure that all co-owners have voluntarily given their consent to the transaction and have authorised the signature of the contract.

Trustees

2.4.2. One trustee alone may sign the contract for sale on behalf of his co-trustees. The solicitor should ensure that all co-trustees have voluntarily given their consent to the transaction and have authorised the signature of the contract.

Partners

2.4.3. Provided that the transaction has been authorised by the partnership, one partner may be given authority to sign the contract on behalf of the partners.

Companies

2.4.4. Provided that the transaction has been authorised by the company, an officer of the company (usually a director or the secretary) may be authorised to sign on behalf of the company.

Attorneys

2.4.5. A person who holds a valid power of attorney on behalf of another may sign the contract on behalf of the donor of the power. The attorney may sign either in his own name or that of the donor. The solicitor acting for the other party should be notified that the contract will be signed by an attorney and a properly certified copy of the power supplied to him so that he may satisfy himself as to the validity of the power and that it contains proper authority for the conduct of the particular transaction (see B7.19 and B.23).

Personal representatives

2.4.6. All proving personal representatives must be parties to the contract and purchase deed.[1]

Occupiers

2.4.7. A non-owning occupier may be joined as a party to the contract in order to give a release of his or her purported interest in the property. Where this occurs the non-owning occupier must sign the contract.[2]

1. Law of Property (Miscellaneous Provisions) Act 1994, s.16.
2. See B3.5.8 for an appropriate form of wording to release rights.

2.5.   **Authority to exchange**

2.5.1.   It may be appropriate to obtain the client's express authority to exchange at the time of signature of the contract (see C4.2).

C3. Insurance

3.1. Risk in the property

3.1.1. At common law and unless the contract provides otherwise, the risk in the property passes to the buyer from the moment of exchange; the buyer thus bears the risk of loss or damage, except where it can be shown that the loss or damage is attributable to the seller's lack of proper care.[1] The buyer should therefore normally insure the property from exchange of contracts onwards.

3.1.2. Since it is impossible to predict at which precise moment exchange will occur, it is essential that the buyer's insurance arrangements have been made in advance of actual exchange so that the policy will be effective immediately upon exchange.

3.1.3. Standard Condition 5.1 provides for the seller to bear the risk in the property until completion and permits rescission if the property is substantially damaged between exchange and completion. This condition permits the seller to cancel his insurance policy (except in certain cases related to the sale of an existing lease) and also excludes Law of Property Act 1925, s.47 which would otherwise give the buyer the right, in certain circumstances, to claim off the seller's policy in the event of damage to the property. However, the buyer's lender will frequently insist that the property is insured in the buyer's name from the date of exchange, in which case Standard Condition 5.1 is excluded by special condition.

3.1.4. Standard Commercial Property Condition 7.1.4 passes risk to the buyer on exchange and provides that the seller is under no obligation to the buyer to insure the property. Condition 10.1.3 applies to leasehold property and in this context may require the seller to maintain his policy if so required by the lease.

3.1.5. A solicitor who fails to advise his client of the consequences of failure to insure, or who fails to carry out his client's instructions to insure the property, will be liable in negligence if the client suffers loss as a result of the lack of insurance.

1. *Clarke* v. *Ramuz* [1891] 2 QB 456; *Phillips* v. *Lamdin* [1949] 2 KB 33.

3.2. Buyer insuring the property from exchange

3.2.1. Where the buyer's solicitor has in force a block policy which covers all properties currently being handled by the firm, the property should be noted on the policy in accordance with the firm's standard procedures and, at the latest, by the morning of the day on which it is anticipated that exchange will occur.

3.2.2. If the buyer is financing his purchase with the assistance of a mortgage, the lender will normally attend to the insurance arrangements on being requested to do so by the buyer's solicitor. The lender's standing instructions to solicitors should be checked to ensure that:

(a) the amount of cover will be adequate;

(b) the property will be put on cover from the time of exchange;

(c) the lender's insurance requirements do not conflict with the terms of the contract or of any lease to which the property is subject.

3.2.3. If neither of the preceding subparagraphs apply the buyer must obtain a policy which will cover the property from exchange.

3.3. The terms of the policy

3.3.1. The terms of the policy should be checked to ensure that:

(a) the amount of cover is adequate;

(b) the sum insured is index linked;

(c) the risks insured against are adequate, e.g. is flood damage covered where the property is situated in a low-lying area?

(d) particular features of the property have been disclosed to the insurance company and are adequately insured, e.g. thatched roofs, garden walls, interior decorative plasterwork;

(e) where the property consists of a flat within a larger building, or is otherwise attached to adjoining property, the insurance cover extends to damage to neighbouring property where practicable.

3.3.2. The client should be alerted to possible exclusions under the policy. In particular damage caused by terrorist activity, environmental contamination and flooding may not be covered; in a leasehold context, in the event of damage by an uninsured risk, the tenant or prospective tenant may remain liable under the terms of the lease, including the covenants to repair and pay rent. Similarly, some policies will not cover damage to empty properties (or to blocks of flats where a resident is claiming social security benefits).

3.4. Property at seller's risk

3.4.1. In some cases, and commonly with property which is in the course of construction, the contract will provide that the property is to remain at the seller's risk until completion. Standard Condition 5.1 also provides for the seller to bear the risk in the property until completion and permits rescission if the property is substantially damaged between exchange and completion. Except in certain cases applicable to the sale of leaseholds, the seller is not obliged by the condition to maintain his own insurance policy after exchange.

3.4.2. Where the risk in the property remains with the seller the buyer need not take out his own policy until completion but should ensure, before exchange, that:

(a) the seller will maintain his policy until completion and the terms of that policy provide sufficient protection for the buyer;

(b) the buyer receives written confirmation that his interest has been noted on the seller's policy;

(c) the contract contains a provision requiring the seller to transfer the property in substantially the same physical condition as it was in at the time of exchange, failing which the buyer is entitled to rescind the contract (Standard Condition 5.1 contains this type of provision). This type of clause is not necessary where the property is in the course of construction because the contract for such a property will normally contain provisions requiring the seller to complete the building in accordance with specifications, failing which the buyer is under no obligation to complete.

3.4.3. Where the property is in the course of construction and the risk is to remain with the seller until completion, the buyer should clarify with the seller whether the word 'completion' is intended to refer only to completion of the building works, or whether it is intended that the seller will retain the risk in the property until actual completion of the transaction.

3.5. Maintenance of seller's policy

3.5.1. Except where the seller is obliged by a condition of his mortgage or lease to maintain his policy, the seller could cancel his insurance policy on exchange of contracts, but in practice he would be ill advised to do so, e.g. in case the buyer failed to complete.

3.5.2. In practice the seller will not usually cancel his policy until after completion; thus for the period between exchange and completion there will often be two policies in force (one having been taken out by the buyer on exchange), both covering the same property against the same risks.

3.5.3. Should the property be damaged or destroyed during the period when the two policies subsist difficulty may sometimes be experienced in obtaining payment from the insurer, since each insurer may maintain that the responsibility for payment lies with the other. This difficulty may be resolved by including a special condition in the contract which requires the buyer to complete, subject to an abatement in the purchase price, leaving the seller to resolve the dispute with his own insurers.

3.6. Damage to the property

3.6.1. Under the common law the buyer will have to bear the cost of any damage caused to the property after exchange unless one of the provisions outlined below can be utilised. Additionally, the buyer's solicitor may be liable to his client in negligence (see C3.1.3).

3.6.2. Law of Property Act 1925, s.47 provides that a buyer may claim his loss from the policy maintained by the seller provided that:

(a) the contract does not exclude the operation of the section;

(b) the buyer pays a proportionate part of the insurance premium; and

(c) the insurance company consents to noting the buyer's interest in the policy.

3.6.3. The contract will normally exclude the operation of section 47, rendering the section ineffective so far as the buyer is concerned. (See Standard Condition 5.1 and Standard Commercial Property Condition 7.1.5.)

3.6.4. Fires Prevention (Metropolis) Act 1774, s.83 allows a person interested in or entitled to a property to require an insurance company to apply the proceeds of the policy towards the reinstatement of the property in the event of its damage by fire. Despite its title, the operation of the Act is not confined to London, but there is no direct authority for the proposition that a buyer under a contract for sale is a 'person interested' under the section.[1]

1. *Rayner* v. *Preston* (1881) 18 Ch 1 suggests *obiter* that a buyer can claim under the Act.

3.7. Other types of insurance

3.7.1. In appropriate cases the buyer should be advised to take out insurance to cover other risks, e.g. house contents, as well as life insurance in accordance with the terms of the mortgage offer.

3.7.2. Steps should be taken before or immediately after exchange to put such policies on foot although they will not normally need to be effective until completion. Advice given by the solicitor to his client about the terms of life insurance policies will be subject to the provisions of Financial Services and Markets Act 2000 (see A4). The seller should be advised not to cancel his house contents or other policies (including life policies linked to his mortgage) until completion.

3.8. **Insurance mediation**

3.8.1. If the solicitor is involved in insurance mediation services with regard to any insurance policy, care must be taken to ensure that the provisions of the Law Society's Scope Rules and Conduct of Business Rules are complied with (see A4).

C4. Exchange of contracts

4.1. The practice of exchange

4.1.1. The physical exchange of contracts between the parties is not a legal requirement for a contract for the sale of land but where a contract is drawn up by solicitors acting for the parties it is usual for the contract to be prepared in two identical parts, one being signed by the seller, the other by the buyer. When the two parts are physically exchanged, so that the buyer receives the part of the contract signed by the seller and vice versa, a binding contract comes into existence. The actual time when the contract comes into being depends on the method which has been employed to effect the exchange (see C4.3).

4.1.2. The practice of exchange was given legal recognition in *Eccles* v. *Bryant and Pollock*[1] where Lord Greene in his judgment stated in relation to the then existing law under Law of Property Act 1925, s.40[2] that the three essential ingredients of a contract for the sale of land were:

(a) compliance with the requirements of Law of Property Act 1925, s.40;[3]

(b) certainty in respect of the existence of the contract; and

(c) certainty in respect of the terms of the contract.

4.1.3. All three of the above requirements are satisfied by the practice of exchange of contracts, because where a contract is to come into existence through exchange both parties have the assurance of knowing that no contract exists until that time, i.e. either party is free to change his mind and withdraw from the negotiations until exchange. In the same way, once exchange has taken place, there is certainty for both parties as to the existence of an enforceable contract, and also certainty over the terms which have been agreed since each party retains a copy of the contract signed by the other in identical form to the one which he himself signed. Where contracts are to be exchanged both parts of the contract must be identical. This includes the filling in of the date of the contract and the date of completion. If this requirement is not met no contract will come into existence whether or not the exchange takes place.[4]

4.1.4. Since exchange is not a legal necessity there is no reason why the contract should not be embodied in a single document which is signed by both parties. In such a case the contract becomes binding and enforceable as soon as the second signature has been put on the document.[5] This situation will not frequently occur and in any event the same solicitor is usually forbidden from acting for both parties by Rule 3.07 Solicitors' Code of Conduct 2007.

4.1.5. An exchange of faxes or e-mails is not an exchange of contracts to satisfy section 2 Law of Property (Miscellaneous Provisions) Act 1989.[6] In *Commission for the New Towns* v. *Cooper (Great Britain) Ltd*[7] an exchange of letters was held not to satisfy section 2.

1. [1948] Ch 93.
2. [1948] Ch 93 at 99.
3. Now replaced by Law of Property (Miscellaneous Provisions) Act 1989, s.2.
4. *Harrison* v. *Battye* [1975] 1 WLR 58.
5. *Smith* v. *Mansi* [1963] 1 WLR 26.
6. *Milton Keynes Development Corporation* v. *Cooper (Great Britain) Ltd* [1993] EGCS 142.
7. [1995] 2 All ER 929, CA.

4.2. Authority to exchange

4.2.1. A solicitor who exchanges contracts without his client's express or implied authority to do so will be liable to the client in negligence. In *Eccles* v. *Bryant and Pollock*[1] Lord Greene said that where a contract was to come into existence using the standard form of contract (now the Standard Conditions of Sale or Standard Commercial Property Conditions), it was implicit that the contract would come into existence on exchange, and that the client therefore impliedly authorised his solicitor to effect an exchange. In *Domb* v. *Isoz*[2] it was held that, once the solicitor has his client's authority to exchange, he has the authority to effect the exchange by whichever method the solicitor thinks most appropriate to the situation.

4.2.2. Although *Eccles* v. *Bryant and Pollock*[3] suggests that a solicitor's authority to exchange may be implied, it is better practice to obtain express authority from the client at the time of signature of the contract. Where an exchange of contracts by telephone is contemplated, it is suggested that, for the avoidance of doubt, express authority to use this method should be obtained. Where Formula C is to be used, it is a requirement of that Formula that express authority be obtained, preferably in writing. The Formula contains a suggested form of wording to meet this situation. Formula C is set out in full with notes for guidance in Appendix II.2.

1. [1948] Ch 93.
2. [1980] Ch 548.
3. [1948] Ch 93.

4.3. Methods of exchange

4.3.1. Whichever method is chosen the exchange is usually initiated by the buyer indicating to the seller that he is now ready to commit himself to a binding contract. Once contracts have been exchanged neither party will be able to withdraw from the contract; it is therefore essential that the parties' solicitors have checked that all necessary arrangements are in order before proceeding to exchange. Also, where the purchase of one property is dependent on the sale of another the solicitor must ensure that the exchange of contracts on both properties is synchronised to avoid leaving his client either owning two houses or being homeless. Failure to synchronise the exchange where the client has instructed that his sale and purchase transactions are interdependent is professional negligence.

Telephone

4.3.2.   Exchange by telephone is now the most common method of effecting an exchange of contracts. Legal recognition of the practice was given by the Court of Appeal in *Domb* v. *Isoz.*[1] With the exception of personal exchange this method represents the quickest way of securing an exchange of contracts and is thus particularly useful in a chain of transactions. The method is not, however, risk free. Where exchange is effected by telephone, the contract between the parties becomes effective as soon as the parties' solicitors agree in the course of a telephone conversation that exchange has taken place. The telephone conversation is usually followed by a physical exchange of documents through the post in the normal way, but the existence of the contract is not dependent on this physical exchange; the contract already exists by virtue of the telephone conversation. If one party were subsequently to change his mind about the contract there is ample scope with this method for disputing the contents of the telephone conversation and thus the existence of the contract itself. Also, neither party is able to check that other's contract is in the agreed form, incorporates all agreed amendments or has been signed by the other party. To avoid the uncertainties arising out of this method of exchange the parties' solicitors must agree prior to exchange that the telephonic exchange will be governed by one of the Law Society's Formulae which were drawn up by the Law Society in response to the decision in *Domb* v. *Isoz.* The text of these Formulae appears in Appendix II.2. An accurate attendance note recording the telephone conversation must also be made as soon as practicable.

Using the Formulae

4.3.3.   (a) The text of the Formulae with their accompanying guidance notes is set out in Appendix II.2 and II.3.

(b) Whichever Formula is used, the client's express authority to exchange must be obtained before the procedure to exchange is commenced.

(c) If any variation to a Formula is to be made, such variation must be expressly agreed and noted in writing by all the solicitors involved before exchange takes place. Any agreement relating to the payment of a less than 10% deposit should be finalised at the preliminary enquiries stage of the transaction and not left until exchange is imminent. Any agreed variation to the Formula which has been made orally must be confirmed in correspondence between the solicitors.

(d) Subject to (c) above, the conditions attached to the Formula being used must be strictly adhered to. In particular, where an undertaking is given to remit a deposit cheque and/or contract to the solicitor acting for the other party, such undertaking must be complied with on the day on which exchange takes place or, if compliance on the same day is not practicable, e.g. because exchange takes place after normal working hours, at the earliest opportunity on the next working day.

(e) To ensure compliance with the conditions attaching to the Formulae it is recommended that only qualified staff be authorised to effect an exchange by telephone.

(f) The Formulae may be used where the other party to the transaction is represented by a licensed conveyancer. The Formulae must never be used where the other party is represented by an unqualified person whose undertaking is not enforceable in the same way as those given by solicitors and licensed conveyancers.

(g) Extreme care needs to be exercised when using Formula C (for use in chain transactions) where, in certain circumstances, a solicitor is required to give an undertaking, the performance of which is outside his direct control, e.g. solicitor A undertakes to solicitor B that solicitor C will send the deposit cheque to solicitor B. The Standard Conditions of Sale only permit a deposit to be used for an exchange of contracts along the chain if that contract contains similar provisions as to the deposit. This almost inevitably means that the second contract must also be made by reference to the Standard Conditions.

(h) Under Formula C the ultimate recipient of the deposit must hold as stakeholder. No other capacity is permitted.

(i) An attendance note recording full details of the exchange by telephone must be made immediately exchange has taken place.

(j) A solicitor's failure to honour an undertaking given in relation to use of one of the Formulae (e.g. failure to send the deposit cheque on the same day as exchange takes place) is professional misconduct but probably does not affect the validity of an otherwise valid contract.[2]

(k) Fax can be used to activate the Formulae.

Personal exchange

4.3.4. By this method the solicitors for the parties meet, usually at the seller's solicitor's office, and the two contracts are physically exchanged. A contract exists from the moment of exchange. Although this type of exchange represents the safest and most instantaneous method of exchange it is frequently not possible to use personal exchange because the physical distance between the offices of the respective solicitors make it impractical to do so. Personal exchange is little used today, but it should be considered for use when the parties' solicitors are located in sufficient geographical proximity to make personal exchange feasible. A personal exchange has the benefit not only of being instantaneous, and thus leaving no uncertainty over the timing of the creation of the contract, but also of enabling both parties to see the other party's part of the contract before exchange actually takes place, so that both may be reassured that the parts of the contract are identical in form and have been properly signed.

Postal exchange

4.3.5. Where exchange is to take place by post the buyer's solicitor will send his client's signed contract and the deposit cheque to the seller's solicitor who on receipt of these documents will post his client's signed contract back to the buyer (see Appendix II.3 for the Law Society's Code for Completion by Post). Generally a contract does not come into being until the buyer has *received* the seller's contract. Exchange of contracts by post forms an exception to this rule and the contract is made when the seller *posts* his part of the contract to the buyer.[3] Posting the contract means that the seller must actually place the letter in the letter box. Handing the letter to a third party with instructions that it should be posted is not sufficient.[4] The postal rules of acceptance may be displaced by contrary intention in the contract itself.[5] It follows from the above that a contract will be formed even if the seller's part of the contract is lost in the post and is thus never received by the buyer. Using the post as a method of exchange is reasonably satisfactory when dealing with a single sale or purchase which is not dependent on another related transaction, but even in this simple scenario some dangers exist. There will inevitably be a delay between the buyer sending his contract to the seller and the seller posting his part back, during which time the buyer is uncertain of whether he has secured the contract. There is also no guarantee that the seller will complete the exchange by posting his part of the contract back to the buyer. Until he actually does so he is free to change his mind and withdraw from the transaction. Although these dangers are minimal where a single sale or purchase is being undertaken, the risks assume a much greater importance where a chain of transactions is involved; thus, the use of postal exchange is not advisable in linked transactions.

Document exchanges

4.3.6. A document exchange would be used to effect an exchange of contracts in a similar way to the normal postal service and is subject to the same risks as are outlined in the preceding subparagraph. The court has approved the use of document exchanges for the service and delivery of documents in non-contentious matters in *John Wilmot Homes* v. *Reed*.[6] The rules on postal acceptance do not apply to document exchanges and unless the contract contains a contrary provision the contract will come into existence when the seller's part of the contract is received by the buyer.[7] Where the Standard Conditions of Sale in each case are used, Condition 2.1 provides that the contract is made when the last copy of the contract is deposited at the document exchange. Standard Commercial Property Condition 2.1 provides to identical effect. If the Standard Conditions of Sale or Standard Commercial Property

Conditions do not form the basis of the contract, the contract probably comes into existence when the last part of the contract is placed in the solicitor's box at the document exchange. There is no decided case on the making of a contract for the sale of land where a document exchange has been used to effect an exchange, and the proposition outlined above would be subject to the rules of the particular document exchange which was being used.

Fax

4.3.7. An exchange of faxes is not a valid exchange of contracts under Law of Property (Miscellaneous Provisions) Act 1989, s.2.[8] The main use of fax is to transmit the messages which activate the Law Society's Formulae. In this context fax is merely a substitute for using the telephone. Standard Condition 1.3.3 and Standard Commercial Property Condition 1.3.3 do not permit fax to be used as a valid method of service of a document where delivery of the original document is essential (as it is with the contract), thus effectively ruling out an *exchange* by this method, although there is no objection to the parties using fax in order to activate the Law Society's Formulae.[9]

E-mail

4.3.8. E-mail can also be used to transmit the messages activating the Law Society's Formulae under both the Standard Conditions of Sale (Condition 1.3) and Standard Commercial Property Conditions (Condition 1.3), provided the relevant e-mail addresses are included in the contract. At present, contracts for the sale of land cannot be entered into electronically via e-mail or the internet.

1. [1980] Ch 548.
2. See *Khan* v. *Hamilton* [1989] EGCS 128.
3. Despite doubts expressed about these rules in *Eccles* v. *Bryant and Pollock* (above), it is generally accepted that the postal rules as established in *Adams* v. *Lindsell* (1818) 1 B & Ald 681 do apply.
4. *Re London and Northern Bank, ex p. Jones* [1900] Ch 220.
5. *Holwell Securities* v. *Hughes* [1974] 1 All ER 161.
6. (1985) 51 P&CR 90.
7. See Standard Conditions 1 and 2 and Standard Commercial Property Conditions 1 and 2.
8. *Milton Keynes Development Corporation* v. *Cooper (Great Britain) Ltd* [1993] EGCS 142. An exchange of faxes was held not to be an exchange of contracts.
9. See *Hastie & Jenkerson (a firm)* v. *McMahon* [1991] 1 All ER 255 where the court, in a contentious case, approved fax as a valid method of service of a document but said that, to be valid as a method of service, the onus was on the sender of the document to prove that the document, in complete and legible form, had arrived at the recipient's terminal.

4.4.   The Protocol

4.4.1. Paragraph 8 of the Protocol (see Appendix II.1 for the full text of the Protocol) provides as follows:

'On exchange, the buyer's solicitor shall send or deliver to the seller's solicitor:

8.1   The signed contract with all names, dates and financial information completed.

8.2 The deposit provided in the manner prescribed in the contract. Under the Law Society's Formula C the deposit may have to be sent to another solicitor nominated by the seller's solicitor.

8.3 If contracts are exchanged by telephone, the procedures laid down by the Law Society's Formulae A, B or C must be used and both solicitors must ensure (unless otherwise agreed) that the undertakings to send documents and pay the deposit on that day are strictly observed.

8.4 The seller's solicitor shall, once the buyer's signed contract and deposit are held unconditionally, having ensured that details of each contract are fully completed and identical, send the seller's signed contract on the day of exchange to the buyer's solicitor in compliance with the undertaking given on exchange.

8.5 Notify the client that contracts have been exchanged.

8.6 Notify the seller's estate agent or property seller of exchange of contracts and the completion date.'

4.5. Standard Conditions of Sale and Standard Commercial Property Conditions

4.5.1. Condition 2.1 of both sets of conditions governs the making of the contract and allows contracts to be exchanged by document exchange, by post, or by telephone using the Law Society's Formulae (see Appendix V.9 and V.10).

C5. After exchange

5.1.	**The effects of exchange**	5.3.	**Protection of the contract**
5.2.	**After exchange**		

5.1. The effects of exchange

5.1.1. A binding contract exists from which normally neither party may withdraw without incurring liability for breach.

5.1.2. The beneficial ownership in the property passes to the buyer who becomes entitled to any increase in value of the property, but also bears the risk of any loss or damage; hence the need to ensure that insurance of the property is effective from the moment of exchange.[1] Standard Condition 5.1 states that the risk in the property is to remain with the seller until completion. However, Standard Commercial Property Condition 7.1.4 passes risk to the buyer on exchange of contracts.

5.1.3. The seller retains the legal title to the property until completion, but holds the beneficial interest on behalf of the buyer. During this period the seller is entitled to remain in possession of the property and to the rents and profits (unless otherwise agreed). He must also discharge the outgoings, e.g. water rates until completion. He owes a duty of care to the buyer and will be liable to the buyer in damages if loss is caused to the property through neglect or wanton destruction.[2] This duty continues so long as the seller is entitled to possession of the property and does not terminate because the seller vacates the property before completion.[3]

5.1.4. From the moment that a binding contract exists between the parties two equitable liens arise, enforceable only through a court order for sale of the property. The seller's lien on the buyer's equitable interest is for the balance of the purchase price and if this is not paid in full on completion the lien attaches to the legal estate in the hands of the buyer. The buyer's lien is on the seller's legal estate for any deposit paid to the seller in the capacity of agent (but not as stakeholder), and in the case of unregistered land would not bind another buyer from the seller unless registered as a Class C(iii) land charge under Land Charges Act 1972. In the case of registered land the lien could be protected by the registration of a notice, although this might not be necessary if the buyer was already in occupation of the property as the lien may then constitute an overriding interest within Land Registration Act 2002.[4] Protection of the lien by registration is not normally considered to be necessary, but should be undertaken immediately if problems arise between the parties in the period between contract and completion.

1. In *National Carriers Ltd* v. *Panalpina (Northern) Ltd* [1981] AC 675 it was held that the doctrine of frustration can, in exceptional cases, apply to leases. Thus if a leasehold property were to be totally

destroyed between exchange and completion, it is arguable that the buyer could not be forced to complete. The same case contains dicta to the effect that the doctrine may also be applicable to freehold land, but to date there has been no decided case where the doctrine has been held to apply, and it is therefore unsafe to assume that the buyer will be discharged from his obligations following total destruction of the property.

2. *Clarke* v. *Ramuz* [1891] 2 QB 456; *Phillips* v. *Lamdin* [1949] 2 KB 33.
3. *Lucie-Smith* v. *Gorman* [1981] CLY 2866.
4. Land Registration Act 2002, Sched.1, para.2 and Sched.3, para.2, and see also *London and Cheshire Insurance Co. Ltd* v. *Laplagrene Property Co. Ltd* [1971] Ch 499.

5.2. After exchange

The seller's solicitor

(a) Inform the client and estate agent that exchange has taken place and enter completion date in diary or file prompt system.

(b) Where, immediately after exchange, the seller is in possession of both copies of the contract, the seller's solicitor should check that both parts of the contract have been dated and bear the agreed completion date. The copy of the contract signed by the seller should immediately be sent to the buyer's solicitor to fulfil any undertaking given in the course of an exchange by telephone.

(c) Any deposit received must immediately be paid into an interest-bearing clients' deposit account.

(d) If any preliminary deposit has been held by an estate agent, the agent should be asked to remit such sum to the seller's solicitor who is normally required under the contract to hold 'the deposit', i.e. the whole of the amount specified in the contract as the contractual deposit (see Standard Condition 2.2 and Standard Commercial Property Condition 2.2). The agent may be reluctant to part with the money, preferring to hold it on account for any commission due to him.

(e) If not already done, the seller should deduce title to the buyer.

The buyer's solicitor

(a) Inform the client and his lender that exchange has taken place and enter completion date in diary or file prompt system.

(b) Where exchange has taken place by telephone, immediately send to the seller (or as directed by him) the signed contract and deposit cheque in accordance with the undertaking given, having first checked that the contract is dated and bears the agreed completion date.

(c) Where the buyer is to insure, inform the insurer that exchange has taken place and check that the insurance policy is in force (see C3).

(d) Where appropriate, protect the contract by registration (see C5.3).

5.3.   **Protection of the contract**

Registered land

5.3.1.   The contract constitutes an interest which needs to be protected by entry of a notice on the register of the title. The contract will then have priority over any future buyer or chargee of the land, but would not take priority over another buyer or chargee who had made an official search before registration of the contract and who lodged his own application for registration within the priority period afforded by his search. Where a buyer is in possession the contract could constitute an overriding interest.[1] In this case protection of the contract by the entry of a notice may not be necessary.

Unregistered land

5.3.2.   The contract is an estate contract within the Class C(iv) category of land charge and will be void against a buyer of the legal estate for money or money's worth if not registered. Registration must be made against the name of the legal estate owner for the time being.[2] Care needs to be exercised when effecting the registration of sub-contracts, where the buyer under the sub-contract needs to register his C(iv) against the current owner of the legal estate who will not be his immediate seller. For example:

> A contracts to sell to B.
>
> Before completion of this contract B contracts to sell to C.
>
> If C seeks to protect his estate contract, he must register a Class C(iv) land charge against A who will be the owner of the legal estate until completion of the contract between himself and B.

5.3.3.   Options to purchase and rights of pre-emption also require registration within this category.

Registration of the contract

5.3.4.   Since the contract is capable of registration, a solicitor who fails to register, thereby causing loss to his client, may be liable in negligence to the client. However, since completion of most contracts occurs within a very short period following exchange, in practice registration of the contract is uncommon. Consideration should always be given to the question of whether or not a particular contract requires protection by registration and the contract should always be registered if any of the circumstances listed in C5.3.5 apply.

Guidelines

5.3.5.   Registration of the contract is desirable in any of the situations listed below. The following is not an exhaustive list of all the circumstances in which registration is desirable. If the solicitor is in any doubt, he should err on the side of caution and register the contract in order to protect his client's interests:

(a) there is to be a long interval (e.g. more than two months) between contract and completion;

(b) there is reason to doubt the seller's good faith;

(c) a dispute arises between the seller and buyer;

(d) the seller delays completion beyond the contractual date;

(e) the purchase price is to be paid by instalments, the conveyance or transfer to be executed after payment of the final instalment;

(f) the transaction is a sub-sale.

1. Land Registration Act 2002, Sched.3, para.2.
2. *Barrett* v. *Hilton Developments Ltd* [1975] Ch 237.

D. TITLE

D1. Deducing title

1.1. Time for deduction of title

1.1.1. Historically the seller deduced title after exchange of contracts but this practice had serious disadvantages because the buyer was committed to a contract without knowing the state of the seller's title. This could cause problems, particularly if the transaction was one of a chain.

1.1.2. Only in exceptional cases should deduction of title be delayed until after contracts have been exchanged.

1.1.3. Where the Protocol is used, by para. 4.4, the seller is required to send evidence of his title to the buyer with the draft contract and other pre-contract documentation.

1.1.4. Standard Condition 4.3.1 and Standard Commercial Property Condition 6.3.1 which both require evidence of title to be supplied 'immediately after making the contract', reflect the traditional practice of supplying the evidence of title after exchange of contracts. Despite these conditions, in most cases deduction of title will in practice take place before exchange of contracts. Standard Condition 4.2.1 and Standard Commercial Property Condition 6.2.1 preclude requisitions on the title shown by the seller before exchange of contracts.

1.2. Seller's obligation

1.2.1. The seller's obligation in relation to the deduction of his title is to supply sufficient documentary evidence to the buyer to prove that the seller is either the outright owner of the land he has contracted to sell or, if not, that he is in a position to compel someone else to transfer the land to the buyer or is a lender whose power of sale has arisen and become exercisable, thus entitling him to sell the land. It is not enough to show that the seller is able to ask a third party to transfer the land to the buyer; the seller must be able to force or oblige the third party to execute the purchase deed, e.g. where the land is held in the name of a company, the seller would need to own a controlling shareholding in that company in order to be able to compel the company to convey to the buyer.[1]

1. See *Re Bryant & Barningham's Contract* (1890) 44 Ch 218; *cf. Elliott v. Pierson* [1948] Ch 452.

1.3.   **Method of deduction in registered land**

1.3.1.   Land Registration Act 1925, s.110 contained detailed provisions as to the documents that a seller was required to supply to the buyer. These provisions have not been carried forward into Land Registration Act 2002. The Act does provide that rules may be made about the obligations of a seller to prove or perfect his title under a contract for the transfer or other disposition for valuable consideration of registered land.[1] No rules have been made, however, and the seller and buyer are free to make their own bargain as to the evidence of title to be deduced.

1.3.2.   The Protocol, Standard Condition 4.1.1 and Standard Commercial Property Condition 6.1.2 all require the seller at his own expense to supply official copy entries of the title to the buyer. Official copy entries of the title should always be supplied since they usually show the up-to-date position of the register. The official copy entries of the title supplied to the buyer must be originals (not photocopies) and of recent date. Later, when making a search at the Land Registry, the buyer will need to search from the date of such an official copy.[2]

1.   Land Registration Act 2002, Sched.10, para.2.
2.   Land Registration Rules 2003, r.131.

1.4.   **Method of deduction in unregistered land**

1.4.1.   The seller will prove his ownership of unregistered land by supplying the buyer with an abstract or epitome of the documents comprising the title. In some cases the evidence supplied will be made up of a combination of these two styles of presentation.

1.4.2.   An abstract of title is in essence a summary of all the documents comprised in the title. The preparation of an abstract in traditional form is a skilled and time-consuming task which has largely been superseded by the practice of supplying an epitome of the title supported by photocopies of all the documents referred to.

1.4.3.   An epitome of title is a schedule of the documents comprising the title. The documents should be numbered and listed in chronological order, starting with the earliest in time. Each document should be identified as to its date, type (e.g. conveyance, assent, etc.), the names of the parties to it, whether a copy of the document is supplied with the epitome, and whether or not the original of the document will be handed to the buyer on completion. Photocopies of the documents which accompany the epitome must be of good quality, marked to show the document's corresponding number on the list shown by the epitome, and any plans included in the documents must be coloured or marked so that they are identical to the original document from which the copy has been made. Before the epitome and copy documents are sent to the buyer the seller's solicitor should check that all the copies are legible and bear the appropriate markings as outlined in the preceding sentence, and that all pages are complete and assembled in the correct sequence. The paper on which the epitome is supplied must be sufficiently permanent and durable to last in a clearly legible state throughout the likely period of its need as evidence of the title. An epitome which is supplied by means of a faxed copy may not at present satisfy these requirements unless the originals of all the documents referred to are to be handed over on completion. Thus if a seller delivers the epitome by fax, in a situation where all of the original documents will not be handed over on completion, he should deliver a further copy of the epitome to the buyer, by post or document exchange, such further copy being produced on non-glossy A4 size durable paper.

Documents to be included in the epitome

Root of title

1.4.4. The epitome must commence with a good root of title, as specified by a special condition in the contract. A good root of title is a document which, at the date of the contract:

(a) is at least 15 years old;[1]

(b) deals with or shows the ownership of the whole legal and equitable interest contracted to be sold;

(c) contains an adequate description of the property; and

(d) contains nothing to cast any doubt on the title.

1.4.5. A conveyance on sale or legal mortgage which satisfies the above requirements is generally acknowledged to be the most acceptable root of title because it effectively offers a double guarantee on the title. The buyer in the present transaction will be investigating the seller's title for a minimum period of 15 years; the buyer under the root conveyance would similarly have investigated title over a period of at least 15 years when he bought the property. Thus the present buyer is provided with the certainty of the soundness of the title over a period of at least 30 years. If there is no conveyance on sale on the title which satisfies the requirements of a good root, a legal mortgage provides an acceptable alternative. Since a lender will not lend money on the security of a property without investigating the title, a legal mortgage used as a root document provides a similar double guarantee of the title to that afforded by a conveyance on sale. In the absence of both a conveyance on sale and a legal mortgage, title may be commenced with either a voluntary conveyance or an assent dated after 1925.[2] Since both of these documents effect gifts of the land, no investigation of prior title would have taken place at the time when they were executed, and they do not therefore provide the double check on the title which is given by the conveyance on sale or the legal mortgage and for this reason are less satisfactory to a buyer when offered as roots of title. They should therefore only be offered as roots of title (and accepted as such by the buyer) where, after investigation of all the title documents available to the seller, no better root can be found. The nature of the root document will be specified by special condition in the contract, and if the buyer does not consider the root being offered to be adequate he must raise this problem with the seller before contracts are exchanged; once contracts have been exchanged, it is too late to vary the terms of the contract. If, however, it transpired that the seller was ultimately unable to prove his title to the property, the buyer could withdraw from the contract.

Less than statutory minimum title is offered

1.4.6. Only in very rare cases will it be found that the seller cannot provide the buyer with a root of title which satisfies the statutory minimum period of 15 years prescribed by Law of Property Act 1925, s.44 (as amended). A buyer who is offered a short title should not accept the situation until he has received a satisfactory explanation for the reasons for the short root from the seller and should be advised that, in accepting less than his statutory entitlement under Law of Property Act 1925, he is also assuming the risk of being bound by incumbrances on the title which he has had no opportunity of discovering or investigating. The risk of being bound by undiscovered incumbrances stretches backwards in time, not just to the statutory 15-year period, but to the date of the first document on the title (however old) which would satisfy the requirements for a good root. A short root should not be accepted by the buyer without a full investigation of the circumstances, the agreement of his lender, and investigation of the possibility of obtaining defective title insurance, preferably at the seller's expense. The acceptance by the buyer of a short root of title may also affect his ability to obtain registration with an absolute title at the Land Registry. At best, the Land Registry may only grant possessory title. An entry may also be made in the register as to any subsisting restrictive covenants or easements affecting the registered estate prior to the short root of title.

Documents to be included in the abstract or epitome

1.4.7. From the root of title, all dealings with the legal and equitable interests in the land down to and including the interests of the present seller must be shown, thus constituting an unbroken chain of ownership stretching from the seller named in the root document to the present day. This includes the following:

(a) conveyances on sale and by gift;

(b) current leases;

(c) evidence of devolutions on death (death certificates, grants of representation, assents);

(d) change of name of an estate owner, e.g. marriage certificate, deed poll or statutory declaration;

(e) mortgages and discharge of legal mortgages;

(f) documents prior to the root which contain details of restrictive covenants which affect the property;

(g)   memoranda endorsed on documents of title, e.g. recording a sale of part, assent to a beneficiary, or severance of a beneficial joint tenancy;

(h)   powers of attorney under which a document within the title has been executed.

Documents which need not be included in the abstract or epitome

1.4.8.   Certain documents need not be included in the abstract or epitome, although in some cases their inclusion will be helpful to the buyer and may forestall queries on the title raised by the buyer. They include:

(a)   documents of record and Land Charges Department search certificates (but it is good practice to include these so that the buyer can see which searches have been correctly made in the past, in which case he need not repeat the search during his own investigation of the title). It is recommended that documents of record should always be abstracted so that the buyer receives a complete picture of the title and one on which he can act immediately. Failure to supply such documents may lead to delay while, e.g. the buyer obtains a document which was not supplied by the seller;

(b)   documents relating to equitable interests which will be overreached on completion of the current transaction (the buyer may discover these charges when he makes his pre-completion searches and if he has already been supplied with information about them he will not need to raise last-minute queries with the seller or to delay completion while he investigates them; therefore as a matter of good practice some notice of their existence should be given to the buyer);

(c)   leases which have expired by effluxion of time (but if the tenant is still in possession of the property, possibly with the benefit of security of tenure, evidence of the terms on which the tenant enjoys the property should be supplied). Although leases which have been surrendered should be abstracted, together with evidence of the surrender, it is common practice not to provide evidence of leases which no longer affect the title;

(d)   documents which pre-date the root of title except where a document within the title refers to the earlier document[3] (note that where a document within the title has been executed under a power of attorney, the power must be abstracted whatever its date);

(e)   documents relating to discharged equitable interests in the land, e.g. receipted equitable mortgages.

1.4.9.   Standard Condition 4.1.3 and Standard Commercial Property Condition 6.1.3 require the seller to produce to the buyer (at the seller's expense) the original of every relevant document, or an abstract, epitome or copy with an original marking by a solicitor of examination either against the original or against an examined abstract or an examined copy.

1.4.10. If the title documents produced by the seller do not adequately show the physical extent of the property or its title, the seller may have to supplement the evidence of title with a statutory declaration. By Standard Condition 4.4 and Standard Commercial Property Condition 6.4.1 the seller is relieved of the obligation to define precisely the boundaries of the property, or to show the ownership of fences, hedges, ditches or walls, or to identify separately parts of the property with different titles, further than he is able to from information in his possession, but the buyer may, if reasonable, call for a statutory declaration as to the facts of these matters. If the land cannot be properly identified or described from its description in the title deeds and contract, the buyer is entitled to call for a plan, to be prepared at the seller's expense. In other cases if the buyer insists on describing the property by means of a plan, he must bear the cost of preparation of the plan himself.

Documents which will not be handed over on completion

1.4.11. The epitome must specify which documents will be handed to the buyer on completion and which will be retained by the seller. The buyer is entitled on completion to take the originals or marked abstracts or marked copies of all the documents within the title except those which relate to an interest in the land which is retained by the seller, e.g. on a sale of part the seller will retain the title deeds in order to be able to prove his ownership of the land retained by him. Similarly, a general power of attorney will be retained because the donee of the power needs to keep the original document in order to deal with other property owned by the donor, and personal representatives will retain their original grant in order to administer the remainder of the deceased's estate.

1. Law of Property Act 1925, s.44, as amended by Law of Property Act 1969.
2. Before 1926 there was no requirement for an assent to be in writing, and an oral assent alone would not have been capable of satisfying the definition of a good root of title.
3. Law of Property Act 1925, s.45.

1.5. Sub-sales

1.5.1. Law of Property Act 1925, s.44 does not appear to apply to a contract for a sub-sale. The buyer of unregistered land will require his immediate seller to deduce title to him as if this section did apply to the transaction, otherwise the buyer will not be sure of purchasing a good title, but the seller, until he completes his own purchase, may not be in a position to deduce such a title to the buyer. In any event the requirements for the deduction of title in these circumstances must be specifically dealt with by a special condition in the contract since there are no common law rules applicable to this situation.[1]

1.5.2. Where the land is registered the requirements for deduction of title must again be dealt with by a special condition in the contract.

1. See also B4 and B14 and see *Urban Manor* v. *Sadiq* [1997] NPC 24, CA.

1.6. Leaseholds

1.6.1. Deduction of title to leaseholds is discussed in section K.

D2. Investigation of title

2.1. Purpose of investigation

2.1.1. The seller having supplied the buyer with evidence of his title, the buyer's task is to investigate that evidence to ensure that the seller is able to transfer that which he has contracted to sell and that there are no defects in that title which would adversely affect the interests of the buyer or his lender.

2.1.2. Any matters which are unclear or unsatisfactory on the face of the documentary evidence supplied by the seller may be raised as queries (requisitions) with the seller within the time limits specified in the contract for raising requisitions (see D3).

2.1.3. Investigation will be carried out by the solicitor on behalf of his buyer and/or lender client. Where the same solicitor is acting for both the buyer and his lender in a simultaneous transaction investigation is carried out only once, bearing in mind the particular requirements of each client (see A11, E3 and section H).

2.1.4. If ultimately the seller cannot show a good title, the buyer is entitled to withdraw from the contract. Prima facie the seller's inability to show title is a breach of contract entitling the buyer to a remedy in damages, but in practice the buyer's right to damages may, in certain circumstances, be curtailed or precluded by express provision in the contract (see D3 and section M).

2.2. Time for investigation

2.2.1. Traditionally investigation of title followed deduction of title as a procedure which is undertaken after exchange of contracts and is subject to time limits imposed by the contract.[1]

2.2.2. In practice the seller will usually supply his evidence of title at the draft contract stage of the transaction (and in Protocol cases must do so) and may, by inclusion of a contractual provision to such effect, prevent the buyer from raising his requisitions after exchange, thus compelling the buyer to carry out his investigation at that stage of the transaction.[2]

1. See Standard Condition 4.3.2 (Appendix V.9) and Standard Commercial Property Condition 6.3.1 (Appendix V.10).
2. See Standard Condition 4.2.1 and Standard Commercial Property Condition 6.2.1.

2.3. Registered land

2.3.1. Investigation of title comprises:

    (a) an examination of the official copy entries of the title supplied by the seller (including a copy of the lease where the title is leasehold and documents which are referred to on the register and evidence relating to matters as to which the register is not conclusive);[1]

    (b) checking for evidence of overriding interests as these are not entered on the register but are binding on the buyer irrespective of notice; and

    (c) pre-completion searches (see E2).

2.3.2. Particular points which may arise out of the examination of the official copy entries of the title are dealt with below.

2.3.3. The existence of most overriding interests can be discovered through:

    (a) pre-contract enquiries of the seller under which the seller will normally be asked to reveal details of adverse interests and occupiers' rights. A seller who did not disclose such matters might be liable to the buyer for non-disclosure (see B5);

    (b) a local land charges search (local land charges not protected on the register are overriding interests);

    (c) inspection of the property before exchange which may reveal, e.g. occupiers, easements, or adverse possession. The buyer may also be advised to re-inspect immediately prior to completion.

2.3.4. The examination of official copy entries of the title in registered land is a relatively quick and simple process. So long as a note is made of any matters on which requisitions need to be raised the method of investigation to be employed with a registered title is a matter to be decided by the solicitor concerned.

Official copy entries of the title

2.3.5. The following points should be checked:

    (a) on the property register:

        (i) the description of the land accords with the contract description;

      (ii)   the title number corresponds with that given on the contract;

      (iii) the estate – is it freehold or leasehold?

      (iv) easements enjoyed by the property (if they are entered on the register) (see B26.5 and B26.6);

      (v)   has any land been removed from the title? If so, does this affect the land being purchased?

  (b) on the proprietorship register:

      (i)   is the class of title correct?

      (ii) is the seller the registered proprietor? If not, who has the ability to transfer the land?

      (iii) the existence and effect of any other entries (restrictions, or pre-Land Registration Act 2002 cautions or inhibitions);

  (c) on the charges register:

      (i)   are there any incumbrances or other entries?

      (ii) how do these affect the buyer?

      (iii) which of them will be removed or discharged on completion and how will their removal be effected?

  (d) on the title plan:

      (i)   is the land being purchased included within the title?

      (ii) check any colourings/hatchings which may indicate rights of way, the extent of covenants or land which has been removed from the title;

  (e) the date of issue of the official copy entries of the title.

Adverse entries in the proprietorship register

2.3.6.   The most commonly found entry on the proprietorship register will be a restriction which regulates the circumstances in which a disposition of a registered estate may be the subject of an entry in the register.[2] The wording of the restriction will indicate what procedure must be followed in order to conduct a valid disposition of the land. The buyer must therefore either follow that procedure (e.g. payment of money to two trustees in the case of land held on a trust of land) or require the seller to procure the removal of the restriction from the register on or before completion. In some cases a pre-Land Registration Act 2002 inhibition will be found on the proprietorship register (usually in connection with the bankruptcy of the proprietor) which will prevent any disposition of the land until it is removed. Similarly, a caution may have been entered on the register before the implementation of Land Registration Act 2002. In the absence of a withdrawal no dealing with the land could be registered until the

Registrar has served notice on the cautioner giving him the opportunity to show cause why the dealing to the buyer should not proceed.

1. See Standard Condition 4.2.1 (Appendix V.9) and Standard Commercial Property Condition 6.3.1 (Appendix V.10).
2. Land Registration Act 2002, s.40(1).

2.4. Unregistered land

2.4.1. Investigation of title comprises:

(a) an examination of the documents supplied in the abstract or epitome to check that:

    (i) the root document is as provided for by the contract or, if none is specified, complies with Law of Property Act 1925, s.44 (see D1). The root document will usually have been specified by special condition of the contract. Once contracts have been exchanged it is too late to object to the date or nature of the deed being offered as a root of title. If the wrong document has been supplied, the buyer is entitled to insist on the correct document being supplied in its place. Both parties may agree to substitute a different document as the root of title;[1]

    (ii) there is an unbroken chain of ownership beginning with the seller in the root document and ending with the present seller;

    (iii) there are no defects in the title which will adversely affect the buyer's title or the interests of his lender;

(b) verification, i.e. inspection of the original deeds (see D2.14);

(c) checking for evidence of occupiers (this is normally done by inspection of the property);

(d) pre-completion searches (see E2);

(e) checking the date when the area became subject to compulsory registration to ensure no event triggering registration has taken place since that date (see Land Registry Practice Guide 51 for the relevant date).

1. The substitution of a different document would constitute a variation of contract and will be subject to Law of Property (Miscellaneous Provisions) Act 1989, s.2. See *McCausland* v. *Duncan Lawrie Ltd* [1996] 4 All ER 995.

2.5. Method of investigation (unregistered land)

2.5.1. Examination of an unregistered title can be a complex and time-consuming business. It is essential that each of the documents within the abstract or epitome is carefully scrutinised to ensure that it is in order and a note made of any irregularities which need to be clarified by way of requisitions with the seller (see D2.6).

2.5.2. To ensure that nothing is overlooked on investigation it is recommended that the solicitor adopts and follows a systematic and thorough method of investigation of an unregistered title and allows himself sufficient time in which to carry out this procedure at an unhurried pace. Except in the simplest cases, written notes of the title should be made while carrying out the investigation so that these notes can be used as the basis for framing requisitions and, if needed, will be available for reference at a later stage of the transaction.

Method

(a) Check each document chronologically starting with the root.

(b) Is the root as provided for in the contract? (See D2.4.1.)

(c) Is there an unbroken chain of title from the root to the present day?

Then, in each document within the abstract or epitome, check the following points, making written notes of any matter which needs to be clarified or rechecked:

(d) **Date**

A deed is not invalid because it is not dated or is wrongly dated, but the date of the document will:

   (i) establish whether a root document is a good root (see D2.4.1);

   (ii) affect the amount of stamp duty payable;

   (iii) affect its vulnerability under Insolvency Act 1986 in the case of a voluntary disposition;

   (iv) assist in making a reasoned judgment on an apparent defect in title, e.g. a technical defect in a document which is over 15 years old may be less detrimental to the title than one contained in a more recent document.

(e) **Stamp duty and SDLT**

   (i) For transactions completed under the Stamp Act 1891 regime (as amended) and subject to impress of stamps on documents, ad valorem and Particulars Delivered stamp should be checked. The amount of duty will depend on the nature of the document, the value of the consideration and the date of the document. The seller must be required to rectify any irregularities of this nature. If no certificate of value is included in the document, stamp duty at full rate should have been paid on the conveyance. In the event of doubt, the buyer should insist that the earlier document is adjudicated and any additional duty, penalties and interest paid (see also D2.13.2–D2.13.5).

   (ii) For transactions subject to SDLT:

   - watchpoints:

       – assignment of lease exempt from SDLT on grant?

       – will the buyer become liable to pay SDLT on remainder of term (as if new grant)?

       – has any relief been claimed by seller or connected party? Will this transaction trigger clawback (e.g. group relief or charities relief)?

       – does the buyer need seller's warranties in respect of SDLT?

       – is there an obligation to file a further tax return following the ascertainment of an uncertain rent?

- if the transaction is not registrable at the Land Registry, has the last buyer made a self-certificate? Is the certified copy available?

(f) Parties

For example, are the seller's names as shown on the previous document?

(g) Description of the property

Does it accord with the contract and is it consistent throughout the epitome?

(h) Acknowledgements for production of earlier deeds

Is there one where necessary, e.g. where deeds are being retained by the seller on a sale of part?

(i) Execution

Have all formalities been observed?

(j) Powers of attorney

Is the disposition by the attorney valid and are subsequent buyers protected?

(k) Endorsements on deeds

Are those that are necessary present, and are there any adverse memoranda?

(l) Incumbrances

What are they? Are they as expected? Is there a chain of indemnity covenants where required?

(m) Easements and rights

Are these as expected? Do they follow down the chain? Have any been added or taken away? (See B26.)

(n) Receipt clause

This is evidence (although not necessarily conclusive evidence) that the seller's lien for the unpaid purchase price has been extinguished.[1]

(o) **Searches supplied with the abstract**

Have searches against all previous estate owners been abstracted or are there gaps? Are the names and periods searched against correct? Did completion take place within the priority period?

(p) **Compulsory registration**

Check:

(i) that there has been no conveyance on sale since the area became one of compulsory registration. The date of the compulsory registration order can be checked from Land Registry Practice Guide 51;

(ii) that there has been no dealing of any kind since 1 April 1998.

If necessary the seller should be required to register before completion.

1. See *London and Cheshire Insurance Co. Ltd* v. *Laplagrene Property Co. Ltd* [1971] Ch 499.

2.6.   Root of title and interpretation of a conveyance

2.6.1.   Documents which are capable of being used as a good root of title are listed in D1.4.

2.6.2.   The document which is to constitute the root will be specified by a special condition in the contract and once contracts have been exchanged cannot be changed except with the consent of both parties (and, where relevant, the buyer's lender) and provided that the variation of the contract meets the requirements of Law of Property (Miscellaneous Provisions) Act 1989, s.2.[1]

2.6.3.   Generally the buyer cannot require evidence of title prior to the root except:[2]

(a) he is always entitled to a copy of a power of attorney under which any abstracted document is executed;

(b) where an abstracted document refers to an earlier document, he may call for that earlier document, e.g. where an abstracted document refers to restrictive covenants imposed by a pre-root conveyance, the document imposing the covenants may be called for;

(c) where an abstracted document describes the property by reference to a plan which is attached to or referred to in an earlier document, that earlier document may be called for so that the plan may be examined;

(d) any document creating any limitation or trust by reference to which any part of the property is disposed of by an abstracted document may be called for even if dated pre-root.

2.6.4.   Where the root document is a conveyance, or the epitome reveals a conveyance elsewhere in the chain of title, the following guidance may assist in the interpretation of the conveyance.

2.6.5. The conveyance will start with the words 'This conveyance' followed by the date and the full names and addresses of all the parties to the deed.

2.6.6. Recitals do not form an operative part of the body of the deed but are more in the nature of a preamble, the function of which is to introduce the nature of and to set the scene for the deed which follows, e.g. by explaining the recent history of the title. Although recitals do not form an operative part of the deed, a party is estopped from later denying the accuracy of a statement of fact made in a recital. Recitals of fact which are contained in a deed which is 20 years old are by Law of Property Act 1925, s.45(6) deemed to be correct. Where there is an ambiguity in an operative part of the deed, recitals may be looked at and used to clarify that ambiguity.[3] Where personal representatives are required to give a statement under Administration of Estates Act 1925, s.36(6) that they have not made any previous assent or conveyance, such statement is usually dealt with by way of recital. Similarly a statement that the survivor of joint tenants is solely and beneficially entitled to the property (required under Law of Property (Joint Tenants) Act 1964) is commonly dealt with in this way.

2.6.7. A consideration and receipt clause will be included (see E1.10.4).

2.6.8. The operative word ('convey(s)') is followed by a statement of title guarantee which imports covenants for title (see section M).

2.6.9. The parcels clause must clearly and adequately describe the land being sold. Where the sale is of part of the seller's land, reference will generally be made to the land which is retained by the seller, such land being identified on the plan annexed to the deed.

2.6.10. Express reference may be made to benefits previously enjoyed by the land which are to pass to the buyer.

2.6.11. Clauses may be included to deal with exceptions, i.e. those matters which are excluded from the land and which do not therefore pass to the buyer, and to reservations, i.e. those matters which (usually on a sale of part) are being regranted by the buyer for the benefit of the seller.

2.6.12. Easements which are to be expressly granted to the buyer (usually only on a sale of part) may be included.

2.6.13. The habendum ('to hold') is followed by express references to the estate conveyed (fee simple) and existing incumbrances, e.g. existing restrictive covenants subject to which the property is sold.

2.6.14. Declarations may be inserted, e.g. on a sale of part to negate the implied grant rules especially in respect of rights of light and air following a contractual provision to this effect (see E1.11.5). Declarations may also be used to define the ownership of party walls.

2.6.15. Where the property is bought by co-owners a statement of their capacity will be included, i.e. as joint tenants or tenants in common. Where the co-owners are tenants in common the division of the beneficial interest between them may be specified either in the conveyance or by separate deed of trust. Since 1 January 1997 it is no longer necessary to include a clause to extend the powers of the trustees to make them co-extensive with those of an absolute owner because these powers are implied by Trusts of Land and Appointment of Trustees Act 1996, s.6.

2.6.16. On a sale of part, new restrictive covenants may be imposed (see E1.11).

2.6.17. Where existing positive covenants or restrictive covenants which are not limited to ownership will continue to bind the land after completion of the sale to the buyer an indemnity covenant will be included in fulfilment of the contractual obligation to that effect.[4]

2.6.18. If any of the documents of title which the seller had were not to be handed over to the buyer on completion, e.g. a grant of probate or all the title deeds on a sale of part, an acknowledgement for their production and undertaking for safe custody will be included in the document. By Law of Property Act 1925, s.64 the acknowledgement gives a right to production of the named document(s) at the cost of the person requiring production. Production may be required, e.g. to satisfy requisition raised by a sub-purchaser. The undertaking gives a right of damages (but no other remedy) if the named document(s) is lost or destroyed otherwise than by fire or inevitable accident. These rights are reiterated by Standard Condition 4.6.5 and Standard Commercial Condition 6.6.5. All sellers will give an acknowledgement for production (where relevant), but only a beneficial owner gives the undertaking for safe custody. Such an undertaking is not appropriate in a situation where the seller is not the true owner of the deeds. If the title deeds which were being retained are not in the seller's possession at the time of completion, e.g. on a sale of part, they may be in the hands of his lender; the seller may give a covenant that he will give an undertaking for safe custody as and when the title deeds come into his possession.

2.6.19. The document concludes with schedules (if any), e.g. of covenants, etc., testimonium (in witness) and attestation clauses. Since 31 July 1990 the attestation clause should contain the words 'signed as a deed' to comply with Law of Property (Miscellaneous Provisions) Act 1989, s.1.

1. See *McCausland* v. *Duncan Lawrie Ltd* [1996] 4 All ER 995.
2. Law of Property Act 1925, s.45.
3. The converse situation is not true. An ambiguous recital cannot be clarified by a statement in the operative part of the deed.
4. See Standard Condition 4.6.4 and Standard Commercial Condition 6.6.4. Also see E1.10.9.

2.7.   **Problem areas**

2.7.1.   The transaction with the seller and any past transactions revealed in the official copies or the epitome should be considered to see if they involve any of the problem areas in D2.8 to D2.12.

2.8.   **Conveyance by trustees to themselves**

2.8.1.   If on the title there is a conveyance by trustees or personal representatives to one of themselves, enquiry must be made into the circumstances of the transaction since, on the face of it, such a conveyance is in breach of trust and is voidable by the beneficiaries without enquiry as to fairness.

2.8.2.   Such a transaction can be justified if one of the following situations exists:

(a)   there is proof of a pre-existing contract to purchase, an option or right of pre-emption in favour of the trustee or personal representative;

(b)   the personal representative was a beneficiary under the will or intestacy of the seller;

(c)   the consent of all the beneficiaries being legally competent was obtained to the transaction;

(d)   the conveyance was made under an order of the court;

(e)   the transaction was sanctioned by the trust instrument.

2.9.   **Particular capacities**

Trustees of land

Registered land

2.9.1.   In registered land, a Form A (or earlier Form 62) restriction may be entered on the proprietorship register indicating what must be done to overreach the beneficial interests. A further restriction may also be entered reflecting any other limitations on the trustees' powers to dispose of the land. Provided the terms of any restriction are complied with the buyer will get good title. Where trustees hold the land on trust for themselves as joint tenants in equity, no restriction is placed on the register and the buyer may safely deal with the survivor on proof of death of the other trustee.

Unregistered land

2.9.2. Such trustees have a wide power of sale,[1] and if consents are required to a sale a buyer is not concerned to see that the consents of more than two persons are obtained and is never concerned with the consents of persons under disability (i.e. minors, persons under mental incapacity).

2.9.3. A buyer paying his money to the trustees, being at least two individuals or a trust corporation, will take the land free from the equitable interests of the beneficiaries, but not otherwise.[2] Thus a conveyance on the title by a sole individual trustee will require investigation.

Personal representatives

Registered land

2.9.4. Personal representatives may apply to become registered as proprietors of the land. In this case, provided the buyer deals with the registered proprietors and complies with any restriction on the register, he will get good title. Personal representatives would not normally register themselves as proprietors unless they intended to hold on to the land without disposing of it for some period of time, e.g. during the minority of a beneficiary. In other cases the personal representatives will produce their grant of representation to the buyer as proof of their authority to deal with the land. Provided the buyer takes a transfer from all the proving personal representatives and submits an office copy or certified copy of the grant with his application for registration, he will obtain a good title.[3] A transfer or assent made by personal representatives must be in the form prescribed.[4]

Unregistered land

2.9.5. Personal representatives have the wide powers of trustees of land. If there is only one proving personal representative he has all the powers of two or more personal representatives and consequently (unlike a sole individual trustee) can convey the land on his own and give a valid receipt for the proceeds of sale. If, however, the grant is made to two or more personal representatives, they must all join in the assent or conveyance, but a sole proving personal representative of an absolute owner is entitled to act on his own. A buyer must therefore call for the grant to see who have been appointed as personal representatives, and must insist that all the personal representatives named in the grant join in the assent or conveyance, or call for evidence of the death of any personal representative who will not be a party to the purchase deed. However, a sole surviving personal representative cannot give a valid receipt for the proceeds of sale.

2.9.6. An assent made by personal representatives must be in writing in order to pass the legal estate in the land to the beneficiary. The beneficiary who is to take the land must be named in the document, which must be signed by the personal representatives. If the document contains covenants given by the beneficiary (e.g. indemnity in respect of existing restrictive covenants) it must be by deed. Even where the beneficiary is also the sole personal representative (as may be the case where a widow is her deceased husband's sole personal representative and sole beneficiary) a written assent is required.[5] A buyer from an assentee (or a subsequent buyer where there is an assent in the chain of title) must check that a memorandum of the assent was endorsed on the grant; otherwise, there is a danger that a later sale by the personal representatives will have deprived the assentee of legal ownership (see D2.9.7).

2.9.7. The effect of Administration of Estates Act 1925, s.36 is that an assent in favour of a beneficiary may be defeated by a later sale of the land by the personal representatives in favour of a buyer who takes from them a written statement that they have made no previous assent or conveyance of the land. However, this will not be the case if either there was an endorsement of a previous assent on the grant or there had been a previous sale by the assentee. It follows that a conveyance on sale by personal representatives should contain a section 36(6) statement and that an assentee (and a buyer) should require an endorsement on the grant. This may be done at the cost of the estate. Where the transaction induces first registration (as it almost always will) an endorsement on the grant is not required.

2.9.8. A disposition by personal representatives should contain an acknowledgement of the right to production of their grant of representation as this is a document of title the inspection of which may be required by subsequent buyers of the land. The grant should be inspected to check for endorsements which have been made on it.

2.9.9. An assent or conveyance by personal representatives of a legal estate is sufficient evidence in favour of a buyer that the person in whose favour it is made is the person entitled to have the legal estate conveyed to him, unless there is a memorandum of a previous assent or conveyance on the grant. This in effect means that a buyer from an assentee of land, having checked the grant and found no adverse endorsements, does not have to look at the deceased's will to check that the assentee was rightly entitled to the land, but this provision will not protect the buyer if it is apparent from some other source (e.g. the assent itself) that it was made in favour of the wrong person.[6]

2.9.10. On a sale by the personal representatives of the survivor of beneficial joint tenants, a statement should be included in the conveyance to the effect that the survivor was solely and beneficially entitled so that the buyer has the protection of Law of Property (Joint Tenants) Act 1964. If such personal representatives did not sell the land but made an assent in favour of a beneficiary, the assent should properly include the above statement in order to protect a buyer from the assentee. If the statement was missing from the assent, consideration should be given to joining the personal representatives of the survivor into the conveyance by the assentee in order to give the statement.

2.9.11. If a sole or sole surviving trustee of a trust of land dies in a case where a buyer cannot rely on the 1964 Act (because the survivor was not solely and benefi- cially entitled), his personal representatives can exercise all the powers of that trustee. If a sole personal representative is appointed in such a situation, he can act on his own in dealing with the deceased's private property (including land), but he must act jointly with another trustee in making a disposition of the trust property under which capital money arises.

Co-owners

2.9.12.   Co-owners hold land on a trust of land and the remarks relating to trustees in D2.9.1, D2.9.2 and D2.9.3 apply.

Registered land

2.9.13.   If the co-owners are tenants in common in equity, there will generally be a restriction on the proprietorship register to the effect that no disposition by a sole proprietor of the registered estate (except a trust corporation) under which capital money arises is to be registered unless authorised by an order of the court. In the event of the death of one or more of the co-owners, so that at the time of sale there is only one surviving trustee, a second trustee must be appointed to join with the survivor in the transfer. Alternatively, the buyer can deal with the survivor alone provided that the restriction is removed from the register, or the survivor provides the buyer with documentary evidence which will enable the restriction to be removed on the buyer's application for registration. Such proof might consist of a statutory declaration by the survivor that in stated circumstances the declarant had become entitled legally and beneficially to the registered estate and that he has not encumbered or dealt with his own share nor has he received notice of any incumbrance on or dealing with the deceased's share. A certificate by the seller's conveyancer will be accepted in place of a declaration if the conveyancer is able to speak from his knowledge of all the relevant facts. In practice, it is better either for the seller to procure the removal of the restriction or to appoint a second trustee to act with the seller.

2.9.14.   If the co-owners are joint tenants in equity, no restriction is placed on the register and a buyer may deal with the survivor of them on proof of the death of the deceased co-owner.

Unregistered land

2.9.15.   Inspection of the conveyance under which the co-owners bought the land will reveal whether they held as joint tenants or tenants in common in equity.

2.9.16.   The sole survivor of tenants in common does not automatically become entitled to the whole equitable estate in the land since a tenancy in common is capable of passing by will or on intestacy. The trust therefore still subsists and a buyer from the survivor should insist on taking a conveyance only from two trustees in order to overreach any beneficial interests which may subsist under the trust. Alternatively, if the survivor has become solely and beneficially entitled to the whole legal and equitable interest in the land, he may convey alone on proof to the buyer of this fact. Such proof would consist of the death certificate of the deceased, a certified or office copy of the grant of representation and an assent made in favour of the survivor.

2.9.17. The survivor of beneficial joint tenants becomes entitled to the whole legal and equitable interest in the land but a buyer from him will only accept a conveyance from the survivor alone if he can be satisfied that he will gain the protection of Law of Property (Joint Tenants) Act 1964. This Act (which is retrospective in operation to 1925) allows the buyer to assume that no severance of the joint tenancy (turning it into a tenancy in common) had occurred before the death of the deceased joint tenant. To gain the protection of the Act the following three conditions must all be satisfied:

   (a)   there must be no memorandum of severance endorsed on the conveyance under which the joint tenants bought the property;

   (b)   there must be no bankruptcy proceedings registered against the names of either of the joint tenants;

   (c)   the conveyance by the survivor must contain a recital stating that the survivor is solely and beneficially entitled to the land.

If any of the above conditions is not met, the survivor must be treated as a surviving tenant in common and the procedure in D2.9.16 followed.

Settled land

2.9.18. Section 2 Trusts of Land and Appointment of Trustees Act 1996 prohibits the creation of new strict settlements (except in limited circumstances). The following sub-paragraphs will generally be relevant only to settlements which were in existence on 1 January 1997.

Registered land

2.9.19. The tenant for life (or, if none, the statutory owners) will be registered as proprietor of the land and an appropriate restriction entered on the register. This restriction will be in Form G, H or I.[7] Provided the buyer complies with the terms of the restriction he will take a good title.

Unregistered land

2.9.20. Where land is settled land within Settled Land Act 1925, the legal estate in the land will be vested in the tenant for life under the Act by a vesting instrument, which will be a vesting deed in the case of an *inter vivos* settlement) and may be a vesting assent by the personal representatives of the deceased where the settlement arises under a will. In exceptional cases, e.g. where the person who would otherwise be tenant for life is a minor, the legal estate will be vested in the trustees of the settlement as statutory owners. Both the tenant for life and the statutory owners have a wide power of sale under the Act (which can be extended by the terms of the settlement itself) but it is provided by Settled Land Act 1925, s.18 that where the land is the subject of a vesting instrument and the trustees of the settlement have not been discharged, any disposition which is not authorised by the Act or by the settlement is void. Further, where capital money arises on a disposition of the land, the disposition is of no effect for the purposes of the Act unless the money is paid to the trustees of the settlement, being at least two individuals or a trust corporation.

2.9.21. A vesting instrument under Settled Land Act 1925 must describe the land, name the person in whose favour it is vested and name the trustees of the settlement for the purposes of the Act. Except in exceptional circumstances, a buyer is bound and entitled to rely on these statements and cannot call for the trust instrument.

Lenders

2.9.22. A power to sell the legal estate vested in the borrower, subject to prior incumbrances but discharged from subsequent ones, is given by Law of Property Act 1925, s.101 to every lender whose mortgage is made by deed. Thus unless expressly excluded the power is available to a lender who has taken a legal mortgage and to one whose equitable mortgage is made by deed. In order actually to convey the legal estate of the borrower to the buyer an equitable lender whose mortgage is not made by deed must adopt some conveyancing device such as an irrevocable power of attorney granted by way of security in his favour by the borrower. An equitable lender whose mortgage is made by deed can apply to the court under Law of Property Act 1925, s.90 for an order for sale and an order appointing a person to convey the land.

2.9.23. In relation to registered land, the proprietor of a registered charge is taken to have the powers of disposition conferred by law on the owner of a legal mortgage in the absence of any entry in the register to the contrary.[8] The owner of a charge which is not substantively registered has no statutory power of sale.

2.9.24. The power of sale arises when the mortgage money becomes due under the mortgage, i.e. on the legal date for redemption which is usually set at an early date in the mortgage term. The power only becomes exercisable by the lender when one of the events specified in Law of Property Act 1925, s.103 has occurred (see B7.7.5). A buyer from the lender must check (by looking at the mortgage deed) that the power of sale has arisen, but is not concerned to enquire whether the power has become exercisable.

2.9.25. The sale must be genuine; a sale to the lender's nominee or to a company controlled by him will not be treated as a valid exercise of the power of sale.

Attorneys

2.9.26. The buyer is entitled to a certified copy of any power of attorney which affects the title (even if in unregistered land the power is dated earlier than the root of title). The buyer must check that the power authorises the transaction and that it has not been revoked before the transaction in question.

2.9.27. Where the seller is a sole legal owner he can delegate his power to sell using a general power under Powers of Attorney Act 1971, s.10. A certified copy of the power should be handed over on completion.

2.9.28. Where co-owners are concerned the requirements vary according to the date of the transaction:

(a) before 1 March 2000 a co-owner who wanted to appoint an attorney to act for him on the sale had to use a specific power of attorney under Trustee Act 1925, s.25. This power was only effective for a period of 12 months. Under a Trustee Act power a co-owner or trustee could not appoint his sole co-trustee to be his attorney. If a co-owner or trustee wished to appoint his sole co-trustee an enduring power of attorney under Enduring Power of Attorney Act 1985 should have been used;

(b) on or after 1 March 2000 a co-owner who has a beneficial interest in the land can use a general power of attorney and can appoint his sole co-trustee to be his attorney (Trustee Delegation Act 1999, s.1);

(c) under Trustee Delegation Act 1999, trustees who are not beneficially entitled to the land may use a general trustee power (Trustee Delegation Act 1999, s.5). However, the general trustee power is only effective for a period of 12 months. The trustee can appoint his sole co-trustee to be his attorney under the general trustee power;

(d) however, whether a general power or general trustee power is used, if a sole co-trustee has been appointed to act as attorney he cannot give a valid receipt for capital money. Overreaching cannot operate in these circumstances. If one of two owners wishes to appoint an attorney to execute the purchase deed, he should therefore appoint a third party to act as attorney. From 1 March 2000, enduring powers of attorney cannot be used to appoint a sole co-trustee to be an attorney.

Registered land

2.9.29. If any document executed by an attorney is delivered to the Land Registry there must be produced to the registrar either the instrument creating the power of attorney or a sufficient copy of the power or a certificate by a solicitor or conveyancer in Form 1.[9]

2.9.30. If the transaction between the attorney and the buyer is not made within 12 months of the date on which the power came into operation, the registrar may require evidence to satisfy him that the power has not been revoked. This may consist of or include a statutory declaration by the buyer or a certificate given by the buyer's conveyancer in Form 2.[10]

2.9.31. For more information on powers of attorney and registered land, see Land Registry Practice Guide 9.

Unregistered land

2.9.32.   A buyer from an attorney holding such a power of attorney under Powers of Attorney Act 1971, s.4 will take good title provided that he had no actual knowledge that the power had been revoked with the attorney's consent.

2.9.33.   A person who buys directly from the attorney will take good title under Powers of Attorney Act 1971, s.5(2) provided he buys in good faith without knowledge of the revocation of the power. The power is revoked automatically if the donor dies, becomes bankrupt or becomes incapable of managing his own affairs. Thus the buyer cannot take good title if he is aware of the death, bankruptcy or incapacity of the donor. A subsequent purchaser gains the protection of Powers of Attorney Act 1971, s.5(4) if either:

    (a)   the dealing between the attorney and his immediate purchaser took place within 12 months of the grant of the power; or

    (b)   the person who buys directly from the attorney makes a statutory declaration within three months of completion of his transaction to the effect that he had no knowledge of the revocation of the power.

2.9.34.   Where a person buys directly from an attorney more than 12 months after the date of the grant of the power, the buyer's solicitor should require his client immediately on completion of the transaction to make the requisite statutory declaration, since this document will be required as evidence of non-revocation on a subsequent disposition of the property. If not made immediately, and the buyer client dies before making the declaration, there will be a defect in title, since the subsequent buyer will not be able to take the protection of Powers of Attorney Act 1971, s.5(4).

2.9.35.   Until the incapacity of the donor the enduring power of attorney takes effect as an ordinary power and the Act contains provisions to protect buyers which are similar to those outlined above. On the incapacity of the donor the attorney's authority to act becomes limited to such acts as are necessary for the protection of the donor and his estate until such time as the power is registered with the Court of Protection. Once registered, the power is incapable of revocation and the attorney's full authority to act is restored. Where a person is buying from an attorney who holds an enduring power he should conduct a search at the Court of Protection to ensure that no application for registration of the power is pending. If the power has already been registered, the attorney should produce the registration certificate to the buyer. An office copy of the power can be produced as evidence both of the contents of the power and of its registration. When Mental Capacity Act 2005 is implemented (see D2.9.36) applications for registration of enduring powers will be dealt with by the Public Guardian instead of the Court of Protection.

2.9.36.   A lasting power of attorney is a new statutory power of attorney created by sections 9–14 Mental Capacity Act 2005. When these sections of the Act are implemented on 1 October 2007, the lasting power will replace the enduring power, although existing enduring powers will not be revoked. Lasting powers will be similar to enduring powers of attorney but can extend to personal welfare matters as well as property and financial affairs and, unlike enduring powers, cannot be validly used by the donee until registered with the new Public Guardian. It is envisaged that a person dealing with a donee of a lasting power will receive protection if he has conducted a search with the Public Guardian which has revealed that lasting power has been registered and he is unaware that the lasting power was invalid or has been revoked. Detailed requirements as to the form, content and registration of a lasting power are set out in the Lasting Powers of Attorney, Enduring Powers of Attorney and Public Guardian Regulations 2007 (SI 2007/1253).

2.9.37. Powers granted before 1 October 1971 are governed by Law of Property Act 1925, ss.126–128 and not by Powers of Attorney Act 1971.

1. Trusts of Land and Appointment of Trustees Act 1996, s.6.
2. Law of Property Act 1925, ss.2 and 27.
3. Land Registration Rules 2003, r.162.
4. Land Registration Rules 2003, r.58.
5. *Re King's Will Trusts* [1964] Ch 542.
6. Administration of Estates Act 1925, s.36.
7. See Land Registration Rules 2003, Sched. 4 as to the wording of the restrictions.
8. Land Registration Act 2002, s.52.
9. Land Registration Rules 2003, r.61 and Sched. 3.
10. Land Registration Rules 2003, r.62 and Sched. 3.

2.10.   Discharged mortgages

Registered land

2.10.1. A mortgage over registered land which has been discharged will be deleted from the charges register of the title and is thus of no further concern to the buyer. As far as the seller's existing mortgage is concerned the buyer should raise a requisition requiring this to be removed on or before completion.

Unregistered land

2.10.2. Discharged legal mortgages should be abstracted by the seller and checked by the buyer's solicitor to ensure that the discharge was validly effected. Discharged equitable mortgages will not normally be abstracted and once discharged no longer affect the title.

2.10.3. Where a sale has been effected by a lender in exercise of his power of sale, the mortgage deed will not bear a receipt.

2.10.4. In the case of a building society mortgage, provided that the receipt (usually endorsed on the mortgage deed) is in the form of wording prescribed by Building Societies Act 1986, and is signed by a person authorised by the particular society, the receipt may be treated as an effective discharge of the mortgage without further enquiry being made.

2.10.5. In other cases, by Law of Property Act 1925, s.115 a receipt endorsed on the mortgage deed (even if the receipt is not executed as a deed) operates to discharge the mortgage provided it is signed by the lender and names the person making repayment. However, where the money appears to have been paid by a person not entitled to the immediate equity of redemption, the receipt will usually operate as a transfer by deed of the mortgage. Thus if the person making repayment is not the borrower named in the mortgage or a personal representative or trustee acting on his behalf, the receipt should make it expressly clear that the receipt is to operate as such and is not intended to be a transfer of the mortgage to the person making payment. If the borrower makes repayment of the mortgage debt, but the receipt is dated later than the date of the conveyance by the borrower to a buyer of the land charged, at the date of the receipt the borrower will not be the person immediately entitled to the equity of redemption under the mortgage, because the mortgage had not been discharged at the date of completion of the sale of the land; thus the buyer will technically have bought the land subject to this incumbrance. In these circumstances the receipt operates to transfer the mortgage to the borrower (and not as a receipt) and it is, in theory, undischarged. In reality, any rights which the borrower has under the mortgage are unlikely to be enforced since he may be estopped from setting up the mortgage against the buyer. The borrower's position is at best that of a puisne mortgagee, since the title deeds will have passed to the buyer on completion of the sale, and unless registered as a Class C(i) or C(iii) land charge would be unenforceable against a subsequent buyer of the land for valuable consideration.[1] A buyer should therefore check the mortgage receipt to see who made repayment and also check that the receipt is dated no later than the date of the next transaction in the chain. If the mortgage receipt appears inadvertently to have transferred the mortgage and not discharged it a requisition should be raised to ensure that the seller or his lender is in possession of the title deeds (so that no mortgage supported by deposit of deeds can have come into existence as a result of the transfer) and the buyer should make a Land Charges Department search against the name of the person who bought from the borrower to ensure that no land charge has been registered against his name. Provided that the present seller or his lender has the deeds and the result of the land charges search reveals no adverse entries the defect can be ignored.

1. See *Cumberland Court (Brighton) Ltd* v. *Taylor* [1964] Ch 29.

2.11.   Transactions at an undervalue

2.11.1. Dispositions which are made by way of gift or at an undervalue (whether *inter vivos* or by assent) are not generally acceptable as roots of title in unregistered land because no investigation of title would have been made by the donee at the time of the transaction. They do not therefore provide the double check on title which is afforded by an arm's length conveyance.

2.11.2. Where a prospective buyer or mortgagee of land, whether registered or not, has notice that the land has been the subject of an undervalue transaction, it may be necessary to consider whether the courts' powers to set aside, under Insolvency Act 1986, s.238 or s.339, apply. An undervalue transaction may be the result of a gift, a partial gift (made for a consideration but a substantially below market value one), financial arrangements following a marriage breakdown, or a deed of variation in relation to an inheritance. If sections 238 or 339 do apply, it will then be necessary to see whether the protection provided by sections 241(2) and 342(2) operates. The courts' sections 238 and 339 powers are exercisable for periods of two or five years, respectively, from the date of the transaction (depending on whether the transferor was a company or an individual), but the Act's provisions protect a person acquiring in good faith and for value during those periods (see D2.11.7). For transactions at an undervalue to defraud creditors, see D2.11.10.

Dispositions by companies

2.11.3. If a company has made a disposition at an undervalue within the last two years, the transaction can be set aside on application from the liquidator or administrator on the company's subsequent insolvency if the transaction was with a person connected with the company, or if the present buyer knows that the company was insolvent at the time of the transaction or knows that the company would have become insolvent as a result of that transaction at an undervalue.

2.11.4. In any dealing where a company has made a transaction at an undervalue more than two years ago, a company search must be carried out as to whether the company went into liquidation or administration within two years of the voluntary disposition.

2.11.5. The term 'connected person' includes a director (Insolvency Act 1986, s.249).

Dispositions by individuals

2.11.6. If an individual becomes bankrupt after having made a disposition at an undervalue, the transaction can be set aside by his trustee in bankruptcy if the transaction was made within the last two years. If the transaction was made within the last five years it can be set aside if the present buyer knows that the donor was insolvent at the time of the transaction or knows that he would have become insolvent as a result of the transaction. It can also be set aside if the transaction at an undervalue was made within the last five years and it was made to an 'associate' of the donor. The word associate is widely defined in Insolvency Act 1986, s.435 to include the donor's spouse, ex-spouse, partner, partner's relatives, employers and employees. Buyers must carry out a Land Charges Department search against the donor in a transaction at undervalue to find out if he has become insolvent within five years.

Protection of the buyer

2.11.7. The courts can set aside transactions at an undervalue against subsequent owners of the property if the insolvency occurred within the two- or five-year periods. Insolvency Act 1986, s.241(2) and s.342(3), provide protection for subsequent buyers. For dispositions made on or before 26 July 1994, the transaction cannot be set aside where the buyer:

(a) was not a party to the transaction at an undervalue;

(b) acted in good faith;

(c) provided value for the purchase (i.e. the open market price) and was without notice that the transaction was at an undervalue.

2.11.8. Where the transaction at an undervalue was made after 26 July 1994, it cannot be set aside where the buyer bought in good faith and for value. Insolvency (No.2) Act 1994 amended s.241(2) and s.342(3) to the effect that the clawback will be limited to cases where either:

(a) the buyer is connected with or is an associate of the donor or donee to the transaction at an undervalue; or

(b) the buyer has notice that the transaction was at an undervalue and that the donor has become insolvent or was about to become insolvent.

If one of these two exceptions in section 241(2A) applies the buyer is rebuttably presumed not to have bought in good faith. Provided the buyer does the appropriate searches and has no knowledge of any insolvency and provided he is not an associate he will be protected from the clawback provisions.

2.11.9. Insolvency (No.2) Act 1994 was passed to deal with difficulties caused by those provisions of Insolvency Act 1986 which apply to undervalue transactions. Various questions had arisen about its effect since it came into force in July 1994. As a result, the Law Society obtained the opinion of leading counsel, Gabriel Moss QC, on certain points. Appendix IV.3 sets out his views.

2.11.10. If the transaction at an undervalue was entered into for the purpose of defrauding creditors (to put assets beyond the reach of someone or to prejudice the interest of someone in relation to a claim they may make), a person who is or is capable of being prejudiced by it can make an application under Insolvency Act 1986, s.423 to have the transaction set aside whether or not the donor is subject to insolvency procedures. Unlike applications under sections 238 and 339, there is no time limit for actions. Section 425(2) provides protection for a subsequent buyer who has acquired the property in good faith, for value and without notice of the relevant circumstances.

2.12. Effect of failure to register land charges (unregistered land)

2.12.1. Charges of Classes C(i), C(ii), C(iii) and F are void against a purchaser of any interest in the land for valuable consideration (including marriage).

2.12.2. Charges of Classes C(iv) and D are void only against a purchaser of a legal estate for money or money's worth.

2.13. Checking stamp duties

Registered land

2.13.1. Once the buyer has become registered as proprietor, the transfer and/or prereg-istration deeds, in general, no longer concern a subsequent buyer.

Unregistered land

2.13.2. Unstamped or incorrectly stamped documents or documents not bearing adju-dication or denoting stamps where these are required by the legislation are not good roots of title, nor good links in the chain. They cannot be produced in evidence in civil proceedings and will not be accepted by the Chief Land Registrar on an application to register the title.

2.13.3. A buyer is entitled to insist that all documents within the title are properly stamped at the expense of the seller. If, therefore, on examination of the title stamping defects are found, the buyer or mortgagee should raise a requisition requiring the seller to remedy the deficiency at his own expense.[1]

2.13.4. Stamp duty may be *ad valorem* or fixed duty, the rates of which vary from time to time. Each document in the title should be checked against a table of stamp duties to ensure that it bears the correct duty in relation to the nature of the instrument, its date, and the amount of its consideration. The presence of a certificate of value in a document may have the effect of reducing the liability to duty or of exempting it from duty altogether. Where VAT has been paid on the consideration, stamp duty is payable on the VAT element of the price.

2.13.5. In addition to stamp duty, conveyances on sale and leases granted for a term of seven years or more and assignments of such leases had to be produced to HM Revenue and Customs under Finance Act 1931. On production a Produced Stamp (Particulars Delivered Stamp) was affixed to the document. The conse-quences of failure to produce a document are the same as for lack of stamp duty and the seller must be required to rectify any deficiency at his own expense.

1. Stamp Act 1891, s.117.

2.14. Verification of title

2.14.1. Verification of title consists of checking the evidence of title supplied by the seller against the original deeds.

2.14.2. In registered land the current state of the register can be confirmed by the buyer when making his pre-completion search at the Land Registry.

2.14.3.   In unregistered land, the abstract or epitome should be checked against the seller's original deeds. The buyer's time limit for making this inspection expires with his time limit for raising requisitions. Verification should therefore be carried out as part of the investigation of title procedure. In most cases, where the title is not complex, and the photocopy documents supplied by the seller are of good quality, the buyer's solicitor postpones his verification until actual completion. If, however, he then finds an error on the title it will be too late to query the error since his time limit for raising requisitions will have expired. If there is any doubt over the validity of the title, or it is of a complex nature, verification should be carried out at the proper time. Unless the contract provides to the contrary the costs of verification are borne by the buyer. Standard Condition 4.1 and Standard Commercial Property Condition 6.1 require the seller to produce to the buyer (without cost to the buyer) the original of every document within the title or, if the original is not available, an abstract, epitome or copy with an original marking by a solicitor of examination either against the original or against an examined abstract or an examined copy.

2.15.   Acting for the lender

2.15.1.   The solicitor will be instructed to ensure that the property has a good and marketable title free from unspecified defects.

2.15.2.   The lender may not be prepared to accept as security any property which is registered with a title other than absolute or any property which is a flying freehold.

2.15.3.   Where the solicitor has been instructed under the terms of the Lenders' Handbook the provisions of the Handbook must be observed. See in particular paragraph 5.4 relating to a good and marketable title.

2.15.4.   Under the Lenders' Handbook specific conditions are applicable to good leasehold titles (paragraph 5.4.2) and to flying freeholds (paragraph 5.5). See Appendix VI.2 for the full text of Part 1 of the Lenders' Handbook.

D3. Requisitions on title

3.1. Purpose of requisitions

3.1.1. The purpose of requisitions on title is to require the seller's solicitor to clarify and if necessary to rectify matters on the title supplied which the buyer's solicitor finds unsatisfactory. In practice they are commonly used also to resolve administrative queries relating to the arrangements for completion.

3.2. Time for raising requisitions

3.2.1. Where title has been deduced following exchange, Standard Condition 4.3.1 and Standard Commercial Property Condition 6.3.1 require written requisitions on the title supplied to be raised within six working days after either the date of the contract or the day of delivery of the seller's evidence of title, whichever is the later. The buyer will lose his right to raise requisitions if he does not do so within the time limits prescribed by these conditions. If the evidence of title is incomplete and this fact is pointed out to the seller within the above period, under Standard Condition 4.3.1 and Standard Commercial Property Condition 6.3.1, the buyer's solicitor has six working days from the supply of additional evidence to raise requisitions on that additional evidence. By Standard Condition 4.3.4 and Standard Commercial Property Condition 6.3.4, this time limit may be adjusted *pro rata* to fit a completion date which is less than 15 working days from the date of the contract.

3.2.2. Where title has been deduced prior to exchange, Standard Condition 4.2.1 and Standard Commercial Property Condition 6.2.1 prevent the raising of requisitions after exchange, but only in relation to matters disclosed by the seller prior to exchange. The buyer may still raise requisitions on previously undisclosed title problems after exchange, so long as he does so within six working days of the problem coming to his attention.[1]

1. See Standard Condition 4.2.2 and Standard Commercial Property Condition 6.2.2.

3.3. Standard form requisitions

3.3.1. A standard form of requisitions (the Completion Information and Requisitions on Title Form) is published by the Law Society for use in Protocol transactions.

Most law stationers produce a standard form of requisitions on title which includes many commonly asked questions, e.g. confirmation that the seller's mortgage on the property will be discharged on or before completion. The seller's solicitor should be asked to confirm that the answers given to enquiries before contract or information volunteered on the Seller's Property Information Form remain correct. Additionally the printed questions frequently deal with the administrative arrangements for completion itself, e.g. method of payment of money. Queries which are specific to the title under consideration may be added to the end of the standard form or typed on a separate sheet. The buyer's solicitor should send two copies of the form to the seller's solicitor who will return one copy with his answers appended, keeping the other copy on his own file for reference. Standard Condition 4.3.1 and Standard Commercial Property Condition 6.3.1 require the seller's solicitor to reply to requisitions within four working days after receiving them from the buyer's solicitor.

3.4.   Further queries

3.4.1.   On receipt of replies from the seller's solicitor, the buyer's solicitor should ensure that the answers given to his queries are satisfactory both in relation to the title and to the client's interests. Any replies which are unsatisfactory should be taken up with the seller's solicitor and further written queries raised until the matter is resolved.

3.4.2.   Standard Condition 4.3.1 and Standard Commercial Property Condition 6.3.1 govern the time limits for raising observations on the seller's replies to requisitions.

3.4.3.   In some cases the replies given to requisitions may be construed as undertakings, e.g. to discharge the seller's outstanding mortgage on the property. Where such an undertaking is given the seller's solicitor should ensure that he has only committed himself to do what is within his power to do; an undertaking to discharge the seller's mortgage(s) on the property or one which is simply worded 'confirmed' or 'noted' will be interpreted as meaning that *all* subsisting charges will be removed. The seller's solicitor should therefore ensure that he is fully aware of the details of all such charges before committing himself to such an undertaking. Alternatively, the seller's solicitor or licensed conveyancer may prefer to undertake to discharge certain named charges only. Similarly, an unqualified promise to send title deeds within a specific time limit should only be given where these deeds are in the possession or control of the seller's solicitor.

3.4.4.   From the buyer's point of view, the buyer's solicitor should ensure that he asks the seller's solicitor to supply a list of all outstanding charges and obtains a specific undertaking in relation to each of them. He should only accept an undertaking from a solicitor or licensed conveyancer, such undertaking being in the form approved by the Law Society, failing which the buyer's solicitor should raise a requisition requiring the mortgages actually to be discharged on or before completion.

3.5.   Restrictions on subject matter of requisitions

3.5.1.   The buyer's solicitor is only entitled to raise requisitions on the title which he has, by contractual condition, agreed to accept. Except where Law of Property Act 1925, s.45 applies, he cannot in the case of unregistered land require production of documents prior to the root of title.[1] The buyer's right to raise requisitions may be curtailed or excluded by a condition in the contract. Such a restriction only takes effect on exchange of contracts and does not preclude the buyer from raising queries in relation to that particular matter before contracts are exchanged. If the seller wishes to curtail or exclude the buyer's right to raise requisitions he must make a full disclosure of all defects in his title. In strict theory, the seller is only obliged to answer requisitions which relate to title, and not those which relate to, e.g. the form of the purchase deed. In practice the distinction between true requisitions on title and those relating to other matters is largely ignored and the seller's solicitor will answer all reasonable queries raised by the buyer's solicitor. Contractual conditions may also require the buyer in certain circumstances to waive a defect in title. At common law the buyer is deemed to accept the seller's title (and thus loses his right to raise requisitions or further requisitions) when he delivers a draft purchase deed to the seller. In practice the draft purchase deed is usually submitted to the seller simultaneously with requisitions and the buyer's right to raise requisitions will be expressly preserved by a contractual condition, e.g. Standard Condition 4.6.1.

1.   See D2.6.

3.6.   Vendor and purchaser summons

3.6.1.   If the seller's solicitor refuses to answer a proper requisition, the buyer can compel an answer by means of the vendor and purchaser summons procedure under Law of Property Act 1925, s.49 which provides a summary method of resolving disputes between the parties. This procedure is intended to be used to resolve an impasse between the parties where agreement cannot be reached over a specific point in relation to the title and not as a general sounding-board to test the validity of the whole title or of the contract.

3.7.   Right to rescind

3.7.1.   Neither the Standard Conditions of Sale (fourth edition) nor the Standard Commercial Property Conditions (second edition) contain clauses entitling the seller to rescind the contract where the buyer raises a requisition with which the seller is unable or unwilling to comply (see D2.3).

3.7.2. If the seller has not answered a requisition by the contractual completion date it might be possible for the buyer to treat the contract as discharged by a breach of condition or to serve a notice to complete under Standard Condition 6.8 or Standard Commercial Property Condition 8.8 (see section M).

E. PRE-COMPLETION

E1. The purchase deed

1.1. Who prepares the deed?

1.1.1. It is normally the buyer's duty to prepare the purchase deed, although the seller may, by Law of Property Act 1925, s.48(1), reserve the right by contractual condition to prepare the deed himself. This right is usually only used in estate conveyancing where the seller commonly supplies an engrossment of the purchase deed in standard form, a draft of the deed having been annexed to the contract. If the seller charges a fee for the engrossment, such fee must be reasonable and is deemed to include VAT unless stated otherwise.

1.2. Time for preparation of deed

1.2.1. Traditionally the purchase deed was prepared after completion of the buyer's investigation of title, but in practice the deed is usually prepared shortly after exchange of contracts and submitted to the seller for his approval with the buyer's requisitions on title. At common law the buyer is deemed to have accepted the seller's title when he submits the purchase deed for approval, and thus the submission of the purchase deed simultaneously with requisitions would preclude the buyer's right to raise requisitions on the seller's title. This problem is solved by Standard Condition 4.6.1 and Standard Commercial Property Condition 6.6.1 which both preserve the buyer's right to raise requisitions in such circumstances. By Standard Condition 4.3.2 and Standard Commercial Property Condition 6.3.2, the buyer is required to submit the draft purchase deed to the seller at least 12 working days before the contractual completion date. Under para. 9.1 of the Protocol the buyer's solicitor is required to submit the draft purchase deed simultaneously with his requisitions on title as soon as possible after exchange of contracts and in any case within the time-limits specified in the contract.

1.3. Form of the deed

1.3.1. The purchase deed must be a deed in order to transfer the legal estate in the land to the buyer.[1]

1.3.2. The purchase deed puts into effect the terms of the contract and so must reflect its terms.

1.3.3. Where the property being transferred is registered land the form of the purchase deed is prescribed by Land Registration Rules 2003.[2] Subject to permitted variations, the prescribed form of wording and layout must also be used.[3]

1.3.4. Land Registry forms may be downloaded free of charge from the Land Registry website at **www.landregistry.gov.uk**. Almost all of the standard Land Registry forms are reproduced by law stationers and these may be used as the basis of the purchase deed. Most of the forms (such as TR1 and TR2) can also be reproduced electronically using commercial forms packages or using the firm's own software.

1.3.5. The Land Registry for Wales will accept a document which is prepared in Welsh and does not require a translation to be supplied.[4]

1.3.6. No prescribed form of wording exists for a conveyance of unregistered land. The buyer is thus free to choose his own form of wording subject to the seller's approval and provided that it accurately reflects the terms of the contract. As the transaction will be submitted for first registration after completion, instead of using a traditional conveyance the buyer will usually prepare his purchase deed as a Land Registry transfer suitably amended.

1. Law of Property Act 1925, s.52.
2. Land Registration Rules 2003, r.58 provides that a transfer of a registered estate must be in Form TP1, TP2, TP3, TR1, TR2, TR5, AS1 or AS3 as appropriate.
3. Land Registration Rules 2003, rr.210 and 211. Detailed guidance on the reproduction of Land Registry forms can be found in Land Registry Practice Guide 46 and see A21.
4. Under the Land Registry's Welsh Language Scheme prepared under Welsh Language Act 1993, s.21(3), the Land Registry will ensure that the English and Welsh languages are treated on a basis of equality in Wales.

1.4. Drafting the deed

1.4.1. When drafting the purchase deed the buyer's solicitor needs to have access to:

(a) the contract – because the purchase deed must reflect the terms of the contract;

(b) the official copy entries of the title/title deeds – because the contract may refer to matters on the title which need to be repeated or reflected in the purchase deed;

(c) except in straightforward cases, a precedent on which to base the deed under preparation.

Using a precedent

1.4.2.   Except in the simplest cases it is advisable to refer to a precedent if only to focus the mind on the types of clauses which will be required in the draft deed. Use the precedent as a guide and not as a model to be followed slavishly. Consider whether a clause is really necessary before copying it from a precedent and check that the law has not altered since the precedent was published.

1.5.   Seller's approval of draft deed

1.5.1.   When the draft has been prepared two copies should be submitted to the seller's solicitor for his approval. A further copy of the draft should be retained by the buyer's solicitor so that amendments can be agreed over the telephone if required. By Standard Condition 4.3.2 and Standard Commercial Property Condition 6.3.2 one of the copies submitted to the seller's solicitor can be of engrossment quality enabling the seller to use this as a top copy for signature in cases where no amendments are needed and where the buyer does not need to sign the deed.

1.5.2.   On receipt of the draft, the seller's solicitor should check it carefully to ensure that the document accurately reflects the terms of the contract. Amendments should be confined to those which are necessary for the fulfilment of the document's legal purpose, bearing in mind that the choice of style and wording is the buyer's prerogative. Minor amendments may be agreed with the buyer's solicitor by telephone in order to save time. More substantial amendments should be clearly marked in a distinct colour on both copies of the draft, one copy being returned to the buyer's solicitor for his consideration, the other being retained in the seller's solicitor's file for reference. By Standard Condition 4.3.2 and Standard Commercial Condition 6.3.2 the seller's solicitor is to approve or return the revised draft document within four working days after delivery of the draft transfer by the buyer's solicitor.

1.6.   Engrossment

1.6.1.   When amendments (if any) to the draft deed have been finalised, the buyer's solicitor should prepare an engrossment of the deed on good quality paper. A deed which is to be submitted to the Land Registry should be engrossed on durable A4 size paper.[1]

1.6.2.   The engrossment must be checked carefully (if necessary by comparing the draft document with the engrossment) to ensure the accuracy of the typing and that all agreed amendments have been incorporated. A copy of the engrossment should be kept on the buyer's solicitor's file for reference.

1.6.3.   The completed engrossment should then be sent to the seller's solicitor for execution by his client. Where the buyer is required to execute the deed it is common practice for the buyer to execute the deed prior to delivery of the deed in escrow to the seller for his signature. The condition attached to the escrow should be defined. By Standard Condition 4.3.2 and Standard Commercial Property Condition 6.3.2 the buyer must deliver the engrossment of the purchase deed to the seller at least five working days before completion.

1. Land Registration Rules 2003, r.210.

1.7.   Execution

1.7.1.   To be valid in law a deed must be clear on the face of it that it is a deed, signed by the necessary parties in the presence of a witness, and delivered.[1] Use of a seal is no longer required either by individuals or bodies corporate. A company seal may, however, still be used and is a valid method of execution of a document.

1.7.2.   Where land is registered, the form of transfer and certain other deeds affecting the land must follow the prescribed form.[2] The forms of words of execution are also prescribed.[3] Land Registry Practice Guide 8 gives further guidance on the execution of deeds.

1.7.3.   Signature by the seller is always required in order to transfer the legal estate.[4]

1.7.4.   The buyer is required to execute the deed if it contains a covenant or declaration on his behalf. Thus execution by the buyer will be needed where the document contains an indemnity covenant in respect of existing restrictive covenants or a declaration by the buyers relating to the trusts on which they hold the property.

1.7.5.   Where other parties are joined in the deed, e.g. to release the property from a mortgage or to give a valid receipt for money paid under the deed, they should also sign the document.

1.7.6.   Signature by an individual must be made by him in person, preferably in ink and it must be signed in the presence of one witness who also signs his name.

1.7.7.   Where an individual is incapable of signing the document himself, e.g. as a result of illness or disability, another person may execute it on his behalf. If necessary the document should be read over to the individual, or its contents clearly explained to him, before signature. Two witnesses are required to the signature.[5]

1.7.8.   Any responsible person may be a witness to the signature of an individual. There is no legal restriction on one party to a document being a witness to the other party's signature nor on one spouse or civil partner being a witness to the signature of the other spouse or civil partner, but an independent witness is preferable since if the validity of the document was ever challenged in court, the independent witness would provide a stronger testimony. The witness should sign his name, and add underneath the signature his address and occupation. If the name of the witness is not clear from the signature it is sensible to ask the witness also to write his full name in block capitals after his signature. Two witnesses are required whenever the document is signed by one person on another's behalf.

1.7.9. Where an individual is capable of signing the document but cannot read it, e.g. because he is blind or the document is in a foreign language, he should familiarise himself with its contents. It is preferable that a solicitor witnesses the signature to confirm that the correct procedure was followed.

1.7.10. A solicitor should always be satisfied before submitting a document for signature that the client understands the nature and contents of the document. Where the solicitor invites his client to sign the purchase deed in the solicitor's presence the deed can be explained to the client before signature, and actually signed in the presence of the solicitor who can then act as a witness to the signature. If this is not possible, the purchase deed may be sent to the client for signature and return. The letter which accompanies the purchase deed should:

    (a)   explain the purpose and contents of the document;

    (b)   contain clear instructions relating to the execution of the deed;

    (c)   specify a date by which the signed document must be returned to the solicitor;

    (d)   request that the client leaves the document undated.

Attorneys

1.7.11. A person who holds a power of attorney on behalf of another may execute a deed on that person's behalf. The attorney may sign either in his own name or in that of the person on behalf of whom he is acting, e.g. '*X* by his attorney *Y*' or '*Y* as attorney on behalf of *X*'.

Companies

1.7.12. A company will normally execute a deed by using its common seal which is impressed on the document in the presence of a director of the company and its secretary (who for this purpose must be two separate individuals) or two directors who will then sign the document to witness the execution by the company. If this is done, then a buyer is, from 15 September 2005, protected by Law of Property Act 1925, s.74(1) (as amended by Regulatory Reform (Execution of Deeds and Documents) Order 2005 (SI 2005/1906)) against any irregularity in the execution.

1.7.13. Alternatively, the document may simply be signed by a director and the secretary or by two directors on behalf of the company. The document must make it clear on the face of it that it is a deed.[6] Use of a common seal is no longer compulsory. If this method is used, due execution by the company may be presumed under Companies Act 1985, s.36A(6) and a buyer (but not a volunteer) need not investigate whether the manner of execution is authorised by the company's articles.

1.7.14. In some cases a company's articles may permit execution of a document by a method different from those outlined above, e.g. signature by an authorised person acting alone. In such a case the procedure prescribed by the articles should be followed and a copy of the signatory's authorisation attached to the deed to prove the validity of its execution. Land Registry Practice Guide 8 contains detailed information on the Land Registry's current requirements.

1.7.15. When Part 4 Companies Act 2006 comes into force, a document will be validly executed if it is signed on behalf of the company by either two authorised signatories (the company's directors and the company secretary) or by a director of the company in the presence of a witness who attests the signature.

1.7.16. The requirements for execution of documents by companies incorporated outside the UK are dealt with in E7.

Other bodies

1.7.17. The requirements for execution of deeds by other bodies, e.g. corporations sole (e.g. a bishop), district councils, government departments or statutory undertakings, will vary depending on the body concerned. The precise procedure for execution should be checked well in advance of execution. The document should then be executed in accordance with the prescribed method, and a copy of the authority of the signatory to sign attached to the deed to prove the validity of its execution. The relaxation on the use of corporate seals which was granted to registered companies by Companies Act 1989 does not extend to these bodies.

Patients

1.7.18. Following Court of Protection Rules 1994, deeds affecting sale and purchase transactions are no longer required to be sealed by the Court of Protection.

Delivery

1.7.19. In addition to signature a deed must be delivered. A deed takes effect on its delivery. When the buyer delivers the engrossment to the seller for execution by him, he does not normally intend the deed to become effective at that time. It is therefore common practice for the buyer to deliver the deed to the seller in escrow, i.e. conditionally, so that the operation of the deed is postponed until completion. In the case of a company, delivery is presumed at the date of execution unless the contrary is proved.[7]

1. Law of Property (Miscellaneous Provisions) Act 1989, s.1.
2. Land Registration Rules 2003, r.206(1) and Sched. 1.
3. Land Registration Rules 2003, r.206(3) and Sched. 9.

4.   Law of Property Act 1925, s.52.
5.   Law of Property (Miscellaneous Provisions) Act 1989, s.1.
6.   Companies Act 1985, s.36A.
7.   Companies Act 1985, s.36AA. The timing of delivery can be expressly postponed by stating in the deed that the document is delivered as at its date.

1.8.   Plans

1.8.1.   If the contract provides for the use of a plan the purchase deed will also refer to the plan. In other cases the buyer is not entitled to demand that a plan is used with the purchase deed unless the description of the property as afforded by the contract and title deeds is inadequate without one. If the buyer wishes to use a plan in circumstances where he is not entitled to demand one, he may do so with the seller's consent but will have to bear the cost of its preparation.

1.8.2.   Where the sale is of the whole of the seller's property use of a plan is not normally considered necessary, and unless very clearly drawn may confuse rather than clarify the deed as well as adding unnecessary expense.

1.8.3.   On a sale of part (including flats and office suites) a plan is highly desirable and where the land is registered generally must be used.[1]

1.8.4.   The plan(s) to be used with the purchase deed should be checked for accuracy, including all necessary colourings and markings, and firmly bound into the engrossment of the deed which should in its wording refer to the use of the plan(s). Measurements must be expressed in metric values.

1.8.5.   In registered land cases the transferor must sign the plan. In unregistered land signature of the plan is not compulsory but is highly desirable. Such signatures need not be witnessed. Where a company seals the purchase deed, it should also seal the plan.

1.8.6.   The preparation and use of plans is further discussed in B21.

1.   Land Registration Rules 2003, r.213.

1.9.   Parties

1.9.1.   Anyone whose concurrence is necessary in order to transfer the legal estate or who is to give a valid receipt for capital money arising out of the transaction must be joined as a party to the deed.

1.9.2.   The seller and buyer will usually be the only parties to the deed, but in view of the principle outlined in E1.9.1 it may be necessary to join, e.g. the trustees of a Settled Land Act settlement or a non-owning occupier.

1.9.3.   Where the seller is bankrupt, his trustee in bankruptcy will transfer the property and the seller is not a party to the deed.[1]

1.9.4.   If the seller is a company which is in liquidation or under receivership, the company itself transfers the property with the receiver or liquidator joining in the deed to give a receipt for the purchase price. In such a case the liquidator actually executes the deed. Exceptionally, if an order has been made by the court under Companies Act 1989 vesting the legal estate of the company's property in the liquidator, the liquidator will be the seller and the company will not be a party to the deed.

1.9.5.   In a sub-sale transaction, the seller transfers the property directly to the sub-purchaser, but the original buyer will join in the document to give implied covenants and, where appropriate, to give a receipt for all or part of the purchase price.

1.9.6.   On a sale of part of registered land which is subject to a mortgage, the lender will not be a party to the purchase deed since he will release the part sold from his charge by using Form DS3. In the same situation in unregistered land the lender may join in the conveyance in order to release the part sold from the mortgage and, where appropriate, to give a receipt for such part of the purchase price as is paid to him. Alternatively, a lender in the case of unregistered land may give a separate deed of release to the buyer. The seller must ascertain from his lender which of these methods of release the lender wishes to employ and inform the buyer accordingly so that the buyer can, if necessary, include appropriate clauses relating to the lender in the draft purchase deed.

1.9.7.   On a sale by a mortgagee in possession the mortgagee will be the seller and the owner will not enter into the deed.

1.   See E6.7.5 as to where a co-owner is bankrupt.

1.10.   Transfer of whole

1.10.1.   A transfer of whole must be in Form TR1 (or, in the case of a transfer under power of sale, TR2).[1] The following paragraphs relate to a transfer to give effect to one sale.

1.10.2.   The title number and short description of the property, i.e. its postal address, may be taken from the official copy entries of the title supplied by the seller.

1.10.3.   The date of the document is inserted on actual completion.

1.10.4.   The amount of consideration must be stated[2] in both words and figures in the consideration panel. The receipt in the consideration panel renders any other form of receipt for the purchase price unnecessary and acts as a sufficient discharge to the buyer.[3] The presence of this receipt also gives the buyer authority to pay the purchase price to the seller's solicitor.[4] The receipt is also evidence, but not necessarily conclusive evidence, that the seller's lien over the property for the unpaid purchase price has been extinguished. The purchase price in the transfer should exclude the amount of any consideration attributable to chattels for which a separate receipt should be prepared.[5]

1.10.5. The seller's name should be inserted as it appears on the proprietorship register of the title. If the seller is not the current registered proprietor, the seller's name should be inserted as it appears in, for example, his transfer.

1.10.6. There is provision on the form for the seller's title guarantee, which will imply covenants for title under Law of Property (Miscellaneous Provisions) Act 1994 (see section M). Any modification of the covenants must be set out expressly on the face of the transfer and must refer to the section of the 1994 Act which is being modified or excluded.

1.10.7. The buyer's full name and address should be inserted. The buyer's address or addresses for service given in the Transfer Form or AP1 (Application to change the register) will be placed on the proprietorship register on registration of the buyer's interest and is the address which will be used by the Chief Land Registrar should it become necessary for him to contact the registered proprietor of the land, e.g. to serve notices on him. The form allows up to three addresses to be given. The addresses given should therefore be ones at which it is certain that the buyer can be contacted.[6] In the case of residential property where the buyer will be moving into the property on completion, one of the addresses should be the address of the property being purchased and not the address at which the buyer is currently living.

1.10.8. Where the sale is subject to existing covenants the contract will usually provide for the purchase deed to include an indemnity covenant to be given by the buyer.[7] An indemnity covenant will be required in respect of positive covenants and restrictive covenants which are not limited to seisin.[8] Where such a covenant is necessary it should be added expressly to the transfer form, there being no such covenant included on the printed forms. A covenant which gives indemnity only is enforceable in breach by an action for damages. One which is 'to observe perform and indemnify' is enforceable by injunction and damages and thus provides fuller protection for the seller. Standard Condition 4.6.4 and Standard Commercial Condition 6.6.4 provides for the full form of covenant to be given. Where there are joint purchasers, the covenant should be given by both or all of them.

1.10.9. Joint purchasers must indicate in the transfer the capacity in which they will hold the equitable interest in the property, i.e. as joint tenants or tenants in common. On registration of the buyers as proprietors a restriction in Form A will automatically be entered on the register unless it is clear that the survivor can give a good receipt for capital monies. Instructions as to the method in which the beneficial ownership is to be held should have been taken by the buyer's solicitor at an early stage in the transaction, and those instructions will now be effected in the transfer. Where the buyers have decided to hold as tenants in common, instructions should also have been obtained in relation to the proportionate shares which each co-owner will hold in the equitable interest. In the absence of evidence to the contrary it will be assumed by the court that they hold the equity in proportion to their original contributions to the property.[9] In order to avoid costly and time-consuming litigation at a later date, it is essential that full details of the beneficial interests of the co-owners are recorded in writing at the time of their purchase. There is provision in the form of transfer to record the respective beneficial interests. Alternatively, a short deed of trust may be drawn up to give effect to the buyers' wishes, in which case it should be referred to in the transfer and kept safely for future reference.

1.10.10. The transfer should provide for execution by all parties in the presence of a witness. The form of attestation is prescribed by Schedule 9 Land Registration Rules 2003 and will vary dependent on the identity of the signatory.[10] See Land Registry Practice Guide 8.

1.10.11. Additional provisions may be required in the deed in accordance with special conditions of the contract. There is a panel in Land Registry forms to include these.

1. Land Registration Rules 2003, r.58.
2. Stamp Act 1891, s.5.
3. Law of Property Act 1925, s.67.
4. Law of Property Act 1925, s.69.
5. The amount of the consideration affects the amount of SDLT payable on the document and, since chattels are not subject to stamp duty, any sum payable for them does not need to be included in the purchase deed. Where VAT is payable the amount of the consideration stated should include the VAT element of the price.
6. Land Registration Rules 2003, r.198 sets out the requirements as to addresses for service. And see G3.11.5.
7. See Standard Condition 4.6.4 and Standard Commercial Property Condition 6.6.4.
8. See *Rhone* v. *Stephens, The Times,* 18 March 1994, HL; *Austerberry* v. *Oldham Corporation* (1885) 29 ChD 750.
9. *Springette* v. *Defoe* (1993) 65 P&CR 1, CA.
10. Land Registration Rules 2003, r. 206(3) and Sched.9.

1.11. Transfer of part

1.11.1. A transfer of part of a registered title must be in Form TP1 (or in the case of a transfer of part under power of sale, TP2).[1] All of the matters referred to in E1.10 will be relevant to a sale of part but the following will also be required either in addition to or in substitution for the above.

1.11.2. At this stage the sale is made by reference to the seller's existing title number. A new title number for the part being sold will be allocated by the Land Registry on registration of the transaction.

1.11.3. A clear description of the land being sold must be included with reference to the plan annexed to the transfer. When necessary, the land retained by the seller should also be expressly defined and identified on the plan. When the postal address of the property is not yet known, the property may be described by the plot number on the seller's approved estate layout plan. However, it will not then be possible to give the property as the buyer's address for service. In this case a care of address may be inserted in the transfer. If the postal address is available when application is made for registration of transfer, it may be inserted in the application Form AP1.

1.11.4.　Where the contract made provision for the grant of easements to the buyer or reservations in favour of the seller, these easements must be expressly inserted into the transfer.

1.11.5.　The contract will usually provide for the exclusion of rights of light and air from the transfer. This contractual provision (Standard Condition 3.4 and Standard Commercial Property Condition 3.3) must be implemented by a declaration to this effect in the transfer.

1.11.6.　New restrictive covenants are frequently imposed in a contract for the sale of part of land; these too must be expressly set out in the transfer. Except where the land forms part of a building scheme, to be enforceable against subsequent owners of the land sold, the covenants must be taken for the benefit of land retained by the seller and the burden annexed to the land sold. Express words to give effect to these principles are advisable.

1.11.7.　Land Registry transfer forms provide sub-headings within the additional provisions panel under which full details of the rights granted and reserved, restrictive covenants, and other matters may be inserted. These sub-headings may be added to, amended, repositioned, or omitted as desired.[2]

1.　Land Registration Rules 2003, r.58.
2.　Land Registration Rules 2003, rr.210 and 211.

1.12.　Conveyance

1.12.1.　As a conveyance of unregistered land will lead to first registration, it is common practice to use a registered land transfer. The only amendments required will be the omission of the title number and a fuller description of the property by reference to a document in the chain of title. In the rare cases where a traditional conveyance is to be used, it will contain similar information but is presented in a different format from a registered land transfer. Each conveyance of unregistered land has slightly different requirements and thus each has to be individually drafted to fit the situation in hand (see D2.6 for guidance on the form and contents of a conveyance).

1.13.　Assent

1.13.1.　Where personal representatives transfer land to a beneficiary they will use an assent. If they sell land to a third party the purchase deed will be a transfer or conveyance depending whether or not the land is registered.

1.13.2.   One exception to the rule that a legal estate can only be conveyed by a deed is an assent by personal representatives which must be in writing but need not be by deed unless it contains a covenant by the assentee, e.g. for indemnity in respect of restrictive covenants.

1.13.3.   An assent of registered land must be in a transfer in Form AS1 or AS3 (prescribed by Land Registration Rules 2003, r.58). An assent of unregistered land is not subject to any restraints on its form or contents except that it must be in writing and must name the person(s) in whose favour it is given.

1.13.4.   On a sale or assent by personal representatives all proving personal representatives must be parties to the document.

1.13.5.   In unregistered land the assent may contain recitals, and will otherwise be similar to an unregistered conveyance. Since the land will be subject to first registration of title following the assent, it may be more convenient to use Form AS1 or AS3 (suitably amended) in preference to an unregistered form of assent. A memorandum of the assent should be noted on the grant after completion, although this is not strictly necessary where the land is to be registered on completion of the assent.

1.14.   Assignment

1.14.1.   An assignment of an existing registered lease is the transfer of a registered estate and the purchase deed will be a Land Registry transfer form. The form is the same as for the transfer of a freehold. An assignment of an unregistered lease is similar in form to a conveyance of unregistered land, subject to some modifications.

1.14.2.   Frequently the contract contains provision modifying the effect of the implied covenants for title in leasehold cases (e.g. Standard Condition 3.3 and Standard Commercial Condition 4) and the purchase deed will contain a provision giving effect to this contractual term. In a transfer, this will appear in the title guarantee panel.

1.14.3.   An express indemnity covenant will be inserted if required by the contract (if any) (see Standard Condition 4.6.4 and Standard Commercial Condition 6.6.4). No indemnity covenant is implied by statute in new leases (granted after 1 January 1996).[1] In leases granted before this date an indemnity covenant is implied except where in unregistered land value is not given by the assignee for the transaction.

1.14.4.   In addition, an unregistered assignment may contain recitals relating to the recent history of the lease, the agreement to sell and, where appropriate, the fact that the landlord has consented to the assignment. The estate transferred will be the unexpired residue of the term, subject to the terms and conditions of the lease itself. The benefit of options should be expressly assigned to ensure that their benefit is transferred to the buyer.

1.   Landlord and Tenant (Covenants) Act 1995, s.14.

1.15.   Sellers' cashback schemes

1.15.1.   These schemes appear to be operated by brokers who, in conjunction with a small number of lenders, participate in enabling a seller to offer an incentive to a buyer. In essence the seller and lender state that, e.g. the property is to be sold for £40,000 but that on completion the seller agrees to pay £5,000 to the buyer. Traditionally the contract discloses the arrangement, but the price inserted in the contract will be the higher figure, e.g. £40,000 rather than £35,000, which is the net price the seller receives from the buyer.

1.15.2.   In these schemes the lender is normally aware of the circumstances, and so the schemes do not, in fact, involve a fraud on the lender in the usual sense. Solicitors (whether acting for sellers or buyers) should always check that the lender is aware of the proposed cashback.

1.15.3.   As the transfer is a matter of public record, it is a solicitor's duty not to be a party to any mis-statement of the sale price. Inserting the higher price would be a mis-statement. If solicitors are instructed in relation to such schemes, they should make it clear from the outset that the figure they will insert in the transfer will be the net figure, and should decline to act if the client instructs otherwise.

1.15.4.   These schemes should be distinguished from cases where the lender gives an incentive 'cashback' to borrowers, as such cashbacks do not affect the price paid to the seller.

E2. Pre-completion searches

2.1.   Who makes the searches?

2.1.1.   In accordance with the *caveat emptor* principle it is up to the buyer to make sure of his bargain. Therefore it is the buyer's solicitor's responsibility to ensure that such pre-completion searches as are relevant to the transaction are carried out and that the results of those searches are satisfactory to his client.

2.1.2.   Where the buyer is purchasing with the assistance of a mortgage, his lender also has an interest in the soundness of the title to the property and some or all of the pre-completion searches may be carried out by the lender's solicitor acting at this stage on behalf of both the lender and the buyer.

2.2.   Reason for making searches

2.2.1.   The principal reason for making pre-completion searches is for the buyer's solicitor to confirm that information obtained about the property prior to exchange remains correct. In some situations searches additional to those which were made before exchange of contracts will also be undertaken at this stage either to verify information received after exchange or where the circumstances were such that the buyer did not have sufficient time to make the relevant search before contracts were exchanged.

2.3.   When to make searches

2.3.1.   The searches must be done in sufficient time to ensure that the results are received by the buyer's solicitor in time for completion to take place on the contractual completion date.

2.3.2.   Pre-completion searches should generally be made about seven days before the contractual completion date but may be left until closer to the completion date if, e.g. a telephone, computer or fax search is to be made. Searches will need to be done earlier than seven days before completion if some delay in the receipt of replies, e.g. through industrial action, is anticipated.

2.3.3. The principal searches which are made at this stage of the transaction (the Land Registry and/or Land Charges Department searches) generally confer protection on the searcher against later entries (i.e. they give a priority period); thus a balance has to be drawn between making the search at the latest moment before completion in order to gain the benefit of a long priority period after completion, and the risk, if a search is submitted at the last moment, of completion being delayed (and compensation payable by the buyer for the delay) because the search result has not been received by the date of completion.

2.4. Which searches to make

2.4.1. The following searches should be made:

    (a) for registered land, search against title number at the Land Registry (see E2.5);

    (b) for unregistered land, including an unregistered reversion to a lease, search at Land Charges Department against names of estate owners of the land (see E2.6);

    (c) if acting for a lender, a bankruptcy search against the name of the borrower (see E2.8);

    (d) such other of the searches listed in E2.9–E2.13 as are applicable to the transaction.

2.5. Land Registry search

2.5.1. When acquiring an interest in a registered estate in land, a pre-completion search should be made at the appropriate Land Registry Office.[1] Guidance on making these searches can be found in Land Registry Practice Guide 12. A fee of £6 per title is payable (£3 if made by Land Registry Direct or NLIS). Fees can be paid by cheque (if the application is lodged by post, DX or in person) or credit account, provided that the applicant's solicitor's key number is quoted in the application.

Official search of the register with priority

2.5.2. An application for an official search with priority can only be made by a 'purchaser'. This term is defined in the Rules as a person who for valuable consideration has entered into or intends to enter into a registrable disposition of a registered estate or registered charge.[2]

Application by post or DX: search of whole

2.5.3. Where the interest being purchased, leased or mortgaged concerns the whole of a registered title, the search application should be made on Form OS1. The application will give details of the title number of the property to be searched, a brief description of its situation, i.e. postal address, county and district, and the names of the registered proprietors. The applicant's name must also be given together with his reason for making the search, i.e. he intends to purchase/lease/ take a charge on the land. Where a solicitor is acting both for a buyer and his lender the search application should be completed in the name of the lender client. If this is done the buyer may take the benefit and protection of the search and a separate search in the buyer's name is unnecessary.

2.5.4. The form requests the registrar to provide information on any adverse entries made in the register or daylist[3] since a specified date. This 'search from' date can be either:

(a) the date shown as the 'subsisting entries' date on an official copy of the register; or

(b) the date shown as the 'subsisting entries' date when register entries were accessed by remote terminal.[4]

2.5.5. The search result contains the applicant's name but where, for example, the clients are both the chargor and chargee and the applicant is the chargee, the chargor's name will not be shown. Further, the result does not contain the address of the property, but it does include an applicant's reference of not more than 25 characters (including spaces). It is therefore suggested that the applicant's reference stated on Form OS1 should include sufficient detail (e.g. applicant's or chargor's name and the address of the property or solicitor's file number) to ensure that the incoming search can be returned to its proper file without delay.

Application by post or DX: search of part

2.5.6. Where the interest being acquired comprises only part of a registered title, the search application is made on Form OS2 and must identify the part of the land against which the search is to be made either by the submission of a clearly marked plan of the land with sufficient detail to identify the land in relation to features shown on the Ordnance Survey plan, or by its plot number where the Land Registry has already approved an estate layout plan. Where the application is made on Form OS2 and an accompanying plan is required, the plan must be delivered in duplicate. It is advisable that the same plan is used for the contract, search application and purchase deed. Care should be taken not to search against more land than is included in the contract as the priority conferred by the search may delay transactions in relation to the additional land. In other respects the application is similar to that made on Form OS1.

Application by fax

2.5.7. This facility is available at all Land Registry offices and further information is contained in Land Registry Practice Guide 44. The facility is only open to credit account holders. No additional fee is charged for this service. Applications may be faxed to the specified fax number at the proper office at any time between 8.00 am Monday and 4.00 pm Friday, except:

- after 4.00 pm on the day before a public holiday; and

- on public holidays; and

- before 8.00 am on the day after a public holiday.

The result of the search cannot be sent by fax but is posted to the applicant in the usual way.

2.5.8. The search must be a search of whole of a title on Form OS1, or a search of part of a title on Form OS2 provided that the applicant can either state the plot number of an approved estate plan and the date of approval of the estate plan or attach a suitable plan. The plan must:

- clearly show the extent of the land to be searched (e.g. by thick black edging, hatching or stippling);

- be drawn to a stated scale of not less than 1/1250;

- be sufficiently detailed to allow accurate plotting to be undertaken on the title plan;

- include a north point; and

- not be endorsed with a statement of disclaimer intending to comply with Property Misdescriptions Act 1991 or stated to be 'for identification only'.

Application by telephone

2.5.9. An application can be made (through the Telephone Service Centre) by an applicant who is or who acts for an intending buyer (including lessee and chargee) and must be for a search of the whole title. Further information is contained in Land Registry Practice Guide 61. The telephone call, using the special number allocated for this service, will only be accepted between 8.30 am and 6.00 pm (Monday to Friday) excluding Christmas Day, Good Friday or a statutory bank holiday and 8.30 am and 1.00 pm on Saturday. The application can only be made by a credit account holder. (Official copy entries can also be obtained by this procedure.) On telephoning the registry the following information must be supplied:

(a) the applicant's key number;

(b) name and address of firm holding the account;

(c) if different from (b) above, the name and address to which the result of search is to be sent;

(d) title number of the land;

(e) the name of the registered proprietor (or applicant for first registration);

(f)   (if requested) the county and district or London borough in which the land is situated;

(g)   where the land is already registered, the date from which the search is to be made;[5]

(h)   the applicant's reference (maximum 25 characters);

(i)   whether the search is intended to protect a purchase lease or charge;

(j)   the name of the applicant on whose behalf the search is being made;

(k)   the name and telephone number of the person making the search telephone call or the person to be contacted if there is an enquiry.

2.5.10.   A paper result of the search is normally dispatched to the applicant's solicitor on the same or following working day. The priority period commences from the time the application is entered on the day list, usually at the time of the telephone call. If the search is 'clear' (if there are no relevant adverse entries in the register or pending applications), a guaranteed result will be given over the telephone. Several search applications may be made during the course of one telephone call including searches of the Land Charges Registers. Informal disclosure of entries revealed by the search can be made over the telephone if so requested by the applicant. Such information is not, however, guaranteed by the Registry. Further, a result of a search of the Land Charge Registers (including a result that reveals no entries) given over the telephone is never guaranteed.

Application by personal attendance

2.5.11.   A buyer or a person acting for a buyer may apply orally for an official search with priority of the whole of the land in a registered title. Application may only be made by the applicant attending a Customer Information Centre at a Land Registry office. Such applications may be made between 8.30 am and 5.00 pm Mondays to Fridays (other than public holidays) and 5.00 pm and 6.00 pm by prior appointment.

Application by Land Registry Direct

2.5.12.   An application can be made through Land Registry Direct by an applicant who is or who acts for an intending buyer (including lessee and chargee) and must be a search of the whole title. A fee of £3 is charged for this service. The application will only be accepted between 7.00 am and 10.00 pm Monday to Friday and 7.00 am and 5.00 pm on Saturdays (excluding public holidays). The application can only be made by a credit account holder who is already connected to Land Registry Direct. (Official copy entries of the title can also be obtained by this procedure.) When making the application the information set out in E2.5.9 must be supplied. Full directions on the use of the service are provided to users on installation.

Application via the National Land Information Service

2.5.13. An applicant can apply via NLIS for any type of search, subject to the usual requirements (see B10.17). An applicant must also provide similar information to that required for an application made by Land Registry Direct.

Sub-sales of whole of a registered title or pending first registration title

2.5.14. Where A has contracted to sell to B, and before B completes his purchase he contracts to resell to C, the sub-purchaser (C) will need to make a search against the title quoting A's name as proprietor since at the time of C's application B will not be the registered proprietor of the land.

Sub-sales of part of a registered title or pending first registration title

2.5.15. Where A has contracted to sell part of his estate to B, and before B completes his purchase he contracts to resell that estate or part of it to C, the sub-purchaser (C) will, to reserve priority, need to make a search. The title to be searched will depend upon whether the application to register B's interest is pending in the Land Registry or not. If the application to register B's interest is pending in the Land Registry, the search should be made against the title number allocated to B's application quoting B as the proprietor. If the application has not been lodged, the search should be made against A's title quoting A as the proprietor.

Official search with priority where application for first registration pending

2.5.16. Where an applicant has applied for first registration of his title and has contracted to sell, lease or charge the land to a third party before completion of the first registration, the third party can make a search as if the land were already registered. A search against the whole of the land in a pending application may be made by post, DX or NLIS on Form OS1 or by using the other methods of searching against the whole of a registered title explained above. A search of part can only be made by post, DX or NLIS on Form OS2. The purpose of the search, in relation to a pending first registration, is to ascertain whether any adverse entry has been made in the daylist (i.e. list of applications received by the Land Registry) since the date of the pending first registration application. The date of the pending first registration application does not have to be specified by the searcher. The effect of the result of search will be to give the searcher priority against any other intervening application if he lodges his own application before the expiry of the priority period.

Result of official search

2.5.17. On completion of the application for the official search with priority, a result of search is issued giving the result of the search as at the date and time that the application was entered on the daylist. The information to be included in the result of an official search is specified in Schedule 6 Land Registration Rules 2003.

Priority period

2.5.18. Currently an official certificate of search issued by the Land Registry following an application for an official search with priority gives a priority period to the searcher of 30 business days.[6] A buyer will also take advantage of this protection where a search was made on his behalf in the name of his lender. The searcher will take priority over any entry made during the priority period provided that a correct application for registration of the transaction is received by the appropriate Land Registry office within the priority period given by the search and the application is completed by registration.

2.5.19. The date of expiry of the priority period is shown on the search certificate and should be marked on the outside of the client's file and entered in the solicitor's diary or file prompt system to ensure that it is not overlooked. The application for registration must actually be delivered to the Land Registry before noon on the date on which the priority expires.

2.5.20. The priority period given by an official search cannot be extended. If completion is delayed and cannot take place within the priority period given by the search, a new search application will have to be made. The new search certificate will give another priority period but does not extend the original priority period from the first search. This means that if a third party has made a search or lodged an application in the intervening period, the third party's interest may have priority.

Withdrawal of official search

2.5.21. A person who has made an application for an official search with priority of a registered title or in relation to a pending first registration application, may withdraw that official search by application to the registrar.[7] Such an application cannot be made if an application for an entry in the register in respect of the purchase made pursuant to that official search has been made and completed.

Official search of the register without priority

2.5.22. The searches with priority are only available for use by a 'purchaser' (see E2.5.2). In other situations or where a priority search is not required an application for a search of the register may be made in the following ways:

(a) by post, DX, fax or NLIS – on Form OS3 for searches of whole or part; and

(b) by telephone, Land Registry Direct or by personal attendance for searches of the whole of a registered title.

2.5.23. A search without priority can be used in the following circumstances, e.g.:

(a) when acting for a buyer of an equitable interest in the land;

(b) a lender who is selling under a power of sale should make a search to discover subsequent incumbrances (if any).

Mortgagee's search for homes rights

2.5.24. This search is of limited application and may only be used by the proprietor of a charge of registered land which consists of or includes a dwelling house. The search is available to any chargees regardless of whether or not the charge is registered. The purpose of the search is for the chargee of a dwelling house to ascertain whether any entry has been made on the register to protect a non-owning spouse's or civil partner's homes rights under Family Law Act 1996. A chargee is required to serve notice on such a person before taking action to enforce his security. The search is made in Form HR3 by post, DX, telephone, Land Registry Direct or NLIS.

Outline applications

2.5.25. An outline application can be used to reserve a period similar to a short period of priority for certain interests that cannot be protected by an official search such as a charging order, a homes right notice or a restriction. The interest claimed must be in existence at the time that the application is made.[8] There is no paper form. An outline application can only be made by telephone, personal attendance, Land Registry Direct and NLIS.[9] Guidance on making outline applications and the interests that can be so protected can be found in Land Registry Practice Guide 12.

1. For address see Appendix VIII.I.
2. Land Registration Rules 2003, r. 131.
3. The daylist is a record of all pending applications and unexpired priority searches kept by the registrar under Land Registration Rules 2003, r.12.
4. Land Registration Rules 2003, r.131.
5. *Ibid.*
6. *Ibid.*
7. *Ibid*, r.150.
8. *Ibid*, r.54(2)(b).
9. *Ibid*, r.54(3).

2.6.   Land Charges Department search

Unregistered land

2.6.1. This search is only of relevance to unregistered land. The register is open to the public and can be searched by anyone subject to the payment of the fee (Land Charges Act 1972, s.9).

Applications

2.6.2.   The search is made by submitting Form K15 to the Land Charges Department at Plymouth with the appropriate fee (see Appendix IX.1 for fee and Appendix VIII.2 for address). Fees can be paid by credit account provided the applicant's solicitor's key number is stated on the application form. An official certificate of result of search confers a priority period of 15 working days on the applicant (see E2.14). The search application can be made by post, or by telephone, telex or fax by a credit account holder. Applications can also be made through Land Registry Direct or NLIS. A personal search of the register can be made but it confers no protection or priority period on the applicant.

Name based system

2.6.3.   The register comprises a list of the names of estate owners of land, with details of charges registered against those names. The search is therefore made not against the land itself but against the names of the estate owners.[1] In the case of unregistered land it is necessary for the search to be made against the names of all the estate owners whose names appear on the abstract or epitome of title supplied by the seller, including those who are merely referred to in the bodies of deeds (as opposed to being parties to the deeds themselves) or in schedules attached to deeds which form part of the title. There is no need to repeat searches where a proper search certificate made against previous estate owners has been supplied with the abstract of title.

Variation in names

2.6.4.   The register is maintained on a computer which will only search against the exact version of the name as shown on the application form. It is therefore important to check that the name inserted on the application form is identical to that shown on the title deeds and that if any variations of that name appear in the deeds, e.g. if Frederick Brown is variously referred to as 'Frederick Brown', 'Frederick Browne' and 'Fred Brown', all the given variations of the name are separately entered on the search form and a separate fee paid in respect of each.[2]

Periods of ownership

2.6.5.   It is only possible for an effective entry to be made against a name in relation to that person's (or company's) period of estate ownership of the land in question. Except as below it is therefore only necessary to search against a name for the period during which the estate owner owned the land. For the purposes of the search form, periods of ownership must be stated in whole years and can be ascertained by looking at the abstract or epitome of title supplied by the seller. If the estate owner's period of ownership is not known, as will be the case when searching against the name of the person who was the seller in the document forming the root of title, the search is in practice made from 1926 (the year when the register was opened).

2.6.6. Where there is a voluntary disposition on the title which is, at the date of the contract, less than five years old, it is necessary to search against the donor's name for a period up to and including the fifth year after the date of the voluntary disposition to ensure that no bankruptcy of the donor occurred during this period. The bankruptcy of the donor during this period could lead to the disposition being set aside by the trustee in bankruptcy. (See D2.11.)

2.6.7. Since it is possible to register a land charge against a deceased estate owner after his death, it is necessary to extend the period of search against the deceased to cover the period between his death and the current date.

Description of the land

2.6.8. Unless a description of the land is inserted on the search application form, the computer will produce entries relating to every person of the given name in the whole of the county or counties specified. In order to avoid having to read through and then reject multiple search entries revealed by the certificate of search, a brief description of the land, which is sufficient to identify it clearly, should be included on the application form.

2.6.9. Although the intention of describing the land is to curtail the number of irrelevant entries produced by the computer, care should be taken in supplying the description, since an inaccurate description of the land may result in a relevant entry not being revealed by the search.[3] Particular care is needed when the abstract shows that the land was formerly part of a larger piece of land, e.g. is one plot on a building estate, since the land may previously have been known by a different description from its current postal address. If the search is limited to the present postal address, entries registered against its former description will not be revealed by the search. In such a case both the present address and former description of the land should be entered on the search application form.

2.6.10. Similarly, there is a possibility that the land was previously situated in a different administrative county from that in which it is now situate. For the reasons given above, both the present and former county must be included in the description of the land given on the search application form. In some cases the postal address of the property differs from its actual address, e.g. the village of Rogate is in the administrative county of West Sussex, but its postal address is Hampshire. In such cases the search must be made against the actual address of the property and not its postal address. Guidance on the names of counties as used by the Land Charges Department is given in Land Registry Practice Guide 63 which also provides advice about land charges applications.

Pre-root estate owners

2.6.11. The buyer is not concerned to search against estate owners who held the land prior to the seller in the root of title supplied to him except in so far as the names of such persons have been revealed to him in documents supplied by the seller.

Conclusiveness of the search

2.6.12. An official certificate of search is conclusive in favour of a 'purchaser' which is defined as anyone taking an interest for valuable consideration.[4] This includes mortgagees, lessees and persons acquiring other legal or equitable interests. The search is only conclusive if it has been correctly made, i.e. it extends over the whole period of the title supplied by the seller and has been made against the correct names of the estate owners for this period, against the correct county or former county, and for the correct periods of ownership of each estate owner. In order to ensure that the buyer gains the protection afforded by the search, and the accompanying priority period, it is vital to check that the search application form is accurately completed.

Priority period

2.6.13. An official certificate of search issued by the Land Charges Department gives a priority period of 15 working days from the date of the certificate. The purchaser will take free of any entries made on the register between the date of the search and the date of completion (except pursuant to a priority notice) provided that completion takes place during the priority period given by the search.[5] The date of expiry of the priority period is shown on the search certificate and should be marked on the outside of the client's file and entered in the solicitor's diary or file prompt system to ensure that it is not overlooked.

2.6.14. The priority period given by land charge searches cannot be extended. If completion is delayed and cannot take place within the priority period given by the search, a new search application will have to be made. The new search certificate will give another priority period but does not extend the original priority period from the first search. This means that if a third party has made a search in the intervening period, the third party may have priority.

Previous search certificates

2.6.15. Where the seller provides previous search certificates as part of the evidence of title, it is not necessary to repeat a search against a former estate owner provided that the search certificate supplied by the seller reveals no adverse entries and was made:

  (a) against the correct name of the estate owner as shown in the deeds;

  (b) for the correct period of ownership as shown in the title deeds; and

  (c) against the correct description of the property as shown in the deeds;

and the next disposition in the chain of title took place within the priority period afforded by the search certificate. If any of the conditions outlined above cannot be met, a further search against the previous estate owner must be made.

Sub-sales

2.6.16. Where A has contracted to sell to B, and before B completes his purchase he contracts to sub-sell to C, the sub-purchaser (C) will need to make a search against A's title since at the time of C's search application B will not be the estate owner of the land. B's name should be included on the search (although B will not be an estate owner in the land within the terms of Land Charges Act 1972) because the search may reveal bankruptcy entries against him. If, however, B does become an estate owner before completing the second sale to C, B's name must also be searched against.

1. Land Charges Act 1972, s.3(1).
2. *Oak Co-operative Building Society* v. *Blackburn* [1968] Ch 730 illustrates the importance of searching against all variations of the relevant names. See also *Diligent Finance Ltd* v. *Alleyne* (1972) 23 P&CR 346 and *Standard Property Investments plc* v. *British Plastics Federation* (1985) 53 P&CR 25.
3. *Horrill* v. *Cooper* (1999) 78 P&CR 336.
4. Land Charges Act 1972, ss.10, 17.
5. Land Charges Act 1972, s.11(5).

2.7. Acting for the lender

2.7.1. The lender is, like the buyer, concerned to ensure that the property being purchased has a good and marketable title.

2.7.2. Where the same solicitor is acting both for the buyer and his lender, pre-completion searches in the Land Charges Department are normally carried out once on behalf of both clients each of whom is able to claim the protection (if any) afforded by the search certificate.

2.7.3. Where a Land Registry search is being made the buyer is able to take the protection of the search if it is made in the name of the lender but not vice versa. It is therefore important in this situation to remember to complete the search application form in the name of the lender client. If the application form is completed in the name of the buyer client a second search must be made on behalf of the lender. The Lenders' Handbook requires the search to be made in the name of the lender.

2.7.4. If the buyer and his lender are separately represented, subject to E2.7.3, the lender will frequently accept the results of searches made by the buyer's solicitor, but in some cases may insist on carrying out the pre-completion searches himself. The lender's requirements in relation to this matter should be ascertained in good time to avoid the duplication of work and expense involved in making two separate sets of searches.

2.7.5. No lender will lend money to a buyer who is bankrupt. The lender will therefore always insist that his solicitor obtains a clear result of a bankruptcy search against the buyer (see E2.8) before releasing the advance.

2.7.6. Some lenders may also insist that a search is made against the buyer's name in the Register of Voluntary Arrangements (see E2.8.5).

2.7.7. Where instructions are being carried out under the terms of the Lenders' Handbook paragraph 5.12 requires that the solicitor must certify that entries revealed by a Land Charges Department search certificate do not apply to the borrower client. If they do, the solicitor must report this to the lender.

2.8.   Bankruptcy search

2.8.1.   Irrespective of whether the transaction relates to registered or unregistered land, a lender will require a clear bankruptcy search against the name of the buyer and also against any guarantor of the buyer for the purposes of the mortgage before releasing the advance.

2.8.2.   Unless a full search of the register has been made on Form K15 (see E2.6) the lender's solicitor should submit Form K16 to the Land Charges Department, completed with the full and correct names of the borrower(s) and guarantor(s) (if applicable). See Appendix IX.1 for fee and Appendix VIII.2 for address.

2.8.3.   A search certificate will be returned by the Department.

2.8.4.   In the event of there being an adverse entry revealed by the search, the solicitor should seek to establish without delay whether or not his client is the person to whom the search entry relates. For this purpose he can obtain an office copy entry, and enquiries of the Official Receiver's office may assist in this investigation. The lender must be informed immediately if the search entry does relate to the borrower client (or guarantor). If there is any doubt about whether the entry does relate to the borrower or guarantor, the lender's instructions should be obtained. The solicitor should only certify the search entry as not relating to the borrower or guarantor if he is absolutely certain that this is the case. A certification is tantamount to a warranty given by the solicitor. The client's self-certification of the entry may not satisfy a lender client.

2.8.5.   Where a mortgage is being taken out independently from the purchase of unregistered land the lender's solicitor should make a full search on Form K15 (see E2.6) against the names of the borrowers and any guarantor(s) to ensure that there are no bankruptcy entries or priority notices registered against them. A bankruptcy only search will not reveal priority notices or deeds of arrangement under Insolvency Act 1986. In respect of the latter a search should be made at the Register of Voluntary Arrangements. This register is maintained by the Insolvency Practitioners Control Unit and a search can be undertaken, without fee, by letter or by telephone (see Appendix VIII.2 for address).

2.9.   Probate and administration

2.9.1.   Where a grant of representation is relevant to the title and it appears from replies given to requisitions on title that the seller cannot produce the original or a marked copy of the grant on completion, the buyer should consider making a pre-completion search at the Principal Probate Registry to ensure that the grant has not been revoked or, in the case of a limited grant, that it has not expired.

Alternatively, where the grant forms a link in the chain of title to unregistered land, the buyer's solicitor may ask the seller's solicitor to produce written evidence (i.e. a clear probate search) on or before completion that the grant was valid at the time of the purported disposition. Where the grant was issued by a District Registry there may be some delay before it is noted at the Principal Registry. Therefore a clear search result may not be conclusive. There is a case for saying that the search should be made in all cases where a grant forms a link in the title but in practice this is not the case.

2.9.2. The protection given to a buyer by Administration of Estates Act 1925, s.27(2) that the payment of money to a personal representative in good faith acts as a good discharge to the payer only operates where the grant is valid and had not been revoked at the time of payment. A probate search confers no priority period on the searcher and if where the buyer is buying directly from personal representatives there is doubt as to the validity of a grant, the buyer may consider whether he should require the seller to insist on the registration of the personal representatives as proprietors at the Land Registry before completion takes place.

2.9.3. The search may be made in person by searching the year book for the year of the issue of the grant. If the grant has been revoked, a note of this fact will be recorded next to the entry recording the issue of the grant.

2.9.4. Alternatively an application may be made by letter for a postal search enclosing the appropriate fee (see Appendix IX.1). The application should specify the full names of the deceased, the date of death, and the last known address of the deceased.

2.10. Company search

2.10.1. The effect of Land Registration Act 2002 is that a buyer is not bound by a charge created by a company unless that charge is registered at the Land Registry, or otherwise protected on the register. However, it is suggested that a company search should still be made even in the case of registered land. The company search might reveal, e.g. impending insolvency or that the company had been struck off the register and therefore no longer exists in law.

2.10.2. When buying unregistered land from a company, a company search ought to be undertaken in order to ensure that there are no adverse entries which would affect the buyer. Adverse entries would include, e.g. fixed or floating charges, or the appointment of a receiver or liquidator.

2.10.3. No official search procedure exists for making a company search which must be made either in person or through an agent by attendance at the Companies Registration office or on-line (see Appendix VIII.2 for address).

2.10.4. The search is made by requisitioning the company's filed documents. For documents filed prior to 31 December 2002, these are available on microfiche but after that date copies must be obtained on-line or by applying for hard copies (available by post or fax). The information obtained from the search is thus dependent on both the extent of the instructions given to the searcher and his diligence in carrying out those instructions. The search will only reveal matters registered against companies which are registered in England and Wales (not foreign companies). Equivalent facilities are available in Scotland for Scottish companies. Since company charges need only be registered within 21 days of creation, and are valid in the intervening period, a company search may not reveal a very recently created charge.[1]

2.10.5.   Where the search is carried out through an agent, care must be taken to instruct the agent fully as to the information which it is desired to obtain from the search.

1.   See *Burston Finance* v. *Speirway* [1974] 3 All ER 735.

2.11.   Enduring powers of attorney

2.11.1.   Where the purchase deed is to be executed by a person who is acting under the authority of an enduring power of attorney a search should be made at the Court of Protection on Form EP4 to check whether or not registration of the power has been effected or is pending. For further details see Court of Protection (Enduring Powers of Attorney) (Amendment) Rules 2002 (SI 2002/832) and for address see Appendix VIII.2.

2.11.2.   If no registration has been made or is pending the transaction may proceed to completion.

2.11.3.   If the power has been registered the attorney may deal with the land and thus, provided the donor is still alive, completion may proceed, since the power is no longer capable of revocation without notification to the Court of Protection.

2.11.4.   While registration is pending the transaction may only proceed if it is within one of the limited categories permitted by Enduring Powers of Attorney Act 1985.

2.11.5.   Note that no new enduring powers of attorney can be created after 30 September 2007.

2.11.6.   See D2.9.36 on lasting powers of attorney.

2.12.   Local land charges search and enquiries

2.12.1.   These searches are invariably made before exchange of contracts and are discussed at B10. Although the local land charges search only shows the state of the register at the time of issue of the search certificate and neither search confers a priority period on the buyer, a repeat of these searches before completion is not normally considered to be necessary provided that completion takes place within a short time after receipt of the search results or (in the case of the local land charges search) adequate insurance has been taken out. Delay in receipt of the replies to these searches also frequently makes it impracticable for them to be repeated at this stage of the transaction.

2.12.2. These searches should, however, be repeated prior to completion if:

(a) there is to be a period of two months or more between exchange of contracts and completion and the search has not been covered by insurance or replaced by insurance;

(b) information received by the buyer's solicitor suggests that a further search may be advisable in order to guard against a recently entered adverse entry on the register;

(c) the contract was conditional on the satisfactory results of later searches;

(d) required under paragraph 5.2 of the Lenders' Handbook.

2.12.3. In the absence of a special condition in the contract the discovery of a late entry on such a search is not a matter of title and will not thus entitle the buyer either to raise requisitions about the entry or to refuse to complete. Where there is to be a long gap between exchange of contracts and the contractual completion date, the buyer should try to negotiate a special condition enabling him to raise requisitions prior to completion in respect of any local land charges or adverse schemes and proposals revealed by a local search and enquiries made prior to completion and not revealed by the searches and enquiries made before exchange. Such a condition may be resisted by the seller.

2.13. Other searches

2.13.1. The buyer's solicitor should check to ensure that all other searches which are relevant to the circumstances of the transaction have been carried out and that their results are satisfactory. A checklist of the most common pre-contract searches appears at B10. These searches should normally have been carried out before exchange of contracts but may be required at this stage of the transaction if either there was insufficient time to make them before exchange or since that time additional information has come to light which indicates that a particular search may be relevant. Inspection of the property is dealt with in E4. It should be noted that paragraph 5.2 of the Lenders' Handbook requires searches which have no priority period attaching to them to be not more than six months old at the date of completion.

2.14. Results of searches

2.14.1. The results of searches must be received by the date when completion is due to take place. Completion cannot proceed until these results have been received and are considered to be satisfactory to the interests of the client.

2.14.2. In the majority of cases the results of searches will either show no subsisting entries or will merely confirm information already known, e.g. an entry on the register protecting the contract between the buyer and the seller or, in the case of unregistered land, the registration of existing restrictive covenants. In such circumstances no further action on the search results is required from the buyer's solicitor.

2.14.3. If an unexpected entry (other than a Class D(ii) protecting restrictive covenants, which cannot generally be removed) is revealed by the search result, the buyer's solicitor should:

    (a) find out exactly what the entry relates to;

    (b) if the entry appears adversely to affect the property, contact the seller's solicitor as soon as possible to seek his confirmation that the entry will be removed on or before completion;

    (c) in the case of a Land Charges Department search, apply for an office copy of the entry using Form K19 (see Appendix IX.1 for fee and Appendix VIII.2 for address). The office copy consists of a copy of the application form which was submitted when the charge was registered and will reveal the name and address of the person with the benefit of the charge who may have to be contacted to seek his consent to its removal;

    (d) keep the client, his lender and, subject to the duty of confidentiality, other solicitors involved in the chain of transactions informed of the situation since negotiations for the removal of the charge may cause a delay in completion.

2.14.4. An application form for the removal of an entry from the register in either registered or unregistered land will generally only be accepted by the Chief Land Registrar if it is signed by the person with the benefit of the charge or a person acting on his behalf. An application form signed by the seller's solicitors or an undertaking given by them on completion to secure the removal of the entry may not therefore suffice unless the seller is the person with the benefit of the entry.[1] In the case of registered land, the cancellation of a registered charge may be made by Form DS1, ENDs or EDs. Withdrawals of cautions and restrictions are effected on Forms WCT and RX4 respectively. The application for cancellation of a unilateral notice must be made in Form UN4. An application for the cancellation of a notice (other than a unilateral notice or a home rights notice) must be in Form CN1. As to bankruptcy entries, evidence needs to be lodged that the bankruptcy no longer affects the property.

2.14.5. Charges which are registered at the Land Charges Department can only be entered against the name of an estate owner in relation to the period during which he was the owner of the land in question. Thus an entry which was made before or after this time cannot prejudice the buyer. The computerised system which is used to process these searches will sometimes throw up entries which are clearly irrelevant to the transaction in hand, particularly where the name searched against is a very common one, e.g. John Smith. Having checked that the entry is irrelevant, it may either be disregarded or the seller's solicitor may at completion be asked to certify the entry as being inapplicable to the transaction. Certification by a solicitor is tantamount to a warranty, the consideration for it being completion of the transaction.

2.14.6. The court has a discretion to remove entries which are redundant but which cannot be removed from the register because the person with their benefit will not consent to their removal or cannot be contacted.

2.14.7. Entries protecting a spouse's or civil partner's homes rights under Family Law Act 1996 can be removed on production of the death certificate of the spouse or civil partner or a decree absolute (unless an order under Family Law Act 1996, s.33(5) has been made and registered) or by an order of the court. In the absence of these items, the charge can only be removed with the consent of the spouse or civil partner who has the benefit of the charge.

2.14.8. An official certificate of search issued by the Land Registry is not conclusive in favour of the searcher who will thus take his interest in the land subject to whatever entries are on the register irrespective of whether or not they were revealed by the search certificate.[2] However, where a person suffers loss as a result of a mistake in an official search he will be able to claim compensation under Land Registration Act 2002, Schedule 8, para.1.

2.14.9. An official certificate of search issued by the Land Charges Department is conclusive in favour of the searcher who will thus take his interest in the land free of any entries which are on the register but which were not revealed by the search certificate. Where a person suffers loss as a result of an error in an official certificate of search he may be able to claim compensation from the Chief Land Registrar, but there is no statutory right to compensation in these circumstances. No liability will attach to the solicitor who made the search provided that a correctly submitted official search was made.[3]

1. See *Holmes* v. *Kennard & Sons* (1985) 49 P&CR 202.
2. *Parkash* v. *Irani Finance Ltd* [1970] Ch 101.
3. Land Charges Act 1972, s.12.

E3. The buyer's mortgage

3.1.   Instructions from lender

3.1.1.   Instructions from the lender to act will usually be received at the same time as an offer of mortgage is made to the buyer, i.e. shortly before exchange of contracts. Since each lender's requirements will differ slightly from another, the precise instructions of the lender for whom the solicitor is acting in the present transaction must be noted and strictly observed. The instructions should comply with Rule 3.19 Solicitors' Code of Conduct 2007 (see Appendix I.1). Any queries which arise in relation to those instructions, whether at the outset of the transaction or during its course, must be immediately clarified with the lender. Where the solicitor is acting also for the buyer, the problems of conflict of interests and confidentiality must be borne in mind. Where the same solicitor is acting for both borrower and lender he owes a duty to both clients.[1] These issues are further discussed in A11. Many lenders require their solicitors to obtain evidence of the client's identity (e.g. a passport) and to keep a copy of the evidence of identity on file.[2]

3.1.2.   Where a mortgage is being taken from an institutional lender over residential property it is likely that the solicitor will be instructed to follow the Lenders' Handbook (see Appendix VI.2). The solicitor must check which specific variations to the Handbook are required by the lender to suit both the lender's own requirements and the transaction in hand.

3.1.3.   See also A4 regarding liability under Financial Services and Markets Act 2000 in respect of arranging and advising upon regulated mortgages.

1. See *Mortgage Express* v. *Bowerman & Partners* (1994) 34 EG 116; and *Bristol & West Building Society* v. *May, May and Merriman* [1997] 3 All ER 206.
2. See paragraph 3.3 of the CML Lenders' Handbook reproduced in Appendix VI.2.

3.2.   Investigation of title

3.2.1.   When instructed to act both for the buyer and his lender, investigation of title on behalf of both clients will be carried out simultaneously, but the particular requirements (if any) of the lender must be considered when carrying out this procedure. Any queries which arise during the course of the investigation should immediately be clarified with the mortgagee client since if they are deferred until a later stage in the transaction some delay in completion may result.

3.2.2. When acting only for the lender, the lender's solicitor should request the buyer's solicitor to send him copies of the following documents as soon as the buyer's solicitor has completed his own investigation of title:

    (a)   all pre-contract searches and enquiries with their results;

    (b)   the contract;

    (c)   evidence of title;

    (d)   requisitions on title with their answers;

    (e)   the draft and subsequently the approved purchase deed;

    (f)   at a later stage, all pre-completion searches with their results;

    (g)   any other documents which are relevant to the acquisition of a good title by the lender or which are specifically required by the lender's instructions.

3.2.3. On receipt of these documents from the buyer's solicitor, the lender's solicitor should conduct his own investigation of the title in accordance with instructions received from his client. Any queries on the title should be raised with the buyer's solicitor who will in turn seek an answer from the seller's solicitor. Investigation must be carried out as quickly as possible so that no delay in completion occurs.

3.3. Report on title

3.3.1. Investigation of title having been completed, the solicitor will be required to make a report on title to his lender client certifying that he has carried out a full investigation in accordance with the lender's instructions and that the title to the property is good and marketable. In residential transactions the report on title will be in the form of the certificate set out in the annex to Rule 3 Solicitors' Code of Conduct 2007 (see Appendix I.1); in other transactions the CLLS Certificate and Short Form Report on Title may be used. At the stage when the Report on Title or Certificate is submitted to the lender, there should be no remaining queries on the title, any such queries having been clarified during the course of investigation of title. Notification of queries at this late stage may well result in completion being delayed pending their resolution. If a plan has been supplied by the lender for verification this must be carefully checked before certification. The solicitor may also be asked to advise whether a further inspection of the property by the lender's surveyor before completion will be required. This is usually only required in connection with property which is in the course of construction.

3.3.2.   If the enquiries before contract indicate that works have been carried out to the property, paragraph 5.3 of the Lenders' Handbook makes it clear that the solicitor must ensure that all the necessary consents are available (i.e. both planning and building regulations consents) and there should be no evidence of any breach of any condition attached to any consent. This should be done before exchange of contracts. Solicitors will rarely be in a position to give an unqualified assurance that all the conditions attached to a planning consent have been complied with.

3.3.3.   Local land charge searches on Form LLC1 will reveal if there are any planning charges and proceedings for building regulation breaches. The reply to question 1 of CON 29R Enquiries of Local Authority (2007) should reveal if proceedings have been authorised for any infringement of building regulations. Enquiries of the seller's solicitors, or the borrower himself if he is in occupation, should reveal whether any notices have been received from the local authority complaining of building regulation or planning breaches.

3.3.4.   Any certificate relating to planning matters by the borrower's solicitor should be limited to matters revealed by the usual local searches and by their enquiries of the seller/borrower. It is suggested that reporting solicitors should decline to certify that they are not aware of any matters which would give rise to a breach of planning conditions or building regulation control. Such a statement might lead a lender to assume that the solicitor has undertaken more extensive enquiries than a solicitor would reasonably be expected to make.

3.3.5.   A reporting solicitor can properly go no further than confirm to the lender that searches and enquiries do not reveal evidence of any breach. This should be done before exchange of contracts.

3.3.6.   A solicitor is liable for a report on title signed by his employee (*Nationwide Building Society* v. *Lewis* [1997] 3 All ER 498).

3.4.   Searches before completion

3.4.1.   Searches before completion are an integral part of the investigation of title procedure and should be strictly carried out before a report on title or certificate is submitted to the lender. If time does not permit this, the report on title or certificate should be qualified by a statement saying that the report is given subject to the results of such searches being satisfactory. The searches which need to be undertaken are identical to those which are conducted on behalf of a buyer, subject to the following modifications, and when the same solicitor is acting both for the buyer and his lender will be carried out once on behalf of both clients. Where two separate solicitors are acting for the buyer and his lender, the lender's solicitor should indicate to the buyer's solicitor whether he will accept the results of pre-completion searches made by the buyer, or whether he wishes to conduct his own searches. Where the title being purchased is registered, the buyer may take the benefit and protection of a search made in the name of the lender; thus only one search application is necessary.[1] The converse is not true, so that if the search application is made in the name of the buyer, a second application must be submitted in the name of the lender. Whether or not the land is registered, the lender will invariably instruct his solicitor to make a Land Charges Department search for bankruptcy against the name of the borrower(s) and to obtain a clear result to that search before releasing the mortgage funds into the buyer's hands. Where the borrower is a company a company search should be made against the borrower both as a safeguard against liquidation, receivership or administration and also for potential incumbrances, e.g. debentures which charge after-acquired property.

3.4.2. All searches, both pre-contract and pre-completion must be no older than six months at completion (Lenders' Handbook, para. 5.2.3).

1. Land Registration Rules 2003, r.151.

3.5. Life policies

3.5.1. The lender's instructions in relation to any life policy which is to protect or act as collateral security to the mortgage must be carried out before completion (see Appendix IV.12). In a case where a solicitor is acting both for the buyer and his lender, in his capacity as buyer's solicitor and irrespective of whether the lender requires an endowment policy to be on foot by actual completion, or whether his instructions permit the policy to be obtained within a certain period after completion has taken place, the solicitor owes a duty to the buyer to ensure that the policy is on foot at the date of actual completion,[1] failing which the solicitor might be liable to the buyer or his personal representatives in negligence for any resulting loss, e.g. if the buyer died after completion so that the mortgage had to be repaid before the policy became effective. It is also usual in the case of a new policy to check that the first premium has been paid and that it states that the age of the insured is admitted. If age is not admitted and the age of the policy holder turns out to be wrong, this could have the effect either of invalidating the policy or of reducing the proceeds which are payable under the policy.

3.5.2. Some lenders require a formal assignment to them of the benefit of the policy, in which case such assignment must be prepared (usually on a standard form supplied by the lender) and executed by the borrower. The assignment should be kept with the title deeds to the mortgaged property and after completion sent to the lender for safe custody or otherwise in accordance with the lender's instructions. The deed of assignment is not submitted to the Land Registry when an application for registration of title is made. Where the lender does not require a formal mortgage or deposit of the policy, the proceeds of the policy will fall into the deceased's estate on his death, and may not therefore be available to pay off the mortgage debt. This problem is particularly relevant where one of two unmarried co-owners dies, and the policy taken out by the deceased will fall into his estate and not into the hands of the surviving co-owner. The consequences of non-assignment or non-deposit of the policy should be explained to the policy holder and to potential beneficiaries under the policy at the time when the policy is taken out.

3.5.3. To preserve the priority of the lender's claim to the benefit of the policy moneys, notice of the assignment of the benefit of the policy should, after completion, be given to the insurance company in accordance with Policies of Assurance Act 1867. If the lender does not supply a standard form on which to make this notification, a letter may be sent to the insurance company informing them of the assignment, the name of the assignee (the lender), and the details of the policy which has been assigned. Two copies of this letter or standard form notice should be sent to the insurance company, requesting them to sign one copy in acknowledgement of its receipt and to return it to the solicitor. The receipted copy must then be placed with the title deeds of the property for safe custody.

3.5.4. The lender may require that an endowment policy is put on risk on or before completion of the mortgage.

1. But see *Lynne* v. *Gordon Doctors & Walton* (1991) 135 SJ (LB) 29.

3.6. The mortgage deed

3.6.1. Where the mortgage is granted by an institutional lender, e.g. a bank or building society, drafts and engrossment copies of the lender's standard form of mortgage will be supplied to the solicitor for completion and execution by the borrower. In other cases the lender's instructions (if any) as to the form and contents of the mortgage must be followed and his approval obtained to the draft deed before engrossment. A legal mortgage must be made by deed to comply with Law of Property Act 1925, s.87. In registered land cases, the mortgage deed must identify the registered land which is to be charged, i.e. by its title number or by reference to a suitable plan. A legal charge of a registered estate may be made in Form CH1.[1]

3.6.2. The mortgage deed will be prepared simultaneously with the purchase deed and will be executed by the borrower prior to completion. The borrower is required to execute the deed in the presence of a witness, but in the case of a legal mortgage the lender does not usually sign the deed. If the mortgage is equitable it will generally be a contract for a disposition of an interest in land within Law of Property (Miscellaneous Provisions) Act 1989, s.2 which is required to be in writing and signed by both contracting parties.

3.6.3. The contents and effect of the mortgage deed must be explained to the borrower before signature to ensure that, e.g. the borrower understands that the lender will be entitled to sell the property if the borrower defaults in his repayments. Any prohibitions contained in the mortgage, e.g. as to letting the property or particular conditions attached to it, must also be explained to the borrower and where the charge is an all-moneys charge the effect of this type of charge should be explained to the client.

3.6.4. The solicitor acting for the lender should take reasonable steps to check that the security effected over the property will be valid and enforceable. Problems can arise where, e.g. a 'friend' of one of the co-borrowers ostensibly pretending to be the co-borrower's wife signs the mortgage deed in the wife's place thus vitiating the security. It would appear that a solicitor does not generally have a duty to ensure that the mortgage deed is validly executed by the named borrower(s) but he should be alert to the issues involved and should do what he can to ensure proper execution by the correct persons. Execution by the borrower(s) in the solicitor's presence is a sensible precaution to take, although even this will not guard against forgery where the identity of the borrowers is not known personally to the solicitor (see A24). The Lenders' Handbook does not specifically require the mortgage deed to be executed in the presence of the solicitor but it does require normally the solicitor to check the identity of signatories to documents and to ensure that the lender is supplied with a fully enforceable first charge by way of legal mortgage over the secured property. The Lenders' Handbook also recommends that the mortgage should be signed in the presence of a solicitor.

3.6.5. The lender's instructions will frequently also require the solicitor to discuss repayment of the mortgage with the borrower and may require the solicitor to obtain a signed banker's standing order for repayments from the borrower.

1.   Land Registration Rules 2003, r.103.

3.7.   Mortgage funds

3.7.1. The effect of any retentions from the mortgage advance must be explained to the buyer in advance of completion and, if necessary, the buyer should be advised to seek estimates for any works which are to be effected on the property.

3.7.2. The lender will not release the mortgage advance to the solicitor until he is satisfied that all conditions attached to the advance have been complied with and he has been requested to release the funds by the solicitor acting for him. Such request is commonly made on the Report on Title Form or Certificate of Title, or on a separate form supplied by the lender. The solicitor should ensure that he is in receipt of cleared funds (in order to avoid any breach of Solicitors' Accounts Rules) by the morning of the day of actual completion. The mortgage advance is clients' money and must be placed in a clients' account. If completion does not take place on the anticipated date, the amount of the mortgage advance must be returned to the lender or dealt with in accordance with his instructions, and a further cheque requested for the re-arranged completion date. If the solicitor pays the advance cheque into his clients' account and completion is delayed the solicitor may be liable to pay interest on the amount of the advance if the cheque is not returned to the lender within the time specified in the lender's instructions. The mortgage advance is held by the solicitor (pending completion) on trust for the lender. If the solicitor deals with the funds during this time, except in accordance with the lender's instructions, a breach of trust will occur.[1]

3.7.3.   Any conditions relating to the discharge of the borrower's existing mortgage(s) over the same or another specified property identified by the lender must be complied with before the mortgage advance is released for his use.

3.7.4.   If it is not possible to synchronise a sale and purchase transaction or in any other situation where it becomes apparent that the mortgage funds will not be available in time to complete the purchase, the buyer must be advised of the consequences of a delayed completion and of any decision to use bridging finance in order to complete the purchase on the due date.

3.7.5.   Where different solicitors are acting for the buyer and his lender, it will be necessary for the two solicitors to liaise in order to ensure that the mortgage funds reach the seller's solicitor's bank account in time for completion.

1. *Target Holdings* v. *Redferns (a firm)* [1995] NPC 136, HL and see *Bristol & West Building Society* v. *May, May and Merrimans* [1997] 3 All ER 206.

3.8.   Duty to lender

3.8.1.   Solicitors who do not apply the advance in the manner required by their instructions or who release it before the lender's title is complete may be liable to repay the advance. Until the mortgage is completed, the solicitor may hold the advance on the borrower's client account but it must be clearly identifiable as coming from the lender and will be returned to the lender on demand.

3.8.2.   Where the lender instructs that separate advice must be given to joint borrowers, the joint borrowers must be seen separately.

3.8.3.   Where the solicitor signs a certificate saying that he has independently advised the borrowers,[1] the lender is not under a duty to enquire as to the nature of the advice given.[2]

1. In *Bank Melli Iran* v. *Samadi-Rad* [1995] 2 FLR 367 the court suggested that advice given by a separate solicitor in the same firm was not considered to be 'independent'.
2. *Bank of Baroda* v. *Rayarel* [1995] NPC 6, and see A10.

3.9.   Completion of the mortgage

3.9.1.   Since it is not possible for the buyer to mortgage a property which he does not own, it follows that formal completion of the mortgage cannot take place until after completion of the purchase, irrespective of the fact that the mortgage funds will have been released to the use of the borrower on completion of the earlier purchase. As soon as completion of the purchase of the property has taken place, the mortgage deed can be completed by insertion of the date of completion and any other formalities which have to be entered in it, e.g. date of first repayment. The lender client may require to be informed that completion has taken place. If there is any doubt over whether vacant possession will be given the client should be advised to inspect the property immediately prior to completion.

3.9.2. Following completion of the mortgage, the lender's charge must be protected by registration on the charges register of the title. The solicitor acting for the lender should take possession of all the necessary documents on completion and should effect the registration on behalf of his client. Where separate solicitors are acting for the buyer and the lender, it is usual for the lender's solicitor to require the buyer's solicitor to hand over on completion completed and signed Land Registry application forms.

3.9.3. Charges created by companies must, in addition to any registration at the Land Registry, be registered at the Companies Registry within 21 days of their creation in accordance with Companies Act requirements. The practice now is to file a memorandum of the charge with the appropriate form at Companies House. Additionally evidence must be lodged at the Land Registry that the charge has been registered at Companies House (see G1.6).

3.10. Custody of deeds

3.10.1. The Lenders' Handbook should be checked to ascertain the precise requirements of the lender in relation to the safe custody of documents.

3.10.2. On completion of the post-completion formalities, any relevant documents, e.g. life policy and assignments and notices relating to it, should normally be sent to the lender for safe custody. The documents to be sent should be listed in triplicate, one copy of the list being retained on the solicitor's file, the remaining two being sent to the lender with the deeds with a request that one copy of the list is signed by the lender and returned to the solicitor as an acknowledgement of their receipt. The deeds should be despatched by a method which ensures their safe arrival at their destination, e.g. registered post, document exchange or insured post. If there is to be any delay in the despatch of the deeds, e.g. because of delays in registration at the Land Registry, the lender should be informed of the delay, the reason for it and its likely duration.

3.11. Costs

3.11.1. The lender's costs in relation to the grant of the mortgage are primarily the lender's responsibility since he is the client who has instructed the solicitor, but the lender commonly seeks indemnity for those costs from the buyer who should be informed of this fact and their likely amount at the outset of the transaction. In other cases the amount to be charged must be agreed between the solicitor and his lender client (see N1).

E4. Preparing for completion

4.1.   Introduction

4.1.1.   In order to ensure that completion proceeds smoothly, both parties need to undertake a number of preparatory steps. Most of these steps have been examined in depth in other areas of this book. The following paragraphs therefore concentrate on summarising the matters to be dealt with at this stage of the transaction by way of checklists with some additional commentary.

4.2.   Seller's checklist

(a) Ensure purchase deed has been approved and requisitions answered.

(b) Receive engrossed purchase deed from buyer – has buyer executed the deed (where appropriate) and plan (if used), or has an acceptable undertaking been given that he will execute after completion?

(c) Get seller to execute purchase deed and return it to solicitor in time for completion.

(d) Obtain redemption figure(s) for seller's mortgage(s) and check that they are correct and ensure that the seller's solicitor is aware of *all* the mortgages which need to be redeemed. The redemption figure will be provided by the seller's mortgage company; see the guidance issued by the Council of Mortgage Lenders and the Law Society in 1992 relating to mortgage redemption statements (see Appendix VI.1). Where the redemption figure relates to a 'flexible mortgage', i.e. one where the borrower's savings and income appear in the one account, it may be necessary to ask for the account to be frozen until the redemption figure has been transferred at completion.

(e) Obtain last receipts, etc., where apportionments are to be made on completion.

(f) Prepare completion statement (where necessary) and send two copies to buyer in good time before completion.

(g) Remind client to organise final readings of meters at the property.

(h) Prepare forms for discharge of land charges where necessary (unregistered land).

(i)   Approve any memorandum which the buyer has requested be placed on retained title deeds or grant of representation (unregistered land).

(j)   Prepare any undertaking which needs to be given on completion (e.g. for discharge of seller's mortgage if also acting for the lender).

(k)   Contact lender to confirm final arrangements for discharge of seller's mortgage, method of payment, etc.

(l)   Prepare authority addressed to tenants relating to payment of future rent (tenanted property).

(m)   Check through file to ensure all outstanding queries have been dealt with.

(n)   Prepare list of matters to be dealt with on actual completion.

(o)   Locate deeds and documents which will need to be inspected/handed over on completion and prepare certified copies for the buyer of those documents which are to be retained by the seller.

(p)   Prepare two copies of schedule of deeds to be handed to buyer on completion.

(q)   Prepare inventory of chattels and receipt for money payable for them.

(r)   Check arrangements for vacant possession and handing over keys.

(s)   Receive instructions from buyer's solicitor to act as his agent on completion and clarify instructions with him if necessary.

(t)   Make final arrangements with buyer's solicitor for time and place of completion.

(u)   Ensure estate agents are aware of completion arrangements.

(v)   Prepare bill for submission to client.

4.3.   Buyer's checklist

(a)   Ensure purchase deed has been approved and requisitions satisfactorily answered.

(b)   Engross purchase and mortgage deeds.

(c)   Get buyer to execute mortgage deed, purchase deed and plan (if necessary) and return it to solicitor.

(d)   Send (executed) purchase deed to seller's solicitor for his client's execution in time for completion. The submission of the deed should be in escrow subject to the express condition that the buyer may withdraw if the seller fails to complete.[1]

(e)   Make pre-completion searches and ensure their results are satisfactory.

(f) Make report on title to lender and request advance cheque in time for completion.

(g) Receive completion statement (where necessary) and copies of last receipts in support of apportionments and check it is correct.

(h) Remind client of arrangements for completion.

(i) Prepare forms for discharge of land charges where necessary (unregistered land).

(j) Obtain seller's approval of the wording of any memorandum which the buyer has requested be placed on retained title deeds or grant of representation (unregistered land).

(k) Prepare and agree the form of wording of any undertaking which needs to be given or received on completion.

(l) Contact lender to confirm final arrangements for completion.

(m) Ensure that any life policy required by the lender is on foot and check with client that any other insurances required for the property (e.g. house contents insurance) have been taken out. Prepare and engross assignments of other insurance policies to the buyer (e.g. for damp treatment) if appropriate.

(n) Check through file to ensure all outstanding queries have been dealt with.

(o) Prepare statement of account and bill for client and submit together with a copy of the completion statement, requesting balance due from client be paid in sufficient time for the funds to be cleared before completion.

(p) Receive advance cheque from lender, pay into clients' account and clear funds before completion.

(q) Receive balance of funds from client and clear through clients' account before completion.

(r) Arrange for final inspection of property if necessary.

(s) Prepare list of matters to be dealt with on actual completion.

(t) Check arrangements for vacant possession and handing over keys.

(u) Instruct seller's solicitor to act as agent on completion if completion not to be by personal attendance.

(v) Make final arrangements with seller's solicitor for time and place of completion.

(w) Ensure estate agents are aware of completion arrangements.

(x) Make arrangements for transmission of completion money to seller's solicitor (or as he has directed).

1. Under Companies Act 1985, s.36AA execution by a company is rebuttably presumed to be delivery of the deed: this re-emphasises the need for execution subject to an express condition in such cases.

4.4. Apportionments

4.4.1.   Where completion does not take place on a date when outgoings on the property fall due, outgoings which attach to the land may be apportioned between the parties on completion, the calculations of the apportioned sums being shown on the completion statement.

4.4.2.   Uniform business rate and water rates can be apportioned but it is normally considered better practice to inform the relevant authority after completion of the change of ownership and request them to send apportioned accounts to seller and buyer.

4.4.3.   Where applicable rent and service charge payments may have to be apportioned. These matters are further dealt with in K1 and K5.

4.4.4.   Standard Condition 6.3 and Standard Commercial Condition 8.3 deal with apportionments and allow a provisional apportionment to be made where exact figures are not available at completion (e.g. in respect of service charges).

4.4.5.   The seller must be asked to produce the last demands or receipts for all sums which are to be apportioned so that the calculations of the amounts due or to be allowed on completion may be made. Copies of these receipts should be sent to the buyer with the completion statement to enable him to check the accuracy of the calculation.

4.5. Completion statement

4.5.1.   A completion statement, to be prepared by the seller's solicitor, showing the amount of money required to complete the transaction and how that figure is calculated, will be requested by the buyer when he submits his requisitions on title.

4.5.2.   It is only necessary to provide the buyer with a completion statement where the sum due on completion includes apportionments or other sums in excess of the balance of the purchase price.[1]

4.5.3.   If not sent to the buyer with the answers to his requisitions on title, the completion statement should be supplied in good time before completion to enable the buyer to check its accuracy and to make arrangements for the amount due to be available.

4.5.4.   The statement should show clearly the total amount due on completion, and how that total sum is made up. Depending on the circumstances it may be necessary to take account of some or all of the following items:

(a) the purchase price, giving credit for any deposit paid;

(b) apportionments of outgoings;

(c) money payable for chattels;

(d) compensation if completion is delayed;

(e) a licence fee if the buyer has been in occupation of the property.

4.5.5. Two copies of the completion statement should be sent to the buyer together with copies of any receipts or demands on which apportioned figures have been based.

1. *Carne* v. *Debono* [1988] 3 All ER 485; *Hanson* v. *South West Electricity Board* [2001] EWCA Civ 1377.

4.6. Statement to client

4.6.1. The buyer's solicitor should prepare and submit to his client a financial statement which shows clearly the total sum which is due from him on completion and how that sum is calculated.

4.6.2. In addition to the matters dealt with on the completion statement, the financial statement should also take account of such of the following matters as are relevant to the transaction:

(a) the mortgage advance and any costs and/or retentions made in respect of it;

(b) disbursements, e.g. SDLT, Land Registry fees, fees payable for registration of notices or search fees;

(c) the solicitor's costs.

4.6.3. The financial statement, accompanied by a copy of the completion statement and the solicitor's properly drawn bill, should be sent to the client in sufficient time before completion to allow the client to forward the required balance of funds to the solicitor in time for those funds to be cleared by completion.

4.7. Money – the buyer

4.7.1. On being informed of the amount required to complete, the buyer's solicitor should check the figures for accuracy, verifying any apportionments made against the copy receipts or demands supplied by the seller. Any discrepancies must be clarified as a matter of urgency.

4.7.2. The solicitor should then make a final calculation of the sums due on completion, preparing his financial statement and bill for submission to the client.

4.7.3. If at this stage it appears that there is any shortfall in funds the client must immediately be informed and steps taken to remedy the shortfall. If bridging finance or a further loan are necessary in order to complete the transaction arrangements must be made to effect such arrangements without delay. An undertaking given by the solicitor to repay bridging finance must only be given where the promise given by the solicitor is wholly capable of performance by him (see B16).

4.7.4. The mortgage advance requested by the solicitor from the lender should be received in sufficient time to permit the funds to be cleared through clients' account before completion.

4.7.5. The client must be asked to put the solicitor in funds for the balance of the completion money (over and above the mortgage advance) in sufficient time to permit the funds to be cleared through clients' account before completion. On receipt of the funds from the client, the cheque should be credited to a ledger account in the name of that client.

4.7.6. On the day of completion arrangements must be made to remit the amount due to the seller's solicitor in accordance with his instructions.

4.8. Completion checklist

4.8.1. When preparing for completion the buyer's solicitor should make a checklist of the matters which need to be dealt with on actual completion to ensure that nothing is overlooked. Where the transaction is complex, the list should be submitted to the seller's solicitor for his agreement as to its contents. Where the buyer instructs a person to act as his agent on completion he should, when instructing the agent, send him a copy of the checklist so that the agent is fully informed as to the matters which need to be dealt with.

4.8.2. Some or all of the items in the following checklist will need to be attended to on actual completion.

4.8.3. The list should contain an itemised list of the documents which need to be inspected/marked/handed over/received at completion.

(a) **Documents to be available at completion**

    (i)   contract;

    (ii)   evidence of title;

    (iii) copy purchase deed;

    (iv) answers to requisitions;

    (v)   completion statement.

(b) **Documents to be inspected by buyer**

    (i)   title deeds where in unregistered land these are not to be handed over on completion (e.g. on a sale of part);

    (ii)   general or enduring power of attorney;

    (iii)   grant of administration;

    (iv)   receipts/demands for apportionments if not previously supplied.

(c) **Documents, etc., to be handed to buyer on completion**

    (i)   title deeds;

    (ii)   original lease;

    (iii)   executed purchase deed;

    (iv)   schedule of deeds;

    (v)   Form DS1/discharged mortgage or undertaking in respect of discharge of mortgage(s);

    (vi)   receipt for money paid for chattels;

    (vii) authority addressed to tenants relating to payment of future rent and original tenancy agreements/leases (tenanted property);

    (viii) keys of the property (if these are not available the seller's solicitor should be asked to telephone the key holder to request the release of the keys);

    (ix)   certified copy of any memorandum endorsed on retained deeds;

    (x)   landlord's licence.

(d) **Documents, etc., to be handed to seller on completion**

    (i)   banker's draft for amount due on completion (unless remitted by direct credit);

    (ii)   executed duplicate purchase deed/counterpart lease/licence (where appropriate);

    (iii)   receipted schedule of deeds received from seller;

    (iv)   release of deposit if held by third party in capacity of stakeholder.

(e) **Endorsements on documents if required by buyer**

    (i)   endorsement of assent or conveyance on grant of representation (unregistered land);

    (ii)   endorsement of sale on most recently dated retained document of title (sale of part of unregistered land);

    (iii)   mark up abstract or epitome as compared against the original deeds (unregistered land in respect of any document the original of which is not handed over on completion).

E5. The buyer in occupation

5.1.   Introduction

5.1.1.   In many cases the seller will be in actual occupation of the property until completion and thus the question of the buyer taking possession before completion does not arise. The seller is entitled to retain possession until completion unless otherwise agreed.

5.1.2.   The buyer's request to enter and occupy the premises before completion should be regarded with some caution by the seller since once the buyer takes up occupation he may lose his incentive to complete on the contractual completion date and, if ultimately he does not complete the transaction at all, it may be difficult to evict the buyer from the property. Where the seller has a subsisting mortgage on the property, his lender's consent should be obtained before the buyer is allowed into occupation.

5.1.3.   It is essential that the nature of the buyer's occupation is a licence and not a tenancy in order to avoid the possibility of the buyer claiming security of tenure against the seller.[1] Even where a licence is granted a court order will always be necessary to remove a residential occupier who does not voluntarily vacate the property,[2] and may be necessary in non-residential cases where the tenant will not peaceably surrender his occupation.

1.   See K12. An outline of the major statutes affecting security of tenure is given in section K.
2.   Protection from Eviction Act 1977, s.2.

5.2.   Conditions to be imposed on buyer

5.2.1.   Where it is agreed to allow the buyer into possession the seller may consider imposing some restrictions or conditions of occupation on the buyer. If the contract does not make provision for occupation by the buyer (e.g. Standard Condition 5.2), the terms of the occupation should be agreed in writing and signed by both parties prior to the commencement of the buyer's occupation.

5.2.2.   Some or all of the following conditions may be considered:

   (a)   the occupation shall be a licence and not a tenancy;[1]

   (b)   payment of a further instalment of the purchase price as a precondition of occupation;

(c)   payment of a licence fee during occupation (frequently this is calculated by reference to the rate at which compensation for late completion
is payable under the general conditions of the contract);

(d)   the licence should be non-assignable;

(e)   restrictions on who may occupy the property;

(f)   restrictions on the use of the property during the buyer's occupation
(including an obligation to comply with the terms of the lease in the case
of leasehold property);

(g)   payment by the buyer of all outgoings on the property;

(h)   the buyer to be responsible for insuring the property and/or paying the
insurance premium;

(i)   the buyer to be responsible for repairs and maintenance;

(j)   prohibition on alterations and improvements;

(k)   provisions for termination of the licence by either party;

(l)   entitlement to the income of the property (if any).

5.2.3.   Some but not all of the above conditions are provided by Standard Condition
5.2 which restricts the occupation of the property to the buyer and his household.

5.2.4.   Alternatively, the seller may consider granting the buyer a licence for access
only, e.g. for measuring up for alterations, such licence to be restricted to access
at specified times and for a specific purpose.

1.   See K12. Where the terms of the original contract do not provide for the buyer's occupation, care must
be exercised in drawing up the terms of the licence agreement. Such an agreement does not fall within
Law of Property (Miscellaneous Provisions) Act 1989, s.2 but for certainty should be in writing and
signed by both parties.

5.3.   Delay

5.3.1.   Where there is a delay in completion and the seller sues for specific performance, the court usually gives the buyer the option either of paying the balance of
the purchase price with interest into court or of giving up possession.[1] This
provision is, however, thought not to apply where the buyer takes possession
under a provision to that effect contained in the contract to purchase the
property, e.g. Standard Condition 5.2.[2]

5.3.2.   The seller has an equitable lien over the property which endures until the
purchase price is paid in full (see section M).

1.   This order is known as a 'Greenwood and Turner' order after the case of that name: *Greenwood* v.
Turner [1891] 2 Ch 144.
2.   *Attfield* v. *DJ Plant Hire and General Contractors Ltd* [1987] Ch 141.

5.4. Common law provisions

5.4.1. The seller's position as quasi-trustee of the property on behalf of the buyer, from which stems the seller's duty to take care of the property pending completion, is not affected by the buyer's occupation. Therefore the seller should expressly pass this duty of care (and to do repairs) on to the buyer as part of the licence to occupy.

5.4.2. The buyer becomes entitled to receive the income of the property and is responsible for outgoings.

5.4.3. Unless the contract provides to the contrary, the buyer, by taking possession, will be deemed to have accepted the seller's title and thus loses his right to object to any defects of which he knew at that time (see C5). Standard Condition 5.2.7 reverses this common law rule by providing that the buyer's right to raise requisitions is unaffected by his occupation of the property.

5.5. The buyer

5.5.1. Since the terms of the occupation agreement will normally be construed as a licence and not a tenancy the buyer's position as occupier is somewhat tenuous and he will face certain eviction if he does not ultimately complete the purchase. The buyer should therefore be advised not to spend money on altering or improving the property until completion has taken place. The terms of the occupation agreement will often prohibit the buyer from altering or improving the property pending completion.

5.5.2. If delay in completion is anticipated, the buyer may seek to protect his contract by applying for registration of a notice (a Class C(iv) estate contract in unregistered land) although this may strictly be unnecessary in registered land cases since by being in occupation the buyer may be able to establish an overriding interest under Land Registration Act 2002.[1]

5.5.3. The terms of the occupation agreement should be fully explained to the buyer. In particular his attention should be drawn to the financial provisions since the buyer is often required to pay a further instalment of the purchase price together with a daily licence fee as one of the terms of his occupation. Where the purchase is being financed by a mortgage, the lender's consent to the terms of the occupation agreement should be obtained.

1. Land Registration Act 2002, Sched. 1, para. 2 and Sched. 3, para. 2.

5.6. Sitting tenants

5.6.1. Where the property is being sold to a sitting tenant there is ample justification for accepting a less than 10% deposit on exchange of contracts, or even for dispensing with the deposit altogether (see B17).

5.6.2.   Although the tenant will already be familiar with the physical condition and structure of the property, he should still consider the merits of a survey of the property. In cases where the landlord is responsible for repairs, the tenant will on completion become responsible for the maintenance and upkeep of the property and will thus need to be aware of any major structural defects in it which might affect his decision to proceed with the purchase or his ability to resell the property at a later date. Even in cases where the tenant is currently responsible for repairs he may still consider it wise to have a survey of the property made.

5.6.3.   Even where the tenant is not raising a mortgage to finance his purchase, full deduction of title by the landlord should be required to ensure that the tenant will become registered with an absolute freehold title and thus able to resell the property should he wish to do so. If the title to the tenant's lease is already registered, an application for merger of the freehold and leasehold titles may be made after completion. If the tenant's leasehold interest in the property is subject to a mortgage which is not discharged on completion of the purchase of the reversion, the freehold and leasehold titles cannot be merged.

5.6.4.   The landlord should include a contractual provision to the effect that the tenant will remain liable on the tenant's covenants contained in the lease until actual completion. Without such a clause it could be argued that the lease under which the tenant currently holds the property comes to an end on the contractual completion date irrespective of whether actual completion occurs then or later. This would mean that the landlord would be unable to enforce covenants or to recover any rent from the tenant during the period between the contractual completion date and actual completion. Alternatively a contractual condition may be inserted to the effect that the sale of the property is subject to the terms of the lease, the lease merging with the freehold on completion. The landlord should consider the effect of the contract for sale on his insurance policy covering the property.

5.6.5.   Standard Condition 5.2 (occupation by buyer) does not apply to a sale to a sitting tenant.

E6. Death and insolvency

6.1.	**Death of a contracting party**	6.7.	**Bankruptcy of seller**
6.2.	**Death of sole seller**	6.8.	**Bankruptcy of buyer**
6.3.	**Death of co-owner**	6.9.	**Appointment of liquidator**
6.4.	**Death of sole buyer**	6.10.	**Appointment of receivers**
6.5.	**Death of joint buyer**		**and administrative receivers**
6.6.	**Service of notices on**	6.11.	**Signature of documents**
	deceased estate owner		

6.1.   Death of a contracting party

6.1.1.   The death of one of the contracting parties between contract and completion does not affect the validity of the contract; the benefit and burden of the contract passes to the deceased's personal representatives who are bound to complete.

6.2.   Death of sole seller

6.2.1.   The seller's personal representatives are bound to complete the contract, but cannot actually do so until issue of the grant of representation. Executors derive their authority from the will, administrators from the grant, but in either case the grant is necessary in order to make title to the buyer. Even in the case of executors, it is unsafe for a person dealing with them to rely on evidence of their appointment other than by production of the grant.

6.2.2.   If completion does not take place on the contractual completion date, a breach of contract will occur (irrespective of whether time was of the essence of the completion date) and remedies, e.g. compensation or damages, will be available to the innocent party (see section M).

6.2.3.   A delay in obtaining the grant of representation will have adverse consequences for a buyer who is involved in a chain of transactions since he may be forced to complete his sale, but unable to complete his purchase simultaneously because of the death of the seller and delay in the issue of the grant of representation. Loss suffered by the buyer, e.g. the cost of temporary accommodation may be claimable as a head of damage against the seller's personal representatives.

6.2.4.   If time was not originally of the essence of the completion date, it can be made so by service of a notice to complete. Such a notice can be served on the executor(s) named in the seller's will (if any) and a separate copy of the notice served on the Public Trustee.

6.2.5.   The practical answer to the problem of the seller's death is for the seller's solicitor immediately to inform the solicitors for the other party (or parties in a chain of transactions) and (with the authority of those concerned) to apply for an expedited grant of probate or letters of administration. Obviously the closer the death to the date of completion, the more acute the problem, but even in a chain transaction the parties may agree in the circumstances to postpone completion until a grant is obtained if assured that this can be done with expedition. In any circumstances where delay in completion is likely, consideration should be given to the protection of the contract by registration by the buyer's solicitor of a notice (registered land) or a Class C(iv) land charge (unregistered land).

6.2.6.   Although generally probate cannot issue within seven days of death (administration within 14 days), there is an exception in case of emergency with leave of two registrars. It is considered that leave would normally be granted in this situation where there is a possibility of damages being awarded against the estate and the Probate Registry will assist with quick responses and advice in such a situation.

6.2.7.   A possible solution to the problems caused by the death of the seller before completion is for the executors named in the will to negotiate to allow the buyer into possession pending formal completion. On taking possession the buyer would normally be required to pay a licence fee under the terms of the contract (see Standard Condition 5.2 and E5) which could be offset against the compensation payable by the personal representatives for late completion.

6.3.   Death of co-owner

6.3.1.   Property owned by beneficial co-owners is held on trust and all the trustees must join in any conveyance of the legal estate.[1] The death of one trustee between contract and completion does not, however, affect the validity of the contract.

6.3.2.   Where following the death there still remain at least two trustees of the legal estate, the transaction can proceed to completion without delay. It will be necessary to produce the death certificate of the deceased in order to provide the buyer with evidence of the death. The purchase deed will need to be redrawn to reflect the change of parties to the transaction.

6.3.3.   Frequently the legal estate is held by only two trustees (e.g. husband and wife) and the death of one of them will leave only one trustee of the legal estate which will prima facie be insufficient to satisfy Law of Property Act 1925, s.27. If the trustees held the property as joint tenants in equity, the surviving joint tenant will become entitled to the deceased's equitable interest through the law of survivorship (*ius accrescendi*) and can deal with the property as a beneficial owner provided that there is no restriction on the proprietorship register of a registered title or, in unregistered land, that the requirements of Law of Property (Joint Tenants) Act 1964 are satisfied.

Surviving beneficial joint tenant

6.3.4. Where the sole surviving joint tenant is to transfer registered land the buyer should:

(a) check that no restriction is entered on the proprietorship register of the title;

(b) redraft the transfer to reflect the change of parties and capacity of the seller;

(c) require the seller to provide evidence of the death,[2] for example, an official copy of the death certificate of the deceased co-owner.

6.3.5. Where the land is unregistered the buyer should:

(a) check the conveyance under which the co-owners *bought* the property to ensure that no memorandum of severance of the joint tenancy has been endorsed on it;

(b) redraft the purchase deed to reflect the change in parties. The conveyance should recite the death and state that the sole seller has become solely and beneficially entitled to the property;

(c) make a Land Charges Department search against the names of both the deceased and the survivor to ensure that no bankruptcy proceedings have been registered against either name.

6.3.6. Steps (a) and (c) immediately above would be done as a matter of course during the normal investigation of title procedure and thus do not put the buyer to extra inconvenience or expense (see D2).

6.3.7. If these conditions are not satisfied, another trustee should be appointed to act with the survivor. Where the survivor has become solely and beneficially entitled to the property, delay in completion should be minimal, but normal remedies for delay would in any event be available (see section M).

Surviving beneficial tenant in common

6.3.8. In all circumstances another trustee should be appointed to act with the surviving tenant in common. This appointment can be effected either by separate deed of appointment or by including the appointment in the purchase deed. In either case the purchase deed will have to be redrafted to reflect the change in parties. The seller's solicitor may act as the second trustee provided that there is no potential conflict of interests between the survivor and other beneficiaries (if any). Alternatively, the other beneficiary (or one of them, being of full age and competence) may be appointed as second trustee of the legal estate.[3] If a dispute arises between the trustees in relation to the sale, delay may occur. The contract is, however, binding and such delay will incur liability to the buyer and the refusal of the new trustee to, e.g. sign the purchase deed will not frustrate the transaction since the buyer could seek specific performance of the contract or serve a notice to complete (see section M).

Settled land

6.3.9. On the death of a sole tenant for life under Settled Land Act 1925 the position depends on whether the land remains settled land after the death. If it does, the trustees of the settlement are entitled to a grant of probate or administration limited to the settled land, and they will be the persons with capacity to make good title. If, however, the settlement ends on the death, the former settled land is included in the grant made to the deceased's ordinary personal representatives who will perform the contract.

1. Law of Property Act 1925, s.27.
2. Land Registration Rules 2003, r.164.
3. See Trusts of Land and Appointment of Trustees Act 1996, s.19 in relation to the appointment of new trustees. See also Land Registry Practice Guide 24.

6.4. **Death of sole buyer**

6.4.1. The personal representatives step into the shoes of the deceased and will be bound to complete the contract. Even in the most straightforward case some delay in completion may be experienced because the purchase deed will have to be redrafted to reflect the change in parties and the personal representatives cannot complete until they obtain the grant of representation. Where the purchase was due to be financed by a mortgage, the death of the borrower (the buyer) will usually mean that the offer of mortgage is revoked and the personal representatives may therefore find themselves with insufficient funds to complete unless an alternative source of finance can be found. Where the deceased buyer intended to purchase the house for his own sole occupation the personal representatives may feel that since the purpose of the transaction has been defeated they no longer wish to proceed with the transaction. Unless they can negotiate a written release with the seller they will, however, be bound to complete (and may then attempt to resell the property) or face an action in damages from the seller.

6.5. **Death of joint buyer**

6.5.1. The survivor remains bound by the contract and can be forced to complete. The joint buyers obtained an equitable interest in the property on exchange of contracts and it is possible that the deceased's share in the property may on his death have passed to a third party (not to the co-purchaser) under his will or intestacy. In order to avoid delay while this matter is resolved it may be advisable to transfer the property into the names of two trustees on completion. In any event the purchase deed will have to be redrafted to reflect the change in parties. Finance may have to be rearranged and a new mortgage deed prepared. Some delay seems to be inevitable and the seller will have a claim against the buyer for loss caused by the delay (see section M). In cases where the surviving buyer (being solely entitled to the benefit of the contract) decides that he/she no longer wishes to proceed with the purchase, an attempt may be made to negotiate a written release with the seller, but he is under no obligation to accede to this request. Failing a negotiated release the buyer will have to proceed with the purchase and then attempt to resell the property.

6.6.   Service of notices on deceased estate owner

6.6.1.   If the person serving the notice is at the time of service unaware of the death, service on the deceased at his last known address is valid.

6.6.2.   If at the time of service the person serving the notice was aware of the death, notice should be served on the deceased and his personal representatives at the deceased's last known address and a copy of the notice served on the Public Trustee (Law of Property (Miscellaneous Provisions) Act 1994, ss.10–14).

6.7.   Bankruptcy of seller

6.7.1.   A buyer will usually only be affected by the bankruptcy of the seller if there is a bankruptcy entry shown on the result of his official search or on official copy entries of the title. Such entry may reveal either the presentation of the petition and/or the making of a bankruptcy order.

6.7.2.   On the bankruptcy of an individual who is the sole proprietor of the land, the legal estate in the property owned by him passes to his trustee in bankruptcy and the buyer must from that time deal only with the trustee and not the seller. The trustee may be forced to complete the sale by an action for specific perform-ance, subject to his right to disclaim under Insolvency Act 1986, s.315. Under that section the trustee may, by the giving of a prescribed notice, disclaim any onerous property, which is defined as 'any unprofitable contract, and any other property comprised in the bankrupt's estate which is unsaleable or not readily saleable or is such that it may give rise to a liability to pay money or perform any other onerous act'. 'Onerous' does not in this context extend to disclaiming the contract simply because the trustee can realise more money by entering into some other contract. The trustee might in an appropriate case take the view that the contract constituted a transaction at an undervalue or a preference, in which event he might refuse to complete the transaction on this ground. Assuming the matter proceeds to completion, the purchase deed will have to be redrafted to show the trustee as the seller and the bankrupt will not be a party to the deed.

6.7.3.   Between the making of a bankruptcy order and the time at which the bankrupt's estate vests in a trustee, the Official Receiver is the receiver and manager of the bankrupt's estate, but under Insolvency Act 1986, s.287 his powers in this period are very limited and it is doubtful whether in most cases he would be entitled to complete the transaction. The Official Receiver has, under Insolvency Act 1986, s.293, 12 weeks following the bankruptcy order in which to decide whether to convene a meeting of creditors to appoint a trustee. If the Official Receiver decides not to summon such a meeting then he must give notice of his decision to the court and to every creditor of the bankrupt known to him or identified in the bankrupt's statement of affairs and as from the giving to the court of such notice the Official Receiver becomes the trustee of the bankrupt's estate (section 293(3)).

6.7.4. If a creditors' meeting is held then a trustee may be appointed at such a meeting.

6.7.5. Trust property, which includes the legal estate in land held by co-owners, does not vest in a bankrupt's trustee. The making of a bankruptcy order effects a severance of a joint tenancy. The bankrupt's beneficial interest in the property will vest in the trustee in bankruptcy. Consequently on the bankruptcy of one co-owner the legal estate is unaffected and completion may proceed, the bankrupt and the co-owner being entitled to convey the legal estate. If the bankrupt will not co-operate it is open to his or her co-trustee to replace the bankrupt on the grounds of the bankruptcy under the provisions of Trustee Act 1925. A buyer should attempt to get the trustee in bankruptcy to join in the purchase deed to give his consent to the sale of the beneficial interest and preferably to give a receipt for the part of the purchase money attributable to the beneficial interest, but cannot insist on this happening, nor can the trustee insist on joining in the deed.

6.7.6. See Land Registry Practice Guide 34 as to the evidence to be lodged on registration of a transfer by a trustee in bankruptcy.

6.8. Bankruptcy of buyer

6.8.1. The benefit of the contract passes to the buyer's trustee in bankruptcy who may complete the transaction subject to his right to disclaim onerous contracts. Where the transaction was to be financed by a mortgage the buyer's mortgage offer will have been revoked by the bankruptcy, and there will obviously be no other available funds to complete the purchase. The trustee is in this situation more likely to disclaim, although he would in so doing forfeit the deposit already paid and be subject to an action brought by the seller against the bankrupt's estate to recover loss suffered. Some delay is inevitable pending the appointment of the trustee and while waiting for his decision whether or not to disclaim. Where one of two or more co-purchasers goes bankrupt, the bankrupt's equitable interest will pass to his trustee.

6.8.2. The remaining buyer(s) may have difficulty in completing on the contractual completion date, or at all, since a joint mortgage offer may have been vitiated by the co-purchaser's bankruptcy. If the non-bankrupt buyer can refinance his purchase he may complete the purchase on his own (he is contractually bound to do so) but would hold the bankrupt's equitable interest in the property on trust for the trustee who might at a later stage wish to sell the property in order to realise this asset for the benefit of the bankrupt's creditors.

6.8.3. A seller who wished to force completion on a buyer's trustee in bankruptcy must give written notice to the trustee requiring him within a period of 28 days (or such longer period specified by the court) in which to perform or disclaim the contract and the property. If the trustee does not disclaim within this period the right to disclaim is lost. The seller may at all times pursue the remedies open to a seller where a buyer defaults, including bringing an action for specific performance.

6.8.4. If the seller completes the transaction with the buyer between the presentation of a petition but before the bankruptcy order is made, but having effected a priority search on which no bankruptcy entry appears, the trustee cannot reclaim the purchase price from the seller: this is probably the case even if he is able to prove that after the making of the priority search the seller became aware of the presentation of a bankruptcy petition.

6.9. Appointment of liquidator

6.9.1. Every disposition of a company's property after presentation of a winding-up petition to the court is void if a winding-up order is subsequently made unless sanctioned by the court. Accordingly where a petition for the compulsory winding up of a company is presented the buyer must insist on obtaining the sanction of the court to the completion of the transaction or he must await the result of the petition. In the case of a voluntary liquidation the directors' powers cease on the appointment of a liquidator whether the liquidation is a members' voluntary liquidation or a creditors' voluntary liquidation. A liquidator can complete a sale on behalf of the company and can bring proceedings to force a buyer to complete a transaction. In the case of a compulsory winding up the liquidator will require the sanction of the court to bring proceedings, but in the case of a voluntary winding up no such sanction is required. When a seller company goes into liquidation the liquidator will normally complete the transaction. The company will normally remain as 'seller' and the liquidator will attest the deed on the company's behalf. The liquidator will only become the 'seller' in the purchase deed if an order vesting the legal estate in him has been made by the court, which happens only very rarely. The formalities of a liquidator's appointment are dealt with by Insolvency Rules 4.100–4.105 and a buyer from a liquidator should ensure that those formalities have been complied with.

6.9.2. Where a liquidator is appointed to a company which is buying land, the liquidator has the power to complete or to disclaim an onerous contract in which latter case the position is the same as already discussed under E6.7.1 in the case of an individual buyer becoming insolvent. Non-availability of funds may present practical problems in proceeding to completion. Where the buyer company is in liquidation and does not complete the seller may exercise his contractual rights, including the ability to forfeit any deposit, and in the converse situation the buyer has the right to recover his deposit from any stakeholder. If the matter does not proceed to completion then any damages will be a provable debt in the liquidation.

6.9.3. For the Land Registry's requirements see Land Registry Practice Guide 35.

6.10. Appointment of receivers and administrative receivers

6.10.1. The amendments made to Insolvency Act 1986 by Enterprise Act 2002 came into force on 15 September 2003. With regard to charges completed on or after 15 September 2003 the lender can usually only appoint an administrator.[1] Where a charge was completed before 15 September 2003 the lender can still appoint an administrative receiver. The appointment of an administrator or administrative receiver between exchange of contracts and completion does not affect the validity of the contract. The powers of the administrators or administrative receivers are those contained in the instrument under which he was appointed and in addition he will have the powers conferred upon him by Schedule 1 Insolvency Act 1986. Most of the powers of the directors will be suspended by virtue of his appointment. The administrator or administrative receiver may join in the purchase deed on sale to give a receipt for the purchase price and will execute the purchase deed on behalf of the company. The company normally remains the 'seller' under the contract or purchase deed since if the administrator or administrative receiver enters the transaction in his own name he will assume personal liability for it. The administrator or administrative receiver is the agent of the company (Insolvency Act 1986, s.14(4)). For this reason, any contract entered into in the name of the company will normally contain a clause excluding the receiver's personal liability and excluding the effect of any implied covenants for title from the purchase deed. Where the company is buying land, the administrator or administrative receiver will execute the purchase deed on behalf of the company, but in this situation the financing of the purchase may have to be re-arranged and this may result in some delay. In practice, the administrator or administrative receiver may be unable to complete because of the lack of available funds. Where completion does take place, a certified copy of the document appointing the administrator or administrative receiver should be handed over on completion.

6.10.2. Administrators are appointed by the court, where a company is likely to become unable to pay its debts. Following the administrator's appointment, he will take over the management of the company and will have authority to use the company seal and execute documents in the name of the company. The administrator has much the same powers as an administrative receiver (see Insolvency Act 1986).

6.10.3. Administrative receivers are appointed by, or on behalf of, holders of debentures or floating charges. Their powers are specified in Insolvency Act 1986,

Sched. 1 and include the power to sell and to grant or accept the surrender of a lease. The administrative receiver's powers can be contractually extended in the debenture under which he is appointed (Insolvency Act 1986, s.42(1)). If a receiver uses a power of attorney to sell under a contractually extended power, his appointment should be by deed rather than under hand.[2] Conventionally administrative receivers are appointed under hand and the appointment is regarded as merely identifying the receiver upon whom the debenture confers the power of attorney.

6.10.4. Receivers may be appointed by debenture holders under Law of Property Act 1925, s.101(1)(iii). However, the powers of administrative receivers do not extend to receivers appointed under section 101(1)(iii). LPA receivers have very limited powers under the Law of Property Act 1925, s.109. Therefore, even if sales are arranged by receivers appointed under Law of Property Act 1925, it is better practice to arrange for the appointing lender to sign the contract once his power of sale has arisen and thereafter for the lender to execute the purchase deed or to transfer as lender.

6.10.5. An LPA receiver appointed by a debenture holder *in writing* has the power to bind a borrower to a conveyance of the legal estate in the property charged by the debenture.[3] The irrevocable authority for the appointment of the receiver as attorney for the company is contained in a debenture executed as a deed by the company, the common law rule requiring that a receiver should be appointed under seal was satisfied. In other words, provided that the company has executed the debenture under seal, the receiver can then validly be appointed by the debenture holder in writing alone.

6.10.6. If an LPA receiver sells with a power of attorney in place of a lender, he will not be able to sell the property free of incumbrances and a deed of release will also need to be executed by the lender and any other charge holders. In this instance, care should be taken to ensure the deed of release is executed by the lender after the execution of the transfer, as otherwise there is a risk that the receiver has no power to sell the property due to the determination of his power of sale and power of attorney under the debenture. However, if the lender sells as outlined above, the property will automatically be sold free of the mortgage and will remove subsequent charges from the title.

6.10.7. For the Land Registry's requirements see Land Registry Practice Guide 36.

1. See Insolvency Act 1986, s.72 for the limited circumstances in which an administrative receiver can still be appointed.
2. *Windsor Refrigerator Co. Ltd* v. *Branch Nominees Ltd* [1968] Ch 88.
3. *Phoenix Properties Ltd* v. *Wimpole Street Nominees Ltd* [1989] Ch 737.

6.11. **Signature of documents**

Trustee in bankruptcy

6.11.1. A trustee in bankruptcy should sign a contract using the following wording: 'trustee in bankruptcy of XY a bankrupt [without personal liability]'.

6.11.2. The attestation clause of the purchase deed can be expressed in the following way: 'signed as a deed by CD in the presence of [*name*] (trustee of the estate of XY, a bankrupt)'.

6.11.3. Many insolvency practitioners seek to limit their liability by adding the words 'without personal liability' to the attestation clause. It is understood that these words imply that the trustee can still be sued *qua* trustee, but that liability in him in his personal capacity is excluded. These words do not preclude negligence liability for which most insolvency practitioners will carry indemnity insurance.

Supervisor of voluntary arrangement

6.11.4. The company, individual or mortgagee will execute the document in the normal way unless the scheme is such that the land has been vested in the supervisor or trustee. If this occurs the supervisor must transfer and execute as a trustee.

6.11.5. A contract signed or transfer executed by a supervisor may use the following wording: 'Supervisor of XY acting in the voluntary arrangement of XY [without personal liability]'.

6.11.6. The words 'without personal liability' have the same effect as is noted in E6.11.3.

Administrative receiver

6.11.7. In the absence of any provision to the contrary, Insolvency Act 1986, s.42 and Sched.1 give power to an administrative receiver to execute deeds and other documents in the name of and on behalf of the company using the company's seal.

Company in administration

6.11.8. A deed should be executed using the common seal of the company in the presence of the administrator, or by the administrator signing in the name of and on behalf of the company (Insolvency Act 1986, Sched.1(8)).

Law of Property Act receiver

6.11.9. A Law of Property Act receiver can sign a contract or execute a transfer provided that the appointing lender delegates this power. The authority from the lender should be in writing but under section 1 Law of Property (Miscellaneous Provisions) Act 1989 does not need to be under seal. A receiver signs a contract as agent for the borrower. It is normal practice in these circumstances for the appointing lender to sign the contract and execute the transfer using his power of sale. The capacity in which the lender sells will affect the nature of the implied covenants for title given to the buyer in the purchase deed.

Debenture holder

6.11.10. A debenture holder can sign in the name of the company provided he holds a valid power of attorney from the company. The attestation clause should read as follows:

Signed as a deed by [*name of company*] acting by [*name of attorney*] duly appointed to execute as an officer of [*name of bank*] pursuant to clause [of a debenture dated …] in the presence of:	Sign here the name of the company and your own name with details of the resolution appointing you [*example:* John Smith Ltd by its attorney Jane Brown duly appointed officer of … Bank by a resolution of … Bank plc dated …]

Company in liquidation

6.11.11. A disposition made by a company in liquidation will be executed by the liquidator, who may either use the common seal, in which case he will sign the document to attest that the seal was affixed in his presence, or the liquidator may sign the deed on behalf of the company.

Signature of contracts

6.11.12. To avoid incurring personal liability, any contracts for the disposal of land should be signed by including the extra words 'without personal liability' in order to ensure that a signatory signs as agent and not principal. The following is a suggested example of how agreements should be signed:

'Signed as agent for ABC Ltd without personal liability	Signature of supervisor/ administrator/ administrative receiver/ liquidator/trustee'

6.11.13. After winding up, or after the presentation of a winding-up petition, a better wording may be:

'Signed in the name of ABC Ltd by its [administrator/administrative receiver] JOHN SMITH ESQ. Without personal liability'	Signature: ABC Ltd [in liquidation]

6.11.14. See Land Registry Practice Guides 8, 35 and 36 as to the Land Registry's requirements for the execution of deeds submitted for registration.

E7. Foreign companies

7.1. What is the status of the foreign company?

7.1.1. If it is recognised as a corporation under its foreign law it will be treated as such by English law.

7.1.2. If the status of the company is not clear from its documents, further evidence of status will be needed before an application for registration of title can be made. This will consist either of an unequivocal certificate by the company's solicitors that it is a corporation validly incorporated under the law of its country of origin or a letter from a lawyer practising in the foreign country confirming that the applicant is a corporation under that law. Confirmation should also be obtained of the corporation's power to enter the particular transaction and of the authenticity of a named person or persons to sign the contract/purchase deed on the corporation's behalf.

7.1.3. The information in E7.1.2 does not apply to companies incorporated in Scotland. Companies registered in the Channel Isles or Isle of Man, however, are foreign companies.

7.1.4. Solicitors acting for the foreign company should ensure that any local consent needed for the transaction is obtained. The documents relating to the transaction should also make it clear which jurisdiction is applicable to the transaction.

7.1.5. If the original documents are not in English or Welsh a certified translation should be supplied with an application to register at the Land Registry.

7.2. What are the powers of the company?

7.2.1. This question is not usually relevant in the case of companies incorporated in the European Union nor where there is evidence that the law of the country of origin contains provisions equivalent to the powers conferred by the Companies Acts on trading companies. In other cases, where the land is registered, any limitation on the power of the company will be reflected on the register of title by an appropriate restriction. The constitution of the company will be perused to see what its powers are and, if not clear, evidence of the powers will be requested.

7.3.   Execution of documents

7.3.1.   Foreign Companies (Execution of Documents) Regulations 1994 (SI 1994/950) have the effect of making Companies Act 1985, s.36(A) (as amended) apply to foreign companies. Section 36(A) abolished the requirement for a company to execute a deed by using its company seal. Prior to 1994 this section was until then of little use to foreign companies, which in many cases did not have company seals of the type used in England and Wales. Although the intention of the Rules is to allow foreign companies to execute deeds by the same method as applies to English companies, thus dispensing with the need for proof of due execution under the jurisdiction of incorporation, the Rules actually deem a deed to be correctly executed by a foreign company if the execution complies with the rules of execution under the jurisdiction of the company's incorporation. It may still therefore be necessary to provide proof that the execution of the document complies with foreign law.

7.3.2.   Schedule 9 Land Registration Rules 2003 contains a form of execution to deal with execution by foreign companies without using a common seal. The prescribed form of execution in Form E is as follows:

Signed as a deed on behalf of [*name of company*] a company incorporated in [*territory*], by [*full name(s) of person(s) signing*], being [a] person[s] who, in accordance with the laws of that territory, [is] [are] acting under the authority of the company.	Signature Authorised signatory [*or* signatories]

7.3.3.   In the case of an overseas company having a common seal, the form of execution appropriate to a company registered under the Companies Acts may be used, with such adaptations as may be necessary, in place of execution by a person or persons acting under the authority of the company. See also Land Registry Practice Guide 8.

7.4.   Disposals by foreign companies

7.4.1.   When a foreign company is disposing of property which it owns the following question is relevant: does the company have power to make the disposition? This will only be of concern where a restriction is already on the register. Provided the terms of the restriction can be complied with the transaction can proceed.

F. COMPLETION

F1. Date and time of completion

1.1.   **Date**   **1.2.**   **Time**

1.1.   Date

1.1.1.   The date of completion will be agreed between the solicitors for the parties (after consultation with their respective clients) shortly before exchange of contracts.

1.1.2.   Where the buyer's purchase is dependent on his sale of another property the completion dates in both contracts must be synchronised. It follows that the completion dates in all transactions in a chain of transactions must also be synchronised if the chain is not to break.

1.1.3.   In residential transactions a completion date 28 days or less from the date of exchange is common. Sufficient time must be allowed between exchange and completion for the respective solicitors to undertake the pre-completion steps in the transaction. If it is anticipated that the clients will wish to complete very quickly after exchange, arrangements can usually be made for some of the pre-completion steps in the transaction to be effected before exchange, e.g. preparation of the purchase deed.

1.1.4.   In the absence of express agreement Standard Condition 6.1.1 and Standard Commercial Property Condition 8.1.1 provide that completion shall take place on the 20th working day after exchange.

1.1.5.   Under Standard Condition 6.1.1 and Standard Commercial Property Condition 8.6.1 time is not of the essence of the completion date (unless a notice to complete has been served). Thus although a delay in completion beyond the date fixed in the contract would give rise to an action in damages at the instigation of the innocent party and would activate the compensation provisions of Standard Condition 7.3 and Standard Commercial Property Condition 9.3, the delay would not of itself entitle the innocent party to withdraw from the contract at that stage (see section M). In the absence of this provision time would be of the essence of the completion date (thus enabling the innocent party to withdraw from the contract if delay occurs) where the common law so provides, e.g. in the case of the sale of a business as a going concern. Since delay in completion can occur for reasons beyond the control of the contracting parties, e.g. postal delays, it is not generally a good idea to make time of the essence of the completion date. If exceptionally it is desired to make time of the essence, this may be done by inserting an express provision to this effect in the contract, e.g. by adding the words 'as to which time shall be of the essence' alongside the insertion of the contractual completion date.

1.2. Time

1.2.1.   Where a buyer's purchase is dependent on the receipt of money from a related sale, the solicitor must ensure that arrangements are made to complete the sale before the purchase to allow funds received from the sale to be utilised in the purchase.

1.2.2.   Where the transaction is part of a chain such arrangements may be complex. Most contracts do not require completion to take place by a certain time, but merely provide that, where the completion money arrives at the nominated bank after a specified time (e.g. 2 pm), it is deemed to have arrived on the next working day for certain purposes (e.g. so as to entitle the seller to compensation). Special conditions may however require completion to take place at a specified time. In practice, particularly if the chain is long, funds will be transferred from the first (time) buyer as early as 9 am and the funds will travel by a series of inter-bank telegraphic transfers until the deadline of 2 pm or even later. Security is maintained in two ways. First each solicitor will not transmit purchase funds until after the sale proceeds reach his bank. Second, the keys to the property being sold will not be released to the buyer or his agent until the seller's solicitor has received the purchase funds.

1.2.3.   Even where a seller has no related purchase, he should ensure that the completion time agreed allows sufficient time for the proceeds of sale to be banked on the day of completion. If the money is not banked or remitted to the mortgagee until the following working day the seller will suffer loss of interest on his money. To this end a completion time later than 2 pm is inadvisable.

1.2.4.   Provided each set of funds reaches its destination before bank closing on the day of completion, the strict timetable of 2 pm is unlikely to be enforced. Nevertheless, Standard Condition 6.1.2 and Standard Commercial Property Condition 8.1.2 provide that if completion does not take place by 2 pm on the day of completion, compensation for late completion becomes payable. It is therefore important for the solicitor to ensure that there is as little delay as possible between receipt of the sale proceeds and release of the purchase money so that his client does not become liable to pay compensation at the contractual interest rate for the delay which he cannot, in turn, recover from his buyer. Standard Condition 6.1.2 and Standard Commercial Property Condition 8.1.2 do not apply where the sale is with vacant possession and the seller has not vacated the property by 2 pm on the date of actual completion.[1]

1.   Standard Condition 6.1.3 and Standard Commercial Property Condition 8.1.3.

F2. Place of completion

2.1.   Place of completion

2.1.1.   By Standard Condition 6.2.2 and Standard Commercial Property Condition 8.2 completion is to take place in England and Wales, either at the seller's solicitor's office or at some other place which the seller reasonably specifies.

2.1.2.   These conditions mirror the convention that the money goes to the deeds.

2.1.3.   Where the seller has an undischarged mortgage over the property and the seller's solicitor is not also acting for the lender, completion may be required to take place at the offices of the seller's lender's solicitors.

2.1.4.   Where there is a complex chain of transactions it may sometimes be convenient for some or all of the solicitors for the parties involved in the chain to meet at a mutually convenient location in order to complete several of the transactions in the chain within a very short interval.

2.1.5.   Under Standard Condition 6.2.2 and Standard Commercial Property Condition 8.2 the choice of venue for completion is given to the seller. If completion is not to take place at the seller's solicitor's office he should give the buyer's solicitor sufficient notice of the chosen venue to allow the buyer's solicitor to make his arrangements for attendance at completion and/or transmission of funds. If possible, the buyer's solicitor should be informed of the venue for completion in the answers given to his requisitions on title.

2.1.6.   Although traditionally the buyer's solicitor attends the seller's solicitor's office in person to effect completion, it is usual (especially in residential transactions) for completion to be effected by using the Law Society's Code for Completion by Post (see Appendix II.3) with the transmission of funds being made directly to the seller's solicitor's bank account. In such cases the actual place of completion is of little significance to the transaction so long as both parties' solicitors are able to contact each other by telephone, fax or email to confirm the transmission and receipt of funds on the day of completion itself.

2.1.7.   If the sale is with vacant possession and the buyer is in doubt whether or not the seller will comply with this condition (e.g. because of the presence of tenants or other non-owning occupiers in the property) he may consider the benefits of insisting on completion taking place at the property itself following an inspection of the property. The buyer may also wish to complete at the property if he, for other reasons, needs to inspect the property or its contents before completion, e.g. to check an inventory of stock or fittings. In such cases the buyer should have included a special condition in the contract stating that completion shall take place at the property, or, if this was not possible, make his request to the seller's solicitor in adequate time before completion to permit the necessary arrangements to be made. Unless such a term is included as a contractual condition, the seller is under no obligation to accede to the buyer's request since the choice of location for completion is, by Standard Condition 6.2.2 and Standard Commercial Property Condition 8.2, given to the seller.

F3. The money

3.1.   Method of payment

3.1.1.   Standard Condition 6.7 and Standard Commercial Property Condition 8.7 provide that the buyer is to pay the money due on completion by direct credit and, if appropriate, by an unconditional release of a deposit held by a stakeholder. Payment by any other method than direct credit requires express amendment to the Conditions.

3.1.2.   Direct credit is a direct transfer (frequently referred to in practice as a telegraphic transfer (TT)) of cleared funds to an account nominated by the seller's solicitor and maintained at a clearing bank. A clearing bank is a bank which is a shareholder in CHAPS Clearing Co. Ltd.

3.1.3.   In the absence of agreement to the contrary, the seller's solicitor is entitled to refuse payment tendered by any method other than those mentioned in the contract. A special condition in the contract is required if payment is to be made in foreign currency or out of the jurisdiction.

3.1.4.   Notes and gold coins are legal tender up to any amount,[1] but other coins are subject to the limits imposed in Coinage Act 1971, s.2. Currently these limits restrict payment by cupro-nickel or silver coins with a value exceeding 10p (including £1 coins) to a maximum face value of £10. Payment by cupro-nickel or silver coins with a face value not exceeding 10p are limited to a maximum of £5, and bronze coins to a maximum of £0.20. Due to the increased liability under Money Laundering Regulations 2003 and Proceeds of Crime Act 2002, solicitors should be wary of accepting cash unless the legitimate source of the funds has been verified.

3.1.5.   Provided the parties agree, payment of money on completion may be made by a solicitor's clients' account cheque or building society cheque, but in practice payment by such methods is uncommon since there is the danger that the cheque could in theory be stopped. A 'stop' on a building society cheque would in practice be very rare and is generally confined to cases of theft, forgery, or fraud.

1.   Currency and Bank Notes Act 1954, s.1.

3.2.   **Banker's draft**

3.2.1.   Where completion is to take place in person payment by banker's draft is the most common method of payment.

3.2.2.   The buyer's solicitor may have the draft drawn in favour of the seller's solicitor (or as he has directed) or may prefer to have the draft drawn to show the buyer's solicitor as payee. In the latter case, the draft will be endorsed in favour of the seller's solicitor at actual completion, but can easily be paid back into the buyer's solicitor's clients' account should completion for some reason not take place on the due date. The draft should not be marked 'account payee only' or 'not negotiable' since the seller's solicitor may wish to endorse the draft to a third party, e.g. to use towards payment in another transaction.

3.2.3.   A banker's draft can be regarded as being analogous to cash. It is therefore sensible to take precautions against forgery and theft of a draft. For this reason it may be considered to be unwise to send a banker's draft through the post and, where completion is to take place through the post or through the attendance of an agent, some other method of transmission of funds should be used.

3.3.   **Direct credit transfer of funds**

3.3.1.   Frequently completion will take place using the Law Society's Code for Completion by Post (see Appendix II.3). In such a case the parties will normally agree to transfer the amount of money needed to complete the transaction through the telegraphic transfer (or similar) system. Payment under a contract governed by the Standard Conditions of Sale or the Standard Commercial Property Conditions must be by way of direct credit (unless the contract has been amended to provide otherwise).

3.3.2.   The seller's solicitor should inform the buyer's solicitor of the amount needed to complete the transaction and of the details of the account to which the funds are to be remitted. This information is normally given in response to the buyer's requisitions on title.

3.3.3.   The buyer's solicitor should instruct his bank to remit funds from the buyer's solicitor's clients' account to the account nominated by the seller's solicitor. Instructions to the bank must be given sufficiently early on the day of completion to ensure that the funds arrive at their destination before the time limit for receipt of funds, as specified in the contract, expires. Some delay in the transmission of funds may be experienced where the funds are to be transmitted from one bank to another as opposed to transfers between different branches of the same bank.

3.3.4.   The seller's bank should be asked to telephone the seller's solicitor to inform him of the receipt of the funds immediately they arrive. Completion may proceed as soon as the seller's solicitor is satisfied as to the arrival of the funds in his clients' account, and it is courteous for him to confirm the safe arrival of the funds to the buyer's solicitor.

3.4. Cleared funds

3.4.1. In order to avoid breach of Rule 22 Solicitors' Accounts Rules 1998, payment of completion money should only be made from cleared funds in client account. This means that the buyer's solicitor must ensure that he is put in funds by his client in sufficient time for those funds to clear through client account before it becomes necessary to draw against them.

3.5. Time for payment

3.5.1. Standard Condition 6.1.2 and Standard Commercial Property Condition 8.1.2 encourage the payment of money on the day of completion by 2 pm in default of which payment is treated (for compensation purposes only) as having been received on the next following working day which may result in the buyer becoming liable to pay compensation for late completion under Condition 7.3 of both sets of conditions. Standard Condition 6.1.2 and Standard Commercial Property Condition 8.1.2 do not apply where the sale is with vacant possession and the seller has not vacated the property by 2 pm on the date of actual completion. See Standard Condition 6.1.3 and Standard Commercial Property Condition 8.1.3.

3.5.2. Where the transaction forms part of a chain of transactions it may be necessary to insert a time limit for the payment of completion money imposing a contractual obligation to complete by this specified time (see F1.2.2). If this is not done, there is a danger that the seller will not receive the funds from his sale in sufficient time to allow him to meet the time limit in his related purchase transaction.

3.6. Chain transactions

3.6.1. As noted in F3.5.2, it will frequently be necessary to insert a special condition relating to the time of completion in order to allow sufficient time for funds to be received by the seller's solicitor and then utilised to complete a purchase transaction later on the same day.

3.6.2. Where it is known that the transaction forms part of a chain arrangements may be made by the solicitors involved for the funds to be sent directly to their ultimate destination. Thus if A is selling to B and buying from C, he may need to use part of the proceeds of sale (to be paid by B) towards payment for his purchase from C. In this case A's solicitor may ask B's solicitor to send a specified part of the sale money direct to C's solicitor, the remainder being sent to A's solicitor in the normal way. C's solicitor must be asked to telephone A's solicitor when he receives the funds from B's solicitor so that the transaction between A and B can be completed. C's solicitor will also be asked to undertake to hold the funds received from B's solicitor to A's order until completion of the transaction between A and C is ready to proceed. Such an arrangement can help to avoid delays in the transmission of funds, since fewer telegraphic transfers are required (particularly in a long chain), and thus it ultimately helps to ensure that all transactions within the chain are completed within their relevant time limits. The solicitors involved must nevertheless be careful to obtain the written authority of the parties since the protection given by Law of Property Act 1925, s.63, only applies where the money is paid to the seller's solicitor. It is a breach of trust for the buyer's solicitor to part with the money without having the title deeds in his possession or without knowing that the seller's solicitor is holding the deeds to the buyer's solicitor's order.

3.7. Discharge of seller's mortgage

3.7.1.   The seller's existing mortgage over the property being sold will frequently be discharged immediately after completion of the sale using part of the proceeds of sale to make payment to the lender.

3.7.2.   The seller's solicitor may choose to ask the buyer to draw separate banker's drafts for completion, one in favour of the lender for the amount needed to discharge the mortgage and the other, for the balance of the money due, in the seller's solicitor's favour.

3.7.3.   Alternatively, where payment is to be made by direct credit transfer, the seller's solicitor may request that a direct transfer is made to the separately represented mortgagee's solicitor, and a second transfer, for the balance of funds due, to the seller's solicitor. The method for achieving this is broadly similar to the method described in F3.6.2.

3.7.4   If the seller had a 'flexible mortgage' on his property the solicitor should have requested that the account be frozen from the time when the mortgage redemption statement was prepared until completion. This is due to the fact that the amount outstanding on such mortgages can vary depending upon the amount of the seller's savings and income in the account. To ensure that the redemption figure is accurate at completion the account must be frozen at the date of the redemption statement.

3.8. Undertakings to remit funds

3.8.1.   In exceptional circumstances the seller's solicitor may be prepared to complete the transaction against the buyer's solicitor's undertaking to remit funds within a specified time, the actual transfer of the money occurring after completion has taken place. The seller's solicitor should only do this if he has his client's authority to do so, and the client understands the consequences of completing against an undertaking. The seller may have an equitable lien over the property for money not paid which should be protected against a subsequent buyer (see M8.1).

3.8.2. Such an undertaking given by the buyer's solicitor is binding on him and should therefore not be given unless the buyer's solicitor is absolutely certain that he will be put in funds in sufficient time to comply with his promise to the seller's solicitor.

3.8.3. If completion does take place on the strength of the buyer's solicitor's undertaking, the seller is bound to complete and may not retain possession of the title deeds and other documents even if the money does not arrive when promised. By Standard Condition 6.5.1 and Standard Commercial Property Condition 8.5.1, the seller is not entitled to a lien over the title deeds after completion.

3.9. Release of deposit

3.9.1. A deposit which is held in the capacity of agent for the seller belongs to the seller and does not need to be released on completion.

3.9.2. Where a deposit is held by some person in the capacity of stakeholder, the buyer's solicitor should on completion provide the seller's solicitor with a written release addressed to the stakeholder, authorising payment of the deposit to the seller or as he directs. Where the deposit is being held by the seller's solicitor as stakeholder, a written release is often neither asked for nor provided, the release being given orally once completion has taken place. If the deposit is being held by a third party, e.g. an estate agent in the capacity of stakeholder, a written release will be required. In the absence of a written release the stakeholder, on being satisfied that the conditions under which he holds the money have been fulfilled, may pay the stake money to the party whom he considers entitled to receive it, subject to his becoming liable to account to the other party if he makes the wrong judgment in relation to the handing over of the money.[1]

1. *Hastingwood Property Ltd* v. *Saunders Bearman Anselm* [1991] Ch 114.

3.10. Retentions from the purchase price

3.10.1. Where it has been agreed that a retention should be deducted from the purchase price on completion, e.g. to cover the cost of outstanding works to be done by the seller, the agreement should be expressly clear as to whether interest is payable on the retained sum and to whom, and whether the buyer is to withhold the sum on completion or, e.g. to pay the full purchase price to the seller's solicitor with the amount of the agreed retention being held by the seller's solicitor in a deposit account opened in the joint names of the seller and buyer until the matter is resolved. It is also desirable to agree that if the obligation secured by the retention money has not been performed by a particular date, the retention money would be remitted back to the buyer to deal with the matter instead, and if it costs more than the retention money to do so, the buyer can claim the deficit from the seller.

3.11.   Money laundering[1]

3.11.1.   Where a transaction is being funded by the client in cash, or via a third party (other than a recognised lender) or from a foreign bank, the solicitor should be alert to the possibilities of money laundering and should take appropriate steps to check the identity of the client and the source of the funds.

1.   See A23.

F4. Completion

4.1. Introduction

4.1.1. The date and time of actual completion will be specified in the contract but may be varied by subsequent agreement between the parties. Similarly the place and method of completion will previously have been agreed by the parties.

4.1.2. Completion may take place by personal attendance by the buyer's solicitor or his agent or through the post using the Law Society's Code for Completion by Post (see Appendix II.3).

4.2. Completion by personal attendance

4.2.1. Personal attendance by the buyer's solicitor on the seller's solicitor or seller's lender's solicitor is the traditional method by which completion takes place but is not commonly used in uncomplicated transactions where, particularly in residential conveyancing, it is now more common for completion to take place through the post.

4.2.2. If the transaction is complex or of a high value, consideration should be given to the benefits of completing the matter in person since, when this method is employed, the buyer's solicitor is able physically to inspect all the relevant documents prior to handing over the purchase price; he takes possession of those documents immediately completion has taken place instead of having to rely on the seller's solicitor's undertaking to forward the documents to him, and there is therefore absolute certainty that all the documents are in order and that completion has taken place at a specific time. Against these benefits may be set the time and expense involved in the buyer's solicitor having to travel to the seller's solicitor's office in order to attend personally at completion.

4.2.3. A few days before the date arranged for completion the buyer's solicitor should telephone the seller's solicitor to arrange a mutually convenient appointment for completion.

4.2.4. On the morning of completion or on the day before completion arrangements should be made for completion money to be sent by direct transfer to the seller's solicitor's bank account (or as agreed under the contract). Alternatively, a banker's draft for the amount required to complete the transaction should be drawn by the buyer's solicitor and kept in a safe place until it is needed (see F3).

4.2.5. The representative from the buyer's solicitors who is to attend completion should take with him to the seller's solicitor's office the following items:

(a) the contract (queries which arise may sometimes be resolved by checking the terms of the contract);

(b) evidence of title (in order to verify the title);

(c) a copy of the approved draft purchase deed and of any other documents which are to be executed by the seller and handed over on completion (in case there is any query over the engrossments);

(d) answers to requisitions on title (some queries which arise, e.g. over who has the keys may be resolved by the answers previously given to requisitions);

(e) the completion checklist and completion statement (see E4);

(f) banker's draft (if this method of payment is to be used);

(g) any documents which are required to be handed over to the seller's solicitor on completion, e.g. release of deposit.

Verifying title

4.2.6. The buyer's time limit for verifying title, i.e. comparing the original deeds against the evidence of title supplied by the seller, expires with the time limit for raising requisitions. Under Standard Condition 4.3.1 and Standard Commercial Property Condition 6.3.1 the buyer must raise his requisitions within six working days after the date of the contract or delivery of evidence of title by the seller, whichever is later. In practice, where title is deduced before exchange of contracts, the right to raise requisitions on certain matters after exchange will be precluded by Standard Condition 4.2.1 and Standard Commercial Property Condition 6.2.1.

4.2.7. Strictly therefore the buyer has no right to verify at this stage. In practice verification is not normally carried out at the requisitions on title stage of the transaction unless the transaction is complicated and the buyer's solicitor will check the evidence of title against the original deeds at completion itself. It should, however, be remembered that since the time limit for verification has now expired, the buyer will have no right to query any defect which he discovers on verification, nor to refuse to complete because of a defect discovered at this stage.

4.2.8. In the case of registered land verification is unnecessary since official copy entries of the title will show the current position of the register.

4.2.9. On a sale by a lender under his power of sale, it is not necessary to obtain discharges relating to subsequent mortgages which will be overreached on the completion of the sale by the selling lender.

4.2.10. When the buyer's solicitor is satisfied as to the title, he should ask the seller's solicitor to hand over the documents necessary to complete the transaction. These documents including the title deeds (in unregistered land) will have been previously agreed in a list drawn up between the parties and itemised on the completion checklist. Except where these documents have recently been checked by verification, the buyer's solicitor should check each document to ensure it is as he expects to find it, and tick each off on his list as he receives it. The purchase deed will be among the documents to be received by the buyer's solicitor and should be dated at completion after being checked by the buyer's solicitor to ensure it has been validly executed and has not been altered since the buyer last saw the document. The seller's solicitor will have prepared a schedule of deeds in duplicate, one copy of which will be handed to the buyer's solicitor to keep; the other should be signed by the buyer's solicitor when he is satisfied that he has received all the documents listed on it, and returned to the seller's solicitor as evidence for his file of the handing over of the deeds.

4.2.11. Depending on the circumstances it may be necessary for the buyer's solicitor to inspect receipts for, e.g. last payment of outgoings where such items have been apportioned on the completion statement. Copies of these receipts should have been supplied to the buyer's solicitor with the completion statement in order to allow him to check the amount of the apportionments. By Standard Condition 6.6 and Standard Commercial Property Condition 8.6 the buyer is required to assume that whoever gave any receipt for the payment of rent, rentcharge or a service charge which the seller produces was the person or agent of the person then entitled to that rent or service charge. In the absence of this condition from the contract Law of Property Act 1925, s.45(2) requires the buyer to make the same assumptions in respect of rent and rentcharges.

4.2.12. Where the sale includes fittings or chattels, a separate receipt for the money paid for those items should be signed by the seller's solicitor and handed to the buyer's solicitor. A copy of the receipt should be retained by the seller's solicitor. The receipt clause in the purchase deed only operates as a receipt for the money paid for the land; therefore a separate receipt for the money paid for chattels is necessary.

Discharge of seller's mortgage

4.2.13. Arrangements for the discharge of the seller's mortgage(s) over the property will have been agreed between the parties at the requisitions on title stage of the transaction. Where the mortgage is a first mortgage of the property in favour of a building society lender, the parties will frequently have agreed to permit the seller to discharge his mortgage after completion takes place by using part of the proceeds of sale to make payment to the lender. In such a case it will have been agreed that the seller's lender's solicitor should hand to the buyer's solicitor on completion an undertaking in the form of wording recommended by the Law Society to discharge the mortgage (F4.2.15) and to forward the receipted deed or Form DS1 to the buyer's solicitor as soon as this is received from the lender. Alternatively an undertaking may be given to discharge the charge by using the Land Registry END or ED systems (see G1.10 and G1.11).

4.2.14. An undertaking to discharge the seller's mortgage should only be accepted from a solicitor or licensed conveyancer because of the difficulties of enforcement of undertakings against unqualified persons.[1] The undertaking should also be in the form of wording approved by the Law Society. The current guidance from the Law Society is that it will not normally be advisable to accept an undertaking if the mortgagee is not a member of the CML, and/or where the amount required to redeem the mortgage exceeds the minimum level of solicitors indemnity insurance (£2 million per claim, £3 million for recognised bodies). In such a case an undertaking should not be accepted and it may be necessary for completion to take place at the lender's solicitors' offices (not the seller's solicitors' offices) or for the lender's solicitor to attend personally at completion in order to discharge the mortgage. If the amount of the mortgage exceeds £2 million consider asking for a warranty from the seller's solicitor that his insurance cover does exceed the amount required to redeem the mortgage. See the Law Society's guidance at Appendix IV.7.

4.2.15. The buyer's solicitor must ensure that any undertaking given mentions every subsisting mortgage on the title. The form of wording recommended by the Law Society for undertakings to discharge building society mortgages is given at Appendix V.3.

4.2.16. When the buyer's solicitor is satisfied as to the documents received from the seller's solicitor and the documents which he has inspected, he should hand to the seller's solicitor any documents which the seller's solicitor requires in accordance with the list agreed prior to completion, e.g. release of deposit, and a banker's draft for the amount specified on the completion statement or otherwise notified to the buyer's solicitor by the seller's solicitor.

4.2.17. Where the banker's draft has been made out in the name of the buyer's solicitor it will have to be endorsed over to the seller's solicitor or as he directs. An endorsement may be general or special. To effect a general endorsement the buyer's solicitor simply signs the reverse of the draft using the payee's name as shown on the front of the draft. To effect a special endorsement the buyer's solicitor writes on the reverse of the draft 'pay to the order of [*name of seller's solicitor or as he directs*]' and then signs the endorsement. In either case the buyer's solicitor must ensure that his signature is in an identical form of wording to that used on the front of the draft where the payee is named. In default of this the endorsement may not be accepted by the bank when the draft is presented for payment.

Release of deposit

4.2.18. An unconditional written release of deposit should be supplied in any situation where the deposit under the contract has been held in the capacity of stakeholder. In practice, where the deposit has been held by the seller's solicitor in that capacity, an oral release will suffice. A written release is only therefore necessary where the deposit has been held by a third party, e.g. an estate agent as stakeholder.

Endorsement of memoranda

4.2.19. Where in unregistered land a document affecting the title is not to be handed over on completion, the buyer may want the seller to endorse a memorandum of the transaction on the deed(s) retained by the seller. The endorsement of such a memorandum protects the buyer against a subsequent mistaken or fraudulent reconveyance of the same property. This is most likely to be needed on the sale of part of unregistered land where the buyer is entitled to insist on the endorsement of the memorandum on the most recent in date of the seller's retained title deeds under Law of Property Act 1925, s.200 (where the seller enters into new restrictive covenants), or where the purchase is from personal representatives of a deceased seller where Administration of Estates Act 1925, s.36(4) gives the buyer the right to insist on the endorsement of a memorandum on the grant of representation.

4.2.20. The form of wording to be used for the endorsement should be drafted by the buyer's solicitor and agreed with the seller's solicitor at the requisitions on title stage of the transaction. A copy of the endorsement should be given to the buyer's solicitor for retention by him as evidence that this has been done. In registered conveyancing this procedure is not necessary.

4.2.21. If in unregistered land the seller is entering into new restrictive covenants he should either retain a copy of the conveyance which imposes those covenants or a copy of the covenants themselves. The covenants will be contained in the purchase deed which will be handed to the buyer on completion and unless a copy is retained by the seller, he will have no documentary evidence of the covenants to produce to a buyer on a subsequent sale of the retained land. An alternative is for the conveyance or transfer to be prepared and executed in duplicate, the seller's solicitor retaining the duplicate on completion.

4.2.22. In some cases the buyer will only be entitled to have copies of documents relating to the seller's title and not the originals. Chiefly this will occur on a sale of part of unregistered land where the seller is entitled to retain the title deeds which relate to the land retained by him. Other examples would include purchases from personal representatives where they are entitled to retain the original grant and purchases from attorneys who hold a general or enduring power. Where a power is a special power, relating only to the sale of this property, the buyer is entitled to the original power.

4.2.23. In any case where an original document relevant to the title is not being handed over, the buyer's solicitor should call for the original document and examine his copy against the original. The copy should then be marked to show that it has been examined against the original and is a true copy of the original document.

4.2.24. On a sale of part of unregistered land all the documents contained in the abstract or epitome of title will have to be so marked and each examined document should bear the wording:

'examined against the original at the offices of [*insert name of seller's solicitors or as appropriate*] signed [*by buyer's solicitor's representative either in his own name or in the name of the firm*] and dated [*insert date of examination*]'.

4.2.25. Where a certified copy of a document will be required by the Land Registry the certification should be carried out by a conveyancer (or such other person as the registrar may permit) by writing on the document clearly and in a conspicuous position the words:

'I certify this to be a true copy of the [*insert type of document*] dated [*insert date of document being certified*] signed [*signature of conveyancer*] and dated [*insert date of certification*]'.

The name and address of the signatory should also be endorsed.[2] This will assist in the event of the certification later having to be checked in a subsequent transaction. It should be noted that under Powers of Attorney Act 1971, s.3(1)(*b*)(ii), a copy of a power of attorney must be certified on every page.

1. See *Patel* v. *Daybells* [2001] EWCA Civ 1229 and Law Society guidance on accepting undertakings on completion following *Patel* v. *Daybells*, Appendix IV.7.
2. See Land Registration Rules 2003, r.217(1) (as amended) as to the definitions of 'certified copy' and 'conveyancer'.

4.3. Completion through the post

4.3.1. In many cases, particularly with simple residential transactions, the buyer's solicitor will not wish to attend completion personally. In such a case arrangements may be made with the seller's solicitor to complete the transaction through the post.

4.3.2. Arrangements to complete through the post should be made at the latest at the requisitions on title stage of the transaction, although it is courteous for the buyer's solicitor to ask the seller's solicitor whether this method of completion will be convenient at an earlier stage so that the seller can if necessary obtain the consent of his lender's solicitor to this procedure.

4.3.3. The Law Society's Code for Completion by Post should be used (see Appendix II.3). The buyer's solicitor should agree any variations to the Code in writing with the seller's solicitor well before completion is due to take place. He should also send written instructions to the seller's solicitor specifying precisely what the buyer's solicitor requires the seller's solicitor to do on the buyer's solicitor's behalf at completion and agreeing a time on the day of completion itself when completion will take place.

4.3.4. The seller's solicitor will effectively act as the buyer's solicitor's agent for the purpose of carrying out the completion procedure. The instructions given by the buyer's solicitor should therefore encompass such of the matters detailed in F4.2 as the buyer's solicitor would have carried out had he attended personally at completion. If the seller's solicitor perceives any difficulty or ambiguity in the instructions received from the buyer's solicitor, he must resolve that query or ambiguity before completion is due to take place.

4.3.5. The buyer's solicitor must either send the banker's draft to the seller's solicitor to arrive in time for completion and to be held by the seller's solicitor to the buyer's solicitor's order until completion takes place, or, more commonly, remit the necessary funds by telegraphic transfer to the seller's solicitor's nominated bank account to arrive there in time for completion to take place at the agreed time.

4.3.6. On being satisfied as to the proper payment of the completion money, either by draft or telegraphic transfer, the seller's solicitor must carry out the buyer's instructions and effect completion on his behalf. He should then immediately telephone (or fax) the buyer's solicitor to inform him that completion has taken place and post to the buyer's solicitor, by first class post or document exchange, the documents which the buyer is entitled to receive on completion. Where documents are required to be marked, certified or endorsed, the seller's solicitor will carry out these operations on behalf of the absent buyer's solicitor.

4.3.7. Under the Law Society's Code, the seller's solicitor is not entitled to make a charge to the buyer's solicitor for acting as his agent in carrying out completion.

4.4. Using an agent

4.4.1. If the buyer's solicitor is unable to attend personally at completion, but does not wish to complete through the post, he may appoint another solicitor to act as his agent, the agent attending completion in person and carrying out the same procedures that the buyer's solicitor would have done had he been present.

4.4.2. The agent will generally be a solicitor who practises within the vicinity of the office where completion is due to take place and should be given instructions to act in good time before actual completion day.

4.4.3. The instructions given to the agent should be full and explicit so that the agent is in no doubt as to what he is required to do. Copies of all the documents which the buyer's solicitor would normally take to completion with him should be supplied with the instructions and the agent should be put in funds either by banker's draft or telegraphic transfer so that he has cleared funds in his own clients' account against which to draw the draft for the completion money.

4.4.4. The agent is entitled to charge a reasonable sum for carrying out his duties as agent. The fee should be agreed in advance between the agent and the buyer's solicitor to avoid any later dispute. The buyer's solicitor is then bound to pay the agent's fee after completion irrespective of whether he has received reimburse-ment from his own client. It should be made clear to the client at the outset of the transaction that if the employment of an agent is required in order to attend completion, the agent's fee will be added as a disbursement on the client's bill (see A8).

4.4.5.   The agent should attend completion in person and carry out the buyer's solicitor's instructions. As soon after completion as possible he should tel-ephone (telex or fax or email) the buyer's solicitor to confirm that completion has taken place and should send the documents which he has received at completion to the buyer's solicitor by first class post or document exchange.

4.5.   Synchronisation

4.5.1.   Where the client is to complete a sale and purchase of property on the same day, it is essential that the sale actually takes place before the purchase so that the proceeds of sale can be utilised in the later purchase transaction. Sufficient time should be allowed between the times of completion of sale and purchase to permit the funds received from the sale transaction to be transmitted to and received by the seller's solicitor in the purchase transaction within the time limits specified in the purchase contract.

4.6.   Deemed late completion

4.6.1.   By Standard Conditions 6.1.2 and 6.1.3 and Standard Commercial Property Conditions 8.1.2 and 8.1.3, where the sale is with vacant possession and the money due on completion is not paid by 2 pm on the day of actual completion (or such other time as may have been agreed by the parties), for compensation purposes completion is deemed to have taken place on the next following working day unless the seller had not vacated the property by 2 pm (or other agreed time). The buyer's solicitor must therefore instruct his bank to remit the completion money in sufficient time to ensure its arrival at its destination bank within the time limit specified in the contract. In default the buyer may find himself liable to pay compensation to the seller under Standard Condition 7.3 or Standard Commercial Property Condition 9.3 (see also M1.4).

4.7.   Lender's requirements

4.7.1.   The buyer's solicitor will often also be acting as solicitor for the buyer's lender. In such a case the buyer's solicitor should check the lender's requirements for completion when he is preparing his checklist and making arrangements for completion. In most cases the lender's requirements will be identical to the buyer's solicitor's own requirements, but a check on the lender's instructions should always be made to ensure that nothing is overlooked.

4.8. Problems with vacant possession

4.8.1. If the buyer's solicitor suspects that there may be practical problems in obtaining vacant possession, he should deal with this matter at an early stage in the transaction. Taking a written release of rights from an occupier and/or joining the occupier as a party to the contract will in most cases resolve the problem, but a signed release is of little comfort if on the day of completion the occupier refuses to vacate the property. If it is suspected that this might happen, the buyer's solicitor may take the precaution of inserting a contractual condition specifying that completion shall take place at the premises themselves so that an inspection of the property can be carried out immediately before completion takes place. Such a condition would have to be inserted into the contract before exchange and it is too late to try to impose such a term just before completion. Standard Condition 6.2.2 and Standard Commercial Property Condition 8.2 give the seller the right to decide where completion will take place.

4.8.2. In the absence of a term allowing completion to take place on the premises themselves, the buyer's solicitor may, in appropriate cases, either inspect the property himself on the day of completion, or ask the client or the client's surveyor to do so and then to telephone the buyer's solicitor to confirm that the premises are vacant before completion proceeds.

4.8.3. Accepting an instruction from a lender that the solicitor acting for the lender will ensure that vacant possession is obtained is a breach of Rule 3.19 Solicitors' Code of Conduct 2007. Such an instruction must therefore be deleted from the lender's instructions.

4.9. Effect of completion

4.9.1. In unregistered land, title in the property passes to the buyer on completion.

4.9.2. In registered land, the legal title does not pass until the buyer has become registered as proprietor of the land.[1]

4.9.3. On completion the contract merges with the purchase deed in so far as the contract and purchase deed cover the same ground; thus after completion it is not possible to bring an action which arises out of one of the terms of the contract unless that provision has been expressly left extant by a term of the contract itself. For this reason it is common for the contract to contain a non-merger clause. Standard Condition 7.4 and Standard Commercial Property Condition 9.4 say that the provisions within the contract do not merge on completion in so far as there is outstanding liability under these provisions.

4.9.4. In the absence of a non-merger provision an action on the contract may not be possible after completion has taken place, but an action in tort or for misrepresentation would still be available since neither of these actions is based on the contract.

4.9.5. The principal remedy available to the buyer after completion is an action on the title guarantee or covenants for title, which is further discussed in M9.

1. Land Registration Act 2002, s.27(1).

G. POST-COMPLETION

G1. After completion

1.1. Seller's checklist

1.1.1. Where appropriate to the transaction the following steps should be taken by the seller's solicitor as soon as possible after completion has taken place:

(a) Where completion has taken place by post, telephone the buyer's solicitor to inform him that completion has taken place.

(b) Telephone the estate agent to inform him of completion and to direct him to release the keys to the buyer.

(c) Inform client that completion has taken place.

(d) Where completion has taken place by post, send purchase deed, title deeds and other relevant documents to buyer's solicitor by first class post or document exchange.

(e) If part of the proceeds of sale are to be used towards the purchase of another property on the same day, make arrangements for the transmission of these funds in accordance with instructions received.

(f) Deal with the discharge of the seller's existing mortgage(s) by sending a clients' account cheque for the amount required (as per redemption statement previously obtained) to the lender together with the engrossment of the Form DS1 (or deed of release relating to unregistered land) requesting him to discharge the mortgage and to forward the receipted Form DS1 to you as quickly as possible.[1] If the mortgage is over unregistered land, the lender will, instead of using a Form DS1, complete the receipt clause on the reverse of the mortgage deed and forward the receipted deed to the seller's solicitor. If in unregistered land the lender is not a building society, the lender should be requested to date the receipt with the date of completion in order to avoid the risk of a transfer of the mortgage under Law of Property Act 1925, s.115. Where necessary, the reassignment of collateral security, e.g. a life policy, should also be dealt with, and a lender who has insured the property will also need to be told to cancel the property insurance cover.

(g) If instructed to do so, pay the estate agent's commission and obtain a receipt for the payment.

(h) Account to the seller's bank for the proceeds of sale in accordance with any undertaking given to them.

(i) Account to the client for the balance of the proceeds of sale in accordance with his instructions.

(j) If not already done, draft and remit bill of costs to the client.

(k) Where money is being held by the solicitor on account of costs, it may be transferred to office account provided that the client has expressly or impliedly agreed to this being done.

(l) If the land is to remain unregistered after completion of this transaction make application for registration of land charges at the Land Charges Department.[2]

(m) On receipt of the completed Form DS1 or receipted mortgage from the lender, check the form or receipt to ensure it is correct, then send it to the buyer's solicitor and ask to be discharged from the undertaking given on completion.

(n) Remind the client of the need to notify the local and water authorities of the change of ownership of the property.

(o) Remind the client to cancel insurance cover over the property (and associated insurances if relevant).

(p) Advise the client about the payment of capital gains tax on assessment.

(q) Deal with the custody of deeds in accordance with the client's instructions. Most, if not all, original deeds will have passed to the buyer's solicitor on actual completion, but the seller will have retained custody of such deeds on a sale of part, or may have, e.g. an original grant of representation or power of attorney.

(r) Check through the file to ensure that all outstanding matters have been dealt with before sending the file for storage.

1. Alternatively the mortgage may be discharged using the END or ED systems (see G1.10 and G1.11).
2. See G3 as to the events giving rise to compulsory first registration.

1.2. Buyer's checklist

1.2.1. Where appropriate to the transaction the following steps should be taken by the buyer's solicitor as soon as possible after completion has taken place:

(a) Inform client and his lender that completion has taken place.

(b) Complete the mortgage deed by insertion of the date and any other information which still has to be completed, e.g. date when first repayment is due.

(c) Complete file copies of the mortgage, purchase deed and other relevant documents.

(d) Ensure that the SDLT return (form SDLT1) is completed and submitted to HM Revenue and Customs, together with the payment of any tax due, within the time limit.

(e) Register any charge created by a company at Companies House within 21 days of its creation in accordance with Companies Act requirements. This time limit is absolute and cannot be extended without an order of the court. Failure to register within the time limit may prejudice the lender's security and will be an act of negligence on the part of the defaulting solicitor.

(f) Account to the buyer's bank for any bridging finance in accordance with any undertaking given to them and ask to be released from that undertaking.

(g) If not already done, draft and remit bill of costs to the client.

(h) Where money is being held by the solicitor on account of costs, it may be transferred to office account provided that the client has expressly or impliedly agreed to this being done.

(i) If the seller's land is to remain unregistered after completion of this transaction make application for registration of land charges at the Land Charges Department within the period given by the previously lodged priority notice, e.g. new restrictive covenants by the seller on a sale of part.

(j) On receipt of the completed Form DS1 or receipted mortgage from the seller's lender's solicitor, check the form or receipt to ensure it is correct, acknowledge its receipt and release the sender from the undertaking given on completion.

(k) Make copies of all documents which are to be sent to the Land Registry to ensure that file copies exist in case requisitions are raised by the Registry or the documents are lost or damaged before registration is complete.

(l) Make copies of any documents where a request is to be made to the registrar for the original to be returned (see G3.11.21).

(m) Certify copy documents which are to be sent to the Land Registry (see G1.8).

(n) Make application for registration of title within the relevant priority period (land already registered) or within two months of completion (application for first registration).

(o)   Make diary or file prompt entry recording the approximate date when the title information document may be expected to be received from the Land Registry and send a reminder if the document is not received by that time.

(p)   Send notice of assignment of a life policy to the insurance company and place their acknowledgement of receipt with the title deeds.

(q)   Give notice to the landlord's solicitors of an assignment, mortgage, etc., in accordance with a requirement to that effect in the lease or in the mortgagee's instructions and place their acknowledgement of receipt with the title deeds.

(r)   Notify tenants of the change of ownership of the property.

(s)   Make application for the discharge of any entry which was lodged to protect the contract. In registered land this will be combined with any application for registration.

(t)   On receipt of the title information document from the Land Registry, check its contents carefully and ask the Registry to correct any errors which have been made.

(u)   Deal with the custody of deeds in accordance with the client's instructions.

(v)   Check through the file to ensure that all outstanding matters have been dealt with before sending the file for storage.

NB: Where a separate solicitor has been instructed to act for the buyer's lender, the lender's solicitor will normally have taken custody of the purchase deed and other title deeds on completion and he will assume responsibility for the presentation of the documents for SDLT and registration of title in place of the buyer's solicitor.

1.3.   **Undertakings**

1.3.1.   Failure to honour an undertaking is professional misconduct. Any undertaking given must therefore be honoured and the obligations promised must be fulfilled without delay.

1.3.2.   A solicitor who has performed his undertaking should formally ask the recipient to release the giver from his undertaking so that the giver has written evidence of the fulfilment of the undertaking. The recipient may either acknowledge the giver's release by letter, or return the original undertaking to the giver, and in either case the evidence of release is to be kept on the giver's file.

1.4.   **Stamp Duty Land Tax**

1.4.1.   The SDLT return form should be submitted to HM Revenue and Customs as soon as possible after the effective date has taken place to ensure that the land transaction return certificate will be returned to the buyer's solicitor in suffi-cient time for an application for registration of title to be made within the appropriate time limits. Forms can be ordered via the HM Revenue and Customs website. Single copies of forms, leaflets and guides can be down-loaded. The land transaction return certificate must be submitted to the Land Registry with the application for registration of the transaction. If the transac-tion does not require notification to HM Revenue and Customs, but requires a self-certificate form signed by the buyer, the original certificate, in the pre-scribed form, must be sent to the Land Registry.

1.4.2. It is not possible to delay the initial application for registration until the land transaction return certificate is available because in doing so the client might lose the protection of the priority period afforded to him by his pre-completion search. However, the Land Registry's rejection policy is to reject applications for registration where the application is not accompanied by one of the follow-ing documents:

- a land transaction return certificate;

- a self-certificate; or

- a letter explaining why neither of the above is required.

1.4.3. Despite the absence of the above documents, the Land Registry will accept the application if an outline application is pending in respect of the transaction or the application clearly states that a land transaction return form has been sent to HM Revenue and Customs and 20 business days or more have passed since completion. In such a case the original transaction document, e.g. the transfer, must accompany the application to the Land Registry. For further information, see Land Registry Practice Guide 49.

1.4.4. Stamp duty only applies to documents dated before 1 December 2003 and to some later transactions (see G2). The Land Registry will reject applications where the transaction document has not been stamped. However, the Land Registry will accept an application where the document has been sent for adjudication, provided a certified copy of the unstamped document and an explanation accompanies the application. The Land Registry will also accept applications where the deed requires *ad valorem* duty but has not yet been stamped, provided that at least 20 business days have passed since completion, a copy of the dated deed is supplied and it is clear that the original deed is missing as it has not yet been returned by the Stamp Office.

1.4.5. The Produced Stamp procedure only applies to transactions before 1 December 2003 and to some later transactions. Where a transfer on sale has to be produced to HM Revenue and Customs under Finance Act 1931, and is certified as not exceeding the relevant stamp duty thresholds, the completed Form L(A)451 (PD) may be sent to the Land Registry with the application for registration of title and the Registry will then stamp the form with the Agency's 'received' stamp before forwarding the Form L(A)451 to HM Revenue and Customs. This procedure circumvents any delay which might otherwise be experienced in separate submission of the document for stamping prior to registration. Leases granted before 1 December 2003 must be presented to the Stamp Office even if no duty is payable.

1.4.6. Depending on the nature of his instructions and report on title, a lender's solicitor may be under a duty to pay SDLT and register at the Land Registry even if the buyer has not put him in funds to do so.

1.5. Registration of title

1.5.1. It is essential that the relevant time limits for submission of an application for registration of the client's title are complied with. Failure to make an application for first registration within two months of completion results in the transfer of the legal estate becoming void and the buyer's title becoming subject to interests from which it would otherwise take free.[1] Failure to make an application for a registration of a dealing within the priority period of 30 business days given by a pre-completion Land Registry search may have the consequence of the client's interest losing priority to another application.[2] In either case, if the client suffered loss as a result of the late application, the solicitor would be liable in negligence.

1.5.2. The Land Registry will accept an application for registration of the buyer's title without a mortgage discharge provided it is marked 'to follow' on the application form or in a covering letter. The Land Registry will allow 20 business days for the discharge to be produced.[3] Before the end of that period an extension can be applied for. The application must state the reason for the delay and give an explanation of the steps taken to obtain the discharge.[4]

1.5.3. Registration of title is further dealt with in G3.

1. Land Registration Act 2002, s.7 and see *Sainsbury's Supermarkets Ltd* v. *Olympia Homes Ltd* [2005] EWHC 1235, ChD.
2. See Land Registration Rules 2003, r.131 for the definition of 'priority period'.
3. *Ibid*, r.16.
4. See Land Registry Practice Guide 50.

1.6. Registration of company charges

1.6.1. Legal charges created by a company are registrable at the Land Registry (or the Land Charges Department in the case of a charge over unregistered land which is not supported by a deposit of title deeds) and, as a separate obligation in relation to any charge on land, at the Companies Registry under Companies Act requirements. Failure to register the charge under the Companies Act 1985 within the 21 days following its creation renders the charge void against a liquidator or another creditor of the company. This time limit can only be extended by an order of the court which is not automatically granted. Fixed equitable charges and floating charges must also be noted on the register if they are to affect registered land.

1.7. Notices of assignment

1.7.1. Where following completion notice has to be given to a landlord of an assignment or mortgage, or notice given to an insurance company of the assignment of a life insurance policy, such notice should be given in duplicate. The recipient of the notice should be requested to sign one copy of the notice in acknowledgement of its receipt, and to return the receipted copy to the sender. The receipted copy will then be kept with the title deeds as evidence of compliance with this requirement.

1.7.2. In the case of the assignment of a life policy, the notice of assignment should be given as soon as possible after completion, since the giving of the notice establishes the priority of charges and is required to be given by Policies of Assurance Act 1867.

1.7.3. Where notice is being given under the terms of a lease, it should be delivered within the time limits specified in the lease together with the appropriate fee.

1.8. Certifying documents

1.8.1. Where a certified copy of a document will be required by the Land Registry the certification should be carried out by a conveyancer (or such other person as the registrar may permit) by writing on the copy clearly and in a conspicuous position the words:

> 'I certify this to be a true copy of the [*insert type of document*] dated [*insert date of document being certified*] signed [*signature of conveyancer*] and dated [*insert date of certification*].'

1.8.2. The name and address of the signatory should also be endorsed.[1] This will assist in the event of the certification later having to be checked in a subsequent transaction.

1.8.3. It should be noted that under Powers of Attorney Act 1971, s.3(1)(b)(ii), a copy of a power of attorney must be certified on every page.

1. See Land Registration Rules 2003, r.217(1) (as amended).

1.9. Custody of deeds

1.9.1. Instructions relating to custody will have been obtained from the client at an earlier stage in the transaction.

1.9.2.   In many cases the client's lender will require custody of the deeds after completion or, if this is not the case, the client may have been advised to deposit the deeds with his bank or in the solicitor's strongroom.

1.9.3.   Where the original deeds are not to be sent to the client himself, it is courteous to photocopy the principal title deeds and send these copies to the client who will thus have immediate access to the relevant information in the case of, e.g. a dispute over a right of way or restrictive covenant.

1.9.4.   Before deeds are sent to a lender (or other third party) for custody, they should be checked for accuracy and a schedule of deeds drawn up in duplicate. The recipient should be asked to acknowledge the receipt of the deeds by signing and returning one copy of the schedule. This signed acknowledgement will then be placed on the buyer's solicitor's file as evidence that the deeds have been sent to the recipient.

1.9.5.   Deeds should normally be sent by recorded delivery, insured post or document exchange to ensure their safe arrival at their destination.

1.9.6.   If deeds are to remain in the solicitor's own strongroom, a schedule of the deeds should be drawn up in duplicate, one copy being placed with the deeds, the other remaining in the solicitor's file. In no circumstances should original deeds be left in the solicitor's file when the file is sent for storage. If deeds are kept in the solicitor's strongroom, the solicitor owes a duty of care to his client and, if the deeds are lost, the solicitor may not charge the client with the cost of replacement.

1.10.   Electronic notification of discharge (END)

1.10.1.   An END is an electronic message sent from an authorised lender to the Land Registry via a computer link using the information supplied on Form END1. This method of discharge is an alternative to Form DS1 in registered land transactions. Like the paper form of discharge, an END does not cause the charge to be cancelled, it must be combined with a formal application to the Land Registry using Form AP1 or DS2, to discharge the charge.

1.10.2.   Form END1 is completed by the borrower's solicitor and sent to the lender as a request for an END to be transmitted to the Land Registry. Lenders will tell you if they belong to the scheme in the redemption statement or when the deeds packet is issued.

1.10.3.   The borrower's solicitors send Form END1 to the lender when they remit the amount required to redeem the mortgage. The lender will then transmit an END to the Land Registry. An authorised lender will normally use the END system in all cases where the whole of the land in a title is discharged from a charge in place of Form DS1.

1.10.4. The lender will send the borrower's solicitors confirmation of receipt of Form END1 or the receipted form.

1.10.5. For further information see Land Registry Practice Guide 31.

1.11. Electronic discharge (ED)

1.11.1. An ED is an electronic message from a lender authorising the discharge of a registered charge. The ED system enables mortgage lenders to discharge mortgages electronically using a direct link to the Land Registry's computer system. No paper application is required.

1.11.2. Lenders will tell you if they belong to the scheme in their redemption statement. You will need to agree on a revised form of undertaking to allow for an ED. Suggested forms of undertaking are at Appendix V.3.

1.11.3. The borrower's solicitors will remit the amount required to redeem the mortgage to the lender. The lender will then send an ED to the Land Registry. On acceptance, the charge entries will be cancelled automatically by the Land Registry's computer system. The lender will then notify the borrower's solicitors that the charge has been discharged.

1.11.4. For further information see Land Registry Practice Guide 31.

G

G2. Stamping documents

2.1. **Introduction**
2.2. **Effect of unstamped documents**

2.3. **Avoidance by inserting false information**

2.1. Introduction

2.1.1. The following paragraphs relate to those documents that continue to require stamping. See A14 for an explanation of Stamp Duty Land Tax (SDLT) and for details on which documents may require stamping.

2.1.2. In circumstances where land transactions remain subject to stamp duty, the relevant instrument must be produced to HM Revenue and Customs for stamping within 30 days of execution or, if delivered subject to conditions, within 30 days of the date when the conditions are fulfilled.

2.1.3. HM Revenue and Customs do not offer a 'local office' service for stamping documents. Postal applications should be made to the Edinburgh Stamp Office, Grayfield House, Spur X, 4 Bankhead Avenue, Edinburgh EH11 4AE. Personal applications should be made to the London Stamp Office, Ground Floor, South West Wing, Bush House, Strand, London WC2B 4QN.

2.2. Effect of unstamped documents

2.2.1. Unstamped or insufficiently stamped documents are not admissible in evidence and it is now the duty of the advocate and the judge to take the point (Stamp Act 1891, s.14(4)). This applies even where the litigant relying upon the document is not a party to it such as a lender seeking to enforce his security. This can provide an expensive surprise and failure to take stamp objections to the other side's documents is a breach of duty to the client.

2.2.2. The Land Registry and Companies Registry will not accept unstamped or incorrectly stamped documents for registration and they may insist that the instrument is presented to HM Revenue and Customs Stamp Taxes Office and adjudicated (Stamp Act 1891, s.17). Duty must therefore normally be paid before an application for registration of title is submitted.

2.2.3. Unstamped or incorrectly stamped documents cannot be used in evidence in civil proceedings. Such a document is not therefore a good root or link in the chain of title to land and since certain documents, including certain contracts for sale, may be subject to stamp duty, these can affect the title to unregistered land.

2.3.   Avoidance by inserting false information

2.3.1.   An agreement to avoid the payment of the correct duty by inserting false information in a document may be a fraud on HM Revenue and Customs which could result in the transaction being declared void as being illegal on the grounds of public policy. This liability extends to the parties' professional advisers involved in the preparation of the documentation (see *Saunders* v. *Edwards* [1987] 2 All ER 651).

G3. Registration of title

3.1.   Introduction

3.1.1.   Registration of title is governed by Land Registration Act 2002 (the Act) and Land Registration Rules 2003 (the Rules), which came into force on 13 October 2003. The Act contains the major principles of law and the supporting details are contained in the Rules.

3.1.2.   Section numbers and rule numbers in this section (G3) correspond to Land Registration Act 2002 and Land Registration Rules 2003 unless otherwise stated.

3.1.3.   The Land Registry has produced Practice Guides and Practice Bulletins relating to the Act and Rules. These are listed in Appendix X.1 and are regularly revised and updated to take account of changes in the law and changes to Land Registry practice. They can be downloaded free of charge from **www. landregistry. gov.uk** or obtained from any Land Registry Office.

3.1.4.   Registration guarantees the title to registered land. Thus, a person who suffers loss as a result of a mistake in the register is normally entitled to be indemnified for that loss (see M7).

3.2.   Compulsory registration

Extension of compulsory registration

3.2.1.   The extension of compulsory registration to the whole of England and Wales became effective on 1 December 1990.[1] The Act extended the events which trigger first registration to include leases granted for more than seven years and leases assigned where they have over seven years left to run (s.4(1)). Most commercial leases are now compulsorily registrable on grant or assignment. The Act also contains provisions enabling the Lord Chancellor, by order, to add to the events that will trigger compulsory first registration (s.5).

When title must be registered

3.2.2. Registration is compulsory on specified types of transfers, leases and mortgages of a qualifying estate, which is defined as either a legal freehold estate or a legal lease with more than seven years to run. Under section 4(1) they are:

    (a) a transfer:

        (i) for valuable or other consideration,[2] by way of gift or in pursuance of a court order; or

        (ii) by means of an assent;

    (b) the grant of a legal lease:

        (i) for a term of more than seven years; and

        (ii) for valuable or other consideration, by way of gift or in pursuance of a court order;

    (c) the grant of a legal lease to take effect in possession more than three months after it is granted;

    (d) the creation of a first legal mortgage where the mortgage is protected by the deposit of documents.

Certain disposals under Housing Act 1985

3.2.3. The following disposals under Housing Act 1985 also trigger compulsory registration:

    (a) the transfer or grant of a legal lease of an unregistered estate where Housing Act 1985, s.171A applies (a disposal by a landlord which leads to a person no longer being a secure tenant); or

    (b) the grant of a 'right to buy' lease under Housing Act 1985, Part 5.

Transfers not subject to compulsory registration

3.2.4. The compulsory registration provisions do not apply to:

    (a) a transfer by operation of law, e.g. the vesting of land in personal representatives (s.4(3));

    (b) an assignment of a mortgage term; or

    (c) a surrender of a lease where the term is to merge into the reversion (s.4(4)).

Duty to apply for registration

3.2.5. Where registration is compulsory, the transferee, lessee or mortgagor is under a duty to apply for first registration (s.6(1)–(3)). In the case of a mortgage, the mortgagee may make an application in the name of the mortgagor whether or not the mortgagor consents (r.21). The application for first registration must be made within two months. This period may be extended by the registrar if he is satisfied that there is a good reason for doing so (s.6(4) and (5)).

Effect of failure to register

3.2.6. Where an application is not lodged within the registration period the transfer, lease or mortgage is void as regards the legal estate (s.7(1)). In the case of a transfer, the legal estate reverts to the transferor. A lease or mortgage takes effect as a contract made for valuable consideration to grant the lease or mortgage concerned (s.7(2)). Although the registration period can be extended, a client is at risk of being registered subject to interests which would not have otherwise bound the land.[3]

Liability for making good void transfers, etc.

3.2.7. If the transaction has to be repeated because of a failure to register, the transferee, lessee or mortgagor:

(a) is liable to the other party for the costs involved; and

(b) must indemnify the other party for any other liability reasonably incurred due to the failure to register (s.8).

1. Registration of Title Order 1989 (SI 1989/1347).
2. If the estate transferred or leased has a negative value it is to be regarded as transferred or leased for valuable or other consideration. Valuable consideration does not include marriage consideration or a nominal consideration in money. See ss.4(6) and 132(1).
3. See, e.g., *Sainsbury's Supermarkets Ltd* v. *Olympia Homes Ltd* [2005] EWHC 1235, ChD.

3.3. **Voluntary registration**

When title may be registered

3.3.1. Under section 3 the following legal estates and interests may be registered under their own title numbers:

(a) a freehold estate;

(b) a lease for a term of which more than seven years are unexpired;[1]

(c) a lease for a discontinuous term whatever its length;

(d) a franchise;

(e) a profit à prendre in gross.

Reasons for voluntary registration

3.3.2. The benefits of the registered system of conveyancing, such as simplified methods of deduction of title, are such that a client should be encouraged to make an application for voluntary registration in appropriate circumstances. This might be particularly appropriate where, for example, an unregistered title is complex; or where the title has minor defects, since on first registration the registrar has a discretion to 'cure' such defects (ss.9(3) and 10(4)). Voluntary applications attract a reduced fee.

1. Where a reversionary lease is to take effect in possession on, or within one month of, the end of the lease in possession, the terms may be treated as one continuous term. If this exceeds seven years, the lease can be registered, see s.3(7).

3.4.   Applications for first registration

3.4.1.   The application for first registration must be made to the proper land registry office. See G3.11 as to the proper office for the receipt of applications and other general matters relating to applications to the Land Registry.

3.4.2.   The application must be made in Form FR1 (r.23). It must be accompanied by (r.24(1)):

(a)   sufficient details, by plan or otherwise, so that the land can be identified clearly on the Ordnance Survey map;[1]

(b)   where the land is leasehold, the lease, if in the control of the applicant, and a certified copy;

(c)   all deeds and documents relating to the title in the control of the applicant;

(d)   a list in duplicate in Form DL of all the documents delivered.

3.4.3.   The registrar needs to investigate title on an application for first registration in order to decide which class of title can be allocated to the title. He therefore needs to have access to all the documents which form the evidence of title to the land. The documents should be individually listed and numbered in chronological sequence in the Form DL. They should include:

(a)   all the documents which formed the evidence of title supplied by the seller's solicitor;

(b)   all the buyer's pre-contract searches and enquiries with their replies (including any variations or further information contained in relevant correspondence);

(c)   the contract;

(d)   requisitions on title with their replies;

(e)   all pre-completion search certificates;

(f)   the purchase deed;

(g)   the seller's mortgage, duly receipted;

(h)   the buyer's mortgage;

(i) where the transaction is leasehold, the original lease and a certified copy;

(j) a land transaction return certificate or self-certificate.

3.4.4. Limitation Act 1980 continues to apply unamended to adverse possession of unregistered land. A person claiming to be in adverse possession of unregistered land may make an application to the Land Registry for first registration on the basis that, under the provisions of section 15 Limitation Act 1980, the documentary title owner is barred from obtaining possession of the land. The application must be accompanied by one or more statutory declarations providing evidence of the adverse occupation for a minimum of 12 years. For further guidance see Land Registry Practice Guide 5.

3.4.5. There is a case for retaining copies of all documents which are to be submitted to the registry on the applicant's solicitor's file pending completion of the registration. The registrar may need to raise requisitions on an application (particularly for first registration) and it assists in the speedy reply to those requisitions if the solicitor has retained copies of the documents which may contain information relevant to the query raised by the registry. A further reason for retaining copies of the documents is so that any queries which arise in relation to the land pending completion of the registration for example, over boundaries or the exercise of a right of way, can be resolved from the copies in the solicitor's possession.

Land charges

3.4.6. On first registration, the Land Registry does not investigate whether restrictive covenants and other land charges may be void for non-registration at the land charges department. Any land charge appearing on the title is noted on the register. This entry, however, does not mean that the land charge is valid.[2]

3.4.7. Application can be made on first registration (or subsequently) to omit (or cancel) notice of a land charge that is void for non-registration. The application should be accompanied by:

(a) the deed or other instrument creating the land charge;

(b) the subsequent conveyance on sale;[3]

(c) any intervening voluntary conveyances or assents; and

(d) an official certificate of the result of search in the land charges department confirming that the land charge has not been registered.[4]

3.4.8. Before making an application the following matters should also be considered:

(a) registration at the land charges department is not required for a land charge created by an instrument dated on or after 27 July 1971 which was compulsorily registrable;[5]

(b) before 1 August 1977, a land charge in favour of a local authority was registrable as a local land charge and may only be revealed by a local land charges search;

(c) before April 1976, the Land Registry sometimes cancelled Class D(ii) (restrictive covenants) land charge entries from the land charges register on first registration of the land burdened by the covenants;[6] and

(d) where the burdened land falls wholly or partly within the former Ridings of Yorkshire, a land charges search made prior to 1 April 1976 may not reveal land charges registered at the Yorkshire Deeds Registry.

Cautions against first registration

3.4.9. Although cautions against dealings with registered land have been abolished, cautions against first registration of unregistered land remain, although there are certain changes. Owners of a registrable estate can no longer register a caution against first registration to protect their own interest against third parties (s.15). The most appropriate course is for such an owner to apply for the first registration of his estate.

3.4.10. The transmission of the cautioner's interest can now be recorded on the register and it is now possible for an application to be made for the cancellation of a caution against first registration in Form CCT (r.44).

3.4.11. A caution against first registration merely entitles the cautioner to be notified of an application for first registration. It does not confer any validity or priority on the interest claimed. Where necessary, such interest should be protected by registration at the Land Charges Department. Land Registry Practice Guide 63 provides advice about land charges applications.

3.4.12. It is important to note that a person must not lodge a caution against first registration without reasonable cause (s.77(1)). A duty of care is owed to any person who suffers damage in consequence of its breach (s.77(2)).

1. On an application to register a rentcharge, franchise or profit à prendre in gross, the land to be identified is the land affected: see Land Registration Rules 2003, r.24(2).
2. Land Registration Act 2002, s.32(3).
3. See Land Charges Act 1972, s.4 and D2.12 as to the effect of failure to register land charges.
4. See E2.6 as to the requirements for the search being correct in every particular.
5. Land Charges Act 1972, s.14(3), and see Land Registry Practice Guide 51 as to the relevant dates of compulsory registration.
6. Enquiry of the appropriate Land Registry office will confirm whether this procedure was carried out in any particular case.

3.5. Classes of title

3.5.1. On first registration the registrar will decide which class of title should be granted to the estate which is being registered. The class of title granted is shown in the proprietorship register of the title (r.8(1)).

Absolute title

3.5.2. The vast majority of titles are registered with absolute title. An absolute title may be approved if the registrar is of the opinion that title to the estate is such that a willing buyer could properly be advised by a competent professional adviser to accept (ss.9(2) and 10(2)(a)). The registrar may disregard a defect in the title if he is of the opinion that the defect will not cause the holding under the title to be disturbed (ss.9(3) and 10(4)). Where the title is leasehold, absolute title is granted where the registrar also approves the lessor's title to grant the lease (s.10(2)(b)).

Qualified title

3.5.3. A person may be registered with qualified title if the registrar is of the opinion that title has been established only for a limited period or subject to certain reservations which cannot be disregarded (ss.9(4) and 10(5)). A qualified title is very rare in practice. It might be approved where, for example, the title submitted for first registration showed that a transaction within the title had been carried out in breach of trust. In this situation the proprietor would take his interest in the land subject to the interests (if any) of the beneficiaries under the trust. Qualified title can be given to either a freehold or a leasehold estate in the land.

Possessory title

3.5.4. Possessory title may be granted where the registrar considers that the applicant is in possession of the land, or in receipt of rents and profits, and there is no other class of title with which he may be registered (ss.9(5) and 10(6)). In practice, a possessory title will be granted where the applicant's title is based on adverse possession or where title cannot be proved satisfactorily because the title deeds have been lost or destroyed. Possessory title can be given to either a freehold or leasehold estate in the land.

Good leasehold title

3.5.5. Registration with good leasehold title will be granted where the registrar is satisfied only as to the title to the leasehold estate (s.10(3)). Such a title will therefore generally only result where the title to the freehold reversion is unregistered and where the applicant for registration of the leasehold interest does not submit evidence of title to the freehold reversion when making his application. A good leasehold title is regarded by some mortgagees as being unsatisfactory, and for this reason is sometimes difficult to sell or mortgage.

3.5.6. The problems of a good leasehold title are discussed in K1. See also Standard Condition 8.2.4 and Standard Commercial Property Condition 10.2.4, which require a seller on the grant of a new lease for over seven years to deduce to a buyer such evidence of title as will enable the buyer to obtain registration of his title with an absolute title.

3.6.   **Effect of first registration**

Freehold estates

3.6.1.   On first registration with absolute title, the legal estate is vested in the proprietor together with all interests subsisting for the benefit of the estate, such as appurtenant implied or prescriptive easements (s.11(3)). The registered estate is subject only to the following interests affecting the estate at the time of registration (s.11(4)):

(a)   interests which are entered in the register (the only interests entered on first registration will be charges, notices and restrictions);

(b)   overriding interests falling within Land Registration Act 2002, Sched.1; and

(c)   interests acquired under the Limitation Act 1980 of which the proprietor has notice.[1]

3.6.2.   Where the proprietor is a trustee, the estate is vested in him subject to the rights of the beneficiaries under the trust of which he has notice (s.11(5)).

3.6.3.   Registration with qualified title has the same effect as registration with absolute title except that it does not affect the enforcement of any estate, right or interest appearing from the register to be excepted from the effect of registration (s.11(6)).

3.6.4.   Registration with possessory title has the same effect as registration with absolute title, except that it does not affect the enforcement of any estate, right or interest, adverse to, or in derogation of, the title subsisting at the time of registration (s.11(7)).

Leasehold estates

3.6.5.   In general terms the registration of a proprietor with absolute, qualified or possessory title to a leasehold estate has the same effect as registration with the corresponding freehold estate. The significant difference is that a leaseholder is also subject to implied and express covenants, obligations and liabilities incident to the leasehold estate. The proprietor, therefore, takes subject to interests such as restrictive covenants contained in the lease (s.12).

3.6.6.   Registration with good leasehold title has the same effect as registration with absolute leasehold title except that it does not affect the enforcement of any estate, right or interest affecting, or in derogation of, the title of the lessor to grant the lease (s.12(6)).

1.   During a three-year transitional period ending on 12 October 2006, a right acquired under Limitation Act 1980 before the coming into force of the 2002 Act was an overriding interest whether or not the proprietor had notice: see Land Registration Act 2002, s.11(4)(b) and (c) and Sched.12, para.7.

3.7. Upgrading title

3.7.1. The registrar has power to upgrade a title in the following circumstances (s.62(1)–(5)):

(a) from possessory or qualified freehold title to absolute freehold title if he is satisfied as to the title to the freehold estate;

(b) from good leasehold title to absolute leasehold title if he is satisfied as to the superior title;

(c) from possessory or qualified leasehold title:

(i) to good leasehold title, if he is satisfied as to the title to the leasehold estate; and

(ii) to absolute leasehold title if he is satisfied both as to the title to the leasehold estate and as to the superior title;

(d) from possessory freehold title to absolute freehold title or from possessory leasehold title to good leasehold title if the title has been registered for at least 12 years and he is satisfied that the proprietor is in possession of the land (see section 131 for meaning given to 'proprietor in possession').

3.7.2. The registrar cannot exercise his power to upgrade a title if there is any outstanding adverse claim under any estate, right or interest whose enforceability is preserved by the existing class of title (s.62(6)). Any adverse claim must be resolved before the title can be upgraded.

3.7.3. An application to upgrade a title must be made in Form UT1 (r.124(1)).

3.8. Dispositions of registered land

Powers of disposition

3.8.1. A registered proprietor is to be taken to have all the powers of an absolute owner unless any limitation of these powers is reflected by an entry on the register (ss.23 and 25), for example, a restriction. The purpose of the statutory provisions is to prevent the title of the buyer being challenged. They do not affect the lawfulness of the sale (s.26). The Law Commission report preceding the Act illustrated the effect of these provisions with the example of trustees who have limited powers of sale, but who failed to enter a restriction on the register to reflect this limitation. If they then sell the land in breach of the terms of the trust they will remain personally liable for this breach. The buyer's title could not be challenged although he might be personally accountable in equity if he knew of the trustee's breach of trust at the time of the sale.

Registrable dispositions

3.8.2. The Act sets out the dispositions that must be completed by registration if they are to operate at law (s.27(1)). These are:

    (a)   a transfer;

    (b)   the grant of a term of years absolute of an estate in land:

        (i)   for a term of more than seven years from the date of the grant;

        (ii)   taking effect in possession after the end of the period of three months beginning with the date of the grant;

        (iii) under which the right to possession is discontinuous;

        (iv) in pursuance of Part 5 Housing Act 1985 (the right to buy); or

        (v)   in circumstances where section 171A of that Act applies (disposal by landlord which leads to a person no longer being a secure tenant);

    (c)   the grant of a lease of a franchise or manor;

    (d)   the express grant or reservation of an easement or other right falling within Law of Property Act 1925, s.1(2)(a), other than one which is capable of being registered under Commons Registration Act 1965;

    (e)   the express grant or a reservation of a rentcharge or right of re-entry falling within Law of Property Act 1925, s.1(2)(b) or (e);

    (f)   the grant of a legal charge; and

    (g)   the transfer or sub-charge of a registered charge (s.27(3)).

3.8.3.   The requirement for registration applies also to transfers by operation of law except for:

    (a)   a transfer on the death or bankruptcy of an individual proprietor;

    (b)   a transfer on the dissolution of a corporate proprietor; and

    (c)   the creation of a legal charge which is a local land charge (s.27(5)).

Effect of dispositions on priority

3.8.4.   The general principle under the Act is that the priority of an interest in registered land is determined by its date of creation and not the date on which it is entered in the register or whether or not it is entered in the register (s.28(1)). There is a major exception, however, in the case of registrable dispositions (such as a transfer or charge) made for valuable consideration. In such cases, on completion of the disposition by registration, the disposition takes priority to an interest whose priority is not protected at the time of registration. The effect of these provisions is that registration of a disposition for valuable consideration takes effect subject only to:

    (a)   a registered charge;

    (b)   an interest the subject of a notice on the register;

    (c)   an overriding interest under Schedule 3 of the Act;

(d) an interest appearing from the register to be excepted from the effect of registration (for example, where the title is less than absolute); and

(e) where the land is leasehold, any interest incident to the leasehold estate, e.g. the covenants contained in the registered lease (s.29).

Relative priority of registered charges

3.8.5. Registered charges rank as between themselves in the order shown in the register (s.48). Any application to alter this priority must be made by, or with the consent of, the proprietor of any postponed registered charge and any other registered charge whose priority is affected by the alteration. But no consent is required from a person who has executed the instrument altering the priority of the charge (r.102(1)). Registration of charges and the priority of further advances are dealt with in more detail in H3.

3.9. **Registered land: applications**

Dispositions

3.9.1. Applications for registration of transfers, charges and other dispositions of registered land must be made on Form AP1 (r.13). This is the 'default' form to be used when no other application form is prescribed.

Transfer of whole

3.9.2. The application for registration of a transfer of the whole of the seller's title (whether freehold or leasehold) should be lodged at the proper office within the 30 business day priority period conferred by the applicant's pre-completion official search certificate (see G3.11.2). It is important to note that the period of protection under the search cannot be extended (although a second search conferring a separate priority period can be made). The application should be accompanied by:

(a) the transfer in Form TR1 (or TR2 if the transfer is under a chargee's power of sale);

(b) the appropriate fee under the current Land Registration Fee Order; and

(c) in appropriate circumstances:

    (i) a completed Form DS1 (or reference in the Form AP1 to the use of the END or ED systems) in respect of the seller's mortgage;

    (ii) where the seller was the personal representative of a sole deceased proprietor an office copy or certified copy of the grant of representation (rr.163(2) and 214);

    (iii) where the transfer has been executed under a power of attorney, the original or a duly certified copy of the power, or a certificate by a conveyancer in Form 1 (r.61(1) and Sched. 3); and where the transfer is not made within one year of the power, appropriate evidence of non-revocation by statutory declaration or in Form 2 (r.62 and Sched. 3);

(iv) a land transaction return certificate or self-certificate.

Transfer of part

3.9.3. The transfer must be in Form TP1 (or TP2 if the transfer is under a chargee's power of sale). The transfer should include a plan signed by the seller identifying the land transferred (r.213). (See B21 for a detailed explanation of the Land Registry's requirements on plans.) The application should be lodged within the priority period referred to in E2.5.18 accompanied by the transfer and such documents listed in that paragraph as are relevant to the transaction.

Charges

3.9.4. A registered proprietor has power to mortgage the land in any way permitted by the general law but not by a mortgage by demise or sub-demise. He may also charge the land at law with the payment of money (s.23). An application to register the charge should be made within the priority period conferred by the pre-completion official search certificate (see E2.5.18) and be accompanied by the charge and any requisite fee. The priority of lenders in registered land is governed by the order shown in the register (s.48).

3.9.5. By far the best way of protecting a lender of registered land is by substantive registration of the charge when the chargee will be entered in the register as the proprietor of the charge (Sched. 2, para. 8). On registration, a registered charge takes effect as a charge by way of legal mortgage and the proprietor of the charge can exercise all the powers of a legal mortgagee (s.51).

3.9.6. Alternatively, a charge can be protected by the entry of notice in the register and any future buyer of the land would take subject to a charge in this way. However, where a charge is not a registered charge, in order to exercise a lender's power of sale, the chargee would need either to register the charge substantively (if it is capable of being registered in its own right), or to obtain an order of the court under Law of Property Act 1925, s.90 and obtain substantive registration pursuant to that order.

3.9.7. Where a lender wishes the Land Registry to note on the register an obligation to make further advances, an application to enter the obligation should be made in Form CH2 unless the form of the charge incorporating the obligation clause has been approved by the registrar or the application is contained in panel 7 of Form CH1 (r.108).

Third party interests

3.9.8. Third party interests in registered land may now only be protected by the entry of either a notice or a restriction. A person must not apply for entry of a notice or restriction without reasonable cause. A duty of care is owed to any person who suffers damage in consequence of its breach (s.77).

3.9.9.   A notice is used to protect interests that will not be overreached on a disposition (for example, restrictive covenants and equitable easements) and will therefore continue to affect the land. A notice may be either an agreed or a unilateral notice. Certain interests are excluded from protection by way of notice (s.33). The main excluded interests are:

(a)   an interest under a trust of land;

(b)   a lease for a term of three years or less which is not required to be registered; and

(c)   a restrictive covenant between lessor and lessee so far as it relates to the property leased.

Where an interest protected by a notice is valid then the notice will protect the priority of that interest. The notice itself does not confer any priority.

3.9.10.   Where a restriction is entered on the register, a disposition cannot be registered otherwise than in accordance with the terms of the restriction. A restriction may be used, for example:

(a)   to reflect any limitations on the proprietor's powers;

(b)   to require that the proceeds of sale of land held on a trust of land are paid to at least two trustees or a trust corporation thus overreaching the beneficial interests under the trust; or

(c)   to ensure that any required consents to a disposition are obtained.

A restriction, however, cannot be entered for the purpose of protecting the priority of an interest which could be protected by notice.

Agreed notices

3.9.11.   An application for an agreed notice is to be made in Form AN1 (r.81). The proprietor's consent is normally required for an application for an agreed notice. An agreed notice may also be used without the proprietor's consent if the registrar is satisfied as to the validity of the claim (s.34(3)). In practice, this might be the case where there is, for example, an application relating to a document signed by the registered proprietor, such as a contract for sale or an equitable charge. If the document contains prejudicial information an application could be made to designate it an exempt information document (see G3.12). Alternatively an application for a unilateral notice may be considered.

3.9.12.   There are some special cases (for example, a home rights notice, or an inheritance tax notice) which can be protected only by agreed notice (r.80).

Unilateral notices

3.9.13.   An application for a unilateral notice must be made on Form UN1 (r.83). The application will be considered on the basis of the statutory declaration or conveyancer's certificate in the Form UN1. The instrument giving rise to the claimed interest need not accompany the application. A unilateral notice is entered without the consent of the registered proprietor. A unilateral notice must indicate that it is such a notice and identify who is the beneficiary of the notice. Where the registrar enters a unilateral notice in the register, notice of the entry will be given to the registered proprietor who may at any time apply for its cancellation using Form UN4. Notice will not be served on the beneficiary of the unilateral notice on registration of a disposition. The unilateral notice remains on the register until such time as it is withdrawn or cancelled.

Restrictions

3.9.14. An application for a restriction is to be made in Form RX1 save where the application is for a standard form of restriction and the application is made in:

(a) the additional provisions panel of Forms TP1, TP2, TP3, TR1, TR2, TR3, TR4, TR5, AS1, AS2 or AS3;

(b) panel 7 of Form CH1;

(c) a charge, the form of which (including the application for the restriction) has first been approved by the registrar; or

(d) clause LR13 of a Prescribed Clauses Lease (see K1.20).

The standard forms of restriction are those listed in Schedule 4 Land Registration Rules 2003 (as amended). Standard form restrictions should be used where possible to avoid the risk of a non-standard restriction being rejected on the grounds that its form is unreasonable or that its application would not be straightforward (s.43(3)).

3.9.15. An application for a restriction must be accompanied by full details of the required restriction. If the restriction requires notice to be given to a person, requires a person's consent or certificate or is a standard form of restriction that refers to a named person, that person's address for service must be provided (r.92).

3.9.16. The application may be made by the registered proprietor or with his consent. A third party who can show a sufficient interest can also make an application (s.43(1) and rr.92 and 93).

3.9.17. The Rules list persons who are to be regarded as having a sufficient interest for this purpose (r.93). These include a person with a beneficial interest under a trust of land, a person who has applied for a freezing order and a person with the benefit of a charging order over a beneficial interest under a trust of land. The corresponding standard forms of restriction are set out in Schedule 4 to the Rules.

3.9.18. For further information see Land Registry Practice Guide 19.

3.10. Adverse possession

3.10.1. Under Schedule 6 Land Registration Act 2002 a squatter on registered land is able to apply for registration if adverse possession has been enjoyed for at least 10 years. The application must be made in Form ADV1 and be accompanied by a statutory declaration complying with the requirements of rule 188 Land Registration Rules 2003.

3.10.2. If the application appears to be in order, notice will be served on the owner, chargee and other interested parties. A person in receipt of a notice has the following options:

(a) he can take no action. If no response is received to the notices, the applicant will be registered as the owner of the registered title;

(b) he may object to the application on the basis that the applicant has not been in adverse possession for 10 years. In the absence of agreement the dispute will need to be resolved judicially (s.73);

(c) he may serve a counter-notice on the registrar requiring that the matter be dealt with under Schedule 6, paragraph 5 of the Act.

3.10.3. Where a counter-notice has been served, the applicant can only be registered if he meets one of three conditions. Summarised, these are that:

(a) an equity by estoppel has arisen by reason of which the applicant should be registered as proprietor;

(b) the applicant is for some other reason entitled be registered as proprietor; or

(c) the squatter is the owner of adjacent land and has been in adverse possession of the land in the application under the reasonable but mistaken belief that the land belonged to him.

3.10.4. Where an application is rejected, then, if still in adverse possession, the squatter may re-apply in two years' time. If the owner has not either evicted the squatter or agreed terms within that period then on re-application the squatter will be registered in place of the owner.

3.10.5. Where a squatter has been in adverse possession of registered land for at least 12 years prior to 13 October 2003, he may apply for registration under the transitional provisions in Land Registration Act 2002 (Sched. 12, para. 18). Such an application is not affected by the new provisions of the Act summarised above.

3.10.6. Further information as to the Land Registry's requirements is contained in Land Registry Practice Guides 4 and 5 and the supplemental notes to Practice Guide 5 in the light of *Beaulane Properties Ltd* v. *Palmer* [2005] All ER (D) 413 and *Pye* v. *UK* (ECHR App. No. 44302/02).

3.11. **Applications generally**

3.11.1. Applications for first registration are dealt with in G3.4. Applications for registration of transfers, charges and other dispositions of registered land are dealt with in G3.9. Applications based on adverse possession are considered in G3.10. This section deals with the more general matters which relate to all applications to the Land Registry.

Delivery of applications

3.11.2. An application for registration must be delivered to the proper Land Registry office (see Appendix VIII.1 and Land Registry Practice Guide 51). Care must be taken to send the application to the proper office (and within the priority period conferred by any official search). Lodging documents at the wrong office may result in loss of priority for the application or at worst no registration at all.

Stamp Duty Land Tax

3.11.3. Applications in respect of land transactions will be rejected unless accompanied by a land transaction return certificate or a self-certificate or, where appropriate, a letter explaining why neither certificate is required. Such a letter is not required, however, where the transaction is, for example, a discharge of charge, legal charge, equitable charge, contract for sale, licence or franchise (see Land Registry Practice Guide 49). These transactions are not normally subject to SDLT.

Time of delivery

3.11.4. An application for registration is to be taken as made at the earlier of:

- (a) the time of the business day that notice of it is entered on the daylist;[1] or

- (b) (i) midnight on the day of receipt (if received before 12 noon on that day); or

  (ii) midnight on the day after receipt (if received at or on the day of receipt after 12 noon) (r.15(1)).[2]

Address for service

3.11.5. A registered proprietor must give the registrar at least one postal address for service, whether or not in the United Kingdom, to which the registrar may send notices and communications to him. Two further addresses for service may be given. They must be either a postal address, inside or outside the United Kingdom, a Document Exchange address in the United Kingdom (provided that delivery can be made on behalf of the Land Registry under existing arrangements between the Land Registry and the service provider), or an electronic address (r.198 and Land Registry Practice Guide 55). It is important that addresses for service are kept up to date.

Duty to disclose overriding interests

3.11.6.   A person applying for either first registration or registration of a registrable disposition must provide the registrar with information as to certain overriding interests which affect the estate. The Act lists separately those interests that override first registration and those that override registered dispositions (see Land Registration Act 2002, Scheds.1 and 3). The information is to be provided in Form DI. See s.71, rr.28 and 57.

3.11.7.   The provision of this information will enable the interests to be noted on the register and they will, as a result, lose their overriding status.

3.11.8.   This disclosure obligation relates only to interests within the actual knowledge of the applicant; and does not extend to, for example:

     (a)   an interest arising under a trust;

     (b)   a lease for a term of three years or less which is not required to be registered;

     (c)   a local land charge;

     (d)   a public right; and

     (e)   on first registration, an interest that is apparent from the deeds and documents of title accompanying the application.

Capacity

3.11.9.   Joint buyers are required to state on their application for registration whether they will hold the land as beneficial joint tenants or beneficial tenants in common. In the latter case a restriction in Form A will be entered in the proprietorship register of the title. Where the parties are to hold as tenants in common, a separate document may have been drawn up prior to completion indicating the proportionate shares which each tenant in common holds in the property because the register will not record the beneficial interests. This document is not submitted to the registry with the application for registration of the title but should be retained safely to avoid later disputes over the shares in the beneficial interests in the property (see E1).

3.11.10.   If a company is registered under the Companies Acts, the application must state the company's registered number (r.181(1)). In other cases, unless agreed with the registry's headquarters, a certified copy of the company's constitution should be lodged. Where the application includes a charge by such a company the applicant must produce to the registrar a certificate that the charge has been registered under section 395 Companies Act 1985 (r.111(1)). In default, the registrar must enter a note in the register that the charge is subject to the provisions of that section (r.111(2)).

3.11.11. In other situations the solicitor may have to satisfy the registrar as to the capacity of the applicant to enter the transaction, for example, housing associations, charities, building societies.

3.11.12. If the transferee of a registered title dies before registration of his interest has been completed, the deceased's equitable interest in the property passes to his personal representatives who may continue the application in their names on production of the grant of representation to the registrar (r.18).

Applications not in order

3.11.13. If an application is not in order the registrar may raise such requisitions as he considers necessary (r.16(1)). Any requisitions raised will:

    (a)   explain what is needed;

    (b)   state when the application will be cancelled if a full reply is not received (the period for complying with the requisitions will be not less than 20 business days from the date of the requisition); and

    (c)   explain what to do if a reply cannot be made by the cancellation date.

3.11.14. Extensions to the cancellation date can be made, particularly when the cause is outside the applicant's control. The Land Registry will need to know:

    (a)   the reason for the delay;

    (b)   what is being done to resolve the problem; and

    (c)   when it is expected that a full reply to the requisition can be supplied.

3.11.15. If an application appears to the registrar to be substantially defective, he may reject it on delivery or he may cancel it at any time thereafter (r.16(3)). Some examples of where this might occur are:

    (a)   applications where the original transfer, lease, charge or other primary document is not lodged and no reasonable explanation for its absence is supplied;

    (b)   dispositions for which a compulsory form is prescribed (for example, TR1 for a transfer of whole) where that form has not been used;

    (c)   applications that have been previously rejected or cancelled if the outstanding points remain unresolved.

3.11.16. For more information on the Land Registry's cancellation and rejection policy, see Land Registry Practice Guides 49 and 50.

Objections

3.11.17. Any person may object to an application to the registrar (s.73(1)). The objection must be in writing, signed by the objector or his conveyancer, state the ground for the objection and give the full name of the objector and the address to which communications may be sent (r.19). The objection must be delivered to the appropriate office.

3.11.18. A person who objects to an application must not do so without reasonable cause; and owes a duty to any person who suffers damage in consequence of its breach (s.77). If the objection is not groundless and cannot be disposed of by agreement it must be referred to the Adjudicator to HM Land Registry (s.73(7)).

3.11.19. See Land Registry Practice Guides 37 (objections and disputes) and 38 (costs).

Completion of applications

3.11.20. Any entry in, removal of an entry from, or alteration of the register made as a result of an application has effect from the time of the making of the application (r.20).

3.11.21. On completion of any application the registrar may retain all or any of the documents that accompanied the application and must return all other such documents to the applicant or as otherwise specified in the application (r.203(1)). If when making the application the applicant or his conveyancer requests the return of any of the documents sent with the application and provides certified copies of those particular documents with the application, the registrar must return the original documents so requested on completion of the application. On first registration, however, an applicant need only provide certified copies of any statutory declaration, subsisting lease, subsisting charge or the latest document of title (r.203(2)–(5)).

3.11.22. A title information document is issued by the Land Registry where an application leads to a change of ownership. The title information document does not constitute a guarantee of title and it does not need to be lodged on the registration of any dealing with the land.

3.11.23. Where panel 10 of the application form AP1 has been completed with the name and address of a third party the Land Registry will send notification of completion of the application to the third party.

3.11.24. The registrar has power to destroy any documents, which accompanied an application and which have been retained by him, if he is satisfied that either he has made and retained a sufficient copy of the document or that its further retention is unnecessary (r.203(6)).

3.11.25. Where, on 13 October 2003, the registrar held a document on which an entry on the register is or was founded, either the person who originally delivered that document to the registrar or, in certain circumstances, the registered proprietor, may within the period to 13 October 2008, ask for the return of the document (r.204(1)–(3)).

3.11.26. After 13 October 2008, the registrar may destroy any document held by him on 13 October 2003 if he is satisfied either that he has made and retained a sufficient copy of the document or that its further retention is unnecessary (r.204(6)).

1. The daylist shows the date and time at which every pending application was made (r.12).
2. See Land Registration Rules 2003, r.15(2) and (3) as to receipt of applications on non-business days and as to the deemed delivery of applications.

3.12. Access to information

3.12.1. Section 66 provides that any person can inspect and make copies of:

(a) the register of title;

(b) any document kept by the registrar which is referred to in the register of title;

(c) any other document kept by the registrar which relates to an application that has been made to him; or

(d) the register of cautions against first registration.

3.12.2. However, any person may apply to the registrar for a document to be designated an exempt information document if he claims that the document contains prejudicial information (r.131).

3.12.3. The application must be made in Forms EX1 (the application form) and EX1A (the reasons in support) and be accompanied by an appropriately certified copy of the document which excludes the prejudicial information (r.136(2)). If the registrar is satisfied that the applicant's claim is not groundless and that completing the application would not prejudice the keeping of the register, he must designate the document an exempt information document (rr.136(3) and (4)).

3.12.4. When so designated, the general right to inspect and make copies relates to a copy of the exempt information document from which the prejudicial information has been excluded (this copy is known as an edited information document (r.131)).

3.12.5. An application can be made for an official copy of an exempt information document. The application must be made in Form EX2. An application can also be made under the provisions of Freedom of Information Act 2000.

3.12.6. The registrar may, on application in Form HC1, provide information about the history of a registered title. Historical editions of the register are available where the register is held in electronic form (r.144).

3.12.7. See also Land Registry Practice Guide 57 (Exempting documents from the right to inspect), Public Guide 1 (Information that can be obtained from the Land Registry) and Public Guide 15 (Freedom of Information Act 2000).

3.13. The Adjudicator to HM Land Registry

3.13.1. The Office of the Adjudicator to HM Land Registry is established by the Act (Part 11 and Sched.9). The Adjudicator is independent of the Land Registry.

3.13.2. The Adjudicator determines references made to him by the Registrar where there is a dispute between a person who has made an application to the Registrar and some other person (s.73(7)). The Adjudicator can decide a matter himself or direct a party to commence proceedings in the court to determine the dispute (s.110).

3.13.3 The Adjudicator also has power, on application, to make any order which the High Court could make for the rectification or setting aside of a document which:

(a) effects a qualifying disposition of a registered estate or charge;

(b) is a contract to make such a disposition; or

(c) effects a transfer of an interest which is the subject of a notice in the register.

A qualifying disposition is a registrable disposition or one which creates an interest which may be the subject of a notice in the register (s.108).

3.13.4. Proceedings before the Adjudicator are governed by Adjudicator to Her Majesty's Land Registry (Practice and Procedure) Rules 2003 (SI 2003/2171).

3.13.5. A requirement made by the Adjudicator is enforceable as an order of the court.

3.13.6. Further information, appropriate application forms and guidance relating to the Office of the Adjudicator to HM Land Registry is available on the website at **www.ahmlr.gov.uk**.

H. LENDERS

H1. Acting for the lender

1.1. Introduction

1.1.1. Matters relating to the solicitor who is acting for a lender client are dealt with in context in other sections of this book. The following paragraphs draw together some of those points in the form of checklists for ready reference.

1.1.2. In many cases the solicitor acting for the lender will also be acting for the borrower in a related sale or purchase transaction. In such a case the principles of conduct relating to conflict of interests and confidentiality must at all times be observed (see A11).

1.2. Instructions to act

1.2.1. Even where instructions are received from a lender for whom the solicitor acts frequently, it should not be assumed that the instructions in the current transaction are identical to those issued on previous occasions.

1.2.2. Instructions to act must be carefully checked in each particular case and any queries clarified with the lender. If at any time during the course of the transaction it appears that compliance with the lender's instructions will not be possible, further instructions must immediately be sought.

1.2.3. In many cases where the loan is connected to residential property the solicitor will be instructed to act in accordance with the terms of the Lenders' Handbook.[1] Part 1 of the Handbook contains provisions which are applicable to all transactions. These provisions may be varied by the specific requirements of an individual lender contained either in Part 2 of the Handbook and/or in special instructions supplied to the solicitor with the lender's letter of instruction. Where applicable, the Lenders' Handbook sets out the terms of the contract between the solicitor and the lender and the conditions must be closely observed.

1.2.4.   A solicitor may only act for a lender where the lender's instructions do not extend beyond the requirements contained in Rule 3.19 Solicitors' Code of Conduct 2007 (see Appendix I.1).

1. Part 1 of the Lenders' Handbook is reproduced in Appendix VI.2. Part 2 of the Handbook is only available online at **www.cml.org.uk**.

1.3.   Creation of new mortgage – checklist

(a)   Check instructions to ensure that all conditions attached to the advance can be complied with by both the solicitor and the borrower and that the instructions comply with Rule 3.19 Solicitors' Code of Conduct 2007.

(b)   If the lender is not a building society, confirm with him the rate of charging for acting for him and who is to be responsible for payment of the solicitor's bill.

(c)   Check that the terms of the contract to purchase are acceptable – does the purchase price in the contract accord with that shown on the lender's instructions?

(d)   If the mortgage is being granted to a sole borrower, what are the lender's instructions relating to non-owning occupiers? Has any relevant consent form been signed?[1]

(e)   Have adequate enquiries been made to ensure that there are no overriding interests over the property which will adversely affect the lender's security?

(f)   Inform lender of exchange of contracts and of contractual completion date if necessary.

(g)   Check that the property will be properly insured from the moment of exchange or completion (as appropriate).

(h)   Has investigation of title been completed satisfactorily (including the results of pre-contract searches and enquiries) – have all the lender's specific requirements been met?

(i)   Engross mortgage deed and obtain borrower's signature(s) to it. Where there are joint borrowers one or more of whom is not known personally to the solicitor, precautions should be taken to verify the signature of the unknown borrower(s) in order to guard against forgery, e.g. by requiring the document to be signed in the presence of the solicitor.[2]

(j)   Engross and obtain borrower's signature to assignment of life policy (where appropriate).

(k)   Ensure that life policy in terms which comply with lender's instructions is in existence.

(l)   Are results of pre-completion searches satisfactory, including a clear result of a bankruptcy search against the names of the borrower(s) and a company search against a company seller?

(m) Send a report on title/certificate of title to the lender and request the advance cheque.[3]

(n) On receipt of advance cheque pay it into clients' account – ensure funds have been cleared before completion.

(o) Make arrangements for completion.

(p) If required, arrange for inspection of property immediately before completion to ensure vacant possession will be given.

(q) Arrange for transmission of funds on day of completion.

(r) Inform lender of completion.

(s) Obtain purchase deed and title deeds from borrower's solicitor on completion with cheque for SDLT and Land Registry fees.

(t) Date and fill in blanks in mortgage deed and related documents.

(u) Send notice of assignment of life policy (in duplicate) to insurance company.

(v) Give notice to prior lender(s) (if second or subsequent mortgage).

(w) Attend to payment of SDLT.

(x) Submit application for registration of title within relevant priority period.

(y) Keep lender informed of the reason for any delays at the Land Registry.

(z) Prepare schedule of deeds for lender.

(za) Send deeds to lender (or as instructed) and request return of receipted schedule of deeds.

1. A signed deed or form of consent must be obtained from all occupants aged 17 or over (Lenders' Handbook, para. 7.3). Also note that the Lenders' Handbook states at para. 8.3 that the solicitor must not advise anyone who is intending to occupy the property regarding the signing of the consent. Arrangements must be made for them to see an independent adviser.
2. See the requirements relating to identification in the Lenders' Handbook, para. 3. The signature must be checked against one of the documents specified in the Handbook.
3. For special procedure on the completion of a mortgage over a new property see I.1.7.

1.4.   Redemption of mortgage – checklist

(a) Request redemption figure from lender and title deeds if unregistered. If the seller has a 'flexible mortgage' ask for the account to be frozen until after completion (see F3.7.4).

(b) Make a search to check if there is a subsequent chargee to whom the title deeds should be handed on completion.

(c) Check instructions from lender on their receipt.

(d) In the case of a related sale prepare epitome of title and send to borrower's solicitor (if unregistered land and lender's solicitor is not also acting for borrower).

(e) In the case of a related sale keep in touch with borrower's solicitor about arrangements for completion.

(f) Prepare Form DS1 or END[1] (or receipt in unregistered land).

(g) Prepare reassignment of life policy (where relevant).

(h) Prepare undertaking for discharge of mortgage to be given to buyer's solicitor on completion.

(i) Prepare forms for discharge of land charges entries (second and subsequent mortgages of unregistered land).

(j) Obtain final redemption figure from lender and inform borrower's solicitor of the figure.

(k) Arrange with borrower's solicitor for actual payment on completion.

(l) On receipt of repayment money, clear draft through clients' account and account to lender in accordance with redemption statement.

(m) Hand over undertaking for discharge of mortgage to buyer's solicitor.

(n) Send Form DS1 or END1 (or receipt in unregistered land) and deed of reassignment of life policy to mortgagee for execution and return. In the case of non-building society lenders, request that documents are dated with the date that completion of the mortgagor's sale took place to avoid problems over inadvertent transfer of the mortgage (see D2.10).

(o) On receipt of executed Form DS1 (or receipt), check it before sending to buyer's solicitor and request to be released from the undertaking given on completion.

(p) Return life policy to borrower.

1. See G1.11 as to electronic discharges.

1.5.   Mortgage not simultaneous with purchase – checklist

(a) Obtain official copy entries of the title/title deeds.

(b) Make relevant pre-contract searches and enquiries including a search to find out whether prior mortgages exist (see B10).

(c) Make enquiries about non-owning occupiers and obtain signature of consent form/release of rights in accordance with lender's instructions (see H1.3).

(d) Investigate title to the property.

(e) Check the state of the prior mortgage account (if relevant).

(f) Ensure compliance with Consumer Credit Act 1974, s.58 where applicable (see H3).

(g) Draft, then engross mortgage deed.

(h) Send report on title/certificate of title to lender with request for advance cheque.

(i) Explain the effect of and obtain borrower's signature to mortgage deed.

(j) Make pre-completion searches, including bankruptcy search against name of borrower, and obtain clear results to searches.

(k) Ensure any conditions attached to offer of advance have been complied with.

(l) Arrange to complete.

(m) On completion hand advance money to mortgagor, date and fill in any blanks in mortgage deed.

(n) Protect lender's security by registration.

(o) Give notice to a prior lender (where relevant).

(p) Advise lender of completion of the mortgage.

1.6. Buy to let mortgages

Occasionally a condition is attached to a buy to let mortgage to the effect that the new tenancy must be agreed and the start date set prior to the completion of the mortgage. This is not always possible to achieve and both the lender and the client must be kept informed of the position and the lender must be requested to withdraw the condition if it becomes clear that it cannot be complied with.

1.7. Incorrect redemption statements

Guidance has been issued jointly by the Law Society and Council of Mortgage Lenders in connection with problems arising out of incorrect redemption statements supplied by lenders (see Appendix VI.2).

H2. Sales by lenders

2.1.	**Power of sale**	2.5.	**Proceeds of sale**
2.2.	**Possession**	2.6.	**Administrative receivers and**
2.3.	**Price**		**administrators**
2.4.	**The sale transaction**	2.7.	**Receiver appointed by lender**

2.1. Power of sale

2.1.1. A lender may sell property over which he enjoys a power of sale and convey in his own name provided his power has both arisen and become exercisable. The existence and exercise of the power are discussed in B7.7.

2.1.2. A first lender sells free of all charges registered subsequent to his own; thus a buyer is not concerned with the discharge of second and subsequent mortgages when a power of sale is exercised by a first lender.[1]

2.1.3. If a second or subsequent lender wishes to sell he must either sell the property subject to any prior charges, or redeem them (thus becoming a first lender) but will overreach all charges which are subsequent to his own.

2.1.4. The lender must exercise his power in good faith for the purpose of obtaining repayment; subject to this, he can exercise his powers even if the exercise is disadvantageous to the borrower.[2] There is no wider duty in negligence.[3]

2.1.5. A lender must not sell to himself or to his nominee.[4] There is no rule that he cannot sell to a person connected with him[5] but the correctness of the price must plainly be beyond doubt, and the lender must have taken and acted on expert advice as to the best method of selling, what steps should reasonably be taken to make the sale a success, and what reserve price should be fixed.

2.1.6. It is usually inadvisable for the sale contract to be conditional or for an option to be granted, since there is a risk that the loan might be repaid and the borrower would then be entitled to a discharge of the mortgage. The borrower's equity of redemption, and his ability to redeem, is only destroyed when there is a binding unconditional contract for sale.[6]

2.1.7. If the mortgage is only over the beneficial interest of a joint owner, the lender will have to make application to the court under section 14 Trusts of Land and Appointment of Trustees Act 1996 for an order for sale. This order will not necessarily be granted by the court.

2.1.8. In the case of an equitable mortgage made by deed, there can be a power of sale provided the power has both arisen and become exercisable. The lender can apply to the court under section 90 Law of Property Act 1925 for an order conveying the property to the buyer or creating and vesting in the lender a legal mortgage to enable the lender to carry out the sale. See G3.9.5 as to the registration of legal charges relating to registered land.

1. Law of Property Act 1925, s.104 and Land Registration Act 2002, s.52.
2. *Kennedy* v. *De Trafford* [1897] AC 180. See also *Meretz Investments NV and Britel Corporation NV* v. *ACP Ltd* [2006] EWHC 74 where it was held that if a lender had mixed motives for exercising his powers of sale and one of the motives was to recover the debt secured by the mortgage, his exercise of the power of sale would not be invalidated.
3. *Downsview Nominees* v. *First City Corp.* [1993] 3 All ER 626.
4. *Farrar* v. *Farrars Ltd* (1888) 40 Ch 395.
5. *Tse Kwong Lam* v. *Wong Chit Sen* [1983] 3 All ER 54, PC.
6. *Property & Bloodstock Ltd* v. *Emerton* [1968] Ch 94.

2.2. Possession

2.2.1. Before selling the lender will normally take possession in order to be able to sell with vacant possession (or subject to any tenancies which bind him).

2.2.2. In the case of residential property it will be necessary to obtain a court order for possession unless the occupier leaves the premises voluntarily.[1]

2.2.3. A buyer from the lender is not concerned to see the court order authorising possession.

1. Protection from Eviction Act 1977, s.2.

2.3. Price

2.3.1. Building societies are under a statutory duty to obtain the best price for the property.[1]

2.3.2. Other lenders must take reasonable precautions to obtain a proper price for the property.[2] Although there is a theoretical distinction between building societies and other lenders in relation to the price which they must obtain for the property, in practice the courts appear to apply similar criteria when applying each test.

2.3.3. Sales by lenders commonly take place by auction but there is no legal requirement to this effect. A sale by auction does not necessarily constitute evidence that the lender has obtained the best possible price for the property,[3] and the lender's duty in this respect is not discharged by placing the property for sale in the hands of reputable agents.[4]

2.3.4. A sale at a sum which is sufficient only to pay off the mortgage would be looked at carefully by the court.[5] Where the mortgage lender fails in its duty and the property is sold at an undervalue, the mortgage lender will have to reimburse the borrower for the loss suffered.[6]

2.3.5.   The fact that the property is resold to a third party shortly after the sale by the lender and at a substantially higher price than that obtained by the lender would also be viewed with suspicion by the court.[7]

2.3.6.   The borrower can challenge the amount of costs claimed by the mortgagee by making an application to the court for the taxation of the lender's costs.[8]

1. Building Societies Act 1986, s.13(7).
2. *Cuckmere Brick Co. Ltd* v. *Mutual Finance Ltd* [1971] Ch 949.
3. *Tse Kwong Lam* v. *Wong Chit Sen* [1983] 3 All ER 54, PC.
4. *Cuckmere Brick Co. Ltd* v. *Mutual Finance Ltd* [1971] Ch 949.
5. *Midland Bank Ltd* v. *Joliman Finance Ltd* (1967) 203 EG 612; *Predeth* v. *Castle Phillips Finance Co. Ltd* [1986] 2 EGLR 144, CA.
6. *Mortgage Express* v. *Mardner* [2004] EWCA 1859.
7. *Bank of Cyprus (London) Ltd* v. *Gill* [1980] 2 Lloyd's Rep 51.
8. *Gomba Holdings (UK) Ltd* v. *Minories Finance (No.2)* [1992] 4 All ER 588.

2.4.   The sale transaction

2.4.1.   The sale follows the normal procedures for the sale of land, subject to any specific requirements or instructions given by the mortgagee client.

2.4.2.   Since the lender will have taken possession of the property (if at all) only shortly before exercising his power of sale, he will have little or no knowledge of the condition of the property and may not therefore be able to answer pre-contract enquiries as fully as the buyer would wish. The buyer should be advised of this fact and of any other special conditions attaching to the sale, e.g. requirement for payment of a full 10% deposit. A selling lender will commonly require the buyer to exchange contracts within a stated period, reserving the right to withdraw from the sale if this condition is not met. This type of condition is imposed because of the lender's duty to obtain the best price for the property. If exchange of contracts became delayed, property values might in the interim period have altered and the lender might find himself liable in an action for breach of trust if he continued with a prospective sale in circumstances where the market price of the property had risen and a better price would be obtainable elsewhere.

2.4.3.   The lender's duty to both the borrower and to subsequent lenders to obtain the best or proper price means that the lender is under an implicit duty to preserve the value of the property by ensuring that it remains in good physical order. For this reason, the buyer should not be allowed access or entry into possession before completion. Standard Condition 5.2 (occupation by the buyer) or any similar provision, should therefore normally be excluded from the contract. If not so excluded a buyer does not have a *right* to occupy; he may only do so with the seller's consent.

2.4.4.   The buyer can demand to see the mortgage deed under which the power of sale is being exercised in order to check the existence of the power and that it has arisen, but is not concerned to enquire whether circumstances exist which entitle the lender to exercise the power.

2.4.5. In the case of registered land, the transfer must be in Form TR2.[1]

2.4.6. The lender will need to consider which covenants for title (if any) he is prepared to give to the buyer in the purchase deed.

2.4.7. On completion of a sale by a lender, the mortgage under which the power is exercised is not 'discharged' although the buyer takes free from it. Where the land is unregistered, the buyer will receive the mortgage deed and other title deeds but not a mortgage receipt. Where the land is registered, the buyer will not receive a Form DS1 or END1 in respect of the mortgage. Forms DS1 or END 1 (mortgage deeds and/or receipts in unregistered land) relating to subsequent mortgages (if any) do not need to be handed over on completion since the sale by the lender overreaches these subsequent charges.

1. Land Registration Rules 2003, r.58 and Sched.1.

2.5. **Proceeds of sale**

2.5.1. The selling lender will discharge the debt owing to him, including interest and the costs of the sale, from the proceeds of sale.

2.5.2. If any surplus then remains, the selling lender holds the surplus on behalf of and must account to a subsequent lender. It is essential that the selling lender makes a search at the Land Registry (registered land) or the Land Charges Department (unregistered land) to discover whether or not subsequent mortgages exist before accounting to the borrower for the surplus proceeds of sale. In registered land, the selling lender is taken to have notice of anything in the register immediately before the transfer.[1] The buyer from the lender is not concerned to see that the lender deals properly with the surplus.

2.5.3. When considering the application of the proceeds of sale, a lender must have regard to any other security he holds for the mortgage debt (e.g. an endowment policy). The lender who sells in possession may not recover his entire debt (or an unfair proportion of it) from one security rather than another, even if he regards the property as his primary security, where this is to the detriment of a second lender who only has one type of security. So, for example, the lender may not take his entire debt from the property and hand the endowment policy back to the borrower, where this would result in the second lender on the property receiving nothing. The selling lender must recover his debt pro rata against all available security in his hands to achieve fairness between himself and any subsequent lender(s) and between subsequent lenders *inter se*.[2]

2.5.4. In the event that there is a shortfall, the lender has a 12-year limitation period in which to bring an action against the borrower to recover the shortfall.

1. Land Registration Act 2002, s.54.
2. For a more detailed discussion of this rather esoteric doctrine of 'marshalling the assets' see *Fisher and Lightwood's Law of Mortgages.*

2.6.   Administrative receivers and administrators

2.6.1.   A properly appointed administrative receiver of a company (this person must be a licensed insolvency practitioner) has power to sell a company's property but is personally liable on all contracts he enters into, unless the contract otherwise provides. He owes a duty to both borrower and lender to take reasonable care to obtain the best price which circumstances permit when selling the assets.[1]

2.6.2.   Where the charge was entered into on or after 15 September 2003 an administrator will be appointed (Enterprise Act 2002). The administrator is appointed by the court and has all the same powers of an administrative receiver and he acts as an agent of the company and an officer of the court in carrying out those duties. An administrator can make distributions to secured and preferential creditors (and with the consent of the court, to unsecured creditors). He can dispose of the floating charge property as if it were not subject to the charge but he must obtain the leave of the court to dispose of other secured property or to acquire property.

2.6.3.   For the Land Registry's requirements see Land Registry Practice Guide 36.

1. *Gosling v. Gaskell* [1897] AC 575.

2.7.   Receiver appointed by lender

2.7.1.   The receiver need not be a licensed insolvency practitioner unless his position is classified as that of an administrative receiver (i.e. his responsibilities extend to substantially the whole of the company's assets and he is appointed under floating as well as fixed charges). The receiver is agent for the borrower company and is personally liable on his contracts unless the contract otherwise provides. The receiver will not automatically take possession of the company's property but is entitled to collect income accruing from it. He must apply that income as directed by section 109 Law of Property Act 1925. Rent collected by and in the hands of the borrower's managing agent may strictly not be classified as 'income' to which the receiver is entitled. To overcome this difficulty the receiver should as soon as practicable after his appointment give notice to all tenants and to the managing agent advising that all rent should be paid to the receiver as from that time. The receiver owes a duty to the borrower to carry out all rent reviews, lease renewals and other acts that a prudent landlord would do.[1] Where a receiver contracts to sell property owned by the borrower, the contract should provide for the purchase deed to be signed by the lender under his power of sale; this procedure will ensure that other interests in the property are overreached on completion.

1. See *Knight v. Lawrence* [1991] 1 EGLR 143.

H3. Second and subsequent mortgages

3.1.   Introduction

3.1.1.   The creation of a second or subsequent mortgage will not necessarily occur simultaneously with the purchase of the property over which the mortgage is taken.

3.1.2.   The solicitor acting for the borrower may also be instructed to act for the lender but not infrequently separate solicitors are instructed to act in this situation.

3.1.3.   The procedures to be followed by the lender's solicitor broadly follow the steps to be taken in a normal purchase transaction (except that there is no contract) since full enquiries about the property and its title must be made on the lender's behalf to ensure that he will obtain a viable security for his loan.

3.1.4.   A checklist of the steps to be taken when acting on a mortgage which is not simultaneous with a purchase is set out in H1.5.

3.1.5.   Mortgages sometimes contain a condition prohibiting the borrower from creating further charges over the property without that lender's consent. In such a case the requisite consent should be sought and obtained at an early stage in the transaction. A mortgage created in breach of such a condition is not itself invalid but will render the borrower vulnerable to repayment of the first charge.

3.2.   Registration of charges

3.2.1.   On completion of a mortgage of registered land the charge must be protected by registration at the Land Registry within the priority period afforded by the lender's search.

3.2.2.   The priority of registered charges in registered land depends on the order in which the charges are registered on the title; therefore registration within the priority period given by a pre-completion search certificate is essential.[1]

3.2.3.   An equitable mortgage must be in writing and signed by both parties in order to satisfy Law of Property (Miscellaneous Provisions) Act 1989, s.2.[2]

3.2.4.   An equitable mortgage of registered land should be protected by registration of a notice at the Land Registry. If not so protected the lender is at risk of losing his priority to the holder of a subsequently created legal charge.[3]

3.2.5.   A charge created by a company, whether fixed or floating and whether over registered or unregistered land, must be registered at the Companies Registry under Companies Act requirements within 21 days of its creation.

3.2.6.   In unregistered land a mortgage which is not accompanied by the deposit of title deeds must be protected by registration at the Land Charges Department by entry of a Class C(i) (for a legal mortgage) or Class C(iii) (for an equitable mortgage) land charge. By Law of Property Act 1925, s.198 registration constitutes actual notice to a third party for all purposes connected with the land; further, the date of registration governs the priority of mortgages. In order to effect registration at the earliest possible opportunity, a priority notice should be lodged at the Land Charges Department at least 15 working days before completion and the application for registration made within 30 working days of lodging the priority notice. This will ensure that registration is effective from the date of completion itself.

3.2.7.   Notice of the mortgage should be given to prior lenders in order to ensure that they are actually aware of the existence of the new charge. The proprietor of a registered charge may make a further advance on the security of that charge ranking in priority to a subsequent charge if he has not received notice of the creation of the subsequent charge (from the subsequent chargee).[4]

1. Land Registration Act 2002, s.48 and see *Mortgage Corporation Ltd* v. *Nationwide Credit Corporation Ltd* [1994] Ch 49, CA.
2. *United Bank of Kuwait plc* v. *Sahib* [1996] NPC 12.
3. Land Registration Act 2002, s.29(1) and (2).
4. *Ibid.*, s.49(1).

3.3.   Power of sale

3.3.1.   Provided that he has a power of sale and that it has both arisen and become exercisable (see B7.7) there is no legal reason why a second or subsequent lender should not sell the property in order to realise his security.

3.3.2.   In practical terms he may experience difficulty in selling the property. Although he will sell free of incumbrances ranking in priority subsequent to his own, he cannot sell free of prior incumbrances (although he may be able to redeem these on completion if the proceeds of sale are sufficient). He should therefore obtain an official copy of the register from the Land Registry (registered land) or make an official search at the Land Charges Department (unregistered land) to establish which incumbrances, if any, have priority over his own.

3.3.3.   The sale of a property which is subject to a subsisting mortgage is not an attractive marketable proposition and the price attainable on such a sale may be low as a reflection of the existence of the mortgage over the property. The selling lender may therefore either have to persuade his prior lender to join with him in exercising the power of sale (assuming that the price obtainable would then be sufficient to discharge both debts) or discharge the prior mortgage out of his own funds before selling thus placing himself in the position of first lender. A contract for sale by a subsequent lender cannot prevent the prior lender selling the property in the meantime. This would put the second lender in breach of his sale contract. He needs to come to an arrangement with the first lender before exchanging contracts. That could either involve him redeeming the first mortgage beforehand out of his own money, or agreeing to discharge it on completion out of the proceeds of sale.

3.4. Consumer Credit Act 1974

3.4.1. Section 58 Consumer Credit Act 1974 is primarily of concern when dealing with the creation of second or subsequent mortgages in favour of finance houses.

3.4.2. The section applies where:

(a) a mortgage is created over land;

(b) the mortgage is not taken out to finance the purchase of the land which is being mortgaged, i.e. a bridging loan or mortgage which is simultaneous with the purchase of land is not within this section;

(c) the lender is not exempt under Consumer Credit Act 1974, s.16 (most building societies, banks and insurance companies are exempt lenders);[1]

(d) the sum secured by the mortgage does not exceed £25,000.[2]

3.4.3. Where this section applies the creditor (lender) must supply the debtor (borrower) with a copy of the prospective mortgage agreement and related documents, e.g. assignment of life policy. Having done this, he must allow seven days to elapse before sending a further copy of the agreement and related documents to the debtor for signature by him. A further period of seven days must then elapse before the creditor is permitted to contact the debtor for any reason. Thus the debtor is given a 14-day 'consideration period' which runs from the date when the first copies of the agreement and related documents are sent to him in which to consider the prospective transaction free of influence from the creditor and if desired to take legal advice. During the whole of this time the creditor must not contact the debtor except to send him the signature copies of the agreement and related documents, although he may speak to or otherwise communicate with the debtor if the debtor contacts him first. Any communication between the creditor and debtor during this period must only be at the instigation of the debtor.

3.4.4. The consideration period can come to an end before the expiry of the 14 days if within that time the debtor signs and returns the agreement to the creditor.

3.4.5.   For the purposes of this section, communications sent to or made with the debtor by the creditor's solicitor would be treated as being communications made by the creditor himself.

3.4.6.   Failure to comply with the section or breach of its provisions renders the agreement improperly executed. This means that it cannot be enforced without a court order under Consumer Credit Act 1974, s.127. Such a court order would not necessarily be granted.

3.4.7.   Because of the seriousness of the consequences of non-compliance with section 58, it is imperative that creditors and their solicitors comply with its requirements and do not contact the debtor while the consideration period is running.

3.4.8.   Where it appears that the loan will be subject to the provisions of section 58, it is best for the parties to be represented by separate solicitors in order to avoid the problems outlined in this paragraph. The section causes particular difficulty where the same solicitor is acting for both parties to the transaction since it means that during the consideration period the solicitor is unable to contact his debtor client, even to advise him about the terms of the loan agreement. It is uncertain whether in such circumstances contact made by the solicitor with the debtor about a matter unrelated to the loan would infringe the terms of the section, but it would seem advisable not to contact the debtor client at all during this period.

3.4.9.   Where the loan is subject to Consumer Credit Act 1974 a proper default notice under section 87 of the Act must be served before enforcement of the security. The court may then make a time order under sections 129–130 of the Act (these sections are similar in their effect to Administration of Justice Act 1970, s.36).[3]

1. Section 16A Consumer Credit Act 1974 gives the Secretary of State the power to provide by order for the exemption of consumer credit agreements from regulation where the debtor has a high net worth. Consumer credit agreements entered into wholly or predominantly for a debtor's business purposes where the credit provided exceeds £25,000 will also be exempted from regulation under section 16B Consumer Credit Act 1974 from a date to be appointed (anticipated 6 April 2008).
2. This financial limit has been repealed by section 2(1)(b) Consumer Credit Act 2006 from a date to be appointed (anticipated 6 April 2008).
3. See *Southern & District Finance* v. *Barnes* [1995] NPC 52.

3.5.   Tacking

3.5.1.   Tacking is the name given to the process by which a lender makes a further advance to the borrower and claims priority for repayment of both the original loan and the further advance over intervening lenders whose mortgages were created after the first loan but before the further advance.

Registered land

3.5.2.   Registered charges are to be taken to rank as between themselves in the order shown in the register.[1] However, this general rule is affected by the provisions contained in Land Registration Act 2002, s.49. Under this section a chargee can make a further advance ranking in priority to a subsequent charge:

(a) if he has not received notice from another chargee that a subsequent charge has been created;[2]

(b) if the advance is made pursuant to an obligation and this obligation is recorded in the register;[3] or

(c) where the parties to the original charge have agreed a maximum amount for which the charge is security and the agreement is entered on the register.[4]

3.5.3. In other cases, tacking is only possible with the agreement of the subsequent chargee.[5]

Unregistered land

3.5.4. Section 94 Law of Property Act 1925 allows a mortgagee to tack a further advance in three cases:

(a) where the intervening lender agrees;

(b) where his mortgage imposes on him an *obligation* to make a further advance;

(c) where he had no notice of the intervening mortgage at the time of making the further advance. The registration of the intervening mortgage (whether legal or equitable) under Land Charges Act is notice for this purpose, except that if the first mortgage was made to secure a current account or other further advances, the mere registration of the intervening mortgage as a land charge is not of itself notice to the first lender to prevent tacking.

3.5.5. It follows from (c) above that a second or subsequent lender of unregistered land should (as well as registering his mortgage as a land charge) give express notice of his mortgage to any prior lender in order to prevent the tacking of further advances by the prior lender.

3.5.6. A further reason for giving such notice is to compel a first (or prior) lender to hand the title deeds to the later lender when the earlier mortgage is discharged. The earlier lender is bound to do this where he has notice of the later mortgage, but the mere registration of the mortgage as a land charge is not notice for this purpose.

1. Land Registration Act 2002, s.48.
2. *Ibid.*, s.49(1) and (2), and see Land Registration Rules 2003, r.107 as to when notice shall be treated as received.
3. Land Registration Act 2002, s.49(3).
4. *Ibid.*, s.49(4).
5. *Ibid.*, s.49(6).

3.6. **Consolidation**

3.6.1. Consolidation is the right of a lender to refuse to allow a mortgage on one property to be redeemed unless a mortgage on another property (or properties) is also redeemed. It is an equitable doctrine, based on the principle that it would be unfair to allow a borrower to redeem a mortgage over a valuable property and leave the lender with security on another property which was not worth the amount of the loan.

3.6.2. As it is an equitable doctrine, the borrower must be seeking to exercise his equitable right to redeem, i.e. the legal date for redemption on all the mortgages sought to be consolidated must have passed, and all the mortgages must originally have been created by the same borrower. At least one of the mortgages must expressly reserve the right to consolidate, i.e. it must expressly exclude the effect of Law of Property Act 1925, s.93 which restricts consolidation.

3.6.3. Provided the conditions set out in H3.6.2 are satisfied, a lender may consolidate provided that all the equities of redemption are in one hand (i.e. owned by the same person) and all the mortgages in another, or, that state of affairs having existed in the past, the equities (only) have become separated.

3.6.4. Because a second mortgage of land is in principle a mortgage of the equity of redemption of the first mortgage, the right, where it exists, can be exercised not only against the transferees of the land, but also against subsequent lenders.

3.6.5. A buyer who is taking land subject to an existing mortgage, or a subsequent lender of the land, should make enquiry as to the existence of mortgages on other land created by the same borrower, since the doctrine operates independently of notice and even the subsequent uniting of mortgages in one hand could cause prejudice to such a person.

3.6.6. A chargee who has a right of consolidation in relation to a registered charge on registered land may apply to the registrar for entry of a notice in the individual register of the registered titles affected to show that the specified registered charges are consolidated. The application must be made in Form CC.[1]

1. Land Registration Act 2002, s.57 and Land Registration Rules 2003, r.110.

H4. Certificates of title

4.1.   Definition

4.1.1.   A certificate of title is written confirmation given by a solicitor or other person qualified in the law of the country in which the property is situated as to the ownership of land or any interest in land.

4.2.   When will a certificate of title be required?

4.2.1.   A certificate of title may be used in any case where confirmation as to the title to property is required and is increasingly requested by mortgage lenders (but see H4.3.5). It may be appropriate to require that a certificate of title be given by or on behalf of the person who owns the land. As an alternative to a certificate it may be possible to deal with the title to the property by means of warranties given by the person owning the property or an investigation and report on the title by lawyers acting on behalf of the person who is seeking to ascertain the quality of the title.

4.2.2.   Examples of situations where a certificate may be appropriate:

(a)   the purchase of shares in a company;

(b)   the purchase of assets from a company;

(c)   flotation, mortgage, debenture or other security arrangements made by companies;

(d)   occasionally on a straightforward house purchase, if required by the mortgage lender.

4.2.3.   In order to avoid a possible breach of Rule 3.07 Solicitors' Code of Conduct 2007, where a seller's solicitor is asked to provide a certificate of title to the buyer's solicitor, it must be made clear that in providing the certificate the seller's solicitor is not acting on behalf of the buyer.

4.3.   Contents of certificate

4.3.1.   The person to whom the certificate is addressed is entitled to rely on its contents; thus the person giving the certificate can be held liable for inaccuracies in its contents. It is therefore important for the person giving the certificate to identify the recipient of the certificate and to know for what purpose the certificate is required. The giver may seek to limit his liability on the certificate to named recipients and/or to limit the validity of the certificate for a specified period, e.g. three months from its date.

4.3.2. The object of certification is not to give evidence of a perfect title but to provide an accurate description of the legal character of the property in question. Any material information or irregularities affecting the property should be stated in a schedule to the certificate.

4.3.3. To be of practical use to the recipient the certificate should deal with the following matters:

(a) ownership of the property;

(b) an adequate description of the property;

(c) its tenure with relevant details;

(d) the name of the current owner of the estate in land;

(e) whether the title to the land is good, marketable and unencumbered;

(f) whether there are any statutory orders, schemes or provisions detrimental to the property or its use;

(g) where appropriate, provisions relating to planning, highways, public health, etc., should be referred to;

(h) appropriate searches which have been made at the Land Registry, the Land Charges Department and the district council, and other relevant searches;

(i) which searches have not been carried out in order to give the recipient a complete picture of the title which he is accepting.

4.3.4. Although the certificate should be positive, a solicitor should qualify it to suit the circumstances where it has not been possible to obtain or to verify all the relevant information.

4.3.5. Where a certificate of title has been requested by a mortgage lender and the form has been provided by the lender, care must be taken to ensure that the certificate does not breach Rules 3.16 to 3.22 Solicitors' Code of Conduct 2007. These Rules apply whenever the solicitor is acting for the lender and borrower, or borrower only, in a standard mortgage as defined in Rule 3.17.

4.3.6. An annex to Rule 3 Solicitors' Code of Conduct 2007 includes an approved certificate of title, which must be used when acting for both lender and borrower in a standard mortgage of property which is to be used as the borrower's private residence only. This certificate is set out in Appendix I.1.

4.4. City of London Law Society certificate of title

4.4.1. The City of London Law Society's (CLLS) standard form certificate of title has been designed to reduce negotiation over the form and content of such certificates. It is designed for use in connection with a number of commercial transactions, including secured loans, acquisitions of companies and businesses, flotations and privatisations. Some lenders insist on the certificate being used.

4.4.2. The sixth edition of the certificate was published in 2007 and is available from the CLLS website **www.citysolicitors.org.uk**.

4.4.3. The Solicitors Regulation Authority has confirmed that the sixth edition of the CLLS certificate is recognised for the purpose of Rule 3.22(2) Solicitors' Code of Conduct 2007.

4.5. Right to buy certificate of title

4.5.1. Where land is being purchased under right to buy legislation, the Land Registry is bound to accept a certificate of title supplied by the seller, the seller being obliged to indemnify the Registry if the certificate turns out to be inaccurate.

I. NEW PROPERTIES

I1. New property

1.1.   Introduction

1.1.1.   A sale of a new property is a more complex transaction than the sale of an existing house or building, and some matters additional to those relevant to a sale of an existing house or building must be considered. The following paragraphs only deal with those matters which are exclusive to new properties.

1.2.   The contract

1.2.1.   Where the property comprises a plot on a new building estate the contract will often be in standard form and the seller will be reluctant to allow substantial amendments to that form.[1] The buyer's solicitor should ensure that the contract does not impose unnecessarily burdensome terms on the buyer, sufficiently protects his client's interests and complies with any conditions required by the buyer's lender. The seller may require the deposit to be paid to him as 'agent' and not as 'stakeholder'. The consequences of this requirement should be explained to the buyer and the lender's consent to such a contractual condition obtained.

1.2.2.   A contract for the sale of a new property will frequently be a sale of part of the seller's existing property and may comprise a plot on a new building estate. In either case adequate provision must be made in the contract for the grant and reservation of easements to the parties and the property being sold will usually be described by reference to a plan which should be prepared in accordance with the Land Registry requirements (see B21 and J1).

1.2.3.   The contract should require the seller to complete the building works in accordance with the agreed specifications, planning permissions and plans submitted to the buyer. It may also contain a 'long stop' completion date requiring the builder to use his reasonable endeavours to complete the building works within a specified period so that, e.g. in the event of a prolonged strike by the workmen on site the buyer has the opportunity to rescind the contract. The buyer and his lender may wish to have a right to inspect the property during and at the completion of the building works.

1.2.4. Where the property being sold is in the course of construction it may not be possible for the seller to agree a definite completion date at the time of exchange since he will not be able to guarantee that the building works will be completed by a specified time. In such a case he may prefer to include a condition in the contract providing for completion of the transaction to take place within a specified number of days after completion of the building works.[2] This type of condition may give rise to difficulties from the buyer's point of view since if he is involved in a chain of transactions such a condition will make it difficult to synchronise the chain, unless similar conditions relating to completion are imposed in every transaction in the chain. The buyer should therefore be advised of this difficulty and warned of the possibility that in the event of the transactions not being synchronised the buyer may either have to complete his dependent sale first and move into temporary accommodation pending completion of the new property, or be prepared to use bridging finance for the completion of the new property pending sale of the old one. Where completion is to take place within a specified number of days of completion of the building works, the buyer's solicitor should also ensure that the number of days provided by the contract gives the buyer's solicitor sufficient time in which to carry out his pre-completion searches and to arrange for the purchase price to be obtained and for a final inspection of the building by the buyer's lender's surveyor. In addition, the contract should provide that notice of the completion date cannot be given unless (as applicable) the home warranty cover note has been issued (see I7.1) and/or a completion certificate has been issued under the Building Regulations.

1.2.5. Provision may be made for the seller to rectify minor defects in the building within a specified time after completion, although where the property is to be covered by a structural defects policy (see I1.5) this matter will usually be covered by such a policy. A contract to build a building is a contract for services within Supply of Goods and Services Act 1982 which implies a condition that the builder will provide his services to a reasonable standard and within a reasonable time if no time is specified in the contract.

1.2.6. The buyer should consider whether the contract should provide for the builder to remove all builder's rubbish from the site before completion, to leave the property in a clean and tidy condition, for the erection of boundary fences, and if appropriate for the landscaping of the gardens and surrounding areas.

1.2.7. New restrictive covenants will frequently be imposed on the buyer by the contract. From the seller's point of view, the imposition of the covenants will be done to allow the seller to maximise his ability to sell the remainder of the houses in the development. From the buyer's point of view, the imposition of such covenants provides the buyer with the certainty that the estate will be developed and will remain in a saleable condition without having to worry about unsightly or undesirable alterations carried out by neighbours to their properties. The wording of the covenants should be checked to ensure that they do not impose an unnecessary or burdensome restriction on the buyer's use and enjoyment of the property and their significance explained to the buyer (see E1).

1.2.8. The plan attached to the purchase deed should be signed by the seller and by or on behalf of the buyer.

1.2.9. Where there is to be a long delay between exchange of contracts and completion, the buyer's contract should be protected by registration (see C5.3).

1. The terms of the contract may be subject to Unfair Terms in Consumer Contract Regulations 1999 (SI 1999/2083) as amended by SI 2001/1186.
2. The building works will be 'complete' on the issue of a certificate of practical completion or on certification by the seller's architect. Habitation certificates are not generally now issued on completion of a building.

1.3. Planning permission

1.3.1. The erection of a new building will normally require both express planning permission and building regulation consent. Copies of the relevant documents should be supplied to the buyer's solicitor prior to exchange of contracts and should be checked by the client or his surveyor to ensure (as far as possible) that the erection of the building complies with the permissions and with any restrictions or conditions attached to them. If on the face of the planning permission there are reserved matters requiring the further consent of the planning authority, compliance with such matters should be checked by the buyer's solicitor. Where there is a short-term condition attached to the permission which affects the right to occupy the property (e.g. the property shall not be occupied until all estate roads have been completed) the contract must be checked to ensure that the completion date specified in the contract can, if necessary, be adjusted to take account of this restriction on occupation. The contract may contain a warranty given by the seller to the effect that he has complied with all restrictions and conditions attached to the planning permission.

1.3.2. In relation to work completed after 1 June 1992 it may be possible to obtain a certificate of completion of the building works from the local authority. The buyer should enquire whether such a certificate is available.

1.4. Roads and drains

Roads

1.4.1. The buyer's solicitor will need to check whether the roads and street lighting adjoining the property are publicly maintained or are intended to be so. Where the property forms part of a new building estate the seller (or developer) will frequently have entered into an agreement with the local highway authority under Highways Act 1980, s.38 whereby the highway authority will, after a certain period of time, adopt the highway and thereafter maintain it at public expense. Such an agreement should be supported by a bond which will guarantee sufficient money to allow the making up of the road to the proper standards required by the highway authority in case of default by the developer.

1.4.2.   Where appropriate a copy of the section 38 agreement and bond should be supplied to the buyer's solicitor with the draft contract and the buyer's solicitor should ask his client whether he wants his surveyor to check the bond to ensure that the amount guaranteed by it is adequate to cover the cost of the outstanding roadworks.

1.4.3.   In practice it is difficult to estimate the cost of the outstanding works and the buyer's solicitor may have to accept the bond which is offered without further investigation. The contract should contain provisions allowing the buyer and his employees, and others authorised by him, a right of access over the road pending its adoption. If no agreement and bond has been entered into, the road will remain in private ownership, maintainable at the expense of the owner. In such a case the buyer's solicitor must ensure that his client is given adequate rights of way to provide access to the property, and should ascertain that proper provisions are being made for the maintenance of the road and the likely cost of maintenance. The buyer and his lender must be advised accordingly.

1.4.4.   Where the property forms part of a small new estate it is common for the roads to remain in the ownership of the seller (or developer). From the buyer's point of view, the contract should then contain a covenant for maintenance by the road owner (at the shared cost of the buyer and owners of other houses on the estate), with provision for the house owners to carry out the work and recover any charges from other liable contributors in the event of default by the road owner. Such a provision may be dealt with by the imposition of an estate rentcharge under Rentcharges Act 1977 (see A25.6).

1.4.5.   In appropriate cases the client should be advised of any potential liability to road charges arising out of section 219 Highways Act 1980 (where advance payments procedure has not been correctly followed by builder and local authority) or arising from the situation where (as is not uncommon) the local authority has released the builder from his bond in relation to part of the development but without formally adopting the roads in the part released.

Drains

1.4.6.   Except where the property is being built in a rural area, the seller will normally have entered into an agreement and bond with the water authority under Water Industry Act 1991, s.104 for the ownership and maintenance of the drains to be transferred to the water authority within a certain time after completion of the building works. Similar considerations apply here as in relation to the maintenance of highways (see I1.4.1). If the drainage system is to remain in private ownership a drainage survey may be desirable to ensure that the system under construction will be adequate to service the property.

1.5. Insurance against structural defects

1.5.1. Most new residential properties will be offered with the benefit of structural defects insurance, e.g. the NHBC 'Buildmark' or similar scheme, which provides the buyer and his successors in title with insurance against structural defects in the property for a number of years after completion of the building. The contract will normally provide for such cover to be obtained by the seller without cost to the buyer and the appropriate insurance policy and other documentation should be supplied to the buyer on or before completion.

1.5.2. The absence of such insurance cover may present the buyer with problems since it will frequently be a condition of the mortgage offer that cover is obtained. Even where the present buyer is not financing his purchase with the assistance of a mortgage, a subsequent buyer who buys the property within the first 10 years after its construction will expect to take the benefit of the policy, and thus the absence of such cover will restrict the potential both to mortgage and to resell the property.

1.5.3. The terms of the policies and their limitations should be examined in each case and their effect explained to the client. The explanatory notes furnished with the scheme documentation should be handed to the client.

1.5.4. It should be noted that subsidence is not generally covered by these schemes and so must be covered by the buyer's buildings insurance policy. The builder's liability under the schemes is often limited to the first two years after completion. After that time, the policy only covers structural defects. A structural survey of the property may be desirable immediately prior to the end of the two-year period.

1.5.5. Where a property is to be covered by a structural defects scheme a full survey may not be necessary, particularly if the property is still in the course of construction so that there is very little for the surveyor actually to survey. However, the usual mining and environmental searches (if applicable) should be undertaken. In some cases a surveyor may be asked to look at the plans for the prospective building to ensure that as far as can be ascertained the building is to be erected in accordance with the client's wishes and expectations.

Assignment of policy

1.5.6. The benefit of the policy can be assigned to a subsequent buyer of the property. NHBC will honour the policy in favour of a subsequent buyer irrespective of whether a formal assignment has taken place between the original and subsequent buyers. A formal assignment of the benefit of the policy may be desirable in other cases.

1.5.7.   Where the property is being constructed under the supervision of an architect
(e.g. under a JCT contract), a lender may accept an architect's certificate of
completion of the building in place of a structural defects policy, although in
such a case it may be desirable from the buyer's point of view for the contract to
contain warranties given by the seller as to the proper design and construction of
the building. The insurance cover carried by architects will only provide
indemnity if the architect has a valid current policy at the time when liability is
notified to the insurers. If therefore the architect has died or ceased to practise
since completion of the building and before liability is discovered there may be
no insurance policy in force to meet the claim and the architect's own assets or
estate may be insufficient to cover the liability.

1.5.8.   Defective Premises Act 1972 implies a term into a contract to purchase a
building in the course of construction that the building when built will be
habitable.

1.6.   Payment of purchase price

1.6.1.   The contract should state clearly whether the buyer is required to pay an
additional price for extras (e.g. a coloured bathroom suite) and, if so, how much.

1.6.2.   Some builders require the purchase price to be paid in stages as the building
works progress. In such a case the buyer's lender must be informed of this fact
and his agreement sought to release the mortgage advance in accordance with
the builder's requirements. For the buyer's protection, he may seek an equitable
charge over the property to the extent of the instalments paid by him. Such a
charge must be registered and the contract to purchase should also be protected
by registration as an estate contract since completion is unlikely to follow
quickly after exchange of contracts in this situation. The lender's consent
should be obtained to the form of the contract prior to exchange.

1.6.3.   Any retention made by the buyer's mortgagee, e.g. in respect of outstanding
roadworks must be discussed with the buyer and arrangements made to cover
the resulting shortfall in time for completion.

1.6.4.   Where the new property is a single building, i.e. not part of an estate development, it may be advantageous for the buyer initially to enter a contract to buy the
site alone, and then to have a second contract for the builder to build the house or
other building. In such a case the builder would expect to take a charge over the
site to secure payment for the building works.

1.7.   Mortgages

1.7.1.   It is usually a condition of the mortgage on a new property that the structural
defects insurance must be in place before completion of the transaction and
release of the mortgage funds. The CML issued a statement in the Gazette (see
Appendix VI.1):

'A lender will not release the mortgage funds for a new property until the buyer's conveyancer has received confirmation in the form of a cover note that the property has received a satisfactory final inspection, and that a full new home warranty will be in place on or before legal completion.

In practice, the new home warranty provider will give the cover note to the builder immediately after the property has passed the final inspection. The builder or the builder's conveyancer will then pass the cover note to the buyer's conveyancer. This revised approach will apply to all transactions involving new properties being built or converted in accordance with a new home warranty scheme and which exchange contracts on or after 1 April 2003. It will not apply to self-build schemes or where the construction or conversion of a property is being supervised by a professional consultant without a new home warranty scheme.'

See Appendix VI.1 for statements from the CML.

1.7.2. The Certificate of Title cannot be sent to the lender until the solicitor has received the appropriate confirmation from the builder. See also paragraph 6.6.2 Lenders' Handbook.

1.7.3. Problems may be encountered when clients want to obtain occupation of the property as early as possible as this new procedure may lead to short delays. Clients should be advised at the outset that completion will not take place until this procedure has been carried out.

1.7.4. Problems may also be encountered in view of the fact that the confirmation will be issued provided there are no 'red' defects in the property. This means that the confirmation will be issued whilst there are still defects in the building, 'green' defects. Solicitors should advise the client that completion may take place despite the existence of minor defects.

1.8. Building estates

1.8.1. This section does not deal in detail with site acquisition and development for which the reader should refer to a specialist work on the subject.

Checklist for seller's solicitor

(a) Has the site been inspected to ascertain the boundaries of each plot and the extent of easements and reservations?

(b) Has planning permission been obtained?

(c) Has a section 38 agreement and bond been obtained in respect of the roads?

(d) Has a section 104 agreement and bond been obtained in respect of sewers?

(e) Who is responsible for building regulation control and who will issue the certificate of completion of the building?

(f) Is the seller to make (and regularly update) pre-contract searches or will this be each buyer's responsibility?

(g) In residential cases will the Protocol be used; if so what variations to it are necessary to meet the present transactions? Remember to notify the buyer's solicitor of such variations.

(h) Will the property be covered by structural defects insurance? Has the builder registered and handed to his solicitor the appropriate documentation? (See I1.5.) Ensure that an unqualified (i.e. unconditional) certificate will be issued.

(i) Has an estate plan been prepared and approved by the Land Registry?

(j) Has the form of transfer been approved by the Land Registry? This is not essential but may save time and requisitions from the Land Registry at a later stage.

(k) Has all the necessary pre-contract documentation been prepared and duplicated for each plot? (See I1.8.2.)

(l) Have arrangements been made with the seller's lender to release the plots from the charge?

(m) Has the builder complied with Construction (Design and Management) Regulations 1994 (SI 1994/3140) (e.g. the appointment of a planning supervisor)?

1.8.2. Documents to be prepared and sent to the prospective buyer's solicitor for each plot on receipt of instructions:

(a) pre-contract enquiries with answers (may include Form TA8 New Home Information);

(b) pre-contract searches with replies (where the seller is to undertake this task);

(c) draft contract in duplicate (with buyer's name left blank);

(d) draft transfer in duplicate with plan attached (annexed to contract, buyer's name left blank);

(e) evidence of title;

(f) requisitions on title with answers;

(g) copies of relevant planning permissions and building regulation approval;

(h) copies of relevant section 104 and section 38 agreements and bonds;

(i) structural defects insurance documentation where appropriate;

(j) a copy of the plan of the property properly marked and coloured in accordance with Land Registry requirements, with a spare copy for search purposes;

(k) if desired, a general information sheet for the buyer containing *inter alia* address of local authorities and other bodies with whom searches may need to be conducted, explanation of the contract terms (including arrangements for deposit and completion), notification of whether the Protocol will be used (residential transactions) and of any variations to it;

(l) covering letter.

12. Defects in new commercial buildings

2.1. Introduction

2.1.1. The owner or tenant of a new commercial building,[1] not being the party for whom the building was constructed or refurbished, will only be in a position to recover the cost of remedying defects to the building from the contractor or professional team (architect, engineer, etc.) if he has a contractual relationship with them.[2] He would, however, be able to sue the contractor or other professional in negligence for damages arising out of personal injury or damage to other property. To enable the subsequent owner to be able to sue the contractor or other professional for the cost of remedial works to the building, he needs to establish an enforceable contractual relationship with the contractor or professional who is to be sued.[3] This can be achieved either by creating new contracts between the subsequent owner/tenant and the contractor/professionals (these are usually called 'collateral warranties') or, where practical, by taking an assignment from the original owner of the building of his original contract(s) with the contractor/professionals. The subsequent owner/tenant might additionally seek a warranty from the original owner as to the condition of the building even in the current market, which may be difficult to obtain; sellers and landlords of new buildings understandably prefer the liability for defects to rest with the contractor/professionals.

Collateral warranties

2.1.2. A buyer or tenant of a new commercial building should, as a term of the contract, require the seller or landlord to procure that on completion collateral warranties in favour of the buyer/tenant are provided by the contractor and all professionals in the form approved by the buyer/tenant. In these the contractor/professionals warrant that they have to date exercised reasonable skill and care and (where work is unfinished at the time of the contract) agree to continue to do so. Other terms are generally included dealing with professional indemnity insurance, the limitation period, assignment and limitations on the warrantor's liability, for example where the defect was partly his fault and partly the fault of other parties.[4]

Assignment of original contracts

2.1.3. Where the whole development is being sold or let the buyer/tenant should consider requiring an assignment of the original contracts with the contractor/ professionals with a view to putting the buyer/tenant in a position to recover under these contracts for any breaches by the contractor/professionals.

2.1.4. In the following paragraphs references to 'A' are to the contractor, architect or other professional, 'B' is the original owner of the building who entered the construction (or as the case may be) contract with A (the 'A–B' contract), and C is the subsequent owner of the building who, having purchased from B, seeks to enforce a term of the A–B contract.

1. I.e. not covered by a structural insurance policy.
2. *Murphy* v. *Brentwood District Council* [1991] 1 AC 398; *Department of the Environment* v. *Thomas Bates & Son Ltd* [1991] 1 AC 499.
3. *Ibid.*
4. E.g. the precedents produced by the British Property Federation.

2.2. Method of assignment

2.2.1. The assignment is a chose in action which, by section 136(1) Law of Property Act 1925 must be in writing (between B and C) and notice of the assignment must be given to A. Notice of the assignment could be given by either B or C, but it is clearly in C's interests to ensure that it is done. A should be asked to sign and return one copy of the notice of assignment served on him in duplicate by C so that tangible evidence exists of the fact that notice was correctly given.

2.3. Types of assignment

2.3.1. The purpose of the assignment is to enable the benefit of the contract between A and B to be transferred to and enforced by C against A.

Novation

2.3.2. Where it is intended that obligations under the A–B contract should be assigned, a novation must take place. The assignment of one party's burdens or obligations can only be done with the consent of the other original contracting party. Therefore, for this to occur, a new contract, made between A, B, and C, will have to be entered into.

Sub-contract

2.3.3. A might enter a sub-contract with D (the sub-contractor) under which D agreed with A to perform some or all of A's obligations to B under the A–B contract. This is effectively an assignment of A's obligations without B's consent, but in this situation A always remains liable to B since the original contract between A and B has been neither novated nor discharged. Any defect in D's performance can therefore be remedied by an action by B against A. The main issue in this situation is whether B is bound to accept D's performance of the contract in A's place. Where the obligations to be performed by A are construed as 'personal services', B cannot be forced to accept performance from anyone other than the original contracting party, i.e. he is entitled to reject D's performance and treat A as being in breach of contract. An obligation to carry out building works has been held to be within the concept of personal services.[1]

Assignment of benefits or rights

2.3.4.   Where there is a prohibition against the assignment of the benefit of the contract, that prohibition is effective to prevent the assignment unless the party with the burden of performance consents to it. Thus an assignment by A to C of the benefit of the A–B contract would require B's consent. This applies irrespective of whether the assignment is of accrued rights (e.g. existing breaches committed by B) or of future rights (e.g. the right to sue for breaches as and when they occur in the future).[2]

2.3.5.   If assignment is not possible (because B will not consent) C's remedy lies in persuading A to take direct action against B. The contract between A and C should contain warranties to this effect given by A. The damages recoverable by A on C's behalf are not restricted to A's losses (which may be nominal since he will no longer have an interest in the property) but can include reimbursement of losses suffered by C.[3] The contract between A and C should also contain a warranty given by A to hold any damages recovered on behalf of C.

1. See *Southway Group Ltd* v. *Wolff* [1991] EGCS 82, CA.
2. *Linden Gardens Trust Ltd* v. *Lenesta Sludge Disposals Ltd*; *St Martins Property Corporation Ltd* v. *Sir Robert McAlpine Ltd* [1993] 3 WLR 408. See also *Darlington Borough Council* v. *Wiltshire Northern Ltd*, *The Times*, 4 July 1994, CA and *Alfred McAlpine Construction Ltd* v. *Panatown Ltd*, *The Times*, 11 February 1998.
3. *Ibid.*

2.4.   **Protection of subsequent owners**

2.4.1.   In view of the uncertainty demonstrated by the general law a subsequent owner of a building needs to ensure that he will have the right to recover his losses in the event of a later defect being discovered.

2.4.2.   In residential property transactions, the property will normally be covered by a structural defects insurance policy which should provide adequate protection for the buyer.

2.4.3.   In commercial situations a buyer from the original owner should ensure that his contract to purchase contains warranties given by the original owner, and that a valid novation or assignment with the contractor's consent takes place. Protection of the subsequent owner is a matter to which attention should be paid when the original owner is entering the original A–B contracts. If at that stage he can ensure that there is no prohibition against assignment in the A–B contract, the benefit of the A–B contract may more easily be assigned to C at a later stage.

2.4.4. The distinction between the assignment of obligations and fruits of performance should not, however, be overlooked since the court seems to apply different rules to these two types of benefits.

2.5. Contracts (Rights of Third Parties) Act 1999

2.5.1. Contracts (Rights of Third Parties) Act 1999 permits a person or company who is not a contracting party to enforce a term of contract, as if he or it were a contracting party, unless the contract indicates that the actual parties did not intend such right of enforcement to arise. The term must be made for the third party's benefit and the third party must be identified in the contract by name, description or implication. The third party does not, however, have to be in existence at the time when the contract is made (e.g. a company not yet incorporated). The provisions of this Act may therefore provide a simpler method of enforcing warranties than that outlined above. Defences and exclusion clauses which would be available to a contracting party can be used against the third party who is seeking to enforce the contract. The Act can be expressly excluded from a contract. It should, however, be noted that where a third party is to benefit under the Act, the contract between the original contracting parties cannot be varied so as to affect the third party without the third party's consent. This provision, too, may be excluded from the contract.

J. SALES OF PART

J1. Sales of part

1.1. Introduction

1.1.1. A sale of part is a more complex transaction than the sale of the whole of the seller's interest in a particular piece of land, and some matters additional to those relevant to a sale of the whole must be considered. The following paragraphs only deal with those matters which are exclusive to sales of part.

1.2. Description of the land

1.2.1. The description of the land in the seller's existing register and/or title deeds may not suffice to describe the part of the land being sold and a new, accurate description of the property must then be devised to describe the land in the particulars of sale of the contract. It will usually be necessary to identify the land by reference to a plan (see B21.2 and J1.6.1 for the Land Registry's requirements). There may be circumstances in which it is useful for the seller's solicitor to inspect the property prior to drafting the contract.

Retained land

1.2.2. Reference will usually have to be made to the land which is to remain in the ownership of the seller after the sale off, e.g. in relation to easements and reservations; such land must therefore also be defined verbally in the contract and marked clearly on the plan attached to the contract.

1.2.3. Where the sale is of part of a registered title and comprises a plot on a building estate, the seller will frequently have deposited an estate plan at the Land Registry and the official copies which are issued will give a certificate of inspection in Form C1 in lieu of a title plan.[1] Where the estate plan procedure is used it is important that it is strictly adhered to in order to avoid difficulties. In addition the solicitor should emphasise to his builder client that if revisions are made on the ground to the layout shown on the approved estate plan, the builder should notify the solicitor immediately so that the solicitor can inform the Land Registry and submit a revised estate plan.

1. Land Registration Rules 2003, rr.134 and 143.

1.3. Grants and reservations

1.3.1. On a sale of part of land Law of Property Act 1925, s.62 and the rule in *Wheeldon* v. *Burrows*[1] may give the buyer as easements certain rights over the land which are continuous and apparent, are necessary for the reasonable enjoyment of the land sold, and which had been and are at the time of the sale used by the seller for the benefit of the part sold. Although Law of Property Act 1925, s.62 and the rule in *Wheeldon* v. *Burrows* will give the buyer such easements and quasi-easements as were previously enjoyed by the land before its division, the existence and extent of these implied rights may not be entirely clear and, for certainty, such matters should be dealt with expressly in the contract. Easements which pass by the operation of these provisions cannot give the buyer any right which the seller has no power to grant, and do not create any better title to any right than the seller is able to transfer. It will therefore usually be necessary to grant new express easements to the buyer, e.g. for a right of way or drainage. Express easements which are to arise in the future must comply with the perpetuity rule.

1.3.2. Section 62 Law of Property Act 1925 and the rule in *Wheeldon* v. *Burrows* only operate in the buyer's favour. There is no reciprocal section or case which entitles the seller to easements over the land being sold off (other than easements of necessity). For this reason it is important to consider what rights the seller will need to exercise over the land being sold, e.g. passage of cables, drainage, etc., and to reserve these expressly in the contract.

1.3.3. Rights of light and air may pass to the buyer under either Law of Property Act 1925, s.62 or the rule in *Wheeldon* v. *Burrows*. The acquisition of such rights by the buyer may have adverse consequences for the seller since the buyer might be able by exercising such rights to prevent the seller from building on his retained land. It is therefore usually considered necessary to exclude the buyer's right to easements of light and air by an express condition in the contract which provides for the insertion of a provision to this effect in the purchase deed.[2] Standard Condition 3.4 and Standard Commercial Property Condition 3.3 both contain a provision to this effect.

1.3.4. Standard Condition 3.3 and Standard Commercial Property Condition 3.3 both provide for the mutual grant of easements and reservations on a sale of part, but the rights given by these conditions are limited and will in most cases be inadequate to deal effectively with the parties' requirements on a sale of part of land.

1.3.5. In registered land, a proprietor who claims the benefit of a legal easement or profit à prendre which has been acquired by implication (or prescription) may apply for it to be registered as appurtenant to the registered estate.[3]

1. (1879) 12 Ch 31.
2. See *Emmet and Farrand on Title*, Chapter 15.
3. Land Registration Rules 2003, r.74.

1.4. Imposition of new covenants

1.4.1. In many cases the seller will wish to impose new covenants on the buyer, e.g. restricting the future use of the land. Provision for the imposition of new restrictions must be made expressly in the contract.

1.4.2. Covenants which are imposed on the sale of a new house on a building estate will usually comply with the terms of a building scheme.[1] In other cases, the enforceability of such restrictions against a subsequent purchaser of the land depends on their being negative in substance, expressly taken for the benefit of the seller's retained land, and protected by the entry of notice in the charges register of the title (or as class D(ii) land charges in unregistered land).[2] Positive covenants may be indirectly enforced through a chain of indemnity covenants but their burden does not run with the land. Where the contract expressly provides for a covenant to benefit a subsequent owner the subsequent owner may be able to enforce the covenant (whether positive or negative) through Contracts (Rights of Third Parties) Act 1999. This Act is not retrospective in operation.

1. See *Re Dolphin's Conveyance* [1970] 1 Ch 654.
2. *Tulk* v. *Moxhay* (1848) 2 Ph 774.

1.5. Consent of seller's lender

1.5.1. Where the land to be sold comprises part of the land which is mortgaged to the seller's lender, the seller must, at the earliest possible opportunity, obtain his lender's consent to the transaction. It should be ascertained from the lender whether the lender requires repayment of the whole or any part of the principal sums owing out of the proceeds of the sale of part and, if part, how much. Arrangements must be made for the lender to discharge the land being sold from the mortgage. In registered land the discharge is in Form DS3 (accompanied by a plan to show the extent of the land being released if not sufficiently defined on the title plan). In unregistered land the lender may either give a deed of release, or he may prefer to be joined as a party to the conveyance in order both to release the land being sold and to give a receipt for the money being paid to him.

1.6. The purchase deed

Registered land

1.6.1. A transfer of part will be drawn up to reflect the contract terms. The transfer must be in Form TP1 or TP2. The seller's title number is used in panel 2 of the transfer form, a new title number being allocated to the land sold off on registration of the sale of part. A transfer of part must have attached to it a plan identifying clearly the land dealt with. However, if the land dealt with is identified clearly on the title plan of the registered title, it may instead be described by reference to that title plan.[1] (See B21 for a detailed explanation of the Land Registry's requirements on plans.) The transfer should be executed by the transferor; and by the transferee if it contains transferee's covenants or declarations or contains an application by the transferee (e.g. for a restriction). In the case of joint transferees, the transfer must be executed by each of them.[2] The transfer plan need only be signed by the transferor.[3] The buyer's pre-completion search at the Land Registry should be made on Form OS2 accompanied by a plan in duplicate or should refer to a Land Registry approved plan and plot number supplied by the seller.

Unregistered land

1.6.2. The conveyance will reflect the terms of the contract. Although a plan is not essential in unregistered land, it is highly desirable in cases where only part of the seller's estate is being sold and should be signed by both parties. Where the transaction will be submitted for first registration after completion, see B21 for a detailed explanation of the Land Registry's requirements on plans. Since the seller will be retaining the documents of title an acknowledgement for production and undertaking for safe custody (where appropriate) of the deeds should be included in the conveyance.[4] Where the seller is selling other than as beneficial owner, only an acknowledgement will be given. The undertaking is not given by owners who are selling in a fiduciary capacity. Where the land is subject to a mortgage the seller may be required to give a covenant that he will give the statutory undertaking for safe custody of the deeds as and when they come into his possession. Where the buyer is entering into a covenant in the deed (whether for indemnity or to observe fresh restrictive covenants) he must execute the purchase deed.

1.6.3. Commonly the draft purchase deed will be prepared by the seller and annexed to the draft contract so that the buyer in fact has limited scope for negotiating its contents.

1. Land Registration Rules 2003, r.213(1) and (4).
2. See the prescribed forms of transfer in Land Registration Rules 2003, Sched.1.
3. Land Registration Rules 2003, r.213(2).
4. See Law of Property Act 1925, s.64 and Standard Condition 4.6.5 and Standard Commercial Property Condition 6.6.5.

1.7.   **Completion and post-completion**

1.7.1. Where the land is unregistered, the seller will not be handing over his title deeds to the buyer on completion; the buyer should therefore verify his abstract or epitome against the original deeds and mark his abstract or epitome as examined against the original (see F4). Where the Protocol is used the seller is required to mark the abstract as examined against the original title deeds before sending it to the buyer. Even where the title to the land bought is to be registered immediately after completion this procedure is necessary so that the buyer can produce proper evidence of the title to the Land Registry with his application for first registration. Additionally, a memorandum of the sale off should be noted on the most recent of the seller's retained title deeds to prevent a second sale of the same land by the seller.[1] A note of any restrictive covenants imposed by the conveyance to the buyer (or a copy of that conveyance) should also be retained by the seller. New restrictive covenants will automatically be entered on the register of the new title on first registration.

1.7.2. Where the seller's title is already registered it is not necessary to provide for an acknowledgement for production of the deeds nor for a memorandum to be endorsed on the seller's deeds since the buyer will obtain his own title number on registration of the sale of part. An acknowledgement is needed where the sale is of part only of a lease or where the purchase deed is to be executed in duplicate. New restrictive covenants imposed or rights reserved by the transfer of part will automatically be entered on the charges register of the new title on registration. Similarly, any new rights granted by the transfer will automatically be entered in the property register.[2]

1.7.3. A lender who has custody of the title deeds will give an acknowledgement for their production. Such an acknowledgement may be contained in the deed of release supplied by the lender but is not necessary when dealing with registered land.

1.7.4. In some cases where new covenants are being imposed the contract will require the buyer to prepare the purchase deed in duplicate, the duplicate copy will be handed to the seller as a record of the transaction. An acknowledgement for production is required in this situation.[3]

1. See Law of Property Act 1925, s.200.
2. Land Registration Rules 2003, r.72(2).
3. See Standard Condition 4.6.5 and Standard Commercial Property Condition 6.6.5.

1.8. Checklist of matters to be considered on sale of part

Easements in the buyer's favour

(a) To what extent will Law of Property Act 1925, s.62 and/or the rule in *Wheeldon* v. *Burrows* imply easements in the buyer's favour?[1]

(b) Is it necessary to extend the implied easements by granting express rights to the buyer?[2]

(c) What does the buyer need, for example:

    (i) rights of way;

    (ii) right to lay new cables/pipelines/drains;

    (iii) right to use/maintain existing or new pipelines/cables/drains?

Rights of way

(a) Will the right be to pass over the land in both directions or should it be restricted to one way only?

(b) Should the right be restricted, e.g. to a particular class of user, e.g. pedestrian only?

(c) Is the exercise of the right to be restricted, e.g. use only for a particular purpose or only at a specified time of day?

All easements

(a) Is the route of the right of way/drain, etc., specified on the plan?

(b) Who is liable for maintenance/repairs?

(c) Will it be necessary for the buyer to enter the seller's land to inspect the state of repair and/or to maintain?

(d) Should the buyer's access to inspect be restricted, e.g. a right to inspect on 24 hours' notice except in case of emergency?

(e) Should the buyer be under an obligation to cause no unnecessary damage and to make good any damage done while inspecting/maintaining?

(f) Where the buyer is to construct a new pipeline/cable, etc., should he be required to finish the construction works within a specified period after completion?

Reservations

(a) Remember the seller generally gets nothing under the implied grant rules.

(b) After completion will the seller need to continue to use a right of way/drain/pipeline/cable passing through the land being sold?

(c) If so, express reservations must be included in the contract by way of special condition. The same considerations in drafting apply as above.

(d) Additionally, to protect the seller, it may be considered necessary to include a general reservations clause in his favour dealing with all easements, quasi-easements, etc., presently enjoyed by the land as a whole.

(e) Should rights of light and air be expressly reserved in order to preserve the seller's freedom to use the retained land in the future?[3]

Existing covenants

Is an indemnity clause required?[4]

New covenants[5]

(a) Should new restrictive covenants be imposed?

(b) If so, what type of restrictions will serve to protect the seller's land without imposing unnecessary constraints on the buyer?

(c) Consider:

    (i) erection of new buildings on the land;

    (ii) use of the land;

    (iii) repair/maintenance of buildings or land;

    (iv) general covenant against nuisance.[6]

(d) Will the covenants be negative in nature?

(e) Do the words used ensure that the covenants will create an enforceable obligation?

Description of the property in the contract

(a) Does the wording of the particulars accurately describe the land being sold?

(b) Has the seller's retained land been precisely defined?[7]

(c) Is there reference in the particulars to a plan?

(d) Is the plan of sufficient size and scale to be able to delineate accurately both the area of land being sold and the routes of easements, etc.?

(e) Does the plan comply with the Land Registry's requirements (see B21)?

Seller's lender

(a) Will it be necessary to obtain the lender's consent to the sale – if so has this been obtained?

(b) How will the lender deal with the release of the land being sold from the mortgage?

Registration of title

The seller should consider including a clause in the contract requiring the buyer's solicitor to supply the seller's solicitor with a copy of the buyer's registered title (when registration has been completed) so that the seller's solicitor may check that all new easements, covenants, etc. have been correctly entered on the new title. The seller may also wish to consider requiring the buyer to complete panel 10 in the application form AP1 with the seller's name and address so that the Land Registry will notify the seller when the transfer application has been completed.

1. Section 62 Law of Property Act 1925 may operate to create easements over retained land where at the time of sale the two tenements are in separate occupation. Further, the rule in *Wheeldon* v. *Burrows* (1879) 12 Ch 31 will impliedly grant to the buyer as easements all rights which are continuous and apparent and reasonably necessary to the reasonable enjoyment of the property sold. These provisions will normally have the effect of giving the buyer fewer easements than he requires, but in some cases may give him more than the seller intends. It is therefore considered safer to negate the effect of these rules in the contract and to deal with easements by way of express grant.
2. Since the extent of the implied easements created by the implied grant rules is not always clear, these matters are better dealt with by way of express condition. Standard Condition 3.4 and Standard Commercial Property Condition 3.3 deal briefly with easements but do not normally give adequate rights to the buyer; hence the need for express special conditions.
3. Standard Condition 3.4 and Standard Commercial Property Condition 3.3 reserve rights of light and air to the seller.
4. Standard Condition 4.6.4 and Standard Commercial Property Condition 6.6.4 require indemnity covenants but it is common to include an indemnity clause by way of special condition in order specifically to draw the requirement to the buyer's attention. See E1.
5. See E1.
6. Nuisance is a tort actionable at common law; therefore the imposition of such a covenant may strictly be unnecessary.
7. Inspection of the property may assist with these matters. It may also be desirable to peg out the boundaries to the property or to ask a surveyor to confirm that it is possible to plot the site.

K. LEASEHOLDS

This section deals only with those matters where the considerations applicable to leasehold property differ from the requirements outlined in other sections of this handbook relating to freehold land.

Some problem areas, e.g. licences to assign, are confined exclusively to the context of leaseholds and these are discussed within this section of the handbook.

A summary of the law relating to security of tenure and the right to buy is included, but the handbook does not contain a comprehensive guide to this topic.

The first group of paragraphs within this section deal with matters which are applicable to most leases, whether short or long and whether of business or residential premises. Then follow paragraphs dealing with a specific type of lease or tenancy and, finally, paragraphs on specific points which affect leasehold land such as the right to buy, options, and liability on covenants.

The Land Registry's requirements are set out in the following Practice Guides, which can be viewed and downloaded from the Land Registry's website **www.landregistry.gov.uk**:

- 25. Leases – when to register
- 26. Leases – determination (and addendum)
- 27. The leasehold reform legislation
- 28. Extension of leases
- 64. Prescribed clauses leases (and addendum)

K1. Acting on grant of lease

1.1. Taking instructions

1.1.1. There are a number of key issues upon which thought, advice and instructions will be needed when acting on the grant or acceptance of a lease. There can be no standard approach; instead the details of the property and letting in question must be carefully considered.

1.1.2. Subject to the above, much of the information required by the landlord's solicitor from his client will be similar to that required from the seller in the case of a freehold transaction.

1.1.3. When acting for a landlord or tenant, a solicitor should draw his client's attention to, and explain, lease provisions which may be of importance to the client and influence the client's decision whether or not to accept the proposed terms.

Code for Leasing Business Premises

1.1.4. In appropriate cases, the client's attention should be drawn to the Code for Leasing Business Premises. The latest version of this voluntary code was introduced in March 2007 and contains 10 recommendations for landlords, a guide for occupiers and model heads of terms.[1]

Model lease clauses

1.1.5. The Law Society forms of Business Leases are set out in Appendix V.1. The British Property Federation and the British Council for Offices have produced a set of 'model lease clauses' for possible use in commercial leases. The clauses cover eight topics: rent, outgoings, repair and maintenance, alterations and signage, disposals, insurance, costs and rent review. They are designed to provide a fair compromise between landlord and tenant.[2]

1. A copy of the Code can be obtained from **www.leasingbusinesspremises.co.uk**.
2. A copy of the model lease clauses can be obtained from **www.bpf.org.uk**.

1.2. Demised premises

1.2.1. The lease must clearly define the extent of the demised premises. A detached building standing in its own ground should cause no problems of description but care is needed when letting parts of a building, e.g. flats or suites of offices. See B21, K1.20 and K6.1.2 for the Land Registry's requirements.

1.2.2. As far as possible express provision should be made relating to the ownership of walls, floors, ceilings, etc.[1] In the absence of express provision the following presumptions apply:

(a) external walls – these are included in the demise even if the landlord is responsible for their repairs;[2]

(b) internal walls – there is no presumption in respect of the internal boundary walls dividing one flat from another or the flat from common parts;

(c) floors and ceilings – the flat includes the ceiling at least to the underside of the floor joists to which the ceiling is attached;[3]

(d) the ownership of the roof area should also be specifically dealt with since if this is not done it may be possible for the tenant of a top floor flat to claim occupation of the roof space and to carry out alterations to the roof space against the landlord's wishes.[4]

1. It is possible to create an 'eggshell' tenancy in which the demise only includes the airspace defined by reference to the area contained within the surfaces of the walls, floors and ceilings. See *Pumperninks of Piccadilly Ltd* v. *Land Securities Ltd* [2002] 21 EG 142.
2. *Sturge* v. *Hackett* [1962] 3 All ER 166.
3. *Ibid.* and see *Phelps* v. *City of London Corporation* [1916] 2 Ch 255. Joists are likely to form part of the structure; see *Marlborough Park Services Ltd* v. *Rowe* [2006] EWCA Civ 436.
4. See *Davies* v. *Yadegar* [1990] 09 EG 67 and *Haines* v. *Florensa* [1989] 09 EG 70.

1.3. Easements – grant

1.3.1. Consideration must then be given to whether the tenant will require easements over the landlord's adjoining property in order to use the demised premises. The tenant might, e.g. need the right to use a private road in order to gain access to the premises or to use conducting media on the landlord's adjoining land to bring services from the mains supply to the demised premises. The tenant of a flat or suite of offices will certainly need such rights over the remainder of the building.[1]

1. Where such rights are not granted this will depress the rent in a commercial lease at renewal under Landlord and Tenant Act 1954 – see *J Murphy & Sons Ltd* v. *Railtrack plc* [2002] 19 EG 148.

1.4.   Easements – reservation

1.4.1.   The landlord will need to consider if he or others claiming title under him will wish to exercise rights over the demised premises because, if so, an express reservation should be included. An example would be part of a driveway which is included within the demised premises but which is required to be used by the landlord and his other tenants.

1.5.   Length of the term to be granted and tax consequences

1.5.1.   Apart from the parties' wishes, consideration must be given to the SDLT consequences of the length of the term and also to the possible effect of security of tenure legislation on the lease which may affect the seller's ability to recover possession at the end of the term (see K5, K7 and K8). Where a short lease of a dwelling is to be granted the effect of the landlord's implied repairing obligations under Landlord and Tenant Act 1985, ss.11–14 must also be borne in mind (see K1.7.2). The term created must be of certain duration but, subject to security of tenure legislation, it may be made determinable on a certain event.[1]

1.5.2.   Rent will usually be taxed as income.[2] Where a premium is charged for the grant of a lease this will be deemed to be a part disposal for Capital Gains Tax (CGT) purposes and liability to this tax may arise. However, where a lease is granted for a term not exceeding 50 years it is treated as a wasting asset for CGT purposes and special rules apply. In these cases a proportion of the premium is charged to tax under Schedule A and the landlord is treated as receiving rent calculated by reference to a formula involving a multiplication of the premium and the length of the term.

1. *Prudential Assurance Co. Ltd* v. *London Residuary Body* [1992] 3 All ER 504.
2. Income Tax (Trading and Other Income) Act 2005, chapters 4, 5 and 6 (individuals); Income and Corporation Taxes Act 1988, Sched. A (companies).

1.6.   Amount of rent and frequency of reviews

1.6.1.   Some statutory limitations on the amount of rent recoverable may be applicable where the lease is an assured tenancy or a protected or statutory tenancy (see K5).

1.6.2.   Rent review provisions should be carefully checked by both landlord and tenant. In commercial leases reviews every five years or so are common. A rent review within, broadly, the first five years will require further SDLT returns to be made (see A14).[1] In long residential leases fixed increment reviews every

25–30 years are more usual. Without an enforceable rent review provision the landlord will not be able to increase the rent during the term of the lease. Rent review provisions in commercial leases are often complex, but they must specify the period at which each review is to take place, and a formula for determining the amount of rent to be paid after each review date with a fall-back procedure (e.g. arbitration) in case of dispute.

1.6.3. A landlord prefers a clause which provides for 'upwards review' only so that the rent payable after the review date can never be less than that which was payable before the review date. The Code for Leasing Business Premises recommends that rent reviews should generally be to open market rent and discourages landlords from automatically inserting upwards only clauses (see K1.1.4). However, the benefit to a tenant of a rent review to open market rent, i.e. one that can fix a new rent more or less than the old rent, can easily be lost if the lease enables only the landlord to initiate the rent review.[2]

1.6.4. It is also common to provide that the new rent, whenever determined, shall be payable as from the review date in question so that where a rent review goes to arbitration and the new rent is not determined until some time after the actual review date, the tenant should be advised to place some money in a deposit account on each rent day so that he will be able to meet the cost of the reviewed rent when it is finally determined. Some leases will have break clauses which are operative in the tenant's favour at review dates, thus enabling the tenant to bring the lease to an end before the contractual term date if the rent payable after the review is more than he can afford to pay. A link between a break right and a rent review clause might impliedly make time of the essence in respect of any time limits that may be contained in the rent review clause.[3]

1. Finance Act 2003, Sched.17A, para.7A provides, in effect, that where a rent review falls in the three months before the end of the fifth year of the term this is treated as taking place after the fifth anniversary for the purposes of SDLT.
2. See *Hemingway Realty Ltd* v. *The Clothworkers' Company* [2005] EWHC 299; [2005] 11 EG 181.
3. *Central Estates Ltd* v. *Secretary of State for the Environment* [1997] 1 EGLR 239; *United Scientific Holdings Ltd* v. *Burnley Borough Council* [1977] 2 All ER 62. The normal presumption that time is not of the essence of a rent review applies to the machinery for fixing a rent on a rent review, not to the date from which the increase is to take effect; see *White* v. *Riverside Housing Association* Ltd [2005] EWCA Civ 1385.

1.7. Common express covenants

To pay rent

1.7.1. The covenant should be clear as to the amount of rent, the intervals of payment, whether payable in advance or in arrear, whether the rent includes outgoings on the property, provisions for increase of the rent and payment of VAT (see A16.7).

To repair

1.7.2. In certain residential cases the landlord will be obliged by statute to keep the structure and exterior of the premises in repair.[1] In all cases, an express covenant to repair should precisely identify the obligations required of the party responsible for undertaking the repairs including, in the case of redecoration obligations, the intervals at which the work is to be undertaken. Where the demised premises form part of a larger building the landlord (or in the case of a flat perhaps a management company) will usually covenant to keep the structure and common parts of the building in repair. See the Law Society Standard Business Leases, of whole clause 5, of part clause 6 (see Appendix V.1).

Gas appliances

1.7.3. Gas Safety (Installation and Use) Regulations 1998 require gas appliances to be installed and maintained by competent personnel and regularly inspected.

Landlords of relevant residential premises are under an obligation to carry out an annual inspection of such appliances (even where the lease places full repairing obligations on the tenant). These provisions apply to leases for a term of less than seven years (including periodic tenancies) and any statutory tenancy arising out of such a lease. The duty also extends to relevant premises held under a licence. A lease which contains a landlord's break clause, exercisable within the first seven years of the term, falls within these provisions but a lease which contains a tenant's option to renew which, if exercised, would extend the term to seven years or more, does not.

Asbestos

1.7.4. Control of Asbestos Regulations 2006, reg. 4 contains a duty relating to the management of asbestos in non-domestic premises.[2] Broadly the duty is imposed on dutyholders (as defined), e.g. those responsible for maintenance of the premises. The duties basically require an assessment as to whether there is asbestos in the premises, a decision as to whether it should be removed or properly maintained, and monitoring. Information has to be provided to those likely to come into contact with the asbestos, for example, contractors and the emergency services.

Fire safety

1.7.5. The Regulatory Reform (Fire Safety) Order 2005 applies to most non-domestic premises. The Order has replaced fire certification under the Fire Precaution Act 1971 with a general duty to take fire precautions.

1.7.6. Responsibility for complying with the Fire Safety Order rests with the 'responsible person'. The primary duty falls on employers, if the workplace is to any extent under their control. Otherwise the duty in Article 3 of the Order is on the person who has control of the premises for the purpose of a trade, business or undertaking (whether or not for profit), which may be the tenant in many instances or, if not, the owner. Article 22 of the Order anticipates there could be more than one 'responsible person' for the same premises, for example, the tenant, landlord and the managing agent in so far as each has responsibility for the maintenance and safety of the building. Responsibility for enforcement will be undertaken by the local fire and rescue service authority. Detailed guides have been published in relation to the application of the Order to various types of properties.[3]

General principles

1.7.7. The extent of the repairing obligations imposed by the lease will vary from lease to lease but the following general principles are relevant:

(a) the wording of the clause must cover every part of the building and of the estate which is intended to be covered. Usually this will mean that the clause(s) must cover five main areas (which may overlap): the demised premises, the structure (including roof, main walls and foundations), the common parts, the common conduits, and the exterior;

(b) the operative words of the clause(s) must be sufficient to cover all foreseeable repair activities. In this respect the wording of the clause should provide for the main areas of maintenance: repairing, cleaning, and decorating. Improvements to the property or major rebuilding effected by the landlord will not necessarily be covered by the wording of a covenant 'to repair' and thus, unless expressly included in the wording of the covenant, a landlord may be unable to recover their cost from the tenants.[4] The word 'repair' is generally regarded as meaning the restoration by renewal or replacement of subsidiary parts of the whole.[5] The courts have drawn a marked contrast between an obligation to 'repair' and one of 'rebuilding' and 'renewal';[6]

(c) the wording of the covenant(s) must leave no grey areas where liability for repair is uncertain, and should not have areas of overlap. Care should be taken with the liability for repair, etc., of walls, ceilings, floors and joists. Clarity in these areas is largely dependent on the wording of the definition of the ownership of the various parts of the walls, floors, ceilings, etc., in the description of the property demised. The obligation to repair can then be defined in relation to ownership of the various parts. In particular, in multi-let buildings the lease should make it expressly clear whether the windows are part of the structure or of the demise;[7]

(d) the wording of the clause must clearly specify the apportionment of liability for repairs, etc., between landlord and tenant;

(e) where the lease requires the premises to be kept in 'good condition' this will require work to be done where the property is in a bad condition even though the property is not in disrepair.[8]

Not to make improvements or alterations

1.7.8. Such a covenant is commonly included in short leases of residential premises and leases of business premises in order to allow the landlord to retain control over his property and to ensure that no alterations are effected in breach of restrictive covenants on the landlord's title, or in breach of planning law or building regulation consent. Some improvements made by a tenant of business premises or agricultural land may commit the landlord to the payment of compensation when the tenant leaves the premises.[9]

1.7.9.	The covenant may be absolute, in which case the tenant is totally prohibited from making improvements or alterations unless the landlord grants a deed of variation of the lease. An absolute covenant is usually considered inappropriate in the context of the grant of a long lease (e.g. exceeding 21 years) of an entire building. A qualified covenant is one where the tenant must seek the landlord's prior consent to the alterations or improvements. A fully qualified covenant is one where the landlord's consent cannot be unreasonably withheld.[10] This may be stated expressly, however, a statutory provision will, in most leases, convert a qualified covenant into a fully qualified one where the alteration amounts to an improvement.[11] An example of the wording of a clause can be seen from the Law Society's Standard Business Leases, clause 5 of whole, clause 6 of part (Appendix V.1).

1.7.10.	Even in the case of an absolute covenant a tenant may seek the court's consent to the proposed improvements or alterations in certain circumstances. Thus if the tenant's works amount to 'improvements' within Part I Landlord and Tenant Act 1927, this Act provides a mechanism whereby the tenant may obtain permission for such improvements even in the face of an absolute prohibition. The Act sets out a procedure whereby, broadly, the tenant must serve notice on the landlord, who may refer the matter to the county court if he wishes to object. If there is no objection or the court consents, the tenant can make the improvement and on leaving he is entitled to compensation.[12]

Disability discrimination

1.7.11.	In outline, Disability Discrimination Act 1995 imposes duties on a number of categories of persons including landlords and employers not to discriminate on the basis of disability.[13] The Act requires employers[14] to take such steps as are reasonable to alter arrangements or physical features of premises if these put a disabled person at a substantial disadvantage in comparison with persons who are not disabled. The Disability Rights Commission has published a Code of Practice on employment and occupation. This discusses the obligations to make reasonable adjustments to premises and includes a consideration of how leases are affected by this obligation.

1.7.12.	One aspect of the 1995 Act which has caused concern to owners of property is in relation to obligations imposed on 'service providers'.[15] These include anyone (landlord or tenant) who provides goods, facilities or services to the public or a section of it. It may therefore include landlords who provide services over common parts to tenants. One element of this obligation is a duty to take reasonable steps to remove or alter a physical barrier which makes it unreasonably difficult for disabled persons to make use of facilities or a service, or to obtain goods offered to others. Alternatively, in appropriate cases, the service provider may provide a reasonable alternative method of making the service, etc., available to the disabled person. Consideration should also be given to the Code of Practice, *Rights of Access – Goods, Facilities, Services and Premises.*[16] A public authority has obligations similar to those imposed on service providers.[17]

1.7.13. By virtue of Disability Discrimination Act 1995, s.27, irrespective of what the lease may actually provide, the lease is deemed to contain provisions permitting a tenant to make any adjustments required by the Act (whether as employer or service provider) with the landlord's consent and any such consent is not to be unreasonably withheld.[18]

1.7.14. Disability Discrimination Act 2005[19] contains further obligations on landlords and those managing residential and commercial property, which are intended to help eliminate discrimination in the letting of property. The 2005 Act amends the 1995 Act[20] so as to make it unlawful for landlords and managers, in relation to premises they wish to let or that are let, to discriminate against a disabled tenant or prospective tenant by failing without justification to comply with a duty to provide a reasonable adjustment for the disabled person. Whilst these new duties are not intended to require the making of any alteration to the physical features of premises by a landlord, nonetheless the provisions would, for example, require a landlord or manager to take reasonable steps to provide an auxiliary aid or service.[21]

1.7.15. Disability Discrimination Act 1995 (as amended)[22] also, essentially, imposes duties on private clubs of more than 25 members, in certain circumstances, to carry out physical alterations to property. So, where a private club has a physical feature which makes it impossible or unreasonably difficult for disabled persons who are members, associates or guests to make use of a benefit, facility or service, the club may be required to take such steps as are reasonable in all the circumstances to alter the premises accordingly.

Covenant restricting user

1.7.16. Some restriction on the tenant's user of the premises is usually considered desirable for the same reasons as are cited in K1.7.8. The covenant may be absolute, in which case the tenant is totally prohibited from changing the use of the property unless the landlord grants a deed of variation of the lease. If the covenant is qualified, a statutory provision implies, in most cases, that no premium can be charged by the landlord for giving consent.[23] There is no implied statutory proviso that the landlord's consent will not be unreasonably withheld. In the context of the lease of a dwelling house it may be appropriate to include an absolute covenant against any use except that as a private residence. In the case of business premises a very restrictive user clause (e.g. a clause which permits one specific type of business only) may have an adverse effect on the saleability of the premises and the amount of rent chargeable for them. A common device to attempt to alleviate the depressive effect on the value of the property for rent review purposes is to provide in the lease for this effect to be disregarded on such a review.

Covenant against alienation

1.7.17.   A covenant restricting the tenant's right to dispose of the property must be carefully drafted since such covenants are construed narrowly by the courts, e.g. a covenant preventing assignment alone will not prevent the tenant from granting a sub-lease of the property. The covenant may be absolute in form, in which case no alienation of the property will be possible unless the landlord specifically grants consent usually by granting a deed of variation of the lease. A qualified covenant is subject to the statutory restrictions and modifications which are explained in K11.[24] Except where the lease provides for payment of a premium as a condition of the granting of consent, no premium is payable for such consent.[25] In the context of the long lease of a dwelling house it is unusual to include a general restriction against alienation except during the last few years of the term. The Lenders' Handbook contains detailed requirements for the content of long term residential leases (see K6.6 and Appendix VI.2). In other cases such a restriction is common and desirable to ensure that the landlord retains some control over the occupiers of his property. In respect of business premises, quite detailed provisions are common.[26] See the Law Society Standard Business Leases, clause 7 (Appendix V.1).

Covenant to give notice of dealings to landlord

1.7.18.   Such a covenant is normally included in order to give the landlord notice of all dealings by the tenant with the property. The obligation for the tenant to give notice of dealings should specify the occasions on which the covenant is to operate, e.g. notice of assignment, sub-lettings, mortgage, change of ownership on death or bankruptcy of the tenant. The tenant is usually required to pay a small registration fee to the landlord with each notice served. See the Law Society Standard Business Leases, clause 7 (Appendix V.1).

Landlord's covenant for quiet enjoyment

1.7.19.   Such a covenant will be implied into the lease by the common law, but it is usual to find an express covenant to this effect. Under this covenant the tenant is entitled to be put into possession of the premises and to remain quietly in possession of them throughout the term. The covenant is broken, for example, by unlawful eviction of the tenant.[27] Damages for mental distress are not recoverable for breach of this covenant.[28]

1. See Landlord and Tenant Act 1985, ss.11–14. Exceptionally a landlord may be under a common law implied duty to repair: see *Liverpool City Council* v. *Irwin* [1977] AC 239; *King* v. *South Northamptonshire District Council* [1992] 1 EGLR 53, CA.
2. Although there is no definition of non-domestic property in the regulations the Health and Safety Executive have produced some guidance. From this it appears that the definition will include some residential properties, for example, in relation to blocks of flats, the common parts will be considered to be non-domestic property. See further www.hse.gov.uk/asbestos/campaign/duty.htm.
3. These can be downloaded from **www.communities.gov.uk**.

4. See *Mullaney* v. *Maybourne Grange (Croydon) Management Ltd* [1986] 1 EGLR 70; *cf. Sutton (Hastoe) Housing Association* v. *Williams* [1988] 16 EG 75.
5. See, e.g. *Minja Properties Ltd* v. *Cussins Property Group plc* [1998] 2 EGLR 52.
6. See, e.g. *Norwich Union Life Insurance Society* v. *British Railways Board* [1987] 2 EGLR 137; *New England Properties* v. *Portsmouth New Shops* [1993] 1 EGLR 84; *Credit Suisse* v. *Beegas Nominees Ltd* [1994] 1 EGLR 76.
7. See *Holiday Fellowship Ltd* v. *Hereford* [1959] 1 All ER 433.
8. *Welsh* v. *Greenwich London Borough Council* [2002] 49 EG 118.
9. Part 1 Landlord and Tenant Act 1927; and see K8.5.17.
10. The Court of Appeal set out a series of principles to be applied in determining whether a refusal of consent is reasonable in *Iqbal* v. *Thakrar* [2004] PLSCS 125.
11. Landlord and Tenant Act 1927, s.19(2) and (4); *Lambert* v. *FW Woolworth & Co. Ltd* [1938] 2 All ER 664.
12. See *Norfolk Capital Group Ltd* v. *Cadogan Estates Ltd* [2004] 1 WLR 1458.
13. Thus a refusal to permit the installation of a chair lift for a disabled tenant may be lawful if the reasons for the landlord's refusal do not relate to the tenant's disability; see *Richmond Court (Swansea) Ltd* v. *Williams* [2006] EWCA Civ 1719. The meaning of disability in Disability Discrimination Act 1995, s.1 is supplemented by the publication, *Guidance on Matters to be Taken into Account in Determining Questions Relating to the Definition of Disability*. Copy from **www.drc-gb.org/the_law.aspx**.
14. See Disability Discrimination Act 1995, s.6.
15. See Disability Discrimination Act 1995, s.19.
16. For details of the code see **www.drc-gb.org/the_law.aspx**. Note also the provisions of Disability Discrimination (Service Providers and Public Authorities Carrying Out Functions) Regulations 2005.
17. See sections 21B to 21F Disability Discrimination Act 1995, and Disability Discrimination (Service Providers and Public Authorities Carrying Out Functions) Regulations 2005 (SI 2005/2901).
18. Further details as to the landlord's consent are contained in Disability Discrimination (Providers of Services) (Adjustment of Premises) Regulations 2001 (SI 2001/3253). Note also that Disability Discrimination Act 2005, s.16 inserts a new section 49G into Disability Discrimination Act 1995 which contains provisions that apply where a tenant seeks consent to make improvement to a let dwelling to facilitate the enjoyment of the premises by a disabled occupier.
19. See, in particular, sections 13, 14 and 16 of the Disability Discrimination Act 2005.
20. See new sections 24A to 24L Disability Discrimination Act 1995.
21. Disability Discrimination Act 1995, s.24J. Further detailed provision is made by Disability Discrimination (Premises) Regulations 2006 (SI 2006/887).
22. See Disability Discrimination Act 1995, s.21F, inserted by Disability Discrimination Act 2005, s.12. These provisions are supplemented by Disability Discrimination (Private Clubs etc.) Regulations 2005 (SI 2005/3258).
23. Landlord and Tenant Act 1927, s.19(3) and (4).
24. See Landlord and Tenant Act 1927, s.19(1) and (4), as amended by Landlord and Tenant Act 1987, and Landlord and Tenant (Covenants) Act 1995.
25. Law of Property Act 1925, s.144.
26. See K7.11.
27. *Miller* v. *Emcer Products Ltd* [1956] Ch 304.
28. *Branchett* v. *Beaney* [1992] 3 All ER 910.

1.8. Service charge

1.8.1. Leases of flats and of commercial premises will frequently require the tenant to pay a service charge for services provided by either the landlord or a management company, e.g. heating or cleaning and repair of the building of which the demised premises form part and the decoration of the common parts. The service charge is usually expressed to be payable as 'additional rent', thus allowing the landlord to distrain[1] for its non-payment. This device also enables the landlord to recover the sum due without the necessity of serving a section 146 notice.

1.8.2. The tenant should ensure that the proportion of the charge which he is required to pay is fair in relation to the amount of the building which he occupies or enjoys rights over, and should ensure that the clause specifies precisely what services are to be supplied in return for the charge. A landlord may wish to provide for an estimate of the service charge to be payable in advance and for there to be a reconciliation at the end of the year.

1.8.3. The landlord may also contemplate setting up a sinking fund to cater for major expenditure on the property. The tenant of a flat may be required to become a member of a residents' association or management company which will have responsibility for providing services and effecting the landlord's repairing covenants under the lease. This allows the tenants to control the expenditure to which they are committing themselves. Membership of a management company is normally restricted to the tenants of the block or estate and the covenant will require the tenant on assignment of his lease to require his assignee to take a transfer of the tenant's share in the management company where this is a company limited by shares. The landlord should be required to assume responsibility for the management company's responsibilities under the lease until the company is set up and shares have been allotted to all the tenants (see further K6.3.5).

1.8.4. Statutory controls over service charges on dwellings are discussed in K6.8. The Lenders' Handbook requirements are considered in K6.6 and Part 1 of the Lenders' Handbook is reproduced in Appendix VI.2. See also the Law Society Standard Business Lease of part clause 3 (reproduced in Appendix V.1).

1.8.5. Tenants are only obliged to pay for items agreed in the lease. The landlord should therefore be careful to include in the service charge provisions all the necessary expenditure which he may incur on the building. The clause must therefore encompass all the obligations which are covered by the landlord's covenants in the lease, e.g. repairs and decoration, insurance, services such as lifts, cleaning common parts, garden maintenance, etc. If the landlord may need in the future to make improvements to the property, this too should be covered by the clause.

1.8.6. Provision for the tenants to contribute to a reserve fund or sinking fund will assist in the financing of major works and eliminate the burden of imposing a very large service charge in one particular year when major items such as a central heating system need to be renewed.

1.8.7. The landlord's expenditure on bank interest and bank charges can only be recovered if the lease so permits.[2] Management charges need only be included where either the landlord will be carrying out his obligations himself or employing independent managing agents to do so. Professional fees are only recoverable under a service charge clause where they are properly incurred in respect of items which are chargeable under the service charge provisions.[3] It is advisable to include a sweeping-up clause to cover any omissions of specific items and to take account of any higher expectations in standards which were not anticipated at the commencement of the term. The Royal Institution of Chartered Surveyors has published a new code of practice, *RICS Code of Practice: Service Charges in Commercial Property*, which is intended for surveyors practising in England and Wales.[4] The code is designed to set best practice for commercial service charges. Its objectives are stated to:

- remove service charges as an area of conflict;

- deliver a budgetable and forecastable part of occupiers' overheads;

- ensure service charges are 'not for profit, not for loss';

- encourage transparency and communication in the relationship between landlords and tenants.

The code came into force on 1 April 2007 for service charges commencing on or after this date.

1. The Tribunals, Courts and Enforcement Bill will, if enacted, abolish distress for rent but will replace it with a modified regime called Commercial Rent Arrears Recovery for recovering rent arrears due under leases of commercial premises only.
2. *Frobisher (Second Investments) Ltd* v. *Kiloran Trust Co. Ltd* [1980] 1 All ER 488.
3. *Holding & Management Ltd* v. *Property Holding & Investment Trust plc* [1988] 2 All ER 702.
4. This can be downloaded from **www.servicechargecode.co.uk**.

1.9. Proviso for forfeiture or re-entry

1.9.1. The landlord's right to forfeit the lease for the tenant's breach of covenant is a valuable remedy which must be expressly included in the lease since such a right is not implied by the common law unless, exceptionally, the lease is made conditional on the due observance of the covenants.[1] Without such a clause the landlord will be unable to remove the tenant from the premises during the currency of the lease term. It is usual to include a clause which gives the landlord the right to forfeit the lease on non-payment of rent by the tenant after a stated period (e.g. 21 days) and for breach of any other covenant in the lease. Forfeiture for the tenant's insolvency is common in non-residential leases but should not be included in the long lease of a dwelling house since such a provision is unacceptable to most mortgagees.[2] Forfeiture for breach of a covenant other than to pay rent must generally be preceded by service of a notice under Law of Property Act 1925, s.146 and may in certain cases be affected by Leasehold Property (Repairs) Act 1938. Repossession of an occupied dwelling house requires a court order.[3] In other cases a court order will be required if re-entry cannot be made peaceably, otherwise an offence may be committed under Criminal Law Act 1977, s.6 (see also K1.9.4). There are further restrictions on the landlord's right to forfeit long residential leases set out in Commonhold and Leasehold Reform Act 2002; see further K6.9.2.

1.9.2. Forfeiture may also occur (even in the absence of an express proviso) where the tenant denies the landlord's title to the property. If a tenant makes a specific allegation that the landlord does not own the property or that a third party has better rights to the property than the landlord, this may be construed as a denial of the landlord's title and result in forfeiture.[4] A general denial of the landlord's title contained in a defence to proceedings brought by the landlord will not have this effect.[5]

1.9.3. A tenant may not apply for relief against forfeiture for breach of covenant other than for non-payment of rent after a landlord has forfeited a lease by court proceedings and entry into possession of the property pursuant to the judgment obtained in those proceedings. Where, however, entry is regained peaceably, the tenant retains his right to apply for equitable relief against forfeiture even after the landlord has taken possession of the property.[6] An equitable assignee from a tenant may claim relief against forfeiture.[7]

1.9.4. Great care must be taken where a landlord chooses to exercise his right to forfeit premises other than a dwelling by peaceable re-entry. If possession is resisted by the tenant when the landlord seeks to re-enter, there is a risk that a criminal offence under Criminal Law Act 1977, s.6 may be committed by the landlord.

1.9.5. Where the landlord seeks to forfeit following breach of a covenant against alienation by the tenant, any section 146 notice should be served on both the assignor (tenant) of the lease and on the purported assignee (person currently in possession).[8]

1.9.6. A notice under Law of Property Act 1925, s.146 is not required before forfeiting for non-payment of rent, and no formal demand for rent need be made if the re-entry clause states that the landlord can re-enter if rent is in arrears 'whether or not formally demanded' or there is wording to similar effect. Where the tenant is in breach of a repairing covenant and the landlord (acting under a power expressly given to him by the lease) effects the repairs himself and then seeks to recover the cost of the repairs from the tenant, it is not necessary to serve a section 146 notice and Leasehold Property (Repairs) Act 1938 does not apply. The action is for recovery of a liquidated sum only.[9]

1.9.7. If the landlord forfeits by legal proceedings, he can include a claim for arrears of rent, mesne profits, and interest.

1.9.8. Where the landlord is forfeiting by action (i.e. legal proceedings) in the county court for non-payment of rent,[10] the tenant can apply to the court for relief against forfeiture under County Courts Act 1984, ss.138–140. In outline, these provisions provide:

(a) for automatic relief if the tenant pays all arrears and costs of the action into court not less than five clear days before the return day of the landlord's proceedings;

(b) that if relief is not obtained as above then the court will make an order for possession on a future date suspended for not less than four weeks. If the tenant pays the arrears and costs within the period of suspension the lease is reinstated;

(c) that even if a possession order is made and the landlord re-enters, the tenant or any person with an interest under the lease derived from the tenant's interest can apply to the court for relief within six months from the landlord's recovery of possession and the court may grant relief on terms it thinks fit.

1.9.9. Where the landlord is forfeiting by action in the High Court the tenant can apply to the court for relief against forfeiture. If there is at least six months' rent in arrears the tenant will obtain automatic relief by paying all arrears and costs to the landlord or to the court before judgment.[11] The tenant's application must be made before the expiration of six months from execution of the judgment for possession.[12] Otherwise relief is still obtainable[13] so that if all the arrears and costs are paid, save in exceptional cases relief will normally be granted. If the tenant owes less than six months' rent he can apply for relief at any time after the possession order has been made. The court has an equitable jurisdiction and will take any delay into account.

1.9.10. The above rules only apply to forfeiture for non-payment of rent and the court has a wider discretion in cases of other breaches of covenant.[14]

1. Law Commission Report, *Termination of Tenancies for Tenant Default* (Law Com No. 303) proposes that the law of forfeiture should be abolished and replaced by a new statutory scheme allowing for termination of tenancies by landlords following a breach of covenant or condition by the tenant.
2. The requirements of the Lenders' Handbook are considered at K6.6 and Part 1 is reproduced in Appendix VI.2.
3. Protection from Eviction Act 1977, s.2. This includes property which is a mixed residential and commercial letting; see *Pirabakaran* v. *Patel* [2006] EWCA Civ 685.
4. *WG Clarke (Properties) Ltd* v. *Dupre Properties Ltd* [1992] Ch 297.
5. *Warner* v. *Sampson* [1959] 1 QB 297. Note also *Abidogun* v. *Frolan Health Care Ltd* [2001] 45 EG 138.
6. *Billson* v. *Residential Apartments* [1992] 1 AC 494, HL.
7. *High Street Investments* v. *Bellshore* [1996] NPC 20.
8. *Fuller* v. *Judy Properties* [1992] 1 EGLR 75 but see *Old Grovebury Manor Farm Ltd* v. *W Seymour Plant Sales & Hire Ltd (No.2)* [1979] 3 All ER 504; and note *Brown & Root Technology* v. *Sun Alliance & London Assurance Co. Ltd* [1997] 18 EG 123.
9. *Jervis* v. *Harris* [1995] NPC 171.
10. Law of Property Act 1925, s.146(2); see, e.g. *Crown Estate Commissioners* v. *Signet Group plc* [1996] 2 EGLR 200.
11. Common Law Procedure Act 1852, s.212.
12. *Ibid.*, s.210.
13. Supreme Court Act 1981, s.38.
14. Law of Property Act 1925, s.146(2); *Crown Estate Commissioners* v. *Signet Group plc* [1996] 2 EGLR 200; also note *Shiryama Shokusan Co.* v. *Danovo* [2005] EWHC 2589.

1.10. **Insurance**

1.10.1. If the landlord is to insure the property (as would generally be the case in a lease of commercial premises) he should ensure that he is able to recover the amount of the premiums from the tenant. The Law Society's Standard Business Lease of Whole does not contain a provision requiring the tenant to reimburse the landlord for the cost of insurance premiums paid by him. In many cases the landlord will require such reimbursement, in which case an amendment to add this requirement should be made. This should be done by attaching an additional page or pages to the lease containing this and any other amendments.

1.10.2. The following statement has been issued by the Law Society:

> 'It has been drawn to the attention of the working party responsible for drafting the Law Society Business Lease that the versions of the 2006 edition for letting the whole of a building (both registered and unregistered) do not require the tenant to reimburse the landlord for the premiums paid to insure the building, as the previous editions of the lease did. As the landlord expressly undertakes to insure, the reservation of an insurance rent would be normal practice. Accordingly, the following addition should be made to the Lease, which the 2006 edition is now treated as including:
>
> "after clause 1(4)(c) insert:
> (d)   insuring the property under this lease"
>
> Arrangements have been made to ensure that the publishers of electronic and printed versions of the Lease do now include this additional provision. The versions of the lease for letting part of a building have not been affected.'

1.10.3. The Law Society's Standard Business Lease of Part provides for reimbursement of the insurance premiums paid by the landlord through the service charge payments. See further Appendix V.1. Where the landlord is to insure, the tenant should ensure that the lease specifies the risks against which the landlord should insure. If the tenant is responsible for repairing all or any part of the property he would also want to ensure that the repairing covenant excepts liability for damage by insured risks. If the tenant is to insure, the covenant should specify the risks against which the landlord wishes the policy to be effected and should give the landlord the right to inspect the policy, to see the receipt for the last premium due, and to insure in the case of the tenant's default.

1.10.4. Where the premises comprise part of a building the lease must provide for both the unit and the common parts of the building to be properly insured. Normally the landlord covenants to insure all the units and the common parts together under a block policy, with a right to recover a proportionate part of the premium from each tenant. Incidental costs are sometimes also recoverable from tenants including the costs of regular valuations for insurance cover. Occasionally the lease may make provision for each tenant to insure his individual unit and for the landlord to insure the common parts of the building, but such an arrangement is not popular since it can lead to situations where not all tenants are insured for the same amounts or against the same risks with consequent difficulties in enforcing claims where it has become necessary for one tenant to claim against another.

1.10.5. The insurance covenant in the lease should provide for an adequate level of cover and of risk to be maintained over the units and common parts, including the full costs of rebuilding or reinstatement and related professional fees, with reputable insurers. Consideration should be given to limiting liability where cover is unavailable in the open market at reasonable rates. Damage caused by certain risks, e.g. terrorist activities is sometimes excluded from cover in which case liability will fall on the party responsible for repair in the event of damage being caused by uninsured losses. In such cases it may be appropriate for the tenant to be entitled to terminate the lease following substantial damage by uninsured risks, unless the landlord elects to reinstate at his own cost. Absolute covenants to insure are strictly construed so that, for example, where a landlord is under an absolute duty to insure against fire risks, he would have to reinstate the property even if the property burns down as a result of an excluded cause such as terrorist action.[1] The tenants should have the right to a copy of the insurance policy or reasonable evidence of its existence and validity, and to inspect the original policy and the receipt (or reasonable evidence of payment) for the last premium due.

1.10.6. A tenant will wish the lease to provide for the landlord to use the proceeds of the policy to reinstate the premises in the event of their damage or destruction by an insured risk. Provision should also be made for the application of the policy money in the event of reinstatement not being possible.

1.10.7. It is also desirable that the landlord should maintain an occupiers' liability insurance policy in a situation where the landlord retains the ownership of common parts of the building.

1.10.8. It is preferable for the landlord to obtain a policy which cannot be vitiated by act or default of the tenants.

1.10.9. Landlords are sometimes able to secure the payment of commission for the placing of insurance cover with a particular insurance company. Except to the extent that the landlord provides services in respect of the insurance, this commission, in principle, belongs to the tenants.[2] Landlords may provide in the lease that they are to be permitted to retain this commission.

1.10.10. If the solicitor is involved in insurance mediation services with regard to any insurance policy, care must be taken to ensure that the provisions of the Law Society's Scope Rules and Conduct of Business Rules are complied with (see A4).

1. See *Enlayde Ltd* v. *Roberts* [1917] 1 Ch 109; *Moorgate Estates Ltd* v. *Trower* [1940] 1 All ER 195.
2. *Williams* v. *Southwark London Borough Council* [2000] EGCS 44.

1.11. **Underleases**

1.11.1. Most of the matters which are relevant when acting for the seller or buyer on grant of a lease will also be applicable to the grant of a sub-lease.

1.11.2. The head-tenant will be liable to his own landlord (the freeholder) on the covenants contained in his lease irrespective of whether the breach is committed by the head- or sub-tenant. To protect himself against liability for a breach committed by the sub-tenant, the head-tenant should impose on the sub-tenant obligations which are at least as onerous as those contained in the head-lease.

1.11.3. A sub-tenant will be directly liable to the freeholder in respect of breach of restrictive covenants which are contained in the head-lease since he will be deemed to know of those covenants through his entitlement to call for the head-lease as part of the evidence of title. Apart from this, the freeholder may choose, as a term of the head-lease or by a condition attached to the grant of any necessary consent to the sub-lease, to require the sub-tenant to enter into a direct covenant with the freeholder. This will put the freeholder in a strong position in relation to the enforcement of covenants contained in the head-lease because it has the effect of establishing the relationship of privity of contract between the freeholder and the sub-tenant. In the case of leases to which Landlord and Tenant (Covenants) Act 1995 applies the landlord may, in any event, sue the sub-tenant directly for breach of certain restrictive covenants under section 3(5).

1.11.4. The existence and validity of a sub-lease is dependent on the existence and validity of the head-lease out of which it is derived. If, therefore, the head-lease is forfeited, the sub-lease is also automatically forfeited[1] although the sub-tenant may have the right to apply directly to the freeholder for relief against forfeiture even in circumstances where the head-tenant is unable to apply for relief. A lender (of the tenant or sub-tenant) has the same right to apply for relief against forfeiture as a sub-tenant.[2]

1.11.5. Where the head-lease requires the prior consent of the freeholder to the grant of a sub-lease, the head-tenant should seek such consent at an early stage in the transaction and should not enter a binding contract for the grant of the sub-lease until it is certain that such consent will be forthcoming. The head-tenant's lender's consent may also be required to the grant of the sub-lease and this too should be obtained at an early stage in the transaction. Obtaining a landlord's consent to a sub-lease or assignment is discussed in K11.

1.11.6. Standard Condition 8.3 and Standard Commercial Property Condition 10.3 require the seller to apply for and pay for any necessary licence, the buyer (subtenant) supplying references and other information. In certain circumstances either party may rescind the contract if the consent is not forthcoming.[3]

1.11.7. In relation to leases granted or entered into on or after 11 May 2000, Contracts (Rights of Third Parties) Act 1999 may allow direct enforcement of covenants between tenants and between a head-landlord and a sub-tenant. The Act can be excluded if required.

1. The sub-lease will also terminate (subject to any rights of continuation under Landlord and Tenant Act 1954) if a superior lease is terminated under a break right. See *Pennell* v. *Payne* [1995] 1 EGLR 6 (confirmed by the House of Lords in *Barrett* v. *Morgan* [2000] 1 All ER 481). See also *PW & Co.* v. *Milton Gate Investments Ltd* [2003] PLSCS 204. A sub-lease will, however, survive the surrender of a head lease (Law of Property Act 1925, s.139).
2. See Law of Property Act 1925, s.146.
3. See for example *Aubergine Enterprises Ltd* v. *Lakewood International Ltd* [2002] PLSCS 50.

1.12. **Title**

1.12.1. Under an open contract in relation to a title which is unregistered, unless the parties are contracting to grant a lease which will trigger first registration, the tenant is not entitled to call for deduction of the freehold reversionary title on the grant of a lease.[1] This rule is unsatisfactory, particularly where a premium is to be paid for the grant of the lease or where a tenant is paying a significant rent for commercial premises. However, where the reversionary title is registered these principles can have no application because the title is open to inspection. The rule has therefore been amended so as not to apply to registered land or to a lease to be derived out of registered land.[2] In a similar way it is disapplied where the contract is to grant a term of years which will require first registration (e.g. for a term of more than seven years).[3] The tenant in such cases is entitled to see the superior title.

1.12.2. These provisions can be varied by contractual provision and in most cases the landlord will contract to deduce his freehold title to the tenant in exactly the same way as if he were selling the freehold and should include a condition in the contract to this effect.[4]

1.12.3. Under an open contract in relation to a title which is unregistered, unless the parties are contracting to grant a lease which will trigger first registration, the rights of a sub-tenant in relation to deduction of title are limited. In such a case the sub-tenant is entitled to call for the head-lease out of which his sub-lease is to be derived and all subsequent assignments under which the lease has been held for the last 15 years. In the absence of a contractual condition to the contrary he is not entitled to call for production of the freehold title.[5]

1.12.4. The sub-tenant's inability in these cases to call for the deduction of the freehold title may cause problems, e.g. if a premium is being demanded for the grant of the sub-lease, or the sub-lease is to be mortgaged. However, as explained in K1.12.1, either where the reversionary title is registered or where the contract is to grant a term of years which will require first registration (e.g. for a term of more than seven years), the tenant is entitled to see the superior title.

1.12.5. A sub-lease will not contain an implied covenant on the part of the landlord that any user clause in the sub-lease is either lawful or complies with a restriction on use in a superior title.[6] A solicitor who accepts a lease or sub-lease without checking the validity of the user clause would be liable to his client in negligence if, as a result, the client suffered loss.

1.12.6. The statutory provisions relating to deduction of title can be varied by contractual provision and in most cases the landlord will contract to deduce such title, which will enable the sub-tenant to apply for registration of his lease with title absolute. Such a clause is contained in the Standard Conditions and the Standard Commercial Property Conditions, and these require the head-tenant to produce the title to the freehold reversion to the sub-tenant on grant of certain sub-leases.[7] A head-tenant who did not call for deduction of the freehold title when he took his own lease may not be able to comply with this standard condition and will have to exclude it by special condition in the contract.

1. Law of Property Act 1925, s.44(4A) inserted by Land Registration Act 2002, s.133, Sched.11, para.2(2).
2. See Law of Property Act 1925, s.44(12) inserted by Land Registration Act 2002, s.133, Sched.11, para.2(1), (4).
3. See Law of Property Act 1925, s.44(4A) inserted by Land Registration Act 2002, s.133, Sched.11, para.2(1), (2).
4. See, for example, Standard Conditions of Sale 8.2.4 and Standard Commercial Property Condition 10.2.4.
5. Law of Property Act 1925, s.44.
6. *Hill* v. *Harris* [1965] 2 QB 601.
7. Standard Conditions of Sale 8.2.4 and Standard Commercial Property Condition 10.2.4.

1.13. Registration

1.13.1. A lease for seven years or less is generally not capable of being registered with its own title at the Land Registry,[1] but the lease will normally take effect as an overriding interest under Land Registration Act 2002.[2] If there is concern about protecting the tenant's interest in the property an application for entry of a notice may be lodged against the landlord's title where the lease is for a term of more than three years from the date of the grant. Alternatively, such a lease may be noted against the landlord's title by the Land Registrar where its existence is disclosed on a dealing with the superior title as a 'disclosable overriding interest'.[3] A lease for a term of three years or less cannot be protected by notice.[4] In unregistered land a purchaser of the reversion will take subject to leases as they are legal estates, but an agreement for a lease must be registered as an estate contract (Class C(iv) land charge) in order to bind purchasers.[5] Should a tenant wish to check that his lease has been noted against a reversionary title where title to the reversion becomes registered subsequent to the grant of a lease, the tenant can ensure that he receives notification of the registration by applying for the registration of a caution against first registration at the Land Registry.[6]

1.13.2. Following completion of the grant of a lease which requires registration the tenant will make application for registration of the lease with a separate title.[7] A notice in respect of the lease will be entered automatically in the register of the landlord's title.[8]

1.13.3. Where a Prescribed Clauses Lease (as to which see K1.20) has been properly completed and registered, [9] on completion of the lease by registration the registrar will (where appropriate and where all relevant title numbers are included in clause LR2) make entries in the relevant individual registers in respect of interests contained in that lease which are of the nature referred to in clauses LR9 (rights of acquisition), LR10 (restrictive covenants given in the lease in respect of land other than the property), LR11 (Easements) or LR12 (Estate rentcharges). It is also possible for an application to be made for the entry of a standard form of restriction in clause LR13. Otherwise an application is necessary for a restriction to be entered against the leasehold title; this should be made in Form RX1 (see G3.9.14).

Easements

1.13.4. On registration of a properly completed Prescribed Clauses Lease where the landlord's title is registered, the Land Registry will automatically enter the benefit and burden of any easements granted and reserved. Where the lease is not registrable, any easements granted do not operate at law until the burden is noted on the landlord's title.[10] The application to note the easements should be made in Form AP1.[11] For more information see Land Registry Practice Guide 62.

Exempt information documents

1.13.5. As a registered lease will be open to public inspection, consideration may need to be given as to whether an application should be made to designate the lease an exempt information document (see G3.12 and K2.3.5).

1. Except leases granted under Housing Act 1985, Part V, and see other exceptions in G3.
2. Land Registration Act 2002, Sched.1, para.1 and Sched.3, para.1.
3. See Land Registration Rules 2003, rr.28 and 57 and Form DI.
4. Land Registration Act 2002, s.33.
5. Such purchasers must fall into the category of those acquiring a legal estate for money or money's worth where a failure to register will render the interest void against them. See Land Charges Act 1972, s.4(6).
6. Where the grant of an underlease is subject to consent (absolute or qualified) of the landlord, the tenant will normally be registered with absolute title. However, if no evidence of the landlord's consent is disclosed, the Land Registry will place a note on the title that none has been shown to the registrar. For further information see **www.landregistry.gov.uk/imp_dev/icp2/**.
7. Land Registration Act 2002, s.15.
8. Land Registration Act 2002, Sched.2 para.3(2)(b).
9. See Land Registration Rules 2003, rr.72A and 92 as amended by Land Registration (Amendment) (No.2) Rules 2005 (SI 2005/1982).
10. Land Registration Act 2002, s.27(1) and (2)(d) and Sched.2, para.7.
11. Land Registration Rules 2003, r.90.

1.14. **Surety**

1.14.1. The landlord may require a surety to the lease as a condition of its grant. Where the proposed tenant is a small private company it is common to find that the directors of the company are asked to guarantee the company's obligations under the lease. In other circumstances a parent company may be asked to guarantee the obligations of a subsidiary company tenant. This gives the landlord additional protection under the lease since the sureties' obligations will be co-extensive with those of the principal debtor. If it is intended to enter a contract prior to the grant of the lease, the sureties should be made parties to that contract.

1.14.2. A buyer's solicitor who is also acting for the sureties to the lease must consider whether any conflict of interests exists or is likely to arise between the interests of his buyer client and the interests of the sureties. It may be in the best interests of the buyer to obtain a lease of the premises, which he can only do if he provides sureties to the lease (a pre-condition imposed by the landlord), but it may not be in the best interests of the sureties to enter into covenants with the landlord to guarantee performance of the buyer's obligations under the lease, e.g. as to payment of rent, repairs, etc., where the enforcement of the sureties' covenants would put the sureties' personal assets, such as a matrimonial home, at risk. Where such a conflict exists or is likely to arise, the sureties should receive independent advice about their potential liability.

1.15. Mortgages

1.15.1. If the freehold reversion is subject to a mortgage, the mortgage deed should be checked to see whether it requires the lender's consent to be obtained prior to the grant of a lease. If so, steps should be taken to obtain the lender's consent before a binding contract to grant the lease is created.

1.15.2. The borrower's powers of leasing can be extended by or excluded from the mortgage by agreement (Law of Property Act 1925, s.99) except in the case of a mortgage of an agricultural holding where they cannot be excluded (Law of Property Act 1925, s.99(13A)) and the mortgage cannot exclude the court's power to order a new tenancy of business premises under Part II Landlord and Tenant Act 1954, s.36(4).

1.15.3. Failure to obtain such consent, where necessary, will put the seller into breach of his mortgage covenants, with the consequence that the principal sum under the mortgage will become due immediately. If consent is not required it should be checked that the lease is within the borrower's powers under Law of Property Act 1925, s.99.

1.15.4. Further, failure to obtain consent will affect the position regarding the tenant's application to register the lease, where applicable. The Land Registry's view is that any lease granted without the consent of a lender is vulnerable to being challenged by the lender. However, the Land Registry is prepared to grant title absolute even though no consent of the lender is lodged, where title absolute would have been granted had there been no charge. However, an entry pointing out that the title is subject to any rights that may have arisen in favour of the lender will be made in the Property Register of the leasehold title.[1]

---

1. However, this does not affect the need for specific consent if a restriction has been registered in favour of the lender requiring consent before a disposition may be registered. In these circumstances its consent will be required before registration can take place. For further information see **www.landregistry.gov.uk/imp_dev/icp2**.

1.16. Sub-sales

1.16.1. By Standard Condition 1.5 and Standard Commercial Property Condition 1.5.1 the buyer is not entitled to transfer the benefit of the contract. Standard Commercial Property Condition 1.5.2 provides that the seller may not be required to transfer the property in parts or to any person other than the buyer. A suitable special condition to this effect would need to be inserted in a contract drawn on the Standard Conditions. For the SDLT provisions which apply to sub-sales, see A14.

1.17. Searches and enquiries before contract

1.17.1. When acting for a tenant on a long lease for a premium or on a commercial lease the same searches and enquiries as are relevant to a freehold purchase should be made. Searches are discussed in B10. In the case of a complex commercial lease it may be convenient to use the Commercial Property Standard Enquiries.

1.17.2. Where a commercial lease is for a very short term at a low rent, or on short-term lettings of residential property, it is not usual for searches and enquiries to be made since the low risk attached to these lettings does not justify the expense of making the searches. The tenant client should be warned of the potential risks involved in not undertaking these. In some cases, however, the prospective tenant may feel it is prudent to make enquiries about the prospective landlord's solvency, particularly where the property is mortgaged, to avoid the risk of the landlord's lender seeking a possession order against the tenant if the landlord does not pay the mortgage.

1.18. The contract

1.18.1. A contract for the grant of the lease is normally entered into in the case of a purchase for a premium of a long-term residential lease but is not generally entered into on short-term lettings of residential premises nor on commercial leases where in both cases the parties directly enter into negotiations on the draft lease. In the case of commercial lettings contracts are used to give early possession on terms, to deal with building work that may be required prior to completion or where in order to achieve quickly a binding commitment a contract is entered into which is expressed to be subject to some contingency, e.g. landlord's consent or grant of planning permission.

1.19. Drafting the lease

1.19.1. A lease for a term of over three years must be granted by deed to vest the legal estate in the tenant. A lease for three years or less, taking effect in possession at the best rent without a fine, may be granted orally or in writing.[1] To ensure certainty of terms between the parties it is recommended that all leases, no matter how short the term, should be in writing (see B1.6).

1.19.2. The lease is normally drafted by the seller's (landlord's) solicitor and annexed to the draft contract submitted to the buyer's (tenant's) solicitor.[2] Except where the lease is to be for a term not exceeding three years, taking effect in possession and with no premium payable for its grant, the contract for the lease must satisfy Law of Property (Miscellaneous Provisions) Act 1989, s.2. Standard Condition 8.2 and Standard Commercial Property Condition 10.2 provide for the lease to be in the form annexed to the draft contract and for the seller to engross the lease and supply the buyer with the engrossment at least five working days before completion date. Law of Property (Miscellaneous Provisions) Act 1989, s.2, requires that the contract must incorporate all its terms (see B1.7). In the case of a contract for a lease the length of the term and its commencement date must be expressly stated on the draft lease which is attached to the contract in order to satisfy Law of Property (Miscellaneous Provisions) Act 1989, s.2, or either or both could be stated in the contract.[3]

1.19.3. Leases which are granted by the same landlord to different tenants of separate units all of which are in the common ownership of the landlord (e.g. flats within a block owned by the landlord) should be uniform in content. If this is not so, difficulty may subsequently be experienced in the management of the property and, where the leases provide for mutual enforceability between tenants, enforcement of covenants against individual tenants. Subject to this, given the diversity of circumstances in which leases are granted, no two leases will ever be identical. It is recommended that the seller's solicitor refers to a suitable precedent before embarking on the drafting of the lease.[4]

1.19.4. Where the lease is of business premises the Law Society Standard Business Leases for the whole or part of premises may be used. The texts of these are set out in Appendix V.1.

1.19.5. Consideration should be given to whether the landlord should give covenants for title on the grant of the lease.[5]

1. Law of Property Act 1925, ss.52–54 and Law of Property (Miscellaneous Provisions) Act 1989, s.2.
2. A lease may describe the property to be let by reference to a plan. For the Land Registry requirements as to plans, see B21.
3. *Marshall* v. *Berridge* (1881) 19 ChD 233.
4. See, e.g. *Encyclopaedia of Forms and Precedents (Vol. 22)*; *Drafting and Negotiating Commercial Leases* by Murray Ross; *Practical Lease Precedents* by Trevor Aldridge; **www.practicallaw.com/ 6-103-0965**.
5. Covenants can be given on the grant of a lease: Law of Property (Miscellaneous Provisions) Act 1994, and see M9.

1.20.   Prescribed Clauses Leases

1.20.1. A standard method for the presentation of certain information applies to registrable leases.[1] The reasons for this include the need to make leases easier to refer to and to use, to assist with the increasing numbers of leases being registered, and to facilitate the move towards e-conveyancing.

1.20.2. In essence, both the lease and counterpart lease must contain certain prescribed clauses and these must appear at the beginning of the document or immediately after any front cover sheet and/or front contents page.

1.20.3. The requirement for leases to contain these prescribed clauses applies to most leases that are granted out of registered land and which are compulsorily registrable, such as leases granted for more than seven years. These leases are called 'Prescribed Clauses Leases'.[2]

1.20.4. There are some exceptions. A lease does not have to be a Prescribed Clauses Lease if it is granted in a form expressly required by any of the following:

(a) an agreement entered into before 19 June 2006;

(b) a court order;

(c) an enactment;

(d) a consent or licence for the grant of the lease, e.g. a superior landlord's consent, given before 19 June 2006.

1.20.5. The prescribed clauses' provisions do not apply to a lease that comes into existence by virtue of a variation of a lease that is a deemed surrender and re-grant.

1.20.6. In many cases the prescribed clause allows a cross-reference to the relevant part of the lease where the provision appears.

1.20.7. One advantage of using a Prescribed Clauses Lease is that, provided the document has been properly drafted, a separate application to register certain matters against other titles affected is not necessary. The registrar is required (where appropriate and where all the relevant title numbers are included in clause LR2) to make entries in the relevant individual register in respect of interests contained in that lease, which are of the nature referred to in clause LR9 (rights of acquisition), LR10 (restrictive covenants), LR11 (easements) or LR12 (rentcharges).[3] In addition a standard form restriction may be applied for in LR13 without the need for a separate application.

The clauses

1.20.8. Set out below is an outline of the prescribed clauses:

(a) LR1. Date of lease;

(b) LR2. Title number(s);

(c) LR2.1. Landlord's title number(s);

(d) LR2.2. Other title numbers. Here it is necessary to insert any existing title numbers against which entries of matters referred to in LR9, LR10, LR11 and LR13 are to be made;

(e) LR3. Parties to the lease;

(f) LR4. Property. Note that in the event of discrepancy between the contents of LR4 and the rest of the lease, the Land Registry will rely solely on the contents of LR4 for registration purposes;

(g)   LR5. Prescribed statements etc.:

    (i)   LR5.1. Statements in leases required by certain statutes. It is necessary to insert here statements prescribed where dispositions are made to a charity,[4] by a charity[5] or where a lease is granted under Leasehold Reform, Housing and Urban Development Act 1993;[6]

    (ii)   LR5.2. Lease made under certain statutes. Certain statements must be inserted where the lease is made under, or by reference to, provisions of Leasehold Reform Act 1967, Housing Act 1985, Housing Act 1988 or Housing Act 1996;

(h)   LR6. Term for which the property is leased;

(i)   LR7. Premium;

(j)   LR8. Prohibitions or restrictions on disposing of the lease. It is only necessary to include a statement as to whether or not the lease contains a provision that prohibits or restricts dispositions;

(k)   LR9. Rights of acquisition etc.:

    (i)   LR9.1. Tenant's contractual rights to renew the lease, to acquire the reversion or another lease of the property, or to acquire an interest in other land;

    (ii)   LR9.2. Tenant's covenant to (or offer to) surrender the lease;

    (iii)   LR9.3. Landlord's contractual rights to acquire the lease;

(l)   LR10. Restrictive covenants given in this lease by the landlord in respect of land other than the property;

(m)   LR11. Easements. In the relevant sub-clause below a reference must be made to the relevant clause, schedule or paragraph of a schedule in the lease where easements are either granted or reserved as appropriate:

    (i)   LR11.1. Easements granted by this lease for the benefit of the property;

    (ii)   LR11.2. Easements granted or reserved by this lease over the property for the benefit of other property;

(n)   LR12. Estate rentcharge burdening the property;

(o)   LR13. Application for standard form of restriction. Note the full text of the standard form restriction must be entered;[7]

(p)   LR14. Declaration of trust where there is more than one person comprising the tenant.

1.20.9.   Full details can be obtained from Land Registry Practice Guide 64.[8]

---

1.   See Land Registration (Amendment) (No.2) Rules 2005.
2.   For details see Land Registration Rules 2003, r.58A(4)(a) and (b), and Land Registry Practice Guide 64.

3. Land Registration Rules 2003, r.72(A).
4. *Ibid.*, r.179.
5. *Ibid.*, r.180.
6. *Ibid.*, r.196.
7. See Land Registry Practice Guide 19 for the wording of the standard restrictions.
8. Available from **www.landregistry.gov.uk**.

1.21. The Protocol

1.21.1. The Protocol does not specifically refer to procedures on the grant of a lease. Since the procedure on grant of a long term residential lease for a premium is very similar to that applicable to a freehold transaction it is recommended that in appropriate cases when dealing with residential property the Protocol procedures are adhered to as closely as circumstances permit.

1.22. Side letters

1.22.1. A side letter (or letter of comfort) is sometimes used by the parties where one of the terms of a proposed lease is to be changed but it is not felt appropriate to vary the lease itself formally. This is sometimes done where the change to the clause in question is intended to be personal to the tenant and therefore intended not to affect assignees. It is important to appreciate that the provisions contained within these letters are likely to be landlord or tenant covenants within the meaning of Landlord and Tenant (Covenants) Act 1995 and will therefore have the same status as a covenant in the lease itself.[1] Such a letter may bind an assignee of the reversion, even if the assignee did not know of the letter or its contents.[2] Where a side letter has been used to vary the terms of a proposed sub-letting this should be disclosed to the landlord on an application for consent to the sub-letting.[3]

1. Landlord and Tenant (Covenants) Act 1995, s.28(1).
2. *System Floors Ltd* v. *Ruralpride Ltd* [1994] EGCS 162.
3. *Allied Dunbar* v. *Homebase* [2002] PLSCS 123.

K2. Acting for the landlord

2.1.   Taking instructions

2.1.1.   Much of the information required by the landlord's solicitor from his client will be similar to that required from the seller in the case of a freehold transaction. These matters are considered in A1 and K1.

2.2.   Drafting the lease

2.2.1.   The lease is normally drafted by the seller's (landlord's) solicitor and annexed to the draft contract submitted to the buyer's (tenant's) solicitor. Except where the lease is to be for a term not exceeding three years, taking effect in possession and with no premium payable for its grant, the contract for the lease must satisfy Law of Property (Miscellaneous Provisions) Act 1989, s.2. Standard Condition 8.2 and Standard Commercial Property Condition 10.2 provide for the lease to be in the form annexed to the draft contract and for the seller to engross the lease and supply the buyer with the engrossment at least five working days before completion date. Law of Property (Miscellaneous Provisions) Act 1989, s.2 requires that the contract must incorporate all its terms (see B1.6 and B1.7). In the case of a contract for a lease the length of the term and its commencement date must be expressly stated in the draft lease which is attached to the contract in order to satisfy Law of Property (Miscellaneous Provisions) Act 1989, s.2, or either or both could be stated in the contract.[1]

2.2.2.   Where the lease is of business premises the Law Society Standard Business Leases for the whole or part of premises may be used. The texts of these are set out in Appendix V.1.

1.   *Marshall* v. *Berridge* (1881) 19 ChD 233.

2.3.   Preparing the package

2.3.1.   Where the lease being granted is of a long-term residential property a sale package is commonly prepared in much the same way as in the sale of a freehold residential property.

Home information pack

2.3.2. In certain circumstances, where certain types of residential property are on the market (e.g. currently homes with three or more bedrooms), a person responsible for marketing the property is subject to the duties relating to home information packs.[1] This means that sellers or their selling agents will be required to have a home information pack when marketing homes for sale,[2] and to make a copy of the pack available to prospective buyers on request. So far as leasehold residential property is concerned, the term 'sale' means, broadly, a disposal, or agreement to dispose, by way of grant or assignment of a long lease. 'Long lease' means:

(a) a lease granted for a term certain exceeding 21 years, whether or not it is (or may become) terminable before the end of that term by notice given by the tenant or by re-entry or forfeiture; or

(b) a lease for a term fixed by law under a grant with a covenant or obligation for perpetual renewal, other than a lease by sub-demise from one which is not a long lease.[3]

The contract

2.3.3. The particulars of sale must state that the property is leasehold and give details of the term to be vested in the tenant. The draft lease should be drafted and annexed to the contract. It is usual to include a condition requiring the tenant to accept the lease in the form annexed to the contract.[4] Incumbrances affecting the freehold title must be disclosed and indemnity taken from the tenant in respect of future breaches. The landlord's solicitor should consider whether or not it is appropriate for his client to offer covenants for title to the tenant (see M9).

Checklist

2.3.4. The landlord's solicitor should normally send to the tenant's solicitor the following documents:[5]

(a) draft contract with draft lease annexed;

(b) evidence of the freehold title;

(c) any relevant planning and building regulation consents;

(d) answers to pre-contract searches and enquiries (including in Protocol cases the Seller's Property Information Form and Seller's Leasehold Information Form), or in the case of a complex commercial property it may be convenient to send replies to the Commercial Property Standard Enquiries;[6]

(e) where appropriate, evidence of the lender's consent to the grant of the lease;

(f) the memorandum and articles of any management company.

Exempt information documents

2.3.5.   A landlord who wishes to apply for the lease to be designated an exempt
information document faces the practical difficulty that the application for
registration of the lease will be made by the tenant. It is only when the tenant
lodges the lease for registration that a leasehold title number is allocated against
which the exemption application can be made. A landlord may want, therefore,
to include a provision in the contract requiring the tenant to lodge the landlord's
exemption application when registering the lease.

1. Housing Act 2004, s.154.
2. A residential property is put on the market when the fact that it is or may become available for sale is,
    with the intention of marketing the property, first made public in England and Wales by or on behalf of
    the seller: Housing Act 2004, s.149.
3. Housing Act 2004, s.177. The details in relation to home information packs are set out in A26.
4. See Standard Condition 8.2.3 and Standard Commercial Property Condition 10.2.3.
5. This list is subject to variation where a home information pack is provided: see A26.
6. Commercial Property Standard Enquiries may be downloaded from **www.bpf.org.uk** or
    www.practicallaw.com.

2.4.   Engrossment and execution of lease

2.4.1.   The lease is normally prepared in two parts (lease and counterpart) both
engrossed by the landlord's solicitor.[1] If the landlord requires the tenant to pay a
fee for the preparation of the engrossment this must be dealt with by special
condition in the contract.

2.4.2.   The counterpart should be sent to the tenant's solicitor at least five days before
contractual completion date[2] for execution by the tenant. The requirements for
execution of a deed are dealt with in section E. The practical difficulties that
stem from the law relating to the execution and delivery of deeds are particularly problematic for landlords in relation to leases. Once the deed is executed
by the landlord and delivered, which can happen by sending it to his solicitor in
certain circumstances,[3] it may be impossible for the landlord to withdraw
unilaterally from the transaction prior to completion even though there is no
contract.[4] Although in most cases delivery will be conditional (or in escrow),
the condition being payment of the purchase price or the handing over of a
counterpart, the signor will still, however, be bound on delivery unless the
condition (escrow) fails. It is possible to show that the executed lease has been
handed by the client to the solicitor for delivery at some later date, e.g. on the
day of completion. In this case withdrawal is possible.[5] As evidence of this
intention, wording is commonly inserted into the lease to show that delivery is
not intended to take place (and therefore the deed is not to be binding) until
completion takes place, or this may be presumed from the surrounding circumstances, e.g. the existence of 'subject to contract' negotiations.[6]

1. Standard Condition 8.2.5 and Standard Commercial Property Condition 10.2.5.
2. *Ibid.*
3. *Venetian Glass Gallery Ltd* v. *Next Properties Ltd* [1989] 2 EGLR 42; *Beesly* v. *Hallwood Estates Ltd*
    [1961] Ch 105; *Johnsey Estates (1990) Ltd* v. *Newport Marketworld Ltd* [1996] EGCS 87.

4. However, the tenant cannot be bound before he has executed the lease, merely because the landlord has delivered the lease in escrow and the escrow conditions are subsequently performed: *Dyment* v. *Boyden* [2004] EWCA 1586.
5. *Longman* v. *Viscount Chelsea* (1989) 58 P&CR 189.
6. *Bolton Metropolitan Borough Council* v. *Torkington* [2003] PLSCS 241.

2.5. Completion and post-completion

2.5.1. On completion in addition to or in substitution for the matters relevant to a freehold transaction the items which the landlord will receive include:

    (a) the counterpart lease executed by the tenant;

    (b) any premium payable for the grant (less any deposit paid on exchange of contracts);

    (c) an apportioned sum representing rent payable in advance under the lease and interim service charge. If the date from which the length of the term is calculated precedes the date of the lease itself, no rent can be recovered for this reason alone in respect of the period between the two dates.

2.5.2. The items which the landlord should give to the tenant include:

    (a) the lease executed by him;

    (b) if not already done, properly marked or certified copies of the freehold title deeds (unregistered land);

    (c) where relevant and if not already done, a certified copy of the consent of the landlord's lender to the transaction;

    (d) where relevant, share certificate relating to the management company.

2.5.3. After completion the landlord may receive notice in duplicate from the tenant, in accordance with the tenant's covenant to do so in the lease, of the tenant's mortgage of the property. One copy of the notice should be placed with the landlord's title deeds, the other receipted on behalf of the landlord and returned to the tenant's solicitor.

2.6. Apportionment of rent

2.6.1. Where the rent reserved by the lease is an annual rent payable quarterly in advance on the usual quarter days and the rent commencement date does not coincide with either the term commencement date or the usual quarter days, it is suggested that the apportionment of rent on completion of the grant of the lease should be made in accordance with the recommended method of calculation set out in Appendix IV.2. The quarter days are 25 March, 24 June, 29 September, and 25 December.

Recommended method of calculation

2.6.2. The Law Society's Conveyancing and Land Law Committee has produced a formula for the calculation of the apportionment of rent. This formula is set out in Appendix IV.2.

2.6.3. For consistency, where the term expires by effluxion of time on a date other than the last day of a term year, the amount of the tenant's final payment of rent should be calculated on a basis similar to the apportionment of his initial payment on the grant of the lease.

2.6.4. Apportionment of rent where the term date does not commence on a rent payment date cannot be made according to the formula explained in Appendix IV.2. In most cases the most appropriate method of calculation in this situation will be what is sometimes called the 'surveyor's method'. This involves simply counting the days to immediately before the next payment date, and applying a daily rate computed on a yearly basis. This is the method provided by the Standard Commercial Property Conditions to apply in all cases. The Standard Conditions of Sale do not specify any formula for the apportionment calculation.

2.6.5. The illogicality of this approach is obvious. A daily rate for rent payable by, e.g. equal quarterly instalments is being calculated on a yearly basis and then applied to the residue of a particular quarter, which does not comprise exactly one-fourth of a year. A variation would be to calculate the daily rate for the particular quarter by reference to the total number of days in that quarter.

2.6.6. On either basis, it will be apparent that, should it be necessary to calculate an apportionment at a later date (e.g. when the lease is assigned or surrendered, or the reversion is transferred), to achieve a fair result it would be necessary to ascertain how much rent was actually paid under the apportionment at the grant of the lease and carry the calculation forward on that basis. This will usually be impractical, and the parties will have to be prepared to adopt each time a more rough and ready approach, such as the 'surveyor's method'.

2.6.7. However, since that method is entirely arbitrary and bears no logical relationship to the term/rent structure of the lease, it is recommended that leases should be drafted so that the term year commences on one of the recurring rent payment dates. Thus if rent is to be payable on the usual quarter days, the term year should commence on a quarter day. This will enable apportionments to be computed on a logical basis as set out in Appendix IV.2.

K3. Acting for the tenant

3.1.   Before exchange

Taking instructions

3.1.1.   The information required by the buyer's (tenant's) solicitor from his client will be similar to that required in a freehold transaction (see A1). The client should be advised about the effect of any security of tenure provisions which may be applicable in the circumstances (see K6, K8, K10).

The draft lease

3.1.2.   The draft lease, prepared by the seller's (landlord's) solicitor, will be supplied to the tenant's solicitor with the draft contract. The contract will normally require the tenant to accept the draft in the form annexed to the contract (see Standard Condition 8.2.3 and Standard Commercial Property Condition 10.2.3); therefore any queries or observations which are to be raised in connection with the lease must be finalised before contracts are exchanged. Even where the lease appears to contain the 'usual' clauses appropriate to the particular transaction in hand, the document must be carefully examined by the tenant's solicitor to ensure that it does contain provisions which are adequate to protect his client's interests and contains no onerous clauses (e.g. in relation to repairing obligations or rent review) which may adversely affect the client. The amount of rent and the length of the term will affect the amount of SDLT payable on the lease by the tenant and this also should be considered.

Checklist

3.1.3.   When checking the lease particular attention should be paid to the provisions relating to the following matters:

(a)   the property to be demised;

(b)   easements and reservations (particularly in the case of flats or other non-detached property: see K1);

(c)   repairing obligations;

(d)   rent and rent review provisions;

(e)   provisions relating to service charges (see K1);

(f)   insurance (who is to insure: landlord or tenant? Do the insurance provisions accord with the tenant's mortgagee's instructions? What is covered by the policy both in terms of premises, amount of cover and risks insured against?);

(g) forfeiture clauses;

(h) covenants restricting alienation of the property;

(i) covenants restricting the use of the property;

(j) provisions relating to a management company or residents' association (is the tenant required to become a member of a management company which is limited by guarantee? Will his liability to the management company terminate on assignment of the lease?);

(k) requirements for a surety or rent deposit scheme;

(l) are any of the covenants onerous?

(m) do the covenants adequately protect the tenant and his lender?

(n) are covenants for title being offered?

(o) requirements of the Lenders' Handbook (see K6.6);

(p) the proper completion of the prescribed clauses where it is a Prescribed Clauses Lease.

A brief summary of the most common express covenants found in leases is contained in K1.

Searches

3.1.4. The tenant's solicitor should usually undertake the same searches and enquiries as if he were buying the freehold (see B10 and E2). Exceptionally, where a short tenancy agreement is being granted, it may be considered unnecessary to do such searches.

Lender's requirements

3.1.5. Where the lease provides security for a loan, the tenant's lender's requirements, contained in the instructions given to the solicitors acting for the lender, must be observed. The tenant's lender will frequently be concerned to see that the following conditions have been satisfied:

(a) the consent of the landlord's lender to the transaction has been obtained (where relevant);

(b) the length of the term to be granted provides adequate security for the loan. The requirements in the Lenders' Handbook are considered at K6.6;

(c) the lease contains adequate insurance provisions relating both to the premises themselves and (where relevant) to common parts of the building and that the insurance provisions coincide with the lender's own requirements for insurance;

(d)   normally title to the freehold reversion should be deduced. This will enable the lease to be registered with an absolute title at the Land Registry (where appropriate);

(e)   the lease contains proper repairing covenants in respect both of the property itself and (where relevant) the common parts of the building;

(f)   in the case of residential leases, that there is no provision for forfeiture on the insolvency of the tenant;

(g)   where the lease is of part of a building or is, e.g. of one house on an estate comprising leasehold houses all owned by the same landlord, that the lease provides for enforceability of covenants as between the tenants (usually by the landlord following a request by a tenant);

(h)   where appropriate the landlord is giving the relevant covenants for title.

3.1.6.   Where the lender's solicitor's instructions are governed by the Lenders' Handbook the requirements of the Handbook must be complied with. This is dealt with at K6.6 and Part 1 of the Lenders' Handbook is reproduced at Appendix VI.2.

Advising the client

3.1.7.   The tenant's obligations under the lease, which are often complex and extensive, should be clearly explained to him. In particular, the tenant (where relevant) should be warned of his continuing liability on the covenants in the lease notwithstanding the subsequent sale of the residue of the term to a third party (see K10) and of the danger of losing the lease through forfeiture for breach of covenant. A pre-contract report may be prepared and given to the client (as in freehold transactions, see C1). The report should explain the main provisions of the terms of the lease and their effect on the tenant.

Protocol and home information pack

3.1.8.   The Protocol does not specifically refer to procedures on the grant of a lease. Since the procedure on grant of a long term residential lease for a premium is very similar to that applicable to a freehold transaction it is recommended that in appropriate cases when dealing with residential property the Protocol procedures are adhered to as closely as circumstances permit.

3.1.9.   The seller or his agent may have supplied the buyer with a home information pack where appropriate. See further A26.

3.2.   **Pre-completion and completion**

3.2.1.   The engrossment of the lease and counterpart will usually be prepared by the landlord's solicitor. The tenant, if the contract so provides, may be required on completion to pay a fee to the landlord for the preparation of the engrossment. By Standard Condition 8.2.5 and Standard Commercial Property Condition 10.2.5 the landlord is to deliver the engrossment of the counterpart lease to the tenant at least five working days before completion and by Standard Condition 8.2.6 and Standard Commercial Property Condition 10.2.6 the tenant is to execute the counterpart lease and deliver it to the landlord on completion. Execution should be made in escrow. Similar points apply in relation to execution of the counterpart as those relating to execution of the lease. This is discussed in K2.4.2 and section E.

3.2.2.   The tenant's solicitor should make pre-completion searches in the same way as if he were buying the freehold (see section E).

3.2.3.   Apportionments on completion may include amounts in respect of rent and service charge payable in advance under the provisions of the lease.

3.2.4.   On completion the tenant should give to the landlord:

    (a)   the duly executed counterpart lease;

    (b)   any money due on completion, e.g. balance of premium (less deposit paid on exchange), apportioned sums payable in respect of rent and service charge, landlord's fee for engrossment of the lease.

3.2.5.   The tenant should on completion receive from the landlord:

    (a)   the duly executed lease;

    (b)   where the landlord's title is unregistered, a marked abstract of the freehold title;

    (c)   where appropriate, consent to the dealing given by the landlord's mortgagee;

    (d)   share certificate and management company documents.

3.3.   Post-completion

Stamp Duty Land Tax

3.3.1.   For every notifiable transaction (see A14) which will include some agreements for lease and the grant of many leases, the tenant must deliver a land transaction return to HM Revenue and Customs within 30 days of the effective date of the transaction. This delivery must include a self-assessment of the liability and payment of the SDLT due (if any).

3.3.2.   The general rule is that the effective date of a land transaction is the date of completion. There are, however, special rules where a contract is substantially performed before it is completed (e.g. where under an agreement lease, occupation is taken by the tenant before completion).[1] These points and matters generally relating to SDLT are explained in A14.

3.3.3.   The lease cannot be registered or noted (if relevant) at the Land Registry without a certificate as to compliance with SDLT (see A14). The certificate will be issued either by HM Revenue and Customs stating that a land transaction return has been delivered or by the buyer (self-certification) that no land transaction return is required.

3.3.4.   The SDLT payable on a premium and on the lease rent are calculated separately (see A14).

Registration of the lease

3.3.5.   Where applicable the lease must be registered at the Land Registry within the relevant priority period, or on first registration within two months of completion. The requirements for registration of a lease are outlined in K1.

Notice to landlord

3.3.6.   The lease will usually contain a covenant requiring the tenant to notify the landlord within a stated period of all dealings with the lease and to pay a fee to the landlord for registration of the notice. The creation of a mortgage by the tenant, depending on the wording of the covenant, may fall within this obligation. Where the tenant is obliged to give notice of dealings, this should be done by sending two copies of the notice, together with a cheque for the appropriate fee, to the landlord's solicitor or other person named in the covenant. The landlord should be asked to sign one copy of the notice and to return it to the tenant so that the receipted notice may be placed with the tenant's title deeds as evidence of compliance with this requirement.

3.3.7.   A tenant's lender may require a signed but otherwise blank stock transfer form and the tenant's share certificate to be lodged with him to ensure that the lender will be able to transfer the tenant's share in the management company in the event of the lender exercising his power of sale.

Registration of certain covenants

3.3.8.   Where the landlord's title is registered, restrictive covenants between landlord and tenant which relate to the demised premises cannot be protected by registration.[2] It is, however, necessary to protect restrictive covenants contained in leases which relate to property other than that demised by means of a notice. If, for example, the landlord has covenanted not to allow another unit in a retail park to trade in competition with a tenant, the tenant should protect the covenant against the landlord's title in respect of land other than the property by means of a notice.[3]

1. Both the contract and the transaction effected on completion are notifiable transactions; see Finance Act 2003, s.44.
2. Land Registration Act 2002, s.33.
3. This may be done by the proper registration of a Prescribed Clauses Lease with details of the restrictive covenants set out in LR10 (see K1.20.8, item (l)) and where all relevant title numbers are included in clause LR2.

K4. Acting for both parties

4.1.   Conflict of interests

4.1.1.   A solicitor must not act where there is a conflict of interest between himself and his clients or between two of his clients (see A10 and A11).

4.2.   Rule 3 Solicitors' Code of Conduct 2007

4.2.1.   Specifically in relation to leasehold conveyancing Rule 3 Solicitors' Code of Conduct 2007 prohibits a solicitor from acting for both landlord and tenant in the grant or assignment of a lease at arm's length. This rule and its exceptions are further discussed in A10 and Rule 3 is reproduced at Appendix I.1.

4.3.   Acting for the client's lender

4.3.1.   Generally, a solicitor may act for his landlord or tenant client and that client's lender provided that no conflict of interests exists or is likely to arise. See A11.

4.3.2.   The Lenders' Handbook also precludes the same fee earner in the same firm acting for the lender and borrower where the borrower is either the fee earner or a member of his or her immediate family. Consent may be given but in this case a separate fee earner of no less standing in the firm must act for the lender.

4.4.   Sureties

4.4.1.   A prospective tenant's solicitor who is also considering acting for the prospective surety to the lease must consider his or her obligations under the Solicitors' Code of Conduct 2007 which provides in Rule 3.01(2) that there is a conflict of interests if:

> 'you owe, or your firm owes, separate duties to act in the best interests of two or more clients in relation to the same or related matters, and those duties conflict, or there is a significant risk that those duties may conflict ...'

However the Code also provides in Rule 3.02(1):

> 'You or your firm may act for two or more clients in relation to a matter in situations of conflict or possible conflict if:

(a)   the different clients have a substantially common interest in relation to that matter or a particular aspect of it; and

(b)   all the clients have given in writing their informed consent to you or your firm acting.'

Where this rule is being relied upon Rule 3.02(4) requires the solicitor to:

'(a)   draw all the relevant issues to the attention of the clients before agreeing to act or, where already acting, when the conflict arises or as soon as is reasonably practicable, and in such a way that the clients concerned can understand the issues and the risks involved;

(b)   have a reasonable belief that the clients understand the relevant issues; and

(c)   be reasonably satisfied that those clietns are of full capacity.'

For example, it may be in the best interests of a prospective tenant to obtain a lease of the premises, which he can only do if he provides a surety to the lease (a pre-condition imposed by the landlord), but, on the face of it, it is not in the best interests of the surety to enter into covenants with the landlord to guarantee performance of the tenant's obligations under the lease, as it is potentially liable for these liabilities of the tenant. However, if the surety is a parent company and the tenant is a wholly owned subsidiary they may have a 'substantially common interest' in the matter proceeding. The position may be completely different if the surety is an individual who becomes potentially liable for the tenant's obligations under the lease where the enforcement of the surety's covenants would put the surety's personal assets, such as a matrimonial home, at risk. It is a matter of judgment in each case whether the situation is one where the interests of both the tenant and the surety are sufficiently 'common' so as to outweigh the extent to which there is a realistic risk of their interests being in conflict. If, in the opinion of the solicitor, he or she feels able to act for both parties then written consent should be obtained in accordance with Rule 3.02. However, where the solicitor feels that there is not a sufficient 'substantial common interest' so as to outweigh the conflict that exists, or is likely to arise, between them, then the surety should be given independent advice about his or her potential liability.

4.4.2.   Where a solicitor does act for a surety or guarantor he owes a duty of care to the surety or guarantor to exercise reasonable skill and care in carrying out the terms of the retainer.[1]

4.4.3.   Under the terms of the Lenders' Handbook the solicitor who is acting for the borrower cannot, generally, also act for a guarantor, any borrower who does not personally benefit from the loan or anyone intending to occupy the property who is to consent to the mortgage. They must be independently advised. See Appendix VI.2.

1.   *Woodward* v. *Wolferstans* [1997] NPC 51.

K5. Short-term residential tenancies

5.1. Grant of lease

5.1.1. A lease for a term of over three years must be granted by deed to vest the legal estate in the tenant. A lease for three years or less, taking effect in possession at the best rent without a fine, may be granted orally or in writing.[1] To ensure certainty of terms between the parties it is recommended that all leases, no matter how short the term, should be in writing.

5.1.2. A contract for the grant of the lease is not generally entered into on short-term lettings of residential premises.

5.1.3. On short-term lettings of residential property it is not usual for searches and enquiries to be made since the low risk attached to these lettings does not justify the expense of making the searches. However, the prospective tenant may feel it is prudent to make enquiries about the prospective landlord's solvency, particularly where the property is mortgaged, to avoid the risk of the landlord's lender seeking a possession order against the tenant if the landlord does not pay the mortgage. No SDLT will normally be payable, nor will such a transaction normally be notifiable (see A14).

5.1.4. Where the lease is to be granted for a short term some of the considerations outlined in K1, K2 and K3 will not be relevant. Frequently a formal contract for the grant of the lease is dispensed with and the landlord's solicitor simply submits a draft lease (sometimes referred to as a tenancy agreement) for approval by the tenant's solicitor. When the form of the lease or agreement is finalised and signed, the tenant will take possession of the premises. No premium is normally taken. In some cases a premium is not permitted by law[2] but, in these cases, a deposit which must not exceed one-sixth of the annual rent may be taken as security against damage to fixtures and fittings.[3] Deposits in relation to assured shorthold tenancies are governed by the tenancy deposit scheme (see K5.5.45).

5.1.5. Where the premises are furnished, an inventory of the contents should be prepared by the landlord and agreed by the tenant.

5.1.6. If the rent is to be payable weekly, a rent book must be provided to the tenant.[4]

5.1.7. The tenant's solicitor will not normally investigate title on his client's behalf, but the risks of omitting this step must be considered in each individual case. The terms of the tenancy agreement must be carefully scrutinised and their effect explained to the client. Particular attention should be paid to the effects of any security of tenure legislation on the tenancy.[5]

5.1.8. A lease of seven years or less is generally not capable of being registered with its own title at the Land Registry,[6] but takes effect as an overriding interest.[7] If there is concern about protecting the tenant's interest in the property a notice may be entered against the landlord's title where the lease is for a term of more than three years from the date of the grant.[8] A lease for a term of three years or less cannot be protected by notice.[9]

5.1.9. Where the title to the reversionary estate is unregistered a purchaser of the reversion will take subject to a lease. An agreement for a lease must be registered as an estate contract (C(iv) land charge) and a caution against first registration may be registered at the Land Registry.

Licences of houses in multiple occupation

5.1.10. Regulations have been introduced in order to improve the standard of rented accommodation, in larger houses which contain tenants who share the facilities of the property, e.g. large nineteenth-century buildings that have been converted into bedsits. This type of property may be classified as a house in multiple occupation (HMO) if it meets the criteria set out in Housing Act 2004, s.77 and ss.254–260.

5.1.11. Part 2 Housing Act 2004 and the regulations made thereunder require the mandatory licensing of certain HMOs.[10]

5.1.12. HMOs are subject to the mandatory licensing scheme, broadly, if the HMO satisfies the following criteria:

    (a) the HMO or any part of it comprises three storeys[11] or more;

    (b) it is occupied by five or more persons; and

    (c) it is occupied by persons living in two or more single households.[12]

However, an HMO may be exempt from mandatory licensing in certain circumstances.[13]

5.1.13. Further regulations make provision for related matters such as:

    (a) application forms and the information to be held on public registers;[14]

    (b) the minimum management standards for HMOs;[15]

    (c) the circumstances in which a local authority may be authorised to take over the management of individual private rented properties that give rise to significant anti-social behaviour problems.[16]

5.1.14.   Where universities and colleges of higher and further education manage and control student accommodation, they are required to comply with a code of management practice in order to secure exception from HMO licensing.[17]

Selective licensing of certain private rented property

5.1.15.   Due to concerns about the activities of some private landlords in areas of declining housing demand who have been offering homes to anti-social tenants.[18] Housing Act 2004, Part 3 enables a local authority to designate an area in England for licensing of private rented accommodation, subject to certain exemptions.[19] Broadly, the local authority will have to be broadly satisfied that the area is, or is likely to become, one of low housing demand and is experiencing a significant problem caused by anti-social behaviour which private sector landlords are failing to address properly.[20]

1.   Section 54(2) Law of Property Act 1925. A legal easement must be created by deed (*Mason* v. *Clarke* [1954] 1 QB 460). Therefore if an easement is contained in a lease of three years or less the lease should be created by a deed.
2.   As in the case of tenancies protected under Rent Act 1977, see Rent Act 1977, Part IX, Sched.1, Pt. II; and K5.3.9.
3.   Rent Act 1977, s.128(1) and see further K5.5.45.
4.   Landlord and Tenant Act 1985, s.4. See *R (on the application of Dewa)* v. *Marylebone Magistrates Court* [2004] EWHC 1002 (Admin), where the section was considered.
5.   The Law Commission has issued a report proposing an entirely new scheme to cover short term residential lettings. This proposes that all these lettings would be controlled by statute and be called 'occupation contracts'. Although there is no immediate proposal to introduce any such legislation, the report may be of interest to anyone advising generally in this area. See Law Com No. 297.
6.   Except leases granted under Housing Act 1985, Part V, see K9.1.6. See exceptions in G3.2.
7.   Land Registration Act 2002, Sched.1, para.1 and Sched.3, para.1.
8.   Note that any easements granted to the tenant should be noted against the landlord's title as these do not operate at law until the burden is noted on the landlord's title; see Land Registration Act 2002, s.27(1) and (2)(d) and Sched.2, para.7. For more information see Land Registry Practice Guide 62.
9.   Land Registration Act 2002, s.33(b).
10.   For further details on the licensing scheme see **www.propertylicence.gov.uk**.
11.   Licensing of Houses in Multiple Occupation (Prescribed Descriptions) (England) Order 2006 (SI 2006/371); Licensing of Houses in Multiple Occupation (Prescribed Descriptions) (Wales) Order 2006 (SI 2006/1712). Paragraph 3(3) of the Orders sets out the conditions to determine which storeys are taken into account depending on their use.
12.   A single household is defined, for the purposes of determining whether a building is an HMO under s.254, by Housing Act 2004, s.258.
13.   If, for example, the property is subject to a temporary exemption notice under Housing Act 2004, s.62, or if it is subject to an interim or final management order under Chapter 1 of Part 4 of the Housing Act 2004. There is power to extend the licensing regime in certain circumstances under Housing Act 2004, s.257 to certain blocks of self-contained flats.
14.   Licensing and Management of Houses in Multiple Occupation and Other Houses (Miscellaneous Provisions) (England) Regulations 2006 (SI 2006/373); Licensing and Management of Houses in Multiple Occupation and other Houses (Miscellaneous Provisions) (Wales) Regulations 2006 (SI 2006/1715).
15.   Management of Houses in Multiple Occupation (England) Regulations 2006 (SI 2006/372); Management of Houses in Multiple Occupation (Wales) Regulations 2006 (SI 2006/1713).
16.   Housing (Interim Management Orders) (Prescribed Circumstances) (England) Order 2006 (SI 2006/369); Housing (Interim Management Orders) (Prescribed Circumstances) (Wales) Order 2006 (SI 2006/1706).
17.   Houses in Multiple Occupation (Specified Educational Establishments) (England) Regulations 2007 (SI 2007/708); Houses in Multiple Occupation (Specified Educational Establishments) (England) (No. 2)

Regulations 2006 (SI 2006/2280); Houses in Multiple Occupation (Specified Educational Establishments) (Wales) Regulations 2006 (SI 2006/1707); Housing (Approval of Codes of Management Practice) (Student Accommodation) (England) Order 2006 (SI 2006/646); Housing (Approval of Codes of Management Practice) (Student Accommodation) (Wales) Order 2006 (SI 2006/1709).

18. See the housing green paper, *Quality And Choice: A Decent Home For All* (December 2000) available on **www.communities.gov.uk**.
19. Selective Licensing of Houses (Specified Exemptions) (England) Order 2006 (SI 2006/370); Selective Licensing of Houses (Specified Exemptions) (Wales) Order 2006 (SI 2006/2824); Selective Licensing of Houses (Additional Conditions) (Wales) Order 2006 (SI 2006/2825).
20. Housing Act 2004, s.80.

5.2. Public sector tenants

5.2.1. Security for public sector tenants is provided by Part IV Housing Act 1985 (as amended by Housing Act 1988) under what are called 'secure tenancies'.

5.2.2. Subject to:

(a) a number of exceptions set out in Schedule 1 (e.g. tenancies granted for over 21 years and business tenancies within Part II Landlord and Tenant Act 1954);

(b) tenancies ceasing to be secure tenancies after the death of the tenant subject to certain limited succession rights;[1] and

(c) tenancies ceasing to be secure tenancies in consequence of an assignment or sub-letting other than one permitted by the Act;[2]

a tenancy under which a dwelling house is let as a separate dwelling is a secure tenancy at any time when the 'landlord condition' and the 'tenant condition' are both satisfied.

5.2.3. The provisions apply to most licences as well as to tenancies.[3]

The 'landlord condition'

5.2.4. The 'landlord condition' is that the interest of the landlord belongs to one of a number of bodies specified in Housing Act 1985, s.80, as modified by Housing Act 1988, s.35. These include local authorities, development corporations and certain housing co-operatives.

The 'tenant condition'

5.2.5. The 'tenant condition' is that the tenant is an individual and occupies the house as his only or principal home or, where the tenancy is a joint tenancy, that each of the joint tenants is an individual and at least one of them occupies the house as his only or principal home.

5.2.6. Where a secure tenancy for a term certain ends by effluxion of time or by an order terminating the tenancy in pursuance of a right of forfeiture, a periodic tenancy arises. A secure tenancy which is either a periodic tenancy or for a term certain but subject to termination by the landlord cannot usually be brought to an end by the landlord except by obtaining a court order for possession. The grounds for possession are set out in Schedule 2 Housing Act 1985.[4] These have been extended by Anti-social Behaviour Act 2003[5] (see K5.4.46). It is also possible for most landlords[6] of secure tenancies to apply to a county court for a demotion order, which can be made if the tenant or a person residing in or visiting the dwelling house has, broadly, either engaged in anti-social behaviour or used the premises for unlawful purposes.[7] If the tenant remains in occupation, a new demoted tenancy will begin on the same date. The terms of a demoted tenancy are set out in the legislation and this may be terminated by the court, provided a prescribed procedure is followed by the landlord.[8]

5.2.7. A secure tenancy ends on the death of the tenant, although provisions for succession to the tenancy after the death of the tenant are contained in Housing Act 1985, ss.87–90.

5.2.8. A secure tenancy cannot generally be assigned, but there are limited exceptions to this rule, e.g. an assignment with the landlord's consent by way of exchange. A secure tenant cannot, without the landlord's consent, sub-let or part with the possession of part only of the house. In this case, the landlord must not unreasonably withhold his consent to the alienation and, if consent is unreasonably withheld, it is treated as having been given. If, however, the tenant sub-lets the whole, the tenancy ceases to be a secure tenancy.[9]

Introductory tenancies

5.2.9. A local housing authority or housing action trust is empowered by Housing Act 1996, s.124 to operate an introductory tenancy regime.

5.2.10. Where the scheme has been adopted by the local authority, the majority of all new periodic tenancies or licences, which would otherwise be secure, granted by the authority will, instead, be 'introductory tenancies'. A new tenancy is one granted to a person (or persons) who immediately before its grant was not a secure tenant of the same or different premises and was not an assured tenant of a registered social landlord of the same or another dwelling house.

5.2.11. An introductory tenancy remains such for a trial period of one year subject to certain earlier termination provisions contained in Housing Act 1996, s.125. If no proceedings are brought within the one-year period, the tenancy will automatically become a secure tenancy.[10]

5.2.12. The landlord can bring an introductory tenancy to an end, after serving notice on the tenant, by obtaining a court order under Housing Act 1996, s.127. The tenant has the right to ask for a review of the landlord's decision to end the tenancy within 14 days of notice of possession proceedings being served on him.[11] Subject to this, the possession ground is mandatory.

5.2.13. Provisions for succession to an introductory tenancy are contained in Housing Act 1996, ss.131–133. An introductory tenancy is not capable of assignment except under certain provisions of the Act which are similar to those for secure tenancies (e.g. assignments under the Matrimonial Causes Act 1973, s.24).

Unfair Terms in Consumer Contracts Regulations 1994

5.2.14. These regulations (despite their title) have been held to apply to certain tenancy agreements entered into by local authorities with individual tenants.[12] The regulations apply to contracts between a supplier or seller and a consumer.

5.2.15. If a term in such a contract is 'unfair' it will be void, although the rest of the contract will subsist. A term will be unfair, broadly, if it causes a significant imbalance in the parties' rights and obligations arising from the contract to the detriment of the consumer. The regulations also require contracts to be drafted in plain English.[13]

1. Housing Act 1985, ss.87–90.
2. *Ibid.*, s.91.
3. *Ibid.*, s.79.
4. On the making of an order for possession, if the tenant is permitted to remain in occupation he becomes a 'tolerated trespasser'; see *Burrows* v. *London Borough of Brent* [1996] 1 WLR 1448; *Newham LBC* v. *Hawkins* [2005] EWCA 451. Note that it is very unlikely that Art.8 of the European Convention on Human Rights will provide a defence to applications for possession orders, where the validity of the law itself is not challenged; see *Leeds City Council* v. *Price*; *Kay* v. *London Borough of Lambeth* [2006] UKHL 10.
5. Section 16(1) inserts a new section 85A into Housing Act 1985. The effect of this is that where the court is considering making a possession order under one of the nuisance grounds for possession, the court must consider the effect of the anti-social behaviour on others.
6. The landlord must be either a local housing authority, a housing action trust or a registered social landlord; see Housing Act 1985, s.82A(1).
7. Housing Act 1985, s.82A(1), (2) and Housing Act 1996, ss.153A or 153B.
8. Anti-social Behaviour Act 2003, s.14(5) and Sched.1 amend Housing Act 1996 and Housing Act 1985 and set out the legal position regarding demoted tenancies.
9. Housing Act 1985, s.95.
10. As to the calculation of this period see *Salford County Council* v. *Garner* [2004] EWCA Civ 364. This period may be extended by a further six months where there are concerns about the conduct of an introductory tenant, including in cases of anti-social behaviour.
11. Should the review lead to the local authority deciding not to proceed, but subsequently there are further breaches, the local authority does not have to serve a second notice: *R (on the application of Stone)* v. *Cardiff City Council* [2003] All ER (D) 379 (Jan), unless the first notice was withdrawn: *R (on the application of Forbes)* v. *Lambeth LBC* [2003] All ER (D) 236 (Feb).
12. *Khatun* v. *Newham London Borough Council* [2004] 3 WLR 417.
13. See further B11.10. The Office of Fair Trading has published various guides to what it believes are unfair terms in various types of contracts, including potentially unfair terms in assured and assured shorthold tenancy agreements. See **www.oft.gov.uk/business/legal/utcc/guidance.htm**.

5.3. Rent Act tenancies

5.3.1. A tenancy under which a dwelling house (including part of a house) was let as a separate dwelling before 15 January 1989 was (and will until termination of the tenancy continue to be) a protected tenancy under Rent Act 1977, unless that tenancy was excluded from the Act (see K5.3.3). Since 14 January 1989 no new

Rent Act tenancies, subject to some minor exceptions, have come into being because on that date Rent Act 1977 was superseded by Housing Act 1988 (see K5.4).

5.3.2. On the termination of a protected tenancy (e.g. by forfeiture or notice to quit), the person who at that time was the protected tenant will become a statutory tenant if and so long as he occupies the house as his residence. Although the terms of the protected tenancy apply to the statutory tenancy so far as they are consistent with the nature of the statutory tenancy, there are a number of differences between the two types of tenancy, such differences deriving from the fact that a protected tenancy is a proprietary right, while a statutory tenancy is merely a personal right of residence. A protected tenancy will vest in a tenant's trustee in bankruptcy and can be disclaimed by him (so ending the tenant's right of residence as against his landlord) but a statutory tenancy does not vest in a trustee in bankruptcy.

Exclusions from protection

5.3.3. These include:[1]

    (a)   tenancies of high value dwellings;

    (b)   tenancies at low rents;

    (c)   holiday lettings;

    (d)   lettings by resident landlords;

    (e)   lettings by local authorities and housing associations;

    (f)   business tenancies within Part II Landlord and Tenant Act 1954; and

    (g)   licences.

Rent control[2]

5.3.4. Unless a rent is registered with the rent officer, a landlord who granted a protected tenancy can initially lawfully recover whatever amount of rent has been agreed between the parties. Such rent can be increased provided that the conditions in the Act relating to the making of a rent agreement are followed.[3] It is open to the tenant to apply to the rent officer for the determination and registration of a 'fair rent', in which case the fair rent will be the maximum legally recoverable amount. An application for revision of the fair rent cannot normally be made within two years of the previous registration.

Recovery of possession

5.3.5. A court order is necessary in order to recover possession from a tenant who has security of tenure under Rent Act 1977.[4] Such an order can only be made where the court[5] is satisfied either that suitable alternative accommodation is available to the tenant or that one or more of the grounds for possession set out in

Schedule 15 Rent Act 1977 has been established. Some of the grounds under Schedule 15 are mandatory and others are discretionary, i.e. the landlord must not only prove the existence of the ground, he must also satisfy the court that it is reasonable in all the circumstances to make an order for possession.

Protected shorthold tenancies

5.3.6. These were introduced by Housing Act 1980, enabling landlords to grant fixed-term tenancies for a minimum period of one year and a maximum period of five years giving the landlord the guaranteed right to possession at the end of the term provided certain conditions were satisfied. The fair rent provisions of Rent Act 1977 apply to such tenancies. No new protected shorthold tenancies have come into existence since 14 January 1989 when these provisions were superseded by Housing Act 1988.

Death of tenant

5.3.7. On the death of the tenant a statutory tenancy may pass to a spouse or civil partner who occupies the property as his or her residence.[6] Otherwise it may pass to a family member who has lived there for at least two years prior to the death,[7] but in this case it is converted to an assured tenancy (see K5.4).

Assignment and sub-letting

5.3.8. Whether or not a protected tenant can assign or sub-let the house or part of it depends on the terms of the tenancy. A statutory tenant cannot assign the lease unless he follows a prescribed statutory procedure.[8] The requirements of this procedure include the need for the assignment to be in writing and for the landlord to be a party to it. The tenant may sub-let in theory, unless the terms of the protected tenancy prohibited this. However, he cannot sub-let in whole without the risk of terminating the statutory tenancy due to cessation of occupation.[9] In a similar way a sub-letting of part risks terminating the statutory tenancy of that part.[10]

Premiums

5.3.9. There is a general prohibition on the taking of a premium as a condition of or in connection with the grant, renewal, continuance, assignment or underletting of a protected tenancy. In relation to long tenancies, these rules are substantially modified by Rent Act 1977, s.127, as amended by Housing Act 1980, s.78 and Housing Act 1988, s.115.

1. See Rent Act 1977, ss.4–16.
2. Parts III and IV Rent Act 1977, as amended by Housing Act 1980.
3. Rent Act 1977, ss.51 and 54.
4. *Ibid.*, s.98.
5. The county court has jurisdiction over all matters under Rent Act 1977.
6. This includes a person living with the tenant as if they were either a spouse or a civil partner; Rent Act 1977, Sched.1, para.2(2) (as amended).

7. Rent Act 1977, Sched.1, para.3. Where more than one person is qualified to succeed they may agree who the successor is to be *(ibid.).* See *Clore* v. *MacNicol* [2004] EWCA Civ 1055.
8. Rent Act 1977, s.3(5), Sched.1, paras.13 and 14.
9. *Smith's Charity Trustees* v. *Wilson* [1983] QB 316. Also note *Moreland Properties (UK) Ltd* v. *Dhokia and Others* [2003] All ER (D) 348 (Oct).
10. *Baron* v. *Phillips* (1979) 28 P&CR 9.

5.4. Assured tenancies

Introduction

5.4.1. The definition of an assured tenancy is set out in Housing Act 1988, s.1. A tenancy under which a dwelling house is let as a separate dwelling will be an assured tenancy, if and so long as all of the following requirements are met:

(a) the tenant or each of joint tenants is an individual; and

(b) the tenant or at least one of joint tenants occupies the dwelling house as his only or principal home; and

(c) the tenancy is not specifically excluded by other provisions of the Act.

5.4.2. From the commencement date of these provisions of the Housing Act 1996 (28 February 1997), most new lettings will be assured shorthold tenancies (see K5.5) and not assured tenancies. However, a shorthold is merely a type of assured tenancy and so must comply with the definition of an assured tenancy as well as the extra requirements which make it a shorthold.

5.4.3. Tenancies which do not satisfy the definition of an assured tenancy (and so cannot be shortholds either) will not be subject to the provisions of Housing Act 1988. Instead, ordinary common law rules as to termination, etc., will apply. They will, however, be subject to Protection From Eviction Act 1977 (see K12.5.1).

Constituent elements of an assured tenancy

Tenancy

5.4.4. There must be a 'tenancy'; licences to occupy dwelling houses are excluded from protection. This distinction is dealt with in K12.

Dwelling house

5.4.5. Housing Act 1988, s.45(1) merely provides that a dwelling house may be a house or part of a house. Therefore it will be a question of fact whether premises can be considered to be a house or not, but any building designed or adapted for living in is capable of forming a dwelling house for these purposes.

Let as a separate dwelling

5.4.6. The premises, as well as being a dwelling house, must be let as a dwelling. So the purpose of the letting is relevant; thus if a building that would otherwise qualify as a dwelling house is let for business purposes, the tenant cannot claim that it is let on an assured tenancy merely because he decides to move in and live there.

5.4.7. There must be a letting as a dwelling. It has been established that this only permits of a singular construction (notwithstanding Interpretation Act 1978).[1] So if the let property comprises two or more residential units, each intended for separate occupation (e.g. the letting of the whole of a house converted into several flats), that tenancy cannot be an assured tenancy. The sub-letting of each of the individual flats could, however, be within the definition.

5.4.8. There must be a separate dwelling. This is intended to exclude lettings of accommodation which lacks some essential feature of a dwelling. The House of Lords has held that the presence of cooking facilities is not an essential feature of a dwelling.[2] However, Housing Act 1988, s.3 makes special provision for the situation where the tenant shares some of the essential features of a dwelling with others. Such a letting is deemed to be an assured tenancy (assuming that all the other conditions are met) even though the absence of essential facilities in the demised property would normally prevent the tenancy from fulfilling the statutory requirements. The tenant must, however, have the exclusive occupation of at least one room (otherwise it cannot be a tenancy), and if the other accommodation is shared with the landlord, the tenancy will be excluded from the definition of an assured tenancy for different reasons. Arrangements where each tenant is given exclusive occupation of his own bed-sitting room, but shares bathroom and kitchen with other tenants, will be deemed to be capable of being assured tenancies.

'If and so long as'

5.4.9. The status of the tenancy is not to be determined once and for all at the commencement of the letting. Whether a tenancy is an assured tenancy can fluctuate according to changed circumstances. For example, one requirement of the definition is that the tenant must be occupying the house as his only or principal home. This may have been the case at the start of the tenancy, and so the tenancy would be assured, but if subsequently the tenant ceases to reside at the premises, the tenancy will no longer be assured. The tenant will thus lose his security of tenure.

The tenant must be an individual

5.4.10. Lettings to companies are excluded from the definition, even though an individual (e.g. a director or employee of the company) may be in occupation of the house. Any sub-letting by a company tenant could, however, qualify as an assured tenancy.

The tenant must occupy as his 'only or principal home'

5.4.11. It is possible for a person to have more than one 'home'. Therefore it is a question of fact as to which is the tenant's principal home. Only a tenancy of the principal home can be an assured tenancy. Although the provision requires 'occupation', this does not mean continuous occupation. A mere temporary absence will not deprive a tenancy of its status as an assured tenancy.

Tenancies excluded from the definition

Tenancies entered into before the commencement of Housing Act 1988

5.4.12. Only lettings entered into on or after 15 January 1989 can be assured tenancies. Any pre-existing tenancy will, if it has any protection at all, still remain subject to the provisions of Rent Act 1977. There are, however, exceptions to this rule in some cases where a succession has taken place in relation to a pre-existing tenancy.

High value properties

5.4.13. For tenancies granted before 1 April 1990, a tenancy of a dwelling house with a rateable value in excess of £750 (£1,500 in Greater London) cannot be an assured tenancy. If the tenancy was granted on or after 1 April 1990, it cannot be an assured tenancy if the rent payable is £25,000 or more per annum.

Tenancies at a low rent

5.4.14. Lettings made before 1 April 1990 cannot be assured if the annual rent is less than two-thirds of the rateable value of the property. For tenancies granted on or after 1 April 1990, the exclusion applies to tenancies in which the rent does not exceed £250 per annum (£1,000 per annum in Greater London).

Business tenancies

5.4.15. A tenancy to which Part II Landlord and Tenant Act 1954 applies cannot be an assured tenancy.[3]

Licensed premises

5.4.16. Premises licensed for the sale of alcohol for consumption on the premises, e.g. a public house, are excluded from the definition of an assured tenancy even if the tenant is residing on the premises.

Tenancies of agricultural land

5.4.17. A tenancy under which agricultural land exceeding two acres is let together with the house cannot be an assured tenancy (Housing Act 1988, Sched.1, para.6).

Tenancies of agricultural holdings

5.4.18.   A tenancy under which a dwelling house is comprised in an agricultural holding (within the meaning of Agricultural Holdings Act 1986) or in a farm business tenancy under Agricultural Tenancies Act 1995, and is occupied by the person responsible for the control of the farming of the holding cannot be an assured tenancy (Housing Act 1988, Sched.1, para.7).

Lettings to students

5.4.19.   Lettings to students by specified educational bodies are outside the definition of an assured tenancy. This exception does not apply to lettings to students by landlords other than the specified universities and colleges.

Holiday lettings

5.4.20.   A letting to confer on the tenant the right to occupy the dwelling house for a holiday cannot be an assured tenancy.

Lettings by resident landlords

5.4.21.   A letting by a resident landlord is excluded from the definition of an assured tenancy provided that certain conditions are satisfied.

Crown, local authority and housing association lettings

5.4.22.   Crown, local authority and certain housing association lettings cannot be assured tenancies.

Rents under assured tenancies

The initial rent

5.4.23.   There is no restriction on the amount of rent which can initially be charged on the grant of an assured tenancy. However, if the landlord subsequently wishes to increase the rent, he may not be able to do so unless he follows the correct procedure.

Statutory increases for assured periodic tenancies

5.4.24.   Statutory increases for assured periodic tenancies are governed by Housing Act 1988, ss.13 and 14 which lay down a complicated procedure requiring the landlord to serve a notice (in the prescribed form) on the tenant. This can then be referred to the Rent Assessment Committee for arbitration if agreement as to the new rent cannot be reached between the parties.[4] The Rent Assessment Committee must determine the rent at which the premises might reasonably be let in the open market. If there is an express term in the tenancy agreement permitting rent increases, this avoids the need to rely on the statutory procedure.

Rent increases for fixed-term assured tenancies

5.4.25. There are no statutory provisions allowing an increase for fixed-term assured tenancies. In the absence of any express provision in the tenancy agreement, the landlord will be unable to increase the rent during the fixed term without the agreement of the tenant.[5] Once the fixed term has ended and the tenant continues in possession as a statutory periodic tenant, then the above provisions of Housing Act 1988, ss.13 and 14 will apply to enable the landlord to increase the rent, even if there is no express provision on the lease.

Prohibition of assignment without consent

5.4.26. If there is no such express provision against assignment in the lease, Housing Act 1988, s.15 may assist the landlord. The section only applies to periodic assured tenancies (including statutory periodic tenancies). It does not apply to fixed-term assured tenancies (including shortholds).

5.4.27. The term implied into a periodic assured tenancy is that the tenant must not without the consent of the landlord:

    (a)   assign the tenancy (in whole or in part); or

    (b)   sub-let or part with possession of all or part of the property.

Landlord and Tenant Act 1927, s.19 does not apply to this implied term and therefore the covenant is not subject to an implied proviso that consent will not be unreasonably withheld.

5.4.28. In the case of a periodic tenancy which is not a statutory periodic tenancy, these prohibitions do not apply if a premium was paid on the grant or renewal of the tenancy. 'Premium' is defined to include any pecuniary consideration in addition to rent and also includes returnable deposits exceeding one-sixth of the annual rent.[6]

Succession on death

5.4.29. On the death of one of joint tenants, the tenancy will vest in the survivor(s). On the death of a sole tenant the tenancy will pass under his will or intestacy. Housing Act 1988, however, contains specific provisions in section 17 dealing with the succession to an assured periodic tenancy on the death of a sole tenant which will override these normal rules.

5.4.30. On the death of a sole periodic tenant the tenancy will vest in the tenant's spouse or civil partner, notwithstanding the terms of the deceased's will, provided that immediately before the deceased tenant's death the spouse or civil partner was occupying the dwelling house as his or her only or principal home. 'Spouse or civil partner' is defined to include a person who was living with the tenant as his or her spouse or civil partner.[7] This provision will not apply if the deceased tenant was himself a 'successor', as defined, i.e. the tenancy became vested in him:

(a) by virtue of this section; or

(b) under the will or intestacy of a former tenant; or

(c) he is the sole survivor of joint tenants; or

(d) he succeeded to the tenancy under the provisions of Rent Act 1977.

5.4.31. Only one statutory succession is possible. If there is no statutory succession, e.g. because there is no qualifying 'spouse or civil partner', or there has already been a succession, or the tenancy is for a fixed term, the tenancy will then pass under the will or intestacy of the deceased in the normal way. However, on the death of a periodic assured tenant in such a situation, the landlord would be able to make use of one of the mandatory grounds in order to obtain possession.

Sub-lettings

5.4.32. Housing Act 1988, s.18 provides that in the case of a house lawfully sub-let on an assured tenancy, on the ending of the head lease the sub-tenancy will still continue. The assured sub-tenant will then become the direct tenant of the head landlord with full security of tenure. However, this only applies to lawful sublettings. In the case of an unlawful sub-letting, the sub-tenant will have no security once the head lease has been determined and the head landlord will thus have an absolute right to possession.

Lettings by resident landlords

Qualifying conditions

5.4.33. Under Part 1 Housing Act 1988, certain tenancies granted by resident landlords are excluded from statutory protection. In order to fall within this category the following conditions must apply to the tenancy:

(a) the dwelling house which is let forms only part of a building; and

(b) the building is not a purpose-built block of flats; and

(c) the tenancy was granted by an individual (i.e. not a limited company) who at the time of the grant occupied another part of the same building as his only or principal home; and

(d) at all times since the tenancy was granted, the interest of the landlord has continued to belong to an individual who continued so to reside.

Continuity of residence

5.4.34. It is not sufficient for the landlord merely to have been in residence at the commencement of the tenancy; he must be in occupation throughout the tenancy. If he ceases to reside then the exception will cease to apply and the letting will once again be capable of being an assured tenancy with full security of tenure.

5.4.35. But if the tenancy was entered into on or after the commencement date of Housing Act 1996, the letting will become an assured shorthold tenancy. However, if the interest of the landlord is vested in two or more individuals, only one of those persons need be in residence at any one time.

Periods of absence disregarded

5.4.36. Certain periods of absence will be disregarded when deciding whether the landlord's occupation has been continuous:

    (a) a period of 28 days beginning with the date on which the interest of the landlord becomes vested at law and in equity in a new owner. If, during this 28 days, the new owner notifies the tenant in writing of his intention to occupy another part of the building as his only or principal home, the disregard will be extended up to six months from the change of ownership; and

    (b) any period not exceeding two years during which the interest of the landlord becomes and remains vested in:

        (i) trustees as such; or

        (ii) the Probate Judge under Administration of Estates Act 1925, s.9; or

        (iii) personal representatives of a deceased person acting in that capacity.

5.4.37. Throughout any period during which absence is disregarded (except in a situation where the house is vested in personal representatives), no order for possession can be made except one which might have been made if the tenancy were an assured tenancy. In other words, during these periods of deemed residence the letting becomes a quasi-assured tenancy and possession can only be obtained against the tenant if assured tenancy grounds can be established. However, as an exception to that rule, personal representatives of a deceased resident landlord will be able to recover possession without proving assured tenancy grounds, provided that the contractual term can be terminated.

Purpose-built blocks of flats

5.4.38. The resident landlord exception does not apply if the building is a purpose-built block of flats and the landlord occupies one flat in the block and lets one (or more) of the others. Such lettings are therefore capable of being assured tenancies.

5.4.39. A building is a purpose-built block of flats if *as constructed* it contained, and still contains, two or more flats.

5.4.40. 'Flat' means a dwelling house which forms only part of a building and is separated horizontally from another dwelling house which forms part of the same building.

5.4.41. Housing Act 1988 makes it clear, however, that if the landlord occupies one flat in a purpose-built block and lets part of that flat, then the resident landlord exception can still apply.

Exceptions

5.4.42. A tenancy will be excluded from the resident landlord provisions if two conditions are both fulfilled:

(a) it was granted to a person who immediately before the grant was an assured tenant of the same house or of another house in the same building; and

(b) the landlord under the new tenancy and under the former tenancy is the same person. If either of the tenancies was granted by two or more persons, it is sufficient for this condition that the same person is the landlord or one of the landlords under each tenancy.

5.4.43. This is an anti-avoidance provision designed to ensure that a landlord does not deprive existing tenants of their protection as assured tenants by taking up possession himself and then granting a new tenancy to those existing tenants.

Security of tenure

Restriction on termination by landlord

5.4.44. An assured tenancy cannot be brought to an end by the landlord otherwise than by obtaining a court order for possession. Thus, in the case of a periodic assured tenancy, a notice to quit is of no effect. On the ending of a fixed-term assured tenancy (including a shorthold) otherwise than by an order of the court or by surrender, the tenant is entitled to remain in possession as a statutory periodic tenant. This statutory periodic tenancy will be on the same terms as the previous fixed-term tenancy.[8]

Obtaining a court order

5.4.45. The landlord will only obtain a court order for possession if he follows the correct procedure and can establish one or more of the grounds for possession set out in Schedule 2 Housing Act 1988. Although some of these grounds are mandatory grounds, i.e. the court must order possession if the ground is established, many of them are discretionary grounds. With these, the court, on proof of the ground, may order possession only if it considers it reasonable to do so. The landlord must serve a notice on the tenant (a 'section 8 notice') in the prescribed form specifying the ground(s) upon which the landlord intends to rely and must give two weeks' notice of the landlord's intention to commence possession proceedings. (Sometimes two months' notice has to be given.) However, if ground 14[9] is specified (whether or not with any other ground), then the proceedings can be commenced as soon as the section 8 notice has been served. The proceedings must then be commenced not earlier than the date specified and not later than 12 months from the date of service of the notice. It is possible for the court to dispense with the requirement for a section 8 notice (unless ground 8 is being relied upon), but only if it considers it just and equitable to do so.[10]

5.4.46. Ground 14 has been extended by Anti-social Behaviour Act 2003. When considering whether it is reasonable to make an order for possession the court is required to consider the effect of anti-social behaviour by the tenant on other people.[11]

5.4.47. A registered social landlord may apply to a county court for a demotion order,[12] which can be made if the tenant or a person residing in or visiting the dwelling house has, broadly, either engaged in anti-social behaviour or used the premises for unlawful purposes.[13] A demotion order will terminate the assured tenancy and, if the tenant remains in occupation of the dwelling house, a demoted tenancy is created.[14] A demoted assured shorthold tenancy can be ended at any time during the demotion period.[15]

5.4.48. In the case of a fixed-term assured tenancy, the landlord cannot normally obtain possession until after the end of the contractual fixed term (assuming that a ground for possession can then be established). However, as an exception to this, certain of the grounds for possession will be available to the landlord during the fixed term provided that the tenancy agreement contains a provision for it to be brought to an end on the ground in question. This provision can take any form at all, including a proviso for re-entry or a forfeiture clause. The grounds on which the landlord can obtain possession in this way during the fixed term are grounds 2, 8 and 10 to 15.

1. *Horford Investments Ltd* v. *Lambert* [1976] Ch 39.
2. *Uratemp Venture Ltd* v. *Collins* [2001] 3 WLR 806.
3. See *Brewer* v. *Andrews* [1997] EGCS 19.
4. A tenant's application to challenge the landlord's notice of increase does not take effect until the Rent Assessment Committee has actually received it: *R (on the application of Lester)* v. *London Rent Assessment Committee* [2003] EWCA Civ 319.
5. Unless the increase is to a very high level designed to be a device to avoid security of tenure: *Bankway Properties* v. *Dunsford* [2001] 1 WLR 1369.
6. Housing Act 1988, s.15(4).
7. *Ibid.*, s.17 (as amended).
8. The type of periodic tenancy will depend on the period of the tenancy for which rent was 'last' payable: Housing Act 1988, s.5(3)(d); see *Church Commissioners for England* v. *Meya* [2006] EWCA Civ 821.
9. Ground 14 relates to the tenant being a nuisance or annoyance or there being illegal or immoral use.
10. As in *Knowsley Housing Trust* v. *Revell* [2003] All ER (D) 137 where possession proceedings were commenced against a tenant who was a secure tenant but who became an assured tenant during the proceedings on the transfer of the landlord's interest to a registered social landlord.
11. Housing Act 1988, s.9A added by Anti-social Behaviour Act 2003, s.16(2). See *London Quadrant Housing Trust* v. *Root* [2005] EWCA Civ 43.
12. Housing Act 1988, s.6A(1), (2).
13. *Ibid.*, s.6A and Housing Act 1996, s.153A or s.153B.
14. Housing Act 1988, s.6A added by Anti-social Behaviour Act 2003, s.15.
15. Housing Act 1988, s.20B added by Anti-social Behaviour Act 2003, s.15.

5.5.   Shorthold tenancies

Introduction

5.5.1.   It is important to distinguish between the two types of shortholds. 'Old' shortholds were entered into before the commencement of section 96 Housing Act 1996 (28 February 1997). 'New' shortholds are those entered into on or after this date unless made pursuant to a contract made before that date.

5.5.2.   In the case of an old shorthold, before the grant of the tenancy the landlord was required to serve a warning notice on the tenant in a prescribed form. An old shorthold was required to be for a fixed term for a minimum duration of at least six months. Providing these criteria were satisfied the landlord had an absolute right to recover possession, provided that he complied with the correct procedure.

5.5.3.   From the commencement of section 96 Housing Act 1996, however, all new lettings (with certain exceptions) are deemed to be shortholds. The old conditions need no longer be complied with; the letting need not be for a fixed term, there is no need for a warning notice, etc. However, the landlord still has the same absolute right to possession as in an old shorthold.

5.5.4.   Note, that 'old' shortholds continue as before and if one fails due to the conditions not having been complied with, e.g. no warning notice was served, the tenancy will still become a fully protected assured tenancy. This means that the conditions for the grant of an old shorthold are still of considerable practical importance even after the introduction of new shortholds.

5.5.5.   The only disadvantage of a shorthold (whether new or old) from a landlord's point of view is the right given to the tenant to refer the rent initially payable to the Rent Assessment Committee. However, this Committee can only reduce the rent if it is 'significantly higher' than the rents under other comparable assured tenancies.

An assured tenancy

5.5.6.   An assured shorthold tenancy must comply with all the requirements of an assured tenancy as it is merely a type of assured tenancy (see K5.4). It is therefore necessary for there to be a letting of a dwelling house to an individual who occupies the house as his only or principal home. In the same way none of the specific exclusions from the definition of an assured tenancy must apply. For example, high rental tenancies and lettings by resident landlords cannot be assured shortholds as they fall outside the definition of an assured tenancy.

5.5.7.   A shorthold cannot be granted to an existing tenant under an ordinary assured tenancy (or to one of joint tenants) if it is granted by the landlord under that existing tenancy. This is so even if the lettings are not of the same premises.

Old shortholds

5.5.8. The qualifying conditions for shortholds entered into before the commencement date of Housing Act 1996 were set out in section 20 Housing Act 1988. It provides that an assured shorthold tenancy is an assured tenancy which:

(a) is a fixed-term tenancy granted for a term of not less than six months; and

(b) contains no power for the landlord to terminate it during the first six months; and

(c) was preceded by the giving to the tenant of the prescribed shorthold notice.[1]

Minimum six-month fixed term

5.5.9. The initial grant of an old shorthold could not be for a periodic term. It was required to be for a fixed term and for a minimum duration of six months. A letting for 'six months and then from month to month' is not a letting for a term certain and so cannot be an old shorthold, even though it is for longer than the minimum six months. There is, however, no maximum length. Many shortholds were granted for the minimum six-month period and, in such a case, care must be taken to ensure that the tenant is given a right to occupy for the minimum period. The six-month period will run from the date on which the tenancy is entered into; it cannot be backdated. So a tenancy granted 'from and including 1 January 1994 until 30 June 1994' but not actually executed until 15 January 1994 would not give the tenant the requisite six months' occupation from the date of grant and so could not be a shorthold.

5.5.10. Problems are likely to arise where a tenancy agreement was drawn up containing a fixed termination date and there was then a delay in the agreement being executed so that by the time that it was executed there then remained less than six months until the prescribed termination date. Such a letting would amount to an ordinary assured tenancy giving the tenant full security of tenure.

No power for landlord to terminate during first six months

5.5.11. Even if a minimum period of six months was granted, any power, however expressed, which would or might allow the landlord to terminate the tenancy within the first six months of the tenancy will prevent the tenancy from amounting to a shorthold. Break clauses exercisable outside that period are not prohibited, but care must be taken with such clauses to ensure that they were only exercisable outside the initial six months; otherwise an ordinary assured tenancy will have been created giving the tenant full security of tenure. Note, however, that a forfeiture clause or a clause allowing termination on assured tenancy grounds 2, 8 and 10 to 15 will not breach this requirement even though it is exercisable during the first six months of the term. A term allowing the tenant to terminate during the first six months could have been validly included. Such a provision, however, will not be implied. A tenant entering into an old shorthold will, therefore, normally be contractually bound to pay the rent and perform the other obligations under the tenancy agreement for the full term entered into.

Preceded by the giving of the prescribed shorthold notice

5.5.12.   As the tenant under an assured shorthold has no security of tenure, he had to be served with a notice prior to the grant of the tenancy warning him of this fact. This notice must have been in the prescribed form.

5.5.13.   The notice must have been served before the tenancy agreement was entered into and not at the same time. Thus, it could not be included in the tenancy agreement itself. It was best to ensure that there was an adequate interval between the service of the notice and the signing of the tenancy agreement to give the tenant the opportunity of digesting the contents of the notice. However, it appears from *Bedding* v. *McCarthy* [1994] 41 EG 151 that an interval of a few hours between the service of the section 20 notice and the tenancy agreement being entered into would be sufficient. In the case of joint tenants, all of the prospective tenants should have been served. Common law rules as to service will apply (and not section 196 of Law of Property Act 1925) and so it is necessary to show that the notice actually came into the tenant's hands. It was advisable for a landlord to serve the notice in duplicate and to require all the prospective tenants to endorse one copy with an acknowledgement of receipt, and the date and time of receipt, and return this to the landlord before the tenancy agreement was entered into. Correct service of the current version of the shorthold notice was vital. The court has no power to dispense with these notice requirements even though it might be just and equitable to do so.

New shortholds

Definition

5.5.14.   Shortholds entered into on or after 28 February 1997 (otherwise than pursuant to a contract made before that date) are governed by Housing Act 1988, s.19A (as inserted by Housing Act 1996). This provides that any assured tenancy entered into on or after the commencement date will be a shorthold unless it falls within one of the specified exceptions.

5.5.15.   There is no need for a shorthold to be for a fixed term and therefore it can be periodic. There is no longer any need for a shorthold to be preceded by a prescribed form of notice. There is also no prohibition on the landlord being able to terminate during the first six months. However, no order for possession using the shorthold ground can be made earlier than six months from the start of the tenancy, whether the tenancy is for a fixed term or is a periodic tenancy. This does not stop possession being obtained during the first six months using an assured tenancy ground because a new shorthold, like an old shorthold, is merely a type of assured tenancy.

Exceptions

5.5.16. All new assured tenancies granted on or after 28 February 1997 (other than those granted pursuant to a contract made before that date) will be shortholds subject to certain exceptions,[2] which will take effect as ordinary assured tenancies. These include:

  (a) tenancies excluded by notice. The landlord may serve a notice on the tenant either before or after the grant of the tenancy stating that the letting is not to be a shorthold;

  (b) tenancies containing a provision stating that the tenancy is not to be a shorthold;

  (c) lettings to existing assured tenants.

5.5.17. Where the landlord (or one of the landlords) under the existing assured tenancy grants a letting to an existing assured (i.e. not shorthold) tenant (whether alone or with others) the new letting will not be a shorthold. However, it is possible for the tenant to serve notice on the landlord before the new tenancy is entered into that he wants it to be a shorthold. This notice must be in a prescribed form.

Duty of landlord to provide a statement of the terms of a shorthold tenancy

5.5.18. Under Housing Act 1988, s.20A (as inserted by Housing Act 1996), the landlord is placed under a duty in certain circumstances to provide a tenant with written details of the following terms provided that they are not already evidenced in writing:

  (a) the commencement date of the tenancy;

  (b) the rent payable and the dates on which it is payable;

  (c) any terms providing for rent review;

  (d) the length of a fixed term tenancy.

The tenant must make a request to the landlord in writing for this information.

5.5.19. It is a criminal offence to fail to provide the information within 28 days, unless the landlord has reasonable excuse.

5.5.20. The right only exists where the terms are not already evidenced in writing. The provision will only apply to tenancies granted orally, or those granted in writing which makes no reference to one or more of the specified matters.

5.5.21. A statement provided by the landlord is not to be regarded as conclusive evidence as to what was agreed between the parties. The statement is the landlord's version of what was agreed; it is still open to the tenant to allege that any particular term was not agreed to by him.

5.5.22. These provisions only apply to new shortholds, i.e. those to which Housing Act 1988, s.19A applies. They do not apply to old shortholds. However, on the ending of an old shorthold any new letting between the same parties will be a new shorthold, and these provisions will then apply.

Rent control

5.5.23. The general principles are the same for both new or old shorthold, but the details differ.

5.5.24. Any existing registration of a 'fair rent' under the provisions of Rent Act 1977 can be ignored, as can any rental figure previously determined by the Rent Assessment Committee under these provisions. Therefore on the granting of the tenancy, the landlord can charge such rent for the premises as the tenant will agree to pay. There is no statutory restriction on the amount of rent chargeable. However, an assured shorthold tenant can apply to the local Rent Assessment Committee for the determination of the rent which, in the Committee's opinion, the landlord might reasonably be expected to obtain under the shorthold tenancy.

5.5.25. If the tenant has an old shorthold, he can apply at any time within the fixed term of the tenancy.

5.5.26. If the tenant has a new shorthold, whether for a fixed term or a periodic letting, he cannot apply if more than six months have elapsed since the beginning of the tenancy. If the tenancy is a 'replacement tenancy', i.e. a second or subsequent shorthold between the same parties and of the same property, the application cannot be made if more than six months have elapsed from the commencement of the first shorthold between the parties.

The effect of a determination by the Rent Assessment Committee

5.5.27. If a rent is determined by the Committee, the effect again differs between old and new shortholds.

5.5.28. The rent assessed will become the maximum rent chargeable for the property throughout the remainder of the fixed term in the case of old shortholds and fixed-term new shortholds, despite anything to the contrary in the tenancy agreement. No matter how long the unexpired term of the tenancy there is no provision for this figure to be increased during the fixed term.

5.5.29. Where a new shorthold is a periodic tenancy, the rent remains fixed throughout the tenancy. Once 12 months have expired, the landlord will be able to make an application under Housing Act 1988, ss.13 and 14 to increase the rent.[3]

5.5.30. With both old and new shortholds, once the rent has been determined by the Committee no further application for the fixing of a different figure can be made by either landlord or tenant. However, the rent determined by the Committee only has relevance to the particular tenancy in question. It will not limit the amount of rent chargeable under any subsequent letting, even if this is between the same parties. Further, in the absence of a further grant, on the ending of a fixed-term shorthold (whether old or new), a statutory periodic tenancy will arise and the provisions of Housing Act 1988, ss.13 and 14 will again apply to allow the landlord to increase the rent.

When is an application to the Rent Assessment Committee not possible?

5.5.31. The restrictions on tenants with new shortholds applying have been dealt with in K5.5.26.

5.5.32. As far as old shorthold tenants are concerned, it is not possible for the tenant to refer the rent to the Rent Assessment Committee once the original term of the shorthold has expired. This is so even if a new letting is entered into between the same parties and irrespective of whether an application was made during the original shorthold.

5.5.33. With both old and new shortholds, only one application to the Committee can be made. Once the rent has been determined by the Committee, it cannot be resubmitted for a further determination, even if the original determination was many years before and open market rents have fallen in the meantime.

What happens when a shorthold expires?

5.5.34. The tenant is allowed to remain in possession as a statutory periodic tenant when a fixed-term tenancy expires. However, the tenant will have no security of tenure. Under Housing Act 1988, s.21(1) the court must still make an order for possession if the landlord follows the correct procedure. This involves the service on the tenant of not less than two months' notice stating that the landlord requires possession.

What happens if a new tenancy is granted?

5.5.35. Although there are differences between new and old shortholds, the basic principle remains the same; if the parties are the same, any new tenancy of the same (or substantially the same) premises will be deemed to be a shorthold unless the landlord serves notice on the tenant that the new letting is not to be a shorthold.

5.5.36. In the case of an old shorthold, the effect of this deeming provision is that the new tenancy will be a shorthold even though it does not comply with the normal requirements for an old shorthold. So no shorthold notice need have been served, the letting need not be for a fixed term, i.e. a periodic shorthold is permissible, and any fixed term need not be for a minimum period of six months. However, the new tenancy must still comply with the normal requirements for an assured tenancy, e.g. the tenant must still be occupying the house as his only or principal home.

5.5.37.   A further feature of a deemed shorthold following an old shorthold is that there is no right to refer the rent to the Rent Assessment Committee. This is the case whether or not an application was made to the Committee during the initial shorthold term. In the case of a tenancy following a new shorthold, the second tenancy will be a 'replacement tenancy' and an application to the Rent Assessment Committee cannot be made more than six months from the commencement of the original tenancy. So in the unlikely event of a new shorthold granted for three months, followed by a replacement tenancy granted for (say) six months, an application to the Rent Assessment Committee could be made during the first three months of that replacement tenancy.

5.5.38.   In any event, if a rent was determined by the Rent Assessment Committee during the initial term this will not limit the amount of rent chargeable by the landlord under the new tenancy agreement.

How does the landlord obtain possession?

5.5.39.   The landlord must apply to the court and obtain an order for possession unless the tenant leaves voluntarily. The court must order possession provided that the landlord follows the correct procedure. This involves the landlord serving a notice on the tenant (the 'section 21 notice') giving the tenant at least two months' notice that he requires possession.

5.5.40.   Possession cannot be obtained using this shorthold procedure during the continuance of a fixed term; possession is only available after its expiry (although the procedure can be set in motion during the fixed term so that possession can be obtained as soon as it has ended). Note also that in the case of a new shorthold possession cannot be obtained within six months of the commencement of the term using the shorthold procedure. This is so whether the tenancy is a fixed-term tenancy or is periodic.

Grounds for possession

5.5.41.   A shorthold is a type of assured tenancy and so, during the term, the mandatory and discretionary grounds which apply to ordinary assured tenancies can also apply. However, in the case of a fixed-term letting, as with other assured tenancies, only certain grounds can be used during the fixed term and only if the tenancy agreement so provides (see K5.4.48).

5.5.42.   In the case of a shorthold which is a periodic tenancy, the ordinary assured tenancy grounds will be available to a landlord without the need for any such provision in the tenancy agreement.

5.5.43.   In the case of a fixed-term shorthold, however, it is always sensible to insert a provision allowing the landlord to terminate the tenancy on the specified grounds. In the case of an old shorthold, this is permissible despite the usual rule that there must be no power for the landlord to terminate within the first six months of the tenancy. This rule does not apply to termination because of a breach of the terms of the tenancy, e.g. non-payment of rent. Similarly, in the case of new shortholds, although possession cannot be obtained using the shorthold procedure within six months of the commencement, possession can be obtained during that period using the ordinary assured grounds provided that they are satisfied.

5.5.44. When the landlord is seeking to obtain possession on one of the ordinary assured grounds, then the procedure relevant to an ordinary assured tenancy should be followed, and not the shorthold procedure. In particular, this will mean that a section 8 notice will have to be served on the tenant before proceedings can be commenced, and not a section 21 notice.

Deposits

5.5.45. A landlord may not take a deposit in respect of an assured shorthold tenancy unless he complies with a 'tenancy deposit scheme'. Until this is done, the landlord will be unable to regain possession of the property using the 'section 21 notice' procedure. There are two types of schemes: a single custodial scheme (where deposits are paid into and held in a separate account); and insurance-based schemes (where any failure to repay the deposit to the tenant is covered by insurance).[4]

1. In some circumstances the notice may be given to the tenant's agent, see *Yenula Properties Ltd* v. *Naida* [2002] EWCA Civ 719. The absence of details of the landlord may not be fatal if the details of the agent are given: *Osborn and Co. Ltd* v. *Dior* [2003] All ER (D) 185.
2. See Schedule 2A Housing Act 1988 as inserted by Housing Act 1996.
3. Rules now enable landlords to specify a date for annual increases; see Regulatory Reform (Assured Periodic Tenancies) (Rent Increases) Order 2003 (SI 2003/259) and Assured Tenancies and Agricultural Occupancies (Forms) (Amendment) (England) Regulations 2003 (SI 2003/260).
4. Housing Act 2004, ss.212–215; Housing (Tenancy Deposit Schemes) Order 2007 (SI 2007/796) and Housing (Tenancy Deposits) (Prescribed Information) Order 2007 (SI 2007/797); Housing (Tenancy Deposits) (Specified Interest Rate) Order 2007 (SI 2007/798). For further information see **www.thedisputeservice.co.uk**.

5.6. Long tenancies at low rents

5.6.1. Rent Act 1977 (as with previous Rent Acts) gave no protection to the tenant where the rent payable under the tenancy was less than two-thirds of the rateable value of the dwelling on the appropriate day (as defined in the Act), with the result that most tenants of dwellings under long tenancies at ground rents had no security of tenure when their contractual tenancies expired. Part I Landlord and Tenant Act 1954 extended to many such tenants the protection of Rent Act 1977 (and its predecessors) when their tenancies expired. Part I applied to a tenancy granted for over 21 years at a rent of less than two-thirds of the rateable value of the property where 'the circumstances (as respects the property comprised in the tenancy, the use of the property, and all other relevant matters) are such that on the coming to an end of the tenancy … the tenant would, if the tenancy had not been one at a low rent, be entitled by virtue of the Rent Acts to retain possession of the whole or part of the property comprised in the tenancy'.

Security of tenure

5.6.2. The current security of tenure provisions for tenants under long leases are contained in Schedule 10 Local Government and Housing Act 1989. This provides that tenants of dwellings who were granted certain long tenancies at a low rent have a right to stay in possession after the end of their leases as assured tenants.

5.6.3. Local Government and Housing Act 1989 applies where the long tenancy was granted after 1 April 1990, and to those granted before this date but which expired after 15 January 1999. Tenants holding under long leases had previously been entitled to security of tenure under Part I Landlord and Tenant Act 1954 (see K5.6.1).

5.6.4. The detailed eligibility criteria are similar to those referred to in K5.6.1. Thus a tenancy is 'long' if, broadly, it is granted for a term of more than 21 years and is at a 'low rent' if the rent is so low that, in effect, it would prevent it being an assured tenancy.[1]

5.6.5. The drawback of these provisions is that the tenant will have to pay a full market rent at the end of the lease. For these reasons other rights of long leaseholders, e.g. to acquire a new long lease or to enfranchise, are often more attractive for such tenants. These are considered in more detail at K9.

1. Housing Act 1988, Sched.1, para.3 and Local Government and Housing Act 1989, Sched.10, para.3.

5.7. Agricultural employees

5.7.1. Security of tenure for farm workers living in accommodation provided by their employers and who are outside the other security of tenure regimes, e.g. because they pay a low rent, is governed by either Rent (Agriculture) Act 1976 or Housing Act 1988, depending on the date of the grant of the tenancy.

5.7.2. To gain the protection of the 1976 Act, the employee must generally have spent two years whole time in agriculture; he then becomes a protected occupier of the house. If as a result of a notice to quit or otherwise he ceases to be a protected occupier, he becomes a statutory tenant of the house under terms laid down by the Act.

5.7.3. The court cannot make an order for possession of a house subject to a protected occupancy or statutory tenancy under the 1976 Act except on the grounds set out in the Act. Special provisions apply to the rehousing of agricultural employees. The provisions for rent control in the Act apply only to statutory tenancies.

5.7.4. Farm workers who enjoyed the protection of Rent Act 1977 (e.g. because they were tenants paying an economic rent) were equated to those protected by the 1976 Act by Rent Act 1977, s.99.

5.7.5. Farm workers with tenancies or licences granted before 15 January 1989 retain their protection under the 1976 Act. Tenancies or licences granted on or after that date are governed by Housing Act 1988. However, those tenants who were previously protected under the 1976 Act will, broadly, continue to enjoy the same regime of protection.[1] This Act introduced the assured agricultural occupancy, which qualifies for protection if it is an assured tenancy or would be such except for the fact that the rent (outside London) is less than £250 per annum or the fact that the house forms part of an agricultural holding and is occupied by the person responsible for the control of the farming. A licence to occupy which confers exclusive occupation and which fulfils the requisite conditions will also qualify. An assured shorthold is excluded from the definition, thus enabling the owner to create a tenancy giving a mandatory right to possession.

5.7.6. In the case of tenancies or licences governed by Housing Act 1988, the main change is in regard to rent. The provisions of the Act in regard to the increase of rents under assured tenancies apply to assured agricultural occupancies, so that on a reference of a notice of increase of rent to a Rent Assessment Committee an open market rent can be fixed.

5.7.7. An occupier of agricultural land may apply to the housing authority concerned (i.e. the local housing authority as defined by Housing Act 1985) to rehouse a tenant on the ground that the land occupier requires the dwelling house to provide accommodation for an agricultural employee, the land occupier being unable to provide the present tenant with suitable alternative accommodation. The housing authority in reaching its decision on whether to rehouse the tenant must have regard to the advice tendered to them by the Agricultural Dwelling House Advisory Committee.[2]

1. Housing Act 1988, s.34(4).
2. See Rent (Agriculture) Act 1976, ss.27–29.

K6. Long-term residential tenancies

6.1. Grant of lease

6.1.1. The grant or assignment of a long lease of a house or flat is similar to the grant or assignment of a lease of other premises. The matters to which particular attention needs to be paid when dealing with this type of lease are merely highlighted here.

6.1.2. The lease of a flat is frequently a complex document which should be specifically drafted to suit the individual requirements of the site. Except in the most straightforward cases, copying a precedent directly from a book or the reuse of a lease drafted for another development will not suffice. The client's attention should be directed to the need for a site inspection before drafting of the lease is commenced so that the following points can be correctly dealt with in the lease:

(a) what is the structure of the building composed of? Repairing covenants must be drafted appropriately so that a covenant, e.g. 'to repair main walls and timbers' will be inappropriate where the building is of concrete construction;

(b) access: the lease must deal with easements of access, e.g. is there a right of way over the drive from the public highway to the entrance of the flats, how does each tenant get from the door of the building to the door of his own flat, is there to be a lift, does each tenant require access to the dustbin area, etc.?

(c) where do the mains services run? Which tenants need easements for pipes, cables, etc., to pass through another flat or common parts on the way to or from their own flat?

(d) amenities: who is to have a garage or parking space, are these to be a part of the demise (i.e. a specific allocated space) or is there to be just a licence to use a garage/parking space (with no guarantee that a space will actually be available), use of gardens, is there communal central heating, is there an entry-phone system, is there a communal television or satellite aerial, are individual aerials to be permitted, is there a caretaker's flat?

(e) service charges: what services are to be included in the charge, will all tenants have the benefit of all the services supplied, should the service charge be split equally between all the tenants or should some pay a greater proportion than others or should different proportions apply to different services?

(f) check site and floor plans against the physical extent of the building both in relation to the whole building and individual flats, are they accurate, which tenants need which plans, and do they comply with Land Registry requirements?[1]

Checklist of items to be sent to buyer's solicitor

6.1.3. The following list is subject to the need to provide a home information pack, which will apply in certain cases (e.g. currently the grant of certain long term residential leases of homes with three or more bedrooms); see A26. Further, not all of the following will be relevant in every transaction:

(a) draft contract in duplicate;

(b) draft lease in duplicate;

(c) copy head lease;

(d) other evidence of superior and reversionary titles;

(e) draft agreement between landlord and management company for transfer of reversion to management company;

(f) copy memorandum and articles of management company;

(g) copy local authority search and enquiries with replies;

(h) copy planning permissions and building regulation consents;

(i) copy indemnity insurance policy covering defects in title, restrictive covenants, etc;

(j) copy approved estate layout plan as deposited at the Land Registry;

(k) copy replies to enquiries before contract;

(l) copy insurance policy and schedules;

(m) copy guarantees, e.g. for repairs to structure;

(n) documentation relating to insurance against structural defects;

(o) estimated service charge calculation;

(p) audited accounts of the management company.

1. See B21 and Land Registry Practice Guide 40.

6.2.   Enforcement of covenants in flats

6.2.1.   The landlord for the time being can almost always enforce covenants in the lease against the tenant for the time being of each flat, because he enjoys privity of estate and in many cases also privity of contract with each tenant. Prima facie there is neither privity of contract nor of estate between the tenants and, although they will each be bound by identical covenants in their leases, without some device in the leases they cannot sue each other directly for breach of the tenants' covenants in their respective leases. It is advisable that the lease contains some method of allowing enforceability of covenants between the tenants, particularly in relation to restrictive covenants concerning use and noise and, in appropriate cases, positive covenants concerning tenant's repairs.

6.2.2.   This can be achieved by taking a covenant in each lease that the landlord will if so requested by a tenant take action to enforce a breach of covenant committed by another tenant in the same block. Such a covenant usually requires the requesting tenant to provide a complete indemnity to the landlord against the costs of the action and provides an effective although cumbersome method of mutual enforceability of covenants. There are other schemes of varying complexity which attempt to ensure that one tenant can sue another. However, in practice none are now considered wholly satisfactory. Where the tenants are responsible for maintenance, insurance and repair of common parts, the Lenders' Handbook requires the key clauses in a lease to be enforceable by the landlord (or the management company) at the request of the tenant (see K6.6). However, these requirements do not apply where the landlord or a management company is responsible for those repairs.

6.3.   Management schemes

6.3.1.   Any management scheme must ensure that the rights and obligations of both the landlord and the tenants under the lease are always enforceable. The landlord's objectives in setting up such a scheme are to provide for the maintenance and repair of the block. The type of scheme employed will depend on the landlord's particular requirements in relation to the flats concerned. It should be borne in mind that tenants have statutory rights in relation to management under Commonhold and Leasehold Reform Act 2002, which are considered in K6.11.

6.3.2.   If the landlord is to retain the reversion of the block he may choose to carry out the landlord's functions personally or through a managing agent. From the landlord's point of view this arrangement has the disadvantage of the work involved and from the tenants' point of view it has the disadvantage that the tenants have only limited control over the way in which their block is managed. As a result tenants may have recourse to their rights under Commonhold and Leasehold Reform Act 2002, which are considered in K6.11.

6.3.3.   Another type of arrangement is for the tenants to covenant with each other by separate deed of covenant to perform the obligations of repairing, etc., the common parts. Such a scheme is not binding on future assignees unless the lease obliges them to enter into similar deeds of covenant as a condition of their assignment.[1] Alternatively, limited use may be made of a letting scheme which can be created to enable tenants to sue each other for breach of restrictive covenants provided the conditions for a development scheme are fulfilled.[2]

6.3.4. Alternatively, the landlord may vest the reversion (with its obligations) in trustees (who would be representatives of the tenants) on trust for the tenants as a whole. This type of scheme is only suitable for the management of small blocks and saves the expense in that situation of setting up and running a management company.

6.3.5. Most larger blocks have schemes which entail the use of a management company. The landlord may transfer his reversion to the management company which will then assume the responsibility for performance of the landlord's covenants in the lease. Until transfer the landlord will be responsible for the management company's duties and should ideally expressly covenant to this effect in the lease. A management company can either be limited by shares or guarantee and is commonly purchased as a ready-made company. The management company may be a party to the lease and enter into direct covenants with the tenant for the performance of the maintenance obligations. Each tenant must be required to become a member of the company and to transfer his share in the company to an assignee on sale of the lease. Such a scheme allows the tenants to have absolute control over the management of their block, but carries with it the responsibility of performance of the maintenance obligations and duties in relation to the company itself under the Companies Acts. The landlord may reserve the right to take over the management company's responsibilities in the event of default by the company.

6.3.6. If maintenance is to be carried out by a maintenance trustee company, the tenant's solicitor should be satisfied as to the integrity of the trustee company. If this has been set up by a third party, the tenant will have no control over the company, and thus needs to be assured that the trustees (and any potential successors to the original trustees) are sound and responsible.

6.3.7. In relation to leases granted on or after 11 May 2000, direct enforcement of the benefit of covenants between tenants may be possible without the device of a management scheme through the operation of Contracts (Rights of Third Parties) Act 1999. However, the Act does not enable the burden of covenants to be passed to successors and is therefore unable to provide a satisfactory solution.

1. Such an obligation may be enforced by means of an appropriate restriction on the land register.
2. See *Williams* v. *Kiley (t/a CK Supermarkets Ltd)* [2003] 06 EG 147.

6.4. Other matters to be considered

6.4.1. The landlord may wish to reserve the right to prepare the engrossment of the lease himself. Such right must be expressly reserved in the contract.

6.4.2.   Where the landlord is to retain the reversion (and the liability for performance of the landlord's covenants in the lease) consideration may be given by the landlord to the appointment of reliable managing agents to carry out the landlord's duties under the lease.

6.4.3.   On completion apportionments of the rent and service charge will have to be made. Apportionments of service charge will at this stage have to be made on an estimated basis and settled at the end of the first accounting period.

6.4.4.   Where a management company is to perform the landlord's covenants under the lease, the company must be set up and share certificates (except where limited by guarantee) and the company books prepared in readiness for completion.

6.4.5.   The term dates of all the leases in a block should commence on the same date (irrespective of the dates of completion of the various leases) otherwise it becomes very difficult to know precisely when performance of some covenants is due, e.g. to decorate.

Apportionment of rent

6.4.6.   The Law Society's Conveyancing and Land Law Committee has prepared a formula for the calculation of the apportionment of rent. See Appendix IV.2.

6.5.   Maisonettes

6.5.1.   Where a maisonette is being purchased, particular care needs to be exercised to ensure that the lease is quite specific as to the ownership and rights over the various parts of the property (especially common parts). Each tenant may be the freeholder of the other tenant's property; they will thus be jointly responsible for the maintenance and upkeep of the structure and common parts. A maintenance trustee company may be set up to deal with maintenance and repair. The Lenders' Handbook sets out specific requirements where there is a freehold flat or where one of the flat owners in the block owns the freehold in whole or in part. In many situations these arrangements may be acceptable to the lender where a building has been converted into not more than four flats (see Lenders' Handbook, para.5.5.3 at Appendix VI.2).

6.6.   Lenders' requirements

6.6.1.   The lenders' requirements may be found in a combination of documents depending on the nature of the transaction and whether the lender is a member of the Council of Mortgage Lenders. These documents are: the Lenders' Handbook England and Wales, the mortgage offer, and instructions to the solicitor.

6.6.2. Part 1 of the Lenders' Handbook is a set of universal instructions to which all CML lenders adhere. Individual lenders issue their own supplemental general instructions to their solicitors by use of Part 2 instructions. The current edition of Part 1 can be found at Appendix VI.2. As the provisions of Part 2 change more regularly than Part 1, these are only available online at **www.cml.org.uk**. Solicitors are also recommended to check the website for the latest version of both Parts. A lender is usually concerned with the following matters:

(a) to ensure that the lease contains proper provision for the enforceability of covenants between tenants (Lenders' Handbook para.5.10.6);

(b) to ensure that the property is leasehold and that the lease contains adequate repairing covenants relating to the flat itself, the exterior structure and the common parts of the building (Lenders' Handbook para.5.10.4);

(c) that the lease contains adequate provision for the insurance of the whole building (Lenders' Handbook paras.5.10.4. and 5.10.5);

(d) that the length of the term of the lease (or unexpired residue in the case of an assignment) is sufficient to permit a resale of the premises on the open market. A common period required by lenders is 55 years unexpired from completion and 30 years unexpired at the end of the mortgage term. Notification may be required if the minimum period is less than 70 years. A term which will have less than 20 years unexpired after the end of the mortgage term may be considered inadequate in the context of normal residential conveyancing;

(e) that the lease contains no provision for forfeiture on the insolvency of the tenant (Lenders' Handbook para.5.10.2);

(f) that the lease contains no restrictions on alienation which may hinder a sale on the open market (Lenders' Handbook para.5.10.3);

(g) that the lease is or will be registered at the Land Registry with an absolute leasehold title;

(h) where the tenant is to become a member of a management company, the mortgagee sometimes requires that a blank form of share transfer (signed by the mortgagor) and the tenant's share certificate is deposited with the lender to enable the lender to transfer that share to a buyer should he need to exercise his power of sale. A copy of the management company's memorandum and articles may also have to be deposited with the lender (Lenders' Handbook para.5.11.2);

(i) that notices have been given to the landlord of the mortgage (Lenders' Handbook para.5.10.11);

(j) that the lease reserves an appropriate ground rent and that receipts are provided for rent and service charge payments (Lenders' Handbook paras.5.10.7 and 5.10.10);

(k) if the property being purchased is held under a sub-lease (so that the landlord's own interest is leasehold), it is desirable that the aggregate ground rents payable by the flats in the block should exceed the amount of rent payable by the landlord to the freeholder. If this is not the case the landlord will have little incentive to pay his own rent, and thus the sub-tenants of the flats would be put at risk from forfeiture of the head-lease. For this reason it is desirable that in any situation where sub-letting is permitted the tenant should be required to enter a covenant with his landlord not to sub-let the whole at a rent lower than that payable under his own lease.

6.7.   The Protocol and home information packs

6.7.1.   The Protocol makes no direct reference to the grant of a lease.

6.7.2.   On the sale of an existing lease paragraph 2.14 of the Protocol requires the seller's solicitor to ask his client to produce, if possible:

(a)   a receipt or evidence from the landlord of the last payment of rent;

(b)   the maintenance charge accounts for the last three years, where appropriate, and evidence of payment;

(c)   details of the buildings insurance policy.

6.7.3.   If any of these are lacking and are necessary to the transaction the solicitor should obtain them from the landlord. Investigation should also be made as to the necessity for a licence to assign, and whether any charge is payable to the management company on the change of ownership. The documents and information obtained in relation to the above matters should be given or communicated to the buyer's solicitor when the pre-contract documentation is sent to him (paragraph 4.4 of the Protocol).

6.7.4.   In certain cases (e.g. currently in relation to certain long term residential leases of homes with three or more bedrooms) the grant of a long term residential lease will require the provision of a home information pack (see A26) when marketing it for sale. The term 'sale' includes a disposal, or agreement to dispose, by way of the grant of a long lease. 'Long lease' means:

(a)   a lease granted for a term certain exceeding 21 years, whether or not it is (or may become) terminable before the end of the term by notice given by the tenant or by re-entry or forfeiture; or

(b)   a lease for a term fixed by law under a grant with a covenant or obligation for perpetual renewal, other than a lease by sub-demise from one which is not a long lease.[1]

6.7.5.   The general details in relation to home information packs are set out in A26. Where the sale involves the grant of a new lease to an appropriate property the Home Information Pack (No.2) Regulations 2007, which require certain documents to be supplied (reg.8) and which specify that only certain documents are authorised for inclusion (reg.9) are modified by regulation 10(3). These are effectively consequential modifications to give effect to the principle that the grant of a new lease as described in K6.7.4 is to be treated as a sale for the purpose of the Home Information Pack Regulations 2007.

6.7.6. The home information pack for the sale of a new leasehold must include documents consisting of or containing information which relates to the following:

    (a)   the terms of the lease that is expected to be granted in order to create the property interest; and

    (b)   estimates of the payment or financial contribution likely to be required of the tenant within 12 months of completion of the sale of the interest towards:

        (i)   service charges;

        (ii)   ground rent;

        (iii)   insurance against damage for the building in which the property is situated (if not to be included in contributions towards service charges); and

        (iv)   insurance for any person in respect of personal injury or death caused by or within the building in which the property is situated (if not to be included in contributions towards service charges).[2]

1.   Housing Act 2004, s.177.
2.   Home Information Pack (No.2) Regulations 2007 (SI 2007/1667), Sched.5, para.4.

6.8.   Service charges

6.8.1. Service charge accounts must be examined carefully and the buyer advised as to his potential liability under the lease.

6.8.2. Statutory provisions relating to service charges are now contained in Landlord and Tenant Act 1985, ss.18–30, as amended. The amendments made to these provisions by Commonhold and Leasehold Reform Act 2002 have significantly enhanced tenants' rights in this respect. For the purposes of these provisions, a service charge is an amount payable by a tenant as part of or in addition to rent:

    (a)   which is payable, directly or indirectly, for services, repairs, maintenance, improvements or insurance or the landlord's costs of management; and

    (b)   the whole or part of which varies or may vary according to the relevant costs.

6.8.3. Provisions in relation to payments to a reserve fund (which allow 'savings' against future expenditure) are contained in Landlord and Tenant Act 1987, ss.42–42B (as amended). These require such payments to be paid into a designated bank account and for the money to be held on trust for the tenants.[1]

6.8.4. The statutory provisions apply to a lease of any dwelling (including houses as well as flats) except that they do not apply to lettings by certain bodies such as local authorities unless the tenancy is a long tenancy as defined in Landlord and Tenant Act 1985, s.26(2).

6.8.5. The statutes impose certain limitations and obligations on landlords which are not set out in detail here but which relate to the following:

(a) limitations on the amount recoverable. The landlord can only recover the costs of providing services to the extent that they are 'reasonable' and only if they are of a 'reasonable standard';[2]

(b) consultations with tenants (failure to do so or to obtain a dispensation from a Leasehold Valuation Tribunal will limit a tenant's service charge contributions);[3]

(c) estimates for work to be done and the giving of notices;

(d) time limits on making demands for service charges;[4]

(e) the tenant's right to receive a statement of account for costs incurred, an accountants certificate and to inspect the landlord's accounts;[5]

(f) the landlord's duty to pass on requests for a summary of the relevant costs to a superior landlord;[6]

(g) the right, in certain circumstances, to withhold a service charge;[7]

(h) service charge contributions to be held in trust;[8]

(i) from 1 October 2007 a demand for service charges must be accompanied by a summary of the rights and obligations of the tenant.[9]

Tenants and landlords also have rights to apply to a leasehold valuation tribunal for an order varying the lease where an administration charge as specified in the lease is unreasonable.[10]

6.8.6. A buyer of the reversion on a lease reserving a service charge and a buyer of a lease subject to such a charge should be aware of the following matters:

(a) the statutory provisions outlined above;

(b) that the obligation to pay a service charge can arise only from an express provision in the lease and the extent of the obligation depends on the wording of such provision. Whether or not the landlord can recover from non-defaulting tenants his legal costs incurred in recovering rent and service charge contributions depends on the wording of the tenant's covenant, and the same is true in respect of a landlord's interest payments on money borrowed to finance the provision of works and services;

(c)   ideally the landlord's obligation should match with the service charge provisions. If the obligations are not matched the landlord may find that he is obliged to provide more services than he can charge for or conversely that the tenants cannot force the landlord to provide them, e.g. carry out repairs because the landlord's covenant does not extend to this matter;

(d)   the manner in which the total service charge is to be apportioned between the various tenants;

(e)   whether or not the landlord can require payment of a charge in advance of expenditure;

(f)   the statutory provisions apply to contribution covenants concerned with improvements as well as repairs;[11]

(g)   where premises are let wholly or mainly as a dwelling for less than seven years, a service charge provision cannot cast on the tenant the cost of matters falling within the landlord's repairing obligation under Landlord and Tenant Act 1985, ss.11–16;

(h)   a provision in the lease enabling the landlord to make an interim service charge is desirable. In the absence of such a provision a landlord may be disinclined to carry out expensive repairs or to provide services since he would have to bear the cost of these matters himself before seeking recovery of the sums from the tenants at a later date.

6.8.7.   The amount of service charge payable will be of particular concern to the buyer of a lease. The Protocol requires production of the maintenance accounts for the last three years which should give some indication of the amounts involved, although sums expended will frequently vary from year to year.[12] A substantial sum recently spent on repairs and redecoration of the exterior of a building may indicate that a similar item should not recur for some time. In each case enquiry should be made of the particular circumstances relating to the building.

6.8.8.   The apportionment of a service charge on a sale may create a problem as the amounts payable may not be determined at the time of completion. Standard Condition 6.3.5 provides that when any sums to be apportioned are not known or easily ascertainable a provisional apportionment is to be made on completion according to the best estimate available. As soon after completion as the amount is known, a final apportionment is to be made and notified to the other party and any resulting balance paid no more than 10 working days later, interest calculated at the contract rate being chargeable for late payment. The Standard Commercial Property Conditions also provide for the seller to provide the buyer with documentation that the buyer will need in order to claim from the tenants the service costs which the seller incurred.

6.8.9.   Sections 45–51 Housing Act 1985 (as amended by Landlord and Tenant Act 1987, s.41) contain restrictions on service charges where a house has been disposed of by a public sector authority other than under a long lease.

6.8.10.   A landlord may not forfeit the lease of a dwelling house for failure to pay a service charge unless the amount of the service charge is agreed or admitted by the tenant or has been determined by a court or tribunal.[13]

1. These provisions are not yet wholly in force. See *St. Mary's Mansions Ltd* v. *Limegate Investment Co. Ltd*, *The Times*, 13 November 2002, CA.
2. Landlord and Tenant Act 1985, ss.19 and 27A.
3. Landlord and Tenant Act 1985, ss.20 and 20ZA; Service Charges (Consultation Requirements) (England) Regulations 2003 (SI 2003/1987); and Service Charges (Consultation Requirements) (Amendment) (No. 2) (England) Regulations 2004 (SI 2004/2939) as amended by Commonhold and Leasehold Reform Act 2002, s.170; and see Commonhold and Leasehold Reform Act 2002 (Commencement Order No.5 and Saving and Transitional Provisions) (England) Order 2004 (SI 2004/3056). Also Service Charges (Consultation Requirements) (Wales) Regulations 2004 (SI 2004/684/W.72) as amended by Service Charges (Consultation Requirements) (Amendment) (Wales) Regulations 2005 (SI 2005/1357). Broadly, where the landlord proposes to incur expenditure on works of repair, maintenance or improvement that would cost an individual service charge payer more than £250. Also there is a requirement to consult before entering into contracts for the provision of long term contracts for services lasting more than 12 months. This will be necessary where the cost per tenant is £100 per year.
4. Where the relevant costs were incurred more than 18 months before a demand for payment of the service charge is served on the tenant, then they are recoverable unless the tenant was notfied about them before this date: see Landlord and Tenant Act 1985, s.20B.
5. Landlord and Tenant Act 1985, ss.21–22. Amendments to section 21, which are not yet in force, require the landlord to provide accounts to tenants automatically.
6. *Ibid.*, s.23 (amendments not yet in force).
7. *Ibid.*, s.21A (not yet in force).
8. When the amendments to Landlord and Tenant Act 1987, ss.42–42B come into force these monies will have to be paid into a separate designated bank account.
9. See Commonhold and Leasehold Reform Act 2002 (Commencement No.6) (England) Order 2007 (SI 2007/1256); Service Charges (Summary of Rights and Obligations, and Transitional Provision) (England) Regulations 2007 (SI 2007/1257); Administration Charges (Summary of Rights and Obligations) (England) Regulations 2007 (SI 2007/1257).
10. Commonhold and Leasehold Reform Act 2002, s.158 and Sched.11.
11. *Ibid.*, s.150 and Sched.9.
12. As to the requirements of the home information pack, see A26.
13. Housing Act 1996, s.81.

6.9.   Limitations on landlords' remedies

6.9.1.   Landlords of long leases as defined in the Commmonhold and Leasehold Reform Act 2002 – generally over 21 years[1]– are required to send the lease-holder a notice requiring payment of ground rent before the sum can be due.[2] Regulations set out the form and content of notices requiring the payment of ground rent.[3]

6.9.2.   There are restrictions on the landlord's rights to forfeit long leases. Thus a landlord under a long lease of a dwelling may not forfeit for failure by a tenant to pay an amount consisting of rent, service charges or administration charges (or a combination of them) unless the unpaid amount exceeds a figure prescribed by regulations or where the amount has been owing for more than a prescribed period.[4] The current prescribed amount is £350 and the prescribed period is three years.[5]

6.9.3.   A landlord of a long lease may not serve a forfeiture notice in respect of a breach of covenant unless the tenant admits the breach, or a court or tribunal has determined that the breach has occurred.[6]

6.9.4. There are restrictions on the landlord's rights to enforce certain insurance covenants in long leases. Where a long lease of a house requires the tenant to insure it with an insurer nominated or approved by the landlord, a tenant may avoid this if he gives a statutory notice of cover to the landlord and meets certain conditions relating to the insurer, the interests and risks covered and the amount of the cover.[7] Regulations prescribe the information that is to be included in a notice of cover.[8]

1. Commonhold and Leasehold Reform Act 2002, ss.76 and 77.
2. *Ibid.*, s.166.
3. Landlord and Tenant (Notice of Rent) (England) Regulations 2004 (SI 2004/3096); Landlord and Tenant (Notices of Rent) (Wales) Regulations 2005 (SI 2005/1355).
4. Commonhold and Leasehold Reform Act 2002, s.167.
5. The Rights of Re-entry and Forfeiture (Prescribed Sum and Period) (England) Regulations 2004 (SI 2004/3086); Rights of Re-entry and Forfeiture (Prescribed Sum and Period) (Wales) Regulations 2005 (SI 2005/1352).
6. Commonhold and Leasehold Reform Act 2002, ss.168 and 169; and see Commonhold and Leasehold Reform Act 2002 (Commencement Order No. 5 and Saving and Transitional Provisions) (England) Order 2004 (SI 2004/3056); Commonhold and Leasehold Reform Act 2002 (Commencement No.3 and Saving and Transitional Provisions) (Wales) Order 2005 (SI 2005/1353).
7. Commonhold and Leasehold Reform Act 2002, s.164.
8. Leasehold Houses (Notice of Insurance Cover) (England) Regulations 2004 (SI 2004/3097), as amended by Leasehold Houses (Notice of Insurance Cover) (England) (Amendment) Regulations 2005 (SI 2005/177); Leasehold Houses (Notice of Insurance Cover) (Wales) Regulations 2005 (SI 2005/1354).

6.10. Appointment of manager

6.10.1. Where a landlord has not complied with his obligations under the terms of the lease, a tenant of a flat may, after serving a preliminary notice on his landlord (and the landlord's lender where relevant), apply to the Leasehold Valuation Tribunal under Part II Landlord and Tenant Act 1987 (as amended by Housing Act 1996) for the appointment of a manager to carry out the landlord's management functions. These provisions apply to premises where the building or part of a building consists of two or more flats except *inter alia* where the landlord is an exempt or resident landlord.

6.11. The right to manage

6.11.1. Commonhold and Leasehold Reform Act 2002 creates a right to manage in favour of the tenants of flats. This right enables tenants to take over the management of their building without having to prove fault on the part of the landlord and without having to pay compensation. The right is exercised through a specific company which must be created in order to manage property, known as an RTM company.

RTM companies[1]

6.11.2. These are defined by the Act in some detail but are essentially private companies limited by guarantee and all qualifying tenants are entitled to be members. Regulations prescribe the content and form of the memorandum and articles of association of these companies.[2]

6.11.3. There are a number of qualifying conditions for exercising the right.

Qualifying conditions

The premises

6.11.4. The premises must, broadly, consist of a self contained building or part, contain two or more flats held by qualifying tenants and the total number of flats held by such tenants must be not less than two-thirds of the total number of flats in the premises.[3]

Excluded premises[4]

6.11.5. In outline this right to manage does not apply to premises if the internal floor area of non-residential parts exceeds 25% of the whole internal floor area.[5] It also does not apply if there is a resident landlord and the premises do not contain more than four units. It does not apply if the local authority is the immediate landlord of any of the qualifying tenants.

Qualifying tenants[6]

6.11.6. A qualifying tenant must be a tenant of a flat under a long lease. However there are some exceptions so that, for example, the right does not apply to tenants of business premises. A long lease is again defined by the Act[7] and is essentially one granted for a term of more than 21 years.

Claiming the right to manage[8]

6.11.7. The right to manage is claimed by the RTM company giving notice inviting participation to those qualifying tenants who are not members of the RTM company. A 'claim notice' is then served on a specified number of interested parties including the landlord. On the date on which the claim notice is served the membership of the RTM company must include a number of qualifying tenants which is not less than half the number of flats.[9] A counter notice may then be served and if the claim is contested an application may be made to a leasehold valuation tribunal for a determination.

1. Commonhold and Leasehold Reform Act 2002, ss.73 and 74.
2. RTM Companies (Memorandum and Articles of Association) (England) Regulations 2003 (SI 2003/2120); RTM Companies (Memorandum and Articles of Association) (Wales) Regulations 2004 (SI 2004/675).
3. Commonhold and Leasehold Reform Act 2002., s.72(1).
4. *Ibid.*, Sched.6.
5. In calculating the percentage of the property used for residential purposes, any part used as such even though part of premises let under a separate commercial lease is included. See *Gaingold Ltd* v. *WHRA RTM Company Ltd* [2006] 1 EGLR 81, Lands Tribunal (LRX/19/2005) available from **www.landstribunal.gov.uk**.

6. Commonhold and Leasehold Reform Act 2002, s.75.
7. *Ibid.*, s.76.
8. *Ibid.*, ss.78 to 87.
9. *Ibid.*, s.79(5).

6.12. Leasehold Advisory Service

6.12.1. LEASE, the Leasehold Advisory Service, provides free legal advice to professional advisers, tenants, landlords, and others on the law affecting residential leasehold and commonhold properties.

6.12.2. LEASE is funded by the government and does not act for any party. The areas on which it provides free advice and assistance include service charges and the right to manage. It will also advise on commonhold, applications to the Leasehold Valuation Tribunal, rights to information, extending the lease and buying the freehold.

6.12.3. LEASE provides a mediation service as an alternative to proceedings before the Leasehold Valuation Tribunal or the court.[1]

1. For further details visit **www.lease-advice.org**.

K7. Business premises

7.1.   Business tenancies

7.1.1.   Part II Landlord and Tenant Act 1954 (as amended) established a comprehensive code of security of tenure for business tenants. The following paragraphs provide only an introduction to this very complex subject.

7.1.2.   The latest amendment to the 1954 Act was made by Regulatory Reform (Business Tenancies) (England and Wales) Order 2003[1] which came into effect on 1 June 2004.

7.1.3.   Broadly, the intent was that the new regime was to be fully effective from that date. Thus, for example, even though a lease was entered into before the start of the new regime, the lease renewal process will follow the new regime. There are, however, some important transitional provisions. These are principally as follows:

(a)   where there is a requirement in a lease to obtain the landlord's consent to a sub-letting with a proviso that the tenant first obtains an order from the court permitting 'contracting out' of the security of tenure provisions of the 1954 Act. In these cases references to the procedures for contracting out are to be construed as references to use of the new procedures, as from 1 June 2004;

(b)   where there is a pre-existing contract to grant a lease on condition that the parties first obtained a court order excluding security of tenure. In these cases the old procedure for joint applications to the court is preserved.

7.1.4.   The Act applies to a tenancy where the property comprised in the tenancy is or includes premises which are occupied by the tenant and are so occupied for the purposes of a business carried on by him or for those and other purposes.[2] It therefore will not apply to a licence (the distinction between licences and tenancies is dealt with in K12).

7.1.5.   The word 'business' is widely defined to include a trade, profession or employment and includes any activity carried on by a body of persons, whether corporate or unincorporate.[3]

1. SI 2003/3096.
2. The degree of occupation by the tenant may be minimal. There is no need for a tenant to be physically present provided the tenant is using the premises for a purpose incidental to the ordinary course of a business; see *Pointon York Group plc* v. *Poulton* [2006] EWCA Civ 1001.
3. Landlord and Tenant Act 1954, s.23(2). See *Hawkesbrook Leisure Ltd* v. *The Reece-Jones Partnership*, 18 November 2003 (Lawtel, 19/11/03). As to mixed use premises see *Broadway Investments Hackney Ltd* v. *Grant* [2006] EWCA Civ 1709.

7.2. Exclusions from the Act

7.2.1. These include:

(a) agricultural holdings;

(b) mining leases;

(c) written service tenancies;

(d) tenancies at will;

(e) fixed term tenancies not exceeding six months unless the tenancy contains provisions for renewing the term or for extending it beyond six months from its beginning. This exception also does not apply if the tenant has been in occupation for a period which, together with any period during which any predecessor in the carrying on of the business carried on by the tenant was in occupation, exceeds twelve months;[1]

(f) tenancies for a term certain where the statutory procedure has been followed to exclude the security of tenure provisions of the Act prior to the commencement of the tenancy.

7.2.2. The procedure referred to in K7.2.1(f) is as follows:

(a) a notice in prescribed form containing a warning must be served on the tenant before the tenant 'enters into the tenancy to which it applies, or (if earlier) becomes contractually bound to do so'. This procedure must therefore be followed before a contract to enter into an excluded lease is made;[2]

(b) either:

(i) not less than 14 days must elapse before the tenant enters into the tenancy. The tenant must then sign a simple, prescribed declaration that he has received the required warning notice and has accepted the consequences of entering into the agreement; or alternatively

(ii) the tenant, or a person duly authorised by him to do so, must, before the tenancy or contract is entered into, make a prescribed statutory declaration. In each case, the forms of notice and declaration are set out in schedules to RRO 2003 (see K7.1);

(c) a reference to the notice and the simple declaration or (if applicable) the statutory declaration must be contained in or endorsed upon the instrument creating the tenancy; and

(d) the agreement to exclude the security of tenure provisions of the Act must be contained in or endorsed upon the instrument creating the tenancy.[3]

7.2.3. Subject to K7.2.1(f), where a tenancy is within the provisions of the Act it is not possible to exclude the operation of the security of tenure provisions of the Act by agreement between the parties.[4]

1. Landlord and Tenant Act 1954, s.43. Considered in *Cricket Ltd* v. *Shaftesbury* [1999] 28 EG 127.
2. It is possible that these provisions may be construed as permitting a conditional agreement for a lease in which compliance with the new procedure is clearly set out to be a precondition of the tenant's obligation to enter into the lease.
3. For a series of articles discussing differing views of some detailed issues relating to this procedure see A. Colby, A. Wallis and K. Fenn, 'Follow the letter of the law', *Estates Gazette* 29 May 2004, 132; K. Fenn, 'Mind the traps', *Estates Gazette* 5 June 2004, 116; K. Fenn, A. Colby and S. Highmore. 'A procedure guaranteed to confuse', *Estates Gazette* 19 June 2004, 166; and A. Colby and K. Fenn, 'No semblance of order', *Estates Gazette* 26 June 2004, 187.
4. Landlord and Tenant Act 1954, s.38.

7.3. Termination of tenancy

7.3.1. A tenancy within the Act can only be determined by one of the methods prescribed by the Act. These include:

(a) forfeiture;

(b) notice to quit given by the tenant;

(c) immediate surrender;[1]

(d) service by the landlord of a notice under Landlord and Tenant Act 1954, s.25;

(e) a tenant's request for a new tenancy under Landlord and Tenant Act 1954, s.26;

(f) notice served under section 27 of the Act.

7.3.2. Where the tenant has a periodic tenancy, his notice to quit will be of the length appropriate to the period of his tenancy (e.g. one month's notice for a monthly tenancy). In the case of a fixed-term tenancy, the tenant may serve a three-month notice under section 27 of the Act to expire on the term date or at any time after the term date. Alternatively, the tenant may vacate before the end of the tenancy.[2]

7.3.3. A tenancy which is not determined by one of the above methods continues to run (despite expiry of a fixed term) on the same terms until terminated by one of these methods.[3]

1. An agreement for the tenant to surrender his tenancy at some future time is void under Landlord and Tenant Act 1954, s.38 except if authorised under the Act. This requires a similar procedure to that authorising contracting out of the security of tenure provisions of the 1954 Act considered in K7.2.1(f).
2. See Landlord and Tenant Act 1954, s.27(1A).
3. In the case of a business lease which was subject to the SDLT regime, further SDLT returns may have to be filed following the extension of the lease by the 1954 Act: see further A14.

7.4. Landlord's notice

7.4.1. A notice to terminate a tenancy served by a landlord under Landlord and Tenant Act 1954, s.25 must be in a prescribed form and must specify a date (not earlier than the term date and not less than six nor more than 12 months ahead) on which the tenancy is to end.[1] If the landlord does not wish to oppose the grant of a new tenancy, he must state in the notice his proposals for the premises, duration, rent and other terms of the new tenancy. If he wishes to oppose the grant of a new tenancy, he must set out which ground or grounds he intends to use (see K7.4.3).

7.4.2. If the tenant wants a new tenancy, he should apply to the court for a new tenancy by the date specified in the landlord's section 25 notice. A tenant's application to the court is a pending land action and should be protected by an entry in the register of pending land actions in the case of unregistered land. Where the land is registered a pending land action should be protected by a notice.[2] Note that even if the tenant is in occupation of registered land his pending land application will not be an overriding interest.[3]

7.4.3. The landlord's grounds for opposing the grant of a new tenancy are contained in Landlord and Tenant Act 1954, s.30 and are briefly as follows:

    (a) breach of repairing obligations by the tenant;

    (b) persistent delay in paying rent;

    (c) substantial breaches of other obligations under the tenancy;

    (d) alternative accommodation;

    (e) possession of whole property required where tenant has a sub-tenancy of part;

    (f) landlord's intention to demolish or reconstruct the property;

    (g) landlord requires possession for his own occupation.[4]

7.4.4. The time limits specified in the Act for service of notices and application to the court are construed strictly and in general no extension of those limits is permitted. Thus if a tenant fails to apply to the court within the prescribed period he will lose his right to a new tenancy unless the landlord has made an application to the court by that date. This period cannot be extended by the court. However, the parties may agree in writing to extend the deadline for making an application to court, providing this agreement is made before the expiry of the statutory period. The agreement cannot be made retrospectively.[5]

1. The form of notice is contained in Landlord and Tenant Act 1954, Part 2 (Notices) Regulations 2004. The methods of service are prescribed by section 66(4) Landlord and Tenant Act 1954 applying to section 23 Landlord and Tenant Act 1927 (as amended by Recorded Delivery Service Act 1962). The most common method used is recorded delivery post. The date of service is deemed to be the date of posting; see *CA Webber (Transport) Ltd* v. *Network Rail Infrastructure Ltd* [2003] All ER (D) 250.
2. Land Registration Act 2002, s.87(1)(a).
3. *Ibid.*, s.87(3).
4. This ground is not available to a landlord whose interest was purchased or created within the five years preceding the termination date of the tenancy as specified in the notice terminating the tenancy (provided that the tenancy or series of tenancies was existing at the time of creation and has continued uninterrupted since that time).
5. Landlord and Tenant Act 1954, s.29.

7.5.   Tenant's request for a new tenancy

7.5.1.   A tenant's request for a new tenancy can be made only if the tenant originally had a tenancy for a term of years certain exceeding one year. It must be in prescribed form and must specify a date (not earlier than the term date and not less than six nor more than 12 months ahead) for the start of the new tenancy. If the landlord wishes to oppose the grant of a new tenancy, he must notify the tenant within two months, stating on which ground(s) he will rely (see K7.4.3). The tenant must then apply to the court for a new tenancy not later than the day before the date specified in the tenant's request[1] (see K7.4.4). A tenant's application to the court is a pending land action and should be protected by an entry in the register of pending land actions in the case of unregistered land. Where the land is registered a pending land action should be protected by a notice. Even if the tenant is in occupation of the land, his application cannot be an overriding interest (see Land Registration Act 2002, s.87(3)).

1. Landlord and Tenant Act 1954, s.29A(2). The form of request is contained in Landlord and Tenant Act 1954, Part 2 (Notices) Regulations 2004.

7.6.   Identifying the parties

7.6.1.   The procedure to terminate the lease by landlord's notice or tenant's request must be carried out between the tenant and the relevant or 'competent' landlord as defined in Landlord and Tenant Act 1954, s.44. The competent landlord is the person who is the owner of that interest in the property that is either the fee simple or a tenancy that will not come to an end within 14 months by effluxion of time.

7.6.2.   To enable the parties to discover the identity of the relevant individuals on whom they should serve notice, the Act contains a provision in section 40 to permit the service of a notice requesting information. This requires the other party to provide information in relation to others who may have an interest in the property. This enables landlords to discover if the tenant has created sub-tenancies, and tenants to discover the nature and extent of their landlord's and superior landlord's and their lender's interests. The section requires the recipient of such a notice to reply within a month, to keep the information up to date for six months and imposes a specific remedy for failing to comply with such a notice. The provision also deals with transfer of ownership of the landlord's or the tenant's interest taking place during the period in which a section 40 notice remains current.

7.7. **Application to the court**

7.7.1. Either the landlord or the tenant can apply to the court for an order determining the terms of the new tenancy. Alternatively, where the landlord is opposing a new tenancy he can apply to the court for an order terminating the current tenancy without the order for a new tenancy.

7.7.2. Unless the landlord can establish one or more of the grounds for possession within section 30(1) Landlord and Tenant Act 1954 (see K7.4.3), a new tenancy must be ordered by the court comprising such holding (i.e. the part of the property occupied by the tenant), at such rent and on such other terms as the court orders (in the absence of agreement between the parties), although the new tenancy cannot, in the absence of agreement, exceed 15 years in length (see ss.32–35 of the Act).

7.8. **Compensation**

7.8.1. If the landlord succeeds in obtaining possession, based on grounds (e), (f), or (g) in K7.4.3, the tenant is entitled to compensation for giving up his tenancy.

7.8.2. In certain circumstances a tenant of business premises may also be entitled to compensation for improvements effected by him under Part I Landlord and Tenant Act 1927. This provision enables a tenant to make improvements if they fall within the classification set out in the Act, which include, for example, certain improvements which add to the letting value of the property, provided, broadly, the tenant serves notice of his intention to do so on the landlord. The landlord then has three months to object when the matter is referred to the county court. If there is no objection or the court consents, the tenant can make the improvement and on leaving he is entitled to compensation equivalent to the increase in value of the premises.[1]

7.8.3. The court may order the landlord to pay the tenant compensation for loss or damage where the court refuses to grant a new tenancy and it subsequently appears that this was due to misrepresentation or concealment of material facts. The court may also award the tenant compensation where the tenant has quit the premises after failing to apply for renewal, or after withdrawing an application for renewal, by reason of misrepresentation or the concealment of material facts.[2]

1. See, for example, *Norfolk Capital Group Ltd* v. *Cadogan Estates Ltd* [2004] 1 WLR 1458.
2. Landlord and Tenant Act 1954, s.37A.

7.9. Rent control

7.9.1. There are no statutory limitations on the rent recoverable on the original grant of a tenancy of business premises, but on a renewal the court can fix a new rent failing agreement by the parties. The court also has power, on application by either party, to fix an interim rent pending the outcome of proceedings.[1] The interim rent is calculated on a valuation based on a tenancy from year to year under the principles laid down in Landlord and Tenant Act 1954, s.24A. As a crude yardstick, it is generally considered that these principles will lead to an interim rent somewhere between 10% to 15% less than the open market valuation. This method of valuation applies where the renewal application is opposed. However, where renewal is uncontested, subject to certain exceptions, the interim rent will simply be the same as the rent for the tenancy once it is renewed.

1. Landlord and Tenant Act 1954, s.24A.

7.10. Buying a business lease

7.10.1. A prospective assignee (purchaser) of a lease of business premises should (in addition to the usual matters to be considered on the assignment of a lease) pay careful attention to the following matters:

    (a)   the rent review provisions contained in the lease;

    (b)   the repairing obligations imposed by the lease;

    (c)   any service charge provisions in the lease;[1]

    (d)   the VAT implications of the transaction;

    (e)   whether the existing tenant has committed any breach of covenant which would give the landlord the right to determine the lease or to refuse a renewal of it;

    (f)   the likelihood of a lease renewal being opposed by a landlord on other grounds, e.g. redevelopment;

    (g)   the provisions relating to alienation of the lease.

1. Note the RICS code of practice, *Service Charges in Commercial Property*. The code is designed to indicate best practice for commercial service charges; see K1.8.7.

7.11. Covenants restricting assignment

7.11.1. It is common for a business lease to prohibit an assignment without the landlord's consent.

7.11.2. Where a lease contains a covenant prohibiting assignment without the landlord's consent, that consent is not to be unreasonably withheld (section 19(1)

Landlord and Tenant Act 1927). Guidelines for testing reasonableness are set out in the Court of Appeal decision in *International Drilling Fluids Ltd* v. *Louisville Investments (Uxbridge) Ltd*:[1]

(a) the purpose of the covenant is to protect the landlord from an undesirable tenant or from an undesirable use being made of the premises;

(b) a landlord cannot, therefore, refuse consent on grounds which have nothing to do with the relationship of landlord and tenant;

(c) as long as the landlord's conclusions were those which a reasonable man might reach he does not have to prove they were justified;

(d) it may be reasonable for a landlord to withhold consent on the grounds of the proposed use of the premises;[2]

(e) normally a landlord need have regard only to his own interests but it may be that the detriment caused to the tenant by withholding consent so outweighs the advantage to the landlord that it is unreasonable for consent to be withheld.

7.11.3. Subject to these considerations, whether a landlord is acting reasonably is a question of fact in each case. A lease which is an 'old tenancy', i.e. one to which Landlord and Tenant (Covenants) Act 1995 does not apply, cannot set out what is to be considered reasonable, although a condition precedent can be imposed.[3] Under Landlord and Tenant Act 1988, a landlord must give consent within a reasonable time unless there is a reason for withholding it. Written reasons for refusal must be given within a reasonable time.[4] A landlord has only a very short time in which to reach a decision once possessed of all the necessary information. What period will be regarded as unreasonable is a question of fact in each case, but it may be a matter of weeks rather than months.[5] The burden of proving that the withholding of consent is reasonable is on the landlord. In appropriate cases a landlord may be penalised for undue delay by an award of exemplary damages.[6]

7.11.4. The above provisions have been amended[7] in relation to assignments of 'new tenancies', i.e. ones to which Landlord and Tenant (Covenants) Act 1995 applies; broadly those granted on or after 1 January 1996 of commercial premises.[8] Paragraphs 7.11.5 to 7.11.8 below set out the new provisions.

7.11.5. A landlord may agree in advance with his tenant:

(a) any circumstance in which he may withhold consent to a proposed assignment; or

(b) any conditions subject to which his consent will be granted;

and if he withholds consent for these reasons he is not acting unreasonably. The agreement has to be made before the application for consent but does not have to be contained in the lease nor made at the same time as the lease.

7.11.6. The 1995 Act distinguishes between factual matters, for example:

(a) the assignee must be a plc;

(b) the assignee must have net assets equal to a specified multiplier of the rent;

(c) the assignee must provide a rent deposit; or

(d) the assignor must enter an AGA;

and discretionary matters, for example the assignee is, in the opinion of the landlord, of equal financial standing to the assignor. In the latter case, the landlord's decision has to be arrived at reasonably, or the tenant must have the right to have the decision reviewed by an independent third party who is identifiable from the agreement and whose decision is conclusive.

7.11.7. The imposition of stringent conditions may have an adverse effect on the assessment of a revised rent or a subsequent review and/or may make it difficult for the tenant to assign the lease. In considering what conditions to impose, landlords are encouraged to have regard to the Code for Leasing Business Premises 2007.[9]

1. [1986] 1 All ER 321.
2. This principle was considered by the House of Lords in *Ashworth Frazer Ltd* v. *Gloucester City Council* [2001] 46 EG 180.
3. See *Bocardo SA* v. *S & M Hotels* [1980] 1 WLR 17; *Vaux Group plc* v. *Lilley* [1991] 04 EG 136.
4. Once the landlord has made a decision this is final and he cannot reconsider this decision within the 'reasonable time' period: *Go West Ltd* v. *Spigarolo* [2003] 07 EG 136.
5. In one case involving an application for consent to underlet, a week after receiving the final piece of information was held to be sufficient: *Blockbuster Entertainment Ltd* v. *Barnsdale Properties Ltd* [2003] EWHC 2912. Note also *NCR Ltd* v. *Riverland Portfolio No.1 Ltd (No.2)* [2004] EWCA Civ 312; [2005] 13 EG 135.
6. *Design Progression Ltd* v. *Thurloe Properties Ltd* [2004] 10 EGCS 184.
7. Landlord and Tenant (Covenants) Act 1995 inserting a new section 19(1A) into Landlord and Tenant Act 1927.
8. This provision applies to leases apart from leases of residential premises or those of agricultural property, see Landlord and Tenant Act 1927, s.19.
9. See K1.1.4.

7.12. Professional arbitration on court terms (PACT)

7.12.1. The Royal Institution of Chartered Surveyors (RICS) and the Law Society have jointly agreed to offer a service providing private determination of lease renewals under the provisions of Landlord and Tenant Act 1954. This is claimed to provide a faster, cheaper and more efficient method of settling lease renewal disputes than in the courts, by professionals who have the expertise to make decisions on technical matters.

7.12.2. The scheme is voluntary with referral by mutual agreement of the landlord and the tenant. Appointments of arbitrators and experts, experienced in landlord and tenant matters, are made by the President of the RICS or the President of the Law Society. Once an application has been made to the court the parties can apply for an agreed adjournment in order to deal with the matter under PACT. Model consent orders are provided to be adapted to cover the needs of the particular case.

7.12.3. The nature of the dispute will dictate the expertise required. Sufficient information on the issue in dispute will be requested from the parties to enable the appropriate President to determine whether the services of a surveyor or solicitor or indeed both are required.

7.12.4. The primary aim is to settle rents where other terms have already been agreed. Other disputes can be referred to the scheme on matters of principle or drafting of a lease.

7.12.5. The tenant will retain the right to reject the tenancy which at present exists under the Act.

7.12.6. Parties will have the option of excluding or retaining a right of appeal to the court from the arbitrator's decision.

7.12.7. The system is designed to be flexible, giving the parties the right to settle their own procedure for determination of a dispute in a way not open to them in litigation.

7.12.8. A summary of the key issues follows:

    (a) Decide with the other party whether it would be advantageous to refer aspects of the lease renewal to a third party solicitor or arbitrator rather than a judge.

    (b) Identify which aspects of the renewal (if any) are agreed.

    (c) Decide which aspects to refer to the third party:

        (i) the interim rent;

        (ii) the new rent;

        (iii) other terms of the lease;

        (iv) the detailed drafting of terms;

        (v) a combination of these.

    (d) Choose which aspects are to be resolved by a third party solicitor and which by a third party surveyor.

    (e) Choose the third party's capacity – arbitrator or expert?

    (f) Draft court application making use of or adapting PACT model orders.

    (g) Apply to court for consent.

    (h) Apply for appointment of person adjudicating (if not agreed).

    (i) Proceed with adjudication.

(j) Receive award subject only to 'cooling off' rights and, in arbitration, any right of appeal.

7.12.9. There have been relatively few referrals to PACT so information as to the effectiveness of the scheme is unavailable. The existence of the new procedures for renewal (see K7.4.4) may mean that parties are more likely to delay the court application by consent, where a negotiated agreement appears likely.

K8. Agricultural tenancies

8.1. Definitions

8.1.1. Many tenants of agricultural holdings which were created before 1 September 1995 enjoy security of tenure under Agricultural Holdings Act 1986. As from 1 September 1995, it is no longer possible to create a new agricultural tenancy which has the protection of the 1986 Act, unless it is a succession tenancy or a contracted in tenancy falling within the limited scope of Regulatory Reform (Agricultural Tenancies) (England and Wales) Order 2006 (SI 2006/2805) which is only relevant to minor boundary changes to the let area in terms of either area or value. K8.2–8.4 only apply to tenancies which are regulated by Agricultural Holdings Act 1986.

8.1.2. The expression 'agricultural holding' is defined as the aggregate of land (whether agricultural land or not) comprised in a contract of tenancy which is a contract for an agricultural tenancy (not being a service tenancy).

8.1.3. In general, 'agricultural land' means land used for agriculture and so used for the purpose of a trade or business.

8.1.4. 'Contract of tenancy' means a letting of land or an agreement for letting land, for a term of years or from year to year.

8.2. Protection of short-term tenants and licensees

8.2.1. Under Agricultural Holdings Act 1986, s.2 an agreement under which any land was let to a person for use as agricultural land for an interest less than a tenancy from year to year, or under which a person was granted a licence to occupy land for use as agricultural land (in circumstances such that if his interest were a tenancy from year to year he would be the tenant of an agricultural holding), took effect (with the necessary modifications) as an agreement for the letting of land for a tenancy from year to year. The licence must not have been gratuitous and must have conferred occupation on the licensee.

8.3. Security of tenure

8.3.1. Subject to a provision dealing with the death of the tenant before the term date[1] a tenancy of an agricultural holding for two years or more continues as a tenancy from year to year unless written notice to quit is given by either party at least one year and not more than two years before the end of the tenancy.[2]

8.3.2. In consequence of Agricultural Holdings Act 1986, ss.2 and 3, a notice to quit is normally necessary to determine an agricultural letting for an interest less than a tenancy from year to year, a licence to occupy agricultural land, and a tenancy for two years or more. The importance of this is that the security of tenure provisions of Agricultural Holdings Act 1986 come into operation where notice to quit (the method of determination of periodic tenancies) is given to the tenant.

8.3.3. In general, if a notice to quit an agricultural holding or part of a holding is given to the tenant he has the right to serve a counter-notice on the landlord, requiring the landlord to obtain the consent of the Agricultural Land Tribunal to the operation of the notice to quit, which consent can only be given on certain grounds. The tenant's right to serve a counter-notice is excluded if the notice to quit is given and is expressed to be given on one of a number of grounds specified in Schedule 3 Agricultural Holdings Act 1986.

1. Agricultural Holdings Act 1986, s.4.
2. Agricultural Holdings Act 1986, s.3.

8.4. Other matters dealt with by Agricultural Holdings Act 1986

8.4.1. Agricultural Holdings Act 1986 deals with a large number of matters regulating the relationship between landlord and tenant, including the right of succession on the death or retirement of the tenant, the tenant's right to compensation for improvements, and arbitration as to rent.

8.5. Agricultural Tenancies Act 1995

8.5.1. Agricultural Tenancies Act 1995 applies to all agricultural tenancies granted after the commencement of the Act on 1 September 1995 (excepting those mentioned at 8.1.1). It is not retrospective in effect and does not affect existing tenancies (or successions to those tenancies) granted under Agricultural Holdings Act 1986.

8.5.2. The words 'agriculture' and 'agricultural' have the same meaning as under the 1986 Act.

8.5.3. Tenancies created under the 1995 Act are called 'farm business tenancies'. Certain conditions must be satisfied for a tenancy to fall within this definition:

(a) **Business**: all or part of the land is farmed for the purposes of a trade or business and has been so farmed since the start of the tenancy.

(b) **Agriculture**: having regard to a number of matters specified in the Act, the character of the tenancy is primarily or wholly agricultural.

(c) **Notice**: as an alternative to the agriculture condition, the parties can, before the grant of the tenancy, exchange written notices identifying the land and stating that the person giving the notice intends that the proposed tenancy is to be and remain a farm business tenancy. Even where such notices are exchanged, the character of the tenancy must be primarily or wholly agricultural at the start of the tenancy.

8.5.4. To be a farm business tenancy, condition (a) above must be satisfied, together with either (b) or (c). If (c) is used, the tenancy will remain a farm business tenancy so long as some part of the land is farmed, but other parts of the land may later be used for other business and non-agricultural purposes.

Exclusions

8.5.5. The following tenancies are excluded:

(a) tenancies granted before the commencement of the Act;

(b) tenancies granted under the succession on death or retirement provisions of the 1986 Act;

(c) tenancies granted to an existing tenant who is protected under the 1986 Act where a variation of the previous tenancy has the effect of an implied surrender and regrant.

Security of tenure

8.5.6. There is no security of tenure or right of renewal given to the tenant under the 1995 Act (other than as provided for in the agreement itself).

Preparation of the agreement

8.5.7. If the tenancy agreement is to be for a fixed term of three years or more, it must be made by deed (under Law of Property Act 1925, s.52) and can only be prepared by 'accredited persons' – a barrister, solicitor, notary public, licensed conveyancer, a full member of the Central Association of Agricultural Valuers, or an Associate or Fellow of ISVA or RICS (Agricultural Tenancies Act 1995, s.35).

Rent and rent review

8.5.8. There are no statutory controls on rent. In relation to rent review, section 10 of the 1995 Act provides for a rent review to take place in accordance with the provisions of that section except where the provisions of section 9 are complied with. Section 9 applies to a tenancy which:

(a) expressly states that the rent is not to be reviewed during the term of the tenancy; or

(b) provides for a rent review at specified times, either:

(i) by or to a specified amount; or

(ii) in accordance with a specified formula (not upwards only) assessed by objective criteria; or

(c) expressly states that Part II of the 1995 Act does not apply and there is nothing that precludes a reduction in the rent; or

(d) provides for an independent expert to make a final determination of the revised rent and there is nothing that precludes a reduction in the rent.[1]

1. Exceptions (c) and (d) were introduced under Regulatory Reform (Agricultural Tenancies) (England and Wales) Order 2006 (SI 2006/2805).

8.5.9. Statutory review under section 10:

(a) either party can call for a review by notice to the other;

(b) the review date must not be less than 12 nor more than 24 months from service of a 'statutory review notice';

(c) if the parties have agreed a specified review date, the review date must be a date as from which rent could be varied under the agreement;

(d) if the parties have agreed in writing that the review date is to be a specified date, the review must be on that date;

(e) if there is no agreement as to the date of the review, the date is the anniversary of the beginning of the tenancy;

(f) subject to any agreement to the contrary, rent reviews may not take place at less than three-yearly intervals.

8.5.10. An independent expert or arbitrator is to be appointed to fix the reviewed rent. In default of agreement, the President of the RICS is to appoint the arbitrator. If the tenancy agreement requires determination by an independent expert, arbitration is excluded.

8.5.11. The reviewed rent on a statutory review is assessed on an open market formula (section 13). Tenant's improvements are broadly disregarded.

Assignment

8.5.12. The 1995 Act does not restrict assignment but section 19 Landlord and Tenant Act 1927 does not apply to these tenancies.

Agricultural covenants

8.5.13. No agricultural covenants are implied by the 1995 Act. Such covenants must be expressly included in the agreement if required.

Repairs and insurance

8.5.14. The 1995 Act does not deal with these matters, thus appropriate clauses to deal with them must be included in the agreement.

Termination

8.5.15. The following apply to termination:

    (a) a fixed-term agreement for two years or less will expire automatically;

    (b) common law rules apply to periodic tenancies except that a yearly tenant needs to be given not less than one year's notice, expiring at the end of a year;

    (c) for a fixed-term tenancy of more than two years, not less than 12 months' notice to terminate on the term day must be given (otherwise the tenancy continues as a tenancy from year to year);

    (d) notices must be in writing.

Compensation

8.5.16. Compensation is payable for the tenant's improvements. These provisions cannot be excluded by the agreement. Improvements are categorised as follows:

    (a) **Intangible advantages**

        something which attaches to the holding and which the tenant has brought to the holding at his own expense, e.g. unimplemented planning permission or a water abstraction licence;

    (b) **Physical improvements**

        (i)   non-routine, e.g. building a shed;

        (ii) routine (section 19(10) of the 1995 Act), e.g. 'tenant's right' (growing crops, etc.).

Conditions for claiming compensation

8.5.17. The landlord's consent must have been obtained (generally before or after the improvement was made). Appeal against the landlord's refusal of consent lies to an arbitrator (but in respect of non-routine physical improvements an appeal can only be lodged before the improvement has been made). There is no appeal against the landlord's refusal of consent to an application by the tenant for planning permission. The arbitrator cannot vary any conditions imposed by the landlord.

Amount of compensation (sections 20–27 of the 1995 Act)

8.5.18. The amount of compensation is the amount attributable to the improvement in the value of the holding at the termination of the tenancy. Appeal lies to an arbitrator under section 22 of the 1995 Act. The landlord and tenant are free to agree an upper limit to the amount of compensation payable at the time consent is given to an improvement. If the concept of a limit is agreed but not the amount of compensation payable, then the amount is the cost to the tenant of making the improvement.

Fixtures

8.5.19. Tenant's fixtures can be removed by the tenant at the end of the tenancy. The tenant is under an obligation not to cause damage and to rectify any damage caused. The tenant need not give notice to the landlord of his intention to remove fixtures. If consent to an improvement was obtained, the tenant could alternatively claim compensation for the fixture as an improvement. The agreement should specify which fixtures are/are not tenant's fixtures.

Dispute resolution

8.5.20. The 1995 Act contains specific provisions for arbitration on rent review, improvements and compensation. Other disputes are to be referred to arbitration unless the parties agree to a different procedure. The arbitrator is appointed with the consent of the parties (either on a joint reference or four weeks' notice by one party unchallenged by the other). In default of agreement, the President of the RICS is to appoint the arbitrator. The court's jurisdiction is not excluded. Arbitration Act 1996 applies to arbitrations under the 1995 Act.

Stamp Duty Land Tax

8.5.21. Under the provisions of section 5 of the 1995 Act landlords and tenants are able to create a rolling tenancy agreement from year to year. The tenant in these circumstances needs to be aware of the ongoing liability to account to HM Revenue and Customs for any SDLT that may be payable under the terms of the transaction (see A14).

Single farm payment

8.5.22. The parties to the tenancy agreement will need to include appropriate clauses to cover the transfer and ownership of any entitlement held by the tenant at the end of the term. Where entitlements are to be leased to the tenant as part of the transaction, consideration should be given to the timing of such transfer. See B8.3.10.

K9. Right to buy

9.1. Public sector

9.1.1. Subject to certain conditions, a secure tenant normally has a right to buy.[1]

9.1.2. 'Right to buy' means:

(a) if the dwelling is a house, and the landlord or a public sector head-landlord owns the freehold, the right to acquire the freehold;

(b) if the landlord does not own the freehold or the dwelling is a flat, the right to be granted a lease of the premises.

9.1.3. To qualify, the tenant must usually have occupied the house or flat as a secure tenant for two years, although there are special provisions in Schedule 4 Housing Act 1985 relating to spouses, civil partners and children. This provision is amended in relation to wholly new tenancies which begin on or after 18 January 2005. In these cases the relevant period of occupation is extended to five years.[2] Schedule 5 Housing Act 1985 (as amended) contains a number of exceptions to the right to buy.

9.1.4. The price payable on exercise of the right is the price which the house would realise if sold on the open market by a willing seller, less any discount to which the buyer is entitled. The amount of the discount depends on the length of occupation of the secure tenant, but cannot usually be less than 32% nor more than 60% in the case of a house, or less than 44% or more than 70% in the case of a flat. This is subject to a maximum amount of the discount imposed by Housing Act 1985, s.131 and related costs incurred in respect of the house.[3] These provisions are amended in relation to wholly new tenancies which begin on or after 18 January 2005. These amendments are consequential to the extension of the initial qualifying period of occupation. Therefore in these cases the amount of the discount previously referred to in this paragraph is amended so that it cannot usually be less than 35% in the case of a house, or less than 50% in the case of a flat.[4]

9.1.5. The Housing Act 2004 enables landlords of secure tenants to seek a court order suspending the right to buy for a specified period in respect of the tenancy on the grounds of anti-social behaviour.[5] In certain circumstances, where an application is pending for a demotion order, a suspension order or a possession order sought on the grounds of anti-social behaviour, a tenant is prevented from being able to enforce his right to buy.[6]

9.1.6. If a tenant who has received a discount sells the property within five years, he will (except in certain specified cases) be required to repay to the landlord a proportionate part of the discount.[7] This liability takes effect as a legal charge on the property. In addition, the purchase deed must grant a right of first refusal to the landlord if the property is sold within 10 years.[8] There are provisions in the legislation governing the form and effect of the conveyance/transfer or lease. There are service charge limits which the buyer can expect to see set out in the conveyance or lease. Where the title to the landlord's property is unregistered, the tenant does not need to examine a landlord's title because the landlord is required to supply the tenant with a certificate of title in the prescribed form, which certificate the Land Registry is bound to accept for the purposes of registration of the tenant's title. A lease taken by a tenant under the right to buy provisions needs to be registered even if for a term of seven years or less since Land Registration Act 2002, s.4(1)(e) applies to it. If application for first registration is not made within two months, the lease will be void as regards the grant of the legal estate.[9] It takes effect as a contract made for valuable consideration to grant the lease concerned.[10] The contract may be protected as an overriding interest if the intended tenant is in occupation.[11]

1. Housing Act 1985, as amended.
2. Housing Act 1985, s.119(1) as amended by Housing Act 2004, s.180.
3. The maximum discount is subject to regulation by Housing (Right to Buy) (Limits on Discount) Order 1998 (as amended).
4. See footnote 2 above.
5. See Housing Act 1985, s.121 as amended by Housing Act 2004, s.192.
6. Housing Act 1985, s.138, as amended by Housing Act 2004, s.193 by inserting new subsections (2A) to (2D).
7. There is a sliding scale which applies to the amount of the discount which must be repaid on early sale which is proportional to the years of occupation at the rate of one-fifth per year; see Housing Act 1985, s.155A, as inserted by Housing Act 2004, s.185.
8. Housing Act 1985, s.156A inserted by Housing Act 2004, s.188(1). Note also: Housing (Right of First Refusal) (England) Regulations 2005 (SI 2005/1917) and Housing (Rights of First Refusal) (Wales) Regulations 2005 (SI 2005/2680).
9. Land Registration Act 2002, s.7(1).
10. *Ibid.*, s.7(2)(b).
11. *Ibid.*, Sched.1, para.2.

9.2. Leasehold Reform Act 1967

9.2.1. Part I Leasehold Reform Act 1967 gives certain tenants the right compulsorily to buy out the landlord's freehold interest (enfranchisement) or to take an extended lease for an additional 50 years. The right to enfranchise can still be exercised after the grant of an extended lease. These provisions have been modified by Leasehold Reform Housing and Urban Development Act 1993, Housing Act 1996 and Commonhold and Leasehold Reform Act 2002 (see K9.3).

Qualifying conditions

9.2.2. For the tenant to qualify, broadly the following factors must be considered:

(a)   his tenancy must be a long tenancy;

(b)   the house must fall within the definition of that word in the 1967 Act;

(c)   the tenant must have held the lease for the last two years;

(d)   the value of the property may be relevant.

Long tenancy

9.2.3.   A long tenancy is one granted for a term certain exceeding 21 years; but there are certain exceptions where shorter leases which have been extended beyond 21 years through renewal will qualify.

House

9.2.4.   A 'house' within the Act includes any building designed or adapted for living in and reasonably so called.[1] The Court of Appeal has held that the question of whether at least a substantial part of the property is designed or adapted for living in should be determined as at the date of the notice served by the tenant of his desire to purchase the freehold.[2] The fact that part of the building is used for business purposes may not exclude the application of the Act.[3] Where a building has been converted into flats or maisonettes, it depends on the structure of the conversion as to whether the converted units fall within the scope of the Act. If the result of the conversion is to produce a building which is divided horizontally, so that each tenant occupies the whole or part of one floor of the building, the units will be classed as flats which do not enjoy the benefit of the Act. If, however, the conversion has been made vertically, so that each tenant occupies a part of each floor of the building from the ground upwards, the individual units will be classed as houses, each of which may utilise the provisions of the Act. This will apply where parts of one overhang the other so that the division is not entirely vertical, providing this is not to a material extent.[4] Flats, whether purpose built or otherwise, are not within the Act.

Value of house

9.2.5.   Originally a tenant was precluded from the right to enfranchise if the house was of high value as defined by the legislation. For the purposes of enfranchisement this requirement has, broadly, been abolished.[5] However, the terms on which the compensation is calculated will be different dependent on the value of the property on certain dates.[6] In the case of the right to a lease extension, the value of the property is still required to be within certain limits set out in Leasehold Reform Act 1967 (as amended).[7]

Residence qualification

9.2.6.   The former residence qualification has essentially been abolished. However, it may be relevant in other circumstances. So, for example, a person may be treated as having been the tenant of a house for two years if it was vested in trustees and he was beneficially entitled and permitted to occupy under the trust.[8] A residence test also exists in order to deal with a situation where a non-resident head-tenant of a house, which is sub-let in parts, might be able to enfranchise and then make a profit if the sub-lessees subsequently exercise their rights under the Leasehold Reform, Housing and Urban Development Act 1993; see K9.3. In this case the head-tenant of the house must, broadly, have been in occupation of part of the house as his or her only or main residence for at least two years in the previous ten years.[9] Also there are special residency rules if the Landlord and Tenant Act 1954, Part II applies to the tenancy.[10]

Registration of notice

9.2.7. A notice served by a qualifying tenant on his landlord of his desire to purchase the freehold or to take an extended lease creates a contract between the parties capable of registration as a notice in registered land or a Class C(iv) land charge in unregistered land. The tenant's rights under the contract, even though he is in occupation, do not constitute an overriding interest in registered land.[11]

Assignment of notice

9.2.8. The benefit of a notice served by a tenant under a lease within the Act can be assigned, but only with the lease itself. Such a provision must be dealt with by special condition in the contract to purchase the lease.[12]

Procedure

9.2.9. Details of the rights and obligations of the parties under the notice and of the procedures to be followed (e.g. form of transfer, etc.) are set out in the Act,[13] which also contains provisions dealing with the acquisition of intermediate reversions where the immediate landlord is not the freeholder.[14] In many cases, however, the strict procedures under the Act are not followed and the procedure following service of the desire notice follows the ordinary steps in a normal purchase transaction. The payment of a deposit is often dispensed with although by written notice the landlord can demand a deposit not exceeding three times the annual rent or £25 whichever is greater. Since the service of notice by the tenant creates a contract between the parties[15] it is not open to the landlord subsequently to draw up a contract on, e.g. the Standard Conditions of Sale Form and to require the tenant to agree to the terms included in the landlord's contract. Where not agreed by the parties the terms of the contract are governed by Leasehold Reform (Enfranchisement and Extension) Regulations 1967.[16] Section 10 of the Act regulates the terms of the conveyance to the tenant. The tenant will take the property subject to legal easements and restrictive covenants of which he has notice, e.g. by registration. The general words implied by Law of Property Act 1925, s.62 cannot be excluded without the tenant's consent and certain more extensive rights as to support and access are implied.[17] The purchase deed must also make reasonable provision for rights of way over and for the benefit of other property belonging to the landlord (where relevant).[18] The landlord is only obliged to give one covenant for title;

namely that he has not himself incumbered the property and must give the statutory acknowledgement relating to retained title deeds (in unregistered land) but need not give an undertaking for safe custody (see M9).

Price formula

9.2.10. The price payable on enfranchisement is the subject of one of two formulae, depending on the rateable/rental value of the property. Failing agreement between the parties the price is settled by the Lands Tribunal. Where premises have been brought into the Act by virtue of Leasehold Reform Housing and Urban Development Act 1993, the tenant must pay compensation to the landlord for loss of development value. Further amendments have been made to the calculation of the value of the property by Commonhold and Leasehold Reform Act 2002. These amendments require the tenant to pay one half of the marriage value except that if the unexpired term of the tenancy is more than 80 years there will be no marriage value.

Rent under extended lease

9.2.11. Where an extended lease is taken, the rent under the extended term represents a ground rent for the property and may be subject to upwards revision after 25 years of the extension.

Costs

9.2.12. The tenant is responsible for payment of the landlord's costs, e.g. of valuation, deduction of title and the purchase deed.

Mortgage

9.2.13. Where the landlord's interest is subject to a mortgage, the lender must, on payment of the purchase price to him, release the property from the mortgage.

Redevelopment

9.2.14. Where the Act applies it is non-excludable, although in certain limited circumstances a landlord may be able to defeat a tenant's claim to an extended lease because he intends to redevelop the premises, or to defeat a claim to enfranchise or to take an extended lease on the ground that he reasonably requires the property for occupation as the only or main residence of himself or an adult member of his family. In each case compensation is payable to the tenant by the landlord.

1. *Tandon* v. *Trustees of Spurgeons Homes* [1982] AC 755; and see *Hareford Ltd* v. *Barnet LBC* [2005] EG 122.
2. *Mallett & Sons (Antiques) Ltd* v. *Grosvenor West End Properties Ltd; Boss Holdings Ltd* v. *Grosvenor West End Properties Ltd and another* [2006] EWCA 594.
3. See K9.2.6.

4. See *Malekshad* v. *Howard de Walden* [2002] All ER (D) 68. Note also *Collins* v. *Howard de Walden Estates Ltd* [2003] EWCA Civ 545.
5. Leasehold Reform Act 1967, s.1A, although there are some exceptions; see s.1AA and, e.g. *Neville* v. *Cowdray Trust Ltd* [2006] EWCA Civ 70. Also see K9.3.1.
6. *Ibid.*, s.1(1), (5) and (6).
7. *Ibid.*
8. *Ibid.*, s.7(3) and (4) as amended by Commonhold and Leasehold Reform Act 2002, s.138(6).
9. *Ibid.*, s.1(1ZB). See *Cadogan* v. *Search Guarantees plc* [2004] EWCA Civ 969 where this provision was interpreted.
10. In this case the Leasehold Reform Act 1967 will only apply in these circumstances: broadly, if the tenancy is for a term certain exceeding 35 years and the tenant has occupied part as his only or main residence for the last 2 years or for periods amounting to 2 years in the last 10 (Leasehold Reform Act 1967, s.1(1ZC)).
11. Leasehold Reform Act 1967, s.5(5) as amended by Land Registration Act 2002, Sched.11, para.8(2).
12. Leasehold Reform Act 1967, s.5(2).
13. A form should be used by landlords to reply to claims. See Leasehold Reform (Notices) (Amendment) (No.2) (England) Regulations 2002 (SI 2002/3209).
14. Leasehold Reform Act 1967, Sched.1.
15. The tenant has a right to withdraw on ascertaining the purchase price: Leasehold Reform Act 1967, s.9(3)(b), as amended.
16. SI 1967/1879 as amended by Leasehold Reform (Enfranchisement and Extension) Regulations 2003 (SI 2003/1989); and Leasehold Reform (Enfranchisement and Extension) (Amendment) (Wales) Regulations 2004 (SI 2004/699/W.74).
17. For an example of how implied rights existing prior to enfranchisement survive, see *Kent* v. *Kavanagh* [2006] EWCA Civ 162.
18. See, for example, *Higgs* v. *Nieroba*, Lands Tribunal (2005) 24 October (LRA/2/2005).

9.3. Leasehold Reform, Housing and Urban Development Act 1993

Introduction

9.3.1. This Act, as amended by Commonhold and Leasehold Reform Act 2002, extends the rights to enfranchise/acquire an extended lease to the owners of flats and removes the rateable value limits which previously applied to houses under Leasehold Reform Act 1967. The Act also deals with some matters relating to public sector housing which are not dealt with in this book.

9.3.2. The majority of the amendments to the 1993 Act are now in force.[1] However the provisions in relation to RTE companies are not yet in force. This text sets out the new law and includes the provisions relating to RTE companies so that these can be dealt with. It therefore assumes that the RTE company provisions are in force. Until that happens the procedure is followed by a group of qualifying tenants known as a 'nominee purchaser'. In most cases this will, in fact, be a company formed by the tenants.

Collective enfranchisement

The right

9.3.3. The right is given to the tenants of a block of flats collectively to acquire the freehold of the block. The freehold is to be conveyed into the name of a company created by the tenants to buy the freehold known as an RTE company. The RTE company (a company limited by guarantee under section 122 Commonhold and Leasehold Reform Act 2002) must be formed before any further steps towards enfranchisement are taken. The RTE company must give notice to all the qualifying tenants under section 12A of the 1993 Act and invite their participation in the proposed enfranchisement. The conveyance can take place without the landlord's consent (subject to certain defences – see K9.3.7). Certain qualifying conditions must be fulfilled (see K9.3.21). Not all the flats in the block need to be let on long leases, nor need all the premises be let exclusively for residential purposes for the Act to apply.

Nature of the collective right

9.3.4. The nature of the collective right is for the tenants to have the freehold of the premises acquired on behalf of the participating qualifying tenants by the nominated RTE company at a price to be determined in accordance with the Act.

Exercise of the collective right

9.3.5. Notice must be served on the reversioner by the RTE company as provided by section 13 of the 1993 Act.

9.3.6. To be entitled to give this notice the RTE company must have members who include a number of qualifying tenants which is not less than one-half of the total number of flats in the premises. Prior to the RTE company provisions being brought into force, in essence, the notice must be given by a number of qualifying tenants which is not less than one-half of the total number of flats.

Landlord's grounds of opposition

9.3.7. The landlord can oppose the tenants' bid to enfranchise if the qualifying conditions are not met by the tenants. He may also oppose on the grounds that he wants to redevelop the whole or a substantial part of the premises but this ground is only available where not less than two-thirds of the long leases in the block are due to terminate within five years and the landlord cannot reasonably carry out the redevelopment without gaining possession.

Qualifications

9.3.8. To qualify, the tenant must be a 'tenant' of a 'flat' under a 'long lease'. However, a tenant who owns three or more of the flats cannot be a qualifying tenant of any of them.

9.3.9. Tenant includes a person holding a lease or tenancy, or an agreement for a lease or tenancy, and includes sub-leases/tenancies. Joint leaseholders are treated as one tenant.

9.3.10.   A flat is defined as a separate set of premises but need not necessarily be all on the same floor level. The premises must form part of a building and be constructed or adapted for use as a dwelling. Additionally, either the whole or some material part of the premises must lie above or below some other part of the building. This definition includes flats above shops, but may not apply to extensions, e.g. granny flats.[2]

9.3.11.   A long lease is one which is granted for a term of years certain exceeding 21 years. Provisions for determination within that period by either party do not affect this. The definition also includes most perpetually renewable leases, leases terminable by death or marriage, and leases granted under right to buy provisions and shared ownership leases where the tenant's total share is 100%, and new leases (of whatever length) granted on the expiry of an old long (i.e. 21 years plus) lease, and continuations under Landlord and Tenant Act 1954, Part 1 or Local Government and Housing Act 1989, Sched.10. Leases for less than 21 years which have been renewed without payment of a premium, taking the total term over 21 years, are also included within this definition.

Excluded tenants

9.3.12.   The following tenancies are excluded from the Act:[3]

(a)   business tenancies;

(b)   where the immediate landlord is a charitable housing trust;

(c)   unlawful sub-lease out of non-qualifying superior lease.

Interests included in the collective right

9.3.13.   Tenants who enfranchise will obtain the freehold of the premises in which the flats are situated and:

(a)   certain other property owned by the same freeholder ('appurtenant property'), e.g. garage, garden;

(b)   intermediate leasehold interests of those premises (but not of any non-residential parts of the building).

Interests excluded from the collective right

9.3.14.   Mineral rights owned by the freeholder are excluded from the collective right.

Interests to be leased back

9.3.15.   The Act contains provisions relating to certain interests which may (or in certain cases must) be leased back to the reversioner. They include the following:

(a)   flats let by the freeholder on secure tenancies;

(b) flats let by housing associations on tenancies other than secure tenancies;

(c) units which are not flats let to qualifying tenants (e.g. commercial parts of the building);

(d) flat occupied by a resident landlord.

9.3.16. The items in (a) and (b) above are subject to mandatory leaseback; (c) and (d) need only be leased back if the freeholder requires them. Schedule 9, Part IV of the Act contains detailed provisions dealing with the terms of the leaseback. Broadly this is to be a 999-year term at a peppercorn rent and will include the usual covenants but there will be no restrictions on alienation where the premises are residential.

Price

9.3.17. The price which the tenants are to pay for the freehold comprises three elements:

(a) market value;

(b) where the unexpired length of the leases held by participating members of the RTE company is 80 years or less, one-half of marriage value;

(c) compensation;

plus landlord's reasonable costs. Where intermediate leases are also to be acquired, the price of each interest has to be separately calculated. A valuer's advice must be sought in relation to this matter.

Market value

9.3.18. Market value is the price which might reasonably be expected to be paid if the property was sold on the open market by a willing seller to an arm's length buyer. The following assumptions also apply:

(a) the seller is selling the freehold subject to any leases subject to which the freeholder's interest is to be acquired by the buyer, but subject to any intermediate or other leases which are to be acquired by the buyer;

(b) that the Act does not apply;

(c) any increase in value caused by the participating tenant's improvements to the premises are to be disregarded.

Marriage value

9.3.19. Marriage value is the increase in the value of the unencumbered freehold over the aggregate values of the freehold and any intermediate leasehold interest when held by the persons from whom they are to be acquired.

Compensation

9.3.20.   Compensation is payable to the freeholder for any loss or damage he may suffer as a result of the enfranchisement. It includes any diminution in the value of any other property owned by the landlord, including loss of development value. Schedule 11 Housing Act 1996 also provides for the tenant to pay compensation to the landlord if an unsuccessful claim is made within two years of the original term date of the lease.

Premises

9.3.21.   The flat must be in premises which either consist of a self-contained building or a self-contained part of a building whether or not the freehold of the whole building or of that part is owned by the same person. Self-contained means structurally detached. Buildings which are divided vertically may qualify under the Act. Premises where more than 25% is occupied or intended to be occupied for non-residential purposes are excluded.[4] This last exclusion means that many flats above shops will not qualify under the Act. Resident landlords are excluded only if there are fewer than four flats in the block and they have owned the premises since their conversion or the block is not a purpose-built block.[5] Further, the building must contain two or more flats held by qualifying tenants; and the total number of flats held by qualifying tenants must be not less than two-thirds of the total number of flats in the building.

Advising in relation to collective enfranchisement

9.3.22.   The first step is for the solicitor to find out whether the tenants and the building qualify under the Act. Information relating to these matters can be obtained by the service of various notices under section 11 of the Act:

    (a)   on the immediate landlord (or person receiving rent on his behalf) to obtain the name and address of the freeholder and any superior leasehold interest;

    (b)   on the freeholder to obtain the name and address of every person who is a tenant of the whole or any part of the building;

    (c)   on the freeholder and/or other tenants to acquire information reasonably required in relation to the enfranchisement claim (e.g. as to how many other tenants qualify).

9.3.23.   Service of these notices does not commit the tenant(s) to proceed and apart from payment for copies of documents the tenants are not required to pay for the provision of this information by the landlord. The landlord must respond to this request for information within 28 days. The tenants have a right to inspect and take copies of documents which might reasonably be required in connection with the enfranchisement claim (e.g. the landlord's title deeds). The landlord is obliged to disclose to the tenant(s) whether he has received initial notices under the Act from any other person.

9.3.24. Having established that the tenants do qualify under the Act an RTE company must be formed and notice served by that company to all the tenants inviting their participation in the enfranchisement.

Costs of enfranchisement

9.3.25. Taking any further steps towards enfranchisement is inevitably going to commit the tenants to the payments of their own solicitor's costs and also the reasonable costs of the landlord. Other expenses, e.g. in connection with the preparation of plans, valuation of the premises, the setting up of a company to purchase the freehold and possibly the expense of a court action to enforce the tenants' rights, will also be incurred. The tenants should be fully advised of the potential liability to costs and an arrangement for the payments of these costs by the qualifying tenants should be made before the matter proceeds further.

Plans

9.3.26. If the tenants decide to proceed with their claim, a plan of the premises will be needed to accompany their initial notice. It may be necessary to have this plan prepared by a surveyor.

Valuation

9.3.27. The provisions for assessment of the price which the tenants have to pay for the freehold are complex and advice will be needed from a surveyor. An estimate of the price which the tenants may have to pay to acquire the freehold should be obtained from a suitably qualified surveyor at an early stage in the transaction to ensure that the tenants collectively will be able to afford to proceed with the transaction.

The initial notice

9.3.28. To exercise rights under the Act the RTE company must serve an initial notice on the reversioner under section 13 of the Act (as revealed in answer to the enquiries noted in K9.3.22). In practice the reason many tenants seek to pursue their rights under the Act is because the landlord fails to carry out its responsibilities and upon enquiry it cannot be located (or identified). The Act contains provisions which enable tenants to apply to the court for a declaration that the reversioner (or one or more of the reversioners) need not be served with a purchase notice and to apply for a vesting order.[6] The section 13 initial notice must be in writing and may be served by post. The Act prescribes the contents of the notice but not its form. Printed forms are available from law stationers. It must:

(a) specify the premises with a plan;

(b) contain a statement of the grounds on which eligibility rests;

(c) specify other freehold or leasehold interests (if any) to be acquired;

(d)   state which flats (if any) are subject to mandatory leaseback provisions;

(e)   specify the proposed purchase price of the freehold and any other interest specified in the notice;

(f)   give the full names of all the qualifying tenants together with details of their leases;

(g)   specify which tenants satisfy the residence qualification and how this is achieved;

(h)   give the name and address of the RTE company;

(i)   specify a date by which the landlord must respond with his counter-notice (not less than two months).

9.3.29.   The initial notice must be registered as an estate contract against the reversioner's title. The right arising under the notice cannot be an overriding interest under Land Registration Act 2002, Scheds. 1 and 3 (interests of persons in actual occupation). A second notice cannot be served while a previously served notice is in force. If the notice is withdrawn (or is deemed to be withdrawn) no further notice can be served for 12 months. Once given, the notice remains in force until a binding contract is entered into or the notice is withdrawn or deemed to be withdrawn. Schedule 3, para. 15 of the Act contains provisions to overcome technical defects in the notice.

RTE company

9.3.30.   The initial notice must specify the name and address of an RTE company through which negotiations for the acquisition of the freehold interest will be conducted and in whose name the freehold interest will ultimately be vested.

Landlord's rights and obligations when an initial notice is served

9.3.31.   Once notice has been served on the reversioner he has the immediate right of access to the premises for the purposes of valuation and to require evidence from the RTE company of title to the qualifying tenants' leases. The RTE company must respond to this request from the landlord within 21 days in default of which the notice is deemed to be withdrawn. The landlord is required to serve a counter-notice on the RTE company within the time limit specified in the initial notice (not less than two months).[7] The counter-notice must either admit or deny the tenants' claim and, if the claim is denied, give the grounds of opposition.[8]

Subsequent procedure

9.3.32.   After service of the landlord's counter-notice, and assuming that the matter is to proceed, negotiations will then ensue between the RTE company and the reversioner for the contract and then for completion of the acquisition. The form of the conveyance is prescribed by section 34 and Schedule 7. Provided the purchase price is paid to the landlord's lender, the property is discharged from the landlord's mortgage.[9] If the landlord fails to serve a counter-notice within the time limit stated in the initial notice (being not less than two months), the tenants may apply to the court within six months for the terms of the acquisition to be determined. If a counter-notice is served and agreement cannot be reached on the terms of the acquisition, an application can be made for a leasehold valuation tribunal to determine the matters in dispute. Any such application must be made not later than the period of six months beginning with the date on which the counter-notice was given to the nominee purchaser.[10]

The Act contains no provisions enabling the time limits prescribed within it to be extended.

Individual acquisition of a long lease

Nature of the right

9.3.33. The tenant has the right to be granted a new lease to expire 90 years after expiry of the existing lease. The rent under the new lease is to be a peppercorn. A premium is payable for the grant.[11] The new lease takes effect immediately in substitution for the tenant's existing lease. This right is available irrespective of the rights to collective enfranchisement.

Entitlement to extension

9.3.34. The right to an extension applies to a qualifying tenant (as defined above) who has had the lease vested in him for at least the previous two years.[12] Tenants who own three or more flats are not excluded in this case.

Landlord's defences

9.3.35. The landlord can oppose the tenant's request on the following grounds:

(a) that the tenant's existing lease is due to expire within five years; and

(b) that the landlord intends to demolish/reconstruct the property and would be unable to do so without being given possession of the premises.[13]

Terms of new lease

9.3.36. The terms of the new lease will be the same as the existing lease except that the new rent is a peppercorn. The new lease takes effect immediately and is for a period which comprises the residue remaining on the old lease plus a further 90 years. Service charge provisions are to be included. The new lease will also contain a statement that the lease has been granted under the Act. Options which were included in the original lease will not be included in the new lease. The new lease will also contain a modification of the landlord's liability under his covenants and modifications to reflect defects in the existing lease. The new lease will include the landlord's right to apply to the court for possession for redevelopment purposes during the last 12 months of the original term or the last five years of the extension, subject to compensation being payable to the tenant.

Premium

9.3.37. The amount of the premium payable by the tenant is the aggregate of:

    (a)   the diminution in the value of the landlord's interest;

    (b)   where the unexpired term of the tenant's existing lease does not exceed 80 years, 50% of the marriage value;

    (c)   compensation to landlord.

Effect of grant of new lease

9.3.38. The grant of a new lease does not preclude a later application for collective enfranchisement. A further claim for another new lease can be brought in relation to any lease granted; subject to this, no security of tenure provisions apply once the original term date has passed.

Acting for a buyer of an individual flat

9.3.39. When acting for a buyer who is buying an existing lease which potentially qualifies under the Act, consideration should be given to raising enquiries of the seller to establish:

    (a)   whether the flat and the lease qualify under the Act;

    (b)   how many qualifying flats and qualifying tenants there are in the block;

    (c)   whether and when any initial notice has been served by an RTE company and if so how far negotiations have reached (a copy of the notice should be requested if not already supplied by the seller's solicitor);

    (d)   whether any steps have been taken by the seller to acquire an extension of his lease under the Act.

1. See the various commencement orders: SI 2002/1912; 2002/3012; 2003/1986; 2003/2377.
2. Leasehold Reform, Housing and Urban Development Act 1993, s.101. Considered in *Cadogan* v. *McGirk* [1996] 3 EG 175 in which a room on the 6th floor was not held to be part of a flat on the 2nd floor.
3. Leasehold Reform, Housing and Urban Development Act 1993, s.5.
4. As to the correct approach to this calculation see *Indiana Investments Ltd* v. *Taylor* [2004] 50 EG 86.
5. See Leasehold Reform, Housing and Urban Development Act 1993, s.4. As to the interpretation of this provision with respect to a trust see *Slamon* v. *Planchon* [2004] EWCA Civ 799.
6. Leasehold Reform, Housing and Urban Development Act 1993, ss.26 and 27.
7. The counter-notice must comply with the requirements of the Leasehold Reform Housing and Urban Development Act 1993, s.21. Where it contains an alternative proposed purchase price this must be made in good faith but does not necessarily have to be a realistic price. See *9 Cornwall Crescent London Ltd* v. *Kensington and Chelsea LBC* [2005] EWCA Civ 324.

8. Failure to specify one of these options will render the counter-notice invalid; see *Burman* v. *Mount Cook Land* [2001] 48 EG 128, CA. Failure to give a counter-notice will entitle the RTE company to apply to the court and acquire the freehold (s.25(1)) and see *Willingale* v. *Globalgrange* [2000] 18 EG 152, CA. The form of notice is specified by the Leasehold Reform (Collective Enfranchisement) (Counter-notices) (England) Regulations 2002 (SI 2002/3208). Failure to adhere to the form of counter-notice will not always be fatal, e.g. failure to declare there was no estate management scheme affecting the property; see *7 Strathray Gardens* v. *Pointstar Shipping and Finance* [2004] EWCA Civ 1669. It is possible for the tenant to waive the requirement for a counter-notice to be served. See *Latifi* v. *Colherne Freehold Ltd* [2003] 12 EG 130.
9. Leasehold Reform, Housing and Urban Development Act 1993, Sched.8, para.2.
10. For details see Leasehold Reform Housing and Urban Development Act 1993, s.24.
11. A tenant must serve a notice specifying the premium he proposes to pay which must be genuine and not just a nominal figure: *Cadogan* v. *Morris* [1999] 1 EGLR 59; *Mount Cook Land Ltd* v. *Rosen* [2003] 10 EG 165.
12. A tenant of a block of flats (each underlet on short leases) may be the 'qualifying tenant' of each flat and therefore entitled to new long leases in respect of all the individual flats. See *Maurice* v. *Holloware Products Ltd* [2005] EWHC 815.
13. Leasehold Reform, Housing and Urban Development Act 1993, s.47. See, e.g. *Majorstake Ltd* v. *Curtis* [2006] EWCA Civ 1171.

9.4. Landlord and Tenant Act 1987

9.4.1. Landlord and Tenant Act 1987 (as amended) gives the tenants of certain premises the right of first refusal where the landlord intends to dispose of his interest in the premises. The Act applies where the landlord of premises which contain two or more flats held by qualifying tenants proposes to make a relevant disposal of the premises and provides that the landlord must first offer to make a disposal to a nominee of the qualifying tenants.

Premises

9.4.2. The provisions of the Act apply to premises consisting of the whole or part of a building which contains two or more flats held by qualifying tenants provided that the number of such flats exceeds 50% of the total number of flats in the building. Since the Act defines a tenancy as including an agreement for a tenancy, it seems that the Act can apply to new blocks as soon as the landlord has exchanged agreements for lease in relation to 50% of the flats. The definition of a flat includes maisonettes and houses which have been converted into flats as well as purpose-built blocks. Premises which are used partly for non-residential purposes may be within the Act subject to a measurement limit. Thus premises which consist of a shop on the ground floor with two or more flats on the upper floors may qualify under the Act provided that the internal floor area of the shop represents less than 50% of the internal area of the whole building[1] and a nominee of the qualifying tenants who purchased the reversion of the flats would also therefore become the landlord of the shop. Where a landlord owns several blocks of flats with communal grounds on an estate development, each block may or may not be a separate building depending on the circumstances.[2]

Landlord

9.4.3. For the purposes of the Act a landlord is the immediate landlord of the qualifying tenants, or the superior landlord if the immediate landlord is himself a tenant under a tenancy for less than seven years or one terminable by his landlord within the first seven years.[3] Certain landlords are exempt and the provisions of the Act do not apply to, e.g. local authorities, urban development corporations or registered housing associations.[4] Resident landlords are also exempted from the provisions of the Act where the three following conditions are satisfied:

(a)   the premises are not a purpose-built block of flats;

(b)   the landlord occupies a flat in the premises as his only or principal residence;

(c)   the landlord has been in occupation for the last 12 months.

Qualifying tenants

9.4.4.   A tenant of a flat (including a company tenant) is a qualifying tenant unless his tenancy is:

(a)   a protected shorthold tenancy;

(b)   a business tenancy within Part II Landlord and Tenant Act 1954;

(c)   an assured tenancy or an assured agricultural occupancy;

(d)   a tenancy terminable on the cessation of the tenant's employment;

(e)   of the flat and by virtue of one or more non-excluded tenancies he is also the tenant of at least two other flats contained in the same building;

(f)   a sub-tenancy and his landlord is a qualifying tenant of the flat in question.

Relevant disposal

9.4.5.   The word 'disposal' is defined in Landlord and Tenant Act 1987, s.4(3) as meaning a disposal whether by the creation or the transfer of an estate or interest. It includes the surrender of a tenancy and the grant of an option or right of pre-emption but excludes a disposal by will or under the intestacy rules.

9.4.6.   A 'relevant disposal' is defined by Landlord and Tenant Act 1987, s.4(1) as a disposal by the landlord of any estate or interest (legal or equitable) in premises to which the Act applies, including a disposal of an interest in any common parts of the premises, other than the grant of a tenancy of a single flat with or without any appurtenant premises and subject to certain exceptions which are listed in K9.4.8.

9.4.7.   A contract to sell is itself a relevant disposal. Further a disposal includes a disposal by the landlord's lender in selling or leasing the property, but not the creation of a mortgage. A conditional contract which is subject to the notice provisions being complied with at a later date is not valid.

Exceptions to 'relevant disposal'

9.4.8. By Landlord and Tenant Act 1987, s.4, the following are excluded from the definition of a relevant disposal:

    (a) a disposal:

        (i)   of an interest of a beneficiary in settled land;

        (ii) by way of the creation of a mortgage;

        (iii) of any incorporeal hereditament;

    (b) a disposal to a trustee in bankruptcy or liquidator;

    (c) a disposal in pursuance of an order under Matrimonial Causes Act 1973, ss.24 or 24A, or Inheritance (Provision for Family and Dependants) Act 1975, s.2 or similar legislative provisions;

    (d) a disposal in pursuance of a compulsory purchase order or agreement in lieu;

    (e) a disposal of any interest by virtue of Leasehold Reform, Housing and Urban Development Act 1993;

    (f) a gift to a member of the landlord's family as defined in section 4(5) or to a charity;

    (g) a disposal of functional land by one charity to another as defined in section 60;

    (h) a disposal of trust property in connection with the appointment or discharge of a trustee;

    (i) a disposal between members of the same family provided that at least one of the original owners still retains an interest;

    (j) a disposal in pursuance of an option or right of pre-emption binding on the landlord before the tenant's right of first refusal arises;

    (k) a surrender of a tenancy in pursuance of any obligation contained in it;

    (l) a disposal to the Crown;

    (m) where the landlord is a body corporate, a disposal to an associated company which has been an associated company of that body for at least two years.

The landlord's offer

9.4.9. Where a landlord proposes to make a relevant disposal of premises to which the Act applies, he must follow the procedure set out in section 5 of the Act which requires him to serve notice on the qualifying tenants of the flats in the premises. Different types of proposed disposals require different prescribed information to be inserted into the notice as set out in s.5A (normal sale by contract), s.5B (sale at auction), s.5C (grant of options and pre-emption rights), s.5D (sale proceeding to completion without contract), and s.5E (wholly or partly for non-monetary consideration). In outline, a notice served under s.5A must:

(a) set out the principal terms proposed including the property and the estate or interest to be disposed of (the 'protected interest') and the consideration required;

(b) state that it constitutes an offer to dispose of the property on those terms which may be accepted by the requisite number of qualifying tenants (the offer is deemed by the Act to be 'subject to contract');

(c) specify a period for acceptance being at least two months beginning with the date of service; and

(d) specify a further period of at least two months beginning with the end of the period of acceptance within which a person or persons may be nominated to take the landlord's interest.

The tenant's acceptance

9.4.10. A tenant's acceptance may take the following forms:

(a) The landlord's offer can be accepted by a simple majority of the qualifying tenants on the basis of one vote per flat let to qualifying tenants in the building. The tenants must nominate a person to deal with the landlord within the periods for acceptance and nomination specified in the landlord's notice.

(b) If a management company structure run by the tenants is already in place in the building, the management company may be nominated to purchase the landlord's interest. In other cases the tenants may consider forming a new company for this purpose.

(c) Acceptance by the qualifying tenants must be by written notice served on the landlord within the period specified in the offer. A single notice is served on behalf of all the accepting tenants which specifies the names and addresses of all the persons serving the notice. If no acceptance notice is served within the acceptance period the landlord is free, for a period of 12 months, to sell to any person at not less than the price offered and on the same terms.[5]

Effects of acceptance

9.4.11. Once the acceptance notice has been served the landlord cannot dispose of the interest described in his offer to anyone other than the tenants' nominees during the 'protected period'. The procedure by which the tenants acquire their landlord's interest is covered by the Act and depends on the nature of the proposed disposal, e.g. sale by auction or not. There are further provisions to deal with the situation where the consideration did not consist wholly or partly of money and to deal with the situation where the landlord requires the consent of a third party to the disposal.[6] The 'protected period' is, in outline, the period beginning with the date of service of the acceptance notice and expiring at the end of the period for nominating a transferee specified in the offer notice (plus a further period covering the subsequent procedure if a transferee is nominated).[7] If no nomination is made the landlord may dispose of his interest during the 12 months following expiry of the nomination period provided that the price is not less than that stated in the offer notice and the other terms of the disposal correspond with the terms of the offer to the tenants. If no disposal occurs within this 12-month period, the landlord must serve a new offer notice on the tenants before attempting to dispose of the property. Acceptance of the offer does not create a binding contract since the offer itself is only subject to contract.

Rejection

9.4.12. If the tenants do not serve an acceptance notice within the period specified for acceptance in the landlord's offer notice or such longer period as may be agreed, the landlord may dispose of his interest during the 12 months following the expiry of that period subject to the same conditions outlined in K9.4.11.

Disposals in breach of the Act

9.4.13. A new landlord who acquires a reversionary interest in flats from a seller who is in breach of the provisions of the Act can be required (on request made by a majority of the qualifying tenants) to supply details of the transaction to a nominee of the qualifying tenants. The qualifying tenants, by serving a purchase notice on the new landlord, can require him to dispose of his interest to a nominee of the qualifying tenants on the same terms as he acquired his interest. If the new landlord's interest is mortgaged, the property is discharged from the mortgage provided that the nominee pays the purchase price to the lender (even if the purchase price is less than the amount of the mortgage). A landlord who disposes of provisions in breach of the Act is also guilty of a criminal offence.[8]

Advice to proposed buyers of reversionary interests

9.4.14. A person who intends to purchase a reversionary interest direct from a landlord must before exchange of contracts check:

(a) whether or not the premises fall within the scope of the Act; and if they do

(b) whether the landlord and any relevant previous owners[9] have served notice on the qualifying tenants as required by the Act; and if so

(c) that either the tenants have rejected the landlord's offer or that the time limits for acceptance have expired and the purchase transaction to the buyer can be completed within 12 months of the expiry of the acceptance period; and

(d) the terms on which the buyer is buying are similar to the terms of the offer which was made to the tenants.

The Standard Commercial Property Conditions contain optional provisions in Part 2 section C providing for warranties covering some of these points (see Appendix V.10).

9.4.15. Section 18 Landlord and Tenant Act 1987 enables a prospective buyer to serve notice on tenants to ensure that rights of first refusal do not arise where it appears to the buyer that the disposal might be a relevant disposal of premises to which the Act applies. The notice must:

(a) set out the principal terms of the proposed disposal;

(b) invite the recipient to serve a notice stating:

(i) whether an offer notice has been served;

(ii) if not, whether he is aware of any reason why he is not entitled to such a notice; and

(iii) whether he would wish to exercise any right of first refusal; and

(c) set out the effect of section 18(3) which says that, provided notices have been served on at least 80% of the tenants, and not more than 50% have replied within two months, or more than 50% have indicated that they do not regard themselves as entitled to an offer notice or would not wish to exercise a right of first refusal, the premises shall be treated as premises to which the Act does not apply.

Auctions

9.4.16. The notice procedures set out in K9.4.9 are modified where the landlord intends to dispose of the property at auction. In outline, such notice must be served on the tenants between four to six months before the auction, giving the tenants at least two months to respond to the notice.[10] The tenants' nominee then has the opportunity to take over the auction contract, after the auction takes place, from the successful bidder. The Standard Commercial Property Conditions contain optional provisions in Part 2 section C covering this (see Appendix V.10).

1. This percentage is subject to alteration by Landlord and Tenant Act 1987, s.1.
2. A 'building' can comprise more than one structure if the occupants of the qualifying flats share the use of the same appurtenant premises; see *Long Acre Securities Ltd* v. *Karet* [2004] 11 EG 138.
3. Landlord and Tenant Act 1987, s.2.
4. *Ibid.*, s.58.
5. *Ibid.*, s.7.
6. *Ibid.*, s.8A to s.8E.
7. *Ibid.*, s.8A.
8. *Ibid.*, s.10A
9. Tenants have broadly six months from receiving a statutory notice from the landlord in respect of a disposal to serve a purchase notice requiring the landlord to transfer the property to them. If no such notice has been served time will not have started to run. Therefore, a purchaser of premises to which the Act potentially applies is concerned with all relevant disposals since the Act came into force (1 February 1988). See Landlord and Tenant Act 1987, s.12B.
10. *Ibid.*, s.5B.

9.5. Compulsory acquisition by tenants of landlord's interest

9.5.1. Where a receiver or manager has been appointed under Part II Landlord and Tenant Act 1987 (see K6.10.1) but this remedy proves to be inadequate, the majority of the qualifying tenants may in certain circumstances apply to the court under Part III Landlord and Tenant Act 1987 for an acquisition order which allows them to acquire their landlord's interest without his consent.[1]

1. An application can also be made if the landlord is in breach of, broadly, his management obligations in respect of the premises under the leases. See Landlord and Tenant Act 1987, s.29.

9.6. Registered social landlords

9.6.1. Certain tenants of a registered social landlord have the right to acquire the dwelling of which they are tenants under Housing Act 1996, s.16. The purchase price may be discounted by the landlord and similar provisions relating to the repayment of discount apply as to public sector tenants (K9.1).

K10. Liability on covenants in leases

10.1. Introduction

10.1.1. The general rule that an original tenant remains liable under his covenants throughout the term of the lease has been abolished by Landlord and Tenant (Covenants) Act 1995 but only in respect of new tenancies (as defined by the 1995 Act). The principle that only a party to a contract can sue or be sued on it has also been abrogated by Contracts (Rights of Third Parties) Act 1999 which affects leases and assignments made on or after 11 May 2000.

New tenancies

10.1.2. A new tenancy is one which is granted on or after 1 January 1996, except those tenancies granted pursuant to:

(a) an agreement made before 1 January 1996; or

(b) a court order made before 1 January 1996; or

(c) an option granted before 1 January 1996.

10.1.3. An overriding lease granted under section 19 Landlord and Tenant (Covenants) Act 1995 (e.g. granted to a former tenant who has discharged the liability of a subsequent assignee) takes its status from that of the original lease.

10.1.4. Some leases granted on or after 1 January 1996 will not be new tenancies. Such a lease should make this clear by including a statement that the lease is not a new lease within the provisions of the 1995 Act.

10.1.5. A variation of a lease sometimes results in a deemed surrender and re-grant, e.g. where:

(a) extra land is included in the tenancy in return for additional rent;[1] or

(b) there is an extension of the term.[2]

The date of the surrender and re-grant will determine whether the lease deemed to be re-granted is a new one.

10.1.6. K10.2–K10.5 inclusive deal with old tenancies (i.e. those to which the 1995 Act does not apply). K10.6 applies to all leases whenever granted. K10.7 onwards deal with new tenancies to which the provisions of the 1995 Act apply.

1. *Jenkin R Lewis* v. *Kerman* [1971] Ch 477.
2. *Baker* v. *Merckel* [1960] 1 QB 657. See also *Friends Provident Life Office* v. *British Railways Board* [1996] 1 All ER 336.

10.2. Old tenancies – liability of original landlord and tenant

10.2.1. Unless released by the landlord the original tenant is liable on all the express and implied covenants in the lease for breaches committed at any time during the term of the lease. His liability is to the landlord for the time being since on a transfer of the reversion all rights of action attached to the reversion pass to the transferee including the right to sue for an existing breach of covenant.[1] The liability of the original tenant to the transferee of the reversion exists even though the tenant assigned the lease before the transfer of the reversion.[2]

10.2.2. The continuing liability of the original tenant may have serious consequences for him if an assignee of the lease cannot meet his obligations to the landlord. The original tenant remains liable for rent due after disclaimer of the lease on an assignee's insolvency,[3] and the release by the landlord of an assignee's surety does not release the original tenant since the latter has primary liability.[4] Although the landlord will normally only pursue the original tenant when the current assignee is unable to fulfil his commitments under the lease, the landlord's right of action against the original tenant is not confined to this situation.[5] The original tenant's liability does not, however, extend to arrears of rent accrued by an assignee during a statutory continuation of the term under Landlord and Tenant Act 1954, Pt. II unless the original tenant's covenant is expressed widely enough to cover this liability.[6]

10.2.3. The original landlord remains contractually bound to the original tenant throughout the term of the lease.[7] If an original landlord is unable through his own act or default (e.g. by transferring the reversion to a third party) to carry out an obligation imposed on him by the lease the landlord may be liable in damages to the tenant.[8]

1. Law of Property Act 1925, s.141 and see *Re King* [1963] Ch 459; *London and County (A & D) Ltd* v. *Wilfred Sportsman Ltd* [1971] Ch 764.

2. *Arlesford Trading Co. Ltd* v. *Servansingh* [1971] 3 All ER 113.
3. *Warnford Investments* v. *Duckworth* [1979] Ch 127; *Hindcastle Ltd* v. *Barbara Attenborough Associates Ltd* [1996] 2 WLR 262; and *Active Estates Ltd* v. *Parness* [2002] 36 EG 147.
4. *Allied London Investments Ltd* v. *Hambro Life Assurance Ltd* (1985) 50 P&CR 207.
5. *Norwich Union Life Insurance Society* v. *Low Profile Fashions Ltd* [1992] 21 EG 104.
6. *London City Corporation* v. *Fell; Herbert Duncan* v. *Cluttons (A Firm)* [1992] NPC 150, CA.
7. *Stuart* v. *Joy* [1904] 1 KB 362.
8. See, e.g. *Eagon* v. *Dent* [1965] 3 All ER 334 where a landlord sold the reversion to a third party and the original tenant who failed in his attempt to exercise an unregistered option against the buyer of the reversion recovered damages from the original landlord for breach of covenant.

10.3. Old tenancies – landlord and tenant for the time being

10.3.1. The relationship between a transferee of the reversion and the tenant for the time being and between an assignee of the lease and the landlord for the time being rests on the doctrine of privity of estate. Liability under this doctrine extends to breaches of covenants which touch and concern the land committed by a transferee of the reversion while he holds the reversion and by an assignee of the lease while the lease is vested in him. This means that an assignee may be liable to the landlord for a breach of covenant giving rise to continuing liability, committed by the assignor.

10.3.2. The doctrine embraces those covenants in the lease which affect the land demised and which also govern the landlord and tenant relationship as such, e.g. payment of rent or repairing covenants. While most covenants in leases will fall within the doctrine, including an option to renew the lease, it does not extend to purely personal obligations or to collateral obligations such as an option to purchase the reversion.[1]

10.3.3. An assignee of the lease will not be liable to the landlord for breaches of covenant committed after the date of an assignment of the lease by him to a third party unless, as is commonly required, he has entered into direct covenants with the landlord, in which case his liability will continue throughout the remainder of the term. In this respect the liability of an assignee is no different from that of an original tenant.

Indemnity

10.3.4. Irrespective of K10.3.3, an assignee of the lease may be called upon to indemnify his assignor in respect of any breach of covenant committed after the date of the assignment to him regardless of whether he has parted with the lease. On the transfer of a registered lease such an indemnity covenant is implied whether or not value was given for the assignment.[2] A similar indemnity provision is implied on the assignment of an unregistered lease, but only where value has been given for the assignment.[3] If the assignment of an unregistered lease is to be made for no valuable consideration an express indemnity covenant will be required by the assignor. At common law an original tenant who is sued by the landlord for a breach of covenant committed by an assignee can pursue a direct claim against that assignee.[4] Standard Condition 4.6.4 and Standard Commercial Property Condition 6.6.4 require the purchase deed to contain an express indemnity covenant except where one is implied by law. A contractual exclusion of Law of Property Act 1925, s.77 does not negate the underlying common law obligation to reimburse.[5]

1. The benefit of an option to purchase the reversion may, however, pass to an assignee of the lease by assignment (see K13).
2. Land Registration Act 2002, Sched.12, para.20. The nature of the liability of the transferee is one of indemnity, not guarantee, and he will remain liable despite any variation in liability of the original tenant: *Scottish & Newcastle plc* v. *Raguz* [2003] 33 EG 62.
3. Law of Property Act 1925, s.77.
4. *Moule* v. *Garrett* (1872) LR & Exch 101.
5. *Re Healing Research Trustee Co. Ltd* [1992] 2 All ER 481.

10.4. Old tenancies – liability between head-landlord and sub-tenant

10.4.1. No privity of estate exists between a head-landlord and a sub-tenant although a contractual relationship will exist between them if the sub-tenant has entered into direct covenants with the head-landlord (e.g. in a licence to sub-let). The sub-tenant will in any event be directly liable to the head-landlord on restrictive covenants in the head-lease of which the former had notice when he took his sub-lease.[1] The sub-tenant is entitled to call for production of the head-lease on grant of the sub-lease to him.[2] Also the head landlord may have the right to sue under Contracts (Rights of Third Parties) Act 1999 (see K1.11).

1. In the case of new tenancies a restrictive covenant is enforceable against a sub-tenant by virtue of Landlord and Tenant (Covenants) Act 1995, s.3(5).
2. The rules relating to deduction of title are set out in K1.12.

10.5. Old tenancies – guarantors and sureties

10.5.1. The liability of a person who guarantees the performance of the tenant's obligations under the lease only arises if the original debtor defaults, but that liability may be extended by the terms of the guarantee to primary liability. The guarantor will have a continuing liability even though the lease has been disclaimed and the tenant's obligations terminated.[1]

10.5.2. The benefit of a tenant's surety's covenant passes automatically to a buyer of the reversion,[2] as does the benefit of a surety's covenant to accept a lease to replace one disclaimed on the tenant's insolvency.[3]

10.5.3. Where an assignee of the lease goes into liquidation and the landlord sues the original tenant for arrears of rent, the latter can pursue an action against the assignee's surety for reimbursement. Although both are liable to the landlord the surety's obligation is prior to that of the original tenant.[4] However, there is no obligation on the landlord to take action against the other parties before proceeding against the original tenant.[5]

1. *Hindcastle Ltd* v. *Barbara Attenborough Associates Ltd* [1996] 2 WLR 262; and *Active Estates Ltd* v. *Parness* [2002] 36 EG 147.
2. *P & A Swift Investments (a firm)* v. *Combined English Stores Group plc* [1989] AC 643. This applies even after the lease is disclaimed following insolvency: *Scottish Widows plc* v. *Tripipatkul* [2003] NPC 106.
3. *Coronation Street Industrial Properties* v. *Ingall Industries plc* [1989] 1 All ER 979.
4. *Becton Dickinson UK Ltd* v. *Zwebner* [1989] QB 208.
5. *Norwich Union Life Insurance Society* v. *Low Profile Fashions Ltd* [1992] 1 EGLR 86.

10.6.   Old and new tenancies – restriction on liability of former tenant or guarantor for rent or service charge

10.6.1.   Where a landlord seeks to recover a 'fixed charge' from a former tenant or guarantor he must serve a written notice on the tenant or guarantor under section 17 Landlord and Tenant (Covenants) Act 1995 within six months of the charge becoming due and in it inform the tenant or guarantor that the charge is now due, and that the landlord intends to recover the sum specified in the notice plus, where payable, interest. The notice must comply with the Notices Regulations made pursuant to Landlord and Tenant (Covenants) Act 1995.[1]

Fixed charge

10.6.2.   A fixed charge is rent, or a service charge as defined by section 18 Landlord and Tenant Act 1985 (but without the statutory restrictions applicable to residential property) or any other liquidated sum payable in the event of a breach of covenant.

Effect of failure to comply

10.6.3.   A landlord who fails to comply will not be able to recover the amounts from either the former tenant or a guarantor.

Amount of fixed charge unknown

10.6.4.   The landlord can only recover the amount stated in the notice. If the rent is in the process of being reviewed, the notice must state that the liability may be greater than that specified, and once the amount is known a further notice must be served claiming the increased amount within three months.[2] The Court of Appeal has held[3] that the correct interpretation of the effect of section 17 is that the landlord must serve a section 17 notice on former tenants or guarantors within six months of a review date where the review remains outstanding. This applies even though at that point there may be no arrears. If this is not done, the landlord will not be able to claim balancing payments from them once the amount of any increase has been settled, should this be necessary. Further, a section 17 notice must be served within six months of every rent review date until the amount is determined and paid.

Restriction of liability of former tenant or his guarantor where tenancy subsequently varied

The effect of variations at common law

10.6.5. A variation may not bind the original tenant following the decision in *Friends Provident Life Office* v. *British Railways Board.*[4] If an assignee agrees a variation with the landlord, the variation does not alter the terms of the contract between the original parties to the lease. The original tenant is not released from liability, but the liability remains governed by the terms of the contract which he entered when he was granted the lease.

Section 18 Landlord and Tenant (Covenants) Act 1995

10.6.6. Section 18 relieves a former tenant of liability for any amount which is referable to a relevant variation made on or after 1 January 1996. A relevant variation need not be contained in a deed. It is a variation which occurs where either a landlord has an absolute right to refuse it, or the lease has been altered after the assignment so as to deprive the landlord of a right of absolute refusal (e.g. a lease which prohibits a change of use without consent). To the extent that a guarantor remains liable despite the variation he will nevertheless not be liable to pay any amount referable to a relevant variation.

Right of former tenant to overriding lease

10.6.7. A person discharging a fixed charge has a right to require the landlord to grant him an overriding lease under Landlord and Tenant (Covenants) Act 1995, s.19. An overriding lease is a reversionary lease granted for the remainder of the term usually plus a short term (e.g. a few days). Its terms are broadly identical to those of the relevant tenancy. It does not contain personal covenants or covenants which are spent, and covenants framed by reference to the beginning of the tenancy, e.g. repairing covenants, should be adjusted.

10.6.8. To obtain an overriding lease the tenant must serve on the landlord a written request specifying the payment and claiming the right to the lease. The request must be made at the time of making the payment or within 12 months. The landlord must grant the lease within a reasonable time. The tenant has to deliver a counterpart and is liable for the landlord's reasonable costs. There is no obligation to grant an overriding lease if the original tenancy has been determined, or if an overriding lease has been granted or a request for one is still outstanding. Two or more requests for overriding leases made on the same day are dealt with in the sequence in which the liability was incurred with a tenant having prior right to a guarantor. A tenant may withdraw his request or may fail to respond to a request from the landlord to take a lease within a reasonable time. In either case, the tenant will be liable for the landlord's costs. A request may be protected by the entry of a notice in registered land (or as an estate contract in unregistered land).

10.6.9. It is possible to have tiers of overriding leases. Whether an overriding lease is a new lease or an old one depends upon the status of the original lease. It should state that it is an overriding lease granted under section 19 Landlord and Tenant (Covenants) Act 1995 and whether or not it is a new tenancy for the purpose of section 1. Any right arising from such a request cannot be an overriding interest.[5] A landlord who fails to grant a reversionary lease may face a claim in tort for breach of statutory duty. A tenant who fails to deliver a counterpart lease cannot exercise rights under the overriding lease. These provisions are binding on mortgagees.

1. SI 1995/2964.
2. Landlord and Tenant (Covenants) Act 1995, s.17(4).
3. *Scottish & Newcastle plc* v. *Raguz* [2007] EWCA 150. The notice should be in Form 1 of Landlord and Tenant (Covenants) Act 1995 (Notices) Regulations 1995. Once the final amount has been determined a further notice in Form 2 of these regulations should be served within three months.
4. [1996] 1 All ER 336; and *Beegas Nominees* v. *BHP Petroleum Ltd* [1998] 31 EG 96.
5. Landlord and Tenant (Covenants) Act 1995, s.20(6) as amended by Land Registration Act 2002, Sched.11, para.33(4).

10.7. New tenancies – covenants to which Landlord and Tenant (Covenants) Act 1995 applies

10.7.1. The 1995 Act applies to all covenants whether they are express, implied or imposed by law and whether or not they 'touch and concern the land'.[1] Most covenants in a lease do touch and concern the land, but not, for example, a covenant by a landlord to repay a deposit to the tenant.[2]

Transmission of the benefit and burden

10.7.2. An assignee under a new tenancy acquires the benefit and takes the burden of all the covenants. The assignor remains liable, and can sue, for breaches occurring before the assignment is made. However, the assignee is not liable in relation to any time prior to the assignment to him, so he is not liable for once-and-for-all breaches of covenant committed by the assignor. An assignor may, however, assign the benefit of a right.[3] The covenants are enforceable by and against any person entitled to the rents and profits and also by and against a mortgagee in possession.

10.7.3. The exceptions are:

(a) personal covenants;

(b) a covenant which does not bind the assignor immediately before the assignment, for example, one that is of limited duration or which has been released;

(c) a covenant which relates to a part of the demised premises which is not included in the assignment;

(d) a covenant which needs to be protected by registration and has not been so protected (e.g. an option).

The landlord's right of re-entry

10.7.4. A landlord's right of re-entry attaches to the reversion and passes on an assignment of it.[4]

1. But not to those imposed pursuant to ss.35, 155 or para.1 of Sched.6A Housing Act 1985, or paras.1 or 3 of Sched.2 Housing Associations Act 1985.
2. *Hua Chiao Commercial Bank Ltd* v. *Chiaphua Industries Ltd* [1987] AC 99, PC.
3. Landlord and Tenant (Covenants) Act 1995, s.23(2).
4. *Ibid.*, s.4.

10.8. New tenancies – tenant's release from covenants

10.8.1. A tenant who assigns the lease will be released from the burden and deprived of the benefit of the covenants from the moment the assignment is made. His guarantor is also released to the same extent.[1] The release is only from future observance of the covenants.

10.8.2. The exceptions are:

    (a) an assignment in breach of covenant or by operation of law (e.g. devolution to PRs) is an 'excluded assignment'. The assignor is not released until the next assignment as long as it is not another excluded one;[2]

    (b) a tenant who has entered an authorised guarantee agreement is similarly not released until the next non-excluded assignment (see K10.9).

1. See Landlord and Tenant (Covenants) Act 1995, s.24(2). It may be possible for the guarantor to guarantee the outgoing tenant's liability under any authorised guarantee agreement he may give. The legal effectiveness of such a provision is unclear and is as yet unresolved by judicial authority.
2. *Ibid.*, s.11(2).

10.9. New tenancies – authorised guarantee agreements

10.9.1. Where a lease contains a restriction on assignment, the landlord can, as a condition of his granting consent to the assignment, require the tenant to enter into an agreement which guarantees the performance of the lease covenants by the immediate assignee (called an 'authorised guarantee agreement'). The terms of the proposed authorised guarantee agreement may be set out in the lease.

10.9.2. The agreement:

    (a) can only guarantee the liability of the assignee;

    (b) must cease when that assignee assigns the lease;

    (c) may impose a primary liability;

    (d) is void to the extent that it imposes obligations beyond those permitted;[1]

(e) may require the tenant to accept a new lease where the old one is disclaimed as long as the tenancy is for no longer a period than the original term and its covenants are no more onerous.

Effect of disclaimers, vesting orders and reversionary leases

10.9.3. Where a tenant is granted a lease following disclaimer, or has a vesting order made in his favour under Insolvency Act 1986, or is granted an overriding lease, he may be required to enter a further authorised guarantee agreement on its assignment.

1. Landlord and Tenant (Covenants) Act 1995, s.16(4)(a) and (b), and s.25.

10.10.   New tenancies – landlord's release from covenants

Need to serve notice

10.10.1. The landlord who assigns the reversion may apply for a release by serving a notice on the tenant either before or within four weeks beginning with the date of the assignment.[1] Note that it is possible to agree in the lease that a landlord will be automatically released from liability on assignment.[2] In default of such agreement the statutory notice procedure must be followed.

Contents of notice

10.10.2. The tenant must be told about the proposed assignment or the fact that it has occurred and that the landlord is seeking a release from his covenants.

Tenant's response

10.10.3. A tenant may object to the landlord's release by serving a notice on the landlord within four weeks beginning with the date of service of the landlord's notice.

Role of the court

10.10.4. Unless the objection is withdrawn, the county court will decide whether it is reasonable for the landlord to be released.

Date of release

10.10.5. A landlord's release takes effect from the date of the assignment. Section 3(3A) Landlord and Tenant Act 1985 still applies: therefore the liability of an assigning landlord is preserved until the tenant is notified of the change of landlord.

Subsequent release

10.10.6. A landlord who has not been released may make a fresh application on the next assignment of the reversion. He should, therefore, take an indemnity covenant from his buyer together with a covenant that the buyer will notify the landlord of his intention to re-sell the reversion.

10.10.7. Notices must comply with the Notices Regulations made pursuant to Landlord and Tenant (Covenants) Act 1995.[3]

1. Landlord and Tenant (Covenants) Act 1995, ss.6–8. Careful consideration needs to be given before taking this step in the case of multi-let properties as obtaining the release by only some of the tenants will leave the landlord in an exposed position.
2. *Avonridge Property Co. Ltd* v. *Mashru* [2005] UKHL 70. Such an agreement does not fall foul of the anti-avoidance provisions of Landlord and Tenant (Covenants) Act 1995, s.25.
3. SI 1995/2964.

10.11. New tenancies – assignment of part

10.11.1. The release of the assignor is only in respect of covenants which relate to the part sold except where the assignment is an excluded assignment.

Apportionment of liability

10.11.2. The assignor and the assignee remain bound by 'non-attributable' covenants, e.g. a covenant to pay rent or a service charge which is charged on the whole property, but they can agree between them how the liability is to be borne. The apportionment may bind the other party to the lease if a notice[1] is served either before or within four weeks beginning with the date of the assignment in question on the other party to the lease. The notice must inform him of the proposed assignment or the fact that it has occurred, the prescribed particulars of the agreement, and the request that the apportionment becomes binding on him. The apportionment will be binding if the recipient fails to serve a written notice[1] of objection within four weeks. If he does object, the parties to the agreement may apply to the county court for a declaration that it is reasonable for the apportionment to bind the other party to the lease. The recipient may also indicate consent to the apportionment or may withdraw a notice of objection. An apportionment which becomes binding does so from the date of the assignment.

Forfeiture or disclaimer limited to part only of demised premises

10.11.3. Where the landlord has a right to forfeit or there is a right for a liquidator or trustee in bankruptcy to disclaim a lease and where part only of the demised premises is affected, the forfeiture or disclaimer relates only to that part vested in the defaulting or insolvent tenant and not to the whole lease.[2]

1. The notices must comply with Landlord and Tenant (Covenants) Act 1995 (Notices) Regulations 1995 (SI 1995/2964).
2. Landlord and Tenant (Covenants) Act 1995, s.21.

10.12. New tenancies – exclusion of the 1995 Act

10.12.1. An agreement to exclude, modify or otherwise frustrate the operation of provisions in the 1995 Act is void.[1]

1.   Landlord and Tenant (Covenants) Act 1995, s.25.

10.13. Contracts (Rights of Third Parties) Act 1999

10.13.1. Contracts (Rights of Third Parties) Act 1999 affects leases and assignments made on or after 11 May 2000 and provides that where a contract made between A and B is intended to benefit C (e.g. a sub-tenant or assignee) C may sue on that contract as if he was an original contracting party. C, the third party, must be identified in the contract made between A and B by name, class or description.[1] This will mean that covenants in a head lease may be directly enforceable as between tenants and as between a head-landlord and sub-tenant or head-landlord and an assignee where previously direct enforcement was not possible because of the doctrines of privity of contract and of estate.[2] The right of enforcement is not for the whole contract but just those terms which are made for the benefit of a third party. In practice the Act is commonly disapplied by the terms of the lease.

1.   See e.g. *Avraamides* v. *Colwill* [2006] EWCA Civ 1533.
2.   In the case of new tenancies a restrictive covenant is enforceable against a sub-tenant by virtue of Landlord and Tenant (Covenants) Act 1995, s.3(5).

K11. Assignment of leases

NB: In this section the word 'lease' should be read to include the word 'sub-lease' where appropriate to the context.

11.1. Taking instructions

11.1.1. The information required by the seller's solicitor and buyer's solicitor will be similar to that needed in a freehold transaction (see A1) with the addition of details of the lease to be sold or bought. Of particular importance is the question of whether the landlord's consent to the transaction will be required (see K11.2.6). The seller's solicitor should check his own title, in particular to ensure that no outstanding breaches of covenant exist, before drafting the contract for sale. A home information pack may be required where relevant; see A26.

11.1.2. The length of the residue of the term should be checked. Where the buyer is to obtain a mortgage on the property his lender will usually require that a minimum stated length of the term remains unexpired at the date of acquisition of the buyer's interest in order to provide the lender with adequate security for his loan (see K6.6). A lease with only a few years left unexpired is a wasting asset in the hands of the tenant and particularly in the case of residential property may prove difficult to sell unless the lease can be extended or enfranchised (see K9).

Seller's solicitor

11.1.3. The seller's solicitor should obtain from his client or, if not available from the client, from the landlord:

   (a)   the receipt for the last rent due under the lease;

   (b)   where relevant, evidence of payment of service charge over the past three years including the receipt for the last payment due;

   (c)   details of the insurance of the property including the receipt for the last premium due;

   (d)   details of any fee payable to a management company on the transfer of the lease (mainly applicable to retirement schemes);

(e) a copy of the memorandum and articles of association of any management company together with a copy of the seller's share certificate;

(f) copies of any side letters made between landlord and tenant which affect the terms of the lease.

As to the information required for the home information pack, see K11.4.

11.1.4. Does the seller's solicitor have in his possession:

(a) evidence of the freehold title?

(b) licence permitting the current assignment and/or use of the property?

(c) insurance policy?

(d) latest rent review memo?

11.1.5. What consents are needed:

(a) from landlord?

(b) from lender?

11.1.6. Consider what statutes affect the current letting and the proposed sale. What impact does this legislation make on the proposed transaction?

11.1.7. Consider the terms of the existing lease, e.g. as to repairs, user, alterations, alienation, forfeiture, because the buyer's solicitor may raise points on these clauses.

11.1.8. Will it be necessary to obtain a release of the current sureties' liability from the landlord, or to obtain a deed of variation of the lease to reflect the current situation as between landlord and tenant?

11.1.9. If the lease to be assigned commenced before 1 January 1996, the assignor should be reminded of his continuing liability under the covenants in the lease.

11.1.10. If the lease to be assigned was granted after 1 January 1996, its terms should be checked to see whether the landlord requires the outgoing tenant to enter into an authorised guarantee agreement on assignment.

Buyer's solicitor

Checking the lease

11.1.11. On receipt of a copy of the lease from the seller's solicitor, the buyer's solicitor should check the lease and lease plan carefully and advise his client about his responsibility under the various covenants in the lease. The lease may require an assignee to enter into direct covenants with the landlord which will create a contractual relationship between the landlord and the assignee and, in the case of 'old tenancies' (as defined by the Landlord and Tenant (Covenants) Act

1995), will make the assignee liable on all of the lease covenants for the remainder of the term, notwithstanding subsequent assignment of the lease to a third party (see K10). The solicitor will also need to check whether the lease, or rights granted by it, have been registered at the Land Registry (e.g. a lease for over seven years, or a lease of part for less than seven years but that grants an easement) where registration was required. The buyer's solicitor should also check whether the circumstances surrounding the payment of SDLT by the original tenant may require the buyer to file a subsequent return during the term, e.g. on a rent review within five years from the grant (see A14).

Landlord's consent

11.1.12. If the landlord's consent to the transfer or assignment will be needed the buyer should be asked to supply his solicitor with the names and addresses of potential referees so that this information may be passed on to the seller's solicitor as quickly as possible in order to avoid any delay in obtaining the licence. References are commonly required from all or some of the following sources:

  (a)   a current landlord;

  (b)   the buyer's bankers;

  (c)   the buyer's employer;

  (d)   a professional person, e.g. accountant or solicitor;

  (e)   a person or company with whom the buyer regularly trades;

  (f)   three years' audited accounts in the case of a company or self-employed person.

11.1.13. A solicitor should only give a reference on behalf of his client if he knows the client well and trusts him. The landlord will rely on the information given in the reference in assessing the suitability of the buyer as a potential tenant and a misstatement made by a solicitor in the course of giving a reference may lead to liability to the landlord under the principles in *Hedley Byrne & Co. Ltd* v. *Heller & Partners Ltd* [1964] AC 465. It is thus common practice for a reference given by a solicitor to exclude liability or responsibility for its contents.

Surety

11.1.14. The landlord may also require a surety to the lease as a condition of the grant of a licence to assign. Consideration should be given as to who should stand surety under the lease. Where the proposed assignee is a company it is common to find that the directors of the company are asked to guarantee the company's obligations under the lease. Although the directors may be happy to do this since, unless they agree, they are unlikely to secure the landlord's consent to the assignment, they should be advised of the considerable personal liability which they are assuming by accepting such a role. This is particularly so if the assignee, by entering direct covenants with the landlord, will be assuming a contingent liability under the lease since the sureties' obligations will be co-extensive with those of the principal debtor. In this situation there may be a conflict between the interests of the company client (the prospective assignee) and those of the sureties (the company directors) and it may be advisable for the sureties to receive independent advice about their responsibilities in relation to the guarantee of the lease obligations.

Buyer's lender

11.1.15. The terms of the lease should be checked to ensure that it will be acceptable to the buyer's lender (see K1) and where appropriate the provisions of the Lenders' Handbook must be observed.

11.2. Covenants against alienation

11.2.1. Covenants against alienation take many forms; they may restrict all or any of the following acts: assignment of the lease, sub-letting, sharing, parting with possession of the whole or any part of the property and creating a mortgage over the property. Such covenants are construed strictly by the courts so that when drafting a covenant it is essential that the covenant is worded to cover precisely the acts which it is intended to restrict, e.g. a covenant which prevents assignment will not restrict sub-letting and vice versa.

Long residential leases

11.2.2. A covenant which restricts assignment of a long lease of a house or flat, except during the final years of its term (e.g. during the last seven years of a 99-year lease), is not generally favoured by either buyers or their lenders since it unnecessarily restricts the saleability of the property and thus has an adverse effect on its market value. See K6.6 for Lenders' Handbook requirements. For this reason such a covenant is uncommon in such a lease and a buyer's solicitor should seek to remove such a restriction from the lease on grant.

11.2.3. Except in long residential leases the inclusion of some type of covenant against alienation is usual and acceptable and provides the landlord with some measure of control over the occupiers of his property. The precise effect of any covenant depends on its wording. The effect of Landlord and Tenant Act 1927, s.19(1)(*b*) on building leases should be noted.[1]

Absolute covenants

11.2.4. If the covenant is absolute, e.g. 'the tenant shall not assign or part with possession of the property', any assignment (or other dealing depending on the wording of the restriction), although effective, will be a breach of covenant by the tenant and may lead to forfeiture of the lease. Although a landlord may be prepared to waive the covenant, such provisions are not popular with tenants since there is no guarantee that the tenant will be able to sell the lease should the need or desire to do so arise. The presence of an absolute covenant may therefore have a deflationary effect on the rent obtainable for the property. Where an absolute covenant exists, there is no objection to the tenant asking the landlord's permission to grant him a variation of the lease to permit assignment (or as the case may be), but there is no obligation on the landlord to accede to the tenant's request or to give reasons for his refusal.

Qualified covenants

11.2.5. A qualified covenant permits the tenant to assign provided that the tenant obtains the prior consent of the landlord to the dealing. This type of covenant is more acceptable to prospective tenants than an absolute covenant but does not give the landlord total control over the occupiers of his property since his discretion to refuse consent to a proposed assignee may be tempered by the application of statutory provisions which, where they apply, are non-excludable.

Consent not to be unreasonably withheld

11.2.6. In the case of a qualified covenant contained in a lease, Landlord and Tenant Act 1927, s.19 adds to the covenant the non-excludable proviso that consent shall not be unreasonably withheld by the landlord.[2] The question of whether a landlord in refusing consent is acting 'unreasonably' presents problems for the tenant. If the tenant does apply for consent and the landlord unreasonably withholds his consent, the tenant may go ahead and assign (or as the case may be) without consent and the dealing will not constitute a breach of covenant by the tenant. The difficulty lies in knowing what is 'unreasonable' since a refusal which may appear to be unreasonable from the tenant's point of view may look very different when considered from the landlord's side.[3] If the landlord does refuse consent the prospective assignee (or as the case may be) is unlikely to wish to proceed with the transaction without consent because he runs the risk of the lease being forfeited against him. One solution is for the tenant to seek a declaration from the court to the effect that the landlord is being unreasonable in withholding his consent but such a course of action is costly and time-consuming. Landlord and Tenant Act 1988 attempts to resolve some of the problems associated with the application of section 19 by providing that the landlord must, after having received a written request for consent, give his consent within a reasonable time unless it is reasonable for him to withhold his consent. He must serve written notice of his decision on the tenant within a reasonable time stating what conditions (if any) are attached to the consent or, if consent is refused, stating his reasons for withholding his consent. Breach of the landlord's duty under the Act is actionable in tort as a breach of statutory duty, giving a remedy to the tenant in damages (see K7.11).

11.2.7. Note that various statutory provisions provide that a refusal to consent based on the grounds of race,[4] sex,[5] disability,[6] religion or sexual orientation[7] will be unlawful in most circumstances.

Offer to surrender

11.2.8. Attached to some covenants against assignment is a proviso that should the tenant wish to assign he should first offer to surrender his lease to the landlord. Such a proviso (commonly known as an 'Adler clause' after the case of that name)[8] was held to be valid in *Bocardo S.A.* v. *S. & M. Hotels*,[9] but the effect of such a clause and the terms of any surrender need to be considered carefully by the tenant, especially since, in the case of business tenancies within Landlord and Tenant Act 1954, Pt. II, section 38 makes void an agreement which has the effect of precluding the tenant from making an application for a new tenancy under the Act. It may therefore be necessary in a commercial lease for landlord and tenant to follow the statutory procedure to 'contract out' of an agreement to surrender.[10] Since Law of Property (Miscellaneous Provisions) Act 1989, s.2 requires a contract for the disposal of an interest in land to be in writing, it is arguable that to create an effective contract for surrender landlord and tenant must both sign a single document incorporating all the terms of the surrender or otherwise comply with the terms of the Act.[11]

Landlord and Tenant (Covenants) Act 1995

11.2.9. In relation to new tenancies (i.e. generally those granted on or after 1 January 1996) of commercial property (section 19(1A) does not apply to residential or agricultural tenancies) the provisions of section 19 of Landlord and Tenant Act 1927 are modified so that a landlord may agree in advance with his tenant:

    (a)   any circumstances in which the landlord may withhold his licence or consent to a proposed assignment; or

    (b)   any conditions subject to which such licence or consent may be granted.

11.2.10. A landlord who withholds consent because of the existence of any such circumstance or who imposes any such condition is not acting unreasonably.

11.2.11. The 1995 Act distinguishes between factual matters, for example:

    (a)   the assignee must be a plc;

    (b)   the assignee must have net assets equal to a specified multiplier of the rent;

    (c)   the assignee must provide a rent deposit; or

    (d)   the assignor must enter an authorised guarantee agreement;

and discretionary matters, for example, the assignee is, in the opinion of the landlord, of equal financial standing to the assignor.

11.2.12. In discretionary matters, the landlord's decision has to be arrived at reasonably, or the tenant must have the right to have the decision reviewed by an independent third party, who is identifiable from the agreement, and whose decision is conclusive.

Demanding a premium for consent

11.2.13. Unless the lease specifically allows the landlord to charge a premium for giving his consent (an uncommon provision in modern leases) the landlord may not attach a condition to his consent requiring a premium to be paid by the tenant.[12]

Undertaking for landlord's costs

11.2.14. The landlord is entitled to ask the tenant to pay the landlord's solicitor's reasonable charges in connection with the preparation of the deed of consent (licence) but may not demand a premium. When the tenant's solicitor approaches the landlord's solicitor asking for consent to be given he should require the landlord's solicitor to provide a firm estimate of the costs of the application which should indicate whether or not VAT and disbursements are included in the estimate and should give a maximum fee which will be charged by the landlord in any event (see A8). A tenant paying the landlord's solicitor's costs is entitled to apply for these costs to be taxed.[13] However, he is not entitled to apply for a remuneration certificate in respect of the landlord's solicitor's costs.[14] In any event, deliberate overcharging is professional misconduct. The Solicitors' Code of Conduct 2007,[15] states that solicitors must not 'use their position as solicitors to take unfair advantage either for themselves or another person'.

11.2.15. It may be difficult for the landlord's solicitor to quote a fixed figure at the outset of the transaction, but he should try to give the tenant's solicitor an accurate estimate of the likely costs and there is no objection to his qualifying the estimate by saying that it is given on the understanding that the matter proceeds to completion without any unforeseen difficulties or delays. The estimate should make it clear whether the tenant is to be responsible for the landlord's costs in any event, i.e. whether or not consent is forthcoming and whether or not the proposed assignment (or as the case may be) proceeds to completion. To assist the landlord in giving an accurate estimate the tenant's solicitor should be prepared to supply the landlord with such information as he requires, e.g. references about the proposed assignee (or as the case may be) as quickly as possible and preferably at the time when the application for consent is first made.

11.2.16. A tenant's solicitor must advise his client of his potential liability to meet the landlord's costs and should not give an unqualified undertaking to meet the landlord's solicitors' costs of preparing the consent since he may be committing his client to an unquantified sum.

11.2.17. An undertaking may be given, provided that the landlord has provided an estimate of costs, and subject to the prior approval of the tenant client (see B16). It is undecided as to whether it is reasonable for a landlord to insist on an undertaking from the tenant's solicitors to pay its reasonable costs before dealing with the application for consent, although it is standard practice for this to be done. Certainly, it is likely to be unreasonable for the landlord to insist on an unlimited undertaking as a precondition for dealing with the application for consent for an indemnity as to costs.[16] Where an undertaking has been given, the tenant's solicitor should obtain money on account from his client to ensure that he will be able to fulfil the undertaking. However, since Landlord and Tenant Act 1988 renders the landlord liable to the tenant in damages if an application for consent is not dealt with within a reasonable time, the landlord's solicitor should be wary of refusing to deal with the matter until such time as he receives an undertaking in respect of his costs.

Standard Conditions of Sale

11.2.18. Standard Condition 8.3 and Standard Commercial Property Condition 10.3 require the seller to apply for the landlord's consent at his own expense and to use his best endeavours to obtain such consent, the buyer providing all information and references reasonably required. Either party may rescind the contract by notice if the consent has not been obtained within a certain time. In the case of the Standard Commercial Property Conditions this period is (broadly) four months after the original completion date. In the case of the Standard Conditions the period is (broadly) three working days before the original completion date. The Standard Conditions do not require the assignee to enter into a direct covenant with the landlord (reversioner). If the lease provides for the assignee to enter into a direct covenant, the contract should contain a condition to this effect.

11.2.19. In view of the difficulties attached to covenants against alienation, it is advisable that contracts for a disposition which is dependent on consent being obtained should not be exchanged until it is certain that the landlord's consent will be forthcoming.

1. The effect of this is, broadly, that if the lease is for more than 40 years and made partly in consideration for construction work, no consent to a dealing is required if this is done more than seven years before the end of the term. See *Vaux Group plc* v. *Lilley* [1991] 04 EG 136.
2. Section 19 does not apply to lettings of certain types of property, e.g. agricultural holdings: see s.19(4).
3. The principles of law which apply to determining the question of reasonableness in these circumstances were set out by the Court of Appeal in *International Drilling Fluids Ltd* v. *Louisville Investments (Uxbridge) Ltd* [1986] Ch 513.
4. Race Relations Act 1976, s.24.
5. Sex Discrimination Act 1975, s.31.
6. Disability Discrimination Act 1995, s.22.
7. Equality Act 2006, s.47.
8. *Adler* v. *Upper Grosvenor Street Investments* [1957] 1 All ER 229.
9. [1980] 1 WLR 17.
10. Landlord and Tenant Act 1954, s.38A(2) and Regulatory Reform (Business Tenancies) (England and Wales) Order 2003, Schedules 1 and 2.
11. *Proudreed Ltd* v. *Microgen Holdings plc* (1995) 72 P&CR 388, CA.
12. Law of Property Act 1925, s.144.
13. Solicitors Act 1974, s.71.
14. Solicitors (Non-Contentious Business) Remuneration Order 1994 (SI 1994/2616).
15. Solicitors' Code of Conduct 2007, rule 10.01.
16. *Dong Bang Minerva* v. *Davina* [1996] 31 EG 87.

11.3. Preparing the package

11.3.1. The seller's solicitor should generally supply the buyer's solicitor with the following documents or information:

    (a) the draft contract;

    (b) a copy of the lease/sub-lease being purchased;

    (c) a plan of the property (where appropriate);

    (d) evidence of the seller's title;

    (e) replies to pre-contract searches;

    (f) details of the insurance of the property (including the receipt for the last premium due);

    (g) details of any management company, including copies of the memorandum and articles of association;

    (h) service charge accounts for the last three years including the receipt for the last sum payable (where appropriate);

    (i) information about what steps have been taken to obtain the landlord's consent to the transaction (where appropriate);

    (j) a request for references or such other information about the buyer as the landlord has indicated that he requires (where appropriate);

    (k) answers to pre-contract enquiries. In Protocol cases the Seller's Property Information Form and Seller's Leasehold Information Form. In the case of complex commercial property replies to the Commercial Property Standard Enquiries should be supplied.[1]

1. The enquiries may be downloaded from **www.bpf.org.uk** or **www.practicallaw.com**. Also see K1.17.1. Also note requirements in relation to home information packs; see K2.3.2.

11.4. The Protocol and home information packs

11.4.1. In the case of appropriate residential leases Protocol applies as in the case of a freehold transaction, but the seller should be asked to produce, if possible, a receipt or evidence from the landlord of the last payment of rent, the maintenance charge accounts for the last three years (where appropriate) and evidence of payment, and details of the buildings insurance policy. If a licence to assign is required, enquiry should be made of the landlord as to what references from the assignee are necessary. A copy of the lease, together with such of the above information as has been obtained and is relevant to the transaction, should be sent to the buyer's solicitor as soon as possible.

11.4.2. In certain cases (e.g. currently in relation to certain residential leases of homes with three or more bedrooms) the assignment of a long term residential lease will require the provision of a home information pack when marketing it for sale.

The term 'sale' includes a disposal or agreement to dispose, by way of the sale of a long lease. 'Long lease' means:

(a)   a lease granted for a term certain exceeding 21 years, whether or not it is (or may become) terminable before the end of that term by notice given by the tenant or by re-entry or forfeiture; or

(b)   a lease for a term fixed by law under a grant with a covenant or obligation for perpetual renewal, other than a lease by sub-demise from one which is not a long lease.[1]

11.4.3.   The details in relation to home information packs are set out in A.26. The additional 'required documents' which must be included in a pack in relation to the sale of a leasehold property are set out in Home Information Pack Regulations 2007, Sched.5, para.1. An outline of these is set out below:

(a)   original or copy lease;

(b)   any regulations or rules made for the purposes of managing the property;

(c)   any statements or summaries of service charges supplied in respect of the property relating to the 36 months preceding the first point of marketing;

(d)   the most recent requests for payment or financial contribution made in respect of the property, relating to the 12 months preceding the first point of marketing, towards:

(i)   service charges;

(ii)   ground rent;

(iii) any separate insurance against damage for the building; and

(iv)   any separate insurance in respect of personal injury or death;

(e)   the names and addresses of:

(i)   the current landlord or proposed landlord;

(ii)   managing agents as are appointed or proposed by the landlord to manage the property; and

(iii) such other persons as manage or are likely to manage the property;

(f)   any amendments as are proposed to the lease; and the regulations or rules; and

(g)   a summary of certain works that are proposed or are being undertaken.

Except for the copy lease the documents referred to above are only those which are in the seller's possession, under his control or to which he can reasonably be expected to have access, taking into account the enquiries that it would be reasonable to make of specified persons. In a similar way, the information required as referred to above is only that which the seller can reasonably be expected to be aware of, taking into account the enquiries that it would be reasonable to make of specified persons.

11.4.4. The additional 'authorised documents' which may be included in a pack in relation to the sale of a leasehold property are set out in Home Information Pack Regulations 2007, Sched.5, para.3. These are documents which contain information relating to, broadly:

(a) any lease, including superior or inferior leases;

(b) any licence of the property;

(c) any freehold estate to which the lease relates including any proposals to buy a freehold interest relating to the property;

(d) the rights or obligations of the tenant under the lease or otherwise, including whether the tenant has complied with such obligations;

(e) the rights or obligations of the landlord under the lease or otherwise, including whether the landlord has complied with such obligations;

(f) the landlord and any information that might affect the tenant's relationship with the landlord;

(g) any agent of the landlord or other manager of the property and any information that might affect the tenant's relationship with them;

(h) the membership or existence of any body of persons corporate or unincorporate which manages the property or building in which the property is situated;

(i) the status or memorandum and articles of association of any company related to the management of the property or building in which the property is situated;

(j) the rent payable for the property, including whether payments for such rent are outstanding;

(k) any service charges payable in respect of the property, including whether payments for such charges are outstanding;

(l) any reserve fund relating to the property for necessary works to it or the building in which the property is situated, including whether payments to such a fund are outstanding;

(m) any planned or recent works to the property or the building in which the property is situated; and

(n) any responsibility for insuring the property or the building in which the property is situated, including the terms of such insurance and whether payments relating to it are outstanding.

1. Housing Act 2004, s.177.

11.5. **Title**

Lease registered with absolute title

11.5.1. By Standard Condition 4.1.2 and Standard Commercial Property Condition 6.1.2, copies supplied must be official copy entries of the title. Since the title to the lease is guaranteed by the Land Registry there is no need for the buyer to investigate the title to the freehold or superior leases.

Lease registered with good leasehold title

11.5.2. By Standard Condition 4.1.2 and Standard Commercial Property Condition 6.1.2 copies supplied must be official copy entries of the title. Registration with a good leasehold title provides no guarantee of the soundness of the title to the reversion(s) and thus the buyer should insist on deduction of the freehold and any intermediate leasehold titles to him. Without deduction of the reversionary title(s) the lease may be unacceptable to the buyer and/or his lender. See G3.5 and note the special requirements in relation to good leasehold title contained in the Lenders' Handbook (Appendix VI.2). The reversionary title(s) will be deduced by the appropriate method applicable to unregistered land (see section D). As the register of title is open to public inspection a prospective tenant will in practice be able to find out a great deal about his proposed landlord's title, assuming it is registered (see G3.12).

Unregistered lease

11.5.3. A special condition should in appropriate cases be added to the contract requiring the seller to deduce the reversionary title to the buyer by the method appropriate to unregistered land (see section D). The Standard Conditions of Sale do not require the seller to deduce a reversionary title in these circumstances.

11.6. **Preparing for completion**

The purchase deed

11.6.1. The purchase deed (an assignment in unregistered land or a transfer in registered land) will be prepared by the buyer's solicitor. Even where the lease was granted informally the assignment must be by deed in order to transfer the legal estate in the land to the buyer.[1] An assignment of an unregistered lease will normally recite the brief history of the lease and the granting of any necessary consent to the present transaction, but is otherwise similar to a conveyance of freehold land. The form of transfer is the same as that used in freehold transactions. Execution of the purchase deed is discussed in E1.

Indemnity

11.6.2. If the assignor is to remain liable on the covenants in the lease after completion of the assignment, the purchase deed should include an express indemnity covenant from the buyer. Where Landlord and Tenant (Covenants) Act 1995 applies so as to release the assignor from future liability, no indemnity covenant is necessary; however, liability is commonly continued by an authorised guarantee agreement. (See also K15.4.7.)

Modification of covenants for title

11.6.3. If a seller is in breach of a repairing covenant in the lease, the lack of repair could involve him in liability to the buyer after completion under the covenants for title which will be implied in the purchase deed.[2] Since liability under the covenants is strict, and it is usual for the contract to contain a provision requiring the buyer to accept the property in its existing state of repair,[3] the contract should also provide for modification of the covenants for title in this respect. Such a contractual condition must be reflected by an express modification of the covenants in the purchase deed itself. A buyer who accepts a condition which restricts the seller's liability under the covenants for title must ensure that he is fully aware of the actual state of repair of the property (e.g. by inspection or survey) before contracts are exchanged since the effect of such a contractual condition is to take away the buyer's right to sue the seller in respect of a breach of repairing covenant.

Pre-completion searches

11.6.4. Where the lease is registered with an absolute title the buyer will make a pre-completion search at the Land Registry in the same way as if he were buying the freehold. Any other searches which would be appropriate to the purchase of a registered freehold should also be undertaken (see E2). Where the title to the lease is unregistered a Land Charges Department search against the names of the estate owners of the leasehold title should be made together with any other searches appropriate to the circumstances of the transaction (see E2). Where the freehold or other reversionary title has been deduced the names revealed through investigation of that title should also be included in the land charges search application. If the lease is registered with a good leasehold title, a search at the Land Registry must be made in respect of the registered title and a Land Charges Department search against the estate owners of an unregistered reversion. A company search should be carried out as necessary, e.g. against the management company.

Landlord's consent

11.6.5. The landlord's solicitor will supply the engrossment of the licence which must be by deed if it is to contain covenants. If the licence requires the buyer to enter into a direct covenant with the landlord (and/or a management company) to observe and perform the covenants in the lease, the licence is usually drawn up in two parts, the landlord executing the original licence which will be given to the seller on completion for onwards transmission to the buyer, the buyer executing the counterpart which will be given to the landlord on completion.

Apportionments

11.6.6. Since it is unlikely that completion will take place on a day when rent and/or service charge become due under the lease it will be necessary for these sums to be apportioned on completion and the seller should supply the buyer with a completion statement which shows the amounts due and explains how they have been calculated. Copies of the rent and service charge receipts or demands should be supplied to the buyer with the completion statement so that the buyer can check the apportioned sums. In many cases it will not be possible to make an exact apportionment of service charge since the figures required in order to make this calculation will not be available. In such a case a provisional apportionment of the sum should be made on a 'best estimate' basis in accordance with Standard Condition 6.3.5 or Standard Commercial Property Condition 8.3.5 (see section F). These conditions, although of most relevance to the apportionment of service charges, are not confined in their application to service charges alone and can be used to make a provisional apportionment of any sums where the amount to be apportioned is not known or easily ascertainable. Where the seller's liability for unascertained service charges may be substantial and there is concern about enforcing his obligation to pay (e.g. where the seller is emigrating), it may be appropriate to negotiate a retention to be held by his solicitors pending the ascertainment of the service charge.

11.6.7. The Law Society's Conveyancing and Land Law Committee has prepared a formula for calculating the apportionment of rent on assignment of a lease. The formula is given at Appendix IV.2.

Shares in management company

11.6.8. Where appropriate the solicitor for the buyer should prepare a stock transfer form to be signed by the seller before completion in order to transfer the seller's management company share(s) to the buyer. If the management company is limited by guarantee (not shares) there will be no share certificate to transfer to the buyer but the buyer will need to write to the company and apply for membership after completion. If the amount of the guarantee is more than nominal the seller's liability under the guarantee continues for a year after he ceases to be a member and he should in such a case take an appropriate indemnity from the buyer.

1. Short leases do not have to be made by deed (Law of Property Act 1925, s.54), but the transfer of a legal estate in land must be by deed by Law of Property Act 1925, s.52. This includes the assignment of a short lease. See *Crago* v. *Julian* [1992] 1 All ER 744.
2. Land Registration Act 2002, Sched.12, para.20; Law of Property Act 1925, s.76; and B7.
3. See Standard Condition 3.2 and Standard Commercial Property Condition 3.2.

11.7.   **Completion**

11.7.1. The procedure on completion follows closely that in a freehold transaction (see section F).

11.7.2. The seller will hand to the buyer such of the following documents as are relevant to the transaction in hand:

    (a) the lease/sub-lease;

    (b) the purchase deed;

    (c) the landlord's licence;

    (d) marked abstract or other evidence of superior titles in accordance with the contract (lease not registered or not registered with absolute title);

    (e) Form DS1 or an appropriate undertaking in respect of the seller's mortgage;

    (f) copies of duplicate notices served by the seller and his predecessors on the landlord in accordance with a covenant in the lease requiring the landlord to be notified of any dispositions;

    (g) insurance policy (or copy if insurance is effected by the landlord) and receipt (or copy) relating to the last premium due;

    (h) rent and service charge receipts;

    (i) management company memorandum and articles;

    (j) seller's share certificate and completed stock transfer form.

11.7.3. The buyer should hand to the seller such of the following items as are appropriate to the transaction:

    (a) money due in accordance with the completion statement;

    (b) duly executed counterpart licence to assign;

    (c) a release of deposit.

Rent receipts

11.7.4. Law of Property Act 1925, s.45(2) provides that on production of the receipt for the last rent due under the lease or sub-lease which he is buying a buyer must assume, unless the contrary appears, that the rent has been paid and the covenants performed under that and all superior leases. The buyer's solicitor should inspect the receipts on completion and also, where appropriate, receipts for payment of service charge. Standard Condition 6.6 and Standard Commercial Property Condition 8.6 entitle a buyer to assume that the correct person gave the receipt.

11.8. **Post-completion**

Stamp Duty Land Tax

11.8.1. Following the assignment of many leases, the tenant must deliver a land transaction return to HM Revenue and Customs within 30 days of the effective date of the transaction. This delivery must include a self-assessment of the liability and where appropriate payment of the SDLT due (see A14).

11.8.2. The general rule is that the effective date of a land transaction is the date of completion. There are, however, special rules where a contract is substantially performed before it is completed and in relation to options and rights of pre-emption. These points and matters generally relating to SDLT are dealt with in A14.

11.8.3. The lease cannot be registered or noted (if relevant) at the Land Registry without a certificate as to compliance with SDLT. The certificate will be issued either by HM Revenue and Customs stating that a land transaction return has been delivered or by the purchaser (self-certification) that no land transaction return is required.

11.8.4. Tax is chargeable on any premium, and is in addition to any tax charged on the rent, and is computed according to the details set out in A14.

Registered lease

11.8.5. Where the lease is already registered at the Land Registry with separate title an application for registration of the transfer to the buyer should be made within the priority period afforded by the buyer's pre-completion search.

Unregistered lease

11.8.6. An unregistered lease or sub-lease which, at the date of the transfer to the buyer, still has over seven years unexpired will need to be registered at the Land Registry within two months of the assignment. An application for first registration of title should therefore be made within this time limit. An absolute title can be granted where:

(a) the registrar is of the opinion that the applicant's title to the lease is such as a willing buyer could properly be advised by a competent professional adviser to accept; and

(b) the registrar approves the lessor's title to grant the lease.[1]

11.8.7. In order to satisfy the Land Registry requirements as to the identification of the premises being assigned, a plan of the premises may be required (see B21). This may be a particular problem where the lease being assigned does not contain an existing plan that meets the Land Registry's criteria (see B21.2.3). In these circumstances a new plan will have to be prepared to meet these criteria and submitted with the application for registration. The parties will need to consider the additional cost implications of obtaining such a plan.

11.8.8. If the title to the reversion is already registered, the lease will be noted against the superior title. In other cases the buyer may consider lodging a caution against first registration against the unregistered superior title in order to protect his interests against a subsequent buyer of the reversion. If the lease has seven years or less unexpired it is generally incapable of registration with separate title but will take effect as an overriding interest.[2] It may be prudent to protect a term for more than three years by the entry of notice in the register of a superior title which is itself registered. A lease for three years or less cannot be so protected.[3]

Notice to landlord

11.8.9. The buyer's solicitor should give notice of the transfer (and of the buyer's mortgage if required) in accordance with any covenant to that effect in the lease. Two copies of the notice together with the appropriate fee should be sent to the landlord's solicitor (or other person specified in the covenant) and the landlord's solicitor should be asked to sign one copy of the notice as an acknowledgement of its receipt and to return the signed copy to the buyer's solicitor. The receipted notice should be kept with the buyer's title deeds as evidence of compliance with this covenant. The fee payable for service of the notice should have been included in the statement of account sent by the buyer's solicitor to his client before completion.

Share transfer

11.8.10. The duly stamped stock transfer form and seller's share certificate should be sent by the buyer's solicitor to the management company who will register the transfer of the share and issue a new share certificate in the buyer's name. The new share certificate should be kept with the buyer's title deeds. It will be necessary to check the requirements of the lender, where appropriate by means of the Lenders' Handbook, to see if the share certificate and other relevant documents should be sent to the lender. Where the management company is limited by guarantee the buyer should write to the company and apply for membership.

Outstanding apportioned sums

11.8.11. As soon as the figures are available the parties' solicitors should make an adjustment of the provisional apportionments which were made on completion. By Standard Condition 6.3.5 and Standard Commercial Property Condition 8.3.5 such outstanding sums must be settled within 10 working days of notification by one party to the other of the adjusted figures. The liability to account for the apportioned sums remains outstanding despite completion having taken place under Standard Condition 7.4 and Standard Commercial Property Condition 9.4 (see also K11.6.6).

1. Land Registration Act 2002, s.10(2).
2. *Ibid.*, Sched.1, para.1 and Sched.3, para.1.
3. *Ibid.*, s.33.

K12. Licence or tenancy

12.1. Importance of the distinction

12.1.1. The principal reason for distinguishing between a licence and a tenancy is that in general a licensee will not enjoy the benefit of security of tenure, whereas a tenant may be protected from eviction at the end of his contractual term by the operation of some statutory provision. It will be a misrepresentation to describe a property as being sold subject to a licence, where in fact the occupier has a business tenancy.[1] A licensee is not protected under:

   (a) Rent Act 1977;

   (b) Housing Act 1988 (assured tenancies);

   (c) Landlord and Tenant Act 1954, Pt. I (long tenancies);

   (d) Local Government and Housing Act 1989, Sched.10 (assured tenancies arising after long tenancies, see K5.6.2);

   (e) Landlord and Tenant Act 1954, Pt. II (business tenancies).

12.1.2. Conversely, licensees do enjoy protection from eviction in the following situations:

   (a) where the licensee would otherwise be a secure tenant under Housing Act 1985, s.79;

   (b) under Rent (Agriculture) Act 1976; and

   (c) generally where a person is granted a licence to occupy land for use as agricultural land under Agricultural Holdings Act 1986, s.2.

1. *Pankhania* v. *Hackney London Borough Council* [2002] All ER (D) 22; and for the decision in relation to quantum of damages see *Pankhania* v. *Hackney London Borough Council and Metropolitan Police Authority* [2004] 1 EGLR 135.

12.2. Licences

12.2.1. It is not always easy to determine whether an arrangement between two parties constitutes a licence or a tenancy. The modern starting point is usually accepted to be *Street* v. *Mountford*[1] where it was held as a general rule that if exclusive possession is given for a term at a rent (although the reservation of a rent is not essential to a tenancy),[2] a tenancy will come into being, whatever the parties chose to call the arrangement and whatever they intended to be the result of that arrangement.

12.2.2. The giving of exclusive possession is essential to the creation of a tenancy, so that if the agreement genuinely denies this to the grantee, no tenancy will come into being. If, therefore, a clause is inserted into an agreement for the occupation of business premises, enabling the grantor to move the location of the grantee's occupied space or stall, such a right, being inconsistent with the creation of a tenancy, would generally ensure that the grantee became a licensee and not a tenant.[3]

12.2.3. The ability of the grantor to move the location of the grantee has more realism in the case of a business arrangement than in the context of residential premises, but in residential cases grantors have sometimes succeeded in denying the existence of a tenancy by using the device of requiring the grantee to share the accommodation either with other tenants or with the grantor himself (i.e. denying exclusive possession to the grantee). The courts will, however, not accept these devices at their face value, and will look into the reality of the situation; thus if a sharing arrangement is patently a sham in order to deprive the grantee of security of tenure, it is unlikely to succeed.[4]

1. [1985] AC 809.
2. *Ashburn Anstalt* v. *Arnold* [1989] Ch 1.
3. *Dresden Estates Ltd* v. *Collinson* (1988) 55 P&CR 47. Note also *Clear Channel UK Ltd* v. *Manchester City Council* [2005] EWCA Civ 1304.
4. See *Antoniades* v. *Villiers* [1988] 3 All ER 1058; *Aslan* v. *Murphy (Nos. 1 & 2)* [1989] 3 All ER 130; *Duke* v. *Wynne* [1989] 3 All ER 130; *AG Securities* v. *Vaughan* [1988] 3 All ER 1058; *Mikeover Ltd* v. *Brady* [1989] 3 All ER 618; *Westminster City Council* v. *Clarke* [1992] 2 AC 288, HL.

12.3. Lodgers

12.3.1. A genuine lodger is a recognised licensee and (apart from the denial of exclusive possession) special circumstances such as a family arrangement may negate a tenancy.

12.4. Possession before completion

12.4.1. In most circumstances a buyer who is let into occupation of the property before completion would be treated as a licensee.[1] Standard Condition 5.2 provides that the buyer takes occupation as a licensee and not as a tenant.

1. But see *Bretherton* v. *Paton* [1986] 1 EGLR 172.

12.5. Notice to terminate

12.5.1. The length of notice necessary to determine a licence which is not protected by statute will normally be settled by agreement between the parties. In the absence of such agreement, reasonable notice must be given. Notice should always be given in writing so that it will be possible, if a dispute arises, to prove the existence and contents of the notice. Some record of posting or delivery should for the same reason be kept. No notice by a landlord or a tenant to quit any premises let as a dwelling or by a licensor or a licensee to determine a periodic licence to occupy premises as a dwelling, is valid unless it is in writing and contains certain prescribed information[1] and it is given not less than four weeks before the date on which it is to take effect.[2] This does not apply if the premises are held on an 'excluded tenancy' or an 'excluded licence'. Protection from Eviction Act 1977 (as amended) sets out a number of situations where a tenancy or licence will be excluded. They principally relate to situations where the licensee or tenant shares accommodation with the landlord or where it is a hostel.[3] Even where the licensee does not have the benefit of security of tenure, it may still be necessary to obtain a court order if the grantor seeks to regain possession.[4]

1. Notices to Quit (Prescribed Information) Regulations 1988 (SI 1988/2201).
2. Protection from Eviction Act 1977, s.5(1), (1A).
3. *Ibid.*, s.3A; Housing Act 1985, s.322 and *Rogerson* v. *Wigan MBC* [2004] EWHC 1677.
4. See, e.g. Protection from Eviction Act 1977, s.2 in the case of residential premises and Housing Act 1988, s.32. This includes property which is a mixed residential and commercial letting. The phrase 'let as a dwelling' in the Protection from Eviction Act 1977, s.2 has been held to mean 'let wholly or partly as a dwelling' and so applied to premises that were let for mixed residential and business purposes. See *Pirabakaran* v. *Patel* [2006] EWCA Civ 685.

K13. Options

13.1. Introduction

13.1.1. An option for the tenant to renew the lease or to purchase the reversion may be included in some leases or may be granted to the tenant independently of the grant of the lease.

13.1.2. It is important that the price or rent to be paid on the exercise of the option is either fixed by the lease itself or is otherwise ascertainable by the operation of some effective formula (e.g. by reference to 'open market value at the time of the exercise of the option') in the absence of which the option may fail for uncertainty.

13.1.3. An option contained in a registrable lease should be protected by the entry of a notice in the register. If the option is protected as an overriding interest by virtue of the tenant's occupation,[1] the option will need to be disclosed on the application to register the reversion.[2] Notice of the option would then be entered in the register.[3]

13.1.4. If a lease out of a registered title is an overriding interest and is not registrable,[4] the option should be protected on the landlord's title by notice. If the tenant is in occupation, the option may be protected as an overriding interest.[5] It would be unwise to rely on protection as an overriding interest in case the tenant went out of occupation for any reason.

13.1.5. A specific application to enter notice of the option in the register of the landlord's title is usually required whether the option is contained in a lease that is being registered or in a separate document. The Land Registry will only automatically note an option in the landlord's title where the option is expressly referred to (usually in form DI as a disclosable overriding interest) on either an application for first registration of the landlord's title or an application to register a registrable disposition in relation to the landlord's title. Where a Prescribed Clauses Lease is used, the option may be automatically noted in the title affected. See K1.20.7.

13.1.6. In unregistered land an option will not bind the buyer of the landlord's reversionary interest unless registered as an estate contract under Land Charges Act 1972. Where an option cannot be enforced against a buyer of the reversion through lack of registration, the tenant may be able to sue the original landlord for damages for breach of contract,[6] who in turn may seek indemnity from the buyer under a contractual provision, e.g. Standard Condition 3.3.2. To protect his own interests the tenant should ensure that his option is registered as soon as possible after completion of its grant (the priority notice procedure may be used to ensure the date of registration is backdated to the date of grant). A landlord may choose to draft the option so that its validity is dependent on its registration within a stated period. Where a lease is granted out of an unregistered reversion, the option must be protected by registration under Land Charges Act 1972 even if the lease granted will itself be registered under Land Registration Act 2002.

13.1.7. The grant of an option is a disposition of an interest in land within Law of Property (Miscellaneous Provisions) Act 1989, s.2 and so must satisfy the requirements for writing specified by that section.[7]

13.1.8. It is unusual to find options contained in long leases of dwellings which are granted at a low rent because, provided the qualifying conditions are satisfied, Leasehold Reform Act 1967 (as amended) or Leasehold Reform Housing and Urban Development Act 1993 will frequently give the tenant the right to an extended lease and/or to purchase the freehold reversion (see K9).

1. Land Registration Act 2002, Sched.1, para.2 and Sched.3, para.2.
2. Land Registration Rules 2003, rr.28 and 57.
3. *Ibid.*, rr.28(4) and 57(5).
4. Land Registration Act 2002, Sched.1, para.1 and Sched.3, para.1.
5. *Ibid.*, Sched.1, para.2 and Sched.3, para.2.
6. *Wright* v. *Dean* [1948] Ch 686.
7. See B11; and note *Spiro* v. *Glencrown Properties Ltd* [1991] 02 EG 167.

13.2. Options to purchase the reversion

13.2.1. The perpetuity rule does not apply to an option to purchase the reversion provided that the option is contained in the lease itself and its exercise is restricted to the tenant and his successors in title either during the term of the lease or no later than one year after the end of the term. Any option which does not satisfy these requirements will fail for perpetuity unless confined within or exercised within 21 years from the date of the grant.[1]

13.2.2. An option to purchase the reversion is not within the doctrine of privity of estate, so that the mere fact that such a relationship exists between the landlord and an assignee of the lease does not automatically mean that the assignee can enforce the option. However, unless the lease restricts the assignability of the option, its benefit may be assigned to a third party,[2] so that an unrestricted option to purchase the reversion at any time during a term in excess of 21 years would fail for perpetuity after 21 years. In such a case the exercise of the option should be restricted to the tenant and his successors in title.

13.2.3. Although the benefit of such an option can be expressly assigned to an assignee of the lease (even after the assignment of the lease itself) and may pass to him by operation of law without express words of assignment,[3] it is recommended that in order to avoid doubt express words assigning the benefit of the option should be included in the document under which the benefit of the lease is transferred to the assignee.

1. Perpetuities and Accumulations Act 1964. Different rules apply to leases granted before this Act came into force.
2. *Re Button's Lease* [1964] Ch 263.
3. *Griffith* v. *Pelton* [1958] Ch 205.

13.3. Options to renew

13.3.1. An option to renew a lease is not subject to the rule against perpetuities[1] but a contract (which by definition includes an option) to renew a lease for a term exceeding 60 years is invalidated by Law of Property Act 1922.

13.3.2. Care must be taken in drafting such an option to ensure that it does not create a perpetually renewable lease, such leases being converted by Law of Property Act 1922 into terms for 2,000 years which are not terminable by a landlord's notice. To avoid the creation of a perpetually renewable lease, the option to renew should be drafted to permit the tenant to renew 'on terms identical to those contained in the present lease *with the exception of the covenant to renew*'. Unless the words which are italicised in the previous sentence are included in the option clause, the new lease will also have to contain a further option to renew, thus creating a perpetually renewable lease.

13.3.3. An option to renew is within the doctrine of privity of estate so that provided the terms of exercise are complied with it can be enforced by the assignee who is in possession of the lease at the date when the option becomes exercisable.

13.3.4. If the exercise of the option is conditional on the tenant's performance of his covenants under the lease, the landlord can insist on strict compliance with the covenants and can refuse to grant the renewal even where the tenant's breach of covenant is merely technical and causes no loss to the landlord.[2] It is common for tenants to limit the strict application of this principle by providing that the breach must be 'material' before it would prevent an option being exercised. 'Material' must be assessed by reference to the ability of the landlord to re-let or sell the property without delay or additional expenditure.[3]

1. See, for example, *Weg Motors Ltd* v. *Hales* [1962] Ch 49.
2. See *West Country Cleaners (Falmouth) Ltd* v. *Saly* [1966] 3 All ER 210. See also *Little Ltd* v. *Courage Ltd, The Times*, 6 January 1995, CA.
3. *Fitzroy House Epworth Street (No. 1) Ltd* v. *The Financial Times Ltd* [2006] EWCA Civ 329.

13.4. Exercise of option

13.4.1. Unless there is provision to the contrary, time is automatically of the essence of the exercise of an option.[1]

13.4.2. Following initial uncertainty Law of Property (Miscellaneous Provisions) Act 1989 has been interpreted as permitting the exercise of an option by a single document signed by the grantee only.[2]

13.4.3. Exercise of an option or even holding-over at the end of a lease term may amount to a further grant for SDLT liability, in which case a return should be made within 30 days and tax paid (see A14).

1. *United Scientific Holdings Ltd* v. *Burnley Borough Council* [1977] 2 All ER 62.
2. *Spiro* v. *Glencrown Properties Ltd* [1991] 1 All ER 600; referred to in *Active Estates Ltd* v. *Parness* [2002] 36 EG 147.

K14. Variation of leases

14.1. Variation of lease

14.1.1. In practice most variations of leases are effected by deed. However, in some cases an informal variation of the terms of the lease (e.g. as to user) is only intended to be effective as between the landlord and tenant for the time being. Such a variation is commonly effected by a side letter or informal agreement.

14.1.2. Where a variation is made to a contract for the lease the variation may fall within the definition of a contract for the disposition of an interest in land within Law of Property (Miscellaneous Provisions) Act 1989, s.2. In essence, in this case the variation agreement must be in writing and signed by both parties and must contain all the terms of the contract between the parties or incorporate the document containing the terms by reference.[1] It is possible for the agreement to be in two identical parts each of which is signed by one of the parties.

14.1.3. Where a side letter varies the terms of a lease after it has been granted it may not have to comply with Law of Property (Miscellaneous Provisions) Act 1989, s.2.[2] In practice it is common for a variation effected by side letter to be personal to the tenant. In any event, the side letter should state whether the variation is to be for the benefit only of the signatories to the letter or is intended to bind and benefit their successors in title. Where the covenant is not personal the benefit and burden may run with the respective landlord and tenant interests.[3]

14.1.4. An application to register the variation of a registered lease must be accompanied by the instrument effecting the variation and evidence to satisfy the registrar that the variation has effect in law.[4]

14.1.5. Where the landlord's title is registered, it is important to register any variation of a registered lease (or one noted against the landlord's title), as otherwise it appears that the variation may not be binding on a purchaser. Although the point is unsettled, the effect of Land Registration Act 2002, s.29 appears to be that a variation must be registered in order to secure its priority and thus bind subsequent purchasers of the reversion and the tenant's estate.[5] However, in many cases the tenant will be in actual occupation of the demised premises. Any interest he has as a result of a variation is presumably capable of having overriding status by virtue of his occupation and therefore it will be binding on purchasers of the reversion.

1. See *Record* v. *Bell* [1991] 1 WLR 853; *McCausland* v. *Duncan Lawrie* [1996] NPC 94. Note generally *Jones* v. *Forest Fencing* [2001] PLSCS 249 and *Grossman* v. *Hooper* [2001] 2 EGLR 82. See also B11.2.3.

2. *Tootal Clothing Ltd* v. *Guinea Properties Management Ltd* [1992] 41 EG 117.
3. See *Lotteryking Ltd* v. *AMEC Properties Ltd* [1995] 2 EGLR 13; *System Floors Ltd* v. *Ruralpride Ltd* [1995] 1 EGLR 48. Personal covenants do not appear to run with the respective landlord and tenant interests. As to this and the effect of Landlord and Tenant (Covenants) Act 1995, see *BHP Petroleum (Great Britain) Ltd* v. *Chesterfield Properties Ltd* [2002] 1 All ER 821.
4. Land Registration Rules 2003, r.78.
5. An article discussing the issues and stating a possible contrary view is 'Off the register' by Alan Riley, *SJ* (26 March 2004).

14.2.   Flats

14.2.1.   Any party to a long lease of a flat may apply to the Leasehold Valuation Tribunal under Part IV Landlord and Tenant Act 1987 as amended by Commonhold and Leasehold Reform Act 2002 for an order for the variation of the lease where the lease fails to make satisfactory provision for:

   (a)   repair or maintenance of the flat or building;

   (b)   insurance of the premises;

   (c)   repair or maintenance of installations;

   (d)   the provision of services;

   (e)   recovery by one party to the lease from another party of expenditure incurred for the benefit of the other party;

   (f)   computation of service charges under the lease.

14.2.2.   The list of provisions which can be varied seemingly only applies to applications under section 35 of the 1987 Act, i.e. individual applications. It appears that applications under section 37, made by a majority of tenants, are not restricted to the items listed above.

14.2.3.   Similar but more limited provisions apply to leases of dwellings other than flats in relation to insurance provisions only.

14.3.   Surrender and re-grant

Where the variation of the lease extends the premises contained in the original demise or extends the length of the original term, it may be deemed to be a surrender of the original lease and a re-grant of a new lease on the varied terms.[1] The new lease created by the variation will be a 'new' tenancy and will therefore be subject to the provisions of Landlord and Tenant (Covenants) Act 1995, even though the former lease was not. It is preferable in these circumstances to execute a new lease rather than a deed of variation. In the new lease the landlord may need to consider whether he should include provisions (in a lease of commercial premises) dealing with a range of matters including the terms on which he will be prepared to consent to an assignment of the lease (including provision for an authorised guarantee agreement) by the tenant.[2] He may also wish to consider whether to exclude the new lease from the renewal provisions of Part II Landlord and Tenant Act 1954.

1. See *Friends Provident Life Office* v. *British Railways Board* [1995] 38 EG 106 and K10.1.5.
2. See Landlord and Tenant (Covenants) Act 1995 and K10.

14.4. Effect of variation on former tenant

14.4.1. Where there has been a variation of a lease which variation the landlord has an absolute right to refuse or where the lease has been altered after an assignment so as to deprive the landlord of an absolute right of refusal (called a 'relevant variation' under section 18 Landlord and Tenant (Covenants) Act 1995), a former tenant is not liable to pay any amounts under the covenants in the lease which are referable to the relevant variation. If, for example, a lease is varied after an assignment and the rent payable under the lease is increased, a former tenant who is sued by the landlord for rent unpaid by the assignee will only be liable for the amount of rent which was payable by the tenant before the variation and the former tenant cannot be held liable for the whole of the increased rent. A guarantor's liability under a variation is co-extensive with that of the tenant whose liability is being guaranteed (see K10.6.5).

14.5. Stamp Duty Land Tax

14.5.1. A variation of a lease may be notifiable and may give rise to liability to stamp duty land tax, particularly where the variation increases the rent but also in other circumstances.[1]

1. Finance Act 2003, Sched.17A paras.13–15A. The SDLT provisions relating to lease variations have been amended on a number of occasions to introduce anti-avoidance measures: see further A14.

K15. Sale of tenanted property

15.1. **Introduction**
15.2. **Disclosure of tenancies**
15.3. **Tenancy terminates before completion**
15.4. **Buyer's solicitor**

15.5. **Completion**
15.6. **After completion**
15.7. **Apportionment on sale of a reversion**

15.1. Introduction

15.1.1. Where a sale is subject to a tenancy, the procedure and steps to be taken equate with those of a vacant possession transaction, but a number of additional matters need to be considered.

15.2. Disclosure of tenancies

15.2.1. It is an implied (and frequently expressed) term of a contract for the sale of land that vacant possession will be given to the buyer on completion. As this will not be the case where the sale is of tenanted property, the contract must include an express term saying that the sale is subject to a tenancy or tenancies, and a copy of the relevant lease or leases (sometimes called tenancy agreements) should be supplied to the buyer with the draft contract. An express condition will also provide that the buyer, having been supplied with copies of the relevant agreements, shall be deemed to purchase with full knowledge of their contents. Standard Condition 3.3.2(a) and Standard Commercial Property Condition 4.1.2 contain provisions to this effect.

15.3. Tenancy terminates before completion

15.3.1. If the tenancy to which the sale is subject comes to an end between contract and completion, the seller should not re-let the property without first consulting the buyer and obtaining his instructions. To re-let the property without the buyer's permission would frequently put the seller in breach of his fiduciary duty to the buyer. Standard Condition 3.3.2(b) provides that the seller is to inform the buyer without delay if any tenancy ends; the seller is then to act as the buyer directs, provided the latter agrees to indemnify the seller against all loss and expense. Standard Condition 3.3.2(c) provides that after the contract is made, the seller is to inform the buyer without delay of any change in the tenancy terms. Standard Commercial Property Conditions 4.1.3 and 4.1.4 contain similar provisions.

15.4. Buyer's solicitor

15.4.1. The matters the buyer's solicitor should check include:

(a) the terms of the lease(s) or agreement(s) supplied by the seller's solicitor;

(b) the effect of any security of tenure legislation on the tenant(s);

(c) details of the landlord's obligations under the lease(s) or agreement(s), and in particular whether or not the seller has complied with such obligations;

(d) whether the tenant has complied with all his obligations under the lease or agreement (e.g. as to payment of rent and service charge) and, if not, what steps the seller has taken to enforce the agreement against the tenant;

(e) what variations have been made to the agreements and/or licences granted;

(f) details of any renewal applications or the exercise of an option made by the tenant;

(g) whether the tenants have a right of first refusal (see K9.4). This is also an important consideration for the seller's solicitor, since it is the seller who will be guilty of an offence if he fails to comply with the 1987 Act.

15.4.2. The buyer should be informed of the matters listed above and advised accordingly. If it is discovered that the landlord is in breach of any of his obligations (e.g. breach of a repairing covenant) the buyer's solicitor should require the seller to remedy the breach before completion. Alternatively the buyer may insist that the contract contains an express term providing that the seller will indemnify the buyer against liability for such breach since, on completion, the buyer will assume the seller's role as landlord and will thus be liable to the tenant for breaches of the landlord's covenants, even though such breach was committed before the buyer became the owner of the property.

15.4.3. If the tenant has the benefit of security of tenure legislation, consideration should be given to the question of whether the buyer, on termination of the contractual tenancy, would be able to recover vacant possession of the property if he so wished. In certain circumstances the buyer may be precluded from relying on some of the statutory grounds for possession, e.g. a landlord who purchases premises which are subject to a business tenancy within Landlord and Tenant Act 1954, Pt. II will be unable to regain possession under section 30(1)(*g*) of that Act until he has owned his interest in the property for a period of five years. On termination of some tenancies the landlord may also be liable to pay compensation to the outgoing tenant, and this contingency should also be discussed with the buyer.

15.4.4. Full enquiries must be made in relation to the amount of rent payable by the tenant, any statutory restrictions on the amount of rent recoverable, and the provisions for review or increase of that rent. Enquiries should also be made to ensure that the rent payable under the lease or agreement has been paid to the date of completion and that no arrears exist. Standard Condition 3.3.2(f) provides that the seller takes no responsibility for whether and how any legislation affects any tenancy and what rent is legally recoverable.

15.4.5. In certain circumstances a landlord who wishes to dispose of his reversionary interest in a block of flats must, before contracting to sell to a third party, first offer the reversion to the 'qualifying tenants'. Where these provisions apply, the buyer must ensure that the seller has correctly fulfilled his obligation to notify the qualifying tenants of their right to purchase the reversion, and that the time limit for the tenants' right to exercise this option has elapsed. See further K9.

15.4.6. Where a tenancy is of a dwelling, and the lease is for a term not exceeding seven years, the landlord may be responsible for repairing the structure and exterior of the premises under Landlord and Tenant Act 1985, ss.11–14. Where these sections apply, they are generally non-excludable and in appropriate cases the buyer should be advised of his potential liability under these provisions (see K1.7.2).

15.4.7. If on an assignment of the reversion the assignor is not to be released from his covenants by the tenant (or there is a possibility that the tenant may refuse to give consent to the landlord's release), the assignor may wish to consider taking an express indemnity covenant from the buyer together with a covenant by the buyer to notify the assignor of the buyer's sale of the reversion to a third party within a specified time of completion of that further sale. This is to enable the first assignor to serve notice on the tenant renewing his request to be released from liability under the landlord's covenants in the lease. The assignor must serve notice on the tenant before or within four weeks after completion of an assignment if he wishes to be released from the landlord's covenants in the lease. The buyer should therefore be required to notify the assignor within seven days of completion of a further sale in order to give the assignor sufficient time to serve his notice on the tenants within the four-week period. It may be possible for a restriction to be entered on the register to prevent registration of a purchase until this has been done. In practice this solution is likely to be impractical (see K10.10).

15.5. Completion

15.5.1. In addition to the usual requirements on completion of the purchase of a freehold property, the buyer should receive:

(a) the original lease(s) or tenancy agreement(s);

(b) an authority signed by the seller and addressed to the tenant(s), authorising the tenant(s) to pay future rent to the buyer.

15.6. After completion

15.6.1. Where the premises which have been purchased consist of a dwelling, Landlord and Tenant Act 1985, s.3 requires the new landlord (the buyer) to give written notice of the assignment and of his name and address to the tenant not later than the next day on which rent is payable, or if that is within two months of the date of the assignment, the end of the period of two months. The seller remains liable for breaches of covenant occurring until written notice of the assignment is given to the tenant by either the seller or the buyer.[1]

15.6.2. Landlord and Tenant Act 1987, s.48 also requires the landlord to provide the tenant with an address in England and Wales for service of notices. This section applies where the premises consist of or include a dwelling (including an agricultural holding)[2] but not to premises to which Landlord and Tenant Act 1954, Pt. II applies. Further, until such notice is given, any rent or service charge under the lease is treated as not being due, and is thus not recoverable by action by the buyer. It is therefore in the interests of both seller and buyer to ensure that such notice is given promptly after completion. Notice should be given to the tenant in duplicate, the tenant being requested to sign one copy and return it to the landlord who will, on receipt of the tenant's signed copy notice, have evidence of compliance with this provision.

15.6.3. Section 47 Landlord and Tenant Act 1987 requires the landlord's name and address to be given on all demands for rent or any other sums payable under the tenancy. This will not satisfy the requirements of section 48.

15.6.4. However, the Act does not make it clear to whom and at what point the notice should be given. The safest course is to give a section 48 notice to the original tenant on the grant of a new lease and to the assignee following every assignment of the lease.

15.6.5. Since most leases contain a covenant by the tenant to give the landlord a notice of assignment within a specified time after the disposition, the section 48 notice should be given to the new assignee as soon as the change of tenant becomes known. Alternatively managing agents or landlords should print the notice on every rent or service charge demand.

15.6.6. Section 48 notices do not have to be served personally on the tenant; delivery by post should be sufficient to meet the requirement that the landlord 'furnishes' the tenant with the information by notice.

1. This notice must also state whether the disposal is one to which the Landlord and Tenant Act 1987 applies (see K9). Failure to do so is a criminal offence; see Landlord and Tenant Act 1985, s.3A.
2. *Dallhold Estates (UK) Pty Ltd* v. *Lindsey Trading Properties Inc., The Times*, 15 December 1993, CA.

15.7. Apportionment on sale of a reversion

15.7.1. The Law Society's Conveyancing and Land Law Committee has prepared a formula for the apportionment of rent on sale of a reversion (see Appendix IV.2).

L. COMMONHOLD

L1. Commonhold

1.1.   Introduction

1.1.1.   Commonhold is a new form of freehold land ownership. It was introduced by Commonhold and Leasehold Reform Act 2002 ('the Act'), Part 1. The commonhold provisions of the Act came into force on 27 September 2004. Commonhold Regulations 2004 ('the Regulations') include the prescribed documentation. Commonhold (Land Registration) Rules 2004 (SI 2004/1830) ('the Rules') are also relevant.

1.1.2.   Commonhold is a system under which land is divided into separate freehold units, with common property owned by a company limited by guarantee, of which the unit owners are members.

1.1.3.   The Act overcomes the need to create a leasehold structure for buildings with multiple ownership by permitting the enforceability of positive obligations in a freehold environment.

1.1.4.   Commonhold was created principally as an alternative for blocks of flats, but it can be applied to various types of schemes. In other jurisdictions similar title systems are used for apartments, offices, industrial and retail parks and hotels.

1.1.5.   Commonhold land may only be created out of land registered with freehold title absolute. Certain land may not be registered as commonhold land, namely certain types of agricultural land, flying freeholds (except where being added to land which is already registered as commonhold) and land which is a contingent estate. Also, an application for registration as commonhold cannot relate to land which is already registered as commonhold.

1.2. **Standard documents**

1.2.1. The key document that creates the rights and obligations of unit-holders and the commonhold association is the commonhold community statement (CCS), which is registered against the title of each unit and the common parts of the commonhold and binds unit-holders, the commonhold association and in some respects tenants. The CCS sets out *inter alia* the percentage of commonhold assessment (service charge) and voting rights allocated to each unit, local rules regarding the use of commonhold units and common parts, and the permitted use for each unit.

1.2.2. The Regulations prescribe a form of CCS and the memorandum and articles of association for commonhold associations. Changes from the standard must be clearly delineated, and the Regulations set out the requirements in this respect. Certain parts of the documents may not be changed.

1.2.3. The Act prohibits certain types of provisions being included in a CCS. For example, a CCS may not prevent or restrict the transfer of a unit. Some changes require special resolutions or the consent of specific persons: for example, an amendment to the permitted use of a commonhold unit requires a special resolution and the prior written consent of the unit-holder.

1.2.4. Any amendment to the CCS will not take effect until the amended CCS is registered at the Land Registry.

1.3. **Creating a commonhold**

1.3.1. The steps involved in creating a commonhold are:

- incorporation of the commonhold association;
- applying for registration of the land as commonhold land; and
- activation of the commonhold.

1.4. **Incorporation of a commonhold association**

1.4.1. A commonhold association is a company limited by guarantee. Each association must have a unique name, which must end with 'Commonhold Association Ltd' or the Welsh equivalent.

1.4.2. The liability of members on a winding up is capped at £1.

1.4.3. On applying for incorporation, the applicant must produce the following to Companies House:

    (a) a statutory declaration that the requirements of Companies Act 1985 have been complied with in regard to registration;

(b)   the memorandum and articles of association; and

(c)   a completed Form 10 – this form sets out the details of the first directors and secretary and the registered office of the commonhold association.

1.4.4.   The memorandum of association must specify the land in respect of which the association is to exercise functions. This should include any land to be brought into the commonhold under phased development.

1.5.   Applying for registration at the Land Registry

1.5.1.   The application to the Land Registry to register land as commonhold land must be made in Form CM1 and must be accompanied by the documents referred to in the form. These include a certified copy of the certificate of incorporation of the commonhold association, and two certified copies of the CCS with the relevant plans. The plans must comply with the Land Registry's technical requirements. The Land Registry offers a free service to have plans approved prior to formal registration.

1.5.2.   The consent of the following parties is required to register land as commonhold land:

(a)   the freeholder;

(b)   any registered mortgagees of the freehold;

(c)   any leaseholders with leases of more than 21 years;

(d)   any mortgagees of such leases; and

(e)   any other prescribed persons.

1.5.3.   The consent of the holder of a lease of 21 years or less is required unless the tenant is given a replacement lease on the same terms. It is necessary to protect the interest of the tenant at the Land Registry by notice as the original lease will be extinguished on registration.

1.5.4.   Consent is required to be given in prescribed form.

1.5.5.   Consent may be dispensed with by court order in limited circumstances, namely where a person:

(a)   cannot be identified after all reasonable efforts have been made to ascertain the identity of the person required to give consent;

(b)   cannot be traced after all reasonable efforts have been made to trace him; or

(c)   has been sent the request for consent and all reasonable efforts have been made to obtain a response but the person has not responded.

There is no right to challenge the reasonableness of refusal to give consent.

1.5.6.   Consents may be given subject to conditions and will lapse if no application is made within 12 months of the giving of consent.

1.5.7.   Compensation is payable to a tenant where a lease is extinguished without the consent of the holder of the lease. The liability rests with the person whose interest is most proximate to the extinguished lease.

1.5.8.   Deregistration is possible where land is improperly registered as commonhold land. This requires a court order. The registered proprietor may also deregister commonhold land during the transitional period. The consent of any party required to register the land as commonhold land must be obtained.

Types of registration

1.5.9.   There are two types of registration, registration without unit-holders and registration with unit-holders.

1.5.10.   A registration without unit-holders is appropriate where a commonhold is set up for a new development and sales are to be completed following registration of the commonhold. It is also appropriate for the conversion of a property to commonhold where the land is owned by a single person.

1.5.11.   A registration with unit-holders is appropriate where a property is already owned or occupied by separate parties and following registration each of those parties is to own one or more units, or for a joint venture where one party provides the land and the intention is that the property will be subdivided in separate ownership immediately on registration.

1.6.   Activation

1.6.1.   For a registration without unit-holders, the commonhold will enter a transitional period on registration. During this time the applicant will remain the registered proprietor of the whole of the freehold estate in the commonhold land and the rights and duties conferred and imposed by the CCS do not apply. The transitional period will come to an end once one (but not all) of the units is transferred to a third party, and when it does the common parts will vest in the commonhold association.

1.6.2.   For a registration with unit-holders, the common parts will vest in the commonhold association and the provisions of the commonhold community statement will apply immediately on registration.

1.6.3.   In either case, a separate title for each of the units and the common parts will be created on registration of the land as commonhold land.

1.7. Conversion

1.7.1. Tenants who wish to convert to a commonhold scheme will first have to enfranchise and subsequently register the land as commonhold land.

1.8. Effect of registration on existing dealings

1.8.1. All leases affecting the land will be extinguished on activation of the commonhold. In the case of a registration without unit-holders this will occur at the end of the transitional period. For a registration with unit-holders this will occur immediately on registration.

1.8.2. Charges over the common parts will be extinguished (to the extent that they relate to the common parts) once the commonhold association is registered as proprietor of the common parts. A charge over the whole of a commonhold unit will survive registration of the commonhold in so far as it relates to the unit. A charge which relates to part of a commonhold unit will however be extinguished on registration to the extent that it relates to that part of the unit.

1.8.3. Other entries such as notices, cautions or easements will continue on registration.

1.9. Acting for the buyer

1.9.1. The buyer's solicitor should review the commonhold documentation, namely the commonhold community statement, and the memorandum and articles of association of the commonhold association. These documents may be obtained from the Land Registry.

1.9.2. If the property is being acquired in joint names, the buyer's solicitor should advise the buyer that only one of them may be recorded as a member of the commonhold association. If no nomination is made, the secretary of the commonhold association will enter as a member the person whose name first appears on the proprietorship register of the commonhold unit.

1.9.3. Within 14 days of completion, the buyer's solicitor should give the secretary of the commonhold association notice of the transfer. Form 10 should be used if the transfer is of the whole of a unit, Form 11 if the transfer is of part of a unit and Form 12 if the transfer occurs by operation of law.

1.9.4. The buyer's solicitor should review the commonhold community statement in detail. Relevant matters for consideration are:

    (a)   the description/identification of the unit;

    (b)   any rights which benefit or burden the unit;

    (c)   the proportion of commonhold assessment and reserve fund assessments allocated to the unit;

    (d)   the votes allocated to the unit;

    (e)   any restrictions on use and duties in respect of maintenance and repair;

    (f)   rules relating to the use of the common parts;

    (g)   insurance provisions; and

    (h)   any development rights.

1.9.5.   The buyer's solicitor should raise enquiries in relation to the operation of the commonhold, and the common parts. Relevant enquiries would include:

    (a)   Financial affairs of the commonhold association:

- What have the previous assessments been? (The buyer's solicitor should note whether there have been any unusually small or large assessments.)

- Are there are outstanding assessments in relation to the unit, or other units? (Outstanding assessments for other units could cause cash flow problems for the association.)

- Have reserve funds been set up? If so, when and what is the balance of these funds? Have these funds been called upon?

    (b)   The administration of the commonhold association:

- Have meetings been held as required by the articles of association?

- Do the minutes identify any disputes?

- Have there been any amendments made to the CCS which are yet unregistered?

- Is there a management agreement in place? If so, what are the terms?

    (c)   Management of the common parts:

- Do the records of the commonhold association identify any defects in the common parts, or necessary repairs?

- What are the terms of the insurance for the common parts? Have there been any claims in relation to the insurance?

1.9.6.   The buyer's solicitor should also ensure that the contract requires the seller to procure a commonhold unit information certificate. The standard CCS permits a unit-holder to give a notice to the commonhold association to provide a commonhold unit information certificate in respect of his unit. This certificate (in Form 9) sets out the arrears of commonhold assessment, reserve fund levies and interest due in respect of the unit. The benefit of the certificate is that the commonhold association may only recover from the buyer the amount specified in the certificate for the period up to and including the date of the certificate.

1.9.7. The buyer's solicitor should ensure that any outstanding monies due to the commonhold association are paid on completion, as subject to the comments above regarding the commonhold unit information certificate, the incoming unitholder will become liable.

1.10. Acting for the seller

1.10.1. The seller's solicitor should ensure that the seller provides all information necessary to answer any enquiries raised by the buyer's solicitor regarding the commonhold. The articles of association permit (subject to any contrary resolution of the commonhold association) a member of the commonhold association to inspect and be provided with a copy of any relevant documents and record of the association upon payment of a reasonable charge for copying.

1.10.2. The seller's solicitor should also ensure that any outstanding monies due to the commonhold association are paid on completion, as the seller will not be released from liability for such arrears on transfer of the unit.

1.11. Acting for the lender

1.11.1. Not all members of CML are prepared to lend on commonhold units. Part 2 of the Lenders' Handbook which sets out the requirements of individual lenders specifies whether a particular member of CML is prepared to accept part of a commonhold as security.

1.11.2. The commonhold specific requirements of the Lenders' Handbook which the solicitor will have to comply with include ensuring that the commonhold association has obtained insurance in accordance with the lender's requirements; a commonhold unit information certificate is obtained; the commonhold assessment is paid to the date of completion; and that the CCS does not include any material restrictions on occupation or use.

1.11.3. The CCS must also contain a provision requiring, in the event of voluntary termination of the commonhold, the termination statement to provide that the unit-holders will ensure that any mortgage secured on the unit is repaid on termination. This provision is not included in the model CCS so solicitors will need to ensure that it has been added.

1.11.4. A company search should be carried out to verify the existence of the commonhold association, that it has not been wound up and that there is no registered indication that it is to be wound up.

1.11.5. Notice of transfer of the commonhold unit and notice of the mortgage should be given to the commonhold association within 14 days of completion.

1.12.   **Leasing**

1.12.1.   Restrictions can apply to the letting of commonhold units.

1.12.2.   A residential commonhold unit (i.e. one which the CCS requires to be used only for residential or for residential and incidental purposes) may not be leased at a premium, for a term longer than seven years, or under an option or agreement which would result in a term of longer than seven years. An exception applies for the grant of a lease of up to 21 years to the holder of a lease which has been extinguished on registration of the land as commonhold land. The lease must be on the same terms as the extinguished lease.

1.12.3.   No restrictions are imposed on lettings of non-residential units. However it is open for a CCS to impose restrictions, such as restrictions on the permitted use.

1.12.4.   A lease of a commonhold unit may not require the tenant to make payments to the commonhold association in discharge of payment due to be made by the unit-holder under the CCS. However, the model CCS includes provisions permitting the diversion of rent where an owner has failed to pay commonhold assessments or reserve fund assessments.

Acting for the landlord

1.12.5.   Before granting a lease of a commonhold unit, the prospective landlord must give the tenant a copy of the CCS (including plans relevant to the unit) and a notice in Form 13 informing the tenant that he will be required to comply with provisions in the CCS on grant of the lease. If the landlord fails to do so, and the tenant suffers loss as a result of an obligation in the CCS being enforced against the tenant, the landlord can be liable to reimburse the tenant unless the obligation is reproduced in the lease.

1.12.6.   A solicitor acting for a landlord should therefore get an acknowledgement from the tenant that the tenant has received these documents before the lease is entered into.

1.12.7.   A solicitor acting for a landlord should also ensure that notice of the tenancy (in Form 14) is given to the commonhold association within 14 days of the grant of the lease.

Acting for the tenant

1.12.8.   A solicitor acting for a tenant should review the terms of the CCS to identify whether:

   (a)   the CCS imposes any conditions in respect of letting;

   (b)   there are any rights attaching to the unit which should be included in the tenancy (for example, limited use rights);

(c) there are any rights granted to the commonhold association in relation to the unit (for example rights of entry, or rights to connect to services in the unit);

(d) there are restrictions on use in the CCS which may interfere with the use permitted under the lease; and

(e) the CCS contains any other provisions which could interfere with the beneficial use and occupation of the property (for example, restrictions on signage or alterations).

1.12.9. The solicitor should in particular bring to the tenant's attention the dispute resolution provisions of the CCS and the provisions dealing with the diversion of rent.

1.12.10. The solicitor should also consider imposing restrictions on the landlord's right to consent to variations to the CCS (for example, amendments to the permitted use) without the consent of the tenant.

Assignment of a lease

1.12.11. Before assigning a tenancy in a commonhold unit, a tenant must give the prospective assignee a copy of the CCS (including plans relevant to the unit) and a notice in Form 15 informing the assignee that he will be required to comply with the provisions in the CCS on assignment of the lease. If the outgoing tenant fails to comply with this and the assignee suffers loss as a result of an obligation in the CCS being enforced against the assignee, the outgoing tenant can be liable to reimburse the assignee unless the obligation is reproduced in the lease.

1.12.12. A solicitor acting for an assignor should therefore get an acknowledgement from the assignee that the assignee has received these documents before the assignment is entered into.

1.13. **Running a commonhold**

1.13.1. A commonhold is managed by the commonhold association, although it will primarily be managed by the board. Some issues must be dealt with by the commonhold association in general meeting. Certain types of transactions and particular amendments require resolutions of the commonhold association in general.

1.13.2. Each commonhold association must hold an annual general meeting each year unless dispensed with under Companies Act 1985. The quorum required for a meeting will be set out in the articles of association.

1.13.3. Members vote either by a show of hands or a poll. A resolution is decided by show of hands unless a poll is demanded before the declaration of the result of the show of hands. On a poll each member has the number of votes allocated in the CCS in respect of the unit. Flying resolutions can be made, without the need for a meeting. Most matters require ordinary resolutions, but some matters require special or unanimous resolutions or special majorities.

1.13.4. A commonhold association has a duty to manage the common parts of its commonhold. It is required to keep the common parts in good repair (including decorating them and putting them into sound condition), and insure them.

1.14. Dealing with the common parts

1.14.1. The commonhold association is free to sell or deal with its interest in the common parts. It may grant easements or leases over common parts. Charges over common parts are not permitted save for legal mortgages approved by unanimous resolution prior to the grant of the mortgage.

1.14.2. Alterations to common parts require the approval of the commonhold association by ordinary resolution.

1.14.3. The commonhold association must insure the common parts to their full rebuilding and reinstatement costs against loss or damage by fire and such other risks specified in paragraph 5 of Annexe 4 of the CCS. The CCS may impose obligations in respect of insurance of commonhold units.

1.15. Financial management

1.15.1. The commonhold association will raise income in the form of commonhold assessments and reserve fund levies. Other sources of income may include rental derived from the letting of common property.

1.15.2. Before raising a commonhold assessment, the directors must give the unit-holders a notice of the proposed commonhold assessment in Form 1. Unit-holders are entitled to make representations to the commonhold association regarding the amount of the assessment within one month of when the notice is given. The directors are required to consider the representations, and are then to issue a notice specifying the payment due.

1.15.3. Reserve funds may be set up to finance the repair and maintenance of common parts. The directors must try to ensure that unnecessary reserves are not accumulated.

1.16. Administration

1.16.1. The commonhold association is required to retain various records including minutes of meetings, a register of members and other registers. Subject to other statutory requirements, the records are required to be kept for a minimum of three years. A commonhold association must maintain financial records in accordance with the requirements of Companies Act 1985. In most cases commonhold associations will not have to have their accounts audited as they will qualify as small companies under Companies Act 1985.

1.16.2. Commonhold associations have to lodge annual returns and lodge notices of any change to the directors or secretary or registered office of the commonhold association. Normal company law rules regarding notice of certain types of resolution also apply.

1.17. **Commonhold units**

1.17.1. A commonhold must consist of at least two commonhold units. The extent of each unit is defined by the CCS and the plans annexed. A commonhold unit may not include the structure and exterior of a building where a building contains all or part of more than one commonhold unit. Therefore in a block of flats the structure and exterior of the building must form part of the common parts. However for a scheme consisting of a series of stand alone buildings, the structure and exterior of the buildings may constitute part of a commonhold unit.

1.17.2. A CCS may not prevent a unit-holder from transferring his unit or place restrictions on such transfer.

1.18. **Further information**

1.18.1. The former Department for Constitutional Affairs published:

- a guidance paper on the drafting of a commonhold community statement: the paper includes specimen local rules and is intended to promote uniformity in the drafting of provisions for individual commonholds;

- non-statutory guidance on Commonhold Regulations 2004.

These are available on the archive of the Department's website at **www.dca. gov.uk**.

1.18.2. Land Registry Practice Guide 60 provides more information on the requirements relating to the registration of commonholds, and dealings in commonhold land.

1.18.3. Where the Protocol is to be used or a home information pack is required, Form TA9 Commonhold Information may be used to supplement the normal pre-contract enquiries.

M. DELAY AND REMEDIES

M1. Delayed completion

1.1. Breach of contract

1.1.1. Any delay in completion beyond the contractual date will be a breach of contract entitling the innocent party to damages for his loss, but will not entitle him immediately to terminate the contract unless time was of the essence of the completion date.[1]

1. *Raineri* v. *Miles* [1981] AC 1050.

1.2. Time of the essence

1.2.1. At common law time is impliedly of the essence of the completion date where the subject matter of the contract makes it so, e.g. on the sale of a business as a going concern, or the sale of a wasting asset.[1] In such cases time will therefore be of the essence unless this implication is expressly negatived by a condition to the contrary in the contract.

1.2.2. By Standard Condition 6.1 and Standard Commercial Property Condition 8.1 time is not of the essence of the contract (but can be made so by express contractual condition) unless a notice to complete has been served.

1. See *Pips (Leisure Productions) Ltd* v. *Walton* (1982) 43 P&CR 415 (sale of a 21-year lease). It was also stated *obiter* in *Raineri* v. *Miles* [1981] AC 1050 that time might be considered to be of the essence in chain transactions.

1.3. Anticipating delay

1.3.1. Delay may occur owing to events outside the immediate control of the parties and their solicitors, e.g. postal delays or late receipt of funds from a lender. In such cases there is usually little doubt that completion will take place but it may be postponed for a few days beyond the contractual completion date.

1.3.2. Where delay is anticipated the client, his lender and the other party's solicitor should be informed of the anticipated delay as soon as possible, and of its likely duration and, subject to the solicitor's duty of confidentiality, of the reason for the delay. This is particularly important in chain transactions where the delay in completion of one link in the chain may have serious consequences on the remainder of the transactions in the chain.

1.3.3.   Any delay in completion may result in an adjustment being made to the repayment figure due on a seller's existing mortgage. This matter must, therefore, be resolved with the solicitors acting for the lender or the lender himself. Similarly, an advance cheque issued by the buyer's lender is usually delivered subject to the condition that it is used to complete the transaction within a stated number of days of its issue, failing which it must be returned to the lender and a fresh advance cheque issued in time for the rearranged completion date. Such an instruction must be observed by the solicitor acting for the buyer's lender.

1.3.4.   Delay in completing one transaction may affect the client's ability to complete a related sale or purchase. If, e.g. completion of the client's sale becomes delayed, he will not have the necessary funds available with which to complete his synchronised purchase transaction, and failure to complete that purchase on the contractual date for completion will be a breach of contract involving the client at the very least in the payment of compensation for the delay. The client should be advised of the delay and of its consequences.

1.3.5.   Although the solicitor should do his best to ensure that any breach of contract is avoided, e.g. by arranging bridging finance so that the purchase transaction can be completed on time, he is also under a duty to act in his own client's best interests, and in these circumstances completion of the purchase with the assistance of bridging finance may not always represent the best course of action for the client to take. In the example under discussion, the client would probably not be able to utilise the advance cheque from his new mortgage to complete the purchase since there will commonly be a condition attached to it that the advance is conditional on the client's existing mortgage first being discharged. Not being able to utilise the new mortgage advance may result in a large sum being needed by way of bridging finance with a possible consequent heavy commitment to interest on the loan. Alternatively the client may choose to use bridging finance to pay off his first mortgage, thus releasing the mortgage funds for his purchase. Secondly, the client will be in the position of owning two houses until the sale of the first is completed, and if the sale transaction is not completed within a short space of time, this too will represent an onerous commitment for the client.

1.3.6.   The reason for the delay on the sale transaction and the likely period of delay in its completion must be taken into account when advising the client whether to complete the purchase on time, or to delay completion of the purchase thereby putting himself into breach of that contract. In the converse situation, where the sale can proceed but the purchase is delayed, completion of the sale transaction on the due date will result in the client becoming homeless for an uncertain length of time with consequent problems relating to alternative accommodation for the period of the delay, storage of furniture and other similar problems.

1.3.7.   Any delay in completion will be a breach of contract for which the innocent party could recover damages but, where the delay is short, the amount of loss sustained by the breach is unlikely to justify the time and expense of an action for breach of contract. Compensation provisions under the contract may provide adequate redress for the innocent party in these circumstances. If not, an action for breach may be brought, but the amount of compensation received under the contract has to be credited against the amount claimed as damages.

1.4. Compensation for delay

1.4.1. The application of the common law provisions relating to payment of compensation for delay might not provide the innocent party with sufficient financial compensation for his loss and are usually replaced by specific contractual provisions providing for compensation. In default of a specific contractual clause dealing with the matter, the common law provisions as set out below would apply.

Common law provisions

1.4.2. In addition to any action for damages, where the delay is the buyer's fault:

(a) the buyer pays the outgoings on the property from the contractual date for completion;

(b) the buyer is entitled to keep the income from the property (if any) from the date of completion;

(c) from the contractual date of completion, the buyer pays interest to the seller on the balance of the purchase price at the general equitable rate.[1]

1.4.3. Where the delay is the seller's fault:

(a) the seller remains responsible for the outgoings on the property;

(b) he is entitled to keep whichever sum is the lesser of:

(i) the net income of the property; or

(ii) the amount of interest payable by the buyer, calculated as under (c) in M1.4.2.

1.4.4. Since there will be no income generated by a property which is being sold with vacant possession, the application of these rules effectively means that the buyer has to pay interest when the delay is his fault, but not when the delay is caused by the seller.

1.4.5. Standard Condition 7.3 provides for the payment of compensation at the 'contract rate' which is defined by Condition 1.1.1(e) as being 'the Law Society's interest rate from time to time in force' (see Appendix IV.13), although the parties are free to substitute a different rate by special condition if they so wish.

1.4.6. Under this condition, compensation is assessed using the 'concept of relative fault', so that whoever is most at fault for the delay pays the compensation; it is not simply a matter of the party who delayed in actual completion being liable to pay compensation. To calculate the liability for compensation, it is necessary to refer to the timetable of events contained in Conditions 4.3.1 and 4.3.2 in order to establish whether the delay in completion has been caused by a delay in carrying out a procedural step earlier in the transaction. Delay occurring before completion is assessed by reference to the definition of a 'working day' contained in Condition 1.1.1(m) but this definition ceases to apply once completion date has passed, after which every day's delay counts towards the liability for compensation. Having apportioned the delay between the parties, the party who is most at fault for the delay pays compensation to the other for the period by which his delay exceeds the delay of the other party. Compensation under this provision is neither additional to nor in substitution for common law damages, but merely on account.

1.4.7. By Standard Conditions 6.1.2 and 6.1.3, where the sale is with vacant possession and the money due on completion is not paid by 2 pm on the day of actual completion (or such other time as may have been agreed by the parties), for the purposes of the compensation provisions only, completion is deemed to have taken place on the next following working day unless the seller had not vacated the property by 2 pm (or other agreed time). If this time limit is not complied with the buyer may find himself liable to pay compensation to the seller under Standard Condition 7.3.

1.4.8. Condition 7.3.4 provides for cases in which the property is tenanted. It allows the seller to recover the income from the property in addition to any compensation to which it may be entitled under condition 7.3.1. While a provision to this effect is commonly encountered in contracts for the sale of commercial property, there is thought to be a risk that, if challenged, it would be struck down as a penalty. A particular source of difficulty is that the object of the compensation is to place the seller in the position it would have been in if the contract had been completed on time: if, however, the contract had been completed on time, the seller would not have received any income from the property following the completion date. The seller may, therefore, need to satisfy the court that the inclusion of the provision is justified by the particular circumstances of the sale.

1.4.9. Standard Commercial Property Condition 9.3 contains the compensation provisions under this form of contract. Condition 9.3 does not operate on the concept of relative fault and effectively only the buyer can be called upon to pay compensation for delayed completion. Where the seller is at fault the buyer is left to his remedy at common law, i.e. an action for damages.

1. According to *Esdaile* v. *Stephenson* (1822) 1 Sim & St 122, the general equitable rate is a mere 4% per annum, but more recently in *Bartlett* v. *Barclays Bank Trust Co. Ltd* [1980] Ch 515 interest was awarded based on the rate allowed on the court's short-term investment account under Administration of Justice Act 1965.

1.5. **Service of a notice to complete**

1.5.1. Where it appears that the delay in completion is not likely to be resolved quickly (or at all), consideration may be given to the service of a notice to complete which will have the effect of making time of the essence of the contract so that if completion does not take place on the new completion date specified in the notice the aggrieved party may then terminate the contract forthwith, forfeit or recover his deposit (as the case may be) with accrued interest and commence an action for damages to recover his loss. This then gives the aggrieved party the certainty of knowing that on a stated date he can make a definite decision either to look for a new property to purchase (if a buyer), or resell the property elsewhere (as a seller). It must, however, be remembered that making time of the essence imposes a condition which binds both parties. If, therefore, between the date of service and new date for completion as specified by the notice, unforeseen events occur which result in the previously aggrieved party being unable to complete on the new date, the previously defaulting party could turn round and terminate the contract, leaving the aggrieved party in breach of contract himself. For this reason a notice to complete should never be served as an idle threat. The server must be sure that he will be able to comply with the new completion date himself before serving the notice.[1]

1.5.2. At common law, the service of a valid notice to complete can only be achieved where the notice specifies a 'reasonable time' for the new completion date, and the party serving the notice is himself ready, able and willing to complete. Both of these conditions present considerable difficulties for the server since it is difficult to assess the 'reasonable time' for the new completion date – a few days ahead may seem quite reasonable to a seller who is anxious to complete the sale, but a few weeks may seem more reasonable to a buyer whose mortgage arrangements have just fallen through. A seller may not be 'ready, able and willing' to complete if he has not discharged his subsisting mortgage over the property.[2] Since it is common practice for a seller to discharge his mortgage after completion, using part of the proceeds of sale with which to make repayment, this condition presents particular difficulties for a seller who wishes to serve a notice on a defaulting buyer. However, a seller will be 'ready, able and willing' to complete even though some of the administrative arrangements have yet to be made.[3] Since the decision in *Behzadi* v. *Shaftesbury Hotels Ltd*[4] it seems that a notice to complete (making time of the essence) can be served immediately contractual completion date passes – there is no need for there to have been 'unreasonable delay'.

1.5.3. The contract normally provides specifically for the service of a notice to complete, such clause being drafted to circumvent the common law problems outlined in the preceding paragraph. Standard Condition 6.8 and Standard Commercial Property Condition 8.8 are such conditions, and provided that the notice expressly refers to the fact that it is served under the provisions of the relevant condition, its service will be valid, the common law requirements being ousted by the specific contractual provisions.

1.5.4.   Standard Condition 6.8.2 and Standard Commercial Property Condition 8.8.2 provide that on service of a notice to complete, completion must take place within 10 working days (exclusive of the date of service) and makes time of the essence of the contract.[5]

1.5.5.   Standard Condition 6.8.3 requires a buyer who has paid less than a 10% deposit to pay the balance of the full 10% immediately on receipt of a notice to complete. No equivalent provision is contained in the Standard Commercial Property Conditions.

1.5.6.   The parties' rights and obligations where a valid notice has been served but not complied with are governed by Standard Conditions 7.5 and 7.6 and Standard Commercial Property Conditions 9.5 and 9.6.

1.5.7.   Once served, a notice to complete cannot be withdrawn.

1.5.8.   If compliance with a first notice to complete is waived there is no reason why a second notice to complete, specifying an extended period for compliance should not be served on expiry of the initial notice, or why the period for compliance, with a first notice should not be extended by mutual agreement (provided it is done in writing so as to comply with Law of Property (Miscellaneous Provisions) Act 1989), but there is some doubt whether time would remain of the essence in such circumstances.

1.5.9.   Non-compliance with a notice to complete gives the aggrieved party the right to terminate the contract, but is not in itself an automatic termination of the contract.

1.5.10.   If it is necessary to serve a notice in a situation where the delay is caused by the death of one of the contracting parties, the notice should be addressed to the deceased and his personal representatives at the deceased's last known address. A further copy of the notice should be served on the Public Trustee.

1. See *Northstar Land Ltd* v. *Maitland Brooks and Jacqueline Brooks* [2006] EWCA Civ 756.
2. *Cole* v. *Rose* [1978] 3 All ER 1121.
3. *Aero Properties* v. *Citycrest* [2002] All ER (D) 77.
4. [1992] Ch 1.
5. In *Northstar* v. *Brooks* an issue was raised as to whether, following the service of a notice to complete, the parties had to complete by the end of normal office hours or had until midnight on the tenth working day. The judge at first instance concluded that, in the absence of a special arrangement, the deadline was 'at 5.30 pm or 6.00 pm or perhaps a few minutes later' (*Northstar Land Ltd* v. *Maitland Brook and Jacqueline Brooks* [2005] EWHC 1919, Ch). In the Court of Appeal, Ward LJ reserved his position on this, stating that he was 'anxious not to give a judgment of this Court which might be taken as a judgment of general and inflexible application to all conveyancing transactions.'

M2. Rescission

2.1. Introduction

2.1.1. The word rescission is used here in the context of contracts which involve a vitiating element, e.g. misrepresentation, fraud, mistake, and refers to the remedy which is available in these circumstances.

2.1.2. Rescission denotes the restoration of the parties to their pre-contract position by 'undoing' the contract and balancing the position of the parties with the payment of compensation by one party to the other. Damages in the conventional sense of that word are not payable since there will have been no breach of contract.

2.1.3. Since rescission is an equitable remedy, its operation is subject to the general equitable bars which are set out in more detail in M4.2.

2.2. Contractual right to rescind

2.2.1. No right to rescind exists except where there is a vitiating element in the contract or a specific contractual right to rescind. Therefore, unless there is a breach of contract entitling one party to terminate his obligations under it, the contract must be performed.

2.2.2. A right to rescind may be given by a specific contractual condition which will specify the circumstances in which the right is to operate and the parties' rights and obligations in the event of rescission taking place. Such a right may be granted, e.g. where the contract is conditional on the fulfilment of a condition.

2.2.3. Under the Standard Conditions of Sale, the right to rescind is available in four situations:

(a) where risk in the property remains with the seller and the property is rendered unusable between contract and completion (Condition 5.1.2);

(b) for misrepresentation (Condition 7.1.3);

(c) where a licence to assign is not forthcoming (Condition 8.3.3);

(d) where either the buyer or the seller has failed to comply with a notice to complete (Condition 7.5 and 7.6).

M

2.2.4.   The Standard Commercial Property Conditions contain similar provisions with the exception of (a) above (see Conditions 9.1, 10.3 and 9.5 and 9.6 respectively).

2.2.5.   Where the right to rescind is exercised under one of the Conditions referred to in M2.2.3 or M2.2.4, the parties' rights on rescission are governed by Standard Condition 7.2 and Standard Commercial Property Condition 9.2 which provide for the repayment of the deposit to the buyer with accrued interest, the return of documents to the seller and the cancellation of any registration of the contract at the buyer's expense.

2.3.   Restrictions on the use of contractual rescission clauses

2.3.1.   A commonly encountered type of contractual rescission clause is one which gives the seller the right to rescind if he is unable or unwilling to answer a requisition raised by the buyer. This type of clause is narrowly construed by the courts who will only permit the seller to rescind where the requisition reveals an incumbrance of which the seller was previously unaware and which he is unable to discharge. They thus provide an emergency escape route for a seller in the event that an unforeseen difficulty with the title arises, and cannot be relied on by a seller who had not taken proper care to investigate his own title before drafting the contract, nor where the seller changes his mind after exchange and decides not to go ahead with the contract.[1] Neither the Standard Conditions of Sale nor the Standard Commercial Property Conditions, however, contain this type of clause.

2.3.2.   This type of clause was examined by the court in *Selkirk* v. *Romar Investments*[2] from which case it appears that the conditions set out below must be satisfied before the court will allow the seller to rely on the clause:

(a)   the seller can show some title; if he can show no title at all his withdrawal from the contract will be a breach entitling the buyer to damages;

(b)   at the date of the contract the seller was unaware of the defect of which the buyer complains;

(c)   the defect is either irremovable or only removable at disproportionate expense;

(d)   the seller relies on the condition definitely and within a reasonable time;

(e)   the seller is reasonable in exercising his right to withdraw.

2.3.3.   The right to rescind under this type of clause can only be exercised in response to requisitions which are raised on the title itself and not in relation to, e.g. the form of the purchase deed or administrative matters relating to completion. Law of Property Act 1925, ss.42, 45 and 125 give the buyer non-excludable rights to raise requisitions about certain matters affecting the title and a contractual rescission clause would not be effective in circumstances affected by one of these sections (see D2).

1. See *Day* v. *Singleton* [1899] 2 Ch 320.
2. [1963] 3 All ER 994.

2.4. Misrepresentation

2.4.1. In certain circumstances rescission may be available for misrepresentation. This remedy is further discussed in M5.

2.5. Misdescription

2.5.1. Misdescription results from an error in the particulars of sale, e.g. misdescribing the tenure of the property or the physical extent of the land to be sold.

2.5.2. If the misdescription is substantial the buyer may ask for rescission of the contract and compensation. A misdescription is substantial if its effect is substantially to deprive the buyer of his bargain.[1]

2.5.3. If the misdescription is not substantial the buyer can be forced to complete but may seek compensation by way of an abatement from the purchase price.

2.5.4. A misdescription of the property will usually also amount to a misrepresentation and it is more common nowadays to pursue a remedy under Misrepresentation Act 1967 than for misdescription.

1. See generally *Watson* v. *Burton* [1957] 1 WLR 19.

2.6. Non-disclosure

2.6.1. Non-disclosure arises out of the seller's failure to comply with his duty of disclosure. The seller's duty of disclosure is discussed in B5.

2.6.2. Where the effect of the non-disclosure is substantial, i.e. its effect is substantially to deprive the buyer of his bargain, the buyer may seek rescission of the contract.

2.6.3. If the non-disclosure is not substantial the buyer can be forced to complete but may seek compensation by way of an abatement to the purchase price.

2.7. Mistake

2.7.1. Where the parties have entered a contract under a fundamental mistake of fact, the contract is void at common law. The transaction will be set aside by the court and the buyer is entitled to recover any money paid. This principle has been applied where the subject matter of the contract had been destroyed before the contract was made,[1] where the buyer unknowingly contracts to buy property which he already owns,[2] where the parties misunderstood the legal effect of the transaction,[3] and where both parties were mistaken as to the meaning of the contract.[4]

2.7.2.   A mistake as to the quality of the subject matter of the contract will not normally have the effect of making the contract void at common law, although equity may in such circumstances refuse specific performance. If the effect of the mistake is to make the subject matter of the contract something entirely different from that which the parties thought it to be, the contract may be avoided.[5]

2.7.3.   A mistake as to the identity of the contracting parties seems not to affect a written contract for the sale of land. The court treats the parties named in the contract as being the correct parties to it and will enforce the contract on that basis.[6]

1. I.e. *res extincta*: see, e.g. *Hitchcock* v. *Giddings* (1817) 4 Price 135.
2. I.e. *res sua*: see, e.g. *Cooper* v. *Phibbs* (1865) 17 I Ch R 73.
3. *Wolff and another* v. *Wolff and others* [2004] All ER (D) 28.
4. *George Wimpey UK Ltd* v. *VI Components Ltd* [2004] EWHC 1374 (Ch), BLD (2506024771).
5. See generally *Bell* v. *Lever Bros Ltd* [1932] AC 161.
6. *Hector* v. *Lyons* (1988) 58 P&CR 156. The principles relating to mistaken identity outlined in *Lewis* v. *Averay (No.2)* [1973] 2 All ER 229 are inapplicable in this situation.

2.8.   Limitation periods

2.8.1.   Where the right to rescind arises out of a contractual provision, it must be exercised within the time limits given within the condition, or if no time is specified within a reasonable time. An action based on a contractual rescission clause is subject to the normal six-year limitation period under Limitation Act 1980 unless the contract was by deed when a 12-year limitation period would be available.

2.8.2.   Actions for rescission arising out of the general law principles, e.g. for misdescription are subject to the equitable doctrine of laches (see M4.3).

M3. Breach of contract

3.1. Introduction

3.1.1. This section is intended as a brief overview of the subject under discussion. It is not intended to be used as a substitute for the advice of an experienced litigation solicitor. Prompt action by someone knowledgeable in the area of litigation is often required where problems arise in relation to a breach of contract.

3.1.2. Remedies for breach of contract depend on whether the breach is of a condition in the contract, entitling the aggrieved party to terminate the contract and/or claim damages, or of a warranty, entitling the aggrieved party to claim damages only.

3.1.3. A term of the contract will be a 'condition' if it is a major or fundamental term. Minor terms are classified as 'warranties'. In some cases it is not possible to classify a term as specifically falling into one or other of these categories until the consequences of the breach can be seen. Where the consequences are serious or far reaching, the unclassified term will be treated as a condition. In the converse situation it will be a warranty only. The terminology or labelling which the parties themselves have attached to the various terms of the contract is not conclusive as to their classification. In conveyancing contracts all terms are usually called 'conditions', but in law some of those terms would only have the status of warranties.[1]

3.1.4. An action on a simple contract, i.e. one not made by deed, has a limitation period under Limitation Act 1980 of six years running from the date of the breach. A limitation period of 12 years applies where the contract was made by deed. A three-year limitation period applies where the amount claimed includes damages for personal injury or death. In some cases, Latent Damage Act 1986 may extend the limitation period.

3.1.5. On completion the terms of the contract merge with the purchase deed in so far as the two documents cover the same ground, and an action on the contract is no longer sustainable after completion except where it is based on a contract term which remains extant despite completion taking place. For this to happen the contract would generally have to contain a non-merger clause (such as Standard

Condition 7.4 or Standard Commercial Property Condition 9.4) which expressly allowed a particular clause or clauses to remain alive after completion,[2] although sometimes the court may imply such an intention from the subject matter of the clause. If an action on the contract cannot be maintained, the buyer may have to attempt to pursue a remedy under the covenants for title or title guarantee (see M9).

3.1.6. In any situation where the buyer suspects that the seller will or may default, consideration should be given to protecting the buyer's contract by entry of a notice (in registered land) or as a Class C(iv) land charge (if the seller's title is unregistered).

1. See *Cehave NV* v. *Bremer Handelsgesellschaft mbH* [1976] QB 44.
2. See Standard Condition 7.4 and Standard Commercial Property Condition 9.4.

3.2.   **Specific performance**

3.2.1. In sale of land cases an action for specific performance may provide an alternative remedy to an action for damages. This remedy is discussed in M4.

3.3.   **Exclusion clauses**

3.3.1. An exclusion clause which purports to exclude liability under the contract must be incorporated in the contract if it is to be valid. In the case of a written contract, an exclusion clause contained within the writing is deemed to be incorporated whether or not the parties have read the document or were capable of reading it. In such circumstances illiteracy or inability to read English is no defence.[1]

3.3.2. Exclusion clauses must be specifically drafted to fit the breach which has occurred; thus a clause which excludes liability for breach of condition will not protect against a breach of warranty and vice versa.[2]

3.3.3. Any ambiguity in the wording of the clause will be construed against the party who is seeking to rely on the clause.

3.3.4. The clause normally only affords protection to the parties to the contract. Therefore an action in tort may be brought against a third party who caused the loss of which the claimant complains. He will be unable to shelter behind the protection of the clause since he does not enjoy privity of contract with the claimant.[3]

3.3.5. Standard Condition 7.1 and Standard Commercial Property Condition 9.1 restrict the remedies available for breach of contract. A buyer is only entitled to damages if there is a material difference in the tenure or value of the property and is only entitled to treat the contract as at an end if the error or omission results from fraud or recklessness, or where he would otherwise be obliged to accept a property differing substantially in quality, quantity or tenure from what he had been led to expect.

3.3.6. Exclusion clauses contained in contracts for the sale of land (except those relating to the exclusion of liability for misrepresentation) are not subject to the reasonableness test in Unfair Contract Terms Act 1977.

1. See *L'Estrange* v. *F Graucob Ltd* [1934] 2 KB 394; *Thompson* v. *London, Midland & Scottish Railway* [1930] 1 KB 41.
2. See *Curtis* v. *Chemical Cleaning and Dyeing Co.* [1951] 1 KB 805.
3. See *Adler* v. *Dickson* [1955] 1 QB 158.

3.4. Delayed completion

3.4.1. Unless time was of the essence of the completion date, or had been made so by service of a notice to complete, a completion which takes place later than the date specified in the contract does not of itself entitle the aggrieved party to terminate the contract.

3.4.2. Late completion will, however, be a breach of warranty entitling the aggrieved party to recover damages for any loss suffered as a result of the delay.[1]

1. *Raineri* v. *Miles; Wiejski (Third Party)* [1981] AC 1050 and see M1.4.

3.5. Damages for breach

3.5.1. Damages for breach of a contract for the sale of land are assessed under the normal contractual principles established in *Hadley* v. *Baxendale*.[1] Thus, subject to establishing causation, damages for losses naturally flowing from the breach may be claimed and in addition reasonably foreseeable consequential loss.

3.5.2. The quantum of damages under the consequential loss head are limited to loss which was reasonably foreseeable by the defaulting party in the light of the facts known by him (or by his agent) at the date when the contract was made (not at the date of the breach of contract).

3.5.3. The starting point for damages for breach of a contract for the sale of land is the difference between the contract and market prices of the property at the date of the breach. To this may be added actual financial loss suffered as a result of the breach, e.g. wasted conveyancing costs, legal costs involved in the purchase of another property, interest payable on a mortgage or bridging loan, costs of removal or storage of furniture, costs of alternative accommodation pending purchase of another property.[2]

3.5.4. Loss of development profit, or loss of profit on a sub-sale, can only be claimed if the defendant was aware of the claimant's proposals for the property at the time the contract was made.[3]

3.5.5. Where the buyer defaults and the seller makes a loss on the resale, that loss can be claimed as damages but, if the seller makes a profit on the resale, he would have to give credit for the amount of the profit in his action since he is only entitled to recover his financial loss and is not entitled to benefit from the buyer's breach. The purpose of contractual damages is to place the parties in the position in which they would have been had the contract been duly performed. There is no punitive element in the assessment of damages.

3.5.6. As a general principle of contractual damages, it is only possible to recover for financial loss, and no claim can be made in respect of mental distress suffered as a result of the defendant's breach. The practice of awarding a nominal sum in respect of damages for mental distress established by *Jarvis* v. *Swans Tours*[4] seems to be confined to leisure and pleasure contracts, e.g. holiday contracts and contracts for leisure activities.

3.5.7. Damages can normally only be claimed in respect of losses which have occurred since the contract was made; thus there is generally no possibility of recovering expenses incurred at the pre-contract stage of the transaction, e.g. for a wasted surveyor's report or search fees.[5]

3.5.8. The claimant must have attempted to mitigate his loss, e.g. by trying to purchase another similar property (as disappointed buyer) or by attempting to resell the property (as disappointed seller). The attempt to mitigate should be made; otherwise the award of damages may be reduced because of the failure to mitigate. If the claimant attempts to mitigate and in so doing increases his loss, the defendant will be liable for the increased loss.

3.5.9. Credit must be given in the claim for damages for any compensation received under Standard Condition 7.3 or Standard Commercial Property Condition 9.3 or for any deposit forfeited by the seller (see M1).

3.5.10. Actions claiming a sum under £50,000 will be brought in the county court; above that limit, the High Court has jurisdiction. Actions brought in the county court for sums not exceeding £1,000 may be referred to arbitration (but not if there is a dispute over a point of law) in which case no costs are normally awarded in the action. In other county court cases, a successful litigant may be penalised as to costs if he does not recover more than £1,000 in his judgment, or does not recover more than the amount paid into court by the defendant prior to the hearing. The question of costs must be fully discussed with the client before the decision to start proceedings is taken, since in some cases the action for breach of contract may not be cost effective for the client.

1. (1854) 9 Exch 341.
2. See, e.g. *Beard* v. *Porter* [1948] 1 KB 321.
3. *Diamond* v. *Campbell-Jones* [1961] Ch 22; *cf. Cottrill* v. *Steyning & Littlehampton Building Society* [1966] 2 All ER 295.
4. [1973] QB 233; and see *Bliss* v. *South-East Thames Regional Health Authority* [1987] ICR 700.
5. But see *Lloyd* v. *Stanbury* [1971] 2 All ER 267 where pre-contract expenditure including money spent on repairs to the property was recovered.

3.6. Action in tort

3.6.1. If an action in contract is not possible, e.g. a valid exclusion clause prevents the claim, an action in tort may be considered. The limitation period for such an action will usually be six years from the time the tort was committed, but a three-year limitation period applies where the claim includes damages for personal injury or death. Actions in tort may also be considered where it is desired to sue a third party who was not privy to the contract. Most actions of this type will lie in negligence which imposes a fairly onerous burden of proof on the claimant. The quantum of damages is assessed using different principles and in general damages for pure economic loss cannot be claimed.[1]

1. Damages are awarded following the principles laid down in *The Wagon Mound* [1961] AC 388. See *Junior Books* v. *The Veitchi Co.* [1983] 1 AC 520 and *Murphy* v. *Brentwood District Council* [1991] 1 AC 398 relating to economic loss.

3.7. Misrepresentation

3.7.1. Where an action on the contract cannot be sustained an action in misrepresentation may still be viable. This remedy is further discussed in M5.

3.8. Freezing order

3.8.1. Although not a conventional sale of land remedy, a freezing order could be obtained if it was suspected that the defendant was intending to remove his assets from the jurisdiction in order to avoid liability. Such an order would not provide a direct remedy but would protect the claimant's position as an interim measure. Prompt action is required. Where the land is registered, a freezing order should be reflected in the register by the entry of a restriction in Form AA.[1] A person who has applied to the court for a freezing order can apply for a restriction in Form CC.[2]

1. Land Registration Rules 2003, r.93 and Sched.4.
2. *Ibid.*, r.93 and Sched.4.

3.9. Frustration

3.9.1. Where the contract has become impossible of performance due to an unforeseen act which is beyond the control of both parties, the contract is frustrated and the parties' rights and obligations are terminated without there being liability for breach on either side. The parties' rights in this situation are, in the absence of specific contractual provision, governed by Law Reform (Frustrated Contracts) Act 1943 which aims to restore the parties to their pre-contract position without imposing penalties. Frustration is usually raised as a defence to an action for breach of contract and, if successfully pleaded, provides an absolute defence to the defendant.

3.9.2. Although the general view is that the doctrine of frustration does not apply to contracts for the sale of land, *dicta* from the House of Lords in *National Carriers Ltd* v. *Panalpina (Northern) Ltd*[1] suggest otherwise. It is therefore possible that the defence of frustration might be allowed in a situation where, e.g. the land which was the subject of the sale was totally destroyed by landslip into the sea between the dates of contract and completion. If the land was destroyed before the date of the contract, the contract would be void for common mistake. Frustration would not apply where the property burned down between contract and completion. Neither does it apply where the property is subject to a compulsory acquisition order.[2]

1. [1981] AC 675.
2. *E Johnson & Co. (Barbados) Ltd* v. *NSR Ltd* [1996] EGCS 133.

3.10. Return of deposit

3.10.1. Where the buyer defaults on completion, the seller will wish to forfeit the deposit, but Law of Property Act 1925, s.49(2) gives the court an absolute discretion to order the return of the deposit to the buyer. A contractual clause attempting to negate the provisions of section 49 is of no effect.[1] If the deposit is more than 10% the buyer may be able to argue that it is not a reasonable amount and is a penalty, in which case the court may order its return to the buyer.

3.10.2. Where the seller defaults on completion the buyer will have to bring an action under Law of Property Act 1925, s.49(2) to recover his deposit.

3.10.3. Under section 49, the court appears to have power to return all of the deposit or none of it to the buyer. There is no discretion to order the return of part of the deposit even where this course of action would represent the most equitable way of dealing with the position between the parties. It seems, however, that the court may be prepared to order the return of the whole deposit to the buyer on condition that the buyer reimburse certain expenses to the seller, which would seem to be a fair way round the restrictions imposed by section 49.[2]

1. *Country & Metropolitan Homes Surrey Ltd* v. *Topclaim Ltd* [1996] 3 WLR 525.
2. See *Universal Corporation* v. *Five Ways Properties* [1979] 1 All ER 552; *James Macara Ltd* v. *Barclay* [1945] KB 148; *cf. Dimsdale Developments (South East) Ltd* v. *De Haan* (1983) 47 P&CR 1. See also *Tennero Ltd* v. *Majorarch Ltd* [2003] EGCS 154 which provides guidance on when the court will exercise its discretion to order the return of the deposit.

3.11. Trade Descriptions Act 1968

3.11.1. Under Trade Descriptions Act 1968, it is an offence to make a false statement in a contract for the supply of services (including land). The Act applies where the seller is acting in the course of a business and so would be applicable where, e.g. a buyer was purchasing land from a builder, but not in an ordinary residential purchase between private individuals. If an action in contract or misrepresentation cannot for some reason be sustained, it may be worth considering reporting a 'false statement', e.g. a misrepresentation about the quality of the property, to the local trading standards office and asking them to pursue a prosecution under the Act. Such a prosecution does not afford a direct remedy for the client. On conviction for the offence it would, however, be possible for the client to ask the court for a compensation order under Powers of Criminal Courts Act 1973, s.35. Where the conviction is obtained in the magistrates' court, the compensation order cannot exceed £2,000 in respect of each offence.[1]

1. See *Breed* v. *Cluett* [1970] 2 QB 459 where such an order was obtained following a builder's conviction under this Act for making false statements about the availability of NHBC protection on a new house.

3.12.   Property Misdescriptions Act 1991

3.12.1.   This Act which came into force on 4 April 1993 creates a criminal offence which is committed where a false or misleading description is applied to certain aspects of the property as listed in regulations made under the Act in the course of an estate agency or property development business. The offence is of strict liability and can be committed by publishing a misleading photograph of property as well as by misdescribing property orally or in writing.[1] An action must generally be brought within three years of the alleged offence. Enforcement of the Act is through criminal proceedings brought by the Trading Standards Department for the area. Some estate agents are now seeking an indemnity from the seller in respect of liability under this Act. The seller should be advised not to accept such a clause.

1. In *Lewin* v. *Barratt Homes Ltd* [1999] EGCS 139 the defendants were held liable under this Act in relation to 'statements' made in photographs and through the display of a show house.

3.13.   MIG policies

3.13.1.   A lender who benefits from the proceeds of a MIG policy does not need to give credit for this sum when quantifying damages.[1]

1. *Europe Mortgage* v. *Halifax Estate Agencies* [1996] NPC 68.

3.14.   Checklist

3.14.1.   A client who is encountering problems with a property transaction will probably first seek the advice of the person who is advising him in the sale or purchase. A checklist of the main points to be considered when discussing the client's problems is set out below. These matters should be taken into consideration when deciding whether and how to pursue a remedy for breach of contract and cover the main points of information which will be needed by the litigation department if the matter is handed to them for further action. In addition to the matters listed below, the person taking instructions should obtain a complete history of the conveyancing transaction from the client, including a detailed timetable of the events leading to the present dispute, and should obtain from the client either the original documents relevant to the matter, or copies of them.

3.14.2. The following is a checklist of the main points to be considered:

(a) Has there been a breach of contract?

(b) If so, what type of breach, i.e. of condition or warranty?

(c) What remedy does the client want, e.g. damages or specific performance?

(d) Is there a valid exclusion clause which might prevent the claim?

(e) When did the limitation period start to run?

(f) What (approximately) is the total of the client's financial loss?

(g) How much of that loss would be recoverable, bearing in mind the rules on remoteness of damage?

(h) Would the costs of an action be justified?

(i) Who should be sued, e.g. other party to the contract, solicitor, surveyor?

(j) If a claim cannot be made in contract, is there a viable alternative action, e.g. in tort or for misrepresentation?

M4. Specific performance

4.1. Introduction

4.1.1. Although this is an equitable remedy which is granted at the discretion of the court, an order for specific performance is not uncommon in sale of land cases where, since no two pieces of land are identical, an award of damages would be inadequate compensation for the injured party's loss.[1]

4.1.2. The claim can be made either on its own, or in conjunction with a claim for damages or rescission, depending on the circumstances.

4.1.3. Specific performance cannot generally be awarded for breach of a contract to grant a loan (whether secured or unsecured).[2] It would not therefore be available where a lender, in breach of contract, withdrew his offer of mortgage.

1. *Hall* v. *Warren* (1804) 9 Ves 605.
2. *Rogers* v. *Challis* (1859) 27 Beav 175.

4.2. General bars to the award

4.2.1. As an equitable remedy, the award of a decree of specific performance is subject to the usual principles of equity. It will not therefore be awarded where:

    (a) an award of damages would adequately compensate for the loss sustained by the breach;

    (b) one of the contracting parties lacks full contractual capacity;

    (c) the contract contains a vitiating element, e.g. mistake, fraud, illegality;

    (d) the enforcement of the order would require the constant supervision of the court;

    (e) a third party has acquired an interest for value in the property;

    (f) the award would cause exceptional hardship to the guilty party;

    (g) the seller cannot make good title.

4.3. Delay

4.3.1. The Limitation Acts do not usually apply to equitable remedies, but the doctrine of laches (lapse of time) does. The remedy may therefore be barred if the innocent party is dilatory in seeking an award.[1]

4.3.2.   Unlike a common law action for breach of contract, the injured party can apply for a decree before a breach of contract has actually occurred (i.e. before contractual completion date) provided that he can show that a serious breach is likely to take place if the court does not intervene.[2]

4.3.3.   Laches will not bar the application where the buyer is already in possession of the property.[3]

1. *Lazard Brothers & Co. Ltd* v. *Fairfield Properties Co. (Mayfair) Ltd* (1977) 121 SJ 793.
2. *Marks* v. *Lilley* [1959] 2 All ER 647; *Hasham* v. *Zenab* [1960] AC 316, PC.
3. *Williams* v. *Greatrex* [1957] 1 WLR 31.

4.4. Damages in lieu

4.4.1.   Subject to the above principles the injured party always has the right to apply for a decree of specific performance, but there is no guarantee that an award will be forthcoming in any given circumstances. If, in a situation where specific performance would otherwise be available to the injured party, the court decides not to make such an order, it may award damages in lieu of specific performance under Supreme Court Act 1981, s.50. Such damages are assessed using normal contractual principles as outlined in M3.

4.4.2.   Where an award of specific performance has been made but has not been complied with, the injured party may return to the court asking the court to withdraw the order and to substitute the decree of specific performance with an award of damages.[1]

1. *Johnson* v. *Agnew* [1980] AC 367.

4.5. Standard Conditions of Sale and Standard Commercial Property Conditions

4.5.1.   Where a notice to complete has been served by the seller under Standard Condition 6.8 or Standard Commercial Property Condition 8.8 and is not complied with, by Standard Condition 7.6 and Standard Commercial Property Condition 9.5, the innocent party's right to apply for a decree of specific performance is not excluded.

M5. Misrepresentation

5.1. **Definition**   5.4. **Imputed knowledge**
5.2. **Fraudulent misrepresentation**   5.5. **Exclusion clauses**
5.3. **Actions under**
      Misrepresentation Act 1967

5.1. Definition

5.1.1. A misrepresentation is an untrue statement of fact which is relied on by the aggrieved party, which induces him to enter the contract, and as a result of which he suffers loss.

5.1.2. The statement must be of fact, not law.[1] A statement of opinion is not actionable unless it can be proved that the opinion was never genuinely held.[2]

5.1.3. A misrepresentation may be fraudulent, i.e. deliberately dishonest within the definition of fraud laid down in *Derry* v. *Peek*,[3] negligent, i.e. made carelessly without having checked the facts, but not necessarily negligent within the tortious meaning of that word, or innocent, i.e. a genuine and innocently made mistake.

5.1.4. The representation can be made by the seller's conduct. In *Taylor* v. *Hamer*[4] the seller was guilty of misrepresentation because her conduct had led the buyer to believe that certain items would be included in the sale. The items were present when the buyer inspected the property but were removed before exchange of contracts.

1. The distinction between fact and law is not always clear; see *Solle* v. *Butcher* [1950] 1 KB 671; and *Pankhania* v. *Hackney London Borough Council* [2002] All ER (D) 22.
2. *Edgington* v. *Fitzmaurice* (1885) 29 Ch 459.
3. (1889) 14 App Cas 337.
4. *Taylor* v. *Hamer* [2002] EWCA Civ 1130.

5.2. Fraudulent misrepresentation

5.2.1. Where the misrepresentation has been made fraudulently, the aggrieved party may bring an action in tort for deceit which may result in rescission of the contract and damages.

5.2.2. The party who alleges fraud must prove fraud. This places a very onerous burden of proof on the claimant in the action and, except where the evidence of fraud is indefeasible, it is more usual to treat the misrepresentation as having been made negligently and to pursue a remedy under Misrepresentation Act 1967.

5.3.   **Actions under Misrepresentation Act 1967**

5.3.1.   The claimant must show that he has an action in misrepresentation as defined in M5.1, after which the burden of proof shifts to the defendant who, in broad terms, has to disprove negligence.

5.3.2.   A misrepresentation is negligent if the defendant cannot prove that he had grounds for belief and did believe the statement he made was true up to the time the contract was made. There is therefore a duty to correct a statement which, although being true at the time when it was made, subsequently becomes untrue.

5.3.3.   The remedies for a negligent misrepresentation are rescission of the contract and damages.

5.3.4.   If the defendant successfully establishes the defence of grounds and belief outlined in M5.3.2, thus showing that the misrepresentation was truly innocent, rescission is available, but not damages.

5.3.5.   Although Misrepresentation Act 1967 allows a party to ask for rescission of the contract, the award of the remedy remains within the equitable jurisdiction of the court and is thus discretionary and subject to the equitable bars.[1]

5.3.6.   If none of the equitable bars applies, but nevertheless the court decides not to grant rescission, it may instead award damages in lieu of rescission to the claimant.[2]

5.3.7.   Damages under Misrepresentation Act 1967 are awarded on a tortious basis[3] under Misrepresentation Act 1967, s.2(2).

5.3.8.   An award of damages can be made under both the subsections of section 2, i.e. an award in lieu of rescission and an award to compensate the claimant for his loss, subject to the overriding principle that the claimant cannot recover more than his actual loss; thus the awards under the two subsections are not cumulative.

5.3.9.   Rescission is only likely to be awarded where the result of the misrepresentation is substantially to deprive the claimant of his bargain.[4]

5.3.10.   An action in misrepresentation does not arise out of the contract, since the misrepresentation is a non-contractual statement which has the effect of inducing the contract. Neither does it arise out of tort. The limitation periods prescribed by Limitation Act 1980 do not therefore apply in this situation and it seems that the limitation period for an action based on misrepresentation relies on the equitable doctrine of laches.

5.3.11.   Where a misrepresentation has become incorporated as a minor term of the contract it is possible by Misrepresentation Act 1967, s.1 to treat the statement as a mere representation and to pursue a remedy under Misrepresentation Act

1967. This option would benefit the claimant by giving him the right to ask for rescission of the contract as well as damages. If his action were confined to breach of a minor contractual term his only available remedy would be damages.

1. The equitable bars are listed in M4.2.
2. Misrepresentation Act 1967, s.2(1).
3. *Chesneau* v. *Interhome, The Times*, 9 June 1983, CA; and see *Royscott Trust* v. *Rogerson* [1991] 2 QB 297.
4. See *Gosling* v. *Anderson, The Times*, 8 February 1972; *cf. Museprime Properties Ltd* v. *Adhill Properties Ltd* (1990) 61 P&CR 111.

5.4. Imputed knowledge

5.4.1. Knowledge gained by a solicitor in the course of a transaction is deemed to be known by the solicitor's client whether or not this is in fact the case. Thus where a solicitor makes an incorrect reply to pre-contract enquiries, basing his reply on an erroneous assessment of the title deeds, the solicitor's knowledge and also his misstatement is attributable to the client who will be liable to the buyer in misrepresentation.[1] In such a situation the solicitor would be liable to his own client in negligence.

5.4.2. The converse situation is also true. If, for example, the seller makes a misrepresentation to the buyer personally, but the misrepresentation is later corrected in correspondence between the seller's solicitors and the buyer's solicitors, the buyer is deemed to know of the correction (even if not actually told by his solicitor) and would not in these circumstances be able to sustain an action for misrepresentation against the seller.[2]

1. *Cemp Properties* v. *Dentsply* [1989] 35 EG 99.
2. *Strover* v. *Harrington* [1988] Ch 390.

5.5. Exclusion clauses

5.5.1. By Misrepresentation Act 1967, s.3, as amended by Unfair Contract Terms Act 1977, s.8, any clause which purports to limit or exclude liability for misrepresentation is only valid in so far as it satisfies the reasonableness test laid down in section 11 and Schedule 2 Unfair Contract Terms Act 1977.

5.5.2. The reasonableness test is applied subjectively, in the light of the circumstances which were known to the parties at the time when the contract was made. It therefore depends on the circumstances of each particular case as to whether the exclusion clause is valid in that situation. There is no guarantee that any given form of wording will satisfy the test unless and until the clause is subjected to the scrutiny of the court. Such clauses therefore require great care in drafting. Fraudulent misrepresentation should (if required) be excluded by express wording to this effect.

5.5.3.   Standard Condition 7.1 and Standard Commercial Property Condition 9.1 purport to limit the seller's liability for, *inter alia*, misrepresentation. The validity of this clause is subject to its satisfying the reasonableness test on the facts of each particular case.

5.5.4.   The majority of misrepresentation actions arising out of property transactions appear to result from erroneous replies to pre-contract enquiries. Some standard forms of pre-contract enquiries (but not the Seller's Property Information Form used in Protocol transactions) have an exclusion clause printed on them. This exclusion clause is also subject to the reasonableness test.[1]

1. See *Walker* v. *Boyle* [1982] 1 All ER 634 where an exclusion clause contained in a then current edition of a standard form of pre-contract enquiries failed the reasonableness test. In the same case, the exclusion clause contained in the 19th edition of the National Conditions of Sale was held to be invalid for the same reason.

M6. Other causes of action

6.1. Introduction

6.1.1. In certain circumstances it may be possible or necessary to seek a remedy from someone other than a party to the contract. Such action will normally have to be brought in tort since no privity of contract will exist between the potential parties to the action.

6.1.2. A non-exhaustive list of suggestions of alternative sources of action which might be relevant if an action on the contract was unavailable is included here.

6.2. Solicitor's liability

6.2.1. A solicitor who is guilty of providing inadequate professional services may be reprimanded by the Legal Complaints Service which additionally may order the solicitor to rectify a mistake at his own expense or to waive his costs or repay costs to the client. The Legal Complaints Service can also order the solicitor to pay compensation of up to £15,000 to the client. For further information, see **www.legalcomplaints.org.uk**.

6.2.2. A solicitor who has been negligent in the conduct of a client's affairs can be sued in negligence (see M10).

6.2.3. If a client has suffered loss as a result of default by a solicitor which loss cannot be recovered from any other source, the Solicitors Regulation Authority's Compensation Fund may be able to assist.

6.2.4. A solicitor's duty of care is owed not only to his own client, but in certain circumstances to third parties as well.[1] It may therefore be possible in some circumstances for an aggrieved buyer to sue his seller's solicitor in negligence[2] although the court has held that in a normal conveyancing transaction the seller's solicitor does not owe a duty of care to the buyer.[3]

6.2.5.   Where the solicitor's own client had been held liable for, e.g. breach of contract in circumstances where the breach was caused by the party's solicitor, the solicitor can be required to indemnify the client against his liability for damages.[4]

1. See *Ross* v. *Caunters* [1980] 1 Ch 297 but see *Murphy* v. *Brentwood District Council* [1991] 1 AC 398.
2. See, e.g. *Wilson* v. *Bloomfield* (1979) 123 SJ 860, CA.
3. *Gran Gelato Ltd* v. *Richcliff Ltd* [1992] Ch 560.
4. E.g. *Cemp Properties* v. *Dentsply* [1989] 35 EG 99.

6.3.   Breach of warranty of authority

6.3.1.   Where an agent acts outside the scope of his authority he will be liable to the third party for breach of warranty of authority.[1]

6.3.2.   A solicitor or estate agent who exceeds his client's authority may thus be sued by a third party.[2]

1. *Yonge* v. *Toynbee* [1910] 1 KB 215.
2. *Suleman* v. *Shahsavari* [1989] 2 All ER 460; *Penn* v. *Bristol & West Building Society* [1997] 3 All ER 470.

6.4.   Estate agents

6.4.1.   Estate agents are regulated by the Estate Agents Act 1979 which sets out the duties agents owe to clients and third parties. The Act also gives the Office of Fair Trading power to issue warning or prohibition notices against persons whom it considers unfit to carry on estate agency work. For further information, contact the Trading Standards Department for the relevant area or the Office of Fair Trading (**www.oft.gov.uk**).

6.4.2.   Liability may also exist if the agent exceeds his authority as under M6.3.

6.4.3.   An estate agent who is authorised to *sell* the property (but not one who is merely empowered to procure a buyer) may have authority to receive the contract deposit.[1]

6.4.4.   As far as pre-contract deposits are concerned, unless there is express authority from the seller to take and hold a pre-contract deposit, such sum must be held on behalf of the buyer. If the pre-contract deposit is lost, e.g. where an estate agent absconds with the money, the loss falls on the buyer except where the agent was expressly authorised to take the pre-contract deposit.[2]

6.4.5.   The estate agent's duty to the seller is similar to the common law duties which exist between an agent and his principal.[3]

6.4.6.   The estate agent's duty is owed to his principal, i.e. the seller client, and generally he owes no duty to the buyer.[4] There may also in some circumstances be a liability in relation to the pre-contract deposit, or in negligence under *Hedley Byrne* v. *Heller* principles.[5]

6.4.7.   Similar remedies to those afforded under Trade Descriptions Act 1968 lie under the Property Misdescriptions Act 1991 against an estate agent (including a solicitor who is acting as an estate agent) who misdescribes a property which he is selling. This Act creates a criminal offence which is committed where a false or misleading description is applied to property in the course of an estate agency or property development business. The offence is of strict liability and can be committed by publishing a misleading photograph of property as well as by misdescribing property orally or in writing. An action must generally be brought within three years of the alleged offence. Enforcement of the Act is through criminal proceedings brought by the Trading Standards Department for the area or the Office of Fair Trading.

6.4.8.   Some estate agents belong to the voluntary Ombudsman for Estate Agents Scheme. This scheme deals with disputes between member agencies and consumers who are buyers or sellers of residential property. The Ombudsman will consider complaints that a member agency has infringed a consumer's legal rights, failed to comply with the Code of Practice, acted unfairly or been guilty of maladministration. The Ombudsman can make compensation awards of up to £25,000. For further information, see **www.oea.co.uk**.[6] The RICS also has a Surveyors Ombudsman Scheme which was extended to the whole of the UK on 4 June 2007 (see **www.rics.org** for further details).

6.4.9.   The Housing Act 2004 makes it mandatory from 1 June 2007 for all estate agents in England and Wales who market homes with HIPs to join an independent complaints handling and redress scheme for dealing with disputes arising over an HIP. The Ombudsman for Estate Agents Scheme (see M6.4.8) is an approved redress scheme for these purposes.

1.   *Boote* v. *RT Shiels & Co.* [1978] 1 NZLR 445.
2.   *Sorrell* v. *Finch* [1977] AC 728.
3.   But see *Luxor* v. *Cooper* [1941] AC 108; *cf. Prebble (PG) & Co.* v. *West* (1969) 211 EG 831.
4.   *McCulloch* v. *Lane Fox, The Times*, 22 December 1995, CA.
5.   [1964] AC 465.
6.   The Consumers, Estate Agents and Redress Bill introduced in Parliament on 16 November 2006 will require all estate agents in the UK to join an independent approved ombudsman scheme (enactment and implementation planned for April 2008).

6.5.   Surveyors

6.5.1.   A surveyor owes his client a duty to perform his contract with reasonable skill and care. This common law duty has been replaced by the implied term to the same effect under Supply of Goods and Services Act 1982, s.13 but the surveyor's duty, and thus his liability, are necessarily limited by the extent of the instructions given to him.

6.5.2.   If the problem with the survey stems from the results of a valuation report, the surveyor will generally have been instructed by the client's lender, and so there will probably be no contractual relationship between the client and the surveyor; thus any liability which does exist will necessarily be in tort. If however the contract between the lender and the valuer contemplates that the buyer will have the benefit of the valuation report, it may be possible for the buyer to sustain an action against the valuer in contract under Contracts (Rights of Third Parties) Act 1999.

6.5.3.   In other cases a contractual relationship between the client and the surveyor will or may exist, giving the choice of action under either contract or tort.

6.5.4.   An exclusion clause purporting to exclude liability for the survey will be construed narrowly against the party seeking to rely on it and will only be valid in so far as it is fair and reasonable in the context of the particular contract in which it is included.[1]

6.5.5.   A surveyor who prepares a valuation report for a lender in the knowledge (express or implied) that the buyer will see the report and may rely on it in deciding whether or not to proceed with his purchase owes a duty of care to the buyer.[2] This duty will not, however, apply in every case. Where, for example, it is reasonable for the surveyor to assume that the buyer would be obtaining his own independent survey – which may be a fair assumption for him to make where the property is at the top end of the property market – or where the buyer is experienced in property matters, the surveyor may be entitled to shelter behind the protection of his exclusion clause and thus avoid liability.[3]

6.5.6.   Where a surveyor is sued, the quantum of damages is usually limited to the difference between what the property was actually worth at the date of the contract and what it would have been worth if the survey report had been accurate (not what the client paid for the property, or the cost of repairs). Thus, in some circumstances, the amount of damages recoverable will not equate with the client's loss. For example, the difference in value may be only a few thousand pounds, but the cost of repairs to put the property right at the date of the action may be huge, and the client can only recover the smaller sum representing the difference in value.[4] Loss in value to the property which is attributable to the fall in value of the property market is not generally recoverable as a head of loss.[5] The lender's contributory negligence (e.g. in relying on the valuation without checking it) may reduce the award made against the surveyor.[6]

6.5.7.   There is no doubt that a valuer owes a duty to the seller to provide a valuation which is as accurate as circumstances allow – a duty of skill and care is owed to the seller. If the valuer's error results in there being an undervalue of the property, the measure of damages will usually be the difference between the sale price and the market value of the property. If on the other hand an over-valuation is given, full contractual damages within *Hadley* v. *Baxendale*[7] principles will be payable to the seller, including loss caused by his inability to sell the property within a reasonable time, if this has been a consequence of the over-valuation.

6.5.8. The cause of action by a lender in respect of a negligent valuation arises when the loss crystallises, i.e. at the date when the security is sold.[8]

6.5.9. The RICS appraisal and valuation manual ('The Red Book') contains mandatory guidelines for surveyors to follow when undertaking surveys and valuations of all types of property. Non-observance of these guidelines may be evidence of negligence.

1. The reasonableness test in Unfair Contract Terms Act 1977, s.11 must be satisfied.
2. *Smith* v. *Eric S Bush (a firm)* [1990] 1 AC 831; and see *Qureshi* v. *Liassides* (unreported) (1995) EG 123 (case comment).
3. *Stevenson* v. *Nationwide Building Society* (1984) 272 EG 663.
4. *Philips* v. *Ward* [1956] 1 All ER 874; and see *Watts* v. *Morrow, The Independent,* 20 August 1991.
5. *Banque Bruxelles Lambert SA* v. *Eagle Star Insurance* [1995] 12 EG 144, CA reversed on appeal to the House of Lords *sub nomine South Australia Asset Management (Pty) Ltd* v. *York Montague* [1996] NPC 100 and see *Platform Home Loans* v. *Oyston* [1999] EGCS 26, HL.
6. *Ibid.*
7. (1854) 9 Exch 341.
8. *First National Commercial Bank* v. *Humberts, The Times,* 27 January 1995, CA.

6.6. Dangerous substances

6.6.1. There may be heavy liability (in financial terms) to third parties in tort, in negligence[1] or under Environmental Protection Act 1990 if, e.g. untreated sewage escapes into a waterway and pollutes the water.

6.6.2. Anyone who is responsible for maintaining or repairing a non-domestic building has a duty to ascertain whether there is asbestos in the building and, if so, to put a risk management process in place. If a tenant is under a covenant to repair the property, the tenant will carry this liability, not the landlord.[2]

1. Subject to foreseeability: *Cambridge Water Co.* v. *Eastern Counties Leather plc* [1994] 1 All ER 53.
2. Control of Asbestos at Work Regulations 2006 (SI 2006/2739).

6.7. Local searches

6.7.1. In certain circumstances compensation may be claimed under Local Land Charges Act 1975, s.10, where there has been an error in an official search (see B10).

6.8. The Land Registry

6.8.1. In certain circumstances compensation may be claimed from the Land Registry where a person suffers loss by reason of a mistake in the register or in an official search (see M7).

6.9.   Covenants in freehold land

6.9.1.   Where restrictive covenants have been validly annexed to land, the person with the benefit of those covenants (who may be a successor in title of the original covenantee) will be able to enforce the covenants by injunction and/or damages against either the present estate owner of the land which bears the burden of the covenants or the original covenantor. The original covenantor may, in turn, be able to recover his loss from his immediate successor in title through an indemnity covenant.

6.9.2.   In certain circumstances it may be possible to make an *ex parte* application to the Lands Tribunal under Law of Property Act 1925, s.84 for the modification or release of an obsolete restrictive covenant and so remove the potential liability under it.

6.9.3.   The burden of positive covenants does not run with freehold land and can only be enforced directly between the original contracting parties.[1] An original covenantor who is held liable in this way may seek to recoup his own loss if an indemnity covenant was taken from his immediate successor in title (see K16).

6.9.4.   Covenants entered into on or after 11 May 2000 and which are clearly expressed to be taken for the benefit of successors in title to the land may be enforceable by successors under Contracts (Rights of Third Parties) Act 1999. This Act applies to both positive and negative covenants.

1.   *Rhone* v. *Stephens, The Times*, 18 March 1994, HL.

6.10.   Covenants in leasehold land

6.10.1.   Although both positive and restrictive covenants are enforceable, liability is limited by the doctrines of privity of contract and of estate. It may not therefore always be possible for a head-landlord to take direct action against a sub-tenant since neither privity of contract nor of estate exist in this situation. However, covenants entered into on or after 11 May 2000 may benefit from Contracts (Rights of Third Parties) Act 1999 which amends the law relating to privity of contract and will allow direct enforcement between e.g. a head-landlord and a sub-tenant.

6.10.2.   Similarly, in the absence of special provisions in the lease, it is not generally possible for one tenant directly to sue a fellow tenant for breach of one of the covenants contained in their leases, and the enforcement of the covenant against the offending tenant frequently has to be brought by the landlord at the request of the injured tenant. However, covenants entered into on or after 11 May 2000 may benefit from Contracts (Rights of Third Parties) Act 1999 which amends the law relating to privity of contract and will allow direct enforcement between tenants.

6.10.3.   Liability on leasehold covenants is further discussed in K6 and K10.

6.11. **Estate agent's commission**

6.11.1. The following points are relevant to the estate agent's entitlement to his commission and when it becomes payable.

6.11.2. The contract between the agent and the seller must be absolutely clear as to what is included in the price. For example does the fee quoted include, e.g. advertising, valuation, agent's expenses, VAT, or are these to be added to the bill?

6.11.3. In the absence of express provision in the contract no charge can be made for abortive work.[1]

6.11.4. As a general principle, an agent's entitlement to his fee depends on his introduction of a ready, able and willing buyer. This means someone who is prepared and able to go ahead to completion not merely a 'subject to contract' offer.[2]

6.11.5. It is in the estate agent's interests to ensure that the contract is quite specific as to the time when his fee for the estate agency work becomes due, and that the fee becomes payable as soon as a binding contract is entered into with the buyer – not on condition that completion takes place. This type of provision (commonly found in estate agent's contracts) ensures that the commission is still payable even if the contract is terminated between exchange and completion or completion fails to take place.[3]

6.11.6. The courts interpret the expressions 'the agent is to find a buyer' or 'the agent is to introduce a buyer' as meaning that the buyer must actually sign the contract before the commission becomes due.[4]

6.11.7. Three conditions must all be satisfied before the agent can claim his commission:

(a) the agent must introduce a person who enters a valid binding contract. This means a contract which satisfies the requirements of Law of Property (Miscellaneous Provisions) Act 1989, s.2 and the contract is not otherwise voidable for mistake, fraud, etc.;

(b) the buyer must be willing and able (financially) to complete. The buyer's ability in this respect is judged at contractual date for completion, so if there is a dispute about the agent's entitlement to his fee the contractual completion date must be allowed to pass before proceedings for the commission are commenced. This is so even if, under the contract with the seller, commission became payable on exchange of contracts;

(c) the agent must be the effective cause of the sale. This means that he must be able to show that his introduction of the buyer led to the formation of the contract of sale between the seller and buyer. An 'introduction' may be nothing more than bringing the property to the buyer's attention (see *Christie, Owen and Davies plc* v. *Rylance* [2005] 18 EG 148 (CS)).

6.11.8. If the buyer fails to complete the contract and is in breach of his contract with the seller, unless commission was expressly due on exchange, no completion means no commission. If, however, the seller successfully claims damages from the buyer for breach, the agent may be entitled to recover a *quantum meruit* out of the seller's damages.[5]

6.11.9. Where two agents are instructed by the seller, there is frequently an argument about which of the agents is entitled to the commission for the sale. The principle here is that commission is payable to the first agent to secure a buyer who enters a binding contract.[6]

6.11.10. If it is the seller who withdraws from the sale, no contract means no commission, unless the contract contains express provision to the contrary. It makes no difference in this situation if the seller rescinds after the contract is made (even if the seller is in breach).

6.11.11. If a sole agency is agreed with the client, it is important that the terms of that agreement are fully and clearly explained to the client so he cannot complain of being misled if things go wrong. The danger as far as the client is concerned is that he does not understand what a sole agency means, instructs a second agent who sells the property and then feels aggrieved because both agents claim to be entitled to commission. If a sole agency agreement is expressed in terms using the phrase 'sole agent', the seller is not entitled to instruct another agent to sell the property, but there is nothing to prevent him from contracting a private sale and in that way depriving the agent of his commission. On the other hand, if the expression 'sole right to sell' is used this prohibits the seller from contracting a private sale on his own initiative. This latter phrase is therefore much more restrictive of the seller's rights than the former and would merit explicit explanation of its implications to the client. The term 'sole selling agent' is construed as meaning 'sole agent', so the seller is not prevented from contracting a private sale if this phrase is used.

6.11.12. If the seller withdraws his instructions from the agent before a sale contract is entered into, this is not a breach of the sole agency contract (the seller is entitled to change his mind and this is a normal and acceptable risk attached to estate agency) but a *sale* contracted elsewhere will be and the sole agent can then claim damages for the breach.

6.11.13. An agent who is himself in breach of his duty to his client may forfeit his right to commission.

6.11.14. Estate Agents (Provision of Information) Regulations 1991 require estate agents to inform their clients in writing of the terms of the agreement between themselves and their clients including, where appropriate, the meaning of 'sole agency' and 'sole selling rights'. The Regulations have adopted definitions of these two phrases which are similar to the explanations contained in M6.11.11.

1. *Lott* v. *Outhwaite* (1893) 10 TLR 76.
2. *Luxor* v. *Cooper* [1941] AC 108.
3. *Poole* v. *Clarke & Co.* [1945] 2 All ER 445; *cf. Midgley Estates Ltd* v. *Hand* [1952] QB 432. See also *Foxtons Ltd* v. *Thesleff* [2005] EWCA Civ 514; [2005] 21 EG 140.
4. *Jones* v. *Lowe* [1945] KB 73.
5. *Boots* v. *E Christopher & Co.* [1952] 1 KB 89.
6. *AA Dickson & Co.* v. *O'Leary* (1979) 254 EG 731 suggests that the seller cannot be made liable to pay commission twice over.

6.12. Timeshare properties

6.12.1. Timeshare Act 1992 gives the prospective buyer of a timeshare property a 14-day 'cooling off' period during which he has the right to cancel the contract.[1] The Act only applies where the buyer is buying from the developer and not to 'second-hand' timeshares.

6.12.2. Notice of the buyer's right to cancel must be given by the seller in prescribed form. Failure to give the correct notice renders the contract unenforceable and the seller is guilty of a criminal offence punishable by a fine. Enforcement of the Act is the responsibility of the local weights and measures office.

6.12.3. Timeshare Regulations 1997 (SI 1997/1081) extend Timeshare Act 1992 to rights acquired as the result of share ownership and rights under collective investment schemes. The Act is also extended to cover properties within the EU, Iceland, Norway, Liechtenstein and Switzerland, where the buyer is a private individual (not acting in the course of a business) who is normally resident in the UK.

6.12.4. A seller is required to provide any person on request with a document containing information on the property. This information will form part of the contract if a contract is subsequently entered into by an individual buyer acting in a private (i.e. non-business) capacity.

6.12.5. The contract must contain certain minimum information relating to the nature of the property, the price and recurring cover and charges. A buyer who is resident in the UK is entitled to have a copy of the contract in English.

1. This period may be extended to three months and 10 days if certain information is not provided to the buyer.

6.13. Squatters

6.13.1. A summary procedure for the eviction of squatters exists under Order 24 County Court Rules or under Criminal Justice and Public Order Act 1994, ss.72–75. The 1994 Act applies to both residential and commercial property.

6.14. Home information packs

6.14.1.   Housing Act (HA) 2004 received Royal Assent on 18 November 2004. Part 5 of HA 2004 (ss.148–178) provides the duties in relation to home information packs. These duties are being brought into force in phases (see A26.2) and the detailed content of home information packs is prescribed by Regulations (see A26.3).

6.14.2.   The person responsible for complying with the Act (a 'responsible person' (HA 2004, s.151)) is the person who markets a property. That is, either the seller or the person 'acting as estate agent' on behalf of the seller.

6.14.3.   The duty to provide a home information pack is enforced by the local Weights and Measures Authority (HA 2004, s.166). It has the power to require the production of a home information pack (s.167) and, in the event of a breach of the duties in HA 2004, ss.155 and 156, it has power to issue a penalty charge notice (s.168 and Sched.8). The penalty charge is £200 (Home Information Pack (No.2) Regulations, reg.35).

6.14.4.   A potential buyer who commissions his own version of any of the prescribed documents because he has not been provided with an authentic copy within the prescribed period may recover any reasonable fee paid by him from the responsible person (HA 2004, s.170).

6.14.5.   Estate agents marketing properties requiring a home information pack are required to belong to an approved redress scheme for the purpose of dealing with complaints related to home information packs.[1] Failure to comply is treated as a breach of duty under HA 2004, Part 5 and may be notified to the Office of Fair Trading.

6.14.6.   There are separate redress schemes for home inspectors and domestic energy assessors and voluntary redress schemes for personal search companies and corporate home information pack providers.

1.   See HA 2004, s.172 and Home Information Pack (Redress Scheme) (No.2) Order 2007 (SI 2007/1946).

6.15. Energy performance of buildings

6.15.1.   Energy Performance of Buildings (Certificates and Inspections) (England and Wales) Regulations 2007 (SI 2007/991)[1] ('the regulations') amend the Building Regulations and place sellers, landlords and builders under an obligation to provide an energy performance certificate (EPC) to prospective buyers and tenants (see A27 for further details as to their requirements and their phased implementation).

6.15.2.   The local Weights and Measures Authority is responsible for the enforcement of the duties. An authorised officer of such an Authority has power to require the production of documents for inspection (reg.39) and, in the event of a breach of duty, has the power to issue a penalty charge notice (reg.40). The amount of the penalty charge is determined according to the category of building and the breach concerned (reg.43). An appeal against such a penalty charge notice lies to the County Court (reg.45).

6.15.3. There is provision to avoid a double penalty where a penalty charge notice has already been given under HA 2004, s.168 for failure to provide a compliant home information pack (reg.41).

6.15.4. An energy assessor must be a member of an accreditation scheme approved by the Secretary of State. Such schemes must contain adequate provision for indemnity arrangements and for facilitating the resolution of complaints (reg.25).

6.15.5. Regulation 14 creates an offence for the unauthorised disclosure of an EPC, recommendation report or any data collected by an energy assessor for the purposes of preparing such a document.

1. As amended by Energy Performance of Buildings (Certificates and Inspection) (England and Wales) (Amendment) Regulations 2007 (SI 2007/1669).

M7. Rectification and indemnity

7.1. Rectification of the contract

7.1.1. Where the parties have reached agreement over a particular matter, but in error that matter is either omitted from the written contract, or is wrongly recorded in the written agreement, an application for rectification of the contract in order to correct the error can be made.[1] Under Law of Property (Miscellaneous Provisions) Act 1989, s.2(4) where rectification is ordered the court has a discretion to determine the date on which the contract comes into operation. If a term is missing from the contract, there is no contract.

1. See *Wright* v. *Robert Leonard Developments Ltd* [1994] EGCS 69.

7.2. Rectification of the purchase deed

7.2.1. Where a term of the contract is either omitted from, or inaccurately represented in, the purchase deed an application for rectification of the deed may be made to the court. Rectification relates back to the date when the original document was executed and there is no need to draw up an amended deed. The order granting rectification is often endorsed on the affected deed.[1] Rectification is an equitable remedy and is thus subject to the equitable bars.

1. For examples of the court's discretion to rectify see, e.g. *Craddock Bros* v. *Hunt* [1923] 2 Ch 136; *Wilson* v. *Wilson* [1969] 3 All ER 945; *Riverlate Properties Ltd* v. *Paul* [1975] Ch 133.

7.3. Rectification of documents by the Adjudicator

7.3.1. The Adjudicator to HM Land Registry[1] has power, on application, to make any order which the High Court could make for the rectification or setting aside of a document which:

(a) effects a qualifying disposition of a registered estate or charge;

(b) is a contract to make such a disposition; or

(c) effects a transfer of an interest which is the subject of a notice in the register.[2]

A qualifying disposition is a registrable disposition or one which creates an interest which may be the subject of a notice in the register.[3]

1. See G3.13 as to other functions of the Adjudicator and his website at **www.ahmlr.gov.uk** for appropriate application forms and guidance notes.
2. Land Registration Act 2002, s.108(2).
3. *Ibid.*, s.108(3).

7.4. **Rectification of the register**

7.4.1. Rectification in Land Registration Act 2002 has a narrower definition than in the previous law. It is limited to an alteration in the register which involves the correction of a mistake and prejudicially affects the title of a registered proprietor.[1] When such rectification occurs, the proprietor may be entitled to indemnity.

7.4.2. The court has power to make an order for rectification of the register:

    (a)   to correct a mistake;

    (b)   to bring the register up to date; or

    (c)   to give effect to any estate, right or interest excepted from the effect of registration.[2]

7.4.3. Rectification cannot be ordered against a proprietor without his consent in relation to land in his possession unless:

    (a)   the proprietor has by fraud or lack of proper care caused or substantially contributed to the mistake; or

    (b)   it would for any other reason be unjust for the alteration not to be made.[3]

Land is in the possession of a proprietor if it is physically in his possession. A proprietor is treated as being in possession of land which is physically in the possession of certain other people, for example, the proprietor's tenant or licensee.[4]

7.4.4. Where the court has power to make an order for rectification it must do so unless there are exceptional circumstances which justify its not doing so.[5]

7.4.5. The registrar has power to rectify the register without the need for the matter to be considered by the court. He can rectify the register for the same purposes, and subject to the same limitations, as the court has power to order it.[6]

1. Land Registration Act 2002, Sched.4, para.1 and see Land Registry Practice Guide 39.
2. Land Registration Act 2002, Sched.4, para.2.
3. *Ibid.*, Sched.4, para.3(2).
4. *Ibid.*, s.131.
5. *Ibid.*, Sched.4, para.3(3).
6. *Ibid.*, Sched.4, paras.5 and 6.

7.5.   Indemnity

7.5.1.   Subject to the exceptions contained in Land Registration Act 2002 a person is entitled to be indemnified by the registrar if he suffers loss by reason of:

    (a)   a rectification of the register;

    (b)   a mistake whose correction would involve rectification of the register;

    (c)   a mistake in an official search;

    (d)   a mistake in an official copy;

    (e)   a mistake in a document kept by the registrar which is not an original and is referred to in the register;

    (f)   the loss or destruction of a document lodged at the registry for inspection or safe custody;

    (g)   a mistake in the cautions register; or

    (h)   failure by the registrar to perform his duty under section 50 Land Registration Act 2002 (duty of notification of overriding statutory charges).[1]

7.5.2.   Indemnity is not payable for any loss suffered by a claimant wholly or partly as a result of his own fraud or lack of proper care.[2]

7.5.3.   No indemnity is payable on account of any mines or minerals, or the existence of any right to work or get mines or minerals, unless it is noted in the register that the title to the registered estate concerned includes the mines or minerals.[3]

7.5.4.   Indemnity may be claimed for costs or expenses reasonably incurred by the claimant with the consent of the registrar.[4]

7.5.5.   For limitation purposes, the claim must be made within six years of the time when the claimant knows, or but for his own default might have known, of the existence of his claim.[5]

7.5.6.   A claim for indemnity should initially be made to the registrar. However, a person may apply to the court for the determination of any question as to whether he is entitled to an indemnity and its amount.[6]

7.5.7.   Where the register is not rectified, the amount of indemnity payable cannot exceed the value of the estate or interest at the time when the mistake which caused the loss was made. Where the register is rectified, the amount of indemnity is limited to the value of the estate or interest immediately before rectification of the register (but as if there were to be no rectification).[7]

7.5.8.   There are provisions for the payment of interest on the amount of any indemnity so paid.[8]

7.5.9. Where an indemnity is paid the registrar is entitled either to recover the amount paid from any person who caused or substantially contributed to the loss by his fraud or to enforce any rights of action for the purpose of recovering the amount paid.[9]

1. Land Registration Act 2002, Sched.8, para.1 and see Land Registry Practice Guide 39.
2. Land Registration Act 2002, Sched.8, para.5.
3. *Ibid.*, Sched.8, para.2 and see Land Registry Practice Guide 65.
4. Land Registration Act 2002, Sched.8, para.3 and see Land Registry Practice Guide 38.
5. Land Registration Act 2002, Sched.8, para.8.
6. *Ibid.*, Sched.8, para.7.
7. *Ibid.*, Sched.8, para.6.
8. Land Registration Rules 2003, r.195.
9. Land Registration Act 2002, Sched.8, para.10.

M8. Liens

8.1.   Seller's lien

8.1.1.   The seller has an equitable lien over the property being sold to the extent of the unpaid purchase price.[1]

8.1.2.   The lien arises immediately there is a binding contract for sale and is discharged on completion to the extent that the purchase price is paid at that time.[2]

8.1.3.   By Law of Property Act 1925, s.68 the presence of a receipt clause in the purchase deed is evidence (but not conclusive evidence) of the discharge of the seller's lien. In registered land, in the absence of an adverse entry on the register of the title (or protection of the lien as an overriding interest) a subsequent purchaser of the land will take free from the lien.[3]

8.1.4.   To protect the lien against a subsequent buyer, it should be registered as a notice in the register of the title in registered land, or as a Class C(iii) land charge in unregistered land pursuant to a priority notice. The lien may take effect as an overriding interest in registered land if (unusually) the person with its benefit is in occupation of the land.[4] An unpaid seller who is in actual occupation may be estopped from claiming that the lien is an overriding interest if he has warranted, in answer to pre-contract enquiries, that vacant possession will be given on completion.[5]

8.1.5.   The lien is enforceable by foreclosure[6] or by a court order for sale of the property.[7]

8.1.6.   If the seller has agreed to permit the buyer to leave part of the purchase price outstanding on mortgage, the purchase deed should not contain a receipt clause. The buyer should enter a covenant to pay the money to the seller and to enter a formal mortgage if required. If the seller has taken a mortgage to secure the outstanding moneys, this will displace the lien. Where it appears from the transfer that further moneys are payable by the buyer to the seller but it is intended that the seller should not have a lien on the property, it is desirable for an express waiver to be included in the transfer. Where the buyer is entering another mortgage to assist with his purchase of the property, care needs to be exercised to ensure that the priorities of the lender's and seller's charges are correctly maintained; a lender will not normally cede priority to the seller's lien. It may be preferable to include a receipt clause in the document and to execute a formal mortgage in the seller's favour.

8.1.7. If the transfer cites the non-payment and contains a provision for a charge over the land, this charge may take priority over a formal mortgage created by the buyer in favour of a third party immediately after completion, but this will depend on priorities and registration.

8.1.8. By Standard Condition 6.5.1 and Standard Commercial Property Condition 8.5.1 the seller is not entitled to a lien over the title deeds after completion. If the seller wishes to reserve such a lien this provision must be expressly excluded by contractual condition.

1. *Mackreth* v. *Symmons* (1808) 15 Ves 329.
2. *London and Cheshire Insurance Co. Ltd* v. *Laplagrene Property Co. Ltd* [1971] Ch 499.
3. Land Registration Act 2002, s.29.
4. *Ibid.*, Sched.1, para.2 and Sched.3, para.2.
5. *UCB Finance* v. *France* [1995] NPC 144.
6. *Hughes* v. *Griffin* [1969] 1 All ER 460.
7. *Williams* v. *Aylesbury & Buckingham Rail Co.* (1874) 9 Ch App 684.

8.2. Buyer's lien

8.2.1. The buyer has a similar lien over the property to the extent of any deposit paid by him. This lien can be registered as a notice in registered land or as a Class C(iii) land charge in unregistered land (see B17.12).

8.3. Solicitor's lien

8.3.1. At common law a solicitor has a lien over his client's property until his costs are paid. He may also ask the court to direct that property recovered by the solicitor in an action brought on the client's behalf should be retained by the solicitor as security against the solicitor's costs.

8.3.2. The common law lien attaches to all deeds, papers and other personal property of the client which come into the solicitor's possession with the client's consent. Such property must have been received by the solicitor in his capacity as solicitor. No lien attaches to a client's will. A buyer's solicitor must have received documents over which he exercises his lien in his capacity as buyer's solicitor and not, e.g. as lender's solicitor.

8.3.3. The lien is restricted to costs due to the solicitor in respect of work done on the client's instructions. The solicitor is entitled to retain the client's property until his costs are paid in full.

8.3.4. The existence of the lien does not entitle the solicitor to sell or otherwise dispose of the client's property.

8.3.5. Despite the existence of a lien the Law Society has power to order a solicitor to hand over papers to one of its officers where there is an intervention in a solicitor's practice under Solicitors Act 1974, Sched.1 and the court also has power to order papers to be delivered.[1]

8.3.6.   On termination of the retainer where the client has instructed another solicitor to act for him, the first solicitor should hand over papers and documents to the second solicitor, subject to obtaining a satisfactory undertaking from the second solicitor in respect of payment of the first solicitor's costs.

8.3.7.   A solicitor has no lien against the official receiver or a trustee in bankruptcy.[2]

8.3.8.   A further type of lien exists by virtue of Solicitors Act 1974, s.73 which empowers the court to make a charging order over real or personal property belonging to the client as security for the solicitor's taxed costs (see N1).

8.3.9.   No lien can be exercised over property which is held by the solicitor in the capacity of stakeholder.[3]

8.3.10.   Under the terms of the Lenders' Handbook the lender's solicitor is not entitled to exercise a lien over the title deeds.

1. Solicitors Act 1974, s.68.
2. See *Re Toleman and England, ex p. Bramble* (1880) 13 Ch 885.
3. *Rockeagle Ltd* v. *Alsop Wilkinson* [1992] Ch 47.

8.4.   **Abortive transactions**

8.4.1.   A draft contract and other papers supplied by the seller's solicitor to the buyer's solicitor belong to the seller until contracts for the transaction are exchanged. If therefore the transaction is aborted before exchange takes place the buyer's solicitor should comply with a request for return of those papers made by the seller's solicitor. This is notwithstanding any contrary instructions issued by the buyer to his own solicitor. For the avoidance of doubt the seller's solicitor may choose to indicate in his covering letter to the buyer's solicitor that he expects such papers to be returned to him on request if the transaction does not proceed to exchange.

M9. Covenants for title

9.1.   Introduction

9.1.1.   On completion of the transaction the contract merges with the purchase deed in so far as the two documents cover the same ground, and in general an action arising out of the contract is not possible after completion has taken place. The principal post-completion remedy available to the buyer will be an action for breach of the title guarantee which was introduced by Law of Property (Miscellaneous Provisions) Act 1994. This applies to all transactions completed on or after 1 July 1995.

9.1.2.   As an exception to the general rule outlined in the preceding paragraph, an action arising out of the contract is sustainable after completion in circumstances where a clause or clauses of the contract have been expressed in such a way that they do not merge with the purchase deed on completion.[1] In appropriate circumstances an action in misrepresentation would also be available since this action does not derive from the contract itself.

9.1.3.   For transactions completed before 1 July 1995 the principal post-completion remedy is an action for breach of the covenants for title. The exact nature of the covenants implied into the purchase deed depends upon the capacity in which the seller transferred the land. The appropriate law is contained in Law of Property Act 1925, s.76 (as modified by Land Registration Act 1925, s.24). If a seller purported to convey in a capacity other than that which he in fact possessed, e.g. a trustee purported to sell as a beneficial owner, it is likely that no covenants of title will have passed in the purchase deed. The benefit of a covenant for title is annexed to and passes with the land. So if A sells to B, B's successor in title can enforce the covenant for title given by A provided the action is brought within the appropriate limitation period of 12 years.

1.   See Standard Condition 7.4 and Standard Commercial Property Condition 9.4.

9.2.   Title guarantee

9.2.1.   The seller can sell with either full or limited title guarantee irrespective of the capacity in which he could have sold the property under the pre 1 July 1995 law, Law of Property (Miscellaneous Provisions) Act 1994. The guarantees apply to the sale of both freehold and leasehold property and on the grant of a lease. They can also be used on the transfer of personal property including intellectual property and rights in shares.

9.2.2. On the front of the Standard Contract form the seller should specify whether he sells with full or limited title guarantee. Should the seller fail to specify the nature of the title guarantee, Standard Condition 4.6.2 and Standard Commercial Property Condition 6.6.2 provide that the seller will sell with full title guarantee.

9.2.3. The warranties given under the full and limited guarantees can be amended in the agreement. If the seller is concerned about incumbrances he should disclose them in the contract and ensure that the buyer agrees to take the property subject to them. See also Standard Condition 4.6.3. Under section 6 of the 1994 Act (as amended by Land Registration Act 2002) the sale of a registered title will also be subject to any matters entered in the register of title at the time of the disposition. As a result any such matters will not be covered by the title guarantee.

9.2.4. If the seller is a beneficial owner, he will usually provide full title guarantee. If the seller is a trustee, personal representative or mortgagee, he will usually provide a limited title guarantee.

Full title guarantee

9.2.5. Where the full guarantee is given the seller warrants that:

(a) he has the right to dispose of the property in the manner purported;

(b) he will at his own cost do all he reasonably can to give his transferee the title he purports to give;

(c) he disposes of his whole interest where that interest is registered;

(d) he disposes of the whole lease where the interest is leasehold;

(e) he disposes of a freehold where it is unclear from the face of the documents whether the interest is freehold or leasehold;

(f) in the case of a subsisting lease he covenants that the lease is still subsisting and that there is no subsisting breach which might result in forfeiture;

(g) in the case of a mortgage of a property which is subject to a rentcharge or lease, that the mortgagor will observe and perform the obligations under the rentcharge or lease;

(h) that the person giving the disposition is disposing of it free from all charges and encumbrances (whether monetary or not) and from all other rights exercisable by third parties, not being rights which the transferor does not and could not reasonably be expected to know about.

9.2.6. Under (b) the seller is promising to put right any defects in title, for example, he will execute any further documents needed to ensure that the buyer receives the title he contracted to buy.

9.2.7. As a result of the warranty in (e) a seller who is selling a leasehold estate must expressly state in the contract that the estate is leasehold. The seller can do this on the front page of the Standard Conditions of Sale form. The warranty in (f) applies on the sale of an existing lease. The seller should modify this covenant to ensure that he will not be liable to the buyer for any breach of any of the tenant's covenants relating to the physical state and condition of the property. Standard Condition 3.2.2 and Standard Commercial Property Condition 3.2.2 modify this implied warranty by providing that the property is sold subject to any subsisting breach of a condition or tenant's obligation relating to the physical state of the property which renders the lease liable to forfeiture. Standard Condition 3.2.3 and Standard Commercial Property Condition 3.2.3 contain a similar provision on the grant of a sub-lease.

9.2.8. The warranty in (h) applies to any encumbrances created by the seller or by his predecessors unless the encumbrances are disclosed in the contract or on the title of a registered property.

Limited title guarantee

9.2.9. Where limited title guarantee is given, all the above warranties apply except for (h), which is replaced with the following:

> (h) that the transferor has not charged or encumbered the property by a charge or encumbrance which still exists, that he has not granted any third party rights which still subsist and that he is not aware that anyone else has done so since the last disposition for value.

9.2.10. The seller therefore warrants that he has not encumbered the property but he does not warrant that his predecessor has not done so.

Assignment of the guarantee

9.2.11. The title guarantee runs with the land and is enforceable by the buyer's successors in title.

Remedies

9.2.12. A breach of title guarantee is actionable as a breach of contract. However, the remedies available may be restricted. Once completion has taken place, or a third party has acquired an interest in the property, e.g. a lender, it is unlikely that rescission will be granted. Damages will therefore be the usual remedy although the seller may be ordered to execute documents to perfect a defective title.

M10. Solicitor's negligence

10.1. **Introduction**
10.2. **Action to be taken by solicitor**

10.1. Introduction

10.1.1. Where a solicitor has been negligent the client must seek redress through a civil action against the solicitor.

10.1.2. Where a client or third party makes a claim against a solicitor (or gives notice of intention to make such a claim) and the claim is one in respect of which indemnity is provided by the solicitor's insurance the solicitor must as soon as practicable notify his insurers and co-operate with them in order to enable the claim to be dealt with in the appropriate manner. Where top-up indemnity cover is maintained the terms of that policy should also be considered.

10.1.3. The Legal Complaints Service can take action against a solicitor providing inadequate professional services (see M6.2).

10.2. Action to be taken by solicitor

10.2.1. If a solicitor discovers an act or omission which would justify a claim by a client (or third party) against him he should:

(a) contact his insurers;

(b) inform the client (or third party) in order to enable him to take independent legal advice;

(c) seek the advice of his insurers as to any further communication with the client (or third party); and

(d) confirm any oral communication in writing.

10.2.2. If a client makes a claim against his solicitor or notifies his intention of doing so, or if the solicitor discovers an act or omission which would justify such a claim, the solicitor is under a duty to inform his client that he should seek independent advice.

10.2.3. If the client refuses to seek independent advice the solicitor should decline to act further for the client unless he is satisfied that no conflict of interest exists.

10.2.4. The solicitor should not admit liability or settle a claim without the consent of his insurers.

10.2.5. Where the solicitor is asked to hand papers over to another solicitor who is giving independent advice to the client about the claim, the solicitor should keep copies of the original documents for his own reference. If the first solicitor has a lien over the client's papers he may, as an alternative to taking copies, ask the second solicitor to give an undertaking for the production of the papers should they be required.

N. COSTS

N1. Costs

1.1.   The basis of charging

1.1.1.   Costs in non-contentious matters including conveyancing are governed by Solicitors' (Non-Contentious Business) Remuneration Order 1994 (see Appendix IX.2).

1.1.2.   Rule 3 Solicitors' (Non-Contentious Business) Remuneration Order 1994 provides that the remuneration shall be 'such sum as may be fair and reasonable having regard to all the circumstances of the case'. The following matters must be taken into account:

(a)   the complexity of the matter or the difficulty or novelty of the questions raised;

(b)   the skill, labour, specialised knowledge and responsibility involved;

(c)   the time spent on the business;

(d)   the number and importance of the documents prepared or perused, without regard to length;

(e)   the place where and the circumstances in which the business or any part thereof is transacted;

(f)   the amount or value of any money or property involved;

(g)   whether any land involved is registered land;

(h)   the importance of the matter to the client; and

(i)   the approval (express or implied) of the entitled person or the express approval of the testator to:

   (i)   the solicitor undertaking all or any part of the work giving rise to the costs; or

   (ii)   the amount of the costs.

1.1.3. On taking instructions the solicitor should give his client the best information he can about the likely cost of the matter including when costs will be charged and whether or not such costs will be deducted from money held by the solicitor on the client's behalf. Where possible an estimate should be given to the client; in other cases the solicitor should give the client a general forecast of the approximate costs to be incurred. Where no estimate has been given and the solicitor has not arranged an agreed fee for the work, the client must be told how the solicitor's charges are to be calculated, e.g. on an hourly rate basis or as a percentage of the value of the transaction. Information should also be given to the client about the nature and cost of disbursements.

1.1.4. Rule 2.03 (information about the cost) and Rule 2.05 (complaints handling) Solicitors' Code of Conduct 2007 and the Law Society's Practice Management Standards should also be followed. Failure to observe these standards is regarded as inadequate professional services by the Legal Complaints Service.

1.1.5. By Supply of Goods and Services Act 1982, s.15 the contract between solicitor and client contains an implied term that the client will pay the solicitor a reasonable sum for his services; however, the matter of costs should be dealt with expressly. It is the solicitor's duty to raise the issue of costs if the client does not enquire.

1.1.6. When confirming the client's instructions the solicitor should record whether a fee has been agreed, and if so what it covers and whether it includes VAT and disbursements.

1.1.7. Where the client has imposed an upper limit on costs, a solicitor who exceeds that limit without the client's authority will not be able to recover his costs in so far as they exceed the agreed maximum sum. The client must be informed as soon as possible if it appears that the limit imposed on the costs will be insufficient and instructions obtained as to whether the client wishes the solicitor to continue with the matter. If the solicitor continues to act and exceeds the limit imposed by the client on the costs to be incurred the amount of the bill in excess of the agreed amount will be disallowed if the client applies for a remuneration certificate or taxation. The solicitor may also be guilty of professional misconduct in these circumstances.

1.1.8. The amount of costs being incurred on a client's behalf should be reviewed regularly. It is recommended that the client should be informed at least every six months of the amount of costs incurred to date and where appropriate an interim bill should be delivered.

1.1.9. A solicitor may, at the outset of the retainer, require the client to make a payment on account of costs and disbursements to be incurred. The solicitor must make his acceptance of the instructions conditional on the client's advance payment. Unless he does this the solicitor will not be able to justify the termination of the retainer if the client does not make the interim payment.

1.1.10. A solicitor may charge interest on the whole or outstanding part of an unpaid bill with effect from one month after delivery of the bill, provided that notice has been given to the client informing him of his right to apply for a remuneration certificate and taxation of the bill. The rate of interest chargeable is that which is payable on judgment debts.

1.1.11. A solicitor must not take advantage of the client by overcharging for work done or to be done. Overcharging the client may be professional misconduct. If a taxing officer allows less than one-half of the sum charged he is under a duty to report the matter to the Law Society. The solicitor is responsible for ensuring that the amount of the bill is fair and reasonable and cannot escape liability by delegating the preparation of the bill to a costs draftsman.

1.1.12. Unless there is an agreement to the contrary, a solicitor is personally responsible for paying the proper costs of any professional agent or other person whom he instructs on behalf of his client, whether or not he receives payment from his client.

1.1.13. Costs which are taken by way of deduction from money which the solicitor is holding on the client's behalf cannot be transferred from clients' account to office account without the consent of the client.

1.1.14. In the absence of agreement to the contrary a solicitor will charge on a *quantum meruit* basis (or for a reasonable sum under Supply of Goods and Services Act 1982, s.15) for abortive work. Reference should be made to the Law Society guidance on Solicitors' Abortive Costs Schemes if the solicitor is offering clients a facility to pay an additional sum to protect them against incurring fees and disbursements for aborted transactions.

1.2. Agreements for charges

1.2.1. Solicitors Act 1974, s.57 allows a solicitor to make an agreement with a client for costs in a non-contentious matter.

1.2.2. In order to be enforceable under the Act, the agreement must fully comply with the provisions of section 57. Thus the agreement must:

    (a) be in writing;

    (b) embody all the terms of the agreement;

    (c) be signed by the party to be charged or his agent, i.e. the client;

    (d) be reasonable in amount and be in lieu of ordinary profit costs.

1.2.3. Remuneration may be by a gross sum, commission, percentage, salary or otherwise, and should state whether the agreed remuneration is to be inclusive of disbursements and VAT. The agreement should specifically set out the method by which the remuneration is to be calculated.

1.2.4.   An agreement which complies with section 57 is enforceable under the ordinary principles of contract law.

1.2.5.   If the costs are ultimately taxed and the client raises an objection to the agreement on the grounds that it is unfair or unreasonable, the taxing officer may enquire into the facts and the court may set the agreement aside or reduce the amount payable and give such consequential directions as it thinks fit.

1.3.   VAT

1.3.1.   When giving an estimate or quotation for costs the solicitor should make it clear to the client whether or not VAT is included in the quoted sum.

1.3.2.   If VAT is not mentioned it is presumed that the quotation or estimate is VAT inclusive.

1.3.3.   Where an individual or firm is registered for VAT the firm's VAT registration number must appear on the bills issued by the firm or, if a separate tax invoice is issued, on the tax invoice.

1.3.4.   The VAT registration number is also required to appear on any bill or fee note produced on a taxation of costs *inter partes*.

1.3.5.   Stamp duties are exempt from VAT (see A14 and A16).

1.3.6.   Where the client's bill is reduced by the amount of commission which a solicitor has earned, e.g. on an endowment policy taken out by the client, VAT should be charged on the gross amount of the bill but in practice is sometimes only charged on the net sum (see A8.8.1).

1.3.7.   Fees for telegraphic transfers, when passed on by a solicitor to his or her client, must bear VAT at the standard rate.

1.4.   Delivery of bill

1.4.1.   A solicitor is under a duty to render a bill of costs to his client within a reasonable time of concluding the matter to which the bill relates.

1.4.2.   It is recommended practice to submit a bill to the client as soon as possible after the conclusion of the transaction and it is particularly important to do so where the solicitor is already holding sums of money on his client's behalf and has chosen to wait for the client's approval of the bill before deducting his costs and accounting to the client for the balance, or where the client has asked for the papers and the solicitor is claiming a lien over them until his costs are met.

1.4.3.   In residential conveyancing purchase transactions the bill is usually submitted to the client before completion on the understanding that the solicitor's charges are paid in full before completion. In sale transactions, the solicitor's costs are usually deducted from money held by the solicitor on the client's behalf before the balance is remitted to the client. If the client refuses to allow payment of costs by deduction the solicitor must nevertheless complete the transaction since he is obliged to fulfil his retainer.

1.4.4. A solicitor's bill of costs should contain sufficient information to identify the matter to which it relates and the period covered.

1.4.5. The form of the bill should comply with Solicitors Act 1974, s.69 and must be signed by the solicitor personally or by one of the partners in the firm. The signature may be either that of the solicitor signing the bill or made in the name of the firm. Alternatively the letter which accompanies and refers to the bill should be so signed. Unless this provision is complied with the solicitor will be unable to sue on the bill. A form of signature such as, e.g. 'signed A. Smith, a partner in A. Smith & Co.' is recommended to ensure that it can be proved in evidence (should it be necessary to sue) that the bill was signed by a solicitor and not merely by an unqualified assistant. Disbursements should be separately itemised in the bill.

1.4.6. A solicitor must not sue or threaten to sue unless he has first informed the client in writing of his right to require a remuneration certificate and of his right to seek taxation of the bill. The form of notice to be given to the client should be in the following wording:

> 'This constitutes notice of your right under paragraph 1 of Article 3 of the Solicitors' (Non-Contentious Business) Remuneration Order 1994 to require me within one month of the receipt hereof to obtain a certificate from the Law Society stating that in their opinion the costs charged are fair and reasonable or, as the case may be, what lesser sum would be fair and reasonable. Also there are provisions in sections 70, 71, and 72 of the Solicitors Act 1974 relating to taxation of costs which give you the right to have the bill checked by an officer of the High Court.'

1.4.7. This notice must be given even where costs are payable by deduction from money already held by the solicitor on behalf of the client.

1.5. **Remuneration certificate**

1.5.1. A client or residuary beneficiary of an estate where all the personal representatives are solicitors who is dissatisfied with his solicitor's bill may require the solicitor to apply to the Legal Complaints Service for a remuneration certificate which will either state that in the opinion of the Legal Complaints Service the sum charged by the solicitor is fair and reasonable, or what lesser sum would be fair and reasonable. If the sum stated in the remuneration certificate is less than the amount of the bill, the client need only pay the amount stated in the certificate. An application for a remuneration certificate is free of charge to the client. A client applying for a remuneration certificate must pay half the costs plus paid disbursements and VAT unless the solicitor agrees to waive this requirement.

1.5.2. The client is not entitled to require a remuneration certificate where:

(a) a period of more than one month has expired after the date on which he was notified of his right to such a certificate; or

(b) a bill has been delivered and paid (otherwise than by deduction without authority); or

(c) the High Court has ordered the bill to be assessed; or

(d) the bill exceeds £50,000, exclusive of VAT and disbursements.

1.5.3. In addition to or as an alternative to a remuneration certificate the client may apply to have his bill assessed by the Supreme Court Costs Office.

1.5.4. Except as below, the right to a remuneration certificate applies to the client in relation to his own solicitor's costs; it is not therefore available to a third party who has agreed to be responsible for another person's solicitor's costs. Where a third party is to pay the solicitor's bill, e.g. where a tenant is to pay his landlord's solicitor's costs, the tenant's solicitor should agree the fee to be paid at the outset of the transaction. Alternatively the third party can apply for a third party taxation within three months of delivery of the bill (see N1.6). A residuary beneficiary of an estate where the personal representatives are all solicitors may apply for a remuneration certificate.

1.6.   Taxation of costs

1.6.1. The right to taxation of the bill by the High Court is in addition to or may be used by the client as an alternative to an application for a remuneration certificate. The costs of an application for taxation must be borne by the client.

1.6.2. If in a non-contentious matter a taxing officer allows less than one-half of the sum charged to the client by the bill, he is under a duty to bring the facts of the case to the attention of the Law Society.

1.6.3. A third party who is responsible for paying the costs of another can apply for a third party taxation within three months of delivery of the bill.

1.7.   Lender's costs

1.7.1. The solicitor should consider making a separate charge for legal work carried out on behalf of the lender client.

1.7.2.   The solicitor should agree his charges with the lender client at the outset of the transaction.

1.7.3.   Under the terms of the Lenders' Handbook the borrower client is responsible for the lender's solicitor's costs (see Appendix VI.2).

1.8.   Commissions, discounts and rebates on disbursements

1.8.1.   Under Rule 2.06 Solicitors' Code of Conduct 2007, a solicitor must normally account to his client for any commission received by him which exceeds £20. Thus where the solicitor introduces a client to an insurance company for the purposes of the client obtaining an insurance policy, and as a result of that introduction the solicitor receives commission from the insurance company, that commission will be subject to Rule 2.06. The solicitor is only entitled to keep a commission which exceeds £20 if, having disclosed the amount to the client, the client agrees that the solicitor may keep the money. If the amount is not known, the solicitor must have disclosed an approximate amount or the basis of the calculation of the commission to the client.

1.8.2.   The rule does not apply where the solicitor acts as agent for a building society or other financial institution and a member of the public, whom the solicitor has not advised as a client about the investment of the money, deposits money with the solicitor.

1.8.3.   Stock Exchange commissions fall within the scope of the rule.

1.8.4.   The amount of any commission earned by the solicitor should be shown on the client's bill.

1.8.5.   Any discount or rebate offered to a solicitor on a search fee or other disbursement which is not a commission falling within Rule 2.06, reduces the cost of that disbursement and must be passed on to the client (see *Guidance on Discounts, Rebates (or 'Commissions') on Search Fees and other Disbursements* issued by the Solicitors Regulation Authority).

1.9.   Recovery of charges

1.9.1.   A solicitor may sue a client who does not pay his solicitor's bill provided that the conditions in the following paragraphs have been complied with.

1.9.2.   A bill of costs in the proper form must have been delivered to the client.

1.9.3.   In a non-contentious matter, a solicitor may not sue the client until the expiration of one month from the delivery of the bill, unless the solicitor had been given leave to do so on the grounds set out in Solicitors Act 1974, s.69. A solicitor must not sue or threaten to sue unless he has first informed the client in writing of his right to require a remuneration certificate and of his right to seek taxation of the bill. A statutory demand in bankruptcy can, however, be made within one month of an unpaid bill being presented.[1]

1.9.4. A lien exists by virtue of Solicitors Act 1974, s.73 which empowers the court to make a charging order over real or personal property belonging to the client as security for the solicitor's taxed costs.

1. *Re A Debtor (No. 88 of 1991)* [1992] 3 All ER 301.

1.10. Court of Protection work

1.10.1. Fixed costs are payable for all conveyancing matters authorised by the Public Guardianship Office.

1.10.2. Two elements will be allowable, as follows:

(a) a sum of £140 in every case to cover correspondence with the Public Guardianship Office, the preparation of the certificate or affidavit of value, and all other work solely attributable to the Court of Protection; together with

(b) a value element of 0.25% of the consideration, with a minimum sum for this element of £385 and a maximum sum of £1,500.

1.10.3. As well as a fee for both the above elements, VAT and disbursements will be allowed.

1.10.4. Fixed costs will apply to conveyancing of all types of property.

1.10.5. If solicitors wish, they may choose to have their costs assessed by the Supreme Court Costs Office, rather than to accept fixed costs. It should, however, be emphasised that agreed costs will not be an option, save in exceptional circumstances.

APPENDICES

APPENDICES

I. PROFESSIONAL RULES

I.1. Solicitors' Code of Conduct 2007 [extracts][1]

This appendix includes the following rules from Solicitors' Code of Conduct 2007, which replaced Solicitors' Practice Rules 1990 on 1 July 2007:

1. Core duties
2. Client relations
3. Conflict of interests
5. Business management in England and Wales
7. Publicity
8. Fee sharing
9. Referrals of business
10. Relations with third parties
18. Property selling
19. Financial services
21. Separate business

RULE 1 – CORE DUTIES

1.01   Justice and the rule of law

You must uphold the rule of law and the proper administration of justice.

1.02   Integrity

You must act with integrity.

1.03   Independence

You must not allow your independence to be compromised.

1.04   Best interests of clients

You must act in the best interests of each client.

1.05   Standard of service

You must provide a good standard of service to your clients.

1. © The Law Society 2007.

1.06 Public confidence

You must not behave in a way that is likely to diminish the trust the public places in you or the profession.

RULE 2 – CLIENT RELATIONS

2.01 Taking on clients

(1) You are generally free to decide whether or not to take on a particular client. However, you must refuse to act or cease acting for a client in the following circumstances:

    (a) when to act would involve you in a breach of the law or a breach of the rules of professional conduct;

    (b) where you have insufficient resources or lack the competence to deal with the matter;

    (c) where instructions are given by someone other than the client, or by only one client on behalf of others in a joint matter, you must not proceed without checking that all clients agree with the instructions given; or

    (d) where you know or have reasonable grounds for believing that the instructions are affected by duress or undue influence, you must not act on those instructions until you have satisfied yourself that they represent the client's wishes.

(2) You must not cease acting for a client except for good reason and on reasonable notice.

2.02 Client care

(1) You must:

    (a) identify clearly the client's objectives in relation to the work to be done for the client;

    (b) give the client a clear explanation of the issues involved and the options available to the client;

    (c) agree with the client the next steps to be taken; and

    (d) keep the client informed of progress, unless otherwise agreed.

(2) You must, both at the outset and, as necessary, during the course of the matter:

    (a) agree an appropriate level of service;

    (b) explain your responsibilities;

    (c) explain the client's responsibilities;

    (d) ensure that the client is given, in writing, the name and status of the person dealing with the matter and the name of the person responsible for its overall supervision; and

    (e) explain any limitations or conditions resulting from your relationship with a third party (for example a funder, fee sharer or introducer) which affect the steps you can take on the client's behalf.

(3) If you can demonstrate that it was inappropriate in the circumstances to meet some or all of these requirements, you will not breach 2.02.

2.03   Information about the cost

(1)   You must give your client the best information possible about the likely overall cost of a matter both at the outset and, when appropriate, as the matter progresses. In particular you must:

    (a)   advise the client of the basis and terms of your charges;

    (b)   advise the client if charging rates are to be increased;

    (c)   advise the client of likely payments which you or your client may need to make to others;

    (d)   discuss with the client how the client will pay, in particular:

        (i)   whether the client may be eligible and should apply for public funding; and

        (ii)   whether the client's own costs are covered by insurance or may be paid by someone else such as an employer or trade union;

    (e)   advise the client that there are circumstances where you may be entitled to exercise a lien for unpaid costs;

    (f)   advise the client of their potential liability for any other party's costs; and

    (g)   discuss with the client whether their liability for another party's costs may be covered by existing insurance or whether specially purchased insurance may be obtained.

(2)   Where you are acting for the client under a conditional fee agreement, (including a collective conditional fee agreement) in addition to complying with 2.03(1) above and 2.03(5) and (6) below, you must explain the following, both at the outset and, when appropriate, as the matter progresses:

    (a)   the circumstances in which your client may be liable for your costs and whether you will seek payment of these from the client, if entitled to do so;

    (b)   if you intend to seek payment of any or all of your costs from your client, you must advise your client of their right to an assessment of those costs; and

    (c)   where applicable, the fact that you are obliged under a fee sharing agreement to pay to a charity any fees which you receive by way of costs from the client's opponent or other third party.

(3)   Where you are acting for a publicly funded client, in addition to complying with 2.03(1) above and 2.03(5) and (6) below, you must explain the following at the outset:

    (a)   the circumstances in which they may be liable for your costs;

    (b)   the effect of the statutory charge;

    (c)   the client's duty to pay any fixed or periodic contribution assessed and the consequence of failing to do so; and

    (d)   that even if your client is successful, the other party may not be ordered to pay costs or may not be in a position to pay them.

(4)   Where you agree to share your fees with a charity in accordance with 8.01(k) you must disclose to the client at the outset the name of the charity.

(5)   Any information about the cost must be clear and confirmed in writing.

(6)   You must discuss with your client whether the potential outcomes of any legal case will justify the expense or risk involved including, if relevant, the risk of having to pay an opponent's costs.

(7)   If you can demonstrate that it was inappropriate in the circumstances to meet some or all of the requirements in 2.03(1) and (5) above, you will not breach 2.03.

2.04   Contingency fees

(1)   You must not enter into an arrangement to receive a contingency fee for work done in prosecuting or defending any contentious proceedings before a court of England and Wales, a British court martial or an arbitrator where the seat of the arbitration is in England and Wales, except as permitted by statute or the common law.

(2)   You must not enter into an arrangement to receive a contingency fee for work done in prosecuting or defending any contentious proceedings before a court of an overseas jurisdiction or an arbitrator where the seat of the arbitration is overseas except to the extent that a lawyer of that jurisdiction would be permitted to do so.

2.05   Complaints handling

(1)   If you are a principal in a firm you must ensure:

   (a)   that the firm has a written complaints procedure and that complaints are handled promptly, fairly and effectively in accordance with it;

   (b)   that the client is told, in writing, at the outset:

      (i)   that, in the event of a problem, the client is entitled to complain; and

      (ii)   to whom the client should complain;

   (c)   that the client is given a copy of the complaints procedure on request; and

   (d)   that once a complaint has been made, the person complaining is told in writing:

      (i)   how the complaint will be handled; and

      (ii)   within what timescales they will be given an initial and/or substantive response.

(2)   If you can demonstrate that it was inappropriate in the circumstances to meet some or all of these requirements, you will not breach 2.05.

(3)   You must not charge your client for the cost of handling a complaint.

2.06   Commissions

If you are a principal in a firm you must ensure that your firm pays to your client commission received over £20 unless the client, having been told the amount, or if the precise amount is not known, an approximate amount or how the amount is to be calculated, has agreed that your firm may keep it.

2.07   Limitation of civil liability by contract

If you are a principal in a firm you must not exclude or attempt to exclude by contract all liability to your clients. However, you may limit your liability, provided that such limitation:

   (a)   is not below the minimum level of cover required by the Solicitors' Indemnity Insurance Rules for a policy of qualifying insurance;

   (b)   is brought to the client's attention; and

   (c)   is in writing.

RULE 3 – CONFLICT OF INTERESTS

3.01   Duty not to act

(1)   You must not act if there is a conflict of interests (except in the limited circumstances dealt with in 3.02).

(2)   There is a conflict of interests if:

     (a)   you owe, or your firm owes, separate duties to act in the best interests of two or more clients in relation to the same or related matters, and those duties conflict, or there is a significant risk that those duties may conflict; or

     (b)   your duty to act in the best interests of any client in relation to a matter conflicts, or there is a significant risk that it may conflict, with your own interests in relation to that or a related matter.

(3)   For the purpose of 3.01(2), a related matter will always include any other matter which involves the same asset or liability.

3.02   Exceptions to duty not to act

(1)   You or your firm may act for two or more clients in relation to a matter in situations of conflict or possible conflict if:

     (a)   the different clients have a substantially common interest in relation to that matter or a particular aspect of it; and

     (b)   all the clients have given in writing their informed consent to you or your firm acting.

(2)   Your firm may act for two or more clients in relation to a matter in situations of conflict or possible conflict if:

     (a)   the clients are competing for the same asset which, if attained by one client, will make that asset unattainable to the other client(s);

     (b)   there is no other conflict, or significant risk of conflict, between the interests of any of the clients in relation to that matter;

     (c)   the clients have confirmed in writing that they want your firm to act in the knowledge that your firm acts, or may act, for one or more other clients who are competing for the same asset; and

     (d)   unless the clients specifically agree, no individual acts for, or is responsible for the supervision of, more than one of those clients.

(3)   When acting in accordance with 3.02(1) or (2) it must be reasonable in all the circumstances for you or your firm to act for all those clients.

(4)   If you are relying on the exceptions in 3.02(1) or (2), you must:

     (a)   draw all the relevant issues to the attention of the clients before agreeing to act or, where already acting, when the conflict arises or as soon as is reasonably practicable, and in such a way that the clients concerned can understand the issues and the risks involved;

     (b)   have a reasonable belief that the clients understand the relevant issues; and

     (c)   be reasonably satisfied that those clients are of full capacity.

3.03   Conflict when already acting

If you act, or your firm acts, for more than one client in a matter and, during the course of the conduct of that matter, a conflict arises between the interests of two or more of those clients, you, or your firm, may only continue to act for one of the clients (or a group of clients between whom there is no conflict) provided that the duty of confidentiality to the other client(s) is not put at risk.

3.04   Accepting gifts from clients

Where a client proposes to make a lifetime gift or a gift on death to, or for the benefit of:

    (a)   you;

    (b)   any principal, owner or employee of your firm;

    (c)   a family member of any of the above,

and the gift is of a significant amount, either in itself or having regard to the size of the client's estate and the reasonable expectations of the prospective beneficiaries, you must advise the client to take independent advice about the gift, unless the client is a member of the beneficiary's family. If the client refuses, you must stop acting for the client in relation to the gift.

3.05   Public office or appointment leading to conflict

You must decline to act where you, a member of your family, or a principal, owner or employee of your firm holds some public office or appointment as a result of which:

    (a)   a conflict of interests, or a significant risk of a conflict, arises;

    (b)   the public might reasonably conclude that you, or your firm, had been able to make use of the office or appointment for the advantage of the client; or

    (c)   your ability to advise the client properly and impartially is inhibited.

3.06   Alternative dispute resolution (ADR)

If you provide ADR services you must not:

    (a)   advise or act for any party in respect of a dispute in which you or any person within your firm is acting, or has acted, as mediator;

    (b)   provide ADR services in connection with a matter in which you or any person within your firm has acted for any party; or

    (c)   provide ADR services where you or any person within your firm has acted for any of the parties in issues not relating to the mediation, unless that has been disclosed to the parties and they consent to your acting.

3.07   Acting for seller and buyer in conveyancing, property selling and mortgage related services

(1)   3.07 to 3.15 apply to the transfer of land for value, and the grant or assignment of a lease or some other interest in land for value. Both commercial and residential conveyancing transactions are covered. The terms 'seller' and 'buyer' include a lessor and lessee. 'You' is defined in 23.01, but is to be construed in 3.07 to 3.15 as including an associated firm (see rule 24 (Interpretation) for the meaning of 'associated firms').

(2)   You must not act for more than one party in conveyancing, property selling or mortgage related services other than as permitted by, and in accordance with, 3.08 to 3.15. 'Property selling'

means negotiating the sale for the seller. 'Mortgage related services' means advising on or arranging a mortgage, or providing mortgage related financial services, for a buyer. 'Mortgage' includes a remortgage.

3.08   Conveyancing transactions not at arm's length

Subject to the prohibition in 10.06(3) and (4), you may act for seller and buyer when the transaction between the parties is not at arm's length, provided there is no conflict or significant risk of conflict.

3.09   Conveyancing transactions at arm's length

Subject to the prohibition in 10.06(3) and (4), you may act for seller and buyer if the conditions set out in 3.10 below are satisfied and one of the following applies:

(a)   both parties are established clients;

(b)   the consideration is £10,000 or less and the transaction is not the grant of a lease; or

(c)   seller and buyer are represented by two separate offices in different localities.

3.10   Conditions for acting under 3.09

In order to act for seller and buyer under 3.09 above, the following conditions must be met:

(a)   the written consent of both parties must be obtained;

(b)   no conflict of interests must exist or arise;

(c)   the seller must not be selling or leasing as a builder or developer; and

(d)   when the seller and buyer are represented by two separate offices in different localities:

    (i)   different individuals (either solicitors or RELs qualified to do conveyancing under regulation 12 of the European Communities (Lawyer's Practice) Regulations 2000 (SI 2000/1119)) who normally work at each office, conduct or supervise the transaction for seller and buyer; and

    (ii)   no office of the firm (or an associated firm) referred either client to the office conducting the transactions.

3.11   Property selling and mortgage related services

Subject to the prohibition in 10.06(3) and (4), you may act for seller and buyer if the conditions set out in 3.13 below are satisfied and one of the following applies:

(a)   the only way in which you are acting for the buyer is in providing mortgage related services; or

(b)   the only way in which you are acting for the seller is in providing property selling services through a Solicitors' Estate Agency Limited (SEAL).

3.12   SEALs and participating firms

A SEAL means a recognised body which:

(a)   does not undertake conveyancing;

(b)   is owned jointly by at least four participating firms which are not associated firms and none of which has majority control;

(c)   is conducted from accommodation physically divided from, and clearly differentiated from that of any participating firm; and (d)　a 'participating firm' means a firm one or more of whose principals (or members if it is an LLP, or owners if it is a company) is part owner of the SEAL.

3.13　Conditions for acting under 3.11

In order to act for seller and buyer under 3.11 above, the following conditions must be met:

(a)　the written consent of both parties must be obtained;

(b)　no conflict of interests must exist or arise;

(c)　the seller must not be selling or leasing as a builder or developer;

(d)　different individuals must conduct the work for the seller and the work for the buyer and, if these individuals need supervision, they must be supervised by different solicitors or RELs who are qualified to do conveyancing under regulation 12 of the European Communities (Lawyer's Practice) Regulations 2000 (SI 2000/1119);

(e)　you must inform the seller in writing, before accepting instructions to deal with the property selling, of any services which might be offered to a buyer, whether through the same firm or any associated firm; and

(f)　you must explain to the buyer, before the buyer gives consent to the arrangement:

(i)　the implications of a conflict of interests arising;

(ii)　your financial interest in the sale going through; and

(iii)　if you propose to provide mortgage related services to the buyer through a SEAL which is also acting for the seller, that you cannot advise the buyer on the merits of the purchase.

3.14　Special circumstances in property selling and conveyancing

If any of the circumstances set out in 3.09 apply (established clients; consideration of £10,000 or less; representation by two separate offices), you may sell the property, provide mortgage related services, and act for seller and buyer in the conveyancing, subject to the prohibition in 10.06(3) and (4) and compliance with the conditions set out in 3.10 and 3.13 as appropriate.

3.15　Conflict arising when acting for seller and buyer

If a conflict arises during the course of a transaction in which you are acting for more than one party, you may continue to act for one of the parties only if the duty of confidentiality to the other party is not at risk.

3.16　Acting for lender and borrower in conveyancing transactions

(1)　3.16 to 3.22 cover the grant of a mortgage of land and are intended to avoid conflicts of interests. 'Mortgage' includes a remortgage. Both commercial and residential conveyancing transactions are covered. 'You' is defined in 23.01, but is to be construed in 3.16 to 3.22 as including an associated firm (see rule 24 (Interpretation) for the meaning of 'associated firms').

(2)　You must not act for both lender and borrower on the grant of a mortgage of land:

(a)　if a conflict of interests exists or arises;

(b)　on the grant of an individual mortgage of land at arm's length;

(c)　if, in the case of a standard mortgage of property to be used as the borrower's private residence only, the lender's mortgage instructions extend beyond the limitations contained in 3.19 and 3.21, or do not permit the use of the certificate of title required by 3.20; or

(d)   if, in the case of any other standard mortgage, the lender's mortgage instructions extend beyond the limitations contained in 3.19 and 3.21.

3.17   Standard and individual mortgages

(1)   A mortgage is a 'standard mortgage' where:

(a)   it is provided in the normal course of the lender's activities;

(b)   a significant part of the lender's activities consists of lending; and

(c)   the mortgage is on standard terms.

An 'individual mortgage' is any other mortgage.

(2)   A mortgage will not be on standard terms if material terms in any of the documents relating to the mortgage transaction are negotiated between the lender's and borrower's lawyers or licensed conveyancers contemporaneously with effecting the mortgage. In commercial transactions, the element of negotiation will often relate to the facility letter or facility agreement rather than the mortgage deed itself.

(3)   Provided there has been no contemporaneous negotiation of material terms between the parties' lawyers or licensed conveyancers, a mortgage will be on standard terms where the lender uses a prescribed form of mortgage deed. Minor variations, such as the usual clause limiting the liability of trustee mortgagors, are not regarded as material and do not alter the nature of these terms as standard.

(4)   In addition to its normal standard terms, a lender may have a different set or sets of standard terms applicable to specialised types of borrower, such as registered social landlords. Provided these terms are applied by the lender to all equivalent specialist borrowers or have been agreed between the lender and a specialist borrower as applicable to all transactions between them, they will constitute standard terms for the purposes of 3.16 to 3.22.

(5)   The lender and the borrower must be separately represented on the grant of an individual mortgage at arm's length (see 3.16(2)(b)). 3.16 to 3.22 are not then applicable.

(6)   You may act for both lender and borrower in a standard mortgage (see 3.16(2)(c) to (d)), provided:

(a)   there is no conflict of interests;

(b)   the mortgage instructions do not go beyond the limits set out in 3.19; and

(c)   in the case of a property to be used solely as the borrower's private residence, the approved certificate of title set out in the annex to rule 3 is used.

(7)   The limitations of 3.19 also apply to a standard mortgage where the lender and the borrower are separately represented (see 3.22(1) which includes certificates of title). However, 3.22(2) allows the borrower's lawyer or licensed conveyancer, in a transaction where the property is not to be used solely as the borrower's private residence, to give a certificate of title in any form recognised by the Board of the Solicitors Regulation Authority. You also remain free to give any other form of certificate which complies with this rule.

(8)   There may be cases where the lapse of time between the mortgage offer and completion (for example, when new properties are added) results in use of an earlier edition of a recognised certificate. That is acceptable.

3.18   Notification of certain circumstances to lender

(1)   If you wish to act for both lender and borrower on the grant of a standard mortgage of land, you must first inform the lender in writing of the circumstances if:

(a)   the prospective borrower is:

(i)   a principal in the firm (or a member if the firm is an LLP, or owner or director if the firm is a company), or a member of their immediate family;

(ii)   a principal in an associated firm (or a member if the firm is an LLP, or owner or director if the firm is a company), or a member of their immediate family; and/or

(iii)   the solicitor or REL conducting or supervising the transaction, or a member of their immediate family; or

(b)   you propose to act for seller, buyer and lender in the same transaction.

(2)   'Immediate family' means spouse, children, parents, brothers and sisters.

3.19   Types of instruction which may be accepted

If acting for both lender and borrower in a standard mortgage, you and the individual solicitor or REL conducting or supervising the transaction may only accept or act upon instructions from the lender which are limited to the following matters:

(a)   (i)   taking reasonable steps to check the identity of the borrower (and anyone else required to sign the mortgage deed or other document connected with the mortgage) by reference to a document or documents, such as a passport, precisely specified in writing by the lender;

(ii)   following the guidance given by the Law Society or the Solicitors Regulation Authority on property fraud and on money laundering;

(iii)   checking that the seller's conveyancers (if unknown to you) appear in a current legal directory or hold practising certificates issued by their professional body; and

(iv)   in the case of a lender with no branch office within reasonable proximity of the borrower, carrying out the money laundering checks precisely specified in writing by the lender;

(b)   making appropriate searches relating to the property in public registers (for example, local searches, commons registration searches, mining searches), and reporting any results specified by the lender or which you consider may adversely affect the lender; or effecting search insurance;

(c)   making enquiries on legal matters relating to the property reasonably specified by the lender, and reporting the replies;

(d)   reporting the purchase price stated in the transfer and on how the borrower says that the purchase money (other than the mortgage advance) is to be provided; and reporting if you will not have control over the payment of all the purchase money (other than a deposit paid to an estate agent or a reservation fee paid to a builder or developer);

(e) reporting if the seller or the borrower (if the property is already owned by the borrower) has not owned or been the registered owner of the property for at least six months;

(f) if the lender does not arrange insurance, confirming receipt of satisfactory evidence that the buildings insurance is in place for at least the sum required by the lender and covers the risks specified by the lender; giving notice to the insurer of the lender's interest and requesting confirmation that the insurer will notify the lender if the policy is not renewed or is cancelled; and supplying particulars of the insurance and the last premium receipt to the lender;

(g) investigating title to the property and appurtenant rights; reporting any defects revealed, advising on the need for any consequential statutory declarations or indemnity insurance, and approving and effecting indemnity cover if required by the lender; and reporting if you are aware of any rights needed for the use or enjoyment of the property over other land;

(h) reporting on any financial charges (for example, improvement or repair grants or Housing Act discounts) secured on the property revealed by your searches and enquiries which will affect the property after completion of the mortgage;

(i) in the case of a leasehold property:

    (i) confirming that the lease contains the terms stipulated by the lender and does not include any terms specified by the lender as unacceptable;

    (ii) obtaining a suitable deed of variation or indemnity insurance if the terms of the lease are unsatisfactory;

    (iii) enquiring of the seller or the borrower (if the property is already owned by the borrower) as to any known breaches of covenant by the landlord or any superior landlord and reporting any such breaches to the lender;

    (iv) reporting if you become aware of the landlord's absence or insolvency;

    (v) making a company search and checking the last three years' published accounts of any management company with responsibilities under the lease;

    (vi) if the borrower is required to be a shareholder in the management company, obtaining the share certificate, a blank stock transfer form signed by the borrower and a copy of the memorandum and articles of association;

    (vii) obtaining any necessary consent to or prior approval of the assignment and mortgage;

    (viii) obtaining a clear receipt for the last payment of rent and service charge; and

    (ix) serving notice of the assignment and mortgage on the landlord;

(j) in the case of a commonhold unit:

    (i) confirming receipt of satisfactory evidence that common parts insurance is in place for at least the sum required by the lender and covers the risks specified by the lender;

    (ii) confirming that the commonhold community statement contains the terms specified by the lender and does not include any restrictions on occupation or use specified by the lender as unacceptable;

    (iii) enquiring of the seller (or the borrower if the property is already owned by the borrower) and the commonhold association as to any known breaches of the commonhold community statement by the commonhold association or any unit-holder, and reporting any such breaches to the lender;

(iv) making a company search to verify that the commonhold association is in existence and remains registered, and that there is no registered indication that it is to be wound up;

(v) obtaining the last three years' published accounts of the commonhold association and reporting any apparent problems with the association to the lender;

(vi) obtaining a commonhold unit information certificate; and

(vii) serving notice of the transfer and mortgage of the commonhold unit on the commonhold association;

(k) if the property is subject to a letting, checking that the type of letting and its terms comply with the lender's requirements;

(l) making appropriate pre-completion searches, including a bankruptcy search against the borrower, any other person in whom the legal estate is vested and any guarantor;

(m) receiving, releasing and transmitting the mortgage advance, including asking for any final inspection needed and dealing with any retentions and cashbacks;

(n) procuring execution of the mortgage deed and form of guarantee as appropriate by the persons whose identities have been checked in accordance with any requirements of the lender under (a) above as those of the borrower, any other person in whom the legal estate is vested and any guarantor; obtaining their signatures to the forms of undertaking required by the lender in relation to the use, occupation or physical state of the property; and complying with the lender's requirements if any document is to be executed under a power of attorney;

(o) asking the borrower for confirmation that the information about occupants given in the mortgage instructions or offer is correct; obtaining consents in the form required by the lender from existing or prospective occupiers of the property aged 17 or over specified by the lender, or of whom you are aware;

(p) advising the borrower on the terms of any document required by the lender to be signed by the borrower;

(q) advising any other person required to sign any document on the terms of that document or, if there is a conflict of interests between that person and the borrower or the lender, advising that person on the need for separate legal advice and arranging for them to see an independent conveyancer;

(r) obtaining the legal transfer of the property to the mortgagor;

(s) procuring the redemption of:

(i) existing mortgages on property the subject of any associated sale of which you are aware; and

(ii) any other mortgages secured against a property located in England or Wales made by an identified lender where an identified account number or numbers or a property address has been given by the lender;

(t) ensuring the redemption or postponement of existing mortgages on the property, and registering the mortgage with the priority required by the lender;

(u) making administrative arrangements in relation to any collateral security, such as an endowment policy, or in relation to any collateral warranty or guarantee relating to the physical condition of the property, such as NHBC documentation;

(v) registering the transfer and mortgage;

(w) giving legal advice on any matters reported on under 3.19, suggesting courses of action open to the lender, and complying with the lender's instructions on the action to be taken;

(x) disclosing any relationship specified by the lender between you and the borrower;

(y) storing safely the title deeds and documents pending registration and delivery to or as directed by the lender; and

(z) retaining the information contained in your conveyancing file for at least six years from the date of the mortgage.

3.20 Using the approved certificate of title

In addition, if acting for both lender and borrower in a standard mortgage of property to be used as the borrower's private residence only:

(a) you must use the certificate of title set out in the annex to rule 3 (below) ('the approved certificate'); and

(b) unless the lender has certified that its mortgage instructions are subject to the limitations contained in 3.19 above and 3.21 below, you must notify the lender on receipt of instructions that the approved certificate will be used, and that your duties to the lender are limited to the matters contained in the approved certificate.

3.21 Terms of rule to prevail

The terms of 3.16 to 3.20 above will prevail in the event of any ambiguity in the lender's instructions, or discrepancy between the instructions and 3.19 or the approved certificate.

3.22 Anti-avoidance

(1) Subject to (2) below, if acting only for the borrower in a standard mortgage of property you must not accept or act upon any requirements by way of undertaking, warranty, guarantee or otherwise of the lender, the lender's solicitor or other agent which extend beyond the limitations contained in 3.19.

(2) Provided the property is not to be used solely as the borrower's private residence, (1) above does not prevent you from giving any form of certificate of title recognised from time to time by the Board of the Solicitors Regulation Authority (a 'recognised certificate'). Additions or amendments which arise from the individual transaction may be made to the text of a recognised certificate but, to the extent to which they create an increased or additional obligation, must not extend beyond the limitations contained in 3.19.

3.23 Waivers

In spite of 22.01(1) (Waivers), the Board of the Solicitors Regulation Authority shall not have power to waive any of the provisions of 3.01 to 3.05.

ANNEX

Certificate of title

Details box

TO: (Lender)
Lender's Reference or Account No:
The Borrower:
Property:
Title Number:
Mortgage Advance:
Price stated in transfer:
Completion Date:
Conveyancer's Name & Address:
Conveyancer's Reference:
Conveyancer's bank, sort code and account number:
Date of instructions:

WE THE CONVEYANCERS NAMED ABOVE CERTIFY as follows:

(1)   If so instructed, we have checked the identity of the Borrower (and anyone else required to sign the mortgage deed or other document connected with the mortgage) by reference to the document or documents precisely specified in writing by you.

(2)   Except as otherwise disclosed to you in writing:

   (i)   we have investigated the title to the Property, we are not aware of any other financial charges secured on the Property which will affect the Property after completion of the mortgage and, upon completion of the mortgage, both you and the mortgagor (whose identity has been checked in accordance with paragraph (1) above) will have a good and marketable title to the Property and to appurtenant rights free from prior mortgages or charges and from onerous encumbrances which title will be registered with absolute title;

   (ii)   we have compared the extent of the Property shown on any plan provided by you against relevant plans in the title deeds and/or the description of the Property in any valuation which you have supplied to us, and in our opinion there are no material discrepancies;

   (iii)   the assumptions stated by the valuer about the title (its tenure, easements, boundaries and restrictions on use) in any valuation which you have supplied to us are correct;

   (iv)   if the Property is leasehold the terms of the lease accord with your instructions, including any requirements you have for covenants by the Landlord and/or a management company and/or by a deed of mutual covenant for the insurance, repair and maintenance of the structure, exterior and common parts of any building of which the Property forms part, and we have or will obtain on or before completion a clear receipt for the last payment of rent and service charge;

   (v)   if the Property is a commonhold unit, the commonhold community statement contains the terms specified by you and does not include any restrictions on occupation or use specified by you as unacceptable, and we have or will obtain on or before completion a commonhold unit information certificate;

(vi) we have received satisfactory evidence that the buildings insurance is in place, or will be on completion, for the sum and in the terms required by you;

(vii) if the Property is to be purchased by the Borrower:

    (a) the contract for sale provides for vacant possession on completion;

    (b) the seller has owned or been the registered owner of the Property for not less than six months; and

    (c) we are not acting on behalf of the seller;

(viii) we are in possession of:

    (a) either a local search or local search insurance; and

    (b) such other searches or search insurance as are appropriate to the Property, the mortgagor and any guarantor, in each case in accordance with your instructions;

(ix) nothing has been revealed by our searches and enquiries which would prevent the Property being used by any occupant for residential purposes; and

(x) neither any principal nor any other solicitor or registered European lawyer in the firm giving this certificate nor any spouse, child, parent, brother or sister of such a person is interested in the Property (whether alone or jointly with any other) as mortgagor.

WE:

(a) undertake, prior to use of the mortgage advance, to obtain in the form required by you the execution of a mortgage and a guarantee as appropriate by the persons whose identities have been checked in accordance with paragraph (1) above as those of the Borrower, any other person in whom the legal estate is vested and any guarantor; and, if required by you:

    (i) to obtain their signatures to the forms of undertaking required by you in relation to the use, occupation or physical state of the Property;

    (ii) to ask the Borrower for confirmation that the information about occupants given in your mortgage instructions or offer is correct; and

    (iii) to obtain consents in the form required by you from any existing or prospective occupier(s) aged 17 or over of the Property specified by you or of whom we are aware;

(b) have made or will make such Bankruptcy, Land Registry or Land Charges Searches as may be necessary to justify certificate no. (2)(i) above;

(c) will within the period of protection afforded by the searches referred to in paragraph (b) above:

    (i) complete the mortgage;

    (ii) arrange for the issue of a stamp duty land tax certificate if appropriate;

    (iii) deliver to the Land Registry the documents necessary to register the mortgage in your favour and any relevant prior dealings; and

    (iv) effect any other registrations necessary to protect your interests as mortgagee;

(d) will despatch to you such deeds and documents relating to the Property as you require with a list of them in the form prescribed by you within ten working days of receipt by us of the title information document from the Land Registry;

(e)   will not part with the mortgage advance (and will return it to you if required) if it shall come to our notice prior to completion that the Property will at completion be occupied in whole or in part otherwise than in accordance with your instructions;

(f)   will not accept instructions, except with your consent in writing, to prepare any lease or tenancy agreement relating to the Property or any part of it prior to despatch of the title information document to you;

(g)   will not use the mortgage advance until satisfied that, prior to or contemporaneously with the transfer of the Property to the mortgagor, there will be discharged:

(i)   any existing mortgage on property the subject of an associated sale of which we are aware; and

(ii)   any other mortgages made by a lender identified by you secured against a property located in England or Wales where you have given either an account number or numbers or a property address;

(h)   will notify you in writing if any matter comes to our attention before completion which would render the certificate given above untrue or inaccurate and, in those circumstances, will defer completion pending your authority to proceed and will return the mortgage advance to you if required; and

(i)   confirm that we have complied, or will comply, with your instructions in all other respects to the extent that they do not extend beyond the limitations contained in the Solicitors' Code of Conduct 2007, 3.19 (Conflict of interests – types of instruction which may be accepted).

OUR duties to you are limited to the matters set out in this certificate and we accept no further liability or responsibility whatsoever. The payment by you to us (by whatever means) of the mortgage advance or any part of it constitutes acceptance of this limitation and any assignment to you by the Borrower of any rights of action against us to which the Borrower may be entitled shall take effect subject to this limitation.

Signature box

SIGNED on behalf of THE CONVEYANCERS	....
NAME of Authorised Signatory	....
QUALIFICATION of Authorised Signatory	....
DATE of Signature	....

RULE 5 – BUSINESS MANAGEMENT IN ENGLAND AND WALES

5.01 Supervision and management responsibilities

(1) If you are a principal in a firm, a director of a recognised body which is a company, or a member of a recognised body which is an LLP, you must make arrangements for the effective management of the firm as whole, and in particular provide for:

(a) compliance with the duties of a principal, in law and conduct, to exercise appropriate supervision over all staff, and ensure adequate supervision and direction of clients' matters;

(b) compliance with the money laundering regulations, where applicable;

(c) compliance by the firm and individuals with key regulatory requirements such as certification, registration or recognition by the Solicitors Regulation Authority, compulsory professional indemnity cover, delivery of accountants' reports, and obligations to co-operate with and report information to the Authority;

(d) the identification of conflicts of interests;

(e) compliance with the requirements of rule 2 (Client relations) on client care, costs information and complaints handling;

(f) control of undertakings;

(g) the safekeeping of documents and assets entrusted to the firm;

(h) compliance with rule 6 (Equality and diversity);

(i) the training of individuals working in the firm to maintain a level of competence appropriate to their work and level of responsibility;

(j) financial control of budgets, expenditure and cashflow;

(k) the continuation of the practice of the firm in the event of absences and emergencies, with the minimum interruption to clients' business; and

(l) the management of risk.

(2) If you are a solicitor or REL employed as the head of an in-house legal department, you must effect supervision and management arrangements within your department to provide for:

(a) adequate supervision and direction of those assisting in your in-house practice;

(b) control of undertakings; and

(c) identification of conflicts of interests.

5.02 Persons who must be 'qualified to supervise'

(1) The following persons must be 'qualified to supervise':

(a) a sole principal;

(b) one of the partners of a partnership;

(c) one of the members of a recognised body which is an LLP;

(d) one of the directors of a recognised body which is a company;

(e) one of the solicitors or RELs employed by a law centre; or

(f)   one in-house solicitor or in-house REL in any department where solicitors and/or RELs, as part of that employment:

   (i)   do publicly funded work; or

   (ii)   exercise or supervise the exercise of any right of audience or right to conduct litigation when advising or acting for members of the public.

(2)   To be 'qualified to supervise' under this paragraph a person:

   (a)   must have completed the training specified from time to time by the Solicitors Regulation Authority for this purpose; and

   (b)   must have been entitled to practise as a lawyer for at least 36 months within the last ten years; and must be able to demonstrate this if asked by the Solicitors Regulation Authority.

5.03   Supervision of work for clients and members of the public

(1)   If you are a principal in a firm, you must ensure that your firm has in place a system for supervising clients' matters.

(2)   If you are an in-house solicitor or in-house REL and you are required to be 'qualified to supervise' under 5.02(1)(e) or (f) above, you must ensure that your law centre or in-house legal department has in place a system for supervising work undertaken for members of the public.

(3)   The system for supervision under 5.03(1) and (2) must include appropriate and effective procedures under which the quality of work undertaken for clients and members of the public is checked with reasonable regularity by suitably experienced and competent persons within the firm, law centre or in-house legal department.

RULE 7 – PUBLICITY

7.01   Misleading or inaccurate publicity

Publicity must not be misleading or inaccurate.

7.02   Clarity as to charges

Any publicity relating to your charges must be clearly expressed. In relation to practice from an office in England and Wales it must be clear whether disbursements and VAT are included.

7.03   Unsolicited visits or telephone calls

(1)   You must not publicise your practice by making unsolicited visits or telephone calls to a member of the public.

(2)   'Member of the public' does not include:

   (a)   a current or former client;

   (b)   another lawyer;

   (c)   an existing or potential professional or business connection; or

   (d)   a commercial organisation or public body.

7.04   International aspects of publicity

Publicity intended for a jurisdiction outside England and Wales must comply with:

    (a)   the provisions of rule 7 (and 15.07, if applicable); and

    (b)   the rules in force in that jurisdiction concerning lawyers' publicity.

Publicity intended for a jurisdiction where it is permitted will not breach 7.04 through being incidentally received in a jurisdiction where it is not permitted.

7.05   Responsibility for publicity

You must not authorise any other person to conduct publicity for your practice in a way which would be contrary to rule 7 (and 15.07, if applicable).

7.06   Application

(1)   Rule 7 applies to any publicity you or your firm conduct(s) or authorise(s) in relation to:

    (a)   your practice;

    (b)   any other business or activity carried on by you or your firm; or

    (c)   any other business or activity carried on by others.

(2)   7.01 to 7.05 apply to all forms of publicity including the name or description of your firm, stationery, advertisements, brochures, websites, directory entries, media appearances, promotional press releases, and direct approaches to potential clients and other persons, and whether conducted in person, in writing, or in electronic form.

7.07   Letterhead

(1)   The letterhead of a firm must bear the words 'regulated by the Solicitors Regulation Authority'.

(2)   (a)   The letterhead of:

       (i)   a sole principal must include the name of the sole principal;

       (ii)   a partnership of 20 or fewer persons must include a list of the partners; and

       (iii)   a recognised body which is a company with a sole director must include the name of the director, identified as director.

    (b)   The letterhead of:

       (i)   a partnership of more than 20 persons must include either a list of the partners;

       (ii)   a recognised body which is an LLP must include either a list of the members, identified as members; and

       (iii)   a recognised body which is a company with more than one director must include either a list of the directors, identified as directors,

    or a statement that the list is open to inspection at the office.

    (c)   (i)   On the letterhead of a recognised body which is an unlimited company; or

       (ii)   in the list of partners referred to in 7.07(2)(a) or (b) if a partnership has an unlimited company as a member; or

(iii)   in the list of members referred to in 7.07(2)(b) if an LLP has an unlimited company as a member;

it must be stated, either as part of the unlimited company's name or otherwise, that the unlimited company is a body corporate.

(3)   In a firm, if the partners (or directors in the case of a company, or members in the case of an LLP) comprise both solicitors and foreign lawyers, the list referred to in 7.07(2)(a) or (b) must:

    (a)   identify any solicitor as a solicitor;

    (b)   in the case of any lawyer or notary of an Establishment Directive state other than the UK:

        (i)   identify the jurisdiction(s) – local or national as appropriate – under whose professional title the lawyer or notary is practising;

        (ii)   give the professional title(s), expressed in an official language of the Establishment Directive state(s) concerned; and

        (iii)   if the lawyer is an REL, refer to that lawyer's registration with the Solicitors Regulation Authority; and

    (c)   indicate the professional qualification(s) as a lawyer and the country or jurisdiction of qualification of any RFL not included in (b) above.

(4)   Whenever an REL is named on the letterhead used by any firm or in-house practice, there must be compliance with 7.07(3)(b).

(5)   In 7.07, 'letterhead' includes a fax heading.

RULE 8 – FEE SHARING

8.01   Fee sharing with lawyers and colleagues

Except as permitted under 8.02 below you may only share or agree to share your professional fees with the following persons:

    (a)   practising members of legal professions covered by the Establishment Directive (other than a member of the English Bar practising in England and Wales);

    (b)   practising members of other legal professions (other than a person who is struck off or suspended from the register of foreign lawyers);

    (c)   bodies corporate wholly owned and directed by lawyers within (a) and (b) above for the purpose of practising law;

    (d)   your partner as permitted by rule 12 (Framework of practice), your retired partner or predecessor, or the dependants or personal representatives of your deceased partner or predecessor;

    (e)   in the case of a recognised body, a retired director, member or shareowner, or the dependants or personal representatives of a deceased director, member or shareowner;

    (f)   your genuine employee (this does not allow you to disguise as 'employment' what is in fact a partnership which rule 12 prohibits);

    (g)   a body corporate through which you practise as permitted by rule 12;

    (h)   your employer, if you are employed by a firm permitted under rule 12, or if you are practising in-house and acting in accordance with rule 13 (In-house practice) or 15.13 (In-house practice overseas);

(i) a law centre or advice service operated by a charitable or similar non-commercial organisation if you are working as a volunteer and receive fees or costs from public funds or recovered from a third party; or

(j) an estate agent who is your sub-agent for the sale of a property; or

(k) a charity (as defined in rule 24 (Interpretation)), provided:

 (i) you remain in compliance with 1.02 (Integrity), 1.03 (Independence) and 1.04 (Best interests of clients);

 (ii) if requested by the Solicitors Regulation Authority to do so, you supply details of all agreements to share fees with a charity;

 (iii) the operation of any such agreement does not result in a partnership;

 (iv) any such agreement does not involve a breach of rule 9 (Referrals of business); and

 (v) if you are employed in-house, you remain in compliance with 13.04 (Pro bono work).

8.02   Fee sharing with other non-lawyers

(1) Except in relation to European cross-border practice, you may share your professional fees with another person or business ('the fee sharer') if:

(a) the purpose of the fee sharing arrangement is solely to facilitate the introduction of capital and/or the provision of services to your firm;

(b) neither the fee sharing agreement nor the extent of the fees shared permits any fee sharer to influence or constrain your professional judgement in relation to the advice which you give to any client;

(c) the operation of the agreement does not result in a partnership prohibited by rule 12 (Framework of practice);

(d) if requested by the Solicitors Regulation Authority to do so, you supply details of all agreements which you have made with fee sharers and the percentage of your firm's annual gross fees which has been paid to each fee sharer; and

(e) your fee sharing agreement does not involve a breach of rule 9 (Referrals of business) or 15.09 (Overseas practice – referrals of business).

(2) 'Fee sharer' means a person or business who or which shares your fees in reliance on (1) above and the expression includes any person or business connected to or associated with the fee sharer.

RULE 9 – REFERRALS OF BUSINESS

9.01   General

(1) When making or receiving referrals of clients to or from third parties you must do nothing which would compromise your independence or your ability to act and advise in the best interests of your clients.

(2) You must draw the attention of potential introducers to this rule and to the relevant provisions of rule 7 (Publicity).

(3) This rule does not apply to referrals between lawyers.

(4) You must not, in respect of any claim arising as a result of death or personal injury, either:

(a) enter into an arrangement for the referral of clients with; or

(b) act in association with,

any person whose business, or any part of whose business, is to make, support or prosecute (whether by action or otherwise, and whether by a solicitor or agent or otherwise) claims arising as a result of death or personal injury, and who, in the course of such business, solicits or receives contingency fees in respect of such claims.

(5) The prohibition in 9.01(4) shall not apply to an arrangement or association with a person who solicits or receives contingency fees only in respect of proceedings in a country outside England and Wales, to the extent that a local lawyer would be permitted to receive a contingency fee in respect of such proceedings.

(6) In 9.01(4) and (5) 'contingency fee' means any sum (whether fixed, or calculated either as a percentage of the proceeds or otherwise howsoever) payable only in the event of success in the prosecution or defence of any action, suit or other contentious proceedings.

9.02 Financial arrangements with introducers

The following additional requirements apply when you enter into a financial arrangement with an introducer:

(a) The agreement must be in writing and be available for inspection by the Solicitors Regulation Authority.

(b) The introducer must undertake, as part of the agreement, to comply with the provisions of this rule.

(c) You must be satisfied that clients referred by the introducer have not been acquired as a result of marketing or publicity or other activities which, if done by a person regulated by the Solicitors Regulation Authority, would be in breach of any of these rules.

(d) The agreement must not include any provision which would:

(i) compromise, infringe or impair any of the duties set out in these rules; or

(ii) allow the introducer to influence or constrain your professional judgement in relation to the advice given to the client.

(e) The agreement must provide that before making a referral the introducer must give the client all relevant information concerning the referral, in particular:

(i) the fact that the introducer has a financial arrangement with you; and

(ii) the amount of any payment to the introducer which is calculated by reference to that referral; or

(iii) where the introducer is paying you to provide services to the introducer's customers:

(A) the amount the introducer is paying you to provide those services; and

(B) the amount the client is required to pay the introducer.

(f)   If you have reason to believe that the introducer is breaching any of the terms of the agreement required by this rule, you must take all reasonable steps to ensure that the breach is remedied. If the introducer continues to breach it you must terminate the agreement.

(g)   Before accepting instructions to act for a client referred under 9.02 you must, in addition to the requirements contained in 2.02 (Client care), 2.03 (Information about the cost) or 2.05 (Complaints handling), give the client, in writing, all relevant information concerning the referral, in particular:

    (i)   the fact that you have a financial arrangement with the introducer;

    (ii)   the amount of any payment to the introducer which is calculated by reference to that referral; or

    (iii) where the introducer is paying you to provide services to the introducer's customers:

        (A)   the amount the introducer is paying you to provide those services; and

        (B)   the amount the client is required to pay the introducer;

    (iv)   a statement that any advice you give will be independent and that the client is free to raise questions on all aspects of the transaction; and

    (v)   confirmation that information disclosed to you by the client will not be disclosed to the introducer unless the client consents; but that where you are also acting for the introducer in the same matter and a conflict of interests arises, you might be obliged to cease acting.

(h)   You must not enter into a financial arrangement with an introducer for the referral of clients in respect of criminal proceedings or any matter in which you will act for the client with the benefit of public funding.

(i)   For the purpose of this rule:

    (i)   'financial arrangement' includes:

        (A)   any payment to a third party in respect of referrals; and

        (B)   any agreement to be paid by a third party introducer to provide services to the third party's customers; and

    (ii)   'payment' includes any other consideration but does not include normal hospitality, proper disbursements or normal business expenses.

9.03   Referrals to third parties

(1)   If you recommend that a client use a particular firm, agency or business, you must do so in good faith, judging what is in the client's best interests.

(2)   You must not enter into any agreement or association which would restrict your freedom to recommend any particular firm, agency or business.

(3)   (2) above does not apply to arrangements in connection with any of the following types of contracts:

    (a)   regulated mortgage contracts;

    (b)   general insurance contracts; or

    (c)   pure protection contracts.

(4)   The terms 'regulated mortgage contracts', 'general insurance contracts' and 'pure protection contracts' in (3) above have the meanings given in 19.01(4).

(5)   Where you refer a client to a firm, agency or business that can only offer products from one source, you must notify the client in writing of this limitation.

(6)   If a client is likely to need an endowment policy, or similar life insurance with an investment element, you must refer them only to an independent intermediary authorised to give investment advice.

RULE 10 – RELATIONS WITH THIRD PARTIES

10.01   Not taking unfair advantage

You must not use your position to take unfair advantage of anyone either for your own benefit or for another person's benefit.

10.02   Agreeing costs with another party

When negotiating the payment of your client's costs by another firm's client or a third party, you must give sufficient time and information for the amount of your costs to be agreed or assessed.

10.03   Administering oaths

You can administer oaths or affirmations or take declarations if you are a solicitor or an REL. You must not do so where you or your firm is acting for any party in the matter.

10.04   Contacting other party to a matter

You must not communicate with any other party who to your knowledge has retained a lawyer or licensed conveyancer to act in a matter, except:

    (a)   to request the name and address of the other party's lawyer or licensed conveyancer;

    (b)   where it would be reasonable to conclude that the other party's lawyer or licensed conveyancer has refused or failed for no adequate reason either to pass on messages to their client or to reply to correspondence, and has been warned of your intention to contact their client direct;

    (c)   with that lawyer or licensed conveyancer's consent; or

    (d)   in exceptional circumstances.

10.05   Undertakings

(1)   You must fulfil an undertaking which is given in circumstances where:

    (a)   you give the undertaking in the course of practice;

    (b)   you are a principal in a firm, and any person within the firm gives the undertaking in the course of practice;

    (c)   you give the undertaking outside the course of practice, but as a solicitor; or

(d)   you are an REL based at an office in England and Wales, and you give the undertaking within the UK, as a lawyer of an Establishment Directive state, but outside your practice as an REL.

(2)   You must fulfil an undertaking within a reasonable time.

(3)   If you give an undertaking which is dependent upon the happening of a future event, you must notify the recipient immediately if it becomes clear that the event will not occur.

(4)   When you give an undertaking to pay another's costs, the undertaking will be discharged if the matter does not proceed unless there is an express agreement that the costs are payable in any event.

10.06   Dealing with more than one prospective buyer in a conveyancing transaction

(1)   Each time a seller of land, other than in a sale by auction or tender, either:

(a)   instructs you to deal with more than one prospective buyer; or

(b)   to your knowledge:

(i)   deals directly with another prospective buyer (or their conveyancer); or

(ii)   instructs another conveyancer to deal with another prospective buyer;

you must, with the client's consent, immediately inform the conveyancer of each prospective buyer, or the prospective buyer if acting in person.

(2)   If the seller refuses to agree to such disclosure, you must immediately stop acting in the matter.

(3)   You must not act for both the seller and any of the prospective buyers.

(4)   You must not act for more than one of the prospective buyers.

10.07   Fees of lawyers of other jurisdictions

(1)   If in the course of practice you instruct a lawyer of another jurisdiction you must, as a matter of professional conduct, pay the lawyer's proper fees unless the lawyer is practising as a solicitor or barrister of England and Wales; or

(a)   you have expressly disclaimed that responsibility at the outset, or at a later date you have expressly disclaimed responsibility for any fees incurred after that date;

(b)   the lawyer is an REL or is registered with the Bar of England and Wales under the Establishment Directive; or

(c)   the lawyer is an RFL based in England and Wales and practising in a firm.

(2)   If in the course of practice you instruct a business carrying on the practice of a lawyer of another jurisdiction you must, as a matter of professional conduct, pay the proper fees for the work that lawyer does, unless:

(a)   you have expressly disclaimed that responsibility at the outset, or at a later date you have expressly disclaimed responsibility for any fees incurred after that date; or

(b)   the business is a firm.

RULE 18 – PROPERTY SELLING

18.01   Standards of property selling services

(1)   When providing property selling services through your firm, you must:

(a)   ensure that you, or the relevant staff, are competent to carry out the work;

(b)   not seek from any prospective buyer a pre-contract deposit in excess of any prescribed limit; and

(c)   promptly send to your client written accurate details of any offer you have received from a prospective buyer in respect of an interest in the property (other than those of a description which your client has indicated in writing that they do not want to receive).

(2)   If you are the person who is responsible for marketing a residential property you must comply with any home information packs regulations made under the Housing Act 2004.

(3)   (a)   In 18.01(1) above:

(i)   'competent' includes meeting any standards of competence set by the Secretary of State under section 22 of the Estate Agents Act 1979; and

(ii)   'prescribed limit' means any limit prescribed by the Secretary of State under section 19 of the Estate Agents Act 1979.

(b)   In 18.01(2) 'the person who is responsible for marketing a residential property' has the meaning used in sections 151–153 of the Housing Act 2004.

18.02   Statement on the cost

(1)   When accepting instructions to act in the sale of a property, you must, at the outset of communication between you and the client, or as soon as is reasonably practicable, and before the client is committed to any liability towards you, give the client a written statement setting out your agreement as to:

(a)   the identity of the property;

(b)   the interest to be sold;

(c)   the price to be sought;

(d)   the amount of your fee or the method of its calculation;

(e)   the circumstances in which your fee is to become payable;

(f)   regarding any payments to be made to others, and charged separately:

(i)   the amount, or the method by which they will be calculated; and

(ii)   the circumstances in which they may be incurred; and

(g)   the incidence of VAT.

(2)   You must also, within the written statement:

(a)   state whether or not you are to have 'sole agency' or 'sole selling rights'. The statement must also include a clear explanation of the intention and effect of those terms, or any similar terms used; and

(b) if the statement refers to a 'ready, willing and able' buyer (or similar term), include a clear explanation of the term.

18.03   Conflict of interests

(1)   In addition to your duties under rule 3 (Conflict of interests), when selling property you must comply with the following requirements.

(a) If you or any connected person has, or is seeking to acquire, a beneficial interest in the property or in the proceeds of sale of any interest in the property, you must promptly inform your client in writing.

(b) If you act in the sale of property, even if not in the conveyancing, you must not act for the buyer in the negotiations.

(c) If a prospective buyer makes an offer for a client's property, you must promptly inform the client in writing if, to your knowledge, you or any connected person has been instructed, or is to be instructed by the buyer to sell an interest in land, and that sale is necessary to enable the buyer to buy from the client or results from that prospective purchase.

(d) If you have, or to your knowledge any connected person has, a beneficial interest in a property or in the proceeds of sale of any interest in it, you must promptly inform in writing any person negotiating to acquire or dispose of any interest in that property. You must make this disclosure before entering into any negotiations with a prospective buyer.

(e) You must not discriminate against a prospective buyer because they are unlikely to instruct you to sell an interest in land, which sale is necessary to enable the buyer to buy from your client or results from that prospective purchase.

(f) When acting for a seller, you must restrict communication with the buyer to your property selling function. In particular:

(i) you must communicate about legal matters so far as possible only through the buyer's solicitor; and

(ii) you must not lead the buyer to believe that they are receiving legal advice from you.

(g) When acting for a seller, if you arrange for a mortgage to be available on the property in order to facilitate the sale, you may inform prospective buyers of the availability of the mortgage (subject to the buyer's status) but, unless exempted by rule 3 (Conflict of interests) you must also inform prospective buyers in writing:

(i) that you cannot advise or act for the prospective buyer in respect of the mortgage;

(ii) that the mortgage may not be the only one available; and

(iii) that the prospective buyer should consult their own lawyer or licensed conveyancer.

(2)   In 18.03(1) above:

(a) 'connected person' means:

(i) spouse, former spouse, reputed spouse, brother, sister, uncle, aunt, nephew, niece, direct descendant, parent or other direct ancestor;

(ii) any employee of your firm, and any member of your employee's family;

    (iii)   any owner or employee of an associated firm defined in rule 24 (Interpretation) or any member of their families;

    (iv)   any company of which you are a director or employee, or any LLP of which you are a member or employee, or any company in which you, either alone or with any other connected person or persons are entitled to exercise, or control the exercise of, one-third or more of the voting power at any general meeting;

    (v)   any company of which any of the persons mentioned in (i) to (iii) above is a director or employee, or any LLP of which any of them is a member or employee, or any company in which any of them, either alone or with any other connected person or persons, is entitled to exercise, or control the exercise of, one-third or more of the voting power at any general meeting; and

    (vi)   any other 'associate' as defined in section 32 of the Estate Agents Act 1979; and

  (b)   'you' includes anyone with whom you carry on a joint property selling practice, and owners of an associated firm as defined in rule 24 (Interpretation).

18.04　Waivers

In spite of 22.01(1) (Waivers), the Board of the Solicitors Regulation Authority shall not have power to waive any of the provisions of this rule.

RULE 19 – FINANCIAL SERVICES

19.01　Independence

(1)   You must not, in connection with any regulated activity:

  (a)   be an appointed representative; or

  (b)   have any arrangement with other persons under which you could be constrained to recommend to clients or effect for them (or refrain from doing so) transactions:

    (i)   in some investments but not others;

    (ii)   with some persons but not others; or

    (iii)   through the agency of some persons but not others; or

  (c)   have any arrangement with other persons under which you could be constrained to introduce or refer clients or other persons with whom you deal to some persons but not others.

(2)   You must not have any active involvement in a separate business which is an appointed representative, unless it is the appointed representative of an independent financial adviser.

(3)   (1)(b) and (c) above shall not apply to arrangements in connection with any of the following types of investments:

  (a)   regulated mortgage contracts;

  (b)   general insurance contracts; or

  (c)   pure protection contracts.

(4)   In this rule:

(a)   'appointed representative' has the meaning given in the Financial Services and Markets Act 2000;

(b)   'general insurance contract' is any contract of insurance within Part I of Schedule 1 to the Financial Services and Markets Act 2000 (Regulated Activities) Order 2001 (SI 2001/544);

(c)   'investment' means any of the investments specified in Part III of the Financial Services and Markets Act 2000 (Regulated Activities) Order 2001 (SI 2001/544);

(d)   'pure protection contract' has the meaning given in rule 8(1) of the Solicitors' Financial Services (Scope) Rules 2001;

(e)   'regulated activity' means an activity which is specified in the Financial Services and Markets Act 2000 (Regulated Activities) Order 2001 (SI 2001/544); and

(f)   'regulated mortgage contract' has the meaning given by article 61(3) of the Financial Services and Markets Act 2000 (Regulated Activities) Order 2001 (SI 2001/544).

RULE 21 – SEPARATE BUSINESSES

21.01   General

(1)   If you are practising from an office in England and Wales as a solicitor or an REL, or as an RFL who is a partner in an MNP, a director of a recognised body which is a company or a member of a recognised body which is an LLP, you must comply with the provisions of this rule in relation to:

(a)   services which may not be provided through a separate business;

(b)   services which may be provided through a separate business or (subject to these rules) through a firm or in-house practice; and

(c)   services which fall outside the scope of a solicitor's practice but which may be provided in conjunction with a firm or in-house practice.

(2)   This rule applies to your involvement in any separate business whether the separate business is in England and Wales or outside the jurisdiction.

(3)   This rule also applies to a recognised body in relation to an interest held in another body corporate which is not a recognised body.

(4)   For the avoidance of doubt, in this rule 'practising' includes practising as an in-house solicitor or an in-house REL.

21.02   Services which may not be provided through a separate business

(1)   Subject to (2) below, you must not provide any of the following services through a separate business:

(a)   the conduct of any matter which could come before a court, tribunal or inquiry, whether or not proceedings are started;

(b)   advocacy before a court, tribunal or inquiry;

(c)   instructing counsel in any part of the UK;

(d)   immigration advice or immigration services;

(e)   any activity in relation to conveyancing, applications for probate or letters of administration, or drawing trust deeds or court documents, which is reserved to solicitors and
others under the Solicitors Act 1974;

(f)   drafting wills;

(g)   acting as nominee, trustee or executor in England and Wales;

(h)   legal advice not included above; or

(i)   drafting legal documents not included above.

Exceptions

(2)   The provisions of (1) above do not apply to prohibit you from providing services through a
separate business:

(a)   which carries on your practice as a lawyer of another jurisdiction;

(b)   which carries on your business as a trade mark agent, patent agent or European patent
attorney;

(c)   which carries on your business as a parliamentary agent;

(d)   which is a wholly owned nominee company operated as a subsidiary but necessary part
of the work of a separate business providing financial services;

(e)   which provides legal advice and/or drafts legal documents within (1)(h) and/or (i)
above, as a subsidiary but necessary part of some other service which is one of the main
services of the separate business; or

(f)   which has no office in England and Wales, does not receive customers directly or
indirectly referred from any firm through which you carry on your practice in England
and Wales, or from any in-house practice you have in England and Wales, does not
provide any services in relation to the UK; and does not provide executor, trustee or
nominee services anywhere.

However, you must comply with the requirements of 21.05 in relation to any such separate business.

21.03   Services which may be provided in conjunction with a firm or in-house practice

(1)   The following services extend beyond, or fall outside, the scope of a solicitor's practice but
you may provide such services in conjunction with a firm or in-house practice:

(a)   practice as a qualified notary public;

(b)   educational activities; and

(c)   authorship, journalism or publishing.

(2)   A service provided in conjunction with a firm or in-house practice of a solicitor, an REL, an
MNP or a recognised body is not provided through a separate business.

21.04   Services which may be provided (subject to these rules) either through a firm or
in-house practice, or through a separate business

(1)   You may provide the following services either (subject to these rules) through a firm or
in-house practice, or through a separate business:

(a)   alternative dispute resolution;

(b)   financial services (except those that cannot form part of a solicitor's practice);

(c)   estate agency;

(d)   management consultancy;

(e)   company secretarial services;

(f)   acting as a parliamentary agent;

(g)   acting as a trade mark agent, patent agent or European patent attorney;

(h)   practising as a lawyer of another jurisdiction;

(i)   acting as a bailiff;

(j)   acting as nominee, trustee or executor outside England and Wales; or

(k)   providing any other business, advisory or agency service which could be provided (subject to these rules) through a firm or in-house practice but is not included in 21.02.

(2)   If you provide any service listed in (1) above through a separate business you must comply with 21.05.

21.05   Safeguards in relation to a separate business

(1)   If you provide services through a separate business you must do nothing in the course of practice, or in the course of making referrals to the business or accepting referrals from the business, which would breach rule 1 (Core duties).

(2)   You must ensure that the following safeguards are in place in relation to a separate business which offers or provides any of the services listed in 21.04(1):

(a)   the separate business must not be held out or described in such a way as to suggest that the separate business is carrying on a practice regulated by the Solicitors Regulation Authority, or that any lawyer connected with your firm is providing services through the separate business as a practising lawyer regulated by the Solicitors Regulation Authority;

(b)   all paperwork, documents, records or files relating to the separate business and its customers must be kept separate from those of any firm or in-house practice, even where a customer of the separate business is also a client of the firm or in-house practice;

(c)   the client account used for any firm or in-house practice must not be used to hold money for the separate business, or for customers of the separate business in their capacity as such;

(d)   if the separate business shares premises, office accommodation or reception staff with any firm or in-house practice:

(i)   the areas used by the firm or in-house practice must be clearly differentiated from the areas used by the separate business; and

(ii)   all customers of the separate business must be informed that it is not regulated by the Solicitors Regulation Authority and that the statutory protections attaching to clients of a lawyer regulated by the Authority are not available to them as customers of that business;

(e)   if you or your firm refer(s) a client to the separate business, the client must first be informed of your interest in the separate business, that the separate business is not regulated by the Solicitors Regulation Authority, and that the statutory protections attaching to clients of a lawyer regulated by the Authority are not available to clients of the separate business; and

(f)   if the separate business is an estate agency, then without prejudice to the provisions of these rules regarding conflicts of interests, neither you nor any firm through which you practise as a principal may act in the conveyance for the buyer of any property sold through the estate agency unless:

   (i)   the firm shares ownership of the estate agency with at least one other business in which neither you nor the firm have any financial interest;

   (ii)   neither you nor anyone else in the firm is dealing with or has dealt with the sale of the seller's property for the separate business; and

   (iii) the buyer has given written consent to you or the firm acting, after your financial interest in the sale going through has been explained to the buyer.

I.2. Solicitors' Accounts Rules 1998: Part C – Interest[1]

Part C – Interest

Rule 24 – When interest must be paid

(1)   When a solicitor holds money in a separate designated client account for a client, or for a person funding all or part of the solicitor's fees, the solicitor must account to the client or that person for all interest earned on the account.

(2)   When a solicitor holds money in a general client account for a client, or for a person funding all or part of the solicitor's fees (or if money should have been held for a client or such other person in a client account but was not), the solicitor must account to the client or that person for a sum in lieu of interest calculated in accordance with rule 25.

(3)   A solicitor is not required to pay a sum in lieu of interest under paragraph (2) above:

   (a)   if the amount calculated is £20 or less;

   (b)   (i)   if the solicitor holds a sum of money not exceeding the amount shown in the left hand column below for a time not exceeding the period indicated in the right hand column:

Amount	Time
£1,000	8 weeks
£2,000	4 weeks
£10,000	2 weeks
£20,000	1 week

   (ii)   if the solicitor holds a sum of money exceeding £20,000 for one week or less, unless it is fair and reasonable to account for a sum in lieu of interest having regard to all the circumstances;

   (c)   on money held for the payment of counsel's fees, once counsel has requested a delay in settlement;

   (d)   on money held for the Legal Services Commission;

   (e)   on an advance from the solicitor under rule 15(2)(b) to fund a payment on behalf of the client in excess of funds held for that client; or

   (f)   if there is an agreement to contract out of the provisions of this rule under rule 27.

(4)   If sums of money are held intermittently during the course of acting, and the sum in lieu of interest calculated under rule 25 for any period is £20 or less, a sum in lieu of interest should still be paid if it is fair and reasonable in the circumstances to aggregate the sums in respect of the individual periods.

---

1. © The Law Society. With consolidated amendments to October 2004.

(5)   If money is held for a continuous period, and for part of that period it is held in a separate designated client account, the sum in lieu of interest for the rest of the period when the money was held in a general client account may as a result be £20 or less. A sum in lieu of interest should, however, be paid if it is fair and reasonable in the circumstances to do so.

(6)   (a)   If a solicitor holds money for a client (or person funding all or part of the solicitor's fees) in an account opened on the instructions of the client (or that person) under rule 16(1)(a), the solicitor must account to the client (or that person) for all interest earned on the account.

     (b)   If a solicitor has failed to comply with instructions to open an account under rule 16(1)(a), the solicitor must account to the client (or the person funding all or part of the solicitor's fees) for a sum in lieu of any net loss of interest suffered by the client (or that person) as a result.

(7)   This rule does not apply to controlled trust money.

Notes

Requirement to pay interest

(i)   The whole of the interest earned on a separate designated client account must be credited to the account. However, the obligation to pay a sum in lieu of interest for amounts held in a general client account is subject to the de minimis provisions in rule 24(3)(a) and (b). Section 33(3) of the Solicitors Act 1974 permits solicitors to retain any interest earned on client money held in a general client account over and above that which they have to pay under these rules. (See also note (viii) to rule 15 on aggregation of accounts.)

(ii)   There is no requirement to pay a sum in lieu of interest on money held on instructions under rule 16(1)(a) in a manner which attracts no interest.

(iii)   Accounts opened in the client's name under rule 16(1)(b) (whether operated by the solicitor or not) are not subject to rule 24, as the money is not held by the solicitor. All interest earned belongs to the client. The same applies to any account in the client's own name operated by the solicitor as signatory under rule 11.

(iv)   Money subject to a trust which is not a controlled trust is client money (see rule 13, note (vii)), and rule 24 therefore applies to it.

De minimis provisions (rule 24(3)(a) and (b))

(v)   The sum in lieu of interest is calculated over the whole period for which money is held (see rule 25(2)); if this sum is £20 or less, the solicitor need not account to the client. If sums of money are held in relation to separate matters for the same client, it is normally appropriate to treat the money relating to the different matters separately, so that, if any of the sums calculated is £20 or less, no sum in lieu of interest is payable. There will, however, be cases when the matters are so closely related that they ought to be considered together – for example, when a solicitor is acting for a client in connection with numerous debt collection matters.

Administrative charges

(vi)   It is not improper to charge a reasonable fee for the handling of client money when the service provided is out of the ordinary.

Unpresented cheques

(vii)   A client may fail to present a cheque to his or her bank for payment. Whether or not it is reasonable to recalculate the amount due will depend on all the circumstances of the case. A reasonable charge may be made for any extra work carried out if the solicitor is legally entitled to make such a charge.

Liquidators, trustees in bankruptcy, Court of Protection receivers and trustees of occupational pension schemes

(viii)   Under rule 9, Part C of the rules does not normally apply to solicitors who are liquidators, etc. Solicitors must comply with the appropriate statutory rules and regulations, and rules 9(3) and (4) as appropriate.

Joint accounts

(ix)   Under rule 10, Part C of the rules does not apply to joint accounts. If a solicitor holds money jointly with a client, interest earned on the account will be for the benefit of the client unless otherwise agreed. If money is held jointly with another solicitors' practice, the allocation of interest earned will depend on the agreement reached.

Requirements for controlled trust money (rule 24(7))

(x)   Part C does not apply to controlled trust money. Under the general law, trustees of a controlled trust must account for all interest earned. For the treatment of interest on controlled trust money in a general client account, see rule 13, note (xi)(b), rule 15(2)(d) and note (vi) to rule 15. (See also note (viii) to rule 15 on aggregation of accounts.)

Rule 25 – Amount of interest

(1)   Solicitors must aim to obtain a reasonable rate of interest on money held in a separate designated client account, and must account for a fair sum in lieu of interest on money held in a general client account (or on money which should have been held in a client account but was not). The sum in lieu of interest need not necessarily reflect the highest rate of interest obtainable but it is not acceptable to look only at the lowest rate of interest obtainable.

(2)   **The sum in lieu of interest** for money held in a general client account (or on money which should have been held in a client account but was not) **must be calculated**:

- **on the balance or balances held over the whole period for which cleared funds are held**

- **at a rate not less than (whichever is the higher of) the following**:

    (i)   the rate of interest payable on a separate designated client account for the amount or amounts held, or

    (ii)   the rate of interest payable on the relevant amount or amounts if placed on deposit on similar terms by a member of the business community

    at the bank or building society where the money is held.

(3)   If the money, or part of it, is held successively or concurrently in accounts at different banks or building societies, the relevant bank or building society for the purpose of paragraph (2) will be whichever of those banks or building societies offered the best rate on the date when the money was first held.

(4)   If, contrary to the rules, the money is not held in a client account, the relevant bank or building society for the purpose of paragraph (2) will be a clearing bank or building society nominated by the client (or other person on whose behalf client money is held).

Notes

(i)   The sum in lieu of interest has to be calculated over the whole period for which money is held – see rule 25(2). The solicitor will usually account to the client at the conclusion of the client's matter, but might in some cases consider it appropriate to account to the client at intervals throughout.

(ii)   When looking at the period over which the sum in lieu of interest must be calculated, it will usually be unnecessary to check on actual clearance dates. When money is received by cheque and paid out by cheque, the normal clearance periods will usually cancel each other out, so that it will be satisfactory to look at the period between the dates when the incoming cheque is banked and the outgoing cheque is drawn.

(iii)   Different considerations apply when payments in and out are not both made by cheque. So, for example, the relevant periods would normally be:

- *from the date when a solicitor receives incoming money in cash until the date when the outgoing cheque is sent;*

- *from the date when an incoming telegraphic transfer begins to earn interest until the date when the outgoing cheque is sent;*

- *from the date when an incoming cheque or banker's draft is or would normally be cleared until the date when the outgoing telegraphic transfer is made or banker's draft is obtained.*

(iv)   The sum in lieu of interest is calculated by reference to the rates paid by the appropriate bank or building society (see rule 25(2) to (4)). Solicitors will therefore follow the practice of that bank or building society in determining how often interest is compounded over the period for which the cleared funds are held.

(v)   Money held in a client account must be immediately available, even at the sacrifice of interest, unless the client otherwise instructs, or the circumstances clearly indicate otherwise. The need for access can be taken into account in assessing the appropriate rate for calculating the sum to be paid in lieu of interest, or in assessing whether a reasonable rate of interest has been obtained for a separate designated client account.

Rule 26 – Interest on stakeholder money

When a solicitor holds money as stakeholder, the solicitor must pay interest, or a sum in lieu of interest, on the basis set out in rule 24 to the person to whom the stake is paid.

Note

For contracting out of this provision, see rule 27(2) and the notes to rule 27.

Rule 27 – Contracting out

(1)   In appropriate circumstances a client and his or her solicitor may by a written agreement come to a different arrangement as to the matters dealt with in rule 24 (payment of interest).

(2)   A solicitor acting as stakeholder may, by a written agreement with his or her own client and the other party to the transaction, come to a different arrangement as to the matters dealt with in rule 24.

Notes

(i)   Solicitors should act fairly towards their clients and provide sufficient information to enable them to give informed consent if it is felt appropriate to depart from the interest provisions. Whether it is appropriate to contract out depends on all the circumstances, for example, the size of the sum involved or the nature or status or bargaining position of the client. It might, for instance, be appropriate to contract out by standard terms of business if the client is a substantial commercial entity and the interest involved is modest in relation to the size of the transaction. The larger the sum of interest involved, the more there would be an onus on the solicitor to show that a client who had accepted a contracting out provision was properly informed and had been treated fairly. Contracting out is never appropriate if it is against the client's interests.

(ii)   In principle, a solicitor-stakeholder is entitled to make a reasonable charge to the client for acting as stakeholder in the client's matter.

(iii)   Alternatively, it may be appropriate to include a special provision in the contract that the solicitor-stakeholder retains the interest on the deposit to cover his or her charges for acting as stakeholder. This is only acceptable if it will provide a fair and reasonable payment for the work and risk involved in holding a stake. The contract could stipulate a maximum charge, with any interest earned above that figure being paid to the recipient of the stake.

(iv)   Any right to charge the client, or to stipulate for a charge which may fall on the client, would be excluded by, for instance, a prior agreement with the client for a fixed fee for the client's matter, or for an estimated fee which cannot be varied upwards in the absence of special circumstances. It is therefore not normal practice for a stakeholder in conveyancing transactions to receive a separate payment for holding the stake.

(v)   A solicitor-stakeholder who seeks an agreement to exclude the operation of rule 26 should be particularly careful not to take unfair advantage either of the client, or of the other party if unrepresented.

Rule 28 – Interest certificates

Without prejudice to any other remedy:

(a)   any client, including one of joint clients, or a person funding all or part of a solicitor's fees, may apply to the Society for a certificate as to whether or not interest, or a sum in lieu of interest, should have been paid and, if so, the amount; and

(b)   if the Society certifies that interest, or a sum in lieu of interest, should have been paid, the solicitor must pay the certified sum.

Notes

(i)   Applications for an interest certificate should be made to the Law Society's Consumer Complaints Service. It is advisable for the client (or other person) to try to resolve the matter with the solicitor before approaching the Consumer Complaints Service.

(ii)   If appropriate, the Law Society will require the solicitor to obtain an interest calculation from the relevant bank or building society.

II. PROTOCOL AND FORMULAE

II.1. National Conveyancing Protocol (fifth edition) for domestic freehold and leasehold property[1]

Acting for the seller

1. The first step

The seller should inform the solicitor as soon as it is intended to place the property on the market so that delay may be reduced after a prospective purchaser is found.

2. Preparing the package: assembling the information

On receipt of instructions, the solicitor should then immediately take the following steps, at the seller's expense:

2.1   Whenever possible instructions should be obtained from the client in person. The Consumer Protection (Distance Selling) Regulations 2000 should not then apply.

2.2   Check the client's identity if the client is not known to you. Comply with money laundering regulations and follow any guidance issued by the Law Society.

2.3   Give the client information as to costs, information relating to the name and status of the person who will be carrying out the work and, if that person is not a partner, the name of the partner who has overall responsibility for the matter. Give any other information necessary to comply with Rule 15 of the Solicitors' Practice Rules 1990 and Solicitors' Costs Information and Client Care Code 1999. If given orally this information should be confirmed in writing.

2.4   Give the seller details of whom to contact in the event of a complaint about the firm's services (Rule 15).

2.5   Consider with client whether to make local authority and other searches so that these can be supplied to the buyer's solicitor as soon as an offer is made. If thought appropriate request a payment on account in relation to disbursements.

2.6   Ascertain the whereabouts of the documents of title and, if not in the solicitor's custody, obtain them and, or if registration or a dealing has taken place after 13 October 2003, apply for an official copy of entries on the register and the title plan.

---

1. The Protocol is under review by the Law Society's TransAction Working Party. This fifth edition was published in 2005 and contains references to *The Guide to the Professional Conduct of Solicitors 1999*, published by the Law Society.

2.7   Ask the seller to complete the Seller's Property Information Form and on its return remind the seller of the need to notify you of any changes in the information supplied prior to completion.

2.8   Obtain such original guarantees with the accompanying specification, planning decisions, building regulation approvals and certificates of completion as are in the seller's possession and copies of any other planning consents that are with the title documents or details of any highway and sewerage agreements and bonds or any other relevant certificates relating to the property (e.g. structural engineer's certificate or an indemnity policy).

2.9   Give the seller the Fixtures, Fittings and Contents Form, with a copy to retain, to complete and return prior to the submission of the draft contract.

2.10   If the title is unregistered make an index map search.

2.11   If so instructed requisition a local authority search and enquiries and any other searches (e.g. mining or commons registration searches).

2.12   Obtain details of all mortgages and other financial charges of which the seller's solicitor has notice including, where applicable, improvement grants and discounts repayable to a local authority. Redemption figures should be obtained at this stage in respect of all mortgages on the property so that cases of negative equity or penalty redemption interest can be identified at an early stage.

2.13   Ascertain the identity of all people aged 17 or over living in the dwelling and ask about any financial contribution they or anyone else may have made towards its purchase or subsequent improvement. All persons identified in this way should be asked to confirm their consent to the sale proceeding.

2.14   In leasehold cases, ask the seller to complete the Seller's Leasehold Information Form and to produce, if possible:

    (1)   A receipt or evidence from the landlord of the last payment of rent.

    (2)   The maintenance charge accounts for the last three years, where appropriate, and evidence of payment.

    (3)   Details of the buildings insurance policy.

If any of these are lacking, and are necessary for the transaction, the solicitor should obtain them from the landlord. At the same time investigate whether a licence to assign is required and, if so, enquire of the landlord what references or deeds of covenant are necessary and, in the case of some retirement schemes, if a charge is payable to the management company on change of ownership. On receipt of the form back from the seller, remind the seller of the need to notify you of any changes in the information supplied prior to completion.

2.15   In commonhold cases:

    (1)   Ask the seller to complete the Seller's Commonhold Information Form, and to produce, if possible

        (i)   Commonhold Association Memorandum and Articles of Association;

        (ii)   Commonhold Community Statement;

        (iii)   Details of the building insurance policy.

    (2)   Make a search at Companies House against the commonhold association.

    (3)   Obtain an official copy of commonhold title for the common parts.

(4) Obtain the account from the commonhold association for the unit and ask if there are

    (i) any other claims or assessments against the unit;

    (ii) details of the annual budget or estimates;

    (iii) any reserve fund; and

    (iv) any restricted use areas.

2.16 Check replies given by the seller on the Seller's Property Information Form and, if appropriate, the Seller's Leasehold Information Form and Seller's Commonhold Information Form from the information in your possession (see the guidance from the Law Society's Conveyancing and Land Law Committee [2003] *Gazette*, 16 October, 43).

3. Preparing the package: the draft documents

As soon as the title documents or official copies of the registered title are available, and the seller has completed the Seller's Property Information Form and, if appropriate, the Seller's Leasehold Information Form and the Seller's Commonhold Information Form, the solicitor shall:

3.1 If the title is unregistered:

    (1) Make a land charges search against the seller and any other appropriate names.

    (2) Make an index map search in the Land Registry (if not already obtained – see 2.10) in order to verify that the seller's title is unregistered and ensure that there are no interests registered at the Land Registry adverse to the seller's title.

    (3) Prepare an epitome of title. Mark copies or abstracts of all deeds which will not be passed to the buyer's solicitor as examined against the original.

    (4) Prepare and mark as examined against the originals copies of all deeds, or their abstracts, prior to the root of title containing covenants, easements, etc., affecting the property.

    (5) Check that all plans on copied documents are correctly coloured.

3.2 If the title is registered, obtain official copy entries of the register, the title plan and copy documents incorporated or referred to in the register entries, if not already obtained (see 2.6).

3.3 Prepare the draft contract and complete and sign the second section of the Seller's Property Information Form and, if appropriate, the Seller's Leasehold Information Form and the Seller's Commonhold Information Form.

3.4 Check contract package is complete and ready to be sent out to the buyer's solicitor.

3.5 Deal promptly with any queries raised by the estate agent.

4. Buyer's offer accepted

When made aware that a buyer has been found the solicitor shall:

4.1 Check with the seller agreement on the price and, if appropriate, that there has been no change in the information already supplied (Seller's Property Information Form, Seller's Leasehold Information Form, Seller's Commonhold Information Form and Fixtures, Fittings and Contents Form). Also check the seller's position on any related purchase. If any part of the purchase price is being apportioned to chattels, which will be in a separate state of severance at completion, advise the seller that apportionment must be a just and reasonable figure, and if in any doubt professional advice from a valuer should be obtained. If appropriate, supply the seller with a copy of the leaflet issued by the Inland Revenue, 'Fixtures and Chattels – Stamp Duty Land Tax'.

4.2   Inform the buyer's solicitor that the Protocol will be used.

4.3   Ascertain the buyer's position on any related sale and in the light of that reply, ask the seller for a proposed completion date.

4.4   Send to the buyer's solicitor as soon as possible the contract package to include:

(1)   Draft contract.

(2)   Official copy entries of the registered title (including official copies of all documents mentioned), the title plan or the epitome of title (including details of any prior matters referred to but not disclosed by the documents themselves) and the index map search.

(3)   The Seller's Property Information Form with copies of all relevant planning decisions, guarantees, etc.

(4)   The completed Fixtures, Fittings and Contents Form. Where this is provided it will form part of the contract and should be attached to it.

(5)   In leasehold cases

(i)   the Seller's Leasehold Information Form, with all information about maintenance charges and insurance and, if appropriate the procedure (including references required) for obtaining the landlord's consent to the sale;

(ii)   a copy of the lease.

(6)   In commonhold cases

(i)   Seller's Commonhold Information Form, with all information obtained under 2.15;

(ii)   a copy of the registered title for the commonhold common parts and a copy of the registered title for the seller's unit.

(7)   If available, the local authority search and enquiries and any other searches made by the seller's solicitor.

If any of these documents are not available the remaining items should be forwarded to the buyer's solicitor as soon as they are available.

4.5   Inform the estate agent or property seller when the draft contract has been submitted to the buyer's solicitor.

4.6   Ask the buyer's solicitor if a 10 per cent deposit will be paid and, if not, what arrangements are proposed.

4.7   If and to the extent that the seller consents to the disclosure, supply information about the position on the seller's own purchase and of any other transactions in the chain above, and thereafter, of any change in circumstances.

4.8   Notify the seller of all information received in response to the above.

4.9   Inform the estate agent of any unexpected delays or difficulties likely to delay exchange of contracts.

Acting for the buyer

5.   The first step

On notification of the buyer's purchase the solicitor should then immediately take the following steps, at the buyer's expense:

5.1   Wherever possible instructions should be obtained from the client in person. The Consumer Protection (Distance Selling) Regulations 2000 should not then apply.

5.2   Check the client's identity if you do not know the client, comply with the Money Laundering Regulations [2003] and follow any guidance issued by the Law Society.

5.3   Give the client information as to costs, information relating to the name and status of the person who will be carrying out the work and, if that person is not a partner, the name of the partner who has overall responsibility for the matter. Give any other information necessary to comply with Rule 15 of the Solicitors' Practice Rules 1990 and Solicitors' Costs Information and Client Care Code 1999. If given orally this information should be confirmed in writing.

5.4   Give the client details of whom to contact in the event of a complaint about the firm's services (Rule 15).

5.5   Request a payment on account in relation to disbursements.

5.6   Confirm to the seller's solicitor that the Protocol will be used.

5.7   Ascertain the buyer's position on any related sale, mortgage arrangements and whether a 10 per cent deposit will be provided.

5.8   If and to the extent that the buyer consents to the disclosure, inform the seller's solicitor about the position on the buyer's own sale, if any, and of any connected transactions, the general nature of the mortgage application, the amount of deposit available and if the seller's target date for completion can be met, and thereafter, of any change in circumstances.

On receipt of the draft contract and other documents:

5.9   Notify the buyer that these documents have been received, check the price and send the client a copy of the Fixtures, Fittings and Contents Form and, if appropriate, a copy of the title plan for checking. If the purchase price is being apportioned between the property and chattels, advise the buyer what constitutes chattels for Stamp Duty Land Tax purposes, that values for the chattels must be just and reasonable, and if in any doubt, professional advice from a valuer should be obtained. If appropriate, supply the buyer with a copy of the leaflet issued by the Inland Revenue 'Fixtures and Chattels – Stamp Duty Land Tax'.

5.10   Subject to 5.20 below, make a local authority search with the usual Part 1 enquiries and any additional enquiries relevant to the property.

5.11   Make a commons registration search, if appropriate.

5.12   Make mining enquiries and drainage enquiries if appropriate and consider any other relevant searches, e.g. environmental searches.

5.13   Check the buyer's position on any related sale and check that the buyer has a satisfactory mortgage offer and all conditions of the mortgage are or can be satisfied.

5.14   Check the buyer understands the nature and effect of the mortgage offer and duty to disclose any relevant matters to the lender.

5.15   Advise the buyer of the need for a survey on the property.

5.16   Check the draft contract to ensure title is satisfactory and add any special conditions necessary to achieve this (e.g. for removal of or consents needed under any restrictions or notices revealed on the title).

5.17   Confirm approval of the draft contract and return it approved as soon as possible, having inserted the buyer's full names and address, subject to any outstanding matters.

5.18   At the same time ask only those specific additional enquiries which are required to clarify some point arising out of the documents submitted or which are relevant to the particular nature or location of the property or which the buyer has expressly requested. Any enquiry, including those about the state and condition of the building, which is capable of being ascertained by the buyer's own enquiries or survey or personal inspection should not be raised. Additional duplicated standard forms should not be submitted; if they are, the seller's solicitor is under no obligation to deal with them nor need answer any enquiry seeking opinions rather than facts.

5.19   If title has been deduced, check the seller's title to the property and raise any requisitions on the title deduced. (See Standard Conditions of Sale (fourth edition) 4.2.1.) Matters relating to the completion arrangements should not be raised at this stage.

5.20   If a local authority search has been supplied by the seller's solicitors with the draft contract, consider the need to make a further local authority search with the usual Part 1 enquiries or raise any of the optional Part 2 enquiries not included in the seller's search or any other additional enquiries relevant to the property. (The local authority search should not be more than three months old at exchange of contracts nor six months old at completion.)

5.21   Ensure that buildings insurance arrangements are in place.

5.22   Check the position over any life policies referred to in the lender's offer of mortgage.

5.23   Check with the buyer if property is being purchased in sole name or jointly with another person. If a joint purchase check whether as joint tenants or tenants in common and advise on the difference in writing.

Both parties' solicitor

6.   Prior to exchange of contracts

If acting for the buyer

When all satisfactory replies received to enquiries, requisitions on title and searches:

6.1   Prepare and send to the buyer a contract report and invite the buyer to make an appointment to call to raise any queries on the contract report and to sign the contract ideally in the presence of a solicitor.

6.2   When the buyer signs the contract check:

(1)   Completion date.

(2)   That the buyer understands and can comply with all the conditions on the mortgage offer if appropriate.

(3)   That all the necessary funds will be available to complete the purchase.

If acting for the seller

6.3   Deal with any requisitions on title raised by the buyer's solicitor.

6.4   Advise the seller on the effect of the contract and ask the seller to sign it, ideally in the presence of the solicitor.

6.5   Check the position on any related purchase so that there can be a simultaneous exchange of contracts on both the sale and purchase.

6.6   Check completion date.

7.   Relationship with the buyer's lender

On receipt of instructions from the buyer's lender:

7.1   Check the mortgage offer complies with Practice Rule 6(3)(c) and (e) and is certified to that effect.

7.2   Check any special conditions in the mortgage offer to see if there are additional instructions or conditions not normally required by Practice Rule 6(3)(c).

7.3   Go through any special conditions in the mortgage offer with the buyer.

7.4   Notify the lender if Practice Rule 6(3)(b) or 1.13 or 1.14 of the CML Lenders' Handbook ('Lenders' Handbook') are applicable.

7.5   Consider whether there are any conflicts of interest which prevent you accepting instructions to act for the lender.

7.6   If you do not know the borrower and anyone else required to sign the mortgage, charge or other document, check evidence of identity (Practice Rule 6(3)(c)(i)).

7.7   Consider whether there are any circumstances covered by the Law Society's:

(1)   Green Card on property fraud

(2)   Blue Card on money laundering

(3)   Pink Card on undertakings

(4)   Money Laundering Guidance.

7.8   If you do not know the seller's solicitor/licensed conveyancer check that they appear in a legal directory or are on the record of their professional body (see Practice Rule 6(3)(c)(i) and the Lenders' Handbook).

7.9   Carry out any other checks required by the lender provided they comply with Practice Rule 6(3)(c).

7.10   Check the lender's requirements as to whether it requires the original mortgage deed to be lodged with it following registration.

7.11   At all times comply with the requirements of Practice Rule 6(3) and the Lenders' Handbook and ensure if a conflict of interest arises you cease to act for the lender.

8.   Exchange of contracts

On exchange, the buyer's solicitor shall send or deliver to the seller's solicitor:

8.1   The signed contract with all names, dates and financial information completed.

8.2   The deposit provided in the manner prescribed in the contract. Under the Law Society's Formula C the deposit may have to be sent to another solicitor nominated by the seller's solicitor.

8.3   If contracts are exchanged by telephone the procedures laid down by the Law Society's Formulae A, B or C must be used and both solicitors must ensure (unless otherwise agreed) that the undertakings to send documents and to pay the deposit on that day are strictly observed.

8.4   The seller's solicitor shall, once the buyer's signed contract and deposit are held unconditionally, having ensured that the details of each contract are fully completed and identical, send the seller's signed contract on the day of exchange to the buyer's solicitor in compliance with the undertaking given on exchange.

8.5   Notify the client that contracts have been exchanged.

8.6   Notify the seller's estate agent or property seller of exchange of contracts and the completion date.

9.   Between exchange and the day of completion

As soon as possible after exchange and in any case within the time limits contained in the Standard Conditions of Sale:

9.1   The buyer's solicitor shall send to the seller's solicitor, in duplicate:

    (1)   Completion Information Form and include any requisitions on title which are necessary and could not be raised prior to exchange of contracts, or ask seller's solicitor to confirm that there is no variation in any replies given prior to exchange.

    (2)   Draft conveyance/transfer or assignment incorporating appropriate provisions for joint purchase.

    (3)   Other documents, e.g. draft receipt for purchase price of fixtures, fittings and contents.

9.2   As soon as possible after receipt of these documents the seller's solicitor shall send to the buyer's solicitor:

    (1)   Replies to Completion Information and Requisitions on Title Form.

    (2)   Draft conveyance/transfer or assignment approved.

    (3)   If appropriate, completion statement supported by photocopy receipts or evidence of payment of apportionments claimed.

    (4)   Copy of licence to assign from the landlord if appropriate.

9.3   The buyer's solicitor shall then:

(1)   Engross the approved draft conveyance/transfer or assignment.

(2)   Explain the effect of that document to the buyer and obtain the buyer's signature to it (if necessary).

(3)   Send it to the seller's solicitor in time to enable the seller to sign it before completion without suffering inconvenience.

(4)   If appropriate prepare any separate declaration of trust, advise the buyer on its effect and obtain the buyer's signature to it.

(5)   Advise the buyer on the contents and effect of the mortgage deed and obtain the buyer's signature to that deed. If possible, and in all cases where the lender so requires, a solicitor should witness the buyer's signature to the mortgage deed.

(6)   Send the certificate of title (complying with Rule 6(3)(d)) to the lender.

(7)   Take any steps necessary to ensure that the amount payable on completion will be available in time for completion including sending to the buyer a completion statement to include legal costs, Land Registry fees and other disbursements and, if appropriate, Stamp Duty Land Tax.

(8)   Make the Land Registry and land charges searches and, if appropriate, a company search.

(9)   Ensure that you have by this stage obtained sufficient information from each buyer to complete the relevant land transaction return, including national insurance numbers, and prepare the return. After checking with the buyer that the information on the form is accurate, advise the buyer that an Inland Revenue enquiry is possible within the following nine months which might result in costs and penalties. Ask the buyer to sign the form in black ink and return it immediately as penalties will be charged by the Inland Revenue unless the form is lodged within 30 days of completion.

(10)   Explain and discuss with the buyer the need to disclose overriding interests in the property and complete Form D1.

9.4   The seller's solicitor shall:

(1)   Request redemption figures for all financial charges on the property revealed by the deeds/official copy entries/land charges search against the seller.

(2)   On receipt of the engrossment of the transfer or assignment, after checking the engrossment to ensure accuracy, obtain the seller's signature to it after ascertaining that the seller understands the nature and contents of the document. If the document is not to be signed in the solicitor's presence the letter sending the document for signature should contain an explanation of the nature and effect of the document and clear instructions relating to the execution of it.

(3)   On receipt of the estate agent's or property seller's commission account obtain the seller's instructions to pay the account on the seller's behalf out of the sale proceeds.

(4)   Consider if the consent of any restrictioner (e.g. a managing agent or management company) who will have a continuing interest is needed and if so, take steps to ensure that such consent will be available on completion.

10.   Relationship with the seller's estate agent or property seller

Where the seller has instructed estate agents or property seller, the seller's solicitor shall take the following steps:

10.1   Inform them when the draft contracts are submitted (see 4.5).

10.2   Deal promptly with any queries raised by them.

10.3   Inform them of any unexpected delays or difficulties likely to delay exchange of contracts (see 4.9).

10.4   Inform them when exchange has taken place and the date of completion (see 8.6).

10.5   On receipt of their commission account send a copy to the seller and obtain instructions as to arrangements for payment (see 9.4(3)).

10.6   Inform them of completion and, if appropriate, authorise release of any keys held by them (see 11.3(1)).

10.7   If so instructed pay the commission (see 9.4(3) and 11.6(2)).

11.   Completion: the day of payment and removals

11.1   If completion is to be by post, the Law Society's Code for Completion shall be used, unless otherwise agreed.

11.2   As soon as practicable and not later than the morning of completion, the buyer's solicitor shall advise the seller's solicitor of the manner and transmission of the purchase money and of steps taken to despatch it.

11.3   On being satisfied as to the receipt of the balance of the purchase money, the seller's solicitor shall:

    (1)   Notify the estate agent or property seller that completion has taken place and authorise release of the keys.

    (2)   Notify the buyer's solicitor that completion has taken place and the keys have been released.

    (3)   Date and complete the transfer.

    (4)   Despatch the deeds including the transfer or the assignment and the licence to assign to the buyer's solicitor with any appropriate undertakings.

11.4   The seller's solicitor shall check that the seller is aware of the need to notify the local and water authorities of the change in ownership.

11.5   After completion, where appropriate, the buyer's solicitor shall give notice of assignment to the lessor.

11.6   Immediately after completion, the seller's solicitor shall:

    (1)   Send to the lender the amount required to release the property sold.

    (2)   Pay the estate agent's or property seller's commission if so authorised.

(3)   Account to the seller for the balance of the sale proceeds.

11.7   Immediately after completion, the buyer's solicitor shall:

(1)   Date and complete the mortgage document and, if appropriate, give notice of any second or subsequent charge to the first chargee.

(2)   Confirm completion of the purchase and the mortgage to the buyer.

(3)   Lodge Form SDLT with the Inland Revenue and pay any Stamp Duty Land Tax that is due. On receipt of the certificate of notification from the Inland Revenue, hold it to lodge with the Land Registry application.

(4)   Consider the need to register a restriction and, if appropriate, complete Form RX1.

(5)   Deal with the registration of the transfer document and mortgage with the Land Registry within the priority period of the search including lodging with the application form (AP1 or FR1) Form D1 and, if appropriate, Form RX1.

(6)   If appropriate, send a notice of assignment of a life policy to the insurance company.

(7)   On receipt of notification from the Land Registry that registration has been completed and a title information document has been supplied, check its contents carefully and supply a copy of that document to the buyer.

(8)   Send the original mortgage deed and/or the title information document to the lender, if appropriate, and deal with any other documents in accordance with its instructions.

(9)   Take the buyer's instructions as to any documents not being held by the lender, and if the documents are to be sent to the buyer or anyone else to hold on the buyer's behalf, inform the buyer of the need to keep the documents safely so that they will be available on a sale of the property.

(10)   If the sale was a sale of part of the land in the registered title, then on completion of the registration of the transfer of part, the seller's solicitor shall check that the title certificate and amended registered plan are accurate and send a copy to the seller.

II.2. The Law Society's formulae for exchanging contracts by telephone, fax or telex[1]

Introduction

It is essential that an agreed memorandum of the details and of any variations of the formula used should be made at the time and retained in the file. This would be very important if any question on the exchange were raised subsequently. Agreed variations should also be confirmed in writing. The serious risks of exchanging contracts without a deposit, unless the full implications are explained to and accepted by the seller client, are demonstrated in *Morris* v. *Duke-Cohan & Co.* (1975) 119 SJ 826.

As those persons involved in the exchange will bind their firms to the undertakings in the formula used, solicitors should carefully consider who is to be authorised to exchange contracts by telephone or telex and should ensure that the use of the procedure is restricted to them. Since professional undertakings form the basis of the formulae, they are only recommended for use between firms of solicitors and licensed conveyancers.

Law Society telephone/telex exchange – Formula A (1986)

(for use where one solicitor holds both signed parts of the contract):

A completion date of […] is agreed. The solicitor holding both parts of the contract confirms that he or she holds the part signed by his or her client(s), which is identical to the part he or she is also holding signed by the other solicitor's client(s) and will forthwith insert the agreed completion date in each part.

Solicitors mutually agree that exchange shall take place from that moment and the solicitor holding both parts confirms that, as of that moment, he or she holds the part signed by his or her client(s) to the order of the other. He or she undertakes that day by first class post, or where the other solicitor is a member of a document exchange (as to which the inclusion of a reference thereto in the solicitor's letterhead shall be conclusive evidence) by delivery to that or any other affiliated exchange, or by hand delivery direct to that solicitor's office, to send his or her signed part of the contract to the other solicitor, together, where he or she is the purchaser's solicitor, with a banker's draft or a solicitor's client account cheque for the deposit amounting to £… .

> *Note:*
>
> *1. A memorandum should be prepared, after use of the formula, recording:*
>
> *(a) date and time of exchange;*
>
> *(b) the formula used and exact wording of agreed variations;*
>
> *(c) the completion date;*

1. Formulae A and B: 9 July 1986, revised January 1996. Formula C: 15 March 1989, revised January 1996. The formulae were previously published in *The Guide to the Professional Conduct of Solicitors 1999* as Annex 25D.

(d)   the (balance) deposit to be paid;

(e)   the identities of those involved in any conversation.

Law Society telephone/telex exchange – Formula B (1986)

(for use where each solicitor holds his or her own client's signed part of the contract):

A completion date of […] is agreed. Each solicitor confirms to the other that he or she holds a part contract in the agreed form signed by the client(s) and will forthwith insert the agreed completion date.

Each solicitor undertakes to the other thenceforth to hold the signed part of the contract to the other's order, so that contracts are exchanged at that moment. Each solicitor further undertakes that day by first class post, or, where the other solicitor is a member of a document exchange (as to which the inclusion of a reference thereto in the solicitor's letterhead shall be conclusive evidence) by delivery to that or any other affiliated exchange, or by hand delivery direct to that solicitor's office, to send his or her signed part of the contract to the other together, in the case of a purchaser's solicitor, with a banker's draft or a solicitor's client account cheque for the deposit amounting to £….

Notes:

1.   *A memorandum should be prepared, after use of the formula, recording:*

   (a)   date and time of exchange;

   (b)   the formula used and exact wording of agreed variations;

   (c)   the completion date;

   (d)   the (balance) deposit to be paid;

   (e)   the identities of those involved in any conversation.

2.   *Those who are going to effect the exchange must first confirm the details in order to ensure that both parts are identical. This means in particular, that if either part of the contract has been amended since it was originally prepared, the solicitor who holds a part contract with the amendments must disclose them, so that it can be confirmed that the other part is similarly amended.*

9 July 1986, revised January 1996

Law Society telephone/fax/telex exchange – Formula C (1989)

Part I

The following is agreed:

Final time for exchange: […] pm

Completion date:

Deposit to be paid to:

Each solicitor confirms that he or she holds a part of the contract in the agreed form signed by his or her client, or, if there is more than one client, by all of them. Each solicitor undertakes to the other that:

(a) he or she will continue to hold that part of the contract until the final time for exchange on the date the formula is used, and

(b) if the vendor's solicitor so notifies the purchaser's solicitor by fax, telephone or telex (whichever was previously agreed) by that time, they will both comply with part II of the formula.

The purchaser's solicitor further undertakes that either he or she or some other named person in his or her office will be available up to the final time for exchange to activate part II of the formula on receipt of the telephone call, fax or telex from the vendor's solicitors.

Part II

Each solicitor undertakes to the other henceforth to hold the part of the contract in his or her possession to the other's order, so that contracts are exchanged at that moment, and to despatch it to the other on that day. The purchaser's solicitor further undertakes to the vendor's solicitor to despatch on that day, or to arrange for the despatch on that day of, a banker's draft or a solicitor's client account cheque for the full deposit specified in the agreed form of contract (divided as the vendor's solicitor may have specified) to the vendor's solicitor and/or to some other solicitor whom the vendor's solicitor nominates, to be held on formula C terms.

'To despatch' means to send by first class post, or, where the other solicitor is a member of a document exchange (as to which the inclusion of a reference thereto in the solicitor's letterhead is to be conclusive evidence) by delivery to that or any other affiliated exchange, or by hand delivery direct to the recipient solicitor's office. 'Formula C terms' means that the deposit is held as stakeholder, or as agent for the vendor with authority to part with it only for the purpose of passing it to another solicitor as deposit in a related property purchase transaction on these terms.

Notes:

1.   Two memoranda will be required when using formula C. One needs to record the use of part I, and a second needs to record the request of the vendor's solicitor to the purchaser's solicitor to activate part II.

2.   The first memorandum should record:

  (a)   the date and time when it was agreed to use formula C;

  (b)   the exact wording of any agreed variations;

  (c)   the final time, later that day, for exchange;

  (d)   the completion date;

  (e)   the name of the solicitor to whom the deposit was to be paid, or details of amounts and names if it was to be split; and

  (f)   the identities of those involved in any conversation.

3.   Formula C assumes the payment of a full contractual deposit (normally 10%).

4.   The contract term relating to the deposit must allow it to be passed on, with payment direct from payer to ultimate recipient, in the way in which the formula contemplates. The deposit must ultimately be held by a solicitor as stakeholder. Whilst some variation in the formula can be agreed this is a term of the formula which must not be varied, unless all the solicitors involved in the chain have agreed.

5.   If a buyer proposes to use a deposit guarantee policy, formula C will need substantial adaptation.

6.   It is essential prior to agreeing part I of formula C that those effecting the exchange ensure that both parts of the contract are identical.

7.   Using formula C involves a solicitor in giving a number of professional undertakings. These must be performed precisely. Any failure will be a serious breach of professional discipline. One of the undertakings may be to arrange that someone over whom the solicitor has no control will do something (i.e. to arrange for someone else to despatch the cheque or banker's draft in payment of the deposit). An undertaking is still binding even if it is to do something outside the solicitor's control.

8.   Solicitors do not as a matter of law have an automatic authority to exchange contracts on a formula C basis, and should always ensure that they have the client's express authority to use formula C. A suggested form of authority is set out below. It should be adapted to cover any special circumstances:

I/We […] understand that my/our sale and purchase of […] are both part of a chain of linked property transactions, in which all parties want the security of contracts which become binding on the same day.

I/We agree that you should make arrangements with the other solicitors or licensed conveyancers involved to achieve this.

I/We understand that this involves each property-buyer offering, early on one day, to exchange contracts whenever, later that day, the seller so requests, and that the buyer's offer is on the basis that it cannot be withdrawn or varied during that day.

I/We agree that when I/we authorise you to exchange contracts, you may agree to exchange contracts on the above basis and give any necessary undertakings to the other parties involved in the chain and that my/our authority to you cannot be revoked throughout the day on which the offer to exchange contracts is made.

15 March 1989, revised January 1996

II.3. The Law Society's code for completion by post[1]

Preamble

The code provides a procedure for postal completion which practising solicitors may adopt by reference. It may also be used by licensed conveyancers.

Before agreeing to adopt this code, a solicitor must be satisfied that doing so will not be contrary to the interests of the client (including any mortgagee client).

When adopted, the code applies without variation, unless agreed in writing in advance.

PROCEDURE

General

1.   To adopt this code, all the solicitors must expressly agree, preferably in writing, to use it to complete a specific transaction.

2.   On completion, the seller's solicitor acts as the buyer's solicitor's agent without any fee or disbursements.

Before completion

3.   The seller's solicitor will specify in writing to the buyer's solicitor before completion the mortgages or charges secured on the property which, on or before completion, will be redeemed or discharged to the extent that they relate to the property.

4.   The seller's solicitor *undertakes*:

    (i)   to have the seller's authority to receive the purchase money on completion; and

    (ii)   on completion to have the authority of the proprietor of each mortgage or charge specified under paragraph 3 to receive the sum intended to repay it,

BUT if the seller's solicitor does not have all the necessary authorities then:

    (iii)   to advise the buyer's solicitor no later than 4pm on the working day before the completion date that they do not have all the authorities or immediately if any is withdrawn later; and

    (iv)   not to complete until he or she has the buyer's solicitor's instructions.

5.   Before the completion date, the buyer's solicitor will send the seller's solicitor instructions as to any of the following which apply:

    (i)   documents to be examined and marked;

---

1. 1984, revised 1998. This code was previously published in *The Guide to the Professional Conduct of Solicitors 1999* as Annex 25E.

(ii)   memoranda to be endorsed;

(iii) undertakings to be given;

(iv)   deeds, documents (including any relevant undertakings) and authorities relating to rents, deposits, keys, etc. to be sent to the buyer's solicitor following completion; and

(v)   other relevant matters.

In default of instructions, the seller's solicitor is under no duty to examine, mark or endorse any document.

6.   The buyer's solicitor will remit to the seller's solicitor the sum required to complete, as notified in writing on the seller's solicitor's completion statement or otherwise, or in default of notification as shown by the contract. If the funds are remitted by transfer between banks, the seller's solicitor will instruct the receiving bank to telephone to report immediately the funds have been received. Pending completion, the seller's solicitor will hold the funds to the buyer's solicitor's order.

7.   If by the agreed date and time for completion the seller's solicitor has not received the authorities specified in paragraph 4, instructions under paragraph 5 and the sum specified in paragraph 6, the seller's solicitor will forthwith notify the buyer's solicitor and request further instructions.

Completion

8.   The seller's solicitor will complete forthwith on receiving the sum specified in paragraph 6, or at a later time agreed with the buyer's solicitor.

9.   When completing, the seller's solicitor *undertakes*:

(i)   to comply with the instructions given under paragraph 5; and

(ii)   to redeem or obtain discharges for every mortgage or charge so far as it relates to the property specified under paragraph 3 which has not already been redeemed or discharged.

After completion

10.   The seller's solicitor *undertakes*:

(i)   immediately completion has taken place to hold to the buyer's solicitor's order every item referred to in (iv) of paragraph 5 and not to exercise a lien over any such item;

(ii)   as soon as possible after completion, and in any event on the same day,

(a)   to confirm to the buyer's solicitor by telephone or fax that completion has taken place; and

(b)   to send written confirmation and, at the risk of the buyer's solicitor, the items listed in (iv) of paragraph 5 to the buyer's solicitor by first class post or document exchange.

Supplementary

11.   The rights and obligations of the parties, under the contract or otherwise, are not affected by this code.

12. (i) References to the seller's solicitor and the buyer's solicitor apply as appropriate to solicitors acting for other parties who adopt the code.

(ii) When a licensed conveyancer adopts this code, references to a solicitor include a licensed conveyancer.

13. A dispute or difference arising between solicitors who adopt this code (whether or not subject to any variation) relating directly to its application is to be referred to a single arbitrator agreed between the solicitors. If they do not agree on the appointment within one month, the President of the Law Society may appoint the arbitrator at the request of one of the solicitors.

NOTES TO THE CODE

1. This code will apply to transactions where the code is adopted after 1st July 1998.

2. The object of this code is to provide solicitors with a convenient means for completion on an agency basis when a representative of the buyer's solicitor is not attending at the office of the seller's solicitor.

3. As with the Law Society's formulae for exchange of contracts by telephone and fax, the code embodies professional undertakings and is only recommended for adoption between solicitors and licensed conveyancers.

4. Paragraph 2 of the code provides that the seller's solicitors will act as agents for the buyer's solicitors without fee or disbursements. The convenience of not having to make a specific appointment on the date of completion for the buyer's solicitors to attend to complete personally will offset the agency work that the seller's solicitor has to do and any postage payable in completing under the code. Most solicitors will from time to time act for both sellers and buyers. If a seller's solicitor does consider that charges and/or disbursements are necessary in a particular case this would represent a variation in the code and should be agreed in writing before the completion date.

5. In view of the decision in *Edward Wong Finance Company Limited* v. *Johnson, Stokes and Master* [1984] AC 1296, clause 4(ii) of the code requires the seller's solicitors to undertake on completion to have authority of the proprietor of every mortgage or charge to be redeemed to receive the sum needed to repay such charge.

6. Paragraph 11 of the code provides that nothing in the code shall override any rights and obligations of the parties under the contract or otherwise.

7. The buyer's solicitor is to inform the seller's solicitor of the mortgages or charges which will be redeemed or discharged (see paragraph 3 above) and is to specify those for which an undertaking will be required on completion (paragraph 5(iii)). The information may be given in reply to requisitions on title. Such a reply may also amount to an undertaking.

8. Care must be taken if there is a sale and sub-sale. The sub-seller's solicitor may not hold the title deeds nor be in a position to receive the funds required to discharge the seller's mortgage on the property. Enquiries should be made to ascertain if the monies or some part of the monies payable on completion should, with either the authority of the sub-seller or the sub-seller's solicitor, be sent direct to the seller's solicitor and not to the sub-seller's solicitor.

9. Care must also be taken if there is a simultaneous resale and completion and enquiries should be made by the ultimate buyer's solicitor of the intermediate seller's solicitor as to the price being

paid on that purchase. Having appointed the intermediate seller's solicitor as agent the buyer's solicitor is fixed with the knowledge of an agent even without having personal knowledge (see the Society's 'green card' warning on property fraud at Annex 25G, p.501).

10.   If the seller's solicitor has to withdraw from using the code, the buyer's solicitor should be notified of this not later than 4pm on the working day prior to the completion date. If the seller's solicitor's authority to receive the monies is withdrawn later the buyer's solicitor must be notified immediately.

These notes refer only to some of the points in the code that practitioners may wish to consider before agreeing to adopt it. Any variation in the code must be agreed in writing before the completion date.

III. WARNING CARDS

III.1. Contaminated Land Warning Card[1]

Warning – To All Solicitors – Contaminated Land Liabilities

The advice contained on this Card is not intended to be a professional requirement for solicitors. Solicitors should be aware of the requirements of Part IIA of the Environmental Protection Act 1990 but they themselves cannot provide their clients with conclusive answers. They must exercise their professional judgement to determine the applicability of this advice to each matter in which they are involved and, where necessary, they should suggest to the client obtaining specialist advice. In the view of the Law Society the advice contained in this Card conforms to current best practice.

Solicitors should be aware that environmental liabilities may arise and consider what further enquiries and specialist assistance the client should be advised to obtain.

Contaminated land

1. The contaminated land regime was brought into effect in England on 1 April 2000. It applies to all land, whether residential, commercial, industrial or agricultural. It can affect owners, occupiers, developers, and lenders. The legislation, which is contained in Part IIA, Environmental Protection Act 1990 and in regulations and statutory guidance issued under it (see Contaminated Land (England) Regulations 2000 SI 2000/227 and DETR Guidance on Contaminated Land April 2000) is retrospective. It covers existing and future contamination.

The National Assembly is expected shortly to introduce similar regulations regarding contaminated land in Wales.

2. Local authorities must inspect and identify seriously contaminated sites. They can issue remediation notices requiring action to remediate contamination, in the absence of a voluntary agreement to do so. In certain cases ('Special Sites') responsibility for enforcement lies with the Environment Agency.

A negative reply to the standard local authority enquiries from the local authority may merely mean the site has not been inspected. It does not necessarily mean there is no problem.

Compliance can be costly, and may result in expenditure which could exceed the value of the property.

Liability falls primarily on those who 'cause or knowingly permit' contamination (a Class A person). If the authority cannot identify a Class A person, liability falls on a Class B person, the current owner, or occupier of the land. Class B persons include lenders in possession. There are complex exclusion provisions for transferring liability from one party to another. Some exclusions apply only on the transfer of land, or the grant of a lease. The applicability of any relevant exclusion needs to be considered before entering such transactions.

In every transaction you must consider whether contamination is an issue.

---

1. © The Law Society June 2001.

Conveyancing transactions

In purchases, mortgages and leases, solicitors should:

1.   Advise the client of potential liabilities associated with contaminated land.

Generally clients should be advised of the possibility and consequences of acquiring interests in contaminated land and the steps that can be taken to assess the risks.

2.   Make specific enquiries of the seller.

In all commercial cases, and if contamination is considered likely to be a risk in residential cases (e.g. redevelopment of brown field land):

3.   Make enquiries of statutory and regulatory bodies.

4.   Undertake independent site history investigation, e.g. obtaining site report from a commercial company.

In commercial cases, if there is a likelihood that the site is contaminated:

5.   Advise independent full site investigation.

6.   Consider use of contractual protections and the use of exclusion tests.

This may involve specific disclosure of known defects, possibly coupled with price reduction, requirements on seller to remedy before completion, and in complex cases the use of warranties and indemnities.

Unresolved problems, consider

7.   Advising withdrawal, and noting advice;

8.   Advising insurance (increasingly obtainable for costs of remediation of undetected contamination and any shortfall in value because of undisclosed problems).

Specific transactions

1.   Leases

Consider if usual repair and statutory compliance clauses transfer remediation liability to tenant, and advise.

2.   Mortgages

Advise lender, if enquiries reveal potential for or existence of contamination, and seek instructions.

In enforcement cases, consider appointment of receivers, rather than steps resulting in lender becoming mortgagee in possession, and so treated as a Class B person.

3.   Share sales and asset purchases

Consider recommending the obtaining of specialist technical advice on potential liabilities, use of detailed enquiries, warranties and indemnities.

Other relevant legislation

Other legislation and common law liabilities (e.g. nuisance) may also be relevant when advising on environmental matters including:

Water Resources Act 1991
Groundwater Regulations 1998
Pollution Prevention and Control (England and Wales) Regulations 2000

Further information

Law Society's *Environmental Law Handbook*
DETR's Website **www.detr.gov.uk**

III.2. Money Laundering Warning Card ('Blue Card')[1]

Be on your guard

Your firm, whatever its size or nature of practice, could be a target for criminals wishing to launder the proceeds of their crime through legal transactions. You might commit a criminal offence if you help them by missing the warning signs.

The Proceeds of Crime Act 2002 means that if you fail to report to the National Criminal Intelligence Service you will be judged by the standard of whether a reasonable solicitor should have been suspicious in all the surrounding circumstances. Learning to spot warning signals is more important than ever before.

The criminal law and regulatory requirements are undergoing rapid change. Keep up to date by reading Law Society guidance and interim updates which can be found at **www.lawsociety.org.uk**.

What does this mean in practice?

You will need to ask your clients more questions. By June 2003 most solicitors will be legally required to establish the identity of most clients. Honest clients should be happy to assist. Make sure you and your colleagues receive some training about money laundering.

Know your client

- Check the identity of new clients and be wary of clients who are reluctant to provide such details.
- Where possible meet new clients in person. Be cautious about third parties introducing clients who you do not meet.

If anything about the circumstances, particularly these warning signals, give cause for concern *then ask more questions*. The answers may deal with your initial cause for concern. If they do not, then the answers may give foundation to a suspicion and you may have to consider whether or not to make a report under the legislation.

Causes for concern can include the following:

Unusual settlement requests

Anything that is unusual or unpredictable or otherwise gives cause for concern should lead you to *ask more questions* about the source of the funds. Remember, proceeds of crime can arrive through the banking system as well.

Think carefully if any of the following are proposed or occur:

- Settlements by cash
- Surprise payments by way of third party cheque

---

1. © The Law Society 2002.

- Money transfers where there is a variation between the account holder or the signatory
- Requests to make regular payments out of client account
- Settlements which are reached too easily

Unusual instructions

- Why has the client chosen your firm? Could the client find the same service nearer their home?
- Are you being asked to do something that does not fit in with the normal pattern of your business?
- Be cautious if instructions change without a reasonable explanation
- Be cautious about transactions which take an unusual turn

Use of your client account

- Using solicitors' client accounts to transmit money is useful to money launderers
- Do not provide a banking facility if you do not undertake any related legal work
- Be cautious if you are instructed to do legal work, receive funds into your client account, but then the instructions are cancelled and you are asked to return the money either to your client or a third party

Remember you may still be assisting a money launderer even though the money does not pass through your firm's bank accounts

Suspect territory

- If you are instructed in transactions with an international element you can refer to the Financial Action Task Force (**www.oecd.org/fatf**) who produce up to date information about different countries
- Be cautious if a client is introduced through an overseas bank or third party based in countries where the production of drugs, drug trafficking, or terrorism may be prevalent
- Take care if funds are being routed into and out of the UK without a logical explanation

Loss making transactions

- Be alert to instructions which could lead to some financial loss to your client or a third party without a logical explanation, particularly where your client seems unconcerned
- Be cautious about confusing movements of funds between different accounts, institutions or jurisdictions without apparent reason

The better you know your client and the full details of and reasons for the transaction before accepting the retainer, and particularly before accepting funds, the less likely you are to become involved in money laundering.

What if you are suspicious?

In many situations, the law will require you to make an official disclosure to:

The National Criminal Intelligence Service
Spring Gardens
Vauxhall
London SE11 5EF

Tel: 020 7238 8282
Fax: 020 7238 8286.

Helpful guidance notes about money laundering are issued by:

The Joint Money Laundering Steering Group
Pinners Hall
105–108 Old Broad Street
London EC2N 1EX

Tel: 020 7216 8800
Fax: 020 7216 8811.

Confidential advice can be obtained from:

The Professional Adviser
Professional Ethics
Solicitors Regulation Authority
Ipsley Court
Berrington Close
Redditch B98 0TD

DX 19114 Redditch
Tel: 0870 6062577
Fax: 0207 320 5897

III.3. Property Fraud Warning Card II ('Green Card')[1]

This card has been updated to take account of knowledge gained from criminal prosecutions and suggestions from the profession.

Could you be involved or implicated?

Could you be unwittingly assisting in a fraud? The general assumption is that if there has been a property fraud a solicitor must have been involved. Solicitors should therefore be vigilant to protect both their clients and themselves. Steps can be taken to minimise the risk of being involved or implicated in a fraud (see below).

Could you spot a property fraud?

The signs to watch for include the following (but this list is not exhaustive):

- **Fraudulent buyer or fictitious solicitors** – especially if the buyer is introduced to your practice by a third party [for example a broker or estate agent] who is not well known to you. Beware of clients whom you never meet and solicitors not known to you.

- **Unusual instructions** – for example a solicitor being instructed by the seller to remit the net proceeds of sale to anyone other than the seller.

- **Misrepresentation of the purchase price** – ensure that the true cash price actually to be paid is stated as the consideration in the contract and transfer and is identical to the price shown in the mortgage instructions and in the report on title to the lender.

- **A deposit or any part of purchase price paid direct** – a deposit, or the difference between the mortgage advance and the price, paid direct, or said to be paid direct, to the seller.

- **Incomplete contract documentation** – contract documents not fully completed by the seller's representative, i.e. dates missing or the identity of the parties not fully described or financial details not fully stated.

- **Changes in the purchase price** – adjustments to the purchase price, particularly in high percentage mortgage cases, or allowances off the purchase price, for example, for works to be carried out.

- **Unusual transactions** – transactions which do not follow their normal course or the usual pattern of events:

    (a) client with current mortgage on two or more properties

    (b) client using alias

    (c) client buying several properties from same person or two or more persons using same solicitor

    (d) client reselling property at a substantial profit, for which no explanation has been provided.

---

1. © The Law Society 2002.

What steps can I take to minimise the risk of fraud?

Be vigilant. If you have any doubts about a transaction, consider whether any of the following steps could be taken to minimise the risk of fraud:

- **Verify the identify and bona fides of your client and solicitor's firm you do not know** – meet the clients where possible and get to know them a little. Check that the solicitor's firm and office address appear in the *Directory of Solicitors and Barristers* or contact the Law Society's Records Office [Tel: 0870 606 2555].

- **Question unusual instructions** – if you receive unusual instructions from your client discuss them with your client fully.

- **Discuss with your client any aspects of the transaction which worry you** – if, for example, you have any suspicion that your client may have submitted a false mortgage application or references, or if the lender's valuation exceeds the actual price paid, discuss with your client. If you believe that the client intends to proceed with a fraudulent application, you must refuse to continue to act for the buyer and the lender.

- **Check that the true price is shown in all documentation** – check that the actual price paid is stated in the contract, transfer and mortgage instructions. Where you are also acting for a lender, tell your client that you will have to cease acting unless the client permits you to report to the lender all allowances and incentives.

- **Do not witness pre-signed documentation** – no document should be witnessed by a solicitor or his or her staff unless the person signing does so in the presence of the witness. If the document is pre-signed ensure that it is pre-signed in the presence of a witness.

- **Verify signatures** – consider whether signatures on all documents connected with a transaction should be examined and compared with signatures on any other available documentation.

- **Make a company search** – where a private company is the seller, or the seller has purchased from a private company in the recent past, and you suspect that the sale may not be on proper arm's length terms, you should make a search in the Companies Register to ascertain the names and addresses of the officers and shareholders, which can then be compared with the names of those connected with the transactions and the seller and buyer.

Remember that, even where investigations result in a solicitor ceasing to act for a client, the solicitors will still owe a duty of confidentiality which would prevent the solicitors from passing on information to the lender. It is only where the solicitor is satisfied that there is a strong *prima facie* case that the client was using the solicitor to further a fraud or other criminal purpose that the duty of confidentiality would not apply.

Any failure to observe these signs and to take the appropriate steps may be used in court as evidence against you if you and your client are prosecuted, or if you are sued for negligence.

Further guidance can be obtained from the Law Society's Practice Advice Service [Tel: 0870 606 2522].

III.4. Undertakings Warning Card ('Pink Card')[1]

Cost to the profession

The giving of sloppy or negligent undertakings is a considerable drain on the Solicitors' Indemnity Fund and the Compensation Fund. SIF estimate that such undertakings cost in excess of £5 million per annum. However, many undertakings may result in a liability within the deductible (i.e. excess) – exposing solicitors to considerable personal liability. Your work is made easier because people know they can rely on a solicitor's undertaking. However, it can be a two-edged sword. The wide and routine use of undertakings can result in a lack of care. The profession can no longer afford to underwrite the bill!

Remember – there is *no* obligation on a solicitor to give an undertaking, even to assist the progress of a client's matter.

Financial guarantees

Think twice before standing guarantor for a client – you could be personally liable for a substantial sum. There can be cases where SIF provides no cover if an undertaking is given which amounts to a bare guarantee of the financial obligations of a client or third party. Moreover, you would have no cover from SIF if you give an undertaking to a lender to repay money which you have borrowed and which you then re-lend to a client who subsequently defaults.

Be **SMART** when giving undertakings – make sure they are:

S Specific

Undertakings should refer to a particular task or action which has been clearly identified and defined. Do not give general or open-ended undertakings, such as an undertaking to discharge 'all outstanding mortgages on a property' or the 'usual undertaking'. Make sure that any undertaking to pay monies out of a fund is qualified by the proviso that the fund comes into your hands, *and* that it is sufficient.

M Measurable

Undertakings should include agreed measures or steps which are understood by both parties and can easily be monitored or checked, so that there can be no dispute as to whether an undertaking has been fully discharged. If an undertaking involves the payment of a sum of money, make sure the amount is clear or that it is easy to calculate. Ambiguous undertakings will be construed in favour of the recipient.

A Agreed

Undertakings should be expressly agreed by both the person giving and the person receiving them and should be confirmed in writing. They may be given orally or in writing and need not necessarily include the word 'undertake' – beware of inadvertent undertakings.

---

1. © The Law Society May 1993

R Realistic

Undertakings should be achievable. Before giving an undertaking consider carefully whether you will be able to implement it. If any events must happen before you will be able to implement your undertaking, it is good practice to spell out those events on the face of the undertaking. An undertaking is still binding even if it is to do something outside your control. As *you* give the undertaking – *you* can stay in control.

T Timed

Undertakings should indicate when, or on the happening of which event, they will be implemented. In the absence of an express term, there is an implied term that an undertaking will be performed within a reasonable time, having regard to its nature.

General points

Costs

- Don't ask other solicitors to provide an undertaking in terms you wouldn't give yourself. This applies particularly to undertakings as to costs: it's unfair to expect another solicitor to give an open-ended undertaking to pay your costs. Be prepared to give an upper limit or agree a basis of charging.

- An undertaking to pay another party's costs is generally discharged if the matter does not proceed to completion. If you intend some other arrangement, make this clear.

Conveyancing

- The Law Society's formulae for exchange of contracts and its Code for Completion by Post contain certain undertakings. Are you sure that you and your staff really know what undertakings they are giving in a normal conveyancing transaction?

- Make sure that each of your replies to requisitions on title concerning mortgages specifies exactly which mortgages or charges you intend to discharge. Vague replies will probably result in you being liable to discharge all charges – whether you know of them or not.

- Do not give unconditional undertakings without sufficient enquiry into the amount owed on prior charges – don't always rely on what your client tells you.

- If your ability to comply with an undertaking depends upon action to be taken by another solicitor, make sure that he or she will be able to comply, e.g. by obtaining an undertaking to a similar effect.

- Beware of bank 'standard form' undertakings – they sometimes go beyond what is in your control – it may be necessary to amend them.

Good management

- Principals are responsible for undertakings given by staff. Clear guidance should be given to staff, specifying those permitted to give undertakings and prescribing the manner in which they can be given. Find out how safe you are by doing an 'undertaking audit' – ask staff to check files for undischarged undertakings. Note how many have been given in a sloppy or negligent manner and calculate the size of the potential claims if things go wrong. Then introduce a system to put things right. This might be to:

    - draw up standard undertakings for use, where possible, by all fee-earners, with any deviation from the norm to be authorised by a partner;

– have all undertakings checked by another fee-earner prior to being given (or at least those which amount to a financial obligation);

– confirm all telephone undertakings (given or received) in writing;

– make sure that undertakings are not overlooked by:

- copying undertakings and attaching them to the file;

- indicating on the file cover, using coloured labels, that an undertaking has been given and its date.

The Guide to the Professional Conduct of Solicitors has a chapter about undertakings which contains useful guidance – please read it!

BE SMART!

IV. PRACTICE INFORMATION

IV.1. Council Statement: Landlords' Solicitors' Costs[1]

Both the Professional Purposes and Non-Contentious Business Departments of The Law Society regularly receive complaints and requests for guidance from solicitors as to the practice where landlords seek to pass liability for their solicitors' costs to a lessee or assignor. The Council hope that this statement will help to resolve the problems that can arise.

Grants of leases

It is, of course, common for a prospective lessee to agree to pay the landlord's solicitor's costs relating to the grant of the lease. The most frequent problem is that the amount of the landlord's solicitor's costs comes as a surprise to the lessee and/or his solicitor. This problem can be mitigated and often avoided if the lessee's solicitor seeks an estimate of the landlord's solicitor's costs at the outset and informs his client forthwith. If it is thought that the estimate is unreasonably high, negotiations can take place immediately, before either party has been involved in any substantial amount of work relating to the grant of the lease.

If a landlord's solicitor is asked for an estimate, then he should do his best to give a firm estimate, although it would usually be reasonable to add that the estimate could be exceeded if matters did not proceed quickly and without unforeseen complications. If the landlord is not prepared to depart substantially from the draft form of lease submitted to the lessee's solicitor, the landlord's solicitor should make this plain and should also state, if it be the case, that his estimate is based on the assumption that attempts will not be made to make substantial changes.

Licences to assign

The second situation where problems arise is where a proposed assignor needs a licence to assign from a superior landlord or a succession of superior landlords. It is sometimes appropriate that the proposed assignor should pay the costs and disbursements of such landlord(s) in relation to such licence(s), especially where the lease itself obliges him to pay (as to which s.144, Law of Property Act 1925 and s.19, Landlord and Tenant Act 1927 are relevant).

The Council express no view on whether in any given case there is a legal obligation on a proposed assignor to bear his landlord's costs. However, where the solicitor for the assignor asks the landlord's solicitor for such a licence, the Council do not regard it as professionally improper for the landlord's solicitor to ask for a professional undertaking that, whether or not the matter proceeds, the assignor's solicitor will pay his costs and disbursements in relation to the required licence. Whether the assignor's solicitor is willing to give the undertaking is a matter for his professional judgment in all the circumstances.

It is often vital to assignors that there should be no delay in obtaining any necessary licences. This will no doubt be a factor in their solicitor's decision whether to give the undertaking. The Council do

1. © The Law Society 1984. This statement first appeared in the Law Society's *Gazette* on 19 December 1984.

emphasise, however, that where solicitors give an undertaking, it will stand to be construed strictly and that compliance with it will be a charge on their resources unless they are put in funds by their client.

It will be prudent for an assignor's solicitor to seek an estimate of the amount of costs and disbursements that are to be covered by his proposed undertaking. It follows that time can be saved if landlords' solicitors include an estimate of the amount when asking for the undertaking. They should certainly do their best to give a firm estimate on request, although again it would usually be reasonable to add that the estimate could be exceeded if matters did not proceed quickly and without unforeseen complications.

Other licences

The principles in the last section of this statement should usually apply also where landlords are asked for licences to underlet, change use, carry out alterations, etc.

Remuneration certificates or taxations of costs

Whether a lease is being granted or a licence has been applied for, the client on whose behalf the relevant costs have been incurred is the landlord. The fact that a third party is liable to pay such costs does not of itself create an entitlement to seek a Remuneration Certificate under the Solicitors' Remuneration Order 1972. As a matter of practice, the Law Society will accept an application for a remuneration certificate in such circumstances, but *only* if the landlord gives his consent. In appropriate cases, the Council would hope that landlords' solicitors will encourage their clients to give such consent.

There is judicial authority for saying that an undertaking to pay reasonable costs means costs to be taxed if not agreed – *Zaniewski* v. *Scales* (1969) 113 SJ 525. If the landlord is unwilling to give his consent, the paying party is entitled to apply to the High Court for a taxation of the bill under s.71, Solicitors Act 1974. The client should be warned of the estimated expense of such an application and as to whether such expense might be disproportionate to the amount of the bill in dispute. Further, the client's attention should be drawn to the provisions of s.70(9) relating to payment of the costs of the taxation proceedings.

IV.2. Apportionment of rent[1]

1.   APPORTIONMENT OF RENT FORMULA

[The following text is reproduced from an article called 'Apportionment of rent' by Philip Freedman, [1990] *Gazette*, 3 October, 35. The article gives the method of calculation for the apportionment of rent formulated by the Law Society's Conveyancing and Land Law Committee.]

The method of calculation is based on the view that, where a lease or tenancy agreement reserves an annual rent, the usual direction to pay the rent by equal quarterly payments will have been inserted for estate management convenience only and will not have been intended to convert the annual rent into a quarterly rent. This is important because the traditional quarters are of unequal duration and hence the daily amount of rent would differ between one quarter and another if it were calculated quarter by quarter.

The example used below to illustrate the methods is for a lease dated 8 March [20—] expressed to grant a term of 'ten years commencing on 29 September [20— (the previous year)]' and expressed to reserve 'a rent of £36,500 per annum payable by equal quarterly payments in advance on the usual quarter days (the first payment being a due proportion thereof for the period from the date hereof to the following quarter day to be paid on the execution hereof)'.

Initial payment

Step 1: Ascertain the 'term year'. In the example, the term year will begin on 29 September in one year and end on 28 September in the following year. If, instead, the term had been expressed as 'a term commencing on the date hereof and expiring on 28 September [in ten years time]', the 'term year' would probably (although it is a matter of intention evidenced by the wording used in the lease) commence on 8 March in one year and end on 7 March in the following year. If the term was expressed to run 'from' a particular date, it would be necessary to consider whether under the particular lease the term began on that date or on the next day, a question discussed in most of the reference books on leases.

Step 2: Count the number of days for which the tenant is liable to pay rent during the first term year. In the example, this would be from 8 March to 28 September inclusive, namely 205 days.

Step 3: Calculate the rent payable for that number of days on an annual basis. In our example, this would be

$$205/365 \times £36,500 = £20,500.$$

Step 4: Calculate the rent that the tenant will have to pay on those rent payment days which will fall between the grant of the lease and the end of the first term year. In our example, there would be two such rent payment days, 25 March and 24 June, on each of which the tenant will have to pay one quarter's rent (£9,125) and therefore the total rent payable on those days will be

$$2 \times £9,125 = £18,250.$$

Step 5: Deduct the sum calculated at step 4 from the sum calculated at step 3. The difference is the amount that the tenant must pay on the grant of the lease. In our example, this is

$$£20,500 - £18,250 = £2,250.$$

---

1. This Appendix is based on two articles published in the Law Society's *Gazette* in October 1990 and June 1992.

(Contrast this with the figure of £1,700 that would have been calculated by simply taking the number of days from 8 March to 24 March inclusive at a daily rate of £100 (calculated on an annual basis) or the figure of £1,723.61 that would have been calculated by taking those days as a fraction of the current quarter.)

Assignment of lease

Assume that the lease is assigned on 31 March [in the second year of the term]. The apportionment as between the assignor and the assignee is to be calculated as follows:

Step 1: Ascertain the term year.

Step 2: Count the number of days for which the present tenant is liable to pay the rent during the current term year down to the date of the assignment. In our example, this is from 29 September [in year 1] to 31 March [in year 2], namely 184 days.

Step 3: Calculate the rent payable for that number of days on an annual basis. In our example, this would be

$$184/365 \times £36,500 = £18,400.$$

Step 4: Ascertain the amount of rent that will have been paid by the present tenant in respect of the current term year. In our example, the present tenant will have paid rent for the current year on 29 September [in year 1], 25 December [in year 1] and 25 March [in year 2], namely

$$3 \times £9,125 = £27,375.$$

Step 5: Compare the figures calculated at steps 3 and 4. If the former exceeds the latter, the present tenant must make an allowance of the difference to the assignee. If the latter exceeds the former, the assignee must make an allowance in favour of the present tenant. In our example, the present tenant has paid more rent than relates to his period of occupation during the current term year by the figure

$$£27,375 - £18,400 = £8,975.$$

This is the amount for which he is to be reimbursed by his assignee. (Contrast this with the sum of £8,400 that would have been calculated by simply applying the daily rate of £100 to the number of days between 31 March and the end of that quarter.)

On sale of reversion

Using our example, suppose that the landlord's interest was transferred to a new landlord on 30 April [in the second year of the term]. The apportionment of rental income between the old landlord and the new landlord is to be calculated as follows:

Step 1: Ascertain the term year.

Step 2: Count the number of days for which the old landlord is entitled to retain the rent received from the tenant in respect of the current term year. In our example, the old landlord is entitled to the rent for the period from 29 September [in year 1] to 30 April [in year 2], namely 214 days.

Step 3: Calculate the rent receivable for that number of days on an annual basis. In our example, this would be

$$214/365 \times £36,500 = £21,400$$

Step 4: Calculate the amount of rent actually received by the old landlord from the tenant in respect of the current term year. In our example, this rent should have been received on 29 September [in year 1], 25 December [in year 1] and 25 March [in year 2], namely

$$3 \times £9,125 = £27,375.$$

Step 5: Compare the figures calculated at steps 3 and 4. If the former exceeds the latter, the new landlord must make an allowance of the difference to the old landlord. If the latter exceeds the former, the old landlord must make an allowance of the difference to the new landlord. In our example, the old landlord has received more rent than relates to his period of ownership by the sum of

$$£27,375 - £21,400 = £5,975.$$

This is the amount which the old landlord must allow to the new landlord on transferring the reversion. (Contrast that with the sum of £5,400 that would have been calculated simply by taking the number of days between 30 April and the end of the current quarter and applying the daily rate of £100.)

For consistency, where the term expires by effluxion of time on a date other than the last day of a term year, the amount of the tenants' final payment of rent should be calculated on a basis similar to the apportionment of his initial payment on the grant of the lease.

2. APPORTIONMENT OF RENT – FURTHER GUIDANCE

[The following text is reproduced from an article called 'Apportionment of rent' prepared by the Law Society's Conveyancing and Land Law Committee, [1992] *Gazette*, 10 June, 22. The article gives further guidance from the Committee on the formula in no.1 above.]

In [1990] *Gazette*, 3 October, 35, an article was published setting out the land law committee's recommended formula ('the standard formula') for the calculation of apportionment of rent.

The application of the standard formula depends on being able to ascertain from the lease a 'term year', and for that term year to commence on a rent payment date (e.g. a quarter day where the rent is payable on quarter days).

To avoid doubt the committee wishes to emphasise that the standard formula cannot be properly applied where the term year runs from a date which is not a rent payment date. Attempting to apply the concept behind the standard formula in that situation usually produces manifestly wrong results. This is because there is a logical nexus where the payment dates for yearly rent are geared to the term year (since this enables one to identify the period to which particular rent payments relate), but not where the rent payment dates bear no relationship to the term year.

For example, take a lease granted for 25 years starting on 11 November 1992 at an initial rent of £365,000 per annum, payable in advance by equal quarterly payments on the usual quarter days. The first 'term year' runs from 11 November 1992 to 10 November 1993 inclusive. How should the first rent payment, payable on the grant of the lease, be calculated? The standard formula cannot be sensibly applied unless it is adjusted on the basis that the payment will fall due on 29 September 1993 (the last rent payment date in the first term year) will only take the rent up to 10 November 1993. That cannot be right, since part of that payment would then have to relate to a period prior to 29 September 1993, in which event the payment would not be 'in advance'.

Therefore in cases where the term is not calculated from a calendar date which is also a recurring rent payment date, the apportionment will have to be made on some other basis. While this may vary according to the precise facts, it is likely that the most appropriate alternative would be what is sometimes called the 'surveyor's method'. This involves simply counting the days to immediately before the next payment date, and applying a daily rate computed on a yearly basis. In this example, the period from 11 November to 24 December 1992 (inclusive) is 44 days, and applying it to the daily rate (calculated by the year) or £1,000 per day produces a figure of £44,000.

This illogicality of this common approach is obvious. A daily rent for rent payable by quarterly instalments is being calculated on a yearly basis and then applied to the residue of a particular quarter, which does not comprise exactly one-fourth of a year. A variation would be to calculate the daily rate for the particular quarter by reference to the total number of days in that quarter, and in this example the daily rate for the September quarter would be £1,061.05, which produces a figure of £46,686.20.

On either basis, it will be apparent that, should it be necessary to calculate an apportionment at a later date (e.g. when the lease is assigned or surrendered, or the reversion is transferred), to achieve a fair result it would be necessary to ascertain how much rent was actually paid under the apportionment at the grant of the lease and carry the calculation forward on that basis. This will usually be impractical, and the parties will have to be prepared to adopt each time a more rough and ready approach, such as the 'surveyor's method'.

However, since that method is entirely arbitrary and bears no logical relationship to the term/rent structure of the lease, the conveyancing and land law committee recommends that leases should be drafted so that the term year commences on one of the recurring rent payment dates. Thus if the rent is to be payable on the usual quarter days, the term year should commence on a quarter day. This will enable apportionments to be computed on a logical basis set out in the standard formula.

IV.3. Insolvency (No.2) Act 1994: counsel's opinion[1]

Section 339 of the 1986 Act gives the court power, on the application of the trustee in bankruptcy, to set aside an undervalue transaction, i.e. a gift or transfer for significantly low consideration, should the maker of the gift or transfer become bankrupt within five years after the date of the undervalue transaction. Section 342 provides protection, in certain conditions, against the use of section 339 powers. However, in its 1986 form, it was too restrictive. It left exposed to the risk of section 339 proceedings not only those who had benefited from undervalue transactions, but also those who had subsequently acquired, in good faith and for value, by way of genuine open market purchases, any property which had previously been the subject of an undervalue transaction. The 1994 Act overcame this problem by removing the 1986 Act's requirement that a buyer of – or, strictly, the acquirer of an interest in – property had to acquire not only in good faith and for value, but also without notice of the previous undervalue transaction, in order to get a title unchallengeable under section 339. With most types of property, a subsequent good faith buyer is unlikely to have notice of a previous undervalue transaction affecting it, and this generally applies to land as long as its title is registered. However, where title is unregistered, a buyer will inevitably have notice of a previous undervalue transaction. There is still a substantial amount of unregistered land in the UK and difficulties caused by section 339 are common. To the extent that the 1994 Act brought about protection for the good faith and for value acquirer, its effect was wholly beneficial. Unfortunately, as the price paid for removing the 'without notice' requirement, section 2(2) of the Act (which inserted new subsection (2A) into section 342 of the 1986 Act) made two exceptions to the improved protection. One of these is of little significance since it applies to an acquirer who is an 'associate of', or is 'connected with' (both terms are defined by the 1986 Act) either the undervalue transferor or transferee. However, the other exception, the 'dual notice' exception, gives rise to the main question which has been raised about the 1994 Act. These are counsel's views on this and other questions about the Act's effect.

Question 1

What is the effect of the 'dual notice' exception on the person who will for convenience be called the 'subsequent acquirer' (i.e. a person acquiring on the open market from the undervalue transferee, and also any further person who later acquires on the open market from that person)? The dual notice exception (section 342(2A) of the 1986 Act as amended by the 1994 Act) says that, where a subsequent acquirer of an interest in property has notice both of a previous undervalue transaction and of bankruptcy proceedings (i.e. a petition which leads to a bankruptcy order; or an actual bankruptcy order) against the undervalue transferor, the acquirer will be presumed to acquire other than in good faith, until he or she shows otherwise. The problem which this exception causes arises thus: A transfers a property at an undervalue to B; B sells on the open market to C who buys in good faith; C, some time later, wants to sell to D, another open market and good faith buyer. C knew of the undervalue transaction between A and B (though, with current land registration rules, this is perhaps unlikely to happen very often) but, at the time when he or she bought, there were no bankruptcy proceedings against A, so C acquired an unquestionably good title. However, by the time C sells to D, bankruptcy proceedings have begun against A, and D knows of the previous undervalue transaction (though this is even more unlikely under the current land registration

1. In 1995 the Law Society obtained the opinion of leading counsel, Gabriel Moss QC. These paragraphs set out his views.

regime). What is D's position as to possible section 339 proceedings? Counsel's view is that D is, in practice, at no risk if he acquires in these circumstances (provided that, in reality, he acts in good faith). Counsel says that this is an issue which must be looked at in context.

The underlying purpose of the legislation is to protect the *bona fide* buyer in good faith and for value, i.e. the buyer in the ordinary course of buying and selling property, while preventing creditors being cheated. Counsel is also confident that no court would deprive D of an interest bought in good faith and for value, for the benefit of the creditors of A, since it would be outrageously unfair to do so. Counsel is also confident that the courts would be concerned to interpret the legislation so as to achieve a fair result. He refers to the observation of Sir Donald Nicholls V-C in *Paramount Airways Ltd (No.2)* [1992] 3 All ER 1 (CA) in support of the view that 'the court will ensure that it does not seek to exercise oppressively or unfairly the very wide jurisdiction conferred by the sections' (in that case, sections 238 to 241). In fact, counsel thinks it highly unlikely that, in practice, any trustee in bankruptcy would even consider trying to challenge D since it would be a waste of the assets of the bankrupt's estate to do so. However, should this unlikely situation occur, counsel's view is that there are three bases on which an application should be resisted.

(i) Under the 'shelter' rule: this rule, which is not widely known, is illustrated in *Wilkes* v. *Spooner* [1911] 2 KB 473 (CA). It says, broadly, that a person who acquires property in good faith and for value can pass on as good a title as he or she has to another person who also acquires in good faith. In *Wilkes* v. *Spooner*, a person acquired land which was subject to various covenants. However, as he had acquired without notice of them, but in good faith and for value, he was not bound by them. By the time he came to sell, the covenants had come to light, but he claimed that, because of the 'shelter' principle, he could sell free of them to another good faith buyer. The Court of Appeal agreed. In counsel's view, this principle applies equally to property in the undervalue transaction context – and, indeed, some of the drafting of section 342 may, he thinks, be a somewhat clumsy attempt to reflect the 'shelter' rule.

(ii) On the grounds that D's title is 'derived' from that of C section 342(2)(a) of the 1986 Act (as amended) says that no order made under section 339 shall prejudice an interest acquired in good faith and for value, nor any interest 'derived' from that interest. What 'derived' means in this context is unclear, but counsel thinks that its use may have been intended to replicate the 'shelter' rule. If this is the effect of the term, D's interest would be protected by reason of being 'derived' from that of C. It is possible, however, that interests such as those of subsequent buyers were not intended to be treated as 'derived' interests and that the term was meant to cover only interests such as those acquired by inheritance.

(iii) On the grounds, simply, that he or she had acquired in good faith and for value. In a normal open market transaction, there would be no question that the buyer had acquired his or her interest in this way. However, new subsection (2A) of section 342 (inserted by the 1994 Act) creates an artificial presumption against good faith where the dual notice exception applies, even in relation to such a transaction. Counsel's view, however, is that a court would ask no more of D, in order to displace this presumption, than to show that his purchase was at arm's length and for value, i.e. that it was a normal, open market purchase. Thus, in the highly unlikely event of a challenge, the presumption against good faith would be easily rebutted. Only where there was actual evidence calling D's good faith into question could there be any prospect of a serious challenge by a trustee. If D had bought on the open market, this would be a highly unusual situation – indeed, it is difficult to imagine its arising.

Question 2

What does 'notice' mean in this context (i.e. as to notice of a previous undervalue transaction but, in particular, notice of bankruptcy proceedings)? Counsel's view is that actual notice is notice in this context, both as to bankruptcy proceedings and previous undervalue transactions. As to statutory notice of bankruptcy proceedings, an acquirer of an interest in unregistered land will have notice of any information recorded either in the register of pending actions or in the register of writs and orders – sections 5 and 6 Land Charges Act 1972. Although there is some question (because of the wording of sections 5 and 6, and also of section 198 Law of Property Act 1925) as to whether this notice would be effective against an acquirer, because it would not be recorded against the name of a bankrupt with any present connection with the property concerned, the prudent view is to assume that it would do so. As to registered land, the acquirer will have notice only of what appears on the land register. Section 59 Land Registration Act 19[2]5 says that a writ, order, etc. has effect against registered land only if lodged as provided by that Act, so that it is shown on the registered title; and section 14 Land Charges Act 1972 excludes that Act's effect as to any matter relating to registered land. Nevertheless, counsel suggests that, where a prospective buyer of registered land has notice of an undervalue transaction – but only then – it would be prudent to carry out a bankruptcy search against the undervalue transferor, if known, as failure to do so might cause difficulties in rebutting the presumption against good faith (section 342(2A)) should the issue arise.

Question 3

What is the effect of the 1994 Act on mortgagees? In counsel's view, exactly the same as on the acquirer of any other kind of interest. A mortgagee acquires an interest in property. In a normal mortgage of domestic property to a bank or building society, the mortgagee clearly acquires its interest in good faith and gives value. The mortgagee's interest is thus protected by section 342(2)(a) as amended. This applies regardless of whether the mortgagor is B, the undervalue transferee; or C, the first subsequent good faith and for value buyer; or D, the next subsequent good faith and for value buyer. Similarly, a mortgagee exercising its power of sale would be able to pass good title to a subsequent acquirer, for the same reasons that a subsequent freehold buyer (C or D) can do so. The Law Society has received queries about the effect of section 339 and the 1994 Act where property which is the subject of an undervalue transaction is transferred subject to an existing mortgage. In this situation, no section 339 issue arises at all, as far as the mortgaged interest is concerned, because the mortgage agreement was entered into before the undervalue transaction took place. Though the trustee in bankruptcy could apply under section 339 for the return of the property itself – in practice, the equity which would have been the subject of an undervalue transaction – the mortgagee's interest would remain intact (as it would have had the mortgage been created after the undervalue transaction, in the event of section 339 proceedings).

Question 4

Where A transfers property at an undervalue to A (self) and B jointly or in common; or A and B transfer jointly either to A or B alone, does the section 342(2)(a) protection operate in relation to C, the subsequent acquirer, or is it disapplied by the exclusion contained in section 342(2)(a) of an interest acquired from 'that individual', i.e. the undervalue transferor. Counsel's view is that C is not excluded from the protection given by section 342(2)(a) because of having acquired from 'that individual'. Where A, as sole owner, transfers to himself and B jointly, what happens is that A transfers the whole of the legal estate in the property, but only that part of his beneficial interest which passes to B. In this context, what Insolvency Act 1986 is concerned with is the beneficial, not the legal, interest in the property which is the subject of an undervalue transaction. Thus, when A and B then sell to C (a good faith and for value buyer), what C acquires is A's beneficial interest which has not been the subject of an undervalue transaction, and B's beneficial interest which has been but which C obviously does not acquire from 'that individual'). Thus, the interest acquired by C comes within the section 342(2)(a) protection to the extent that it is acquired from B, and is outside section 339 altogether to the extent that it is acquired from A. Similarly, when A and B transfer jointly owned property to B, and B then sells to C, the same principle applies. That is, since the only transfer to which section 339 and section 342(2)(a) are material is that of A's beneficial interest to B and, as C is acquiring from B and not A, he or she is not affected by the 'other than that individual' exclusion.

IV.4. Dealing with licensed conveyancers[1]

A solicitor may normally deal with a licensed conveyancer as if the conveyancer were a solicitor, subject to the best interests of the solicitor's client.

1.   Licensed conveyancers are permitted to practise in partnership with other licensed conveyancers, or with other persons (although not with solicitors). Licensed conveyancers may also practise through the medium of a 'recognised body', i.e. a body corporate recognised by the Council for Licensed Conveyancers.

2.   The identity of firms of licensed conveyancers can be checked in the *Directory of Solicitors and Barristers*. In cases of doubt contact the Council for Licensed Conveyancers [16 Glebe Road, Chelmsford, Essex CM1 1QG. DX 121925 Chelmsford 6. Tel: 01245 349599. Fax: 01245 341300].

3.   Licensed conveyancers are subject to conduct and accounts rules similar to those which apply to solicitors. They are covered by compulsory indemnity insurance and contribute to a compensation fund. In dealings with licensed conveyancers, it should normally be possible to proceed as if the licensed conveyancer were a solicitor and bound by the same professional obligations. For example, if it is agreed to use the Law Society's code for exchange of contracts by telephone, it is understood that any failure to respect the code would expose the licensed conveyancer to disciplinary proceedings; this also applies to the Society's code for completion by post, and reliance on undertakings. Since licensed conveyancers may practise in partnership or association with others, it is important to ensure that the other party's representative is a licensed conveyancer, or a person working immediately under the supervision of a licensed conveyancer.

IV

---

1. © The Law Society. The following text was previously published as principle 25.06 in *The Guide to the Professional Conduct of Solicitors 1999*.

IV.5. Dealing with unqualified conveyancers[1]

Effect of section 22 of the Solicitors Act 1974

1. Section 22 of the Solicitors Act 1974 (see Annex 2A at p.45 in the Guide) makes it an offence for an unqualified person to draw or prepare, *inter alia*, a contract for sale or a transfer, conveyance, lease or mortgage relating to land in expectation of fee, gain or reward. Qualified persons under this section are solicitors, barristers, notaries public, licensed conveyancers, some public officers and, for unregistered conveyancing, Scottish solicitors.

2. It is inevitable that an unqualified person who undertakes a conveyancing transaction in the course of a conveyancing business will commit an offence under section 22, unless the drawing or preparation of the relevant documents is undertaken by a qualified person. In such circumstances, the unqualified conveyancer's client is likely, albeit unwittingly, to be guilty of aiding and abetting the offence. The solicitor acting for the other party could also be guilty of procuring the commission of an offence by inviting or urging the unqualified person to provide a draft contract or transfer or to progress the transaction.

3. Solicitors should therefore refuse to have any dealings with any unqualified person carrying on a conveyancing business unless there is clear evidence that offences under section 22 will not be committed.

4. It is recommended that, at the outset of any transaction, the solicitor should write to the unqualified conveyancer drawing attention to this guidance and saying that the solicitor cannot enter into any dealings with him or her unless there is clear evidence that no offences will be committed. An example of satisfactory evidence would be a letter from a qualified person confirming that he or she will prepare the relevant documents. The solicitor should also immediately report to his or her own client and explain why he or she cannot deal with the unqualified conveyancer unless clear evidence is forthcoming.

Draft letter to unqualified conveyancer

'We are instructed to act for the seller/buyer in connection with the above transaction and understand that you have been instructed by the buyer/seller. Please confirm that you are a solicitor or licensed conveyancer. If not, please state who will prepare the contract/conveyance/transfer for you; we need to receive written confirmation from a qualified person that he or she will personally settle the contract/conveyance/transfer.

As you know, it is an offence for an unqualified person to prepare a contract for sale or a transfer, conveyance or mortgage relating to land in expectation of fee, gain or reward. We have been advised by the Law Society that we should not deal with an unqualified person carrying on a conveyancing business unless clear evidence is provided that offences under section 22 of the Solicitors Act 1974 will not be committed. The written confirmation referred to above, if explicit and unequivocal, could provide such evidence.

---

1. © The Law Society. The following text was previously published as Annex 25A in *The Guide to the Professional Conduct of Solicitors 1999*. Cross references to paragraphs in the *Guide* include page references from the *Guide*.

We regret that unless you are a solicitor or licensed conveyancer, we cannot deal with you until the evidence required above is provided.'

Draft letter to client of solicitor

'Thank you for your instructions relating to the above transactions. There is unfortunately a problem. The buyer/seller appears to have instructed an unqualified conveyancer to act for him/her and this could lead to the conveyancer, his/her client and myself being involved in the commission of criminal offences under the Solicitors Act 1974. The Law Society, my professional body, has advised solicitors not to deal with unqualified conveyancers because of the possibility of committing criminal offences.

I have therefore written to the firm acting for the buyer/seller asking for confirmation whether or not they are unqualified conveyancers and, if they are, whether they will be making arrangements to prevent the commission of such offences. If they cannot satisfy me about this, the buyer/seller will have to instruct a solicitor or licensed conveyancer, or deal with me direct.'

Further help

1.   Solicitors should first check with the Council for Licensed Conveyancers whether a person is a licensed conveyancer, since a licensed conveyancer can normally be dealt with as if a solicitor (see **25.06**, p.472 in the Guide).

2.   The Society can help practitioners dealing with unqualified conveyancers if the above guidance and the practice notes below do not cover the situation. Telephone calls and written requests for guidance should be made to the Practice Advice Service – for contact details see p.xv.

3.   The Professional Adviser (for contact details, see p.xv) has responsibility for investigating and prosecuting non-solicitors who appear to be in breach of the Solicitors Act 1974. Solicitors are asked to report (without submitting their files) any case where there is *prima facie* evidence of breaches of the Solicitors Act.

4.   For assistance in those cases where the solicitor has clear evidence that no offences under section 22 will be committed, there is set out below a series of practice notes relating to the problems which might arise in a transaction in which the other party is represented by an unqualified conveyancer. These practice notes give advice only and it is for solicitors to decide for themselves what steps should properly be taken in any particular situation.

PRACTICE NOTES

(applicable only where evidence is provided of compliance with section 22)

General

1.   Any undertaking which unqualified agents may offer in the course of a transaction is not enforceable in the same way as an undertaking given by a solicitor or licensed conveyancer. Solicitors should therefore never accept such undertakings.

2.   Solicitors are under no duty to undertake agency work by way of completions by post on behalf of unqualified persons, or to attend to other formalities on behalf of third parties who are not clients, even where such third parties offer to pay the agent's charges.

3.   The Council also suggests that in cases where a solicitor is dealing with an unqualified conveyancer, the solicitor should bear in mind the line of decisions starting with *Hedley Byrne* v.

Heller [1964] AC 465, which extends the duty of care owed by a solicitor to persons who are not clients, but who rely and act on the solicitor's advice to his or her knowledge.

4. Solicitors must decide in each case whether special provisions should be incorporated in the draft contract to take account of the problems which arise by reason of the other party having no solicitor or licensed conveyancer, e.g. that the seller should attend personally at completion if represented by an unqualified agent. All such matters must be considered prior to exchange of contracts since contractual conditions cannot, of course, be imposed subsequently.

5. The protection provided by section 69 of the Law of Property Act 1925 only applies when a document containing a receipt for purchase money is handed over by a solicitor or licensed conveyancer or the seller himself or herself. Thus it should be considered whether the contract should provide either for the seller to attend personally at completion, or for an authority signed by the seller, for the purchase money to be paid to his or her agent, to be handed over on completion.

Acting for the seller: buyer not represented by a solicitor or licensed conveyancer

Completion

6. It is important to ensure that the deeds and keys are passed to the person entitled to receive them, i.e. the buyer. If an authority on behalf of the buyer is offered to the seller's solicitor, it is for the solicitor to decide whether or not to accept it, bearing in mind that no authority, however expressed, can be irrevocable. Again it is worth considering at the outset whether the point should be covered by express condition in the contract (see practice note 4 above).

Acting for the buyer: seller not represented by a solicitor or licensed conveyancer

Preliminary enquiries and requisitions on title

7. It may be prudent to require and ensure that replies to all preliminary enquiries and requisitions are signed by the seller.

Payment of deposit

8. Difficulties may arise in connection with payment of the deposit where there is no estate agent involved to whom the deposit may be paid as stakeholder in the ordinary way. The deposit may be paid direct to the seller, but this cannot be recommended since it is equivalent to parting with a portion of the purchase money in advance of investigation of the title and other matters.

9. Some unqualified agents insist that the deposit be paid to them. The Council does not recommend this. If a solicitor is obliged to pay the deposit to unqualified agents, he or she should inform the client of the risks involved, and obtain specific instructions before proceeding.

10. An alternative is for the deposit to be paid to the buyer's solicitor as stakeholder. The buyer's solicitor should insist on this where possible. If the seller will not agree to this, it may be possible to agree to place the deposit in a deposit account in the joint names of the buyer's solicitor and the seller, or in a deposit account in the seller's name, with the deposit receipt to be retained by the buyer's solicitor.

Payment of purchase money

11. As referred to in practice note 5 above, the buyer's solicitor should ensure that all the purchase money, including any deposit, is paid either to the seller or to the seller's properly authorised agent.

Matters unresolved at completion

12.   Whilst it is unusual to leave any issues revealed by searches and other enquiries outstanding at completion, undertakings relating to their discharge or resolution may on occasions be given between solicitors or licensed conveyancers. Such undertakings should not be accepted from unqualified agents for the reason mentioned in practice note 1 above.

Power of attorney

13.   Unqualified agents sometimes obtain a power of attorney to enable themselves or their employees to conduct certain aspects of the transaction. It is clearly important to ensure that such powers are valid, properly granted, and effective for all relevant purposes.

Acting for the lender: borrower not represented by a solicitor or licensed conveyancer

14.   The lender's solicitor often finds himself or herself undertaking much of the work which a borrower's solicitor would do. Whilst the client's interests are paramount, the solicitor must ensure that he or she does not render the unqualified agent additional assistance in a way which might establish a solicitor/client relationship either with the unqualified conveyancer or with the borrower, or leave the solicitor open to a negligence claim either from the solicitor's lender client or from the borrower.

Advances

15.   As regards the drafting and preparation of the instrument of transfer by the borrower's representative, the lender's solicitor is not obliged to undertake work which would normally be done by the borrower's solicitor. Solicitors are reminded, however, that it is of paramount importance to their lender client that good title is conveyed to the borrower.

16.   The importance of paying mortgage advances only to those properly entitled to receive them is a reason for insisting either that the borrower attends personally on completion, or that a signed authority from the borrower in favour of his or her agent is received on completion. Section 69 of the Law of Property Act 1925 is a relevant consideration in this context (see practice note 5 above).

Redemptions

17.   On completion, cheques or drafts should be drawn in favour of solicitors or licensed conveyancers or their clients, and not endorsed over to some intermediate party. The deeds should normally be handed over to the borrower personally, unless he or she provides a valid authority for them to be handed to a third party.

18.   Any issues of doubt or difficulty must be referred to the lender/client for detailed instructions. Where the lender is a building society and its solicitor considers that the totality of the work involved justifies a charge in excess of the building society's guideline fee, he or she should seek the approval of the lender/client, supported if necessary by a bill of costs containing sufficient detail of the work and the time spent on it.

16th March 1988, revised December 1995

IV.6. Tax on bank and building society interest – practice information[1]

Since April 1996, savings income received by an individual, the estate of a deceased person or an interest in possession trust has been taxable at the lower rate (20%), unless in the case of an individual his or her total income makes him or her liable to higher rate tax, rather than the basic rate of tax (section 73 of the Finance Act 1996 inserting a new section 1A into the Income and Corporation Taxes Act 1988). This is relevant to the tax treatment of bank and building society interest received by solicitors.

The Solicitors' Accounts Rules 1998, Part C

Under this part of the rules ('the interest provisions'), a solicitor who is required to account for interest to a client may do so by either of two methods. He or she may:

(a) account to the client for the interest earned on the client's money in a separate designated client account; or

(b) pay to the client a sum in lieu of interest when the money is held in a general client account.

These two procedures are referred to as Method A and Method B respectively.

Deduction of tax at source

The tax deduction at source rules apply, broadly, to separate designated client accounts, e.g. accounts held for individuals who are ordinarily resident in the UK.

Interest on general client accounts, whether with a bank or a building society, is paid gross.

When opening any separate designated client account the solicitor must provide the necessary information for the bank or building society to decide whether or not deduction of tax at source is appropriate.

Tax treatment of interest – Method A

Method A applies to separate designated client accounts. Where tax is deducted at source by the bank or building society interest will be received by the solicitor net, and he or she will simply pass it on to the client net – no tax deduction certificate is required. Interest from separate designated client accounts is taxable as savings income. The client, when making his or her tax return, will declare the interest as having been received under deduction of tax, and will only be liable to be assessed in relation to higher rate tax in respect of it (since he or she will have a tax credit for the lower rate of tax). If the client is for any reason not liable to income tax, he or she can recover any tax deducted from the interest. In those circumstances the solicitor must, on being required by the client, obtain a certificate of deduction of tax from the bank or building society and deliver this to the client. The client's position is, therefore, for practical purposes, the same as that which arises where he or she receives interest from a building society or bank on a deposit of his or her own.

---

1. © The Law Society. This information was previously published in Annex 28D in *The Guide to the Professional Conduct of Solicitors 1999*.

Where the client is not liable to tax or is not ordinarily resident (NOR) in the UK the bank or building society will pay the interest gross provided that it holds the relevant declaration. Declarations of non-ordinary residence can be completed by either the solicitor or the client but declarations of non-liability by UK residents will normally be completed by the client. However, in view of the difficulty of obtaining complete information about an overseas client, solicitors may feel that it is more appropriate for the client concerned to make the declaration, especially since it contains an undertaking to notify the bank or building society should circumstances change.

Where the tax deduction at source rules do not apply, the solicitor will receive interest from the bank or building society gross and may account to the client for it gross, even if the client is non-resident. The client will be assessed on the gross receipt (but a non-resident client may, by concession – not be assessed) and (unless the solicitor has been acting as the client's agent for tax purposes – see below under 'Solicitors as agents') the solicitor himself or herself will not be assessed in respect of the interest.

Tax treatment of interest – Method B

Where Method B is used, deduction of tax at source does not apply to the solicitor's general client account at either a bank or building society, and interest is therefore paid to the solicitor gross. When making a payment to the client of a sum in lieu of interest under the interest provisions, the solicitor should make the payment gross even if the client is not ordinarily resident. The Revenue's view is that such payments may be treated as within Case III of Schedule D, so that the lower rate of tax on savings income may apply where appropriate. The client will be assessed to income tax on his or her receipt, but a non-resident may, by concession, not be assessed.

Wherever payments are made by solicitors to clients under Method B they can, in practice, be set off against the solicitor's Case III assessment on gross interest received on general client account deposits; if the payments exceed the interest received, a Case II deduction can be claimed for the excess.

Stake money

Since 1st June 1992, stake money has been included in the definition of 'client money'. Interest will be payable to the person to whom the stake is paid using either Method A or B above. But there will still be circumstances in which payment is not possible until a later tax year. Where this situation looks likely to arise, e.g. if the stake is held pending the outcome of litigation, the deposit would normally be placed in a general client account until it is established to whom the stake is to be paid. Because, in the meantime, interest will be included in the solicitor's Case III assessment, it is again important to make provision for the tax liability to be met out of the interest as it arises.

Tax treatment of interest – money paid into court

The position of money paid into court is covered by the Supreme Court Funds Rules as amended. Where any order for payment out of money paid into court is made, the order should provide for the disposal of any interest accrued to the date of the judgment or order, and for interest accruing thereafter up to the date the money is paid out in accordance with the order. In the absence of such provision, interest accruing between the date of the payment into court, and its acceptance or the judgment or order for payment out, goes to the party who made the payment in, and interest from the date of the judgment or order follows the capital payment.

Where interest is paid to a party to proceedings in respect of money held in court, it should be paid to the client gross, even if he or she is non-resident. The client will normally be assessable under Case III, but the solicitor will not, unless exceptionally he or she is assessable as the client's agent.

Solicitors as agents

Where a solicitor acts for tax purposes as agent for a non-resident client, the solicitor will remain liable to be assessed on behalf of the client in relation to interest earned in a separate designated client account, where Method A is used, unless he or she is an agent without management or control of the interest, in which case, under Extra Statutory Concession B13, no assessment will be made on him or her. Where the solicitor is assessable, the charge may, if appropriate, be to higher rate tax, so the solicitor will need to retain tax at the client's marginal rate of income tax from interest received gross from a bank or building society before remitting it to the client. This is the case even though the account would not be subject to deduction of tax at source since the client would have completed a declaration of non-liability due to his or her non-residence. No question of the solicitor being taxed as an agent will arise where the interest in question has been earned in a general client account, or on stake money, but it could very exceptionally do so in relation to money held in court.

Determination of whether a solicitor has management or control for the purposes of the extra statutory concession will depend on the nature of the solicitor's relationship with the client. Under the Finance Act 1995, a person not resident in the UK is assessable and chargeable to income tax in the name of an agent if the agent has management or control of the interest. Acting as a solicitor in giving advice or in conducting a transaction on the client's instructions will not of itself give management or control nor usually would the holding of a power of attorney on behalf of the client for a specific purpose, e.g. concluding a specified purchase or sale. If a client had no fixed place of business in the UK, and his or her solicitor had, and habitually exercised, an authority to conclude contracts on behalf of the client, this would give rise to the client having a permanent establishment in the UK, and accordingly the client would be taxable. In essence, the solicitor would be deemed to have management and control if he or she were effectively carrying on the client's business in the UK, rather than merely acting as a solicitor, even regularly. Therefore, in order for the agency principle to apply, the solicitor/client relationship would normally have to go beyond a solicitor's usual representative capacity. It should be noted that where interest arises in connection with the receipt of rents on behalf of the non-resident, the solicitor would be chargeable as agent in relation to the rent.

For a more detailed analysis of when solicitors can be taxed as agents, see [1991] *Gazette*, 1 May, 15 (article by John Avery Jones).

If a solicitor is assessable on behalf of the client, he or she has a general right to reimbursement, out of the client's money coming into his or her hands, for any tax for which the client is liable and in respect of which the solicitor has been charged. For the exercise of this right see the Finance Act 1995.

Trusts

Deduction of tax at source may apply depending upon the type of trust and where the investment is held. But it can only apply where money is held in a separate designated client account. The income of trusts where none of the beneficiaries is ordinarily resident in the UK will not be subject to deduction of tax at source, even if a separate designated client account is used, provided that the appropriate declaration has been made.

Administration of estates

Interest on money held for UK resident personal representatives will, if placed in a separate designated client account, be subject to deduction of tax at source unless a declaration is made by the solicitor or the personal representatives that the deceased was not resident in the UK immediately before his death.

AIDE-MEMOIRE OF NORMAL SITUATIONS

Type of account	Payment of interest by bank or building society	Consequences
A Designated – where subject to tax deduction	Net	Pay net to client, who gets basic rate tax credit. No further tax deductions for residents (unless solicitor is assessable as an agent).
B Designated – where paid gross (client money generally)	Gross	Pay gross to client who is assessable on payment as gross income. No deduction of tax for non-residents (unless the solicitor is assessable as agent).
C Bank and building society general client account – always paid gross (client money generally and stake money)	Gross	Pay gross to client who in turn is assessable on payment as gross income; in practice solicitor assessed on interest after setting-off this payment. No deduction of tax for non-residents.

4th March 1992, revised February 1999

IV.7. Accepting undertakings on completion following the Court of Appeal decision in Patel v. Daybells[1]

Accepting undertakings on completion

The first instance decision in *Patel* v. *Daybells* [2000] All ER(D) 1004 caused consternation among conveyancers. It held that it was negligent for a buyer's solicitor to accept an undertaking for Form 53 (now DS1), save in exceptional circumstances. The Court of Appeal ([2001] EWCA Civ 1229) has now upheld the decision that the solicitor in the case was not negligent, but reversed the reasoning – the acceptance of a solicitor's undertaking for a DS1 will not normally be negligent. But does this mean a return to business as usual?

The Court of Appeal held that 'conformity to a common (or even universal) professional practice is not an automatic defence against liability; the practice must be demonstrably reasonable and responsible'. This involves considering the risks involved and how to avoid them. The Court of Appeal was satisfied that the legal profession had considered the risks of accepting an undertaking and that in the standard case it was reasonable to rely on the existence of compulsory insurance, the Compensation Fund and the summary procedure for enforcing undertakings when assessing the extent of that risk. Other relevant factors were: the Council of Mortgage Lenders' advice to its members to discharge a mortgage even where insufficient funds were sent, if this was due to the lender's error; and the problems which would ensue if the buyer's solicitor had to communicate directly with the seller's lender.

Exceptional cases

The 'exceptional circumstances' in which it might be negligent for a buyer's solicitor to accept an undertaking were not specified by the Court of Appeal, although the court made it clear that the fact that the seller's solicitor was a sole practitioner did not make the transaction exceptional.

The court referred in detail to the expert evidence on behalf of the buyer's solicitor that it would not be normal or advisable to rely on an undertaking in two situations, but did not expressly endorse these as the relevant 'exceptional circumstances'. The two situations mentioned are:

- Where the amount required to redeem the seller's mortgage exceeds the minimum level of solicitors' indemnity insurance (currently [£2m] per claim); or

- Where the mortgagee is not a member of the Council of Mortgage Lenders.

Minimising the risks in exceptional cases

The risk of accepting an undertaking for a DS1 is that it might not be forthcoming (e.g. because of the fraud or negligence of the seller's solicitor or because of problems in identifying the amount required to redeem the mortgage). Default by the seller's solicitor is dealt with by the requirement for compulsory insurance and, ultimately, the Compensation Fund. Only where the figures exceed

---

1. © The Law Society. Prepared by the Law Society's Conveyancing and Land Law Committee in May 2002.

the compulsory level of insurance might the buyer's solicitor need to take additional steps to deal with that risk. The risk of a dispute with the lender should not normally be a problem where the lender is a member of the CML. Even disputes not covered by the CML's advice may not put the buyer's solicitor at risk: the Law Society's recommended form of undertaking puts an absolute obligation on the seller's solicitor to discharge the relevant mortgage. It is therefore the seller's solicitor who is at risk if the DS1 is not forthcoming: his obligations can be summarily enforced and are backed by compulsory insurance and in certain cases, the Compensation Fund.

In each of the exceptional cases mentioned in *Patel* v. *Daybells* the matter comes back to the safeguards put in place by the profession. The only variable is the level of insurance cover and that is only relevant in the case of large mortgages. Normally the buyer's solicitor does not know the amount of the debt (and the Court of Appeal disapproved of the idea that the buyer's solicitor should have to make such enquiries). It is common to ask in preliminary enquiries for confirmation that the sale price exceeds the amount secured on the mortgage. Provided the sale price is not more than [£2m], such confirmation should give the buyer's solicitor the necessary comfort to accept an undertaking from the seller's solicitor. In larger transactions the buyer's solicitor may wish to take additional steps before or instead of accepting an undertaking.

- The buyer's solicitor could ask the seller's solicitor to get express written confirmation from the lender that he has been appointed the lender's agent for the receipt of the redemption money. This places the risk of default or dispute with the lender and avoids the buyer having to investigate either the details of the mortgage or the seller's solicitor's insurance.

- The buyer's solicitor could insist on sending the redemption money direct to the lender. The buyer's solicitor should ask to see the redemption statement as independent evidence of the figure. The Court of Appeal disapproved of the buyer making such enquiries in the standard case but in an exceptional case, where large sums are involved, this may be inevitable. As this information is confidential to the seller, the seller's solicitor should get instructions before revealing it. However, this solution does not deal with the problem of a dispute over the amount required to redeem. It may also be difficult to arrange in the case of an 'all moneys' mortgage. If this course is followed, Standard Condition 6.7 should be amended (or, if using the Standard Commercial Property Conditions, expand condition 6.7). In either case, the issue must be addressed before exchange (or if using the Standard Commercial Property Conditions, expand condition 8.7).

- Where the amount of the mortgage debt exceeds the minimum indemnity insurance (as will often be the case in commercial transactions), a buyer's solicitor might only accept an undertaking for DS1 if coupled with a warranty from the seller's solicitor that his insurance cover exceeds the amount required to redeem the mortgage.

- Finally, there is no obligation to accept an undertaking in place of performance of the obligation. Indeed, solicitors have often been unwilling to accept an undertaking for the DS1 in the case of a mortgage to a non-institutional or overseas lender or in the case of a private loan. However, if that is the buyer's solicitor's position, a contract condition that the DS1 must be available on completion will be necessary. In many cases this will not be a realistic option as institutional lenders' procedures do not include issuing the DS1 in escrow.

Before the buyer's solicitor accepts an undertaking where the expert evidence in *Patel* v. *Daybells* stated it would not be normal practice to do so, it is essential to explain the risks to the buyer and get clear instructions that the buyer is willing to take them.

Even where the lender is separately represented, the buyer's solicitor should consider whether there are any exceptional circumstances making it unwise (or potentially negligent) to accept an undertaking (or at least without evidence of the lender's solicitor's authority to accept the redemption money).

ENDs

The use of Electronic Notifications of Discharge (END) presents a particular problem as there is never a paper DS1 to be handed over: the buyer's solicitor is always reliant on an undertaking by the seller's solicitor to forward the redemption money and the END form to the lender, who then sends the discharge notification directly to the Land Registry. Even where the transaction might fall into the category of exceptional cases the buyer's solicitor will ultimately have no choice but to accept the undertaking and will have to take such steps as are available (e.g. split payments, evidence of the seller's solicitor's authority, evidence of sufficient insurance cover).

IV.8. Undue influence – solicitors' duties post Etridge[1]

Introduction

Many negligence claims have arisen as a result of solicitors viewing their role in the execution of third party charge documentation as little more than a formality. The important House of Lords decision in *Royal Bank of Scotland* v. *Etridge* was delivered on 11th October 2001 and as a result all conveyancing lawyers should consider carefully their procedures when faced with a transaction where a third party provides security for another person's borrowing. The risk to solicitors' professional indemnity cover remains acute. *Etridge* involved a wife claiming that she had charged her interest in the matrimonial home as a result of the undue influence of her husband. Whilst the decision has to some extent clarified the scope of the solicitors' duties and set out what is required of the lender this arrangement does still present all parties with exposure to risk and this has not in any way been reduced following the House of Lords decision.

Can you advise?

Whilst *Etridge* does contemplate that the same solicitor can act for both parties and the lender in an administrative capacity, the first decision for the solicitor is whether he or she should be acting at all. The risk of conflict is extreme when attempting to reconcile Lord Nicholls' comments concerning the provision of full information with a client who in many cases may not wish for the documentation to be fully explained. When the third party realises that the home will be at risk to secure the other person's borrowing, there may be some reluctance to sign.

If advising the third party the solicitor will be acting for the third party alone and so must consider carefully whether there is a conflict of duty or interest and whether it would be in the best interests of that client to accept the instructions. If the third party is a wife she may well have an interest in supporting the husband's business as it is the source of the family's income. In such cases the wife may, despite the risks, have a good reason to sign the charge.

Many solicitors will, however, be reluctant to advise in such circumstances. The Law Lords stressed the importance of bank finance in the business world and stated that 'finance raised by second mortgages on the principal's home is a significant source of capital for the start up of small businesses'. So in order to facilitate the development of embryonic businesses, solicitors will no doubt still be asked to witness charge documentation. What steps should the solicitor take to ensure that the obligation of independent advice is properly discharged?

Who is your client?

The solicitor must ensure that the client wishes and intends to instruct the solicitor. It must be established that there is no conflict of interest and that it is the third party (and not the borrower) who is the client.

---

1. © The Law Society. Prepared by the Law Society's Conveyancing and Land Law Committee in May 2002.

Full financial information

The solicitor must obtain full financial information concerning the borrower's account. This will normally include (para 79 of Lord Nicholls' judgment) information on the purpose for the new facility, the current indebtedness, the amount of the current overdraft facility, and the amount and terms of any new borrowing together with a copy of any application form. Lord Nicholls stated that:

> '...it should become routine practice for banks if relying on confirmation from a solicitor for their protection to send to the solicitor the necessary financial information'.

Expertise

The solicitor must be satisfied that he or she has the necessary expertise to interpret or advise on the detailed financial information.

Advice

The solicitor must explain to the client the purpose for which the solicitor has become involved and that the bank, should it ever become necessary, will rely upon the solicitor's involvement to counter any suggestion that the client did not properly understand the implications of the transaction (para 64). After explaining the documents, it is the client's rather than the solicitor's decision as to whether or not to proceed.

Core Minimum Requirements

Lord Nicholls summarised at paragraph 65 of the judgment the core minimum requirements for advice which typically will include:

- the nature of the documents and the risk that the client will lose the home if the borrower's business does not prosper, and even the possibility that the client could be made bankrupt;

- the seriousness of the risks involved by reference to the purpose, amount and terms of the new facility and whether the client understands the value of the property being charged and if there are any other assets out of which repayment could be made if the business fails;

- the fact that the lender may alter the terms of the loan including increasing the amount borrowed without reference to the client;

- asking whether the client is content for the solicitor to write to the bank confirming that the solicitor has explained the nature of the documents to the client and the practical implications they may have;

- discussing whether the client wishes the solicitor to negotiate with the bank on the terms of the transaction (e.g. limitation on the amount borrowed);

- providing the advice at a face to face meeting in the absence of the borrower and giving the advice using non-technical language;

- explaining that the client does have a choice on whether to sign the charge/guarantee or to consent to mortgage with the decision being up to the client alone.

However, it must be appreciated that additional requirements may become appropriate depending on the specific facts of the case. It should be appreciated by the solicitor that 'the solicitor's task is an important one. It is not a formality' (Lord Nicholls, para 65). To comply properly with the House of Lord's judgment guidance is likely to take several chargeable hours.

Confirmation

The advice given should be recorded in a full attendance note and confirmed in detail in writing in a letter sent promptly after the meeting. A draft letter is available on the Law Society website [and is reproduced in Appendix V.11].

Summary

All conveyancing solicitors should be certain that before advising on third party charges:

(1)   they have the necessary expertise.

(2)   there is no conflict.

(3)   there is no suspicion of undue influence or impropriety.

(4)   the bank provides full financial information.

(5)   the advice covers, at the very least, the core minimum requirements.

(6)   the advice is confirmed in writing.

In addition the solicitor should check if the firm's indemnity insurers have any additional requirements or have issued any guidance.

Finally it is up to the solicitor to exercise his or her skill and judgement in each individual case to decide whether to act. A solicitor who is acting for the borrower should not agree to advise the third party if there is a real possibility that the advice would be that the third party should not execute the charge/guarantee or consent to mortgage.

IV.9. Anti-money laundering guidance for solicitors undertaking property work[1]

Introduction

1.   Solicitors conducting conveyancing are at risk of money laundering because property transactions can involve any stage of the money laundering process, see paragraph 1.13 of the Guidance. As the property itself can be 'criminal property' for the purposes of POCA, solicitors can still be involved in money laundering even if no money changes hands, see paragraph 3 below.

2.   Conveyancing transactions can be attractive to money launderers who are trying to disguise the audit trail of the proceeds of their crimes. However, a criminal may also want to buy a property simply to live in themselves. This would also involve an offence or offences of money laundering under the wide definition in section 340(11) of POCA. Solicitors who defend clients charged with criminal offences should be particularly alert to the danger of money laundering if their firms also undertake property work.

3.   Solicitors should also be aware that information about tax evasion or welfare benefit fraud may come to light in conveyancing matters. The notional proceeds of tax evasion, that is an amount of money equal to the saving in tax, are 'criminal property' under section 340(3) and (6). Although the law on notional criminal property is unclear and it is uncertain how such property can be identified, solicitors are advised to act cautiously and treat assets, including bank balances, acquired in whole or in part after the date of any obtaining of a pecuniary advantage by tax evasion, as being or including criminal property. Depending on the date when notional property is obtained through tax evasion, real property may be regarded as 'criminal property' either at the time of the purchase or later if mortgage payments in respect of that property are made from a bank account that should be treated as itself being or including criminal property. Any subsequent sale of the property for the 'suspected party' would amount to money laundering. In such cases, the client may not even realise that their conveyancing instructions amount to money laundering. Solicitors should remain alert to situations of this kind and should speak to their client and, if appropriate, should make a money laundering report, see paragraph 31 onwards below.

4.   Conveyancers should be alert to instructions which are a deliberate attempt to avoid assets being dealt with in the way intended by a court, or through the usual legal process, for example solicitors may sometimes suspect that instructions are being given to avoid the property forming part of a bankruptcy, or forming part of assets subject to confiscation. Although money laundering reports may not necessarily arise, in such circumstances solicitors should consider their duties in conduct, in particular Principle 12.02 which prevents solicitors acting if instructions would involve the solicitor in a breach of the law or a breach of the principles of professional conduct.

---

1. © The Law Society. Prepared by the Money Laundering Task Force and Conveyancing and Land Law Committee on 22 December 2005.

5.   The case of *Bowman* v. *Fels* (2005) EWCA Civ 226 has drastically altered how conveyancers should deal with knowledge or suspicion of money laundering which they form in the course of their work, especially how they should balance their duties to inform clients with the reporting obligations under POCA. This has in turn affected solicitors' duties to their Lender clients. This recent change centres upon the increased importance of legal professional privilege, and an increased reliance on the defence to the tipping off offences which applies to professional legal advisers.

Money Laundering Regulations 2003

6.   Conveyancing, and indeed any legal work connected to 'real property', is 'relevant business' for the purposes of the ML Regulations (2003) ('the Regulations'). The Regulations require the appointment of a Nominated Officer (Money Laundering Reporting Officer, MLRO), training of relevant employees, record-keeping, and client identification, see paragraph 3.16 of the Guidance. Chapter 3 of the Guidance provides guidance on methods of compliance with the Regulations, including how to identify clients who solicitors don't meet in person, see paragraphs 3.91–3.94 and paragraph 15 below.

Note:

The Regulations came into force for solicitors on 1 March 2004. If a solicitor formed a 'business relationship' with a client before that date there will not usually be a need to identify the client, however solicitors are advised to exercise caution and check clients' identity if they have not undertaken any work for the client for some time.

7.   Identification checks should be undertaken 'as soon as reasonably practicable' after contact is first made between solicitors and their clients, see paragraph 3.29 of the Guidance. Given the money laundering risk posed by conveyancing, and the speed of some transactions, it may be preferable to make the necessary checks prior to starting work, and usually before accepting any money. In most cases the person or entity who needs to be identified will be the solicitors' own client, but in some circumstances solicitors will consider Regulation 4(3)(d) and identify parties providing funding, see note to paragraph 18 below and Money Laundering Regulations 4 and 5.

Note:

Solicitors may be asked by others subject to the Regulations and involved in the transaction, to confirm they have undertaken identity checks, e.g. house building companies acting as Estate Agents regularly ask solicitors acting for purchasers to provide such confirmation. Solicitors are advised to ensure that if they provide information they do not accept liability for the compliance with the Regulations by others.

8.   Commonly solicitors who undertake conveyancing also act for a Lender. However, the Lender client will usually not need to be identified if the exception from the identification requirement in Regulation 5(2) applies, see paragraph 3.42 of the Guidance and Money Laundering Regulations 4 and 5.

Note:

In some circumstances, solicitors conducting fixed fee conveyancing may not fall within the definition of 'business relationship' in Regulation 2(2) because the total amount of any payments may be capable of being ascertained at the outset, see paragraph 3.33 of the Guidance. However, even if fixed fee conveyancing is defined as 'one off', the client identification requirement will still apply unless the transaction involves less than approximately 15,000 Euro in total, see paragraph 3.44 of the Guidance.

9.   In addition to the identification checks required under Regulation 4, Regulation 3 requires 'systems' to prevent money laundering. For conveyancers compliance with this Regulation is likely to be achieved if the solicitor is reasonably comfortable about what they are being asked to do by the client and why. Some firms will choose to ask all clients for some basic information before accepting instructions, but this is not an absolute requirement and other firms will take a different approach. The important point is that higher risk transactions are identified and acted upon. Usually the most effective way of ensuring this is a sufficient level of training and awareness amongst staff, ongoing supervision by the MLRO, and detailed record-keeping about additional questions posed and responses received in particular cases.

10.   Chapter 6 of the Guidance encourages solicitors to take a risk based approach which should avoid solicitors wasting resources on low risk matters and allow greater focus of resources on higher risk transactions. Higher risk work may require broader checks to be made beyond basic identification, the extent of which will depend upon the level of risk. However, conveyancing instructions automatically include obtaining significant information about both the client and the proposed transaction, especially if instructions are also received from a Lender. For example, a solicitor conducting conveyancing is already likely to know about their client's occupation, especially if they also act for the Lender. This information will help the solicitor judge whether the amount of private funding available to the client makes sense, or whether they need to ask more questions. All information which is already available should be considered before other enquiries are made, especially as this will avoid repetition and enable the solicitor to determine what additional questions to ask. If additional enquiries are to be made it is usually helpful to consider whether there are any reasons for concern about the provenance of funds used either in the original purchase of a property about to be sold, and/or to be used in a current property purchase, i.e. is there any reason to know or suspect that those funds could constitute 'criminal property'.

11.   Solicitors should consider whether it is preferable to collect in all of the money needed for the purchase before exchange of contracts takes place to avoid unexpected matters arising at a later stage when they can be much more difficult to deal with. This method is likely to be of most use if a solicitor is uncertain about the information they have been given by a client including what the client has said about where the monies are coming from.

12.   Solicitors acting for purchasers will usually make sufficient checks about their client, and transfer the funds to the seller's solicitors. In effect, the purchaser's solicitors act as a filter, which gives the seller's solicitors additional comfort. For this reason solicitors acting for sellers should try and avoid accepting money direct from the purchaser if possible, although in some instances this will be unavoidable, e.g. if the purchaser is unrepresented.

Warning signs

13.   Both sales and purchases of domestic, commercial, and agricultural property can have money laundering implications under POCA, and so solicitors conducting such transactions need to remain alert. Solicitors should take care not to be deterred from making the necessary checks because instructions are given urgently as this may be a tactic designed to draw the focus away from making the necessary checks.

14.   Attention should also be paid to the Law Society's green warning card, Property Fraud II (see Annex 15 of the Guidance), the blue warning card (see Annex 5 of the Guidance) , and paragraphs 6.14–6.34 of the Guidance. The additional comments below may also be of assistance to conveyancers specifically.

15.   Many conveyancers receive instructions from clients whom they never meet and who may live and/or work a considerable distance away from their solicitor, perhaps because the client is

introduced by an intermediary or because of online conveyancing. The anti-money laundering requirements are not intended to restrict the development of innovative business practices. However, where solicitors do not meet their clients, they should consider how they check their client's identity and minimise any increased risk of money laundering. If an intermediary is involved they may be able to provide information which could allay concerns. Regulation 4(3)(b) also refers to the need to take into account the greater potential for money laundering which arises when the client is not physically present when being identified.

Ownership issues

16.   In the absence of any logical explanation properties owned by nominee companies, multiple owners may be used as sophisticated money laundering vehicles designed to disguise the true owner and/or confuse the audit trail. Solicitors also need to be alert to quick or unexplained changes in ownership.

17.   For example, a solicitor may know or suspect that a third party is providing the funding for a purchase, but that the property is being registered in somebody else's name. There may be legitimate reasons for this, such as a family arrangement, but it is important that solicitors are alert to the possibility that they are being misled about the true ownership and consider Regulation 4(3)(d).

Methods of funding

18.   Many properties are bought with a combination of deposit, mortgage, and/or equity from a current property. Usually solicitors will have information about how their clients intend to fund the transaction, and will expect to be updated if those details change, e.g. if a mortgage offer falls through and new funding is obtained. Obtaining this information will help firms with their risk assessment, and decision whether they need to know more. As well as assisting with anti-money laundering procedures, this information may prevent difficulties linking payments received into client account with particular clients.

> *Note:*
>
> *Third parties often assist others with purchases, e.g. relatives of a first time buyer. Solicitors may be asked to receive funds direct from those third parties. Whether, and to what extent, any checks need to be undertaken in relation to the third parties will be a matter of judgement for the solicitor dependent upon the level of risk and whether there are suspicions that in fact the client is not the true owner, Regulation 4(3)(d). Relevant risk factors may be what is known about the actual client and/or the third party – including the relationship between them, the proportion of the funding being provided by the third party, and whether any warning signs are apparent. In some circumstances identification checks of the third parties, and/or information about provenance of funds they are providing, should be obtained. Solicitors should also consider their obligations to Lenders in these circumstances as there is generally a requirement to advise Lenders if the purchasers are not funding the balance of the price from their own resources.*

Cash payments

19.   Most commonly purchase funds are made up of some private funding, with the majority of the purchase price being provided by way of a mortgage. Transactions are likely to be a higher risk if they do not involve mortgages. However, concerns over such transactions may be allayed by the solicitor simply asking the client for an explanation, and assessing whether in their view the explanation is valid, e.g. money received from an inheritance, or from the sale of another property. In such higher risk situations it may be prudent for the solicitor to ask some questions about the

provenance of the private funding. 'Provenance' is not limited to the whereabouts of the monies, but goes beyond that to how the client has come by the money. However, solicitors are not required to become detectives, but to prevent money laundering.

20.   Payments made through the mainstream banking system are not guaranteed to be of clean 'provenance', although the fact that a client has successfully opened and maintained an account with a mainstream financial institution may be one of the factors solicitors take into consideration in their risk assessment. If payments may be made from an individual's personal funds, or collected from a number of individuals or other sources, solicitors should consider whether they would feel more comfortable proceeding only after asking some questions about where the money has come from and also consider Regulation 4(3)(d). For example, large amounts of money provided by clients who only have relatively low incomes may be a cause to ask more questions. It is good practice to make a file note both of the questions posed and the responses received. However, if there are concerns about money laundering the circulation of these notes will need to be carefully managed, e.g. not provided to clients if they ask for their files.

21.   Large payments made in actual cash can also give rise to money laundering suspicions. Firms can avoid this difficulty by having a clear office policy on not accepting cash at the office or direct into their bank account, see paragraph 6.2 of the Guidance. However, clients may attempt to circumvent such a policy, and avoid paying a bank fee, by depositing cash direct into the solicitor's client account at a branch of the solicitor's bank. If possible solicitors should try and avoid this by controlling the manner and circumstance of the disclosure of their client account details, and when doing so making it clear that an electronic method of transfer of the funds is expected. Having said that, it is accepted that account details are readily available on client account cheques. Solicitors may also wish to arrange with their bank that such cash deposits should never be accepted by the bank. Ultimately if a cash deposit is received solicitors will have to consider what they know about their clients and the overall circumstances to assess whether or not they are suspicious of money laundering.

22.   Solicitors may form knowledge or suspicion that cash has changed hands directly between a seller and purchaser, e.g. where money has changed hands at a rural auction. If a solicitor is openly informed about this payment, they may be requested to bank the cash payment into their client account. This places the solicitor in a difficult position as the source of the cash is not their own client, which can make checking more difficult. The auction house may be able to assist because of checks they must make themselves under the Regulations, but ultimately the solicitor may feel more comfortable not banking the cash into their account and would prefer their client to do so. Again, this is where a firm's cash policy can be helpful. If the solicitor is not openly informed but forms knowledge or suspicion that there has been a direct payment between a seller and purchaser's solicitors, the solicitor will need to consider whether there is any reason for concern, or whether the documentation will include the true purchase price, so that there are no concerns about tax evasion, see paragraph 30 below.

23.   On the other hand solicitors may feel that, although their instructions are that money has changed hands directly, in fact it has not done so. The motivation for such a misrepresentation could be to encourage a mortgage Lender to lend more than they would ordinarily do so, because they are under the impression that private funds will also be put into the purchase when in fact this is not the case. Solicitors in this situation who act for the Lender need to consider their duties to their Lender, see paragraph 24 onwards below.

Lender issues

24.   Solicitors may form knowledge or suspicion that a lay client is attempting to mislead a Lender client to improperly inflate a mortgage advance, e.g. misrepresentations about the potential

borrower's income, or that a seller and purchaser are conspiring to overstate a sale price, see paragraph 25 below. Transactions which are not 'arm's length' may warrant particularly close consideration, see paragraph 4 above. However, until the improperly obtained mortgage advance is received there will not be any 'criminal property' for the purposes of reporting obligations under POCA.

25.   Where a solicitor acting for purchaser suspects that their client may be making a misrepresentation to a mortgage they must either dissuade their client from doing so, or terminate their retainer. Even if the solicitor no longer acts in these circumstances they may still be under a duty to advise the mortgage company.

> *Note:*
>
> *Although principles of client confidentiality would usually mean that the lay client would need to waive their confidentiality before the mortgage company could be informed, in these circumstances because there was not a valid retainer because of the crime/fraud exception, which means that the solicitor can tell the mortgage company without their client's permission. If knowledge or suspicion is formed during the course of the retainer with the mortgage company the solicitor will have a duty to advise the Lender because the information is relevant to the Lender's decision to make the loan.*

26.   If knowledge or suspicion is formed that a mortgage advance has already been improperly obtained a solicitor may advise the mortgage Lender that they were misled. In fact if a solicitor is acting in a remortgage and forms knowledge or suspicion about a previous mortgage there may be a duty to advise the Lender, especially if the remortgage is with the same Lender. It may also be necessary to consider reporting to NCIS as there is 'criminal property', namely the improperly obtained mortgage advance. If the client has purposefully decided to make a misrepresentation on their mortgage application it is likely that the crime/fraud exception to legal professional privilege would apply, meaning that no waiver to confidentiality will be needed before a report is made, but solicitors will need to consider matters on a case by case basis, and if necessary seek guidance from Professional Ethics or take independent legal advice.

27.   Naturally solicitors will be concerned about whether speaking to their Lender client conflicts with the tipping off offences. A key element of these offences is likelihood of prejudicing an investigation, and this may be a small risk when making disclosures to reputable Lenders. Also if the Lender is the solicitor's client the exception in s.333(3)(a) and s.342(4)(a) may apply, relating to professional legal advisers giving advice to their clients, see paragraph 2.61 of the Guidance, and the guidance about the case of *Bowman* v. *Fels.*

Unusual instructions

28.   It may be important to know why instructions have been received. Asking for that information may help deter potential money launderers.

29.   Transactions which abort without good apparent cause and/or which lead a solicitor to be unexpectedly asked to transfer funds back to their source, may be suspicious. Firms may wish to have a policy on only sending money back to clients, or to the original source. Such a policy also avoids a breach of Rule 15 of the Solicitors' Accounts Rules (note (ix)), see paragraph 6.24 of the Guidance and Money Laundering Regulations 4 and 5.

Tax issues

30.   Tax evasion of any type, by whatever means, whether committed by a client or the other party to a transaction, can lead to a solicitor committing a section 328 arrangements offence, see paragraph 2.17 of the Guidance. Abuse of the new Stamp Duty Land Tax procedure may also give rise to money laundering implications, e.g. through misleading apportionment of the purchase price. If a client gives a solicitor instructions which offend the Stamp Duty Land Tax procedure the solicitor must consider their position under Principle 12.02. If a solicitor discovers the evasion after it has occurred they may have a reporting obligation, see paragraph 31 onwards below.

Reporting issues

31.   If a solicitor continues to act in a conveyancing matter which has a money laundering element, this may amount to the commission of a section 328 arrangements offence, see paragraph 2.17 of the Guidance. However a defence is available if a report is made and 'appropriate consent' obtained, see paragraph 2.23 of the Guidance.

32.   The recent case of *Bowman* v. *Fels* has drastically altered how conveyancers should approach this area and careful attention should be paid to the full Law Society guidance about the implications of this case. Essentially, if a conveyancer forms knowledge or suspicion of money laundering he should first consider whether the information on which that knowledge or suspicion is based was received in legally privileged circumstances; if it was, he cannot make a report to NCIS without the client's authority. In *Three Rivers District Council and others* v. *Governor and Company of the Bank of England* (2004) UKHL 48 at 111 common law privilege was described as covering 'all communications between a solicitor and his client relating to a transaction in which the solicitor has been instructed for the purpose of obtaining legal advice... notwithstanding that they do not contain advice on matters of law and construction, provided that they are directly related to the performance by the solicitor of his professional duty as legal adviser of his client.' Communications to which the crime/fraud exception applies will not be covered by legal professional privilege and conveyancers must be particularly careful in this regard, see paragraphs 5.11 and 5.12 of the *Bowman* v. *Fels* guidance.

33.   Section 6 of the *Bowman* v. *Fels* guidance covers the exception to the tipping off offences for professional legal advisers. Solicitors who cannot make reports because of legal professional privilege need to consider whether they would prefer not to act, or use this exception to speak to clients about reporting. Weighing up the options can be very difficult, and will need to be approached by MLROs on a case by case basis, although Professional Ethics can help. (The Professional Ethics helpline telephone number is **0870 606 2577**.)

34.   Solicitors conducting conveyancing transaction often feel they could benefit from speaking to the solicitor acting for the other side in a transaction. The exceptions to the tipping off offences applies to communications with clients, which may either be the lay client or Lender client. The exceptions also apply to disclosures made to 'any person in connection with the giving by the adviser of legal advice to the client', see paragraphs 5.6–5.10 of the *Bowman* v. *Fels* guidance. In any event a key element of the tipping off offences is 'likely to prejudice an investigation', and it may be unlikely that speaking to another solicitor who is also under a duty not to tip off would fulfil this test.

35.   In urgent cases where appropriate consent is required faster than the usual statutory timetable, perhaps because suspicions are formed when a transaction is at an advanced stage and a Notice to Complete has been received the NCIS fast track procedure may be used, see paragraphs 7.18–7.21 of the Guidance. Reliance cannot be placed on others already having made a report. However, a key advantage achieved by the judgment is that a solicitor who makes a report would be able to continue

work on the transaction short of transferring funds or taking some other irrevocable step without committing a section 328 offence, see section 3 of the *Bowman* v. *Fels* guidance, especially paragraph 3.3. However, for other professional reasons solicitors who report pre-exchange should not exchange until 'appropriate consent' has been received.

In case of difficulties solicitors are advised to call the Professional Ethics helpline: 0870 606 2577

Money Laundering Task Force
Conveyancing and Land Law Committee

IV.10. Statement of demands and needs when arranging/ recommending contracts of insurance – a compliance checklist[1]

Solicitors who arrange and/or recommend contracts of insurance for a client must comply with the Solicitors' Financial Services (Conduct of Business) Rules 2001 and provide their client with a statement of demands and needs in most cases. This guidance contains information about when a statement of demands and needs must be prepared and what ought to be in it.

1   When is it necessary to provide a statement of demands and needs?

Where a firm recommends that a client enters into a particular insurance contract, or arranges such a contract for the client, it must provide the client with a written demands and needs statement. This is to comply with Appendix 1 to the Solicitors' Financial Services (Conduct of Business) Rules 2001.

2   Are there any circumstances in which a statement of demands and needs is not needed?

A statement of demands and needs is not needed in the following circumstances:

- where the firm acts on the renewal or amendment of a contract of insurance if the information given to the client in relation to the original contract is still accurate;

- where the firm does no more than introduce the client to an authorised person and takes no further part in arranging the contract of insurance

- where the firm is acting for a commercial client and the insurance is for large risks as specified in paragraph 4 of Appendix 1.

3   At what point in the transaction must the statement be given?

The statement must be given before the contract is finalised except in the following circumstances:

- where the information is provided orally at the client's request;

- where immediate cover is required;

- where the contract is concluded by telephone.

The information must, however, be provided to the client in writing immediately after the conclusion of the contract of insurance.

---

1. © The Law Society. This guidance was issued by Professional Ethics in March 2006.

4   What are the requirements if the firm arranges a contract of insurance on an execution-only basis?

This requires a more limited statement; the document need only identify the contract of insurance requested by the client, confirm that no advice has been given, and state that the firm is undertaking the arrangement at the client's specific request.

5   Has the Law Society produced precedent statements for use by solicitors?

The Law Society has not produced precedent documents. This is because the statement must be tailored to the needs of the individual client and reflect the complexity of the insurance contract being proposed.

There is no prescribed wording which must be used. However, the checklist below may assist practitioners to identify the information which ought to appear in the statement:

	Question	*Yes*	*No*
1	Does the statement identify why the client needs the particular type of insurance contract?		
2	Has the client identified any existing policy which may be of use? (e.g. does the client have any existing home contents policy which may include legal expenses insurance)		
3	Does the statement include an explanation about what the client needs to disclose to the insurance provider?		
4	Does the statement include an assessment by the firm as to whether the level of cover is sufficient for the risks which the client wishes to insure?		
5	Does the statement identify and include an assessment of the relevance of any exclusions, excesses, limitations or conditions?		
6	If the firm has recommended the policy, does the statement include an explanation for the firm recommending that particular insurance contract?		

IV.11. Mortgages, insurance, the FSA and solicitors[1]

Practitioners will be aware that the Financial Services Authority (FSA) is the single statutory regulator of financial services in the UK. Under the Financial Services and Markets Act 2000 (the FSMA), firms which carry on regulated activities must be regulated by the FSA.

Part XX of the FSMA makes provision for professional firms which do not carry on mainstream regulated activities but which may carry on regulated activities in the course of the professional services which they provide to their clients. For example, Part XX enables solicitors which meet certain conditions to be treated as exempt professional firms and to carry on exempt regulated activities. These firms do not need to be authorised by the FSA but are able to carry on exempt regulated activities under the supervision of and regulation by the Law Society which is a Designated Professional Body (DPB).

As a DPB, the Law Society is required to make rules governing the carrying on of regulated activities by its members. The Solicitors' Financial Services (Scope) Rules 2001 (Scope Rules) set out the scope of the activities which may be undertaken by firms under the Part XX exemption. A firm which cannot fulfil the requirements of Part XX and wishes to conduct regulated activities must be authorised by the FSA. In addition, the Solicitors' Financial Services (Conduct of Business) Rules (the COB Rules) regulate the way in which these firms carry on exempt regulated activities.

The FSA has expanded its regulatory regime to mortgages and general insurance contracts. Regulation of mortgages and long-term care insurance contracts began on **31 October 2004** and general insurance contracts began on **14 January 2005**.

The Law Society has amended its rules to take account of the new activities. Without these amendments firms would not have been able to carry on these activities after the commencement dates without being directly authorised by the FSA. The Solicitors' Financial Services (Insurance and Mortgages) Amendment Rules 2004 were made on 8 June 2004. They amend the Scope Rules and the COB Rules.

Mortgages

Since 31 October 2004, the FSA has regulated activities relating to regulated mortgage contracts. These are contracts which meet the following conditions at the time they are entered into:

- the borrower is an individual or a trustee;

- the lender takes a first legal charge over property in the UK; and

- at least 40% of the property is, or is intended to be, occupied by the borrower (or, where trustees are the borrower, by an individual who is a beneficiary of the trust) or a member of his immediate family.

The scope of the activities available to firms operating under the DPB regime (assuming that they can satisfy the basic conditions in the Scope Rules) are:

- arranging a regulated mortgage contract/making arrangements with a view to a person entering into a regulated mortgage contract;

1. © The Law Society. This guidance was issued in March 2006.

- advising on a regulated mortgage contract, but not recommending a client to enter into a regulated mortgage contract except where that advice consists of an endorsement of a recommendation given to the client by an authorised person;

- advising on varying a RMC *except* where the advice relates to varying the terms of a contract entered into before 31 October 2004 and the variation to the old contract is so fundamental that it amounts to recommending a client to enter into a new RMC *or* where the advice relates to varying the terms of a RMC entered into by the client on or after 31 October 2004 in such a way as to vary the client's obligations under the RMC.

- entering into and/or administering a regulated mortgage contract *but only where* the firm acts as a trustee or personal representative, provided that the borrower is a beneficiary under the trust, will or intestacy; and

- agreeing to carry on any of the above activities.

The Scope Rules have been amended to reflect the regulation of regulated mortgage contracts as follows:

- rule 3(l) has been added to prohibit an exempt professional firm from entering into a regulated mortgage contract as lender unless this is in the firm's capacity as a trustee or personal representative and the borrower is a beneficiary under the trust, will or intestacy; and

- rule 5(7) has also been added to attach a restriction on the making of a recommendation to a client to enter into a particular mortgage contract. A firm must not recommend a client to enter as borrower into a regulated mortgage contract but can endorse a recommendation given by an authorised person with permission to advise on regulated mortgage contracts or an exempt person in relation to the giving of such advice; and

- the definition of regulated mortgage contract has been included in rule 8.

Insurance mediation

The other area into which the regulatory regime has extended is general insurance contracts. Regulation of long-term care insurance contracts began on 31 October 2004 and general contracts of insurance began on 14 January 2005.

The extension of the regulatory regime has a significant impact on solicitors as most contracts of insurance are now regulated. Solicitors have dealings with a variety of insurance contracts in the course of practice; after the event insurance in litigation, restrictive covenant and defective title indemnity and life policies in conveyancing, long-term care insurance with elderly clients and missing beneficiary indemnity in probate matters, etc.

The regulated activities will be known as insurance mediation activities. The term 'mediation' has caused confusion for many practitioners. It is used in connection with the regulated activities carried on in respect of contracts of insurance.

Firms working from within the DPB regime are able to carry on the following insurance mediation activities provided that they can satisfy the basic conditions in the Scope Rules:

- dealing as agent in contracts of insurance;

- arranging/making arrangements with a view to a person entering into a contract of insurance;

- assisting in the administration and performance of contracts of insurance;

- advising on the merits of buying or selling a contract of insurance (other than the buying of a life policy or other investment based contract of insurance);

- agreeing to carry on any of the above activities.

The Scope Rules have been amended to reflect the extension of regulation to contracts of insurance as follows:

- rule 5(6) has been added to make it a requirement that any firm carrying on insurance mediation activities must be registered in the FSA Register and must appoint a compliance officer;

- insurance mediation activity, FSA Register and compliance officer and other defined terms have been included in rule 8.

All firms carrying on insurance mediation activities (whether they are authorised by the FSA or not) must be included in the FSA Register and appoint a compliance officer. Firms should satisfy themselves that they are on the FSA Register before they carry on any insurance mediation activities. They can inspect the FSA Register on the FSA's website (**www.fsa.gov.uk**) where their details should appear on the EPF (exempt professional firms) Register unless they are authorised directly by the FSA. If firms are not registered, and they intend to carry on insurance mediation activities, they must submit their details (including the name of their compliance officer) to the Law Society's Customer Applications Team (**www.customerapplications@lawsociety.org.uk**) for onward transmission to the FSA.

The COB Rules apply to all firms within the DPB regime and regulate the way in which they carry on exempt regulated activities. Amendments to these rules have been necessary because of the extension of regulation to contracts of insurance, as follows:

- rule 3 (status disclosure) has been amended. When firms carry on an insurance mediation activity, the fact that they are included on the FSA Register does not mean that the firm is authorised by the FSA. The FSA requires such firms to include a standard statement to this effect in its status disclosure information. The agreed form of wording has been included at rule 3(3);

- rule 8A and appendix 1 have been inserted so that there are the following requirements on firms where they carry on insurance mediation activities from within the DPB regime. They must:

    (1) take reasonable steps to communicate information to their clients in a way that is clear, fair and not misleading, including the need to relay information about whether or not they have given advice on the basis of a fair analysis of the market; and

    (2) before they recommend a contract of insurance (although note that firms operating under the DPB regime are prohibited from recommending that their clients buy a particular life policy), consider their client's demands and needs and provide a written demands and needs statement; but

    (3) in specific circumstances the written demands and needs statement can be delayed until after the conclusion of the contract or not provided at all;

    (4) paragraph 5 of appendix 1 implements passporting rights and allows firms on the FSA Register to exercise these rights in another EEA State.

The amended rules and detailed guidance on the changes is available online at **www.lawsociety. org.uk** (please search under 'financial services').

IV.12. Mortgages and life policies[1]

1.   Life policies and certain mortgage contracts are investments which are regulated by the Financial Services Authority (FSA).

2.   Under the Financial Services and Markets Act 2000 (FSMA), firms carrying on regulated activities, as defined by the Financial Services and Markets Act 2000 (Regulated Activities) Order 2001 (RAO), need to be regulated by the FSA. However, Part XX of FSMA makes special provision for professional firms which do not carry on mainstream investment business but which may carry on regulated activities in the course of other work such as conveyancing services. Part XX enables firms of solicitors which meet certain conditions to be treated as exempt professional firms and to carry on activities known as exempt regulated activities. These firms do not need to be regulated by the FSA but are able to carry on exempt regulated activities under the supervision of and regulation by the Law Society which is a Designated Professional Body (DPB). As a DPB the Law Society has made the Solicitors' Financial Services (Scope) Rules 2001 (the Scope Rules) which govern the carrying on of regulated activities by its members.

3.   Solicitors who are working from within the DPB regime can carry on the following regulated activities (usually referred to as insurance mediation activities), in respect of life policies provided that they can comply with the Scope Rules:

*   deal as an agent in the buying or selling of the life policy;

*   make arrangements with a view to a person entering into a life policy;

*   assist in the administration and performance of the life policy;

*   advising on the merits of buying and selling (but not recommending a client to buy a life policy);

*   agreeing to carry on any of the above activities.

4.   Solicitors within the DPB regime cannot recommend that their client buys a particular life policy. However, the solicitor can explain the transaction to the client and give advice provided that the advice does not amount to a recommendation to enter into the transaction; give negative advice (i.e. advise the client not to buy the life policy); obtain advice from and/or endorse a recommendation given by an authorised or exempt person.

5.   Where clients may need life insurance, solicitors should introduce the client to an independent intermediary who is authorised by the FSA. See rule 12 of the Solicitors' Practice Rules 1990 and also section 4 of the Solicitors' Introduction and Referral Code 1990.

6.   Solicitors will need to consider their duty to act in the best interests of their client. For example, where the independent intermediary has persuaded the client to enter into an obviously inappropriate contract, then whilst there is no duty to re-advise, or to offer investment advice, there may be a general duty in relation to the conveyancing retainer to give advice on the legal implications of the recommendation. See *The Guide to the Professional Conduct of Solicitors 1999*, chapter 25, 25.10 note 5.

---

1. . © Law Society 2005. This guidance was issued by Professional Ethics in May 2005. It contains references to Solicitors' Practice Rules 1990 and associated codes, which have now been repealed.

7.   Since 31 October 2004, regulated mortgage contracts (RMCs) have been investments regulated by the FSA. This is defined in the RAO as a contract which, at the time it is entered into, satisfies the following conditions:

- the lender provides credit to an individual or trustees (the 'borrower'); and

- it is secured by a first legal mortgage on land which is in the United Kingdom; and

- at least 40% of the land is, or is to be, used as a dwelling by the borrower or, where the borrower is a trustee, by a beneficiary of the trust, or by a related person.

8.   Solicitors who rely on the DPB regime can carry on the following regulated activities provided that they can comply with the basic conditions in the Scope Rules:

- arrange RMCs or make arrangements for a person to vary the terms of a RMC;

- make arrangements with a view to a person entering into a RMC;

- advise a client on entering into or varying a RMC (but not recommend a particular RMC);

- enter into a RMC as a lender, but only in their capacity as a trustee or personal representative and where the borrower is a beneficiary under the trust or will in question;

- administer a RMC, but again only in their capacity as a trustee or personal representative and where the borrower is a beneficiary under the trust or will in question;

- agreeing to carry on any of the above.

9.   This means that solicitors are no longer able to secure bridging finance, loans to clients etc by way of first legal charge over their client's residential property unless it is in the circumstances described above (and they are able to comply with the Scope Rules) or unless they are authorised by the FSA.

10.   Under the DPB Rules, solicitors cannot recommend a client to enter as borrower into a particular RMC but they can explain the RMC to the client and give advice (provided that the advice does not amount to a recommendation); obtain advice from and/or endorse a recommendation given by an authorised person; give negative advice; and give advice on varying a RMC. This is except where that advice relates to varying the terms of a contract entered into before 31 October 2004 and the variation is so fundamental that it amounts to recommending that a client enters into a new RMC or where the advice relates to varying the terms of a RMC entered into by the client on or after 31 October 2004 in such a way as to vary the client's obligations under the RMC.

11.   If the best interests of the client requires it, a solicitor may refer a client requiring a mortgage to a tied agent, provided that the client is informed that the agent offers products from only one company. See rule 12 of the Solicitors' Practice Rules 1990 and section 4 of the Solicitors' Introduction and Referral Code 1990.

12.   Solicitors who act as mortgage intermediaries, i.e. who advise clients on which mortgage to apply for after reviewing a range of mortgage products, need to be authorised by the FSA. The FSA Handbook contains requirements as to financial promotions etc which mortgage intermediaries must observe. It is no longer necessary for mortgage intermediaries to register with the Mortgage Code Register of Intermediaries and to comply with the Mortgage Code. This is because the Mortgage Code was disapplied on 31 October 2004 and the Mortgage Code Compliance Board (MMCB) has ceased its regulatory operations.

13.   Mortgage based equity release schemes are regulated by the FSA. These are also known as lifetime mortgages. These are schemes where a borrower takes out a loan where repayment of the capital (and in some cases the interest) is not required until the property is sold, usually on the borrower's death. Home reversion schemes under which a property owner sells some or all of his interest in the property for a lump sum and a right to reside at the property for the rest of his life are not currently regulated by the FSA. However, the Treasury has consulted on regulating these home reversion schemes and has decided to bring forward legislation to achieve this as soon as the Parliamentary timetable allows.

14.   However, with both lifetime mortgages and home reversion schemes, there is an element of risk and, so far as they can, solicitors should dissuade clients from entering into any scheme of this kind without expert and independent advice. Reference may be made to *Using Your Home as Capital* by Cecil Hinton and Mark Goodale published by Age Concern (**www.ageconcern.org.uk**) for an account of these schemes.

15.   Solicitors who introduce clients to third parties for advice on life policies and RMCs may receive commission or other pecuniary reward from the introducer. In order to comply with the DPB regime, it will be necessary to account to their clients in accordance with rule 4(c) of the Scope Rules. This is similar to rule 10 of the Solicitors' Practice Rules 1990 but there is no *de minimus* provision and the solicitors must account for all commission however small the amount in question.

16.   Further information on life policies, RMCs and the DPB regime is contained in the information pack 'Financial Services and Solicitors' (September 2004) available from professional ethics. Further guidance is available on the Law Society's website (**www.lawsociety.org.uk**) and from the FSA (**www.fsa.gov.uk**).

IV.13. The Law Society interest rate

The Law Society interest rate is the 'contract rate' in the Standard Conditions of Sale first published in 1990. The Law Society interest rate is 4% above Barclays Bank base rate. Rates are as at close of business on the day indicated.

This information is provided for your use and it is your responsibility to check its accuracy and application. No liability is accepted to third parties.

Please note: For the current rate ring the Library Enquiry Line on 0870 606 2511. A message giving the current rate is accessible even when the Library is closed.

05 July 2007	9.75%
10 May 2007	9.50%
11 January 2007	9.25%
09 November 2006	9.00%
03 August 2006	8.75%
04 August 2005	8.50%
05 August 2004	8.75%
10 June 2004	8.50%
06 May 2004	8.25%
05 February 2004	8.00%
06 November 2003	7.75%
10 July 2003	7.50%
06 February 2003	7.75%
08 November 2001	8.00%
04 October 2001	8.50%
18 September 2001	8.75%
02 August 2001	9.00%
10 May 2001	9.25%
05 April 2001	9.50%
08 February 2001	9.75%
10 February 2000	10.00%
13 January 2000	9.75%
04 November 1999	9.50%

08 September 1999	9.25%
10 June 1999	9.00%
08 April 1999	9.25%
04 February 1999	9.50%
07 January 1999	10.00%
11 December 1998	10.25%
05 November 1998	10.75%
09 October 1998	11.25%
04 June 1998	11.50%
06 November 1997	11.25%
07 August 1997	11.00%
10 July 1997	10.75%
06 June 1997	10.50%
06 May 1997	10.25%
30 October 1996	10.00%
06 June 1996	9.75%
08 March 1996	10.00%
18 January 1996	10.25%
13 December 1995	10.50%
02 February 1995	10.75%
07 December 1994	10.25%
12 September 1994	9.75%
08 February 1994	9.25%
23 November 1993	9.50%
26 January 1993	10.00%
13 November 1992	11.00%
16 October 1992	12.00%
22 September 1992	13.00%
17 September 1992	14.00%
16 September 1992	16.00%
05 May 1992	14.00%
04 September 1991	14.50%
12 July 1991	15.00%
24 May 1991	15.50%

12 April 1991	16.00%
22 March 1991	16.50%
27 February 1991	17.00%
13 February 1991	17.50%
08 October 1990	18.00%
30 April 1990	19.00%

V. FORMS AND PRECEDENTS

V.1. Standard Business Leases (of whole and of part, registered and unregistered)

Licences

The Law Society holds the copyright in the leases and grants licences to print the documents. The printed forms are available from law stationers. However, it is intended that solicitors who wish to do so will be licensed to produce the leases on their word processors but it is on the understanding that:

1.   The format of the standard leases is adopted as closely as practicable in the form of the printed lease.

2.   No alterations or additions whatsoever are to be made to the text of the standard clauses. This means that cll 1 to 14.4 of the lease of the whole building and cll 1 to 18 of the lease of part of the building are to be reproduced without any amendment whatsoever.

3.   The lease must contain a statement that it is in the form of the Law Society Business Lease.

4.   All variations, whether being amendments or additional clauses, must be set out at the end of the document in an additional page to be attached to the lease which will deal with all alterations and variations to the standard clauses and any additional provisions required. It is essential that neither alterations nor deletions are made to the text itself.

5.   The licence to reproduce the lease does not extend to printing the lease. Local law societies will be granted a licence to print both forms of the leases on favourable terms should they wish to do so.

6.   Photocopies of the leases must not be used other than as file copies.

The Law Society business leases (whole and part of building) are set out on the following pages.

The Law Society

The Law Society Business Lease (Whole of Building) (Registered) 2006

LR1.   DATE OF LEASE _____ 20____

LR2.   TITLE NUMBER(S)

LR2.1   LANDLORD'S TITLE NUMBER(S) _____

LR2.2   OTHER TITLE NUMBERS   _____

LR3.   PARTIES TO THIS LEASE

        LANDLORD   _____

                ADDRESS _____

                _____ POSTCODE _____

                COMPANY NO. _____

        TENANT   _____

                ADDRESS _____

                _____ POSTCODE _____

                COMPANY NO. _____

        GUARANTOR   _____

                ADDRESS _____

                _____ POSTCODE _____

                COMPANY NO. _____

LR4.   PROPERTY   _____

                _____

                _____ POSTCODE _____

                In the case of a conflict between this clause and the remainder of this lease then, for the purposes of registration, this clause shall prevail.

LR5.   PRESCRIBED STATEMENTS ETC.   None

LR6.   TERM FOR WHICH THE PROPERTY IS LEASED

                From and including _____ 20____

                To and including _____ 20____

LR7.   PREMIUM   None

LR8.   PROHIBITIONS OR RESTRICTIONS ON DISPOSING OF THIS LEASE

                This lease contains a provision that prohibits or restricts dispositions.

1   LS2 (Whole)(Reg) 2006

LR9.	RIGHTS OF ACQUISITION ETC.	
LR9.1	TENANT'S CONTRACTUAL RIGHTS TO RENEW THIS LEASE, TO ACQUIRE THE REVERSION OR ANOTHER LEASE OF THE PROPERTY, OR TO ACQUIRE AN INTEREST IN OTHER LAND	None
LR9.2	TENANT'S COVENANT TO (OR OFFER TO) SURRENDER THIS LEASE	None
LR9.3	LANDLORD'S CONTRACTUAL RIGHTS TO ACQUIRE THIS LEASE	None
LR10.	RESTRICTIVE COVENANTS GIVEN IN THIS LEASE BY THE LANDLORD IN RESPECT OF LAND OTHER THAN THE PROPERTY	None
LR11.	EASEMENTS	
LR11.1	EASEMENTS GRANTED BY THIS LEASE FOR THE BENEFIT OF THE PROPERTY	None
LR11.2	EASEMENTS GRANTED OR RESERVED BY THIS LEASE OVER THE PROPERTY FOR THE BENEFIT OF OTHER PROPERTY	None
LR12.	ESTATE RENTCHARGE BURDENING THE PROPERTY	None
LR13.	APPLICATION FOR STANDARD FORM OF RESTRICTION	None
[LR14.	DECLARATION OF TRUST WHERE THERE IS MORE THAN ONE PERSON COMPRISING THE TENANT	

The Tenant is more than one person. They are to hold the property on trust for themselves as [joint tenants] [tenants in common in equal shares]]

USE ALLOWED

_____

or any other use to which the Landlord consents (and the Landlord is not entitled to withhold that consent unreasonably)

RENT

_____ Pounds

(£_____) a year, subject to increase under clause 8 from every rent review date

FIRST PAYMENT DATE

The _____ 20 _____

MONTHLY PAYMENT DATE

The _____ day of every month

RENT REVIEW DATES

Every _____ anniversary of the start of the lease term

The Landlord lets the property to the Tenant for the lease term at the rent and on the terms in clauses 1 to 14 and in any additional clauses.

2

TENANT'S OBLIGATIONS

1 PAYMENTS

1. The Tenant is to pay the Landlord:

1.1 the rent, which is to be paid by the following instalments:

    (a) on the first payment date, a proportionate sum from that date to the next monthly payment date

    (b) on each monthly payment date, one-twelfth of the annual rent

1.2 a fair proportion (decided by a surveyor whom the Landlord nominates) of the cost of repairing, maintaining and cleaning: party walls, party structures, yards, gardens, roads, paths, gutters, drains, sewers, pipes, conduits, wires, cables and things used or shared with other property

1.3 the cost (including professional fees) of any works to the property which the Landlord does after the Tenant defaults

1.4 the costs and expenses (including professional fees) which the Landlord incurs in:

    (a) dealing with any application by the Tenant for consent or approval, whether it is given or not

    (b) preparing and serving a notice of a breach of the Tenant's obligations, under section 146 of the Law of Property Act 1925, even if forfeiture of this lease is avoided without a court order

    (c) preparing and serving schedules of dilapidations either during the lease term or recording failure to give up the property in the appropriate state of repair when this lease ends

    (d) insuring the property under this lease

1.5 interest at the Law Society's interest rate on any of the above payments when more than fourteen days overdue, to be calculated from its due date and in making payments under this clause:

    (a) nothing is to be deducted or set off

    (b) any value added tax payable is to be added

2 The Tenant is also to make the following payments, with value added tax where payable:

2.1 all periodic rates, taxes and outgoings relating to the property, including any imposed after the date of this lease (even if of a novel nature), to be paid on the due date to the appropriate authorities

2.2 the cost of the grant, renewal or continuation of any licence or registration for using the property for the use allowed, to be paid to the appropriate authority

2.3 a registration fee of £40 for each document which this lease requires the Tenant to register, to be paid to the Landlord's solicitors when presenting the document for registration

3 USE

3. The Tenant is to comply with the following requirements as to the use of the property and any part of it, and is not to authorise or allow anyone else to contravene them:

3.1 to use the property, except any residential accommodation, only for the use allowed

3.2 to use any residential accommodation only as a home for one family

3.3 not to do anything which might invalidate any insurance policy covering any part of the property or which might increase the premium

3.4 not to hold an auction in the property

3.5 not to use the property for any activities which are dangerous, offensive, noxious, illegal or immoral, or which are or may become a nuisance or annoyance to the Landlord or to the owner or occupier of any neighbouring property

3.6 not to display any signs or advertisements on the outside of the property or which are visible from outside the property unless the Landlord consents (and the Landlord is not entitled to withhold that consent unreasonably)

3.7 not to overload any part of the property

3.8 to comply with every statutory obligation authorising or regulating how the property is used, and to obtain, comply with the terms of, renew and continue any licence or registration which is required

4 ACCESS

4. The Tenant is to give the Landlord, or anyone with the Landlord's written authority, access to the property:

4.1 for these purposes:

    (a) inspecting the condition of the property, or how it is being used

    (b) doing works which the Landlord is permitted to do under clause 5.7

    (c) complying with any statutory obligation

    (d) viewing the property as a prospective buyer, tenant or mortgagee

    (e) valuing the property

    (f) inspecting, cleaning or repairing neighbouring property, or any sewers, drains, pipes, wires or cables serving the property or any neighbouring property

4.2 and only on seven days' written notice except in an emergency

4.3 and during normal business hours except in an emergency

4.4 and the Landlord is promptly to make good all damage caused to the property and any goods there in exercising these rights

5 CONDITION AND WORK

5. The Tenant is to comply with the following duties in relation to the property:

5.1 to maintain the state and condition of the property, but the Tenant need not alter or improve it except as required in clause 5.6

5.2 to decorate the inside and outside of the property:

    (a) in every fifth year of the lease term

    (b) in the last three months of the lease term (however it ends) except to the extent that it has been decorated in the previous year

and on each occasion the Tenant is to use the colours and the types of finish used previously

5.3 not to make any structural alterations, external alterations or additions to the property

5.4 not to make any other alterations unless the Landlord gives written consent in advance (and the Landlord is not entitled to withhold that consent unreasonably)

5.5 to keep any plate glass in the property insured for its full replacement cost with reputable insurers, to give the Landlord details of that insurance on request, and to replace any plate glass which becomes damaged

5.6 to do any work to the property required under a statute even if it alters or improves the property. The work is to be done on the following conditions:

    (a) before doing it, the Tenant is to obtain the Landlord's written consent (and the Landlord is not entitled to withhold that consent unreasonably)

    (b) the Landlord is to contribute a fair proportion of the cost, taking into account any value of the work to the Landlord

and any dispute is to be decided by arbitration under clause 14.3

5.7 if the Tenant fails to do any work which this lease requires and the Landlord gives the Tenant written notice to do it, to do that work. In such a case, the Tenant is to start the work within two months, or immediately in case of emergency, and proceed diligently with it. In default, the Tenant is to permit the Landlord to do the work.

5.8   However, this clause only requires the Tenant to make good damage caused by an insured risk to the extent that the insurance money has not been paid because of any act or default of the Tenant

6   TRANSFER ETC.

6.   The Tenant is to comply with the following:

6.1   the Tenant is not to share occupation of the property and no part of it is to be transferred, sublet or occupied separately from the remainder

6.2   the Tenant is not to transfer or sublet the whole of the property unless the Landlord gives written consent in advance, and the Landlord is not entitled to withhold that consent unreasonably

6.3   any sublease is to be on terms which are consistent with this lease, but is not to permit the sub-tenant to underlet

6.4   within four weeks after the property is transferred, mortgaged or sublet, the Landlord's solicitors are to be notified and a copy of the transfer, mortgage or sublease sent to them for registration with the fee payable under clause 2.3

6.5   if the Landlord reasonably requires, a tenant who transfers the whole of the property is to give the Landlord a written guarantee, in the terms set out in the Guarantee Box, that the transferee will perform the tenant's obligations

7   OTHER MATTERS

7.   The Tenant:

7.1   is to give the Landlord a copy of any notice concerning the property or any neighbouring property as soon as it is received

7.2   is to allow the Landlord, during the last six months of the lease term, to fix a notice in a reasonable position on the outside of the property announcing that it is for sale or to let

7.3   is not to apply for planning permission relating to the use or alteration of the property unless the Landlord gives written consent in advance

7.4   in occupying, using and doing work on the property, is to comply with all statutory requirements

8   RENT REVIEW

8.1   On each rent review date, the rent is to increase to the market rent if that is higher than the rent applying before that date

8.2   The market rent is the rent which a willing tenant would pay for the property on the open market, if let on the rent review date by a willing landlord on a lease on the same terms as this lease without any premium and for a term equal to the remainder of the lease term, assuming that at that date:

    (a)   no account is taken of any goodwill belonging to anyone who had occupied the property

    (b)   the property is vacant and had not been occupied by the Tenant or any sub-tenant

    (c)   the property can immediately be used

    (d)   the property is in the condition required by this lease and any damage caused by any of the risks insured under clause 11 has been made good

    (e)   no tenant or sub-tenant has previously during the lease term done anything to the property to increase or decrease its rental value. In this paragraph "anything" includes work done by the Tenant to comply with clause 5.6, but nothing else which the Tenant was obliged to do under this lease

8.3   If the Landlord and the Tenant agree the amount of the new rent, a statement of that new rent, signed by them, is to be attached to this lease

8.4   If the Landlord and the Tenant have not agreed the amount of the new rent two months before the rent review date, either of them may require the new rent to be decided by arbitration under clause 14.3

8.5   (a)   The Tenant is to pay rent at the rate applying before the rent review date until the next rent day after the new rent is agreed or decided

    (b)   Starting on that rent day, the Tenant is to pay the new rent

    (c)   On that rent day, the Tenant is also to pay any amount by which the new rent since the rent review date exceeds the rent paid, with interest on that amount at 4% below the Law Society's interest rate

9   DAMAGE

9.   If the property is damaged by any of the risks required to be insured under clause 11 and as a result of that damage the property, or any part of it, cannot be used for the use allowed:

9.1   the rent, or a fair proportion of it, is to be suspended for three years or until the property is fully restored, if earlier

9.2   if at any time when it is unlikely that the property will be fully restored either within three years from the date of the damage, or (if sooner) before the end of the lease term, the Landlord (so long as he has not wilfully delayed the restoration) or the Tenant may end this lease by giving one month's notice to the other in which case

    (a)   the insurance money belongs to the Landlord and

    (b)   the Landlord's obligation to make good damage under clause 11 ceases

9.3   a notice is only effective if given within three years from the date of the damage

9.4   If the insurers refuse to pay all or part of the insurance money because of the Tenant's act or default:

    (a)   to the extent of that refusal, the Tenant cannot claim the benefit of clause 9.1

    (b)   the Tenant cannot serve notice under clause 9.2

9.5   Any dispute under any part of this clause is to be decided by arbitration under clause 14.3

LANDLORD'S OBLIGATIONS AND FORFEITURE RIGHTS

10   QUIET ENJOYMENT

10.   The Landlord is to allow the Tenant to possess and use the property without lawful interference from the Landlord, anyone who derives title from the Landlord or any trustee for the Landlord

11   INSURANCE

11.   The Landlord is to:

11.1   keep the property (except the plate glass) insured with reputable insurers to cover:

    (a)   full rebuilding, site clearance, professional fees, value added tax and three years' loss of rent

    (b)   against fire, lightning, explosion, earthquake, landslip, subsidence, heave, riot, civil commotion, aircraft, aerial devices, storm, flood, water, theft, impact by vehicles, damage by malicious persons and vandals and third party liability and other risks reasonably required by the Landlord

so far as cover is available at normal insurance rates for the locality and subject to reasonable excesses and exclusions

11.2   take all necessary steps to make good as soon as possible all damage to the property by insured risks except to the extent that the insurance money is not paid because of the act or default of the Tenant

11.3   give the Tenant on request once a year particulars of the policy and evidence from the insurer that it is in force

12   FORFEITURE

12.   This lease comes to an end if the Landlord forfeits it by entering any part of the property, which the Landlord is entitled to do whenever:

    (a)   payment of any rent is fourteen days overdue, even if it was not formally demanded

4

(b) the Tenant has not complied with any of the terms of this lease

(c) the Tenant if an individual (and if more than one, any of them) is adjudicated bankrupt or an interim receiver of the Tenant's property is appointed

(d) the Tenant if a company (and if more than one, any of them) goes into liquidation (unless solely for the purpose of amalgamation or reconstruction when solvent), or has an administrative receiver appointed or has an administration order made in respect of it or the directors of the Tenant give notice of their intention to appoint an administrator

The forfeiture of this lease does not cancel any outstanding obligation of the Tenant or a Guarantor

13 END OF LEASE

13. When this lease ends the Tenant is to:

13.1 return the property to the Landlord leaving it in the state and condition in which this lease requires the Tenant to keep it

13.2 (if the Landlord so requires) remove anything the Tenant fixed to the property and make good any damage which that causes

GENERAL

14 PARTIES' RESPONSIBILITY

14.1 Whenever more than one person or company is the Landlord, the Tenant or the Guarantor, their obligations can be enforced against all or both of them jointly and against each individually

SERVICE OF NOTICE

14.2 The rules about serving notices in section 196 of the Law of Property Act 1925 (as since amended) apply to any notice given under this lease

ARBITRATION

14.3 Any matter which this lease requires to be decided by arbitration is to be referred to a single arbitrator under the Arbitration Act 1996. The Landlord and the Tenant may agree the appointment of an arbitrator, or either of them may apply to the President of the Royal Institution of Chartered Surveyors to make the appointment

HEADINGS

14.4 The headings do not form part of this lease

GUARANTEE BOX

The terms in this box only take effect if a guarantor is named in clause LR.3 and then only until the Tenant transfers this lease with the Landlord's written consent. The Guarantor must sign this lease.

The Guarantor agrees to compensate the Landlord for any loss incurred as a result of the Tenant failing to comply with an obligation in this lease during the lease term or any statutory extension of it. If the Tenant is insolvent or this lease ends because it is disclaimed, the Guarantor agrees to accept a new lease, if the Landlord so requires, in the same form but at the rent then payable. Even if the Landlord gives the Tenant extra time to comply with an obligation, or does not insist on strict compliance with terms of this lease, the Guarantor's obligation remains fully effective.

THIS DOCUMENT CREATES LEGAL RIGHTS AND LEGAL OBLIGATIONS. DO NOT SIGN IT UNTIL YOU HAVE CONSULTED A SOLICITOR. THERE IS A CODE OF PRACTICE CONCERNING COMMERCIAL LEASES IN ENGLAND AND WALES PUBLISHED UNDER THE AUSPICES OF THE DEPARTMENT FOR COMMUNITIES AND LOCAL GOVERNMENT.

If a party to this lease is a company, either two directors or a director and the company secretary must sign on behalf of the company.

Signed as a deed by/on behalf of the
Landlord and delivered in the presence of:

Landlord

Witness

Witness's occupation and address

Signed as a deed by/on behalf of the
Tenant and delivered in the presence of:

Tenant

Witness

Witness's occupation and address

Signed as a deed by/on behalf of the
Guarantor and delivered in the presence of:

Guarantor

Witness

Witness's occupation and address

5

LS2 (Whole)(Reg) 2006

The Law Society

The Law Society Business Lease (Whole of Building) (Unregistered) 2006

DATE OF LEASE _____ 20 _____

PARTIES TO
THIS LEASE

    LANDLORD _____

    ADDRESS _____

    _____ POSTCODE _____

    COMPANY NO. _____

    TENANT _____

    ADDRESS _____

    _____ POSTCODE _____

    COMPANY NO. _____

    GUARANTOR _____

    ADDRESS _____

    _____ POSTCODE _____

    COMPANY NO. _____

PROPERTY

    _____

    _____

    _____ POSTCODE _____

TERM FOR WHICH
THE PROPERTY IS
LEASED

    From and including _____ 20 _____

    To and including _____ 20 _____

USE ALLOWED

    _____

    or any other use to which the Landlord consents (and the Landlord is not entitled to withhold that consent unreasonably)

RENT

    _____ Pounds

    (£ _____) a year, subject to increase under clause 8 from every rent review date

FIRST PAYMENT
DATE

    The _____ 20 _____

MONTHLY
PAYMENT
DATE

    The _____ day of every month

RENT REVIEW
DATES

    Every _____ anniversary of the start of the lease term

    The Landlord lets the property to the Tenant for the lease term at the rent and on the terms in clauses 1 to 14 and in any additional clauses.

     1   **LS2 (Whole)(Unreg) 2006**

TENANT'S OBLIGATIONS

1 PAYMENTS

1. The Tenant is to pay the Landlord:

1.1 the rent, which is to be paid by the following instalments:

(a) on the first payment date, a proportionate sum from that date to the next monthly payment date

(b) on each monthly payment date, one-twelfth of the annual rent

1.2 a fair proportion (decided by a surveyor whom the Landlord nominates) of the cost of repairing, maintaining and cleaning: party walls, party structures, yards, gardens, roads, paths, gutters, drains, sewers, pipes, conduits, wires, cables and things used or shared with other property

1.3 the cost (including professional fees) of any works to the property which the Landlord does after the Tenant defaults

1.4 the costs and expenses (including professional fees) which the Landlord incurs in:

(a) dealing with any application by the Tenant for consent or approval, whether it is given or not

(b) preparing and serving a notice of a breach of the Tenant's obligations, under section 146 of the Law of Property Act 1925, even if forfeiture of this lease is avoided without a court order

(c) preparing and serving schedules of dilapidations either during the lease term or recording failure to give up the property in the appropriate state of repair when this lease ends

(d) insuring the property under this lease

1.5 interest at the Law Society's interest rate on any of the above payments when more than fourteen days overdue, to be calculated from its due date and in making payments under this clause:

(a) nothing is to be deducted or set off

(b) any value added tax payable is to be added

2 The Tenant is also to make the following payments, with value added tax where payable:

2.1 all periodic rates, taxes and outgoings relating to the property, including any imposed after the date of this lease (even if of a novel nature), to be paid on the due date to the appropriate authorities

2.2 the cost of the grant, renewal or continuation of any licence or registration for using the property for the use allowed, to be paid to the appropriate authority

2.3 a registration fee of £40 for each document which this lease requires the Tenant to register, to be paid to the Landlord's solicitors when presenting the document for registration

3 USE

3. The Tenant is to comply with the following requirements as to the use of the property and any part of it, and is not to authorise or allow anyone else to contravene them:

3.1 to use the property, except any residential accommodation, only for the use allowed

3.2 to use any residential accommodation only as a home for one family

3.3 not to do anything which might invalidate any insurance policy covering any part of the property or which might increase the premium

3.4 not to hold an auction in the property

3.5 not to use the property for any activities which are dangerous, offensive, noxious, illegal or immoral, or which are or may become a nuisance or annoyance to the Landlord or to the owner or occupier of any neighbouring property

3.6 not to display any signs or advertisements on the outside of the property or which are visible from outside the property unless the Landlord consents (and the Landlord is not entitled to withhold that consent unreasonably)

3.7 not to overload any part of the property

3.8 to comply with every statutory obligation authorising or regulating how the property is used, and to obtain, comply with the terms of, renew and continue any licence or registration which is required

4 ACCESS

4. The Tenant is to give the Landlord, or anyone with the Landlord's written authority, access to the property:

4.1 for these purposes:

(a) inspecting the condition of the property, or how it is being used

(b) doing works which the Landlord is permitted to do under clause 5.7

(c) complying with any statutory obligation

(d) viewing the property as a prospective buyer, tenant or mortgagee

(e) valuing the property

(f) inspecting, cleaning or repairing neighbouring property, or any sewers, drains, pipes, wires or cables serving the property or any neighbouring property

4.2 and only on seven days' written notice except in an emergency

4.3 and during normal business hours except in an emergency

4.4 and the Landlord is promptly to make good all damage caused to the property and any goods there in exercising these rights

5 CONDITION AND WORK

5. The Tenant is to comply with the following duties in relation to the property:

5.1 to maintain the state and condition of the property, but the Tenant need not alter or improve it except as required in clause 5.6

5.2 to decorate the inside and outside of the property:

(a) in every fifth year of the lease term

(b) in the last three months of the lease term (however it ends) except to the extent that it has been decorated in the previous year

and on each occasion the Tenant is to use the colours and the types of finish used previously

5.3 not to make any structural alterations, external alterations or additions to the property

5.4 not to make any other alterations unless the Landlord gives written consent in advance (and the Landlord is not entitled to withhold that consent unreasonably)

5.5 to keep any plate glass in the property insured for its full replacement cost with reputable insurers, to give the Landlord details of that insurance on request, and to replace any plate glass which becomes damaged

5.6 to do any work to the property required under a statute even if it alters or improves the property. The work is to be done on the following conditions:

(a) before doing it, the Tenant is to obtain the Landlord's written consent (and the Landlord is not entitled to withhold that consent unreasonably)

(b) the Landlord is to contribute a fair proportion of the cost, taking into account any value of the work to the Landlord

and any dispute is to be decided by arbitration under clause 14.3

5.7 if the Tenant fails to do any work which this lease requires and the Landlord gives the Tenant written notice to do it, to do that work. In such a case, the Tenant is to start the work within two months, or immediately in case of emergency, and proceed diligently with it. In default, the Tenant is to permit the Landlord to do the work.

2

5.8 However, this clause only requires the Tenant to make good damage caused by an insured risk to the extent that the insurance money has not been paid because of any act or default of the Tenant

6   TRANSFER ETC.

6.   The Tenant is to comply with the following:

6.1   the Tenant is not to share occupation of the property and no part of it is to be transferred, sublet or occupied separately from the remainder

6.2   the Tenant is not to transfer or sublet the whole of the property unless the Landlord gives written consent in advance, and the Landlord is not entitled to withhold that consent unreasonably

6.3   any sublease is to be on terms which are consistent with this lease, but is not to permit the sub-tenant to underlet

6.4   within four weeks after the property is transferred, mortgaged or sublet, the Landlord's solicitors are to be notified and a copy of the transfer, mortgage or sublease sent to them for registration with the fee payable under clause 2.3

6.5   if the Landlord reasonably requires, a tenant who transfers the whole of the property is to give the Landlord a written guarantee, in the terms set out in the Guarantee Box, that the transferee will perform the tenant's obligations

7   OTHER MATTERS

7.   The Tenant:

7.1   is to give the Landlord a copy of any notice concerning the property or any neighbouring property as soon as it is received

7.2   is to allow the Landlord, during the last six months of the lease term, to fix a notice in a reasonable position on the outside of the property announcing that it is for sale or to let

7.3   is not to apply for planning permission relating to the use or alteration of the property unless the Landlord gives written consent in advance

7.4   in occupying, using and doing work on the property, is to comply with all statutory requirements

8   RENT REVIEW

8.1   On each rent review date, the rent is to increase to the market rent if that is higher than the rent applying before that date

8.2   The market rent is the rent which a willing tenant would pay for the property on the open market, if let on the rent review date by a willing landlord on a lease on the same terms as this lease without any premium and for a term equal to the remainder of the lease term, assuming that at that date:

    (a) no account is taken of any goodwill belonging to anyone who had occupied the property

    (b) the property is vacant and had not been occupied by the Tenant or any sub-tenant

    (c) the property can immediately be used

    (d) the property is in the condition required by this lease and any damage caused by any of the risks insured under clause 11 has been made good

    (e) no tenant or sub-tenant has previously during the lease term done anything to the property to increase or decrease its rental value. In this paragraph "anything" includes work done by the Tenant to comply with clause 5.6, but nothing else which the Tenant was obliged to do under this lease

8.3   If the Landlord and the Tenant agree the amount of the new rent, a statement of that new rent, signed by them, is to be attached to this lease

8.4   If the Landlord and the Tenant have not agreed the amount of the new rent two months before the rent review date, either of them may require the new rent to be decided by arbitration under clause 14.3

8.5   (a) The Tenant is to pay rent at the rate applying before the rent review date until the next rent day after the new rent is agreed or decided

    (b) Starting on that rent day, the Tenant is to pay the new rent

    (c) On that rent day, the Tenant is also to pay any amount by which the new rent since the rent review date exceeds the rent paid, with interest on that amount at 4% below the Law Society's interest rate

9   DAMAGE

9.   If the property is damaged by any of the risks required to be insured under clause 11 and as a result of that damage the property, or any part of it, cannot be used for the use allowed:

9.1   the rent, or a fair proportion of it, is to be suspended for three years or until the property is fully restored, if earlier

9.2   if at any time when it is unlikely that the property will be fully restored either within three years from the date of the damage, or (if sooner) before the end of the lease term, the Landlord (so long as he has not wilfully delayed the restoration) or the Tenant may end this lease by giving one month's notice to the other in which case

    (a) the insurance money belongs to the Landlord and

    (b) the Landlord's obligation to make good damage under clause 11 ceases

9.3   a notice is only effective if given within three years from the date of the damage

9.4   If the insurers refuse to pay all or part of the insurance money because of the Tenant's act or default:

    (a) to the extent of that refusal, the Tenant cannot claim the benefit of clause 9.1

    (b) the Tenant cannot serve notice under clause 9.2

9.5   Any dispute under any part of this clause is to be decided by arbitration under clause 14.3

LANDLORD'S OBLIGATIONS AND FORFEITURE RIGHTS

10   QUIET ENJOYMENT

10.   The Landlord is to allow the Tenant to possess and use the property without lawful interference from the Landlord, anyone who derives title from the Landlord or any trustee for the Landlord

11   INSURANCE

11.   The Landlord is to:

11.1   keep the property (except the plate glass) insured with reputable insurers to cover:

    (a) full rebuilding, site clearance, professional fees, value added tax and three years' loss of rent

    (b) against fire, lightning, explosion, earthquake, landslip, subsidence, heave, riot, civil commotion, aircraft, aerial devices, storm, flood, water, theft, impact by vehicles, damage by malicious persons and vandals and third party liability and other risks reasonably required by the Landlord

so far as cover is available at normal insurance rates for the locality and subject to reasonable excesses and exclusions

11.2   take all necessary steps to make good as soon as possible all damage to the property by insured risks except to the extent that the insurance money is not paid because of the act or default of the Tenant

11.3   give the Tenant on request once a year particulars of the policy and evidence from the insurer that it is in force

12   FORFEITURE

12.   This lease comes to an end if the Landlord forfeits it by entering any part of the property, which the Landlord is entitled to do whenever:

    (a) payment of any rent is fourteen days overdue, even if it was not formally demanded

3

(b) the Tenant has not complied with any of the terms of this lease

(c) the Tenant if an individual (and if more than one, any of them) is adjudicated bankrupt or an interim receiver of the Tenant's property is appointed

(d) the Tenant if a company (and if more than one, any of them) goes into liquidation (unless solely for the purpose of amalgamation or reconstruction when solvent), or has an administrative receiver appointed or has an administration order made in respect of it or the directors of the Tenant give notice of their intention to appoint an administrator

The forfeiture of this lease does not cancel any outstanding obligation of the Tenant or a Guarantor

13 END OF LEASE

13. When this lease ends the Tenant is to:

13.1 return the property to the Landlord leaving it in the state and condition in which this lease requires the Tenant to keep it

13.2 (if the Landlord so requires) remove anything the Tenant fixed to the property and make good any damage which that causes

GENERAL

14 PARTIES' RESPONSIBILITY

14.1 Whenever more than one person or company is the Landlord, the Tenant or the Guarantor, their obligations can be enforced against all or both of them jointly and against each individually

SERVICE OF NOTICE

14.2 The rules about serving notices in section 196 of the Law of Property Act 1925 (as since amended) apply to any notice given under this lease

ARBITRATION

14.3 Any matter which this lease requires to be decided by arbitration is to be referred to a single arbitrator under the Arbitration Act 1996. The Landlord and the Tenant may agree the appointment of an arbitrator, or either of them may apply to the President of the Royal Institution of Chartered Surveyors to make the appointment

HEADINGS

14.4 The headings do not form part of this lease

GUARANTEE BOX

The terms in this box only take effect if a guarantor is named above and then only until the Tenant transfers this lease with the Landlord's written consent. The Guarantor must sign this lease.

The Guarantor agrees to compensate the Landlord for any loss incurred as a result of the Tenant failing to comply with an obligation in this lease during the lease term or any statutory extension of it. If the Tenant is insolvent or this lease ends because it is disclaimed, the Guarantor agrees to accept a new lease, if the Landlord so requires, in the same form but at the rent then payable. Even if the Landlord gives the Tenant extra time to comply with an obligation, or does not insist on strict compliance with terms of this lease, the Guarantor's obligation remains fully effective.

THIS DOCUMENT CREATES LEGAL RIGHTS AND LEGAL OBLIGATIONS. DO NOT SIGN IT UNTIL YOU HAVE CONSULTED A SOLICITOR. THERE IS A CODE OF PRACTICE CONCERNING COMMERCIAL LEASES IN ENGLAND AND WALES PUBLISHED UNDER THE AUSPICES OF THE DEPARTMENT FOR COMMUNITIES AND LOCAL GOVERNMENT.

If a party to this lease is a company, either two directors or a director and the company secretary must sign on behalf of the company.

Signed as a deed by/on behalf of the
Landlord and delivered in the presence of:

Landlord

Witness

Witness's occupation and address

Signed as a deed by/on behalf of the
Tenant and delivered in the presence of:

Tenant

Witness

Witness's occupation and address

Signed as a deed by/on behalf of the
Guarantor and delivered in the presence of:

Guarantor

Witness

Witness's occupation and address

4

    LS2 (Whole)(Unreg) 2006

The Law Society

LR1.	DATE OF LEASE	_____ 20_____
LR2.	TITLE NUMBER(S)	
LR2.1	LANDLORD'S TITLE NUMBER(S)	_____
LR2.2	OTHER TITLE NUMBERS	_____
LR3.	PARTIES TO THIS LEASE	

LANDLORD   _____

                ADDRESS _____

                _____ POSTCODE _____

                COMPANY NO. _____

TENANT   _____

                ADDRESS _____

                _____ POSTCODE _____

                COMPANY NO. _____

GUARANTOR   _____

                ADDRESS _____

                _____ POSTCODE _____

                COMPANY NO. _____

LR4.	PROPERTY	_____

shown edged red on the attached plan being part of the Building known as

_____

_____ POSTCODE _____

In the case of a conflict between this clause and the remainder of this lease then, for the purposes of registration, this clause shall prevail.

LR5.	PRESCRIBED STATEMENTS ETC.	None
LR6.	TERM FOR WHICH THE PROPERTY IS LEASED	

        From and including _____ 20_____

        To and including _____ 20_____

LR7.	PREMIUM	None
LR8.	PROHIBITIONS OR RESTRICTIONS ON DISPOSING OF THIS LEASE	

        This lease contains a provision that prohibits or restricts dispositions.

1   **LS1 (Part)(Reg) 2006**

The Law Society Business Lease (Part of Building) (Registered) 2006

LR9.	RIGHTS OF ACQUISITION ETC.	
LR9.1	TENANT'S CONTRACTUAL RIGHTS TO RENEW THIS LEASE, TO ACQUIRE THE REVERSION OR ANOTHER LEASE OF THE PROPERTY, OR TO ACQUIRE AN INTEREST IN OTHER LAND	None
LR9.2	TENANT'S COVENANT TO (OR OFFER TO) SURRENDER THIS LEASE	None
LR9.3	LANDLORD'S CONTRACTUAL RIGHTS TO ACQUIRE THIS LEASE	None
LR10.	RESTRICTIVE COVENANTS GIVEN IN THIS LEASE BY THE LANDLORD IN RESPECT OF LAND OTHER THAN THE PROPERTY	None
LR11.	EASEMENTS	
LR11.1	EASEMENTS GRANTED BY THIS LEASE FOR THE BENEFIT OF THE PROPERTY	See clause 16.1
LR11.2	EASEMENTS GRANTED OR RESERVED BY THIS LEASE OVER THE PROPERTY FOR THE BENEFIT OF OTHER PROPERTY	See clause 16.2
LR12.	ESTATE RENTCHARGE BURDENING THE PROPERTY	None
LR13.	APPLICATION FOR STANDARD FORM OF RESTRICTION	None
[LR14.	DECLARATION OF TRUST WHERE THERE IS MORE THAN ONE PERSON COMPRISING THE TENANT	

The Tenant is more than one person. They are to hold the property on trust for themselves as [joint tenants] [tenants in common in equal shares]]

USE ALLOWED	.... or any other use to which the Landlord consents (and the Landlord is not entitled to withhold that consent unreasonably)
PARKING	No more than _____ vehicles (see clause 16.1(d))
RENT	.... Pounds (£ _____) a year, subject to increase under clause 9 from every rent review date
FIRST PAYMENT DATE	The .... 20 _____
MONTHLY PAYMENT DATE	The .... day of every month
RENT REVIEW DATES	Every .... anniversary of the start of the lease term

The Landlord lets the property to the Tenant for the lease term at the rent and on the terms in clauses 1 to 18 and in any additional clauses.

2

TENANT'S OBLIGATIONS

1 PAYMENTS

1. The Tenant is to pay the Landlord:

1.1 the rent, which is to be paid by the following instalments:

    (a) on the first payment date, a proportionate sum from that date to the next monthly payment date

    (b) on each monthly payment date, one-twelfth of the annual rent

1.2 the service charge in accordance with clause 3, and whenever a sum is overdue the Landlord is entitled to recover it by distraint as if it were rent in arrear

1.3 a fair proportion (decided by a surveyor whom the Landlord nominates) of the cost of repairing, maintaining and cleaning: party walls, party structures, yards, gardens, roads, paths, gutters, drains, sewers, pipes, conduits, wires, cables and things used or shared with other property

1.4 the cost (including professional fees) of any works to the property which the Landlord does after the Tenant defaults

1.5 the costs and expenses (including professional fees) which the Landlord incurs in:

    (a) dealing with any application by the Tenant for consent or approval, whether it is given or not

    (b) preparing and serving a notice of a breach of the Tenant's obligations, under section 146 of the Law of Property Act 1925, even if forfeiture of this lease is avoided without a court order

    (c) preparing and serving schedules of dilapidations either during the lease term or recording failure to give up the property in the appropriate state of repair when this lease ends

1.6 interest at the Law Society's interest rate on any of the above payments when more than fourteen days overdue, to be calculated from its due date and in making payments under this clause:

    (a) nothing is to be deducted or set off

    (b) any value added tax payable is to be added

2 The Tenant is also to make the following payments, with value added tax where payable:

2.1 all periodic rates, taxes and outgoings relating to the property, including any imposed after the date of this lease (even if of a novel nature), to be paid on the due date to the appropriate authorities

2.2 the cost of the grant, renewal or continuation of any licence or registration for using the property for the use allowed, to be paid to the appropriate authority

2.3 a registration fee of £40 for each document which this lease requires the Tenant to register, to be paid to the Landlord's solicitors when presenting the document for registration

3 SERVICE CHARGE

3. The Landlord and the Tenant agree that:

3.1 the service charge is the Tenant's fair proportion of each item of the service costs

3.2 the service costs:

    (a) are the costs which the Landlord fairly and reasonably incurs in complying with obligations under clauses 12 and 13

    (b) include the reasonable charges of any agent, contractor, consultant or employee whom the Landlord engages to provide the services under clauses 12 and 13

    (c) include interest at no more than the Law Society's interest rate on sums the Landlord borrows to discharge his obligations under clauses 12 and 13

3.3 the Tenant is to pay the Landlord interim payments on account of the service charge within 21 days of receiving a written demand setting out how it is calculated

3.4 an interim payment is to be the Tenant's fair proportion of what the service costs are reasonably likely to be in the three months following the demand

3.5 the Landlord is not entitled to demand interim payments more than once every three months

3.6 the Landlord is to keep full records of the service costs and at least once a year is to send the Tenant an account setting out, for the period since the beginning of the lease term or the last account as the case may be:

    (a) the amount of the service costs

    (b) the service charge the Tenant is to pay

    (c) the total of any interim payments the Tenant has paid

    (d) the difference between the total interim payments and the service charge

3.7 within 21 days after the Tenant receives the account, the amount mentioned in clause 3.6(d) is to be settled by payment between the parties, except that the Landlord is entitled to retain any overpayment towards any interim payments already demanded for a later accounting period

3.8 the Landlord is either:

    (a) to have the account certified by an independent chartered accountant, or

    (b) to allow the Tenant to inspect the books, records, invoices and receipts relating to the service costs

3.9 disagreements about the amounts of the service charge or the service costs are to be decided by arbitration under clause 17.3

4 USE

4. The Tenant is to comply with the following requirements as to the use of the building and any part of it, and is not to authorise or allow anyone else to contravene them:

4.1 to use the property only for the use allowed

4.2 not to obstruct any part of the building used for access to the property or to any other part of the building

4.3 not to do anything which might invalidate any insurance policy covering any part of the building or which might increase the premium

4.4 not to hold an auction in the property

4.5 not to use any part of the building for any activities which are dangerous, offensive, noxious, illegal or immoral, or which are or may become a nuisance or annoyance to the Landlord or to the owner or occupier of any neighbouring property

4.6 not to display any signs or advertisements on the outside of the property or which are visible from outside the property unless the Landlord consents (and the Landlord is not entitled to withhold that consent unreasonably)

4.7 not to overload any part of the property

4.8 to comply with every statutory obligation authorising or regulating how the property is used, and to obtain, comply with the terms of, renew and continue any licence or registration which is required

5 ACCESS

5. The Tenant is to give the Landlord, or anyone with the Landlord's written authority, access to the property:

5.1 for these purposes:

    (a) inspecting the condition of the property, or how it is being used

    (b) doing works which the Landlord is permitted to do under clauses 6.9 or 13

    (c) complying with any statutory obligation

    (d) viewing the property as a prospective buyer, tenant or mortgagee

    (e) valuing the property

3

(f) inspecting, cleaning or repairing neighbouring property, or any sewers, drains, pipes, wires or cables serving the building or any neighbouring property

5.2 and only on seven days' written notice except in an emergency

5.3 and during normal business hours except in an emergency

5.4 and the Landlord is promptly to make good all damage caused to the property and any goods there in exercising these rights

6 CONDITION AND WORK

6. The Tenant is to comply with the following duties in relation to the property, and for this purpose the inside of the property includes all ceilings, floors, doors, door frames, windows and window frames and the internal surfaces of all walls but excludes joists immediately above the ceilings and supporting the floors:

6.1 to maintain the state and condition of the inside of the property, but the Tenant need not alter or improve it except as required in clause 6.8

6.2 to decorate the inside of the property:

(a) in every fifth year of the lease term

(b) in the last three months of the lease term (however it ends) except to the extent that it has been decorated in the previous year

6.3 where the property has a shop front, to maintain and decorate it

6.4 when decorating, to use the colours and the types of finish used previously

6.5 not to make any structural alterations or additions to the property

6.6 not to make any other alterations unless the Landlord gives written consent in advance (and the Landlord is not entitled to withhold that consent unreasonably)

6.7 to keep any plate glass in the property insured for its full replacement cost with reputable insurers, to give the Landlord details of that insurance on request, and to replace any plate glass which becomes damaged

6.8 to do any work to the property required under a statute even if it alters or improves the property. The work is to be done on the following conditions:

(a) before doing it, the Tenant is to obtain the Landlord's written consent (and the Landlord is not entitled to withhold that consent unreasonably)

(b) the Landlord is to contribute a fair proportion of the cost, taking into account any value of the work to the Landlord

and any dispute is to be decided by arbitration under clause 17.3

6.9 if the Tenant fails to do any work which this lease requires and the Landlord gives the Tenant written notice to do it, to do that work. In such a case, the Tenant is to start the work within two months, or immediately in case of emergency, and proceed diligently with it. In default, the Tenant is to permit the Landlord to do the work

6.10 However, this clause only requires the Tenant to make good damage caused by an insured risk to the extent that the insurance money has not been paid because of any act or default of the Tenant

7 TRANSFER ETC.

7. The Tenant is to comply with the following:

7.1 the Tenant is not to share occupation of the property and no part of it is to be transferred, sublet or occupied separately from the remainder

7.2 the Tenant is not to transfer or sublet the whole of the property unless the Landlord gives written consent in advance, and the Landlord is not entitled to withhold that consent unreasonably

7.3 any sublease is to be on terms which are consistent with this lease, but is not to permit the sub-tenant to underlet

7.4 within four weeks after the property is transferred, mortgaged or sublet, the Landlord's solicitors are to be notified and a copy of the transfer, mortgage or sublease sent to them for registration with the fee payable under clause 2.3

7.5 if the Landlord reasonably requires, a tenant who transfers the whole of the property is to give the Landlord a written guarantee, in the terms set out in the Guarantee Box, that the transferee will perform the tenant's obligations

8 OTHER MATTERS

8. The Tenant:

8.1 is to give the Landlord a copy of any notice concerning the property or any neighbouring property as soon as it is received

8.2 is to allow the Landlord, during the last six months of the lease term, to fix a notice in a reasonable position on the outside of the property announcing that it is for sale or to let

8.3 is not to apply for planning permission relating to the use or alteration of the property unless the Landlord gives written consent in advance

8.4 in occupying and doing work on the property, and in using any part of the building, is to comply with all statutory requirements

9 RENT REVIEW

9.1 On each rent review date, the rent is to increase to the market rent if that is higher than the rent applying before that date

9.2 The market rent is the rent which a willing tenant would pay for the property on the open market, if let on the rent review date by a willing landlord on a lease on the same terms as this lease without any premium and for a term equal to the remainder of the lease term, assuming that at that date:

(a) no account is taken of any goodwill belonging to anyone who has occupied the property

(b) the property is vacant and has not been occupied by the Tenant or any sub-tenant

(c) the property can immediately be used

(d) the property is in the condition required by this lease and any damage caused by any of the risks insured under clause 12 has been made good

(e) no tenant or sub-tenant has previously during the lease term done anything to the property to increase or decrease its rental value. In this paragraph "anything" includes work done by the Tenant to comply with clause 6.8, but nothing else which the Tenant was obliged to do under this lease

9.3 If the Landlord and the Tenant agree the amount of the new rent, a statement of that new rent, signed by them, is to be attached to this lease

9.4 If the Landlord and the Tenant have not agreed the amount of the new rent two months before the rent review date, either of them may require the new rent to be decided by arbitration under clause 17.3

9.5 (a) The Tenant is to pay rent at the rate applying before the rent review date until the next rent day after the new rent is agreed or decided

(b) Starting on that rent day, the Tenant is to pay the new rent

(c) On that rent day, the Tenant is also to pay any amount by which the new rent since the rent review date exceeds the rent paid, with interest on that amount at 4% below the Law Society's interest rate

10 DAMAGE

10. If the property is, or the common parts are, damaged by any of the risks required to be insured under clause 12 and as a result of that damage the property, or any part of it, cannot be used for the use allowed:

10.1 the rent, or a fair proportion of it, is to be suspended for three years or until the property or the common parts are fully restored, if earlier

4

10.2 if at any time when it is unlikely that the damage will be fully repaired either within three years from the date of the damage, or (if sooner) before the end of the lease term, the Landlord (so long as he has not wilfully delayed the restoration) or the Tenant may end this lease by giving one month's notice to the other in which case

(a) the insurance money belongs to the Landlord and

(b) the Landlord's obligation to make good damage under clause 12 ceases

10.3 a notice is only effective if given within three years from the date of the damage

10.4 If the insurers refuse to pay all or part of the insurance money because of the Tenant's act or default:

(a) to the extent of that refusal, the Tenant cannot claim the benefit of clause 10.1

(b) the Tenant cannot serve notice under clause 10.2

10.5 Any dispute under any part of this clause is to be decided by arbitration under clause 17.3

LANDLORD'S OBLIGATIONS AND FORFEITURE RIGHTS

11 QUIET ENJOYMENT

11. The Landlord is to allow the Tenant to possess and use the property without lawful interference from the Landlord, anyone who derives title from the Landlord or any trustee for the Landlord

12 INSURANCE

12. The Landlord is to:

12.1 keep the building (except the plate glass) insured with reputable insurers to cover

(a) full rebuilding, site clearance, professional fees, value added tax and three years' loss of rent

(b) against fire, lightning, explosion, earthquake, landslip, subsidence, heave, riot, civil commotion, aircraft, aerial devices, storm, flood, water, theft, impact by vehicles, damage by malicious persons and vandals and third party liability and other risks reasonably required by the Landlord so far as cover is available at normal insurance rates for the locality and subject to reasonable excesses and exclusions

12.2 take all necessary steps to make good as soon as possible all damage to the building by insured risks except to the extent that the insurance money is not paid because of the act or default of the Tenant

12.3 give the Tenant on request once a year particulars of the policy and evidence from the insurer that it is in force

13 SERVICES

13. The Landlord is to comply with the following duties in relation to the building:

13.1 to maintain the state and condition (including the decorations) of:

(a) the structure, outside, roof, foundations, joists, floor slabs, load bearing walls, beams and columns of the building and any plant, machinery and fixtures required to provide the services listed in clause 18

(b) those parts of the building which tenants of more than one part can use ("the common parts")

13.2 to decorate the common parts and the outside of the building every five years, using colours and types of finish reasonably decided by the Landlord

13.3 to pay promptly all periodic rates, taxes and outgoings relating to the common parts, including any imposed after the date of this lease (even if of a novel nature)

13.4 to pay or contribute to the cost of repairing, maintaining and cleaning party walls, party structures, yards, gardens, roads, paths, gutters, drains, sewers, pipes, conduits, wires, cables and other things used or shared with other property

13.5 to provide the services listed in clause 18, but the Landlord is not to be liable for failure or delay caused by industrial disputes, shortage of supplies, adverse weather conditions or other causes beyond the control of the Landlord

14 FORFEITURE

14. This lease comes to an end if the Landlord forfeits it by entering any part of the property, which the Landlord is entitled to do whenever:

(a) payment of any rent is fourteen days overdue, even if it was not formally demanded

(b) the Tenant has not complied with any of the terms of this lease

(c) the Tenant if an individual (and if more than one, any of them) is adjudicated bankrupt or an interim receiver of the Tenant's property is appointed

(d) the Tenant if a company (and if more than one, any of them) goes into liquidation (unless solely for the purpose of amalgamation or reconstruction when solvent), or had an administrative receiver appointed or had an administration order made in respect of it or the directors of the Tenant give notice of their intention to appoint an administrator

The forfeiture of this lease does not cancel any outstanding obligation of the Tenant or a Guarantor

15 END OF LEASE

15. When this lease ends the Tenant is to:

15.1 return the property to the Landlord leaving it in the state and condition in which this lease requires the Tenant to keep it

15.2 (if the Landlord so requires) remove anything the Tenant fixed to the property and make good any damage which that causes

PROPERTY RIGHTS

16 FACILITIES

16.1 The Tenant is to have the following rights for the Tenant and visitors, whether or not exclusive:

(a) to come and go to and from the property over the parts of the building designed or designated to afford access to the property

(b) shelter and support of the property as is now enjoyed

(c) to use the existing service wires, pipes and drains, and

(d) to use the parking area for parking the number of vehicles specified above

16.2 The Landlord is to have the following rights for the Landlord, tenants of other parts of the building and visitors over the property:

(a) to come and go to and from other parts of the building over the parts of the property designated for that purpose

(b) shelter and support as is now enjoyed

(c) to use the existing service wires, pipes and drains

GENERAL

17 PARTIES' RESPONSIBILITY

17.1 Whenever more than one person or company is the Landlord, the Tenant or the Guarantor, their obligations can be enforced against all or both of them jointly and against each individually

SERVICE OF NOTICE

17.2 The rules about serving notices in section 196 of the Law of Property Act 1925 (as since amended) apply to any notice given under this lease

5

ARBITRATION

17.3 Any matter which this lease requires to be decided by arbitration is to be referred to a single arbitrator under the Arbitration Act 1996. The Landlord and the Tenant may agree the appointment of an arbitrator, or either of them may apply to the President of the Royal Institution of Chartered Surveyors to make the appointment

HEADINGS

17.4 The headings do not form part of this lease

18 SERVICES

These are the services mentioned in clause 13.5 (delete or add as required):

  Cleaning of the common parts
  Lighting of the common parts
  Heating of the common parts
  Lift maintenance
  Hot and cold water to wash hand basins in the common parts
  Porterage
  Fire extinguishers in the common parts
  Heating in the property
  Window cleaning for the building
  Furnishing the common parts

GUARANTEE BOX

The terms in this box only take effect if a guarantor is named in clause LR.3 and then only until the Tenant transfers this lease with the Landlord's written consent. The Guarantor must sign this lease.

The Guarantor agrees to compensate the Landlord for any loss incurred as a result of the Tenant failing to comply with an obligation in this lease during the lease term or any statutory extension of it. If the Tenant is insolvent or this lease ends because it is disclaimed, the Guarantor agrees to accept a new lease, if the Landlord so requires, in the same form but at the rent then payable. Even if the Landlord gives the Tenant extra time to comply with an obligation, or does not insist on strict compliance with terms of this lease, the Guarantor's obligation remains fully effective.

THIS DOCUMENT CREATES LEGAL RIGHTS AND LEGAL OBLIGATIONS. DO NOT SIGN IT UNTIL YOU HAVE CONSULTED A SOLICITOR. THERE IS A CODE OF PRACTICE CONCERNING COMMERCIAL LEASES IN ENGLAND AND WALES PUBLISHED UNDER THE AUSPICES OF THE DEPARTMENT FOR COMMUNITIES AND LOCAL GOVERNMENT.

If a party to this lease is a company, either two directors or a director and the company secretary must sign on behalf of the company.

Signed as a deed by/on behalf of the
Landlord and delivered in the presence of:

Landlord

Witness

Witness's occupation and address

Signed as a deed by/on behalf of the
Tenant and delivered in the presence of:

Tenant

Witness

Witness's occupation and address

Signed as a deed by/on behalf of the
Guarantor and delivered in the presence of:

Guarantor

Witness

Witness's occupation and address

6

LS1 (Part)(Reg) 2006

The Law Society

DATE OF LEASE	_____ 20_____
PARTIES TO THIS LEASE	
	LANDLORD _____
	ADDRESS _____
	_____ POSTCODE _____
	COMPANY NO. _____
	TENANT _____
	ADDRESS _____
	_____ POSTCODE _____
	COMPANY NO. _____
	GUARANTOR _____
	ADDRESS _____
	_____ POSTCODE _____
	COMPANY NO. _____
PROPERTY	shown edged red on the attached plan being part of the Building known as
	_____ POSTCODE _____
TERM FOR WHICH THE PROPERTY IS LEASED	From and including _____ 20_____
	To and including _____ 20_____
PARKING	No more than _____ vehicles (see clause 16.1(d))
USE ALLOWED	
	or any other use to which the Landlord consents (and the Landlord is not entitled to withhold that consent unreasonably)
RENT	_____ Pounds
	(£_____) a year, subject to increase under clause 9 from every rent review date
FIRST PAYMENT DATE	The _____ 20_____
MONTHLY PAYMENT DATE	The _____ day of every month
RENT REVIEW DATES	Every _____ anniversary of the start of the lease term

The Landlord lets the property to the Tenant for the lease term at the rent and on the terms in clauses 1 to 18 and in any additional clauses.

    1   **LS1 (Part)(Unreg) 2006**

TENANT'S OBLIGATIONS

1 PAYMENTS

1. The Tenant is to pay the Landlord:

1.1 the rent, which is to be paid by the following instalments:

(a) on the first payment date, a proportionate sum from that date to the next monthly payment date

(b) on each monthly payment date, one-twelfth of the annual rent

1.2 the service charge in accordance with clause 3, and whenever a sum is overdue the Landlord is entitled to recover it by distraint as if it were rent in arrear

1.3 a fair proportion (decided by a surveyor whom the Landlord nominates) of the cost of repairing, maintaining and cleaning: party walls, party structures, yards, gardens, roads, paths, gutters, drains, sewers, pipes, conduits, wires, cables and things used or shared with other property

1.4 the cost (including professional fees) of any works to the property which the Landlord does after the Tenant defaults

1.5 the costs and expenses (including professional fees) which the Landlord incurs in:

(a) dealing with any application by the Tenant for consent or approval, whether it is given or not

(b) preparing and serving a notice of a breach of the Tenant's obligations, under section 146 of the Law of Property Act 1925, even if forfeiture of this lease is avoided without a court order

(c) preparing and serving schedules of dilapidations either during the lease term or recording failure to give up the property in the appropriate state of repair when this lease ends

1.6 interest at the Law Society's interest rate on any of the above payments when more than fourteen days overdue, to be calculated from its due date and in making payments under this clause:

(a) nothing is to be deducted or set off

(b) any value added tax payable is to be added

2 The Tenant is also to make the following payments, with value added tax where payable:

2.1 all periodic rates, taxes and outgoings relating to the property, including any imposed after the date of this lease (even if of a novel nature), to be paid on the due date to the appropriate authorities

2.2 the cost of the grant, renewal or continuation of any licence or registration for using the property for the use allowed, to be paid to the appropriate authority

2.3 a registration fee of £40 for each document which this lease requires the Tenant to register, to be paid to the Landlord's solicitors when presenting the document for registration

3 SERVICE CHARGE

3. The Landlord and the Tenant agree that:

3.1 the service charge is the Tenant's fair proportion of each item of the service costs

3.2 the service costs:

(a) are the costs which the Landlord fairly and reasonably incurs in complying with obligations under clauses 12 and 13

(b) include the reasonable charges of any agent, contractor, consultant or employee whom the Landlord engages to provide the services under clauses 12 and 13

(c) include interest at no more than the Law Society's interest rate on sums the Landlord borrows to discharge his obligations under clauses 12 and 13

3.3 the Tenant is to pay the Landlord interim payments on account of the service charge within 21 days of receiving a written demand setting out how it is calculated

3.4 an interim payment is to be the Tenant's fair proportion of what the service costs are reasonably likely to be in the three months following the demand

3.5 the Landlord is not entitled to demand interim payments more than once every three months

3.6 the Landlord is to keep full records of the service costs and at least once a year is to send the Tenant an account setting out, for the period since the beginning of the lease term or the last account as the case may be:

(a) the amount of the service costs

(b) the service charge the Tenant is to pay

(c) the total of any interim payments the Tenant has paid

(d) the difference between the total interim payments and the service charge

3.7 within 21 days after the Tenant receives the account, the amount mentioned in clause 3.6(d) is to be settled by payment between the parties, except that the Landlord is entitled to retain any overpayment towards any interim payments already demanded for a later accounting period

3.8 the Landlord is either:

(a) to have the account certified by an independent chartered accountant, or

(b) to allow the Tenant to inspect the books, records, invoices and receipts relating to the service costs

3.9 disagreements about the amounts of the service charge or the service costs are to be decided by arbitration under clause 17.3

4 USE

4. The Tenant is to comply with the following requirements as to the use of the building and any part of it, and is not to authorise or allow anyone else to contravene them:

4.1 to use the property only for the use allowed

4.2 not to obstruct any part of the building used for access to the property or to any other part of the building

4.3 not to do anything which might invalidate any insurance policy covering any part of the building or which might increase the premium

4.4 not to hold an auction in the property

4.5 not to use any part of the building for any activities which are dangerous, offensive, noxious, illegal or immoral, or which are or may become a nuisance or annoyance to the Landlord or to the owner or occupier of any neighbouring property

4.6 not to display any signs or advertisements on the outside of the property or which are visible from outside the property unless the Landlord consents (and the Landlord is not entitled to withhold that consent unreasonably)

4.7 not to overload any part of the property

4.8 to comply with every statutory obligation authorising or regulating how the property is used, and to obtain, comply with the terms of, renew and continue any licence or registration which is required

5 ACCESS

5. The Tenant is to give the Landlord, or anyone with the Landlord's written authority, access to the property:

5.1 for these purposes:

(a) inspecting the condition of the property, or how it is being used

(b) doing works which the Landlord is permitted to do under clauses 6.9 or 13

(c) complying with any statutory obligation

(d) viewing the property as a prospective buyer, tenant or mortgagee

(e) valuing the property

2

(f) inspecting, cleaning or repairing neighbouring property, or any sewers, drains, pipes, wires or cables serving the building or any neighbouring property

5.2 and only on seven days' written notice except in an emergency

5.3 and during normal business hours except in an emergency

5.4 and the Landlord is promptly to make good all damage caused to the property and any goods there in exercising these rights

6 CONDITION AND WORK

6. The Tenant is to comply with the following duties in relation to the property, and for this purpose the inside of the property includes all ceilings, floors, doors, door frames, windows and window frames and the internal surfaces of all walls but excludes joists immediately above the ceilings and supporting the floors:

6.1 to maintain the state and condition of the inside of the property, but the Tenant need not alter or improve it except as required in clause 6.8

6.2 to decorate the inside of the property:

(a) in every fifth year of the lease term

(b) in the last three months of the lease term (however it ends) except to the extent that it has been decorated in the previous year

6.3 where the property has a shop front, to maintain and decorate it

6.4 when decorating, to use the colours and the types of finish used previously

6.5 not to make any structural alterations or additions to the property

6.6 not to make any other alterations unless the Landlord gives written consent in advance (and the Landlord is not entitled to withhold that consent unreasonably)

6.7 to keep any plate glass in the property insured for its full replacement cost with reputable insurers, to give the Landlord details of that insurance on request, and to replace any plate glass which becomes damaged

6.8 to do any work to the property required under a statute even if it alters or improves the property. The work is to be done on the following conditions:

(a) before doing it, the Tenant is to obtain the Landlord's written consent (and the Landlord is not entitled to withhold that consent unreasonably)

(b) the Landlord is to contribute a fair proportion of the cost, taking into account any value of the work to the Landlord

and any dispute is to be decided by arbitration under clause 17.3

6.9 if the Tenant fails to do any work which this lease requires and the Landlord gives the Tenant written notice to do it, to do that work. In such a case, the Tenant is to start the work within two months, or immediately in case of emergency, and proceed diligently with it. In default, the Tenant is to permit the Landlord to do the work

6.10 However, this clause only requires the Tenant to make good damage caused by an insured risk to the extent that the insurance money has not been paid because of any act or default of the Tenant

7 TRANSFER ETC.

7. The Tenant is to comply with the following:

7.1 the Tenant is not to share occupation of the property and no part of it is to be transferred, sublet or occupied separately from the remainder

7.2 the Tenant is not to transfer or sublet the whole of the property unless the Landlord gives written consent in advance, and the Landlord is not entitled to withhold that consent unreasonably

7.3 any sublease is to be on terms which are consistent with this lease, but is not to permit the sub-tenant to underlet

7.4 within four weeks after the property is transferred, mortgaged or sublet, the Landlord's solicitors are to be notified and a copy of the transfer, mortgage or sublease sent to them for registration with the fee payable under clause 2.3

7.5 if the Landlord reasonably requires, a tenant who transfers the whole of the property is to give the Landlord a written guarantee, in the terms set out in the Guarantee Box, that the transferee will perform the tenant's obligations

8 OTHER MATTERS

8. The Tenant:

8.1 is to give the Landlord a copy of any notice concerning the property or any neighbouring property as soon as it is received

8.2 is to allow the Landlord, during the last six months of the lease term, to fix a notice in a reasonable position on the outside of the property announcing that it is for sale or to let

8.3 is not to apply for planning permission relating to the use or alteration of the property unless the Landlord gives written consent in advance

8.4 in occupying and doing work on the property, and in using any part of the building, is to comply with all statutory requirements

9 RENT REVIEW

9.1 On each rent review date, the rent is to increase to the market rent if that is higher than the rent applying before that date

9.2 The market rent is the rent which a willing tenant would pay for the property on the open market, if let on the rent review date by a willing landlord on a lease on the same terms as this lease without any premium and for a term equal to the remainder of the lease term, assuming that at that date:

(a) no account is taken of any goodwill belonging to anyone who has occupied the property

(b) the property is vacant and has not been occupied by the Tenant or any sub-tenant

(c) the property can immediately be used

(d) the property is in the condition required by this lease and any damage caused by any of the risks insured under clause 12 has been made good

(e) no tenant or sub-tenant has previously during the lease term done anything to the property to increase or decrease its rental value. In this paragraph "anything" includes work done by the Tenant to comply with clause 6.8, but nothing else which the Tenant was obliged to do under this lease

9.3 If the Landlord and the Tenant agree the amount of the new rent, a statement of that new rent, signed by them, is to be attached to this lease

9.4 If the Landlord and the Tenant have not agreed the amount of the new rent two months before the rent review date, either of them may require the new rent to be decided by arbitration under clause 17.3

9.5 (a) The Tenant is to pay rent at the rate applying before the rent review date until the next rent day after the new rent is agreed or decided

(b) Starting on that rent day, the Tenant is to pay the new rent

(c) On that rent day, the Tenant is also to pay any amount by which the new rent since the rent review date exceeds the rent paid, with interest on that amount at 4% below the Law Society's interest rate

10 DAMAGE

10. If the property is, or the common parts are, damaged by any of the risks required to be insured under clause 12 and as a result of that damage the property, or any part of it, cannot be used for the use allowed:

3

10.1 the rent, or a fair proportion of it, is to be suspended for three years or until the property or the common parts are fully restored, if earlier

10.2 if at any time when it is unlikely that the damage will be fully repaired either within three years from the date of the damage, or (if sooner) before the end of the lease term, the Landlord (so long as he has not wilfully delayed the restoration) or the Tenant may end this lease by giving one month's notice to the other in which case

    (a) the insurance money belongs to the Landlord and

    (b) the Landlord's obligation to make good damage under clause 12 ceases

10.3 a notice is only effective if given within three years from the date of the damage

10.4 If the insurers refuse to pay all or part of the insurance money because of the Tenant's act or default:

    (a) to the extent of that refusal, the Tenant cannot claim the benefit of clause 10.1

    (b) the Tenant cannot serve notice under clause 10.2

10.5 Any dispute under any part of this clause is to be decided by arbitration under clause 17.3

LANDLORD'S OBLIGATIONS AND FORFEITURE RIGHTS

11 QUIET ENJOYMENT

11. The Landlord is to allow the Tenant to possess and use the property without lawful interference from the Landlord, anyone who derives title from the Landlord or any trustee for the Landlord

12 INSURANCE

12. The Landlord is to:

12.1 keep the building (except the plate glass) insured with reputable insurers to cover

    (a) full rebuilding, site clearance, professional fees, value added tax and three years' loss of rent

    (b) against fire, lightning, explosion, earthquake, landslip, subsidence, heave, riot, civil commotion, aircraft, aerial devices, storm, flood, water, theft, impact by vehicles, damage by malicious persons and vandals and third party liability and other risks reasonably required by the Landlord

so far as cover is available at normal insurance rates for the locality and subject to reasonable excesses and exclusions

12.2 take all necessary steps to make good as soon as possible all damage to the building by insured risks except to the extent that the insurance money is not paid because of the act or default of the Tenant

12.3 give the Tenant on request once a year particulars of the policy and evidence from the insurer that it is in force

13 SERVICES

13. The Landlord is to comply with the following duties in relation to the building:

13.1 to maintain the state and condition (including the decorations) of:

    (a) the structure, outside, roof, foundations, joists, floor slabs, load bearing walls, beams and columns of the building and any plant, machinery and fixtures required to provide the services listed in clause 18

    (b) those parts of the building which tenants of more than one part can use ("the common parts")

13.2 to decorate the common parts and the outside of the building every five years, using colours and types of finish reasonably decided by the Landlord

13.3 to pay promptly all periodic rates, taxes and outgoings relating to the common parts, including any imposed after the date of this lease (even if of a novel nature)

13.4 to pay or contribute to the cost of repairing, maintaining and cleaning party walls, party structures, yards, gardens, roads, paths, gutters, drains, sewers, pipes, conduits, wires, cables and other things used or shared with other property

13.5 to provide the services listed in clause 18, but the Landlord is not to be liable for failure or delay caused by industrial disputes, shortage of supplies, adverse weather conditions or other causes beyond the control of the Landlord

14 FORFEITURE

14. This lease comes to an end if the Landlord forfeits it by entering any part of the property, which the Landlord is entitled to do whenever:

    (a) payment of any rent is fourteen days overdue, even if it was not formally demanded

    (b) the Tenant has not complied with any of the terms of this lease

    (c) the Tenant if an individual (and if more than one, any of them) is adjudicated bankrupt or an interim receiver of the Tenant's property is appointed

    (d) the Tenant if a company (and if more than one, any of them) goes into liquidation (unless solely for the purpose of amalgamation or reconstruction when solvent), or had an administrative receiver appointed or had an administration order made in respect of it or the directors of the Tenant give notice of their intention to appoint an administrator

The forfeiture of this lease does not cancel any outstanding obligation of the Tenant or a Guarantor

15 END OF LEASE

15. When this lease ends the Tenant is to:

15.1 return the property to the Landlord leaving it in the state and condition in which this lease requires the Tenant to keep it

15.2 (if the Landlord so requires) remove anything the Tenant fixed to the property and make good any damage which that causes

PROPERTY RIGHTS

16 FACILITIES

16.1 The Tenant is to have the following rights for the Tenant and visitors, whether or not exclusive:

    (a) to come and go to and from the property over the parts of the building designed or designated to afford access to the property

    (b) shelter and support of the property as is now enjoyed

    (c) to use the existing service wires, pipes and drains, and

    (d) to use the parking area for parking the number of vehicles specified above

16.2 The Landlord is to have the following rights for the Landlord, tenants of other parts of the building and visitors over the property:

    (a) to come and go to and from other parts of the building over the parts of the property designated for that purpose

    (b) shelter and support as is now enjoyed

    (c) to use the existing service wires, pipes and drains

GENERAL

17 PARTIES' RESPONSIBILITY

17.1 Whenever more than one person or company is the Landlord, the Tenant or the Guarantor, their obligations can be enforced against all or both of them jointly and against each individually

SERVICE OF NOTICE

17.2 The rules about serving notices in section 196 of the Law of Property Act 1925 (as since amended) apply to any notice given under this lease

4

ARBITRATION

17.3 Any matter which this lease requires to be decided by arbitration is to be referred to a single arbitrator under the Arbitration Act 1996. The Landlord and the Tenant may agree the appointment of an arbitrator, or either of them may apply to the President of the Royal Institution of Chartered Surveyors to make the appointment

HEADINGS

17.4 The headings do not form part of this lease

18 SERVICES

These are the services mentioned in clause 13.5 (delete or add as required):

Cleaning of the common parts

Lighting of the common parts

Heating of the common parts

Lift maintenance

Hot and cold water to wash hand basins in the common parts

Porterage

Fire extinguishers in the common parts

Heating in the property

Window cleaning for the building

Furnishing the common parts

GUARANTEE BOX

The terms in this box only take effect if a guarantor is named above and then only until the Tenant transfers this lease with the Landlord's written consent. The Guarantor must sign this lease.

The Guarantor agrees to compensate the Landlord for any loss incurred as a result of the Tenant failing to comply with an obligation in this lease during the lease term or any statutory extension of it. If the Tenant is insolvent or this lease ends because it is disclaimed, the Guarantor agrees to accept a new lease, if the Landlord so requires, in the same form but at the rent then payable. Even if the Landlord gives the Tenant extra time to comply with an obligation, or does not insist on strict compliance with terms of this lease, the Guarantor's obligation remains fully effective.

THIS DOCUMENT CREATES LEGAL RIGHTS AND LEGAL OBLIGATIONS. DO NOT SIGN IT UNTIL YOU HAVE CONSULTED A SOLICITOR. THERE IS A CODE OF PRACTICE CONCERNING COMMERCIAL LEASES IN ENGLAND AND WALES PUBLISHED UNDER THE AUSPICES OF THE DEPARTMENT FOR COMMUNITIES AND LOCAL GOVERNMENT.

If a party to this lease is a company, either two directors or a director and the company secretary must sign on behalf of the company.

Signed as a deed by/on behalf of the
Landlord and delivered in the presence of:

....
Landlord

....
Witness

....
Witness's occupation and address

Signed as a deed by/on behalf of the
Tenant and delivered in the presence of:

....
Tenant

....
Witness

....
Witness's occupation and address

Signed as a deed by/on behalf of the
Guarantor and delivered in the presence of:

....
Guarantor

....
Witness

....
Witness's occupation and address

5

LS1 (Part)(Unreg) 2006

V.2. Form of undertaking agreed with banks[1]

FORM NO. 4 (BRIDGING FINANCE)

Undertaking by solicitor (with form of authority from client) to account to bank for net proceeds of sale of the existing property, the bank having provided funds in connection with the purchase of the new property.

Authority from client(s)

[*Date*]

To [*name and address of solicitors*]

I/We hereby irrevocably authorise and request you to give an undertaking in the form set out below and accordingly to pay the net proceeds of sale after deduction of your costs to […] Bank plc […] Branch.

Signature of client(s) ....

Undertaking

[*Date*]

To […] Bank plc

If you provide facilities to my/our client […] for the purchase of the freehold/leasehold property (the new property) [*description of property*] pending the sale by my/our client of the freehold/leasehold property (the existing property) [*description of property*]

I/we undertake:

1. That any sums received from you or your customer will be applied solely for the following purposes:

    (a) in discharging the present mortgage(s) on the existing property [*delete if not applicable*];

    (b) in acquiring a good marketable title to the new property, subject to the mortgage mentioned below [*delete if not applicable*];

    (c) in paying any necessary deposit, legal fees, costs and disbursements in connection with the purchase.

The purchase price contemplated is £[…] gross.

---

1. © The Law Society 1999.

I/We are informed that a sum of £[…] is being advanced on mortgage by […] [*delete if not applicable*]. The amount required from my/our client for the transaction including the deposit and together with costs, disbursements and apportionments is not expected to exceed £[…]

2.   To hold to your order when received by me/us the documents of title of the existing property pending completion of the sale (unless subject to any prior mortgage(s)) and of the new property (unless subject to any prior mortgage(s)).

3.   To pay to you the net proceeds of sale of the existing property when received by me/us. The sale price contemplated is £[…] and the only deductions which will have to be made at present known to me/us are:

    (i)   the deposit (if not held by me/us),

    (ii)   the estate agents' commission,

    (iii)   the amount required to redeem any mortgages and charges, which so far as known to me/us at present do not exceed £[…],

    (iv)   the legal fees, costs and disbursements relating to the transaction.

4.   To advise you immediately of any subsequent claim by a third party upon the net proceeds of sale of which I/we have knowledge.

Notes:

(1)   If any deductions will have to be made from the net proceeds of sale other than those shown above, these must be specifically mentioned.

(2)   It would be convenient if this form of undertaking were presented in duplicate so that a copy could be retained by the solicitor.

V.3. Recommended form of undertaking for discharge of building society mortgages

'In consideration of your today completing the purchase of [...] WE HEREBY UNDERTAKE forthwith to pay over to the [...] Building Society the money required to redeem the mortgage/legal charge dated [...] and to forward the receipted mortgage/legal charge to you as soon as it is received by us from the [...] Building Society.'[1]

Suggested form of undertaking for use by solicitors on the redemption of a mortgage and lodgement of an electronic discharge at HM Land Registry[2]

In consideration of your today completing the purchase of [property] we hereby undertake forthwith (1) to pay over to [the lender] the money required to discharge the legal charge dated [date]; (2) to forward a form END1 to [the lender]; (3) and to forward to you a copy of the written confirmation or acknowledgement from the lender that an Electronic Notification of Discharge of the registered charge has been sent to Land Registry as soon as it is received by us.

---

1. The following text appears in *The Guide to the Professional Conduct of Solicitors 1999* as Annex 25B.
2. Crown copyright 2005. This suggested form of undertaking is reproduced from Land Registry Practice Guide 31 (Discharge of Charges).

V.4. Letter to lender if lender's instructions do not contain a certificate that it complies with Rule 3.19[1]

To [*Lender*]

Re: Application Number:
Property:
Borrower:

Dear Sir,

Thank you for your instructions of [...] relating to this matter. Since it is intended that we should act on behalf of the borrower as well as yourselves, the provisions of Solicitors' Code of Conduct 2007, Rule 3.19 will apply. Under the terms of this rule, unless a lender's mortgage instructions contain a certificate given by the lender that such instructions are subject to the limitations contained in Solicitors' Code of Conduct 2007, Rules 3.19 and 3.21, we are under an obligation to give you a notification which limits our responsibilities to you.

We have read your instructions and cannot see the certificate referred to above. Accordingly, we notify you that our duties to you under your instructions will be limited to the matters contained in the approved certificates set out in the annex to Rule 3 and no more. We must draw to your attention the final paragraph of the certificate which states as follows:

'Our duties to you are limited to the matters set out in this certificate and we accept no further liability or responsibility whatsoever. The payment by you to us (by whatever means) of the mortgage advance or any part of it constitutes acceptance of this limitation and any assignment to you by the borrower of any rights of action against us to which the borrower may be entitled shall take effect subject to this limitation.'

You will understand that we are professionally bound by the requirements of this rule and are unable to depart from the requirement. Accordingly, if you are unable to accept this limitation we regret that you will have to instruct somebody else to act on your behalf. Will you please confirm your acceptance of the position.

Yours faithfully,

1. © The Law Society 1999. This letter was first published as Appendix A to 'Practice rule 6(3) solicitor acting for lender and borrower' (see [1999] *Gazette*, 29 September). It has been updated to refer to Solicitors' Code of Conduct 2007.

V.5. Letter to lender if lender's instructions (either general or specific to the transaction) appear to go beyond the limitations of Rule 3.19[1]

To [*Lender*]

Application Number:
Property:
Borrower:

Dear Sir,

Thank you for your instructions of [...] related to this matter, in accordance with which we shall be pleased to act.

As you will be aware, as solicitors we are bound by the requirements of Solicitors' Code of Conduct 2007, Rule 3.19 which limits the duties which we can undertake to a lender in cases (such as this one) where we are also acting for the borrower.

Although you have certified that your mortgage instructions are subject to the limitations contained in Rules 3.19 and 3.21, we are concerned that your instructions may fall outside the terms of the rule in certain respects which we mention in this letter.

We draw to your attention that since this is a residential property, the certificate of title will be in the form set out in the annex to Rule 3, the concluding paragraph of which reads as follows:

'Our duties to you are limited to the matters set out in this certificate and we accept no further liability or responsibility whatsoever. The payment by you to us (by whatever means) of the mortgage advance or any part of it constitutes acceptance of this limitation and any assignment to you by the borrower of any rights of action against us to which the borrower may be entitled shall take effect subject to this limitation.'

You will understand that we are professionally bound by the requirements of this rule and are unable to depart from the same. Accordingly, we respectfully point out that the instructions referred to below appear to us to conflict with Rule 3.19. The contractual effect of your certificate is to exclude any obligation (even if it is specifically stated in your instructions) which goes beyond the limitations of Rule 3.19. The certificate of title will be accordingly given subject to such exclusion.

List of offending conditions: [*insert list here*]

Yours faithfully,

---

1. © The Law Society 1999. This letter was first published as Appendix B to 'Practice rule 6(3) solicitor acting for lender and borrower' (see [1999] *Gazette*, 29 September). It has been updated to refer to Solicitors' Code of Conduct 2007.

V.6. CON 29DW Standard Drainage and Water Enquiries (2007)[1]

Public sewer map

1 Where relevant, please include a copy of an extract from the public sewer map.

Foul water

2 Does foul water from the property drain to a public sewer?

Surface water

3 Does surface water from the property drain to a public sewer?

Public adoption of sewers and lateral drains

4 Are any sewers or lateral drains serving or which are proposed to serve the property the subject of an existing adoption agreement or an application for such an agreement?

Public sewers within the boundaries of the property

5 Does the public sewer map indicate any public sewer, disposal main or lateral drain within the boundaries of the property?

Public sewers near to the property

6 Does the public sewer map indicate any public sewer within 30.48 metres (100 feet) of any buildings within the property?

Building over a public sewer, disposal main or drain

7 Has a sewerage undertaker approved or been consulted about any plans to erect a building or extension on the property over or in the vicinity of a public sewer, disposal main or drain?

Map of waterworks

8 Where relevant, please include a copy of an extract from the map of waterworks.

---

1. © The Law Society 2007.

CON 29DW Standard drainage and water enquiries (2007)

This search form must be submitted with the appropriate fee and a copy of the location plan.

A. Name and address of water company

(For use by water company only)

B. Address of the land/property

UPRN(s)

House name/number

Street

Locality

Town

County

Postcode

If the enquiries are made of a plot of land or of a property less than 5 years old:

Name of developer

Plot no.

Site name and phase

C. Your details

Signed ....

Name/contact name

Company name

Date

Your reference

Telephone

Fax

Email

Account no.

D. Fees

Search	Fee
CON 29DW Standard drainage and water enquiries 2007	
Total	

E. Reply to

DX

Notes

The standard drainage and water enquiries are listed on page 2 of this form. These enquiries comply with the Home Information Pack (No.2) Regulations 2007.

Completing and submitting this form to a water company indicates an acceptance of that water company's terms and conditions. Terms and conditions may vary between water companies. Request a copy of the terms and conditions from the water company or see its website for details.

A. Ensure that search forms are sent to the correct water company, see www.drainageandwater.co.uk for details.

B. Enter the address of the property. Please give the Unique Property Reference Number if known. If the enquiries are made of a plot of land or the property is less than 5 years old, please give the developer's details.

C. Sign, date and enter your details. Account customers of water companies may enter their account number.

D. Enter the fee for the enquiries. Fees may differ between water companies. Consult the water company or see www.drainageandwater.co.uk for the current fees.

E. Enter the name and address/DX address of the person or company conducting this enquiry.

Adoption of water mains and service pipes

9   Is any water main or service pipe serving or which is proposed to serve the property the subject of an existing adoption agreement or an application for such an agreement?

Sewerage and water undertakers

10   Who are the sewerage and water undertakers for the area?

Connection to mains water supply

11   Is the property connected to mains water supply?

Water mains, resource mains or discharge pipes

12   Are there any water mains, resource mains or discharge pipes within the boundaries of the property?

Current basis for sewerage and water charges

13   What is the current basis for charging for sewerage and water services at the property?

Charges following change of occupation

14   Will the basis for charging for sewerage and water services at the property change as a consequence of a change of occupation?

Surface water drainage charges

15   Is a surface water drainage charge payable?

Water meters

16   Please include details of the location of any water meter serving the property.

Sewerage bills

17   Who bills the property for sewerage services?

Water bills

18   Who bills the property for water services?

Risk of flooding due to overloaded public sewers

19   Is the dwelling-house which is or forms part of the property at risk of internal flooding due to overloaded public sewers?

Risk of low water pressure or flow

20   Is the property at risk of receiving low water pressure or flow?

Water quality analysis

21   Please include details of a water quality analysis made by the water undertaker for the water supply zone in respect of the most recent calendar year.

Authorised departures from water quality standards

22   Please include details of any departures –

    (a)   authorised by the Secretary of State under Part 6 of the 2000 Regulations from the provisions of Part 3 of those Regulations; or

    (b)   authorised by the National Assembly for Wales under Part 6 of the 2001 Regulations from the provisions of Part 3 of those Regulations.

Sewage treatment works

23   Please state the distance from the property to the nearest boundary of the nearest sewage treatment works.

NOTES

(i)   Copyright in enquiries 1–23 belongs to the Crown. The enquiries are reproduced from Sched.8, Part 2 of the Home Information Pack (No.2) Regulations 2007.

(ii)   The terms used in these enquiries have the meaning given to them by the Home Information Pack (No.2) Regulations 2007, Sched.8, Part 1.

(iii)   The report prepared by a water company in response to these enquiries will include those enquiries and replies which are relevant to the property. The numbering and order of enquiries may differ between this form and a report.

V.7. CON 29R Enquiries of Local Authority (2007) and CON 29O Optional Enquiries of Local Authority (2007)[1]

CON 29R Enquiries of Local Authority (2007)

PLANNING AND BUILDING REGULATIONS

1.1. Planning and building decisions and pending applications

Which of the following relating to the property have been granted, issued or refused or (where applicable) are the subject of pending applications?

(a) a planning permission

(b) a listed building consent

(c) a conservation area consent

(d) a certificate of lawfulness of existing use or development

(e) a certificate of lawfulness of proposed use or development

(f) building regulations approval

(g) a building regulation completion certificate and

(h) any building regulations certificate or notice issued in respect of work carried out under a competent person self-certification scheme

1.2. Planning designations and proposals

What designations of land use for the property or the area, and what specific proposals for the property, are contained in any existing or proposed development plan?

ROADS

2. Roadways, footways and footpaths

Which of the roads, footways and footpaths named in the application for this search (via boxes B and C) are:

(a) highways maintainable at public expense

(b) subject to adoption and, supported by a bond or bond waiver

(c) to be made up by a local authority who will reclaim the cost from the frontagers

(d) to be adopted by a local authority without reclaiming the cost from the frontagers

---

1. © The Law Society 2007. Reproduced with the kind permission of Oyez Straker.

CON 29R Enquiries of local authority (2007)

The Law Society

A duplicate plan is required for all searches submitted directly to a local authority.
If submitted manually, this form must be submitted in duplicate. Please type or use BLOCK LETTERS

A.

Local authority name and address	Search No:..
	Signed:..
	On behalf of: .... Local authority/private search company/ member of the public (indicate as applicable)
	Dated: ....

B.

Address of the land/property

UPRN(s):

Secondary name/number:

Primary name/number:

Street:

Locality/village:

Town:

Postcode:

C.

Other roadways, footways and footpaths in respect of which a reply to enquiry 2 is required

D.

Fees

£_____ is enclosed/is paid by NLIS transfer (delete as applicable)

Signed:

Dated:

Reference:

Telephone No:

Fax No:

E-mail:

E. (For HIPs regulations compliance only)

Names of those involved in the sale (this box is only completed when the replies to these enquiries are to be included in a Home Information Pack)

Name of vendor:

Name of estate agents:

Name of HIP provider:

Name of solicitor/conveyancer:

Your personal data – name and address – will be handled strictly in accordance with the requirements of the Data Protection Act. It is required to pass on to the relevant authority(ies) in order to carry out the necessary searches.

Notes

A. Enter name and address of appropriate Council. If the property is near a local authority boundary, consider raising certain enquiries (e.g. road schemes) with the adjoining Council.
B. Enter address and description of the property. Please give the UPRN(s) (Unique Property Reference Number) where known. **A duplicate plan is required for all searches submitted directly to a local authority.** The search may be returned if land/property cannot easily be identified.
C. Enter name and/or mark on plan any other roadways, footways and footpaths abutting the property (in addition to those entered in Box B) to which a reply to enquiry 2 is required.
D. Details of fees can be obtained from the Council, your chosen NLIS channel or search provider.
E. Box E is only to be completed when the replies to these enquiries are to be included in a Home Information Pack. Enter the name of the individual(s) and firms involved in the sale of the property.
F. Enter the name and address/DX address of the person or company lodging or conducting this enquiry.

F.

Reply to

DX address:

Oyez 7 Spa Road, London SE16 3QQ   © Law Society 2007   4.2007 F7618   5033382

Conveyancing 29R (Enquiries)

OTHER MATTERS

3.1. Land required for public purposes

Is the property included in land required for public purposes?

3.2. Land to be acquired for road works

Is the property included in land to be acquired for road works?

3.3. Drainage agreements and consents

Do either of the following exist in relation to the property?

(a) an agreement to drain buildings in combination into an existing sewer by means of a private sewer

(b) an agreement or consent for (i) a building, or (ii) extension to a building on the property, to be built over, or in the vicinity of a drain, sewer or disposal main

3.4. Nearby road schemes

Is the property (or will it be) within 200 metres of any of the following?

(a) the centre line of a new trunk road or special road specified in any order, draft order or scheme

(b) the centre line of a proposed alteration or improvement to an existing road involving construction of a subway, underpass, flyover, footbridge, elevated road or dual carriageway

(c) the outer limits of construction works for a proposed alteration or improvement to an existing road involving

    (i) construction of a roundabout (other than a mini roundabout), or

    (ii) widening by construction of one or more additional traffic lanes;

(d) the outer limits of

    (i) construction of a new road to be built by a local authority,

    (ii) an approved alteration or improvement to an existing road involving construction of a subway, underpass, flyover, footbridge, elevated road or dual carriageway,

    (iii) construction of a roundabout (other than a mini roundabout) or widening by construction of one or more additional traffic lanes

(e) the centre line of the proposed route of a new road under proposals published for public consultation

(f) the outer limits of

    (i) construction of a proposed alteration or improvement to an existing road involving construction of a subway, underpass, flyover, footbridge, elevated road or dual carriageway,

    (ii) construction of a roundabout (other than a mini roundabout),

    (iii) widening by construction of one or more additional traffic lanes, under proposals published for public consultation

3.5.   Nearby railway schemes

Is the property (or will it be) within 200 metres of the centre line of a proposed railway, tramway, light railway or monorail?

3.6.   Traffic schemes

Has a local authority approved but not yet implemented any of the following for the roads, footways and footpaths (named in Box B) which abut the boundaries of the property?

   (a)   permanent stopping up or diversion

   (b)   waiting or loading restrictions

   (c)   one way driving

   (d)   prohibition of driving

   (e)   pedestrianisation

   (f)   vehicle width or weight restriction

   (g)   traffic calming works including road humps

   (h)   residents parking controls

   (i)   minor road widening or improvement

   (j)   pedestrian crossings

   (k)   cycle tracks

   (l)   bridge building

3.7.   Outstanding notices

Do any statutory notices which relate to the following matters subsist in relation to the property other than those revealed in a response to any other enquiry in this form?

   (a)   building works

   (b)   environment

   (c)   health and safety

   (d)   housing

   (e)   highways

   (f)   public health

3.8.   Contravention of building regulations

Has a local authority authorised in relation to the property any proceedings for the contravention of any provision contained in Building Regulations?

3.9.   Notices, orders, directions and proceedings under Planning Acts

Do any of the following subsist in relation to the property, or has a local authority decided to issue, serve, make or commence any of the following?

   (a)   an enforcement notice

   (b)   a stop notice

(c)   a listed building enforcement notice

(d)   a breach of condition notice

(e)   a planning contravention notice

(f)   another notice relating to breach of planning control

(g)   a listed building repairs notice

(h)   in the case of a listed building deliberately allowed to fall into disrepair, a compulsory purchase order with a direction for minimum compensation

(i)   a building preservation notice

(j)   a direction restricting permitted development

(k)   an order revoking or modifying planning permission

(l)   an order requiring discontinuance of use or alteration or removal of building or works

(m)   a tree preservation order

(n)   proceedings to enforce a planning agreement or planning contribution

3.10.   Conservation area

Do the following apply in relation to the property?

(a)   the making of the area a conservation area before 31st August 1974

(b)   an unimplemented resolution to designate the area a conservation area

3.11.   Compulsory purchase

Has any enforceable order or decision been made to compulsorily purchase or acquire the property?

3.12.   Contaminated land

Do any of the following apply (including any relating to the land adjacent to or adjoining the property which has been identified as contaminated land because it is in such a condition that harm or pollution of controlled waters might be caused on the property)?

(a)   a contaminated land notice

(b)   in relation to a register maintained under section 78R of the Environmental Protection Act 1990

(i)   a decision to make an entry

(ii)   an entry

(c)   consultation with the owner or occupier of the property conducted under section 78G(3) of the Environmental Protection Act 1990 before the service of a remediation notice

3.13.   Radon gas

Do records indicate that the property is in a 'Radon Affected Area' as identified by the Health Protection Agency?

NOTES:

(1)   References to the provisions of particular Acts of Parliament or Regulations include any provisions which they have replaced and also include existing or future amendments or re-enactments.

(2)   The replies will be given in the belief that they are in accordance with information presently available to the officers of the replying Council, but none of the Councils or their officers accept legal responsibility for an incorrect reply, except for negligence. Any liability for negligence will extend to the person who raised the enquiries and the person on whose behalf they were raised. It will also extend to any other person who has knowledge (personally or through an agent) of the replies before the time when he purchases, takes a tenancy of, or lends money on the security of the property or (if earlier) the time when he becomes contractually bound to do so.

(3)   This Form should be read in conjunction with the guidance notes available separately.

(4)   Area means any area in which the property is located.

(5)   References to the Council include any predecessor Council and also any council committee, sub-committee or other body or person exercising powers delegated by the Council and their approval includes their decision to proceed. The replies given to certain enquiries cover knowledge and actions of both the District Council and County Council.

(6)   Where relevant, the source department for copy documents should be provided.

CON 29O Optional Enquiries of Local Authority (2007)

ROAD PROPOSALS BY PRIVATE BODIES

4.   What proposals by others, still capable of being implemented, have the Council approved for any of the following, the limits of construction of which are within 200 metres of the property?

   (a)   the construction of a new road

   (b)   the alteration or improvement of an existing road, involving the construction, whether or not within existing highway limits, of a subway, underpass, flyover, footbridge, elevated road, dual carriageway, the construction of a roundabout (other than a mini roundabout) or the widening of an existing road by the construction of one or more additional traffic lanes

This enquiry refers to proposals by bodies or companies (such as private developers) other than the Council (and where appropriate the County Council) or the Secretary of State. A mini roundabout is a roundabout having a one-way circulatory carriageway around a flush or slightly raised circular marking less than 4 metres in diameter and with or without flared approaches.

PUBLIC PATHS OR BYWAYS

5.1.   Is any footpath, bridleway, restricted byway or byway open to all traffic which abuts on, or crosses the property, shown in a definitive map or revised definitive map prepared under Part IV of the National Parks and Access to the Countryside Act 1949 or Part III of the Wildlife and Countryside Act 1981?

5.2.   If so, please mark its approximate route on the attached plan.

CON 29O Optional enquiries of local authority (2007)

The Law Society

A duplicate plan is required for all searches submitted directly to a local authority.
If submitted manually, this form must be submitted in duplicate. Please type or use BLOCK LETTERS

A.

Local authority name and address	Search No:...
	Signed:...
	On behalf of: Local authority/private search company/ member of the public (indicate as applicable)
	Dated:...

B.

Address of the land/property

UPRN(s):

Secondary name/number:

Primary name/number:

Street:

Locality/village:

Town:

Postcode:

C.

Optional enquiries (please tick as required)

- [ ] 4. Road proposals by private bodies
- [ ] 5. Public paths or byways
- [ ] 6. Advertisements
- [ ] 7. Completion notices
- [ ] 8. Parks and countryside
- [ ] 9. Pipelines
- [ ] 10. Houses in multiple occupation
- [ ] 11. Noise abatement
- [ ] 12. Urban development areas
- [ ] 13. Enterprise zones
- [ ] 14. Inner urban improvement areas
- [ ] 15. Simplified planning zones
- [ ] 16. Land maintenance notices
- [ ] 17. Mineral consultation areas
- [ ] 18. Hazardous substance consents
- [ ] 19. Environmental and pollution notices
- [ ] 20. Food safety notices
- [ ] 21. Hedgerow notices
- [ ] 22. Common land, town and village greens

D.

Fees

£_____ is enclosed/is paid by NLIS transfer (delete as applicable)

Signed:

Dated:

Reference:

Telephone No:

Fax No:

E-mail:

Notes

A. Enter name and address of appropriate Council. If the property is near a local authority boundary, consider raising certain enquiries (e.g. road schemes) with the adjoining Council.

B. Enter address and description of the property. Please give the UPRN(s) (Unique Property Reference Number) where known. **A duplicate plan is required for all searches submitted directly to a local authority.** The search may be returned if land/property cannot easily be identified.

C. Questions 1-3 appear on CON 29O Enquiries of local authority (2007).

D. Details of fees can be obtained from the Council, your chosen NLIS channel or search provider.

E. Enter the name and address/DX address of the person or company lodging or conducting this enquiry.

E.

Reply to

DX address:

Oyez 7 Spa Road, London SE16 3QQ

© Law Society 2007   4.2007 F7619

5033384

Conveyancing 290 (Optional Enquiries)

ADVERTISEMENTS

Entries in the register

6.1.   Please list any entries in the register of applications, directions and decisions relating to consent for the display of advertisements.

6.2.   If there are any entries, where can that register be inspected?

Notices, proceedings and orders

6.3.   Except as shown in the official certificate of search:

(a)   has any notice been given by the Secretary of State or served in respect of a direction or proposed direction restricting deemed consent for any class of advertisement

(b)   have the Council resolved to serve a notice requiring the display of any advertisement to be discontinued

(c)   if a discontinuance notice has been served, has it been complied with to the satisfaction of the Council

(d)   have the Council resolved to serve any other notice or proceedings relating to a contravention of the control of advertisements

(e)   have the Council resolved to make an order for the special control of advertisements for the area

COMPLETION NOTICES

7.   Which of the planning permissions in force have the Council resolved to terminate by means of a completion notice under s.94 of the Town and Country Planning Act 1990?

PARKS AND COUNTRYSIDE

Areas of outstanding natural beauty

8.1.   Has any order under s.82 of the Countryside and Rights of Way Act 2000 been made?

National Parks

8.2.   Is the property within a National Park designated under s.7. of the National Parks and Access to the Countryside Act 1949?

PIPELINES

9.   Has a map been deposited under s.35 of the Pipelines Act 1962, or Schedule 7 of the Gas Act 1986, showing a pipeline laid through, or within 100 feet (30.48 metres) of the property?

HOUSES IN MULTIPLE OCCUPATION

10.   Is the property a house in multiple occupation,or is it designated or proposed to be designated for selective licensing of residential accommodation in accordance with the Housing Act 2004?

NOISE ABATEMENT

Noise abatement zone

11.1.   Have the Council made, or resolved to make, any noise abatement zone order under s.63 of the Control of Pollution Act 1974 for the area?

Entries in register

11.2.   Has any entry been recorded in the noise level register kept pursuant to s.64 of the Control of Pollution Act 1974?

11.3.   If there is any entry, how can copies be obtained and where can that register be inspected?

URBAN DEVELOPMENT AREAS

12.1.   Is the area an urban development area designated under Part XVI of the Local Government, Planning and Land Act 1980?

12.2.   If so, please state the name of the urban development corporation and the address of its principal office.

ENTERPRISE ZONES

13.   Is the area an enterprise zone designated under Part XVIII of the Local Government, Planning and Land Act 1980?

INNER URBAN IMPROVEMENT AREAS

14.   Have the Council resolved to define the area as an improvement area under s.4 of the Inner Urban Areas Act 1978?

SIMPLIFIED PLANNING ZONES

15.1.   Is the area a simplified planning zone adopted or approved pursuant to s.83 of the Town and Country Planning Act 1990?

15.2.   Have the Council approved any proposal for designating the area as a simplified planning zone?

LAND MAINTENANCE NOTICES

16.   Have the Council authorised the service of a maintenance notice under s.215 of the Town and Country Planning Act 1990?

MINERAL CONSULTATION AREAS

17.   Is the area a mineral consultation area notified by the county planning authority under Schedule 1 para 7 of the Town and Country Planning Act 1990?

HAZARDOUS SUBSTANCE CONSENTS

18.1.   Please list any entries in the register kept pursuant to s.28 of the Planning (Hazardous Substances) Act 1990.

18.2.   If there are any entries:

    (a)   how can copies of the entries be obtained

    (b)   where can the register be inspected

ENVIRONMENTAL AND POLLUTION NOTICES

19.   What outstanding statutory or informal notices have been issued by the Council under the Environmental Protection Act 1990 or the Control of Pollution Act 1974? (This enquiry does not cover notices under Part IIA or Part III of the EPA, to which enquiries 3.12 or 3.7 apply).

FOOD SAFETY NOTICES

20.   What outstanding statutory notices or informal notices have been issued by the Council under the Food Safety Act 1990 or the Food Hygiene Regulations 2006?

HEDGEROW NOTICES

21.1.   Please list any entries in the record maintained under regulation 10 of the Hedgerows Regulations 1997.

21.2.   If there are any entries:

    (a)   how can copies of the matters entered be obtained

    (b)   where can the record be inspected

COMMON LAND, TOWN AND VILLAGE GREENS

22.1.   Is the property, or any land which abuts the property, registered common land or town or village green under the Commons Registration Act 1965 or the Commons Act 2006?

22.2.   If there are any entries, how can copies of the matters registered be obtained and where can the register be inspected?

NOTES:

(1)   References to the provisions of particular Acts of Parliament or Regulations include any provisions which they have replaced and also include existing or future amendments or re-enactments.

(2)   The replies will be given in the belief that they are in accordance with information presently available to the officers of the replying Council, but none of the Councils or their officers accept legal responsibility for an incorrect reply, except for negligence. Any liability for negligence will extend to the person who raised the enquiries and the person on whose behalf they were raised. It will also extend to any other person who has knowledge (personally or through an agent) of the

replies before the time when he purchases, takes a tenancy of, or lends money on the security of the property or (if earlier) the time when he becomes contractually bound to do so.

(3)   This form should be read in conjunction with the guidance notes available separately.

(4)   Area means any area in which the property is located.

(5)   References to the Council include any predecessor Council and also any council committee, sub-committee or other body or person exercising powers delegated by the Council and their approval includes their decision to proceed. The replies given to certain enquiries cover knowledge and actions of both the District Council and County Council.

(6)   Where relevant, the source department for copy documents should be provided.

V.8. CON 29M (2006) Coal Mining and Brine Subsidence Claim Search (including Guidance Notes)

LAW SOCIETY GUIDANCE NOTES 2006

1. Introduction

1.1 A coal mining and brine subsidence claim search should be made by solicitors when acting on the occasion of any dealing with land in coal mining and brine subsidence claim areas ('affected areas'), including purchase, mortgage, further advance or before any development takes place.

1.2 For those solicitors not using the National Land Information Service (NLIS) or other electronic means, the enquiry should be made using form CON 29M which has been extended to include enquiries covering brine subsidence claims. This revised CON 29M (2006) is approved by the Law Society, the Coal Authority and the Cheshire Brine Subsidence Compensation Board ('the Brine Board'). The search should be made before the exchange of contracts or any binding obligation is entered into.

1.3 Whilst the Brine Board will retain control, liability and responsibility for the accuracy of the Brine data and be available to deal with any technical non-service related follow-up enquiries, the combined CON 29M coal and brine report service will be provided by the Coal Authority.

1.4 Where reports are provided by the Coal Authority on its own and on behalf of the Brine Board following a CON 29M search, there is no need for the applicant to supply evidence of the authority from the seller or seller's solicitor to the release of the information (if any) on the brine register. However, where a property is purchased that is subject of a pending brine claim, clients need to complete a notice of purchase. These are available from the Brine Board on 0845 002 0562.

1.5 Solicitors are recommended to submit a plan of the property with every postal search enquiry. Plans should be marked with the full boundary of the property and not just the property building footprint or other lesser area. Solicitors should retain a copy of the search form and plan.

1.6 These Guidance Notes should be read in conjunction with the Coal Authority and Brine Board's Terms and Conditions 2006 and User Guide 2006.

2. Preliminary enquiries

2.1 If the property is in an affected area (see User Guide 2006, paragraph 2), a solicitor should make a search on form CON 29M and raise an additional preliminary enquiry of the seller. The enquiry should ask whether during the ownership of the seller, or to the seller's knowledge his predecessors in title, the property has sustained subsidence damage related to coal mining or brine pumping and if so how any claim was resolved (by repair or payment in respect of the cost of remedial, merged or redevelopment works or otherwise).

2.2 If the report discloses a current 'Stop Notice' concerning the deferment of remedial works or repairs affecting the property, or the withholding of consent to a request for preventive works

CON 29M (2006) COAL MINING AND BRINE SUBSIDENCE CLAIM SEARCH

A cheque with the appropriate fee MUST be sent with the printed form unless charged to an appropriate account. A location plan should be included with all search requests to avoid delay. Users should retain a copy of the form and the location plan.

The Coal Authority
Mining Reports
200 Lichfield Lane
Mansfield
Nottinghamshire
NG18 4RG

DX 716176 MANSFIELD 5

(For Coal Authority Use Only)

Complete each applicable box below. Use type or BLOCK LETTERS.

Notes

Reply to: DX	Enter the name, firm/organisation and DX number to which the report is to be returned. If you are not a member of the DX system please enter your name, firm/organisation and the full address, including postcode, to which the report is to be returned.
Email (if applicable):	Only insert your email address when you wish the report to be returned by email in a secure PDF file.
Telephone number:	Insert your telephone number so that the Authority may contact you if necessary regarding this search.
Account number (if applicable):	See the User Guide 2006
Report type requested (tick box): Residential Property Search ☐ Non-Residential Property or Site Search ☐	Please tick the appropriate box and ensure that the correct fee is enclosed for the report type requested (see Notes overleaf). It is inappropriate to request a Residential Property Search for non-residential property or development sites and any such requests will be returned for resubmission and the correct fee. A Residential Property Search includes enquiries 1-12 overleaf. A Non-Residential or Site Search includes enquiries 1-15 overleaf.
Expedited Search required (delete as applicable): **YES/NO** **Fax number:**	Expedited Search Reports can be ordered and returned by fax within 48 hours. The full fee, including the expedite element, is payable in advance (see Notes overleaf). Only insert your fax number when you wish the report to be returned by fax or you are requesting an expedited search.
Request date:	Insert the date on which this search form is sent.
Address of the land/site/property: Address Street Locality Town/Village County Postcode	The Address field may be used for house and flat names and numbers. Include the complete address if possible. Always include the postcode where the property has a postal address. Where the land, site or property does not have a postal address, use any fields provided to include a description sufficient for the property to be identified.
Location plan enclosed (delete as applicable): **YES/NO**	Searches may be returned unanswered or delayed if a plan is not enclosed (see Notes overleaf).
Customer reference:	Insert your own file reference number.

TERMS AND CONDITIONS - These enquiries are made and the replies prepared in accordance with the Coal Authority's and the Cheshire Brine Subsidence Compensation Board's Terms and Conditions 2006, User Guide 2006 and Law Society's Guidance Notes 2006. These are available to view at www.miningreports.co.uk or by contacting the Coal Authority's Mining Reports Helpline on 0845 762 6848 or by email to miningreports@coal.gov.uk. These terms and conditions apply regardless of the method used to order and receive reports.

© Law Society 2006

CON 29M (2006) COAL MINING AND BRINE SUBSIDENCE CLAIM SEARCH

RESIDENTIAL PROPERTY SEARCH ENQUIRIES

1.   Past underground coal mining

Is the property within the zone of likely physical influence on the surface of past underground coal workings? If yes, indicate the number of seams involved, their depth and approximate last date of working.

For the purpose of this enquiry "zone of likely physical influence" will be based on the principle of 0.7 times the depth of the working allowing for seam inclination.

2.   Present underground coal mining

Is the property within the zone of likely physical influence on the surface of present underground coal workings? If yes, indicate the seams involved.

3.   Future underground coal mining

(a)   Is the property within any geographical area for which the Coal Authority is determining whether to grant a licence to remove coal by underground methods?

(b)   Is the property within any geographical area for which a licence to remove coal by underground methods has been granted? If yes, when was the licence granted?

(c)   Is the property within the zone of likely physical influence on the surface of planned future underground coal workings? If yes, indicate the seams involved and approximate date of working.

(d)   Has any notice of proposals relating to underground coal mining operations been given under section 46 of the Coal Mining Subsidence Act 1991? If yes, supply the date and details of the last such notice.

For the purpose of this enquiry "geographical area" means the surface area directly above a licence being determined or granted.

4.   Shafts and adits (mine entries)

Are there any shafts and adits or other entries to underground coal mine workings within the property or within 20 metres of the boundary of the property? If yes, supply a plan showing the approximate recorded location and any relevant information, where available, regarding any treatment carried out to such shafts, adits or entries.

5.   Coal mining geology

Is there any record of any fault or other line of weakness due to coal mining at the surface within the boundary of the property that has made the property unstable?

6.   Past opencast coal mining

Is the property situated within the geographical boundary of an opencast site from which coal has been removed in the past by opencast methods?

7.   Present opencast coal mining

Is the property within 200 metres of the boundary of an opencast site from which coal is being removed by opencast methods?

8.   Future opencast coal mining

(a)   Is the property within 800 metres of the boundary of an opencast site for which the Coal Authority are determining whether to grant a licence to remove coal by opencast methods?

(b)   Is the property within 800 metres of the boundary of an opencast site for which a licence to remove coal by opencast methods has been granted? If yes, when was the licence granted?

9.   Coal mining subsidence claims

(a)   Has any damage notice or claim for alleged coal mining subsidence damage to the property been given, made or pursued since 1 January 1984? If yes, supply the date of such notice or claim.

(b)   In respect of any such notice or claim has the responsible person given notice agreeing that there is a remedial obligation or otherwise accepted that a claim would lie against him?

(c)   In respect of any such notice or acceptance has the remedial obligation or claim been discharged? If yes, state whether such remedial obligation or claim was discharged by repair or payment, or a combination thereof.

(d)   Does any current "Stop Notice" delaying the start of remedial works or repairs affect the property? If yes, supply the date of the notice.

(e)   Has any request been made under section 33 of the 1991 Act to execute preventive works before coal is worked, which would prevent the occurrence or reduce the extent of subsidence damage to any buildings, structures or works? If yes, has any person withheld consent or failed to comply with any such request to execute preventive works?

10.   Mine gas emissions

Does the Coal Authority have record of any mine gas emission within the boundary of the property being reported that subsequently required action by the Authority to mitigate the effects of the mine gas emission?

11.   Emergency Surface Hazard Call Out incidents

Have the Coal Authority carried out any work on or within the boundaries of the property following a report of an alleged hazard related to coal mining under the Authority's Emergency Surface Hazard Call Out procedures?

12.   Cheshire brine subsidence compensation claims

(a)   Is the property situated within the Cheshire Brine Compensation District prescribed by the Cheshire Brine Pumping (Compensation for Subsidence) Act 1952?

(b)   If yes, is the property situated within a Consultation Area prescribed by the Cheshire Brine Board under the provisions of section 38(1) of the 1952 Act?

(c)   Has a Notice of Damage been filed in respect of the property? If yes, was the claim accepted and how was the claim discharged?

(d)   Have any claims in respect of the property been commuted by a once and for all payment of compensation?

(e)   Would the compensation provisions of the Cheshire Brine Pumping (Compensation for Subsidence) Acts of 1952 and 1964 apply should the property be affected at some future date by subsidence due to brine pumping?

ADDITIONAL ENQUIRIES FOR NON-RESIDENTIAL PROPERTY OR SITE SEARCH IN COAL MINING AREAS

13.   Withdrawal of support

(a)   Does the land lie within a geographical area in respect of which a notice of entitlement to withdraw support has been published? If yes, supply the date of the notice.

(b)   Does the land lie within a geographical area in respect of which a revocation notice has been given under section 41 of the Coal Industry Act 1994? If yes, supply the date of the notice.

14.   Working facilities orders

Is the property within a geographical area subject to an order in respect of the working of coal under the Mines (Working Facilities and Support) Acts of 1923 and 1966 or any statutory modification or amendment thereof? If yes, supply the date and title of the order.

15.   Payments to owners of former copyhold land

(a)   Has any relevant notice, which may affect the property, been given?

(b)   If yes, has any notice of retained interests in coal and coal mines been given?

(c)   If yes, has any acceptance notice or rejection notice been served?

(d)   If any such acceptance notice has been served, has any compensation been paid to a claimant?

NOTES

(A)   Advice and information on coal mining and brine subsidence searches

For information on procedure, turnaround and current fees, account facilities or further to a specific search, contact the Coal Authority Mining Reports Helpline on 0845 762 6848 or by email to miningreports@coal.gov.uk or visit www.miningreports.co.uk There is a higher fee for the Non-Residential Property or Site Search and an additional fee for Expedited Searches. Searches having incorrect fees will be returned uncompleted.

(B)   Refunds

No refund or transfer of any fee (or part of a fee) will be made once a search has been logged onto the Authority's MRSDS computer systems for report production.

(C)   Expedited searches

Select 'YES' against Expedited Search and add your fax number in full. This service is only available to credit account customers or where the full fee, including the expedite element, is paid in advance by credit/debit card (over the telephone 0845 762 6848) or by cheque (postal enquiries).

(D)   Affected areas

A directory of places where a CON 29M (2006) search is required can be found on the Authority's website at www.miningreports.co.uk together with a useful search by postcode facility.

(E)   Ordering CON 29M reports

Reports can be ordered by telephone, and ordered and returned by post, fax or electronically via the internet and email (www.miningreports.co.uk). A fully electronic link to the National Land Information Service (NLIS) provides a further channel for customers to order and receive searches.

(F)   Terms and Conditions, User Guide and Law Society's Guidance

These Notes should be read in conjunction with the Coal Authority's and the Cheshire Brine Board's Terms and Conditions 2006, User Guide 2006, and the Law Society's Guidance Notes 2006, under which all replies to these enquiries are made. These terms apply regardless of the method used to order and receive reports. The Terms and Conditions and User Guide have been approved by the Law Society following consultation with key stakeholders including the CML and RICS, and apply to all searches made including those using the CON 29M search form. Copies of these documents can be found on the Coal Authority's website at www.miningreports.co.uk

(G)   Plans

If a plan is not submitted there may be difficulties and delays in identifying the property and its extent, in which case the Coal Authority may request that a plan be supplied before the search can be completed.

affecting the property, it is recommended that a solicitor should ask preliminary enquiries of the seller as to the present position.

3. Reproduction of forms

3.1   Copyright in the form CON 29M and enquiries belong to the Law Society, which has granted to solicitors a non-exclusive licence to reproduce them. Any such form must follow precisely and in all respects the printed version.

3.2   The Coal Authority (as operator of the service) will reject any reproduction of the CON 29M enquiry form which does not comply with these requirements.

4. Mining surveys and site investigation

4.1   Disclosure of a disused mine shaft or mine adit in a report, the existence of recorded shallow coal workings or possible unrecorded coal workings reported as believed to be at or close to the surface (such that future ground movement may still subsequently occur) and/or any other coal mining related hazard identified within the report, should be brought to the attention of the client. If further information or advice is required in addition to that available from the Coal Authority (e.g. further to that contained within a Coal Authority Interpretive Report, see paragraph 19 of the User Guide 2006), then solicitors should in these circumstances explain to clients that there are experienced mining surveyors and structural engineers able to advise as to what further enquiries, surveys or investigation should be made.

4.2   If a lender is involved in the transaction, solicitors should establish that the surveyor or engineer selected is acceptable to the lender and make arrangements to provide a copy of the search to them.

4.3   In most cases, but not all, the Coal Authority and not the adjacent surface landowner will own any coal shaft or adit. Clients should be advised accordingly and reminded that in these cases the permission of the Coal Authority must be sought before carrying out any works to locate, treat or in any other way interfere with former coal workings including disused coal mine shafts or adits.

5. Dealing with lenders

5.1   If domestic property which is the subject of a CON 29M search is to be charged as security for a loan, a copy of the report should be sent to the lender as soon as received. Whether or not this is appropriate depends on the result of the search and the lender's instructions. The solicitor should not comment substantively on the replies within the report but should recommend that they be referred to the lender's valuer for review and information.

5.2   Provided that a copy of the mining report has been so provided, solicitors are not obliged to make any other reference to the replies in any report on title to a lender save to refer to the existence of the CON 29M search and the report.

5.3   With regard to non-domestic property a similar procedure should be adopted. Solicitors should, however, refer to the replies to the additional enquiries included in the mining reports for non-residential, commercial or development sites as these deal with legal matters (namely the withdrawal of support, the existence of working facilities orders and payments to owners of former copyhold land).

5.4   When also acting for the lender it is suggested that solicitors should, in all cases, check whether the instructions from that lender require the solicitor to deal with the replies to the CON 29M report in any other manner. If so, it is suggested that the solicitor should explain to the lender the basis upon which the solicitor is recommended by these paragraphs to proceed. It is important that solicitors should not attempt to perform the function of the client's valuer or surveyor with regard to the replies to the CON 29M report.

6.   Implementation of Form CON 29M (2006)

6.1   Form CON 29M (2006) will be available from 31 October 2006. The Coal Authority will continue to accept the 2003 form until 31 December 2006.

6.2   From 31 October 2006, all CON 29M reports requested from the Coal Authority will be prepared in accordance with the Law Society's Guidance Notes 2006, the User Guide 2006 and the Coal Authority's and the Brine Board's Terms and Conditions 2006.

V.9. Standard Conditions of Sale (fourth edition) (including Explanatory Notes)[1]

CONTRACT

(Incorporating the Standard Conditions of Sale (Fourth Edition))

Date	:
Seller	:
Buyer	:
Property (freehold/leasehold)	:
Title Number/root of title	:
Specified incumbrances	:
Title guarantee (full/limited)	:
Completion date	:
Contract rate	:
Purchase price	:
Deposit	:
Chattels price (if separate)	:
Balance	:

The seller will sell and the buyer will buy the property for the purchase price.

WARNING	**Signed**
This is a formal document, designed to create legal rights and legal obligations. Take advice before using it.	Seller/Buyer

---

1. © 2003 Oyez (The Solicitors' Law Stationery Society Ltd) and the Law Society.

STANDARD CONDITIONS OF SALE (FOURTH EDITION)
(NATIONAL CONDITIONS OF SALE 24TH EDITION, LAW SOCIETY'S CONDI-
TIONS OF SALE 2003)

1 GENERAL

1.1 Definitions

1.1.1 In these conditions:

    (a) 'accrued interest' means:

        (i) if money has been placed on deposit or in a building society share account, the interest actually earned

        (ii) otherwise, the interest which might reasonably have been earned by depositing the money at interest on seven days' notice of withdrawal with a clearing bank

        less, in either case, any proper charges for handling the money

    (b) 'chattels price' means any separate amount payable for chattels included in the contract

    (c) 'clearing bank' means a bank which is a shareholder in CHAPS Clearing Co. Limited

    (d) 'completion date' has the meaning given in condition 6.1.1

    (e) 'contract rate' means the Law Society's interest rate from time to time in force

    (f) 'conveyancer' means a solicitor, barrister, duly certified notary public, licensed conveyancer or recognised body under sections 9 or 23 of the Administration of Justice Act 1985

    (g) 'direct credit' means a direct transfer of cleared funds to an account nominated by the seller's conveyancer and maintained by a clearing bank

    (h) 'lease' includes sub-lease, tenancy and agreement for a lease or sub-lease

    (i) 'notice to complete' means a notice requiring completion of the contract in accordance with condition 6

    (j) 'public requirement' means any notice, order or proposal given or made (whether before or after the date of the contract) by a body acting on statutory authority

    (k) 'requisition' includes objection

    (l) 'transfer' includes conveyance and assignment

    (m) 'working day' means any day from Monday to Friday (inclusive) which is not Christmas Day, Good Friday or a statutory Bank Holiday.

1.1.2 In these conditions the terms 'absolute title' and 'official copies' have the special meanings given to them by the Land Registration Act 2002.

1.1.3 A party is ready, able and willing to complete:

    (a) if he could be, but for the default of the other party, and

    (b) in the case of the seller, even though the property remains subject to a mortgage, if the amount to be paid on completion enables the property to be transferred freed of all mortgages (except any to which the sale is expressly subject).

1.1.4 These conditions apply except as varied or excluded by the contract.

1.2   Joint parties

If there is more than one seller or more than one buyer, the obligations which they undertake can be enforced against them all jointly or against each individually.

1.3   Notices and documents

1.3.1   A notice required or authorised by the contract must be in writing.

1.3.2   Giving a notice or delivering a document to a party's conveyancer has the same effect as giving or delivering it to that party.

1.3.3   Where delivery of the original document is not essential, a notice or document is validly given or sent if it is sent:

    (a)   by fax, or

    (b)   by e-mail to an e-mail address for the intended recipient given in the contract.

1.3.4   Subject to conditions 1.3.5 to 1.3.7, a notice is given and a document is delivered when it is received.

1.3.5   (a)   A notice or document sent through a document exchange is received when it is available for collection

    (b)   A notice or document which is received after 4.00 pm on a working day, or on a day which is not a working day, is to be treated as having been received on the next working day

    (c)   An automated response to a notice or document sent by e-mail that the intended recipient is out of the office is to be treated as proof that the notice or document was not received.

1.3.6   Condition 1.3.7 applies unless there is proof:

    (a)   that a notice or document has not been received, or

    (b)   of when it was received.

1.3.7   A notice or document sent by the following means is treated as having been received as follows:

    (a)   by first-class post: before 4.00 pm on the second working day after posting

    (b)   by second-class post: before 4.00 pm on the third working day after posting

    (c)   through a document exchange: before 4.00 pm on the first working day after the day on which it would normally be available for collection by the addressee

    (d)   by fax: one hour after despatch

    (e)   by e-mail: before 4.00 pm on the first working day after despatch.

1.4   VAT

1.4.1   An obligation to pay money includes an obligation to pay any value added tax chargeable in respect of that payment.

1.4.2   All sums made payable by the contract are exclusive of value added tax.

1.5 Assignment

The buyer is not entitled to transfer the benefit of the contract.

2 FORMATION

2.1 Date

2.1.1 If the parties intend to make a contract by exchanging duplicate copies by post or through a document exchange, the contract is made when the last copy is posted or deposited at the document exchange.

2.1.2 If the parties' conveyancers agree to treat exchange as taking place before duplicate copies are actually exchanged, the contract is made as so agreed.

2.2 Deposit

2.2.1 The buyer is to pay or send a deposit of 10 per cent of the total of the purchase price and the chattels price no later than the date of the contract.

2.2.2 If a cheque tendered in payment of all or part of the deposit is dishonoured when first presented, the seller may, within seven working days of being notified that the cheque has been dishonoured, give notice to the buyer that the contract is discharged by the buyer's breach.

2.2.3 Conditions 2.2.4 to 2.2.6 do not apply on a sale by auction.

2.2.4 The deposit is to be paid by direct credit or to the seller's conveyancer by a cheque drawn on a solicitor's or licensed conveyancer's client account.

2.2.5 If before completion date the seller agrees to buy another property in England and Wales for his residence, he may use all or any part of the deposit as a deposit in that transaction to be held on terms to the same effect as this condition and condition 2.2.6.

2.2.6 Any deposit or part of a deposit not being used in accordance with condition 2.2.5 is to be held by the seller's conveyancer as stakeholder on terms that on completion it is paid to the seller with accrued interest.

2.3 Auctions

2.3.1 On a sale by auction the following conditions apply to the property and, if it is sold in lots, to each lot.

2.3.2 The sale is subject to a reserve price.

2.3.3 The seller, or a person on his behalf, may bid up to the reserve price.

2.3.4 The auctioneer may refuse any bid.

2.3.5 If there is a dispute about a bid, the auctioneer may resolve the dispute or restart the auction at the last undisputed bid.

2.3.6 The deposit is to be paid to the auctioneer as agent for the seller.

3 MATTERS AFFECTING THE PROPERTY

3.1 Freedom from incumbrances

3.1.1 The seller is selling the property free from incumbrances, other than those mentioned in condition 3.1.2.

3.1.2 The incumbrances subject to which the property is sold are:

(a) those specified in the contract

(b) those discoverable by inspection of the property before the contract

(c) those the seller does not and could not reasonably know about

(d) entries made before the date of the contract in any public register except those maintained by the Land Registry or its Land Charges Department or by Companies House

(e) public requirements.

3.1.3 After the contract is made, the seller is to give the buyer written details without delay of any new public requirement and of anything in writing which he learns about concerning a matter covered by condition 3.1.2.

3.1.4 The buyer is to bear the cost of complying with any outstanding public requirement and is to indemnify the seller against any liability resulting from a public requirement.

3.2 Physical state

3.2.1 The buyer accepts the property in the physical state it is in at the date of the contract unless the seller is building or converting it.

3.2.2 A leasehold property is sold subject to any subsisting breach of a condition or tenant's obligation relating to the physical state of the property which renders the lease liable to forfeiture.

3.2.3 A sub-lease is granted subject to any subsisting breach of a condition or tenant's obligation relating to the physical state of the property which renders the seller's own lease liable to forfeiture.

3.3 Leases affecting the property

3.3.1 The following provisions apply if any part of the property is sold subject to a lease.

3.3.2 (a) The seller having provided the buyer with full details of each lease or copies of the documents embodying the lease terms, the buyer is treated as entering into the contract knowing and fully accepting those terms.

(b) The seller is to inform the buyer without delay if the lease ends or if the seller learns of any application by the tenant in connection with the lease; the seller is then to act as the buyer reasonably directs, and the buyer is to indemnify him against all consequent loss and expense.

(c) Except with the buyer's consent, the seller is not to agree to any proposal to change the lease terms nor to take any step to end the lease.

(d) The seller is to inform the buyer without delay of any change to the lease terms which may be proposed or agreed.

(e) The buyer is to indemnify the seller against all claims arising from the lease after actual completion; this includes claims which are unenforceable against a buyer for want of registration.

(f) The seller takes no responsibility for what rent is lawfully recoverable, nor for whether or how any legislation affects the lease.

(g) If the let land is not wholly within the property, the seller may apportion the rent.

3.4 Retained land

Where after the transfer the seller will be retaining land near the property:

(a) the buyer will have no right of light or air over the retained land, but

(b) in other respects the seller and the buyer will each have the rights over the land of the other which they would have had if they were two separate buyers to whom the seller had made simultaneous transfers of the property and the retained land.

The transfer is to contain appropriate express terms.

4. TITLE AND TRANSFER

4.1 Proof of title

4.1.1 Without cost to the buyer, the seller is to provide the buyer with proof of the title to the property and of his ability to transfer it, or to procure its transfer.

4.1.2 Where the property has a registered title the proof is to include official copies of the items referred to in rules 134(1)(a) and (b) and 135(1)(a) of the Land Registration Rules 2003, so far as they are not to be discharged or overridden at or before completion.

4.1.3 Where the property has an unregistered title, the proof is to include:

(a) an abstract of title or an epitome of title with photocopies of the documents, and

(b) production of every document or an abstract, epitome or copy of it with an original marking by a conveyancer either against the original or an examined abstract or an examined copy.

4.2 Requisitions

4.2.1 The buyer may not raise requisitions:

(a) on the title shown by the seller taking the steps described in condition 4.1.1 before the contract was made

(b) in relation to the matters covered by condition 3.1.2.

4.2.2 Notwithstanding condition 4.2.1, the buyer may, within six working days of a matter coming to his attention after the contract was made, raise written requisitions on that matter. In that event, steps 3 and 4 in condition 4.3.1 apply.

4.2.3 On the expiry of the relevant time limit under condition 4.2.2 or condition 4.3.1, the buyer loses his right to raise requisitions or to make observations.

4.3 Timetable

4.3.1   Subject to condition 4.2 and to the extent that the seller did not take the steps described in condition 4.1.1 before the contract was made, the following are the steps for deducing and investigating the title to the property to be taken within the following time limits:

Step		**Time limit**
1.	The seller is to comply with condition 4.1.1	Immediately after making the contract
2.	The buyer may raise written requisitions	Six working days after either the date of the seller's evidence of title on which the contract or the date of delivery of the requisitions are raised whichever is the later
3.	The seller is to reply in writing to any requisitions raised	Four working days after receiving the requisitions
4.	The buyer may make written observations on the seller's replies	Three working days after receiving the replies

The time limit on the buyer's right to raise requisitions applies even where the seller supplies incomplete evidence of his title, but the buyer may, within six working days from delivery of any further evidence, raise further requisitions resulting from that evidence.

4.3.2   The parties are to take the following steps to prepare and agree the transfer of the property within the following time limits:

Step		**Time limit**
A.	The buyer is to send the seller a draft transfer	At least twelve working days before completion date
B.	The seller is to approve or revise that draft and either return it or retain it for use as the actual transfer	Four working days after delivery of the draft transfer
C.	If the draft is returned the buyer is to send an engrossment to the seller	At least five working days before completion date

4.3.3   Periods of time under conditions 4.3.1 and 4.3.2 may run concurrently.

4.3.4   If the period between the date of the contract and completion date is less than 15 working days, the time limits in conditions 4.2.2, 4.3.1 and 4.3.2 are to be reduced by the same proportion as that period bears to the period of 15 working days. Fractions of a working day are to be rounded down except that the time limit to perform any step is not to be less than one working day.

4.4 Defining the property

4.4.1   The seller need not:

    (a)   prove the exact boundaries of the property

    (b)   prove who owns fences, ditches, hedges or walls

    (c)   separately identify parts of the property with different titles further than he may be able to do from information in his possession.

4.4.2   The buyer may, if it is reasonable, require the seller to make or obtain, pay for and hand over a statutory declaration about facts relevant to the matters mentioned in condition 4.4.1. The form of the declaration is to be agreed by the buyer, who must not unreasonably withhold his agreement.

4.5   Rents and rentcharges

The fact that a rent or rentcharge, whether payable or receivable by the owner of the property, has been, or will on completion be, informally apportioned is not to be regarded as a defect in title.

4.6   Transfer

4.6.1   The buyer does not prejudice his right to raise requisitions, or to require replies to any raised, by taking any steps in relation to preparing or agreeing the transfer.

4.6.2.   Subject to condition 4.6.3, the seller is to transfer the property with full title guarantee.

4.6.3   The transfer is to have effect as if the disposition is expressly made subject to all matters covered by condition 3.1.2.

4.6.4   If after completion the seller will remain bound by any obligation affecting the property which was disclosed to the buyer before the contract was made, but the law does not imply any covenant by the buyer to indemnify the seller against liability for future breaches of it:

    (a)   the buyer is to covenant in the transfer to indemnify the seller against liability for any future breach of the obligation and to perform it from then on, and

    (b)   if required by the seller, the buyer is to execute and deliver to the seller on completion a duplicate transfer prepared by the buyer.

4.6.5   The seller is to arrange at his expense that, in relation to every document of title which the buyer does not receive on completion, the buyer is to have the benefit of:

    (a)   a written acknowledgement of his right to its production, and

    (b)   a written undertaking for its safe custody (except while it is held by a mortgagee or by someone in a fiduciary capacity).

5 PENDING COMPLETION

5.1   Responsibility for property

5.1.1   The seller will transfer the property in the same physical state as it was at the date of the contract (except for fair wear and tear), which means that the seller retains the risk until completion.

5.1.2   If at any time before completion the physical state of the property makes it unusable for its purpose at the date of the contract:

    (a)   the buyer may rescind the contract

    (b)   the seller may rescind the contract where the property has become unusable for that purpose as a result of damage against which the seller could not reasonably have insured, or which it is not legally possible for the seller to make good.

5.1.3   The seller is under no obligation to the buyer to insure the property.

5.1.4   Section 47 of the Law of Property Act 1925 does not apply.

5.2   Occupation by buyer

5.2.1.   If the buyer is not already lawfully in the property, and the seller agrees to let him into occupation, the buyer occupies on the following terms.

5.2.2.   The buyer is a licensee and not a tenant. The terms of the licence are that the buyer:

    (a)   cannot transfer it

    (b)   may permit members of his household to occupy the property

    (c)   is to pay or indemnify the seller against all outgoings and other expenses in respect of the property

    (d)   is to pay the seller a fee calculated at the contract rate on a sum equal to the purchase price and the chattels price (less any deposit paid) for the period of the licence

    (e)   is entitled to any rents and profits from any part of the property which he does not occupy

    (f)   is to keep the property in as good a state of repair as it was in when he went into occupation (except for fair wear and tear) and is not to alter it

    (g)   is to insure the property in a sum which is not less than the purchase price against all risks in respect of which comparable premises are normally insured

    (h)   is to quit the property when the licence ends.

5.2.3   On the creation of the buyer's licence, condition 5.1 ceases to apply, which means that the buyer then assumes the risk until completion.

5.2.4   The buyer is not in occupation for the purposes of this condition if he merely exercises rights of access given solely to do work agreed by the seller.

5.2.5   The buyer's licence ends on the earliest of: completion date, rescission of the contract or when five working days' notice given by one party to the other takes effect.

5.2.6   If the buyer is in occupation of the property after his licence has come to an end and the contract is subsequently completed he is to pay the seller compensation for his continued occupation calculated at the same rate as the fee mentioned in condition 5.2.2(d).

5.2.7   The buyer's right to raise requisitions is unaffected.

6. COMPLETION

6.1   Date

6.1.1   Completion date is twenty working days after the date of the contract but time is not of the essence of the contract unless a notice to complete has been served.

6.1.2   If the money due on completion is received after 2.00 pm, completion is to be treated, for the purposes only of conditions 6.3 and 7.3, as taking place on the next working day as a result of the buyer's default.

6.1.3   Condition 6.1.2 does not apply and the seller is treated as in default if:

    (i)   the sale is with vacant possession of the property or any part of it, and

    (ii)   the buyer is ready, able and willing to complete but does not pay the money due on completion until after 2.00 pm because the seller has not vacated the property or that part by that time.

6.2   Arrangements and place

6.2.1   The buyer's conveyancer and the seller's conveyancer are to co-operate in agreeing arrangements for completing the contract.

6.2.2   Completion is to take place in England and Wales, either at the seller's conveyancer's office or at some other place which the seller reasonably specifies.

6.3   Apportionments

6.3.1   Income and outgoings of the property are to be apportioned between the parties so far as the change of ownership on completion will affect entitlement to receive or liability to pay them.

6.3.2   If the whole property is sold with vacant possession or the seller exercises his option in condition 7.3.4, apportionment is to be made with effect from the date of actual completion; otherwise, it is to be made from completion date.

6.3.3   In apportioning any sum, it is to be assumed that the seller owns the property until the end of the day from which apportionment is made and that the sum accrues from day to day at the rate at which it is payable on that day.

6.3.4   For the purpose of apportioning income and outgoings, it is to be assumed that they accrue at an equal daily rate throughout the year.

6.3.5   When a sum to be apportioned is not known or easily ascertainable at completion, a provisional apportionment is to be made according to the best estimate available. As soon as the amount is known, a final apportionment is to be made and notified to the other party. Any resulting balance is to be paid no more than ten working days later, and if not then paid the balance is to bear interest at the contract rate from then until payment.

6.3.6   Compensation payable under condition 5.2.6 is not to be apportioned.

6.4   Amount payable

The amount payable by the buyer on completion is the purchase price and the chattels price (less any deposit already paid to the seller or his agent) adjusted to take account of:

    (a)   apportionments made under condition 6.3

    (b)   any compensation to be paid or allowed under condition 7.3.

6.5   Title deeds

6.5.1   As soon as the buyer has complied with all his obligations on completion the seller must hand over the documents of title.

6.5.2   Condition 6.5.1 does not apply to any documents of title relating to land being retained by the seller after completion.

6.6   Rent receipts

The buyer is to assume that whoever gave any receipt for a payment of rent or service charge which the seller produces was the person or the agent of the person then entitled to that rent or service charge.

6.7   Means of payment

The buyer is to pay the money due on completion by direct credit and, if appropriate, an unconditional release of a deposit held by a stakeholder.

6.8   Notice to complete

6.8.1   At any time on or after completion date, a party who is ready, able and willing to complete may give the other a notice to complete.

6.8.2   The parties are to complete the contract within ten working days of giving a notice to complete, excluding the day on which the notice is given. For this purpose, time is of the essence of the contract.

6.8.3   On receipt of a notice to complete:

(a)   if the buyer paid no deposit, he is forthwith to pay a deposit of 10 per cent

(b)   if the buyer paid a deposit of less than 10 per cent, he is forthwith to pay a further deposit equal to the balance of that 10 per cent.

7. REMEDIES

7.1   Errors and omissions

7.1.1   If any plan or statement in the contract, or in the negotiations leading to it, is or was misleading or inaccurate due to an error or omission, the remedies available are as follows.

7.1.2   When there is a material difference between the description or value of the property, or of any of the chattels included in the contract, as represented and as it is, the buyer is entitled to damages.

7.1.3   An error or omission only entitles the buyer to rescind the contract:

(a)   where it results from fraud or recklessness, or

(b)   where he would be obliged, to his prejudice, to accept property differing substantially (in quantity, quality or tenure) from what the error or omission had led him to expect.

7.2   Rescission

If either party rescinds the contract:

(a)   unless the rescission is a result of the buyer's breach of contract the deposit is to be repaid to the buyer with accrued interest

(b)   the buyer is to return any documents he received from the seller and is to cancel any registration of the contract.

7.3 Late completion

7.3.1   If there is default by either or both of the parties in performing their obligations under the contract and completion is delayed, the party whose total period of default is the greater is to pay compensation to the other party.

7.3.2   Compensation is calculated at the contract rate on an amount equal to the purchase price and the chattels price, less (where the buyer is the paying party) any deposit paid, for the period by which the paying party's default exceeds that of the receiving party, or, if shorter, the period between completion date and actual completion.

7.3.3   Any claim for loss resulting from delayed completion is to be reduced by any compensation paid under this contract.

7.3.4   Where the buyer holds the property as tenant of the seller and completion is delayed, the seller may give notice to the buyer, before the date of actual completion, that he intends to take the net income from the property until completion. If he does so, he cannot claim compensation under condition 7.3.1 as well.

7.4 After completion

Completion does not cancel liability to perform any outstanding obligation under this contract.

7.5 Buyer's failure to comply with notice to complete

7.5.1   If the buyer fails to complete in accordance with a notice to complete, the following terms apply.

7.5.2   The seller may rescind the contract, and if he does so:

(a)   he may

 (i)   forfeit and keep any deposit and accrued interest

 (ii)   resell the property and any chattels included in the contract

 (iii)   claim damages

(b)   the buyer is to return any documents he received from the seller and is to cancel any registration of the contract.

7.5.3   The seller retains his other rights and remedies.

7.6 Seller's failure to comply with notice to complete

7.6.1   If the seller fails to complete in accordance with a notice to complete, the following terms apply.

7.6.2   The buyer may rescind the contract, and if he does so:

(a)   the deposit is to be repaid to the buyer with accrued interest

(b)   the buyer is to return any documents he received from the seller and is, at the seller's expense, to cancel any registration of the contract.

7.6.3   The buyer retains his other rights and remedies.

8 LEASEHOLD PROPERTY

8.1 Existing leases

8.1.1 The following provisions apply to a sale of leasehold land.

8.1.2 The seller having provided the buyer with copies of the documents embodying the lease terms, the buyer is treated as entering into the contract knowing and fully accepting those terms.

8.1.3. The seller is to comply with any lease obligations requiring the tenant to insure the property.

8.2 New leases

8.2.1 The following provisions apply to a contract to grant a new lease.

8.2.2 The conditions apply so that:

'seller' means the proposed landlord

'buyer' means the proposed tenant

'purchase price' means the premium to be paid on the grant of a lease.

8.2.3 The lease is to be in the form of the draft attached to the contract.

8.2.4 If the term of the new lease will exceed seven years, the seller is to deduce a title which will enable the buyer to register the lease at the Land Registry with an absolute title.

8.2.5 The seller is to engross the lease and a counterpart of it and is to send the counterpart to the buyer at least five working days before completion date.

8.2.6 The buyer is to execute the counterpart and deliver it to the seller on completion.

8.3 Consent

8.3.1 (a) The following provisions apply if a consent to let, assign or sub-let is required to complete the contract

    (b) In this condition 'consent' means consent in the form which satisfies the requirement to obtain it.

8.3.2 (a) The seller is to apply for the consent at his expense, and to use all reasonable efforts to obtain it

    (b) The buyer is to provide all information and references reasonably required.

8.3.3 Unless he is in breach of his obligation under condition 8.3.2, either party may rescind the contract by notice to the other party if three working days before completion date (or before a later date on which the parties have agreed to complete the contract):

    (a) the consent has not been given, or

    (b) the consent has been given subject to a condition to which a party reasonably objects. In that case, neither party is to be treated as in breach of contract and condition 7.2 applies.

9. COMMONHOLD LAND

9.1 Terms used in this condition have the special meanings given to them in Part 1 of the Commonhold and Leasehold Reform Act 2002.

9.2 This condition applies to a disposition of commonhold land.

9.3 The seller having provided the buyer with copies of the current versions of the memorandum and articles of the commonhold association and of the commonhold community statement, the buyer is treated as entering into the contract knowing and fully accepting their terms.

9.4 If the contract is for the sale of property which is or includes part only of a commonhold unit:

(a) the seller is to apply for the written consent of the commonhold association at his expense and is to use all reasonable efforts to obtain it

(b) either the seller, unless he is in breach of his obligation under paragraph (a), or the buyer may rescind the contract by notice to the other party if three working days before completion date (or before a later date on which the parties have agreed to complete the contract) the consent has not been given.

In that case, neither party is to be treated as in breach of contract and condition 7.2 applies.

10. CHATTELS

10.1 The following provisions apply to any chattels which are included in the contract, whether or not a separate price is to be paid for them.

10.2 The contract takes effect as a contract for sale of goods.

10.3 The buyer takes the chattels in the physical state they are in at the date of the contract.

10.4 Ownership of the chattels passes to the buyer on actual completion.

SPECIAL CONDITIONS

1 (a) This contract incorporates the Standard Conditions of Sale (Fourth Edition).

(b) The terms used in this contract have the same meaning when used in the Conditions.

2 Subject to the terms of this contract and to the Standard Conditions of Sale, the seller is to transfer the property with either full title guarantee or limited title guarantee, as specified on the front page.

3 The chattels which are on the property and are set out on any attached list are included in the sale and the buyer is to pay the chattels price for them.

4 The property is sold with vacant possession.

(or)

4 The property is sold subject to the following leases or tenancies:

Seller's conveyancers*:

Buyer's conveyancers*:

*Adding an e-mail address authorises service by e-mail: see condition 1.3.3(b).

EXPLANATORY NOTES

General

The fourth edition of the Standard Conditions of Sale (the SCS) takes effect on 13 October 2003, being the date on which the main provisions of the Land Registration Act 2002 come into force. The fourth edition takes account of the changes made by that Act, and also anticipates the coming into force in early 2004 of the provisions relating to commonhold in Part I of the Commonhold and Leasehold Reform Act 2002.

The SCS are intended primarily for use in residential sales and in the sale of small business premises. For more complex commercial transactions, conveyancers are likely to find the Standard Commercial Property Conditions (the SCPC) better suited to their needs. A second edition of the SCPC is planned for later in 2003.

The fourth edition of the SCS represents the 24th Edition of the National Conditions of Sale and the Law Society's Conditions of Sale 2003.

'Contract'

Previous editions of the SCS have distinguished between 'the agreement' (meaning the contractual document which contains the individually negotiated terms and incorporates the SCS) and 'the contract' (meaning the whole bargain, including the SCS). Some users of the SCS have found this distinction confusing, and it has been abandoned in the present edition, which refers only to 'the contract'.

It should, however, be noted that condition 1.1.4 of the SCS embodies a new general provision to the effect that the SCS apply except as varied or excluded by the contract, so ensuring that, where there is a conflict, the individually negotiated terms will prevail over the SCS.

Condition 1.1.4 will also ensure that the general provisions of the SCS which determine the completion date (conditions 1.1.1(d) and 6.1.1), the contract rate (condition 1.1.1(e)) and the title guarantee to be given in the transfer (condition 4.6.2) will automatically take effect subject to any individually negotiated terms which deal with these matters. For that reason, these provisions no longer include words making them expressly subject to the particular terms of the agreement.

Front and back pages: specified incumbrances

The back page no longer contains a special condition stating that the property is sold subject to the incumbrances set out on the front page. However, condition 3.1.2(a) provides that the property is sold subject to the incumbrances specified in the contract, and the front page includes space for specifying any incumbrances to which the sale is expressly made subject. The sale will, therefore, continue to take effect subject to any incumbrances there set out.

Chattels

The SCS now make fuller provision for cases in which a separate price is agreed for any chattels included in the sale. In such a case, the 'purchase price' will refer to the price agreed for the property and the 'chattels price' (as defined in condition 1.1.1(b)) will refer to the price separately agreed for the chattels. The SCS provide for the deposit to be 10 per cent of the total of the purchase price and the chattels price (condition 2.2.1). They also provide for the chattels price to be taken into account in calculating any licence fee payable where the buyer goes into occupation before completion (condition 5.2.2(d)), in working out the amount payable on completion (condition 6.4) and in working out any compensation payable on late completion (condition 7.3.2).

It should, however, be noted that condition 10 will apply to any chattels included in the sale whether or not a separate price is payable for them.

'Conveyancer'

In this edition, 'conveyancer' has replaced 'solicitor' as the defined term used to refer to the various categories of persons who may lawfully carry out conveyancing work for reward (condition 1.1.1(f)). Note, however, that, in a case where the property is being sold otherwise than at auction and the deposit is paid by cheque, the cheque may be drawn only on a solicitor's or licensed conveyancer's client account (conditions 2.2.3 and 2.2.4). This requirement reflects the fact that solicitors and licensed conveyancers (in contrast, for example, to barristers) hold money on client account and can be expected to have taken steps to comply with their obligations under the general law and professional rules to ensure that their client accounts are not being used for money-laundering purposes.

Payment by direct credit

In the light of developments in conveyancing practice, the present edition of the SCS no longer gives the buyer the option of paying the deposit by banker's draft, or of paying the money due on completion by banker's draft or legal tender. The current position is that, unless the property is being sold by auction, the deposit must be paid either by direct credit or (as noted above) by cheque drawn on a solicitor's or licensed conveyancer's client account (conditions 2.2.3 and 2.2.4). The money due on completion may now be paid only by direct credit, coupled where appropriate with the release of any deposit held by a stakeholder (condition 6.7). For these purposes, 'direct credit' is defined in condition 1.1.1(g) as meaning a direct transfer of cleared funds to an account nominated by the seller's conveyancer and maintained by a 'clearing bank', that is to say, a bank which is a shareholder in CHAPS Clearing Co. Ltd (condition 1.1.1(c)).

Ready, able and willing to complete

Condition 1.1.3 contains a new general provision stating when a party is ready, able and willing to complete. The provision is relevant in applying conditions 6.1.3 and 6.8.1.

Notices and documents

Condition 1.3.6 now makes it clear that the presumed times of receipt set out in condition 1.3.7 may be displaced not only by proof of the actual time at which a notice or document was received, but also by proof that the notice or document was not received at all.

Condition 1.3.3(b) is a new provision, which enables a notice or document to be sent by e-mail where delivery of the original is not essential. It is important to appreciate that condition 1.3.3(b) permits notices or documents to be sent in this way if, but only if, an e-mail address for the intended recipient is given in the contract. Thus, a party's conveyancers should not include their e-mail address in the contract unless they are prepared to accept service by e-mail at that address.

Two further provisions relevant to the use of e-mail should be noted. First, condition 1.3.5(c) provides that, where a notice or document sent by e-mail prompts an automated response that the intended recipient is out of the office, the response (while in reality establishing that the message has reached its intended destination) is to be treated as proof that the notice or document has not been received. The sender may, therefore, need to consider other means for sending the notice or document to its intended recipient (e.g., hand delivery or fax). Secondly, condition 1.3.7(e) provides that (in the absence of proof to the contrary under condition 1.3.6) a notice or document sent by e-mail is treated as having been received before 4.00 pm on the first working day after dispatch. It will be noted that this is later than the time of receipt presumed by condition 1.3.7(d) for a notice or document sent by fax (one hour after despatch). The reason for this is that the receipt of an e-mail may on occasion be delayed for several hours without the delay in transmission being readily apparent to the sender.

Assignment

Condition 1.5 now contains a general prohibition on the transfer by the buyer of the benefit of the contract. The specific prohibitions which formerly applied to the transfer of contracts for the grant or assignment of a lease or sub-lease have accordingly been deleted.

Auctions

Condition 2.3.6 now follows the SCPC in providing that, on a sale by auction, the deposit is to be paid to the auctioneer as agent for the seller.

Proof of title

Condition 4.1.1 requires the seller to provide the buyer with proof of his title to the property and of his ability to transfer it or to procure its transfer (the latter alternative applying, for example, to a sub-sale).

Where the title is registered, the effect of condition 4.1.2 is that the proof must include official copies of the individual register and any title plan referred to in it, and of any document referred to in the register and kept by the registrar (unless the document is to be discharged or overridden at or before completion).

Requisitions

Previous editions of the SCS have allowed the buyer to raise requisitions after the making of the contract, whether or not title was deduced beforehand. The fourth edition recognises that where the seller deduces title before the contract is made (as he normally will, at least where the title is registered), the buyer should ensure that any concerns about the title so shown are raised before contract and, where necessary, appropriately provided for in the special conditions. Accordingly, condition 4.2.1(a) now bars the buyer from raising any requisitions on the title shown by the seller before the making of the contract. The buyer, however, retains the right to raise requisitions on matters coming to his attention for the first time after the contract is made (condition 4.2.2).

In cases where the seller deduces title (either in whole or in part) after the contract is made, condition 4.3.1 continues to allow the buyer to raise requisitions within six working days of the date of the contract or delivery of the seller's proof of title on which the requisitions are raised.

Completion after 2.00 pm

Conditions 6.1.2 and 6.1.3 clarify the position where the money due on completion is received after 2.00 pm. Condition 6.1.2 states the normal rule that, in such a case, apportionments are to be worked out as if completion had taken place on the next working day, and compensation is to be calculated as if completion had been deferred to that day as a result of the buyer's default. It would, however, be unfair to adopt that approach where completion has been delayed because the seller has failed to vacate the property by 2.00 pm. Condition 6.1.3 therefore disapplies condition 6.1.2 in a case where the sale is with vacant possession and the buyer is ready, able and willing to complete (as to which, see condition 1.1.3(a)) but does not pay the money due on completion because the seller has not vacated the property by 2.00 pm. In such a case, condition 6.1.3 provides that the seller is to be treated as in default, so that compensation will be calculated on that basis under condition 7.3.

Consent

Condition 8.3.1(a) ensures that condition 8.3 now applies not only in cases where the landlord's consent is required for the assignment of an existing lease or the creation of a sub-lease but also in cases where consent is required for the creation of a new lease of freehold land.

Two changes to condition 8.3 have been made in the light of the decision of the Court of Appeal in *Aubergine Enterprises Ltd* v. *Lakewood International Ltd* [2002] 1 WLR 2149. First, condition 8.3.1(b) confirms that any necessary consent must be in the form which satisfies the requirement to obtain it. Secondly, condition 8.3.3 now provides that, where the parties agree to complete the contract after the contractual completion date, the right to rescind will not arise unless the consent has not been obtained by three working days before the later date agreed for completion.

Commonhold

The new commonhold regime is made the subject of express provision in two ways. First, the seller is required to provide the buyer with current copies of the memorandum and articles of the commonhold association and the commonhold community statement. If the buyer then enters into the contract, he is treated as doing so knowing and accepting their terms (condition 9.3, and cf. condition 3.3.2(a), which makes similar provision with regard to the terms of leases affecting the property). Secondly, cases in which the consent of the commonhold association is required to the sale of part only of a commonhold unit are dealt with (in condition 9.4) in a way which parallels the provision made in conditions 8.3.2(a) and 8.3.3 for cases in which a consent to let, assign or sub-let is required to complete the contract.

V.10. Standard Commercial Property Conditions of Sale (second edition) (including Explanatory Notes)[1]

CONTRACT

(Incorporating the Standard Commercial Property Conditions (Second Edition))

Date	:
Seller	:
Buyer	:
Property (freehold/leasehold)	:
Title Number/Root of title	:
Specified incumbrances	:
Completion date	:
Contract rate	:
Purchase price	:
Deposit	:

The seller will sell and the buyer will buy:

    (a)   the property, and

    (b)   any chattels which, under the special conditions, are included in the sale

for the purchase price

WARNING	**Signed**
This is a formal document, designed to create legal rights and legal obligations. Take advice before using it.	Authorised to sign on behalf of Seller/Buyer

---

1. © 2004 Oyez (The Solicitors' Law Stationery Society Ltd) and the Law Society.

STANDARD COMMERCIAL PROPERTY CONDITIONS
(SECOND EDITION)

Part 1

1. GENERAL

1. Definitions

1.1.1   In these conditions:

(a) 'accrued interest' means:

    (i)   if money has been placed on deposit or in a building society share account, the interest actually earned

    (ii)   otherwise, the interest which might reasonably have been earned by depositing the money at interest on seven days' notice of withdrawal with a clearing bank

less, in either case, any proper charges for handling the money

(b) 'apportionment day' has the meaning given in condition 8.3.2

(c) 'clearing bank' means a bank which is a shareholder in CHAPS Clearing Co. Limited

(d) 'completion date' has the meaning given in condition 8.1.1

(e) 'contract rate' is the Law Society's interest rate from time to time in force

(f) 'conveyancer' means a solicitor, barrister, duly certified notary public, licensed conveyancer or recognised body under sections 9 or 23 of the Administration of Justice Act 1985

(g) 'direct credit' means a direct transfer of cleared funds to an account nominated by the seller's conveyancer and maintained at a clearing bank

(h) 'election to waive exemption' means an election made under paragraph 2 of Schedule 10 to the Value Added Tax Act 1994

(i) 'lease' includes sub-lease, tenancy and agreement for a lease or sublease

(j) 'notice to complete' means a notice requiring completion of the contract in accordance with condition 8

(k) 'post' includes a service provided by a person licensed under the Postal Services Act 2000

(l) 'public requirement' means any notice, order or proposal given or made (whether before or after the date of the contract) by a body acting on statutory authority

(m) 'requisition' includes objection

(n) 'transfer' includes conveyance and assignment

(o) 'working day' means any day from Monday to Friday (inclusive) which is not Christmas Day, Good Friday or a statutory Bank Holiday.

1.1.2   In these conditions the terms 'absolute title' and 'official copies' have the special meanings given to them by the Land Registration Act 2002.

1.1.3   A party is ready, able and willing to complete:

(a) if it could be, but for the default of the other party, and

(b)   in the case of the seller, even though a mortgage remains secured on the property, if the amount to be paid on completion enables the property to be transferred freed of all mortgages (except those to which the sale is expressly subject).

1.1.4 (a)   The conditions in Part 1 apply except as varied or excluded by the contract.

(b)   A condition in Part 2 only applies if expressly incorporated into the contract.

1.2   Joint parties

If there is more than one seller or more than one buyer, the obligations which they undertake can be enforced against them all jointly or against each individually.

1.3   Notices and documents

1.3.1   A notice required or authorised by the contract must be in writing.

1.3.2   Giving a notice or delivering a document to a party's conveyancer has the same effect as giving or delivering it to that party.

1.3.3   Where delivery of the original document is not essential, a notice or document is validly given or sent if it is sent:

(a)   by fax, or

(b)   by e-mail to an e-mail address for the intended recipient given in the contract.

1.3.4   Subject to conditions 1.3.5 to 1.3.7, a notice is given and a document delivered when it is received.

1.3.5 (a)   A notice or document sent through the document exchange is received when it is available for collection

(b)   A notice or document which is received after 4.00 p.m. on a working day, or on a day which is not a working day, is to be treated as having been received on the next working day

(c)   An automated response to a notice or document sent by e-mail that the intended recipient is out of the office is to be treated as proof that the notice or document was not received.

1.3.6   Condition 1.3.7 applies unless there is proof:

(a)   that a notice or document has not been received, or

(b)   of when it was received.

1.3.7   Unless the actual time of receipt is proved, a notice or document sent by the following means is treated as having been received as follows:

(a)   by first class post: before 4.00 pm on the second working day after posting

(b)   by second-class post: before 4.00 pm on the third working day after posting

(c)   through a document exchange: before 4.00 pm on the first working day after the day on which it would normally be available for collection by the addressee

(d)   by fax: one hour after despatch

(e)   by e-mail: before 4.00 pm on the first working day after despatch.

1.3.8   In condition 1.3.7, 'first class post' means a postal service which seeks to deliver posted items no later than the next working day in all or the majority of cases.

1.4 VAT

1.4.1   The seller:

    (a)   warrants that the sale of the property does not constitute a supply that is taxable for VAT purposes

    (b)   agrees that there will be no exercise of the election to waive exemption in respect of the property, and

    (c)   cannot require the buyer to pay any amount in respect of any liability to VAT arising in respect of the sale of the property, unless condition 1.4.2 applies.

1.4.2   If, solely as a result of a change in law made and coming into effect between the date of the contract and completion, the sale of the property will constitute a supply chargeable to VAT, the buyer is to pay to the seller on completion an additional amount equal to that VAT in exchange for a proper VAT invoice from the seller.

1.4.3   The amount payable for the chattels is exclusive of VAT and the buyer is to pay to the seller on completion an additional amount equal to any VAT charged on that supply in exchange for a proper VAT invoice from the seller.

1.5   Assignment and sub-sales

1.5.1   The buyer is not entitled to transfer the benefit of the contract.

1.5.2   The seller may not be required to transfer the property in parts or to any person other than the buyer.

2. FORMATION

2.1   Date

2.1.1   If the parties intend to make a contract by exchanging duplicate copies by post or through a document exchange, the contract is made when the last copy is posted or deposited at the document exchange.

2.1.2   If the parties' conveyancers agree to treat exchange as taking place before duplicate copies are actually exchanged, the contract is made as so agreed.

2.2   Deposit

2.2.1   The buyer is to pay a deposit of 10 per cent of the purchase price no later than the date of the contract.

2.2.2   Except on a sale by auction the deposit is to be paid by direct credit and is to be held by the seller's conveyancer as stakeholder on terms that on completion it is to be paid to the seller with accrued interest.

2.3 Auctions

2.3.1   On a sale by auction the following conditions apply to the property and, if it is sold in lots, to each lot.

2.3.2   The sale is subject to a reserve price.

2.3.3   The seller, or a person on its behalf, may bid up to the reserve price.

2.3.4   The auctioneer may refuse any bid.

2.3.5   If there is a dispute about a bid, the auctioneer may resolve the dispute or restart the auction at the last undisputed bid.

2.3.6   The auctioneer is to hold the deposit as agent for the seller.

2.3.7   If any cheque tendered in payment of all or part of the deposit is dishonoured when first presented, the seller may, within seven working days of being notified that the cheque has been dishonoured, give notice to the buyer that the contract is discharged by the buyer's breach.

3. MATTERS AFFECTING THE PROPERTY

3.1   Freedom from incumbrances

3.1.1   The seller is selling the property free from incumbrances, other than those mentioned in condition 3.1.2.

3.1.2   The incumbrances subject to which the property is sold are:

(a)   those specified in the contract

(b)   those discoverable by inspection of the property before the contract

(c)   those the seller does not and could not reasonably know about

(d)   matters, other than monetary charges or incumbrances, disclosed or which would have been disclosed by the searches and enquiries which a prudent buyer would have made before entering into the contract

(e)   public requirements.

3.1.3   After the contract is made, the seller is to give the buyer written details without delay of any new public requirement and of anything in writing which he learns about concerning a matter covered by condition 3.1.2.

3.1.4   The buyer is to bear the cost of complying with any outstanding public requirement and is to indemnify the seller against any liability resulting from a public requirement.

3.2   Physical state

3.2.1   The buyer accepts the property in the physical state it is in at the date of the contract unless the seller is building or converting it.

3.2.2   A leasehold property is sold subject to any subsisting breach of a condition or tenant's obligation relating to the physical state of the property which renders the lease liable to forfeiture.

3.2.3   A sub-lease is granted subject to any subsisting breach of a condition or tenant's obligation relating to the physical state of the property which renders the seller's own lease liable to forfeiture.

3.3   Retained land

Where after the transfer the seller will be retaining land near the property:

(a)   the buyer will have no right of light or air over the retained land, but

(b)   in other respects the seller and the buyer will each have the rights over the land of the other which they would have had if they were two separate buyers to whom the seller had made simultaneous transfers of the property and the retained land.

The transfer is to contain appropriate express terms.

4. LEASES AFFECTING THE PROPERTY

4.1   General

4.1.1   This condition applies if any part of the property is sold subject to a lease.

4.1.2   The seller having provided the buyer with full details of each lease or copies of documents embodying the lease terms, the buyer is treated as entering into the contract knowing and fully accepting those terms.

4.1.3   The seller is not to serve a notice to end the lease nor to accept a surrender.

4.1.4   The seller is to inform the buyer without delay if the lease ends.

4.1.5   The buyer is to indemnify the seller against all claims arising from the lease after actual completion; this includes claims which are unenforceable against a buyer for want of registration.

4.1.6   If the property does not include all the land let, the seller may apportion the rent and, if the lease is a new tenancy, the buyer may require the seller to apply under section 10 of the Landlord and Tenant (Covenants) Act 1995 for the apportionment to bind the tenant.

4.2   Property management

4.2.1   The seller is promptly to give the buyer full particulars of:

(a)   any court or arbitration proceedings in connection with the lease, and

(b)   any application for a licence, consent or approval under the lease.

4.2.2   Conditions 4.2.3 to 4.2.8 do not apply to a rent review process to which condition 5 applies.

4.2.3   Subject to condition 4.2.4, the seller is to conduct any court or arbitration proceedings in accordance with written directions given by the buyer from time to time (for which the seller is to apply), unless to do so might place the seller in breach of an obligation to the tenant or a statutory duty.

4.2.4   If the seller applies for directions from the buyer in relation to a proposed step in the proceedings and the buyer does not give such directions within 10 working days, the seller may take or refrain from taking that step as it thinks fit.

4.2.5   The buyer is to indemnify the seller against all loss and expense resulting from the seller's following the buyer's directions.

4.2.6   Unless the buyer gives written consent, the seller is not to:

  (a)   grant or formally withhold any licence, consent or approval under the lease, or

  (b)   serve any notice or take any action (other than action in court or arbitration proceedings) as landlord under the lease.

4.2.7   When the seller applies for the buyer's consent under condition 4.2.6:

  (a)   the buyer is not to withhold its consent or attach conditions to the consent where to do so might place the seller in breach of an obligation to the tenant or a statutory duty

  (b)   the seller may proceed as if the buyer has consented when:

     (i)   in accordance with paragraph (a), the buyer is not entitled to withhold its consent, or

     (ii)   the buyer does not refuse its consent within 10 working days.

4.2.8   If the buyer withholds or attaches conditions to its consent, the buyer is to indemnify the seller against all loss and expense.

4.2.9   In all other respects, the seller is to manage the property in accordance with the principles of good estate management until completion.

4.3   Continuing liability

At the request and cost of the seller, the buyer is to support any application by the seller to be released from the landlord covenants in a lease to which the property is sold subject.

5. RENT REVIEWS

5.1   Subject to condition 5.2, this condition applies if:

  (a)   the rent reserved by a lease of all or part of the property is to be reviewed,

  (b)   the seller is either the landlord or the tenant,

  (c)   the rent review process starts before actual completion, and

  (d)   no reviewed rent has been agreed or determined at the date of the contract.

5.2   The seller is to conduct the rent review process until actual completion, after which the buyer is to conduct it.

5.3   Conditions 5.4 and 5.5 cease to apply on actual completion if the reviewed rent will only be payable in respect of a period after that date.

5.4   In the course of the rent review process, the seller and the buyer are each to:

  (a)   act promptly with a view to achieving the best result obtainable,

  (b)   consult with and have regard to the views of the other,

  (c)   provide the other with copies of all material correspondence and papers relating to the process,

    (d)   ensure that its representations take account of matters put forward by the other, and

    (e)   keep the other informed of the progress of the process.

5.5   Neither the seller nor the buyer is to agree a rent figure unless it has been approved in writing by the other (such approval not to be unreasonably withheld).

5.6   The seller and the buyer are each to bear their own costs of the rent review process.

5.7   Unless the rent review date precedes the apportionment day, the buyer is to pay the costs of a third party appointed to determine the rent.

5.8   Where the rent review date precedes the apportionment day, those costs are to be divided as follows:

    (a)   the seller is to pay the proportion that the number of days from the rent review date to the apportionment day bears to the number of days from that rent review date until either the following rent review date or, if none, the expiry of the term, and

    (b)   the buyer is to pay the balance.

6. TITLE AND TRANSFER

6.1   Proof of title

6.1.1   Without cost to the buyer, the seller is to provide the buyer with proof of the title to the property and of his ability to transfer it, or to procure its transfer.

6.1.2   Where the property has a registered title the proof is to include official copies of the items referred to in rules 134(1)(a) and (b) and 135(1)(a) of the Land Registration Rules 2003, so far as they are not to be discharged or overridden at or before completion.

6.1.3   Where the property has an unregistered title, the proof is to include:

    (a)   an abstract of title or an epitome of title with photocopies of the documents, and

    (b)   production of every document or an abstract, epitome or copy of it with an original marking by a conveyancer either against the original or an examined abstract or an examined copy.

6.2   Requisitions

6.2.1   The buyer may not raise requisitions:

    (a)   on the title shown by the seller taking the steps described in condition 6.1.1 before the contract was made

    (b)   in relation to the matters covered by condition 3.1.2.

6.2.2   Notwithstanding condition 6.2.1, the buyer may, within six working days of a matter coming to his attention after the contract was made, raise written requisitions on that matter. In that event steps 3 and 4 in condition 6.3.1 apply.

6.2.3   On the expiry of the relevant time limit under condition 6.2.2 or condition 6.3.1, the buyer loses his right to raise requisitions or to make observations.

6.3 Timetable

6.3.1 Subject to condition 6.2 and to the extent that the seller did not take the steps described in condition 6.1.1 before the contract was made, the following are the steps for deducing and investigating the title to the property to be taken within the following time limits:

Step	Time limit
1. The seller is to comply with condition 6.1.1	Immediately after making the contract
2. The buyer may raise written requisitions	Six working days after either the date of the seller's evidence of title on which the contract or the date of delivery of the requisitions are raised whichever is the later
3. The seller is to reply in writing to any requisitions raised	Four working days after receiving the requisitions
4. The buyer may make written observations on the seller's replies	Three working days after receiving the replies

The time limit on the buyer's right to raise requisitions applies even where the seller supplies incomplete evidence of its title, but the buyer may, within six working days from delivery of any further evidence, raise further requisitions resulting from that evidence.

6.3.2 The parties are to take the following steps to prepare and agree the transfer of the property within the following time limits:

Step	Time limit
A. The buyer is to send the seller a draft transfer	At least twelve working days before completion date
B. The seller is to approve or revise that draft and either return it or retain it for use as the actual transfer	Four working days after delivery of the draft transfer
C. If the draft is returned the buyer is to send an engrossment to the seller	At least five working days before completion date

6.3.3 Periods of time under conditions 6.3.1 and 6.3.2 may run concurrently.

6.3.4 If the period between the date of the contract and completion date is less than 15 working days, the time limits in conditions 6.2.2, 6.3.1 and 6.3.2 are to be reduced by the same proportion as that period bears to the period of 15 working days. Fractions of a working day are to be rounded down except that the time limit to perform any step is not to be less than one working day.

6.4 Defining the property

6.4.1 The seller need not, further than it may be able to do from information in its possession:

    (a) prove the exact boundaries of the property

    (b) prove who owns fences, ditches, hedges or walls

    (c) separately identify parts of the property with different titles.

6.4.2   The buyer may, if to do so is reasonable, require the seller to make or obtain, pay for and hand over a statutory declaration about facts relevant to the matters mentioned in condition 6.4.1. The form of the declaration is to be agreed by the buyer, who must not unreasonably withhold its agreement.

6.5   Rents and rentcharges

The fact that a rent or rentcharge, whether payable or receivable by the owner of the property, has been or will on completion be, informally apportioned is not to be regarded as a defect in title.

6.6   Transfer

6.6.1   The buyer does not prejudice its right to raise requisitions, or to require replies to any raised, by taking steps in relation to the preparation or agreement of the transfer.

6.6.2   Subject to condition 6.6.3, the seller is to transfer the property with full title guarantee.

6.6.3   The transfer is to have effect as if the disposition is expressly made subject to all matters covered by condition 3.1.2.

6.6.4   If after completion the seller will remain bound by any obligation affecting the property and disclosed to the buyer before the contract was made, but the law does not imply any covenant by the buyer to indemnify the seller against liability for future breaches of it:

    (a)   the buyer is to covenant in the transfer to indemnify the seller against liability for any future breach of the obligation and to perform it from then on, and

    (b)   if required by the seller, the buyer is to execute and deliver to the seller on completion a duplicate transfer prepared by the buyer.

6.6.5   The seller is to arrange at its expense that, in relation to every document of title which the buyer does not receive on completion, the buyer is to have the benefit of:

    (a)   a written acknowledgement of the buyer's right to its production, and

    (b)   a written undertaking for its safe custody (except while it is held by a mortgagee or by someone in a fiduciary capacity).

7. INSURANCE

7.1   Responsibility for insuring

7.1.1   Conditions 7.1.2 and 7.1.3 apply if:

    (a)   the contract provides that the policy effected by or for the seller and insuring the property or any part of it against loss or damage should continue in force after the exchange of contracts, or

    (b)   the property or any part of it is let on terms under which the seller (whether as landlord or as tenant) is obliged to insure against loss or damage.

7.1.2   The seller is to:

    (a)   do everything required to continue to maintain the policy, including the prompt payment of any premium which falls due

    (b)   increase the amount or extent of the cover as requested by the buyer, if the insurers agree and the buyer pays the additional premium

(c)   permit the buyer to inspect the policy, or evidence of its terms, at any time

(d)   obtain or consent to an endorsement on the policy of the buyer's interest, at the buyer's expense

(e)   pay to the buyer immediately on receipt, any part of an additional premium which the buyer paid and which is returned by the insurers

(f)   if before completion the property suffers loss or damage:

  (i)   pay to the buyer on completion the amount of policy moneys which the seller has received, so far as not applied in repairing or reinstating the property, and

  (ii)   if no final payment has then been received, assign to the buyer, at the buyer's expense, all rights to claim under the policy in such form as the buyer reasonably requires and pending execution of the assignment, hold any policy moneys received in trust for the buyer

(g)   on completion:

  (i)   cancel the insurance policy

  (ii)   apply for a refund of the premium and pay the buyer, immediately on receipt, any amount received which relates to a part of the premium which was paid or reimbursed by a tenant or third party. The buyer is to hold the money paid subject to the rights of that tenant or third party.

7.1.3   The buyer is to pay the seller a proportionate part of the premium which the seller paid in respect of the period from the date when the contract is made to the date of actual completion, except so far as the seller is entitled to recover it from a tenant.

7.1.4   Unless condition 7.1.2 applies:

(a)   the seller is under no obligation to the buyer to insure the property

(b)   if payment under a policy effected by or for the buyer is reduced, because the property is covered against loss or damage by an insurance policy effected by or for the seller, the purchase price is to be abated by the amount of that reduction.

7.1.5   Section 47 of the Law of Property Act 1925 does not apply.

8. COMPLETION

8.1   Date

8.1.1   Completion date is twenty working days after the date of the contract but time is not of the essence of the contract unless a notice to complete has been served.

8.1.2   If the money due on completion is received after 2.00 pm, completion is to be treated, for the purposes only of conditions 8.3 and 9.3, as taking place on the next working day as a result of the buyer's default.

8.1.3   Condition 8.1.2 does not apply if:

(a)   the sale is with vacant possession of the property or a part of it, and

(b)   the buyer is ready, willing and able to complete but does not pay the money due on completion until after 2.00 pm because the seller has not vacated the property or that part by that time.

8.2 Place

Completion is to take place in England and Wales, either at the seller's conveyancer's office or at some other place which the seller reasonably specifies.

8.3 Apportionments

8.3.1 Subject to condition 8.3.6 income and outgoings of the property are to be apportioned between the parties so far as the change of ownership on completion will affect entitlement to receive or liability to pay them.

8.3.2 The day from which the apportionment is to be made ('apportionment day') is:

    (a) if the whole property is sold with vacant possession or the seller exercises its option in condition 9.3.4, the date of actual completion, or

    (b) otherwise, completion date.

8.3.3 In apportioning any sum, it is to be assumed that the buyer owns the property from the beginning of the day on which the apportionment is to be made.

8.3.4 A sum to be apportioned is to be treated as:

    (a) payable for the period which it covers, except that if it is an instalment of an annual sum the buyer is to be attributed with an amount equal to 1/365th of the annual sum for each day from and including the apportionment day to the end of the instalment period

    (b) accruing –

        (i) from day to day, and

        (ii) at the rate applicable from time to time.

8.3.5 When a sum to be apportioned, or the rate at which it is to be treated as accruing, is not known or easily ascertainable at completion, a provisional apportionment is to be made according to the best estimate available. As soon as the amount is known, a final apportionment is to be made and notified to the other party. Subject to condition 8.3.8, any resulting balance is to be paid no more than ten working days later, and if not then paid the balance is to bear interest at the contract rate from then until payment.

8.3.6 Where a lease of the property requires the tenant to reimburse the landlord for expenditure on goods or services, on completion:

    (a) the buyer is to pay the seller the amount of any expenditure already incurred by the seller but not yet due from the tenant and in respect of which the seller provides the buyer with the information and vouchers required for its recovery from the tenant, and

    (b) the seller is to credit the buyer with payments already recovered from the tenant but not yet incurred by the seller.

8.3.7 Condition 8.3.8 applies if any part of the property is sold subject to a lease and either:

    (a)   (i) on completion any rent or other sum payable under the lease is due but not paid

        (ii) the contract does not provide that the buyer is to assign to the seller the right to collect any arrears due to the seller under the terms of the contract, and

        (iii) the seller is not entitled to recover any arrears from the tenant, or

    (b)   (i)   as a result of a rent review to which condition 5 applies a reviewed rent is agreed or determined after actual completion, and

            (ii)   an additional sum then becomes payable in respect of a period before the apportionment day.

8.3.8 (a)   The buyer is to seek to collect all sums due in the circumstances referred to in condition 8.3.7 in the ordinary course of management, but need not take legal proceedings or distrain.

    (b)   A payment made on account of those sums is to be apportioned between the parties in the ratio of the amounts owed to each, notwithstanding that the tenant exercises its right to appropriate the payment in some other manner.

    (c)   Any part of a payment on account received by one party but due to the other is to be paid no more than ten working days after the receipt of cash or cleared funds and, if not then paid, the sum is to bear interest at the contract rate until payment.

8.4   Amount payable

The amount payable by the buyer on completion is the purchase price (less any deposit already paid to the seller or its agent) adjusted to take account of:

    (a)   apportionments made under condition 8.3

    (b)   any compensation to be paid under condition 9.3

    (c)   any sum payable under condition 7.1.2 or 7.1.3.

8.5   Title deeds

8.5.1   As soon as the buyer has complied with all its obligations on completion the seller must hand over the documents of title.

8.5.2   Condition 8.5.1 does not apply to any documents of title relating to land being retained by the seller after completion.

8.6   Rent receipts

The buyer is to assume that whoever gave any receipt for a payment of rent which the seller produces was the person or the agent of the person then entitled to that rent.

8.7   Means of payment

The buyer is to pay the money due on completion by direct credit and, if appropriate, by an unconditional release of a deposit held by a stakeholder.

8.8   Notice to complete

8.8.1   At any time on or after completion date, a party who is ready, able and willing to complete may give the other a notice to complete.

8.8.2   The parties are to complete the contract within ten working days of giving a notice to complete, excluding the day on which the notice is given. For this purpose, time is of the essence of the contract.

9. REMEDIES

9.1   Errors and omissions

9.1.1   If any plan or statement in the contract, or in the negotiations leading to it, is or was misleading or inaccurate due to an error or omission, the remedies available are as follows.

9.1.2   When there is a material difference between the description or value of the property as represented and as it is, the buyer is entitled to damages.

9.1.3   An error or omission only entitles the buyer to rescind the contract:

    (a)   where the error or omission results from fraud or recklessness, or

    (b)   where the buyer would be obliged, to its prejudice, to accept property differing substantially (in quantity, quality or tenure) from that which the error or omission had led it to expect.

9.2   Rescission

If either party rescinds the contract:

    (a)   unless the rescission is a result of the buyer's breach of contract the deposit is to be repaid to the buyer with accrued interest

    (b)   the buyer is to return any documents received from the seller and is to cancel any registration of the contract

    (c)   the seller's duty to pay any returned premium under condition 7.1.2(e) (whenever received) is not affected.

9.3   Late completion

9.3.1   If the buyer defaults in performing its obligations under the contract and completion is delayed, the buyer is to pay compensation to the seller.

9.3.2   Compensation is calculated at the contract rate on the purchase price (less any deposit paid) for the period between completion date and actual completion, but ignoring any period during which the seller was in default.

9.3.3   Any claim by the seller for loss resulting from delayed completion is to be reduced by any compensation paid under this contract.

9.3.4   Where the sale is not with vacant possession of the whole property and completion is delayed, the seller may give notice to the buyer, before the date of actual completion, that it will take the net income from the property until completion as well as compensation under condition 9.3.1.

9.4   After completion

Completion does not cancel liability to perform any outstanding obligation under the contract.

9.5   Buyer's failure to comply with notice to complete

9.5.1   If the buyer fails to complete in accordance with a notice to complete, the following terms apply.

9.5.2   The seller may rescind the contract, and if it does so:

(a) it may

    (i)   forfeit and keep any deposit and accrued interest

    (ii)   resell the property

    (iii) claim damages

(b) the buyer is to return any documents received from the seller and is to cancel any registration of the contract.

9.5.3   The seller retains its other rights and remedies.

9.6   Seller's failure to comply with notice to complete

9.6.1   If the seller fails to complete in accordance with a notice to complete, the following terms apply:

9.6.2   The buyer may rescind the contract, and if it does so:

(a) the deposit is to be repaid to the buyer with accrued interest

(b) the buyer is to return any documents it received from the seller and is, at the seller's expense, to cancel any registration of the contract.

9.6.3   The buyer retains its other rights and remedies.

10. LEASEHOLD PROPERTY

10.1   Existing leases

10.1.1   The following provisions apply to a sale of leasehold land.

10.1.2   The seller having provided the buyer with copies of the documents embodying the lease terms, the buyer is treated as entering into the contract knowing and fully accepting those terms.

10.1.3   The seller is to comply with any lease obligations requiring the tenant to insure the property.

10.2   New leases

10.2.1   The following provisions apply to a contract to grant a new lease.

10.2.2   The conditions apply so that:

       'seller' means the proposed landlord

       'buyer' means the proposed tenant

       'purchase price' means the premium to be paid on the grant of a lease.

10.2.3   The lease is to be in the form of the draft attached to the contract.

10.2.4   If the term of the new lease will exceed seven years, the seller is to deduce a title which will enable the buyer to register the lease at the Land Registry with an absolute title.

10.2.5   The seller is to engross the lease and a counterpart of it and is to send the counterpart to the buyer at least five working days before completion date.

10.2.6   The buyer is to execute the counterpart and deliver it to the seller on completion.

10.3   Consents

10.3.1(a)   The following provisions apply if a consent to let, assign or sub-let is required to complete the contract

(b)   In this condition 'consent' means consent in a form which satisfies the requirement to obtain it.

10.3.2(a)   The seller is to:

(i)   apply for the consent at its expense, and to use all reasonable efforts to obtain it

(ii)   give the buyer notice forthwith on obtaining the consent

(b)   The buyer is to comply with all reasonable requirements, including requirements for the provision of information and references.

10.3.3   Where the consent of a reversioner (whether or not immediate) is required to an assignment or sub-letting, then so far as the reversioner lawfully imposes such a condition:

(a)   the buyer is to:

(i)   covenant directly with the reversioner to observe the tenant's covenants and the conditions in the seller's lease

(ii)   use reasonable endeavours to provide guarantees of the performance and observance of the tenant's covenants and the conditions in the seller's lease

(iii)   execute or procure the execution of the licence

(b)   the seller, in the case of an assignment, is to enter into an authorised guarantee agreement.

10.3.4   Neither party may object to a reversioner's consent given subject to a condition:

(a)   which under section 19(1A) of the Landlord and Tenant Act 1927 is not regarded as unreasonable, and

(b)   which is lawfully imposed under an express term of the lease.

10.3.5   If any required consent has not been obtained by the original completion date:

(a)   the time for completion is to be postponed until five working days after the seller gives written notice to the buyer that the consent has been obtained or four months from the original completion date whichever is the earlier

(b)   the postponed date is to be treated as the completion date.

10.3.6   At any time after four months from the original completion date, either party may rescind the contract by notice to the other, if:

(a)   consent has still not been given, and

(b)   no declaration has been obtained from the court that consent has been unreasonably withheld.

10.3.7   If the contract is rescinded under condition 10.3.6 the seller is to remain liable for any breach of condition 10.3.2(a) or 10.3.3(b) and the buyer is to remain liable for any breach of condition 10.3.2(b) or 10.3.3(a). In all other respects neither party is to be treated as in breach of contract and condition 9.2 applies.

10.3.8   A party in breach of its obligations under condition 10.3.2 or 10.3.3 cannot rescind under condition 10.3.6 for so long as its breach is a cause of the consent's being withheld.

11. COMMONHOLD

11.1   Terms used in this condition have the special meanings given to them in Part 1 of the Commonhold and Leasehold Reform Act 2002.

11.2   This condition applies to a disposition of commonhold land.

11.3   The seller having provided the buyer with copies of the current versions of the memorandum and articles of the commonhold association and of the commonhold community statement, the buyer is treated as entering into the contract knowing and fully accepting their terms.

11.4   If the contract is for the sale of property which is or includes part only of a commonhold unit:

(a)   the seller is, at its expense, to apply for the written consent of the commonhold association and is to use all reasonable efforts to obtain it

(b)   either the seller, unless it is in breach of its obligation under paragraph (a), or the buyer may rescind the contract by notice to the other party if three working days before completion date (or before a later date on which the parties have agreed to complete the contract) the consent has not been given. In that case, neither party is to be treated as in breach of contract and condition 9.2 applies.

12. CHATTELS

12.1   The following provisions apply to any chattels which are included in the contract.

12.2   The contract takes effect as a contract for the sale of goods.

12.3   The buyer takes the chattels in the physical state they are in at the date of the contract.

12.4   Ownership of the chattels passes to the buyer on actual completion but they are at the buyer's risk from the contract date.

Part 2*

*The conditions in Part 2 do not apply unless expressly incorporated. See condition 1.1.4(b).

A. VAT

A1   Standard rated supply

A1.1   Conditions 1.4.1 and 1.4.2 do not apply.

A1.2   The seller warrants that the sale of the property will constitute a supply chargeable to VAT at the standard rate.

A1.3   The buyer is to pay to the seller on completion an additional amount equal to the VAT in exchange for a proper VAT invoice from the seller.

A2   Transfer of a going concern

A2.1   Condition 1.4 does not apply.

A2.2   In this condition 'TOGC' means a transfer of a business as a going concern treated as neither a supply of goods nor a supply of services by virtue of article 5 of the Value Added Tax (Special Provisions) Order 1995.

A2.3   The seller warrants that it is using the property for the business of letting to produce rental income.

A2.4   The buyer is to make every effort to comply with the conditions to be met by a transferee under article 5(1) and 5(2) for the sale to constitute a TOGC.

A2.5   The buyer will, on or before the earlier of:

    (a)   completion date, and

    (b)   the earliest date on which a supply of the property could be treated as made by the seller under this contract if the sale does not constitute a TOGC, notify the seller that paragraph (2B) of article 5 of the VAT (Special Provisions) Order 1995 does not apply to the buyer.

A2.6   The parties are to treat the sale as a TOGC at completion if the buyer provides written evidence to the seller before completion that it is a taxable person and that it has made an election to waive exemption in respect of the property and has given a written notification of the making of such election in conformity with article 5(2) and has given the notification referred to in condition A2.5.

A2.7   The buyer is not to revoke its election to waive exemption in respect of the property at any time.

A2.8   If the parties treat the sale at completion as a TOGC but it is later determined that the sale was not a TOGC, then within five working days of that determination the buyer shall pay to the seller:

    (a)   an amount equal to the VAT chargeable in respect of the supply of the property, in exchange for a proper VAT invoice from the seller; and

    (b)   except where the sale is not a TOGC because of an act or omission of the seller, an amount equal to any interest or penalty for which the seller is liable to account to HM Customs and Excise in respect of or by reference to that VAT.

A2.9   If the seller obtains the consent of HM Customs and Excise to retain its VAT records relating to the property, it shall make them available to the buyer for inspection and copying at reasonable times on reasonable request during the six years following completion.

B.   CAPITAL ALLOWANCES

B1   To enable the buyer to make and substantiate claims under the Capital Allowances Act 2001 in respect of the property, the seller is to use its reasonable endeavours to provide, or to procure that its agents provide:

    (a)   copies of all relevant information in its possession or that of its agents, and

(b)   such co-operation and assistance as the buyer may reasonably require.

B2.1   The buyer is only to use information provided under condition B1 for the stated purpose.

B2.2   The buyer is not to disclose, without the consent of the seller, any such information which the seller expressly provides on a confidential basis.

B3.1   On completion, the seller and the buyer are jointly to make an election under section 198 of the Capital Allowances Act 2001 which is consistent with the apportionment in the Special Conditions.

B3.2   The seller and the buyer are each to submit the amount fixed by that election to the Inland Revenue for the purposes of their respective capital allowance computations.

C. REVERSIONARY INTERESTS IN FLATS

C1   No tenants' rights

C1.1   In this condition, sections refer to sections of the Landlord and Tenant Act 1987 and expressions have the special meanings given to them in that Act.

C1.2   The seller warrants that:

(a)   it gave the notice required by section 5,

(b)   no acceptance notice was served on the landlord or no person was nominated for the purposes of section 6 during the protected period, and

(c)   that period ended less than 12 months before the date of the contract.

C2   Tenants' right of first refusal

C2.1   In this condition, sections refer to sections of the Landlord and Tenant Act 1987 and expressions have the special meanings given to them in that Act.

C2.2   The seller warrants that:

(a)   it gave the notice required by section 5, and

(b)   it has given the buyer a copy of:

(i)   any acceptance notice served on the landlord and

(ii)   any nomination of a person duly nominated for the purposes of section 6.

C2.3   If the sale is by auction:

(a)   the seller warrants that it has given the buyer a copy of any notice served on the landlord electing that section 8B shall apply,

(b)   condition 8.1.1 applies as if 'thirty working days' were substituted for 'twenty working days',

(c)   the seller is to send a copy of the contract to the nominated person as required by section 8B(3), and

(d)   if the nominated person serves notice under section 8B(4):

(i)   the seller is to give the buyer a copy of the notice, and

(ii)   condition 9.2 is to apply as if the contract had been rescinded.

SPECIAL CONDITIONS

1.   This contract incorporates the Standard Commercial Property Conditions (Second Edition).

2.   The property is sold with vacant possession.

(or)

2.   The property is sold subject to the leases or tenancies set out on the attached list but otherwise with vacant possession on completion.

3.   The chattels at the Property and set out on the attached list are included in the sale. [The amount of the purchase price apportioned to those chattels is £[…]]

4.   The conditions in Part 2 shown against the boxes ticked below are included in the contract:

- Condition A1 (VAT: standard rate)

[or]

- Condition A2 (VAT: transfer of a going concern)
- Condition B (capital allowances). The amount of the purchase price apportioned to plant and machinery at the property for the purposes of the Capital Allowances Act 2001 is £
- Condition C1 (flats: no tenants' rights of first refusal)

[or]

- Condition C2 (flats: with tenants' rights of first refusal).

Seller's Conveyancers*:

Buyer's Conveyancers*:

*Adding an e-mail address authorises service by e-mail: see condition 1.3.3(b).

EXPLANATORY NOTES

General

The second edition of the Standard Commercial Property Conditions (the SCPC) takes effect on 1 June 2004. It takes account of the Land Registration Act 2002 and also anticipates the coming into force in the summer of 2004 of the provisions relating to commonhold in Part I of the Commonhold and Leasehold Reform Act 2002. In addition, it covers a number of other developments.

The SCPC are intended primarily for use in more complex commercial transactions. Conveyancers are likely to find that, for residential sales and the sale of small business premises, the Standard Conditions of Sale (the SCS) are better suited to their needs.

The fourth edition of the SCS came into effect on 13 October 2003 and represents the 24th Edition of the National Conditions of Sale and the 2003 revision of the Law Society's Conditions of Sale. It should be noted that the second edition of the SCPC does not represent a further edition or revision of either of those sets of conditions. References in existing legal documents to 'the current' edition of the National Conditions of Sale or the Law Society Conditions of Sale accordingly continue to have effect as references to the fourth edition of the SCS.

Front page and special conditions

In contrast to the first edition of the SCPC (which provided for any amount payable for chattels to be stated separately from the purchase price for the property), the purchase price to be entered on the front page is now the total sum payable both for the property and for any chattels which are included in the sale. Special condition 3 makes provision for chattels included in the sale to be set out on an attached list, and, if part of the purchase price has been apportioned to the chattels, for that amount to be stated.

The special conditions no longer provide that the property is sold subject to the incumbrances set out on the front page. Instead, condition 3.1.2(a) provides that the property is sold subject to the incumbrances specified in the contract, and the front page includes space for specifying any incumbrances to which the sale is expressly made subject. The sale will, therefore, continue to take effect subject to any incumbrances there set out.

'Conveyancer'

In this edition, 'conveyancer' has replaced 'solicitor' as the defined term used to refer to the various categories of persons who may lawfully carry out conveyancing work for reward (condition 1.1.1(f)).

Ready, able and willing to complete

Condition 1.1.3 contains a new general provision stating when a party is ready, able and willing to complete. The provision is relevant in applying conditions 6.1.3 and 6.8.1.

Part 1 and Part 2

The new edition is in two parts. Part 1 is an updated and expanded version of the first edition. Part 2 is new, and contains a number of optional further conditions which the parties may wish to incorporate in particular cases.

As is apparent from condition 1.1.4, the conditions in Part 1 apply except as varied or excluded by the contract, whereas a condition in Part 2 will not apply unless expressly incorporated into the contract by a special condition.

A particular effect of condition 1.1.4(a) is that the general provisions in Part 1 which determine the completion date (conditions 1.1.1(d) and 8.1.1), the contract rate (condition 1.1.1(e)) and the title guarantee to be given in the transfer (condition 6.6.2) will automatically take effect subject to any individually negotiated terms which deal with these matters. For that reason, these provisions no longer include words making them expressly subject to the particular terms of the agreement.

Notices and documents

Condition 1.3.6 now makes it clear that the presumed times of receipt set out in condition 1.3.7 may be displaced not only by proof of the actual time at which a notice or document was received, but also by proof that the notice or document was not received at all.

Condition 1.3.3(b) is a new provision, which enables a notice or document to be sent by e-mail where delivery of the original is not essential. It is important to appreciate that condition 1.3.3(b) permits notices or documents to be sent in this way if, but only if, an e-mail address for the intended recipient is given in the contract. Thus, a party's conveyancers should not include their e-mail address in the contract unless they are prepared to accept service by e-mail at that address.

Two further provisions relevant to the use of e-mail should be noted. First, condition 1.3.5(c) provides that, where a notice or document sent by e-mail prompts an automated response that the intended recipient is out of the office, the response (while in reality establishing that the message has reached its intended destination) is to be treated as proof that the notice or document has not been received. The sender may, therefore, need to consider other means for sending the notice or document to its intended recipient (e.g., hand delivery or fax). Secondly, condition 1.3.7(e) provides that (in the absence of proof to the contrary under condition 1.3.6) a notice or document sent by e-mail is treated as having been received before 4.00 pm on the first working day after dispatch. This is later than the time of receipt presumed by condition 1.3.7(d) for a notice or document sent by fax (one hour after despatch), because the receipt of an e-mail may on occasion be delayed for several hours without the delay in transmission being readily apparent to the sender.

VAT

Condition 1.4 now includes a warranty by the seller that the sale of the property (as distinct from any chattels) is exempt from VAT and an agreement by the seller not to elect to waive that exemption before completion. In a case where it is intended either that the sale is to be standard rated for VAT, or that it is to be treated as the transfer of a going concern, condition 1.4 should be excluded, either partly or completely, by special condition. In such cases, users may wish to adopt condition A1 or A2 in Part 2 (see below), which have the effect of partly or wholly excluding condition 1.4, as appropriate.

Leases affecting the property

Condition 4 corresponds to condition 3.3 in the first edition, but has been expanded and rationalised. Condition 4.1, preserves the former condition 3.3.1 and 3.3.2, which specified the circumstances in which the condition applied and provided that the seller should provide the buyer with details of leases affecting the property before exchange and the buyer should then be treated as knowing and accepting the terms of each lease. It expands the terms previously found in condition 3.3.6 by providing not only that the seller is debarred from serving a notice to end the lease but also that it must not accept a surrender (condition 4.1.3). It is then provided that the seller is to inform the buyer if the lease ends (condition 4.1.4). Conditions 4.1.5 and 4.1.6 adopt the previous conditions 3.3.7 and 3.3.8 relating to the indemnity to be given by the buyer to the seller and the apportionment of the rent.

Provisions relating to the management of the property are then gathered together in condition 4.2. The information which the seller must give the buyer now extends to court or arbitration proceedings as well as to applications, and relevant applications are identified as applications for a licence, consent or approval (condition 4.2.1). Conditions 4.2.3 to 4.2.8 (which do not, however, apply to a rent review process governed by condition 5) distinguish between the conduct of court or arbitration proceedings and the taking of other steps in connection with the lease.

As regards court or arbitration proceedings, condition 4.2.3 requires the seller to conduct the proceedings in accordance with the buyer's directions (for which the seller must apply), unless the seller might thereby be placed in breach of an obligation to the tenant or a statutory duty. If the buyer fails to give directions with regard to a proposed step in the proceedings within 10 working days, the seller can decide for itself whether or not to take that step (condition 4.2.4). Where directions are given, the buyer must indemnify the seller against all loss or expense which it incurs by following those directions (condition 4.2.5).

As regards other steps in connection with the lease, condition 4.2.6 provides that the written consent of the buyer is required before the seller may grant or formally withhold any licence, consent or approval under the lease or take any other action as landlord under the lease. The previous provision prohibiting a buyer from refusing consent or attaching conditions where to do so might place the seller in breach of an obligation or statutory duty is now in condition 4.2.7(a), and additionally the seller is entitled to proceed as if the buyer has consented when the buyer is not entitled to refuse consent or, if so entitled, has not in fact refused consent within 10 working days. The buyer must indemnify the seller against loss and expense resulting from the refusal of consent or the attaching of conditions to consent (condition 4.2.8).

The general obligation to manage the property in accordance with the principles of good estate management is retained and now appears in condition 4.2.9.

A new condition (condition 4.3) has been included obliging the buyer, at the request and cost of the seller, to support any application by the seller to be released from the landlord covenants in the lease (see sections 6 to 8 of the Landlord and Tenant (Covenants) Act 1995).

Rent reviews

Condition 5 is new, and makes specific provision for cases in which a rent review is in progress during some or all of the period between the date of the contract and actual completion. As will be apparent from condition 5.1(a), the condition applies whether the seller's position is that of landlord or tenant: condition 5.4(a) will normally oblige the parties to press for the highest rent in the former case and the lowest rent in the latter.

The general rule is that condition 5 will continue to apply after actual completion if the rent review process has not been concluded by then. If the reviewed rent will be payable only in respect of a period which will begin after actual completion (so that the seller has no interest in the amount of the reviewed rent), the obligation to conduct the review in accordance with conditions 5.4 and 5.5 will cease to apply on actual completion (condition 5.2). Accordingly, the buyer will be a free agent in conducting the review process from then on.

The seller and buyer will each bear their own costs of the rent review process (condition 5.6). Where a third party is appointed to determine the rent, the buyer is to pay the third party's costs, except that, if the rent review date precedes the apportionment date, those costs are to divided between the buyer and seller in accordance with condition 5.8.

Where the seller is the landlord and a new rent is not agreed or determined until after actual completion, conditions 8.3.7(b) and 8.3.8 make provision for any additional rent which becomes due in respect of the period before the completion date to be collected by the buyer and paid to the seller.

Proof of title

Condition 6.1.1 requires the seller to provide the buyer with proof of its title to the property and of its ability to transfer it or to procure its transfer (the latter alternative applying, for example, to a sub-sale).

Where the title is registered, the effect of condition 6.1.2 is that the proof must include official copies of the individual register and any title plan referred to in it, and of any document referred to in the register and kept by the registrar (unless the document is to be discharged or overridden at or before completion).

Requisitions

The first edition of the SCPC allowed the buyer to raise requisitions after the making of the contract, whether or not title was deduced beforehand. The present edition recognises that where the seller deduces title before the contract is made (as it normally will, at least where the title is registered), the buyer should ensure that any concerns about the title so shown are raised before contract and, where necessary, appropriately provided for in the special conditions. Accordingly, condition 6.2.1(a) now bars the buyer from raising any requisitions on the title shown by the seller before the making of the contract. The buyer, however, retains the right to raise requisitions on matters coming to its attention for the first time after the contract is made (condition 6.2.2). The prohibition in condition 6.2.1(a) will not prevent the buyer from making enquiries about the seller's arrangements for discharging any mortgages because these enquiries relate to matters of conveyance rather than matters of title and are not, strictly speaking, requisitions.

In cases where the seller deduces title (either in whole or in part) after the contract is made, condition 6.3.1 continues to allow the buyer to raise requisitions within six working days of the date of the contract or delivery of the seller's proof of title on which the requisitions are raised.

Insurance

The old condition 5, which was entitled 'Pending completion' has been radically amended by the removal of the provisions relating to the occupation of the property by the buyer. The view was taken that in the commercial context such occupation would be upon terms specifically negotiated and the general provisions of condition 5.2 were unlikely to be used to a significant extent. The material then remaining in the condition related to the insurance of the property, and so condition 7 (as it is now) has been re-titled 'Insurance'. The provisions themselves have also been considerably revised.

Condition 7.1.4 maintains the general principle that the seller is under no obligation to the buyer to insure the property. However, in the circumstances specified in condition 7.1.1 (namely, where the contract provides for the seller's policy to continue after exchange or where the seller is obliged by the terms of a lease to continue to insure), the general rule is displaced and the position is governed by conditions 7.1.2 and 7.1.3. The obligations in relation to insurance which the seller then comes under are generally similar to those which previously applied, but it is now expressly provided that to the extent that the policy proceeds are applied in repairing or reinstating insured property which has been damaged, the seller is not obliged to pay the proceeds to the buyer (condition 7.1.2(f)). The provisions for the situation on completion which were formerly contained separately in condition 5.1.3 are now incorporated in condition 7.1.2 as paragraph (g). The buyer is still obliged to pay the seller a proportionate part of the premium paid by the seller for the period between contract and completion, but an exception has been introduced for the case in which the seller is entitled to recover the premium from a tenant (condition 7.1.3).

Section 47 of the Law of Property Act 1925 continues to be excluded, now by condition 7.1.5.

Completion after 2.00 pm

Conditions 8.1.2 and 8.1.3 clarify the position where the money due on completion is received after 2.00 pm. Condition 8.1.2 states the normal rule that, in such a case, apportionments and compensation are to be worked out as if completion had taken place on the next working day as a result of the buyer's default. It would, however, be unfair to adopt that approach where completion has been delayed because the seller has failed to vacate the property by 2.00 pm. Condition 8.1.3 therefore disapplies condition 8.1.2 in a case where the sale is with vacant possession and the buyer is ready, able and willing to complete (as to which, see condition 1.1.3(a)) but does not pay the money due on completion because the seller has not vacated the property by 2.00 pm.

Apportionments

Condition 8.3.2 identifies the day (called the 'apportionment day') from which income and outgoings are to be apportioned. That day will be the date of actual completion where the whole property is being sold with vacant possession or where (in a case where completion of tenanted property is delayed through the buyer's default) the seller opts to take the net income from the property until completion as well as compensation from the buyer. In any other case, the apportionment day will be the completion date.

Condition 8.3.4 explains how the apportionment is to be carried out. For these purposes, condition 8.3.4(a) provides that a sum to be apportioned is to be treated as payable for the period which it covers (so that, for example, a monthly rent will be treated as paid for the relevant month, however many days it may contain, and not as an equal twelfth part of the rent that would be payable over a complete year). Where, however, the sum is an instalment of an annual sum (e.g. a yearly rent payable by twelve monthly instalments), condition 8.3.4(a) will require the buyer to be credited or debited with 1/365th of the annual sum for each day from and including the apportionment day to the end of the instalment period. Thus, where, for example, the seller receives a quarterly instalment of rent and the apportionment day falls 10 days before the end of the relevant quarter, the buyer will be treated as entitled to so much of the instalment as corresponds to 10/365ths of the annual rent. It is thought that this accords with normal commercial practice. Condition 8.3.4(b) provides that sums are to be treated as accruing from day to day and at the rate applicable from time to time. Accordingly, changes in the daily rate occurring at any time during the period covered by the payment will need to be taken into account.

Condition 8.3.6 is no longer limited to service charge payments, but covers any expenditure on goods or services incurred, or to be incurred, by the seller in its capacity as landlord under a lease of the property. Under condition 8.3.6(a), the buyer's obligation to reimburse the seller for expenditure already incurred but not yet due from the tenant is dependent on the provision by the seller of the information and vouchers which the buyer will need to recover the expenditure from the tenant.

Seller's right to net income and compensation

Condition 9.3.4 (formerly condition 7.3.4) provides for cases in which the property is tenanted. It allows the seller to recover the income from the property in addition to any compensation to which it may be entitled under condition 9.3.1. While a provision to this effect is commonly encountered in contracts for the sale of commercial property, there is thought to be a risk that, if challenged, it would be struck down as a penalty. A particular source of difficulty is that the object of the compensation is to place the seller in the position it would have been in if the contract had been completed on time: if, however, the contract had been completed on time, the seller would not have received any income from the property following the completion date. The seller may, therefore, need to satisfy the court that the inclusion of the provision is justified by the particular circumstances of the sale.

Consent

The consent provisions of condition 10.3 (formerly condition 8.3) have undergone some significant amendment. Condition 10.3.1(a) ensures that condition 10.3 now applies not only in cases where the landlord's consent is required for the assignment of an existing lease or the creation of a sub-lease but also in cases where consent is required for the creation of a new lease of freehold land (e.g. from a mortgagee). In the light of the decision of the Court of Appeal in *Aubergine Enterprises Ltd* v. *Lakewood International Ltd* [2002] 1 WLR. 2149, condition 10.3.1(b) confirms that any necessary consent must be in a form which satisfies the requirement to obtain it.

Condition 10.3.2(b) now obliges the buyer to comply with all reasonable requirements, including requirements for the provision of information and references (thereby slightly rephrasing the obligation under the old condition 8.3.3(a) to use reasonable endeavours to provide promptly all information and references). This obligation applies whether the consent is required for a new lease or for an assignment or for a sub-letting. The further obligations which applied to the buyer in the case of an assignment or sub-letting under the previous edition are now included in condition 10.3.3. As regards the seller's obligations, these remain unchanged in content, but the seller's obligations in connection with applying for consent and giving notice to the buyer apply in all cases (condition 10.3.2(a)), whereas condition 10.3.3(b) now expressly provides that an authorised guarantee agreement may be required only in cases of assignment.

The remaining provisions of the old condition 8.3 appear in the new condition 10.3, subject to minor drafting amendments and a change in the order of the provisions.

Commonhold

The new commonhold regime is made the subject of express provision in two ways. First, the seller is required to provide the buyer with current copies of the memorandum and articles of the commonhold association and the commonhold community statement. If the buyer then enters into the contract, it is treated as doing so knowing and accepting their terms (condition 11.3, and cf. condition 4.1.2, which makes similar provision with regard to the terms of leases affecting the property). Secondly, in cases in which the consent of the commonhold association is required to the sale of part only of a commonhold unit, condition 11.4 places the onus on the seller to apply for the association's consent and to use all reasonable efforts to obtain it; a right of rescission will normally be available to either party if the association's consent has not been given three working days before completion date.

Part 2

As already noted, Part 2 consists of optional provisions which the parties may wish to incorporate by special condition in particular cases.

Conditions A1 and A2 offer two alternatives to the provision for VAT made in condition 1.4 of Part 1 (which assumes that the sale will be exempt from VAT). Condition A1 is designed for cases where the purchase price will attract VAT at the standard rate (either because exemption is not available or because it has been waived). Condition A2 is designed for cases where (i) the seller is using the property for the business of letting to produce a rental income, (ii) the seller has waived the exemption from VAT or for some other reason the sale attracts VAT (e.g. where the property consists of a newly constructed building) and (iii) it is intended that the sale should be treated as the transfer of a going concern (so that it will not be treated as the supply of either goods or services for VAT purposes).

Condition B is offered for use in cases where the seller has claimed capital allowances in respect of plant and machinery at the property and it is intended that, on completion, the parties will make an election under section 198 of the Capital Allowances Act 2001 which will determine the amount of the sale price which is to be treated as expenditure incurred by the buyer on the provision of the plant and machinery. It should be noted that condition B3.1 assumes that the special conditions will include an apportionment of part of the total price to plant and machinery.

Condition C contains two alternative provisions which may be relevant if the seller is selling a reversionary interest in a building which contains flats held by tenants who qualify for the right of first refusal conferred by the Landlord and Tenant Act 1987. Condition C1 is intended for use in cases where the seller, having served an offer notice on the tenants under section 6 of the Act, is free to proceed with the sale to the buyer (i.e. because the tenants did not accept the offer, or failed to nominate a person to take a transfer of the property, within the relevant time limits). Condition C2 is intended for use in cases where, at the date of the contract, the qualifying tenants have exercised, or may yet exercise, the right of first refusal conferred by the 1987 Act. Condition C2.3 makes provision for cases in which the sale is by auction. Among other things, it caters for the possibility that, following the auction, a person nominated by the tenants exercises the right under section 8B(4) to take over the contract: should that happen, the consequences as between the seller and the buyer will be the same as if the contract had been rescinded.

Error on first print of SCPC 2nd edition

Condition 10.3.4 should refer to section 19(1A), not section 19A, of the Landlord and Tenant Act 1927.

V.11. Model letter to wife where charging home to secure loan to husband or his business[1]

To be amended as necessary

Dear [...]

This letter confirms the advice that [I] [we] gave you at our meeting [today] in respect of the proposal that your [freehold][leasehold] property known as [...] (the Property) is to be mortgaged to [...] (the Lender) to secure a loan from the Lender to [...] (the Borrower).

The Lender requires that you are given this advice so that, if you sign [the mortgage] [and related documents] [a consent to mortgage] you will not be able to claim afterwards that you are not legally bound by [it] [them].

(1)   The Property is owned [in your sole name] [in the Borrower's sole name] [in the joint names of yourself and [...]] and you [both] will be required to sign [the mortgage] [and related documents] [the consent to mortgage] in favour of the Lender.

(2)   Enclosed is a copy of the form of mortgage [and the mortgage conditions that are incorporated into it] [and related documents], which please read carefully and ask [me] [us] if you have any questions. The following is a summary of the main provisions and implications, but does not cover everything.

(3)   The mortgage is [initially] required to give the Lender security for a loan [of £...] [a loan facility of up to £...] to be provided to the Borrower.

[However, the mortgage will be on 'all monies' terms and will also give the Lender security over the Property for:

    (1)   any further loan or increased facility that the Borrower (individually or jointly with you or anyone else) may in future obtain from the Lender while the mortgage remains in existence, even if this is done without your knowledge or consent;

    (2)   any existing loans from the Lender to the Borrower (individually or jointly with you or anyone else), even if you do not know about them;

    (3)   any existing or future loans that you yourself may obtain (individually or jointly with anyone else) from the Lender while the mortgage remains in existence;

    (4)   any sums owing to the Lender, at any time while the mortgage remains in existence, by any other person or company if you or the Borrower has already given, or shall in future give, a guarantee for those sums to the Lender, and even if the Borrower has given or shall give such a guarantee without your knowledge and consent;

---

1. This model letter was issued by the Law Society's Conveyancing and Land Law Committee in May 2002. It was first published as an appendix to the guidance – 'Undue influence – solicitors' duties post *Etridge*', which is reproduced here as Appendix IV.8.

    (5)   interest on all such sums as charged by the Lender;

    (6)   [*anything else*].]

According to the terms of the loan the Lender can demand repayment at [any time,] [on fixed dates,] [by instalments,] [*set out repayment requirements*] .

(4)   During the subsistence of the mortgage, [you] [the Borrower] must:

    (1)   keep the Property insured in accordance with the Lender's requirements;

    (2)   keep the Property in good repair;

    (3)   not make any structural alterations or changes of use without the Lender's consent;

    (4)   not let the Property or take in lodgers without the Lender's consent;

    (5)   comply with all covenants and restrictions affecting the Property ;

    (6)   [*anything else*].

(5)   The mortgage will give the Lender a [first] charge over the Property as security for all the sums mentioned in paragraph (3) above. You could lose the Property if the Borrower's business does not prosper, or if the borrowing is increased unwisely. This is because, if any loan repayment or interest charge is not paid on time, the Lender would be entitled to enforce the mortgage by taking court proceedings to evict you and any other occupiers from the Property and sell the Property in order to obtain repayment. Alternatively the Lender could appoint a receiver to take possession of the Property from you and any other occupiers.

(6)   [The Lender reserves the right to transfer the benefit of the mortgage to another lender.]

(7)   [In addition, the mortgage will contain a covenant by you to pay all sums falling within paragraph (3) above if the Borrower fails to pay them [up to a maximum of £[…] plus interest charged by the Lender]. This means that [up to that level] you will be a guarantor for the liabilities of the Borrower to the Lender, you will be personally liable for those sums, you could be sued by the Lender for them and, if the value of the Property and your other assets is insufficient to meet those sums, you could be made bankrupt as well as losing the Property.]

(8)   [*Any other features of the mortgage needing comment?*]

The above legal advice relates to the effect of the proposed mortgage documents and the types of risks that arise. [However, [I am] [we are] not qualified to assess the likelihood of those risks actually materialising. That depends largely on the financial standing and prospects of the Borrower [and his business], although you should also consider whether the sums secured could be repaid from the sale value of the Property and your other assets. Therefore, before you decide whether to agree to sign [the mortgage] [the consent to mortgage], you should get help on assessing the risks by taking advice on those important financial aspects from a chartered accountant or other qualified professional financial adviser who should be independent of the Borrower.]

You do not have to agree to these arrangements at all if you consider that the risks are too great or if you think that these arrangements are of no advantage to you. If you are generally willing but find particular terms unacceptable, it may be possible to negotiate variations of those terms with the Lender in order to make them acceptable to you. These decisions are yours and yours alone.

[As you know, [I am] [my firm is] also acting for the Borrower in this matter [and also for the Lender in an administrative capacity] but I have given you this advice independently. Nevertheless you should consider whether you want further legal advice from a completely separate solicitor before you make a final decision in connection with the mortgage.]

Please sign paragraph (A) at the end of the enclosed copy of this letter to acknowledge that you have been given, and have understood, this advice.

If and when you decide that you will enter into the mortgage and will not require the Lender to vary any of the terms, please also sign paragraph (B) to confirm that decision and to allow the Lender to be told that you have received this advice.

Yours […]

ACKNOWLEDGEMENTS

(A)   I confirm that I have read this letter and have received and understood the advice given in it.Signed: .... Date: ....

(B)   I confirm that that I have decided, of my own free will, to enter into the mortgage, I do not require the Lender to vary any of the terms, [I do not require any further legal advice,] and I agree that the Lender may be told that I have received the advice in this letter.

Signed: .... Date: ....

V.12. Report on proposed purchase (domestic)[1]

Of the property known as
15 High Hill, Harkley, Herts

prepared for Mr and Mrs Harvey Hart

1. The Property

The Property is known as 15 High Hill, Harkley, Herts HH1 2ZZ. A copy of the Land Registry entries and title plan is attached [*not produced in this book*] showing the extent of the property edged in red.

Land Registry title plans are to a small scale and are not intended to show the precise location of each boundary; these should be checked on site and any significant discrepancies referred to us so that we can seek clarification from the sellers.

2. Title

The Property is freehold. The title number is HH123456. It is registered at the Land Registry with 'absolute' title, which means that ownership is guaranteed by the Registry. You should inspect the property to ensure that it is only occupied by the seller and his immediate family and let us know if this is not the case. The property is being sold to you with full vacant possession on completion.

3. Rights passing with the Property

The Property has the benefit of a right of way over the alleyway at the rear of the Property, marked in brown on the Land Registry plan, leading to the road known as Hall Hollow. This right is on foot only, so there is no right to drive vehicles (or ride bicycles or horses) along it. The deeds do not make provision for any person to be responsible for maintaining or clearing the alleyway but do provide for the owner of the Property to pay a fair contribution towards any expenditure on such matters. The sellers state that they are not aware of anyone carrying out such works and have not been asked to pay anything in this regard. If the alleyway needs maintaining so that you can walk along it, as a matter of general law the right of way would give you the right to do necessary maintenance, but wholly at your own cost.

4. Rights over the Property

The owner of the property known as 13 High Hill has a right of way on foot across the south-west corner of the rear garden of the Property, to enable him to pass between the end of his garden and the alleyway. The route is marked in blue on the Land Registry plan. This right was apparently granted because the alleyway stops level with the west boundary of the Property and does not run behind the garden of number 13. The sellers state that the neighbour has never exercised this right during their 8 years of ownership of the Property; however, this does not mean that the right has legally lapsed.

5. Covenants

A number of restrictive covenants were imposed on the owner of the Property when the plot was sold to the original house builder in 1898. It appears that similar covenants were imposed on all the

---

1. This Report has been written by Frances Silverman and the Editorial Board of the Conveyancing Handbook.

plots in the street, and these covenants may still be enforceable by one house owner against another; if you purchase the Property, you may be obliged to observe them, and you may be entitled to require the neighbouring owners to observe them. The following is a summary of those that may still be relevant:

(1)   not to park any caravan or similar vehicle on the Property;

(2)   not to erect more than one single house on the Property, apart from a greenhouse or other usual outbuilding;

(3)   not to use any house for business use but only as a private dwelling;

(4)   not to cause nuisance or annoyance to neighbours.

Even if these covenants are not strictly enforceable in law, planning restrictions imposed by the local authority may in practice have a similar effect.

A positive covenant was also imposed in 1898, requiring the owner of the Property to maintain the fence on the east boundary of the Property. We have marked this fence with the letter 'T' on the attached copy of the Land Registry plan. Whilst it is unlikely that anyone could legally enforce compliance with this covenant, in practice you should be prepared to maintain this fence, and the other fences bounding the Property, at your own cost.

6.   Information from the Sellers

The solicitors acting for the sellers, Henry and Hetty Hodgson, have supplied us with a package of information under the Law Society TransAction scheme. We attach copies of the following items supplied to us in that package:

(a) Seller's Property Information Form

This gives information about boundaries, disputes, notices, guarantees, services, rights and other matters. Our comments are:

(1)   the information on boundaries must be read subject to our comment about the eastern fence, in paragraph 5 of this Report;

(2)   the building work mentioned in reply to question 10.3 of the Form did not need planning permission, but future enlargement of the building might.

(b) List of Fixtures Fittings and Contents

This indicates which items at the Property are included in the sale and which are not. Please let us know if anything stated to be excluded was in fact supposed to be included, or if you reach agreement with the sellers to buy any of the excluded items.

We understand that this sale is dependent upon the sellers buying another property, but their solicitors tell us that this is progressing well and they hope to be in a position to exchange contracts on both transactions at the end of next month.

7.   Information from the Local Authority, etc.

We have made a search in the Register of Local Land Charges and have raised enquiries with the local council, and have obtained the following information which relates to the property which you are intending to buy. A separate search would be needed to obtain information relating to neighbouring properties:

(1)   High Hill and Hall Hollow are publicly maintained roads, but the rear alleyway is not;

(2)   there are no current plans for road improvements or new roads within 200 metres of the Property;

(3) foul drainage is believed to be connected to the public sewer but the means of connection is not known (a drain running between a house and the public sewer is not maintained at public expense and you should consult your surveyor as to the likelihood of your having to repair or maintain any drain connected to the property).

None of the other replies by the council to our enquiries need to be drawn to your attention.

Because of the location of the Property, we have also made a search with British Coal in order that you or your surveyor can assess the risk of future subsidence due to coal extraction beneath the Property. A statutory compensation scheme is available if you suffer damage as a result of mining works. British Coal has given the following response:

(1) Two seams of coal have been mined at an approximate depth of 200 metres under or near the Property, the last working being in 1990.

(2) There are presently no workings taking place within influencing distance of the Property.

(3) Although coal exists unworked, British Coal states that the possibility of future working is considered unlikely.

8. Outgoings

The Property is in band F for council tax purposes. The annual water charge (currently £XXX) is payable to Hartford Water Company. The water supply at the Property is not metered.

9. The Purchase Contract

This is in a form incorporating the Standard Conditions of Sale, which are widely used for this type of transaction. The main provisions of the contract are:

(1) The purchase price is £XXX,XXX. (No VAT will be payable on this.) The price includes the items shown on the list attached to the contract, which corresponds with the list of Fixtures, Fittings and Chattels mentioned above.

(2) On exchange of contracts, you must pay a deposit of £XX,XXX. If we cannot complete your purchase of the Property due to the Hodgsons' default, you will become entitled to the return of the deposit (and may be able to claim damages for your loss). However, under the Standard Conditions of Sale, all or part of the deposit money can be used by Mr and Mrs Hodgson to pay the deposit on their new property, and only the remainder, if any, will be retained by their solicitors as 'stakeholder' until we satisfactorily complete the purchase. Whilst this arrangement has become common practice, we must warn you that in the event of the matter not completing, it may be more difficult to obtain repayment of deposit money which has been used by the Hodgsons in that way, than if the whole deposit was retained by their solicitors until completion; on the other hand, very few house purchases totally fail to complete (though completion is occasionally delayed), and you may be prepared to take this risk rather than insisting that the Hodgsons incur the expense of obtaining separate bridging finance for the deposit on their new property. Please discuss this with us if you are concerned about it.

(3) The completion date will be inserted just before contracts are exchanged. We will discuss it with you at that time so that a date acceptable to both you and the Hodgsons can be fixed. This date will then be the date on which the transaction is to be completed: the Hodgsons must vacate the Property on that date, if they do not vacate earlier, and we must send the completion money to their solicitors to reach their bank account by 2 pm that afternoon. You will be liable to pay daily interest at X% per year above bank base rate if cleared funds are not made available to us in time to remit the completion money

early enough, so we will need to receive the funds (other than the loan from your Building Society, mentioned below) from you either by cheque in favour of this firm reaching us at least five working days before the completion date, or by bank transfer into this firm's bank account preferably on the day before the completion date. Nearer the time, we will let you know how much we require; this will include a sum to cover our fees, disbursements paid or payable by us (including stamp duty of £X,XXX and registration fees of £XXX) and VAT.

(4) You are buying the Property in its actual state and condition. You must be satisfied about this from your own inspection of the Property and from your surveyor's report. If you expect the sellers to remedy (or pay for the remedy of) any defects, this will have to be agreed with them before contracts are exchanged and special provisions added to the contract. Your lender has asked us to point out to you that the valuation undertaken by their surveyor may not reveal all the defects in the Property.

(5) The Property remains at the sellers' risk until completion, and the sellers must hand it over in its present condition, except for fair wear and tear. You would be entitled to withdraw from the transaction, with the return of your deposit, if the Property was so badly damaged before the completion date as to make it unusable, and the sellers would have a similar right if the damage was caused by a risk against which they could not have been expected to insure.

10. Mortgage

We have received instructions from the Highland Building Society to act for them on a mortgage loan to assist you in buying the Property. We have to report to them on the result of our investigations about the Property and also on any discrepancies between the details of the transaction known to us and the details you gave the Society with your mortgage application (e.g. as to the purchase price). So far, the documents supplied to us do not show any such discrepancies.

The main terms of the proposed mortgage are:

(1) The loan will be £XX,XXX.

(2) Interest is variable at the discretion of the Society, but will initially be at the rate of X% per year.

(3) The loan is repayable, with interest, over XX years, by monthly instalments comprising a mixture of capital and interest. Initially the instalments will be £XXX per month, but this is variable and the Society will recalculate the amount as a result of changes in the rate of interest. You will be required to pay the instalments by bank standing order. Failure to pay any instalments will entitle the Society to call for immediate repayment of the entire loan.

(4) The loan will be to both of you, and you will both be individually legally responsible for ensuring that the instalment payments are duly made and that the other provisions of the mortgage, mentioned below, are observed.

(5) The loan and interest will be secured on a first legal mortgage over the Property. This will give the Society various rights if you fail to pay the instalments, including the right to apply to the court to evict you and your family so that the Society can sell the Property in order to recoup the outstanding loan and any unpaid interest. If the sale proceeds exceed the amount due to the Society, the surplus will be paid to you (or to any second lender), but if there is a shortfall the Society can sue you for it.

(6) The mortgage will impose a number of standard obligations and restrictions, the most important being:

(a)   you must keep the Property in good repair;

(b)   you must insure the Property with insurers agreed between you and the Society;

(c)   you must not alter the Property, or change its use, without the Society's prior consent;

(d)   you must not let any part of the Property without the Society's prior consent;

(e)   no second or subsequent mortgage must be taken out without the Society's prior consent.

(7)   The mortgage will be security for any future loans you may borrow from the Society, as well as for the loan mentioned above.

The full text of the mortgage terms are set out in the enclosed book from the Society, and we recommend that you read them.

11.   Environmental matters

We have/have not made enquiries relating to environmental matters affecting the property. [Our enquiries revealed the following information [*set out details*].]

Please ask us if you have any queries about this report or on any other aspect of this transaction.

12.   Joint purchase

[*Where there are two or more buyers explain the difference between joint tenancy and tenancy in common and request the buyers to confirm their choice to you.*]

[*Name of solicitors*]

V.13. Explanatory notes to the TransAction forms 2007 [extracts]¹

The TransAction forms 2007

The new TransAction forms are listed below and may be viewed at www.hips.lawsociety.org.uk. The forms marked with an asterisk are intended exclusively for use with the preparation of a HIP:

TA1   Home information pack index*

TA2   Sale statement*

TA3   Required leasehold information*

TA4   Required commonhold information*

TA5   Proof of requests for missing documents and information*

TA6   Property information form

TA7   Leasehold information form

TA8   New home information form

TA9   Commonhold information form

TA10   Fittings and contents

TA11   Additional property information

TA12   Buyer Information

TA13   Completion information and requisitions on title

TA14   Leasehold information request*

TA15   Commonhold information request*

The TransAction forms will be available to purchase from the Law Society's licensed providers, including:

- Oyez Straker
- Laserform International

---

1. © The Law Society 2007.

- Shaw and Sons
- Peapod Solutions.

It is anticipated that the new TransAction forms will be reviewed in the future so that they can be developed to meet the new and changing requirements of the profession. Solicitors will for a time need to refer to the detail of the regulations to ensure that the forms deal appropriately with the case in hand, but it is hoped that the forms will meet wide acceptance in the property industry.

Any feedback on the forms from the profession would be gratefully received by the Law Society. Please write with your comments to: The Publications Manager, Law Society Publishing, 113 Chancery Lane, London WC2A 1PL.

KEY CHANGES TO TRANSACTION FORMS

The new forms are designed for use by solicitors and have been made as easy to use as is possible bearing in mind the complexities and permutations that can arise under the new procedure for HIPs.

Titles of the forms

Whilst, so far as possible, the look of the existing TransAction forms has been preserved it has proved necessary to change the titles of the forms. It may in future be easier to refer to the forms by reference to their numbers rather than the titles which are tied in to the Regulations nomenclature.

Notes to clients

As many of the forms are designed to be included in a HIP it was not appropriate to include within the forms explanatory notes for buyers and sellers. However, every effort has been made to ensure the forms are written in language that makes it possible for them to be sent to clients.

It will be for the seller's solicitor to obtain the information needed from his client and to complete the form whether for inclusion in a HIP or to be supplied separately. Where forms are given to sellers to complete, some commentary will be needed from the solicitor to tailor the form to the situation in hand.

Part II of the Seller's Property Information Form

The Seller's Property Information Form was divided into Part I and Part II. An equivalent of Part II has not been included in the new TransAction forms. The Seller's Property Information Form is replaced by TA11 for non HIP transactions and where there is a HIP in existence then the standard information for a freehold can be provided through use of form TA8 and/or form TA11.

COMMENTARY ON THE FORMS

In order to explain the rationale for the new forms, these notes will explain each form by reference to what it is intended to cover and draw attention to those situations where special care must be taken to refer to both sets of regulations and to the facts of the particular case as well as the circumstances and needs of the particular client.

In addition to forms which have been specifically prepared for use in a HIP as 'Required' documents or as 'Authorised' documents the full suite contains forms which can be used outside the HIP environment. Those forms could be used to provide information alongside, or 'in close proximity' to the HIP, in early negotiations or could be delivered with a draft contract in a case where a HIP has not been relevant. Where a HIP has been produced, then it is to be expected that the buyer or the buyer's solicitor may have some interest in the HIP documentation although the principle of caveat emptor remains paramount.

It is important to bear in mind when using the forms that there is an overlap between the two sets of regulations and that the Energy Regulations and the Amended Energy Regulations have their own requirements that, in relation to marketing constraints, go beyond the requirements of the HIP legislation.

Home Information Pack Index (TA1)

A HIP must be compliant with the HIP Regulations at the first date of marketing (r.3) and specified documents must be included in the HIP at that date, and others may be added later. The Responsible Person cannot proceed to marketing of the property without a compliant pack (s.149 HA 2004). It should be borne in mind that the seller can be deemed to be a Responsible Person in addition to any estate agent appointed to market the property.

The Home Information Pack Index must always be included in the HIP and is the responsibility of the Responsible Person. It must contain the elements described in Schedule 1 of the HIP Regulations.

The Home Information Pack Index provides a checklist for compiling a HIP and gives a list of its contents. Pagination can be inserted if required. The Home Information Pack Index also provides an audit trail for enforcement purposes.

Part A of the form lists the possible content of the HIP that falls within the category of Required documents and information:

- the Home Information Pack Index
- the Energy Performance Certificate and recommendation (EPC) or Predicted Energy Assessment
- the Sale Statement
- the Official Copies of the Title Register and Title Plan
- a certificate of an Official Index Map Search for unregistered title
- documents sufficient to deduce unregistered title
- searches and enquiries (local land charges, local enquiries, drainage and water enquiries)
- any leases and licences for parts of the property not sold with vacant possession.

The EPC must be the second document in the HIP but like other Required documents and information that are not available at the first day of marketing may be added later so long as the procedure in Regulations 18 and 19 is followed. This procedure is overridden during the transitional phase lasting until 31 December 2007 (see the section on the transitional arrangements above).

Order of documents

Documents do not need to appear in any order in the HIP itself save in the case of the EPC and recommendation or Predicted Energy Assessment which must always be placed as the second document in the HIP.

Not all categories of Required documents will be relevant in each case. Land will either be registered or unregistered, although it is possible that the title could include both. There is the further situation to consider where a new title is being created such as on the grant of a lease. Here the HIP Regulations require that the HIP should be prepared on the basis that the new interest is already in existence.

Incomplete HIPs

Particular care ought to be taken in respect of Required documents which are 'missing' at the date when the HIP is delivered to the Responsible Person. The Home Information Pack Index must be completed to show the particulars which have been specified in the column headings. Additionally, evidence must be included in the HIP of the facts which are specified in relation to the missing document (rr.18 and 19). A form has been devised to enable this 'proof of request' to be completed and included in the HIP. The details of this form (TA5) are set out below.

Updating the HIP (r.21)

At the point of delivery of the HIP to the Responsible Person, whether the seller or an estate agent acting in the marketing of the property, it will be appropriate for the solicitor to ask the seller to check it and also to explain to the Responsible Person both the content of the HIP and the requirements in relation to its use and updating.

Whenever a HIP is updated the Home Information Pack Index must be revised.

Where Required documents or information become out of date or are superseded, the HIP must be updated. The old HIP must be withdrawn, old items removed and new items inserted, and the Home Information Pack Index must be updated.

Energy Performance Certificate (EPC) or Predicted Energy Assessment

The EPC is a certificate and a recommendation report complying with Paragraphs 10 and 11 of the Energy Regulations. A full EPC may be prepared by a Home Inspector or Domestic Energy Assessor and is Required in respect of a property which is 'physically complete'.

The Predicted Energy Assessment is relevant where a property is not 'physically complete' and, on physical completion of the property, must be replaced (and the Home Information Pack Index updated) by a full EPC and recommendation report (r.22). It must be prepared in accordance with the HIP Regulations but may be prepared by any person (not necessarily a Domestic Energy Assessor or Home Inspector).

If despite all reasonable efforts an EPC is unobtainable before the 'first point of marketing' then, under Regulation 16, the HIP can be published without it. However, the first point of marketing is deferred until 14 days after the request for the EPC has been made. In other words there is a waiting period of 14 days after making a request for an EPC.

Regulation 17 makes provision for other documents or information that is not available at the first point of marketing, but is expected within 28 days of the first point of marketing. No waiting period is required in the case of a local search or leasehold information or any other Required document that is missing and for which a proof of request can be filed in the HIP.

In summary, the HIP Regulations and the Home Information Pack Index contain provisions for an EPC to be missing at the first point of marketing but, in practice, this relaxation of the regulations should be treated with extreme care.

There are additional restrictions on marketing arising from the operation of Paragraphs 5 and 6 of the Energy Regulations. Here it is provided that no written information can be given to a prospective buyer of a property and no viewing of a property can be arranged unless a free copy of the EPC is made available to the prospective buyer/viewer. Written particulars (as defined) require the EPC to be attached to them or, at least, the asset rating section if not the whole certificate. The asset rating consists of the two graphs that appear within the EPC. (See also the section on transitional arrangements above).

Solicitors will need to take particular care in relation to this concession under Regulation 16 and to make it clear to a Responsible Person that the delivery of a 'complete' HIP without an EPC does not enable the Responsible Person to market the property in the normal way (save where Regulation 34 applies as stated in the section on transitional arrangements above). Also the HIP will need to be updated as soon as the EPC is delivered and the Home Information Pack Index must be amended.

Proof of missing documents and information

The Home Information Pack Index must set out the matters required by Paragraphs 1(e) and (f) of Schedule 1 of the HIP Regulations. Proof of requests for missing documents and information must be recorded in the Home Information Pack Index and must be included in the HIP.

As soon as a missing item becomes available it must be placed in the HIP and the Home Information Pack Index must be updated.

Practitioners are urged to look carefully at the provisions of Regulation 19 that set out the method for calculating the date when the request is deemed to be delivered.

Evidence of title

Official Copies of the Register and Title Plan must always be included in the HIP at the first point of marketing and for unregistered land the requirement is met by inclusion of the Official Index Map Search certificate.

Part B Required leasehold documents and information

In respect of Required leasehold documents and information Form TA3 should be used. As an alternative the required information can be inserted in the pack in such other form or format as may exist. For example, summaries of works could be contained in a letter from the landlord or managing agents and in such cases that letter may be included in the pack.

Part C Required commonhold documents and information

Although commonhold precedes leasehold in the order of the regulations the order has been reversed in these forms to reflect current usage. Form TA4 should be used or alternatively the document(s) containing the information can be used, as described for leaseholds.

Part D Missing documents and information

The HIP regulations stipulate that the Home Information Pack Index must include specified information about missing documents. A separate proof of request must also be included in the HIP and form TA5 has been designed for the purpose of containing the confirmation required by Regulation 18. As a precaution, provision has been made to identify the Responsible Person in this form.

Sale Statement (TA2)

This document requires a brief description of various particulars as described in Schedule 3 of the HIP Regulations. The Sale Statement must always be included in the HIP and is the responsibility of the Responsible Person.

The Sale Statement must be carefully completed, particularly in the case of land that is both registered and unregistered, or freehold and leasehold. There is also a special category where a new interest has been created.

Form TA2 provides for the situation envisaged by s.171(2) Housing Act 2004 where part of the property is let or occupied, so that the details can be given. The HIP Regulations are not prescriptive as to the amount of detail to be included.

Required leasehold information (TA3)

This is HIP document that, as it states at the top, contains some (but not all) of the required content for leaseholds. Other Required content will be in original documents that must be included in the HIP. Examples are the lease itself and service charge statements and demands.

Required commonhold information (TA4)

This is the commonhold version of TA3. Again, some of the required information will be in original documents.

Proof of requests for missing documents and information (TA5)

TA5 is a vital form if the HIP is to be provided to the marketing agent or seller at a time when it is incomplete. There is a box for the date to be inserted when the form is prepared or updated. This anticipates that missing documents/information will not all arrive at the same time. This document along with the Home Information Pack Index may need to be revised on a number of occasions as the HIP becomes complete.

Practitioners need to be aware that missing documents must be added to the HIP as soon as they arrive. It is not permitted to wait until all missing documents are available and then update the HIP in one exercise.

The columns in form TA5 distil the information needed. Regulation 19 describes how to calculate the delivery date of each request by reference to how the request was delivered. Practitioners will also need to bear in mind the 28 day period for obtaining missing documents. Again this form and the Home Information Pack Index will need to be amended if it is likely that a missing document or information is going to take longer than 28 days to arrive.

Property information form (TA6)

Schedule 10 of the HIP Regulations sets out those matters considered relevant and of interest to a buyer that may be included in the HIP. Communities and Local government put out to consultation their own version of a form based in many ways upon the concept of the existing TransAction forms. It has now been decided that there will be no prescribed forms.

However the government have acknowledged that TransAction forms will be an acceptable method of delivering Authorised information.

The new form TA6 is an authorised document that has derived from the well known Seller's Property Information Form. It has been adapted to provide information that may be useful at the marketing stage of a transaction rather than 'post offer'. Although it could be used at any stage.

It is envisaged that forms TA11 Additional property information and TA12 Buyer information (see below) will be used to pick up on additional enquiries that may be considered relevant to some buyers after an offer has been accepted.

In this way it is hoped that the TransAction forms will provide a seamless progression from the HIP used at the time of marketing to the conveyancing that proceeds once an offer has been accepted.

TA7 Leasehold information form (TA7)

This form provides a vehicle for additional information to be given about a leasehold property.

It assumes that this information will be required at the stage when an offer for the property has been accepted. It can be completed at the same time as other forms or whilst the property is being marketed to assist in avoiding delays and additional costs.

New home information form (TA8)

Although many of the previous regulations relating to homes under construction have been omitted from the HIP Regulations made on 11 June 2007, there is good deal of information that buyers want and developers and builders may wish to provide at an early stage. This form has been devised to accommodate this anticipated need.

Solicitors are reminded that a full EPC is required once a property is 'physically complete' and also that, under the Energy Regulations, contracts cannot be exchanged until a free copy of the EPC has been provided to the buyer (see also the section on transitional arrangements above).

Commonhold information form (TA9)

This is the commonhold version of the above form TA7. It closely follows the previous Commonhold Information Form.

Fittings and contents (TA10)

This form closely follows the form that most solicitors are used to with an additional column for comments on the contents.

The government had proposed that this form would be a required element in the HIP but its inclusion is now a matter of choice for the seller. The form can be introduced at any stage of the process. Solicitors may wish to obtain the seller's signature to this form where it is to form part of the contract.

Additional property information (TA11)

The latest incarnation of the HIP provided for by the 11 June Regulations is a comparatively 'thin' dossier on a property with much less information than was originally envisaged by the previous 2006 HIP Regulations. Some sellers may wish to supplement the information available to buyers to speed up a sale. This form can be used to give further Authorised information and can be delivered at an early stage in the process.

In the main, however, it is expected this form will be used once terms have been agreed 'subject to contract' and a draft contract is being submitted to the proposed buyer of the property.

It can also be used for transactions where no HIP is required. Excepted properties are described in Regulations 25-32. Thus the form can be used to deliver information once an offer is accepted and a draft contract is submitted. It is to that extent a replacement for the Seller's Property Information Form.

In cases where there is a HIP, form TA11 can be used to supplement the HIP and add to the information in form TA6, if that has been used. This new form also includes a schedule of information about the supply of services, reflecting the trend of recent years for this information to be requested as it is practical information of interest to buyers.

The certification of information in the form prescribed by Part II of the Seller's Property Information Form has been omitted in TA11 but this does not affect the legal responsibility of any person acting on behalf of the seller. In those cases where further or additional verification is needed it will be matter for the buyer to raise separately.

Buyer information (TA12)

This form is designed to pick up on any additional information that may be required for a particular buyer or property. It is anticipated this will be sent by the buyer's solicitor once a draft contract has been submitted.

Completion information and requisitions on title (TA13)

The first point to draw to practitioners' attention is that requisitions 4.2 and 6.2 are regarded as undertakings.

It also provides space for additional requisitions to be raised for particular transactions.

Leasehold information request (TA14)

Extensive and detailed information is required for leasehold property. Sellers may not have such information available and enquiries of third parties may be necessary. These forms have been devised to be sent to sellers, landlords or managing agents, or indeed all of them (at the same time), in order to obtain missing information.

It is NOT a form for inclusion in the HIP as it may include information that is neither required nor authorised for inclusion. The form asks for some limited insurance information and as this is not 'required' it may be deleted. Other information requests could be added, especially if the seller can anticipate the further information that may be wanted at a later stage in the transaction when a buyer has been found. Thus time and further fees may be avoided.

Commonhold information request (TA15)

The commonhold version of TA14, again, is not for inclusion in the HIP.

VI. COUNCIL OF MORTGAGE LENDERS GUIDANCE

VI.1. Mortgage redemption statements[1]

The guidance set out below has been issued jointly by the Law Society and Council of Mortgage Lenders in connection with problems arising out of incorrect redemption statements supplied by lenders.

GUIDANCE NOTES

Problems relating to mortgage redemption statements have caused difficulties for lenders and solicitors (this expression to include licensed conveyancers) for a number of years. In 1985 the Building Societies Association and the Law Society issued detailed advice to their respective members on this subject because of the difficulties which were apparent at that time.

The advice comprised paras. 9 to 13 of BSA circular No. 3155. Those paragraphs are now replaced by the new guidance set out below.

In recent months, the Council of Mortgage Lenders (CML) has received a number of enquiries in respect of redemption statements provided by lenders to solicitors acting for the lender (who will often also act for the seller). This guidance refers to some of the circumstances which can produce errors and problems, and the consequences which this can have for the solicitor in the conveyancing transaction. It also suggests certain practical measures designed to reduce problems in this area. Accordingly, it is of importance to all lenders and covers:

    (a) the function and importance of solicitors' undertakings;

    (b) the general principle that lenders should seal a discharge where a redemption statement was incorrect;

    (c) ways in which lenders might overcome the difficulty caused when the borrower prematurely stops payments;

    (d) similar proposals as to the problem of dishonoured cheques;

    (e) suggestions for overcoming difficulties sometimes presented by multiple mortgage accounts;

    (f) information to be provided to banks for inclusion in telegraphic transfers; and

    (g) the importance of returning the sealed discharge promptly.

Terms of reference

This guidance applies to England and Wales; separate guidance for Scotland and Northern Ireland will follow, if necessary.

---

1. Joint guidance from the Law Society and the Council of Mortgage Lenders issued on 29 April 1992.

Redemption on sale

The guidance applies primarily to redemption of a mortgage on sale of the security and, consequently, the lender's/seller's solicitor is required to give an undertaking to the buyer's solicitor that the charge will be discharged.

Remortgages

It is appreciated that an undertaking will also be given on a remortgage and that, accordingly, the guidance should be interpreted as including this situation.

Simple redemption

Much of the guidance is inapplicable to a straightforward redemption (without sale or remortgage) as no undertaking is given. However, even in redemption per se, solicitors and lenders will no doubt wish to provide accurate information and deal promptly with their respective responsibilities.

Solicitors' undertakings

The solicitor acting for the seller will need, on completion, to satisfy the buyer's solicitor that the mortgage on the property being sold has been or will be discharged. In theory the buyer's solicitor will wish to see the mortgage discharged before the purchase money is paid. However, where the monies to repay the mortgage are being provided wholly or partly by the proceeds of sale, then the mortgage cannot be paid off until after completion.

Most lenders will not seal the discharge (this expression to include sealing the vacating receipt on a mortgage deed or sealing of Form DS1) until they receive the redemption money. This leaves the buyer's solicitor with a problem in that he or she has to be satisfied that the mortgage will be discharged and that he or she will obtain the receipted mortgage or Land Registry Form DS1 or END1. This problem is solved by the use of the solicitor's undertaking.

On completion, the seller's/lender's solicitor will provide the buyer's solicitor with a written undertaking to redeem the mortgage(s) in a form recommended by the Law Society similar to that set out below:

> 'In consideration of your today completing the purchase of [...] we hereby undertake forthwith to pay over to [...] [*the lender*] the money required to redeem the mortgage/legal charge dated [...] and to forward the receipted mortgage/legal charge to you as soon as it is received by us from [...] [*the lender*].'

Incorrect redemption statements

Before completion of a sale, the lender's seller's solicitor will obtain a redemption statement calculated to the date of redemption. He or she will sometimes request the daily figure for interest which will be added if completion is delayed. If the lender supplies an incorrect redemption statement, the solicitor is likely to forward insufficient money to redeem the mortgage. The lender might be unwilling to discharge the mortgage and, if the solicitor is not holding more funds on behalf of the borrower, the solicitor would be in breach of his or her undertaking.

Problem areas

Problems with redemption statements can arise for a number of reasons:

(a) a lender might simply make a mistake in calculating the redemption figure;

(b) difficulties could be caused by the cancellation of standing orders or direct debit payments or by borrowers' cheques being dishonoured; and

(c) there might be misunderstanding between a lender and the solicitor.

Some of the more common practical problems are outlined below.

Cancellation

A difficulty arises if the mortgage payments are made by standing order and, shortly before completion, the borrower stops the payments without notice to the lender. There will be a shortfall if the lender assumed, without making this assumption clear, that the next payment would be paid and made the redemption figure calculation accordingly.

If this is the case, and the solicitor has acted in good faith and with no knowledge that a payment has been or is likely to be cancelled, the view of the CML is that the lender should seal the discharge. This is to avoid the solicitor being in breach of his or her undertaking to the buyer's solicitor. (The lender would then have to recoup the money from the borrower.)

This difficulty is less likely to arise where payments are made by direct debit because the lender is the originator of the debit and therefore has control over the raising of any future direct debits from the borrower's bank account.

However, there is no guarantee that direct debits will be honoured and they may be returned on the grounds of insufficient funds or that the customer has closed his or her account or instructed his or her bank to cancel the direct debit.

Some lenders overcome this problem by excluding any future payments due when calculating the redemption figure. In other words, they 'freeze' the account balance at the day of the redemption calculation. The disadvantages of this are that (if the payment has not been cancelled) the borrower has to pay a higher redemption figure and the lender has to make a refund to the borrower after redemption.

An alternative is for the lender on the redemption statement to make it clear to the solicitor that it is assumed that the next payment will be made and that, if it is not paid, the mortgage will not be discharged until the balance is received. This gives the solicitor an early chance to address his or her and his or her borrower client's mind to this situation and to ensure that sufficient monies will be available to redeem the mortgage. Indeed, this would also serve as a reminder to the solicitor to warn the borrower client of the importance of continuing the payments in the normal way up to completion.

Uncleared cheques

This is a very similar situation to that of standing orders and direct debits. The CML's view is that if the lender does not notify the solicitor that it is assumed that the borrower's cheque will clear then, provided that the solicitor acts in good faith and without knowledge that the cheque would be or is likely to be dishonoured, the lender should seal the discharge. Exceptions to this are if the lender:

(a) prepares the redemption statement on the assumption that the cheque will not clear and informs the solicitor of this, probably, in a note on the statement. This has the disadvantages described above, or

(b) notifies the solicitor that a cheque has been received and that, if it does not clear by the date of redemption, the mortgage will not be discharged until the balance is received.

Separate loan account

The lender may have more than one loan secured on the property. For example, in addition to the principal mortgage, there could be a secured personal loan which is a regulated agreement under Consumer Credit Act 1974 and/or a further advance conducted on a separate account basis. In such cases, there will be more than one account number.

On a sale, as all mortgage accounts will be repaid, multiplicity of accounts should not present a problem unless the solicitor does not know and is unable to specify every account and has no notice or cause to query the matter and the lender fails to cross-check the matter internally.

However, it is possible, for example, on certain remortgages, that it is the intention of the borrower and the lender that not all mortgages will be discharged and replaced. If so, when requesting the redemption statement, the solicitor should make it clear to the lender which mortgages the borrower wishes to redeem. The solicitor should inform the lender of any mortgages of which he or she is aware which are outstanding with the lender but which are not being redeemed. The solicitor should also quote all relevant account numbers if known as far as possible and ensure that the redemption statement received from the lender includes all the mortgages which are intended to be redeemed.

The lender should have its own internal cross-checking system but it is vital that the solicitor (who will, after all, be acting for the lender in most cases) is as clear as possible about the mortgage account(s) being redeemed. It is suggested that the solicitor should if possible, and time permits, send a copy of the redemption statement to the borrower to check agreement on the amount shown as due to the lender. Solicitors should be encouraged to ask for a statement at the earliest possible date.

Telegraphic transfers

Lenders could request that solicitors adopt procedures to assist in the identification of telegraphic transfers. When mortgages are being redeemed the telegraphic transfer which a lender receives is often difficult to identify and to match to a particular account.

The administrative difficulties which are caused by the inability to identify the money would be overcome if solicitors provided to the bank the information to be included in the telegraphic transfer, i.e. the borrower's mortgage account number and the firm's name and address.

Delay

Lenders are sometimes criticised for delay in providing a form of discharge after redemption of the mortgage. It is recognised that most lenders can and do return the receipted mortgage or Form DS1 promptly and that solicitors can apply for registration to protect priority. However, unless there is good reason for the delay, e.g. a solicitor sending the form to the wrong office of the lender, lenders will no doubt deal promptly with this important procedure.

It is suggested that lenders should aim to return the receipted mortgage or Form DS1 within seven days, and if there is likely to be a delay beyond that period they should notify the seller's solicitor. This would enable the buyer's solicitor to lodge an application with the Land Registry pending receipt of receipted mortgage or sealed Form DS1, although it is hoped that this would only be necessary in exceptional circumstances.

The CML view

Many of the difficulties described above would be reduced if as a matter of course solicitors gave lenders correct information about the borrower, the property, the account number(s), etc., and lenders, in turn, operated internal cross-checking systems and provided accurate and complete redemption statements showing clearly the last payment to be taken into account and, systems permitting, details of all the borrower's accounts relating to the property which represent mortgages to be discharged.

If the solicitor, relying on an incorrect redemption statement provided by the lender, sends insufficient money to redeem a mortgage, the lender should discharge the mortgage. (However, the lender might wish to make it clear that the release was not intended to discharge the borrower from his or her outstanding personal liability. This might prevent the borrower from successfully claiming estoppel against the lender.)

Such cases do not occur frequently; when they do, it is generally because of a clerical or administrative error on the part of the lender, such as by omitting one month's interest or an insurance premium, and the amount is usually small. Nevertheless, where it appears that there has been an error, the solicitor should immediately draw this to the lender's notice and should pursue his or her borrower client actively for any shortfall.

Very rare cases could arise where general guidance of this kind is inapplicable, for example, if there is such a major discrepancy in the redemption figure that the borrower, and, perhaps, his or her solicitor, could not reasonably have believed in the accuracy of the statement.

Conclusion

Where there is an incorrect redemption statement, which is clearly due to an error by the lender or lack of clarification, it is unreasonable that a solicitor should be put in breach of his or her undertaking. The undertaking given to the buyer's solicitor is a vital part of the conveyancing process. It is the CML's view, in such cases, that the lender should seal the discharge.

The Law Society and the Council for Licensed Conveyancers agree with the views expressed in these paragraphs. It is hoped that some of the practical measures referred to above will be implemented to avoid difficulties on redemption.

VI.2. The CML Lenders'Handbook for England and Wales (second edition) Part 1[1]

Part 1 of the CML Lenders' Handbook for England and Wales is reproduced in this appendix with the kind permission of the Council of Mortgage Lenders. Part 2 of the Handbook for England and Wales and the editions of the Handbook for Scotland and the Isle of Man are only available online (at www.cml.org.uk). Solicitors are advised to always check the CML website for the latest version of the Handbook.

PART 1 – INSTRUCTIONS AND GUIDANCE

Those lenders who instruct using the CML Lenders' Handbook certify that these instructions have been prepared to comply with the requirements of Rule 6 (3) of the Solicitors' Practice Rules 1990 (or when applicable to the Solicitors' Code of Conduct 2007).

1. GENERAL

1.1   The CML Lenders' Handbook is issued by the Council of Mortgage Lenders. Your instructions from an individual lender will indicate if you are being instructed in accordance with the Lenders' Handbook. If you are, the general provisions in part 1 and any specific requirements in part 2 must be followed.

1.2   References to 'we', 'us' and 'our' means the lender from whom you receive instructions.

1.3   The Lenders' Handbook does not affect any responsibilities you have to us under the general law or any practice rule or guidance issued by your professional body from time to time.

1.4   The standard of care which we expect of you is that of a reasonably competent solicitor or licensed conveyancer acting on behalf of a mortgagee.

1.5   The limitations contained in rule 6(3)(c) and (e) of the Solicitors' Practice Rules 1990 (and when applicable the Solicitors' Code of Conduct 2007) apply to the instructions contained in the Lenders' Handbook and any separate instructions. This does not apply to licensed conveyancers following clause 3B.

1.6   You must also comply with any separate instructions you receive for an individual loan.

1.7   If the borrower and the mortgagor are not one and the same person, all references to 'borrower' shall include the mortgagor. Check part 2 to see if we lend in circumstances where the borrower and the mortgagor are not one and the same.

---

1. With consolidated amendments to 1 June 2007.

1.8   References to 'borrower' (and, if applicable, 'guarantor' or, expressly or impliedly, the mortgagor) are to each borrower (and guarantor or mortgagor) named in the mortgage instructions/offer (if sent to the conveyancer). This applies to references in the Lenders' Handbook and in the certificate of title.

1.9   References to 'mortgage offer' include any loan agreement, offer of mortgage or any other similar document.

1.10   If you are instructed in connection with any additional loan (including a further advance) then you should treat references to 'mortgage' and 'mortgage offer' as applying to such 'additional loan' and 'additional loan offer' respectively.

1.11   In any transaction during the lifetime of the mortgage when we instruct you, you must use our current standard documents in all cases and must not amend or generate them without our written consent. We will send you all the standard documents necessary to enable you to comply with our instructions, but please let us know if you need any other documents and we will send these to you. Check part 2 to see who you should contact. If you consider that any of the documentation is inappropriate to the particular facts of a transaction, you should write to us (see part 2) with full details and any suggested amendments.

1.12   In order to act on our behalf your firm must be a member of our conveyancing panel. You must also comply with any terms and conditions of your panel appointment.

1.13.1   If you or a member of your immediate family (that is to say, a spouse, civil partner, co-habitee, parent, sibling, child, step-parent, step-child, grandparent, grandchild, parent-in-law, or child-in-law) is the borrower and you are a sole practitioner, you must not act for us.

1.13.2   Your firm or company must not act for us if the partner or fee earner dealing with the transaction or a member of his immediate family is the seller, unless we say your firm may act (see part 2) and a separate fee earner of no less standing or a partner within the firm acts for us.

1.14   Your firm or company must not act for us if the partner or fee earner dealing with the transaction or a member of his immediate family is the borrower, unless we say your firm may act (see part 2) and a separate fee earner of no less standing or a partner within the firm acts for us.

1.15   If there is any conflict of interest, you must not act for us and must return our instructions.

1.16   Nothing in these instructions lessens your duties to the borrower.

1.17   In addition to these definitions any reference to any regulation, legislation or legislative provision shall be construed as a reference to that regulation, legislation or legislative provision as amended, re-enacted or extended at the relevant time.

2. COMMUNICATION

2.1   All communication between you and us should be in writing quoting the mortgage account or roll number, the surname and initials of the borrower and the property address. You should keep copies of all written communication on your file as evidence of notification and authorisation. If you use PC fax or e-mail, you should retain a copy in readable form.

2.2   If you require deeds or information from us in respect of a borrower or a property then you must first of all have the borrower's authority for such a request. If there is more than one borrower, you must have the authority of all the borrowers.

2.3   If you need to report a matter to us, you must do so as soon as you become aware of it so as to avoid any delay. If you do not believe that a matter is adequately provided for in the Handbook, you should identify the relevant Handbook provision and the extent to which the issue is not covered by it. You should provide a concise summary of the legal risks and your recommendation on how we should protect our interest. After reporting a matter you should not complete the mortgage until you have received our further written instructions. We recommend that you report such matters before exchange of contracts because we may have to withdraw or change the mortgage offer.

3. SAFEGUARDS

A   This section relates to solicitors and those working in practices regulated by the Solicitors Regulation Authority only

A3.1.1   You must follow the guidance in the Law Society's Green Card (mortgage fraud) and Pink Card (undertakings).

A3.1.2   You must follow the Law Society's guidance relating to money laundering and comply with the current money laundering regulations and the Proceeds of Crime Act 2002 to the extent that they apply.

A3.2   If you are not familiar with the seller's solicitors or licensed conveyancers, you must verify that they appear in a legal directory or they are currently on record with the Law Society or Council for Licensed Conveyancers as practising at the address shown on their note paper. If the seller does not have legal representation you should check part 2 to see whether or not we need to be notified so that a decision can be made as to whether or not we are prepared to proceed.

A3.3   Unless you personally know the signatory of a document, you must ask the signatory to provide evidence of identity, which you must carefully check. You should check the signatory's identity against one of the documents from list A or two of the documents in list B:

List A

–   a valid full passport; or

–   a valid H M Forces identity card with the signatory's photograph; or

–   a valid UK Photo-card driving licence; or

–   any other document listed in the additional list A in part 2.

List B

–   a cheque guarantee card, credit card (bearing the Mastercard or Visa logo), American Express or Diners Club card, debit or multi-function card (bearing the Switch or Delta logo) issued in the United Kingdom with an original account statement less than three months old; or

–   a firearm and shot gun certificate; or

–   a receipted utility bill less than three months old; or

–   a council tax bill less than three months old; or

- a council rent book showing the rent paid for the last three months; or

- a mortgage statement from another lender for the mortgage accounting year just ended; or

- any other document listed in the additional list B in part 2.

A3.4   You should check that any document you use to verify a signatory's identity appears to be authentic and current, signed in the relevant place. You should take a copy of it and keep the copy on your file. You should also check that the signatory's signature on any document being used to verify identity matches the signatory's signature on the document we require the signatory to sign and that the address shown on any document used to verify identity is that of the signatory.

B   This section applies to licensed conveyancers' practices only

B3.1   You must follow the professional guidance of the Council for Licensed Conveyancers relating to money laundering and comply with the current money laundering regulations and the Proceeds of Crime Act 2002 to the extent that they apply and you must follow all other relevant guidance issued by the Council for Licensed Conveyancers.

B3.2   If you are not familiar with the seller's solicitors or licensed conveyancers, you must verify that they appear in a legal directory or they are currently on record with the Law Society or Council for Licensed Conveyancers as practising at the address shown on their note paper. If the seller does not have legal representation you should check part 2 to see whether or not we need to be notified so that a decision can be made as to whether or not we are prepared to proceed.

B3.3   Unless you personally know the signatory of a document, you must ask the signatory to provide evidence of identity, which you must carefully check. You must satisfy yourself that the person signing the document is the borrower, mortgagor or guarantor (as appropriate). If you have any concerns about the identity of the signatory you should notify us immediately.

B3.4   You should check that any document you use to verify a signatory's identity appears to be authentic and current, signed in the relevant place. You should take a copy of it and keep the copy on your file. You should also check that the signatory's signature on any document being used to verify identity matches the signatory's signature on the document we require the signatory to sign and that the address shown on any document used to verify identity is that of the signatory.

4. VALUATION OF THE PROPERTY

4.1   Valuation

4.1.1   Check part 2 to see whether we send you a copy of the valuation report or if you must get it from the borrower.

4.1.2   You must take reasonable steps to verify that there are no discrepancies between the description of the property as valued and the title and other documents which a reasonably competent conveyancer should obtain, and, if there are, you must tell us immediately. The requirements in this clause and clause 4.1.3 apply to valuation reports and home condition reports. Where there is both a valuation report and a home condition report the requirements apply to both.

4.1.3   You should take reasonable steps to verify that the assumptions stated by the valuer (and where applicable a home inspector) about the title (for example, its tenure, easements, boundaries and restrictions on its use) in the valuation and home condition report are correct. If they are not, please let us know as soon as possible (see part 2) as it will be necessary for us to check with the valuer whether the valuation needs to be revised. We are not expecting you to assume the role of valuer. We are simply trying to ensure that the valuer has valued the property based on correct information.

4.1.4   When a home condition report is not provided we recommend that you should advise the borrower that there may be defects in the property which are not revealed by the inspection carried out by our valuer and there may be omissions or inaccuracies in the report which do not matter to us but which would matter to the borrower. We recommend that, if we send a copy of a valuation report that we have obtained, you should also advise the borrower that the borrower should not rely on the report in deciding whether to proceed with the purchase and that he obtains his own more detailed report on the condition and value of the property, based on a fuller inspection, to enable him to decide whether the property is suitable for his purposes.

4.2   Re-inspection

Where the mortgage offer states that a final inspection is needed, you must ask for the final inspection at least 10 working days before the advance is required (see part 2). Failure to do so may cause delay in the issue of the advance. Your certificate of title must be sent to us in the usual way (see part 2).

5. TITLE

5.1   Surrounding Circumstances

5.1.1   Please report to us (see part 2) if the owner or registered proprietor has been registered for less than six months or the person selling to the borrower is not the owner or registered proprietor unless the seller is:

5.1.1.1   a personal representative of the registered proprietor; or

5.1.1.2   an institutional mortgagee exercising its power of sale; or

5.1.1.3   a receiver, trustee-in-bankruptcy or liquidator; or

5.1.1.4   developer or builder selling a property acquired under a part-exchange scheme.

5.1.2   If any matter comes to your attention, which you should reasonably expect us to consider important in deciding whether or not to lend to the borrower (such as whether the borrower has given misleading information to us or the information which you might reasonably expect to have been given to us is no longer true) and you are unable to disclose that information to us because of a conflict of interest, you must cease to act for us and return our instructions stating that you consider a conflict of interest has arisen.

5.2   Searches and Reports

5.2.1   In carrying out your investigation, you must ensure that all usual and necessary searches and enquiries have been carried out. You must report any adverse entry to us but we do not want to be sent the search itself. We must be named as the applicant in the Land Registry search.

5.2.2   In addition, you must ensure that any other searches which may be appropriate to the particular property, taking into account its locality and other features are carried out.

5.2.3   All searches except where there is a priority period must not be more than six months old at completion.

5.2.4   You must advise us of any contaminated land entries revealed in the local authority search. Check part 2 to see if we want to receive environmental or contaminated land reports (as opposed to contaminated land entries revealed in the local authority search). If we do not, you do not need to make these enquiries on our behalf.

5.2.5   Check part 2 to see if we accept:

5.2.5.1   personal searches; or

5.2.5.2   search insurance.

5.2.6   If we do accept personal searches or search insurance, check part 2 to see our requirements as to such searches. If no requirements are specified in part 2, you must ensure:

5.2.6.1   a suitably qualified search agent carries out the personal search and has indemnity insurance that adequately protects us; or

5.2.6.2   the search insurance policy adequately protects us.

5.2.7   You must be satisfied that you will be able to certify that the title is good and marketable.

5.3   Planning and Building Regulations

5.3.1   You must by making appropriate searches and enquiries take all reasonable steps (including any further enquiries to clarify any issues which may arise) to ensure the property has the benefit of any necessary planning consents (including listed building consent) and building regulation approval for its construction and any subsequent change to the property (see part 2) or its current use; and

5.3.2   there is no evidence of any breach of the conditions of that or any other consent or certificate affecting the property; and

5.3.3   that no matter is revealed which would preclude the property from being used as a residential property or that the property may be the subject of enforcement action.

5.3.4   If there is such evidence and all outstanding conditions will not be satisfied by completion, then this must be reported to us (see part 2). Check part 2 to see if copies of planning permissions, building regulations and other consents or certificates should be sent to us.

5.3.5   If the property will be subject to any enforceable restrictions, for example under an agreement (such as an agreement under section 106 of the Town and Country Planning Act 1990) or in a planning permission, which, at the time of completion, might reasonably be expected materially to affect its value or its future marketability, you should report this to us (see part 2).

5.4   Good and Marketable Title

5.4.1   The title to the property must be good and marketable free of any restrictions, covenants, easements, charges or encumbrances which, at the time of completion, might reasonably be expected to materially adversely affect the value of the property or its future marketability (but excluding any matters covered by indemnity insurance) and which may be accepted by us for mortgage purposes. Our requirements in respect of indemnity insurance are set out in paragraph 9. You must also take reasonable steps to ensure that, on completion, the property will be vested in the borrower.

5.4.2   Good leasehold title will be acceptable if:

5.4.2.1   a marked abstract of the freehold and any intermediate leasehold title for the statutory period of 15 years before the grant of the lease is provided; or

5.4.2.2   you are prepared to certify that the title is good and marketable when sending your certificate of title (because, for example, the landlord's title is generally accepted in the district where the property is situated); or

5.4.2.3   you arrange indemnity insurance. Our requirements in respect of indemnity insurance are set out in paragraph 9.

5.4.3.1   A title based on adverse possession or possessory title will be acceptable if the seller is or on completion the borrower will be registered at the Land Registry as registered proprietor of a possessory title or there is satisfactory evidence by statutory declaration of adverse possession for a period of at least 12 years. In the case of lost title deeds, the statutory declaration must explain the loss satisfactorily;

5.4.3.2   we will also require indemnity insurance where there are buildings on the part in question or where the land is essential for access or services;

5.4.3.3   we may not need indemnity insurance in cases where such title affects land on which no buildings are erected or which is not essential for access or services. In such cases, you must send a plan of the whole of the land to be mortgaged to us identifying the area of land having possessory title. We will refer the matter to our valuer so that an assessment can be made of the proposed security. We will then notify you of any additional requirements or if a revised mortgage offer is to be made.

5.5   Flying Freeholds, Freehold Flats, other Freehold Arrangements and Commonhold

5.5.1   If any part of the property comprises or is affected by a flying freehold or the property is a freehold flat, check part 2 to see if we will accept it as security.

5.5.2   If we are prepared to accept a title falling within 5.5.1:

5.5.2.1   (unless we tell you not to in part 2) you must report to us that the property is a freehold flat or flying freehold; and

5.5.2.2   the property must have all necessary rights of support, protection, and entry for repair as well as a scheme of enforceable covenants that are also such that subsequent buyers are required to enter into covenants in identical form; and

5.5.2.3   you must be able to certify that the title is good and marketable; and

5.5.2.4   in the case of flying freeholds, you must send us a plan of the property clearly showing the part affected by the flying freehold.

If our requirements in 5.5.2.2 are not satisfied, indemnity must be in place at completion (see paragraph 9).

Other freehold arrangements

5.5.3   Unless we indicate to the contrary (see part 2), we have no objection to a security which comprises a building converted into not more than four flats where the borrower occupies one of those flats and the borrower or another flat owner also owns the freehold of the building and the other flats are subject to long leases.

5.5.3.1   If the borrower occupying one of the flats also owns the freehold, we will require our security to be:

5.5.3.1.1   the freehold of the whole building subject to the long leases of the other flats; and

5.5.3.1.2   any leasehold interest the borrower will have in the flat the borrower is to occupy.

5.5.3.2   If another flat owner owns the freehold of the building, the borrower must have a leasehold interest in the flat the borrower is to occupy and our security must be the borrower's leasehold interest in such flat.

5.5.3.3   The leases of all the flats should contain appropriate covenants by the tenant of each flat to contribute towards the repair, maintenance and insurance of the building. The leases should also grant and reserve all necessary rights and easements. They should not contain any unduly onerous obligations on the landlord.

5.5.4   Where the security will comprise:

5.5.4.1   one of a block of not more than four leasehold flats and the borrower will also own the freehold jointly with one or more of the other flat owners in the building; or

5.5.4.2   one of two leasehold flats in a building where the borrower also owns the freehold reversion of the other flat and the other leaseholder owns the freehold reversion in the borrower's flat;

check part 2 to see if we will accept it as security and if so, what our requirements will be.

Commonhold

5.5.5   If any part of the property comprises of commonhold, check part 2 to see if we will accept it as security.

5.5.6   If we are prepared to accept a title falling within 5.5.5, you must:

5.5.6.1   ensure that the commonhold association has obtained insurance for the common parts which complies with our requirements (see 6.13);

5.5.6.2   obtain a commonhold unit information certificate and ensure that all of the commonhold assessment in respect of the property has been paid up to the date of completion;

5.5.6.3   ensure that the commonhold community statement does not include any material restrictions on occupation or use (see 5.4 and 5.6);

5.5.6.4   ensure that the commonhold community statement provides that in the event of a voluntary termination of the commonhold the termination statement provides that the unit holders will ensure that any mortgage secured on their unit is repaid on termination;

5.5.6.5   make a company search to verify that the commonhold association is in existence and remains registered, and that there is no registered indication that it is to be wound up; and

5.5.6.6   within 14 days of completion, send the notice of transfer of a commonhold unit and notice of the mortgage to the commonhold association.

5.6   Restrictions on Use and Occupation

You must check whether there are any material restrictions on the occupation of the property as a private residence or as specified by us (for example, because of the occupier's employment, age or income), or any material restrictions on its use. If there are any restrictions, you must report details to us (see part 2). In some cases, we may accept a restriction, particularly if this relates to sheltered housing or to first time buyers.

5.7   Restrictive Covenants

5.7.1   You must enquire whether the property has been built, altered or is currently used in breach of a restrictive covenant. We rely on you to check that the covenant is not enforceable. If you are unable to provide an unqualified certificate of title as a result of the risk of enforceability you must ensure (subject to paragraph 5.7.2) that indemnity insurance is in place at completion of our mortgage (see paragraph 9).

5.7.2   We will not insist on indemnity insurance:

5.7.2.1   if you are satisfied that there is no risk to our security; and

5.7.2.2   the breach has continued for more than 20 years; and

5.7.2.3   there is nothing to suggest that any action is being taken or is threatened in respect of the breach.

5.8   First Legal Charge

On completion, we require a fully enforceable first charge by way of legal mortgage over the property executed by all owners of the legal estate. All existing charges must be redeemed on or before completion, unless we agree that an existing charge may be postponed to rank after our mortgage. Our standard deed or form of postponement must be used.

5.9   Other Loans

You must ask the borrower how the balance of the purchase price is being provided. If you become aware that the borrower is not providing the balance of the purchase price from his own funds and/or is proposing to give a second charge over the property, you must report this to us if the borrower agrees (see part 2), failing which you must return our instructions and explain that you are unable to continue to act for us as there is a conflict of interest.

5.10   Leasehold Property

5.10.1   Our requirements on the unexpired term of a lease offered as security are set out in part 2.

5.10.2   There must be no provision for forfeiture on the insolvency of the tenant or any superior tenant.

5.10.3   The only situations where we will accept a restriction on the mortgage or assignment (whether by a tenant or a mortgagee) of the lease is where the person whose consent needs to be obtained cannot unreasonably withhold giving consent. The necessary consent for the particular transaction must be obtained before completion. If the lease requires consent to an assignment or mortgage to be obtained, you must obtain these on or before completion (this is particularly important if the lease is a shared ownership lease). You must not complete without them.

5.10.4   You must take reasonable steps to check that:

5.10.4.1   there are satisfactory legal rights, particularly for access, services, support, shelter and protection; and

5.10.4.2   there are also adequate covenants and arrangements in respect of the following matters, buildings insurance, maintenance and repair of the structure, foundations, main walls, roof, common parts, common services and grounds (the 'common services').

5.10.5   You should ensure that responsibility for the insurance, maintenance and repair of the common services is that of:

5.10.5.1   the landlord; or

5.10.5.2   one or more of the tenants in the building of which the property forms part; or

5.10.5.3   the management company – see paragraph 5.11.

5.10.6   Where the responsibility for the insurance, maintenance and repair of the common services is that of one or more of the tenants;

5.10.6.1   the lease must contain adequate provisions for the enforcement of these obligations by the landlord or management company at the request of the tenant.

5.10.6.2   In the absence of a provision in the lease that all leases of other flats in the block are in, or will be granted in, substantially similar form, you should take reasonable steps to check that the leases of the other flats are in similar form. If you are unable to do so, you should effect indemnity insurance (see paragraph 9). This is not essential if the landlord is responsible for the maintenance and repair of the main structure.

5.10.6.3   We do not require enforceability covenants mutual or otherwise for other tenant covenants.

5.10.7   We have no objection to a lease which contains provision for a periodic increase of the ground rent provided that the amount of the increased ground rent is fixed or can be readily established and is reasonable. If you consider any increase in the ground rent may materially affect the value of the property, you must report this to us (see part 2).

5.10.8   You should enquire whether the landlord or managing agent foresees any significant increase in the level of the service charge in the reasonably foreseeable future and, if there is, you must report to us (see part 2).

5.10.9   If the terms of the lease are unsatisfactory, you must obtain a suitable deed of variation to remedy the defect. We may accept indemnity insurance (see paragraph 9). See part 2 for our requirements.

5.10.10   You must obtain on completion a clear receipt or other appropriate written confirmation for the last payment of ground rent and service charge from the landlord or managing agents on behalf of the landlord. Check part 2 to see if it must be sent to us after completion. If confirmation of payment from the landlord cannot be obtained, we are prepared to proceed provided that you are satisfied that the absence of the landlord is common practice in the district where the property is situated, the seller confirms there are no breaches of the terms of the lease, you are satisfied that our security will not be prejudiced by the absence of such a receipt and you provide us with a clear certificate of title.

5.10.11   Notice of the mortgage must be served on the landlord and any management company immediately following completion, whether or not the lease requires it. If you cannot obtain receipt of the notice then, as a last resort, suitable evidence of the service of the notice on the landlord should be provided. Check part 2 to see if a receipted copy of the notice or evidence of service must be sent to us after completion.

5.10.12   We will accept leases which require the property to be sold on the open market if rebuilding or reinstatement is frustrated provided the insurance proceeds and the proceeds of sale are shared between the landlord and tenant in proportion to their respective interests.

5.10.13   You must report to us (see part 2) if it becomes apparent that the landlord is either absent or insolvent. If we are to lend, we may require indemnity insurance (see paragraph 9). See part 2 for our requirements.

5.10.14   If the leasehold title is registered but the lease has been lost, we are prepared to proceed provided you have checked a Land Registry produced copy of the registered lease. Whilst this will not be an official copy of the lease you may accept it as sufficient evidence of the lease and its terms when approving the title for mortgage purposes provided it is, on its face, a complete copy.

5.11   Management Company

5.11.1   In paragraph 5.11 the meanings shall apply:

- 'management company' means the company formed to carry out the maintenance and repair of the common parts;

- 'common parts' means the structure, main walls, roof, foundations, services grounds and any other common areas serving the building or estate of which the property forms part.

If a management company is required to maintain or repair the common parts, the management company should have a legal right to enter the property; if the management company's right to so enter does not arise from a leasehold interest, then the tenants of the building should also be the members of the management company.

If this is not the case, there should be a covenant by the landlord to carry out the obligations of the management company should it fail to do so.

5.11.1.1   For leases granted before 1 September 2000:

If the lease does not satisfy the requirements of paragraph 5.11.1 but:

you are nevertheless satisfied that the existing arrangements affecting the management company and the maintenance and repair of the common parts are sufficient to ensure the adequate maintenance and repair of the common parts; and

you are able to provide a clear certificate of title,

then we will rely on your professional judgement.

5.11.2   You should make a company search and verify that the company is in existence and registered at Companies House. You should also obtain the management company's last three years' published accounts (or the accounts from inception if the company has only been formed in the past three years). Any apparent problems with the company should be reported to us (see part 2). If the borrower is required to be a shareholder in the management company, check part 2 to see if you must arrange for the share certificate, a blank stock transfer form executed by the borrower and a copy of the memorandum and articles of association to be sent to us after completion (unless we tell you not to). If the management company is limited by guarantee, the borrower (or at least one of them if two or more) must become a member on or before completion.

5.12   Insolvency Considerations

5.12.1   You must obtain a clear bankruptcy search against each borrower (and each mortgagor or guarantor, if any) providing us with protection at the date of completion of the mortgage. You must fully investigate any entries revealed by your bankruptcy search against the borrower (or mortgagor or guarantor) to ensure that they do not relate to them.

5.12.2   Where an entry is revealed against the name of the borrower (or the mortgagor or guarantor):

5.12.2.1   you must certify that the entry does not relate to the borrower (or the mortgagor or guarantor) if you are able to do so from your own knowledge or enquiries; or

5.12.2.2   if, after obtaining office copy entries or making other enquiries of the Official Receiver, you are unable to certify that the entry does not relate to the borrower (or the mortgagor or guarantor) you must report this to us (see part 2). We may as a consequence need to withdraw our mortgage offer.

5.12.3   If you are aware that the title to the property is subject to a deed of gift or a transaction at an apparent undervalue completed within five years of the proposed mortgage then you must be satisfied that we will acquire our interest in good faith and will be protected under the provisions of the Insolvency (No 2) Act 1994 against our security being set aside. If you are unable to give an unqualified certificate of title, you must arrange indemnity insurance (see paragraph 9).

5.12.4   You must also obtain clear bankruptcy searches against all parties to any deed of gift or transaction at an apparent undervalue.

5.13   Powers of Attorney

5.13.1.1   If any document is being executed under power of attorney, you must ensure that the power of attorney is, on its face, properly drawn up, that it appears to be properly executed by the donor and that the attorney knows of no reason why such power of attorney will not be subsisting at completion.

5.13.1.2   Where there are joint borrowers the power should comply with section 25 of the Trustee Act 1925, as amended by section 7 of the Trustee Delegation Act 1999, or with section 1 of the Trustee Delegation Act 1999 with the attorney making an appropriate statement under section 2 of the 1999 Act.

5.13.1.3   In the case of joint borrowers, neither borrower may appoint the other as their attorney.

5.13.2   A power of attorney must not be used in connection with a regulated loan under the Consumer Credit Act 1974.

5.13.3   Check part 2 to see if:

5.13.3.1   the original or a certified copy of the power of attorney must be sent to us after completion;

5.13.3.2   where the power of attorney is a general power of attorney and was completed more than 12 months before the completion of our mortgage, you must send us a statutory declaration confirming that it has not been revoked.

5.14   Title Guarantee

Whilst we recommend that a borrower should try to obtain a full title guarantee from the seller, we do not insist on this. We, however, require the borrower to give us a full title guarantee in the mortgage deed. The mortgage deed must not be amended.

5.15   Affordable Housing: Shared ownership and shared equity

Housing associations, other social landlords and developers sometimes provide schemes under which the borrower will not have 100% ownership of the property and a third party will also own a share or will be taking a charge over the title. In these cases you must check with us to see if we will lend and what our requirements are unless we have already provided these (see part 2).

6.   THE PROPERTY

6.1   Mortgage Offer and Title Documents

6.1.1   The loan to the borrower will not be made until all relevant conditions of the mortgage offer which need to be satisfied before completion have been complied with and we have received your certificate of title.

6.1.2   You must check your instructions and ensure that there are no discrepancies between them and the title documents and other matters revealed by your investigations.

6.1.3   You should tell us (see part 2) as soon as possible if you have been told that the borrower has decided not to take up the mortgage offer.

6.2   Boundaries

These must be clearly defined by reference to a suitable plan or description. They must also accord with the information given in the valuation report, if this is provided to you. You should check with the borrower that the plan or the description accords with the borrower's understanding of the extent of the property to be mortgaged to us. You must report to us (see part 2), if there are any discrepancies.

6.3   Purchase Price

6.3.1   The purchase price for the property must be the same as set out in our instructions. If it is not, you must tell us (unless we say differently in part 2).

6.3.2   You must tell us (unless we say differently in part 2) if the contract provides for or you become aware of any arrangement in which there is:

6.3.2.1   a cashback to the buyer; or

6.3.2.2   part of the price is being satisfied by a non-cash incentive to the buyer; or

6.3.2.3 any indirect incentive (cash or non cash) or rental guarantee.

Any such arrangement may lead to the mortgage offer being withdrawn or amended.

6.3.3 You must report to us (see part 2) if you will not have control over the payment of all of the purchase money (for example, if it is proposed that the borrower pays money to the seller direct) other than a deposit held by an estate agent or a reservation fee of not more than £1,000 paid to a builder or developer.

6.4 Vacant Possession

Unless otherwise stated in your instructions, it is a term of the loan that vacant possession is obtained. The contract must provide for this. If you doubt that vacant possession will be given, you must not part with the advance and should report the position to us (see part 2).

6.5 Properties Let at Completion

6.5.1 Unless it is clear from the mortgage offer that the property is let or is to be let at completion then you must check with us whether we lend on 'buy to let' properties and that the mortgage is for that purpose (see part 2).

6.5.2 Where the property, or part of it, is already let, or is to be let at completion, then the letting must comply with the details set out in the mortgage offer or any consent to let we issue. If no such details are mentioned, you must report the position to us (see part 2).

6.5.3 Check part 2 for whether counterparts or certified copies of all tenancy agreements and leases in respect of existing tenancies must be sent to us after completion.

6.5.4 Where the property falls within the definition of a house in multiple occupation under the Housing Act 2004 see part 2 as to whether we will accept this as security and if so what our requirements are.

6.6 New Properties – Building Standards Indemnity Schemes

6.6.1 If the property has been built or converted within the past ten years or is to be occupied for the first time, you must ensure that it was built or converted under a scheme acceptable to us (see part 2 for a list of schemes acceptable to us and our requirements).

6.6.2 Where the cover under a scheme referred to in clause 6.6.1 is not yet in place before you send us the certificate of title, you must obtain a copy of a new home warranty provider's cover note from the developer. The cover note must confirm that the property has received a satisfactory final inspection and that the new home warranty will be in place on or before completion. This does not apply to self-build schemes. Check part 2 to see what new home warranty documentation should be sent to us on completion.

6.6.3 We do not insist that notice of assignment of the benefit of the new home warranty agreement be given to the builder in the case of a second and subsequent purchase(s) during the period of the insurance cover. Check part 2 to see if any assignments of building standards indemnity schemes which are available should be sent to us after completion.

6.6.4 Where the property does not have the benefit of a scheme under 6.6.1 and has been built or converted within the past 6 years check part 2 to see if we will proceed and, if so, whether you must satisfy yourself that the building work is being monitored (or where the work is completed was monitored) by a professional consultant. If we do accept monitoring you should ensure that the professional consultant has provided the lender's Professional Consultant's Certificate which forms an appendix to this Handbook or such other form as we may provide. The professional consultant should also confirm to you that he has appropriate experience in the design or monitoring of the construction or conversion of residential buildings and has one or more of the following qualifications:

6.6.4.1   fellow or member of the Royal Institution of Chartered Surveyors (FRICS or MRICS); or

6.6.4.2   fellow or member of the Institution of Structural Engineers (FI Struct.E or MI Struct.E); or

6.6.4.3   fellow or member of the Chartered Institute of Building (FCIOB or MCIOB); or

6.6.4.4   fellow or member of the Architecture and Surveying Institute (FASI or MASI); or

6.6.4.5   fellow or member of the Association of Building Engineers (FB.Eng or MB.Eng); or

6.6.4.6   member of the British Institute of Architectural Technologists (MBIAT); or

6.6.4.7   architect registered with the Architects Registration Board (ARB). An architect must be registered with the Architects Registration Board, even if also a member of another institution, for example the Royal Institute of British Architects (RIBA); or

6.6.4.8   fellow or member of the Institution of Civil Engineers (FICE or MICE).

6.6.5   At the time he issues his certificate of practical completion, the consultant must have professional indemnity insurance in force for each claim for the greater of either:

6.6.5.1   the value of the property once completed; or

6.6.5.2   £250,000 if employed directly by the borrower or, in any other case, £500,000.

If we require a collateral warranty from any professional adviser, this will be stated specifically in the mortgage instructions.

6.6.6   Check part 2 to see if the consultant's certificate must be sent to us after completion.

6.7   Roads and Sewers

6.7.1   If the roads or sewers immediately serving the property are not adopted or maintained at public expense, there must be an agreement and bond in existence or you must report to us (see part 2 for who you should report to).

6.7.2   If there is any such agreement, it should be secured by bond or deposit as required by the appropriate authority to cover the cost of making up the roads and sewers to adoptable standards, maintaining them thereafter and procuring adoption.

6.7.3   If there is an arrangement between the developer and the lender whereby the lender will not require a retention, you must obtain confirmation from the developer that the arrangement is still in force.

6.7.4   Where roads and sewers are not adopted or to be adopted but are maintained by local residents or a management company this is acceptable providing that in your reasonable opinion appropriate arrangements for maintenance repairs and costs are in place.

6.8   Easements

6.8.1   You must take all reasonable steps to check that the property has the benefit of all easements necessary for its full use and enjoyment. All such rights must be enforceable by the borrower and the borrower's successors in title. If they are not check part 2 for our requirements.

6.8.2   If the borrower owns adjoining land over which the borrower requires access to the property or in respect of which services are provided to the property, this land must also be mortgaged to us.

6.9   Release of Retentions

6.9.1   If we make a retention from an advance (for example, for repairs, improvements or road works) we are not obliged to release that retention, or any part of it, if the borrower is in breach of any of his obligations under the mortgage, or if a condition attached to the retention has not been met or if the loan has been repaid in full. You should, therefore, not give an unqualified undertaking to pay the retention to a third party.

6.9.2   Check part 2 to see who we will release the retention to.

6.10   Neighbourhood Changes

The local search or the enquiries of the seller's conveyancer should not reveal that the property is in an area scheduled for redevelopment or in any way affected by road proposals. If it is, please report this to us (see part 2).

6.11   Rights of Pre-emption and Restrictions on Resale

You must ensure that there are no rights of pre-emption, restrictions on resale, options or similar arrangements in existence at completion which will affect our security. If there are, please report this to us (see part 2).

6.12   Improvement and Repair Grants

Where the property is subject to an improvement or repair grant which will not be discharged or waived on completion, check part 2 to see whether you must report the matter to us.

6.13   Insurance

Where we do not arrange the insurance, you must:

6.13.1   report to us (see part 2) if the property is not insured in accordance with our requirements (one of our requirements, see part 2, will relate to whether the property is insured in the joint names of us and the borrower or whether our interest may be noted);

6.13.2   arrange that the insurance cover starts from no later than completion;

6.13.3   check that the amount of buildings insurance cover is at least the amount referred to in the mortgage offer. If the property is part of a larger building and there is a common insurance policy, the total sum insured for the building must be not less than the total number of flats multiplied by the amount set out in the mortgage offer for the property – check part 2 for our requirements on this;

6.13.4   ensure that the buildings insurance cover is index linked;

6.13.5   ensure that the excess does not exceed the amount set out in part 2;

6.13.6   Check part 2 to see if we require you to confirm that all the following risks are covered in the insurance policy:

6.13.6.1   fire;

6.13.6.2   lightning;

6.13.6.3   aircraft;

6.13.6.4   explosion;

6.13.6.5   earthquake;

6.13.6.6   storm;

6.13.6.7   flood;

6.13.6.8   escape of water or oil;

6.13.6.9   riot;

6.13.6.10   malicious damage;

6.13.6.11   theft or attempted theft;

6.13.6.12   falling trees and branches and aerials;

6.13.6.13   subsidence;

6.13.6.14   heave;

6.13.6.15   landslip;

6.13.6.16   collision;

6.13.6.17   accidental damage to underground services;

6.13.6.18   professional fees, demolition and site clearance costs; and

6.13.6.19   public liability to anyone else.

6.13.7   Check part 2 to see if we require you to obtain before completion the insurer's confirmation that the insurer will notify us if the policy is not renewed or is cancelled or if you do not obtain this, report to us (see part 2).

6.13.8   Check part 2 to see if we require you to send us a copy of the buildings insurance policy and the last premium receipt to us.

7. OTHER OCCUPIERS

7.1   Rights or interests of persons who are not a party to the mortgage and who are or will be in occupation of the property may affect our rights under the mortgage, for example as overriding interests.

7.2   If your instructions state the name of a person who is to live at the property, you should ask the borrower before completing the mortgage that the information given by us in our mortgage instructions or mortgage offer about occupants is correct and nobody else is to live at the property.

7.3   Unless we state otherwise (see part 2), you must obtain a signed deed or form of consent from all occupants aged 17 or over of whom you are aware who are not a party to the mortgage before completion of the mortgage.

7.4   We recognise that in some cases the information given to us or you by a borrower may be incorrect or misleading. If you have any reason to doubt the accuracy of any information disclosed, you should report it to us (see part 2) provided the borrower agrees; if the borrower does not agree, you should return our instructions.

8. SEPARATE REPRESENTATION

8.1   Unless we otherwise state (see part 2), you must not advise:

8.1.1   any borrower who does not personally benefit from the loan; or

8.1.2   any guarantor; or

8.1.3   anyone intending to occupy the property who is to execute a consent to the mortgage,

and you must arrange for them to seek independent legal advice.

8.2   If we do allow you to advise any of these people, you must only do so after recommending in the absence of any other person interested in the transaction that such person obtains independent legal advice. Any advice that you give any of these people must also be given in the absence of any other person interested in the transaction. You should be particularly careful if the matrimonial home or family home is being charged to secure a business debt. Any consent should be signed by the person concerned. A power of attorney is not acceptable.

9. INDEMNITY INSURANCE

You must effect an indemnity insurance policy whenever the Lenders' Handbook identifies that this is an acceptable or required course to us to ensure that the property has a good and marketable title at completion. This paragraph does not relate to mortgage indemnity insurance. The draft policy should not be sent to us unless we ask for it. Check part 2 to see if the policy must be sent to us after completion. Where indemnity insurance is effected:

9.1   you must approve the terms of the policy on our behalf; and

9.2   the limit of indemnity must meet our requirements (see part 2); and

9.3   the policy must be effected without cost to us; and

9.4   you must disclose to the insurer all relevant information which you have obtained; and

9.5   the policy must not contain conditions which you know would make it void or prejudice our interests; and

9.6   you must provide a copy of the policy to the borrower and explain to the borrower why the policy was effected and that a further policy may be required if there is further lending against the security of the property; and

9.7   you must explain to the borrower that the borrower will need to comply with any conditions of the policy and that the borrower should notify us of any notice or potential claim in respect of the policy; and

9.8   the policy should always be for our benefit and, if possible, for the benefit of the borrower and any subsequent owner or mortgagee. If the borrower will not be covered by the policy, you must advise the borrower of this.

10. THE LOAN AND CERTIFICATE OF TITLE

10.1   You should not submit your certificate of title unless it is unqualified or we have authorised you in writing to proceed notwithstanding any issues you have raised with us.

10.2   We shall treat the submission by you of the certificate of title as a request for us to release the mortgage advance to you. Check part 2 to see if the mortgage advance will be paid electronically or by cheque and the minimum number of days notice we require. See part 2 for any standard deductions which may be made from the mortgage advance.

10.3.1   You are only authorised to release the loan when you hold sufficient funds to complete the purchase of the property and pay all stamp duty land tax and registration fees to perfect the security as a first legal mortgage or, if you do not have them, you accept responsibility to pay them yourself.

10.3.2   Before releasing the loan when the borrower is purchasing the property you must either hold a properly completed and executed stamp duty land tax form or you must hold an appropriate authority from the borrower allowing you to file the necessary stamp duty land tax return(s) on completion.

10.3.3   You must ensure that all stamp duty land tax returns are completed and submitted to allow registration of the charge to take place in the priority period afforded by the search.

10.3.4   You must hold the loan on trust for us until completion. If completion is delayed, you must return it to us when and how we tell you (see part 2).

10.4   You should note that although your certificate of title will be addressed to us, we may at some time transfer our interest in the mortgage. In those circumstances, our successors in title to the mortgage and persons deriving title under or through the mortgage will also rely on your certificate.

10.5   If, after you have requested the mortgage advance, completion is delayed you must telephone or fax us immediately after you are aware of the delay and you must inform us of the new date for completion (see part 2).

10.6   See part 2 for details of how long you can hold the mortgage advance before returning it to us. If completion is delayed for longer than that period, you must return the mortgage advance to us. If you do not, we reserve the right to require you to pay interest on the amount of the mortgage advance (see part 2).

10.7   If the mortgage advance is not returned within the period set out in part 2, we will assume that the mortgage has been completed, and we will charge the borrower interest under the mortgage.

11. THE DOCUMENTATION

11.1   The Mortgage

The mortgage incorporates our current mortgage conditions and, where applicable, loan conditions. If the mortgage conditions booklet is supplied to you with your instructions you must give it to the borrower before completion of the mortgage.

11.2   Explanation

You should explain to each borrower (and any other person signing or executing a document) his responsibilities and liabilities under the documents referred to in 11.1 and any documents he is required to sign.

11.3   Signing and Witnessing of Documents

It is considered good practice that the signature of a document that needs to be witnessed is witnessed by a solicitor, legal executive or licensed conveyancer. All documents required at completion must be dated with the date of completion of the loan.

12. INSTALMENT MORTGAGES AND MORTGAGE ADVANCES RELEASED IN INSTALMENTS

12.1   Introduction

12.1.1   If the cost of the building is to be paid by instalments as work progresses (for example, under a building contract) the amount of each instalment which we will be able to release will be based on a valuation made by our valuer at the time. Whilst we will not be bound by the terms of any building contract we will meet the reasonable requirements of the borrower and the builder as far as possible.

12.1.2   The borrower is expected to pay for as much work as possible from his own resources before applying to us for the first instalment. However, we may, if required, consider advancing a nominal sum on receipt of the certificate of title to enable the mortgage to be completed so long as the legal estate in the property is vested in the borrower.

12.1.3   The borrower is responsible for our valuer's fees for interim valuations as well as the first and final valuations.

12.2   Applications for Part of the Advance

As in the case of a normal mortgage account, funds for instalment mortgages may be sent to you. However, instalments (apart from the first which will be sent to you to enable you to complete the mortgage) can be sent directly to the borrower on request. We may make further payments and advances without reference to you.

12.3   Requests for Intermediate Funds

To allow time for a valuation to be carried out, your request should be sent to us (see part 2) at least 10 days before the funds are required.

12.4   Building Contract as Security

We will not lend on the security of a building contract unless we tell you to the contrary. As a result the mortgage must not be completed and no part of the advance released until the title to the legal estate in the property has been vested in the borrower.

13. MORTGAGE INDEMNITY INSURANCE OR HIGHER LENDING CHARGE

You are reminded to tell the borrower that we (and not the borrower) are the insured under any mortgage indemnity or similar form of insurance policy and that the insurer will have a subrogated right to claim against the borrower if it pays us under the policy. Different lenders call the various schemes of this type by different names. They may not involve an insurance policy.

14. AFTER COMPLETION

14.1   Registration

14.1.1.1   You must register our mortgage as a first legal charge at the Land Registry. Before making your Land Registry application for registration, you must place a copy of the results of the Official Search on your file together with certified copies of the transfer, mortgage deed and any discharges or releases from a previous mortgagee.

14.1.1.2   Where the borrower or mortgagor is a company an application to register the charge must be lodged at Companies House within the required time period.

14.1.2   Our mortgage conditions and mortgage deed have been deposited at the Land Registry and it is therefore unnecessary to submit a copy of the mortgage conditions on an application for registration.

14.1.3   Where the loan is to be made in instalments or there is any deferred interest retention or stage release, check part 2 to see whether you must apply to Land Registry on form CH2 for entry of a notice on the register that we are under an obligation to make further advances. If the mortgage deed states that it secures further advances, and that the lender is under an obligation to make them, there is no need to submit a form CH2 provided the mortgage deed also states that application is made to the Registrar for a note to be entered on the register to that effect and the mortgage deed bears a Land Registry MD reference at its foot..

14.1.4   The application for registration must be received by the Land Registry during the priority period afforded by your original Land Registry search made before Completion and, in any event, in the case of an application for first registration, within two months of completion. Please check part 2 to see if we require the original mortgage deed to be returned to us.

14.2   Title Deeds

14.2.1   All title deeds, official copies of the register (where these are issued by the Land Registry after registration), searches, enquiries, consents, requisitions and documents relating to the property in your possession must be held to our order and you must not create or exercise any lien over them. Check part 2 for our requirements on what you should do with these documents following registration. If registration at the Land Registry has not been completed within three months from completion, you should advise us in writing with a copy of any correspondence with the Land Registry explaining the delay.

14.2.2   You must only send us documents we tell you to (see part 2). You should obtain the borrower's instructions concerning the retention of documents we tell you not to send us.

14.3   Your Mortgage File

14.3.1   For evidential purposes you must keep your file for at least six years from the date of the mortgage before destroying it. Microfiching or data imaging is suitable compliance with this requirement. It is the practice of some fraudsters to demand the conveyancing file on completion in order to destroy evidence that may later be used against them. It is important to retain these documents to protect our interests.

14.3.2   Where you are processing personal data (as defined in the Data Protection Act 1998) on our behalf, you must:

14.3.2.1   take such security measures as are required to enable you to comply with obligations equivalent to those imposed on us by the seventh data protection principle in the 1998 Act; and

14.3.2.2   process such personal data only in accordance with our instructions. In addition, you must allow us to conduct such reasonable audit of your information security measures as we require to ensure your compliance with your obligations in this paragraph.

14.3.3   Subject to any right of lien or any overriding duty of confidentiality, you should treat documents comprising your file as if they are jointly owned by the borrower and us and you should not part with them without the consent of both parties. You should on request supply certified copies of documents on the file or a certified copy of the microfiche to either the borrower or us, and may make a reasonable charge for copying and certification.

15. LEGAL COSTS

Your charges and disbursements are payable by the borrower and should be collected from the borrower on or before completion. You must not allow non-payment of fees or disbursements to delay the payment of stamp duty land tax, the lodging of any stamp duty land tax return and registration of documents. For solicitors the Law Society recommends that your costs for acting on our behalf in connection with the mortgage should, in the interest of transparency, be separately identified to the borrower.

16. TRANSACTIONS DURING THE LIFE OF THE MORTGAGE

16.1   Requests for Title Documents

All requests for title documents should be made in writing and sent to us (see part 2). In making such a request you must have the consent of all of the borrowers to apply for the title documents.

16.2   Further Advances

Our mortgage secures further advances. Consequently, when a further advance is required for alterations or improvements to the property we will not normally instruct a member of our conveyancing panel but if you are instructed the appropriate provisions of this Handbook will apply.

16.3   Transfers of Equity

16.3.1   You must approve the transfer (which should be in the Land Registry's standard form) and, if we require, the deed of covenant on our behalf. Check part 2 to see if we have standard forms of transfer and deed of covenant. When drafting or approving a transfer, you should bear in mind that:

16.3.1.1   although the transfer should state that it is subject to the mortgage (identified by date and parties), it need give no details of the terms of the mortgage;

16.3.1.2   the transfer need not state the amount of the mortgage debt. If it does, the figure should include both principal and interest at the date of completion, which you must check (see part 2 for where to obtain this);

16.3.1.3   there should be no statement that all interest has been paid to date.

16.3.2   You must ensure that every person who will be a borrower after the transfer covenants with us to pay the money secured by the mortgage, except in the case of:

16.3.2.1   an original party to the mortgage (unless the mortgage conditions are being varied); or

16.3.2.2   a person who has previously covenanted to that effect.

16.3.3   Any such covenant will either be in the transfer or in a separate deed of covenant. In a transfer, the wording of the covenant should be as follows, or as close as circumstances permit: 'The new borrower agrees to pay the lender all the money due under the mortgage and will keep to all the terms of the mortgage.' If it is in the transfer, you must place a certified copy of the transfer with the deeds (unless we tell you not to in part 2).

16.3.4   If we have agreed to release a borrower or a guarantor and our standard transfer form (if any) includes no appropriate clause, you must add a simple form of release. The release clause should be as follows, or as close as circumstances permit: 'The lender releases ... from [his/her/their] obligations under the mortgage.' You should check whether a guarantor who is to be released was a party to the mortgage or to a separate guarantee.

16.3.5   You must obtain the consent of every guarantor of whom you are aware to the release of a borrower or, as the case may be, any other guarantor.

16.3.6   You must only submit the transfer to us for execution if it releases a party. All other parties must execute the transfer before it is sent to us. See part 2 for where the transfer should be sent for sealing. Part 2 also gives our approved form of attestation clause.

16.4   Properties to be Let after Completion (other than 'Buy to Let')

16.4.1   If after completion the Borrower informs you of an intention to let the property you should advise the borrower that any letting of the property is prohibited without our prior consent. If the borrower wishes to let the property after completion then an application for consent should be made to us by the borrower (see part 2). Check part 2 to see whether it is necessary to send to us a copy of the proposed tenancy when making the application.

16.4.2   If the application for our consent is approved and we instruct you to act for us, you must approve the form of tenancy agreement on our behalf in accordance with our instructions.

16.4.3   Please also note that:

16.4.3.1   an administration fee may be payable for our consideration of the application whether or not consent is granted; and

16.4.3.2   the proposed rent should cover the borrower's gross mortgage payments at the time; and

16.4.3.3   you should draw the borrower's attention to the fact that, under the terms of the mortgage, we may reserve the right to charge a higher rate of interest to the borrower or change the terms of the mortgage.

16.5   Deeds of Variation, etc.

16.5.1   If we consent to any proposal for a deed of variation, rectification, easement or option agreement, we will rely on you to approve the documents on our behalf.

16.5.2   Our consent will usually be forthcoming provided that you first of all confirm in writing to us (see part 2) that our security will not be adversely affected in any way by entering into the deed. If you are able to provide this confirmation then we will not normally need to see a draft of the deed. If you cannot provide confirmation and we need to consider the matter in detail then an additional administration fee is likely to be charged.

16.5.3   Whether we are a party to the deed or give a separate deed or form of consent is a matter for your discretion. It should be sent to us (see part 2) for sealing or signing with a brief explanation of the reason for the document and its effect together with your confirmation that it will not adversely affect our security.

16.6   Deeds of Postponement or Substitution

If we agree to enter into an arrangement with other lenders concerning the order of priority of their mortgages, you will be supplied with our standard form of deed or form of postponement or substitution. We will normally not agree to any amendments to the form. In no cases will we postpone our first charge over the property.

17. REDEMPTION

17.1   Redemption Statement

17.1.1   When requesting a redemption statement you should quote the expected repayment date and whether you are acting for the borrower or have the borrower's authority to request the redemption statement in addition to the information mentioned in paragraph 2.1. You should request this at least five working days before the expected redemption date. You must quote all the borrower's mortgage account or roll numbers of which you are aware when requesting the repayment figure. You must only request a redemption statement if you are acting for the borrower or have the borrower's written authority to request a redemption statement.

17.1.2   To guard against fraud please ensure that if payment is made by cheque then the redemption cheque is made payable to us and you quote the mortgage account number or roll number and name of the borrower.

17.2   Discharge

On the day of completion you should send the discharge and your remittance for the repayment to us (see part 2). Check part 2 to see if we discharge via a DS1 form or direct notification to the Land Registry.

APPENDIX 1 – PROFESSIONAL CONSULTANT'S CERTIFICATE

Return to:
Name of Applicant(s)
Full address of the property

I certify that:

1.   I have visited the site at appropriate periods from the commencement of construction to the current stage to check generally:

    (a) progress, and

    (b) conformity with drawings, approved under the building regulations, and

    (c) conformity with drawings/instructions properly issued under the building contract.

2.   At the stage of my last inspection on […], the property had reached the stage of […].

3.   So far as could be determined by each periodic visual inspection, the property has been generally constructed:

    (a) to a satisfactory standard, and

    (b) in general compliance with the drawings approved under the building regulations.

4.   I was originally retained by […] who is the applicant/builder/developer in this case (delete as appropriate).

5.   I am aware this certificate is being relied upon by the first purchaser […] of the property and also by […] (name of lender) when making a mortgage advance to that purchaser secured on this property.

6.   I confirm that I will remain liable for a period of 6 years from the date of this certificate. Such liability shall be to the first purchasers and their lenders and upon each sale of the property the remaining period shall be transferred to the subsequent purchasers and their lenders.

7.   I confirm that I have appropriate experience in the design and/or monitoring of the construction or conversion of residential buildings.

Name of Professional Consultant:
Qualifications:
Address:
Telephone No.:
Fax No.:
Professional Indemnity Insurer:

8.   The box below shows the minimum amount of professional indemnity insurance the consultant will keep in force to cover his liabilities under this certificate […] for any one claim or series of claims arising out of one event.

Signature:

Date:

VII. STAMP DUTY LAND TAX AND VAT

VII.1. Inland Revenue Statement of Practice on the sale of new houses[1]

SALE OF LAND WITH ASSOCIATED CONSTRUCTION, ETC., CONTRACT

We have been asked how to determine the chargeable consideration for Stamp Duty Land Tax purposes where V agrees to sell land to P and V also agrees to carry out work (commonly works of construction, improvement or repair) on the land sold. Our view is that the decision in *Prudential Assurance Co Ltd* v. *IRC* [1992] STC 863 applies for the purposes of Stamp Duty Land Tax as it does for stamp duty. This is because the basis of the decision was the identification of the subject matter of the transaction and this is as relevant for Stamp Duty Land Tax as it is for stamp duty.

It follows that SP8/93 will be applied for Stamp Duty Land Tax as it was for stamp duty. The paragraphs on 'contracts already entered into' and 'procedure for submitting documents' are, however, not relevant to Stamp Duty Land Tax.

Where, however, the sale of land and the construction, etc., contract are in substance one bargain (as they were in the *Prudential* case) there must be a just and reasonable apportionment of the total consideration given for all elements of the bargain in order to arrive at the chargeable consideration for Stamp Duty Land Tax purposes.

The SDLT Manual will be amended in due course to reflect this.

STAMP DUTY: NEW BUILDINGS

This Statement sets out the practice the Board of Inland Revenue will apply in relation to the stamp duty chargeable in certain circumstances on the conveyance or lease of a new or partly constructed building. It affects transactions where, at the date of the contract for sale or lease of a building plot, building work has not commenced or has been only partially completed on that site but where that work has started or has been completed at the time the conveyance or lease is executed.

This Statement reflects the advice the Board have received on this subject in the light of the decision in the case of *Prudential Assurance Company Limited* v. *IRC* ([1993] 1 WLR 211). The Statement does not apply to the common situation where the parties have entered into a contract for the sale of a new house and that contract is implemented by a conveyance of the whole property. This Statement replaces the Statements of Practice issued in 1957 and 1987 (SP 10/87) on this subject which are now withdrawn.

The Board are advised that, whilst each case will clearly depend on its own facts, the law is as follows:

1.   Two transactions/two contracts

Where the purchaser or lessee is entitled under the terms of a contract to a conveyance or lease of land alone in consideration of the purchase price or rent of the site and a second genuine contract for

---

1. 12 July 1993 (amended in 2003).

building works is entered into as a separate transaction, the ad valorem duty on the conveyance or lease will be determined by the amount of the purchase price or rent which the purchaser or lessee is obliged to pay under the terms of the first contract. In these circumstances it does not matter whether any building work has commenced at the date of the conveyance or lease. The consideration chargeable to ad valorem duty will still be only that passing for the land.

2.   One transaction/two contracts

Where there is one transaction between the parties but this is implemented by two contracts, one for the sale or lease of the building plot and one for the building works themselves, the amount of ad valorem duty charged on the instrument will depend on the amount of the consideration, which in turn will depend on whether those contracts can be shown to be genuinely independent of each other.

    (i)   If the two contracts are so interlocked that they cannot be said to be genuinely capable of independent completion (and in particular where if default occurs on either contract, the other is then not enforceable) ad valorem duty will be charged on the total consideration for the land and buildings, whether completed or not, as if the parties had entered into only one contract.

    (ii)   If the two contracts are shown to be genuinely independent of each other, ad valorem duty will be charged by reference to the consideration paid or payable for the land and any building works on that land at the date of execution of the instrument. It follows that, where the instrument is executed after the building works are completed, ad valorem duty will be charged on the consideration for the land and the completed building(s).

3.   Sham or artificial transactions

This Statement does not apply to cases where the transaction concerned, or any part of it, involves a sham or artificial transaction.

[Paragraphs 4 and 5 are deleted as they are not relevant to Stamp Duty Land Tax.]

VII.2. Stamp Duty Form 22: Apportionment of consideration under agreement for sale

	A		B
Amount of consideration payable in Cash or Bills	£	Legal Estates in Freehold Property	£
Amount of consideration payable in Shares, Debentures etc.	£	Fixed Plant and Machinery in Freehold Property	£
Liabilities assumed by the Purchaser:		Legal Estates in Leasehold Property	£
Amounts due on mortgages of Freeholds and/or Leaseholds, including interest to date of sale	£	Fixed Plant and Machinery in Leasehold Property	£
Hire Purchase Debts for Goods acquired	£	Equitable interests in Freehold or Leasehold Property	£
Other liabilities of the Vendor	£	Loose Plant and Machinery, Stock-in-Trade and other Chattels	£
		(Only Plant and Machinery in an actual state of severance, i.e. not fixed to the premises at the date of the Agreement for Sale, must be included in this figure)	
Any other consideration	£	Goods, Wares and Merchandise subject to Hire Purchase Agreements (Written Down Value)	£
		Goodwill and Benefit of Contracts	£
		Patents, Designs, Trade Marks, Licences, etc.	£
		Book Debts	£
		Cash in Hand and at Bank on Current Account	£
		Cash on Deposit	£
		Shares, Debentures and other investments	£
Please note that Column A should equal Column B.		Other property viz	£
	£		£

I hereby certify that the particulars shown in this form are in every respect fully and truly stated according to the best of my judgment and belief, and that the Loose Plant and Machinery included in the above apportionment were in a state of severance at the date of the sale agreement.

This certificate should be signed by the Vendor or Purchaser (the Secretary in the case of a Company) or by an Accountant or Solicitor acting in the sale.

Signed .... Address ....

Date ....

VII.3. HM Revenue and Customs SDLT Manual – Fixtures and fittings[1]

For an item to be regarded as a fixture or part of the land and therefore chargeable to tax, as opposed to a chattel or moveable in Scotland which is not chargeable, it must be annexed to the property.

The issue will then turn on the degree and purpose of the annexation, with emphasis being placed in many cases to purpose.

Where a purchaser agrees to buy a property for a price that includes an amount properly attributed to chattels or moveables, that amount will not be charged to stamp duty land tax.

Under stamp duty land tax a purchaser is responsible for the accurate completion of their land transaction return, including the entry for the consideration of the land transaction at box 10 in form SDLT1.

By virtue of FA03/SCH4/PARA4 a just and reasonable apportionment is required where a price is paid partly for a land transaction and partly for a non-land transaction such as the purchase of chattels.

It does not matter that the parties to a transaction may agree a particular apportionment which is then documented in the contract. The apportionment will not be correct unless it was arrived at on a just and reasonable basis.

HM Revenue and Customs has the right to make enquiries into the accuracy of a land transaction return. See SDLTM80800+.

The apportionment of the purchase price may well be one aspect on which an enquiry may be opened.

Similarly it is quite possible that we will also undertake enquiries into cases where a deduction has been made for chattels to confirm that those items properly fall within the definition of chattels.

HM Revenue and Customs is unable to provide a comprehensive list of items that are accepted as chattels or moveables. This is because each case must be considered on its own merits and because this is an area of the law that continues to evolve.

The following items are, however, confirmed as being assets that will normally be regarded as chattels

- carpets (fitted or otherwise)
- curtains and blinds
- free standing furniture
- kitchen white goods
- electric and gas fires (provided that they can be removed by disconnection from the power supply without causing damage to the property)

---

1. Crown copyright.

- light shades and fittings (unless recessed)

On the other hand, the following items will not normally be regarded as chattels

- fitted kitchen units, cupboards and sinks

- agas and wall mounted ovens

- fitted bathroom sanitary ware

- central heating systems

- intruder alarm systems

Externally, any plants, shrubs or trees growing in the soil which forms part of the land, are not to be regarded as chattels.

A deduction would, however, be appropriate for amounts properly apportioned to any plants growing in pots or containers.

The above guidance is written primarily in the context of sales of residential property.

HM Revenue and Customs is advised that the same principles will apply when considering the purchase of industrial or commercial property in which the sale may also involve the acquisition of plant, machinery or equipment.

Tenants fixtures

The question of whether plant or machinery is a fixture or a chattel is determined in the same way as for any other asset.

In particular tenants fixtures in England, Wales and Northern Ireland are fixtures and therefore part of the land, notwithstanding that a tenant may have a right to sever them.

The tenant's right of severance is also a chargeable interest within the meaning of FA03/S48(1).

While each case depends on its own facts it is unlikely that plant or machinery that can be relatively easily severed from the property to which it is fixed, for example by the simple expedient of removing some bolts securing it to the floor or walls, will be a fixture.

Alternatively heavy plant or machinery that is integral to a building, or plant or machinery whose removal would damage the building or land, is likely to be a fixture.

It follows therefore that escalators and elevators, boilers, furnaces, walk-in refrigerators and restaurant cooking stations are likely to be fixtures.

VII.4. Stamp Duty (Exempt Instruments) Regulations 1987 (SI 1987/516)[1]

1987 No. 516

TAXES

The Stamp Duty (Exempt Instruments) Regulations 1987

Made 24th March 1987
Laid before the House of Commons 26th March 1987
Coming into force 1st May 1987

Note. – FA 1985, s. 87 (2) provides that instruments which would otherwise be chargeable with stamp duty of a fixed amount under any provision specified in regulations shall not be so charged if they are of a kind specified in regulations and certified to be instruments of that kind.

These regulations specify the provisions under which, subject to conditions, that duty shall not be charged; specify the instruments (executed on or after 1 May 1987) in relation to which the exemption is available; and provide for the certification requirements.

Regulation 1 provides the title and commencement date.

Regulation 2 provides the conditions for the exemption.

Regulation 3 provides for the requirements for the certificate and the conditions which have to be fulfilled.

Regulation 4 introduces the Schedule which specifies the instruments which may qualify for the exemption provided by regulation 2.

Regulation 5 dispenses with the requirement of adjudication in accordance with the Stamp Act 1891, s. 12 as required by FA 1985, ss. 82(5) and 84(9).

The Treasury, in exercise of the powers conferred on them by section 87(2) of the Finance Act 1985, hereby make the following regulations:

1. These regulations may be cited as the Stamp Duty (Exempt Instruments) Regulations 1987 and shall come into force on 1st May 1987.

In these Regulations 'life policy' means –

(a) any policy of insurance on a human life, or on the happening of a contingency dependent upon a human life, except a policy of insurance for a payment only upon the death of a person otherwise than from a natural cause, or

(b) a grant or contract for the payment of an annuity upon a human life.

---

1. Incorporating amendments made by Stamp Duty (Exempt Instruments) (Amendments) Regulations 1999 (SI 1999/2539) and Tax and Civil Partnership (No.2) Regulations 2005 (SI 2005/3230).

2.   (1)   An instrument which –

   (a)   is executed on or after 1st May 1987,

   (b)   is of a kind specified in the Schedule hereto for the purposes of this regulation, and

   (c)   is certified by a certificate which fulfils the conditions of regulation 3 to be an instrument of that kind,

shall be exempt from duty under the provisions specified in paragraph (2) of this regulation.

   (2)   The provisions specified are –

   (a)   the following paragraphs of Part III of Schedule 13 to the Finance Act 1999 –

   (i)   paragraph 16 (conveyance or transfer otherwise than on sale),

   (ii)   paragraph 17 (declaration of use or trust),

   (iii)   paragraph 18 (dispositions in Scotland);

   (b)   sections 83(2) and 84(8) of the Finance Act 1985.

3.   The certificate –

   (a)   shall be in writing and –

   (i)   be included as part of the instrument, or

   (ii)   be endorsed upon or, where separate, be physically attached to the instrument concerned;

   (b)   shall contain a sufficient description of –

   (i)   the instrument concerned where the certificate is separate but physically attached to the instrument, and

   (ii)   the category in the Schedule hereto into which the instrument falls;

   (c)   (i)   shall be signed by the transferor or grantor or by his solicitor or duly authorised agent, and

   (ii)   where it is not signed by the transferor or grantor or by his solicitor, it shall contain a statement by the signatory of the capacity in which he signs, that he is authorised so to sign and that he gives the certificate from his own knowledge of the facts stated in it.

4.   The Schedule to these regulations shall have effect for the specification of instruments for the purposes of regulation 2.

5.   An instrument which is certified in accordance with these regulations shall not be required under section 82(5) or section 84(9) of the Finance Act 1985 to be stamped in accordance with section 12 of the Stamp Act 1891 with a particular stamp denoting that it is duly stamped or that it is not chargeable with any duty.

SCHEDULE

Regulation 4

An instrument which effects any one or more of the following transactions only is an instrument specified for the purposes of regulation 2 –

A.   The vesting of property subject to a trust in the trustees of the trust on the appointment of a new trustee, or in the continuing trustees on the retirement of a trustee.

B.   The conveyance or transfer of property the subject of a specific devise or legacy to the beneficiary named in the will (or his nominee).

C.   The conveyance or transfer of property which forms part of an intestate's estate to the person entitled on intestacy (or his nominee).

D.   The appropriation of property within section 84(4) of the Finance Act 1985 (death: appropriation in satisfaction of a general legacy of money) or section 84(5) or (7) of that Act (death: appropriation in satisfaction of any interest of surviving spouse or civil partner and in Scotland also of any interest of issue).

E.   The conveyance or transfer of property which forms part of the residuary estate of a testator to a beneficiary (or his nominee) entitled solely by virtue of his entitlement under the will.

F.   The conveyance or transfer of property out of a settlement in or towards satisfaction of a beneficiary's interest, not being an interest acquired for money or money's worth, being a conveyance or transfer constituting a distribution of property in accordance with the provisions of the settlement.

G.   The conveyance or transfer of property on and in consideration only of marriage to a party to the marriage (or his nominee) or to trustees to be held on the terms of a settlement made in consideration only of the marriage.

GG.   The conveyance or transfer of property on and in consideration only of the formation of a civil partnership to a party to the civil partnership (or his nominee) or to trustees to be held on the terms of a settlement made in consideration only of the civil partnership.

H.   The conveyance or transfer of property within section 83(1) or (1A) of the Finance Act 1985 (transfers in connection with divorce or dissolution of civil partnership etc.).

I.   The conveyance or transfer by the liquidator of property which formed part of the assets of the company in liquidation to a shareholder of that company (or his nominee) in or towards satisfaction of the shareholder's rights on a winding-up.

J.   The grant in fee simple of an easement in or over land for no consideration in money or money's worth.

K.   The grant of a servitude for no consideration in money or money's worth.

L.   The conveyance or transfer of property operating as a voluntary disposition inter vivos for no consideration in money or money's worth nor any consideration referred to in section 57 of the Stamp Act 1891 (conveyance in consideration of a debt etc.).

M.   The conveyance or transfer of property by an instrument within section 84(1) of the Finance Act 1985 (death: varying disposition).

N.   The declaration of any use or trust of or concerning a life policy, or property representing, or benefits arising under, a life policy.

VII.5. HM Customs Statement of Practice: variations of leases of commercial property[1]

HM Customs and Excise have published the following revised Statement of Practice which will apply in circumstances where a deemed surrender and re-grant occur by operation of law.

'(A)   Where there is no monetary consideration passing from lessor to lessee as a result of or in connection with the variation, then Customs Policy is that there is no surrender of the old lease for non-monetary consideration when:

   (i)   the new lease is for the same building (or the same part of the building) but the new lease is for an extended term; or

   (ii)   the new lease is for a larger part of the same building than the old lease but the term is for the same or an extended term; or

   (iii) the new lease is for the same land and for an extended term.

   However, (i)–(iii) above do not embrace 'new for old' ground leases or building leases, i.e. leases granted on condition that the lessee will undertake development. Very often, the negotiations between the parties will result in agreement for demolition of an old building and the construction of a new one, or partial demolition and reconstruction or enlargement. In the case of these ground/building leases and in any other cases not covered above, Customs would expect to find that the terms of the new lease will be more favourable to the lessee as a result of the surrender of the old lease. They would be likely to rule that the old lease was being surrendered in consideration of the grant of the new on favourable terms and that the surrender supply by the lessee should be valued at its open market value. Where there is doubt, the position should be discussed with Customs.

(B)   Where the surrender and re-grant involves ground leases or building leases, i.e. leases granted on condition that the lessee will undertake development, very often the negotiations between the parties will result in demolition of an old building and the construction of a new one, or partial demolition and reconstruction or enlargement. Customs may find that the terms of the new lease will be more favourable to both the lessee and the lessor but do not consider this in itself indicates that the old lease was surrendered in consideration of the grant of the new one. However, if the lessee receives a direct benefit in return for undertaking the construction works (e.g. a rent-free period, or reduced rent for a period) Customs are likely to see a consideration passing from the lessee to the lessor in return for the benefit. In cases where there is doubt you should agree the position with Customs.

(C)   Where monetary consideration passes from lessor to lessee, Customs would normally regard the monetary consideration as the sole consideration for the surrender.

---

1. First published [1991] *Gazette*, 1 May, 16, and revised version published as A16.9.3 in the Law Society's *Conveyancing Handbook*, seventh edition.

Where monetary consideration passes to the lessor from the lessee Customs would normally see this as consideration for the grant of the new lease which would be exempt subject to the lessor's election to waive exemption (option to tax). However, the circumstances may indicate that the payment is consideration for the lessor's supply of the acceptance of the surrender of an onerous lease from the lessee (sometimes known as a reverse surrender). From 1 March 1995, we say these payments are for an exempt supply, with the option to tax. When the payment received by the lessor is seen as consideration for the grant of a new lease, there would be no surrender by the lessee.'

VIII. DIRECTORY

VIII.1. Land Registry addresses

The Land Registry will reject applications that are sent to the wrong office. To determine which area is served by which office, see Land Registry Practice Guide 51 (available at **www.landregistry.gov.uk**).

Land Registry Head Office

32 Lincoln's Inn Fields
London WC2A 3PH

Tel: 020 7917 8888
Fax (for correspondence only): 020 7955 0110
DX: 1098 London/Chancery Lane

Birkenhead (Rosebrae)

Land Registry
Birkenhead (Rosebrae) Office
Rosebrae Court
Woodside Ferry Approach
Birkenhead
Merseyside CH41 6DU

Tel: 0151 472 6666
Fax: 0151 472 6789
DX: 24270 Birkenhead (4)

Birkenhead (Old Market)

Land Registry
Birkenhead (Old Market) Office
Old Market House
Hamilton Street
Birkenhead
Merseyside CH41 5FL

Tel: 0151 473 1110
Fax: 0151 473 0251
DX: 14300 Birkenhead (3)

Coventry

Land Registry
Coventry Office
Leigh Court
Torrington Avenue
Tile Hill
Coventry CV4 9XZ

Tel: 024 7686 0860
Fax: 024 7686 0021
DX: 18900 Coventry (3)

Croydon

Land Registry
Croydon Office
Sunley House
Bedford Park
Croydon CR9 3LE

Tel: 020 8781 9103
Fax: 020 8781 9110
DX: 2699 Croydon (3)

Durham (Boldon)

Land Registry
Durham (Boldon) Office
Boldon House
Wheatlands Way
Pity Me
Durham DH1 5GJ

Tel: 0191 301 2345
Fax: 0191 301 2300
DX: 60860 Durham (6)

VIII

Durham (Southfield)

Land Registry
Durham (Southfield) Office
Southfield House
Southfield Way
Durham DH1 5TR

Tel: 0191 301 3500
Fax: 0191 301 0020
DX: 60200 Durham (3)

Gloucester

Land Registry
Gloucester Office
Twyver House
Bruton Way
Gloucester GL1 1DQ

Tel: 01452 511111
Fax: 01452 510050
DX: 7599 Gloucester (3)

Harrow

Land Registry
Harrow Office
Lyon House
Lyon Road
Harrow
Middlesex HA1 2EU

Tel: 020 8235 1181
Fax: 020 8862 0176
DX: 4299 Harrow (4)

Kingston Upon Hull

Land Registry
Kingston Upon Hull Office
Earle House
Colonial Street
Hull HU2 8JN

Tel: 01482 223244
Fax: 01482 224278
DX: 26700 Hull (4)

Lancashire

Land Registry
Lancashire Office
Wrea Brook Court
Lytham Road
Warton
Lancashire PR4 1TE

Tel: 01772 836700
Fax: 01772 836970
DX: 721560 Lytham St Annes (6)

Leicester

Land Registry
Leicester Office
Westbridge Place
Leicester LE3 5DR
Tel: 0116 265 4000

Fax: 0116 265 4008
DX: 11900 Leicester (5)

Lytham

Land Registry
Lytham Office
Birkenhead House, East Beach
Lytham St Annes
Lancashire FY8 5AB

Tel: 01253 849849
Fax: 01253 840001
DX: 14500 Lytham St Annes (3)

Nottingham (East)

Land Registry
Nottingham (East) Office
Robins Wood Road
Nottingham NG8 3RQ

Tel: 0115 906 5353
Fax: 0115 936 0036
DX: 716126 Nottingham (26)

Nottingham (West)

Land Registry
Nottingham (West) Office
Chalfont Drive
Nottingham NG8 3RN

Tel: 0115 935 1166
Fax: 0115 935 0038
DX: 10298 Nottingham (3)

Peterborough

Land Registry
Peterborough Office
Touthill Close
City Road
Peterborough PE1 1XN

Tel: 01733 288288
Fax: 01733 280022
DX: 12598 Peterborough (4)

Plymouth

Land Registry
Plymouth Office
Plumer House
Tailyour Road
Crownhill
Plymouth PL6 5HY

Tel: 01752 636000
Fax: 01752 636161
DX: 8299 Plymouth (4)

Portsmouth

Land Registry
Portsmouth Office
St Andrew's Court
St Michael's Road
Portsmouth
Hampshire PO1 2JH

Tel: 023 9276 8888
Fax: 023 9276 8768
DX: 83550 Portsmouth (2)

Stevenage

Land Registry
Stevenage Office
Brickdale House
Swingate
Stevenage
Hertfordshire SG1 1XG

Tel: 01438 788889
Fax: 01438 785460
DX: 6099 Stevenage (2)

Swansea (Titles in England)

Land Registry
Swansea Office
Ty Bryn Glas
High Street
Swansea SA1 1PW

Tel: 01792 458877
Fax: 01792 473236
DX: 33700 Swansea (2)

Telford

Land Registry
Telford Office
Parkside Court
Hall Park Way
Telford TF3 4LR

Tel: 01952 290355
Fax: 01952 290356
DX: 28100 Telford (2)

Tunbridge Wells

Land Registry
Tunbridge Wells Office
Forest Court
Forest Road
Tunbridge Wells
Kent TN2 5AQ

Tel: 01892 510015
Fax: 01892 510032
DX: 3999 Tunbridge Wells (2)

Wales/Cymru (Titles in Wales)

Land Registry
Wales Office
Ty Cwm Tawe
Phoenix Way
Llansamlet
Swansea SA7 9FQ

Tel: 01792 355000
Fax: 01792 355055
DX: 82800 Swansea (2)

Weymouth

Land Registry
Weymouth Office
Melcombe Court
1 Cumberland Drive
Weymouth
Dorset DT4 9TT

Tel: 01305 363636
Fax: 01305 363646
DX: 8799 Weymouth (2)

York

Land Registry
York Office
James House
James Street
York YO10 3YZ

Tel: 01904 450000
Fax: 01904 450086
DX: 61599 York (2)

VIII.2. All other addresses

AIG Europe (UK) Ltd

The AIG Building
58 Fenchurch Street
London EC3M 4AB

Tel: 020 7954 7000
Fax: 020 7954 7001
www.aigeurope.co.uk

Association of British Insurers

51 Gresham Street
London EC2V 7HQ

Tel: 020 7600 3333
Fax: 020 7696 8999
www.abi.org.uk

BRB (Residuary) Ltd (formerly British Railways Board)

Whittles House
14 Pentonville Road
London N1 9HF

Tel: 020 7904 5079
www.brb.gov.uk

British Gas

Head Office

Centrica plc
Millstream
Maidenhead Road
Windsor
Berkshire SL4 5GD

Tel: 01753 494 000
Fax: 01753 494 001
www.centrica.co.uk

British Geological Survey

Kingsley Dunham Centre
Keyworth
Nottingham NG12 5GG

Tel: 0115 936 3100
Fax: 0115 936 3200
www.bgs.ac.uk

British Property Federation

7th Floor
1 Warwick Row
London SW1E 5ER

Tel: 020 7828 0111
Fax: 020 7834 3442
www.bpf org.uk

British Sugar plc

Sugar Way
Peterborough PE2 9AY

Tel: 01733 563 171
Fax: 01733 422 967
www.britishsugar.co.uk

British Waterways Board (BWB)

Head Office

Willow Grange
Church Road
Watford
Herts WD17 4QA

Tel: 01923 201 120
Fax: 01923 201 400
www.britishwaterways.co.uk

Regional Offices

London
British Waterways London
1 Sheldon Square
Paddington Central
London W2 6TT

Tel: 020 7985 7200
Fax: 020 7985 7201

Northern
East Midlands
The Kiln
Mather Road
Newark NG24 1FB

Tel: 01636 704 481
Fax: 01636 705 584

VIII

North West
Waterside House
Waterside Drive
Wigan WN3 5AZ

Tel: 01942 405700
Fax: 01942 405710

Wales and Border Counties
Navigation Road
Northwich
Cheshire CW8 1BH

Tel: 01606 723800
Fax: 01606 871471

Yorkshire
Fearns Wharf
Neptune Street
Leeds LS9 8PB

Tel: 0113 281 6800
Fax: 0113 281 6886

Southern
South East
Ground Floor
Witan Gate House
500–600 Witan Gate
Milton Keynes MK9 1BW

Tel: 01908 302500
Fax: 01908 302510

South West
Harbour House
West Quay
The Dock
Gloucester GL1 2LG

Tel: 01452 318000
Fax: 01452 318076

West Midlands
Peel's Wharf
Lichfield Street
Fazeley
Tamworth
Staffordshire B78 3QZ

Tel: 01827 252 000
Fax: 01827 288 071

The Charity Commission

Charity Commission Direct
PO Box 1227
Liverpool L69 3UG

Tel: 0845 3000 218
Fax: 0151 7031 555
www.charity-commission.gov.uk

Chatham House

10 St James's Square
London SW1Y 4LE

Tel: 020 7957 5700
Fax: 020 7957 5710
www.chathamhouse.org.uk

Cheshire Brine Subsidence Compensation Board

Cheshire County Council Property
Management Services,
Richard House
80 Lower Bridge Street
Chester CH1 1FW

Tel: 01244 602 576
DX: 717532 Chester (15)

Church Commissioners for England

Church House
Great Smith Street
Westminster
London SW1P 3AZ

Tel: 020 7898 1000
www.cofe.anglican.org/about/
churchcommissioners/

Coal Authority

Mining Reports Dept
200 Lichfield Lane
Mansfield
Nottinghamshire NG18 4RG

Tel: 0845 762 6848
www.coal.gov.uk
www.coal.gov.uk/services/miningreports/
index.cfm

Companies House

Contact Centre
Tel: 0870 3333 636

Main Office

Companies House
Crown Way
Maindy
Cardiff CF14 3UZ

DX: 33050 Cardiff
www.companieshouse.gov.uk

Cornish Mines and Property Surveys Ltd

22 New Bridge Street
Truro
Cornwall TR1 2AA

Tel/Fax: 01872 272 720

Cornwall Consultants Ltd

Parc Vean House
Coach Lane
Redruth
Cornwall TR15 2TT

Tel: 01209 313 511
Fax: 01209 313 512
www.cornwallconsultants.co.uk

Council for Licensed Conveyancers

16 Glebe Road
Chelmsford
Essex CM1 1QG

Tel: 01245 349 599
Fax: 01245 341 300
DX: 121925 Chelmsford (6)
www.theclc.gov.uk

Council of Mortgage Lenders

Bush House
North West Wing
Aldwych
London WC2B 4PJ

Tel: 0845 373 6771 (switchboard)
Tel: 020 7438 8956 (consumer information)
Fax: 0845 373 6778
www.cml.org.uk

Countrywide Legal Indemnities

St Crispins
Duke Street
Norwich NR3 1PD

Tel: 01603 617 617
Fax: 01603 622 933
DX: 5261 Norwich
www.countrywidelegal.co.uk

Court of Protection

Public Guardianship Office
Court of Protection
Archway Tower
2 Junction Road
London N19 5SZ

Tel: 0845 330 2900
Fax: 0870 739 5780
DX: 141150 Archway (2)
www.guardianship.gov.uk

Crown Estate

Headquarters
16 New Burlington Place
London W1S 2HX

Tel: 020 7851 5000
Fax: 020 7851 5125
www.crownestate.co.uk

Document Exchange

DX Network Services Ltd
DX House
Ridgeway
Iver
Buckinghamshire SL0 9JQ

Tel: 01753 630 630
Fax: 01753 631 631
DX: Iver (1)
www.thedx.co.uk

Domestic Energy Assessor (DEA) Accreditation

Buildings Research Establishment (BRE)
Bucknalls Lane
Watford WD25 9XX

Tel: 01923 664000
www.breassessor.co.uk

Elmhurst Energy Systems Ltd
Unit 16
St Johns Business Park
Lutterworth
Leicestershire LE17 4HB

Tel: 08700 850490
www.elmhurstenergy.co.uk

NHER
National Energy Centre
Davy Avenue
Knowhill
Milton Keynes MK5 8NA

Tel: 01908 540605
www.nher.co.uk

Northgate Information Solutions
Peoplebuilding 2
Peoplebuilding Estate
Maylands Avenue
Hemel Hempstead
Hertfordshire HP2 4NW

Tel: 01442 232 424
www.northgate-ispublicservices.com

Royal Institution of Chartered Surveyors
12 Great George Street
Parliament Square
London SW1P 3AD

Tel: 0870 333 1600
www.rics.org/hips

Drinking Water Inspectorate

55 Whitehall
London SW1A 2EY

Tel: 020 7082 8024
Fax: 020 7082 8028
www.dwi.gov.uk

Duchy of Cornwall

10 Buckingham Gate
London SW1E 6LA

Tel: 020 7834 7346
Fax: 020 7931 9541
www.duchyofcornwall.org

Duchy of Lancaster

Lancaster Place
Strand
London WC2E 7ED

Tel: 020 7269 1700
Fax: 020 7269 1710
www.duchyoflancaster.org.uk

**Electricity companies – General informa-
tion on energy network sector**

Energy Networks Association
18 Stanhope Place
Marble Arch
London W2 2HH

Tel: 020 7706 5100
www.energynetworks.org

Electricity distribution companies

CE Electric UK

www.ceelectricuk.com

Northern Electricity Distribution Ltd
Manor House
Station Road
New Penshaw
Houghton-le-Spring DH4 7LA
Tel: 0845 070 7172

Yorkshire Electricity Distribution
161 Gelderd Road
Leeds LS1 1QZ

Tel: 0845 602 4454

edf energy networks
40 Grosvenor Place
Victoria
London SW1X 7EN

Tel: 020 7242 9050
www.edfenergy.com

e-on/central networks
Central Networks
Herald Way
Pegasus Business Park
East Midlands Airport
Castle Donington DE74 2TU

Tel: 0800 096 3080 (Eastern Region)
Tel: 08457 353 637 (Western Region)
www.eon-uk.com

Manx Electricity Authority
PO Box 177
Douglas
Isle of Man IM99 1PS

Tel: 01624 687 687
Fax: 01624 687 612
www.gov.im/mea

Powergen
PO Box 7750
Nottingham NG1 6WR

Tel: 0800 052 0346
www.powergen.co.uk

RWE npower
Windmill Hill Business Park
Whitehill Way
Swindon
SN5 6PB

Tel: 01793 877 777
Fax: 01793 892 525
www.rwenpower.com

Scottish and Southern Energy plc
Inveralmond House
200 Dunkeld Road
Perth PH1 3AQ

Tel: 01738 456 000
www.scottish-southern.co.uk

Scottish Power Energy Networks (For England
and Wales)
Sp EnergyNetworks
PO Box 168
Prenton CH26 9AY

Tel: 0845 272 4444
www.spenergynetworks.net

United Utilities
Haweswater House
Lingley Mere Business Park
Great Sankey
Warrington WA5 3LP

Tel: 01925 237 000
Fax: 01925 237 073

Western Power Distribution
Avonbank
Feeder Road
St Philip's
Bristol BS2 0TB

Tel: 0117 933 2000
www.westernpower.co.uk

Energy Watch

Head Office

4th Floor
Artillery House
Artillery Row
London SW1P 1RT

Tel: 0845 906 0708
Fax: 020 7799 8341
www.energywatch.org.uk

Regional Offices

Central
Civic House
156 Great Charles Street
Birmingham B3 3HN

Tel: 0845 906 0708

South
5th Floor
Heron House
8–10 Christchurch Road
Bournemouth BH1 3NA

Tel: 0845 906 0708

Wales
5th Floor (West Wing)
St David's House
Wood Street
Cardiff CF10 1ER

Tel: 0845 906 0708

London & South East
3rd Floor
Artillery House
Artillery Row
London SW1P 1RT

Tel: 0845 906 0708

North East (business enquiries)
8th Floor
Percy House
Percy Street
Newcastle upon Tyne NE1 4PW

Tel: 0845 906 0708

Scotland
Delta House
50 West Nile Street
Glasgow G1 2NP

Tel: 0845 906 0708

Environment Agency

National Customer Contact Centre (NCCC)
PO Box 544
Templeborough
Rotherham S60 1BY

Tel: 08708 506 506
www.environment-agency.gov.uk

GroundSure Ltd

Level 7
New England House
New England Street
Brighton BN1 4GH

Tel: 01273 819 500
Fax: 01273 819 550
DX: 30262 Brighton Preston Rd
www.groundsure.com

Health Protection Agency (HPA)

Central Office
7th Floor
Holborn Gate
330 High Holborn
London WC1V 7PP

Tel: 020 7759 2700/1
Fax: 020 7759 2733
www.hpa.org.uk

Home Information Pack providers and organisations

Association of Home Information Pack Providers (AHIPP)
55 The Ridgeway
Market Harborough
Leicestershire
LE16 7HG

Tel: 0870 950 7739
www.hipassociation.co.uk

Independent Property Codes Adjudication Scheme (IPCAS)
24 Angel Gate
City Road
London EC1V 2PT

Tel: 020 7520 3810
www.idrs.ltd.uk

Law Society Home Information Pack
113 Chancery Lane
London WC2A 1PL

Tel: 0870 606 2522
www.hips.lawsociety.org.uk

Property Codes Compliance Board (PCCB)
212 Piccadilly
London W1J 9HG

Tel: 020 7917 1817
www.propertycodes.org.uk

Home Inspector Register and Certification Schemes

Buildings Research Establishment (BRE)
Bucknalls Lane
Watford WD25 9XX

Tel: 01923 664000
www.bre.co.uk

Royal Institution of Chartered Surveyors
12 Great George Street
Parliament Square
London SW1P 3AD

Tel: 0870 333 1600
www.rics.org/hips

SAVA Certification Scheme
The National Energy Centre
Davy Avenue
Knowlhill
Milton Keynes MK5 8NA

Tel: 01908 540605
www.sava-cs.org.uk

HM Courts Service Headquarters

Customer Service Unit
5th Floor
Clive House
Petty France
London SW1H 9HD

Tel: 020 7189 2000/0845 456 8770
Fax: 020 7189 2732

HM Revenue and Customs (Capital Taxes)

Ferrers House
PO Box 38
Castle Meadow Road
Nottingham NG2 1BB

Tel: 0845 302 0900
DX: 701201 Nottingham-4 (non-cash)
DX: 701205 Nottingham-4 (cash)
DX: 701202 Nottingham-4 (pre-grant)
www.hmrc.gov.uk/cto/iht.htm

HM Revenue and Customs Stamp Offices

Land Transaction Returns

HMRC Stamp Taxes
Comben House
Farriers Way
Netherton
Merseyside L30 4RN

DX: 725593 Bootle (9)

Stamp Taxes General Correspondence

Customer Service Manager
Birmingham Stamp Office
9th Floor
City Centre House
30 Union Street
Birmingham B2 4AR

Tel: 0845 603 0135
Fax: 0121 643 8381
DX: 15001 Birmingham (1)
www.hmrc.gov.uk/so/contact/index.htm

SDLT

Customer Service Manager
Birmingham Stamp Office
9th Floor
City Centre
30 Union Street
Birmingham B2 4AR

Tel: 0845 603 0135
Fax: 0121 643 8381
DX: 15001 Birmingham (1)
www.hmrc.gov.uk/so/contact/index.htm

Written Enquiries on Complex Transactions and COP 10 Ruling

Stamp Taxes Complex Transaction Unit
Upper Fifth Floor
Royal Exchange
Exchange Street
Manchester
M2 7EB

Tel: 0161 834 8109/8024
DX: 719821 Manchester (2)

Pre-December 2003 stamp duty

Edinburgh Stamp Office
Grayfield House
Spur X
4 Bankhead Avenue
Edinburgh EH11 4BF

Tel: 0131 442 3161
Fax: 0131 442 3038
DX: ED543303 Edinburgh (33)

VIII

Local Offices

Birmingham Stamp Office
See under Stamp Taxes General Correspondence, *above*

Bristol Stamp Office
The Pithay
All Saints Street
Bristol BS1 2NY

Tel: 0117 927 2022
DX: 7899 Bristol (1)

Edinburgh Stamp Office
See under Pre-December 2003 stamp duty

Manchester Stamp Office
See under Written Enquiries on Complex Transactions etc, above

Newcastle Stamp Office
15th Floor
Cale Cross House
156 Pilgrim Street
Newcastle upon Tyne NE1 6TF

Tel: 0191 261 7839
Fax: 0191 261 7644
DX: 61021 Newcastle upon Tyne (1)

Imerys Minerals Ltd

Par Moor Centre
Par Moor Road
Par PL24 2SQ

Tel: 01726 818 093
www.imerys.com

Insolvency Practitioners Control Unit

The Insolvency Service
5th Floor
Ladywood House
45/46 Stephenson Street
Birmingham B2 4UZ

Tel: 0121 698 4000
Fax: 0121 698 4095
DX: 713895 Birmingham (37)
www.insolvency.gov.uk

Institute of Legal Executives

Kempston Manor
Kempston MK42 7AB

Tel: 01234 841 000
Fax: 01234 840 373
DX: 124780 Kempston (2)
www.ilex.org.uk

Kaolin and Ball Clay Association Ltd

Tehidy Centre
Burngullow Lane
High Street
St Austell PL26 7TQ

Tel: 01726 828 517
Fax: 01726 828 523

LABC New Home Warranty

MD Insurance Services Ltd
Haymarket Court
Hinson Street
Birkenhead
Wirral CH41 5BX

Tel: 0845 054 0505
www.labcnewhomewarranty.co.uk

Land Charges Department (the Land Registry)

Plumer House
Tailyour Road
Crownhill
Plymouth PL6 5HY

Tel: 01752 636 666
Fax: 01752 636 699
DX: 8249 Plymouth (3)
www.landreg.gov.uk

Landmark Information Group Ltd

5–7 Abbey Court
Eagle Way
Sowton Industrial Estate
Exeter EX2 7HY

Tel: 01392 441 700
Fax: 01392 441 709
DX: 149460 Exeter (23)
www.landmark-information.co.uk

Land Registry, Independent Adjudicator

The Adjudicator to HM Land Registry
Procession House
55 Ludgate Hill
London EC4M 7JW

Tel: 020 7029 9860
Fax: 020 7029 9801
www.ahmlr.gov.uk

Lands Tribunal

In person

Procession House
110 New Bridge Street
London EC4V 6JL

By post

Procession House
55 Ludgate Hill
London EC4M 7JW

Tel: 020 7029 9780
Fax: 020 7029 9781
www.landstribunal.gov.uk

Law Society of England and Wales

113 Chancery Lane
London WC2A 1PL

Tel: 020 7242 1222 (switchboard)
Tel: 0870 606 2522 (practice advice)
DX: 56 London/Chancery Lane
www.lawsociety.org.uk

Legal Complaints Service

Victoria Court
8 Dormer Place
Leamington Spa
Warwickshire CV32 5AE

Tel: 01926 820 082
Fax: 01926 431 435
www.legalcomplaints.org.uk

Local Government Association

Local Government House
Smith Square
London SW1P 3HZ

Tel: 020 7664 3131
Fax: 020 7664 3030
www.lga.gov.uk

Mutual Societies Registration

Financial Services Authority
25 The North Colonnade
Canary Wharf
London E14 5HS

Tel: 020 7066 1000
Fax: 020 7066 1099
www.fsa.gov.uk

National Archives

Kew
Richmond
Surrey TW9 4DU

Tel: 020 8876 3444
www.nationalarchives.gov.uk

National Association of Estate Agents

Arbon House
21 Jury Street
Warwick CV34 4EH

Tel: 01926 496 800
Fax: 01926 400 953
www.naea.co.uk

National House Building Council (NHBC)

Main Offices

Buildmark House
Chiltern Avenue
Amersham HP6 5AP

Tel: 01494 735 363
Fax: 01494 723 530
DX: 50712 Amersham
www.nhbc.co.uk

VIII

NHBC House
Davy Avenue
Knowlhill
Milton Keynes MK5 8FP

Tel: 0870 241 4302
Fax: 0870 241 4759

Satellite Office

London
Candlewick House
120 Cannon Street
London EC4N 6AS

Tel: 0207 648 4040
Fax: 0207 648 4041

Network Rail

40 Melton Street
London NW1 2EE

Tel: 020 7557 8000
Fax: 020 7557 9000
www.networkrail.co.uk

National Land Information Service (NLIS)

Council for the National Land Information Service (C-NLIS)
25 Southampton Buildings
London WC2A 1AL

Tel: 0203 043 8880
www.c-nlis.org.uk/

Jordans Property (NLIS Channel)
21 St Thomas Street
Bristol BS1 6JS

Tel: 0117 923 0600
www.jordansproperty.co.uk

MDA SearchFlow Limited (NLIS Channel)
Nepicar House
London Road
Wrotham Heath
Kent TN15 7RS

Tel: 0870 787 7625
www.searchflow.com

TM Property Service Limited (NLIS Channel)
Delta 200
Delta Business Park
Swindon
Wiltshire SN5 7XP

Tel: 0870 740 7833
www.tmsearch.co.uk

Ordnance Survey

Customer Service Centre
Romsey Road
Southampton SO16 4GU

Tel: 08456 05 05 05
Fax: 023 8079 2615
www.ordnancesurvey.co.uk

Pollution Legal Liability

Environment Impairment Liability
(EIL) Dept
AIG Europe (UK) Ltd
The AIG Building
58 Fenchurch Street
London EC3M 4AB

Tel: 020 7954 7000
Fax: 020 7954 7001
www.aigeurope.co.uk

Premier Guarantee

MD Insurance Services Ltd
Haymarket Court
Hinson Street
Birkenhead CH41 5BX

Tel: 0151 650 4343
Fax: 0151 650 4344
DX: 17864 Birkenhead
www.premierguarantee.co.uk

Probate Service

Principal Registry
First Avenue House
42–49 High Holborn
London WC1V 6NP

Tel: 020 7947 6000
DX: 396 Lond/Chancery Ln
www.hmcourts-service.gov.uk/cms/wills.htm
(for complete list of probate registries)

Public Guardianship Office

Archway Tower
2 Junction Road
London N19 5SZ

Tel: 0845 330 2900
Fax: 0870 739 5780
DX: 141150 Archway (2)
www.guardianship.gov.uk

Residential Property Tribunal Service

Corporate Unit
10 Alfred Place
London WC1E 7LR

Tel: 020 7446 7751/2
Fax: 020 7580 5684
www.rpts.gov.uk

Eastern Rent Assessment Panel
Residential Property Tribunal Service
Great Eastern House
Tenison Road
Cambridge CB1 2TR

Tel: 01223 505112/0845 100 2616
Fax: 01223 505116

London Rent Assessment Panel
Residential Property Tribunal Service
10 Alfred Place
London WC1E 7LR

Tel: 020 7446 7700
Fax: 020 7637 1250

Midlands Rent Assessment Panel
Residential Property Tribunal Service
2nd Floor
East Wing
Ladywood House
45–46 Stephenson Street
Birmingham B2 4DH

Tel: 0121 643 8336/0845 100 2615
Fax: 0121 643 7605

Northern Rent Assessment Panel
Residential Property Tribunal Service
First Floor
26 York Street
Manchester M1 4JB

Tel: 0845 100 2614
Fax: 0161 237 3656/9491

Southern Rent Assessment Panel
Residential Property Tribunal Service
1st Floor
1 Market Avenue
Chichester PO19 1JU

Tel: 01243 779 394/0845 100 2617
Fax: 01243 779 389

Royal Courts of Justice

The Strand
London WC2A 2LL

Tel: 020 7947 6000
(No general Fax)
DX: 44450 Strand

Royal Institute of British Architects

66 Portland Place
London W1B 1AD

Tel: 020 7580 5533
Fax: 020 7255 1541
www.riba.org

Royal Institution of Chartered Surveyors

RICS Contact Centre
Surveyor Court
Westwood Way
Coventry CV4 8JE

Tel: 0870 333 1600
Fax: 0207 334 3811
www.rics.org

Rural Payments Agency

Headquarters
Kings House
33 Kings Road
Reading RG1 3BU

Tel: 0118 958 3626
Fax: 0118 959 7736

Milk Quotas
PO Box 277
Exeter EX5 1WB

Tel: 01392 266466
Fax: 01392 266489
www.rpa.gov.uk

SearchFlow

Nepicar House
London Road
Wrotham Heath
Sevenoaks TN15 7RS

Tel: 0870 220 3086
Fax: 0870 990 9949
www.transaction-online.co.uk

Serious Organised Crime Agency (SOCA)

PO Box 8000
London SE11 5EF

Tel: 020 7238 8000
Fax: 020 7238 8446
www.soca.gov.uk

Solicitors Regulation Authority (SRA)

Ipsley Court
Berrington Close
Redditch B98 0TD

Tel: 0870 606 2555
www.sra.gov.uk

Spacia

1 Eversholt Street
London NW1 2DN

Tel: 0800 830 840
www.spacia.co.uk

Sugar Bureau

Duncan House
Dolphin Square
London SW1V 3PW

Tel: 020 7828 9465
Fax: 020 7821 5393
www.sugar-bureau.co.uk

Tenancy deposit protection schemes

The Deposit Protection Service (The DPS)
The Pavilions
Bridgwater Road
Bristol BS99 6AA

Tel: 0870 7071 707
www.depositprotection.com

Tenancy Deposit Solutions Limited
3rd Floor
Kingmaker House
Station Road
New Barnet
Hertfordshire EN5 1NZ

Tel: 0871 703 0552
www.mydeposits.co.uk

The Tenancy Deposit Scheme
The Dispute Service Ltd
PO Box 541
Amersham
Bucks HP6 6ZR

Tel: 0845 226 7837
www.thedisputeservice.co.uk

TSol (formerly Treasury Solicitor)

1 Kemble Street
London WC2B 4TS

Tel: 020 7210 3000
DX: 123242 Kingsway
www.tsol.gov.uk

Water and Sewerage Companies (Head Offices)

Anglian Water Services Ltd
Anglian House
Ambury Road
Huntingdon PE29 3NZ

Tel: 01480 323 000
Fax: 01480 323 115
www.anglianwater.co.uk

Northumbrian Water Ltd
Abbey Road
Pity Me
Durham DH1 5FJ

Tel: 0870 608 4820
Fax: 0191 384 1920
www.nwl.co.uk

Severn Trent Water Ltd
2297 Coventry Road
Sheldon
Birmingham B26 3PU

Tel: 0121 722 4000
Fax: 0121 722 4800
www.stwater.co.uk

South West Water Ltd
Peninsula House
Rydon Lane
Exeter EX2 7HR

Tel: 01392 446 688
Fax: 01392 434 966
www.southwestwater.co.uk

Southern Water Services Ltd
Southern House
Yeoman Road
Worthing
West Sussex BN13 3NX

Tel: 01903 264 444
Fax: 01903 262 185
www.southernwater.co.uk

Thames Water Utilities Ltd
Clearwater Court
Vastern Road
Reading RG1 8DB

Tel: 0845 9200 888
Fax: 01793 424 291
www.thameswater.co.uk

United Utilities Water plc
Haweswater House
Lingley Mere Business Park
Lingley Green Avenue
Great Sankey
Warrington WA5 3LP

Tel: 01925 237 000
Fax: 01925 237 073
www.unitedutilities.com

Welsh Water/Dwr Cymru Cyfyngedig
Pentwyn Road
Nelson
Treharris
Mid Glamorgan CF46 6LY

Tel: 01443 452 300
Fax: 01443 452 323
www.dwrcymru.co.uk

Wessex Water Services Ltd
Claverton Down Road
Claverton Down
Bath BA2 7WW

Tel: 01225 526 000
Fax: 01225 528 000
www.wessexwater.co.uk

Yorkshire Water Services Ltd
Western House
Western Way
Bradford BD6 2LZ

Tel: 01274 691 111
Fax: 01274 604 764
www.yorkshirewater.com

Water Only Companies (Head Offices)

Albion Water Ltd
71 Clarence Road
Teddington
Middlesex TW11 0BN

Tel: 020 8977 3055
Fax: 020 8977 3185
www.albionwater.co.uk

Bournemouth & West Hampshire Water plc
George Jessel House
Francis Avenue
Bournemouth BH11 8NB

Tel: 01202 591 111
Fax: 01202 597 022
www.bwhwater.co.uk

Bristol Water plc
PO Box 218
Bridgwater Road
Bristol BS99 7AU

Tel: 0117 966 5881
Fax: 0117 963 4576
www.bristolwater.co.uk

Cambridge Water Company plc
90 Fulbourn Road
Cambridge CB1 9JN

Tel: 01223 403 000
Fax: 01223 214 052
www.cambridge-water.co.uk

Cholderton & District Water Company Ltd
Estate Office
Cholderton
Salisbury SP4 0DR

Tel: 01980 629 203
Fax: 01980 629 307

Dee Valley Water plc
Packsaddle
Wrexham Road
Rhostyllen
Wrexham LL14 4EH

Tel: 01978 846 946
Fax: 01978 846 888
www.deevalleygroup.com/DVW/DVW.htm

Essex & Suffolk Water Company
(now part of Northumbrian Water)
Hall Street
Chelmsford CM2 0HH

Tel: 01245 491 234
Fax: 01245 212 345
www.eswater.co.uk

Folkestone & Dover Water Services Ltd
Cherry Garden Lane
Folkestone CT19 4QB

Tel: 01303 298 800
Fax: 01303 276 712
www.fdws.co.uk

Hartlepool Water plc
(now part of Anglian Water Services Ltd)
3 Lancaster Road
Hartlepool TS24 8LW

Tel: 01429 858 050
Fax: 01429 858 000
www.hartlepoolwater.co.uk

Mid Kent Water Ltd plc
PO Box 45
High Street
Snodland ME6 5AH

Tel: 01634 240 313
Fax: 01634 242 764
www.midkentwater.co.uk

Portsmouth Water plc
PO Box 8
West Street
Havant PO9 1LG

Tel: 023 9249 9888
Fax: 023 9245 3632
www.portsmouthwater.co.uk

South East Water plc
3 Church Road
Haywards Heath RH16 3NY

Tel: 01444 448 200
Fax: 01444 413 200
www.southeastwater.co.uk

South Staffordshire Water plc
Green Lane
Walsall WS2 7PD

Tel: 01922 638 282
Fax: 01922 723 631
www.south-staffs-water.co.uk

Sutton & East Surrey Water plc
London Road
Redhill RH1 1LJ

Tel: 01737 772 000
Fax: 01737 766 807
www.waterplc.com

Tendring Hundred Water
Services Ltd
Mill Hill
Manningtree CO11 2AZ

Tel: 01206 399 200
Fax: 01206 399 210
www.thws.co.uk

Three Valleys Water plc
PO Box 48
Bishops Rise
Hatfield AL10 9HL

Tel: 01707 268 111
Fax: 01707 277 333
www.3valleys.co.uk

Zurich Insurance Company

Building Guarantee
6 Southwood Crescent
Farnborough GU14 0NL

Tel: 01252 377 474
www.zurich.co.uk/buildingguarantee/home/
intro.htm

IX. STATUTORY MATERIALS

IX.1. Land Charges Fees Rules 1990 (SI 1990/327)[1]

1990 No. 327

LAND CHARGES

The Land Charges Fees Rules 1990

Made 21st February 1990
Coming into force 2nd April 1990

The Lord Chancellor, with the concurrence of the Treasury, in exercise of the powers conferred on him by sections 9(1), 10(2), 16(1) and 17(1) of the Land Charges Act 1972 hereby makes in the following rules:

1.   (1)   These Rules may be cited as the Land Charges Fees Rules 1990 and shall come into force on 2nd April 1990.

   (2)   In these Rules, unless the context otherwise requires –

   'the Act' means the Land Charges Act 1972;

   'credit account' means an account authorised by the Registrar for the purpose of providing credit facilities for the payment of fees;

   'fee' means a fee specified in Schedule 1;

   'Schedule' means a schedule to these Rules;

   'written application' in Schedule 1 does not include an application made by teleprinter or facsimile transmission.

2.   The fees specified in Schedule 1 shall be payable under the Act.

3.   Every fee which accompanies an application is to be paid in money in accordance with the Land Charges (Fees) Order 1990 and shall, except as mentioned in Rule 4 or as the Registrar may otherwise allow, be paid in cash or by means of a postal order crossed and made payable to HM Land Registry.

4.   (1)   Any person or firm having a credit account may request the Registrar, on any application, to debit the requisite fee to that account.

   (2)   When a person or firm having a credit account makes an application which is not accompanied by any fee and does not contain a request for the fee to be debited to that account, the Registrar may, if he thinks fit, nevertheless accept the application and debit the fee to that person's or that firm's account.

---

1. Incorporating amendments made by the Land Charges Fees (Amendment) Rules 1994 (SI 1994/286).

(3) If the Registrar debits a fee to a credit account, this shall be treated as due payment of that fee.

(4) Credit accounts shall be authorised and maintained in accordance with the provisions set out in Schedule 2.

5. The Land Charges Fees Order 1985 so far as made under powers conferred by the Act is hereby revoked.

Mackay of Clashfern, C.
Dated 16th February 1990

We concur

David Lightbown
Stephen Dorrell
Two of the Lord Commissioners of Her Majesty's Treasury
Dated 21st February 1990

SCHEDULE 1

Rule 2

	Service		*Amount of Fee*
1.	Registration, renewal, rectification or cancellation of an entry in any register	per name	£1
2.	Certificate of cancellation	per name	£1
3.	Entry of priority notice	per name	£1
4.	Inspection of an entry in the register	per entry	£1
5.	Office copy of an entry in the register (including any plan) whether the application is made in writing or by telephone or teleprinter or facsimile transmission or to the registrar's computer system by means of the applicant's remote terminal	per copy	£1
6.	Official search in the index (including issue of printed certificate of result):–		
	written application	per name	£1
	telephone application	per name	£2
	teleprinter application	per name	£2
	facsimile transmission application	per name	£2
	application made to the registrar's computer system by means of the applicant's remote terminal	per name	£2
7.	Official search in the index (including visual display of result of search and issue of printed certificate of such result)	per name	£2

SCHEDULE 2

Provision of credit accounts

Rule 4(4)

1.   The Registrar may, as he thinks fit, authorise any person or firm to use a credit account for the purpose of the payment of fees but may withdraw or suspend any such authorisation at any time without giving any reason therefor.

2.   The Registrar may also at any time terminate or suspend all credit accounting facilities generally.

3.   A statement of account shall be sent by the Registrar to each account holder at the end of each calendar month or at such other period as the Registrar shall direct either in any particular case or generally.

4.   On receipt of the statement and if no question arises thereon the account holder shall pay by cheque any sum due on his account promptly, and in any event within ten days of its receipt.

5.   Cheques shall be made payable to HM Land Registry and sent to the Accounts Section, Land Charges Department, Burrington Way, Plymouth, PL5 3LP or at such other address as the Registrar shall direct.

IX.2. Solicitors' (Non-Contentious Business) Remuneration Order 1994 (SI 1994/2616)

1994 No. 2616

SOLICITORS

The Solicitors' (Non-Contentious Business) Remuneration Order 1994

Made 5th October 1994
Laid before Parliament 10th October 1994
Coming into force 1st November 1994

The Lord Chancellor, the Lord Chief Justice, the Master of the Rolls, the President of the Law Society, the president of Holborn law society and the Chief Land Registrar (in respect of business done under the Land Registration Act 1925), together constituting the committee authorised to make orders under section 56 of the Solicitors Act 1974, in exercise of the powers conferred on them by that section and having complied with the requirements of section 56(3), hereby make the following Order:

Citation, commencement and revocation

1. (1) This Order may be cited as the Solicitors' (Non-Contentious Business) Remuneration Order 1994.

    (2) This Order shall come into force on 1st November 1994 and shall apply to all non-contentious business for which bills are delivered on or after that date.

    (3) The Solicitors' Remuneration Order 1972 is hereby revoked except in its application to business for which bills are delivered before this Order comes into force.

Interpretation

2. In this Order:
    'client' means the client of a solicitor;
    'costs' means the amount charged in a solicitor's bill, exclusive of disbursements and value added tax, in respect of non-contentious business or common form probate business;
    'entitled person' means a client or an entitled third party;
    'entitled third party' means a residuary beneficiary absolutely and immediately (and not contingently) entitled to an inheritance, where a solicitor has charged the estate for his professional costs for acting in the administration of the estate, and *either*

    (a) the only personal representatives are solicitors (whether or not acting in a professional capacity); or

    (b) the only personal representatives are solicitors acting jointly with partners or employees in a professional capacity;

'paid disbursements' means disbursements already paid by the solicitor;

'recognised body' means a body corporate recognised by the Council under section 9 of the Administration of Justice Act 1985;

'remuneration certificate' means a certificate issued by the Council pursuant to this Order;

'residuary beneficiary' includes a person entitled to all or part of the residue of an intestate estate;

'solicitor' includes a recognised body [and shall apply to registered European lawyers (SI 2000/1119)];

'the Council' means the Council of the Law Society.

Solicitors' costs

3.   A solicitor's costs shall be such sum as may be fair and reasonable to both solicitor and entitled person, having regard to all the circumstances of the case and in particular to:

(a)   the complexity of the matter or the difficulty or novelty of the questions raised;

(b)   the skill, labour, specialised knowledge and responsibility involved;

(c)   the time spent on the business;

(d)   the number and importance of the documents prepared or perused, without regard to length;

(e)   the place where and the circumstances in which the business or any part thereof is transacted;

(f)   the amount or value of any money or property involved;

(g)   whether any land involved is registered land;

(h)   the importance of the matter to the client; and

(i)   the approval (express or implied) of the entitled person or the express approval of the testator to:

    (i)   the solicitor undertaking all or any part of the work giving rise to the costs; or

    (ii)   the amount of the costs.

Right to certification

4.   (1)   Without prejudice to the provisions of sections 70, 71, and 72 of the Solicitors Act 1974 (which relate to taxation of costs), an entitled person may, subject to the provisions of this Order, require a solicitor to obtain a remuneration certificate from the Council in respect of a bill which has been delivered where the costs are not more than £50,000.

(2)   The remuneration certificate must state what sum, in the opinion of the Council, would be a fair and reasonable charge for the business covered by the bill (whether it be the sum charged or a lesser sum). In the absence of taxation the sum payable in respect of such costs is the sum stated in the remuneration certificate.

Disciplinary and other measures

5.   (1)   If on a taxation the taxing officer allows less than one half of the costs, he must bring the facts of the case to the attention of the Council.

(2)   The provisions of this Order are without prejudice to the general powers of the Council under the Solicitors Act 1974.

Commencement of proceedings against a client

6.   Before a solicitor brings proceedings to recover costs against a client on a bill for non-contentious business he must inform the client in writing of the matters specified in article 8, except where the bill has been taxed.

Costs paid by deduction

7.   (1)   If a solicitor deducts his costs from monies held for or on behalf of a client or of an estate in satisfaction of a bill and an entitled person objects in writing to the amount of the bill within the prescribed time, the solicitor must immediately inform the entitled person in writing of the matters specified in article 8, unless he has already done so.

   (2)   In this article and in article 10, 'the prescribed time' means:

   (a)   in respect of a client, three months after delivery of the relevant bill, or a lesser time (which may not be less than one month) specified in writing to the client at the time of delivery of the bill; or

   (b)   in respect of an entitled third party, three months after delivery of notification to the entitled third party of the amount of the costs, or a lesser time (which may not be less than one month) specified in writing to the entitled third party at the time of such notification.

Information to be given in writing to entitled person

8.   When required by articles 6 or 7, a solicitor shall inform an entitled person in writing of the following matters:

   (a)   where article 4(1) applies:

   (i)   that the entitled person may, within one month of receiving from the solicitor the information specified in this article or (if later) of delivery of the bill or notification of the amount of the costs, require the solicitor to obtain a remuneration certificate; and

   (ii)   that (unless the solicitor has agreed to do so) the Council may waive the requirements of article 11(1), if satisfied from the client's written application that exceptional circumstances exist to justify granting a waiver;

   (b)   that sections 70, 71 and 72 of the Solicitors Act 1974 set out the entitled person's rights in relation to taxation;

   (c)   that (where the whole of the bill has not been paid, by deduction or otherwise) the solicitor may charge interest on the outstanding amount of the bill in accordance with article 14.

Loss by client of right to certification

9.   A client may not require a solicitor to obtain a remuneration certificate:

   (a)   after a bill has been delivered and paid by the client, other than by deduction;

   (b)   where a bill has been delivered, after the expiry of one month from the date on which the client was informed in writing of the matters specified in article 8 or from delivery of the bill if later;

   (c)   after the solicitor and client have entered into a non-contentious business agreement in accordance with the provisions of section 57 of the Solicitors Act 1974;

(d) after a court has ordered the bill to be taxed;

(e) if article 11(2) applies.

Loss by entitled third party of right to certification

10. An entitled third party may not require a solicitor to obtain a remuneration certificate:

(a) after the prescribed time (within the meaning of article 7(2)(b)) has elapsed without any objection being received to the amount of the costs;

(b) after the expiry of one month from the date on which the entitled third party was (in compliance with article 7) informed in writing of the matters specified in article 8 or from notification of the costs if later;

(c) after a court has ordered the bill to be taxed.

Requirement to pay a sum towards the costs

11. (1) On requiring a solicitor to obtain a remuneration certificate a client must pay to the solicitor the paid disbursements and value added tax comprised in the bill together with 50% of the costs unless:

(a) the client has already paid the amount required under this article, by deduction from monies held or otherwise; or

(b) the solicitor or (if the solicitor refuses) the Council has agreed in writing to waive all or part of this requirement.

(2) The Council shall be under no obligation to provide a remuneration certificate, and the solicitor may take steps to obtain payment of his bill, if the client, having been informed of his right to seek a waiver of the requirements of paragraph (1), has not:

(a) within one month of receipt of the information specified in article 8, either paid in accordance with paragraph (1) or applied to the Council in writing for a waiver of the requirements of paragraph (1); or

(b) made payment in accordance with the requirements of paragraph (1) within one month of written notification that he has been refused a waiver of those requirements by the Council.

Miscellaneous provisions

12. (1) After an application has been made by a solicitor for a remuneration certificate the client may pay the bill in full without invalidating the application.

(2) A solicitor and entitled person may agree in writing to waive the provisions of sub-paragraphs (a) or (b) of articles 9 or 10.

(3) A solicitor may take from his client security for the payment of any costs, including the amount of any interest to which the solicitor may become entitled under article 14.

Refunds by solicitor

13. (1) If a solicitor has received payment of all or part of his costs and a remuneration certificate is issued for less than the sum already paid, the solicitor must immediately pay to the entitled person any refund which may be due (after taking into account any other sums which may properly be payable to the solicitor whether for costs, paid disbursements, value added tax or otherwise) unless the solicitor has applied for an order for taxation within one month of receipt by him of the remuneration certificate.

(2) Where a solicitor applies for taxation, his liability to pay any refund under paragraph (1) shall be suspended for so long as the taxation is still pending.

(3) The obligation of the solicitor to repay costs under paragraph (1) is without prejudice to any liability of the solicitor to pay interest on the repayment by virtue of any enactment, rule of law or professional rule.

Interest

14. (1) After the information specified in article 8 has been given to an entitled person in compliance with articles 6 or 7, a solicitor may charge interest on the unpaid amount of his costs plus any paid disbursements and value added tax, subject to paragraphs (2) and (3) below.

(2) Where an entitlement to interest arises under paragraph (1), and subject to any agreement made between a solicitor and client, the period for which interest may be charged may run from one month after the date of delivery of a bill, unless the solicitor fails to lodge an application within one month of receipt of a request for a remuneration certificate under article 4, in which case no interest is payable in respect of the period between one month after receiving the request and the actual date on which the application is lodged.

(3) Subject to any agreement made between a solicitor and client, the rate of interest must not exceed the rate for the time being payable on judgment debts.

(4) Interest charged under this article must be calculated, where applicable, by reference to the following:

(a) if a solicitor is required to obtain a remuneration certificate, the total amount of the costs certified by the Council to be fair and reasonable plus paid disbursements and value added tax;

(b) if an application is made for the bill to be taxed, the amount ascertained on taxation;

(c) if an application is made for the bill to be taxed or a solicitor is required to obtain a remuneration certificate and for any reason the taxation or application for a remuneration certificate does not proceed, the unpaid amount of the costs shown in the bill or such lesser sum as may be agreed between the solicitor and the client, plus paid disbursements and value added tax.

Application by solicitor

15. A solicitor, when making an application for a remuneration certificate in accordance with the provisions of this Order, must deliver to the Council the complete relevant file and working papers, and any other information or documentation which the Council may require for the purpose of providing a remuneration certificate.

EXPLANATORY NOTE

(*This note is not part of the Order*)

Section 56 of the Solicitors Act 1974 establishes a Committee with power to make general orders regulating the remuneration of solicitors in respect of non-contentious business. Paragraph 22(2) of Schedule 2 to the Administration of Justice Act 1985 modifies the section so that references to solicitors include references to recognised bodies (solicitors' incorporated practices recognised under section 9 of the Administration of Justice Act 1985). This Order sets out the rights of solicitors' clients and residuary beneficiaries of certain estates to require the solicitor charging the client or estate to obtain a certificate from the Law Society as to the reasonableness of his costs. The Order prescribes requirements in relation to information to be given in writing to clients and beneficiaries who are entitled to require a solicitor to obtain a certificate, and lays certain obligations on clients, beneficiaries and solicitors.

IX.3. Land Registration Fee Order 2006 (SI 2006/1332)

2006 No. 1332

LAND REGISTRATION, ENGLAND AND WALES

The Land Registration Fee Order 2006

Made 15th May 2006
Laid before Parliament 15th May 2006
Coming into force 7th August 2006

The Lord Chancellor makes the following Order in exercise of the powers conferred on him by sections 102 and 128 of the Land Registration Act 2002.

In accordance with section 102 of that Act, he has received the advice and assistance of the Rule Committee, appointed under section 127 of that Act.

Also in accordance with section 102 of that Act, the Treasury has consented to the making of this Order.

PART 1

General

Citation, commencement and interpretation

1. (1) This Order may be cited as the Land Registration Fee Order 2006 and shall come into force on 7 August 2006.

   (2) In this Order unless the context otherwise requires –

   'account holder' means a person or firm holding a credit account,

   'the Act' means the Land Registration Act 2002, 'CLRA' means the Commonhold and Leasehold Reform Act 2002,

   'charge' includes a sub-charge,

   'common parts' has the same meaning as in the CLRA,

   'a commonhold' has the same meaning as in the CLRA,

   'commonhold association' has the same meaning as in the CLRA, 'commonhold community statement' has the same meaning as in the CLRA,

   'commonhold land' has the same meaning as in the CLRA, 'commonhold unit' has the same meaning as in the CLRA,

   'credit account' means an account authorised by the registrar under article 14(1), 'developer' has the same meaning as in the CLRA,

'large scale application' has the same meaning as in article 6(1)(b),

'monetary consideration' means a consideration in money or money's worth (other than a nominal consideration or a consideration consisting solely of a covenant to pay money owing under a mortgage),

'premium' means the amount or value of any monetary consideration given by the lessee as part of the same transaction in which a lease is granted by way of fine, premium or otherwise, but, where a registered leasehold estate of substantially the same land is surrendered on the grant of a new lease, the premium for the new lease shall not include the value of the surrendered lease,

'profit' means a profit à prendre in gross,

'remote terminal' means a remote terminal communicating with the registrar's computer system in accordance with a notice given under Schedule 2 to the rules,

'rent' means the largest amount of annual rent the lease reserves within the first five years of its term that can be quantified at the time an application to register the lease is made,

'the rules' means the Land Registration Rules 2003 and a rule referred to by number means the rule so numbered in the rules,

'Scale 1' means Scale 1 in Schedule 1,

'Scale 2' means Scale 2 in Schedule 2,

'scale fee' means a fee payable in accordance with a scale set out in Schedule 1 or 2 whether or not reduced in accordance with article 2(6),

'scale fee application' means an application which attracts a scale fee, or which would attract such a fee but for the operation of article 6,

'share', in relation to land, means an interest in that land under a trust of land,

'surrender' includes a surrender not made by deed,

'unit-holder' has the same meaning as in the CLRA,

'voluntary application' means an application for first registration (other than for the registration of title to a rentcharge, a franchise or a profit) which is not made wholly or in part pursuant to section 4 of the Act (when title must be registered).

(3) Expressions used in this Order have, unless the contrary intention appears, the meaning which they bear in the rules.

PART 2

Scale fees

Applications for first registration and applications for registration of a lease by an original lessee

2. (1) The fee for an application for first registration of an estate in land is payable under Scale 1 on the value of the estate in land comprised in the application assessed under article 7 unless the application is –

(a) for the registration of title to a lease by the original lessee or his personal representative, where paragraph (2) applies,

(b) a voluntary application, where either paragraph (6) or article 6(3) applies, or

(c) a large scale application or a large area application, where article 6 applies.

(2) The fee for an application for the registration of title to the grant of a lease by the original lessee or his personal representative is payable under Scale 1 –

(a) on an amount equal to the sum of the premium and the rent, or

(b) where

(i) there is no premium, and

(ii) either there is no rent or the rent cannot be quantified at the time the application is made,

on the value of the lease assessed under article 7 subject to a minimum fee of £40, unless either of the circumstances in paragraph (3) applies.

(3) Paragraph (2) shall not apply if the application is –

(a) a voluntary application, where paragraph (6) applies, or

(b) a large scale application, where article 6 applies.

(4) The fee for an application for the first registration of a rentcharge is £40.

(5) The fee for an application for the first registration of a franchise or a profit is payable under Scale 1 on the value of the franchise or the profit assessed under article 7.

(6) The fee for a voluntary application (other than a large scale application, where article 6(3) applies) is the fee which would otherwise be payable under paragraph (1) or (2) reduced by 25 per cent and, where the reduced fee would be a figure which includes pence, the fee must be adjusted to the nearest £10.

(7) In paragraph (2) 'lease' means –

(a) a lease which grants an estate in land whether or not the grant is a registrable disposition, or

(b) a lease of a franchise, profit or manor the grant of which is a registrable disposition.

Transfers of registered estates for monetary consideration, etc.

3. (1) Subject to paragraphs (2), (3) and (4), the fee for an application for the registration of –

(a) a transfer of a registered estate for monetary consideration,

(b) a transfer for the purpose of giving effect to a disposition for monetary consideration of a share in a registered estate,

(c) a surrender of a registered leasehold estate for monetary consideration, other than a surrender to which paragraph (3) of Schedule 4 applies,

is payable under Scale 1 on the amount or value of the consideration.

(2) Paragraph (1) shall not apply if the application is –

(a) a large scale application, where article 6 applies, or

(b) for the registration of a transfer of a registered estate made pursuant to an order of the Court under the Matrimonial Causes Act 1973 or the Civil Partnership Act 2004, where article 4(1)(h) applies.

(3)   Where a sale and sub-sale of a registered estate are made by separate deeds of transfer, a separate fee is payable for each deed of transfer.

(4)   Where a single deed of transfer gives effect to a sale and a sub-sale of the same registered estate a single fee is assessed upon the greater of the monetary consideration given by the purchaser and the monetary consideration given by the sub-purchaser.

(5)   The fee for an application to cancel an entry in the register of notice of an unregistered lease which has determined is payable under Scale 1 on the value of the lease immediately before its determination assessed under article 7.

Transfers of registered estates otherwise than for monetary consideration, etc.

4.   (1)   Unless the application is a large scale application (where article 6 applies), the fee for an application for the registration of –

(a)   a transfer of a registered estate otherwise than for monetary consideration (unless paragraph (2) applies),

(b)   a surrender of a registered leasehold estate otherwise than for monetary consideration,

(c)   a transfer of a registered estate by operation of law on death or bankruptcy, of an individual proprietor,

(d)   an assent of a registered estate (including a vesting assent),

(e)   an appropriation of a registered estate,

(f)   a vesting order or declaration to which section 27(5) of the Act applies,

(g)   an alteration of the register, or

(h)   a transfer of a registered estate made pursuant to an order of the Court under the Matrimonial Causes Act 1973 or the Civil Partnership Act 2004,

is payable under Scale 2 on the value of the registered estate which is the subject of the application, assessed under article 7, but after deducting from it the amount secured on the registered estate by any charge subject to which the registration takes effect.

(2)   Where a transfer of a registered estate otherwise than for monetary consideration is for the purpose of giving effect to the disposition of a share in a registered estate, the fee for an application for its registration is payable under Scale 2 on the value of that share.

Charges of registered estates or registered charges

5.   (1)   The fee for an application for the registration of a charge is payable under Scale 2 on the amount of the charge assessed under article 8 unless it is an application to which paragraphs (2), (3) or (4) apply.

(2)   No fee is payable for an application to register a charge lodged with or before the completion of either a scale fee application or an application to which paragraph (17) in Part 1 of Schedule 3 applies ('the primary application') that will result in the chargor being registered as proprietor of the registered estate included in the charge unless –

(a)   the charge includes a registered estate which is not included in the primary application, where paragraph (4) applies, or

(b) the primary application is a voluntary application, in which case this paragraph shall apply only if the application to register the charge accompanies the primary application.

(3) No fee is to be paid for an application to register a charge made by a predecessor in title of the applicant that is lodged with or before completion of an application for first registration of the estate included in the charge.

(4) Where a charge also includes a registered estate which is not included in the primary application ('the additional property') any fee payable under Scale 2 is to be assessed on an amount calculated as follows:

$$\frac{\text{Value of the additional property}}{\text{Value of all the property included in the charge}} \times \text{Amount secured by the charge}$$

(5) The fee for an application for the registration of –

(a) the transfer of a registered charge for monetary consideration, or

(b) a transfer for the purpose of giving effect to the disposition for monetary consideration of a share in a registered charge,

is payable under Scale 2 on the amount or value of the consideration.

(6) The fee for an application for the registration of the transfer of a registered charge otherwise than for monetary consideration is payable under Scale 2 on –

(a) the amount secured by the registered charge at the time of the transfer or,

(b) where the transfer relates to more than one charge, the aggregate of the amounts secured by the registered charges at the time of the transfer.

(7) The fee for an application for the registration of a transfer for the purpose of giving effect to a disposition otherwise than for monetary consideration of a share in a registered charge is payable under Scale 2 on:

(a) the proportionate part of the amount secured by the registered charge at the time of the transfer or,

(b) where the transfer relates to more than one charge, the proportionate part of the aggregate of the amounts secured by the registered charges at the time of the transfer.

(8) This article takes effect subject to article 6 (large scale applications).

Large scale applications, etc.

6. (1) In this article –

(a) 'land unit' means –

(i) the land registered under a single title number other than, in the case of an application to register a charge, any estate under any title number which is included in a primary application within the meaning of article 5(2), or

(ii) on a first registration application, a separate area of land not adjoining any other unregistered land affected by the same application.

(b) 'large scale application' means a scale fee application which relates to 20 or more land units, other than an application to register a disposition by the developer affecting the whole or part of the freehold estate in land which has been registered as a freehold estate in commonhold law, or a low value application,

    (c)   'low value application' means a scale fee application, other than an application for first registration, where the value of the land or the amount of the charge to which it relates (as the case may be) does not exceed £30,000.

(2)   Subject to paragraph (3), the fee for a large scale application is the greater of –

    (a)   the scale fee, and

    (b)   a fee calculated on the following basis –

        (i)   where the application relates to not more than 500 land units, £10 for each land unit, or

        (ii)   where the application relates to more than 500 land units, £5,000 plus £5 for each land unit in excess of 500, up to a maximum of £40,000.

(3)   If a large scale application is a voluntary application, the fee payable under paragraph (2) is reduced by 25 per cent and, where the reduced fee would be a figure which includes pence, the fee must be adjusted to the nearest £10.

PART 3

Valuation

Valuation (first registration and registered estates)

7.   (1)   The value of the estate in land, franchise, profit, manor or share is the maximum amount for which it could be sold in the open market free from any charge –

    (a)   in the case of a surrender, at the date immediately before the surrender, and

    (b)   in any other case, at the date of the application.

(2)   As evidence of the amount referred to in paragraph (1), the registrar may require a written statement signed by the applicant or his conveyancer or by any other person who, in the registrar's opinion, is competent to make the statement.

(3)   Where an application for first registration is made on –

    (a)   the purchase of a leasehold estate by the reversioner,

    (b)   the purchase of a reversion by the leaseholder, or

    (c)   any other like occasion,

and an unregistered interest is determined, the value of the land is the combined value of the reversionary and determined interests assessed in accordance with paragraphs (1) and (2).

Valuation (charges)

8.   (1)   On an application for registration of a charge, the amount of the charge is –

    (a)   where the charge secures a fixed amount, that amount,

    (b)   where the charge secures further advances and the maximum amount that can be advanced or owed at any one time is limited, that amount,

(c)   where the charge secures further advances and the total amount that can be advanced or owed at any one time is not limited, the value of the property charged,

(d)   where the charge is by way of additional or substituted security or by way of guarantee, an amount equal to the lesser of –

     (i)   the amount secured or guaranteed, and

     (ii)   the value of the property charged,

(e)   where the charge secures an obligation or liability which is contingent upon the happening of a future event ('the obligation'), and is not a charge to which subparagraph (d) applies, an amount equal to –

     (i)   the maximum amount or value of the obligation, or

     (ii)   if that maximum amount is greater than the value of the property charged, or is not limited by the charge, or cannot be calculated at the time of the application, the value of the property charged.

(2)   Where a charge of a kind referred to in paragraph (1)(a) or (1)(b) is secured on unregistered land or other property as well as on a registered estate or registered charge, the fee is payable on an amount calculated as follows –

$$\frac{\text{Value of the registered estate or registered charge}}{\text{Value of all the property charged}} \times \text{Amount of the charge}$$

(3)   Where one deed contains two or more charges made by the same chargor to secure the same debt, the deed is to be treated as a single charge, and the fee for registration of the charge is to be paid on the lesser of –

(a)   the amount of the whole debt, and

(b)   an amount equal to the value of the property charged.

(4)   Where one deed contains two or more charges to secure the same debt not made by the same chargor, the deed is to be treated as a separate single charge by each of the chargors and a separate fee is to be paid for registration of the charge by each chargor on the lesser of –

(a)   the amount of the whole debt, and

(b)   an amount equal to the value of the property charged by that chargor.

(5)   In this article 'value of the property charged' means the value of the registered estate or the amount of the registered charge or charges affected by the application to register the charge, less the amount secured by any prior registered charges.

PART 4

Fixed fees and exemptions

Fixed fees

9.   (1)   Subject to paragraphs (2) and (3) and to article 10, the fees for the applications and services specified in Schedule 3 shall be those set out in that Schedule.

(2) The fee for an application under rule 140 shall be the aggregate of the fees payable for the services provided, but the maximum fee for any one application shall be £200.

(3) Where an application is one specified in paragraphs (1), (2) or (10) in Part 1 of Schedule 3 affecting the whole or part of the freehold estate in land which has been registered as a freehold estate in commonhold land registered in the name of the developer under more than one title number, the fee is to be assessed as if the application affects only one title.

Exemptions

10. No fee is payable for any of the applications and services specified in Schedule 4.

PART 5

General and administrative provisions

Cost of surveys, advertisements and special enquiries

11. The applicant is to meet the costs of any survey, advertisement or other special enquiry that the registrar requires to be made or published in dealing with an application.

Applications not otherwise referred to

12. The fee payable for an application in respect of which no other fee is payable under this Order shall be £40.

Method of payment

13. (1) Except where the registrar otherwise permits, every fee shall be paid by means of a cheque or postal order crossed and made payable to the Land Registry.

(2) Where there is an agreement with the applicant, a fee may be paid by direct debit to such bank account of the Land Registry as the registrar may from time to time direct.

(3) Where the amount of the fee payable on an application is immediately quantifiable, the fee shall be payable on delivery of the application.

(4) Where the amount of the fee payable on an application is not immediately quantifiable, the applicant shall pay the sum of £40 towards the fee when the application is made and shall lodge at the same time an undertaking to pay on demand the balance of the fee due, if any.

(5) Where an outline application is made, the fee payable shall be the fee payable under paragraph (9) of Part 1 of Schedule 3 in addition to the fee otherwise payable under this Order.

Credit accounts

14. (1) Any person or firm may, if authorised by the registrar, use a credit account in accordance with this article for the payment of fees for applications and services of such kind as the registrar shall from time to time direct.

(2) To enable the registrar to consider whether or not a person applying to use a credit account may be so authorised, that person shall supply the registrar with such information and evidence as the registrar may require to satisfy him of that person's fitness to

hold a credit account and the ability of that person to pay any amounts which may become due from time to time under a credit account.

(3) To enable the registrar to consider from time to time whether or not an account holder may continue to be authorised to use a credit account, the account holder shall supply the registrar, when requested to do so, with such information and evidence as the registrar may require to satisfy him of the account holder's continuing fitness to hold a credit account and the continuing ability of the account holder to pay any amounts which may become due from time to time under the account holder's credit account.

(4) Where an account holder makes an application where credit facilities are available to him, he may make a request, in such manner as the registrar directs, for the appropriate fee to be debited to the account holder's credit account, but the registrar shall not be required to accept such a request where the amount due on the account exceeds the credit limit applicable to the credit account, or would exceed it if the request were to be accepted.

(5) Where an account holder makes an application where credit facilities are available to him, and the application is accompanied neither by a fee nor a request for the fee to be debited to his account, the registrar may debit the fee to his account.

(6) The registrar shall send a statement of account to each account holder at the end of each calendar month or such other interval as the registrar shall direct.

(7) The account holder must pay any sums due on his credit account before the date and in the manner specified by the registrar.

(8) The registrar may at any time and without giving reasons terminate or suspend any or all authorisations given under paragraph (1).

(9) In this article 'credit limit' in relation to a credit account authorised for use under paragraph (1) means the maximum amount (if any) which is to be due on the account at any time, as notified by the registrar to the account holder from time to time, by means of such communication as the registrar considers appropriate.

Revocation

15. The Land Registration Fee Order 2004 and the Land Registration Fee (Amendment) Order 2004 are revoked.

Signed by the authority of the Lord Chancellor

Cathy Ashton
Parliamentary Under Secretary of State, Department for Constitutional Affairs

Dave Watts
Frank Roy
Two of the Lord Commissioners of Her Majesty's Treasury

Dated 15th May 2006

SCHEDULE 1

Articles 2 and 3

SCALE 1

NOTE 1: Where the amount or value is a figure which includes pence, it must be rounded down to the nearest £1.

NOTE 2: The third column, which sets out the reduced fee payable where article 2(6) (voluntary registration: reduced fees) applies, is not part of the scale.

Amount or value £	Fee £	Reduced fee where article 2(6) (voluntary registration: reduced fees) applies £
0–50,000	40	30
50,001–80,000	60	45
80,001–100,000	100	75
100,001–200,000	150	110
200,001–500,000	220	165
500,001–1,000,000	420	315
1,000,001 and over	700	525

SCHEDULE 2

Articles 4 and 5

SCALE 2

NOTE: Where the amount or value is a figure which includes pence, it may be rounded down to the nearest £1.

Amount or value £	Fee £
0–100,000	40
100,001–200,000	50
200,001–500,000	70
500,001–1,000,000	100
1,000,001 and over	200

SCHEDULE 3

Articles 9 and 14

PART 1

Fixed fee applications

	Fee
(1) To register:	
(a) a standard form of restriction contained in Schedule 4 to the rules, or	
(b) a notice (other than a notice to which section 117(2)(b) of the Act applies), or	
(c) a new or additional beneficiary of a unilateral notice	
– total fee for up to three registered titles affected	£40
– additional fee for each subsequent registered title affected	£20
Provided that no such fee is payable if, in relation to each registered title affected, the application is accompanied by a scale fee application or another application which attracts a fee under this paragraph.	
(2) To register a restriction in a form not contained in Schedule 4 of the rules – for each registered title	£80
(3) To register a caution against first registration (other than a caution to which section 117(2)(a) of the Act applies)	£40
(4) To alter a cautions register – for each individual cautions register	£40
(5) To close or partly close a registered leasehold or a registered rentcharge title other than on surrender – for each registered title closed or partly closed	£40
Provided that no such fee is payable if the application is accompanied by a scale fee application.	
(6) To upgrade from one class of registered title to another	£40
Provided that no such fee is payable if the application for upgrading is accompanied by a scale fee application.	
(7) To cancel an entry in the register of notice of an unregistered rentcharge which has determined – for each registered title affected	£40
Provided that no such fee is payable if the application is accompanied by a scale fee application.	
(8) To enter or remove a record of a defect in title pursuant to section 64(1) of the Act	£40
Provided that no such fee is payable if the application is accompanied by a scale fee application.	
(9) An outline application made under rule 54:	
(a) where delivered from a remote terminal	£2

	Fee
(b) where delivered by any other permitted means	£4
Such fee is payable in addition to any other fee which is payable in respect of the application.	
(10) For an order in respect of a restriction under section 41(2) of the Act – for each registered title affected	£40
(11) To register a person in adverse possession of a registered estate – for each registered title affected	£100
(12) For registration as a person entitled to be notified of an application for adverse possession	
– for each registered title affected	£40
(13) For the determination of the exact line of a boundary under rule 118 – for each registered title affected	£80
(14) To register a freehold estate in land as a freehold estate in commonhold land which is not accompanied by a statement under section 9(1)(b) of the Commonhold and Leasehold Reform Act 2002:	
(a) up to 20 commonhold units	£40
(b) for every 20 commonhold units, or up to 20 commonhold units, thereafter	£10
(15) To add land to a commonhold:	
(a) adding land to the common parts title	£40
(b) adding land to a commonhold unit	£40
(c) adding commonhold units – up to 20 commonhold units	£40
– for every 20 commonhold units, or up to 20 commonhold units, thereafter	£10
(16) To apply for a freehold estate in land to cease to be registered as a freehold estate in commonhold land during the transitional period, as defined in the CLRA	£40
(17) To register a freehold estate in land as a freehold estate in commonhold land, which is accompanied by a statement under section 9(1)(b) of the CLRA – for each commonhold unit converted	£40
(18) To register an amended commonhold community statement which changes the extent of the common parts or any commonhold unit:	
(a) for the common parts	£40
(b) for up to three commonhold units	£40
(c) for each subsequent commonhold unit	£20
Provided that no such fee shall be payable if, in relation to each registered title affected, the application is accompanied by a scale fee application or another application that attracts a fee under this Part.	
(19) To register an amended commonhold community statement, which does not change the extent of a registered title within the commonhold	£40

IX

		Fee
	Provided that no such fee shall be payable if, in relation to each registered title affected, the application is accompanied by a scale fee application or another application that attracts a fee under this Part.	
(20)	To register an alteration to the Memorandum or Articles of Association of a commonhold association	£40
(21)	To make a termination application – for each registered title affected	£40
(22)	To note the surrender of a development right under section 58 of the CLRA	£40

PART 2

Services – inspection and copying

Note: In this Part 'lease' means a lease or a copy of a lease.

			Fee
(1)	Inspection, from a remote terminal:		
	(a)	for each individual register	£3
	(b)	for each title plan	£3
	(c)	for any or all of the documents (other than leases) referred to in an individual register – for each registered title	£5
	(d)	for each lease referred to in an individual register	£10
	(e)	for the individual register and title plan of a commonhold common parts title – for each registered title	£3
	(f)	for each individual caution register	£3
	(g)	for each caution plan	£3
	(h)	for any other document kept by the registrar which relates to an application to him	
		– for each document	£5
(2)	Inspection (otherwise than under paragraph (1)):		
	(a)	for each individual register	£6
	(b)	for each title plan	£6
	(c)	for any or all of the documents (other than leases) referred to in an individual register	
		– for each registered title	£10
	(d)	for each lease referred to in an individual register	£20
	(e)	for the individual register and title plan of a commonhold common parts title – for each registered title	£6
	(f)	for each individual caution register	£6
	(g)	for each caution plan	£6

					Fee

(h) for any other document kept by the registrar which relates to an application to him

      – for each document   £10

(3) Official copy in respect of a registered title:

    (a) for each individual register

        (i) where an official copy in electronic form is requested from a remote terminal   £3

        (ii) where an official copy in paper form is requested by any permitted means   £6

    (b) for each title plan:

        (i) where an official copy in electronic form is requested from a remote terminal   £3

        (ii) where an official copy in paper form is requested by any permitted means   £6

    (c) for each commonhold common parts register and title plan:

        (i) where an official copy in electronic form is requested from a remote terminal   £3

        (ii) where an official copy in paper form is requested by any permitted means   £6

(4) Official copy in respect of a cautions register

    (a) for each individual caution register:

        (i) where an official copy in electronic form is requested from a remote terminal   £3

        (ii) where an official copy in paper form is requested by any permitted means   £6

    (b) for each caution plan

        (i) where an official copy in electronic form is requested from a remote terminal   £3

        (ii) where requested by any other permitted means   £6

(5) Official copy of any or all of the documents (other than a lease) referred to in an individual register – for each registered title:

    (a) where an official copy in electronic form is requested from a remote terminal   £5

    (b) where an official copy in paper form is requested by any other permitted means   £10

(6) Official copy of a l ease referred to in an individual register – for each lease

    (a) where an official copy in electronic form is requested from a remote terminal and a copy of the lease is held in electronic form by the registrar   £10

	Fee
(b) where an official copy in electronic form is requested from a remote terminal and a copy of the lease is not held in electronic form by the registrar	£20
(c) where an official copy in paper form is requested by any permitted means.	£20
(7) Official copy of any other document kept by the registrar which relates to an application to him – for each document	
(a) where an official copy in electronic form is requested from a remote terminal and a copy of the document is held in electronic form by the registrar	£5
(b) where an official copy in electronic form is requested from a remote terminal and a copy of the document is not held in electronic form by the registrar	£10
(c) where an official copy in paper form is requested by any permitted means	£10
(8) Copy of an historical edition of a registered title (or of part of the edition where rule 144(4) applies) – for each title	£8
(9) Subject to paragraph (14) of Schedule 4, application to the registrar to ascertain the title number or numbers (if any) under which the estate is registered where the applicant seeks to inspect or to be supplied with an official copy of an individual register or of a title plan and the applicant has not supplied a title number, or the title number supplied does not relate to any part of the land described by the applicant – for each title number in excess of ten disclosed	£4

PART 3

Services – searches

	Fee
(1) An official search of an individual register or of a pending first registration application made to the registrar from a remote terminal – for each title	£3
(2) An official search of an individual register by a mortgagee for the purpose of section 56(3) of the Family Law Act 1996 made to the registrar from a remote terminal – for each title	£3
(3) An official search of an individual register or of a pending first registration application other than as described in paragraphs (1) and (2) – for each title	£6
(4) The issue of a certificate of inspection of a title plan – for each registered title affected	£6
(5) Subject to paragraph (15) of Schedule 4, an official search of the index map – for each registered title in excess of ten in respect of which a result is given	£4

		Fee
(6)	Search of the index of proprietors' names – for each name	£10
(7)	An official search of the index of relating franchises and manors – for each administrative area:	
	(a) where the application is made by means of a remote terminal	£3
	(b) where the application is made by any other permitted means	£6

PART 4

Services – Other information

		Fee
(1)	Application to be supplied with the name and address of the registered proprietor of a registered title identified by its postal address – for each application	£4
(2)	Application for return of a document under rule 204	£8
(3)	Application that the registrar designate a document an exempt information document	£20

SCHEDULE 4

Article 10

Exemptions

No fee is payable in respect of:

(1) reflecting a change in the name, address or description of a registered proprietor or other person referred to in the register, or in the cautions register, or changing the description of a property,

(2) giving effect in the register to a change of proprietor where the registered estate or the registered charge, as the case may be, has become vested without further assurance (other than on the death or bankruptcy of a proprietor) in some person by the operation of any statute (other than the Act), statutory instrument or scheme taking effect under any statute or statutory instrument,

(3) registering the surrender of a registered leasehold estate where the surrender is consideration or part consideration for the grant of a new lease to the registered proprietor of substantially the same premises as were comprised in the surrendered lease and where a scale fee is paid for the registration of the new lease,

(4) registering a discharge of a registered charge,

(5) registering a home rights notice, or renewal of such a notice, or renewal of a home rights caution under the Family Law Act 1996,

(6) entering in the register the death of a joint proprietor,

(7)   cancelling the registration of a notice (other than a notice in respect of an unregistered lease or unregistered rentcharge), caution against first registration, caution against dealings, including a withdrawal of a deposit or intended deposit, inhibition, restriction, or note,

(8)   the removal of the designation of a document as an exempt information document,

(9)   approving an estate layout plan or any draft document with or without a plan,

(10)   an order by the registrar (other than an order under section 41(2) of the Act),

(11)   deregistering a manor,

(12)   an entry in the register of a note of the dissolution of a corporation,

(13)   registering a restriction in form A in Schedule 4 to the rules,

(14)   an application to ascertain the title number or numbers (if any) under which the estate is registered where the applicant seeks to inspect or to be supplied with an official copy of an individual register or of a title plan and the applicant has not supplied a title number, or the title number supplied does not relate to any part of the land described by the applicant, provided the number of registered titles supplied does not exceed ten,

(15)   an official search of the index map where either no part of the land to which the search relates is registered, or, where the whole or part is registered, the number of registered titles disclosed does not exceed ten,

(16)   an application for day list information on any one occasion from a remote terminal,

(17)   an application to lodge a caution against first registration or to make a register entry where in either case the application relates to rights in respect of the repair of a church chancel.

IX.4. Practice Note: Ancillary relief orders – Conveyancing for mentally incapacitated adults[1]

1. This Practice Note is issued by the Official Solicitor to the Supreme Court. It gives his understanding of the law and practice applying to the implementation of property adjustment orders and orders for sale in ancillary relief proceedings under Part II of the Matrimonial Causes Act 1973 (MCA 1973) or Section 72 and Schedule 5 of the Civil Partnership Act 2004 (CPA 2004) where one of the parties is under mental incapacity. It has been seen in draft and approved by the Master of the Court of Protection and the Senior District Judge at the Principal Registry of the Family Division of the High Court.

2. A petitioner or respondent who lacks capacity to conduct matrimonial proceedings or civil partnership proceedings for himself or herself will require to be represented through a next friend or guardian ad litem. If he or she lacks capacity to conduct the proceedings, he or she is likely also to lack capacity to sign a contract for sale of a property, a transfer or other conveyance arising from an order made in those proceedings. Capacity is issue specific, so medical evidence establishing incapacity to conduct the litigation may have to be supplemented by specific evidence as to capacity to execute the conveyancing documents.

Powers of the family court

3. On or after granting a decree of divorce, nullity or judicial separation in matrimonial proceedings or, in civil partnership proceedings, making a dissolution, nullity or separation order, the court may make an order for the transfer of the family home or other property from one party to the other, or other orders for property adjustment, under MCA 1973, s.24 or CPA 2004, Sch. 5, para. 7 (as the case may be). Further, where the court makes such an order or makes an order for secured periodical payments or for the payment of a lump sum under MCA 1973, s.23 or CPA 2004, Sch.5, para. 2, it may make an order for the sale of any property in which, or in the proceeds of which, either party has an interest. However, for any such order to be put into effect where one of the parties is under mental incapacity, it will be necessary to obtain either an authority of the Court of Protection or, where that party is a trustee of a jointly owned property, an order providing for a substitute trustee to be made (see s.22 Law of Property Act 1925 which is explained in paragraph 8 below).

4. Only the persons listed in s.94 Mental Health Act 1983 may give any approval or make any order required for the management of property and affairs of a patient under Part VII of that Act. These persons are the nominated judges of the Court of Protection (High Court judiciary of the Chancery and Family divisions), the Master of the Court of Protection and his nominated officers.

5. Section 39 of the Supreme Court Act 1981 (applied in County Courts by s.38 of the County Courts Act 1984) authorises the (High or County) Court to order that a person (usually the District Judge) may sign the conveyance on behalf of a litigant, where that litigant '*neglects or refuses*' to comply with an order. In the opinion of the Official Solicitor, a mentally incapacitated person who lacks capacity to sign a conveyance has neither neglected nor refused to comply with an order, hence

---

1. Issued by the Official Solicitor on 3 January 2006.

this provision may not be used to avoid the need to obtain an authority of the Court of Protection or appoint a substitute trustee.

Where the patient is sole owner of the property

6.   Where a receiver has been appointed, it is generally for the receiver to liaise with the Court of Protection and to obtain the necessary authority of that court to the sale (or any purchase). See Court of Protection Practice Note 4.

7.   Where no receiver has been appointed, it is necessary to apply to the Court of Protection for a person to be authorised to carry the terms of the family court order into effect on behalf of the patient. The authority can be drafted to extend to ancillary documentation, such as surrender of an endowment policy. Where the Official Solicitor is acting as next friend or guardian ad litem, he can apply for authority and, once granted, will be able to sign the documentation on behalf of the patient to enable the transaction to proceed. The costs of this application should be provided for in the family court order as these will not be paid by any CLS funding that is available to the patient. The application to the Court of Protection must be supported by medical evidence in form CP3.

Patient as joint owner of the property

8.   If a patient is a co-owner of property with another then s.22(2) of the Law of Property Act 1925 prevents the disposition of the legal estate in land so long as one trustee is a patient. It will therefore be necessary to replace the patient as trustee before a sale can proceed (unless there is a registered Enduring Power of Attorney).

9.   The appointment of a new trustee can be made by the family court under ss.41 and 44 of the Trustee Act 1925. Where the Official Solicitor is acting as next friend or guardian ad litem, his family litigation division can provide precedent documentation for the appointment of the Official Solicitor as new trustee in the patient's place.

10.   The county court has jurisdiction under section 41 where the trust or estate or fund to be dealt with in the court does not exceed the county court limit, currently £30,000 (see s.63A Trustee Act 1925). This jurisdictional limit may be exceeded by agreement of the parties (s.24 County Courts Act 1984).

11.   Once the order appointing a substitute trustee has been made, the sale can proceed, the sellers being the co-owner and the new trustee (usually the Official Solicitor). No mention of the patient should appear on the contract nor on the transfer. A copy of the order providing for the new trustee will need to be produced to HM Land Registry with the transfer documentation. The costs of the new trustee should be provided for in the family court order and should generally be met from the gross proceeds of sale.

Property jointly owned to be jointly transferred to one party

12.   If the family court orders the patient's share of jointly owned property to be transferred to the other joint owner it will usually be necessary for an application to be made to the Court of Protection for authority for the Official Solicitor (or some other party) to take all necessary steps in the name and on behalf of the patient to secure the transfer of all his/her legal and beneficial interest in the property. Similarly, where the share of the spouse with capacity is to be transferred to the patient, authority of the Court of Protection will be needed for any covenants to be executed on behalf of the patient as transferee. In either case, while awaiting the authority, the wording of the transfer should be agreed. The Official Solicitor has a form of transfer which may be used in such circumstances. Once the authority is received, the documentation can be completed. Provision will need to be made in the matrimonial court order for the costs of any application to the Court of Protection.

IX.5 Home Information Pack (No.2) Regulations 2007 (SI 2007/1667) [extracts]

PART 3

Contents of home information packs

Required pack documents

8.   Subject to regulations 10, 11, 12 and Parts 4 and 5, the home information pack must include the following –

(a)   an index to the home information pack complying with Schedule 1 (the home information pack index);

(b)   an energy performance certificate and its accompanying recommendation report for a property which is physically complete before or at the first point of marketing;

(c)   a predicted energy assessment complying with Schedule 2 if the property is not physically complete before or at the first point of marketing;

(d)   a document complying with Schedule 3 (the sale statement);

(e)   if the property interest is or includes the whole or part of a registered estate –

    (i)   an official copy of the individual register relating to that estate; and

    (ii)   an official copy of the title plan relating to that estate;

(f)   if the property interest is or includes the whole or part of an estate, the title to which is not entered in the register of title –

    (i)   a certificate of an official search of the index map issued under rule 145(4) of the Land Registration Rules 2003 in relation to the parcel of land to which the property interest relates; and

    (ii)   such other documents on which the seller can reasonably be expected to rely in order to deduce title to that estate for the purposes of its sale;

(g)   if the property interest is or includes the whole or part of a freehold estate in commonhold land –

    (i)   the documents described in paragraph 1 of Schedule 4; and

    (ii)   documents consisting of or containing information about the matters described in paragraph 2 of that Schedule;

(h)   if the property interest is or includes the whole or part of a leasehold interest –

    (i)   the documents described in paragraph 1 of Schedule 5; and

    (ii)   documents consisting of or containing information about the matters described in paragraph 2 of that Schedule;

(i) if the property interest is or includes the whole or part of an interest in dwelling-houses to which Part 5 of the 2004 Act applies by virtue of section 171(2) of that Act, such leases or licences –

    (i) to which the dwelling-houses are subject or are expected to be subject at the time of, or following completion of the sale of the property interest; and

    (ii) as have not been included in the pack under paragraph (h) of this regulation;

(j) a search report which relates to the property and which records the results of a search of all parts of the appropriate local land charges register –

    (i) in the form of an official search certificate, in the case of an official search made pursuant to section 9 of the Local Land Charges Act 1975; or

    (ii) in any other form but made in accordance with Parts 1 and 2 of Schedule 6, in the case of a personal search made pursuant to section 8 of that Act;

(k) a search report which –

    (i) is made in accordance with Parts 1 and 2 of Schedule 6 and with Schedule 7; and

    (ii) records the results of a search of records held by or derived from a local authority (local enquiries); and

(l) a search report which is made in accordance with Parts 1 and 2 of Schedule 6 and with Schedule 8 (drainage and water enquiries).

Authorised pack documents

9. Subject to regulations 10, 11, 12 and Parts 4 and 5, the home information pack may include documents consisting of or containing any of the following –

(a) a home condition report which complies with Schedule 9;

(b) documentary evidence of any safety, building, repair or maintenance work as has been carried out in relation to the property since the date of any home condition report included in the pack under paragraph (a);

(c) any warranty, policy or guarantee for defects in the design, building, or completion of the property, or its conversion for residential purposes;

(d) information about the design or standards to which a property has been or is being built;

(e) an accurate translation in any language of any pack document;

(f) an additional version of any pack document in another format, such as Braille or large print;

(g) a summary or explanation of any pack document, including legal advice on the content of the pack or any pack document;

(h) information identifying the property including a description, photograph, map, plan or drawing of the property;

(i) information about a pack document, about information contained within a pack document or about the home information pack, relating to –

    (i) its source or supply; or

    (ii) complaints or redress procedures arising from it;

(j) if the property interest is or includes the whole or part of a registered estate, official copies of any documents referred to in the individual register, including any edited information documents derived from such exempt information documents as are referred to in the register;

(k) if the property interest is or includes the whole or part of a freehold estate in common-hold land, information which –

    (i)   relates to one or more of the matters described in paragraph 3 of Schedule 4; and

    (ii)   would be of interest to potential buyers of the property interest;

(l) if the property interest is or includes the whole or part of a leasehold interest, information which –

    (i)   relates to one or more of the matters described in paragraph 3 of Schedule 5; and

    (ii)   would be of interest to potential buyers of the property interest;

(m) one or more of the following search reports which must be made in accordance with Part 1 of Schedule 6 and may be made in accordance with Part 2 of that Schedule, which records the results of a search relating to the property and relating to any of the following matters –

    (i)   information held by or derived from a local authority, and dealing with matters supplementary to those contained in the search reports required by regulation 8(j) (search of the local land charges register) or 8(k) (local enquiries);

    (ii)   common land or town or village greens;

    (iii) rights of access to, over or affecting the property interest;

    (iv) ground stability, the effects of mining or extractions or the effects of natural subsidence;

    (v)   actual or potential environmental hazards, including the risks of flooding or contamination from radon gas or any other substance;

    (vi) telecommunications services;

    (vii) sewerage, drainage, water, gas or electrical services;

    (viii) the potential or actual effects of transport services, including roads, waterways, trams and underground or over-ground railways; or

    (ix) liabilities to repair or maintain buildings or land not within the property interest;

(n) where it would be of interest to potential buyers of the property interest, a document which –

    (i)   records the results of a search relating to other premises in the vicinity of the property; and

    (ii)   would otherwise be a report of the type required by regulation 8(j) (search of the local land charges register), 8(k) (local enquiries) or 8(l) (drainage and water enquiries) or authorised by paragraph (m) of this regulation, if references in those provisions and in Schedules 6, 7 and 8 to 'property', 'land' and 'land on which the property is or will be situated' were references to those other premises;

(o) any documents referred to in a search report included in the pack under regulation 8(j) (search of the local land charges register), 8(k) (local enquiries), 8(l) (drainage and water enquiries) (subject to paragraph 2(4)(b) of Schedule 8) or paragraphs (m) or (n) of this regulation; and

(p) information which –

      (i)   relates to one or more of the matters described in Schedule 10; and

      (ii)   would be of interest to potential buyers of the property interest.

Creation of interests

10.   (1)   Subject to regulation 12 and Parts 4 and 5, where the sale involves –

      (a)   the whole or part of a commonhold unit, which at the first point of marketing has not been registered by the Chief Land Registrar as a freehold estate in commonhold land; or

      (b)   a leasehold property interest, which at the first point of marketing has not yet been created,

      regulations 8 and 9 apply as respects that freehold estate or leasehold interest, as modified by this regulation.

   (2)   Where paragraph (1)(a) applies –

      (a)   the sale statement must be completed as if the freehold estate had been registered by the Chief Land Registrar;

      (b)   regulations 8(e) (evidence of title for registered estates), 8(f) (evidence of title for unregistered estates) and 9(j) (documents referred to in the individual register) apply as if for 'is or includes' in each paragraph, there were substituted 'to be registered as a freehold estate in commonhold land arises from';

      (c)   paragraphs 1 and 2 of Schedule 4 (required commonhold information) do not apply;

      (d)   regulation 9(k) and paragraph 3 of Schedule 4 (authorised commonhold information) must be construed by reference to the information expected to be relevant to the interest to be registered as a freehold estate in commonhold land; and

      (e)   the home information pack must include documents consisting of or containing information which relates to the matters described in paragraph 4 of Schedule 4.

   (3)   Where paragraph (1)(b) applies –

      (a)   the sale statement must be completed as if the leasehold interest had been created;

      (b)   regulations 8(e) (evidence of title for registered estates), 8(f) (evidence of title for unregistered estates) and 9(j) (documents referred to in the individual register) apply as if for 'is or includes' in each paragraph, there were substituted 'is to be created from';

      (c)   paragraphs 1 and 2 of Schedule 5 (required leasehold information) do not apply;

      (d)   regulation 9(l) and paragraph 3 of Schedule 5 (authorised leasehold information) must be construed by reference to the information expected to be relevant to the interest to be created; and

      (e)   the home information pack must include documents consisting of or containing information which relates to the matters described in paragraph 4 of Schedule 5.

SCHEDULE 5

regulations 8(h), 9(l) and 10(3)

Leasehold information

Required leasehold documents

1. (1) Subject to sub-paragraph (2), the documents referred to in regulation 8(h)(i) are –

    (a) the lease in the form of –

        (i) an official copy;

        (ii) the original lease (or a copy of it in accordance with regulation 6); or

        (iii) an edited information document if, despite all reasonable efforts and enquiries by the responsible person, the lease can only be obtained by him in that form;

    (b) such regulations or rules as are made for the purposes of managing the property by –

        (i) the current lessor or proposed lessor;

        (ii) such managing agents as are appointed or proposed for appointment by the lessor to manage the property; and

        (iii) such other persons as manage or are likely to manage the property,

        and their predecessors (if any);

    (c) statements or summaries of service charges supplied in respect of the property under section 21 of the Landlord and Tenant Act 1985 or otherwise, and relating to the 36 months preceding the first point of marketing; and

    (d) the most recent requests for payment or financial contribution where made in respect of the property, relating to the 12 months preceding the first point of marketing, towards such of the following as are relevant to the property –

        (i) service charges;

        (ii) ground rent;

        (iii) insurance against damage for the building in which the property is situated (if made separately from the request relating to service charges included under sub-paragraph (i)); and

        (iv) insurance for any person in respect of personal injury or death caused by or within the building in which the property is situated (if made separately from the request relating to service charges included under sub-paragraph (i)).

    (2) Except for the documents specified in sub-paragraph (1)(a), the documents required by that sub-paragraph are only those which are in the seller's possession, under his control or to which he can reasonably be expected to have access, taking into account the enquiries that it would be reasonable to make of –

    (a) the lessee (unless the seller is the lessee); and

    (b) the persons described in sub-paragraph (1)(b) and their predecessors (if any).

Required leasehold information

2.   (1)   Subject to sub-paragraph (2), the matters referred to in regulation 8(h)(ii) are –

      (a)   the names and addresses of –

          (i)   the current lessor or proposed lessor;

          (ii)   such managing agents as are appointed or proposed for appointment by the lessor to manage the property; and

          (iii) such other persons as manage or are likely to manage the property;

      (b)   such amendments as are proposed to the following –

          (i)   the lease; and

          (ii)   the regulations or rules described in paragraph 1(1)(b); and

      (c)   where section 20 of the Landlord and Tenant Act 1985 applies to any qualifying works or qualifying long term agreement in respect of the property, a summary of –

          (i)   such works or agreements in relation to which a relevant contribution (or any part of a relevant contribution) has not been paid by the first point of marketing;

          (ii)   the total or estimated total cost of such works or agreements;

          (iii) the expected remaining relevant contribution of a lessee of the property;

          (iv)   the date or estimated date that such works or agreements will be concluded; and

          (v)   the date or estimated date that the remaining relevant contribution will be required of a lessee of the property.

    (2)   The information required by sub-paragraph (1) is only that which the seller can reasonably be expected to be aware of, taking into account the enquiries that it would be reasonable to make of –

      (a)   the lessee (unless the seller is the lessee); and

      (b)   the persons described in paragraph 1(1)(b)(i) and their predecessors (if any).

Authorised leasehold information

3.   The matters referred to in regulation 9(1) are –

    (a)   any lease of the property, including those that are superior or inferior to the property interest;

    (b)   any licence relating to the property;

    (c)   any freehold estate to which the lease relates including any proposals to buy a freehold interest relating to the property;

    (d)   the rights or obligations of the lessee under the lease or otherwise, including whether the lessee has complied with such obligations;

    (e)   the rights or obligations of the lessor under the lease or otherwise, including whether the lessor has complied with such obligations;

    (f)   the lessor of the property and any information that might affect the lessee's relationship with the lessor;

(g) any agent of the lessor or other manager of the property and any information that might affect the lessee's relationship with such persons;

(h) the membership or existence of any body of persons corporate or unincorporate which manages the property or building in which the property is situated;

(i) the status or memorandum and articles of association of any company related to the management of the property or building in which the property is situated;

(j) the rent payable for the property, including whether payments for such rent are outstanding;

(k) any service charges payable in respect of the property, including whether payments for such charges are outstanding;

(l) any reserve fund relating to the property for necessary works to it or the building in which the property is situated, including whether payments to such a fund are outstanding;

(m) any planned or recent works to the property or the building in which the property is situated; and

(n) any responsibility for insuring the property or the building in which the property is situated, including the terms of such insurance and whether payments relating to it are outstanding.

Creation of leasehold interests

4. The matters referred to in regulation 10(3)(e) are –

(a) the terms of the lease that will or is expected to be granted in order to create the property interest; and

(b) estimates of the payment or financial contribution likely to be required of the lessee within 12 months of completion of the sale of the property interest towards –

(i) service charges;

(ii) ground rent;

(iii) insurance against damage for the building in which the property is situated (if not to be included in contributions towards service charges); and

(iv) insurance for any person in respect of personal injury or death caused by or within the building in which the property is situated (if not to be included in contributions towards service charges).

SCHEDULE 10

regulation 9(p)

Additional relevant information

The matters referred to in regulation 9(p)(ii) are –

(a) energy performance, environmental impact or sustainability;

(b) potential or actual environmental hazards that might affect the property or its occupants;

(c)   the price at which –

    (i)   the property is available for sale; or

    (ii)   was previously sold;

(d)   the length of time the property has been available for sale either generally or through a particular person;

(e)   location or address;

(f)   aspect, view, outlook or environment;

(g)   proximity and identity of local services, facilities or amenities;

(h)   Welsh speaking communities in the local area;

(i)   the use of the Welsh language;

(j)   the property's contents, fixtures or fittings;

(k)   history of the property, including age, ownership or use of the property or land on which it is or will be situated;

(l)   tenure or estate;

(m)   application of any statutory provision which restricts the use of land or which requires it to be preserved or maintained in a specified manner;

(n)   existence or nature of any restrictive covenants, or of any restrictions on resale, restrictions on use or pre-emption rights;

(o)   existence of any easements, servitudes or wayleaves;

(p)   any information held or provided by the Chief Land Registrar relating to the property;

(q)   equitable interests in the property;

(r)   rights of way or access to or over –

    (i)   the property (not including any ancillary land); or

    (ii)   land outside the property;

(s)   rights of way or access to or over any ancillary land to the property including –

    (i)   obligations to maintain such land; or

    (ii)   whether any payments for maintaining such land are outstanding;

(t)   obligations to maintain the boundaries of the property;

(u)   communications from any public authority or person with statutory functions, that affect or might affect the property, including whether any request made by them (under any enactment or otherwise) has been complied with;

(v)   acquisition of any land by a public authority or person with statutory functions that affects or might affect the property;

(w)   standards of safety, building, repair or maintenance to which the property, its contents or the building in which it is situated ought to comply, and whether such standards have been complied with;

(x)   the property's suitability or potential suitability for occupancy by a disabled person;

(y)   alterations or other works relating to the property and –

(i)   the date or approximate date they occurred;

(ii)   whether any necessary permissions for such alterations or works have been obtained; or

(iii)   whether relevant consultations have been conducted;

(z)   identity of a person by whom the property, its fixtures or components were designed, constructed, built, produced, treated, processed, repaired, reconditioned or tested;

(aa)   measurements of the property;

(bb)   use or occupation of the property or use or occupation of other premises which affects or might affect the property;

(cc)   insurance policies, warranties, certificates or guarantees for the property or its contents;

(dd)   utility services connected to the property;

(ee)   taxes, levies or charges relating to the property; and

(ff)   information of any type mentioned in this Schedule relating to neighbouring, adjoining or nearby land or premises.

IX.6. Sample energy performance certificate[1]

Energy Performance Certificate

S A P

© Crown copyright 2007

17 Any Street,
Any Town,
County,
YY3 5XX

Dwelling type:	Detached house
Date of assessment:	02 February 2007
Date of certificate:	[dd mmmm yyyy]
Reference number:	0000-0000-0000-0000-0000
Total floor area:	166 m²

This home's performance is rated in terms of the energy use per square metre of floor area, energy efficiency based on fuel costs and environmental impact based on carbon dioxide (CO₂) emissions.

Energy Efficiency Rating

	Current	Potential

Very energy efficient - lower running costs

- (92-100) **A**
- (81-91) **B**
- (69-80) **C** — 73
- (55-68) **D**
- (39-54) **E** — 37
- (21-38) **F**
- (1-20) **G**

Not energy efficient - higher running costs

England & Wales — EU Directive 2002/91/EC

The energy efficiency rating is a measure of the overall efficiency of a home. The higher the rating the more energy efficient the home is and the lower the fuel bills will be.

Environmental Impact (CO₂) Rating

	Current	Potential

Very environmentally friendly - lower CO₂ emissions

- (92-100) **A**
- (81-91) **B**
- (69-80) **C** — 69
- (55-68) **D**
- (39-54) **E**
- (21-38) **F** — 31
- (1-20) **G**

Not environmentally friendly - higher CO₂ emissions

England & Wales — EU Directive 2002/91/EC

The environmental impact rating is a measure of a home's impact on the environment in terms of carbon dioxide (CO₂) emissions. The higher the rating the less impact it has on the environment.

Estimated energy use, carbon dioxide (CO₂) emissions and fuel costs of this home

	Current	Potential
Energy Use	453 kWh/m² per year	178 kWh/m² per year
Carbon dioxide emissions	13 tonnes per year	4.9 tonnes per year
Lighting	£81 per year	£65 per year
Heating	£1173 per year	£457 per year
Hot water	£219 per year	£104 per year

Based on standardised assumptions about occupancy, heating patterns and geographical location, the above table provides an indication of how much it will cost to provide lighting, heating and hot water to this home. The fuel costs only take into account the cost of fuel and not any associated service, maintenance or safety inspection. This certificate has been provided for comparative purposes only and enables one home to be compared with another. Always check the date the certificate was issued, because fuel prices can increase over time and energy saving recommendations will evolve.

To see how this home can achieve its potential rating please see the recommended measures.

Remember to look for the energy saving recommended logo when buying energy-efficient products. It's a quick and easy way to identify the most energy-efficient products on the market.

For advice on how to take action and to find out about offers available to help make your home more energy efficient, call **0800 512 012** or visit **www.energysavingtrust.org.uk/myhome**

Page 1 of 6

---

1. Crown copyright.

17 Any Street, Any Town, County, YY3 5XX
[certificate date] RRN: 0000-0000-0000-0000-0000

Energy Performance Certificate

About this document

The Energy Performance Certificate for this dwelling was produced following an energy assessment undertaken by a qualified assessor, accredited by [scheme name], to a scheme authorised by the Government. This certificate was produced using the RdSAP 2005 assessment methodology and has been produced under the [regulations]. A copy of the certificate has been lodged on a national register.

Assessor's accreditation number:	[accredition number]
Assessor's name:	[assessor name]
Company name/trading name:	[company name]
Address:	[company address]
	[address continued]
Phone number:	[phone]
Fax number:	[fax]
E-mail address:	[e-mail]
Related party disclosure:	[disclosure]

If you have a complaint or wish to confirm that the certificate is genuine

Details of the assessor and the relevant accreditation scheme are on the certificate. You can get contact details of the accreditation scheme from our website at [website address] together with details of their procedures for confirming authenticity of a certificate and for making a complaint.

About the bulding's performance ratings

The ratings on the certificate provide a measure of the building's overall energy efficiency and its environmental impact, calculated in accordance with a national methodology that takes into account factors such as insulation, heating and hot water systems, ventilation and fuels used. The average energy efficiency rating for a dwelling in England and Wales is band E (rating 46).

Not all buildings are used in the same way, so energy ratings use 'standard occupancy' assumptions which may be different from the specific way you use your building. Different methods of calculation are used for homes and for other buildings. Details can be found at www.communities.gov.uk.

Buildings that are more energy efficient use less energy, save money and help protect the environment. A building with a rating of 100 would cost almost nothing to heat and light and would cause almost no carbon emissions. The potential ratings in the certificate describe how close this building could get to 100 if all the cost effective recommended improvements were implemented.

About the impact of buildings on the environment

One of the biggest contributors to global warming is carbon dioxide. The way we use energy in buildings causes emissions of carbon. The energy we use for heating, lighting and power in homes produces over a quarter of the UK's carbon dioxide emissions and other buildings produce a further one-sixth.

The average household causes about 6 tonnes of carbon dioxide every year. Adopting the recommendations in this report can reduce emissions and protect the environment. You could reduce emissions even more by switching to renewable energy sources. In addition there are many simple every day measures that will save money, improve comfort and reduce the impact on the environment, such as:

- Check that your heating system thermostat is not set too high (in a home, 21°C in the living room is suggested) and use the timer to ensure you only heat the building when necessary.
- Make sure your hot water is not too hot - a cylinder thermostat need not normally be higher than 60°C.
- Turn off lights when not needed and do not leave appliances on standby. Remember not to leave chargers (e.g. for mobile phones) turned on when you are not using them.

Visit the Government's website at www.communities.gov.uk to:

- Find how to confirm the authenticity of an energy performance certificate
- Find how to make a complaint about a certificate or the assessor who produced it
- Learn more about the national register where this certificate has been lodged
- Learn more about energy efficiency and reducing energy consumption

---

Page 2 of 6

Recommended measures to improve this home's energy performance

17 Any Street,
Any Town,
County,
YY3 5XX

Date of certificate: [dd mmmm yyyy]
Reference number: 0000-0000-0000-0000-0000

Summary of this home's energy performance related features

The following is an assessment of the key individual elements that have an impact on this home's performance rating. Each element is assessed against the following scale: Very poor / Poor / Average / Good / Very good.

Element	Description	Current performance	
		Energy Efficiency	Environmental
Walls	Cavity wall, as built (no insulation)	Poor	Poor
Roof	Pitched, 250 mm loft insulation	Good	Good
Floor	Solid, no insulation (assumed)	–	–
Windows	Partial double glazing	Poor	Poor
Main heating	Boiler and radiators, mains gas	Average	Average
Main heating controls	Programmer, room thermostat and TRVs	Average	Average
Secondary heating	None	–	–
Hot water	From main system, no cylinderstat	Poor	Poor
Lighting	Low energy lighting in 75% of fixed outlets	Very good	Very good
Current energy efficiency rating		F 37	
Current environmental impact (CO_2) rating			F 31

Page 3 of 6

17 Any Street, Any Town, County, YY3 5XX
[certificate date] RRN: 0000-0000-0000-0000-0000

Recommendations

Recommendations

The measures below are cost effective. The performance ratings after improvement listed below are cumulative, that is they assume the improvements have been installed in the order that they appear in the table.

Lower cost measures (up to £500)	Typical savings per year	Performance ratings after improvement	
		Energy efficiency	Environmental impact
1 Cavity wall insulation	£411	E 53	E 46
2 Low energy lighting for all fixed outlets	£11	E 53	E 46
Sub-total	£422		
Higher cost measures (over £500)			
3 Hot water cylinder thermostat	£102	D 58	E 51
4 Replace boiler with Band A condensing boiler	£323	C 73	C 69
Total	£847		

Potential energy efficiency rating	C 73
Potential environmental impact (CO$_2$) rating	C 69

Further measures to achieve even higher standards

The further measures listed below should be considered in addition to those already specified if aiming for the highest possible standards for this home.

5 Replace single glazed windows with low-E double glazing	£40	C 75	C 71
6 Solar photovoltaics panels, 25% of roof area	£49	C 77	C 74

Enhanced energy efficiency rating	C 77
Enhanced environmental impact (CO$_2$) rating	C 74

Improvements to the energy efficiency and environmental impact ratings will usually be in step with each other. However, they can sometimes diverge because reduced energy costs are not always accompanied by a reduction in carbon dioxide (CO$_2$) emissions.

Page 4 of 6

About the cost effective measures to improve this home's performance ratings

Lower cost measures (typically up to £500 each)

These measures are relatively inexpensive to install and are worth tackling first. Some of them may be installed as DIY projects. DIY is not always straightforward, and sometimes there are health and safety risks, so take advice before carrying out DIY improvements.

1 Cavity wall insulation

Cavity wall insulation, to fill the gap between the inner and outer layers of external walls with an insulating material, reduces heat loss. The insulation material is pumped into the gap through small holes that are drilled into the outer walls, and the holes are made good afterwards. As specialist machinery is used to fill the cavity, a professional installation company should carry out this work, and they should carry out a thorough survey before commencing work to be sure that this type of insulation is right for this home. They should also provide a guarantee for the work and handle any building control issues. Further information can be obtained from National Cavity Insulation Association (http://dubois.vital.co.uk/database/ceed/cavity.html).

2 Low energy lighting

Replacement of traditional light bulbs with energy saving recommended ones will reduce lighting costs over the lifetime of the bulb, and they last up to 12 times longer than ordinary light bulbs. Also consider selecting low energy light fittings when redecorating; contact the Lighting Association for your nearest stockist of Domestic Energy Efficient Lighting Scheme fittings.

Higher cost measures (typically over £500 each)

3 Cylinder thermostat

A hot water cylinder thermostat enables the boiler to switch off when the water in the cylinder reaches the required temperature; this minimises the amount of energy that is used and lowers fuel bills. The thermostat is temperature sensor that sends a signal to the boiler when the required temperature is reached. To be fully effective it needs to be sited in the correct position and hard wired in place, so it should be installed by a competent plumber or heating engineer.

4 Band A condensing boiler

A condensing boiler is capable of much higher efficiencies than other types of boiler, meaning it will burn less fuel to heat this property. This improvement is most appropriate when the existing central heating boiler needs repair or replacement, but there may be exceptional circumstances making this impractical. Condensing boilers need a drain for the condensate which limits their location; remember this when considering remodelling the room containing the existing boiler even if the latter is to be retained for the time being (for example a kitchen makeover). Building Regulations apply to this work, so your local authority building control department should be informed, unless the installer is registered with a competent persons scheme[1], and can therefore self-certify the work for Building Regulation compliance. Ask a qualified heating engineer to explain the options.

About the further measures to achieve even higher standards

Further measures that could deliver even higher standards for this home.

5 Double glazing

Double glazing is the term given to a system where two panes of glass are made up into a sealed unit. Replacing existing single-glazed windows with double glazing will improve comfort in the home by reducing draughts and cold spots near windows. Double-glazed windows may also reduce noise, improve security and combat problems with condensation. Building Regulations apply to this work, so either use a contractor who is registered with a competent persons scheme[1] or obtain advice from your local authority building control department.

---

[1] For information on competent persons schemes enter "existing competent person schemes" into an internet search engine or contact your local Energy Saving Trust advice centre on 0800 512 012.

6 Solar photovoltaics (PV) panels

A solar PV system is one which converts light directly into electricity via panels placed on the roof with no waste and no emissions. This electricity is used throughout the home in the same way as the electricity purchased from an energy supplier. The Solar Trade Association has up-to-date information on local installers who are qualified electricians and any grant that may be available. . Planning restrictions may apply in certain neighbourhoods and you should check this with the local authority. Building Regulations apply to this work, so your local authority building control department should be informed, unless the installer is registered with a competent persons scheme[1], and can therefore self-certify the work for Building Regulation compliance. Ask a suitably qualified electrician to explain the options.

---

[1] For information on competent persons schemes enter "existing competent person schemes" into an internet search engine or contact your local Energy Saving Trust advice centre on 0800 512 012.

Page 6 of 6

X. THE LAND REGISTRY

X.1. Land Registry Practice Guides

The Land Registry publishes the following Practice Guides at **www.landregistry.gov.uk**. Land Registry forms, fact sheets and bulletins are also available from this website.

Code	Name
LRPG001	First registrations
LRPG002	First registration of title where deeds have been lost or destroyed
LRPG003	Cautions against first registration
LRPG004	Adverse possession of registered land under the new provisions of the Land Registration Act 2002
LRPG005	Adverse possession of unregistered land and transitional provisions for registered land in the Land Registration Act 2002 (see Practice Guide 5 flyer and addendum for additional practice)
LRPG005 Flyer	Adverse possession of unregistered land and transitional provisions for registered land in the Land Registration Act 2002
LRPG006	Devolution on the death of a registered proprietor
LRPG007	Entry of price paid or value stated on the register
LRPG008	Execution of deeds
LRPG009	Powers of attorney and registered land
LRPG010	Official searches of the Index Map
LRPG011	Inspection and applications for official copies
LRPG012	Official searches and outline applications
LRPG013	Official searches of the index relating to franchises and manors
LRPG014	Charities
LRPG015	Overriding interests and their disclosure
LRPG016	Profits à prendre in gross
LRPG017	Souvenir land
LRPG018	Franchises
LRPG019	Notices, restrictions and the protection of third party interest in the register
LRPG020	Applications under the Family Law Act 1996
LRPG021	Using transfer forms for less straightforward applications
LRPG022	Manors
LRPG023	Electronic lodgement of applications to change the register

Code	Name
LRPG024	Private trusts of land
LRPG025	Leases – when to register
LRPG026	Leases – determination
LRPG026 Addendum	Leases determination
LRPG027	The Leasehold Reform Legislation
LRPG028	Extension of leases
LRPG029	Registration of legal charges and deeds of variation of charge
LRPG030	Approval of mortgage documentation
LRPG031	Discharges of charges
LRPG032	Applications affecting one or more Land Registry office
LRPG033	Large scale applications (calculation of fees)
LRPG034	Personal insolvency
LRPG035	Corporate insolvency
LRPG036	Administration and receivership
LRPG037	Objections and disputes – A guide to Land Registry practice and procedures
LRPG038	Costs
LRPG039	Rectification and indemnity
LRPG040	Land Registry plans: A summary of Land Registry plans records, pre-registration requirements, other plans related services
LRPG041	Developing estates – registration services
LRPG041-S1	Developing estates – registration services. Supplement 1 Estate boundary approval
LRPG041-S2	Developing estates – registration services. Supplement 2 Estate plan approval
LRPG041-S3	Developing estates – registration services. Supplement 3 Approval of draft transfers and leases
LRPG041-S4	Developing estates – registration services. Supplement 4 Plot sales, transfers and leases
LRPG041-S5	Developing estates – registration services. Supplement 5 Detailed plan requirements and surveying specifications – guidance for surveyors
LRPG041-S6	Developing estates – registration services. Supplement 6 Voluntary application to note overriding interests
LRPG042	Upgrading the class of title
LRPG043	Applications in connection with court proceedings, insolvency and tax liability
LRPG044	Fax facilities
LRPG045	Receiving and replying to notices by e-mail
LRPG046	Land Registry forms
LRPG047	Transfers of public housing estates
LRPG048	Implied covenants

Code	Name
LRPG049	Rejection of applications for registration
LRPG050	Requisition and cancellation procedures
LRPG051	Areas served by Land Registry offices
LRPG052	Easements claimed by prescription
LRPG053	Scheme titles
LRPG054	Acquisition of land by general vesting declaration under the Compulsory Purchase (Vesting Declarations) Act 1981
LRPG055	Address for service
LRPG056	Formal apportionment and redemption of a rent or a rentcharge that affects a registered estate
LRPG057	Exempting documents from the general right to inspect and copy
LRPG058	Land Registry's Welsh Language Scheme – register format
LRPG059	Receiving and replying to requisitions by email
LRPG060	Commonhold
LRPG060 Addendum	Commonhold
LRPG061	Telephone Services (credit account holders only)
LRPG062	Easements
LRPG063	Land Charges – Applications for registration, office copy and cancellation
LRPG064	Prescribed clauses leases
LRPG064 Addendum	Prescribed clauses leases – addendum to Practice Guide 64
LRPG065	Registration of mines and minerals
LRPG066	Overriding interests losing automatic protection in 2013

Index

Home Information Pack
The professional solution

A range of HIP solutions to match how you work

The Law Society offers a range of flexible Home Information Pack (HIP) services, designed to suit the different approaches solicitors have taken in preparing HIPs.

The Law Society online HIP

- An easy-to-use, web-based solution
- Create and monitor the status of packs online
- Order any Required and Authorised HIP components quickly and conveniently
- Packs are available in a professionally bound hard copy, online or on CD

The Law Society bureau HIP

- Order key HIP components by telephone, fax or email
- Provides Energy Performance Certificates, any Required or Authorised searches, title documents and more
- You take care of any leasehold, commonhold or unregistered items
- Ordered components are available in hard copy and electronic format
- A sturdy, high quality Law Society binder is also provided in which to house the completed HIP

The Law Society's starter kit is also available if you're producing HIPs in-house. Providing a sturdy, high quality binder in which to house the completed HIP, you can also order the Law Society's industry standard TransAction forms.

Visit **www.hips.lawsociety.org.uk** to find out more about the Law Society's range of HIP solutions